The Who's Who
of Nobel
Prize Winners
1901–2000

The Who's Who of Nobel Prize Winners 1901–2000

Fourth Edition

Louise S. Sherby
Foreword by Wilhelm Odelberg

ORYX PRESS

Westport, CT • London

The rare Arabian Oryx is believed to have inspired the myth of the unicorn. This desert antelope became virtually extinct in the early 1960s. At that time, several groups of international conservationists arranged to have nine animals sent to the Phoenix Zoo to be the nucleus of a captive breeding herd. Today, the Oryx population is over 1000, and over 500 have been returned to reserves in the Middle East.

Library of Congress Cataloging-in-Publication Data

The Who's who of Nobel Prize winners 1901–2000 / [edited by] Louise S. Sherby ; foreword by Wilhem Odelberg.—4th ed.

    p. cm.

  Includes index.

  ISBN 1–57356–414–1 (alk. paper)

  1. Nobel Prizes. 2. Biography—20th century—Dictionaries. I. Sherby, Louise S. II. Odelberg, Wilhelm.

AS911.N9W53 2002

001.4′4—dc21   2001050029

British Library Cataloguing in Publication Data is available.

Library of Congress Catalog Card Number: 2001050029

ISBN: 1–57356-414–1

First published in 2002

Oryx Press, 88 Post Road West, Westport, CT 06881

An imprint of Greenwood Publishing Group, Inc.

www.oryxpress.com

Printed in the United States of America

The paper used in this book complies with the Permanent Paper Standard issued by the National Information Standards Organization (Z39.48–1984).

10 9 8 7 6 5 4 3 2 1

Contents

Foreword
Alfred Nobel: The Man and His Prizes

by Wilhelm Odelberg

It came to pass in 1907 that the famous physicist Albert Abraham Michelson set off from America for the wilds of Stockholm to collect that year's Nobel Prize for Physics. He took the Atlantic steamer from New York to Southampton, went by train to Harwich, from there to Esbjerg in Denmark, and so to Sweden. An English gentleman who boarded the boat at Harwich happened to be given a seat at the same dining table as Michelson. During the voyage a somewhat heated discussion ensued between the two of them. The English gentleman spoke disparagingly of American science and military might— Michelson was on the teaching staff of the Annapolis Naval College—and Michelson in turn was critical of the exercise of power in the British Empire. They parted in the express hope of never setting eyes on one another again. But they did meet again, and sooner than either of them expected.

During the early years of the Nobel Prizes, up until the First World War, the rule was that only a few people were to be informed of the identity of the year's Laureates before they actually appeared in the Banqueting Hall of the Royal Academy of Music to receive their prizes from the King of Sweden. So you can imagine the mutual astonishment of our two fighting cocks on discovering that both of them were Nobel Laureates, the English gentleman being one Rudyard Kipling. His citation read: "In consideration of the power of observation, originality of imagination, virility of ideas and remarkable talent for narration which characterise the creations of this famous author." Michelson's citation referred to "his optical precision instruments and the spectroscopic and metrological investigations, carried out with their aid." Michelson's granddaughter, who includes this anecdote in a biography of her grandfather, is unable to tell us whether or not Kipling and Michelson were reconciled

afterwards. In any event, this was neither the first nor the last instance of a Nobel Prize generating controversy.

When the first Nobel Prize for Literature came up in 1901, the literary world expected one of the current giants of literature to be selected for the honor. They were wrong. The Nobel Committee of the Swedish Academy chose French author Sully Prudhomme "in special recognition of his poetic composition, which gives evidence of lofty idealism, artistic perfection and a rare combination of qualities of both heart and intellect." Prudhomme was unquestionably a brilliant poet, but his true fame was 40 years past. Young writers in Sweden were furious with the Academy, a gathering of old fogeys, and a letter, signed by most of Sweden's most eminent authors, was sent to Leo Tolstoy, deploring the fact that he had not been made the first recipient.

The task of the Swedish Academy, of course, is a difficult and touchy one, because the prize has to take in the whole of the world's literature. And so, not infrequently, the choice turns out to be somebody who is not all that well known to the general public, thereby confounding all manner of conjecture. Graham Greene, for example, has been rumored on several occasions to be chosen, while in actual fact the prize has gone to a Greek, Italian, or Japanese poet. The choice of Laureate has often been criticized in literary journals or in the daily papers.

There have also been political ramifications. The 1958 Prize for Literature went to Soviet author Boris Pasternak "for his important achievement both in contemporary lyrical poetry and the field of the great Russian epic tradition." For ideological reasons which are not altogether clear, Pasternak was out of favor with the regime at that time and was forced to decline the prize. Today, 29 years after his death, he has been restored to

Wilhelm Odelberg, Ph.D, is former head librarian for Stockholm University, a member of the Royal Swedish Academy of Sciences, and former vice-president of the Royal Academy of Military Sciences. He is author of several books and articles on modern history, biographies, and history of science. He served from 1968 to 1988 as editor of *Les Prix Nobel,* the yearbook of the Nobel Foundation.

grade and his books are once more being printed in Russia-though not, as yet, the most remarkable one of all: *Doctor Zhivago.*

When the 1953 prize went to Sir Winston Churchill ''for his mastery of historical and biographical description as well as for his brilliant oratory in defending exalted human values,'' there were probably quite a few people who felt that the distinction ought to have gone to a fiction writer instead. But most people in the free world welcomed this tribute to civilization. When, in 1970, the prize went to Alexander Solzhenitsyn ''for the ethical force with which he has pursued the indispensable traditions of Russian literature,'' this was another choice that did not go over well with the rulers of the Soviet Union. His autobiography and Nobel lecture were secretly conveyed out of the country for publication in the Year Book of the Nobel Foundation. But several years were to elapse before, exiled from his native country, he was able to visit Stockholm and collect his prize.

The science prizes, that is, the prizes for Physics, Chemistry, and Physiology or Medicine, have come in for less criticism on the whole. Experts have generally approved of the awards and felt that they have gone to the right people. But some scathing remarks have been passed on occasions, for example in the journals *Nature* and *Science.* I remember that when Sir Martin Ryle and Antony Hewish from Cambridge shared the prize for their remarkable discoveries in astrophysics, it was pointed out that one of the most vital contributions had been made by an assistant at the observatory whom the Nobel Committee for Physics had overlooked.

The most controversial prize of all, of course, has been the Nobel Peace Prize, awarded by the Nobel Committee Norwegian Storting (Parliament). The Peace Prize has often gone to organizations, or representatives of organizations, that have been felt to play an important part in the cause of peace. Quite naturally, the first recipient in this category, in 1901, was Henri Dunant, founder of the International Red Cross.

On quite a number of occasions the Peace Prize has gone to people who have been in the political limelight, have irked the wielders of power but have campaigned for human dignity and reconciliation. The first really startling instance came in 1936, when the Peace Prize was awarded to the German Carl von Ossietsky, a radical pacifist and journalist. At that time he was imprisoned in one of Hitler's concentration camps, and der Führer was so enraged by the Norwegian Committee's decision that he forbade any Germans to accept Nobel Prizes in the future. The Nobel Committees, unmoved, persistently awarded prizes to Germans. For example, the 1939 Prize for Physiology or Medicine went to Gerhard Domagk ''for the discovery of the antibacterial effects of prontosil.''

Domagk was, of course, ordered to decline the prize, but after the War he was able to collect his medal and diploma, though not the money.

There are plenty of other peace Laureates who have caused tempers to flare in one place or another: Martin Luther King, Andrei Sakharov (another Russian dissident who was reinstated before his death), President Anwar Sadat of Egypt and Israeli Prime Minister Menachem Begin, Lech Walesa, and South African Archbishop Desmond Tutu, to mention but a few.

Sweden and Norway, and the events that take place there, do not often attract attention in the international press. A remarkable exception from this rule is the announcements of the year's Nobel Prizes, which are usually made in October, and the events surrounding the award ceremony on December 10. It is only natural that interest should at that time be directed also at the man who was the cause of all this attention.

ALFRED NOBEL, THE DONOR

Alfred Nobel was very much an international figure. He was born in Stockholm in 1833, grew up in St. Petersburg, Russia, lived the greater part of his life in Paris, and died in San Remo, Italy, in 1896.

Even at an early age, he began to take an interest in the explosives industry. In this, he was inspired by his father, who manufactured mines in St. Petersburg during the Crimean War. After studies in various countries, he founded, in 1864, Nitroglycerin AB and set up factories outside Stockholm and Hamburg. The foundation of Alfred Nobel's operation was his invention of primary detonation with a percussion cap, which made it possible in practice to release the detonative force of nitroglycerine and other explosive substances subsequently invented by Nobel.

Since nitroglycerine proved to be highly dangerous in transit (numerous deaths had occurred, and nitroglycerine had acquired a bad reputation), Nobel set about producing a more suitable explosive, and in 1866 he invented dynamite, which is produced by mixing nitroglycerine and kieselguhr, or fossil meal. A subsequent improvement on this was explosive gelatin, invented by Nobel in 1875, which consists of nitroglycerine converted into a gelatinous form by the solution in it of nitrocellulose of a lesser degree of nitrification, i.e., collodion cotton. Now, powerful and inexpensive explosives such as gelignite and extra-dynamite were produced by the admixture of nitrates and pollen, etc. The invention of extra-dynamite saved huge sums in blasting. When the St. Gotthard tunnel was blasted, 20 million francs were saved and the time taken considerably reduced.

In 1893, Nobel began to take an interest in the Swedish arms industry and established himself in Bofors, in Värmland, in the western part of central Sweden. During the closing period of his life he visited Bofors every year and stayed in his manor there, which is known as Björkborn. A large research laboratory was also set up in Bofors for the study, above all, of smokeless powder, that is to say smokeless nitroglycerine—nitrocellulose powder, ballistite, or "Nobel" powder. Numerous engineers were employed at his laboratory, including Ragnar Sohlman, who later became managing director of the Nobel Foundation. Nobel was also responsible for real inventions in a variety of different fields, including the invention of artificial silk and leather, and gutta-percha. He registered no fewer than 355 patents in different countries. The management of Bofor's now world-famous arms factory has paid outstanding tribute to Nobel's memory. In 1983, the manor of Björkborn and the old laboratory nearby were converted into a museum to mark the 150th anniversary of Alfred Nobel's birth. The laboratory has been reconstructed as it was in Nobel's day. The manor now houses the greater part of Nobel's personal library.

Through his inventions, mainly in the field of explosives, and the revenues from the companies he had founded, Nobel built up a considerable fortune, which amounted at his death to SEK 33 million, or in current terms some $5 million.

At the personal level, Nobel lived a very retired life, and for his circumstances a very simple one. He was unmarried, and posterity's eager delvings into his erotic relationships have produced fairly scanty results. His emotional life was sublimated into the thought of new inventions. To him, a day without any new ideas taking shape was a day wasted. "But," he said, "if only a few out of a hundred such ideas ever bear fruit, I consider I have gained a rich result." Nobel thus had an unusual capacity for work. He spoke and wrote five languages, and was an extremely witty correspondent. He received, of course, numerous honors.

THE WILL

On November 25, 1895, Nobel drew up his will in Paris. There has been a great deal of speculation as to Nobel's thoughts before he made his final wishes known. He had corresponded a great deal over the years with the well-known Austrian author and apostle of peace Bertha von Suttner. Probably this correspondence gave him the inspiration for what was to be the Nobel Peace Prize.

Nobel had two brothers, Ludvig and Robert, who settled in Russia and developed, with great success, the oil finds in Baku on the Caspian Sea. They, too, became extremely wealthy and have been referred to in literature as the "Rockefellers of Europe." Alfred Nobel had some interests in the Russian companies headed by his brother Ludvig. Ludvig Nobel died in Cannes, France, in 1888. The French press reported his death, but a paper in Paris confused Ludvig with Alfred and ran the headline: "Le marchand de la mort est mort" or "The merchant of death is dead." We can assume that Alfred Nobel, faced with this headline, wondered whether this was the sort of obituary he would get when his own time came. It has also been suggested that Nobel entertained radical-liberal political views close to those of Social Democracy.

Anyway, without really discussing the matter with anyone—he had been let down by lawyers before and decided not to employ one this time—Nobel drew up his will and deposited it in a bank in Stockholm. Its contents were a vast surprise to his relatives, colleagues, and the general public in Sweden:

> The whole of my remaining realizable estate shall be dealt with in the following way:
>
> The capitol shall be invested by my executors in safe securities and shall constitute a fund, the interest on which shall be annually distributed in the form of prizes to those who, during the preceding year, shall have conferred the greatest benefit on mankind. The said interest shall be divided into five equal parts, which shall be apportioned as follows: one part to the person who shall have made the most important discovery of invention within the field of physics; one part to the person who shall have made the most important chemical discovery or improvement; one part to the person who shall have made the most important discovery within the domain of physiology or medicine; one part to the person who shall have produced in the field of literature the most outstanding work of an idealistic tendency; and one part to the person who shall have done the most or the best work for fraternity among nations, for the abolition or reduction of standing armies and for the holding and promotion of peace congresses.
>
> The prizes for physics and chemistry shall be awarded by the Swedish Academy of Sciences; that for physiology or medical works by the Karolinska Institute in Stockholm; that for literature by the Academy in Stockholm; and that for champions of peace by a committee of five persons to be elected by the Norwegian Storting. It is my express wish that in awarding the prizes no consideration whatever shall be given to the nationality of the candidates, so that the most worthy shall receive the prize, whether he be a Scandinavian or not.

His relatives were quite naturally disappointed, but the foremost of these, Immanuel Nobel, assisted the executor of the will, Ragnar Sohlman, in every possible way. Many people regarded the will as reflecting a lack of patriotic feeling. The French state, for its part, was keenly interested in the question of whether Alfred Nobel's fortune had its legal domicile In France or Sweden. What decided the issue was that Nobel had transferred to Sweden his famous carriage horses, Orloff horses from Russia, which he had received from his brother Ludvig. By French custom, wherever the carriage horses were, there the estate inventory had to be drafted.

The disposal of Nobel's various shareholding's, and the transfer of his fortune to Sweden, proved to be a complicated affair. Difficulties were also experienced in persuading the institutions that Nobel had wished to be responsible for the awards in their respective fields to undertake their duties. Finally, however, the organizational details were settled, and the first prizes could be awarded in 1901.

To coordinate the provisions of the will and generally further the purposes of the donor, and to administer Nobel's fortune, the Nobel Foundation was created. Since the will only indicated the intentions of the donor in general terms, it became necessary to create firm procedures for the administration of the donation; this was done in the Foundation's Statutes, which were ratified in 1900 and approved by the government. Special statutes were also drawn up to regulate the award of prizes through the Swedish award bodies, namely the royal Swedish Academy of Sciences for the prizes in physics and chemistry, the Karolinska Institute for the prize in physiology or medicine, and the Swedish Academy for the prize in literature. In 1968, a further prize was added, in the economic sciences, through a donation made to celebrate the tercentenary of the Swedish National Bank (Riksbank). In contradistinction from the prizes instituted by Alfred Nobel himself, this is known as the ''Alfred Nobel Memorial Prize.''

CHOOSING LAUREATES

There were thus five Nobel prizes, and there are now six, if we count the Alfred Nobel Memorial Prize in Economics. At the time Alfred Nobel wrote his will, Sweden and Norway were joined in a Political union, which was dissolved in 1905. Nobel decided that the Peace Prize should be awarded through the Norwegian Parliament, the Storting, which subsequently delegated the decision to a special Norwegian Nobel Committee.

The Board of the Nobel Foundation consists of a chairperson, appointed by the Swedish government, and four members, chosen for a term of two years by the 15 electors appointed by the prize awarding bodies. The electors who also serve for two years, can put forward proposals or make statements on proposals, for amendments to the basic Statutes. This has been done on several occasions.

The Nobel Foundation's capital has grown since it was first acquired. [Editor's Note: As of 2001 it has grown to around SEK 4 billion, corresponding to approximately $369 million. The prize sum in 2001 was SEK 10 million, corresponding to $900,000.]

By the terms of the Nobel Foundation's Statutes, a prize can be equally divided between two achievements, or awarded jointly to two or more persons for work they have done together. The Peace Prize can also be awarded to an institution or association. In any given year, all the prizes are of an identical amount. On the other hand, they vary in size from year to year, depending on the yield on the fund on which they are based. That it has been possible to increase the yield more or less in step with inflation is due largely to the fact that the Nobel Foundation is now exempt from State tax, and therefore escapes the capital gains tax that has been such a burden in all capital administration in Sweden.

By the terms of the Statutes, proposals shall be submitted prior to February 1 of the year in which the award is to be made. Decisions are regularly made by the Swedish award bodies during the period from October 1 to November 15. The Norwegian Nobel Committee makes its decision on the Peace Prize between September 1 and November 15.

Of great importance in the evaluation of candidates worthy of the Nobel Prize is the fact that so many people have the right to submit nominations. Previous Laureates, and the officials and members of academies, along with universities and other scientific institutions throughout the world are all entitled to nominate candidates.

An important rule is that the right to propose candidates is assigned to individuals, not to academies and university faculties as such, or corporations. This rule was established in order to avoid public discussion. If it becomes clear that prizes cannot be awarded—and awards were suspended for a number of years during the two World Wars—the sums are reserved and allocated to the main fund; a certain part of the sum reserved, however, can be allocated to a special fund. The yield on this latter fund can be used to promote the purposes of the Nobel Foundation other than through the prizes.

Traditionally, the prize-giving takes place with due ceremony in Stockholm and Oslo on December 10 each year—Nobel Day—the day on which Alfred Nobel died. Apart from the money prize, each Laureate receives a diploma, executed in the case of Laureates elected by the Academy of Sciences and the Swedish Academy by a well-known Swedish artist, and a gold medal of generous size-the value of the gold in 1990 was around SEK 20,000 or $3,425. In Sweden, the practice is for H.M. the King to hand over the prizes in the Stockholm concert hall, after which a banquet is held for some 1,300 persons in the Stockholm City Hall. In Oslo, the Peace Prize is presented by the chairman of the Storting's Nobel Committee in the university auditorium, traditionally in the presence of the royal family. By the terms of the basic Statutes, a Laureate is required within six months of the award ceremony to give a so-called Nobel lecture; this is usually delivered on acceptance of the prize.

Work on the election of Laureates continues practically all year round. The committees for the various prizes are required to take previous proposals into consideration and to note new proposals. In 1989 nominations for prizes totaled 208 for physics, 261 for chemistry, 189 for physiology or medicine, 188 for literature, 97 for the Peace Prize, and 131 for the Memorial Prize in economic sciences. Naturally, many of these nominations recur from year to year.

To acquire as all-round a picture as possible, the committees have commissioned specialists to investigate the weight and significance of the research performed by the various potential candidates for prizes. These investigators, who present their reports to the committee in question, can be up to 20 in number and are naturally required to observe the strictest confidentiality. Since the number of proposals is so great, the committee has to reach agreement as to what particular field it will interest itself in on this occasion; whether, for example, in physics, priority is to be accorded to ''solid state'' or ''particle physics.'' Similar deliberations have to be made in chemistry; for example, whether to give priority to organic or inorganic chemistry.

By late summer the committees have usually put together their proposals, which now have to be scrutinized by the royal Academy of Sciences' respective classes for physics and chemistry. The physics class is chaired by the Academy's permanent secretary and consists at present of 28 members. Once the class has scrutinized the proposal and held its meeting, the nomination is submitted for a decision to a plenary session of the Academy. By the time the session is held, the proposal will have been available for a couple of weeks to members of the Academy, all of whom have taken a pledge of secrecy. Finally, the decision is taken by the Academy, which, in the case of the prizes in physics and chemistry, usually takes about a day. The procedure starts with the committee's secretary presenting a general survey of those research inputs that have been regarded as the most interesting and have been studied by the special investigators. Finally, the secretary reports which scientist or group of scientists should, in the opinion of the committee, be awarded the year's Nobel Prize. The president of the Academy then describes the position taken by the respective class within the Academy to the committee's proposals. A specialist on the committee then presents a detailed account of the research performed by the proposed candidate and, where applicable, his co-worker or co-workers.

Discussions arise usually relating to the problem of rewarding a team of researchers for a given discovery. It may be, for example, that candidate A has made a remarkable research finding but the significance of the finding was first established by candidate B and the discovery was then decisively developed by candidate C. The question can then be put as follows. Is candidate A to receive the entire award? If this is thought inappropriate, should the prize be split into three equal parts? We must add that not more than three Laureates may be selected in one and the same subject. When a secret ballot has been taken and the Academy has made its decision, a special press conference is given, after which the Laureate in question is informed of the decision and invited to the award ceremony in Stockholm. The Nobel Foundation also pays the travel costs and living expenses in Stockholm for a very limited number of close relatives.

The procedure followed by the Karolinska Institute, the Swedish Academy and the Storting Nobel Committee in Oslo is roughly the same. In the case of the Karolinska Institute, where it is the teaching staff who decides on the prize in physiology or medicine, the situation until the early 1970s was that discussions were confidential as in the case of other prize-awarding bodies. Unlike the academies, however, the Karolinska Institute is a state organization, and certain new regulations meant that its activities would be subject to complete public insight. So, when affairs relating to the Nobel Prizes are discussed, the college of professors is converted into a special ''Nobel Assembly'' of a private nature, into which outsiders have no insight.

The Nobel Prizes have attracted an enormous amount of attention ever since they were introduced. The choices made by the prize-awarding bodies have attracted both praise and blame. It is above all, perhaps, the prize in literature and the Peace Prize, that have come in for criticism, due, of course, to these being subjects on which everyone can have an opinion. The other prizes are usually commented on in *Nature* and *Science* in a more initiated manner, although some fairly waspish remarks have been made there too from time to time.

CONCLUSION

The first time Alfred Nobel seems to have considered writing a will was in March 1889. People have been disposed to regard the absence of detailed instructions as a consequence of Nobel's habit of giving trusted assistants only the merest indication of what he wanted done. It was their business to work out the means to the end. This is perhaps a correct surmise, but the fund was to be administered by people about whom Nobel knew nothing. The actual choice of Laureates, it is true, was entrusted to three institutions and a committee appointed by the Norwegian Storting, but not even in this case did Nobel give any thought to the procedural details.

There was a touch of flamboyant gesture about Nobel's will as he cast his millions into the air, without inquiring too closely where they were going to land. The main thing was that they should not get into the pockets of his legal heirs. This massive donation was probably one of innumerable ideas, and Nobel's imagination seems to have been extra prolific at the time when his will was drawn up. He oscillated from phonographs and telephones to projectiles of various kinds. He simply did not have time to work out his ideas in more detail, and his last will and testament, like several of provisional patent applications, remained an evanescent sketch.

Of one thing, however, we can be relatively certain: It was people with ideas he wanted to reward, people with inspiration. In other words, people of his own kind. This is why the prizes had to refer to achievements during the past year. There is no prize for technology, because Nobel knew from his own experience that a successful invention is often rewarded through the patent system. But a medical or chemical discovery was something different; there was nothing to guarantee that the person making the discovery would have a share in the resultant profit.

Although interest in the Nobel Prizes has fluctuated with the years, the prizes have become internationally established in the way in which Alfred Nobel intended. They are astonishingly well known in large parts of the world. Interest in Alfred Nobel personally has also been sustained, perhaps partly because he was such a complicated and unusual personality. There is no formula or slogan with which he can be pinned down.

Preface

SCOPE AND CONTENTS

The Who's Who of Nobel Prize Winners 1901–2000 is the fourth edition of a book conceived to give users quick access to basic information about all Nobel Laureates and their achievements. With the retirement of the editors of the previous three editions, Bernard S. Schlessinger and June H. Schlessinger, the fourth edition of *The Who's Who of Nobel Prize Winners 1901–2000* became my sole responsibility. Because I had served as an associate editor for the first three editions, I was familiar with the organization of the volume and its purpose. Along with the previous editors I believe that there is a need for a "ready-reference" book, providing a one-stop place to look for basic biographical information on each winner in a consistent format and independently verified. Often information is included here that does not appear on Web sites, including the Nobel e-museum, or that is difficult to find easily. Also included is a list of additional sources to locate more information about the winners, and the book concludes with four useful indexes.

This fourth edition of *The Who's Who of Nobel Prize Winners* contains revised entries for Nobel Prize Winners from 1901–1995 and 62 new entries for the winners from 1996–2000, totaling 720 entries. Each of the 658 entries from the third edition was reviewed and updated by the editor, with approximately 70 percent of the previous entries changing. In most cases, new biographical information was available, Nobel laureates continued to win awards that marked their achievements, or personal information changed. To the extent possible, all entries are accurate through January 1, 2001. The year 2001 is a special one for the Nobel Prize, as it marks the 100th anniversary of the awarding of the Nobel Prize. The Centennial Year will be marked by many special events and exhibitions culminating in the Centennial Week in December, to which all living Laureates have been invited to participate.

Entries for the prizewinners from 1996–2000 were researched and written by the editor. Every entry was checked against the standard biographical resources, newspaper and magazine accounts of their awards, and in many specialized resources relevant to the particular subject discipline for the award. For the first time, many resources were available to the editor in electronic format but all entries required significant cross-checking of facts. One source that was of particular importance is the Nobel e-Museum http://www.nobel.se/. The Nobel Foundation has created an online Web site that provides useful information about the Nobel Prize, including historical and background information. It also provides biographical or autobiographical information on the winners, the winner's acceptance speech and/or Nobel lecture, and, for the more recent winners, the press release announcing the awards, video clips, and links to other resources on the individual laureates.

As with the first three editions, each entry is composed of 15 fields of biographical and bibliographical information. See "Using This Book" for complete information on the kinds of information to be found in each entry. Entries are arranged by prize: Chemistry, Economics, Literature, Medicine and Physiology, Peace and Physics. Within each section, entries are arranged chronologically. Information has been included in each of the 15 fields when available. In cases where the information could not be verified independently, it was left out. Readers should also note that, due to events such as war and/or lack of suitable candidates, prizes were not awarded in some years.

In addition to the chronological arrangement of the prize winners, four other indexes are included to help readers access the entries: (1) Name Index, an alphabetical listing of all winners; (2) Education Index, a listing of post-secondary educational institutions and the winners who received degrees from them; (3) Nationality or Citizen Index, a listing of winners by their nationality or citizenship (some laureates are thus listed under more than one nationality or citizenship category); and (4) Religion Index, a listing of winners by religion. This includes only those laureates whose religious affiliations have been definitely ascertained.

In spite of all my best efforts, it is possible that errors were made in some entries. Therefore I ask readers of this edition to notify me of any corrections, suggestions, and updates so that they can be incorporated in future editions. Please send all queries to Louise S. Sherby, in care of the Oryx Press, 4041 N. Central Ave., Phoenix, Arizona 85012–3397.

NOBEL PRIZE WINNERS 2001

Chemistry
William Knowles, United States
K. Barry Sharpless, United States
Ryoji Noyori, Japan

Economics
George A. Akerlof, United States
A. Michael Spence, United States
Joseph E. Stiglitz, United States

Literature
V.S. Naipaul, Great Britain

Medicine
Leland H. Hartwell, United States
R. Timothy Hunt, Great Britain
Paul M. Nurse, Great Britain

Peace
United Nations and U.N. Secretary-General Kofi Annan, Ghana

Physics
Eric A. Cornell, United States
Carl E. Wieman, United States
Wolfgang Ketterle, Germany

ACKNOWLEDGMENTS

Last, but not least, I wish to thank Bernie Schlessinger and June Schlessinger for their help in making this edition happen and for their confidence in me. I also want to thank my editor, Eleanora S. von Dehsen, of the Oryx Press, who has been most helpful and patient as I took on this new responsibility. My thanks, too, to Dr. Anita Ondrusek, Science Reference Librarian at the Hunter College Libraries, whose superb searching skills found citations to publications when needed.

I hope that this fourth edition will prove to be as useful and valuable as the previous three editions and that it will be a resource of first choice when looking for basic biographical information on Nobel Prize winners.

Louise S. Sherby
Associate Dean and Chief Librarian
Hunter College, New York City

Using This Book

Each entry in this book is composed of 15 fields of information. The format of each field, and some further information about the nature of each field, are explained here.

NAME

The most complete name found for the individual has been used. If a pseudonym was found, it is included in parentheses. If a person's name changed, the former name is included in parentheses. The last name is always given first. Also included as part of the name are titles of nobility, when applicable. Examples of entries are

Angell, Norman, Sir (Lane, Ralph Norman Angell)

Agnon, Shmuel Yosef (Czaczkes, Shmuel Yosef)

Sienkiewicz, Henryk Adam Aleksandr Pius (Litwos)

All such name variations are included in the Name Index of this book, with ''see'' references given to direct the user to the main name entry.

PRIZE

The prize awarded is listed, followed by the year in which the award was won. Thus, this field appears as follows:

Peace, 1931

In those cases where a prize was awarded posthumously or the laureate refused the prize, a notation to that effect is included in the entry. Multiple winners are listed under each applicable category, with ''see'' references given to direct the user to the first full listing for the winner. In years when no prize was given, there is no entry.

BIRTH AND DEATH DATES

The birth and death dates (when applicable) of each Nobel Prize winner are listed, along with birthplace and location of death (when applicable). States in the United States are abbreviated with the standard two-letter codes. Otherwise, the fullest information is presented, as can be seen here:

January 27, 1903; Melbourne, Australia

September 26, 1888; St. Louis, MO

For individuals who were born in political regions no longer in existence, such as the Austro-Hungarian Empire prior to 1918, place of birth is given as region of the empire (i.e., Poland or Czechoslovakia), rather than Austria-Hungary.

FOUNDED

In the case of corporate or institutional winners, the date when and location in which the institution or corporation was established is included.

PARENTS

The names of the winner's father and mother in the fullest form found are included. Mothers' names especially were often difficult to find. The absence of a first or maiden name indicates that only an incomplete name could be found. If no record was found, the phrase ''no record found'' is used. Thus, an entry such as the one shown below can be considered to be complete.

Father, Ezra Flory; Mother, Martha Brumbaugh Flory

However, entries will also be found in less complete forms, such as these:

Father, Muhammed El-Sadat; Mother, no record found

Father, Panayiotis Alepoudelis; Mother, Maria Alepoudelis

NATIONALITY OR CITIZENSHIP

In cases where the laureate was born and remained in the country of birth throughout his or her career, a single notation is given, as in the following example:

German

If the laureate was born in one country, then later moved to and became a citizen of another country, the country of birth is given first, followed by a notation for the country to which the laureate moved and became a citizen. An example is:

German; later American citizen

In cases where laureates spent significant parts of their lives in several countries and obtained multiple citizenships, each of those is identified in the entry:

German; later Swiss and American citizen

In cases where it is known that a laureate resided in a certain country, but citizenship for that country cannot be determined, the entry is arranged as follows:

Dutch; later French resident and American citizen

RELIGION

Of all the fields in this book, this was by far the most difficult for which to locate definitive information. Whether the Nobel Prize winner was in Literature, Peace, Economics, Medicine and Physiology, Chemistry, or Physics, there was scant data on religious preference and oftentimes contradictory data. The Literature and Peace were more likely to have religion identified; but even in these cases, it was more often a passing (and sometimes puzzling) reference, rather than a clear statement (e.g., "Jewish/Evangelical" or "Freethinker; from Lutheran background"). Unless a specific narrow religious preference was stated in the literature consulted, generic terms (such as "Christian") were used. In instances where we were fairly certain of religion, but not positive, we used the phrase "Most probably." When not even a good guess could be made, we used the notation, "No record found." Where a person's religious preference changed, we used statements such as "Agnostic; from Christian background." Also, in some cases, the laureate's parents were of different religious persuasions; that fact has been noted, when known, in the field. Here is an example:

Areligious; from Anglican/Methodist background.

Even when the literature consulted was definite about religious preference, there is still some question as to religious affiliation in some instances because of the highly personal and variable nature of a person's preference in this area. The user should read all entries with that thought in mind. Any new information made available will be included in later editions.

The Religion Index contains only the winners whose religious affiliation was definite. A citation for "Most probably Jewish," for example, will not be found in the Religion Index under "Jewish."

EDUCATION

In citing the university name and the degree name, the format found in the sources consulted was followed. For universities in the United States, the abbreviation of the state in which the university is located is used. For universities outside the United States, the country of location is given. Some country identifications may look odd, as may some spellings, but it must be remembered that both geographic locations and spelling customs changed markedly between 1901 and 2000. Our rule was that we used the data presented in the sources consulted unless an obvious error would thus result. Where the laureate did not receive any degree, the entry reads "No college degrees."

SPOUSE

The full name of the spouse is presented, followed by as full a date of marriage as was available. If the person married more than once, the death or divorce of the previous spouse is noted, with a date, if available. Where it was not possible to determine whether the previous spouse had died or been divorced, that information was omitted. In some cases, the term "dissolved" (used in some sources) is carried into this book as well. If the person did not marry, the notation "None" is used. If it was impossible to determine whether a marriage had occurred, the notation "No record found" is used.

CHILDREN

Where names of children were found, the name plus the term "son" or "daughter" are included. If numbers of children were found, but no names, the numbers are given, sometimes as totals and sometimes broken down by daughters and sons, as available. Interestingly, where names were not found, it was most often the names of daughters; in some cases, sons' names were given, but daughters' names were omitted! Where applicable, and where such information is available, adopted children, stepchildren, and stillborn children are listed as well.

CAREER

In its most complete form, career information is presented this way:

> Organization name, geographic location, title, years of employment.

The career entry generally begins with the first ''professional'' position held by the winner. Thus, for most science-oriented laureates, the first position listed will be after the year of the terminal degree. For academics, the title ''Professor'' is used, no matter what the rank or distribution between teaching, research, and service. In the case of the Literature winners, where the person's sole involvement was in writing, the title ''Writer'' is used. In the case of the Peace winners, where the person's career was spent in a variety of activist and political roles, appropriate general titles such as ''Political Activist'' or ''political posts'' are used. For military career years, no specific titles are given.

Many laureates have periods in their careers where they occupied concurrent positions. In these cases, the principal position, as interpreted by the editors, is listed, except in a few extraordinary entries. Occasionally, there will be a gap in coverage, often due to a return to educational pursuit.

OTHER AWARDS

The listings for this field are those taken directly from the sources consulted. Where dates were available, they are included. The awards are listed in chronological order. Knighthood is noted where appropriate, but peerages are not.

SELECTED PUBLICATIONS

For all entries, the publications listed are not exhaustive or comprehensive, but representative of the winners' works. They represent the work for which the laureate was awarded or are representative of the career work of the laureate. In a few cases, either the winners did not write any works or no titles attributed to them could be found.

We found that the Literature and Peace winners' bibliographic listings were more complete than those for the laureates in Economics, Medicine and Physiology, Chemistry, and Physics. For the laureates in Literature and Peace, the total significant output was limited in numbers of titles because it was not uncommon to find one laureate with a production of several hundred works.

The titles of works included are given in the most complete form available.

For books, both the English title and the original-language title, if applicable, are given as presented in standard cataloging sources. For periodical material, the most complete article information and periodical name available in the standard indexing sources consulted are included. If a ''Collected Works'' was found, it was listed as one of the bibliographic entries. Bibliographic items in this field are in chronological order, and the laureate's name, as author, is not included.

BIOGRAPHICAL SOURCES

Where a book-length biography or autobiography on the winner was available, it has been listed in this field. For these laureates, usually in Literature or Peace, for whom several biographies were found, these titles are limited.

For many of the science laureates, especially those of more recent vintage, no book-length biographical treatment was found. In those cases, the listings are of either journal articles about the person, the publicity attending the receipt of the Prize, or a specialty encyclopedia's treatment of the individual.

Bibliographic items in this field are arranged in alphabetical order. If the title is autobiographical, the author is not listed. For those sources (e.g., a *New York Times* article), where the title would be a headline such as ''Nobel Prize Announced,'' the title has been omitted.

COMMENTARY

The commentary provides a brief explanation of why the laureate received his or her Prize, as well as summarizes other important contributions made by the individual. In this field, the laureate is referred to by his or her familiar name rather than the full name used to head the entry. Where the language of the Academy's citation was available (either in the Nobel Academy's publications or in such standard sources as the *New York Times* or *The Times*), it has been included. Each commentary concludes with a parenthetical abbreviation of the entry editor's name. The complete listing of abbreviations and full editor names can be found in the ''List of Contributors'' in this volume.

List of Contributors

A.C.—Dr. Ana Cleveland, Professor, Texas Woman's U., Denton, TX

A.D.—Dr. Anne Day, Professor, Clarion U. of PA, Clarion, PA

A.D.J.—Dr. Ada D. Jared, Librarian, Louisiana State U., Alexandria, LA

A.J.—Alice Johnson, Librarian, Texas Woman's U., Denton, TX

A.N.—Dr. Al Nicosia, Professor, Texas Woman's U., Denton, TX

A.S.—Alison Staton, Librarian, McKinney Public Library, McKinney, TX

B.E.—Barbara Edmanson, Texas Woman's U., Denton, TX

B.E.M.—Barbara E. Mooschekian, Librarian, Infomart, Dallas, TX

B.F.—Brenda Flowers, Librarian, Blower Mound, TX

B.I.M.—Barbara I. McNutt, Librarian, Monmouth County Library, Freehold, NJ

B.L.—Dr. Bullit Lowry, Professor, North Texas State U., Denton, TX

B.L.W.—Bryan L. Wagner, Student, Clarion U. of PA, Clarion, PA

B.M.—Barbara McCracken, Librarian, Tarrant County Community College, Fort Worth, TX

B.N.L.—Barbara N. List, Librarian, Columbia U., New York, New York

B.R.W.—Beverly R. Wester, Librarian, Health Sciences Library, U. of Maryland, Baltimore, MD

B.S.—Barbara Spencer, Texas Woman's U., Denton, TX

B.S.S.—Dr. Bernard S. Schlessinger, Professor, Texas Woman's U., Denton, TX

B.W.—Brenda Westbrook, Library Consultant, Fort Worth, TX

C.B.—Dr. Charles Bruce, Professor, Texas Woman's U., Denton, TX

C.B.B.—Charlotte B. Brown, Librarian, Franklin and Marshall College, Lancaster, PA

C.C.—Cheryl Chan, Librarian, Texas Woman's U., Denton, TX

C.D.—Connie Dowell, Librarian, U. of California, Santa Barbara, CA

C.E.—Carlyle Edwards, Librarian, Cumberland County Public Library, Fayetteville, NC

C.G.—Carole Godt, Librarian, U. of Michigan, Ann Arbor, MI

C.H.W.—Carol H. Wing, Librarian, Rhode Island College, Providence, RI

C.M.—Carolyn Meanley, Librarian, Jacobs Engineering, Houston, TX

C.N.B.—Cheryl N. Broome, Librarian, Texas Woman's U., Denton, TX

C.R.L.—Charles Logan, Librarian, Naval Underwater Systems Center, New London, CT

C.S.—Carol Somers, Student, Clarion U. of PA, Clarion, PA

C.T.—Clarabel Tanner, Library Consultant, Fort Worth, TX

D.B.—Dr. Daniel Bergen, Professor, U. of Rhode Island, Kingston, RI

D.C.—Dr. Donald Cleveland, Professor, North Texas State U., Denton, TX

D.C.S.—Dr. Darrel C. Sheraw, Professor, Clarion U. of PA, Clarion, PA

D.E.S.—Doreen E. Stevens, Librarian, Cleburne Public Library, Cleburne, TX

D.G.—Diane Grund, Librarian, Moraine Valley Community College, Palos Hills, IL

D.H.—Diane Hudson, Librarian, Texas Woman's U. Denton, TX

D.K.—Deborah Kane, Librarian, Dallas Transportation System, Dallas, TX

Editor's Note: This list refers to the contributors to the first three editions of *The Who's Who of Nobel Prize Winners* (1986, 1991, and 1996).

D.N.S.—Dr. David N. Shavit, Professor, Northern Illinois U., De Kalb, IL

D.N.W.—David N. Weatherby, Professor, Clarion U. of PA, Clarion, PA

D.O.F.—Dr. Darlene O. Ford, Adjunct Professor, North Texas State U., Denton, TX

D.P.—Dolores Payette, Librarian, Bartlett Public Library, Bartlett, IL

D.P.K.—David P. Karp, Student, Clarion U. of PA, Clarion, PA

D.P.N.—Darlene P. Nichols, Librarian, U. of Michigan, Ann Arbor, MI

D.R.—Dorothy Riemenschneider, Librarian, Columbia U., New York, NY

D.S.—Delbye Sessions, Librarian, Norwich U., Norwich, VT

D.T.—Diane Tilson, Student, Texas Woman's U., Denton, TX

D.V.—Dr. Don Vann and Dolores Vann, Professors, North Texas State U., Denton, TX

D.W.—Diane Whit, Librarian, De Soto, Inc., Des Plaines, IL

E.B.—Dr. Edra Bogle, Professor, North Texas State U., Denton, TX

E.E.G.—Dr. Elizabeth E. Gunter, Professor, North Texas State U., Denton, TX

E.G.—Elizabeth Gwyn, Librarian, Bridgeport Public Library, Bridgeport, CT

E.L.—Elaine Lowenthal, Librarian, Flossmoor Public Library, Flossmoor, IL

F.K.—Frank Kellerman, Librarian, Brown U., Providence, RI

F.L.T.—Dr. Frank L. Turner, Professor, Texas Woman's U., Denton, TX

F.R.P.—Dr. Francisco R. Perez, Professor, Southwestern Texas State U., San Marcos, TX

G.E.M.—Glenn E. Mensching, Librarian, U. of Michigan, Ann Arbor, MI

G.K.—Dr. Gerald Kirk, Professor, North Texas State U., Denton, TX

G.N.W.—G. Neale Weber, Phoenix, AZ

G.R.—Graciela Reyna, Librarian, U. of Texas, Southwestern Medical Center, Dallas, TX

G.S.—Dr. Gene Sessions, Professor, Norwich U., Norwich, VT

G.W.—Dr. George Wollaston, Professor, Clarion U. of PA, Clarion, PA

H.J.W.—Henry J. Watkin, Librarian, Columbia U., New York, NY

H.L.F.—Dr. Howard L. Ford, Professor, North Texas State U., Denton, TX

I.H.G.—I. Helen Gross, Librarian, Texas Woman's U., Denton, TX

I.S.Z.—Irwin S. Zeidman, Librarian, Columbia U., New York, NY

J.A.—John Adcox, Student, North Texas State U., Denton, TX

J.A.S.—Joanne A. Saale, Student, Texas Woman's U., Denton, TX

J.B.—Dr. Joni Bodard, Professor, Emporia State U., Emporia, KS

J.B.T.—Dr. Julie B. Todaro, Professor, U. of Michigan, Ann Arbor, MI

J.C.—Joyce Chesher, Student, Texas Woman's U., Denton, TX

J.C.H.—John C. Hepner, Librarian, Texas Woman's U., Denton, TX

J.E.H.—Dr. James E. Hardcastle, Professor, Texas Woman's U., Denton, TX

J.F.—John Ferguson, Professor, Richland Community College, Dallas, TX

J.F.K.—Dr. Jake F. Kobler, Professor, North Texas State U., Denton, TX

J.G.—Dr. James Galloway, Librarian, Texas Woman's U., Denton, TX

J.H.—Joyce Hughes, Librarian, Lewisville Public Schools, Lewisville, TX

J.H.S.—Dr. June H. Schlessinger, Professor, U. of North Texas, Denton, TX

J.J.S.—Joel J. Schlessinger, M.D., U. of Alabama, Birmingham, AL

J.L.—Dr. James Lee, Professor, U. of North Texas, Denton, TX

J.L.K.—J. Lawrence Kelland, Librarian, U. of Rhode Island, Kingston, RI

J.M.S.—Jeanne M. Stevens, Librarian, Hamline U. School of Law, St. Paul, MN

J.N.B.—Jill N. Bergahn, Student, Texas Woman's U., Denton, TX

J.N.F.—Janice N. Franklin, Student, Texas Woman's U., Denton, TX

J.N.L.—Jeanne N. Leader, Librarian, Bozeman Public Library, Bozeman, MT

J.N.S.—Janice N. Sieburth, Librarian, U. of Rhode Island, Kingston, RI

J.P.—Jeanette Prasifka, Librarian, Anderson Accounting, Dallas, TX

J.S.—Dr. John Smith, Professor, North Texas State U., Denton, TX

J.V.—June Vanderryst, Librarian, Richardson Public Library, Richardson, TX

J.V.S.—Junko V. Stuveras, Librarian, Columbia U., New York, NY

J.W.—Jack Weigel, Librarian, Columbia U., New York, NY

K.C.—Dr. Katherine Cveljo, Professor, North Texas State U., Denton, TX

K.F.—Kay Frey, Librarian, Northern Michigan U., Marquette, MI

K.G.—Kathleen Gunning, Librarian, U. of Houston, Houston, TX

K.H.—Kay Harvey, Librarian, East Texas State U., Commerce, TX

K.J.H.—Kathleen J. Haynes, Librarian, Texas Woman's U., Denton, TX

K.M.—Keith McReary, North Texas State U., Denton, TX

K.N.M.—Kathleen N. Murray, Librarian, Mount Prospect Public Library, Mount Prospect, IL

L.A.—Linda Arny, Librarian, U. of Massachusetts, Amherst, MA

L.B.—Louise Blalock, Librarian, Darien Public Library, Darien, CT

L.B.W.—Dr. L.B.Woods, Library Director, Henderson State U., Arkedelphia, AR

L.C.—Linda Clary, Student, Texas Woman's U., Denton, TX

L.C.B.—Linda C. Bradley, Student, Texas Woman's U., Denton, TX

L.D.—Lisa Dalton, Librarian, U. of North Carolina, Chapel Hill, NC

L.I.S.—Louise I. Saul, Librarian, Texas Woman's U., Denton, TX

L.I.W.—Lisa I. White, Librarian, Duncanville Public Library, Duncanville, TX

L.H.—Leah Harrick, Librarian, Texas Woman's U., Denton, TX

L.K.—Lisa Kammerlocher, Librarian, North Texas State U., Denton, TX

L.M.—Lynda Maceachron, Student, Texas Woman's U., Denton, TX

L.M.W.—Dr. Lucille M. Wert, Librarian, U. of Illinois, Champaign, IL

L.N.W.—Laura N. Windsor, Librarian, U. of Michigan, Ann Arbor, MI

L.P.—Dr. Lloyd Parks, Professor, North Texas State U., Denton, TX

L.R.S.—Dr. L. Robert Stevens, Professor, North Texas State U., Denton, TX

L.S.—Leslie Sandlin, Librarian, Mount Pleasant Public Library, Mount Pleasant, TX

L.S.S.—Louise S. Sherby, Assistant Director for Public Services, U. of Missouri-Kansas City, MO

L.T.—Linda Tashbook, Librarian, Texas Woman's U., Denton, TX

L.W.—Loralyn Whitney, Librarian, Villa Maria College Library, Erie, PA

M.A.V.C.—Mary Ann Van Cura, Librarian, Hamline U. School of Law, St. Paul, MN

M.B.—Martha Babula, Student, Northern Illinois U., De Kalb, IL

M.C.—Mary Coleson, Student, Texas Woman's U., Denton, TX

M.D.C.—Mary Ducca Carrick, Teacher, Cortez High School, Phoenix, AZ

M.E.T.—Mary E. Teasdale, Student, Texas Woman's U., Denton, TX

M.F.—Maurice Fortin, Librarian, North Texas State U., Denton, TX

M.F.L.—Maureen F. Logan, Teacher, Westerly High School, Westerly, RI

M.G.R.—Dr. Martha G. Randiro, Professor, Texas Woman's U., Denton, TX

M.H.—Marguerite Horn, Librarian, Brown U., Providence, RI

M.J.B.—Marsha J.Blair, Librarian, East Texas State U., Commerce, TX

M.J.H.—Mary Jane Hilburger, Librarian, Northeastern Illinois U., Chicago, IL

M.K.—Mona Kerby, Librarian, Arlington District, Arlington, TX

M.L.—Marlene Latuch, Librarian, Somerset District, Somerset PA

M.L.L.—Marlene L. Lopes, Librarian, Rhode Island College, Providence, RI

M.N.—Metta Nicewarmer, Librarian, Texas Woman's U., Denton, TX

M.N.C.—Mary N. Cargill, Librarian, Columbia U., New York, NY

M.N.K.—Mary N. Kay, Librarian, Columbia U., New York, NY

M.P.—Mary Porrett, Librarian, Texas Woman's U, Denton, TX

N.H.—Nancy Humphreys, Librarian, U. of Wisconsin, Whitewater, WI

N.L.—Nolan Lushington, Librarian, Greenwich Public Library, Greenwich, CT

N.R.H.—Nancy R. Hessler, Librarian, Moraine Valley Community College, Palos Hills, IL

P.A.C.—Patricia A. Cannon, Librarian, Amarillo Public Library, Amarillo, TX

P.A.G.—Dr. Pete A. Gunter, Professor, North Texas State U., Denton, TX

P.E.J.—Dr. Patricia E. Jensen, Professor, U. of Rhode Island, Kingston, RI

P.H.—Phillip Hight, Librarian, Northeastern Illinois U., Chicago, IL

P.K.—Dr. Parvin Kujoory, Professor, Prairie View A & M U, Prairie View, TX

P.M.—Patricia Montrose, Student, Texas Woman's U., Denton, TX

P.P.—Patricia Peak, Librarian, Texas Woman's U., Denton, TX

P.P.F.—Pamela P. Feather, Librarian, Oswego Public Library, Oswego, IL

P.P.H.—Dr. Pamela P. Hufnagel, Professor, Pennsylvania State U., Dubois, PA

P.S.—Patricia Squires, Librarian, Northern Telecom, Dallas, TX

R.A.—Dr. Reynaldo Ayala, Professor, U. of San Diego, Calexico, CA

R.J.—Ralph Johnson, Librarian, North Texas State U., Denton, TX

R.K.—Dr. Rashelle Karp, Professor, Clarion U. of PA, Clarion, PA

R. P.—Robert Peden, Librarian, Infomart, Dallas, TX

R.R.—Richard Russell, Librarian, Glenville State College, Glenville, WV

R.S.L.—Dr. Robert S. La Forte, Professor, North Texas State U., Denton, TX

R.W.S.—Robert W. Sears, Librarian, Dallas Public Library, Dallas, TX

S.B.—Sharon Charette, Librarian, Texas Woman's U., Denton, TX

S.D.—Sara Davis, Librarian, Jacobs Engineering, Houston, TX

S.D.S.—Sarah D. Smith, Librarian, Indian Trails Public Library, Wheeling, IL

S.G.—Sandy Gallup, Librarian, Brown U., Providence, RI

S.H.S.—Sarah H. Spurgin, Librarian, Columbia U., New York, NY

S.K.—Stephen Dochoff, Librarian, Columbia U., New York, NY

S.K.A.—Sheila K. Arestad, Librarian, Franklin and Marshall College, Lancaster, PA

S.M.—Dr. Samuel Marino, Professor, Texas Woman's U., Denton, TX

S.O.—Dr. Solveig Olsen, Professor, North Texas State U., Denton, TX

S.R.—Susan Roosth, Librarian, Southern Methodist U., Dallas, TX

S.W.—Dr. Steve Wood, Professor, U. of Rhode Island, Kingston, RI

S.W.C.—Sarah W. Cogan, Librarian, U. of Michigan, Ann Arbor, MI

S.L.—Steven Lin, Librarian, Dallas Public Library, Dallas, TX

T.B.—Teresa Bungard, Librarian, U. of Michigan, Ann Arbor, MI

T.K.—Taissa Kuzman, Librarian, American Mathematical Society, Providence, RI

T.M.—Thomas McGinty, Librarian, LTV Corporation, Dallas, TX

T.N.B.—Thomas N. Booker, Student, Texas Woman's U., Denton, TX

T.S.—Tony Stankus, Library, Holy Cross College, Worcester, MA

T.S.K.—Dr. Turner S. Kobler, Professor, Texas Woman's U., Denton, TX

V.A.H.—Virginia A. Hooton, Librarian, U. of Texas at Dallas, Dallas, TX

V.B.—Veronica Beasley, Student, Texas Woman's U., Denton, TX

V.C.—Victoria Clayton, Librarian, Queens College, Flushing, New York

V.V.M.—Dr. Vandelia Van Meter, Professor, University of Southern Mississippi, Hattiesburg, MS

W.E.W.—Wynne E. Weiss, Librarian, Des Plaines Public Library, Des Plaines, IL

W.G.—Wendy Graham, Librarian, Montana State Library, Helena , MT

W.K.—Dr. William Kamman, Professor, North Texas State U., Denton, TX

W.L.N.—Dr. W. Lee Nahrgang, Professor, North Texas State U., Denton, TX

MAIN ENTRY SECTION

Chemistry

1901

Van't Hoff, Jacobus Henricus   1

Prize: Chemistry, 1901. *Born:* August 30, 1852; Rotterdam, Netherlands. *Death:* March 1, 1911; Berlin, Germany. *Parents:* Father, Jacobus Henricus Van't Hoff; Mother, Alida Jacoba Kalff Van't Hoff. *Nationality:* Dutch. *Religion:* No organized religion; most probably Christian/Protestant background. *Education:* Polytechnic School, Netherlands, technology diploma, 1871; Univ. of Utrecht, Netherlands, doctorate, 1874. *Spouse:* Johanna Francina Mees, married 1878. *Children:* Johanna Francina, daughter; Aleida Jacoba, daughter; Jacobu Henricus, son; Govert Jacob, son. *Career:* Veterinary College, Utrecht, Netherlands, Professor, 1876–77; Univ. of Amsterdam, Netherlands, Professor, 1877–78; Univ. of Leipzig, Germany, Professor, 1878–96; Univ. of Berlin, Germany, Professor, 1896–1911. *Other Awards:* Davy Medal, 1893; Chevalier de la Legion d'Honneur, 1894; Helmholtz Medal, Prussian Academy of Sciences, 1911.

Selected Publications: La Chimie dans l'Espace. Rotterdam: P.M. Bazendijk, 1875. *Ansichten über die Organische Chemie.* 2 volumes. Braunschweis, Germany: F. Viewes, 1878–81. *Etudes de Dynamique Chimique.* Amsterdam: F. Muller & Co., 1884. *Lois de l'Equilibre Chimique dans l'Etate Dilue, Gazeux on Dissous.* Stockholm: P.A. Norstedt, 1886. *Vorlesunsen über Theoretischen und Physikalischen Chemie.* 3 volumes. Braunschweig, Germany: F. Vieweg und Sohn, 1898–1900.

For More Information See: Cohen, E. *Jacobus Henricus Van't Hoff. Sein Leben und Werken.* Leipzig, Germany: Akademische Verlags-gesellschaft, 1912. *Dictionary of Scientific Biography.* New York: Scribner's, 1976 (Volume 13), 575–81.

Commentary: Jacobus Van't Hoff was awarded the Nobel Prize "in recognition of the extraordinary services he has rendered by the discovery of the laws of chemical dynamics and osmotic pressure in solutions." In addition to this work, he was also noted for his research on structural formulas in space (stereochemistry) and on chemical equilibrium. (W.G.)

1902

Fischer, Hermann Emil   2

Prize: Chemistry, 1902. *Born:* October 9, 1852; Euskirchen, Germany. *Death:* July 15, 1919; Berlin, Germany. *Parents:* Father, Laurenz Fischer; Mother, Julie Poensgen Fischer. *Nationality:* German. *Religion:* Protestant. *Education:* Univ. of Bonn, Germany, B.S., 1871; Univ. of Strasbourg, France, Ph.D., 1874. *Spouse:* Agnes Gerlach, married 1888. *Children:* Hermann Otto Laurenz, son; 2 other sons. *Career:* Univ. of Munich, Germany, Professor, 1875–82; Univ. of Erlangen, Germany, Professor, 1882–85; Univ. of Wurzberg, Germany, Professor, 1885–92; Univ. of Berlin, Germany, Professor, 1892–1919. *Other Awards:* Davy Medal, 1890; Hoffman Medal, German Chemical Society, 1906; Elliot Cresson Gold Medal, Franklin Institute, Philadelphia, PA, 1913.

Selected Publications: Anleitung zur Darstellung Organischer Präparate. Würzburg, Germany: Verlag der Stahel'schen kgl. Hof-und Universitäts-Buch und Kunstbandlung, 1893. *Untersuchungen über Aminosäuren, Polypeptide, und Proteine, 1899–1906.* Berlin: Springer, 1906. *Untersuchungen in der Puringrupp, 1882–1906.* Berlin: Springer, 1907. *Untersuchungen über Triphenylmethanfarbstoffe, Hydrazine, und Indole.* Berlin: Springer, 1924.

For More Information See: Aus Meinem Leben. Berlin: Verlang Julius Springer, 1921. *Dictionary of Scientific Biography.* New York: Scribner's, 1972 (Volume 5), 1–5. Forster, Martin Onslow. "Emil Fischer Memorial Lecture." *Journal of the Chemical Society* 117 (1920): 1157–1201. Hoesch, Kurt. *Emil Fischer, Sein Leben und Sein Werk.* Berlin: Verlag Chemie, 1921.

Commentary: Emil Fischer was awarded the Nobel Prize for his work with the carbohydrate and purine chemical groups. In addition, he was recognized for his work in the areas of enzyme chemistry and aniline dyestuffs, his syntheses of previously unknown amino acids, and the fatty acid esterification of glycerol to produce margarine. Fischer greatly expanded the science of biochemistry by elucidating basic chemical structures, clarifying structural relationships within chemical groups, and synthesizing new variations and configurations of organic substances. A practical aspect of his research was the development of laboratory principles which were applicable in the technological production of synthetic chemicals and foodstuffs. (D.O.F.)

1903

Arrhenius, Svante August   3

Prize: Chemistry, 1903. *Born:* February 19, 1859; Wik, Sweden. *Death:* October 2, 1927; Stockholm, Sweden. *Parents:* Father, Svante Gustav Arrhenius; Mother, Carolina Christina Thunberg Arrhenius. *Nationality:* Swedish. *Religion:* Lutheran. *Education:* Univ. of Uppsala, Sweden, B.S., 1878; Univ. of Uppsala, Sweden, Ph.D., 1884. *Spouse:* Sofia Rudbeck, married 1894; Maria Johansson, married 1905. *Children:* Olof, son; Sven, son; Ester, daughter; Anna-Lisa, daughter. *Career:* Univ. of Uppsala, Sweden, Professor, 1884–91; Univ. of Stockholm, Sweden, Professor and Administrator, 1891–1905; Nobel Institute for Physical Chemistry, Sweden, Director, 1905–27. *Other Awards:* Davy Medal, Royal Society, 1902; Willard Gibbs Medal, United States, 1911; Faraday Medal, 1914.

Selected Publications: Lehrbuch der Elektrochemie. Leipzig, Germany: Quandt & Handell, 1901 (*Textbook on Electrochemistry.* Tr. by John McCrae. New York: Longmans

Green & Co., 1902). *Theorien der Chemie*. Leipzig, Germany: Akademische Verlagsegesellschaft, 1906 (*Theories of Chemistry*. Tr. by T. Slater Price. New York: Longmans Green & Co., 1907). *The World in the Making: Evolution of the Universe*. New York: Harper & Brothers, 1908. *The Silliman Lectures and Theories of Solutions*. New Haven, CT: Yale Univ. Press, 1912. *The Quantitative Laws in Biological Chemistry*. London: G. Bell & Sons, 1915.

For More Information See: Dictionary of Scientific Biography. New York: Scribner's, 1973 (Volume 1), 296–302. *The Legacy of Svante Arrhenius: Understanding the Greenhouse Effect*. Stockholm: Royal Swedish Academy of Sciences, Stockholm University, 1998. Solovev, I. *Svante Arrhenius, 1859–1927*. Moscow, Russia: Nauka, 1990. "Svante August Arrhenius." *Zeitschrift für Physikalische Chemie* 69 (1909): 5–20. *Svenst Biografiskt Lexikon*. Stockholm: Albert Bonniers Forlag, 1920 (Volume 2), 287–301.

Commentary: Svante Arrhenius received the Nobel "in recognition of the extraordinary services he has rendered to the advancement of chemistry by his electrolytic theory of dissociation." He was also notable for his work in electrical conductivity, in serology and immunochemistry, and in physical processes in the universe. Arrhenius participated actively in nonscientific affairs and was instrumental in negotiating the release of German-Austrian scientists who were prisoners of war in World War I. (B.S.S.)

1904

Ramsay, William, Sir   **4**
Prize: Chemistry, 1904. *Born:* October 2, 1852; Glasgow, Scotland. *Death:* July 23, 1916; High Wycombe, Buckinghamshire, Glasgow, Scotland. *Parents:* Father, Robertson W. Ramsay; Mother, Catherine Robertson Ramsay. *Nationality:* Scottish. *Religion:* Calvinist. *Education:* Univ. of Tübingen, Germany, Ph.D., 1872. *Spouse:* Margaret Stevenson Buchanan, married August 1881. *Children:* 1 son; 1 daughter. *Career:* Anderson College, Glasgow, Scotland, Professor, 1872–74; Univ. of Glasgow, Scotland, Professor, 1874–80; Bristol Univ., England, Professor, 1880–87; Univ. of London, England, Professor, 1887–1913. *Other Awards:* Davy Medal, Royal Society, 1895; Hodgkins Prize, Smithsonian Institution, 1895; French Academy of Scientists Prize, 1895; Knighthood, 1902; A.W. Hoffman Medal, German Chemical Society, 1903; Prussian Order of Merit; Commander of the Crown of Italy.

Selected Publications: The Gases of the Atmosphere: The History of Their Discovery. New York: Macmillan, 1896. *Modern Chemistry: Theoretical*. London: J. Dent, 1900. *Modern Chemistry: Systematic*. London: J. Dent, 1900. *Introduction to the Study of Physical Chemistry*. London: Joseph Black, 1904. *Essays Biographical and Chemical*. London: A. Constable & Co., 1908. *Elements and Electrons*. New York: Harper, 1912.

For More Information See: Dictionary of Scientific Biography. New York: Scribner's, 1973 (Volume 11), 277–84. Travers, Morris W. *A Life of William Ramsay*. London: Edward Arnold, 1956.

Commentary: William Ramsay's Nobel was "in recognition of his services in the discovery of the inert gaseous elements in air, and his determination of their place in the periodic system." His interests, however, were far-ranging

and included significant work on the pyridine bases, on evaporation and dissociation, on molecular surface energy, and on radioactivity. (B.S.S.)

1905

Von Baeyer, Adolf Johann Friedrich Wilhelm   **5**
Prize: Chemistry, 1905. *Born:* October 31, 1835; Berlin, Germany. *Death:* August 20, 1917; Starnberg, Bavaria, Germany. *Parents:* Father, Johann Jakob Baeyer; Mother, Eugenie Hitzig Baeyer. *Nationality:* German. *Religion:* Jewish/Evangelical. *Education:* Univ. of Berlin, Germany, Ph.D., 1858. *Spouse:* Adelheid Bendemann, married 1868. *Children:* Eugenie, daughter; Hans, son; Otto, son. *Career:* Kekule Laboratory, Heidelberg, Germany, Researcher, 1858–60; Trade Academy, Berlin, Germany, Professor, 1860–66; Univ. of Berlin, Germany, Professor, 1866–69; War Academy, Germany, Professor, 1869–72; Univ. of Strausberg, Germany, Professor, 1872–75; Univ. of Munich, Germany, Professor, 1875–1913. *Other Awards:* Davy Medal, Royal Society, 1881.

Selected Publications: Adolph von Baeyer's Gesammelte Werke (*Collected Works*). 2 volumes. Brunswick, Germany: F. Viewig und Sohn, 1905.

For More Information See: Dictionary of Scientific Biography. New York: Scribner's, 1970 (Volume 2), 389–91. Rupe, H. *Adolf von Baeyer als Lehrer und Forscher*. Stuttgart, Germany: F. Enke, 1932. Schmorl, Karl. *Adolf von Baeyer, 1835–1917*. Stuttgart: Wissenschaftliche Verlagsgesellschaft, 1952.

Commentary: Adolf von Baeyer was granted the Nobel "in recognition of his services in the advancement of organic chemistry and the chemical industry, through his work on organic dyes and hydroaromatic compounds." One of the fathers of organic chemistry, Baeyer's work encompassed the study of uric acid, barbituric acid, indigo, indole, indigotin, zinc-dust distillation, condensation reactions, the phthaleins, acetylene, polyacetylene, organic peroxides, oxonium compounds, benzene and cyclic terpene. (B.S.S.)

1906

Moissan, Henri   **6**
Prize: Chemistry, 1906. *Born:* September 28, 1852; Paris, France. *Death:* February 20, 1907; Paris, France. *Parents:* Father, no record found; Mother, Mitelle Moissan. *Nationality:* French. *Religion:* Jewish. *Education:* Univ. of Paris, France, baccalaureate, 1874; Univ. of Paris, France, licence, 1877; Univ. of Paris, France, docteur es sciences physiques, 1880. *Spouse:* Leonie Lugan, married 1882. *Children:* Louis, son. *Career:* École Superieure de Pharmacie, France, Professor, 1879–83, 1886–1900; Univ. of Sorbonne, France, Professor, 1900–07. *Other Awards:* Lacaze Prize, Academy of Sciences, 1887; Davy Medal, Royal Society, 1896; Hoffman Medal, German Chemical Society, 1903.

Selected Publications: Le Four Electrique. Paris: G. Steinheil, 1897. *Le Fluor et ses Composes*. Paris: G. Steinheil, 1900. *Le Chimie Minerale, ses Relations avec les Autres Sciences*. Paris: G. Steinheil, 1904. *Traite de Chimie Minerale*. Paris: Masson, 1904–06.

For More Information See: Dictionary of Scientific Biography. New York: Scribner's, 1970 (Volume 9), 450–52. Gutbier, Alexander. *Zur Erinnerung an Henrie Moissan*.

Erlangen: M. Mencke, 1908. Lebeau, Paul. "Henri Moissan." *Bulletin de la Societe Chimique de France* (4th series) 3 (1908): 1–38.

Commentary: Henri Moissan was awarded the Nobel Prize "in recognition of the great services rendered by him in his investigation and isolation of the element fluorine, and for the adoption in the service of science of the electric furnace called after him." Moissan used the high temperatures attainable in the electric furnace he developed to prepare numerous new compounds and to vaporize substances previously regarded as infusible. In addition, he discovered silicon carbide (carborundum), produced artificial diamonds, and devised a commercially profitable method of producing acetylene. The development of high-temperature chemistry was greatly inspired by his electric furnace. (D.R.)

1907

Buchner, Eduard 7

Prize: Chemistry, 1907. *Born:* May 20, 1860; Munich, Germany. *Death:* August 13, 1917; Focsani, Rumania. *Parents:* Father, Ernst Buchner; Mother, Friederike Martin Buchner. *Nationality:* German. *Religion:* Most probably Christian/Protestant. *Education:* Univ. of Munich, Germany, Ph.D., 1888. *Spouse:* Lotte Stahl, married 1900. *Children:* 2 sons; 1 daughter. *Career:* Univ. of Munich, Germany, Professor, 1889–93; Univ. of Kiel, Germany, Professor, 1893–96; Univ. of Tübingen, Germany, Professor, 1896–98; Agricultural College, Berlin, Germany, Professor, 1898–1908; Univ. of Breslau, Germany, Professor, 1908–11; Univ. of Würzburg, Germany, Professor, 1911–17.

Selected Publications: Die Zymassegarung (Zymosis). Munich: R. Oldenbourg, 1903 (with H. Buchner and M. Hahn).

For More Information See: Biographical Dictionary of Scientists. London: A. and C. Black, 1969, 87–88. *Dictionary of Scientific Biography.* New York: Scribner's, 1970 (Volume 2), 560–63.

Commentary: Eduard Buchner was awarded the Nobel Prize in chemistry in 1907 "for his biochemical researches and his discovery of cell-free fermentation," the turning point for the study of enzymes and the beginning of modern enzyme chemistry. By grinding yeast cells with sand at a controlled temperature, he was able to prepare a cell-free extract that would ferment sucrose to ethanol. He called the active, fermentation-producing agent of the expressed fluid "zymase." The work showed that living yeast cells were not essential for fermentation as others had supposed. Buchner's revolutionary discoveries in biochemistry overshadowed his work in preparative organic chemistry, one result of which was the syntheses of cycloheptatriene and cycloheptanecarboxylic acid. (D.R.)

1908

Rutherford, Ernest, Sir 8

Prize: Chemistry, 1908. *Born:* August 30, 1871; Nelson, New Zealand. *Death:* October 19, 1937; Cambridge, England. *Parents:* Father, James Rutherford; Mother, Martha Thompson Rutherford. *Nationality:* British. *Religion:* Protestant. *Education:* Canterbury College, New Zealand, B.A., 1892; Canterbury College, New Zealand, M.A., 1893; Canterbury College, New Zealand, B.Sc., 1894. *Spouse:* Mary Georgina Newton, married 1900. *Children:* Eileen, daughter. *Career:* McGill Univ., Canada, Professor, 1898–1907; Victoria Univ., Manchester, England, Professor, 1907–19; Cambridge Univ., England, Professor, 1919–37. *Other Awards:* Rumford Medal, Royal Society, 1904; Bressa Prize, 1910; Knighthood, 1914; Copley Medal, Royal Society, 1922; Order of Merit, 1925; Albert Medal, Royal Society of Arts, 1928; Faraday Medal, 1930.

Selected Publications: Radioactivity. Cambridge: Cambridge Univ. Press, 1904. *Radioactive Transformations.* London: A. Constable, 1906. *Radioactive Substances and Their Radiations.* Cambridge: Cambridge Univ. Press, 1913. *Radiations from Radioactive Substances.* Cambridge: Cambridge Univ. Press, 1930 (with J. Chadwick and C.D. Ellis). *The Newer Alchemy.* New York: Macmillan, 1937. *Collected Papers of Lord Rutherford of Nelson.* 3 volumes. New York: Interscience Publishers, 1962–65.

For More Information See: Dictionary of Scientific Biography. New York: Scribner's, 1975 (Volume 12), 25–36. Feather, Norman. *Lord Rutherford.* London: Blackie and Son, Ltd., 1940. *Obituary Notices of the Royal Society of London.* Cambridge: Royal Society, 1938 (Volume 2), 395–423.

Commentary: Ernest Rutherford was honored by the Academy "for his investigations into the disintegration of the elements, and the chemistry of radioactive substances." While still in New Zealand, Rutherford studied the magnetic properties of iron in high-frequency discharges and designed a time-measuring device. In England, he invented an electromagnetic wave detector and studied x-ray bombardment and uranium radiations. During his time in Canada, he continued his studies of radioactivity and radon. Back in England, his further studies on radioactivity led to his concept of nuclear structure and eventually to the bombardment studies that elaborated this, and produced transmutations. In addition to his own work, he developed a multitude of great researchers. (L.K.)

1909

Ostwald, Friedrich Wilhelm 9

Prize: Chemistry, 1909. *Born:* September 2, 1853; Riga, Latvia. *Death:* April 4, 1932; Grossbothen, Germany. *Parents:* Father, Gottfried Ostwald; Mother, Elizabeth Leuckel Ostwald. *Nationality:* Latvian; later German citizen. *Religion:* Christian. *Education:* Univ. of Dorpat, Latvia, baccalaureate, 1875; Univ. of Dorpat, Latvia, M.A., 1876; Univ. of Dorpat, Latvia, Ph.D., 1878. *Spouse:* Helene von Reyher, married April 24, 1880. *Children:* Carl Wilhelm Wolfgang, son; Grete, daughter; 2 other sons; 1 other daughter. *Career:* Riga Polytechnic Institute, Latvia, Professor, 1881–87; Univ. of Leipzig, Germany, Professor, 1887–1906. *Other Awards:* Faraday Medal, Royal Society, 1904.

Selected Publications: Lehrbuch der Allgemeinen Chemie. Leipzig, Germany: Engleman, 1891–1902. *Hand-und Hilfsbuch zur Ausfuhrung Physikochemischer Messungen.* Leipzig, Germany: W. Englemann, 1893. "Über Physikochemische Messmethoden." *Zeitschrift für Physikalische Chemie* 17 (1895): 427–45. *Grundlinien der Anorganischen Chemie.*

Leipzig, Germany: W. Englemann, 1900. "Über Katalyse." *Verhandlungen der Gesellschaft Deutsch Naturforscher und Arzte* 73 (1901): 184–201.

For More Information See: *Dictionary of Scientific Biography.* New York: Scribner's, 1978 (Volume 15), 455–69. *Lebenslinien.* 3 volumes. Berlin: Klasing and Co., 1926–27. Ostwald, Grete. *Wilhelm Ostwald, Mein Vater.* Stuttgart, Germany: Berliner Union, 1953.

Commentary: The Nobel Prize was presented to Wilhelm Ostwald "for his work on catalysis and on the conditions of chemical equilibrium and velocities of chemical reactions." Ostwald's early research on chemical dynamics and his efforts to develop new methods of measurement prompted his emergence as one of the central figures in the development of the new field of physical chemistry. His studies of catalysis, seminal in this field, led to his patenting of the Ostwald process of oxidizing ammonia to nitric acid. Ostwald's writings were basic to the developing fields of inorganic, analytical, and physical chemistry. His later philosophical and "universal" scientific writings were equally important. (L.K.)

1910

Wallach, Otto   **10**

Prize: Chemistry, 1910. **Born:** March 27, 1847; Königsberg, Germany. **Death:** February 26, 1931; Göttingen, Germany. **Parents:** Father, Gerhard Wallach; Mother, Otillia Thoma Wallach. **Nationality:** German. **Religion:** Jewish. **Education:** Univ. of Göttingen, Germany, Ph.D., 1869. **Spouse:** None. **Children:** None. **Career:** Aktiengesellschaft für Anilinfabrikation, Germany, Researcher, 1871–73; Univ. of Bonn, Germany, Professor, 1873–89; Univ. of Göttingen, Germany, Professor, 1889–1915. **Other Awards:** Davy Medal, 1912; German Royal Order of the Crown, 1915.

Selected Publications: "Zur Kentniss de Terpene und Atherischen Oele IV." *Justus Liebigs Annalen der Chemie* 238 (1887): 78–89. "Zur Constitutionsbestimmung des Terpineols." *Berichte der Deutschen Chemischen Gesellschaft* 28 (1895): 1773–77. *Die Terpene und Campher.* Leipzig, Germany: Veit, 1909.

For More Information See: *Dictionary of Scientific Biography.* New York: Scribner's (Volume 14), 141–42. Partridge, William S., and Schierz, Ernest R. "Otto Wallach: The First Organizer of the Terpenes." *Journal of Chemical Education* 24 (1947): 106–08.

Commentary: The Nobel Award to Otto Wallach was "in recognition of his services to organic chemistry and the chemical industry by his pioneer work in the field of alicyclic compounds." Although he was also responsible for some of the key research on organic structure determination and on organic syntheses and transformations, his research in the area of oils and perfumes is usually cited because of its impetus in the development of a major industry. (J.H.)

1911

Curie, Marie (Sklodowska, Maria)   **11**

Prize: Physics, 1903 [SEE REF]; Chemistry, 1911. **Born:** November 7, 1867; Warsaw, Poland. **Death:** July 4, 1934; Sancellemoz, France. **Parents:** Father, Wladyslaw Sklodowska; Mother, Bronislawa Boguska Sklodowska. **Nationality:** Polish; later French citizen. **Religion:** Anticlerical; from Catholic background. **Education:** Univ. of Paris-Sorbonne, France, licence es sciences physiques, 1893; Univ. of Paris-Sorbonne, France, licence es sciences mathematiques, 1894; Univ. of Paris-Sorbonne, France, Ph.D., 1904. **Spouse:** Pierre Curie, married July 25, 1895. **Children:** Irene, daughter; Eve, daughter. **Career:** Governess, 1885–91; École Normale Supérieur, Sèvres, France, Professor, 1900; Univ. of Sorbonne, France, Professor, 1904–34. **Other Awards:** Bertholet Medal, Académie des Sciences, 1902; Gegner Prize, 1902; Davy Medal, Royal Society, 1903; Elliott Cresson Medal, 1909.

Selected Publications: *Recherches sur les Substances Radioactives.* Paris: Gauthier-Villars, 1904. *Traité de Radioactivité.* 2 volumes. Paris: Gauthier-Villars, 1910. "Les Mesures en Radioactivité et l'Etalon du Radium." *Journal de Physique* 2 (1912): 715. *Oeuvres de Marie Sklodowska-Curie.* Warsaw: Panstwowie Widawnictwo Naukowe, 1954.

For More Information See: Cotton, Eugene. *Les Curies.* Paris: Seghers, 1963. Curie, Eve. *Madame Curie.* Paris: Gallimard, 1939. *Dictionary of Scientific Biography.* New York: Scribner's, 1971 (Volume 3), 497–503.

Commentary: Marie Curie was the first woman to win a Nobel Prize and the first person to receive two Nobel Prizes. She shared the first Nobel, in Physics, with her husband, Pierre, and A. H. Becquerel "in recognition of the special services rendered by them in the work they jointly carried out in investigating the phenomena of radiation discovered by Professor Becquerel." Her second, unshared Nobel Prize, in Chemistry, came "in recognition of the services rendered by her to the development of chemistry: by her discovery of the elements radium and polonium, by her determination of the nature of radium and isolation of it in a metallic state, and by her investigations into the compounds of this remarkable element." (V.C.)

1912

Grignard, François Auguste Victor   **12**

Prize: Chemistry, 1912. **Born:** May 6, 1871; Cherbourg, France. **Death:** December 13, 1935; Lyons, France. **Parents:** Father, Theophile Henri Grignard; Mother, Marie Hebert Grignard. **Nationality:** French. **Religion:** Most probably Christian/Protestant. **Education:** Univ. of Lyons, France, Licencie es Sciences Mathematiques, 1893; Univ. of Lyons, France, Licencie es Sciences Physiques, 1898; Univ. of Lyons, France, Docteur es Sciences, 1901. **Spouse:** Augustine Marie Boulant, married 1910. **Children:** Roger, son; 1 daughter. **Career:** Univ. of Lyons, France, Professor, 1894–1905; Univ. of Besançon, France, Professor, 1905–06; Univ. of Lyons, France, Professor, 1906–09; Univ. of Nancy, France, Professor, 1909–20; Univ. of Lyons, France, Professor, 1920–32. **Other Awards:** Cahours Prize (Institute de France), 1901 and 1902; Bertholet Medal, 1902; Prix Jecker, 1905; Lavoisier Medal, 1912.

Selected Publications: "Sur Quelques Nouvelles Combinasions Organometalliques du Magnesium et Leur Application a des Syntheses d'Alcohols et d'Hydrocarbures." *Comptes Rendus de l'Académie des Sciences* 126 (1898): 1322. "Sur les Combinasions Organomagnesiennes Mixtes et Leur Application a des Syntheses d'Acides, d'Alcohols, et d'Hydrocarbures." *Annales de l'Universite de Lyon* 6

(1901): 1–116. *Traite de Chimie Organique*. Paris: Masson, 1935–59.

For More Information See: *Dictionary of Scientific Biography*. New York: Scribner's, 1972 (Volume 5), 540–41. "Victor Grignard." *Journal of the American Chemical Society* 59 (1937): 17–19.

Commentary: The award to Victor Grignard was "for the discovery of the so-called Grignard reagent, which in recent years has greatly advanced the progress of organic chemistry." He first studied ethyl beta-isopropylacetobutyrate, the diisopropylbutenedicarboxylic acids and branched unsaturated hydrocarbons, moving on then to the organomagnesium compounds. After preparation of the magnesium alkyl halides, he used them to prepare alcohols, ketones, keto-esters, nitriles, terpene compounds, and fulvenes. Grignard also studied hydrocarbon cracking and catalytic hydrogenation and dehydrogenation. (M.E.T.)

Sabatier, Paul 13

Prize: Chemistry, 1912. **Born:** November 5, 1854; Carcassone, France. **Death:** August 14, 1941; Toulouse, France. **Parents:** Father, Alexis Sabatier; Mother, Pauline Guilham Sabatier. **Nationality:** French. **Religion:** Catholic. **Education:** École Normale Supérieure, France, Agrege in Physical Sciences, 1877; Collège de France, Doctor of Science, 1880. **Spouse:** Germaine Herail, married 1884. **Children:** 4 daughters. **Career:** Lycée de Nimes, France, Professor, 1877–78; College de France, Professor, 1878–80; Univ. of Bordeaux, France, Professor, 1880–82; Univ. of Toulouse, France, Professor, 1882–1929. **Other Awards:** Prix La Caze, Academy of Sciences, 1897; Prix Jecker, Academy of Sciences, 1905; Davy Medal, Royal Society, 1915; Royal Medal, Royal Society, 1918; Special Award, American Chemical Society, 1926; Franklin Medal, Franklin Institute of Philadelphia, 1933; Commander, Legion d'Honneur.

Selected Publications: *Leçons Elementaires de Chimie Agricole* (*Elementary Lessons in Agricultural Chemistry*). Paris: G. Masson, 1890. *La Catalyse en Chimie Organique* (*Catalysis in Organic Chemistry*). Paris: Beranger, 1913. "How I Have Been Led to the Direct Hydrogenation Method by Metallic Catalysts." *Industrial and Engineering Chemistry* 18 (October 1926): 1005–08.

For More Information See: *Biographical Memoirs of the Fellows of the Royal Society*. London: Royal Society, 1942–44 (Volume 4), 63–66. *Dictionary of Scientific Biography*. New York: Scribner's, 1975 (Volume 12), 46–47. "Paul Sabatier, 1854–1941." *Nature* 174 (November 6, 1954): 859–60. Wojtkowiak, Bruno. *Paul Sabatier, un Chimiste indépendant (1854–1941): Naissance de l'hydrogénation catalytique*. Elbeuf-sur-Andelle, Argueil (France, Seine Maritime): Jonas éditeur, 1989.

Commentary: Recognized early for his work in physical chemistry, Paul Sabatier expanded his studies to include organic processes and molecular structure, culminating in the Nobel Prize awarded "for his method of hydrogenating organic compounds in the presence of finely divided metals whereby the progress of organic chemistry has been greatly advanced in recent years." In 1897, in collaboration with the Abbé Jean-Baptiste Senderens, he initiated over 30 years of research and refinement of the chemical theory involved. He

elaborated on his hypothesis in *La Catalyse en Chimie Organique*, considered a fundamental work in organic catalysis. Sabatier sparked broader provincial participation in French scientific institutions and, through his advocacy of new techniques, expanded scientific accomplishment. (P.A.C.)

1913

Werner, Alfred 14

Prize: Chemistry, 1913. **Born:** December 12, 1866; Mulhausen, France. **Death:** November 15, 1919; Zürich, Switzerland. **Parents:** Father, Jean-Adam Werner; Mother, Salome Jeannette Tesche Werner. **Nationality:** French; later Swiss citizen. **Religion:** Catholic. **Education:** Zürich Polytechnic, Switzerland, baccalaureate, 1889; Univ. of Zürich, Switzerland, doctorate, 1890. **Spouse:** Emma Wilhelmine Giesker, married 1894. **Children:** Alfred, son; Charlotte, daughter. **Career:** Zürich Polytechnikum, Switzerland, Professor, 1889–91; College de France, 1891–92; Zürich Polytechnikum, Switzerland, Professor, 1892–93, Univ. of Zürich, Switzerland, Professor, 1893–1919. **Other Awards:** Leblanc Medal, Société Chimique; Officier de l'Instruction Publique, Société Chimique.

Selected Publications: "Bieträge Zur Theorie der Affinität und Valenz." *Vierteljahrsschrift der Naturforschenden Gesellschaft in Zürich* 36 (1891): 129–69. *Lehrbuch der Stereochemie* (*Textbook of Stereo-Chemistry*). Jena, Germany: G. Fischer, 1904. *Neuere Anschauungen auf dem Gebiete der Anorganischen Chemie*. Brunswick, Germany: Viewig and Son, 1905.

For More Information See: *Dictionary of Scientific Biography*. New York: Scribner's, 1976 (Volume 14), 264–72. Kaufmann, G.B. *Alfred Werner, Founder of Coordination Chemistry*. New York: Springer-Verlag, 1966.

Commentary: Alfred Werner was awarded the Nobel Prize "in recognition of his work on the linkage of atoms in molecules, by which he has thrown fresh light on old problems and opened up new fields of research, particularly in inorganic chemistry." Having established an early reputation in organic chemistry by extending LeBel and Van't Hoff's ideas and questioning Kekulé's concept of valences, Werner developed a comprehensive coordination theory. When, after nearly 20 years of application, he discovered optically active inorganic compounds predicted by the theory, its wide applicability was recognized. (P.A.C.)

1914

Richards, Theodore William 15

Prize: Chemistry, 1914. **Born:** January 31, 1868; Germantown, PA. **Death:** April 2, 1928; Cambridge, MA. **Parents:** Father, William T. Richards; Mother, Anna Matlack Richards. **Nationality:** American. **Religion:** Protestant. **Education:** Haverford College, PA, S.B., 1885; Harvard Univ., MA, A.B., 1886; Harvard Univ., MA, A.M., Ph.D., 1888. **Spouse:** Miriam Stuart Thayer, married May 28, 1896. **Children:** Grace Thayer, daughter; William Theodore, son; Greenough Thayer, son. **Career:** Harvard Univ., MA, Professor, 1894–1928. **Other Awards:** Davy Medal, Royal Society, 1910; Faraday Medal, Chemical Society, 1911; Willard Gibbs Medal, American Chemical Society, 1912;

Franklin Medal, Franklin Institute of Philadelphia, 1916; Lavoisier Medal, Paris, 1922; Le Blanc Medal, Paris, 1922.

Selected Publications: "The Relative Values of the Atomic Weights of Hydrogen and Oxygen." *Proceedings of the American Academy of Arts and Sciences* 23 (1887): 149 (with J. Cooke, Jr.). "A Revision of the Atomic Weights of Sodium and Chlorine." *Journal of the American Chemical Society* 27 (1905): 459 (with R.C. Wells). "The Atomic Weight of Lead of Radioactive Origin." *Journal of the American Chemical Society* 36 (1914): 1329.

For More Information See: *Biographical Memoirs of the National Academy of Sciences.* Washington, DC: National Academy of Sciences, 1974 (volume 44), 251–86. *Dictionary of Scientific Biography.* New York: Scribner's, 1975 (Volume 11), 416–18. "Theodore William Richards Memorial Lecture." *Journal of the American Chemical Society* (1930): 1930–68.

Commentary: The Academy cited Theodore Richards "in recognition of his accurate determinations of the atomic weight of a large number of chemical elements." Richards developed the techniques and determined 30 atomic weights, including such fundamental atomic weights as those of oxygen, silver, chlorine, bromine, iodine, potassium, sodium, nitrogen, and sulfur. He was also a notable researcher in the areas of crystal growth, gas expansion, electrical resistance, and spectra. (B.S.S.)

1915

Willstäter, Richard Martin 16
Prize: Chemistry, 1915. *Born:* August 13, 1872; Karlsruhe, Germany. *Death:* August 3, 1942; Locarno, Switzerland. *Parents:* Father, Max Willstäter; Mother, Sophie Ulmann Willstäter. *Nationality:* German. *Religion:* Jewish. *Education:* Univ. of Munich, Germany, Ph.D., 1894. *Spouse:* Sophie Lesen, married 1903. *Children:* Ludwig, son; Ida Margarete, daughter. *Career:* Univ. of Munich, Germany, Professor, 1896–1905; Federal Institute of Technology, Germany, Professor, 1905–12; Univ. of Berlin, Germany, Professor and Administrator, 1912–16; Univ. of Munich, Germany, Professor, 1916–25. *Other Awards:* Davy Medal, 1932; Gibbs Medal, 1933.

Selected Publications: *Untersuchungen über Chlorophyll.* Berlin: J. Springer, 1913 (with Arthur Stoll). *Untersuchungen über die Assimilation der Kohlensaure.* Berlin: J. Springer, 1918 (with Arthur Stoll). *Untersuchungen über Enzyme.* 2 volumes. Berlin: J. Springer, 1928.

For More Information See: *Aus Meinem Leyben.* Weinheim, Germany: Verlag Chemie, 1948. *Dictionary of Scientific Biography.* New York: Scribner's, 1976 (Volume 14), 411–12.

Commentary: The Nobel Award to Richard Willstäter was "for his research on plant pigments, especially chlorophyll" and recognized his contribution in elaborating the structure and function of chlorophyll. He was equally noted for his work on plant pigments, especially the study of the blue and red pigments of flowers, and for the studies of carbonic acid assimilation by plants, of enzymes, and of synthesis and structure of atropine and cocaine. His development of the techniques of partition chromatography changed the nature of research in organic chemistry. (J.H.)

1918

Haber, Fritz 17
Prize: Chemistry, 1918. *Born:* December 9, 1868; Breslau, Germany. *Death:* January 29, 1934; Basel, Switzerland. *Parents:* Father, Siegfried Haber; Mother, Paula Haber. *Nationality:* German. *Religion:* Jewish. *Education:* Technische Hochschule, Germany, Ph.D., 1891. *Spouse:* Clara Immewhar, married 1901, died 1914; Charlotta Nathan, married 1917, divorced 1927. *Children:* Herman, son; Ludwig, son; Eva, daughter. *Career:* Univ. of Jena, Germany, Researcher, 1892–94; Technische Hochschule, Karlsruhe, Germany, Professor, 1894–1911; Kaiser Wilhelm Institute, Dahlem, Germany, Director, 1911–33. *Other Awards:* Rumford Medal, Royal Society, 1932.

Selected Publications: *Experimentelle Untersuchungen über Zertsetzgung und Verbrennung von Kohlenwasserstoffen.* Munich: R. Oldenbourg, 1896. *Grundriss der Technischen Elektrochemie auf Theoretischer Grundlage.* Munich: R. Oldenbourg, 1898. *Thermodynamik Technisher Gasreaktionen Vorlesungen.* Munich: R. Oldenbourg, 1905. "Processes for the Preparation of Ammonia." U.S. Patent 971501, 1910 (with R. Le Rossignol). "Production of Synthetic Ammonia." U.S. Patent 1, 149, 510, 1915 (with K. Bosch and A. Mittasch).

For More Information See: *Dictionary of Scientific Biography.* New York: Scribner's, 1972 (Volume 5), 620–23. Goran, Morris. *The Story of Fritz Haber.* Norman, OK: Univ. of Oklahoma Press, 1967. Stoltzenberg, D. *Fritz Haber.* New York: VCH, 1994

Commentary: Fritz Haber received the Nobel Prize for his development of the Haber process, which combined nitrogen and hydrogen under pressure with an iron catalyst, producing ammonia, which could be used in production of fertilizer or explosives. His productive career also included a number of other pioneering contributions: the development of the glass pH electrode, the study of chemical reactions in a flame, the applications of chemicals in gas warfare, and his research into catalysis. (C.N.B.)

1920

Nernst, Walther Hermann 18
Prize: Chemistry, 1920. *Born:* June 25, 1864; Briesen, Germany. *Death:* November 18, 1941; Muskau, Germany. *Parents:* Father, Gustav Nernst; Mother, Ottilie Nerger Nernst. *Nationality:* German. *Religion:* Christian. *Education:* Univ. of Würzburg, Germany, Ph.D., 1887. *Spouse:* Emma Lohmeyer, married 1892. *Children:* 2 sons; 3 daughters. *Career:* Univ. of Leipzig, Germany, Researcher, 1887–90; Univ. of Göttingen, Germany, Professor, 1890–1904; Univ. of Berlin, Germany, 1904–33.

Selected Publications: *Theoretische Chemie vom Standpunkte der Avogadroschen Regel und der Thermodynamik.* Göttingen, Germany: F. Enke, 1893 (*Theoretical Chemistry from the Standpoint of Avogadro's Rule and Thermodynamics.* Tr. by Prof. Charles Skeele Palmer. New York: Macmillan and Co., 1895). *Einfuhrung in die Mathematische Behandlung der Naturwissenschaften-Kurzgefasstes Lehrbuch der Differential-und Integralrechnung mit Besonderer Berucksichtigung der Chemie.* Munich: Dr. E. Wolff, 1895. *Experimental and Theoretical Applications of Thermodynamics to Chemistry.* New York: C.

Scribner's Sons, 1907. *Die Theoretischen und Experimentellen Grundlagen des Neuen Warmesatzes.* Halle-Salle, Germany: W. Knapp, 1918. *Das Weltgebaude im Lichte der Neueren Forschung.* Berlin: Julius Springer, 1921.

For More Information See: Barkan, Diana K. *Walther Nernst and the Transition to Modern Physical Science.* Cambridge; New York: Cambridge University Press, 1999. Bodenstein, Max. "Walther Nernst." *Berichte der Deutschen Chemischen Gesellschaft* 75 (1942): 79–104. *Dictionary of Scientific Biography.* New York: Scribner's, 1978 (Volume 15), 432–53. Mendelsohn, Kurt. *The World of Walther Nernst. The Rise and Fall of German Science, 1864–1941.* New York: Macmillan, 1973.

Commentary: Walther Nernst received the Nobel Prize "in recognition of his work in thermochemistry." Nernst's early research was in electrochemistry. During this period, he formulated the theory of galvanic cells. This was followed by his famous heat theorem, also known as the Third Law of Thermodynamics, which became the basis for the solution of many industrial problems. He participated in the development of quantum theory, especially with his determination of specific heats at low temperature and vapor densities at high temperature. Nernst's studies of photochemistry led him to the atom chain reaction theory. His later research was in astrophysical theories. (L.K.)

1921

Soddy, Frederick　　　　　　　　　　　**19**
Prize: Chemistry, 1921. *Born:* September 2, 1877; Eastbourne, Sussex, England. *Death:* September 22, 1956; Brighton, England. *Parents:* Father, Benjamin Soddy; Mother, Hannah Green Soddy. *Nationality:* British. *Religion:* Calvinist. *Education:* Oxford Univ., England, B.A., 1898; Oxford Univ., England, M.A., 1910. *Spouse:* Winifred Moller Beilloy, married March 3, 1908. *Children:* 3 children. *Career:* McGill Univ., Montreal, Canada, Researcher, 1900–02; Univ. of London, England, Researcher, 1903–04; Univ. of Glasgow, Scotland, Professor, 1904–14; Aberdeen Univ., Scotland, Professor, 1914–19; Oxford Univ., England, Professor, 1919–36. *Other Awards:* Cannizzaro Prize, Academia dei Lincei, Rome, 1913.

Selected Publications: Radio-Activity: An Elementary Treatise from the Standpoint of the Disintegration Theory. London: The Electrician Printing and Publishing, 1904. *The Interpretation of Radium.* London: J. Murray, 1908. *The Chemistry of the Radio-Elements.* London: Longmans, Green, 1911–14. *Science and Life.* London: J. Murray, 1920.

For More Information See: Biographical Memoirs of the Fellows of the Royal Society. London: Royal Society, 1957 (Volume 3), 203–16. *Dictionary of Scientific Biography.* New York: Scribner's, 1981 (Volume 12), 504–09. Howorth, Muriel. *Pioneer Research on the Atom, Rutherford and Soddy in a Glorious Chapter of Science, the Life of Frederick Soddy.* London: New World Publications, 1958. Kaufman, George B. *Frederick Soddy: Early Pioneer in Radiochemistry.* London: Reidel, 1986. Merricks, Linda. *The World Made New: Frederick Soddy, Science, Politics, and Environment.* Oxford; New York: Oxford University Press, 1996.

Commentary: The award to Frederick Soddy was "for his contributions to our knowledge of the chemistry of radioactive substances, and his investigations into the origin and nature of isotopes." Soddy worked with Lord Rutherford on the theory of radioactive decay. His work on helium and other elements helped clarify the relations of elements in the periodic table. Throughout his career, but especially after his retirement in 1936, Soddy was also outspoken regarding social issues. He blamed scientists for their disregard for the social consequences of their work, including radioactivity. (F.K.)

1922

Aston, Francis William　　　　　　　　**20**
Prize: Chemistry, 1922. *Born:* September 1, 1877; Harborne, Birmingham, England. *Death:* November 20, 1945; Cambridge, England. *Parents:* Father, William Aston; Mother, Fanny Charlotte Hallis Aston. *Nationality:* British. *Religion:* Anglican. *Education:* Malvern College, England, B.S., 1893; Cambridge Univ., England, B.A., 1912. *Spouse:* None. *Children:* None. *Career:* British Brewery, Chemist, 1900–03; Univ. of Birmingham, England, Researcher, 1903–09; Cambridge Univ., England, Researcher, 1909–14; Royal Aircraft Establishment, England, Researcher, 1914–18; Cambridge Univ., England, Researcher, 1919–45. *Other Awards:* Mackenzie Davidson Medal, Roentgen Society, 1920; Hughes Medal, Royal Society, 1922; John Scott Medal, Franklin Institute, PA, 1923; Paterno Medal, 1923; Royal Medal, Royal Society, 1938; Duddell Medal, Physical Society, 1941.

Selected Publications: "Constitution of Atmospheric Neon." *Philosophical Magazine* 39 (1920): 449–55. "The Mass Spectra of Chemical Elements." *Philosophical Magazine* 40 (1920): 628–34. *Isotopes.* London: E. Arnold and Co., 1922. *Structural Units of the Material Universe.* London: Oxford Univ. Press, 1925. *Mass-Spectra and Isotopes.* London: Arnold, 1933. "Masses of Some Light Atoms Measured by Means of a New Mass Spectrometer." *Nature* 137 (1936): 357–58.

For More Information See: Dictionary of Scientific Biography. New York: Scribner's, 1970 (Volume 1), 320–22. *Obituary Notices of Fellows of the Royal Society.* Cambridge: Royal Society, 1945–48 (Volume 5), 635–51.

Commentary: Francis Aston's Nobel Prize was granted "for his discovery, by means of his mass spectrograph, of isotopes in a large number of non-radioactive elements, and for his enunciation of the whole-number rule." Beginning in the field of optical properties of organic compounds and in brewery chemistry, Aston moved on to study phenomena in gas discharge tubes and discovered the Aston Dark Space. His studies of positive rays led him to the identification of two isotopes of neon and eventually to the invention of the mass spectrograph. With this instrument, Aston identified 212 naturally occurring isotopes and stated the Whole Number Rule, which says that all isotopes have very nearly whole number masses relative to the defined mass of the oxygen isotope. (B.S.S.)

1923

Pregl, Fritz　　　　　　　　　　　　　**21**
Prize: Chemistry, 1923. *Born:* September 3, 1859; Laibach, Austria. *Death:* December 13, 1930; Graz, Austria. *Parents:* Father, Raimund Pregl; Mother, Friderike Schlacker

Pregl. *Nationality:* Austrian. *Religion:* Catholic. *Education:* Univ. of Graz, Austria, M.D., 1894. *Spouse:* None. *Children:* None. *Career:* Univ. of Graz, Austria, Professor, 1893–1907; Medico-Chemical Institute, Graz, Austria, Forensic Chemist, 1907–10; Univ. of Innsbruck, Austria, Professor, 1910–13; Univ. of Graz, Austria, Professor, 1913–30. *Other Awards:* Lieben Prize, Imperial Academy of Science, Vienna, Austria, 1914.

Selected Publications: Die Quantitative Organische Mikroanalyse (Quantitative Organic Microanalysis). Berlin: J. Springer, 1917.

For More Information See: Dictionary of Scientific Biography. New York: Scribner's, 1975 (Volume 11), 128–29. "Fritz Pregl." *Berichte der Deutschen Chemischen Gesellschaft* 64A (1931): 113.

Commentary: Fritz Pregl's Nobel Prize was "for his invention of the method of micro-analysis of organic substances," a result of his dissatisfaction with the lengthy, complicated, and inexact analytical methods for organic chemistry of his time. The use of very small quantities for analysis made possible the progress in many areas of biochemistry. (P.H.)

1925

Zsigmondy, Richard Adolf 22

Prize: Chemistry, 1925. *Born:* April 1, 1865; Vienna, Austria. *Death:* September 24, 1929; Göttingen, Germany. *Parents:* Father, Adolf Zsigmondy; Mother, Irma von Szakmary Zsigmondy. *Nationality:* Austrian; later German resident. *Religion:* Most probably Christian/Protestant. *Education:* Univ. of Munich, Germany, Ph.D., 1890. *Spouse:* Laura Louise Muller, married 1903. *Children:* Annemarie, daughter; Kathe, daughter. *Career:* Univ. of Berlin, Germany, Researcher, 1891–92; Technische Hochschule, Graz, Austria, Professor, 1893–97; Schott und Genossen, Jena, Germany, Researcher, 1897–1900; Personal Researcher, 1900–07; Univ. of Göttingen, Germany, Professor and Administrator, 1907–19.

Selected Publications: Zur Erkenntnis der Kolloide (Colloids and the Ultramicroscope). Jena, Germany: G. Fischer, 1905. *Kolloidchemie: ein Lehrbuch (The Chemistry of Colloids).* Leipzig, Germany: Otto Spamer, 1912. *Das Kolloid Gold (Colloidal Gold).* Leipzig, Germany: Akademische Verlagsgesellschaft, 1925 (with P.A. Thiessen).

For More Information See: Asimov's Biographical Encyclopedia of Science and Technology. Garden City, NY: Doubleday, 1982, 603–04. *Dictionary of Scientific Biography.* New York: Scribner's, 1976 (Volume 14), 632–34.

Commentary: Richard Zsigmondy won the Nobel Prize for his "elucidation of the heterogeneous nature of colloidal solutions." He started on this path early in his career, when he became interested in the colors produced by organic solutions of gold. Later, he worked in a related area, studying properties of colored glass. He formulated a variety of white glass, called milk glass, which became famous. These investigations led to work on colloids. With H.F.W. Siedentopf, Zsigmondy invented the ultramicroscope, a tool which enabled him to study the movement of colloidal particles, to determine their quantity in a particular solution, and to learn something of their shape, all of which was impossible before his discoveries. (P.H.)

1926

Svedberg, Theodor H. E. 23

Prize: Chemistry, 1926. *Born:* August 30, 1884; Flerang, Valbo, Sweden. *Death:* February 25, 1971; Orebro, Sweden. *Parents:* Father, Elias Svedberg; Mother, Augusta Alstermark Svedberg. *Nationality:* Swedish. *Religion:* Lutheran. *Education:* Univ. of Uppsala, Sweden, B.S., 1905; Univ. of Uppsala, Sweden, Ph.D., 1907. *Spouse:* Andrea Andreen, married 1909; Jane Frodi, married 1916; Ingrid Bloomquist, married 1938; Margit Hallen, married 1948. *Children:* 6 sons; 6 daughters. *Career:* Univ. of Uppsala, Sweden, Professor, 1912–49; Gustaf Werner Institute of Nuclear Chemistry, Sweden, Director, 1949–67. *Other Awards:* Scheele Award, Royal Swedish Academy of Sciences, 1907, 1916; Oscar II Reward, Univ. of Uppsala, Sweden, 1908; Edlund Award, Royal Swedish Academy of Sciences, 1909; Bergstedt Reward, Royal Society of Sciences, Sweden, 1910; Wallmark Award, Royal Swedish Academy of Sciences, 1910; Bjorken Prize, 1913, 1923, 1926; Berzelius Medal, 1941; Medal, City of Uppsala, Sweden, 1948; Franklin Medal, Franklin Institute, PA, 1949; Gustaf Adolf Medal, 1964.

Selected Publications: Die Methoden zur Herstellung Kolloider Losungen Anorganischer Stoffe. Dresden, Germany: T. Steinkopff, 1909. *Die Existenz der Molekule.* Leipzig, Germany: Academische Verlagsgesellschaft, 1912. *Colloid Chemistry.* New York: Chemical Catalog Company, 1924. *The Ultracentrifuge.* Oxford: Clarendon Press, 1940 (with K.O. Pedersen). "The Osmotic Balance." *Nature* 153 (1944): 523 (with I. Jullander). "The Cellulose Molecule. Physical-Chemical Studies." *Journal of Physical and Colloid Chemistry* 51 (1947): 1–18.

For More Information See: Biographical Memoirs of the Fellows of the Royal Society. Cambridge: Royal Society, 1972 (Volume 18), 595–627. *Dictionary of Scientific Biography.* New York: Scribner's, 1976 (Volume 13), 158–64.

Commentary: Theodor Svedberg was given the Nobel Prize for his lifelong involvement with colloidal chemistry in its various forms. His early research dealt with the preparation and study of colloidal suspensions of metals. Svedberg developed the ultracentrifuge so that he could use centrifugal force to separate colloidal particles from solution and used it to characterize and study protein molecules. It was later adapted to the study of polymers. With Tiselius, he also later developed the techniques of electrophoresis. (C.N.B.)

1927

Wieland, Heinrich Otto 24

Prize: Chemistry, 1927. *Born:* June 4, 1877; Pforzheim, Germany. *Death:* August 5, 1957; Starnberg, Germany. *Parents:* Father, Theodor W. Wieland; Mother, Elise Blum Wieland. *Nationality:* German. *Religion:* Christian. *Education:* Univ. of Munich, Germany, Ph.D., 1901. *Spouse:* Josephine Bartmann, married 1908. *Children:* Wolfgang, son; Theodor, son; Otto, son; Eva, daughter. *Career:* Univ. of Munich, Germany, Professor, 1901–13; Technische Hochschule, Munich, Germany, Professor, 1913–21; Univ. of Freiburg, Germany, Professor, 1921–25; Univ. of Munich, Germany, Professor, 1925–50. *Other Awards:* Lavoisier

Medal, France, 1938; Order Pour le Mérite, 1952; Otto Hahn Prize, 1955.

Selected Publications: Die Hydrazine. Stuttgart, Germany: F. Enke, 1913. "Die Chemie der Gallensauren." *Zeitschrift für Angewandte Chemie und Zentralblate für Technische Chemie* 42 (1929): 421–24. "Recent Researches on Biological Oxidation." *Journal of the Chemical Society* (1931): 1055–64. *On the Mechanism of Oxidation.* New Haven, CT: Yale Univ. Press, 1932.

For More Information See: "Autobiography." *Nachrichten aus Chemie und Technik* (1955): 222–23. *Dictionary of Scientific Biography.* New York: Scribner's, 1976 (Volume 14), 334–35. Lunde, Gulbrand. "The 1927 and 1928 Nobel Chemistry Prize Winners, Wieland and Windaus." *Journal of Chemical Education* 7 (1930): 763–71.

Commentary: Heinrich Wieland's Nobel Prize was awarded "for his investigations of the constitution of the bile acids and related substances." Wieland's earlier work dealt with organic nitrogen-containing compounds, moving from studies of nitrogen oxide reactions with olefins and aromatic compounds through studies of polymerization and synthesis to production and characterization of short-lived radicals. His later research was on the chemistry of natural substances such as morphine, strychnine, the alkaloids, crystalline cyclopeptides, and pterin compounds. Wieland's major contributions were the study of bile acids which led to the recognition of the carbon framework of the steroids and the study of oxidation processes in living cells. (R.J.)

1928

Windaus, Adolf Otto Reinhold   **25**

Prize: Chemistry, 1928. *Born:* December 25, 1876; Berlin, Germany. *Death:* June 9, 1959; Göttingen, Germany. *Parents:* Father, Adolf Windaus; Mother, Margarete Elster Windaus. *Nationality:* German. *Religion:* Most probably Christian. *Education:* Univ. of Berlin, Germany, medical license, 1897; Univ. of Freiburg, Germany, Dr. phil., 1900. *Spouse:* Elizabeth Resau, married 1915. *Children:* Gunter, son; Gustav, son; Margarete, daughter. *Career:* Univ. of Berlin, Germany, Researcher, 1900–01; Univ. of Freiburg, Germany, Professor, 1901–13; Innsbruck Univ., Austria, Professor, 1913–15; Univ. of Göttingen, Germany, Professor, 1915–44. *Other Awards:* Pasteur Medal, 1938; Goethe Medal, 1941; Grand Order of Merit, 1951; Order Pour le Mérite, 1952; Grand Order of Merit with Star, 1956.

Selected Publications: "Die Konstitution des Cholesterins." *Nachrichten Gesellschaft d. Wissenschaften.* Göttingen, Germany: 1919. "Anwendungen der Spannungstheorie." *Nachrichten Gesellschaft d. Wissenschaften.* Göttingen, Germany: 1921. "Ultra-violet Bestrahlung von Ergasterin." *Nachrichten Gesellschaft d. Wissenschaften, Göttingen* (1929): 45–59 (with others). "Chemistry of Irradiated Ergosterol." *Proceedings of the Royal Society* B 108 (1931): 568–75.

For More Information See: Butenandt, Adolf. *Proceedings of the Chemical Society* (1961): 131–38. *Dictionary of Scientific Biography.* New York: Scribner's, 1976 (Volume 14), 443–46.

Commentary: Adolf Windaus was cited by the Academy "for the services rendered through his research into the constitution of the sterols and their connection with the vitamins." Windaus, in accordance with his view that sterols were parents to other groups of natural substances, converted cholesterol to cholanic acid, proving the relationship of sterols to bile acids. He also showed that histidine, a protein component, was an imidazole alanine, and discovered histamine. His later research centered around the antirachitic and antineuritic vitamins, whose structural components he investigated; the stereochemistry of hydrogenated rings; and chemotherapy. (B.S.S.)

1929

Euler-Chelpin, Hans Karl August Simon von   **26**

Prize: Chemistry, 1929. *Born:* February 15, 1873; Augsburg, Germany. *Death:* November 6, 1964; Stockholm, Sweden. *Parents:* Father, Rigas von Euler-Chelpin; Mother, Gabrielle Furtner von Euler-Chelpin. *Nationality:* German; later Swedish citizen. *Religion:* Most probably Christian/Protestant. *Education:* Univ. of Munich, Germany, doctorate, 1895. *Spouse:* Astrid Cleve, married 1902, divorced 1912; Elizabeth Baroness Ugglas, married 1913. *Children:* 9 children. *Career:* Researcher, 1895–1906; Univ. of Stockholm, Sweden, Professor, 1906–41. *Other Awards:* Lindblom Prize, Germany, 1898; Grand Cross for Federal Services with Star, Germany, 1959.

Selected Publications: Chemie der Hefe und der Alkoholischen Gärung. Leipzig, Germany: Akademische Verlagsgesellschaft, 1915 (with Paul Lindner). *Chemie der Enzyme.* Munich: J.F. Bergman, 1920–27. *Biokatalysatoren.* Stuttgart, Germany: F. Enke, 1930. *Biochemie der Tumoren.* Stuttgart, Germany: Enke, 1942 (with Bol Skarzynski).

For More Information See: Dictionary of Scientific Biography. New York: Scribner's, 1971 (Volume 4), 485–86. "Hans von Euler-Chelpin." *Bayerische Akademie der Wissenschaften, Jahrbuch* (1965): 206–12.

Commentary: Hans von Euler-Chelpin won the Nobel (along with Arthur Harden) for his "investigation on the fermentation of sugar and fermentative enzymes." Euler-Chelpin's initial interest was in catalysis. He moved on to study the chemistry of plants, the chemistry of fungi, and the chemistry of enzymes. In addition, he played an important part in explaining the chemistry of vitamins and the biochemistry of tumors. His German patriotism was reflected in his voluntary service in both world wars. (L.C.B.)

Harden, Arthur, Sir   **27**

Prize: Chemistry, 1929. *Born:* October 12, 1865; Manchester, England. *Death:* June 17, 1940; Bourne End, England. *Parents:* Father, Albert Tyas Harden; Mother, Eliza MacAlister Harden. *Nationality:* British. *Religion:* Christian. *Education:* Univ. of Manchester, England, B.S., 1885; Univ. of Erlangen, Germany, Ph.D., 1888. *Spouse:* Georgina Sydney Bridge, married 1900. *Children:* None. *Career:* Univ. of Manchester, England, Researcher, 1888–97; British Institute of Preventive Medicine, Professor, 1897–1930. *Other Awards:* Knighthood, 1926; Davy Medal, Royal Society, 1935.

Selected Publications: An Elementary Course of Practical Organic Chemistry. London: Longmans, Green, 1897 (with F.C. Garrett). *Inorganic Chemistry for Advanced Students.* London: Macmillan and Co., 1899 (with H.E.

Roscoe). "The Alcoholic Ferment of Yeast Juice." *Proceedings of the Royal Society* 77B (1907): 405–20 (with W.J. Young). *Alcoholic Fermentations.* London: Longmans, Green, and Company, 1911.

For More Information See: Dictionary of Scientific Biography. New York: Scribner's, 1972 (Volume 6), 110–12. *Obituary Notices of Fellows of the Royal Society.* Cambridge: Royal Society, 1942–44 (Volume 4), 3–14. Smedley-Maclean, Ida. "Arthur Harden (1865–1940)." *Biochemical Journal* 35 (1941): 1071–81.

Commentary: Arthur Harden and Hans von Euler-Chelpin shared the Nobel Prize "for their investigations on the fermentation of sugar and fermentative enzymes." Harden's early research was on the effect of light on chlorine mixtures with carbon dioxide and on biological reactions such as bacterial action and alcoholic fermentation. His classic work was on sugar fermentation by yeast juice—work which added much to later studies of metabolic processes in life. He also studied vitamins. (L.K.)

1930

Fischer, Hans   28
Prize: Chemistry, 1930. *Born:* July 27, 1881; Hochstam-Main, Germany. *Death:* March 31, 1945; Munich, Germany. *Parents:* Father, Eugen Fischer; Mother, Anna Herdegen Fischer. *Nationality:* German. *Religion:* Most probably Christian/Protestant. *Education:* Univ. of Marburg, Germany, doctorate, 1904; Univ. of Munich, Germany, M.D., 1908. *Spouse:* Wiltrud Haufe, married 1935. *Children:* None. *Career:* Univ. of Berlin, Germany, Researcher, 1908–10; Univ. of Munich, Germany, Professor, 1910–16; Univ. of Innsbruck, Austria, Professor, 1916–18; Univ. of Vienna, Austria, Professor, 1918–21; Technische Hochschule, Germany, Professor, 1921–45. *Other Awards:* Liebig Memorial Medal, 1929; Davy Medal, Royal Society, 1937.

Selected Publications: Die Chemie des Pyrrols. 3 volumes. Leipzig, Germany: Akademische Verlagsgesellschaft, 1934–40 (with H. Orth). *Vorlesungen über Organische Chemie.* 2 volumes. Munich: P. Beleg, 1950.

For More Information See: Biographical Dictionary of Scientists. New York: John Wiley, 1982, 181. *Dictionary of Scientific Biography.* New York: Scribner's, 1978 (Volume 15), 157–58.

Commentary: Hans Fischer won the Nobel Prize "for his works on the structural composition of the coloring matter of blood, and of leaves, and for his synthesis of hemin." Later he worked out the structural formulas for both biliverdin and bilirubin, and in 1942 he synthesized biliverdin, with the synthesis of bilirubin following in 1944. He also worked out the complete structure of chlorophylls, demonstrating that chlorophylls were substituted porphins with an atom of magnesium at the center, thus paving the way for their synthesis by his pupils following his untimely death. (K.H.)

1931

Bergius, Friedrich Karl Rudolph   29
Prize: Chemistry, 1931. *Born:* October 11, 1884; Goldschmieden, Germany. *Death:* March 30, 1949; Buenos Aires, Argentina. *Parents:* Father, Heinrich Bergius; Mother, Marie Haase Bergius. *Nationality:* German. *Religion:* Protestant. *Education:* Univ. of Leipzig, Germany, Ph.D, 1907. *Spouse:* Ottilie Krazert, married (no date found). *Children:* 2 sons; 1 daughter. *Career:* Technical Univ., Hanover, Germany, Professor, 1909–14; Goldschmidt Company, Essen, Germany, Research Director, 1914–45; Argentine Ministry of Industries, Researcher, 1946–49. *Other Awards:* Liebig Medal, Germany.

Selected Publications: Die Anwendung Hoher Drucke bei Chemischen Vorgangen und Eine Nachbildung des Entstehungsprozesses der Steinkohle. Halle, Germany: W. Knapp, 1913. "Die Verflussigung der Kohle." *Zeitschrift des vereins Deutscher Ingenieure* 69 (1926). "Gewinnung von Alkohol und Glucose aus Holz." *Chemical Age (London)* 29 (1933): 481–83.

For More Information See: Dictionary of Scientific Biography. New York: Scribner's, 1970 (Volume 2), 3–4. Stranges, A. "Friedrich Bergius and the Rise of the German Synthetic Fuel Industry." *ISIS* 75 (December 1984): 643–67.

Commentary: Friedrich Bergius was awarded the Nobel for his "services regarding the invention and development of chemical high-pressure methods." Beginning with his work on the dissociation of calcium peroxide, he developed methods for laboratory work at high pressures and applied them to the liquefaction of coal. After successfully commercializing this process, he solved the problem of obtaining sugar from the cellulose in wood. (M.P.)

Bosch, Carl   30
Prize: Chemistry, 1931. *Born:* August 27, 1874; Cologne, Germany. *Death:* April 26, 1940; Heidelberg, Germany. *Parents:* Father, Carl Bosch; Mother, Paula Liebst Bosch. *Nationality:* German. *Religion:* Most probably Christian/Protestant. *Education:* Univ. of Leipzig, Germany, Ph.D., 1898. *Spouse:* Else Schibach, married 1902. *Children:* 1 daughter; 1 son. *Career:* Badische Anilin-und Sodafabrik, Germany, Researcher and Administrator, 1899–1925; I.G. Farben Industrie, Researcher and Administrator, 1925–40. *Other Awards:* Liebig Medal, Germany; Bunsen Medal, Germany; Siemens Ring, Germany; Exner Medal, Austria; Carl Lueg Medal, Germany.

Selected Publications: "Verfahren zur Herstellung von Ammoniak aus Seinen Elementen mit Hilfe von Katalysatoren." *Chemisches Zentralblatt* (1913): 195. "Stickstoff in Wihtschaft und Technik." *Naturwissenschaften* 8 (1920): 867–68. "Probleme Grosstechnischer Hydrierung-Verfahren." *Chemische Fabrik* 7 (1934): 1–10.

For More Information See: "Carl Bosch, 1874–1940." *Chemische Berichte* 90 (1957): 19–39. *Dictionary of Scientific Biography.* New York: Scribner's, 1970 (Volume 2), 323–24. Holdermann, Karl. *Im Banne der Chemie: Carl Bosch, Leben und Werk.* Düsseldorf: Econ-Verlag, 1954.

Commentary: Carl Bosch received the Nobel Prize for his "discovery and development of chemical high-pressure methods," most particularly for the work he did in fixing of nitrogen. Beginning with the production of barium cyanide, he succeeded in commercializing the high-pressure synthesis of ammonia. He then developed the methods for practical production of nitrogen fertilizers. (M.P.)

1932

Langmuir, Irving 31

Prize: Chemistry, 1932. *Born:* January 31, 1881; Brooklyn, NY. *Death:* August 16, 1957; Falmouth, MA. *Parents:* Father, Charles Langmuir; Mother, Sadie Comings Langmuir. *Nationality:* American. *Religion:* Protestant. *Education:* Columbia Univ., NY, B.S., 1903; Univ. of Göttingen, Germany, Ph.D., 1906. *Spouse:* Marion Mersereau, married April 27, 1912. *Children:* Kenneth, son; Barbara, daughter. *Career:* Stevens Institute of Technology, Hoboken, NJ, Professor, 1906–09; General Electric Research Laboratory, Schenectady, NY, Researcher and Administrator, 1909–50. *Other Awards:* Hughes Medal, Royal Society, 1918; Rumford Medal, 1920; Nichols Medal, American Chemical Society, 1920; Gibbs Medal, 1930; Franklin Medal, 1934; Faraday Medal, Chemical Society, 1938; Faraday Medal, Institute of Electrical Engineers, 1943; Medal for Merit, Univ. S. Army and Navy, 1948; John Carty Medal, National Academy of Sciences, 1950.

Selected Publications: The Collected Works of Irving Langmuir. New York: Pergamon Press, 1962.

For More Information See: Biographical Memoirs of the National Academy of Sciences. Washington, DC: National Academy of Sciences, 1974 (Volume 45), 215–47. *Dictionary of American Biography.* New York: Scribner's, 1980 (Supplement 6), 363–65. Reich, Leonard. "I. Langmuir and the Pursuit of Science and Technology in the Corporate Environment." *Technology and Culture* 24 (1983): 199–221. Rosenfeld, Albert. *The Quintessence of Irving Langmuir.* Volume 12 of *Collected Works.* New York: Pergamon Press, 1962.

Commentary: Irving Langmuir was cited by the Academy "for his discoveries and researches in the field of surface chemistry." Langmuir, in the course of pursuing theoretical studies in chemistry, physics, and engineering, managed to provide some of the major practical advances of the twentieth century. His achievements included the development of the gas-filled light bulb, the high-vacuum radio tube, the atomic hydrogen welding torch, and many other electronic devices. The general theory of absorbed films was another of his contributions, as was the initial work on production of artificial rainfall. (L.C.B.)

1934

Urey, Harold Clayton 32

Prize: Chemistry, 1934. *Born:* April 29, 1893; Walkerton, IN. *Death:* January 5, 1981; La Jolla, CA. *Parents:* Father, Samuel Clayton Urey; Mother, Cora Rebecca Reinoehl Urey. *Nationality:* American. *Religion:* Christian. *Education:* Univ. of Montana, B.S., 1917; Univ. of California, Ph.D., 1923. *Spouse:* Frieda Daum, married June 12, 1926. *Children:* Gertrude Elizabeth, daughter; Frieda Rebecca, daughter; Mary Alice, daughter; John Clayton, son. *Career:* Univ. of Copenhagen, Denmark, Researcher, 1923–24; Johns Hopkins Univ., MD, Professor, 1924–29; Columbia Univ., NY, Professor and Administrator, 1929–42; Manhattan Project, United States, Director of War Research, 1940–45; Univ. of Chicago, IL, Professor, 1945–58; Univ. of California, San Diego, Professor, 1958–70. *Other Awards:* Gibbs Medal, American Chemical Society, 1934; Davy Medal,

Royal Society, 1940; Franklin Medal, Franklin Institute, PA, 1943; Medal for Merit, 1946; Distinguished Service Award, Phi Beta Kappa, 1950; Cordoza Award, 1954; Priestley Award, Dickenson College, PA, 1955; Hamilton Award, Columbia Univ., NY, 1961; Remsen Award, 1963; Medal, Univ. of Paris, 1964; National Medal of Science for Astronomy, 1964; Achievement Award, American Academy, 1966; Gold Medal, Royal Astronomical Society, 1966; Leonard Medal, Meteoritical Society, 1969; Day Award, Geological Society of America, 1969; Chemical Pioneer Award, American Institute of Chemists, 1969; Linus Pauling Award, Oregon State Univ., 1970; Johann Kepler Medal, American Society for the Advancement of Science, 1971; Gold Medal, American Institute of Chemists, 1972; Priestley Medal, American Chemical Society, 1973; Exceptional Scientific Achievement Award, NASA, 1973; Knight of Malta, 1973; Headliner Award, San Diego Press Club, 1974; Goldschmidt Medal, Geochemical Society, 1975.

Selected Publications: Atoms, Molecules and Quanta. New York: McGraw-Hill, 1930 (with A.E. Ruark). *The Planets: Their Origin and Development.* New Haven, CT: Yale Univ. Press, 1952. *Production of Heavy Water.* New York: McGraw-Hill, 1955 (with others). *Reprints.* La Jolla, CA: Univ. of California, San Diego, 1990. *Some Cosmochemical Problems.* University Park, PA: Pennsylvania State Univ. Press, 1963.

For More Information See: Current Biography Yearbook. New York: H.W. Wilson, 1960, 441–42. *New York Times* (January 7, 1981): 1+.

Commentary: Harold Clayton Urey was awarded the Nobel Prize for Chemistry in 1934 "for his discovery of heavy hydrogen" known as deuterium, a key factor in the development of the atomic bomb. He was also known for his research on thermodynamic properties of gases, atomic structure, absorption spectra and structure of molecules, properties and separation of isotopes, exchange reactions, measurement of paleotemperature, and chemical problems relative to the origin of the earth, meteorites, the moon, and the solar system. (D.R.)

1935

Joliot-Curie, Frédéric 33

Prize: Chemistry, 1935. *Born:* March 19, 1900; Paris, France. *Death:* August 14, 1958; Paris, France. *Parents:* Father, Henri Joliot; Mother, Émilie Roederer Joliot. *Nationality:* French. *Religion:* Atheist; from Protestant background. *Education:* École de Physique et de Chimie Industrielle, France, engineering degree, 1923; École de Physique et de Chimie Industrielle, France, licencié-és science, 1927; Univ. of Paris, France, docteur-és-sciences, 1930. *Spouse:* Irène Curie, married October 9, 1926. *Children:* Héléne, daughter; Pierre, son. *Career:* Radium Institute, Paris, France, Researcher, 1925–31; Caisse Nationale des Sciences, Researcher, 1931–37; Collège de France, Professor, 1937–44; Centre National de la Recherche Scientifiques, Director, 1944–46; Atomic Energy Commission, France, Commissioner, 1946–50; Univ. of Paris, France, Professor and Researcher, 1956–58. *Other Awards:* Henri Wilde Prize, France, 1933; Marquet Prize, France, 1934; Barnard Gold Medal, Columbia Univ., 1940.

Selected Publications: Oeuvres Scientifiques Completes. Paris: Presses Universitaires de France, 1961.

For More Information See: Current Biography Yearbook. New York: H.W. Wilson, 1946, 294–96. *Dictionary of Scientific Biography.* New York: Scribner's, 1973 (Volume VII), 151–57. Goldsmith, Maurice. *Frédéric Joliot-Curie, A Biography.* London: Laurence and Wishart, 1976. Pinault, Michel. *Frédéric Joliot-Curie.* Paris: O. Jacob, 2000.

Commentary: This joint award to Frédéric and Irène Joliot-Curie (the fifth Nobel for the Curie extended family) was made "for their jointly performed synthesis of the new radioactive elements," referring to experiments in which alpha-particle bombardment produced radioactive phosphorus from aluminum, radioactive nitrogen from boron, and radioactive silicon from magnesium. The team had previously produced neutrons by bombardment of beryllium. Frédéric's earlier work was on the electrochemical properties of radioactive elements. He was later involved with producing high-energy particles, with the theory of nuclear fission, and with the development of France's Atomic Energy Commission, on which he served as high commissioner. In his nonscientific endeavors, he became a hero of the underground resistance during the Second World War, an active member of the French Communist Party, and a prime mover in the World Peace Movement. (L.B.W.)

Joliot-Curie, Irène 34

Prize: Chemistry, 1935. *Born:* September 12, 1897; Paris, France. *Death:* March 17, 1956; Paris, France. *Parents:* Father, Pierre Curie; Mother, Marie Sklodowska Curie. *Nationality:* French. *Religion:* Atheist; from Catholic (mother) and Protestant (father) background. *Education:* Collège Sévigné, France, baccalauréat, 1914; Univ. of Paris, France, licentiate, 1920; Univ. of Paris, France, Sc.D., 1925. *Spouse:* Frédéric Joliot, married October 9, 1926. *Children:* Héléne, daughter; Pierre, son. *Career:* Curie Laboratory, Paris, France, Researcher, 1921–35; Caisse Nationale de la Recherche, Researcher, 1935–36; Univ. of Paris and Radium Institute, France, Researcher, 1937–56. *Other Awards:* Henri Wilde Prize, France, 1933; Marquet Prize, France, 1934; Barnard Gold Medal, Columbia Univ., NY, 1940.

Selected Publications: Oeuvres Scientifiques Complètes. Paris: Presses Universitaires de France, 1961.

For More Information See: Current Biography Yearbook. New York: H.W. Wilson, 1940, 435–36. McKown, Robin. *She Lived for Science: Irene Joliot-Curie.* New York: Messner, 1961. Vare, Ethlie Ann. *Mothers of Invention.* New York: Morrow, 1988, 143–48.

Commentary: The joint award of the Nobel Prize to Irène and Frédéric Joliot-Curie was made "for their jointly performed synthesis of the new radioactive elements," referring to the experiments in which alpha-particle bombardment produced radioactive phosphorus from aluminum, radioactive nitrogen from boron, and radioactive silicon from magnesium. The team had previously produced neutrons by bombardment of beryllium. Irene later demonstrated the splitting of uranium. Together, the Joliot-Curies were also instrumental in developing atomic energy in France, and were active in the underground of the Second World War, in Communist activities, and in the World Peace Movement. (L.B.W.)

1936

Debye, Peter Josephus Wilhelmus 35

Prize: Chemistry, 1936. *Born:* March 24, 1884; Maastricht, Netherlands. *Death:* November 2, 1966; Ithaca, NY. *Parents:* Father, Wilhelmus Debye; Mother, Maria Reumkens Debye. *Nationality:* Dutch; later American citizen. *Religion:* Catholic. *Education:* Aachen Institute of Technology, Germany, electrical technology degree, 1905; Univ. of Munich, Germany, Ph.D., 1908. *Spouse:* Mathilde Alberer, married April 10, 1913. *Children:* Peter Paul Rupprecht, son; Mathilde Maria, daughter. *Career:* Aachen Technological Institute, Germany, Researcher, 1905–06; Univ. of Munich, Germany, Researcher, 1906–10; Univ. of Zürich, Switzerland, Professor, 1910–12; Univ. of Utrecht, Netherlands, Professor, 1912–14; Univ. of Göttingen, Germany, Professor, 1914–20; Univ. of Zürich, Switzerland, Professor, 1920–27; Univ. of Leipzig, Germany, Professor, 1927–34; Univ. of Berlin, Germany, Professor, 1934–39; Cornell Univ., NY, Professor, 1939–52. *Other Awards:* Rumford Medal, Royal Society; Franklin Medal, Philadelphia, PA; Faraday Medal; Lorentz Medal, Royal Netherlands Academy; Willard Gibbs Medal, 1949; Max Planck Medal, West German Physical Society, 1950; Kendall Award, 1957; Nichols Medal, 1961; Priestley Medal, American Chemical Society, 1963; American Physics Society High-Polymer Physics Prize, Ford Motor Co., 1965; Madison Marshall Award, American Chemical Society, 1965; National Medal of Science, 1965.

Selected Publications: The Dipole Moment and Chemical Structure. London: Blakiston, 1932. "Energy Absorption in Dielectrics with Polar Molecules." *Faraday Society* 30 (1934): 679–84. *Collected Papers.* New York: Interscience, 1954.

For More Information See: Biographical Memoirs of National Academy of Sciences. Washington, DC: National Academy of Sciences, 1975 (Volume 46), 23–68. Davies, Mansel. *Journal of Chemical Education* 45 (1968): 467–73. *Dictionary of Scientific Biography.* New York: Scribner's, 1971 (Volume 3), 617–21.

Commentary: The Academy honored Peter Debye "for his contributions to our knowledge of molecular structure through his investigations on dipole moments and on the diffraction of x-rays and electrons in gases." By utilizing techniques of measuring dipole moments and of electron and x-ray diffraction, Debye established invaluable tools for structure determination. Debye also made significant contributions in the areas of specific heats of bodies at various temperatures, magnetic cooling, crystal structure determination, the theory of solutions, and polymer size determinations. (B.S.S.)

1937

Haworth, Walter Norman, Sir 36

Prize: Chemistry, 1937. *Born:* March 19, 1883; Chorley, Lancashire, England. *Death:* March 19, 1950; Birmingham, England. *Parents:* Father, Thomas Haworth; Mother, Hannah Haworth. *Nationality:* British. *Religion:* Christian. *Education:* Univ. of Manchester, England, baccalaureate, 1906; Univ. of Göttingen, Germany, Ph.D., 1910; Univ. of Manchester, England, D.Sc., 1911. *Spouse:* Violet Chilton Dobbie, married 1922. *Children:* James, son; David, son. *Career:*

Univ. of London, England, Professor, 1911–12; Univ. of St. Andrews, Scotland, Professor, 1912–20; Univ. of Durham, England, Professor, 1920–25; Univ. of Birmingham, England, Professor and Administrator, 1925–48. *Other Awards:* Longstaff Medal, 1933; Davy Medal, 1934; Royal Medal, 1942; Knighthood, 1947.

Selected Publications: The Constitution of Sugars. London: E. Arnold & Company, 1929. "The Constitution of Some Carbohydrates." *Chemische Berichte* (1932): 43–65. "Synthesis of Ascorbic Acid." *Chemistry and Industry* (1933): 2790–2806 (with E.L. Hirst). "Starch." *Journal of the Chemical Society* (1946): 543–49. "The Structure, Function and Synthesis of Polysaccharides." *Proceedings of the Royal Society* (1946): 1–9.

For More Information See: Dictionary of Scientific Biography. New York: Scribner's, 1972 (Volume 6), 184–85. *Obituary Notices of Fellows of the Royal Society.* Cambridge: Royal Society, 1950–51 (Volume 7), 373–404. "Walter Norman Haworth." *Journal of the Chemical Society* (1951): 2790–2806.

Commentary: Walter Haworth received the Nobel Prize "for his researches into the constitution of carbohydrates and vitamin C." His elaborations of the structure of the simple sugars, his studies in cellulose chemistry, and his investigations of vitamin C were all pioneer landmark efforts. In addition, he took part in the chemical work of the atomic energy project in World War II. (B.E.)

Karrer, Paul 37

Prize: Chemistry, 1937. *Born:* April 21, 1889; Moscow, Russia. *Death:* June 18, 1971; Zürich, Switzerland. *Parents:* Father, Paul Karrer; Mother, Julie Lerch Karrer. *Nationality:* Russian; later Swiss citizen. *Religion:* Protestant. *Education:* Univ. of Zürich, Switzerland, doctorate, 1911. *Spouse:* Helene Frolich, married April 14, 1914. *Children:* Jurg, son; Heinz, son. *Career:* Univ. of Zürich, Switzerland, Researcher, 1911–12; Georg Speyer Haus, Frankfurt-am-Main, Germany, Researcher and Administrator, 1912–18; Univ. of Zürich, Switzerland, Professor and Administrator, 1918–59. *Other Awards:* Marcel Benoist Prize, Switzerland, 1923; Cannizzaro Prize, Italy, 1935; Officier de la Legion d'Honneur, 1954.

Selected Publications: Einführung in die Chemie der Polymeren Kohlehydrate, ein Grundiss der Chemie der Starke, des Glykogen, der Zellulose und Anderer Polysaccharide. Leipzig, Germany: Akademische Verlagsgesellschaft, 1925. *Lehrbuch der Organischen Chemie.* Leipzig, Germany: Thieme, 1928. *Die Carotenoids.* Basel, Switzerland: Birkhäuser, 1948 (with E. Jucker).

For More Information See: Biographical Memoirs of the Fellows of the Royal Society. London: Royal Society, 1978 (Volume 24), 244–321. *Dictionary of Scientific Biography.* New York: Scribner's, 1978 (Volume 15), 257–58.

Commentary: Paul Karrer was awarded the Nobel prize "for his researches into the constitution of carotenoids, flavins and vitamins A and B2." He synthesized vitamin E; isolated vitamin K1, determined its structure, and synthesized it; contributed greatly to an understanding of the structure and function of nicotin-amide-adenine dinucleotide (NAD); worked on many of the carotenoids; carried out the total synthesis of carotene hydrocarbons; synthesized and determined the structure of toxiferine and related alkaloids;

and synthesized canthaxanthin from B-carotene. In addition, he also founded two important foundations for the advancement of science: the Fritz Hoffman-La Roche Foundation for the advancement of interdisciplinary study groups in Switzerland and the Foundation for Scholarships in Chemistry. (K.H.)

1938

Kuhn, Richard 38

Prize: Chemistry, 1938. *Born:* December 3, 1900; Vienna, Austria. *Death:* August 1, 1967; Heidelberg, Germany. *Parents:* Father, Hofrat Richard Clemens Kuhn; Mother, Angelika Rodler Kuhn. *Nationality:* Austrian; later German citizen. *Religion:* Most probably Christian/Protestant. *Education:* Univ. of Munich, Germany, Ph.D., 1922. *Spouse:* Daisy Hartman, married 1928. *Children:* 2 sons; 4 daughters. *Career:* Univ. of Munich, Germany, Professor, 1925–26; Eidgenossische Technische Hochschule, Zürich, Switzerland, Professor, 1926–28; Univ. of Heidelberg, Germany, Professor, 1928–67. *Other Awards:* Pour le Mérite für Wissenschaften und Kunste, 1958.

Selected Publications: "Materials of Living Nature." *Naturwissenschaften* 25 (1937): 225–31. "Fertilizing (Gamones) and Sex-Determining Substances (Termones) in Plants and Animals." *Angewandte Chemie* 53 (1940): 1–6. "Carotene Dyes." German Patent 719845 (March 26, 1942) (with H. Bielig). "Vitamins and Medicines." *Die Chemie* 55 (1942): 1–6.

For More Information See: Biographical Encyclopedia of Scientists. New York: Facts on File, 1981, 455. *Dictionary of Scientific Biography.* New York: Scribner's, 1973 (Volume 7), 517–18. Oberkofler, G. *Richard Kuhn.* Innsbruck, Austria: Das Archiv, 1992.

Commentary: Richard Kuhn was awarded the Nobel "for his work on carotenoids and vitamins." He began his career working on enzyme specificity in carbohydrate metabolism and moved on to study optical stereochemistry. Among the many areas in which he worked were additions to ethylene bonds, the diphenyls, the diphenylpolyenes, colored hydrocarbons, crocetin, bixin, carotene, water-soluble vitamins, and factors effective against infection. (M.F.)

1939

Butenandt, Adolf Friedrick Johann 39

Prize: Chemistry, 1939. *Born:* March 24, 1903; Bremerhaven-Lehe, Germany. *Death:* January 18, 1995; Munich, Germany. *Parents:* Father, Otto Louis Max Butenandt; Mother, Wilhelmina Thomfohrde Butenandt. *Nationality:* German. *Religion:* Most probably Christian/Protestant. *Education:* Univ. of Göttingen, Germany, Ph.D., 1927. *Spouse:* Erika von Ziegner, married February 28, 1931. *Children:* Ina, daughter; Otfrid, son; Heide, daughter; Eckart, son; Anke, daughter; Imme, daughter; Maike, daughter. *Career:* Schering Corporation, Germany, Researcher, 1927–31; Univ. of Göttingen, Germany, Professor, 1931–33; Technische Hochschule, Danzig, Germany, Professor, 1933–36; Kaiser-Wilhelm Institute for Biochemistry, Berlin, Germany, Director, 1936–45; Max-Planck Institute for Biochemistry, Germany, Professor and Administrator, 1945–85. *Other Awards:* Von Harnack Medal, 1973, 1983.

Selected Publications: Untersuchungen über das Weibliche Sexualhormon (Follikel-oder Brunsthormon). Berlin: Weidmannsche Buchhandlung, 1931. *Die Biologische Chemie im Dienste der Volkagesundheit.* Berlin: W. de Gruyter, 1941. *Über die Biochemische Analyse einer Gen-Wirkkette der Pigmentbildung bei Insekten.* Debrecen, Hungary: Tisza Istvan-Tudomanyegyetemi Nyomda, 1943. *Zur Feinstruktur des Tabakmosaik-Virus.* Berlin: Akademie der Wissenschaften, W. de Gruyter, 1944.

For More Information See: "Adolf Butenandt." *Journal of Chemical Education* 26 (February 1949): 91. *Asimov's Biographical Encyclopedia of Science and Technology.* Garden City, NY: Doubleday, 1982, 792. Karlson, O. *Adolf Butenandt.* Stuttgart, Germany: Wissenschaftliche Verlagsgesselschaft, 1990.

Commentary: The award to Adolf Butenandt was "for his work on sex hormones." He was forced by the German government to refuse the prize but was able to accept the honor later in 1949. In 1929, Butenandt isolated estrone, one of the hormones responsible for female sexual development and functioning; in 1931, androsterone, a male sex hormone; and in 1934, the hormone progesterone, which plays an important part in the female reproductive cycle. He also studied the interrelationships of sex hormones and their possible carcinogenic properties. (C.D.)

Ruzicka, Leopold Stephen 40

Prize: Chemistry, 1939. *Born:* September 13, 1887; Vukovar, Yugoslavia. *Death:* September 26, 1976; Zürich, Switzerland. *Parents:* Father, Stjepan Ruzicka; Mother, Ljubica Sever Ruzicka. *Nationality:* Yugoslavian; later Swiss citizen. *Religion:* Christian. *Education:* Technische Hochschule, Germany, Dr. Ing., 1910. *Spouse:* Anna Hausman, married 1912, divorced 1950; Gertrud Frei Acklin, married July 1951. *Children:* None. *Career:* Federal Institute of Technology, Zürich, Switzerland, Professor, 1923–26; Univ. of Utrecht, Netherlands, Professor, 1926–29; Federal Institute of Technology, Zürich, Switzerland, Professor, 1929–57.

Selected Publications: Über den Bau der Organischen Materie; Antrittarede Gehalten am 10. Utrecht, Netherlands: Aula der Reichsuniversitat, 1926. *Über Konstitution und Zusammenhange in der Sesquiterpenreihe.* Berlin: Gebruder Borntraeger, 1928. *Conferenze di Chimica Organica, Tenute Nell'Instituto Chimico dell'Universita di Roma.* Rome: Academia Nazionale dei Lincei, 1951. "The Isoprene Rule and the Biogenesis of Terpenic Compounds." *Experimentia* 9 (1953): 357–65.

For More Information See: Asimov's Biographical Encyclopedia of Science and Technology. Garden City, NY: Doubleday, 1982, 712. *Biographical Memoirs of the Fellows of the Royal Society.* London: Royal Society, 1980 (Volume 26), 411–501. "Dr. Leopold Ruzicka Dies in Switzerland at Age 89; Won Nobel in Chemistry." *The New York Times* (September 27, 1976): 34.

Commentary: The award to Leopold Ruzicka was "for his work on polymethylenes and higher terpenes." In 1916, he began researching natural odoriferous compounds, which culminated in the discovery that the molecules of muskone and civetone, important to the perfume industry, contain rings of 15 and 17 carbon atoms respectively. Prior to his work, rings with more than eight atoms were thought to be unstable, if they did exist. By 1933/34, Ruzicka was able to

offer the first complete proof of the constitution of a sex hormone and accomplish the first artificial production of a sex hormone. His patent for the preparation of testosterone from cholesterol earned him a fortune as well as international acclaim. (C.D.)

1943

Hevesy, George Charles von (Hevesy, George Charles De) 41

Prize: Chemistry, 1943. *Born:* August 1, 1885; Budapest, Hungary. *Death:* July 5, 1966; Freiburg, Germany. *Parents:* Father, Louis de Hevesy; Mother, Eugenie Schosberger de Hevesy. *Nationality:* Hungarian; later German resident, Danish resident, and Swedish citizen. *Religion:* Jewish. *Education:* Univ. of Freiburg, Germany, Ph.D., 1908. *Spouse:* Pia Riis, married September 26, 1924. *Children:* George Louis, son; Jenny, daughter; Ingrid, daughter; Pia, daughter. *Career:* Technical High School, Zürich, Switzerland, Teacher, 1908–10; Austrian-Hungarian Government Worker, 1910–12; Univ. of Budapest, Hungary, Professor, 1912–20; Institute of Theoretical Physics, Copenhagen, Denmark, Researcher, 1920–26; Univ. of Freiburg, Germany, Professor, 1926–34; Institute of Theoretical Physics, Copenhagen, Denmark, Researcher, 1934–43; Univ. of Stockholm, Sweden, Professor, 1943–55. *Other Awards:* Canizzaro Prize, Academy of Sciences, Rome, 1929; Copley Medal, 1949; Faraday Medal, 1950; Bailey Medal, 1951; Sylvanus Thompson Medal, 1955; Atoms for Peace Award, United Nations, 1959; Niels Bohr Medal, 1961; Rosenberger Medal, Univ. of Chicago, 1961.

Selected Publications: Adventures in Radioisotope Research: The Collected Papers of George Hevesy. New York: Pergamon Press, 1962.

For More Information See: Current Biography Yearbook. New York: H.W. Wilson, 1959, 186–88. *Dictionary of Scientific Biography.* New York: Scribner's, 1972 (Volume 6), 365–67. Levi, Hilde. *George de Hevesy.* Stockholm: Hilger, 1985.

Commentary: George von Hevesy received the Nobel Prize "for his work on the use of isotopes as tracer elements in researches on chemical processes." Early in his career he attempted unsuccessfully to separate radium-D from lead and instead used the radioactivity of the radium-D to follow the reactions of lead, introducing the concept of radioactive labeling and tracing. Hevesy was instrumental later in achieving physical separations and applying tracer techniques in biology. He also was the codiscoverer of the element hafnium. (M.F.)

1944

Hahn, Otto 42

Prize: Chemistry, 1944. *Born:* March 8, 1879; Frankfurt-am-Main, Germany. *Death:* July 28, 1968; Göttingen, Germany. *Parents:* Father, Heinrich Hahn; Mother, Charlotte Stutzmann Giese Hahn. *Nationality:* German. *Religion:* Protestant. *Education:* Univ. of Marburg, Germany, Ph.D., 1901. *Spouse:* Edith Junghans, married March 22, 1913. *Children:* Hanno, son. *Career:* Univ. of Berlin, Germany, Professor, 1907–33; Kaiser Wilhelm Institute of Chemistry, Germany, Professor, 1928–45; Max Planck Society for the Advancement of Science, Germany, President, 1946–60.

Other Awards: Grand Cross of the Order of Merit, Germany, 1959; Fermi Award, United States Atomic Energy Commission, 1966.

Selected Publications: Applied Radiochemistry. Ithaca, NY: Cornell Univ. Press, 1936. *New Atoms, Progress and Some Memories: A Collection of Papers.* New York: Elsevier, 1950.

For More Information See: Dictionary of Scientific Biography. New York: Scribner's, 1972 (Volume 6), 14–17. Hoffman, K. *Schuld und Verantwortung.* Berlin, Germany: Springer-Verlag, 1993. *My Life: The Autobiography of a Scientist* (tr. *Mein Leben*). New York: Herder and Herder, 1970. *Otto Hahn: A Scientific Autobiography.* New York: Scribner's, 1966.

Commentary: Otto Hahn received the Nobel "for his discovery of the fission of heavy nuclei." Hahn's early discoveries included the identification of radiothorium and protactinium, research which laid the foundation for the new field of radiochemistry. His interest in the effects of thermal neutrons on uranium and thorium led to the recognition of the theory of fission. Hahn was exceedingly concerned over the application of his discoveries in atomic energy and was responsible for the "Mainau Declaration" in 1955, which warned of the dangers in misusing atomic energy. In 1957, he was one of 18 eminent German scientists who publicly protested any German acquisition of nuclear weapons. (J.L.)

1945

Virtanen, Arturi Ilmari   **43**
Prize: Chemistry, 1945. *Born:* January 15, 1895; Helsinki, Finland. *Death:* November 11, 1973; Helsinki, Finland. *Parents:* Father, Kaarlo Virtanen; Mother, Serafüna Isotalo Virtanen. *Nationality:* Finnish. *Religion:* Most probably Christian. *Education:* Univ. of Helsinki, Finland, M.Sc., 1916; Univ. of Helsinki, Finland, Ph.D., 1919. *Spouse:* Lilja Moisio, married 1920. *Children:* Kaarlo, son; Arturi, son. *Career:* Central Laboratory of Industry, Finland, Researcher, 1916–17; Government Butter and Cheese Control Station, Finland, Researcher, 1919; Finnish Cooperative Dairies Association, Researcher, 1919–24; Univ. of Helsinki, Finland, Professor, 1924–48; Academy of Finland, President, 1948–63. *Other Awards:* Friesland Prize, Netherlands, 1967; Atwater Prize, 1968; Siegfried Thannhauser Medal, 1969; Gold Medal, Germany, 1971; Gold Medal and Prize, Spain, 1972; Uovo d'oro, Italy, 1973.

Selected Publications: Cattle, Fodder and Human Nutrition: With Special Reference to Biological Nitrogen Fixation. Cambridge: Cambridge Univ. Press, 1938. *Kirjaka-uppojen Liiketalous ja Kannattavuus, 1952.* Helsinki: Liiketalous tieteellinen Tutkimuslaitos, 1954. *On Nitrogen Metabolism in Milking Cows.* Helsinki: Suomalainen Tiedeakatemia, 1968. *Fundamental Studies of Organic Compounds in Plants, Especially Vegetables and Fodder Plants, and Their Enzymic and Chemical Splitting Products Which Often Have Physiological Effects, in Order to Improve the Utilization Potential for Their Products, Final Report.* Helsinki: Biochemical Research Institute, 1969.

For More Information See: Biographical Encyclopedia of Scientists. New York: Facts on File, 1981, 812. *Dictionary of Scientific Biography.* New York: Scribner's, 1976 (Volume 14), 454–56. Miettinen, Jormak, Tor-Magnus Enari,

Marjatta Kivimaki-Majanen. *A.I. Virtanen Työtoverien Silmin.* Helsinki: Kemian Kustannus, 1994.

Commentary: Arturi Virtanen received the Nobel Prize for "his researches and inventions in agricultural and nutritive chemistry, especially for his method of fodder preservation." He studied the process of fermentation that occurs in stored green fodder and determined that acidifying the fodder to a pH level slightly under 4 would halt the deterioration of the forage. Tests showed that the acidified fodder not only kept well but also continued to be satisfactory in taste and nutrition. This discovery was particularly important for countries with long winters, as it ensured a constant supply of feed regardless of the time of harvest. Virtanen did additional research on leguminous, nitrogen-fixing plants; the chemical composition of higher plants; and on the methods by which plants synthesize vitamins. (L.D.)

1946

Northrop, John Howard   **44**
Prize: Chemistry, 1946. *Born:* July 5, 1891; Yonkers, NY. *Death:* May 27, 1987; Wickenberg, AZ. *Parents:* Father, John I. Northrop; Mother, Alice Belle Rich Northrop. *Nationality:* American. *Religion:* Protestant. *Education:* Columbia Univ., NY, B.S., 1912; Columbia Univ., NY, M.A., 1913; Columbia Univ., NY, Ph.D., 1915. *Spouse:* Louise Walker, married June 26, 1917. *Children:* Alice, daughter; John, son. *Career:* Rockefeller Institute, NY, Professor, 1916–62; Univ. of California, Berkeley, Professor, 1949–62. *Other Awards:* Stevens Prize, Columbia Univ., 1931; Daniel Giraud Elliot Medal, National Academy of Sciences, 1939; Certificate of Merit, United States, 1948; Alexander Hamilton Award, Columbia Univ., 1961.

Selected Publications: "Crystalline Pepsin." *Science* 69 (1929): 580. "Crystalline Pepsin.I. Isolation and Tests of Purity." *Journal of General Physiology* 13 (1930): 739–66. "The Isolation of Crystalline Pepsin and Trypsin." *Scientific Monthly* 35 (1932): 333–40. "Concentration and Partial Purification of Bacteriophage." *Science* 84 (1936): 90–91. *Crystalline Enzymes.* New York: Columbia Univ. Press, 1939 (with others).

For More Information See: Biographical Encyclopedia of Scientists. New York: Facts on File, 1981, 599–600. *Current Biography Yearbook.* New York: H.W. Wilson, 1947, 472–74. *The Excitement and Fascination of Science.* Palo Alto, CA: Annual Reviews, Inc., Vol. 1, 335–44. *New York Times Biographical Service* (July 16, 1987): 693.

Commentary: John Northrop shared the Nobel Prize for his contributions to the "preparation of enzymes and virus proteins in a pure form." His major efforts dealt with the crystallization of a number of enzymes and the proof of their protein nature. The techniques he developed were used in his laboratory to isolate pepsin, trypsin, chymotripsin, ribonuclease, and deoxyribonuclease. He worked later with isolation and characterization of a bacterial virus and also studied temperature effects on life span. (J.B.)

Stanley, Wendell Meredith   **45**
Prize: Chemistry, 1946. *Born:* August 16, 1904; Ridgeville, IN. *Death:* June 15, 1971; Salamanca, Spain. *Parents:* Father, James G. Stanley; Mother, Claire Plessinger Stanley. *Nationality:* American. *Religion:* Most probably Christian.

Education: Earlham College, IN, B.S., 1926; Univ. of Illinois, M.A., 1927; Univ. of Illinois, Ph.D., 1929. *Spouse:* Marian Staples Jay, married June 15, 1929. *Children:* Wendell Meredith, Jr., son; Marjorie Jean, daughter; Dorothy Claire, daughter; Janet Elizabeth, daughter. *Career:* Univ. of Illinois, Professor, 1929–30; Univ. of Munich, Germany, Researcher, 1930–31; Rockefeller Institute, NY, Professor, 1931–48; Univ. of California, Professor and Administrator, 1948–71. *Other Awards:* American Association for the Advancement of Science Prize, 1937; Isaac Adler Award, Harvard Univ., MA, 1938; Rosenburger Medal, Univ. of Chicago, IL, 1938; Scott Award, Philadelphia, PA, 1938; Gold Medal, American Institute of New York, 1941; Copernican Citation, 1943; Nichols Medal, American Chemical Society, 1946; Gibbs Medal, American Chemical Society, 1947; Franklin Medal, Franklin Institute, Philadelphia, PA, 1948; Certificate of Merit, United States, 1948; Modern Medicine Award, 1958; Distinguished Service Medal, American Cancer Society, 1963; Scientific Achievement Award, American Medical Association, 1966.

Selected Publications: "Chemical Studies on the Virus of Tobacco Mosaic. VI. The Isolation from Diseased Turkish Tobacco Plants of a Crystalline Protein Possessing the Properties of Tobacco-Mosaic Virus." *Phytopathology* 26 (1936): 305–20. "The Isolation of a Crystalline Protein Possessing the Properties of Ancuba-Mosaic Virus." *Journal of Bacteriology* 31 (1936): 52–53. "The Isolation of Crystalline Tobacco Mosaic Virus Protein from Diseased Tomato Plants." *Science* 83 (1936): 85 (with H.S. Loring).

For More Information See: Asimov's Biographical Encyclopedia of Science and Technology. Garden City, NY: Doubleday, 1982, 801–02. *Current Biography Yearbook.* New York: H.W. Wilson, 1947, 604–07. *National Cyclopedia of American Biography.* Clifton, NJ: James T. White, 1977 (Volume 57), 161–63.

Commentary: Wendell Stanley won his Nobel Prize for his contributions to the "preparation of enzymes and virus proteins in a pure form." Stanley used John Northrop's techniques to crystallize tobacco mosaic virus, which retained its infective properties. Later, he isolated the influenza virus and prepared a vaccine against it. (J.B.)

Sumner, James Batcheller   **46**
Prize: Chemistry, 1946. *Born:* November 19, 1887; Canton, MA. *Death:* August 12, 1955; Buffalo, NY. *Parents:* Father, Charles Sumner; Mother, Elizabeth Rand Kelly Sumner. *Nationality:* American. *Religion:* Unitarian. *Education:* Harvard Univ., MA, B.A., 1910; Harvard Univ., MA, M.A., 1913; Harvard Univ., MA, Ph.D., 1914. *Spouse:* Bertha Louise Ricketts, married 1915, divorced 1930; Agnes Paulina Lundquist, married 1931, divorced 1942; Mary Morrison Beyer, married 1943. *Children:* Roberta Rand, daughter; Prudence Avery, daughter; Nathanial, son; James Cosby Ricketts, son; Frederick Overton Burnley, son; John Increase, son; Samuel Beyer, son. *Career:* Cornell Univ., NY, Professor, 1914–55. *Other Awards:* Scheele Medal, Sweden, 1937.

Selected Publications: "The Isolation and Crystallization of the Enzyme Urease." *Journal of Biological Chemistry* 69 (1926): 435–41. *Textbook of Biological Chemistry.* New York: Macmillan Company, 1927. "Crystalline Catalase." *Journal of Biological Chemistry* 121 (1937):

417–24. *Chemistry and Methods of Enzymes.* New York: Academic Press, 1943. *The Enzymes, Chemistry and Mechanism of Action.* 2 volumes. New York: Academic Press, 1950–52 (with K. Myrback).

For More Information See: Biographical Memoirs of the National Academy of Sciences. Washington, DC: National Academy of Sciences, 1958 (Volume 31), 376–96. *Current Biography Yearbook.* New York: H.W. Wilson, 1947, 620–22. *Dictionary of Scientific Biography.* New York: Scribner's, 1976 (Volume 13), 152–53.

Commentary: James Sumner shared the Nobel Prize "for his discovery that enzymes can be crystallized," stemming from his work with urease. His work also included the crystallization of catalase and contributions to the chemistry of the peroxidases and lipoxidase. (J.B.)

1947

Robinson, Robert, Sir   **47**
Prize: Chemistry, 1947. *Born:* September 13, 1886; Chesterfield, Derbyshire, England. *Death:* February 8, 1975; Great Missenden, Bucks, England. *Parents:* Father, W. B. Robinson; Mother, Jane Davenport Robinson. *Nationality:* British. *Religion:* Freethinker; from Congregationalist background. *Education:* Univ. of Manchester, England, baccalaureate, 1906; Univ. of Manchester, England, D.Sc., 1910. *Spouse:* Gertrude Maud Walsh, married 1922, died 1954; Stearn Sylvia Hershey Hillstrom, married 1957. *Children:* Marion, daughter; Michael, son. *Career:* Univ. of Sydney, Australia, Professor, 1912–15; Univ. of Liverpool, England, Professor, 1915–20; British Dyestuffs Corporation, Director of Research, 1920; Univ. of St. Andrews, Scotland, Professor, 1921; Univ. of Manchester, England, Professor, 1922–28; Univ. of London, England, Professor, 1928–30; Oxford Univ., England, Professor, 1930–55. *Other Awards:* Davy Medal, 1930; Royal Medal, 1932; Knighthood, 1939; Copley Medal, 1942; Franklin Medal, PA, 1947.

Selected Publications: "A Synthesis of Tropinone." *Journal of the Chemical Society* 111 (1917): 762–68. "A Theory of the Mechanism of the Phytochemical Synthesis of Certain Alkaloids." *Journal of the Chemical Society* 111 (1917): 876–99. "An Electrochemical Theory of the Mechanism of Organic Reactions." *Inst. Internat. Chim. Solvay Conseil Chim* 4e Conseil, Brussels (1932): 423–50.

For More Information See: Biographical Memoirs of the Fellows of the Royal Society. London: Royal Society, 1976, 415–527. *Memoirs of a Minor Prophet.* New York: Elsevier, 1976. Williams, T. *Robert Robinson, Chemist Extraordinary.* Oxford, England: Clarendon Press, 1990.

Commentary: The Nobel Prize was granted to Robert Robinson "for research on certain vegetable products of great biological importance, particularly alkaloids." His contributions included important research on sterols, pyrimidine analogs, the artificial sex hormones, and penicillin. (B.E.)

1948

Tiselius, Arne Wilhelm Kaurin   **48**
Prize: Chemistry, 1948. *Born:* August 10, 1902; Stockholm, Sweden. *Death:* October 29, 1971; Stockholm, Sweden. *Parents:* Father, Hans Abraham Jason Tiselius; Mother,

Rosa Kaurin Tiselius. *Nationality:* Swedish. *Religion:* Lutheran. *Education:* Univ. of Uppsala, Sweden, M.A., 1924; Univ. of Uppsala, Sweden, Ph.D., 1930. *Spouse:* Ingrid Margareta Dalén, married November 26, 1930. *Children:* Per, son; Eva, daughter. *Career:* Univ. of Uppsala, Sweden, Researcher and Professor, 1925–68. *Other Awards:* Bergstedt Prize, Royal Swedish Scientific Society, 1926; Paterno Medal, 1954; Hoffman Medal, 1955; Franklin Medal, 1956; Mookerjee Medal, 1959; Karrer Medal, 1961; Messel Medal, 1962.

Selected Publications: "A New Method for Determination of the Mobility of Proteins." *Journal of the American Chemical Society* 48 (September 1926): 2272–78 (with T. Svedberg). "The Moving Boundary Method of Studying the Electrophoresis of Proteins." *Nova Acta Regiae Societatis Scientarium Upsaliensis* 4th series, 7 (1930): 100–07. "Adsorption and Diffusion in Zeolite Crystals." *Journal of Physical Chemistry* 40 (February 1936): 223–32. "A New Apparatus for Electrophoretic Analysis of Colloidal Mixtures." *Transactions of the Faraday Society* 33 (1937): 524–31. "Electrophoresis of Serum Globulin II. Electrophoretic Analysis of Normal and Immune Sera." *Biochemical Journal* 31 (July 1937): 1464–77. "Separation and Fractionation of Macromolecules and Particles." *Science* 141 (July 1963): 13–20 (with J. Parath and P.A. Albertsson).

For More Information See: Biographical Memoirs of the Fellows of the Royal Society. London: Royal Society, 1974 (Volume 20), 401–28. *Current Biography Yearbook.* New York: H.W. Wilson, 1949, 603–04. *Dictionary of Scientific Biography.* New York: Scribner's, 1976 (Volume 13), 418–22. *The Excitement and Fascination of Science.* Palo Alto, CA: Annual Reviews, Inc., 1978, Vol. 2, 549–72.

Commentary: Arne Tiselius received the Nobel Prize for his work with two methods of biochemical study of proteins and other large molecules: electrophoresis and adsorption analysis. The awards committee specifically cited his use of electrophoretic methods to separate the proteins of blood serum; Tiselius had developed an apparatus which separated albumin from globulin and led to the discovery of alpha, beta, and gamma globulins and the immunoglobulins (antibodies). He later worked with adsorption methods for separating substances and through this work made major contributions to the field of protein chromatography. (D.O.F. and H.L.F.)

1949

Giauque, William Francis   49

Prize: Chemistry, 1949. *Born:* May 12, 1895; Niagara Falls, Ontario, Canada. *Death:* March 29, 1982; Berkeley, CA. *Parents:* Father, William Tecumseh Sherman Giauque; Mother, Isabella Jane Duncan Giauque. *Nationality:* American. *Religion:* Most probably Christian. *Education:* Univ. of California, B.S., 1920; Univ. of California, Ph.D., 1922. *Spouse:* Murill Francis Ashley, married July 19, 1932. *Children:* William Francis Ashley, son; Robert David Ashley, son. *Career:* Univ. of California, Berkeley, Professor, 1922–62. *Other Awards:* Pacific Division Prize, American Association for the Advancement of Science, 1929; Medal, Chandler Foundation, Columbia Univ., NY, 1936; Elliot

Cresson Medal, Franklin Institute, 1937; Gibbs Medal, American Chemical Society, 1951; Lewis Medal, 1956.

Selected Publications: "Thermodynamic Treatment of Certain Magnetic Effects: A Proposed Method of Producing Temperatures Considerably Below 1° Absolute." *Journal of the American Chemical Society* 49 (1927): 1864–70. "Temperatures Below 1° Absolute." *Industrial and Engineering Chemistry* 28 (1936): 743–45.

For More Information See: The Annual Obituary, 1982. New York: St. Martin's Press, 1983, 143–45. *Biographical Memoirs of National Academy of Sciences.* Washington, DC: National Academy of Sciences, 1996 (Volume 69), 1–21. *Current Biography Yearbook.* New York: H.W. Wilson, 1950, 170–72.

Commentary: William Francis Giauque won the Nobel Prize "for his contributions in the field of chemical thermodynamics, particularly concerning the behaviour of substances at extremely low temperatures." Beginning with his interest during his Ph.D. research, he embarked on research that would cool elements to zero degrees absolute and then tested their molecular order. In 1933, he first approached his goal, having invented most of the equipment needed to measure and test at such low temperatures. In the course of his experiments, he discovered two new isotopes of oxygen (17 and 18). Giauque also was a key worker in the area of statistical mechanics and the measurement of entropies at low temperatures. (L.T.)

1950

Alder, Kurt   50

Prize: Chemistry, 1950. *Born:* July 10, 1902; Königshuette, Germany. *Death:* June 20, 1958; Cologne, Germany. *Parents:* Father, Joseph Alder; Mother, Maria Alder. *Nationality:* German. *Religion:* Most probably Christian. *Education:* Univ. of Kiel, Germany, Ph.D., 1926. *Spouse:* No record found. *Children:* No record found. *Career:* Univ. of Kiel, Germany, Professor, 1930–36; I.G. Farben Industrie, Administrator, 1936–40; Univ. of Cologne, Germany, Professor and Administrator, 1940–58. *Other Awards:* Emil Fischer Memorial Medal, Association of German Chemists, 1938.

Selected Publications: "Synthesen in der Hydroaromatischen Reihe. I. Mitteilung, Anlagerungen von 'Di-en'-kohlenwasserstoffen." *Annalen die Chemie* 460 (1928): 98–122 (with O. Diels). "Die Methode der Dien-Synthese." *Handbuch der Biologischen Arbeitsmethoden.* Berlin: Urban and Schwartzenburg, 1933 (Volume 2), 3171. *Neuere Methoden der Praeparativen Organischen Chemie.* Berlin: Verlag Chemie, 1943. "Über den Sterischen Verlauf von Dien-Synthesen mit Acyclischen Dienen. Die Allgemeine Sterische Formel." *Annalen die Chemie* 571 (1951): 157–66.

For More Information See: Dictionary of Scientific Biography. New York: Scribner's, 1970 (Volume 1), 105–06. Guenzl-Schumacher, M. "Kurt Alder." *Chemikerzeitung* 82 (1958): 489–90.

Commentary: Kurt Alder was awarded the Nobel Prize for his contributions to the "discovery and development of the diene synthesis," which involves addition of unsaturated compounds with alternating double bonds to compounds with a double bond activated by a carbonyl or carboxyl group in near proximity to form a new compound. Alder continued to study the conditions and applications of the Diels-Alder reaction throughout his career. He also had an industrial interest in production of synthetic rubbers, and he showed his interest in the external world by joining in the Nobel laureate renunciation of war in 1955. (T.K.)

Diels, Otto Paul Herman 51

Prize: Chemistry, 1950. *Born:* January 23, 1876; Hamburg, Germany. *Death:* March 7, 1954; Kiel, Germany. *Parents:* Father, Hermann Diels; Mother, Bertha Duebell Diels. *Nationality:* German. *Religion:* Most probably Christian. *Education:* Univ. of Berlin, Germany, Ph.D., 1899. *Spouse:* Paula Geyer, married 1909. *Children:* 3 sons; 2 daughters. *Career:* Univ. of Berlin, Germany, Professor, 1899–1916; Univ. of Kiel, Germany, Professor and Administrator, 1916–48. *Other Awards:* Gold Medal, St. Louis Exposition, MO, 1906; Adolf von Baeyer Memorial Medal, Society of German Chemists, 1931.

Selected Publications: "Über das Kohlensuboxyd I." *Berichte der Deutschen Chemischen Gesellschaft* 39 (1906): 689 (with B. Wolf). *Einfuhrung in die Organische Chemie.* Leipzig, Germany: Weinheim, 1907. "Synthesen in der Hydroaromatischen Reihe. I. Mitteilung, Anlagerungen von'si-en-'kohlenwasserstoffen." *Annalen die Chemie* 460 (1927): 98–122 (with K. Alder).

For More Information See: *Dictionary of Scientific Biography.* New York: Scribner's, 1971 (Volume 4), 90–92. Olsen, S. "Otto Diels." *Chemische Berichte* 95 (1962): 5–46.

Commentary: Otto Diels shared the Nobel Prize for his work in the "discovery and development of the diene synthesis," in which an organic compound with a set of double-bonded carbons around a single-bonded set combines with an organic compound that contains a double bond activated by a nearby carbonyl or carboxyl group to form a new compound. Diels continued to study Diels-Alder reactions and their applications throughout his career. He also isolated, earlier in his career, carbon suboxide, and developed a method for removing hydrogen from steroids, using selenium. (T.K.)

1951

McMillan, Edwin Mattison 52

Prize: Chemistry, 1951. *Born:* September 18, 1907; Redondo Beach, CA. *Death:* September 7, 1991; El Cerrito, CA. *Parents:* Father, Edwin Harbaugh McMillan; Mother, Anne Marie Mattison McMillan. *Nationality:* American. *Religion:* Christian. *Education:* California Institute of Technology, B.S., 1928; California Institute of Technology, M.S., 1929; Princeton Univ., NJ, Ph.D., 1932. *Spouse:* Elsie Walford Blumer, married June 7, 1941. *Children:* Ann, daughter; David, son; Stephen, son. *Career:* Univ. of California, Berkeley, Professor, 1932–73. *Other Awards:* Research Corporation Scientific Award, 1951; Atoms for Peace Award, 1963; Alumni Distinguished Service Award, California Institute of Technology, 1966; Centennial Citation, Univ. of California, Berkeley, 1968; National Medal of Science, 1990.

Selected Publications: "The Synchrotron—A Proposed High-Energy Particle Accelerator." *Physical Review* 68

(September 1945): 143–44. *Lecture Series in Nuclear Physics.* Washington, DC: United States Government Printing Office, 1947. "Production of Mesons by X-rays." *Science* 110 (1949): 579–83 (with J. Peterson and R. White).

For More Information See: *Current Biography Yearbook.* New York: H.W. Wilson, 1952, 382–84. *National Cyclopedia of American Biography.* New York: J. T. White, 1952 (Volume H), 236–37. *New York Times Biographical Service* (September 9, 1991): 941. *Physics Today* 45 (1992):118.

Commentary: Edwin McMillan won the 1951 Nobel Prize for chemistry for "his discovery of element 93, neptunium, the first element beyond uranium." He shared the prize with Glenn Seaborg, who had been instrumental in discovering elements 94–102. McMillan was involved also in the wartime work on radar, sonar, and the atomic bomb, and devised the theory of phase stability used in the construction of high-energy atom-smashing equipment. (B.F.)

Seaborg, Glenn Theodore 53

Prize: Chemistry, 1951. *Born:* April 19, 1912; Ishpeming, MI. *Death:* February 25, 1999; Lafayette, CA. *Parents:* Father, Herman Theodore Seaborg; Mother, Selma Erickson Seaborg. *Nationality:* American. *Religion:* Protestant. *Education:* Univ. of California, Los Angeles, A.B., 1934; Univ. of California, Ph.D., 1937. *Spouse:* Helen Lucille Griggs, married 1942. *Children:* Peter, son (dec.); David, son; Stephen, son; John Eric, son; Lynne, daughter; Diane, daughter. *Career:* Univ. of California, Berkeley, Professor and Administrator, 1937–99. *Other Awards:* Award in Pure Chemistry, 1947; John Ericsson Gold Medal, 1948; Nichols Medal, 1948; John Scott Award, 1953; Medal of City of Philadelphia, 1953; Perkin Medal, 1957; Enrico Fermi Award, United States Atomic Energy Commission, 1959; Priestley Memorial Award, 1960; Franklin Medal, 1963; Charles Lathrop Parsons Award, 1964; Chemistry Pioneer Award, 1968; Gold Medal Award, 1973; Arches of Science Award, 1968; John R. Kuebler Award, Alpha Chi Sigma, 1978; Priestley Medal, American Chemical Society, 1979; Henry DeWolf Smyth Award, American Nuclear Society, 1982; Actinide Award, 1984; Bush Award, 1988; National Medal of Science, 1991.

Selected Publications: *The Chemistry of the Actinide Elements.* New York: Wiley, 1958 (with Joseph J. Katz). *The Transuranium Elements.* New Haven, CT: Yale Univ. Press, 1958. *Education and the Atom.* New York: McGraw-Hill, 1964 (with Daniel M. Wilkes). *Man and Atom.* New York: E. P. Dutton, 1971 (with William R. Corliss). *Nuclear Milestones.* San Francisco, CA: W.H. Freeman, 1972. *Transuranium Elements: Products of Modern Alchemy.* New York: Academic Press, 1978 (with others).

For More Information See: *Asimov's Biographical Encyclopedia of Science and Technology.* Garden City, NY: Doubleday, 1982, 842–43. *Biographical Encyclopedia of Scientists.* New York: Facts on File, 1981, 721–22. *Chemist in the White House.* Washington, DC: American Chemical Society, 1998. *Current Biography Yearbook.* New York: H.W. Wilson, 1961, 413–15.

Commentary: Glenn Seaborg's Nobel Prize (shared with Edwin McMillan) came "for discoveries in the chemistry of the transuranium elements." Of the 13 such elements known in the 70s, he was involved in the identification of nine (atomic numbers 94 through 102). He also studied the chemistry and physics of the actinide series, especially of neptunium and plutonium. In addition, Seaborg was an active scientist outside of the laboratory and served a term as chair of the Atomic Energy Commission. (B.F.)

1952

Martin, Archer John Porter   **54**

Prize: Chemistry, 1952. *Born:* March 1, 1910; London, England. *Parents:* Father, William Archer Porter Martin; Mother, Lillian Kate Brown Martin. *Nationality:* British. *Religion:* Most probably Christian/Protestant. *Education:* Cambridge Univ., England, B.A., 1932; Cambridge Univ., England, M.A., 1935; Cambridge Univ., England, Ph.D., 1936. *Spouse:* Judith Bagenal, married January 9, 1943. *Children:* 2 sons; 3 daughters. *Career:* Cambridge Univ., England, Researcher, 1933–38; Wool Industries Research Association, Leeds, England, Researcher, 1938–46; Boots Pure Drug Company, Nottingham, England, Researcher, 1946–48; Medical Research Council, England, Researcher, 1948–52; National Institute for Medical Research, London, England, Researcher, 1952–56; Consultant, England, 1956–59; Abbotsbury Laboratories, England, Director, 1959–70; Wellcome Foundation, England, Consultant, 1970–73; Univ. of Houston, TX, Professor, 1974–79. *Other Awards:* Berzelius Gold Medal, Swedish Medical Society, 1951; John Scott Award, 1958; John Price Wetherill Medal, 1959; Franklin Institute Medal, 1959; Leverhulme Medal, 1963; Kolthoff Medal, 1969; Callendar Medal, 1971; Achievement Award, The Worshipful Company of Scientific Instrument Makers, 1972; Randolf Major Medal, 1979; Fritz Pregl Medal, 1985.

Selected Publications: "A New Form of Chromatography Employing Two Liquid Phases." *Biochemical Journal* 35 (1941): 1358–68 (with R. Synge). "Identification of Lower Peptides in Complex Mixtures." *Biochemical Journal* (February 1947): 595–96 (with R. Consden and A. Gordon). "Separation of the C12-C13 Fatty Acids by Reversed-Phase Partition Chromatography." *Biochemical Journal* (May 1950): 532–38 (with G. Howard).

For More Information See: Campbell, W. A., and Greenwood, N. N. *Contemporary British Chemists.* London: Taylor and Francis, 1971. *Current Biography Yearbook.* New York: H.W. Wilson, 1953, 417–19.

Commentary: A. J. P. Martin was awarded the Nobel Prize for his invention of partition chromatography, which combines the principles of countercurrent solvent extraction and chromatography. Small quantities of closely related chemical substances can be separated from one another by partition chromatography. Martin also was instrumental in the development of paper chromatography and gas chromatography. (J.H.)

Synge, Richard Laurence Millington   **55**

Prize: Chemistry, 1952. *Born:* October 28, 1914; Liverpool, England. *Death:* August 18, 1994: Norwich, England. *Parents:* Father, Laurence Millington Synge; Mother, Katharine Charlotte Swan Synge. *Nationality:* British. *Religion:* Most probably Christian/Protestant. *Education:* Cambridge Univ., England, baccalaureate, 1936; Cambridge Univ., England,

Ph.D., 1941. *Spouse:* Ann Stephen, married 1943. *Children:* Jane, daughter; Elizabeth, daughter; Charlotte, daughter; Mary, daughter; Thomas Millington, son; Matthew Millington, son; Patrick Millington, son. *Career:* Wool Industries Research Association, Leeds, England, Researcher, 1941–43; Lister Institute of Preventive Medicine, London, England, Researcher, 1943–48; Rowett Research Institute, Aberdeen, Scotland, Researcher and Administrator, 1948–67; Food Research Institute, Researcher, Norwich, England, 1967–76; Univ. of East Anglia, England, Professor, 1967–84. *Other Awards:* John Price Wetherill Medal, Franklin Institute, Philadelphia, PA, 1959.

Selected Publications: "A New Form of Chromatography Employing Two Liquid Phases." *Biochemical Journal* 35 (1941): 1358–68 (with A. Martin). *Science in Society.* London: Edward Arnold, 1969.

For More Information See: *A Biographical Encyclopedia of Scientists.* New York: Facts on File, 1981, 769. *Current Biography Yearbook.* New York: H.W. Wilson, 1953, 611–12. *London Daily Telegraph* (October 10, 1994): 21.

Commentary: The Nobel Prize was awarded to R. L. M. Synge for the research that led to the development of partition chromatography. Synge immediately used this technique to separate the 20 closely related amino acids of which proteins are composed. Also, Synge used chromatographic techniques in his "elegant investigation" of the chemical structure of the antibiotic gramicidin. In later years, he was a translator of notable Russian scientific textbooks and a tireless worker in various peace movements. (L.D. and J.H.)

1953

Staudinger, Hermann   **56**

Prize: Chemistry, 1953. *Born:* March 23, 1881; Worms, Germany. *Death:* September 8, 1965; Freiburg-im-Breisgau, Germany. *Parents:* Father, Franz Staudinger; Mother, Auguste Wench Staudinger. *Nationality:* German. *Religion:* Most probably Christian. *Education:* Univ. of Halle, Germany, Ph.D., 1907. *Spouse:* Magda Woit, married 1927. *Children:* None. *Career:* Technische Hochschule, Karlsruhe, Germany, Professor, 1907–12; Federal Technical Institute, Zürich, Switzerland, Professor, 1912–26; Univ. of Freiburg, Germany, Professor and Administrator, 1926–56. *Other Awards:* Emil Fisher Medal, 1930; Le Blanc Medal, 1931; Cannizzaro Prize, Reale Academia Nazionale dei Lincei, Rome, Italy, 1933.

Selected Publications: *Die Ketene (Ketenes).* Stuttgart, Germany: Enke, 1912. *Anleitung zur Organischen Qualitativen Analyse (Introduction to Organic Qualitative Analysis).* Berlin: Springer, 1923. *Die Hochmolekularen Organischen Verbindungen, Kautschuk und Cellulose (The High-Molecular Organic Compounds, Rubber and Cellulose).* Berlin: Springer, 1932. *Organische Kolloid Chemie (Organic Colloid Chemistry).* Braunschweig, Germany: Vieweg, 1940. *Makromolekulare Chemie und Biologie (Macromolecular Chemistry and Biology).* Basel, Switzerland: Wepf and Co., 1947.

For More Information See: *Arbeitserrinnerungen (Working Memoirs).* Heidelberg, Germany: A. Huthig, 1961.

Dictionary of Scientific Biography. New York: Scribner's, 1976 (Volume 13), 1–4.

Commentary: Hermann Staudinger was cited by the Academy "for his discoveries in the field of macromolecular chemistry." His work, which was the foundation of much of macromolecular chemistry, was concentrated mostly on cellulose, rubber, and isoprene, but there were significant contributions as well to the chemistry of ketenes, oxalyl chloride, outoxidation, aliphatic diazo-compounds, explosions, and insecticides. (T.K.)

1954

Pauling, Linus Carl 57

Prize: Chemistry, 1954; Peace, 1962 [SEE REF]. *Born:* February 28, 1901; Portland, OR. *Death:* August 19, 1994; Big Sur, CA. *Parents:* Father, Herman Henry William Pauling; Mother, Lucy Isabelle Darling Pauling. *Nationality:* American. *Religion:* No religious practice; from Christian background. *Education:* Oregon State College, B.Sc., 1922; California Institute of Technology, Ph.D., 1925. *Spouse:* Ava Helen Miller, married 1923; died 1981. *Children:* Linus Carl, Jr., son; Peter Jeffress, son; Linda Helen, daughter; Edward Crellin, son. *Career:* Oregon State College, Corvallis, Professor, 1919–20; California Institute of Technology, Professor, 1925–64; Center for Study of Democratic Institutions, Professor, 1964–67; Univ. of California, San Diego, Professor, 1967–69; Stanford Univ., CA, Professor, 1969–74; Linus Pauling Institute, 1974–92. *Other Awards:* Langmuir Prize, American Chemical Society, 1931; Nichols Medal, 1941; Davy Medal, Royal Society, 1947; Medal for Merit, 1948; Pasteur Medal, Biochemical Society of France, 1952; Addis Medal, National Nephrosis Federation, 1955; Phillips Memorial Award, American College of Physicians, 1956; Avogadro Medal, Italian Academy of Science, 1956; Fermat Medal, 1957; Sabatier Medal, 1957; International Grotius Medal, 1957; Order of Merit, Republic of Italy, 1965; Medal, Academy of Rumanian People's Republic, 1965; Linus Pauling Medal, 1966; Silver Medal, Institute of France, 1966; Supreme Peace Sponsor, World Fellowship of Religion, 1966; International Lenin Peace Prize, 1971; Martin Luther King, Jr., Medal, 1972; National Medal of Science, 1974; Priestley Medal, 1984; American Chemical Society Award in Chemical Education, 1987; Bush Award, 1989; Tolman Medal, 1991.

Selected Publications: Introduction to Quantum Mechanics. New York: McGraw-Hill, 1935 (with E. B. Wilson, Jr.). *The Nature of the Chemical Bond.* Ithaca, NY: Cornell Univ. Press, 1939. *No More War!* New York: Dodd, Mead, 1958. *The Architecture of Molecules.* San Francisco, CA: W. H. Freeman, 1964 (with R. Hayward). *Vitamin C and the Common Cold.* San Francisco, CA: W. H. Freeman, 1970.

For More Information See: Current Biography Yearbook. New York: H. W. Wilson, 1964, 339–42. *The Excitement and Fascination of Science.* Palo Alto, CA: Annual Reviews, Inc., 1965, Vol. 1, 347–60; and 1990, Vol. 3, Part 1, 541–49. Hager, Thomas. *Force of Nature: the Life of Linus Pauling.* New York: Simon & Schuster, 1995. *The Roots of Molecular Medicine: A Tribute to Linus Pauling.* New York: W. H. Freeman, 1986. Serafini, A. *Linus Pauling.* New York: Paragon House, 1991. White, F. M. *Linus*

Pauling: Scientist and Crusader. New York: Walker and Co., 1980.

Commentary: Linus Pauling was the first person to receive two unshared Nobel Prizes in two different fields. His prize in chemistry was granted for his work on chemical bonds and molecular structure, while his peace prize cited his writings and lectures warning against the dangers of radioactive fallout in weapons testing and war. Pauling's applications of quantum mechanics to chemistry began his career, but it ventured far afield, investigating such varying areas as crystal structure, bonding, the resonance theory, protein structure, antibodies, hereditary diseases, anesthesia, and Vitamin C therapy. Since World War II, Pauling also devoted large amounts of time to the cause of peace and disarmament, in debates, lectures, articles, petitions, and books. (M.E.T. and B.S.S.)

1955

Du Vigneaud, Vincent 58

Prize: Chemistry, 1955. *Born:* May 18, 1901; Chicago, IL. *Death:* December 11, 1978; White Plains, NY. *Parents:* Father, Alfred Joseph Du Vigneaud; Mother, Mary Theresa O'Leary Du Vigneaud. *Nationality:* American. *Religion:* Most probably Christian. *Education:* Univ. of Illinois, B.Sc., 1923; Univ. of Illinois, M.Sc., 1924; Univ. of Rochester, NY, Ph.D., 1927. *Spouse:* Zella Zon Ford, married June 12, 1924. *Children:* Vincent Jr., son; Marilyn Renée, daughter. *Career:* DuPont Laboratory, DE, Researcher, 1924; Philadelphia General Hospital, PA, Researcher, 1924–25; Univ. of Rochester, NY, Researcher, 1925–27; Johns Hopkins Univ., MD, Researcher, 1927–28; Univ. of Illinois, Professor, 1929–32; George Washington Univ., Washington, DC, Professor, 1932–38; Cornell Univ., NY, Professor, 1938–75. *Other Awards:* Hildebrand Award, Washington Chemical Society, 1936; Mead-Johnson Vitamin B Complex Award, American Institute of Nutrition, 1942; Nichols Medal, New York Section, American Chemical Society, 1945; Borden Award, American Association of American Medical Colleges; Lasker Award, American Public Health Association, 1948; Award of Merit for War Research, 1948; Osborne and Mendel Award, 1953; John Scott Medal and Award, American Pharmaceutical Manufacturers' Association, 1954; Chandler Medal, 1955; Passano Foundation Award, 1955; Willard Gibbs Medal, American Chemical Society, 1956.

Selected Publications: A Trail of Research in Sulphur Chemistry and the Metabolism and Related Fields. Ithaca, NY: Cornell Univ. Press, 1952. "Tritiation of Oxytocin by the Wilzbach Method and the Synthesis of Oxytocin from Tritium-Labeled Leucine." *Journal of the American Chemical Society* 84 (1962): 409–13 (with others). "The Hormones of the Posterior Pituitary Gland with Special Reference to Their Milk-Ejecting Ability." *Bulletin of the New York Academy of Medicine* 41 (1965): 802–03.

For More Information See: Biographical Encyclopedia of Scientists. New York: Facts on File, 1981, 222. *Current Biography Yearbook.* New York: H.W. Wilson, 1956, 160–62. *New York Times Biographical Service* (August 27, 1994): 1252.

Commentary: Vincent Du Vigneaud was cited by the Academy "for his work on biochemically important sulphur compounds, especially for the first synthesis of a polypeptide hormone." Du Vigneaud began his research on the sulphur of insulin, studied other sulphur-containing compounds and the role of the methyl group in biology, and contributed to the knowledge about biotin, coenzyme R, and penicillin. His later research centered on oxytocin and vasopressin, two pituitary hormones. (L.T.)

1956

Hinshelwood, Cyril Norman, Sir 59

Prize: Chemistry, 1956. *Born:* June 19, 1897; London, England. *Death:* October 9, 1967; London, England. *Parents:* Father, Norman Macmillan Hinshelwood; Mother, Ethel Frances Smith. *Nationality:* British. *Religion:* Most probably Christian/Protestant. *Education:* Oxford Univ., England, B.A., 1920; Oxford Univ., England, M.A., 1924. *Spouse:* None. *Children:* None. *Career:* Oxford Univ., England, Professor, 1921–64. *Other Awards:* Lavoisier Medal, Société Chimique de France, 1935; Davy Medal, Royal Society, 1943; Royal Medal, Royal Society, 1947; Longstaff Medal, Chemical Society, 1948; Knighthood, 1948; Guldberg Medal, Univ. of Oslo, 1952; Faraday Medal, Chemical Society, 1953; Order of the Republic, Italy, 1956; Avogadro Medal, Accademia dei Lincei, 1956; Leverhulme Medal, Royal Society, 1960.

Selected Publications: Kinetics of Chemical Change in Gaseous Systems. Oxford: Clarendon Press, 1926. *Thermodynamics for Students of Chemistry.* London: Methuen, 1926. *The Reaction Between Hydrogen and Oxygen.* Oxford: Clarendon Press, 1934 (with A. T. Williamson). *The Chemical Kinetics of the Bacterial Cell.* London: Clarendon Press, 1947. *The Structure of Physical Chemistry.* Oxford: Clarendon Press, 1951. *Growth, Function and Regulation in Bacterial Cells.* Oxford: Clarendon Press, 1966 (with A.C.R. Dean).

For More Information See: Current Biography Yearbook. New York: H.W. Wilson, 1957, 259–60. *Dictionary of Scientific Biography.* New York: Scribner's, 1972 (Volume 6), 404–05.

Commentary: The Nobel Prize was awarded to Sir Cyril Hinshelwood (and Nikolai Semenov) for "their researches into the mechanism of chemical reactions." Working independently, each discovered that a series of molecules could react in one sequence without the addition of new outside energy but could also be forced to so react. By speeding up changes in the structure of molecules, the resulting chain reactions could produce sudden or controlled violent explosions. These discoveries paved the way for more efficient automobile engines and for the modern plastics industry. Later work by Hinshelwood centered on investigation of chemical reactions in living organisms. (B.M.)

Semenov, Nikolai Nikolaevich 60

Prize: Chemistry, 1956. *Born:* April 16, 1896; Saratov, Russia. *Death:* September 25, 1986; Moscow, Russia. *Parents:* Father, Nikolai Alex Semenov; Mother, Elena Dmitrieva Semenov. *Nationality:* Russian. *Religion:* Most probably Eastern Orthodox. *Education:* Leningrad State Univ., USSR, graduate, 1917. *Spouse:* Natalia Nikolaevna Burtseva, married September 15, 1924. *Children:* Yurii Nikolaevich, son; Ludmilla Nikolaevna, daughter. *Career:* Leningrad Poly-Technical Institute, USSR, Professor, 1920–31; Institute of

Chemical Physics of the Academy of Sciences, USSR, Director, 1932–86. *Other Awards:* Stalin Prize; Order of the Red Banner of Labor; Order of Lenin (7 times); Lomonosov Gold Medal, USSR.

Selected Publications: Chain Reactions. Tr. by Prof. Frenkel and Judviga Smidt-Chernysheff. Oxford: Clarendon Press, 1935. *Chemical Kinetics and Chain Reactions.* Tr. by Prof. Frenkel and Judviga Smidt-Chernysheff. Oxford: Clarendon Press, 1935. *Some Problems of Chemical Kinetics and Reactivity.* Tr. by Michel Boudart. Princeton, NJ: Princeton Univ. Press, 1958–59.

For More Information See: Biographical Memoirs of the Fellows of the Royal Society. London: Royal Society, 1990 (Volume 36), 527. *Current Biography Yearbook.* New York: H.W. Wilson, 1957, 498–500. *New York Times* (November 2, 1956): 1.

Commentary: Nikolai Semenov was the first Soviet citizen living in his homeland to win the Nobel Prize. His research on chemical processes led him to believe physics might be the key to many of the problems of chemistry. In pursuing this idea, he developed the science of chemical kinetics. In 1956, Semenov, with Sir Cyril Hinshelwood, was awarded the Nobel Prize in Chemistry for "researches into the mechanism of chemical reactions." Some contend that their work led to the capability of controlled atomic chain reactions; it is more generally agreed that their work paved the way for the development of more efficient automobile engines and the foundation of the plastics industry. Semenov's early work dealt with molecular physics and the splitting off of electrons by electrical force. As early as 1927, he developed a theory of the thermal explosion of gaseous mixtures. (B.M.)

1957

Todd, Alexander Robertus, Sir 61

Prize: Chemistry, 1957. *Born:* October 2, 1907; Glasgow, Scotland. *Death:* January 10, 1997; Cambridge, England. *Parents:* Father, Alexander Todd; Mother, Jane Lowrie Todd. *Nationality:* British. *Religion:* Christian. *Education:* Glasgow Univ., Scotland, baccalaureate, 1928; Univ. of Frankfurt, Germany, Ph.D., 1931; Oxford Univ., England, Ph.D., 1933. *Spouse:* Alison Sarah Dale, married January 10, 1937. *Children:* Alexander Henry, son; Helen Jean, daughter; Hilary Alison, daughter. *Career:* Edinburgh Univ., Scotland, Researcher, 1934–36; Lister Institute for Preventive Medicine, England, Researcher, 1936–38; Manchester Univ., England, Professor, 1938–44; Cambridge Univ., England, Professor, 1944–78. *Other Awards:* Lavoisier Medal, French Chemical Society, 1948; Davy Medal, Royal Society, 1949; Knighthood, 1954; Royal Medal, 1955; Cannizzaro Medal, Italian Chemical Society, 1958; Longstaff Medal, Chemical Society of London, 1963; Copley Medal, Royal Society, 1970; Ordre Pour Le Mérite, Federal Republic of Germany; Second Class Order of Rising Sun, Japan; Lomonosov Gold Medal, USSR, 1979; Hanbury Medal, 1986.

Selected Publications: "Chemical Structure and Properties of Tocopherol (Vitamin E). I. Chemistry." *Soc. Chem. Ind., Food Group* (April 1939): 3–8. "Vitamins of the B Group." *Journal of the Chemical Society* (1941): 427–32.

"Synthesis in the Study of Nucleotides." *Journal of the Chemical Society* (1946): 647–53. "Synthesis of Nucleotides." *Bull. Soc. Chem. France* (1948): 933–38. "A Hundred Years of Organic Chemistry." *Advancement of Science* 8 (1952): 393–96. *Perspectives in Organic Chemistry*. New York: Interscience, 1956.

For More Information See: Current Biography Yearbook. New York: H.W. Wilson, 1958, 437–39. *New York Times* (January 15, 1997): Sect. B, 7. *A Time to Remember: The Autobiography of a Chemist*. Cambridge: Cambridge Univ. Press, 1983.

Commentary: Alexander Todd was awarded the Nobel Prize for his contributions to biochemistry and to the understanding of the gene. At the beginning of his impresssive career, Todd synthesized and determined the structure of vitamin B-1 and also studied vitamins E and B-12, as well as isolating the active entity from Cannabis. He later synthesized and determined the structures of the purine and pyrimidine bases in nucleic acids, synthesized coenzymes related to the nucleic acid systems, and synthesized the energy-transfer compounds (adenosine diphosphate and adenosine triphosphate). (C.T.)

1958

Sanger, Frederick 62

Prize: Chemistry, 1958; Chemistry, 1980 [SEE REF]. *Born:* August 13, 1918; Rendcomb, Gloucestershire, England. *Parents:* Father, Frederick Sanger; Mother, Cicely Crewdson Sanger. *Nationality:* British. *Religion:* Agnostic; from Quaker/Anglican background. *Education:* Cambridge Univ., England, B.A., 1940; Cambridge Univ., England, Ph.D., 1943. *Spouse:* Margaret Joan Howe, married 1940. *Children:* Robin, son; Peter Frederick, son; Sally Joan, daughter. *Career:* Cambridge Univ., England, Professor, 1944–83. *Other Awards:* Corday-Morgan Medal and Prize, Chemical Society, 1951; Gairdner Foundation Annual Award, 1971, 1979; William Bate Hardy Prize, Cambridge Philosophical Society, 1976; Copley Medal, Royal Society, 1977; Wheland Award, 1978; Horwitz Prize, 1979; Lasker Award, 1979.

Selected Publications: "The Free Amino Groups of Insulin." *Biochemical Journal* 39 (1945): 507–15. "The Amino-Acid Sequence in the Glycyl Chain of Insulin. The Identification of Lower Peptides from Partial Hydrolysates." *Biochemical Journal* 53 (1953): 353–66 (with E.O.P. Thompson). "DNA Sequencing with Chain-Terminating Inhibitors." *Proceedings of the National Academy of Sciences, USA* 74 (1977): 5463–67 (with A. R. Coulson and S. Nicklen). "Nucleotide Sequence of Bacteriophage Phi X174 DNA." *Nature (London)* 265 (1977): 687–95 (with others).

For More Information See: Current Biography Yearbook. New York: H.W. Wilson, 1981, 354–56. Silverstein, A. *Frederick Sanger*. New York: Day, 1969.

Commentary: Frederick Sanger, the recipient of two Nobel Prizes in Chemistry, received the first "for his work on the structure of proteins, especially that of insulin" and the second for his work in determining the base sequences of nucleic acids. The methods which Sanger developed in painstaking years of effort were successfully used by others in determining the structures of complicated compounds. In his work on DNA, Sanger also found two cases of genes located within genes, previously thought to be impossible. (M.B.)

1959

Heyrovsky, Jaroslav 63

Prize: Chemistry, 1959. *Born:* December 20, 1890; Prague, Czechoslovakia. *Death:* March 27, 1967; Prague, Czechoslovakia. *Parents:* Father, Leopold Heyrovsky; Mother, Clara Hanlova Heyrovsky. *Nationality:* Czechoslovakian. *Religion:* Christian. *Education:* Univ. of London, England, B.Sc., 1913; Charles Univ., Czechoslovakia, Ph.D., 1918; Charles Univ., Czechoslovakia, D.Sc., 1921. *Spouse:* Marie Karanova, married February 22, 1926. *Children:* Michael, son; Judith Cěrny, daughter. *Career:* Univ. of London, England, Professor, 1913–14; Charles Univ., Prague, Czechoslovakia, Professor and Administrator, 1919–54; Institute of Physical Chemistry, Prague, Czechoslovakia, Director, 1926–54; Central Polarographic Institute, Prague, Czechoslovakia, Director, 1950–63. *Other Awards:* First State Prize, Czechoslovakia, 1951; Order of the Czechoslovak Republic, 1955.

Selected Publications: "Electrolysis with a Dropping Mercury Cathode, Part I. Deposition of Alkali and Alkaline Earth Metals." *Philosophical Magazine* 45 (1923): 303–14. "Researches with the Dropping Mercury Cathode, Part II. The Polarograph." *Recueil des Travaux Chimiques des Pays-Bas* 44 (1925): 496–98 (with M. Shikata). *A Polarographic Study of the Electrokinetic Phenomena of Adsorption, Electroreduction and Overpotential Displayed at the Dropping Mercury Cathode*. Paris: Hermann, 1934. *Polarographie: Theoretische Grundlagen, Praktische Ausfuhrung und Anwendungen der Elektrolyse mit der Tropfenden Quecksilberelektrode*. Vienna: Springer, 1941. *Bibliography of Publications Dealing with the Polarographic Method*. 5 volumes. Prague: Nakladatelství Cěskoslovenské akademie véd, 1960–1964.

For More Information See: Current Biography Yearbook. New York: H.W. Wilson, 1961, 202–04. *Dictionary of Scientific Biography*. New York: Scribner's, 1975 (Volume 6), 370–76. Koryta, J. *Jaroslav Heyrovsky*. Prague, Czechoslovakia: Melantrich, 1990.

Commentary: Jaroslav Heyrovsky was cited by the Academy as "the originator of one of the most important methods of contemporary chemical analysis." At the presentation it was said "your polarograph . . . can be used for the most diverse purposes. Steadily your method has won the confidence of analytical chemists." Heyrovsky's career was unusual in that he spent it entirely on the study of the polarograph, the device that he invented, and on its application in polarography, the electrochemical means of determining the chemical composition of oxidizable substances. (D.W.)

1960

Libby, Willard Frank 64

Prize: Chemistry, 1960. *Born:* December 17, 1908; Grand Valley, CO. *Death:* September 8, 1980; Los Angeles, CA. *Parents:* Father, Ora Edward Libby; Mother, Eva May Rivers Libby. *Nationality:* American. *Religion:* Most probably Christian/Protestant. *Education:* Univ. of California,

B.S., 1931; Univ. of California, Ph.D., 1933. *Spouse:* Leonor Hickey, married 1940, divorced 1966; Leona Woods Marshall, married 1966. *Children:* Janet Eva, daughter; Charlotte, daughter. *Career:* Univ. of California, Berkeley, Professor, 1933–45; Univ. of Chicago, IL, Professor, 1945–54; United States Atomic Energy Commission, 1954–59; Univ. of California, Los Angeles, Professor and Administrator, 1959–80. *Other Awards:* Research Corporation Award, 1951; Chandler Medal, Columbia Univ., 1954; Remsen Memorial Lecture Award, 1955; Bicentennial Lecture Award, City College of New York, 1956; Nuclear Applications in Chemistry Award, 1956; Cresson Medal, Franklin Institute, 1957; Willard Gibbs Medal, 1958; Priestley Memorial Award, Dickinson College, 1959; Albert Einstein Medal Award, 1959; Day Medal, Geological Society of America, 1961; Gold Medal, American Institute of Chemists, 1970; Lehman Award, New York Academy of Science, 1971.

Selected Publications: "Stability of Uranium and Thorium for Natural Fission." *Physical Review* 55 (1939): 1269. *Radiocarbon Dating.* Chicago: Univ. of Chicago Press, 1952. "Chemistry and the Peaceful Uses of the Atom." *Chemical and Engineering News* 35 (1957): 14–17.

For More Information See: Current Biography Yearbook. New York: H.W. Wilson, 1954, 406–07. *The Excitement and Fascination of Science.* Palo Alto, CA: Annual Reviews, Inc., 1965, Vol. 1, 241–46. *New York Times* (September 10, 1980): D23.

Commentary: The award to Willard Libby was made "for his method to use carbon-14 for age determination in archaeology, geology, geophysics, and other branches of science." He developed sensitive techniques to detect the amount of carbon-14 activity in a sample, and by relating the amount found to the constant amount when the substance was a living plant or animal, he determined the age of the sample. Libby also participated in the Manhattan Project during World War II as part of the group that developed the gaseous-diffusion method of separating uranium isotopes, and he was an important member of the Atomic Energy Commission in its deliberations in the 50s. (G.W.)

1961

Calvin, Melvin 65

Prize: Chemistry, 1961. *Born:* April 8, 1911; St. Paul, MN. *Death:* January 8, 1997; Berkeley, CA. *Parents:* Father, Elias Calvin; Mother, Rose Hervitz Calvin. *Nationality:* American. *Religion:* Jewish. *Education:* Michigan College of Mining and Technology, B.S., 1931; Univ. of Minnesota, Ph.D., 1935. *Spouse:* Genevieve Jemtegaard, married 1942, died 1986. *Children:* Noel, son; Elin, daughter; Karole, daughter. *Career:* Univ. of Manchester, England, Researcher, 1935–37; Univ. of California, Berkeley, Professor, 1937–80. *Other Awards:* Davy Medal, Royal Society, 1964; Priestley Medal, American Chemical Society, 1978; Gold Medal, American Institute of Chemists, 1979; Lynen Medal, 1983; Hendricks Medal, 1983; Calvin Medal, 1985; National Medal of Science, 1989; Ericsson Award, 1991.

Selected Publications: "The Path of Carbon in Photosynthesis." *Science* 107 (1948): 476. *The Path of Carbon in Photosynthesis.* Englewood Cliffs, NJ: Prentice-Hall, 1957

(with J.A. Bassham). "Quantum Conversion in Photosynthesis." *Journal of Theoretical Biology* 1 (1961): 258. *Photosynthesis of Carbon Compounds.* New York: W.A. Benjamin, 1962.

For More Information See: Asimov's Biographical Encyclopedia of Science and Technology. Garden City, NY: Doubleday, 1982, 837. *Current Biography Yearbook.* New York: H.W. Wilson, 1962, 68–70. *Following the Trail of Light.* Washington, DC: American Chemical Society, 1992. *New York Times* (January 10, 1997): Sect. B, 6.

Commentary: Melvin Calvin's Nobel Prize was earned "for his research on the carbon dioxide assimilation in plants," the process of photosynthesis. He pioneered the use of radioactive isotopes, particularly carbon-14, in the tracing of the metabolism of chemical substances in biochemical pathways. His research on the metal chelate compounds and in the area of biology was also significant. (J.E.H.)

1962

Kendrew, John Cowdery, Sir 66

Prize: Chemistry, 1962. *Born:* March 24, 1917; Oxford, England. *Death:* August 23, 1997; Cambridge, England. *Parents:* Father, Wilfrid George Kendrew; Mother, Evelyn May Graham Sandberg Kendrew. *Nationality:* British. *Religion:* Agnostic. *Education:* Cambridge Univ., England, B.A., 1939; Cambridge Univ., England, M.A., 1943; Cambridge Univ., England, Ph.D., 1949; Cambridge Univ., England, D.Sc., 1962. *Spouse:* None. *Children:* None. *Career:* British Military Service, 1939–46; Cambridge Univ., England, Researcher and Professor, 1947–74; European Molecular Biology Laboratory, Heidelberg, Germany, Director, 1975–82. *Other Awards:* Order of the British Empire, 1963; Royal Medal, Royal Society, 1965; Knighthood, 1974; Order of the Madara Horsemen, Bulgaria, 1980.

Selected Publications: "The Crystal Structure of Horse Myoglobin." *Haemoglobin (Symposium on Conference at Cambridge in Memory of Joseph Barcroft)* (June 1948): 131–49. "The Crystal Structure of Horse Metmyoglobin I. General Features: The Arrangement of the Polypeptide Chains." *Proceedings of the Royal Society (London)* A201 (1950): 62–89. "A Three-Dimensional Model of the Myoglobin Molecule Obtained by X-ray Analysis." *Nature* 181 (1958): 666 (with others). "The Molecular Structures of Myoglobin and Hemoglobin." *New Perspectives in Biology, Proceedings of the Symposium, Rehovoth, Israel* (1963): 18–27.

For More Information See: Biographical Encyclopedia of Scientists. New York: Facts on File, 1981, 434. *Current Biography Yearbook.* New York: H.W. Wilson, 1963, 215–17. *New York Times* (August 30, 1997):A52. *Thinkers of the Twentieth Century.* Detroit, MI: Gale, 1983, 292–93.

Commentary: John Kendrew shared the Nobel Prize for his contributions to the "studies of the structures of globular proteins," using x-ray crystallography. Kendrew determined the structure of myoglobin, a protein containing approximately 2,600 atoms. Another major interest was the highly respected *Journal of Molecular Biology*, which he founded in 1959, and for which he served as editor throughout the remainder of his career. (J.E.H.)

Perutz, Max Ferdinand   **67**
Prize: Chemistry, 1962. *Born:* May 19, 1914; Vienna, Austria. *Parents:* Father, Hugo Perutz; Mother, Adele Goldschmidt Perutz. *Nationality:* Austrian; later British citizen. *Religion:* Jewish. *Education:* Cambridge Univ., England, Ph.D., 1940. *Spouse:* Gisela Clara Peiser, married March 28, 1942. *Children:* Robin, son; Vivien, daughter. *Career:* Cambridge Univ., England, Researcher and Professor, 1939–79. *Other Awards:* Royal Medal, Royal Society, 1971; Copley Medal, Royal Society, 1979.

Selected Publications: Proteins and Nucleic Acids: Structure and Function. New York: Elsevier Publishing Company, 1962. *Haemoglobin and Myoglobin* (Atlas of Molecular Structures in Biology Series: No. 2). New York: Oxford Univ. Press, 1981 (with G. Fermi).

For More Information See: Biographical Encyclopedia of Scientists. New York: Facts on File, 1981. *Current Biography Yearbook.* New York: H.W. Wilson, 1963, 324–26. *Is Science Necessary?* Oxford, England: Oxford Univ. Press, 1991.

Commentary: Max Perutz shared the Nobel Prize for his contribution to the "studies of the structures of globular proteins." In particular, Perutz determined the structure of hemoglobin, using X-ray diffraction analysis of hemoglobin crystals. His research interests centered on molecular biology, and his discoveries led to a greater understanding of the relationship between the structure and function of macromolecules in living systems. (J.E.H.)

1963

Natta, Giulio   **68**
Prize: Chemistry, 1963. *Born:* February 26, 1903; Imperia, Italy. *Death:* May 1, 1979; Bergamo, Italy. *Parents:* Father, Francesco Natta; Mother, Elena Crespi Natta. *Nationality:* Italian. *Religion:* Catholic. *Education:* Polytechnic Institute, Italy, Ph.D., 1924. *Spouse:* Rosita Beati, married April 25, 1935. *Children:* Franca, daughter; Giussepe, son. *Career:* Polytechnic Institute, Milan, Italy, Professor, 1924–33; Univ. of Pavia, Italy, Professor and Administrator, 1933–35; Univ. of Rome, Italy, Professor and Administrator, 1935–37; Polytechnic Institute, Turin, Italy, Professor and Administrator, 1937–74. *Other Awards:* Gold Medal, Milan, Italy, 1960; Gold Medal, President of Italy, 1961; Gold Medal, Synthetic Rubber Industry, 1961; Stas Medal, Belgian Chemical Society, 1962; Gold Medal, Society of Plastic Engineers, NY, 1963; Perrin Medal, French Chemical Physical Society, 1963; Lavoisier Medal, French Chemical Society, 1963; Perkin Gold Medal, English Society of Dyers and Colourists, 1963; John Scott Award, Philadelphia, PA, 1964; Lomonosov Gold Medal, Academy of Sciences, USSR, 1969.

Selected Publications: "The Kinetics of the Stereospecific Polymerization of A-Olefins." *Advances in Catalysis* 11 (1959): 1–66 (with I. Pasquon). "Organometallic Complexes As Catalysts in Ionic Polymerization." *Tetrahedron* 8 (1960): 86–100 (with G. Mazzanti). "Precisely Constructed Polymers." *Scientific American* 205 (August 1961): 33–41. "Alternating Copolymer of Dimethylketene with Acetone." *Macromolecular Syntheses* 4 (1972): 73–75 (with G.F. Pregaglia and M. Binaghi). *Polymerization Reactions.* New York: Springer, 1975 (with others). *Structure and Behavior of 3-Dimensional Molecules. An Introduction to Stereochemistry.* Weinheim, Germany: Verlag Chemie, 1976 (with Mario Farino).

For More Information See: Current Biography Yearbook. New York: H.W. Wilson, 1964, 312–14. "Giulio Natta: Biography." *Rubber Chem. Technology* 57 (May/June 1984): 658–61

Commentary: Giulio Natta's life as a teacher, administrator, and researcher spanned over 50 years of work in industrial and chemical engineering, which resulted in the discovery of basic chemical techniques and their practical applications for business and industry. Natta's major research focus in macromolecular chemistry was the study of petrochemicals, specifically olefins. Working independently but cooperatively with Karl Ziegler, and using his background in polymers, Natta discovered the process of stereospecific polymerization. For these studies, for discoveries in polymerization, for "bridging the gap between natural and synthetic macromolecules, and for developing practical methods for linking simple atoms into complex molecular networks," Natta and Ziegler won the Nobel Prize. (J.B.T.)

Ziegler, Karl   **69**
Prize: Chemistry, 1963. *Born:* November 26, 1898; Helsa, Oberhausen, Germany. *Death:* August 11, 1973; Mulheim, Germany. *Parents:* Father, Karl Ziegler; Mother, Luise Rall Ziegler. *Nationality:* German. *Religion:* Lutheran. *Education:* Univ. of Marburg, Germany, Ph.D., 1920. *Spouse:* Maria Kurtz, married 1923. *Children:* Erhart, son; Marianne, daughter. *Career:* Marburg Univ., Germany, Professor, 1923–27; Heidelberg Univ., Germany, Professor, 1927–36; Univ. of Halle, Germany, Professor and Administrator, 1936–43; Kaiser Wilhelm Institute, Germany, Director, 1943–69. *Other Awards:* Leibig Medal, 1935; Lavosier Medal, 1955; Swinburne Medal, 1964.

Selected Publications: "Catalysis of the Polymerization of Unsaturated Hydrocarbons by Alkali Organic Compounds." *Annalen* 511 (1934): 45–63 (with L. Jakob). "The Importance of Alkali Metallo-organic Compounds for Synthesis." *Angewandte Chemie* 49 (1936): 455–60. "The Polymerization of Butadiene and the Production of Artificial Rubber." *Rubber Chem. Tech* 11 (1938): 501–07. "Organoalkali Compounds. XV. Controlled 1,2- and 1,4-Polymerization of Butadiene." *Annalen* 542 (1940): 90–122 (with H. Grimm and R. Willer). *Praparative Organische Chemie.* Wiesbaden, Germany: Dieterichsche Verlags, 1948. "The Polymerization of Ethylene." *Bull. Soc. Chim. France* (1956): 1–6.

For More Information See: Biographical Memoirs of the Fellows of the Royal Society. London: Royal Society, 1975 (Volume 21), 569. *Chemical and Engineering News* 41 (November 11, 1963): 22. "Karl Ziegler: Biography." *Rubber Chemistry and Technology* 57 (May/June 1984): G49-G57.

Commentary: Karl Ziegler shared the Nobel Prize for his work on catalysis of polymerization. His early research centered on the Grignard reactions, which prompted his interest in metallo-organic compounds. In the 1950s, Ziegler discovered that he could use aluminum- or titanium-imbedded resins as catalysts in the production of polyethylene, producing a stronger, unbranched polymer. He and his colaureate, Giulio Natta, continued to develop this fertile field of chemistry over the course of their careers. (R.P.)

1964

Hodgkin, Dorothy Crowfoot   **70**

Prize: Chemistry, 1964. *Born:* May 12, 1910; Cairo, Egypt. *Death:* July 29, 1994; Shipston-on-Stour, England. *Parents:* Father, John Winter Crowfoot; Mother, Grace Mary Hood Hodgkin. *Nationality:* British. *Religion:* Most probably Christian/Protestant. *Education:* Oxford Univ., England, baccalaureate, 1932; Cambridge Univ., England, Ph.D., 1937. *Spouse:* Thomas L. Hodgkin, married December 16, 1937, died 1982. *Children:* Luke, son; Tobias, son; Elizabeth, daughter. *Career:* Oxford Univ., England, Professor, 1934–77; Bristol University, England, Professor and Administrator, 1970–88. *Other Awards:* Royal Medal, Royal Society, 1957; Order of Merit, 1965; Copley Medal, Royal Society, 1976; Mikhail Lomonosov Gold Medal, 1982; Dmitrov Prize, 1984; Lenin Prize, 1987.

Selected Publications: "X-ray Analysis and Protein Structure." *Cold Spring Harbor Symposia on Quantitative Biology* 14 (1949): 79–84. "X-ray Analysis of the Structure of Penicillin." *Advancement Sci* 6 (1949): 85–89. "X-ray Crystallographic Study of the Structure of Vitamin B-12." *Bull. Soc. Franc. Mineral et Cryst* 78 (1955): 106–15. *Wandering Scientists*. New Delhi: Indian Council for Cultural Relations, 1974. *Structural Studies on Molecules of Biological Interest*. New York: Oxford Univ. Press, 1981.

For More Information See: *Asimov's Biographical Encyclopedia of Science and Technology*. Garden City, NY: Doubleday, 1982, 834. *Biographical Encyclopedia of Scientists*. New York: Facts on File, 1981, 386–87. Ferry, Georgina. *Dorothy Hodgkin: a Life*. London: Granta Books, 1998. *New York Times Biographical Service* (August 1, 1994): 1150.

Commentary: Dorothy Hodgkin spent her career working on the determination of the structure of complex organic molecules and was awarded the Nobel Prize for her structural determination on vitamin B-12. She was the first to use the computer successfully in such work to determine the structure of penicillin (1949) and later also studied the structure of insulin. Hodgkin was also an inveterate traveler, an avocation inherited from her archaeologist father, and a worker for peace and communication between nations. (J.L.)

1965

Woodward, Robert Burns   **71**

Prize: Chemistry, 1965. *Born:* April 10, 1917; Boston, MA. *Death:* July 8, 1979; Cambridge, MA. *Parents:* Father, Arthur Chester Woodward; Mother, Margaret W. Burns Woodward. *Nationality:* American. *Religion:* Protestant. *Education:* Massachusetts Institute of Technology, B.S., 1936; Massachusetts Institute of Technology, Ph.D., 1937; Wesleyan Univ., CT, D.Sc., 1945. *Spouse:* Irji Pullman, married July 30, 1938; Eudoxia M.M. Muller, married September 14, 1946. *Children:* Siiri Anne, daughter; Jean Kirsten, daughter; Crystal Elisabeth, daughter; Eric Richard Arthur, son. *Career:* Harvard Univ., MA, Professor, 1937–79. *Other Awards:* John Scott Medal, Franklin Institute, 1945;

Ledlie Prize, Harvard Univ., MA, 1955; Davy Medal, Royal Society, 1959; Pius XI Gold Medal, Pontifical Academy of Sciences, 1961; Roger Adams Medal, American Chemical Society, 1961; Priestley Medallion, Dickinson College, NJ, 1962; National Medal of Science, USA, 1964; Willard Gibbs Medal, American Chemical Society, 1967; Lavoisier Medal, Société Chimique de France, 1968; Decorated Order of the Rising Sun, Japan, 1970; Science Achievement Award, American Medical Association, 1971; Arthur C. Cope Award, American Chemical Society, 1973; Copley Medal, Royal Society, 1978.

Selected Publications: "Total Synthesis of Quinine." *Journal of the American Chemical Society* 66 (1944): 849 (with W. E. Doering). "Total Synthesis of a Steroid." *Journal of the American Chemical Society* 73 (1951): 2403–04 (with others). "The Total Synthesis of Cholesterol." *Journal of the American Chemical Society* 73 (1951): 3548 (with F. Sondheimer and D. Taub). "The Total Synthesis of Cortisone." *Journal of the American Chemical Society* 73 (1951): 4057 (with F. Sondheimer and D. Taub). "The Total Synthesis of Reserpine." *Journal of the American Chemical Society* 78 (1956): 2023–25 (with others). "Total Synthesis of Vitamin B-12." *Pure and Applied Chemistry* 33 (1973): 145–77.

For More Information See: *Biographical Memoirs of the Fellows of the Royal Society* . London: Royal Society, 1981 (Volume 27), 629–95. Bowden, M. *Robert Burns Woodward and the Art of Organic Synthesis*. Philadelphia, PA: Beckman Center, 1992. *Current Biography Yearbook*. New York: H.W. Wilson, 1952, 647–49.

Commentary: Robert Woodward's Nobel recognized "his meritorious contributions to the art of chemical synthesis." A brilliant laboratory worker, Woodward developed techniques for total synthesis and achieved total synthesis of quinine (1944), penicillin (1945), strychnine (1947), cholesterol and cortisone (1951), lysergic acid (1954), reserpine (1956), tetracycline (1962), chlorophyll (1966), and vitamin B-12 (1971). (E.G.)

1966

Mulliken, Robert Sanderson   **72**

Prize: Chemistry, 1966. *Born:* June 7, 1896; Newburyport, MA. *Death:* October 31, 1986; Arlington, VA. *Parents:* Father, Samuel Parsons Mulliken; Mother, Katherine Wilmarth Mulliken. *Nationality:* American. *Religion:* Unitarian. *Education:* Massachusetts Institute of Technology, B.S., 1917; Univ. of Chicago, IL, Ph.D., 1921. *Spouse:* Mary Helen Noe, married December 24, 1929; died 1975. *Children:* Lucia Maria, daughter; Valerie Noe, daughter. *Career:* Bureau of Mines, United States, Engineer, 1917; United States Army, 1918–19; Univ. of Chicago, IL, Professor, 1919–26; New York Univ., Professor, 1926–28; Univ. of Chicago, IL, 1928–84. *Other Awards:* Medal, Univ. of Liege, 1948; Lewis Gold Medal, American Chemical Society, 1960; Richards Gold Medal, 1960; Debye Award, 1963; Kirkwood Medal, 1964; Willard Gibbs Gold Medal, 1965; Baskerville Medal, CCNY, 1965; Priestley Medal, 1983.

Selected Publications: "The Assignment of Quantum Numbers for Electrons in Molecules." *Physics Review* 32 (1928): 186–222. "The Assignment of Quantum Numbers for Electrons in Molecules. II. Correlation of Molecular and Atomic Electron States." *Physics Review* 32 (1928): 761–72. "Electronic States of Diatomic Carbon, and the C-C Bond." *Physics Review* 56 (1939): 778–81. "Quantum-Mechanical Methods and the Electronic Spectra and Structure of Molecules." *Chemical Reviews* 41 (1947): 201–06.

For More Information See: Biographical Encyclopedia of Scientists. New York: Facts on File, 1981, 752–53. *Biographical Memoirs of the Fellows of the Royal Society.* London: Royal Society, 1990 (Volume 35), 327. *Current Biography Yearbook.* New York: H.W. Wilson, 1967, 307–09. Mulliken, R.S. and Ransil, B.J. *Life of a Scientist.* Berlin; New York: Springer-Verlag, 1989.

Commentary: Robert Mulliken's Nobel was presented "for his fundamental work concerning chemical bonds and the electronic structure of molecules by the molecular-orbital method." Mulliken, over a long and fruitful career, developed the theory and interpretation of molecular spectra and applied quantum theory to the electronic states of molecules, eventually providing the molecular orbital theory of electrons moving in a field produced by all the nuclei present. He also worked in the areas of isotope separation by evaporative centrifuging and in electronegativity. (P.P.)

1967

Eigen, Manfred 73

Prize: Chemistry, 1967. *Born:* May 9, 1927; Bochum, Germany. *Parents:* Father, Ernst Eigen; Mother, Hedwig Feld Eigen. *Nationality:* German. *Religion:* Lutheran. *Education:* Univ. of Göttingen, Germany, Doctor Rerum Naturalium, 1951. *Spouse:* Elfriede Müller, married 1952. *Children:* Gerald, son; Angela, daughter. *Career:* Univ. of Göttingen, Germany, Researcher, 1951–53; Max Planck Institut, Germany, Professor and Administrator, 1953-. *Other Awards:* Bodenstein Prize, 1956; Otto Hahn Prize, German Chemical Society, 1962; Kirkwood Medal, 1963. Harrison Howe Award, 1965; Carus Medal, 1967; Linus Pauling Medal, 1967; Faraday Medal, 1977; Max Planck Forschungs-Preis, 1994; Paul Ehrlich Award, 1996.

Selected Publications: "Methods for Investigation of Ionic Reactions in Aqueous Solutions with Half Times as Short as 10^{-9} Sec.: Application to Neutralization and Hydrolysis Reactions." *Discussions of the Faraday Society* 17 (1954): 194–205. "Kinetics of Neutralization." *Zeitschrift für Elektrochemie* 59 (1955): 986–93 (with Leo De Maeyer). "Potential-Impulse Method for the Investigation of Very Rapid Ionic Reactions in Aqueous Solution." *Zeitschrift für Elektrochemie* 59 (1955): 483–94 (with J. Schoen). "A Temperature-Jump Method for the Examination of Chemical Relaxation." *Zeitschrift für Elektrochemie* 63 (1959): 652–61 (with G. Czerlinski). "Eine Kinetische Methode zur Untersuchung Schneller Prototroper Tautomerisierungsreaktionen." *Chemische Berichte* 98 (May 1965): 1623–38 (with G. Ilgenfritz and W. Kruse).

For More Information See: Contemporary Authors. Detroit, MI: Gale Research Company, 1983 (Volume 108), 140. *Science* 158 (November 10, 1967): 748–68.

Commentary: Manfred Eigen was awarded the Nobel Prize for developing techniques to measure rapid chemical reactions. Ronald G.W. Norrish and George Porter jointly shared the other half of the prize. The relaxation methods developed by Eigen, beginning in the mid-1950s, revolutionized chemical research by making possible the study of chemical reactions with half times from one second to fractions of a millimicrosecond. By disturbing the equilibrium of a solution and electronically measuring the time necessary for the solution to return to equilibrium, Eigen provided a way to study the reaction rates of previously unmeasurable chemical processes. (J.C.H.)

Norrish, Ronald George Wreyford 74

Prize: Chemistry, 1967. *Born:* November 9, 1897; Cambridge, England. *Death:* June 7, 1978; Cambridge, England. *Parents:* Father, Herbert Norrish; Mother, Amy Norrish. *Nationality:* British. *Religion:* Most probably Christian/Protestant. *Education:* Cambridge Univ., England, baccalaureate, 1921; Cambridge Univ., England, Ph.D., 1924. *Spouse:* Anne Smith, married 1926. *Children:* 2 daughters. *Career:* British Army, 1916–19; Cambridge Univ., England, Professor, 1925–65. *Other Awards:* Liversidge Medal, Chemical Society, 1958; Davy Medal, Royal Society, 1958; Bernard Lewis Gold Medal, Combustion Institute, 1964; Faraday Medal, Chemical Society, 1965; Longstaff Medal, Chemical Society, 1969.

Selected Publications: "Chemical Reactions Produced by Very High Light Intensities." *Nature* 164 (1949): 658 (with G. Porter). "The Application of Flash Techniques to the Study of Fast Reactions." *Discussions of the Faraday Society* 17 (1954): 40–46 (with G. Porter). "The Gas Phase Oxidation of n-Butenes." *Proceedings of the Royal Society (London)* Series A272 (1963): 164–91 (with K. Porter). "The Kinetics and Analysis of Very Fast Reactions." *Chemistry in Britain* 1 (1965): 289–311.

For More Information See: Biographical Memoirs of the Fellows of the Royal Society. London: Royal Society, 1981 (Volume 27), 379–424. *The Excitement and Fascination of Science.* Palo Alto, CA: Annual Reviews, Inc., 1978, Vol. 2, 483–506. "Obituary R. G. W. Norrish, 1897–1978." *Nature* 275 (September 7, 1978): 78–79.

Commentary: Ronald Norrish was awarded the prize for his "studies of extremely fast chemical reactions, effected by disturbing the equilibrium by means of very short pulses of energy." The chemical reactions studied lasted only for one-billionth of a second, but the techniques developed allowed for the observation of short-lived intermediate species, such as free radicals, and for complete elaborations of reaction kinetics. The techniques of flash photolysis have been used in liquids, gases, and for the study of biological materials. Norrish also further developed the theory of photochemical reactions. (M.F.)

Porter, George, Sir 75

Prize: Chemistry, 1967. *Born:* December 6, 1920; Stainforth, England. *Parents:* Father, John Smith Porter; Mother, Alice Ann Roebuck Porter. *Nationality:* British. *Religion:* Agnostic; from Methodist background. *Education:* Univ. of Leeds, England, B.Sc., 1941; Cambridge Univ., England, M.A., 1947; Cambridge Univ., England, Ph.D., 1949. *Spouse:* Stella Jean Brooke, married August 12, 1949. *Children:* John Brooke, son; Andrew Christopher, son. *Career:* British Navy, 1941–45; Cambridge Univ., England, Professor,

1949–55; Univ. of Sheffield, England, Professor, 1955–66; Royal Institution, England, Professor and Administrator, 1966–85; Imperial College, England, Researcher and Administrator, 1990-. *Other Awards:* Corday-Morgan Medal, Chemical Society, 1955; Silvanus Thompson Medal, 1969; Davy Medal, Royal Society, 1971; Knighthood, 1972; Kalinga Prize, 1977; Robertson Prize, National Academy of Sciences, 1978; Rumford Medal, Royal Society, 1978; Communications Award, European Physical Society, 1978; Faraday Medal, Chemical Society, 1979; Longstaff Medal, 1981; Faraday Award, 1991; Copley Medal, 1992.

Selected Publications: "Chemical Reactions Produced by Very High Light Intensities." *Nature* 164 (1949): 658 (with R. Norrish). "The Application of Flash Techniques to the Study of Fast Reactions." *Discussions of the Faraday Society* 17 (1954): 40–46 (with R. Norrish). *Chemistry for the Modern World.* New York: Barnes and Noble, 1962. *Progress in Reaction Kinetics.* New York: Pergamon Press, 1965.

For More Information See: Biographical Encyclopedia of Scientists. New York: Facts on File, 1981, 647–48. *Science* 158 (November 10, 1967): 746–48.

Commentary: George Porter shared the Nobel for his "studies of extremely fast chemical reactions, effected by disturbing the equilibrium by means of very short pulses of energy." The chemical reactions studied lasted only for one-billionth of a second, but the techniques that were developed became standard for observing short-lived intermediates that permitted elucidating chemical reaction kinetics. Flash photolysis was used in important studies of gases, liquids, and biochemical systems. (M.F.)

1968

Onsager, Lars   76
Prize: Chemistry, 1968. *Born:* November 27, 1903; Oslo, Norway. *Death:* October 5, 1976; Coral Gables, FL. *Parents:* Father, Erling Onsager; Mother, Ingrid Kirkeby Onsager. *Nationality:* Norwegian; later American citizen. *Religion:* Protestant. *Education:* Norges Tekniske Hogskale, Norway, Chem. E., 1925; Yale Univ., CT, Ph.D., 1935. *Spouse:* Margarete Arledter, married September 7, 1933. *Children:* Inger Marie, daughter; Erling Frederick, son; Hans Tanberg, son; Christian Carl, son. *Career:* Brown Univ., Providence, RI, Professor, 1928–33; Yale Univ., New Haven, CT, Professor, 1933–72; Univ. Miami, Professor, 1972–76. *Other Awards:* Rumford Medal, American Academy of Sciences, 1953; Lorentz Medal, 1958; G. N. Lewis Medal, 1962; J. G. Kirkwood Medal, 1962; Willard Gibbs Medal, 1962; T. W. Richards Medal, 1964; Debye Award, 1965; Belfer Award, 1966; National Science Medal, 1969.

Selected Publications: "Reciprocal Relations in Irreversible Processes." *Physical Review* 37 (1931): 405–26. "Reciprocal Relations in Irreversible Processes." *Physical Review* 38 (1931): 2265–79. "Initial Recombination of Ions." *Physical Review* 54 (1938): 554–57. "de Haas-van Alphen Effect in Zinc." *Physical Review* 74 (1948): 1235 (with J. E. Robinson). "Fluctuations and Irreversible Processes." *Physical Review* 91 (1953): 1505–12 (with S. Machlup).

For More Information See: Biographical Memoirs of the Fellows of the Royal Society. London: Royal Society, 1978 (Volume 24), 445. *Current Biography Yearbook.* New York: H.W. Wilson, 1958, 321–23.

Commentary: Lars Onsager was awarded the Nobel Prize "for the discovery of the reciprocal relations bearing his name which are fundamental for the thermodynamics of irreversible processes." His theoretical treatments provided the foundation for the study of nonequilibrium thermodynamics. Earlier in his career, he also modified the Debye-Huckel equations for ion motion in solution to include the effect of Brownian motion. (W.G.)

1969

Barton, Derek Harold Richard, Sir   77
Prize: Chemistry, 1969. *Born:* September 8, 1918; Gravesend, Kent, England. *Death:* March 16, 1998; College Station, TX. *Parents:* Father, William Thomas Barton; Mother, Maude Henrietta Lukes Barton. *Nationality:* British. *Religion:* Christian. *Education:* Imperial College, England, B.Sc., 1940; Imperial College, England, Ph.D., 1942; Univ. of London, England, D.Sc., 1949. *Spouse:* Jeanne Wilkins, married December 20, 1944, divorced 1965; Christiane Cognet, married November 5, 1969, died 1992; Judith Von-Leuenberger Cobb, married August 15, 1993. *Children:* William Godfrey Lukes, son. *Career:* British Government Service, Researcher, 1942–45; Imperial College, England, Professor, 1945–49; Harvard Univ., MA, Professor, 1949–50; Univ. of London, England, Professor, 1950–55; Univ. of Glasgow, Scotland, Professor, 1955–57; Imperial College, England, Professor, 1957–78; Institute of Chemistry and Natural Substances, France, Director, 1978–85; Texas A & M, Professor, 1985–98. *Other Awards:* Hoffman Prize, Imperial College, England, 1940; Harrison Memorial Prize, Chemical Society, 1948; Corday-Morgan Medal, Chemical Society, 1951; Fritzsche Award, American Chemical Society, 1956; Roger Adams Award, American Chemical Society, 1959; Davy Medal, Royal Society, 1961; Knighthood, 1972; Royal Medal, 1972; Longstaff Medal, 1972; Priestley Medal, 1995.

Selected Publications: "The Conformation of the Steroid Nucleus." *Experienta* 6 (1950): 316–20. "The Stereochemistry of Cyclohexane Derivatives." *Journal of the Chemical Society* (1953): 1027–40. "The Inaugural Simonsen Lecture. Some Aspects of Sesquiterpenoid Chemistry." *Proceedings of the Chemical Society* (1958): 61–66. "Recent Progress in Conformational Analysis." *Theoret Org. Chem., Papers Kekule Symposium, London* (1958): 127–43. "Recent Progress in Conformational Analysis." *Suomen Kemistilehte* 32A (1959): 27–33.

For More Information See: The Biographical Dictionary of Scientists: Chemists. New York: Bedrick, 1984, 14–15. *Chemical and Engineering News* 47 (November 10, 1969): 11. *Science* 166 (November 7, 1969): 715–22. *Some Recollections of Gap Jumping.* Washington, DC: American Chemical Society, 1991.

Commentary: Derek Barton shared the Nobel Prize with Odd Hassel for contributions "to the development of the concept of conformation and its application in chemistry." Barton's landmark paper proposed that functional group orientations in space affect the reaction rates in isomers. He applied his views to six-membered organic rings and explained the stability of cyclohexane, building on Hassel's work. Barton's later work dealt with steroids, terpenes, and oxyradicals. (J.R.F.)

Hassel, Odd   78

Prize: Chemistry, 1969. *Born:* May 17, 1897; Oslo, Norway. *Death:* May 15, 1981; Oslo, Norway. *Parents:* Father, Ernst Hassel; Mother, Mathilde Klaveness Hassel. *Nationality:* Norwegian. *Religion:* Lutheran. *Education:* Univ. of Oslo, Norway, Candidate Real degree, 1920; Univ. of Berlin, Germany, D. Phil., 1924. *Spouse:* None. *Children:* None. *Career:* Univ. of Oslo, Norway, Professor, 1925–64. *Other Awards:* Fridtjof Nansen Award, 1946; Knight Order of St. Olav; Gunnerus Medal, 1964; Guldberg Waage Medal, 1964.

Selected Publications: Crystal Chemistry. London: Heinemann, 1935. *U.S. Dept. Com., Office Tech. Serv.* AD267293 (1961): 1–37. "Weak Intermolecular Bonds in Solids." *Dansk. Tidsskr. Farm* 36 (1962): 41–54. "Investigation of Molecular Structures." *Selected Topics in Structure Chemistry.* Oslo: Universitetsforlaget, 1967.

For More Information See: Chemical and Engineering News 47 (November 10, 1969): 11. *Science* 166 (November 7, 1969): 715–22.

Commentary: Odd Hassel and Derek Barton shared the Nobel Prize for their contributions "to the development of the concept of conformation and its application in chemistry." Hassel's early career centered on the investigation of silver halide photosensitization by organic dyes, in the course of which he discovered adsorption indicators. However, it was his landmark papers on conformational analysis of cyclohexane (which showed the chair form of the compound to be more stable than the boat form) that brought him to prominence. His later studies of charge-transfer bonding were also important. (J.R.F.)

1970

Leloir, Luis Federico   79

Prize: Chemistry, 1970. *Born:* September 6, 1906; Paris, France. *Death:* December 2, 1987; Buenos Aires, Argentina. *Parents:* Father, Federico R. Leloir; Mother, Hortensia Aguirre Leloir. *Nationality:* Argentinian. *Religion:* Catholic. *Education:* Univ. of Buenos Aires, Argentina, M.D., 1932. *Spouse:* Amelie Zuherbuhler, married November 26, 1943. *Children:* Amelia, daughter. *Career:* Univ. of Buenos Aires, Argentina, Researcher, 1932–35; Cambridge Univ., England, Researcher, 1935–37; Institute of Physiology, Argentina, Researcher, 1937–44; United States, Exile, 1944–47; Biochemical Research Institute, Argentina, Researcher, 1947–87. *Other Awards:* Gairdner Award; Louisa Gross Horowitz Award.

Selected Publications: "The Enzymic Transformation of Uridine Diphosphate into a Galactose Derivative." *Arch. Biochem. Biophys* 33 (1951): 186–90. "Carbohydrate Metabolism." *Ann. Rev. Biochem* 22 (1953): 179–210 (with C.E. Cardini). "Uridine Coenzymes." *Proc. 3rd Intern. Congr. Biochem., Brussels* (1955): 154–62. "Nucleotide and Saccharide Synthesis." *Conf. on Polysaccharides in Biol., Trans* (1958): 155–234.

For More Information See: Biographical Memoirs of the Fellows of the Royal Society. London: Royal Society, 1990 (Volume 35), 201. *Chemical and Engineering News* 48

(November 2, 1970): 13. *The Excitement and Fascination of Science.* Palo Alto, CA: Annual Reviews, Inc., 1990, Vol. 3, Part 1, 367–81 *Science* 170 (November 6, 1970): 604–09.

Commentary: Luis Leloir was awarded the Nobel Prize for "his discovery of sugar nucleotides and their role in the biosynthesis of carbohydrates." Leloir, working in simple circumstances, isolated uridine diphosphate glucose and showed that it was incorporated into glycogen in the presence of a liver enzyme. He also worked out the mechanism of synthesis of starch. Leloir's discoveries—that the sugar nucleotides are principal actors in interconversion of sugars and polysaccharide formation—led to additional research in carbohydrate metabolism and on the medical implications of the discoveries. (C.N.B.)

1971

Herzberg, Gerhard   80

Prize: Chemistry, 1971. *Born:* December 25, 1904; Hamburg, Germany. *Death:* March 3, 1999; Ottawa, Ontario, Canada. *Parents:* Father, Albin Herzberg; Mother, Ella Biber Herzberg. *Nationality:* German; later Canadian citizen. *Religion:* Jewish. *Education:* Darmstadt Institute of Technology, Germany, Doctor of Engineering, 1928. *Spouse:* Luise H. Oettinger, married December 29, 1929, died 1971; Monika Tenthoff, married March 21, 1972. *Children:* Paul Albin, son; Agnes Margaret, daughter. *Career:* Darmstadt Institute of Technology, Germany, Professor, 1930–35; Univ. of Saskatchewan, Canada, Professor, 1935–45; Univ. of Chicago, IL, Professor, 1945–48; National Research Council, Canada, Researcher and Administrator, 1949–94. *Other Awards:* Univ. of Liege Medal, 1950; Henry Marshall Tory Medal, Canadian Royal Society, 1953; Jay Kissen Mookerjee Gold Medal, Indian Association for the Cultivation of Science, 1957; Frederic Ives Medal, Optical Society of America, 1964; Willard Gibbs Medal, American Chemical Society, 1969; Faraday Medal, Chemical Society of London, 1970; Royal Medal, Royal Society, 1971; Linus Pauling Medal, American Chemical Society, 1971; Plyler Prize, 1985.

Selected Publications: Atomic Spectra and Atomic Structure. New York: Prentice-Hall, 1937. *Molekulspektren und Molekulstructur. Zweiatomige Molekule.* Dresden, Germany: T. Steinkopff, 1939. *Infrared and Roman Spectra of Polyatomic Molecules.* New York: D. Van Nostrand, 1945. "The Electronic Structure of the Nitrogen Molecule." *Physical Review* 69 (1946): 362–65. "Lamb Shift of the 1(2)S Ground State of Deuterium." *Proceedings of the Royal Society of London* 234A (1956): 516–28.

For More Information See: Chemical and Engineering News 49 (November 1, 1971): 5. *Current Biography Yearbook.* New York: H.W. Wilson, 1973, 185–87.

Commentary: The Nobel Prize was given to Gerhard Herzberg for his "contributions to the knowledge of electronic structure and geometry of molecules, particularly free radicals." Herzberg was responsible for development of techniques and measurement and interpretation of the spectra of molecules, including hydrogen, oxygen, nitrogen, and CO. He also measured the Lamb shifts in D, He, and Li (+) and the spectra of interstellar gas. His work was used in the explanation of the properties of free radicals and ions present as intermediates in chemical reactions. (L.I.S.)

1972

Anfinsen, Christian Boehmer   **81**

Prize: Chemistry, 1972. *Born:* March 26, 1916; Monessen, PA. *Death:* May 14, 1995, Randallstown, MD. *Parents:* Father, Christian Boehmer Anfinsen; Mother, Sophie Rasmussen Anfinsen. *Nationality:* American. *Religion:* Most probably Christian. *Education:* Swarthmore College, PA, B.A., 1937; Univ. of Pennsylvania, M.S., 1939; Harvard Univ., MA, Ph.D., 1943. *Spouse:* Florence Bernice Kenenger, married November 29, 1941, divorced 1978; Libby Esther Shulman Ely, married 1979. *Children:* Carol, daughter; Margot, daughter; Christian, son. *Career:* Univ. of Pennsylvania, Professor, 1938–39; Carlsberg Univ., Denmark, Researcher, 1939–40; Harvard Univ., MA, Professor, 1941–50; National Heart Institute, Researcher, 1950–62; Harvard Univ., MA, Professor, 1962–63; National Institute of Arthritis, Metabolism, and Digestive Diseases, Researcher, 1963–81; Johns Hopkins Univ., MD, Professor, 1982–95. *Other Awards:* Public Service Award, Rockefeller Foundation, 1954; Myrtle Wreath, Hadassah, 1977.

Selected Publications: "Method for the Specific Proteolytic Cleavage of Protein Chains." *Archives of Biochemistry and Biophysics* 65 (1956): 156–63 (with Michael Sela and Harold Tritsch). "Reductive Cleavage of Disulfide Bridges in Ribonuclease." *Science* 125 (1957): 691–92 (with Michael Sela and Frederick H. White). *The Molecular Basis of Evolution.* New York: Wiley, 1959. "The Ribonucleases-Occurrence, Structure and Properties." In *Enzymes.* New York: Academic Press, 1961 (Volume 5), 95–122.

For More Information See: "The 1972 Nobel Prize for Chemistry." *Science* (November 3, 1972): 492–93. "Nobel Winners in Physics, Chemistry." *New York Times* (October 21, 1972) 1: L14.

Commentary: The Nobel citation commends Christian Anfinsen's "work on ribonuclease, especially concerning the connection between the amino acid sequence and the biologically active conformation." His pioneering work on enzymes relating protein organization and function and on the genetic basis of protein organization have been landmark studies in the field. (A.S.)

Moore, Stanford   **82**

Prize: Chemistry, 1972. *Born:* September 4, 1913; Chicago, IL. *Death:* August 23, 1982; Manhattan, NY. *Parents:* Father, John Howard Moore; Mother, Ruth Fowler Moore. *Nationality:* American. *Religion:* Catholic. *Education:* Vanderbilt Univ., TN, A.B., 1935; Univ. of Wisconsin, Ph.D., 1938. *Spouse:* None. *Children:* None. *Career:* Rockefeller Institute for Medical Research, NY, Professor, 1939–42; Office of Scientific Research and Development, Washington, DC, Researcher, 1942–45; Rockefeller Institute for Medical Research, NY, Professor, 1945–82. *Other Awards:* Founder's Medal, Vanderbilt Univ., TN, 1935; Chromatography Award, American Chemical Society, 1964; Richards Medal, American Chemical Society, 1972; Linderstrom-Lang Medal, Copenhagen, Denmark, 1972.

Selected Publications: "Structure and Activity of Pancreatic Ribonuclease." *Soc. Chim. Biol., Celebration Cinquantenaire, Conf. Rappt., Paris* (1964): 189–94. "Amino Acid Analysis: Aqueous Dimethyl Sulfoxide as Solvent for the Ninhydrin Reaction." *Journal of Biological Chemistry* 243 (1968): 6281–83. "Chemical Structures of Pancreatic Ribonuclease and Deoxyribonuclease." *Science* 180 (1973): 458–64 (with William H. Stein). "The Precision and Sensitivity of Amino Acid Analysis." *Kagaku No Ryoiki Zokan* 106 (1976): 136–75.

For More Information See: *Science* 178 (November 3, 1972): 492–93. *Science News* 102 (October 28, 1972): 276. *Biographical Memoirs. National Academy of Sciences.* Washington, DC: National Academy Press, 1987, Volume 56, 355.

Commentary: Stanford Moore, with his colaureate William Stein, received the Nobel Prize for painstaking, lengthy research which established the amino-acid sequence of the enzyme ribonuclease. In the process, they developed an invaluable tool for later research—the automatic amino acid analyzer—as well as identifying critical solvents and techniques for use in such work. Moore and Stein also identified the most likely active site on the ribonuclease molecule. (M.N.)

Stein, William Howard   **83**

Prize: Chemistry, 1972. *Born:* June 25, 1911; New York, NY. *Death:* February 2, 1980; New York, NY. *Parents:* Father, Fred M. Stein; Mother, Beatrice Borg Stein. *Nationality:* American. *Religion:* Jewish. *Education:* Harvard Univ., MA, B.S., 1933; Columbia Univ., NY, Ph.D., 1938. *Spouse:* Phoebe L. Hockstader, married June 22, 1936. *Children:* William Howard, Jr., son; David F., son; Robert J., son. *Career:* Rockefeller Institute, NY, Researcher, 1938–80. *Other Awards:* Award in Chromatography and Electrophoresis, 1964; Theodore Richards Medal, 1972.

Selected Publications: "Amino-Acid Composition of Human Hemoglobin." *Biochimica et Biophysica Acta* 24 (1957): 640–42 (with others). "Chemical Modifications of Ribonuclease." *Brookhaven Symposia in Biology* 13 (1960): 104–14. "Relations Between Structure and Activity of Ribonuclease." *Proc. Intern. Congr. Biochem., 5th, Moscow* 4 (1961): 33–38 (with Stanford Moore). "Structure-Activity Relations in Ribonuclease." *Federation Proceedings* 23 (1964): 599–608. "Structure and the Activity of Ribonuclease." *Israel Journal of Medical Science* 1 (1965): 1229–43.

For More Information See: *Chemical and Engineering News* 50 (October 30, 1972): 2–3. *Dictionary of Scientific Biography.* Supplement II. New York: Scribner's, 851–55. *Science* 178 (November 3, 1972): 492–93. *Biographical Memoirs. National Academy of Sciences.* Washington, DC: National Academy Press, 1987, Volume 56, 415.

Commentary: William Stein was awarded the Nobel Prize for his careful elucidation, with Stanford Moore, of the amino-acid sequence of the enzyme ribonuclease. Stein devised an automatic amino acid analyzer and chromatographic methods for determining the hydrolysis products of proteins and used the technology he had developed to solve the puzzle of the amino-acid sequence. (J.A.S.)

1973

Fischer, Ernst Otto   **84**

Prize: Chemistry, 1973. *Born:* November 10, 1918; Muchen-Solln, Germany. *Parents:* Father, Karl Tobias Fischer; Mother, Valentine Danzer Fischer. *Nationality:* German.

Religion: Lutheran. *Education:* Univ. of Munich, Germany, Dipl. Chem., 1949; Univ. of Munich, Germany, Doctor Rerum Naturalium, 1952. *Spouse:* None. *Children:* None. *Career:* Univ. of Munich, Germany, Professor, 1954-. *Other Awards:* Göttingen Academy Prize, 1957; Alfred Stock-Gedachtnis Prize, 1959.

Selected Publications: "The Nomenclature of Metal Compounds Containing Two Cyclopentadienyl Rings." *Z. Naturforsch* 9b (1954): 619–20. "New Results on Aromatic Metal Carbonyls." *Journal of Inorganic and Nuclear Chemistry* 8 (1958): 268–72. *Metal (pi)-Complexes.* New York: Elsevier, 1966 (with H. Werner). "Transition Metal Carbonyl Carbene Complexes." *Pure and Applied Chemistry* 30 (1972): 353–72.

For More Information See: Biographical Encyclopedia of Scientists. New York: Facts on File, 1981, 264–65. *Science* 182 (November 16, 1973): 699–700.

Commentary: The award to Ernst Otto Fischer was "for his pioneering research in organometallic chemistry . . . in particular, his independent and imaginative efforts in the development of the chemistry of sandwich complexes of the transition metals." His work on the structure of ferrocene gave impetus to the study of sandwich complexes. His later work on transition metal complexes with organic compounds was prolific and notable. (L.I.W.)

Wilkinson, Geoffrey   85
Prize: Chemistry, 1973. *Born:* July 14, 1921; Todmorden, England. *Death:* September 26, 1996; London, England. *Parents:* Father, Henry Wilkinson; Mother, Ruth Crowther Wilkinson. *Nationality:* British. *Religion:* Agnostic; from Anglican and Methodist background. *Education:* Univ. of London, England, B.Sc., 1941; Univ. of London, England, Ph.D., 1946. *Spouse:* Lise Sölver Schou, married July 17, 1951. *Children:* Anne Marie, daughter; Pernille Jane, daughter. *Career:* National Research Council of Canada, Scientific Officer, 1943–46; Univ. of California, Berkeley, Researcher, 1946–50; Massachusetts Institute of Technology, Professor, 1950–51; Harvard Univ., MA, Professor, 1951–55; Univ. of London, England, Professor, 1956–88. *Other Awards:* Inorganic Chemistry Award, American Chemical Society, 1966; Lavoisier Medal, French Chemical Society, 1968; Transition Medal Chemistry Award, Royal Society, 1972; Hiroshima Univ. Medal, Japan, 1978; Royal Medal, Royal Society, 1981; Galileo Medal, Univ. of Pisa, Italy, 1983; Longstaff Medal, 1987; Polyhedron Prize, Royal Society, 1989; Messel Medal, 1990.

Selected Publications: "The Structure of Iron Biscyclopentadienyl." *Journal of the American Chemical Society* 74 (1952): 2125–26 (with M. Rosenblum, M. C. Whiting, and R. B. Woodward). *Advanced Inorganic Chemistry.* New York: Interscience, 1962 (with F. A. Cotton). "Catalytically Active Rhodium (I) Complexes." German Patent 2, 136, 470 (February 10, 1972). "Hexamethyltungsten." U.S. Patent 3, 816, 491 (June 11, 1974). *Basic Inorganic Chemistry.* New York: Wiley, 1976 (with F. A. Cotton).

For More Information See: "The 1973 Nobel Prize for Chemistry." *Science* (November 16, 1973): 699–701. "Three Win Nobel Physics Prize and Two the Chemistry Award." *New York Times* (October 24, 1973) 1: L1, L26.

Commentary: Geoffrey Wilkinson was cited by the Academy for his "pioneering work, performed independently, on the chemistry of the organometallic so-called sandwich compounds." His earlier work on the preparation and elaboration of structure of iron biscyclopentadienyl was followed by other important work on the preparation and structure of transition metal compounds with organic entities, such as hexamethyltungsten. His later work on the catalytic activity of rhodium (II) complexes is another step in developing manufactured compounds that may have far-reaching consequences in the use of metal-based industrial materials. (A.S.)

1974

Flory, Paul John   86
Prize: Chemistry, 1974. *Born:* June 19, 1910; Sterling, IL. *Death:* September 8, 1985; Big Sur, CA. *Parents:* Father, Ezra Flory; Mother, Martha Brumbaugh Flory. *Nationality:* American. *Religion:* Protestant. *Education:* Manchester College, IN, B.Sc., 1931; Ohio State Univ., M.S., 1931; Ohio State Univ., Ph.D., 1934. *Spouse:* Emily Catharine Tabor, married March 7, 1936. *Children:* Susan, daughter; Malinda, daughter; Paul, Jr., son. *Career:* DuPont Experimental Station, DE, Researcher, 1936–38; Univ. of Cincinnati, OH, Professor, 1938–40; Standard Oil Development, OH, Researcher, 1940–43; Goodyear Tire and Rubber, OH, Administrator, 1943–48; Cornell Univ., NY, Professor, 1948–56; Mellon Institute, Pittsburgh, PA, Administrator, 1956–61; Stanford Univ., CA, Professor, 1961–85. *Other Awards:* Sullivant Medal, 1945; Baekeland Award, 1947; Cowyn Medal, 1954; Nichols Medal, 1962; High-Polymer Physics Prize, 1962; International Award in Plastics, 1967; Goodyear Medal, 1968; Debye Award, 1968; Chandler Medal, 1970; First Award for Excellence, 1971; Cresson Medal, 1971; Kirkwood Medal, 1971; Gibbs Medal, 1973; National Medal of Science, 1974; Priestley Medal, 1974.

Selected Publications: Principles of Polymer Chemistry. Ithaca, NY: Cornell Univ. Press, 1953. *Statistical Mechanics of Chain Molecules.* New York: Interscience Publishers, 1969. *Selected Works of Paul J. Flory.* Stanford, CA: Stanford Univ. Press, 1985.

For More Information See: Biographical Encyclopedia of Scientists. New York: Facts on File, 1981, 271–72. *Current Biography Yearbook.* New York: H.W. Wilson, 1975, 127–30.

Commentary: The award to John Flory was for his "fundamental achievements, both theoretical and experimental, in the field of macromolecules." Flory used statistical mechanics early in his career to develop expressions for the chain-length distribution in polymer molecules. He later presented a theory of nonlinear polymer structure and introduced the idea of a Flory temperature, at which polymer properties can be measured. His work on the elasticity of polymer materials was also noteworthy. Flory spent his later years as a leading spokesperson for activist groups working to protect Soviet scientists. (J.A.S.)

1975

Cornforth, John Warcup, Sir   87
Prize: Chemistry, 1975. *Born:* September 7, 1917; Sydney, Australia. *Parents:* Father, John William Cornforth; Mother,

Hilda Eipper Cornforth. *Nationality:* British. *Religion:* Protestant. *Education:* Univ. of Sydney, Australia, B.S., 1937; Univ. of Sydney, Australia, M.Sc., 1938; Oxford Univ., England, D.Phil., 1941. *Spouse:* Rita H. Harradence, married September 27, 1941. *Children:* John, son; Brenda, daughter; Philippa, daughter. *Career:* Medical Research Council, London, England, Researcher, 1946–62; Shell Research Laboratory, Kent, England, Director, 1962–75; Univ. of Sussex, Brighton, England, Professor, 1975–82. *Other Awards:* Corday-Morgan Medal, Chemistry Society, 1953; Flintoff Medal, Chemistry Society, 1966; CIBA Medal, 1966; Stouffer Prize, 1967; Davy Medal, Royal Society, 1968; Ernest Guenther Award, American Chemical Society, 1969; Prix Roussel, 1972; Royal Medal, Royal Society, 1976; Knighthood, 1977; Copley Medal, Royal Society, 1982; Order of Australia, 1991.

Selected Publications: The Chemistry of Penicillin. Princeton, NJ: Princeton Univ. Press, 1949 (with others). "Absolute Configuration of Cholesterol." *Nature* 173 (1954): 536 (with I. Youhotsky and G. Popjack). "Total Synthesis of Steroids." *Progress in Organic Chemistry* 3 (1955): 1–43. "Stereoselective Synthesis of Squalene." *Journal of the Chemical Society* (1959): 2539–47 (with R. H. Cornforth and K. K. Mathew). "Absolute Stereochemistry of Some Enzymic Processes." *Biochemical Journal* 86 (1963): 7.

For More Information See: Biographical Encyclopedia of Scientists. New York: Facts on File, 1981, 163. *Science* 190 (November 21, 1975): 772–73.

Commentary: The award to John Cornforth was "for his researches on the stereochemistry of enzyme-catalyzed reactions." Cornforth began his research with work on the structure of penicillin but was most noted for his elucidation of the steps in the biosynthesis of cholesterol from acetic acid. His synthesis of alkenes, oxazoles, and abscisic acid was also notable. (L.I.W.)

Prelog, Vladimir   **88**

Prize: Chemistry, 1975. *Born:* July 23, 1906; Sarajevo, Bosnia, Yugoslavia. *Death:* January 7, 1998; Zurich, Switzerland. *Parents:* Father, Milan Prelog; Mother, Mara Cettolo Prelog. *Nationality:* Yugoslavian; later Swiss citizen. *Religion:* Agnostic; from Catholic background. *Education:* Institute of Technology and School of Chemistry, Czechoslovakia, doctorate, 1929. *Spouse:* Kamila Vitek, married October 31, 1933. *Children:* Jan, son. *Career:* G. Z. Driza Laboratories, Prague, Czechoslovakia, Researcher, 1929–35; Univ. of Zagreb, Yugoslavia, Professor, 1935–42; Eidgenossische Technische Hochschule, Switzerland, Professor, 1942–76. *Other Awards:* Werner Medal, 1945; Stas Medal, 1962; Medal of Honor, Rice Univ., 1962; Marcel Benoist Award, 1965; A.W. Hofman Medal, 1968; Davy Medal, Royal Society, 1968; Roger Adams Award, 1969; Paracelsus Medal, 1976.

Selected Publications: "Conformation and Reactivity of Medium-sized Ring Compounds." *Pure Applied Chemistry* 6 (1963): 545–60. "Constitution of Rifamycins." *Pure Applied Chemistry* 7 (1963): 551–64. "Role of Certain Microbial Metabolites as Specific Complexing Agents." *Pure Applied Chemistry* 25 (1971): 197–210. "Chiral Ionophores." *Pure Applied Chemistry* 50 (1978): 893–904. "Structure and Properties of Boromycin and Products of Its Degradation." *Front. Bioorg. Chem. Mol. Biol* (1979): 87–96.

For More Information See: Biographical Encyclopedia of Scientists. New York: Facts on File, 1981, 651–52. *Chemical and Engineering News* 53 (October 27, 1975): 4–5.

Commentary: Vladimir Prelog received the Nobel Prize for his contributions in the area of the "stereochemistry of organic molecules and reactions," specifically for the techniques and rules which can determine whether a partially asymmetric compound is dextra or levo. His early research included notable advances in the areas of the structure of the alkaloids, microorganism metabolites, the discovery of boromycin, the stereospecificity of microorganisms, and the relationship between conformation and chemical activity of medium-sized ring structures. (J.P.)

1976

Lipscomb, William Nunn, Jr.   **89**

Prize: Chemistry, 1976. *Born:* December 9, 1919; Cleveland, OH. *Parents:* Father, William Nunn Lipscomb; Mother, Edna Patterson Porter Lipscomb. *Nationality:* American. *Religion:* Christian. *Education:* Univ. of Kentucky, B.S., 1941; California Institute of Technology, Ph.D., 1946. *Spouse:* Mary Adele Sergeant, married May 20, 1944, divorced August 14, 1983; Jean Craig Evans, married August 1983. *Children:* Dorothy Jean, daughter; Jenna, daughter; James Sargent, son. *Career:* United States Office of Scientific Research and Development, Chemist, 1942–46; Univ. of Minnesota, Professor, 1946–59; Harvard Univ., MA, Professor, 1959–90. *Other Awards:* Harrison Howe Award, American Chemical Society, 1958; Distinguished Service Award, American Chemical Society, 1968; George Ledlie Prize, Harvard Univ., MA, 1971; Peter Debye Award, American Chemical Society, 1973; Evans Award, Ohio State Univ.; Remsen Award, American Chemical Society, Maryland Section, 1976; Alexander von Humboldt-Stiftung, 1979.

Selected Publications: "Valence in the Boron Hydrides." *Journal of Physical Chemistry* 61 (1957): 23–27. "Boron Hydrides." *Advances in Inorganic Chemistry and Radiochemistry* 1 (1959): 117–56. *Boron Hydrides.* New York: W.A. Benjamin, 1963. "Geometrical Theory of Boron Hydrides." *Inorganic Chemistry* 3 (1964): 1683–85. *Nuclear Magnetic Resonance Studies of Boron Hydrides and Related Compounds.* New York: W.A. Benjamin, 1969.

For More Information See: Chemistry 49 (December 1976): 2. *Science* 194 (November 1976): 709–10.

Commentary: William Lipscomb, Jr., received his Nobel for research that explained the molecular structure and chemical bonding in the boranes, using the concept of two electrons binding together three atoms. He went on to study chemical effects in nuclear magnetic resonance studies of complex molecules and the quantum mechanics of large molecules. Lipscomb used low-temperature x-ray diffraction to research the structure of other crystals and compounds, including biochemical substances. (L.C.)

1977

Prigogine, Ilya   **90**

Prize: Chemistry, 1977. *Born:* January 25, 1917; Moscow, Russia. *Parents:* Father, Roman Prigogine; Mother, Julia Wichmann Prigogine. *Nationality:* Russian; later Belgian citizen and American resident. *Religion:* Jewish. *Education:* Université Libre de Bruxelles, Belgium, baccalaureate, 1939; doctorate, 1941. *Spouse:* Marina Prokopowicz, married February 25, 1961. *Children:* Yves, son; Pascal, son. *Career:* Universite Libre de Bruxelles, Belgium, Professor and Administrator, 1947–87; Univ. of Texas, Austin, Professor and Administrator, 1967–87. *Other Awards:* Prix Van Laar, 1947; Prix A. De Potter, 1950; Prix A. Wetrems, 1950; Prix Francqui, 1955; Prix Solvay, 1965; Order of Leopold, 1968; Arrhenius Gold Medal, 1969; Belgian First Class Civilian Medal, 1972; Bourke Medal, Chemical Society, England, 1972; Cothenius Gold Medal, 1975; Rumford Medal, Royal Society, 1976; Karcher Medal, American Crystallographic Association, 1978; Descartes Medal, Univ. of Paris, France, 1979; Honda Prize, 1983; Artificial Intelligence Award, 1990.

Selected Publications: *Thermodynamique Chimique Conformement aux Methodes de Gibbs et De Donder.* Liège, Belgium: Desoer, 1944–51 (*Treatise on Thermodynamics Based on the Methods of Gibbs and De Donder.* London: Longmans, Green, 1954) (with R. Defay). *Introduction to Thermodynamics of Irreversible Processes.* New York: Interscience, 1962 (with A. Bellemans and V. Mathot). *Order Out of Chaos.* New York: Bantam Books, 1984.

For More Information See: *Chemical and Engineering News* 55 (October 17, 1977): 4. *Current Biography Yearbook.* New York: H.W. Wilson, 1987, 447–50. *Physics Today* 30 (December 1977): 79–80.

Commentary: Ilya Prigogine was awarded the Nobel Prize for "his successful development of a satisfactory theory of nonlinear thermodynamics in states which are far removed from equilibrium." The "generalized, nonlinear and irreversible thermodynamics," especially the method used by Prigogine to study the stability of the dissipative structures which "live in their symbiosis with their environment," has possible applications in a very wide range of problems; his researches have created "theories to bridge the gaps between chemical, biological and social scientific fields of inquiry." He has been called "the poet of thermodynamics" for his elegant and lucid presentation of innovative theories. (J.V.S.)

1978

Mitchell, Peter Dennis   91

Prize: Chemistry, 1978. *Born:* September 29, 1920; Mitcham, Surrey, England. *Death:* April 10, 1992; Bodmin, England. *Parents:* Father, Christopher Gibbs Mitchell; Mother, Kate Beatrice Dorothy Taplin Mitchell. *Nationality:* British. *Religion:* Atheist; from Atheist/Agnostic Christian background. *Education:* Cambridge Univ., England, B.A., 1943; Cambridge Univ., England, Ph.D., 1950. *Spouse:* Patricia Helen Mary French, married November 1, 1958. *Children:* Jeremy, son; Daniel, son; Jason, son; Gideon, son; Julia, daughter; Vanessa, daughter. *Career:* Cambridge Univ., England, Professor, 1943–55; Univ. of Edinburgh, Scotland, Professor, 1955–63; Glynn Research Institute, England, Director, 1964–87. *Other Awards:* CIBA Medal and Prize, Biochemical Society, England, 1973; Warren Triennial Prize, Massachusetts General Hospital, 1974; Louis and Bert Freedman

Foundation Award, New York Academy of Sciences, 1974; Wilhelm Feldberg Foundation Prize, Anglo/American Science Exchange, 1976; Lewis S. Rosenstiel Award, Brandeis Univ., 1977; Medal, Federal European Biochemistry Society, 1978; Copley Medal, Royal Society, 1981.

Selected Publications: *Chemiosmotic Coupling in Oxidative and Photosynthetic Phosphorylation.* Bodmin, Cornwall, England: Glynn Research, 1966. *Chemiosmotic Coupling and Energy Transduction.* Bodmin, Cornwall, England: Glynn Research, 1968. *Chemiosmotic Proton Circuits in Biological Membranes.* Reading, MA: Addison-Wesley, 1981 (with P. C. Hinkle and V. P. Skulachev).

For More Information See: *Biographical Encyclopedia of Scientists.* New York: Facts on File, 1981, 564. *Biographical Memoirs of the Fellows of the Royal Society.* London: Royal Society, 1994 (Volume 40), 281. *Science* 202 (December 8, 1978): 1174–76.

Commentary: Peter Mitchell was awarded the Nobel Prize in Chemistry for his once-controversial chemiosmotic theory regarding energy coupling oxidation and photosynthetic phosphorylation. He proposed that hydrogen ions are transported across the membranes of a cell's mitochondria during the production of adenosine triphosphate (ATP) through the creation of an electrochemical gradient. Previously, it was thought that energy was transported down the respiratory chain by an elusive high-energy intermediate compound generated during oxidation. Mitchell was also unconventional in his creation of his own laboratory, in its architecture, and in his interest in local affairs, building restoration, and history. (L.C.)

1979

Brown, Herbert Charles (Brovarnik, Herbert Charles)   92

Prize: Chemistry, 1979. *Born:* May 22, 1912; London, England. *Parents:* Father, Charles Brovarnik; Mother, Pearl Gorinstein Brovarnik. *Nationality:* British; later American citizen. *Religion:* Jewish. *Education:* Wright Junior College, IL, A.S., 1935; Univ. of Chicago, IL, B.S., 1936; Univ. of Chicago, IL, Ph.D., 1938. *Spouse:* Sarah Baylen, married February 6, 1937. *Children:* Charles Allan, son. *Career:* Univ. of Chicago, IL, Professor, 1936–43; Wayne State Univ., MI, Professor, 1943–47; Purdue Univ., IN, Professor, 1947–78. *Other Awards:* Purdue Sigma Xi Research Award, 1951; Nichols Medal, American Chemical Society, 1959; American Chemical Society Award for Creative Research in Synthetic Organic Chemistry, 1960; H. N. McCoy Award, 1965; Linus Pauling Medal, 1968; National Medal of Science, 1969; Roger Adams Medal, 1971; Charles Frederick Chandler Medal, 1973; Madison Marshall Award, 1975; Chemical Pioneer Award, 1975; CCNY Scientific Achievement Award Medal, 1976; Elliot Cresson Medal, 1978; C. K. Ingold Medal, 1978; Priestley Medal, 1981; Perkin Medal, 1982; Kosolapoff Medal, 1987; NAS Award, 1987; Oesper Award, 1990; H.C. Brown Award, 1998.

Selected Publications: *Hydroboration.* New York: W.A. Benjamin, 1962. *Boranes in Organic Chemistry.* Ithaca, NY: Cornell Univ. Press, 1972. *Organic Syntheses via*

Boranes. New York: Wiley-Interscience, 1975 (with others). *The Nonclassical Ion Problem.* New York: Plenum Press, 1977.

For More Information See: Asimov's Biographical Encyclopedia of Science and Technology. Garden City, NY: Doubleday, 1982, 843. *Biographical Encyclopedia of Scientists.* New York: Facts on File, 1981, 114.

Commentary: Herbert C. Brown received the Nobel Prize for his "discovery and exploration of borohydrides and organoboranes." Beginning with the development of a practical method for diborane synthesis, Brown later produced sodium borohydride, used extensively in organic chemistry. He was responsible for the introduction of a new class of compounds, the organoboranes, which also became valuable in organic chemistry. His work on steric effects was also noteworthy. (I.S.Z.)

Wittig, Georg Friedrich Karl   93

Prize: Chemistry, 1979. *Born:* June 16, 1897; Berlin, Germany. *Death:* August 26, 1987; Heidelberg, Germany. *Parents:* Father, Gustav Wittig; Mother, Martha Dombrowski Wittig. *Nationality:* German. *Religion:* Christian. *Education:* Univ. of Marburg, Germany, Ph.D., 1923. *Spouse:* Waltraut Ernst, married 1930, died 1978. *Children:* 2 daughters. *Career:* Univ. of Marburg, Germany, Professor, 1926–32; Technische Hochschule, Braunschweig Institute of Technology, Germany, Professor, 1932–37; Univ. of Freiburg, Germany, Professor, 1937–44; Univ. of Tübingen, Germany, Professor, 1944–56; Univ. of Heidelberg, Germany, Professor, 1956–67. *Other Awards:* Adolf von Baeyer Medal, Society of German Chemists, 1953; Silver Medal, Univ. of Helsinki, 1957; Dannie Heineman Award, Göttinger Academy of Sciences, 1965; Otto Hahn Prize, Germany, 1967; Silver Medal, City of Paris, 1969; Paul Karrer Medal, Univ. of Zürich, 1972; Medal of the Bruylants Chair, Univ. of Leuwen, 1972; Roger Adams Award, American Chemical Society, 1973; Karl Ziegler Prize, Society of German Chemists, 1975; Ordens Grosses Verdienstkreuz, 1980.

Selected Publications: "Course of Reactions of Pentaphenylphosphorus and Certain Derivatives." *Annalender Chemie, Justus Liebigs* 580 (1953): 44–57. "Triphenylphosphinemethylene as an Olefin-forming Reagent." *Chemisches Berichte* 87 (1954): 1318–30. "Triphenylphosphinemethylenes as Olefin-forming Reagents." *Chemisches Berichte* 88 (1955): 654–66. "Metallizability of Quaternary Ammonium and Phosphonium Salts." *Annalender Chemie, Justus Liebigs* 562 (1956): 177–78.

For More Information See: Biographical Dictionary of Scientists, Chemists. New York: Peter Bedrick Books, 1983, 148–49. *Modern Scientists and Engineers.* 3 volumes. New York: McGraw-Hill, 1980 (Volume 3), 341–42.

Commentary: Georg Wittig won the Nobel Prize for "the discovery of the rearrangement reaction that bears his name," which caused phosphorusylides to react with ketones and aldehydes to form alkenes. The reactions, commonly known as the Wittig reaction, introduced double bonds between carbons in specified locations and led to the synthesis of pharmaceuticals and other complex organic substances, including Vitamin A, Vitamin D derivatives, prostaglandin, and insect pheromones. (M.B.)

1980

Berg, Paul   94

Prize: Chemistry, 1980. *Born:* June 30, 1926; New York, NY. *Parents:* Father, Harry Berg; Mother, Sarah Brodsky Berg. *Nationality:* American. *Religion:* Jewish. *Education:* Pennsylvania State Univ., B.S., 1948; Case Western Reserve Univ., OH, Ph.D., 1952. *Spouse:* Mildred Levy, married September 13, 1947. *Children:* John Alexander, son. *Career:* Washington Univ., St. Louis, MO, Professor, 1955–59; Stanford Univ., CA, Professor, 1959-. *Other Awards:* Eli Lilly Award, 1959; California Scientist of the Year, 1964; V.D. Mattia Prize, Roche Institute for Molecular Biochemistry, 1972; Sarasota Medal, 1979; N.Y. Academy of Science Award, 1980; Albert Lasker Medical Research Award, 1980; Gairdner Foundation Award, 1980; National Medal of Science, 1983

Selected Publications: "Contributions of Nucleic Acids to the Specificity of Protein Synthesis." *Probl. Neoplastic Disease; Symp., New York* (1962): 15–34. "Viral Genome in Transformed Cells." *Proceedings of the Royal Society, Series B* (1971): 65–76. "Potential Biohazards of Recombinant DNA Molecules." *Proceedings of the National Academy of Sciences U.S.A.* (1974): 2593–94 (with others).

For More Information See: New York Times Biographical Service (October 1980): 1359. *Science* 210 (November 21, 1980): 887–89.

Commentary: Paul Berg was cited for "his fundamental studies of the biochemistry of nucleic acids, with particular regard to recombinant DNA," and for his development of the new technology of genetic engineering. He had been one of the leaders in studying the molecular biology of nucleic acids throughout his career. His work on bacterial protein synthesis was followed by his studies of gene expression in higher organisms. He was also notable for leading molecular biologists in calling for a cessation of recombinant DNA research until the risks could be assessed. (P.P.)

Gilbert, Walter   95

Prize: Chemistry, 1980. *Born:* March 21, 1932; Boston, MA. *Parents:* Father, Richard V. Gilbert; Mother, Emma Cohen Gilbert. *Nationality:* American. *Religion:* Jewish. *Education:* Harvard Univ., MA, B.A., 1953; Harvard Univ., MA, A.M., 1954; Cambridge Univ., England, D. Phil., 1957. *Spouse:* Celia Stone, married December 29, 1953. *Children:* John Richard, son; Kate, daughter. *Career:* Harvard Univ., MA, Professor, 1957–82; Biogen, Inc., MA, Researcher, 1982–84; Harvard Univ., MA Professor, 1984-. *Other Awards:* U.S. Steel Foundation Award, National Academy of Sciences, 1968; Ledlie Prize, Harvard Univ., MA, 1969; Warren Triennial Prize, Massachusetts General Hospital, 1977; Louis and Bert Freedman Foundation Award, New York Academy of Sciences, 1977; Prix Charles-Leopold Mayer, Académie des Sciences, France, 1977; Louisa Gross Horwitz Prize, Columbia Univ., NY, 1979; Gairdner Prize, 1979; Albert Lasker Basic Science Award, 1979.

Selected Publications: "Protein Synthesis in Escherichia Coli." *Cold Spring Harbor Symposium on Quantitative Biology* 28 (1963): 287–97. "Isolation of the Lac Repressor." *Proceedings of the National Academy of Sciences U.S.* 56 (1966): 1891–98 (with Benno Mueller-Hill). "DNA Replication. The Rolling Circle Model." *Cold Spring Harbor Symposium on Quantitative Biology* 33 (1968): 473–84 (with David Dressler). "The Lac Operator in DNA." *Proceedings of the National Academy of Sciences U.S.* 58 (1968): 2415–21 (with Benno Mueller-Hill). "Repressors and Genetic Control." *Neurosci: Second Study Program* (1970): 946–54.

For More Information See: New York Times (November 12, 1996): C1. *Physics Today* 34 (January 1981): 17–18. *Science* 210 (November 21, 1980): 887–89.

Commentary: Walter Gilbert shared the Nobel Prize for his work on determination of the sequence of bases in DNA by a method applicable to single- and double-stranded DNA. He was equally well-known for his use of equilibrium dialysis to isolate the lac repressor, the element in the Monod-Jacob model that determined whether or not the gene in Escherichia coli would cause production of the enzyme beta-galactosidase, which is dependent on the presence or absence of lactose. (B.S.S.)

Sanger, Frederick *See* entry **62**

1981

Fukui, Kenichi   **96**

Prize: Chemistry, 1981. *Born:* October 4, 1918; Nara, Japan. *Death:* January 9, 1998; Kyoto, Japan. *Parents:* Father, Ryokichi Fukui; Mother, Chie Fukui. *Nationality:* Japanese. *Religion:* No record found. *Education:* Kyoto Imperial Univ., Japan, Bachelor's in Engineering, 1941; Kyoto Imperial Univ., Japan, Ph.D., 1948. *Spouse:* Tomoe Horie, married 1947. *Children:* Tetsuya, son; Miyako, daughter. *Career:* Japanese Army Fuel Laboratory, Researcher, 1941–44; Kyoto Imperial Univ., Japan, Professor, 1944–82; Kyoto Univ. of Industrial Arts, Japan, President, 1982–88; Institute for Fundamental Chemistry, Director, 1988–98. *Other Awards:* Japan Academy Medal, 1962; Order of Culture, Japan, 1981; Person of Cultural Merit, Japan, 1981.

Selected Publications: "Developments in Quantum-Mechanical Interpretation of the Reactivity of Unsaturated Hydrocarbons." *Journal of Japanese Chemistry* 6 (1952): 379–85. "Further Studies on the Frontier Electrons." *Journal of Japanese Chemistry* 8 (1954): 73–74. "Molecular Orbital Theory of Orientation in Aromatic, Heteroaromatic, and Other Conjugated Molecules." *Journal of Chemical Physics* 22 (1954): 1433–42 (with others). "Theoretical Reactivity Index of Addition in the Frontier Electron Theory." *Bulletin of the Chemical Society of Japan* 34 (1961): 230–32 (with others).

For More Information See: Chemical and Engineering News 59 (October 26, 1981): 6–7. *Science* 214 (November 6, 1981): 627–29. *New York Times* (January 12, 1998): B8.

Commentary: Kenichi Fukui was cited by the Academy "for his frontier orbital theory of chemical reactivity," which stated that the progress of a reaction depends on the geometries and relative energies of the highest occupied molecular orbital of one reactant and the lowest unoccupied molecular orbital of the other. His theory was extended by his colaureate Roald Hoffman, while Fukui continued to work on calculations and applications to many specific reactions during his career. (D.P.N.)

Hoffmann, Roald (Hoffmann, Ronald)   **97**

Prize: Chemistry, 1981. *Born:* July 18, 1937; Zloczow, Poland. *Parents:* Father, Hillel Safran; Stepfather, Paul Hoffmann; Mother, Clara Rosen Safran Hoffmann. *Nationality:* Polish; later American citizen. *Religion:* Jewish. *Education:* Columbia Univ., NY, B.A., 1958; Harvard Univ., MA, M.A., 1960; Harvard Univ., MA, Ph.D., 1962. *Spouse:* Eva Borjesson, married April 30,1960. *Children:* Hillel Jan, son; Ingrid Helena, daughter. *Career:* Harvard Univ., MA, Researcher, 1962–65; Cornell Univ., NY, Professor, 1965-. *Other Awards:* American Chemical Society Award, 1969; Fresenius Award, 1969; Harrison Howe Award, 1970; Annual Award of International Academy of Quantum Molecular Sciences, 1970; Arthur C. Cope Award, American Chemical Society, 1973; Linus Pauling Award, 1974; Nichols Medal, 1980; Inorganic Chemistry Award, American Chemical Society, 1982; National Medal of Science, 1983; Priestley Medal, 1990; Centennial Medal, Harvard University, 1994; Jawarharlal Nehru Birth Centenary Award, 1998.

Selected Publications: "Orbital Symmetries and Endo-exo Relationships in Concerted Cycloaddition Reactions." *Journal of the American Chemical Society* 87 (1965): 4388–89 (with R.B. Woodward). "Orbital Symmetries and Orientational Effects in a Sigmatropic Reaction." *Journal of the American Chemical Society* 87 (1965): 4389–90 (with R.B. Woodward). "Selection Rules for Concerted Cycloaddition Reactions." *Journal of the American Chemical Society* 87 (1965): 2046–48 (with R.B. Woodward). "Stereochemistry of Electrocyclic Reactions." *Journal of the American Chemical Society* 87 (1965): 395–97 (with R.B. Woodward). *Conservation of Orbital Symmetry.* Weinheim, Germany: Verlag Chemie, 1970 (with R.B. Woodward). "Theoretical Aspects of the Coordination of Molecules to Transition Metal Centers." *Pure Applied Chemistry* 50 (1978): 1–9 (with T.A. Albright and D.L. Thorn).

For More Information See: Biographical Encyclopedia of Scientists. New York: Facts on File, 1981, 387–88. *Chemistry Imagined.* Washington, D.C.: Smithsonian Institute Press, 1993. *Old Wine, New Flasks.* New York: W.H. Freeman, 1997. *The Same and Not the Same.* New York: Columbia University Press, 1995. *Science* 214 (November 6, 1981): 627–29.

Commentary: Roald Hoffmann's Nobel was granted for his applications of molecular orbital theory to chemical reactions. He and Robert Woodward formulated the Woodward-Hoffmann rules of orbital symmetry, which permitted predictions of reaction results. Hoffmann continued in the study of chemical reactions, as affected by the interactions between the molecular orbitals of reactants and products. (J.P.)

1982

Klug, Aaron   **98**

Prize: Chemistry, 1982. *Born:* August 11, 1926; Zelvas, Lithuania. *Parents:* Father, Lazar Klug; Mother, Bella Silin Klug. *Nationality:* South African; later British resident. *Religion:* Jewish. *Education:* Univ. of Witwatersrand, South Africa, B.Sc., 1946; Univ. of Cape Town, South Africa, M.Sc., 1947; Cambridge Univ., England, Ph.D., 1949. *Spouse:* Liebe Bobrow, married 1948. *Children:* Adam, son; David, son. *Career:* Cambridge Univ., England, Professor, 1949–53; Birkbeck College, London, England, Professor and Administrator, 1954–61; Cambridge Univ., England, Professor and Administrator, 1962-. *Other Awards:*

Heineken Prize, Royal Netherlands Academy of Science, 1979; Louisa Gross Horowitz Prize, Columbia Univ., 1981; Gold Medal of Merit, Univ. of Cape Town, 1983; Copley Medal, 1985; Harden Medal, 1985: Baly Medal, 1987; Knighthood, 1988; Order of Merit, 1995.

Selected Publications: "Reaggregation of the A-protein of Tobacco Mosaic Virus." *Biochim. et Biophys. Acta* 23 (1957): 199–201 (with R.E. Franklin). "Joint Probability Distributions of Structure Factors and the Phase Problem." *Acta Cryst* 11 (1958): 515–43. "Architecture of Plant Viruses." *Biochemical Journal* 88 (1963): 24. "An Optical Method for the Analysis of Periodicities in Electron Micrographs, and Some Observations on the Mechanism of Negative Staining." *Journal of Molecular Biology* 10 (1964): 565–69 (with J. Berger).

For More Information See: Chemical and Engineering News 60 (October 25, 1982): 4–5. *Nobel Prize Winners: Chemistry.* Pasadena, CA: Salem Press, 1990 (Volume 3), 1079–86. *Science* 218 (November 12, 1982): 653–55.

Commentary: Aaron Klug was cited by the Academy "for his development of crystallographic electron microscopic techniques and for elucidation of biologically important nucleic acid-protein complexes." Klug's work refined electron microscopy so that it could be used quantitatively to permit three-dimensional images. His structural research included time spent successfully with transfer-RNA, tobacco mosaic virus, chromatin, and the structures within the purple membrane of a selected bacterium. (S.B.)

1983

Taube, Henry   99

Prize: Chemistry, 1983. *Born:* November 30, 1915; Neudorf, Saskatchewan, Canada. *Parents:* Father, Samuel Taube; Mother, Albertina Tiledetzki Taube. *Nationality:* Canadian; later American citizen. *Religion:* Lutheran. *Education:* Univ. of Saskatchewan, Canada, B.S., 1935; Univ. of Saskatchewan, Canada,, M.S., 1937; Univ. of California, Berkeley, Ph.D., 1940. *Spouse:* Mary Alice Wesche, married November 27, 1952. *Children:* Linda, daughter; Marianna, daughter; Heinrich, son; Karl, son. *Career:* Univ. of California, Berkeley, Professor, 1940–41; Cornell Univ., NY, Professor, 1941–46; Univ. of Chicago, IL, Professor, 1946–61; Stanford Univ., CA, Professor, 1962–86. *Other Awards:* American Chemical Society Award for Nuclear Applications, 1955; Harrison Howe Award, 1960; Chandler Medal, Columbia Univ., NY, 1964; Kirkwood Award, Yale Univ. and American Chemical Society, 1966; Distinguished Service in Advancement of Inorganic Chemistry Award, 1967; Nichols Medal, 1971; Willard Gibbs Medal, 1971; F.P. Dwyer Medal, Australia, 1973; National Medal of Science, 1977; T.W. Richards Medal, 1980; Linus Pauling Award, 1981; Monsanto Co. Award, 1981; Welch Award, 1983; Bailar Medal, 1983; National Academy of Sciences Award, 1983; Priestley Medal, 1985; Oesper Award, 1986; Achievement Award, International Precious Metals Institute, 1986; Kosolapoff Award, 1990; Brazilian Order of Science Merit Award, 1993.

Selected Publications: "Rates and Mechanisms of Substitution in Inorganic Complexes in Solution." *Chemical Reviews* 50 (1952): 69–126. "Evidence for a Bridged Activated Complex for Electron Transfer Reactions." *Journal of the American Chemical Society* 76 (1954): 2103–11 (with Howard Myers). "Electron-Transfer Reactions of Ruthenium Ammines." *Inorganic Chemistry* 7 (1968): 2369–79 (with T.J. Meyer). "A Direct Approach to Measuring the Franck-Codon Barrier to Electron Transfer Between Metal Ions." *Journal of the American Chemical Society* 91 (1969): 3988–89 (with C. Creutz). *Electron Transfer Reactions of Complex Ions in Solution.* New York: Academic Press, 1970. "Redetermination of the Hexaaminecobalt (III/II) Electron-Self-Exchange Rate." *Inorganic Chemistry* 23 (1984): 979–82 (with Anders Hammershoi and Daniel Geselowitz).

For More Information See: "Electron-Transfer Work Earns Taube a Nobel." *Chemical Week* (October 26, 1983): 15–16. "The 1983 Nobel Prize in Chemistry." *Science* (December 1983): 986–87. "Nobel Prize Winner Henry Taube Discusses His Research." *Science* (January 9, 1984): 43–44.

Commentary: Henry Taube received the Nobel Prize for "his work in the mechanism of electron transfer reactions, especially in metal complexes." His career research answered the question of how an electron moves from one place to another, via a "chemical bridge." Taube also studied the transfers of electrons in metals through chemical reactions as exemplified in the formation of rust and other oxidations. His research had great applicability in industry. (B.W.)

1984

Merrifield, Robert Bruce   100

Prize: Chemistry, 1984. *Born:* July 15, 1921; Fort Worth, TX. *Parents:* Father, George E. Bruce Merrifield; Mother, Lorene Lucas Merrifield. *Nationality:* American. *Religion:* Methodist. *Education:* Univ. of California, Los Angeles, B.A., 1943; Univ. of California, Los Angeles, Ph.D., 1949. *Spouse:* Elizabeth Furlong, married June 20, 1949. *Children:* Nancy, daughter; James, son; Betsy, daughter; Cathy, daughter; Laurie, daughter; Sally, daughter. *Career:* Philip R. Park Research Foundation, Researcher, 1943–44; Univ. of California, Los Angeles, Medical School, Researcher, 1948–49; Rockefeller Institute for Medical Research, NY, Researcher, 1949–57; Rockefeller Univ., NY, Professor, 1957–92. *Other Awards:* Lasker Award, 1969; Gairdner Award, 1970; Intra-Science Award, 1970; Award for Creative Work in Synthetic Organic Chemistry, American Chemical Society, 1972; Nichols Medal, 1973; Alan E. Pierce Award, American Peptide Symposium, 1979; Rudinger Award, 1990; Hirschmann Award in Peptide Chemistry, 1990; Glenn Seaborg Award, 1993; Chemistry Pioneer Award, 1993; Association of Biomolecular Resource Facilities Award, 1998.

Selected Publications: "Solid-Phase Peptide Synthesis: The Synthesis of a Tetrapeptide." *Journal of the American Chemical Society* 85 (1963): 2149–54. "Solid-Phase Synthesis of the Cyclododecadepsipeptide Valinomycin." *Journal of the American Chemical Society* 91 (1969): 2691–95 (with B.F. Gisin and D.C. Tosteson). "An Assessment of Solid Phase Peptide Synthesis." *Peptides: Structural Function, Proceedings of the American Peptide Symposium, 8th* (1983): 33–44. "SN2 Deprotection of Synthetic Peptides with a Low Concentration of Hydrogen Fluoride in Dimethyl

Sulfide: Evidence and Application in Peptide Synthesis." *Journal of the American Chemical Society* 105 (1983): 6442–55 (with James P. Tam and William F. Heath). "Solid-Phase Synthesis of Cecropin A and Related Peptides." *Proceedings of the National Academy of Sciences USA* 80 (1983): 6475–79 (with D. Andreu and H.G. Boman).

For More Information See: Current Biography Yearbook. New York: H.W. Wilson, March 1985, 20–22. "The 1984 Nobel Prize in Chemistry." *Science* (December 7, 1984): 1151–53. "R. Bruce Merrifield: Designer of Protein-Making Machine." *Chemical and Engineering News* August 2, 1971): 22–26.

Commentary: Robert Bruce Merrifield was awarded the Nobel Prize for his development of a "simple and ingenious automated laboratory technique for rapidly synthesizing peptide chains in large quantities on a routine basis, called 'solid-phase peptide synthesis.'" The technique has aided in the treatment and prevention of a number of diseases and genetic disorders and has greatly stimulated progress in genetic engineering. (B.W.)

1985

Hauptman, Herbert Aaron   101

Prize: Chemistry, 1985. *Born:* February 14, 1917; Bronx, NY. *Parents:* Father, Israel Hauptman; Mother, Leah Rosenfeld Hauptman. *Nationality:* American. *Religion:* Jewish. *Education:* City College of New York, B.S., 1937; Columbia Univ., NY, M.A., 1939; Univ. of Maryland, Ph.D., 1955. *Spouse:* Edith Citrynell, married November 10, 1940. *Children:* Barbara, daughter; Carol, daughter. *Career:* United States Census Bureau, Statistician, 1940–42; United States Air Force, 1942–43, 1946–47; United States Naval Research Laboratory, Researcher, 1947–70; Medical Foundation of Buffalo (now Hauptman-Woodward Medical Research Institute), NY, Administrator, 1970-. *Other Awards:* Belden Prize, 1935; Pure Science Award, Sigma Xi, 1959; A.L. Patterson Award, American Crystallographic Association, 1984; Jewish Academy Arts and Sciences Award, 1986; Schoelkopf Award, 1986; Gold Plate Award, American Academy of Achievement, 1986; National Library of Medicine Medal, 1986; Law School Award, Maimonides Chabad House, 1986.

Selected Publications: "The Phases and Magnitudes of the Structure Factors." *Acta Cryst* 3 (1950): 181–87 (with J. Karle). "Solution of Structure-Factor Equations." *Acta Cryst* 4 (1951): 188–89 (with J. Karle). *Solution of the Phase Problem. I. The Centrosymmetric Crystal.* Ann Arbor, MI: American Crystallographic Association, 1953 (with J. Karle). "A Theory of Phase Determination for the Four Types of Non-centrosymmetric Space Groups." *Acta Cryst* 9 (1956): 635–51 (with J. Karle). *Table of All Primitive Roots for Primes Less than 5000.* Washington, DC: Naval Research Laboratory, 1970. *Crystal Structure Determination: The Role of the Cosine Seminvariants.* New York: Plenum Press, 1972.

For More Information See: New York Times (October 27, 1985): 1. *Nobel Prize Winners: Chemistry.* Pasadena, CA: Salem Press, 1990 (Volume 3): 1113–18. *Science* 231 (January 24, 1986): 362–64.

Commentary: Now considered one of the "founders of a new era in research on molecular structure," Herbert

Hauptman was cited by the Academy for the "development of direct methods for the determination of crystal structures." The original work was considered "unaccepted and controversial" for more than 15 years after its publication. By analyzing the intensity of the structure of a molecule directly, it is now possible to quickly analyze the three-dimensional structure of the molecule. Adapting these techniques for use by computers, scientists are now able to determine the structure of complex molecules in just a few days. (L.S.S.)

Karle, Jerome   102

Prize: Chemistry, 1985. *Born:* June 18, 1918; Brooklyn, NY. *Parents:* Father, Louis Karfunkle Karle; Mother, Sadie Kun Karle. *Nationality:* American. *Religion:* Jewish. *Education:* City College of New York, B.S., 1937; Harvard Univ., MA, A.M., 1938; Univ. of Michigan, Ph.D., 1943. *Spouse:* Isabella Helen Lugoski, married June 4, 1942. *Children:* Louise Isabella, daughter; Jean Marianne, daughter; Madeline Diane, daughter. *Career:* Manhattan Project, Chicago, IL, Researcher, 1943–44; United States Navy Project, MI, Researcher, 1944–46; Naval Research Laboratory, MD, Researcher and Administrator, 1946-. *Other Awards:* Pure Science Award, Sigma Xi, 1959; Navy Distinguished Civilian Service Award, 1968; Hillebrand Award, American Chemical Society, 1969; Robert Dexter Conrad Award, 1976; A.L. Patterson Award, American Crystallographic Association, 1984; National Research Laboratory Lifetime Achievement Award, 1993.

Selected Publications: "The Phases and Magnitudes of the Structure Factors." *Acta Cryst* 3 (1950): 181–87 (with H. Hauptman). "Solution of Structure-Factor Equations." *Acta Cryst* 4 (1951): 188–89 (with H. Hauptman). *Solution of the Phase Problem. I. The Centrosymmetric Crystal.* Ann Arbor, MI: American Crystallographic Association, 1953 (with H. Hauptman). "A Theory of Phase Determination for the Four Types of Non-centrosymmetric Space Groups." *Acta Cryst* 9 (1956): 635–51 (with H. Hauptman).

For More Information See: New York Times October 27, 1985): 1. *Science* 231 (January 24, 1986): 362–64.

Commentary: Jerome Karle, whose work was not accepted until the mid-1960s, was cited by the Academy for "the development of direct methods for the determination of crystal structures." The mathematical techniques allowed the use of x-ray crystallography for directly determining the structure of three-dimensional molecules, particularly hormones, vitamins, and antibiotics. (L.S.S.)

1986

Herschbach, Dudley Robert   103

Prize: Chemistry, 1986. *Born:* June 18, 1932; San Jose, CA. *Parents:* Father, Robert Dudley Herschbach; Mother, Dorothy Edith Beer Herschbach. *Nationality:* American. *Religion:* From Protestant background. *Education:* Stanford Univ., CA, B.S., 1954; Stanford Univ., CA, M.S., 1955; Harvard Univ., MA, M.A., 1956; Harvard Univ., MA, Ph.D., 1958. *Spouse:* Georgene Lee Botyos, married December 26, 1964. *Children:* Lisa Marie, daughter; Brenda Michele, daughter. *Career:* Harvard Univ., Researcher, 1957–59; Univ. of California, Berkeley, Professor, 1959–63; Harvard Univ., MA, Professor, 1963-. *Other Awards:* Pure Chemistry Award,

American Chemical Society, 1965; Spiers Medal, 1976; Centenary Medal, British Chemical Society, 1977; Linus Pauling Medal, 1978; Polanyi Medal, 1981; Langmuir Prize, 1983; National Medal of Science, 1991; Heyrovsky Medal, 1992; Sierra Nevada Distinguished Chemist Award, 1993; Kosolapoff Medal, 1994; William Faulkner Prize, 1994.

Selected Publications: "Molecular Beam Kinetics: Evidence for Preferred Geometry in Interhalogen Exchange Reactions." *Journal of Chemical Physics* 51 (1969): 455–56. "Supersonic Molecular Beams of Alkali Dimers." *Journal of Chemical Physics* 54 (1971): 2393–2409. "Molecular Beam Kinetics: Reactions of Hydrogen and Deuterium Atoms with Diatomic Alkali Molecules." *Journal of Chemical Physics* 54 (1971): 2410–23. *Chemical Kinetics.* London: Butterworths, 1976.

For More Information See: New York Times (October 16, 1986): B19+. *Physics Today* 40 (1987): 17–19. *Research and Development* 28 (1986): 37–38.

Commentary: Dudley Herschbach shared the Nobel for research that provided "a much more detailed understanding of how chemical reactions take place." Herschbach developed the approach of crossed molecular beams, in which two beams of molecules are accelerated and collide under controlled and known conditions, and the products of the collision are investigated. The process can be used to study all types of chemical reactions in a way very different from previous gross studies of reactions and has led to a much more detailed understanding of reaction dynamics. (G.R.)

Lee, Yuan Tseh 104

Prize: Chemistry, 1986. *Born:* November 29, 1936; Hsinchu, Taiwan. *Parents:* Father, Tse Fan Lee; Mother, Pei Tsai Lee. *Nationality:* Chinese; later American citizen. *Religion:* None, from Buddhist background. *Education:* National Taiwan Univ., B.S., 1959; National Tsinghua Univ., Taiwan, M.S., 1961; Univ. of California, Berkeley, Ph.D., 1965. *Spouse:* Bernice Chinli Wu, married June 28, 1963. *Children:* Ted, son; Sidney, son; Charlotte, daughter. *Career:* Univ. of Chicago, IL, Professor, 1968–74; Univ. of California, Berkeley, Professor, 1974–94; Academia Sinica, Taiwan, President, 1994-. *Other Awards:* Ernest Orlando Lawrence Award, 1981; Harrison E. Howe Award, 1983; Peter Debye Award, 1986; National Medal of Science, 1986.

Selected Publications: "Molecular Beam Kinetics: Evidence for Preferred Geometry in Interhalogen Exchange Reactions." *Journal of Chemical Physics* 51 (1969): 455–56. "Molecular Beam Kinetics: Reaction of Hydrogen and Deuterium Atoms with Diatomic Alkali Molecules." *Journal of Chemical Physics* 54 (1971): 2410–23. "Studies with Crossed Laser and Molecular Beams." *Physics Today* 33 (1980): 52–59. "Molecular Beam Studies of Elementary Chemical Processes." *Science* 236 (1987): 793–98.

For More Information See: Current Biography. New York: H.W. Wilson, 1987, 167. *New York Times* (October 16, 1986): B19+. *Science* 234 (1986): 673–74.

Commentary: Yuan Tseh Lee shared the Nobel for "contributions concerning the dynamics of elementary chemical processes." Lee replaced his colaureate Herschbach's surface ionization hot-wire detector, which was limited to study of alkali-atom-containing entities, with a universally applicable, specially designed mass spectrometer that could separate and identify reaction products. His later work

explored the reactions of larger molecules and combustion chemistry. (G.R.)

Polanyi, John Charles 105

Prize: Chemistry, 1986. *Born:* January 23, 1929; Berlin, Germany. *Parents:* Father, Michael Polanyi; Mother, Magda Elizabeth Kemeny Polanyi. *Nationality:* German; later English; now Canadian citizen. *Religion:* Christian (from Jewish background). *Education:* Manchester Univ., England, B.S., 1949; Manchester Univ., England, M.Sc., 1950; Manchester Univ., England, Ph.D., 1952. *Spouse:* Anne Ferrar Davidson, married 1958. *Children:* Margaret Alexandra, daughter; Michael Ferrar, son. *Career:* National Research Council, Canada, Researcher, 1952–54; Princeton Univ., NJ, Researcher, 1954–56; Univ. of Toronto, Canada, Professor, 1956-. *Other Awards:* Marlow Medal, 1962; Steacie Prize, 1965; Centenary Medal, British Chemical Society, 1965; Noranda Award, 1967; Mack Award, 1969; British Chemical Society Award, 1971; Henry Marshall Tory Medal, 1977; Remsen Award, 1978; Companion of the Order of Canada, 1979; Wolf Prize, 1982; Killam Memorial Prize, 1988; Royal Medal, 1989; Polanyi Award, 1992; Bakerian Award, 1994.

Selected Publications: "Quenching and Vibrational-energy Transfer of Excited Iodine Molecules." *Canadian Journal of Chemistry* 36 (1958): 121–30. "Energy Distribution Among Reagents and Products of Atomic Reactions." *Journal of Chemical Physics* 31 (1959): 1338–51. "An Infrared Maser Dependent on Vibrational Excitation." *Journal of Chemical Physics* 34 (1961): 347–48. "Some Concepts in Reaction Dynamics." *Science* 236 (1987): 680–90.

For More Information See: Chemical Week 139 (1986): 8–10. *Maclean's* 99 (1986): 60. *Science* 234 (1986): 673–74.

Commentary: The Nobel Prize was shared by John Polanyi for "contributions concerning the dynamics of elementary chemical reactions." Unlike his two colaureates who developed the molecular beam method for studying chemical reactions, Polanyi used infrared chemiluminescence to follow the excited products of reactions, progressing from the relatively simple hydrogen-chlorine reaction to much more complicated reactions. His work also led into the development of chemical lasers. (G.R.)

1987

Cram, Donald James 106

Prize: Chemistry, 1987. *Born:* April 22, 1919; Chester, VT. *Parents:* Father, William Moffet Cram; Mother, Joanna Shelley Cram. *Nationality:* American. *Religion:* Christian. *Education:* Rollins College, FL, B.S., 1941; Univ. of Nebraska, M.S., 1942; Harvard Univ., MA, Ph.D., 1947. *Spouse:* Jean Turner, married 1941, divorced 1968; Jane L. Maxwell, married November 25, 1969. *Children:* None. *Career:* Merck and Company, NJ, Researcher, 1942–45; Univ. of California, Los Angeles, Professor, 1947–90. *Other Awards:* American Chemical Society Award, 1953 and 1965; Herbert Newby McCoy Award, 1965 and 1975; Society of Chemical Manufacturing Association Award, 1965; Arthur C. Cope Award, 1974; California Scientist of the Year, 1974; Gold Medal, Royal Institute of Chemistry, 1976; Roger Adams Award, 1985; Willard Gibbs Award, 1985; Tolman Medal, 1985; Seaborg Award, 1989; National

Medal of Science, 1993; Univ. of California, Los Angeles Medal, 1993.

Selected Publications: "Chiral, Hinged, and Functionalized Multiheteromacrocycles." *Journal of the American Chemical Society* 95 (1973): 2691–92. "Chiral Recognition in Molecular Complexing." *Journal of the American Chemical Society* 95 (1973): 2692–93. "Host-Guest Chemistry." *Science* 183 (1974): 803–09. "The Design of Molecular Hosts, Guests, and Their Complexes." *Science* 240 (1988): 760–67.

For More Information See: From Design to Discovery. Washington, DC: American Chemical Society, 1990. *New York Times.* (October 15, 1987): A14. *Science* 238 (1987): 611–12.

Commentary: The Chemistry Nobel was shared by Donald Cram for his part in "elucidating mechanisms of molecular recognition, which are fundamental to enzymic catalysis, regulation, and transport." Cram extended his colaureate Pedersen's work on one-dimensional crown ether hosts and alkali-metal guests to three-dimensional cyclic compounds that exhibited a permanently rigid structure and could accept substrates in a structurally preorganized cavity. He called the compounds cavitands, whereas colaureate Lehn referred to his new structures as cryptands. (G.R./B.S.S.)

Lehn, Jean-Marie Pierre   107

Prize: Chemistry, 1987. *Born:* September 30, 1939; Rosheim, Bas Rhin, France. *Parents:* Father, Pierre Lehn; Mother, Marie Salomon Lehn. *Nationality:* French. *Religion:* No record found. *Education:* Univ. of Strasbourg, France, B.S., 1960; Univ. of Strasbourg, France, Ph.D., 1963. *Spouse:* Sylvie Lederer, married 1965. *Children:* David, son; Mathias, son. *Career:* National Center for Scientific Research, France, Researcher, 1960–66; Univ. of Strasbourg, France, Professor, 1966–69; Univ. Louis Pasteur, France, Professor, 1970–79; College of France, Paris, Professor, 1979-. *Other Awards:* Gold Medal, Italy, 1981; Paracelsus Prize, 1982; von Humboldt Prize, 1983; Karl-Ziegler Prize, 1989; Vermeil Medal, Paris, 1989; Bonner Chemiepreis, 1993; Ettore Majorana-Erice Peace Prize, 1994; Gold Medal, Society Academy Arts, Sciences, Lettres, 1995; Davy Medal, 1997; Lavoisier Medal, 1997; A.R. Day Award, 1998.

Selected Publications: "Kinetic and Conformational Studies by Nuclear Magnetic Resonance. XI. Ring Inversion in Tetrahydro-1, 3-Oxazines." *Bulletin Soc. Chim. France* 3 (1968): 1172–77. "Cryptates, Cation Exchange Rates." *Journal of the American Chemical Society* 92 (1970): 2916–18. "Cation and Cavity Selectivities of Alkali- and Alkaline-Earth Cryptates." *Journal of the Chemical Society D.* (1971): 440–41. "Cryptates." *Recherche* 2 (1971): 276–77.

For More Information See: New York Times (October 15, 1987): A14. *Science* 238 (1987): 611–12.

Commentary: Jean-Marie Lehn shared the Nobel Prize in Chemistry for his part in "elucidating mechanisms of molecular recognition, which are fundamental to enzymic catalysis, regulation, and transport." Lehn extended his colaureate Pedersen's work on one-dimensional crown ether hosts and alkali metal-ion guests to three-dimensional stacked-layer polycyclic compounds that exhibited a rigid structure, and could bind a variety of molecules in the "crypts" that were produced in the structure, while changing that structure

in some ways. Lehn referred to the activity as supramolecular, since the interaction was transient in nature and not as permanent as ordinary covalent bonds. (G.R./B.S.S.)

Pedersen, Charles John   108

Prize: Chemistry, 1987. *Born:* October 3, 1904; Pusan, Korea. *Death:* October 26, 1989; Salem, NJ. *Parents:* Father, Brede Pedersen; Mother, Takino Yasui Pedersen. *Nationality:* American; born in Korea. *Religion:* Catholic. *Education:* Univ. of Dayton, OH, B.S., 1926; Massachusetts Institute of Technology, M.S., 1927. *Spouse:* Susan J. Ault, married 1947, died 1983. *Children:* Shirley, daughter; Barbara, daughter. *Career:* duPont Company, DE, Researcher, 1927–69. *Other Awards:* American Chemical Society Award, 1968.

Selected Publications: "Macrocyclic Polyethers with Aromatic Groups and Their Cationic Complexes." French Patent 1, 440, 716 (June 3, 1966). "Cyclic Polyethers and Their Complexes with Metal Salts." *Journal of American Chemical Society* 89 (1967): 7017–36. "Macrocyclic Polyethers." British Patent 1, 149, 229 (April 16, 1969). "Macrocyclic Polyether Compounds and Their Ionic Complexes." German Patent 1, 963, 528 (July 2, 1970).

For More Information See: New York Times. (October 15, 1987): A14. *Science* 238 (1987): 611–12.

Commentary: The Nobel Prize in Chemistry was shared by Charles Pedersen for his part in "elucidating mechanisms of molecular recognition, which are fundamental to enzymic catalysis, regulation, and transport." Pedersen found that alkali metal ions could be bound by crown ethers, converting the flexible ether ring into a more rigid, layered structure, in which the alkali metal ion was bound into the center of the ring. Pedersen's work initiated the field of what is known as host-guest chemistry. (G.R./B.S.S.)

1988

Deisenhofer, Johann   109

Prize: Chemistry, 1988. *Born:* September 30, 1943; Zusamaltheim, Germany. *Parents:* Father, Johann Deisenhofer; Mother, Thekla Magg Deisenhofer. *Nationality:* German; later American resident. *Religion:* Christian. *Education:* Technical Univ., Munich, Germany, M.S., 1971; Max Planck Institute for Biochemistry, Germany, Ph.D., 1974. *Spouse:* Kirsten Fischer-Lindahl, married June 19, 1989. *Children:* No record found. *Career:* Max Planck Institute for Biochemistry, Germany, Researcher, 1974–88; Univ. of Texas Southwestern Medical Center, Professor, 1988-. *Other Awards:* Biological Physics Prize, American Physical Society, 1986; Otto-Bayer Prize, 1988.

Selected Publications: "X-ray Structure of a Membrane Protein Complex." *Journal of Molecular Biology* 180 (1984): 385–98. "Structure of the Protein Subunits in the Photosynthetic Reaction Center of *Rhodopseudomonas viridis* at 3 Angstrom Resolution." *Nature* 318 (1985): 19–26. "Experience with Various Techniques for the Refinement of Protein Structures." *Methods Enzymol* (1985): 115.

For More Information See: Chemical Week 143 (1988): 11–12. *New York Times* (October 20, 1988): B12.

Commentary: The Nobel in Chemistry was shared by Johann Deisenhofer for his part in work that "revealed the three-dimensional structure of closely-linked proteins that are essential to photosynthesis." After colaureate Michel crystallized the membrane-bound protein photosynthetic reaction center of the *Rhodopseudomonas viridis* bacterium, Deisenhofer and his other colaureate Huber used x-ray crystallography to elucidate the positions of the approximately 10,000 atoms in the protein complex. In addition to its importance in the understanding of photosynthesis, the work had other applications, since membrane-bound proteins are also important in many disease states. (G.R./B.S.S.)

Huber, Robert   110

Prize: Chemistry, 1988. *Born:* February 20, 1937; Munich, Germany. *Parents:* Father, Sebastian Huber; Mother, Helene Kebinger Huber. *Nationality:* German. *Religion:* Christian. *Education:* Technical Univ., Munich, Germany, B.S., 1960; Technical Univ., Munich, Germany, Ph.D., 1963. *Spouse:* Christa Essig, married 1960. *Children:* Martin, son; Robert, son; Ulrike, daughter; Julia, daughter. *Career:* Technical Univ., Munich, Germany, Professor, 1968-; Max Planck Institute of Biochemistry, Germany, Director, 1972-. *Other Awards:* E.K. Frey Prize, 1972; Otto Warburg Medal, 1977; Emil von Behring Prize, 1982; Keilin Medal, 1987; Richard Kuhn Medal, 1987; Frey-Werle Medal, 1989; Kone Award, 1990; Krebs Medal, 1992.

Selected Publications: "X-ray Structure of a Membrane Protein Complex." *Journal of Molecular Biology* 180 (1984): 385–98. "Structure of the Protein Subunits in the Photosynthetic Reaction Center of *Rhodopseudomonas viridis* at 3 Angstrom Resolution." *Nature* 318 (1985): 19–26. "Structural Basis for Antigen-Antibody Recognition." *Science* 233 (1986): 702–03.

For More Information See: *New York Times* (October 20, 1988): A1. *Physics Today* 42 (1989): 17–18.

Commentary: Robert Huber shared the Nobel in Chemistry for his part in work that revealed "the three-dimensional structure of closely-linked proteins that are essential to photosynthesis." After colaureate Michel crystallized the membrane-bound protein photosynthetic reaction center of the *Rhodopseudomonas viridis* bacterium, Huber and his other colaureate Deisenhofer used x-ray crystallography to elucidate the positions of the approximately 10,000 atoms in the protein complex. In addition to its importance in the understanding of photosynthesis, the work had other applications since membrane-bound proteins are also important in many disease states. (G.R./B.S.S.)

Michel, Hartmut   111

Prize: Chemistry, 1988. *Born:* July 18, 1948; Ludwigsburg, Germany. *Parents:* Father, Karl Michel; Mother, Frieda Kachler Michel. *Nationality:* German. *Religion:* Protestant. *Education:* Univ. of Tubingen, Germany, B.S., 1974; Univ. of Würzburg, Germany, Ph.D., 1977. *Spouse:* Ilona S. Leger-Michel, married 1979. *Children:* Andrea, daughter; Robert, son. *Career:* University of Würzburg, Germany, Researcher 1977–79; Max Planck Institute of Biochemistry, Germany, Researcher, 1979–87; Max Planck Institute of Biophysics, Germany, Director, 1987-. *Other Awards:* Biophysics Prize, American Physical Society, 1986; Otto Klung Prize, 1986; Leibniz Prize, 1986; Otto Bayer Prize, 1988.

Selected Publications: "Crystallization of Membrane Proteins." *Trends in Biochemical Science* 8 (1983): 56–59. "X-ray Structure of a Membrane Protein Complex." *Journal of Molecular Biology* 180 (1984): 385–98. "Structure of the Protein Subunits in the Photosynthetic Reaction Center of *Rhodopseudomonas viridis* at 3 Angstrom Resolution." *Nature* 318 (1985): 19–26.

For More Information See: *New York Times* (October 20, 1988); B12. *Science* 242 (1988): 672–73.

Commentary: Hartmut Michel was awarded a share of the Nobel for his part in work that revealed "the three-dimensional structure of closely-linked proteins that are essential to photosynthesis." Michel invested four years of effort in trying to fully crystallize bacterial membrane protein before succeeding with the membrane-bound protein photosynthetic reaction center of the *Rhodopseudomonas viridis* bacterium. He then joined with his colaureates in a successful two-year effort to map the protein complex structure using x-ray crystallography. The work was an important key to understanding photosynthesis and many disease states. (G.R./B.S.S.)

1989

Altman, Sidney   112

Prize: Chemistry, 1989. *Born:* May 7, 1939; Montreal, Canada. *Parents:* Father, Victor Altman; Mother, Ray Arlin Altman. *Nationality:* Canadian; later American citizen. *Religion:* Jewish. *Education:* Massachusetts Institute of Technology, B.S., 1960; Univ. of Colorado, Ph.D., 1967. *Spouse:* Ann Korner, married 1972. *Children:* Daniel, son; Leah, daughter. *Career:* Harvard Univ., MA, Researcher, 1967–69; Medical Research Council Laboratory, Cambridge, England, Researcher, 1969–71; Yale Univ., CT, Professor and Administrator, 1971-. *Other Awards:* Rosenstiel Award, 1989

Selected Publications: *Transfer RNA.* Cambridge, MA: Massachusetts Institute of Technology Press, 1978. "Transfer-RNA Processing Enzymes." *Cell* 23 (1981): 3–4. "Gene Coding for a Protamine-like Protein." *Cell* 26 (1981): 299–304. "Aspects of Biochemical Catalysis." *Cell* 36 (1984): 237–39.

For More Information See: *New York Times* (October 13, 1989): A10. *Science* 246 (October 20, 1989): 325–26.

Commentary: The Nobel Prize was shared by Sidney Altman for "discoveries about the active role of RNA in chemical cell reactions." The laureates proved independently that RNA (ribonucleic acid) could act as a catalyst for reactions in the cell. It was previously thought that all enzymes, the catalysts of reactions inside cells, were proteins. The research showed that RNA could serve as an enzyme (a ribozyme), in addition to its role as a transmitter of the DNA genetic codes. Specifically, Altman demonstrated that the RNA molecule could rearrange itself, producing different products, an act that was thought to be dependent on the presence of an enzyme. The research has potential application for treatment of disease states. (G.R./B.S.S.)

Cech, Thomas Robert   113

Prize: Chemistry, 1989. *Born:* December 8, 1947; Chicago, IL. *Parents:* Father, Robert Franklin Cech; Mother, Annette

Marie Cerveny Cech. *Nationality:* American. *Religion:* From Methodist background. *Education:* Grinnell College, IA, B.A., 1970; Univ. of California, Berkeley, Ph.D., 1975. *Spouse:* Carol Lynn Martinson, married 1970. *Children:* Allison E., daughter; Jennifer N., daughter. *Career:* Massachusetts Institute of Technology, Resident, 1975–77; Univ. of Colorado, Professor, 1978–99; Howard Hughes Medical Institute, MD, President, 2000-. *Other Awards:* Passano Foundation Award, 1984; Harrison Howe Award, 1984; Pfizer Award, 1985; U.S. Steel Award, 1987; V.D. Mattia Award, 1987; Newcombe-Cleveland Award, 1988; Heineken Prize, 1988; Horwitz Prize, 1988; Gairdner Foundation Award, 1988; Lasker Research Award, 1988; Molecular Biology Award, National Academy of Sciences, 1988; Rosenstiel Award, 1989; Warren Prize, 1989; Hopkins Medal, 1992; Feodor Lynen Medal, 1995; National Science Medal, 1995; Mike Hogg Award, 1997; Wright Prize, 1998; Bonfils-Stanton Award, 1990.

Selected Publications: "RNA as an Enzyme." *Scientific American* 255 (November 1986): 64–74. "The Chemistry of Self-splicing RNA and RNA Enzymes." *Science* 236 (June 19, 1987): 1532–40. "Ribozymes and Their Medical Implications." *Journal of the American Medical Association* (November 25, 1988): 3030–35. "Defining the Inside and Outside of a Catalytic RNA Molecule." *Science* 245 (July 21, 1989): 276–83.

For More Information See: *New York Times* (October 13, 1989): A10. *Science* 246 (October 20, 1989): 325–26.

Commentary: Thomas Cech shared the Nobel Prize for "discoveries about the active role of RNA in chemical cell reactions." The laureates proved independently that RNA (ribonucleic acid) could act as a catalyst for reactions in the cell. It was previously thought that all enzymes, the catalysts of reactions inside cells, were proteins. The research showed that RNA could serve as an enzyme (a ribozyme) in addition to its role as a transmitter of the DNA genetic codes. Specifically, Cech demonstrated the independent catalytic function of RNA, leading to the discovery of many ribozymes. The research has potential application for treatment of disease states. (G.R./B.S.S.)

1990

Corey, Elias James   114

Prize: Chemistry, 1990. *Born:* July 12, 1928; Methuen, MA. *Parents:* Father, Elias Corey; Mother, Fatina (Tina) Hasham Corey. *Nationality:* American. *Religion:* From Catholic background. *Education:* Massachusetts Institute of Technology, B.S., 1948; Massachusetts Institute of Technology, Ph.D., 1951. *Spouse:* Claire Higham, married September 14, 1961. *Children:* David, son; John, son; Susan, daughter. *Career:* Univ. of Illinois, Professor, 1951–59; Harvard Univ., MA, Professor, 1959-. *Other Awards:* Pure Chemistry Award, 1960; Intrascience Foundation Award, 1968; Ernest Guenther Award, 1968; Fritzche Award, 1968; Award for Creative Work in Synthetic Organic Chemistry, 1971; Harrison Howe Award, 1971; Ciba Foundation Medal, 1972; Evans Award, Ohio State Univ., 1972; Linus Pauling Award, 1973; Dickson Prize, 1973; George Ledlie Prize, 1973; Remsen Award, 1974; A.C. Cope Award, 1976; Nichols Medal, 1977; Buchman Award, 1978; Franklin Medal, 1978; Science Achievement Award, CCNY, 1979; C.S. Hamilton Award, 1980; J.G. Kirkwood Award, 1980; Chemistry Pioneer Award, 1981; Madison Marshall Award, 1985; V.D. Mathia Award, 1985; Silliman Award, 1986; Wolf Prize, 1986; National Medal of Science, 1988; R. Robinson Award, 1988; Japan Prize, 1989; Gold Medal Award, AIC, 1990; Roger Adams Award, 1993.

Selected Publications: "General Methods for the Construction of Complex Molecules." *Pure and Applied Chemistry* 14 (1967): 19–37. "Total Synthesis of Humulene." *Journal of the American Chemical Society* 89 (1967): 2758–59. "Total Syntheses of Prostaglandins." *Proceedings of the Robert A. Welch Foundation Conference on Chemical Research* 12 (1968): 51–79. *The Logic of Chemical Synthesis.* New York: Wiley, 1989.

For More Information See: *New York Times* (October 18, 1990): A12. *Science* 250 (October 26, 1990): 510–11.

Commentary: Elias Corey won the Nobel Prize for "his development of the theory and methodology of organic synthesis." Particularly noteworthy were his syntheses of terpenes, hydrocarbons found in natural plant oils, and precursors of biologically active proteins; his syntheses of several prostaglandin hormones; and the synthesis of an active substance extracted from the ginkgo tree that is used for blood circulation disorders and asthma. (B.S.S.)

1991

Ernst, Richard Robert   115

Prize: Chemistry, 1991. *Born:* August 14, 1933; Winterhur, Zürich, Switzerland. *Parents:* Father, Robert Ernst; Mother, Irma Brunner Ernst. *Nationality:* Swiss. *Religion:* From Protestant background. *Education:* ETH—Zürich, Diploma, Chemistry, 1956; D.Sc., 1962. *Spouse:* Magdalena Kielholz, married October 9, 1963. *Children:* Anna Magdalena, daughter; Katharina Elisabeth, daughter; Hans-Martin Walter, son. *Career:* Varian Associates, CA, Researcher, 1963–68; Federal Institute of Technology (ETH-Zurich), Switzerland, Researcher, 1968-. *Other Awards:* Silver Medal, ETH-Zurich, 1962; Ruzicka Prize, 1968; Gold Medal, Society of Magnetic Resonance, 1983; Benoist Prize, 1986; Kirkwood Medal, 1989; Ampere Prize, 1990; Wolf Prize, 1991; Horwitz Prize, 1991; Achievements in Magnetic Resonance EAS Award, 1992

Selected Publications: "Recent Developments in Fourier Spectroscopy." *Pulsed Nucl. Magn. Resonance Spin Dyn. Solids, Proc. Spec. Colloq. Ampere 1st* (1973): 40–52 "Two-dimensional Spectroscopy." *Chimia* 29 (1975): 179–83; "Recent Advances in Two-dimensional Spectroscopy." *Proc. Colloq. Spectrosc. Int., Invited Lect., 20th* 2 (1977): 175–81

For More Information See: *Chemical and Engineering News* 69 (October 21, 1991): 4; *Science* 254 (October 25, 1991): 518

Commentary: Richard Ernst won the Nobel Prize for his "contributions to the development of the methodology of high-resolution nuclear magnetic resonance spectroscopy." His most cited contributions are the Fourier-transform, two-dimensional, and tomographic methodologies—all based on applications of advanced mathematical/graphical analysis of results obtained using refined instrumentation. (B.S.S./J.H.S.)

1992

Marcus, Rudolph Arthur   **116**

Prize: Chemistry, 1992. *Born:* July 21, 1923; Montreal, Canada. *Parents:* Father, Myer Marcus; Mother, Esther Cohen Marcus. *Nationality:* Canadian; later U.S. Citizen, 1958. *Religion:* Jewish. *Education:* McGill Univ., Canada, B.Sc., 1943; Ph.D., 1946. *Spouse:* Laura Hearne, married August 27, 1949. *Children:* Alan Rudolph, son; Kenneth Hearne, son; Raymond Arthur, son. *Career:* National Research Council, Canada, Researcher, 1946–48; Univ. of North Carolina, Chapel Hill, NC, Researcher, 1949–51; Polytechnic Institute of Brooklyn, NY, Professor, 1951–64; Univ. of Illinois, Professor, 1964–78; California Institute of Technology, Professor, 1978-. *Other Awards:* Langmuir Award, 1978; Robinson Medal, 1982; Chandler Medal, 1983; Wolf Prize, 1985; Faraday Medal, 1988; Centenary Medal, Royal Society of Chemistry, 1988; Debye Award, 1988; Gibbs Medal, 1988; National Medal of Science, 1989; T.W. Richards Medal, 1990; Evans Award, 1990; E.F. Smith Award, 1991; Remsen Memorial Award, 1991; Pauling Medal, 1991; Hirschfelder Prize, 1993; Golden Plate Award, 1993; Lavoisier Medal, 1994; Auburn-Kosolapoff Award, 1996; Theoretical Chemistry Award, 1997; Oesper Award, 1997.

Selected Publications: "Theory of Oxidation-Reduction Reactions Involving Electron Transfer." *J. Chem. Phys.* 24 (1956): 966–78; "Theory of Electrochemical and Chemical Electron-transfer Processes." *Can. J. Chem.* 37 (1959): (155–63); "Theory of Electron-transfer Reactions and of Related Phenomena." *Exchange Reactions, Proc. Symp. Upton, NY.* (1965): 1–6

For More Information See: Physics Today 46 (January 1993): 16–20; *Science* 258 (October 23, 1992): 544.

Commentary: Rudolph Marcus won the Nobel Prize "for his contributions to the theory of electron transfer reactions in chemical systems." Marcus developed a mathematical analysis of the jumps of electrons from one molecule to another. The Committee noted that the Nobelist's work has helped in the explanation of phenomena such as photosynthesis, electrically conducting polymers, chemiluminescence, and corrosion. Marcus also worked in the areas of unimolecular reactions and intramolecular dynamics, semiclassical theories of bound vibrational states and of collisions, and reaction dynamics. (B.S.S./J.H.S.)

1993

Mullis, Kary Banks   **117**

Prize: Chemistry, 1993. *Born:* December 28, 1944; Lenoir, NC. *Parents:* Father, Cecil Banks Mullis; Mother, Bernice Alberta Barker Fredericks Mullis. *Nationality:* American. *Religion:* Most probably Christian. *Education:* Georgia Institute of Technology, B.S., 1966; Univ. of California, Berkeley, Ph.D., 1973. *Spouse:* Richards Haley, married 1964, dissolved, no date; Gail Hubbell, married, no date, dissolved, no date; Cynthia Gibson, married 1976, divorced 1981; Nancy Lier Cosgrove, married March 21, 1998. *Children:* Christopher, son; Jeremy, son; Louise, daughter *Career:* Cetus Corp., CA, Researcher, 1979–86; Xytronyx, Inc., CA, Researcher, 1986–88; Consultant, 1988–92; StarGene, Inc., CA, Chairman, 1992-; Vyrex, Inc., CA,

Administrator, 1996-. *Other Awards:* Preis Award, 1990; Allan Award, 1990; Gairdner Foundation Award, 1991; National Biotech Award, 1991; Koch Award, 1992; Chiron Corp. Award, 1992; Japan Prize, 1993; Clinical Chemistry Award, 1993; Gustavus Esselen Award, 1994.

Selected Publications: "Transcription Termination at the Tryptophan Operon Attenuator is Decreased In Vitro by an Oligomer Complementary to a Segment of the Leader Transcript." *Proc. Natl. Acad. Sci. USA* 79 (1982): 2181–5; "Isolation of a cDNA Clone for the Human HLA-DR Antigen Alpha Chain by Using a Synthetic Oligonucleotide as a Hybridization Probe." *Proc. Natl. Acad. Sci. USA* 79 (1982): 5966–70; "Enzymic Amplification of Beta-globin Genomic Sequences and Restriction Site Analysis for Diagnosis of Sickle Cell Anemia." *Science* 230 (1985): 1350–4.

For More Information See: Dancing Naked in the Mind Field. New York: Pantheon Books, 1998. *Chemical and Engineering News 71* (October 18, 1993): 6; *New Scientist* 140 (October 23, 1993): 4

Commentary: Kary Mullis shared the Nobel with Michael Smith for "fundamental contributions to the establishment of oligonucleotide-based, site-directed mutagenesis and its development for protein studies." Mullis devised the technique of the polymerase chain reaction, which allowed duplication of a single gene fragment. The technique has been used for copying DNA in forensic applications and in molecules remaining in fossil material. Mullis left the organized world of science in 1988 for surfing, rollerblading, consulting, and thinking. (B.S.S./J.H.S.)

Smith, Michael   **118**

Prize: Chemistry, 1993. *Born:* April 26, 1932; Blackpool, England. *Death:* October 4, 2000; Vancouver, British Columbia, Canada. *Parents:* Father, Rowland Smith; Mother, Mary Agnes Smith. *Nationality:* English; later Canadian citizen. *Religion:* Atheist; from Anglican background. *Education:* Univ. of Manchester, England, B.Sc., 1953; Ph.D., 1956. *Spouse:* Helen Wood, married August 6, 1960; separated December, 1982. *Children:* Tom, son; Ian, son; Wendy, daughter. *Career:* Univ. of Wisconsin, Researcher, 1960–61; Vancouver Laboratory Fisheries Board, Canada, Researcher, 1961–66; Univ. of British Columbia, Canada, Researcher, 1966–97; Genome Sequencing Center, British Columbia, Canada, Admininstrator, 1997–2000. *Other Awards:* Gairdner Foundation Award, 1986.

Selected Publications: "Cellular Adaptation to the Environment." *Environ. Physiol. Anim.* (1976): 231–58; "The First Complete Nucleotide Sequencing of an Organism's DNA." *Am. Sci.* 67 (1979): 57–67; "Applications of Synthetic Oligodeoxyribonucleotides to Problems in Molecular Biology." *Nucleic Acids Symp. Ser.* 7 (1980): 387–95.

For More Information See: Chemical and Engineering News 71 (October 18, 1993): 6; *New Scientist* 140 (October 23, 1993): 4; *New York Times* (October 6, 2000): A31.

Commentary: Michael Smith was awarded the Nobel Prize for work in the field of genetics. Smith developed oligonucleotide-based, site-directed mutagenesis, by which foreign genetic segments can be spliced into an organism's genetic molecule, modifying the proteins produced by the organism. The technique has found use in genetic engineering of agricultural plants. (B.S.S./J.H.S.)

1994

Olah, George Andrew   **119**

Prize: Chemistry, 1994. *Born:* May 22, 1927; Budapest, Hungary. *Parents:* Father, Julius Olah; Mother, Magda Krasznai Olah. *Nationality:* Hungarian; later U.S. citizen. *Religion:* Most probably Christian. *Education:* Technical Univ. of Budapest, Hungary, Ph.D., 1949. *Spouse:* Judith Agnes Lengyel, married July 9, 1949. *Children:* George John, son; Ronald Peter, son. *Career:* Technical Univ. of Budapest, Hungary, Professor, 1949–54; Central Chemical Research Institute, Hungary, Researcher, 1954–56; Dow Chemical Co., Canada and U.S., Researcher, 1957–65; Case Western Reserve Univ., OH, Professor, 1965–77; Univ. of Southern California, Professor, 1977–. *Other Awards:* Petroleum Chemistry Award, 1964; Baekeland Award, 1966; Morley Medal, 1970; Humboldt Award, 1979; Synthetic Organic Chemistry Award, 1979; Roger Adams Award, 1989; California Scientist of the Year, 1989; Mendeleev Medal, 1992; Pioneer of Chemistry Award, 1993; Kapitsa Medal, 1995.

Selected Publications: Carbonium Ions. New York: Interscience Publishers, 1969–76; *Carbocations and Electrophilic Reactions.* New York: Wiley, 1973; *Superacids.* New York: Wiley, 1984; *Hydrocarbon Chemistry.* New York: John Wiley, 1995.

For More Information See: Chemical and Engineering News 72 (October 17, 1994): 4. *A Life in Magic Chemistry.* New York: Wiley, 2000. *New York Times Biographical Service* (1994): 1570.

Commentary: The Nobel Prize was granted to George Olah for his work in developing a technique to disassemble and rebuild hydrocarbons. Olah used superacids (like HF and S_6F_5) to break up hydrocarbons and form carbocations that could be stabilized in very cold solvents. The work resulted in the development of higher-octane gasoline and new fuels. (B.S.S./J.H.S.)

1995

Crutzen, Paul Josef   **120**

Prize: Chemistry, 1995. *Born:* December 3, 1933; Amsterdam, Netherlands. *Parents:* Father, Josef Crutzen; Mother, Anna Gurk Crutzen. *Nationality:* Dutch, later German resident. *Religion:* Most probably Christian. *Education:* Middelbare Technische School, Netherlands, civil engineering degree, 1958; Univ. of Stockholm, Sweden, M.S., 1963; Ph.D, 1968; D.Sc., 1973. *Spouse:* Terttu Soininen, married February 1958. *Children:* Ilona, daughter; Sylvia, daughter *Career:* Bridge Construction Bureau of Amsterdam, Netherlands, Engineer, 1954–58; House Construction Bureau, Sweden, Engineer, 1958–59; Univ. of Stockholm, Sweden, Researcher and Professor, 1959–74; National Center for Atmospheric Research (NCAR), Colorado, Researcher, 1974–80; Max Planck Institute for Chemistry, Germany, 1980-. *Other Awards:* Special Achievement Award, NOAA, 1977; Rolex-Discover Scientist of the Year, 1984; Szilard Prize, 1985; Tyler Prize, 1989; Volvo Prize, 1991; German Environmental Prize, 1994; Max-Planck-Forschungpreis, 1994; U.N. Environment Ozone Award, 1995.

Selected Publications: "SST's Threat to the Earth's Ozone Shield," *Ambio* 1 (1972): 41–51; "Estimates of Possible Variations in Total Ozone Due to Natural Causes and Human Activities," *Ambio* 3 (1974): 201–10; "Upper Limits on Atmospheric Ozone Reductions Following Increased Application of Fixed Nitrogen to the Soil," *Geophys. Res. Lett.* 3 (1976): 169–72; *Atmospheric Change,* New York: W. H. Freeman, 1993. *Atmosphere, Climate, and Change.* New York: Scientific American Library, 1995.

For More Information See: New York Times (October 12, 1995): A1

Commentary: Paul Crutzen shared the Nobel Prize with Mario Molina and F. Sherwood Rowland for work that "contributed to our salvation from a global environmental problem that could have catastrophic consequences [and made it] possible to make far-reaching decisions on prohibiting the release of gases that destroy ozone." Crutzen's contributions trace back to his work in the 1970s which showed how nitrogen oxides resulting from human activity accelerated the rate of ozone depletion in the atmosphere. (B.S.S./J.H.S.)

Molina, Mario Jose   **121**

Prize: Chemistry, 1995. *Born:* March 19, 1943; Mexico City, Mexico. *Parents:* Father, Roberto Molina-Pasquel; Mother, Leonor Henriquez de Molina. *Nationality:* Mexican, later U.S. citizen. *Religion:* None; from Catholic background. *Education:* Univ. Nacional Autónoma de Mexico, B.A., 1965; Univ. of Freiburg, Germany, M.A., 1967; Univ. of California, Berkeley, Ph.D., 1972. *Spouse:* Luisa Y. Tan, married July 12, 1973. *Children:* Felipe, son. *Career:* Univ. Nacional Autonoma de Mexico, Professor, 1967–68; Univ. of California, Berkeley, Professor, 1972–73; Univ. of California, Irvine, Professor, 1973–82; Jet Propulsion Laboratory, MD, Researcher, 1982–89; Massachusetts Institute of Technology, Professor, 1989-. *Other Awards:* Tyler Award, 1983; Esselen Award, 1987; Newcomb-Cleveland Prize, 1988; NASA Medal, 1989; U.N. Environmental Programme Global 500 Award, 1989.

Selected Publications: "Stratospheric Sink for Chlorofluoromethanes, Chlorine Atom-Catalyzed Destruction of Ozone." *Int. Conf. Environ. Impact Aerosp. Oper. High Atmos., 2nd,* (1974): 99–104; *Nature (London)* 249 (1974): 810–12 (with F. Rowland); "Unmeasured Chlorine Atom Reaction Rates Important for Stratospheric Modeling of Atom-Catalyzed Removal of Ozone." *J. Phys. Chem.* 79 (1975): 667–9 (with F. Rowland)

For More Information See: New York Times (October 12, 1995): A1.

Commentary: The Nobel Prize was awarded to Mario Molina, F. Sherwood Rowland, and Paul Crutzen for the work that "contributed to our salvation from a global environmental problem that could have catastrophic consequences [and made it] possible to make far-reaching decisions on prohibiting the release of gases that destroy ozone." Molina and Rowland, in 1974, cautioned that chlorofluorocarbons, commonly used in spray cans, refrigeration, and many industrial applications, could destroy the ozone layer that protects the planet from ultraviolet radiation. (B.S.S./J.H.S.)

Rowland, Frank Sherwood   **122**

Prize: Chemistry, 1995. *Born:* June 28, 1927; Delaware, OH. *Parents:* Father, Sidney A. Rowland; Mother, Lois

Drake Rowland. *Nationality:* American. *Religion:* Most probably Christian. *Education:* Ohio Wesleyan Univ., A.B., 1948; Univ. of Chicago, IL, M.S., 1951, Ph.D., 1952. *Spouse:* Joan E. Lundberg, married June 7, 1952. *Children:* Jeffrey Sherwood, son; Ingrid Drake, daughter. *Career:* Princeton Univ., NJ, Professor, 1952–56; Univ. of Kansas, Professor, 1956–64; Univ. of California, Irvine, Professor, 1964-. *Other Awards:* Wiley Jones Award, 1975; Tolman Medal, 1976; Billard Award, 1977; Leo Szilard Award, 1979; Zimmerman Award, 1980; Environmental Science and Technology Award, 1983; Tyler Prize, 1983; Esselen Award, 1987; Dana Award, 1987; Wadsworth Award, 1989; Japan Prize, 1989; Medal, Univ. of California, Irvine, 1989; Silver Medal, Royal Institute of Chemistry, 1989; Dickson Prize, 1991; Debye Award, 1993; Revelle Medal, 1994; Albert Einstein Prize, 1994; Alumni Medal, Univ. of Chicago, 1997; Nevada Medal, 1997.

Selected Publications: "Stratospheric Sink for Chlorofluoromethanes, Chlorine Atom-catalyzed Destruction of Ozone." *Int. Conf. Environ. Impact Aerosp. Oper. High Atmos., 2nd,* (1974): 99–104; *Nature* (London), 249 (1974): 810–12 (with M. Molina); "Unmeasured Chlorine Atom Reaction Rates Important for Stratospheric Modeling of Atom-catalyzed Removal of Ozone." *J. Phys. Chem* 79 (1975): 667–9 (with M. Molina).

For More Information See: New York Times (October 12, 1995): A1.

Commentary: F. Sherwood Rowland shared the Nobel with Mario Molina and Paul Crutzen for the work that "contributed to our salvation from a global environmental problem that could have catastrophic consequences [and made it] possible to make far-reaching decisions on prohibiting the release of gases that destroy ozone." Rowland and Molina, in 1974, cautioned that chlorofluorocarbons, commonly used in spray cans, refrigeration, and many industrial applications, could destroy the ozone layer that protected the planet from ultraviolet radiation. (B.S.S./J.H.S.)

1996

Curl, Robert Floyd, Jr.   123

Prize: Chemistry, 1996. *Born:* August 23, 1933; Alice, Texas. *Parents:* Father, Robert Floyd Curl; Mother, Lessie Merritt Curl. *Nationality:* American. *Religion:* Methodist. *Education:* Rice Univ., TX, B.A., 1954; Univ. of California, Berkeley, Ph.D., 1957. *Spouse:* Jonel Whipple, married December 12, 1955. *Children:* Michael, son; David, son. *Other Awards:* Clayton Prize, Institution of Mechanical Engineers, 1958; von Humboldt Award, 1984; APS International New Materials Prize, 1992; Order of Golden Plate, 1997; Achievement in Carbon Science Award, 1997; Texas Distinguished Scientist Award, 1997; Johannes Marcus Marci Award, 1998; Madison Marshall Award, 1998; Space Act Award, 1998; Centenary Medal, Royal Society of Chemistry, 1999.

Selected Publications: "Probing C60," *Science* 242 (November 18, 1988): 1017–22 (with R.E. Smalley). "Probing Chemical Reaction: Evidence for Exploration of an Excited Potential Energy Surface at Thermal Energies," *Science* (1993)(with others). "The Reaction of NH2 with O," *Journal of Physical Chemistry* (1994) (with others).

For More Information See: Journal of Physical Chemistry 94 (October 4, 1990): 7743–53 (with R.E.Smalley). *New York Times* (October 10, 1996): D21. *Science News*, 150 (October 19, 1996): 247.

Commentary: Robert Curl, Harold Kroto and Richard Smalley shared the Nobel Prize for "their discovery of fullerenes." In 1985, the three researchers discovered a new form of the element carbon arranged in the form of a ball whose structure was similar to the geodesic dome designed by the American architect R. Buckminster Fuller in 1967. Thus, they named the carbon structure buckminsterfullerene, or buckyball, after him. The number of carbon atoms in the shell can vary but they were able primarily to produce clusters of 60 or 70 carbon atoms with C60 being most prevalent. This discovery subsequently led to the development of a new branch of chemistry, "with consequences in such diverse areas as astrochemistry, superconductivity and materials chemistry/physics." (L.S.S.)

Kroto, Harold Walter, Sir   124

Prize: Chemistry, 1996. *Born:* October 7, 1939; Wisbech, Cambridgeshire, England. *Parents:* Father, Heinz Kroto; Mother, Edith Kroto. *Nationality:* British. *Religion:* Atheist, from Jewish background. *Education:* Univ. of Sheffield, England, B.S., 1961; Univ. of Sheffield, England, Ph.D., 1964. *Spouse:* Margaret Henrietta Hunter, married 1963. *Children:* Stephen, son; David, son. *Career:* National Research Council, Canada, Researcher, 1964–66; Bell Telephone Labs, NJ, Researcher, 1966–67; Univ. of Sussex, England, Professor, 1968-. *Other Awards:* Sunday *Times* Book Jacket Design Competition, 1964; APS International New Materials Prize, 1992; Italgas Prize, 1992; Longstaff Medal, 1993; Hewlett Packard Europhysics Prize, 1994; Science pour L'art Prize, Moet Hennessy Louis Vuitton Prize, 1994; Knighthood, 1996.

Selected Publications: "Space, Stars, C60, and Soot," *Science* 242 (November 25, 1988): 1139–45. "C60: Buckminsterfullerene, the Celestial Sphere That Fell to Earth," *Chemistry*, International Edition, 1992. *The Fullerenes.* NY: Pergamon Press, 1993 (with J.E. Fischer and D.E. Cox).

For More Information See: New York Times (October 10, 1996): D21. *Financial Times* (London) (October 10, 1996): 4.

Commentary: Harold Kroto shared the Nobel Prize with Robert Curl and Richard Smalley for their discovery of a third form of carbon, C60, in the shape of a geodesic dome, thus the name buckminsterfullerene or buckyball. The other forms of carbon were diamond and graphite. Kroto had been studying the analysis of gas in space and was particularly interested in carbon-rich giant stars and their long-chain molecules. Kroto, Curl and Smalley planned to investigate carbon vaporisation. Instead they found carbon clusters, C60, in the shape of a "truncated (cut off) icosahedron." This discovery has led to the development of a whole new chemistry "to manipulate the fullerene structure, and the properties of fullerenes can be studied systematically." (L.S.S.)

Smalley, Richard Errett   125

Prize: Chemistry, 1996. *Born:* June 6, 1943; Akron, Ohio. *Parents:* Father, Frank Dudley Smalley, Jr.; Mother, Esther

Virginia Rhoads Smalley. *Nationality:* American. *Religion:* Probably Christian. *Education:* Univ. of Michigan, B.S., 1965; Princeton Univ., NJ, M.A., 1971; Princeton Univ., NJ, Ph.D., 1973. *Spouse:* Judith Grace Sampierj, married May 4, 1968, divorced July 1979; Mary Lynn Chapieski, married July 10, 1980, divorced November 1994; JoNell Marie Chauvin, married March 1, 1997, divorced June 1998. *Children:* Chad Richard, son; Preston, son. *Career:* Shell Chemical Company, NJ, Researcher, 1965–68; Univ. of Chicago, IL, Researcher, 1973–76; Rice Univ., TX, Professor, 1976-. *Other Awards:* Langmuir Prize, 1991; APS International New Materials Prize, 1992; William H. Nichols Medal, 1993; S.W. Regional Award, American Chemical Society, 1992; Harrison Howe Award, 1994; Madison Marshall Award, 1995; Franklin Medal, 1996.

Selected Publications: "Probing C60," *Science* 242 (November 18, 1988): 1017–22 (with R.F. Curl). "Doping Bucky: Formation and Properties of Boron-Doped Buckminsterfullerene," *Journal of Physical Chemistry* (1991). "Formation of Fullerides and Fullerene-Based Heterostructure," *Science* (1991) (with others). "Great Balls of Carbon," *The Sciences* (March/April 1991) (with T. Guo and C. Jin).

For More Information See: "The All-Star of Buckyball," *Scientific American* 269 (September 1993): 46+. *New York Times* (October 10, 1996): D21.

Commentary: Richard Smalley shared the Nobel prize with Robert Curl and Harold Kroto for their discovery of a new form of carbon, called fullerenes. Fullerenes are formed when "vaporised carbon condenses in an atmosphere of inert gas." When intense pulses of laser light are directed at a carbon surface, the released carbon atoms mix with helium gas and form clusters of carbon atoms, predominantly in clusters of 60 atoms or C60 clusters. When cooled at very low temperatures, the carbon balls can be studied using mass spectrometry. The discovery of the fullerenes "has influenced our conception of such widely separated scientific problems as the galactic carbon cycle and classical aromaticity" but no practical applications have yet been discovered. (L.S.S.)

1997

Boyer, Paul Delos　　126

Prize: Chemistry, 1997. *Born:* July 31, 1918; Provo, Utah. *Parents:* Father, Daryl Dell Delos Boyer; Mother, Grace Guymon Boyer. *Nationality:* American. *Religion:* Atheist, from Christian background. *Education:* Brigham Young Univ., UT, B.S., 1939; Univ. of Wisconsin, WI, M.S., 1941; Univ. of Wisconsin, WI, Ph.D., 1943. *Spouse:* Lyda Mae Whicker, married August 31, 1939. *Children:* Gail Anne, daughter; Marjorie Lynne, daughter; Douglas, son. *Career:* Stanford Univ., CA, Researcher, 1943–45; U.S. Navy, 1945–46; Univ. of Minnesota, MN, Professor, 1946–63; Univ. of California, Los Angeles, CA, Professor, 1963–89. *Other Awards:* Enzyme Chemistry Award, 1955; McCoy Award for Chemical Research, 1976; Tolman Award, 1984; Rose Award, 1989.

Selected Publications: Enzymes. New York: Academic Press, 1975, 3rd ed. "Oxygen-18 probes of enzymic reactions of phosphate compounds," *Methods in Enzymology* 64 (1980): 60–83 (with D.D. Hackney and K.E. Stempel). "The

binding change mechanism for ATP synthase—Some probabilities and possibilities," *Biochimica et Biophysica Acta* 1140 (1993):215–250. "The ATP synthase—a splendid molecular machine," *Annual Review in Biochemistry* 66 (1997):717–749. "From human serum albumin to rotational catalysis by ATP synthase," *The FASEB Journal* 9 (April 1995): 559–561.

For More Information See: New York Times (October 16, 1997): A16.

Commentary: Paul Boyer and John Walker shared half the Nobel Prize for "their elucidation of the enzymatic mechanism underlying the synthesis of adenosine triphosphate." ATP functions as a carrier of energy in all living organisms, including plants, bacteria, animals and humans. Boyer won the prize for showing how "ATP synthase functions and particularly how it uses energy to create new ATP." (L.S.S.)

Skou, Jens Christian　　127

Prize: Chemistry, 1997. *Born:* October 8, 1918; Lemvig, Denmark. *Parents:* Father, Magnus Martinus Skou; Mother, Ane Margrethe Jensen Knak Skou. *Nationality:* Danish. *Religion:* Probably Christian. *Education:* Univ. of Copenhagen, Denmark, M.D., 1944; Aarhus Univ., Denmark, Dr. Med. Sci., 1954. *Spouse:* Ellen-Margrethe Nielsen, married May 17, 1947. *Children:* Hanne, daughter; Karen, daughter. *Career:* Hjorring Hospital, Denmark, Intern and Resident, 1944–46; Hospital Aarhus, Netherlands, Orthopedist, 1946–47; Aarhus Univ., Netherlands, Professor, 1947–88. *Other Awards:* Leo Prize, 1954; Novo Prize, 1965; Consul Carlsen Prize, 1973; A. Retzius Gold Medal, 1977; E.K. Fernstroom Big Nordic Prize, 1985; Prokash Dotta Medal, 1985.

Selected Publications: "The influence of some cations on an adenosine triphosphatase from peripheral nerves," *Biochimica et Biophysica Acta* 23 (1957): 394–401. "The Na, K-ATPase," *Journal of Bioenergetics and Biomembranes* 24 (1992): 249–261 (with M. Esmann).

For More Information See: New York Times (October 16, 1997): A16.

Commentary: Jens Skou received half of the Nobel Prize "for the first discovery of an ion-transporting enzyme, NA+,K+-ATPase." He discovered the enzyme sodium, potassium-stimulated adenosine triphosphatase (NA+,K+-ATPase), which "maintains the balance of sodium and potassium ions in the living cell." The cell acts like a pump maintaining a balance in the cells. If the pump stops, the cell can swell and it can lead to unconsciousness from a lack of oxygen to the brain. This has led to the discovery of other ion pumps with similar structures and functions. (L.S.S.)

Walker, John Ernest　　128

Prize: Chemistry, 1997. *Born:* January 7, 1941; Halifax, Yorkshire, England. *Parents:* Father, Thomas Ernest Walker; Mother, Elsie Lawton Walker. *Nationality:* British. *Religion:* Probably Christian. *Education:* St. Catherine's College, England, B.A., 1964; Oxford Univ., England, Ph.D., 1969. *Spouse:* Christina Jane Westcott, married 1963. *Children:* Esther, daughter; Miriam, daughter. *Career:* Univ. of Wisconsin, WI, Researcher, 1969–71; CNRS, France, Researcher, 1971–72; Pasteur Institute, France, Researcher,

1972–74; Cambridge Medical Research Council, England, Researcher and Administrator, 1974-. *Other Awards:* A.T. Clay Gold Medal, 1959; Johnson Foundation Prize, 1994; CIBA Medal, 1996; Peter Mitchell Medal, 1996; Gaetano Quagliariello Prize, 1997; Knight Bachelor, 1999.

Selected Publications: "The Mitochondrial Transporter Family," *Current Opinion in Structural Biology* 2 (1992): 519–526. "The Mechanism of ATP Synthesis," *The Biochemist* 16 (1994): 31–35. "The Regulation of Catalysis in ATP Synthase," *Current Opinion in Structural Biology* 4 (1994): 912–918. "Structure at 2.8 Å resolution of F 1 - ATPase from bovine heart mitochondria," *Nature* 370 (1994): 621–628 (with others).

For More Information See: *New York Times* (October 16, 1997): A16.

Commentary: John Walker shared half of the Nobel Prize with Paul Boyer for establishing the structure of the enzyme ATP and verifying the mechanism of how it worked proposed by Boyer. ATP has been termed the "cell's energy currency" and is one of the most universal enzymes found in living cells. (L.S.S.)

1998

Kohn, Walter   129

Prize: Chemistry, 1998. *Born:* March 9, 1923; Vienna, Austria. *Parents:* Father, Salomon Kohn; Mother, Gittel Rappaport Kohn. *Nationality:* Austrian; later Canadian citizen, then American citizen. *Religion:* Jewish. *Education:* Univ. of Toronto, Canada, B.A., 1945; Univ. of Toronto, Canada, M.A., 1946; Harvard Univ., MA, Ph.D., 1948. *Spouse:* Lois Mary Adams Kohn, married, 1948, dissolved, no date; Mara Schiff, married, 1978. *Children:* J. Marilyn, daughter; Ingrid E., daughter; E. Rosalind, daughter *Career:* Sutton Horsley Co., Canada, Researcher, 1941–43; Koulomzine, Canada, Geophysicist, 1944–46; Harvard Univ., MA, Professor, 1948–50; Carnegie-Mellon Univ., PA, Professor, 1950–60; Univ. of California, San Diego, CA, Professor, 1960–79; Univ. of California, Santa Barbara, Professor, 1979–91. *Other Awards:* Buckley Prize, 1960; Davisson-Germer Prize, 1977; National Medal of Science, 1988; Feenberg Medal, 1991; Niels Bohr/UNESCO Gold Medal, 1998.

Selected Publications: "Theory of the Insulating State," *Phys. Rev.* 133 (1964): A171. "Quantum Density Oscillations in an Inhomogeneous Electron Gas," *Phys. Rev.* 137 (1965):A1697 (with L. J. Sham). "Wannier Functions and Self-Consistent Metal Calculations," *Phys. Rev.* 382 (1974):B10. "Local Density-Functional Theory of Frequency-Dependent Linear Response," *Phys. Rev. Lett.* 55 (1985):2850 (with E. K. U. Gross).

For More Information See: *New York Times* (October 14, 1998): A16.

Commentary: Walter Kohn shared the Nobel Prize "for his development of the density-functional theory," a simpler method of calculating the properties of molecules. Kohn showed that it was not necessary "to consider the motion of each individual electron: it suffices to know the average number of electrons located at any one point in space." This simpler method makes it possible to study very large molecules and has been used to calculate the geometrical structure of molecules to mapping chemical reactions. (L.S.S.)

Pople, John Anthony   130

Prize: Chemistry, 1998. *Born:* October 31, 1925; Burnham, Somerset, England. *Parents:* Father, Herbert Keith Pople; Mother, Mary Frances Jones Pople. *Nationality:* British; later American resident. *Religion:* Probably Christian. *Education:* Cambridge Univ., England, B.A., 1946; Cambridge Univ. England, M.A., 1950; Cambridge Univ., England, Ph.D., 1951. *Spouse:* Joy Cynthia Bowers, married September 22, 1952. *Children:* Hilary Jane, daughter; Adrian John, son; Mark Stephen, son; Andrew Keith, son. *Career:* Cambridge Univ., England, Researcher and Professor, 1951–58; National Physical Laboratory, England, Researcher, 1958–64; Carnegie Institute of Technology, PA, Professor, 1961–62; Carnegie-Mellon Univ., PA, Professor, 1964–93; Northwestern Univ., IL, Professor, 1986-. *Other Awards:* Mayhew Prize, 1948; Smith Prize, 1950; Marlow Medal, 1958; Langmuir Award, 1970; Pittsburgh Award, 1975; Harrison Howe Award, 1971; Gilbert Newton Lewis Prize, 1973; Linus Pauling Award, 1977; Sr. Scientist Award, Humboldt Foundation, 1981; G. Willard Wheland Award, 1981; Evans Award, 1982; Oesper Award, 1984; Davy Medal, 1988; Computers in Chemistry Award, 1991; Wolf Prize, 1992; Kirkwood Medal, 1994; J.O. Hirschfelder Prize, 1994.

Selected Publications: *High Resolution Nuclear Magnetic Resonance.* New York: McGraw Hill, 1959. *Approximate Molecular Orbital Theory.* New York: McGraw Hill, 1970 (with D.L. Beveridge). *Ab Initio Molecular Orbital Theory.* New York: Wiley, 1986 (with others).

For More Information See: *Journal of Physical Chemistry* 94 (July 12, 1990): 5431–34. *New York Times* (October 14, 1998): A16.

Commentary: John Pople shared the Nobel Prize with Walter Kohn for his "development of computational methods in quantum chemistry" which has made possible "the theoretical study of molecules, their properties and how they act together in chemical reactions." Pople developed a computer program called GAUSSIAN-70 that is now widely used. This program and Pople's continuing refinements have led to a "well-documented model chemistry" that have allowed the study of increasingly complex molecules. (L.S.S.)

1999

Zewail, Ahmed Hassan   131

Prize: Chemistry, 1999. *Born:* February 26, 1946; Damanhour, Egypt. *Parents:* Father, Hassan A. Zewail; Mother, Rawhia Dar Zewail. *Nationality:* Egyptian; later American citizen. *Religion:* No record found. *Education:* Alexandria Univ., Egypt, B.S., 1967; Alexandria Univ., Egypt, M.S., 1969; Univ. of Pennsylvania, Ph.D., 1974. *Spouse:* Dema Zewail, married, no date *Children:* Maha; Amani, son; Nabeel; Hani. *Career:* Univ. of California, Berkeley, Researcher, 1974–76; California Institute of Technology, Professor, 1976-. *Other Awards:* von Humboldt Award, 1983; Buck-Whitney Medal, 1985; Guggenheim Memorial Foundation Award, 1987; King Faisal International Prize, 1989; Harrison Howe Award, 1989; Hoechst Prize, 1990; NASA Award, 1991; AMM Achievement Award, 1991; Nobel Laureate Signature Award, 1992; Carl Zeiss Award, 1992; Cairo University Medal, 1992; University of Qatar Medal, 1993; E.K. Plyler Prize, 1993; Wolf

Prize, 1993; Royal Netherlands Academy of Arts & Sciences Medal, 1993; Niles Award, 1994; Leonardo Da Vinci Award, 1995; H.P. Broida Prize, 1995; Chemistry Science Award, 1996; Kirkwood Medal, 1996; Peking University Medal, 1996; Peter Debye Award, 1997; Linus Pauling Medal, 1997; E.B. Wilson Award, 1997; R.A. Welch Award, 1997; Pittsburgh Spectroscopy Award, 1997; William H. Nichols Award, 1998; Richard Tolman Award, 1998; Franklin Medal, 1999; Paul Karrer Gold Medal, 1999; Roentgen Prize, 1999; E.O. Lawrence Award, 1999; Merski Award, 1999.

Selected Publications: "The Birth of Molecules" *Scientific American* (December 1990): 40–46. "The Validity of the Diradical Hypothesis: Direct Femtosecond Studies of the Transition-State Structures," *Science* 266 (1994): 1359–1364 (with S. Pedersen and J.L. Herek).

For More Information See: New York Times (October 13, 1999): A8.

Commentary: Ahmed Zewail received the Nobel Prize "for his studies of the transition states of chemical reactions using femtosecond spectroscopy." Using a "slow motion" laser "camera," Zewail was able to study "actual chemical reactions on the time scale on which the reactions actually occur." Femtochemistry allows one to observe the "love," "hate" and "divorce" of molecules as they come together, bond, and break apart. The Nobel Committee notes Zewail's contributions have "brought about a revolution in chemistry and adjacent sciences, since this type of investigation allows us to understand and predict important reactions." (L.S.S.)

2000

Heeger, Alan Jay 132

Prize: Chemistry, 2000. *Born:* January 22, 1936; Sioux City, Iowa. *Parents:* Father, Peter J. Heeger; Mother, Alice Minkin Heeger. *Nationality:* American. *Religion:* Probably Christian. *Education:* Univ. of Nebraska, B.S., 1957; Univ. of California, Berkeley, Ph.D., 1961. *Spouse:* Ruthann Chudacoff, married August 11, 1957. *Children:* Peter S., son; David J., son. *Career:* Univ. of Pennsylvania, PA, Professor, 1962–82; Univ. of California, Santa Barbara, CA, Professor and Administrator, 1982-; UNIAX Corp., CA, Founder & Administrator, 1990–2000. *Other Awards:* John Scott Medal, 1989; Oliver P. Buckley Prize, 1983; Balzan Foundation Prize, 1995.

Selected Publications: "Synthesis of electrically conducting organic polymers: Halogen derivatives of polyacetylene (CH)n," *The Journal of Chemical Society, Chemical Communications* (Summer 1977)(with A. MacDiarmid and H.Shirakawa). "Synthesis of Highly Conducting Films of Derivatives of Polyacetylene, (CH)x," *Journal of the American Chemical Society* 100 (1978): 1013 (with others).

For More Information See: New York Times (October 11, 2000): A16.

Commentary: Alan Heeger and his colaureates shared the Nobel Prize "for the discovery and development of conductive polymers." Heeger, Alan MacDiarmid and Hideki Shirakawa discovered that plastics, after some modifications, can conduct electrical current. Plastics are polymers,

made up of long molecules that resemble a chain. In order for the polymer to be able to conduct electricity, it must be "doped," which means that electrons are either removed or introduced. This creates "holes" which allows extra electrons to move along the molecule thus becoming electrically conductive. (L.S.S.)

MacDiarmid, Alan Graham 133

Prize: Chemistry, 2000. *Born:* April 14, 1927; Masterton, New Zealand. *Parents:* No record found. *Nationality:* New Zealander; later American citizen. *Religion:* Probably Christian. *Education:* Univ. of New Zealand, B.Sci., 1948; M. Sci., 1950; Univ. of Wisconsin, WI, M.S., 1952; Ph.D., 1953; Cambridge Univ., England, Ph.D., 1955. *Spouse:* married, 1954. *Children:* 4 children *Career:* Univ. of Pennsylvania, PA, Professor, 1955-. *Other Awards:* Francis J. Clamer Medal, 1993; American Chemical Society Award in Materials Chemistry, 1999.

Selected Publications: "Synthesis of electrically conducting organic polymers: Halogen derivatives of polyacetylene (CH)n," *The Journal of Chemical Society, Chemical Communications* (Summer 1977)(with A. Heeger and H.Shirakawa). "Synthesis of Highly Conducting Films of Derivatives of Polyacetylene, (CH)x," *Journal of the American Chemical Society* 100 (1978): 1013 (with others). "Plastics That Conduct Electricity," *Scientific American* 106 (February 1988)(with R.B. Kaner).

For More Information See: New York Times (October 11, 2000): A16.

Commentary: Alan MacDiarmid shared the Nobel Prize with Alan Heeger and Hideki Shirakawa for discovering that plastics, after certain modifications, can conduct electricity. Plastics, or polymers, can be modified by either removing electrons (through oxidation) or adding electrons (through reduction) that allows the extra electrons to move along the molecule and become electrically conductive. The Nobel Committee notes "we stand at the threshold to a plastic-electronics revolution with exciting implications in chemistry and physics as well as information technology." (L.S.S.)

Shirakawa, Hideki 134

Prize: Chemistry, 2000. *Born:* 1936; Tokyo, Japan. *Parents:* No record found. *Nationality:* Japanese. *Religion:* No record found. *Education:* Tokyo Institute of Technology, Japan, Ph.D., 1966. *Spouse:* Married, no further record found. *Children:* No record found. *Career:* Tokyo Institute of Technology, Japan, Researcher; Univ. of Pennsylvania, PA, Researcher; Univ. of Tsukuba, Japan, Professor, 1966-.

Selected Publications: "Synthesis of Electronically Conducting Organic Polymers: Halogen derivatives of polyacetylene (CH)n," *Journal of Chemical Society, Chemical Communications* (Summer 1977) (with A. Heeger and A. MacDiarmid). "Synthesis of Highly Conducting Films of Derivatives of Polyacetylene, (CH)x," *Journal of the American Chemical Society* 100 (1978): 1013 (with others).

For More Information See: New York Times (October 11, 2000): A16.

Commentary: Hideki Shirakawa, along with Alan Heeger and Alan MacDiarmid, received the Nobel Prize "for the discovery and development of conductive polymers." Plastics are generally considered as insulation, covering copper wires used in electricity. They found that after certain modifications, plastics, or polymers, could become electrically conductive. Practical applications include antistatic coating on photographic film, luminous signs, and the development of other antistatic materials for use in places where static electricity should be avoided. (L.S.S.)

Economics

1969

Frisch, Ragnar Kittil, Anton   **135**
Prize: Economics, 1969. *Born:* March 3, 1895; Oslo, Norway. *Death:* January 31, 1973; Oslo, Norway. *Parents:* Father, Anton Frisch; Mother, Ragna Fredrikke Kittilsen Frisch. *Nationality:* Norwegian. *Religion:* Jewish. *Education:* Univ. of Oslo, Norway, B.A., 1919; Univ. of Oslo, Norway, Ph.D., 1926. *Spouse:* Marie Smedal, married April 28, 1920, died 1952; Astrid Johannessen, married 1953. *Children:* Ragna, daughter. *Career:* Univ. of Oslo, Norway, Professor, 1931–71. *Other Awards:* Schumpeter Prize, Harvard Univ., MA, 1955; Antonio Feltrinelli Prize, Academia Nacionale dei Lincei, Rome, Italy, 1961.

    Selected Publications: Maxima and Minima. Theory and Economic Applications. Tr. by Express Translation Service. Chicago: Rand McNally, 1966. *Economic Planning Studies.* Dordrecht, Netherlands: D. Reidel, 1976. *New Methods of Measuring Marginal Utility.* Philadelphia, PA: Porcupine Press, 1978. *Foundations of Modern Econometrics.* Brookfield, VT: Edward Elgar Publishers, 1995.

    For More Information See: "Ragnar Frisch and Business Cycle Research during the Interwar Years." *History of Political Economy* 13 (1981): 695–725. *Science* 166 (1969): 715–17. *Thinkers of the Twentieth Century.* Detroit, MI: Gale, 1983, 184–85.

    Commentary: Ragnar Frisch was awarded the Nobel Prize for his contributions in establishing the subjects of econometrics and mathematical economics. Frisch's research was important in establishing theories for: models of whole economics, production, consumer behavior, index numbers, and planning. His work was not restricted to economics, since his statistical and mathematical methodologies could be applied elsewhere as well. (J.F.)

Tinbergen, Jan   **136**
Prize: Economics, 1969. *Born:* April 12, 1903; The Hague, Netherlands. *Death:* June 9, 1994; Amsterdam, Netherlands. *Parents:* Father, Dirk Cornelis Tinbergen; Mother, Jeanette Van Eek Tinbergen. *Nationality:* Dutch. *Religion:* Agnostic; from Protestant background. *Education:* Leiden Univ., Netherlands, Ph.D., 1929. *Spouse:* Tine Johanna de Wit, married July 19, 1929, died 1994. *Children:* Adriaan M., daughter; Elsje, daughter; Hanneke, daughter; Marianne, daughter. *Career:* Central Bureau of Statistics, Netherlands, Statistician, 1929–36; League of Nations Secretariat, Statistician, 1936–38; Central Bureau of Statistics, Netherlands, Statistician, 1938–45; Central Planning Bureau, Netherlands, Director, 1945–55; Netherlands School of Economics, Professor, 1933–73; Leiden Univ., Netherlands, Professor, 1973–75. *Other Awards:* Erasmus Prize, 1967; Order of the Lion; Order of Orange Nassau; Four Freedoms Award, 1992.

    Selected Publications: An Economic Approach to Business Cycle Problems. Paris: Hermann, 1937. *Statistical Testing of Business Cycle Theories.* Geneva: League of Nations, 1939. *Business Cycles in the United Kingdom, 1870–1914.* Amsterdam: North-Holland, 1951. *On the Theory of Economic Policy.* Amsterdam: North-Holland, 1952. *Economic Policy: Principles and Design.* Amsterdam: North-Holland, 1956. *Production, Income and Welfare.* Lincoln, NE: Univ. of Nebraska Press, 1985.

    For More Information See: New York Times Biographical Service (June 14, 1994): 882. *Science* 166 (1969): 715–17. *Thinkers of the Twentieth Century.* Detroit, MI: Gale, 1983, 567–68.

    Commentary: Jan Tinbergen was awarded the Nobel Prize for his work in econometrics, the mathematical representation of economic theory. During his impressive career, he worked with statistical models of economies, the mathematical analysis of economic cycles, and several theories: of income distribution, of economic growth, of economic planning, and of economic development. (J.F.)

1970

Samuelson, Paul Anthony   **137**
Prize: Economics, 1970. *Born:* May 15, 1915; Gary, IN. *Parents:* Father, Frank Samuelson; Mother, Ella Lipton Samuelson. *Nationality:* American. *Religion:* Jewish. *Education:* Univ. of Chicago, IL, B.A., 1935; Harvard Univ., MA, M.A., 1936; Harvard Univ., MA, Ph.D., 1941. *Spouse:* Marion Crawford, married July 2, 1938, died 1978; Risha Eckaus, married 1981. *Children:* Jane Kendall, daughter; Margaret Wray, daughter; William Frank, son; Robert James, son; John Crawford, son; Paul Reid, son; Susan Miller, stepdaughter. *Career:* Massachusetts Institute of Technology, Professor, 1940–85. *Other Awards:* David Wells Prize, Harvard Univ., 1941; John Bates Clark Medal, American Economic Association, 1947; Guggenheim Fellow, 1948; Ford Foundation Fellow, 1958; Medal of Honor, Univ. of Evansville, IL, 1970; Albert Einstein Commemorative Award, 1971; Distinguished Service Award, National Association of Investment Clubs, 1974; Alumni Medal, Univ. of Chicago, IL, 1983; Britannica Award, 1989; Medal of Honor, Valencia, Spain, 1990; Gold Scanno Prize, Naples, Italy, 1990; National Medal of Science, 1996.

    Selected Publications: Foundations of Economic Analysis. Cambridge, MA: Harvard Univ. Press, 1947. *Economics: An Introductory Analysis.* New York: McGraw-Hill, 1948. *Linear Programming and Economic Analysis.* New York: McGraw-Hill, 1958 (with Robert Dorfman and Robert Solow). *The Collected Scientific Papers of Paul A. Samuelson.* 5 volumes. Cambridge, MA: Harvard Univ. Press, 1966–86.

    For More Information See: Current Biography Yearbook. New York: H.W. Wilson, 1965, 356–59. *Science* 170 (November 13, 1970): 720–21. Silk, Leonard. *The Economists.* New York: Basic Books, 1976, 3–43.

    Commentary: The Nobel Committee cited Paul Samuelson for doing "more than any other contemporary economist to raise the level of scientific analysis in economic theory." Most contemporaries would probably agree that this is because of Samuelson's ability to express in mathematical terms and lucid prose the economic theories of the day. However, his greatest impact has been through his classic textbook, *Economics*, and his popular writings which have educated the general public to the world of economics. (B.S.S.)

1971

Kuznets, Simon Smith   138

Prize: Economics, 1971. *Born:* April 30, 1901; Kharkov, Russia. *Death:* July 9, 1985; Cambridge, MA. *Parents:* Father, Abraham Kuznets; Mother, Pauline Friedman Kuznets. *Nationality:* Russian; later American citizen. *Religion:* Jewish. *Education:* Columbia Univ., NY, B.A., 1923; Columbia Univ., NY, M.A., 1924; Columbia Univ., NY, Ph.D., 1926. *Spouse:* Edith Handler, married June 5, 1929. *Children:* Paul Kuznets, son; Mrs. Norman Stein, daughter. *Career:* National Bureau of Economic Research, Researcher, 1927–30; Univ. of Pennsylvania, Professor, 1930–54; Johns Hopkins Univ., MD, Professor, 1954–60; Harvard Univ., MA, Professor, 1960–71. *Other Awards:* Robert Troup Paine Prize, 1970; Francis A. Walker Medal, 1977.

Selected Publications: Commodity Flow and Capital Formation. New York: National Bureau of Economic Research, 1938. *National Product Since 1869.* New York: National Bureau of Economic Research, 1946. *Economic Change.* New York: Norton, 1953. *Capital in the American Economy.* Princeton, NJ: Princeton Univ. Press, 1961. *Economic Growth of Nations: Total Output and Production Structure.* Cambridge, MA: Harvard Univ. Press, 1971. *National Income and Its Composition, 1919–1935.* New York: National Bureau of Economic Research, 1971.

For More Information See: Nobel Laureates in Economic Sciences. New York: Garland, 1984, 143–59. *Science* 174 (October 27, 1971): 481–83. "Simon Kuznets' Contribution to Economics." *Swedish Journal of Economics* 73 (December 1971): 444–61.

Commentary: Simon Kuznets was recognized for his "empirically founded interpretation of economic growth" and "for illuminating with facts—and explaining through analysis—the economic growth from the middle of the last century." His contribution consisted of developing a system for national income accounting and applying statistical methods to measure the sources and uses of the annual production of a country. Later in his career, Kuznets studied the changing roles of capital, labor, and productivity in the United States economy and became a leader in socioeconomic theory. (B.S.S.)

1972

Arrow, Kenneth Joseph   139

Prize: Economics, 1972. *Born:* August 23, 1921; New York, NY. *Parents:* Father, Harry I. Arrow; Mother, Lillian Greenberg Arrow. *Nationality:* American. *Religion:* Jewish. *Education:* City College of New York, B.S., 1940; Columbia Univ., NY, M.A., 1941; Columbia Univ., NY, Ph.D., 1951. *Spouse:* Selma Schweitzer, married August 31, 1947. *Children:* David Michael, son; Andrew Seth, son.

Career: Cowles Commission for Research in Economics, Univ. of Chicago, IL, Researcher, 1947–49; Stanford Univ., CA, Professor, 1949–68; Harvard Univ., MA, Professor, 1968–79; Stanford Univ., CA, Professor, 1979–91. *Other Awards:* John Bates Clark Medal, American Economic Association, 1957; Von Neumann Prize, 1986; Kempe de Feriet Medal, 1998; Medal, Univ. of Paris, 1998.

Selected Publications: Social Choice and Individual Values. New York: Wiley, 1951. *Studies in Linear and Nonlinear Programming.* Stanford, CA: Stanford Univ. Press, 1958 (with others). *Studies in the Mathematical Theory of Inventory and Production.* Stanford, CA: Stanford Univ. Press, 1958. *Essays in the Theories of Risk-Bearing.* Chicago: Markham Publishing Co., 1971. *Studies in Resource Allocation.* New York: Cambridge Univ. Press, 1977. *Social Choice and Justice: Collected Papers of Kenneth J. Arrow.* Oxford: Blackwell, 1984.

For More Information See: Arrow and the Foundations of the Theory of Economic Policy. London: Macmillan, 1987. *Nobel Laureates in the Economic Sciences.* New York: Garland, 1989, 9–30. *Science* 178 (November 3, 1972): 487–89.

Commentary: The Nobel Prize was awarded to Kenneth Arrow for his "pioneering work on the theory of general economic equilibrium." Arrow's doctoral research was on social choice and individual values (the title of his dissertation), and he continued over the course of his career to apply economic theory to all types of social problems—medical care, education, water resources, etc. His later research concerned the role of information in the behavior of businesspeople and consumers. Arrow was also heavily involved with students at all levels and with university affairs wherever he taught. (B.S.S.)

Hicks, John Richard, Sir   140

Prize: Economics, 1972. *Born:* April 8, 1904; Leamington Spa, England. *Death:* May 20, 1989; London, England. *Parents:* Father, Edward Hicks; Mother, Dorothy Stephens Hicks. *Nationality:* British. *Religion:* Baptist. *Education:* Oxford Univ., England, B.A., 1927; Oxford Univ., England, M.A., 1931. *Spouse:* Ursula Kathleen Webb, married 1935, died 1985. *Children:* None. *Career:* London School of Economics, England, Professor, 1926–35; Cambridge Univ., England, Professor, 1935–38; Univ. of Manchester, England, Professor, 1938–46; Oxford Univ., England, Professor, 1946–65. *Other Awards:* Knighthood, 1964.

Selected Publications: The Theory of Wages. London: Macmillan, 1932. *Value and Capital: An Inquiry into Some Fundamental Principles of Economic Theory.* Oxford: Clarendon Press, 1939. *The Social Framework: An Introduction to Economics.* Oxford: Clarendon Press, 1942. *A Contribution to the Theory of the Trade Cycle.* Oxford: Clarendon Press, 1950. *Capital and Growth.* Oxford: Clarendon Press, 1965. *The Crisis in Keynesian Economics.* Oxford: Basil Blackwell, 1974. *Methods of Dynamic Economics.* Oxford: Oxford Univ. Press, 1987.

For More Information See: Baumol, William J. "John R. Hicks' Contribution to Economics." *The Swedish Journal of Economics* 74 (December 1972): 503–27. *John R. Hicks.* Oxford, England: Blackwell, 1993. Morgan, Brian. "Sir John Hicks's Contributions to Economic Theory." In *Twelve Contemporary Economists.* New York: John Wiley, 1981,

108–40. Reid, G.C., and Wolfe, J.N. "Hicks, John R." *International Encyclopedia of the Social Sciences*. New York: Free Press, 1979 (Volume 18), 300–02.

Commentary: Although honored for his "pioneering contributions to general economic equilibrium theory and welfare theory," the work of John Hicks also influenced such areas as monetary theory and stability analysis, as his writings became the foundation for much of the economic thought of the time. Hicks was perhaps best known for *Value and Capital* (1939), in which he set forth his general economic equilibrium theory. Considered an economic classic, few works had such a profound effect on the basic structure of economic theory. (R.W.S.)

1973

Leontief, Wassily W. 141

Prize: Economics, 1973. *Born:* August 5, 1906; St. Petersburg, Russia. *Death:* February 5, 1999; New York, NY. *Parents:* Father, Wassily Leontief; Mother, Eugenia Bekker Leontief. *Nationality:* Russian; later American citizen. *Religion:* Eastern Orthodox. *Education:* Leningrad State Univ., USSR, Learned Economist, 1925; Univ. of Berlin, Germany, Ph.D., 1928. *Spouse:* Estella Helena Marks, married December 25, 1932. *Children:* Svetlana Eugenia Alpers, daughter. *Career:* Univ. of Kiel, Germany, Research Economist, 1927–30; National Bureau of Economic Research, NY, Research Associate, 1931; Harvard Univ., MA, Professor, 1931–75; New York Univ., Professor and Administrator, 1975–91. *Other Awards:* Guggenheim Fellowship, 1940, 1950; Bernhard-Harms Prize, Germany, 1970; Takemi Memorial Award, Japan, 1991; Harry Edmonds Award for Life Achievement, 1995.

Selected Publications: "Quantitative Input and Output Relations in the Economic System of the United States." *Review of Economic Statistics* 18 (August 1936): 105–25. *The Structure of the American Economy, 1919–1929: An Empirical Application of Equilibrium Analysis.* Cambridge, MA: Harvard Univ. Press, 1941. "Exports, Imports, Domestic Output and Employment." *Quarterly Journal of Economics* 60 (February 1946): 171–93. "Factor Proportions and the Structure of American Trade: Further Theoretical and Empirical Analysis." *Review of Economics and Statistics* 38 (November 1956): 386–407. "The Economic Impact—Industrial and Regional—of an Arms Cut." *Review of Economics and Statistics* 47 (August 1965): 217–41. "The Distribution of Work and Income." *Input-Output Economics.* New York: Oxford Univ. Press, 1966. *Scientific American* (September 1982): 188–190+.

For More Information See: Dorfman, Robert. "Wassily Leontief's Contribution to Economics." *Swedish Journal of Economics* 75 (December 1973): 442–49. Samuelson, Paul A. "Nobel Laureate Leontief." *Newsweek* (November 5, 1973): 94. Seligman, Ben B. *Main Currents in Modern Economics: Economic Thought Since 1870.* New York: Free Press of Glencoe, 1962, 434–41. Silk, Leonard. *The Economists.* New York: Basic Books, 1976, 151–90.

Commentary: Wassily Leontief won his award for the "development of the input-output method of economic analysis, used in various forms in more than 50 industrialized countries for planning and forecasting." He has used his methods to study the effects of various factors on the U.S.

economy—the end of World War II, military spending, environment, and world development. (N.H.)

1974

Hayek, Friedrich August Von 142

Prize: Economics, 1974. *Born:* May 8, 1899; Vienna, Austria. *Death:* March 23, 1992; Freiberg, Germany. *Parents:* Father, August Von Hayek; Mother, Felicitas von Juraschek Von Hayek. *Nationality:* Austrian; later British, American, and German resident. *Religion:* Catholic. *Education:* Univ. of Vienna, Austria, Dr. Jur., 1921; Univ. of Vienna, Austria, Ph.D., 1923. *Spouse:* Helene von Fritsch, married 1926, divorced 1950; Helene Bitterlich, married 1950. *Children:* Christine, daughter; Lawrence, son. *Career:* Austrian Institute of Economic Research, Director, 1927–31; Univ. of London, England, Professor, 1931–50; Univ. of Chicago, IL, Professor, 1950–62; Univ. of Freiburg, Germany, 1962–70; Univ. of Salzburg, Austria, Professor, 1970–77. *Other Awards:* Ordre Pour le Mérite; Medal of Honor, Austria, 1976; Companion of Honor, 1984.

Selected Publications: *Geldtheorie und Konjunkturtheorie.* Vienna: Hoelder-Pichler-Tempsky, 1929 (*Monetary Theory and the Trade Cycle.* London: Harcourt, 1933). *Prices and Production.* London: G. Routledge, 1933. *The Pure Theory of Capital.* London: G. Routledge, 1941. *The Road to Serfdom.* Chicago: Univ. of Chicago Press, 1944. *Individualism and Economic Order.* Chicago: Univ. of Chicago Press, 1949. *The Counter-Revolution of Science.* Chicago: Univ. of Chicago Press, 1952. *The Constitution of Liberty.* Chicago: Univ. of Chicago Press, 1960. *Denationalization of Money.* London: Institute of Economic Affairs, 1976. *New Studies in Philosophy, Politics, Economics and the History of Ideas.* Chicago: Univ. of Chicago Press, 1985.

For More Information See: *Contemporary Authors.* Detroit, MI: Gale, 1980 (Volumes 93–96), 218–19. *Current Biography Yearbook.* New York: H.W. Wilson, 1945, 271–73. Ebenstein, Alan O. *Friedrich Hayek: A Biography.* New York: St. Martin's Press, 2000. *Hayek on Hayek.* Chicago: Univ. of Chicago Press, 1989.

Commentary: Friedrich Hayek shared the Nobel Prize for "pioneering work in the theory of money and economic fluctuations" and for "penetrating analysis of the interdependence of economic, social, and institutional phenomena." Beginning with work on theoretical economic thought, Hayek later combined these writings with analyses of the viability of different economic systems that made him a world figure. His firm belief in free-market economics was said to have influenced Milton Friedman and the economic policies of Margaret Thatcher and Ronald Reagan. (S.K.)

Myrdal, Karl Gunnar 143

Prize: Economics, 1974. *Born:* December 6, 1898; Gustafs Parish, Sweden. *Death:* May 17, 1987; Stockholm, Sweden. *Parents:* Father, Karl Adolf Myrdal; Mother, Anna Sophia Carlson Myrdal. *Nationality:* Swedish. *Religion:* Lutheran. *Education:* Univ. of Stockholm, Sweden, law degree, 1923; Univ. of Stockholm, Sweden, doctorate, 1927. *Spouse:* Alva Riemer, married October 8, 1924. *Children:* Jan, son; Kaj, daughter; Sissela, daughter. *Career:* Stockholm, Sweden, Attorney, 1923–27; Univ. of Stockholm, Sweden, Professor, 1927–38; Carnegie Corp., NY, Researcher, 1938–42;

then Writer and Political Activities. *Other Awards:* Peace Prize, West Germany, 1970; Seidman Award, Memphis, TN, 1973; Felix Newburgh Award, Sothonburg, Sweden, 1977; Nehru Award for International Understanding, 1981.

Selected Publications: Population: A Problem for Democracy. Cambridge, MA: Harvard Univ. Press, 1940. *An American Dilemma: The Negro Problem and Modern Democracy.* New York: Harper & Brothers, 1944. *Challenge to Affluence.* New York: Pantheon, 1963. *Asian Drama: An Inquiry into the Poverty of Nations.* New York: Pantheon, 1968.

For More Information See: Assarsson-Rizzi, Kerstin and Bohin, Harald. *Gunnar Myrdal: A Bibliography, 1919–1981.* New York: Garland, 1983. *Current Biography Yearbook.* New York: H.W. Wilson, 1975, 295–98. *New York Times Biographical Service* (May 18, 1987): 476. *Nobel Laureates in Economic Sciences.* New York: Garland, 218–28.

Commentary: Gunnar Myrdal received the Nobel Prize for his "pioneering work in the theory of money and economic fluctuations" and for his "penetrating analysis of the interdependence of economic, social and institutional phenomena." Myrdal's studies of and influence on economic and social affairs began in Sweden and extended to the United States. His treatments of economic policy in both countries and his study of the population question in Sweden and the race issue in America were classics. He was also an active United Nations worker, especially in Asia, and a campaigner for peace. (S.K.)

1975

Kantorovich, Leonid Vital'evich 144

Prize: Economics, 1975. *Born:* January 19, 1912; St. Petersburg, Russia. *Death:* April 6, 1986; Moscow, Russia. *Parents:* Father, Vitalij M. Kantorovich; Mother, Pauline G. Saks Kantorovich. *Nationality:* Russian. *Religion:* Jewish. *Education:* Leningrad State Univ., USSR, B.A., 1930; Leningrad State Univ., USSR, Ph.D., 1935. *Spouse:* Natalja Vladimirovna Ilyina, married March 11, 1938. *Children:* Ien, son; Vselovod, daughter. *Career:* Leningrad State Univ., USSR, Professor, 1934–60; Academy of Sciences, USSR, Administrator, 1960–71; Institute of National Economy Control, Moscow, USSR, Administrator, 1971–76; Academy of Sciences, USSR, Administrator, 1976–86. *Other Awards:* State Prize, USSR, 1949; Lenin Prize, USSR, 1965; Order of Lenin, USSR, 1967, 1982.

Selected Publications: Mathematicheskie Metody Organizatsii i Planirovaniia Proizvodstva. Leningrad: Leningrad State Univ., 1939. "Mathematical Methods of Organizing and Planning Production." *Management Science* 6 (July 1960): 366–422. *Ekonomicheskii Raschet Nailuschshego Ispol'zogvaniia Resursov.* Moscow: Izdvo Akademii Nauk SSSR, 1959 (*The Best Use of Economic Resources.* Tr. by P.F. Knightsfield. Cambridge, MA: Harvard Univ. Press, 1965). *Optimal'nye Resheniia v Ekonomike* (*Optimal Solution in Economics*). Moscow: Nauka, 1972 (with A.V. Gorstko). *Funktsionalyi Analiz* (*Functional Analysis*). Moscow: Nauka, 1977 (with G.P. Akilov).

For More Information See: Johansen, Leif. "L.V. Kantorovich's Contribution to Economics." *The Scandinavian Journal of Economics* 78 (1976): 61–80. Stuart, Robert

C. "Leonid Vitalevich Kantorovich." In *Soviet Leaders.* New York: Thomas Y. Crowell, 1967, 187–93.

Commentary: Leonid Kantorovich won the Nobel Prize for his "contributions to the theory of optimum allocation of resources." His 1939 treatise, *Mathematical Methods of Organizing and Planning Production*, introduced linear programming as a solution to the problems of resource allocation. Received unfavorably by the Soviet government, his theories were not recognized until the publication in the 1950s of works such as *The Best Use of Economic Resources*. (R.W.S.)

Koopmans, Tjalling Charles 145

Prize: Economics, 1975. *Born:* August 28, 1910; Graveland, Netherlands. *Death:* February 26, 1985; New Haven, CT. *Parents:* Father, Sjoerd Koopmans; Mother, Wijkje van der Zee Koopmans. *Nationality:* Dutch; later American citizen. *Religion:* Christian. *Education:* Univ. of Utrecht, Netherlands, M.A., 1933; Univ. of Leiden, Netherlands, Ph.D., 1936. *Spouse:* Truus Wanningen, married 1936. *Children:* Anne W., daughter; Helen J., daughter; Henry S., son. *Career:* Netherlands School of Economics, Professor, 1936–38; League of Nations, Specialist Financial Secretary, 1938–40; Princeton Univ., NJ, Researcher, 1940–41; Penn Mutual Life Insurance Company, Economist, 1941–42; Combined Shipping Adjustment Board, Statistician, 1942–44; Univ. of Chicago, IL, Professor, 1944–55; Yale Univ., CT, Professor, 1955–85.

Selected Publications: Three Essays on the State of Economic Science. New York: McGraw-Hill, 1957. *Scientific Papers of Tjalling C. Koopmans.* New York: Springer-Verlag, 1970, V-VII, 595–600.

For More Information See: New York Times Biographical Service (1975): 1285–86. *Nobel Laureates in Economic Sciences.* New York: Garland, 136–43. *Science* 190 (November 14, 1975): 649, 710–12.

Commentary: Tjalling Koopmans received the Nobel Prize for his contributions to the theory of optimum allocation of resources. Beginning with his work on efficient use of shipping facilities, Koopmans applied brilliant mathematical techniques to develop the complicated equations of this field. His work in econometrics and mathematical programming developed entire new areas of economic studies. (M.C.)

1976

Friedman, Milton 146

Prize: Economics, 1976. *Born:* July 31, 1912; Brooklyn, NY. *Parents:* Father, Jeno Saul Friedman; Mother, Sarah Ethel Landau Friedman. *Nationality:* American. *Religion:* Jewish. *Education:* Rutgers Univ., NJ, A.B., 1932; Univ. of Chicago, IL, A.M., 1933; Columbia Univ., NY, Ph.D.; 1946. *Spouse:* Rose Director, married June 25, 1938. *Children:* Janet, daughter; David, son. *Career:* National Resources Committee, Washington, DC, Assistant Economist, 1935–37; National Bureau of Economic Research, NY, Researcher, 1937–45; Univ. of Minnesota, Professor, 1945–46; Univ. of Chicago, IL, Professor, 1946–83. *Other Awards:* Clark Medal, American Economic Association, 1951; Chicagoan of the Year, Chicago Press Club, 1972; Private Enterprise Exemplar Medal, Freedoms Foundation, 1978; Presidential

Medal of Freedom, 1988; National Medal of Science, 1988; Prize in Moral-Cultural Affairs, 1993; Goldwater Award, 1997.

Selected Publications: Friedman, Milton. *Capitalism and Freedom.* Chicago: Univ. of Chicago Press, 1962. Friedman, Milton, and Schwartz, Anna Jacobson. *A Monetary History of the United States, 1867–1960.* Princeton, NJ: Princeton Univ. Press, 1963. Friedman, Milton. *The Counter-Revolution in Monetary Theory.* London: Institute of Economic Affairs, 1970. Friedman, Milton, and Director, Rose. *Free to Choose.* New York: Harcourt, Brace, Jovanovich, 1980.

For More Information See: Current Biography Yearbook. New York: H.W. Wilson Co., 1969, 151–54. Shackleton, J.R. "Milton Friedman, Superstar?" *Political Quarterly* 51 (July/September 1980): 349–54. Tobin, James, and Johnson, Harry. "Nobel Milton." *The Economist* 261 (October 23, 1976): 94–95. Viorst, Milton. *Hustlers and Heroes.* New York: Simon and Schuster, 1971.

Commentary: The Nobel citation notes Milton Friedman's work, *Capitalism and Freedom,* but also states that it is "very rare for an economist to wield such influence, directly or indirectly, not only on the direction of scientific research but also on the actual practice." His clear statements in conservative economics and in the areas of monetary and quantity theory have influenced economists and policy makers in the United States and throughout the world. (M.J.B.)

1977

Meade, James Edward   147

Prize: Economics, 1977. *Born:* June 23, 1907; Swanage, Dorset, England. *Death:* December 22, 1995; Cambridge, England. *Parents:* Father, Charles Hippisley Meade; Mother, Kathleen Cotton-Stapleton Meade. *Nationality:* British. *Religion:* Most probably Christian/Protestant. *Education:* Oxford Univ., England, B.A., 1930. *Spouse:* Elizabeth Margaret Wilson, married March 14, 1933. *Children:* Thomas Wilson, son; Charlotte Elizabeth, daughter; Bridget Ariane, daughter; Carol Margaret, daughter. *Career:* Oxford Univ., England, Professor, 1930–37; League of Nations, Economist, 1938–47; London School of Economics, Professor, 1947–57; Cambridge Univ., England, Professor, 1957–68. *Other Awards:* Companion of the Order of Bath, 1947.

Selected Publications: The Theory of International Economic Policy. 2 volumes. London: Oxford Univ. Press, 1951–55. *A Geometry of International Trade.* London: Allen & Unwin, 1952. *A Neo-Classical Theory of Economic Growth.* London: Allen & Unwin, 1962. *The Principles of Political Economy.* 4 volumes. Albany, NY: State Univ. of New York Press, 1965–76. *The Intelligent Radical's Guide to Economic Policy.* London: Allen & Unwin, 1975. *Alternate Systems of Business Organization and of Workers' Remuneration.* London: George Allen and Union, 1986. *The Collected Papers of James Meade.* London: Unwin Hyman, 1990.

For More Information See: Science 198 (1977): 813–14+. *Twentieth Century Culture: A Biographical Companion.* New York: Harper and Row, 1983.

Commentary: James Meade won the Nobel Prize for his work as a pioneer in the area of macroeconomics, the economic behavior of large systems. A prolific writer, Meade's influence was felt primarily through his books and his work on important British committees studying the economy. His books that dealt with foreign trade in an "open" world economy and with the dangers, as well as benefits, of employers' associations and trade unions, are representative of his influence. (J.F.)

Ohlin, Bertil Gotthard   148

Prize: Economics, 1977. *Born:* April 23, 1899; Klippan, Sweden. *Death:* August 3, 1979; Northern Sweden. *Parents:* Father, Elis Vilhelm Ohlin; Mother, Ingeborg Sandberg Ohlin. *Nationality:* Swedish. *Religion:* Lutheran. *Education:* Lund Univ., Sweden, B.A., 1917; Harvard Univ., MA, M.A., 1923; Univ. of Stockholm, Sweden, Ph.D., 1924. *Spouse:* Evy Kruse, married May 2, 1931. *Children:* Helen, daughter; Thomas, son; Anne Marie, daughter. *Career:* Univ. of Copenhagen, Denmark, Professor, 1925–30; Stockholm School of Economics, Sweden, Professor, 1930–65; Sweden, Member of Parliament, 1938–70. *Other Awards:* Commander with the Great Cross, Royal North Star, Sweden, 1961; Commander, First Order of the Dannebrogen, Denmark.

Selected Publications: Handelns Teori (*The Theory of Trade*). Stockholm: Centraltryckeriet, 1924. *The Course and Phases of the World Economic Depression; Report Presented to the Assembly of the League of Nations.* Geneva: The Secretariat of the League of Nations, 1931. *Interregional and International Trade.* Cambridge, MA: Harvard Univ. Press, 1933. *The Problem of Economic Stabilization.* New York: Columbia Univ. Press, 1949. *Bertil Ohlin's Memoarer* (*Bertil Ohlin's Memoirs*). Stockholm: Bonnier, 1972.

For More Information See: Blaug, Mark. *Bertil Ohlin (1899–1979).* Aldershot, Hants, England; Brookfield, VT: E. Elgar, 1992. *International Encyclopedia of the Social Sciences Biographical Supplement.* New York: The Free Press, 1979, 603–07. Lundberg, Erik. "Portrait: Bertil Ohlin." *Challenge* 23 (September-October 1980): 54–57. Samuelson, Paul A. "Bertil Ohlin: 1899–1979." *Journal of International Economics Supplement* (January 1982): 31–49.

Commentary: Bertil Ohlin received the Nobel award for his "pathbreaking contribution to the theory of international trade and international capital movements." Although a prominent economist and a member of the Swedish Academy of Science, Ohlin was probably better known in his native Sweden as a politician and a journalist. For more than two decades he was the leader of the Swedish Liberal Party and served as the Minister of Trade at the close of World War II. Ohlin produced the majority of the economic work for which the prize was awarded prior to the start of his political career, but beginning in the 1920s and continuing until his death, he regularly contributed material on economic policy to the Swedish daily newspapers. (D.G.)

1978

Simon, Herbert Alexander   149

Prize: Economics, 1978. *Born:* June 15, 1916; Milwaukee, WI. *Parents:* Father, Arthur Simon; Mother, Edna Merkel Simon. *Nationality:* American. *Religion:* Unitarian; from

Jewish background. *Education:* Univ. of Chicago, IL, A.B., 1936; Univ. of Chicago, IL, Ph.D., 1943. *Spouse:* Dorothea Pye, married December 25, 1937. *Children:* Katherine, daughter; Barbara, daughter; Peter Arthur, son. *Career:* Univ. of Chicago, IL, Researcher, 1936–38; International City Managers Association, Chicago, IL, Editor, 1938–39; Univ. of California, Berkeley, Administrator, 1939–42; Illinois Institute of Technology, Professor, 1942–49; Carnegie-Mellon Univ., PA, Professor and Administrator, 1949–93. *Other Awards:* Administrator's Award, American College of Hospital Administrators, 1957; Distinguished Scientific Contributions Award, American Psychological Association, 1969; Frederick Mosher Award, American Society for Public Administration, 1974; Turing Award, Association for Computing Machinery, 1975; Proctor Prize, 1980; Dow-Jones Award, 1983; Scholarly Contributions Award, Academy of Management, 1983; James Madison Award, American Political Science Association, 1984; National Medal of Science, United States, 1986; Gold Medal, American Psychology Foundation, 1988; Von Neumann Theory Award, 1988; Lifetime Contribution Award, American Psychological Association, 1993; Dwight Waldo Award, 1995; Research Excellence Award, International Joint Conference Artificial Intelligence, 1995.

Selected Publications: Administrative Behavior: A Study of Decision-Making Processes in Administrative Organization. New York: Macmillan Co., 1947. *Models of Man: Social and Rational; Mathematical Essays on Rational Human Behavior in a Social Setting.* New York: Wiley, 1957. *Organizations.* New York: Wiley, 1958 (with J.G. March and H. Guetzkow). *New Science of Management Decision.* New York: Harper, 1960. *Human Problem Solving.* Englewood Cliffs, NJ: Prentice-Hall, 1972 (with Allen Newell). *Reason in Human Affairs.* Stanford, CA: Stanford Univ. Press, 1983.

For More Information See: Contemporary Authors. New Revision Series. Detroit, MI: Gale, 1983 (Volume 9), 456–57. *Current Biography Yearbook.* New York: H.W. Wilson Co., 1971, 358–61. *Models of My Life.* New York: Basic Books, 1991.

Commentary: Thirty years after he published his research results in the now classic text *Administrative Behavior*, Herbert Simon received the Nobel Prize in recognition of his "pioneering research into the decision making process in economic organization." His concept of "bounded rationality" acknowledged the human element in problem solving and showed that decision makers choose not the optimum solution but rather the first alternative "good enough" to meet predefined needs. Later, Simon, working with Allen Newell, used computer simulation to study problem solving and thereby became a pioneer in the field of artificial intelligence. Described as a true Renaissance man because of the variety and scope of his knowledge and talents, Simon has written on subjects ranging from economics and political science to psychology and computers. (M.L.L.)

1979

Lewis, William Arthur, Sir   150

Prize: Economics, 1979. *Born:* January 23, 1915; Castries, St. Lucia. *Death:* June 15, 1991; Barbados, West Indies.

Parents: Father, George F. Lewis; Mother, Ida Barton Lewis. *Nationality:* St. Lucian; later British and American resident. *Religion:* Anglican. *Education:* St. Mary's College, British West Indies, Bachelor degree, 1929; London School of Economics, England, Bachelor of Commerce, 1937; Ph.D., 1940. *Spouse:* Gladys Isabel Jacobs, married May 5, 1947. *Children:* Elizabeth Anne, daughter; Barbara Jean, daughter. *Career:* London School of Economics, England, Lecturer, 1938–48; Univ. of Manchester, England, Professor, 1948–58; Univ. of West Indies, Professor and Administrator, 1959–63; Princeton Univ., NJ, Professor, 1963–83. *Other Awards:* Knighthood, 1963.

Selected Publications: Economic Survey, 1919–39. Philadelphia, PA: Blakiston Co., 1950. *Development Planning.* New York: Harper and Row, 1966. *Aspects of Tropical Trade, 1883–1965.* Stockholm: Almqvist and Wiksell, 1969. *The Evolution of the International Economic Order.* Princeton, NJ: Princeton Univ. Press, 1978. *Selected Economic Writings of W. Arthur Lewis.* New York: New York Univ. Press, 1983.

For More Information See: Crittenden, Ann. "1979 Nobel Economics Award Shared by Two Experts on Poorer Nations." *New York Times* (October 17, 1979): 1+. *New York Times Biographical Service* (June 16, 1991): 605. "Nobel Laureate Sir William Arthur Lewis 1980." *Black Enterprise* 10 (July 1980): 34. Ranis, Gustan. "The 1979 Nobel Prize in Economics." *Science* 206 (December 1979): 1389–91.

Commentary: Sir William Arthur Lewis is most noted for his models for developing the economics of Third World nations, based on work with the developing nations in Africa and the English-speaking Caribbean. The Nobel Prize award was a recognition of his "lifelong concerns with poverty and growth, agricultural and human development in developing countries," in contrast to other years, when the award was given strictly for theoretical breakthroughs. Lewis was the first Black to receive a Nobel Prize in a category other than Peace. (E.L.)

Schultz, Theodore William   151

Prize: Economics, 1979. *Born:* April 30, 1902; Arlington, SD. *Death:* February 26, 1998; Evanston, IL. *Parents:* Father, Henry Edward Schultz; Mother, Anna Elizabeth Weiss Schultz. *Nationality:* American. *Religion:* Most probably Christian/Protestant. *Education:* South Dakota State College, B.S., 1927; Univ. of Wisconsin, M.S., 1928; Univ. of Wisconsin, Ph.D., 1930. *Spouse:* Esther Florence Werth, married 1930. *Children:* Elaine, daughter; Margaret, daughter; T. Paul, son. *Career:* Iowa State College, Professor, 1930–43; Univ. of Chicago, IL, Professor, 1943–72. *Other Awards:* Francis A. Walker Medal, American Economic Association, 1972; Leonard Elmhirst Medal, International Agriculture Economic Association, 1976.

Selected Publications: The Economic Value of Education. New York: Columbia Univ. Press, 1963. *Transforming Traditional Agriculture.* New Haven, CT: Yale Univ. Press, 1964. *Economic Growth and Agriculture.* New York: McGraw-Hill, 1968. *Investments in Human Capital: The Role of Education and of Research.* New York: Macmillan Co., 1971. *Distortions of Agricultural Incentives.* Bloomington, IN: Indiana Univ. Press, 1978. *Investing in People:*

The Economics of Population Quality. Berkeley, CA: Univ. of California Press, 1981.

For More Information See: *Biographical Memoirs of National Academy of Sciences*. Washington, DC: National Academy of Sciences, 1999 (Volume 77), 303–17. *New York Times Biographical Service* (October 1979): 1414. *Science* 206 (December 21, 1979): 1389–91.

Commentary: Theodore Schultz was awarded the Nobel Prize in recognition of his work which stressed the importance of human resources in agriculture. The citation noted his importance in pointing out that there "has been a considerably higher yield on human capital than on physical capital in the American economy." His thinking was a prime factor in the development of human resources in the United States and developing countries. (M.C.)

1980

Klein, Lawrence Robert 152

Prize: Economics, 1980. ***Born:*** September 14, 1920; Omaha, NE. ***Parents:*** Father, Leo Byron Klein; Mother, Blanche Monheit Klein. ***Nationality:*** American. ***Religion:*** Most probably Jewish. ***Education:*** Univ. of California, Berkeley, B.A., 1942; Massachusetts Institute of Technology, Ph.D., 1944; Oxford Univ., England, M.A., 1957. ***Spouse:*** Sonia Adelson, married February 15, 1947. ***Children:*** Hannah, daughter; Rebecca, daughter; Rachel, daughter; Jonathan, son. ***Career:*** Univ. of Chicago, IL, Researcher, 1944–47; National Bureau of Economic Research, Researcher, 1948–50; Univ. of Michigan, Professor, 1949–54; Oxford Univ., England, Researcher, 1954–58; Univ. of Pennsylvania, Professor, 1958-. ***Other Awards:*** John Bates Clark Medal, American Economic Association, 1959; William F. Butler Award, New York Association of Business Economists, 1975; Golden Slipper Club Award, 1977; President's Medal, Univ. of Pennsylvania, 1980.

Selected Publications: *The Keynesian Revolution*. New York: Macmillan, 1947. *Economic Fluctuations in the United States, 1921–1941*. New York: Wiley, 1950. *A Textbook of Econometrics*. Evanston, IL: Row, Peterson, 1953. *An Econometric Model of the United States, 1929–1952*. Amsterdam: North-Holland Publishing Company, 1955 (with A.S. Goldberger). *An Introduction to Econometrics*. Englewood Cliffs, NJ: Prentice-Hall, 1962. *Economic Theory and Econometrics*. Philadelphia, PA: Univ. of Pennsylvania Press, 1985.

For More Information See: Ball, R.J. "On Lawrence R. Klein's Contributions to Economics." *Scandinavian Journal of Economics* 83 (1981): 81–95. Maugh, Thomas H., II. "The 1980 Nobel Memorial Prize in Economics." *Science* 210 (November 14, 1980): 758–59.

Commentary: Citing Lawrence Klein as the leading researcher in the field of econometrics, the Academy acknowledged three decades of achievement by awarding him the Nobel Prize for "the creation of econometric models and their application to the analysis of economic fluctuations and economic policies." Not the first to study the relationship of individual variables within a total economy, Klein revived Jan Tinbergen's 1930s model, added a system of equations based upon the economic theory of John Maynard Keynes, applied modern statistical analysis and computer technology, and therewith pioneered a practical instrument that could both forecast business fluctuations and portray economic interrelationships. Klein's writings clarified theory; his projects became training grounds for economists and government officials throughout the world. (M.L.L.)

1981

Tobin, James 153

Prize: Economics, 1981. ***Born:*** March 5, 1918; Champaign, IL. ***Parents:*** Father, Louis Michael Tobin; Mother, Margaret Anketell Edgerton Tobin. ***Nationality:*** American. ***Religion:*** Most probably Christian. ***Education:*** Harvard Univ., MA, A.B., 1939; Harvard Univ., MA, M.A., 1940; Harvard Univ., MA, Ph.D., 1947. ***Spouse:*** Elizabeth Fay Ringo, married September 14, 1946. ***Children:*** Margaret Ringo, daughter; Louis Michael, son; Hugh Ringo, son; Roger Gill, son. ***Career:*** Office of Price Administration, Economist, 1941–42; U.S. Navy, Lieutenant, 1942–46; Harvard Univ., MA, Professor, 1946–50; Yale Univ., CT, Professor, 1950–88. ***Other Awards:*** Clark Medal, American Economics Association, 1955; Centennial Medal, Harvard Univ., 1989.

Selected Publications: *National Economic Policy*. New Haven, CT: Yale Univ. Press, 1966. *Essays in Economics*. Volume 1, Macroeconomics. Chicago: Markham, 1972. *The New Economics: One Decade Older*. Princeton, NJ: Princeton Univ. Press, 1974. *Essays in Economics*. Volume 2, Consumption and Economics. New York: Elsevier, 1975. *Asset Accumulation and Economic Activity*. Chicago: Univ. of Chicago Press, 1980. *Essays in Economics*. Volume 3, Theory and Policy. Cambridge, MA: MIT Press, 1982. *A Keynesian View of the Stagnation of the 1980's*. Wolfeboro, NH: Longwood Publishing Group, 1985.

For More Information See: *Current Biography Yearbook*. New York: H.W. Wilson Co., 1984, 393–96. *Econometric Theory*, 15 (1999):867–900. *The National Cyclopedia of American Biography*. New York: James T. White and Co., 1964 (Volume J), 280–81. Samuelson, Paul A. "1981 Nobel Prize in Economics." *Science* (October 30, 1981): 520–22.

Commentary: James Tobin's award citation noted that he had provided "a basis for understanding how subjects actually behave when they acquire different assets and incur debts" by his statement of the "portfolio selection theory" of investment. His work was in the areas of economic theory, econometrics, monetary theory, and policy and consumer behavior, but his major concern was to modify, in terms of the later U.S. economy, the original Keynesian theory that the federal government should pursue an aggressive fiscal and monetary policy to attain rapid growth and full employment. (B.E.M.)

1982

Stigler, George Joseph 154

Prize: Economics, 1982. ***Born:*** January 17, 1911; Renton, WA. ***Death:*** December 1, 1991; Chicago, IL. ***Parents:*** Father, Joseph Stigler; Mother, Elizabeth Hungler Stigler. ***Nationality:*** American. ***Religion:*** Most probably Christian. ***Education:*** Univ. of Washington, BBA, 1931; Northwestern Univ., IL, MBA, 1932; Univ. of Chicago, IL, Ph.D.,

1938. *Spouse:* Margaret L. Mack, married December 26, 1936, died 1970. *Children:* Stephen, son; David, son; Joseph, son. *Career:* Iowa State Univ., Professor, 1936–38; Univ. of Minnesota, Professor, 1938–46; Brown Univ., RI, Professor, 1946–47; Columbia Univ., NY, Professor, 1947–57; Center for Advanced Studies in Behavioral Sciences, Fellow, 1957–58; Univ. of Chicago, IL, Professor, 1958–81. *Other Awards:* National Medal of Honor, 1987

Selected Publications: Production and Distribution Theories. New York: Macmillan, 1941. *The Theory of Price.* New York: Macmillan, 1942. *Five Lectures on Economic Problems.* New York: Longmans Green, 1949. *The Citizen and the State: Essays on Regulation.* Chicago: Univ. of Chicago Press, 1975. *The Economist as Preacher.* Chicago: Univ. of Chicago Press, 1982. *The Organization of Industry.* Chicago: Univ. of Chicago Press, 1983. *The Intellectual and the Marketplace.* Cambridge, MA: Harvard Univ. Press, 1984.

For More Information See: The Essence of Stigler. Stanford, CA: Hoover Press, 1986. "George Stigler's Contributions to Economics." *Scandinavian Journal of Economics* 85: 1 (1983): 77–86. *Memoirs of an Unregulated Economist.* New York: Basic Books, 1988. *New York Times Biographical Service* (December 3, 1991): 1299. *Science* 218 (November 12, 1982): 655–57.

Commentary: George Stigler was awarded the Nobel Prize for his "seminal studies of industrial structures, functioning of markets and the causes and effects of public regulations. His studies of the forces which give rise to regulatory legislation have opened up a completely new area of economic research," the Academy's citation said. The Academy also praised his work in explaining price variations and his explanations of the effect in the marketplace of households and companies making similar economic decisions with different amounts of information. (V.B.)

1983

Debreu, Gerard   155

Prize: Economics, 1983. *Born:* July 4, 1921; Calais, France. *Parents:* Father, Camille Debreu; Mother, Fernande Decharne Debreu. *Nationality:* French; later American citizen. *Religion:* Most probably Christian. *Education:* École Normale Supérieure, France, Agrégé de l'Université, 1946; Univ. of Paris, France, D.Sc., 1956. *Spouse:* Françoise Bled, married June 14, 1945. *Children:* Chantal, daughter; Florence, daughter. *Career:* French Army, 1944–45; Center National de la Rocherche Scientifique, Paris, France, Researcher, 1946–48; Rockefeller Fellow, U.S., Sweden, and Norway, 1948–50; Univ. of Chicago, IL, Researcher, 1950–55; Yale Univ., CT, Professor, 1955–61; Univ. of California, Berkeley, Professor, 1962–91. *Other Awards:* Chevalier de Légion d'Honneur, 1976; Senior U.S. Scientist Award, Alexander von Humboldt Foundation, 1977; Commander de l'Ordre Nationale du Mèrite, 1984; Berkeley Citation, 1991; Legion d'Honneur, 1993.

Selected Publications: Theory of Value: An Axiomatic Analysis of Economic Equilibrium. New Haven, CT: Yale Univ. Press, 1959. *Professor Debreu's "Market Equilibrium" Theorem: An Expository Note.* West Lafayette, IN: Purdue Univ. Press, 1973. *Mathematical Economics: Twenty*

Papers of Gerard Debreu. Cambridge, MA: Cambridge Univ. Press, 1983.

For More Information See: Arrow and the Ascent of Modern Economic Theory. London: Macmillan, 1987, 243–57. Samuelson, Paul. "The 1983 Nobel Prize in Economics." *Science* 222 (December 2, 1983): 987–89. Varian, Hal. "Gerhard Debreu's Contributions to Economics." *Scandinavian Journal of Economics* 86 (1984): 4–14.

Commentary: Gerard Debreu was awarded the Nobel Prize for three decades of work on one of the most basic of economic problems: the equilibrium between prices in a free-market economy and what producers supplied and consumers demanded. Debreu's work, though little known outside of the economic community, is the basis on which many other economists concerned with micro-economics have built their own work. The Academy said Debreu's book, *The Theory of Value,* is "a classic both for its universality and for its elegant analytical approach." They further stated that Debreu's theoretical contributions lent themselves to "far-reaching interpretations and applications." (V.B.)

1984

Stone, John Richard Nicholas, Sir   156

Prize: Economics, 1984. *Born:* August 30, 1913; London, England. *Death:* December 6, 1991; Cambridge, England. *Parents:* Father, Gilbert Stone; Mother, Elsie Stone. *Nationality:* British. *Religion:* Most probably Christian/Protestant. *Education:* Cambridge Univ., England, baccalaureate, 1935; Cambridge Univ., England, M.A., 1938; Cambridge Univ., England, D.Sc., 1957. *Spouse:* Winifred Mary Jenkins, married 1936, divorced 1940; Feodora Leontinoff, married 1941, died 1956; Giovanna Saffi Croft-Murray, married 1960. *Children:* 1 daughter. *Career:* C.E. Heath and Co., London, England, Economist, 1936–39; British Government Offices, Economist, 1939–45; Cambridge Univ., England, Professor, 1945–80. *Other Awards:* Knighthood, 1978.

Selected Publications: Quantity and Price Indexes in National Accounts. Paris: Organization for Economic Cooperation and Development, 1956. *Mathematics in the Social Sciences and Other Essays.* London: Chapman & Hall, 1966. *Demographic Accounting and Model Building.* Paris: Organization for Economic Cooperation and Development, 1971. *National Income and Expenditure.* London: Bowes & Bowes, 1977.

For More Information See: "Bibliography of Richard Stone's Works." *Scandinavian Journal of Economics* 87 (1) (1985): 33–43. *New York Times Biographical Service* 15 (1984): 1397–98. *Nobel Laureates in Economic Sciences.* New York: Garland, 294–304. *Science* 227 (1985): 20–22.

Commentary: Richard Stone's achievements which earned him the Nobel Prize lay in developing complex economic models, particularly those which led to accounting systems that could be used to chart the economic activity of nations. His work was responsible for standardization of national income reports throughout the world and by the United Nations. Early in his career, Stone developed statistical techniques for economics and studied consumer reaction to changes in income and prices. (J.F.)

1985

Modigliani, Franco   **157**

Prize: Economics, 1985. ***Born:*** June 18, 1918; Rome, Italy. ***Parents:*** Father, Enrico Modigliani; Mother, Olga Flaschel Modigliani. ***Nationality:*** Italian; later American citizen. ***Religion:*** Jewish. ***Education:*** Univ. of Rome, Italy, law degree, 1939; New School for Social Research, NY, Ph.D., 1944. ***Spouse:*** Serena Calabi, married May 22, 1939. ***Children:*** Andre, son; Sergio, son. ***Career:*** New Jersey College for Women, Professor, 1942; Bard College, NY, Professor, 1942–44; New School for Social Research, NY, Professor, 1944–48; Univ. of Illinois, Professor, 1948–52; Carnegie-Mellon Univ., PA, Professor, 1952–60; Northwestern Univ., IL, Professor, 1960–62; Massachusetts Institute of Technology, Professor, 1962–88. ***Other Awards:*** Graham and Dodd Award, 1975, 1980; Cavaliere Di Gran Croce, Italy, 1985; Premio Coltura, Italy, 1988; Premio APE Award, 1988; Lord Foundation Prize, 1989; Italy Premio Columbus, 1989; Italy Premio Guido Dorso, 1989; Italy Premio Stivale D'oro, 1991; Italy Premio Campione D'Italia, 1992; Premio Scanno, 1997.

Selected Publications: *The Collected Papers of Franco Modigliani*. 3 volumes. Cambridge, MA: MIT Press, 1980. *The Debate over Stabilization Policies, Lectures and Other Macroeconomic Issues*. Cambridge: Cambridge Univ. Press, 1986.

For More Information See: *Adventures of an Economist*. London: Texere, 2000. *Business Week* (October 28, 1985): 32. *New York Times Biographical Service* (October 16, 1985): 1259–60. *Nobel Laureates in Economic Sciences* New York: Garland, 203–17.

Commentary: Franco Modigliani was given the Nobel Prize for two major theories. The first, on personal finance, stated that persons save when their income is highest to allow for financial security throughout life. The second, on corporate finance, noted that a company's market value was not altered by the distribution of shares or bonds in its balance sheet. The two theories are well accepted in economic circles and provide the basis for much work in the field. (D.P.K.)

1986

Buchanan, James McGill, Jr.   **158**

Prize: Economics, 1986. ***Born:*** October 3, 1919; Murfreesboro, Tennessee. ***Parents:*** Father, James McGill Buchanan; Mother, Lila Scott Buchanan. ***Nationality:*** American. ***Religion:*** Most probably Christian. ***Education:*** Middle Tennessee State Teachers College, B.A., 1940; Univ. of Tennessee, M.S., 1941; Univ. of Chicago, IL, Ph.D., 1948. ***Spouse:*** Anne Bakke, married October 5, 1945. ***Children:*** None. ***Career:*** Univ. of Tennessee, Professor, 1948–51; Florida State Univ., Professor, 1951–56; Univ. of Virginia, Professor, 1956–68; Univ. of California, Los Angeles, 1968–69; Virginia Polytechnic Institute, Professor, 1969–83; George Mason Univ., VA, Professor, 1983–99. ***Other Awards:*** Frank E. Seidman Award, 1984.

Selected Publications: *Public Principles of Public Debt*. Homewood, IL: R.D. Irwin, 1958. *The Calculus of Consent: Logical Foundations of Constitutional Democracy*. Ann Arbor, MI: Univ. of Michigan Press, 1962. *Cost and Choice:*

An Inquiry in Economic Theory. Chicago: Markham Publishing Co., 1969. *The Limits of Liberty: Between Anarchy and Leviathan*. Chicago: Univ. of Chicago Press, 1975. *The Reason of Rules* (with G. Brennan). Cambridge; NY: Cambridge Univ. Press, 1985. *Liberty, Market and State*. NY: New York Univ. Press, 1986.

For More Information See: "Better Than Plowing." *Banca Nazionale del Lavoro Quarterly Review* 159 (1986): 359–75. Katz, Bernard S. *Nobel Laureates in Economic Sciences*. New York: Garland, 1989, 30–39. *New York Times* (October 17, 1986), D1.

Commentary: The Nobel Prize was a recognition of James Buchanan's "development of the contractual and constitutional bases for the theory of economic and political decision-making." His leadership in the area known as public choice theory resulted in a bridge between the disciplines of economics and political science. The basic idea of public choice theory is that not only are individuals motivated by self-interest, but so also are politicians and all of society. As a result of this theory an idea has developed that individual self-interest generally produces benefits for society while political self-interest generally results in negative effects on the economy. (L.H./B.S.S.)

1987

Solow, Robert Merton   **159**

Prize: Economics, 1987. ***Born:*** August 23, 1924; Brooklyn, NY. ***Parents:*** Father, Milton Henry Solow; Mother, Hanna Gertrude Sarney Solow. ***Nationality:*** American. ***Religion:*** Jewish. ***Education:*** Harvard Univ., MA, B.A., 1947; Harvard Univ., MA, M.S. 1949; Harvard Univ., MA, Ph.D., 1951. ***Spouse:*** Barbara Lewis, married August 19, 1945. ***Children:*** John Lewis, son; Andrew Robert, son; Katherine, daughter. ***Career:*** Army Signal Corps, 1942–45; Massachusetts Institute of Technology, Professor, 1949–95; New York Univ., 1996–97. ***Other Awards:*** David A. Wells Prize, 1951; John Bates Clark Medal, 1961; Faculty Achievement Award, Massachusetts Institute of Technology, 1978; Seidman Award, 1983; National Medal of Science, 2000.

Selected Publications: *Capital Theory and the Rate of Return*. Chicago: Rand-McNally, 1965. *Price Expectations and the Behavior of the Price Level: Lectures Given in the University of Manchester*. United Kingdom: Manchester Univ. Press, 1969. *The Great Society: Lessons for the Future*. New York: Basic Books, 1974. *Alternative Approaches to Macroeconomic Theory: A Partial View*. Albuquerque, NM: Institute for Economic Research, 1979. *Linear Programming and Economic Analysis*. New York: Dover Publishing, 1987. *The Consequences of Economic Rhetoric*. Cambridge, England: Cambridge Univ. Press, 1988.

For More Information See: Klamer, Arjo. *Conversations with Economists*. Totowa, NJ: Rowman and Allanheld, 1983, 127–48. *Science* 238 (November 6, 1987): 754–55.

Commentary: Robert Solow was awarded the Nobel Prize "for his contributions to the theory of economic growth." His pioneering work in measurement of technological change's effect on economic growth resulted in the development of a mathematical model demonstrating the dependence of long-term growth on technological advancement, which was in direct opposition to the theory that stated that the accumulation of capital was the most important factor in economic growth. Solow also was a proponent of government involvement in markets to maintain a healthy economic policy. (L.H./B.S.S.)

1988

Allais, Maurice Felix   160
Prize: Economics, 1988. *Born:* May 31, 1911; Paris, France. *Parents:* Father, Maurice Allais; Mother, Louise Caubet Allais. *Nationality:* French. *Religion:* Most probably Christian. *Education:* École Polytechnique, France, baccalauréat, 1933; École Nationale Supérieure des Mines de Paris, France, graduate, 1936; Univ. of Paris, D.Eng., 1949. *Spouse:* Jacqueline Bouteloup, married September 6, 1960. *Children:* Christine, daughter. *Career:* Department of Mines and Quarries, France, Researcher, 1937–43; École Nationale Supérieure des Mines de Paris, France, Professor, 1944–88. *Other Awards:* Dupin Prize, 1954; Lanchester Prize, 1958; Dutens Prize, 1959; Galabert Prize, 1959; Great Prize of Atlantic Community, 1959; Gravity Research Foundation Prize, 1959; Grand Prix Andre Arnoux, 1968; Gold Medal, Société d'Encouragement pour l'Industrie Nationale, France, 1970; Gold Medal, Centre National de la Recherche Scientifique, France, 1978; Prix Robert Blanche, 1983; Grand Prix Zerilli Marimo, 1984; Prix Special du Jury, 1987; Medal, Univ. of Paris, 1989; Gold Medal, City of Paris, 1989; Gold Medal, Etoile Civique, 1990.

Selected Publications: A la Recherche d'une Discipline Economique. Paris: Ateliers Industria, 1943. *Economie et Interet*. Paris: Imprimerie Nationale, 1947. "The Role of Capital in Economic Development." In *The Economic Approach to Economic Development*. Amsterdam: North-Holland, 1965. "Growth and Inflation." *Journal of Money, Credit and Banking* 1 (August 1969): 355–426. "Theories of General Economic Equilibrium and Economic Efficiency." In *Equilibrium and Disequilibrium in Economic Theory*. Dordrecht: Reidel, 1971. "The Psychological Rate of Interest." *Journal of Money, Credit and Banking* 6 (August 1974): 285–331. "The So-called Allais Paradox and Rational Decisions under Uncertainty." In *Expected Utility Hypotheses and the Allais Paradox*. Dordrecht: Reidel, 1979.

For More Information See: Autoportraits. Paris: Montchrestien, 1989. *New York Times* (October 19, 1988): D1+. *Nobel Laureates in Economic Sciences*. New York: Garland, 1989, 1–9.

Commentary: Maurice Allais, the first Frenchman to win the Nobel in economics, was honored "for his pioneering development of theories to better understand market behavior and the efficient use of resources." The laureate developed the theoretical foundation for determining a socially acceptable and efficient optimum price, not only in a free marketplace, but also in monopolies, including large state monopolies. His work was extended by two other former laureates and colleagues, Gerard Debreu and Kenneth Arrow. Allais is also known for his Allais Paradox, which argues against the concept that individuals make decisions based on differences between risks and rewards, and instead advances the argument that the decisions are based, not only on differences, but also on factors that are the same for both choices. (L.H./B.S.S.)

1989

Haavelmo, Trygve Magnus   161
Prize: Economics, 1989. *Born:* December 13, 1911; Skedsmo, Norway. *Death:* July 26, 1999; Oslo, Norway. *Parents:* No record found. *Nationality:* Norwegian. *Religion:* Most probably Christian. *Education:* Univ. of Oslo, Norway, B.A., 1933; Univ. of Oslo, Norway, Ph.D., 1946. *Spouse:* No record found. *Children:* No record found. *Career:* Institute of Economics, Univ. of Oslo, Norway, Researcher, 1933–38; Univ. of Aarhus, Norway, Professor, 1938–39; Norwegian Government, Researcher, 1940–45; Univ. of Chicago, IL, Researcher, 1945–47; Norwegian Trade Commission, Researcher, 1947–48; Univ. of Oslo, Norway, Professor, 1948–79. *Other Awards:* Fridtjof Nansen Award, 1979.

Selected Publications: "The Statistical Implications of a System of Simultaneous Equations." *Econometrica* 11 (January 1943): 1–12. "Multiplier Effects of a Balanced Budget." *Econometrica* 13 (October 1945): 311–18. *A Study in the Theory of Economic Evolution*. Amsterdam: North-Holland, 1954. *A Study in the Theory of Investment*. Chicago: University of Chicago Press, 1960.

For More Information See: The New Palgrave. London: Macmillan Press, 1987, Volume 2, 580. *New York Times Biographical Service*. (1989): 1000.

Commentary: Trygve Haavelmo won the Nobel because his "pioneering work in methods for testing economic theories helped pave the way for modern economic forecasting." His early contributions helped found the study of econometrics based on probability theory. His later work focused on the need for a developed theoretical approach in economics, on growth theory, and on the microeconomic basis of the macroeconomic theory of investment demand. (B.S.S.)

1990

Markowitz, Harry M.   162
Prize: Economics, 1990. *Born:* August 24, 1927; Chicago, IL. *Parents:* Father, Morris Markowitz; Mother, Mildred Gruber Markowitz. *Nationality:* American. *Religion:* No record found. *Education:* Univ. of Chicago, IL, Ph.B., 1947; Univ. of Chicago, IL, M.A., 1950; Univ. of Chicago, IL, Ph.D., 1954. *Spouse:* Barbara Gay, married (no date found). *Children:* 2 children. *Career:* Rand Corporation, CA, Researcher, 1952–63; Consolidated Analysis Centers, CA, Researcher, 1963–68; Univ. of California, Los Angeles, Professor, 1968–69; Arbitrage Management, NY, President, 1969–72; Consultant, New York, 1972–74; IBM, New York, Researcher, 1974–83; Baruch College, City Univ. of New York, Professor, 1982–93. *Other Awards:* John von Neumann Prize, 1989

Selected Publications: Portfolio Selection. New Haven, CT: Yale Univ. Press, 1971 reprint. *Mean Variance Analysis in Portfolio Choice and Capital Markets*. New York: Basil Blackwell, 1990.

For More Information See: New York Times (October 16, 1990): A1. *New York Times* (October 17, 1990): C5. *Science* 250 (October 26, 1990): 509.

Commentary: Harry Markowitz shared the Nobel in Economics "for developing the theory of portfolio choice." His study of combinations of different types of assets, for example, stocks of different industries or companies with different product lines, indicated that combinations of different assets of differing risks could decrease the overall risk of investment. (B.S.S.)

Miller, Merton Howard 163

Prize: Economics, 1990. *Born:* May 16, 1923; Boston, MA. *Death:* June 3, 2000; Chicago, IL. *Parents:* Father, Joel L. Miller; Mother, Sylvia F. Starr Miller. *Nationality:* American. *Religion:* Most probably Jewish. *Education:* Harvard Univ., MA, A.B., 1943; Johns Hopkins Univ., MD, Ph.D., 1952. *Spouse:* Eleanor Miller, married (no date), deceased 1969; Katherine, married 1970. *Children:* Margot, daughter; Pamela, daughter; Louise, daughter. *Career:* U.S. Treasury Department, Researcher, 1944–47; U.S. Federal Reserve Board, Researcher, 1947–49; Ph.D. study, 1949–52; London School of Economics, Professor, 1952–53; Carnegie Institute of Technology, PA, Professor, 1953–61; Univ. of Chicago, IL, Professor, 1961–96.

Selected Publications: Theory of Finance. Hinsdale, IL: Dryden, 1972; *Macroeconomics: A Neoclassical Introduction.* Chicago, IL: Univ. of Chicago Press, 1986 reprint. *Financial Innovations and Market Volatility.* Cambridge, MA: Blackwell, 1991.

For More Information See: New York Times (October 16, 1990): A1. *Science* 250 (October 26, 1990): 509.

Commentary: The Nobel in Economics was awarded to Merton Miller "for his fundamental contributions to the theory of corporate finance." Miller developed different methods of looking at a company's absolute value. His research showed that companies might increase absolute value more effectively, for example, by investing the profits in the business, instead of paying the profits out to the shareholders as dividends. (B.S.S.)

Sharpe, William Forsyth 164

Prize: Economics, 1990. *Born:* June 16, 1934; Boston, MA. *Parents:* Father, Russell Thornley Sharpe; Mother, Evelyn Forsyth Jillson Maloy Sharpe. *Nationality:* American. *Religion:* No record found. *Education:* Univ. of California, Los Angeles, A.B., 1955; Univ. of California, Los Angeles, M.A., 1956; Univ. of California, Los Angeles, Ph.D., 1961. *Spouse:* Roberta Ruth Branton, married July 2, 1954, divorced 1986; Kathryn Dorothy Peck, married April 5, 1986. *Children:* Jonathan Forsyth, son; Deborah Ann, daughter. *Career:* Rand Corp., Researcher, 1957–61; Univ. of Washington, Professor, 1961–68; Univ. of California, Irvine, Professor, 1968–70; Stanford Univ., CA, Professor, 1970–89, 1992–99; concurrently William F. Sharpe Associates, President, 1986–92; Financial Engines, Inc., CA, Chairman, 1996-. *Other Awards:* Graham and Dodd Award, 1972, 1973, 1986, 1988; Nicholas Molodovsky Award, 1989, UCLA Medal, 2000.

Selected Publications: Economics of Computers. New York: Columbia Univ. Press, 1969. *Introduction to Managerial Economics.* New York: Columbia Univ. Press, 1973. *Investments* (with G.J. Alexander and J.V. Bailey). 6th ed. Upper Saddle River, NJ: Prentice Hall, 1999. *Fundamentals of Investments.* (with G.J. Alexander and J.V. Bailey) 3rd ed. Upper Saddle River, NJ: Prentic Hall, 2001.

For More Information See: New York Times (October 17, 1990): C5. *Science* 250 (October 26, 1990): 509.

Commentary: William Sharpe was awarded the Nobel "for his contributions to the theory of price formation for financial assets, the so-called Capital Asset Pricing Model." Sharpe said that "the bottom line . . . concluded in 1964 is that portfolios composed of stocks with high market risks—like those of airlines, which can tank in a recession, are expected by investors to earn more over the long run than less risky stocks, such as utilities." Sharpe also devised the beta coefficient, a measure of a stock's risk factor. (B.S.S.)

1991

Coase, Ronald Harry 165

Prize: Economics, 1991. *Born:* December 29, 1910; Willesden, England. *Parents:* Father, Henry Joseph Coase; Mother, Rosalie Giles Coase. *Nationality:* British; came to U.S. in 1951. *Religion:* No religion. *Education:* London School of Economics, England, B. of Commerce, 1932; D.Sc., 1951. *Spouse:* Marian Ruth Hartung, married August 7, 1937. *Children:* None. *Career:* Dundee School of Economics, Scotland, Professor, 1932–34; Univ. of Liverpool, England, Professor, 1934–35; London School of Economics, Professor, 1935–51; Univ. of Buffalo, NY, Professor, 1951–58; Univ. of Virginia, Professor, 1958–64; Univ. of Chicago, IL, Professor, 1964–82.

Selected Publications: "The Nature of the Firm." *Economica* 4 (1937): 368; *British Broadcasting, a Study in Monopoly.* London, England: Longman's Green, 1950; "The Problem of Social Cost." *J. Law Ec.* 3 (1960): 1; *The Firm, the Market, and the Law.* Chicago, IL: Univ. of Chicago Press, 1990; *Essays on Economics and Economists.* Chicago, IL: Univ. of Chicago Press, 1994.

For More Information See: Medema, S. *Ronald H. Coase* . New York: St. Martin's Press, 1994; *New York Times Biographical Service* (October 16, 1991): 1094; *Science* 254 (October 25, 1991): 519–20.

Commentary: Ronald Coase received the Nobel for his explanations of why companies exist and why the marketplace can be more efficient than government intervention in solving social problems. Earlier in his career, Coase also introduced the idea that access to portions of the radio spectrum should be treated as a form of property. (B.S.S./J.H.S.)

1992

Becker, Gary Stanley 166

Prize: Economics, 1992. *Born:* December 2, 1930; Pottsville, PA. *Parents:* Father, Louis William Becker; Mother, Anna Siskind Becker. *Nationality:* American. *Religion:* Jewish. *Education:* Princeton Univ., NJ, A.B., 1951; Univ. of Chicago, IL, A.M., 1953; Ph.D., 1955. *Spouse:* Doria Slote, married September 19, 1954; died 1970; Guity Nashat, married October 31, 1979. *Children:* Judith Sarah, daughter; Catherine Jean, daughter; Michael Claffey, stepson; Cyrus Claffey, stepson. *Career:* Univ. of Chicago, IL, Professor, 1954–57; Columbia Univ., NY, Professor, 1957–70; Univ. of Chicago, IL, Professor, 1970-. *Other Awards:* Clark Medal, 1967; Woytinsky Award, 1967; Seidman Award, 1985; Merit Award, National Institutes of Health, 1986; Commons Award, 1987; Lord Foundation Award, 1995; Irene Taueber Award, 1997.

Selected Publications: "Crime and Punishment." *Journal of Political Economy* 76 (March-April 1968): 169–217. *Economics of Discrimination.* Chicago, IL: Univ. of Chicago Press, 1971. *A Treatise on the Family.* Cambridge, MA: Harvard Univ. Press, 1991. *Human Capital.* Chicago, IL: Univ. of Chicago Press, 1993. *Accounting for Tastes.* Cambridge, MA: Harvard Univ. Press, 1996. *Economics of Life.* New York: McGraw-Hill, 1997. *Social Economics* (with Kevin M. Murphy). Cambridge, MA: Belknap Press, 2000.

For More Information See: *Business Week* (October 26, 1992): 36; *New York Times Biographical Service* (October 14, 1992): 1321.

Commentary: The Nobel Prize was given to Gary Becker for "having extended the domain of economic theory to aspects of human behavior which had previously been dealt with—if at all—by other social science disciplines." Becker has been noted for his applications of traditional economics to unusual subjects (e.g., child-bearing, binge drinking, discrimination, crime, and the family). (B.S.S./J.H.S.)

1993

Fogel, Robert William   167

Prize: Economics, 1993. *Born:* July 1, 1926; New York, NY. *Parents:* Father, Harry Gregory Fogel; Mother, Elizabeth Mitnik Fogel. *Nationality:* American. *Religion:* Most probably from Jewish background. *Education:* Cornell Univ., NY, A.B., 1948; Columbia Univ., NY, A.M., 1960; Johns Hopkins Univ., MD, Ph.D., 1963. *Spouse:* Enid Cassandra Morgan, married April 2, 1949. *Children:* Michael Paul, son; Steven Dennis, son. *Career:* Univ. of Rochester, NY, Professor, 1960–64; Univ. of Chicago, IL, Professor, 1964–75; Harvard Univ., MA, Professor, 1975–81; Univ. of Chicago, IL, Professor, 1981-. *Other Awards:* Cole Prize, 1968; Schumpeter Prize, 1971; Bancroft Prize, 1975; Myers Prize, 1990.

Selected Publications: *Railroads and American Economic Growth.* Baltimore, MD: Johns Hopkins Press, 1964. *The Reinterpretation of American Economic History.* New York: Harper, 1971. *Time on the Cross.* New York: Little, Brown, 1974. *Without Consent or Contract.* New York: Norton, 1989. *The Fourth Great Awakening & the Future of Egalitarianism.* Chicago: Chicago Univ. Press, 2000.

For More Information See: *New York Times Biographical Service* (October 14, 1993): 1410; *Science* 262 (October 22, 1993): 508; *Two Pioneers of Cliometrics.* Oxford, OH: Cliometric Society, 1994

Commentary: Robert Fogel shared the Nobel Prize with Douglass North, both of whom were cited for "applying economic theory and quantitative methods" to history. Their work led to cliometrics, the study of economics of the past by quantitative means. Fogel has been the subject of much controversy for his assertions that railroads were not critical driving forces of the American economy and that slavery in the U.S. was economically efficient. (B.S.S./J.H.S.)

North, Douglass Cecil   168

Prize: Economics, 1993. *Born:* November 5, 1920; Cambridge, MA. *Parents:* Father, Henry Emerson North; Mother, Edith Saitta North. *Nationality:* American. *Religion:* Most probably Christian. *Education:* Univ. of California, Berkeley, B.A., 1942; Ph.D., 1952. *Spouse:* 1st wife, married 1944, dissolved, no date; Elisabeth Willard Case, married September 28, 1972 *Children:* Douglass Alan, son; Christopher, son; Malcolm Peter, son *Career:* Univ. of Washington, Professor, 1950–83; Washington Univ., MO, Professor, 1983-.

Selected Publications: *Economic Growth of the United States.* Boston: Norton and Co., 1966. *The Economics of Public Issues.* New York: Harper and Row, 1971. *Growth and Welfare in the American Past.* Englewood Cliffs, NJ: Prentice-Hall, 1974. *Structure and Change in Economic History.* Boston: W. W. Norton and Co. 1982. *Institutions, Institutional Change and Economic Performance.* Cambridge: Cambridge Univ. Press, 1990. *Empirical Studies in Institutional Change.* Cambridge; New York: Cambridge Univ. Press, 1996. *Rise of the Western World.* Cambridge: Cambridge Univ. Press, 1999, 1973.

For More Information See: *New York Times Biographical Service* (October 14, 1993): 1410; *Science* 262 (October 22, 1993): 508; *Two Pioneers of Cliometrics.* Oxford, OH: Cliometric Society, 1994.

Commentary: Douglass North was granted the Nobel jointly with Robert Fogel, both of whom were cited for "applying economic theory and quantitative methods" to history. Their work led to cliometrics, the study of economics of the past by quantitative methods. North is noted for his theoretical work, which provides a methodology for study of institutions and how they develop over time. The Nobelist has studied the interactions of political and economic institutions and has pointed out that a macro-economic policy, to be successful, must also have a body of law "that gives people the right incentives to engage in economic activity." (B.S.S./J.H.S.)

1994

Harsanyi, John Charles   169

Prize: Economics, 1994. *Born:* May 29, 1920; Budapest, Hungary. *Death:* August 9, 2000; Berkeley, CA. *Parents:* Father, Charles Harsanyi; Mother, Alice Harsanyi. *Nationality:* Born Hungarian; emigrated to U.S., 1961. *Religion:* Catholic, from Jewish background. *Education:* Univ. of Budapest, Hungary, Dr. Phil., 1947; Sydney Univ., Australia, M.A., 1953; Stanford Univ., CA, Ph.D., 1959. *Spouse:* Anne Klauber, married January 2, 1951. *Children:* Tom Peter, son. *Career:* Univ. Institute of Sociology, Hungary, Professor, 1947–48; Factory worker, Australia, 1950–53; Univ. of Queensland, Australia, Professor, 1954–56; Stanford Univ., CA, Professor, 1956–58; Australian National Univ., Researcher, 1958–61; Wayne State Univ., MI, Professor, 1961–63; Univ. of California, Berkeley, Professor, 1964–90.

Selected Publications: *Rational Behavior and Bargaining Equilibrium.* Cambridge: Cambridge Univ. Press, 1977; *Papers in Game Theory.* Boston: D. Reidel Publishing Co., 1982; *A General Theory of Equilibrium Selection in Games.* Cambridge, MA: Massachusetts Institute of Technology Press, 1988 (with Reinhard Selten).

For More Information See: *New York Times Biographical Service* (1994): 1572; *Science* 266 (October 21, 1994): 368.

Commentary: John Harsanyi won the Nobel Prize for his work on game theory, which explores how entities like businesses or countries make decisions in competitive situations. Harsanyi built upon John Nash's equilibrium theory, which explained why entities cease bargaining, to allow for situations where knowledge of information was not equal between the participants. The Nobelist also studied how individuals decide to take ethical positions or make moral judgments. (B.S.S./J.H.S.)

Nash, John Forbes 170

Prize: Economics, 1994. *Born:* June 13, 1928; Bluefield, WV. *Parents:* Father, John F. Nash; Mother, Margaret Virginia Martin Nash. *Nationality:* American. *Religion:* Most probably Christian. *Education:* Carnegie Institute of Technology, PA, B.S., M.S., 1948; Princeton Univ., NJ, Ph.D., 1950. *Spouse:* Alicia Larde, married 1957, divorced 1963. *Children:* J. C. M., son. *Career:* Princeton Univ., NJ, Professor, 1950–51; Massachusetts Institute of Technology, Professor, 1951–59; Princeton Univ., NJ, Visiting Research Collaborator, 1959-. *Other Awards:* Von Neumann Medal, 1978; *Business Week* Award, Erasmus Univ., 1998; Leroy P. Steele Prize, 1999; President's Award, National Alliance for the Mentally Ill, 1999.

Selected Publications: "Equilibrium Points in n-Person Games." *Proc. Nat. Acad. Sci. USA* 36 (1950): 155–62. "The Bargaining Problem," *Econometrica* 18 (1950): 155–62; "Non-Cooperative Games," *Annals of Mathematics* 54 (1951): 286–92; "Two-person Cooperative Games," *Econometrica* 21 (1953): 128. "Analyticity of the Solutions of Implicit Function Problems with Analytic Data." *Annals of Mathematics* 84 (1966): 345–55.

For More Information See: Mathematical Intelligencer. 17 (Summer 1995): 11–17. *New York Times Biographical Service* (1994): 1572. *Science* 266 (October 21, 1994): 368.

Commentary: The Nobel Prize was awarded to John Nash for his pioneering work which resulted in a thesis that presented the foundations of game theory. Game theory explores the interactions and decisions of entities in competition. Nash first distinguished between cooperative and noncooperative games and formulated an equilibrium theory for noncooperative games. His later work dealt with parabolic and elliptic equations, Riemannian manifolds, and solutions of implicit function problems. (B.S.S./J.H.S.)

Selten, Reinhard 171

Prize: Economics, 1994. *Born:* October 5, 1930; Breslau, Germany. *Parents:* Father, Adolf Selten; Mother, Kathe Luther Selten. *Nationality:* German. *Religion:* From Jewish/Protestant background. *Education:* Univ. of Frankfurt, Germany, B.A., 1957; Ph.D., 1961. *Spouse:* Elisabeth Amalie Langreiner, married February, 1959. *Children:* None. *Career:* Univ. of Frankfurt am Main, Germany, Professor, 1957–67; Univ. of California, Berkeley, Professor, 1967–68; Free Univ. of Berlin, Germany, Professor 1969–72; Univ. of Bielefeld, Germany, Professor 1972–84; Univ. of Bonn, Germany, Professor, 1984–96.

Selected Publications: General Equilibrium with Price-Making Firms. New York: Springer-Verlag, 1974. *A General Theory of Equilibrium Selection in Games.* Cambridge, MA: Massachusetts Institute of Technology Press, 1988

(with John Harsanyi). *Models of Strategic Rationality.* Boston: Kluwer Academic Publishers, 1988. *Game Theory and Economic Behaviour.* 2 vols. Cheltenham, UK; Northampton, MA: Edward Elgar, 1999.

For More Information See: New York Times Biographical Service (1994): 1572; *Science* 266 (October 21, 1994): 368.

Commentary: Reinhard Selten's Nobel Prize was granted in recognition of his study of the planning mechanisms ("players' strategies") that are a critical part of game theory. His research elaborates on the work of both of his colaureates, John Nash and John Harsanyi, who developed the mathematical formulations that describe how entities (i.e., persons, businesses, or countries) make decisions while in competitive situations. (B.S.S./J.H.S.)

1995

Lucas, Robert Emerson, Jr. 172

Prize: Economics, 1995. *Born:* September 15, 1937; Yakima, WA. *Parents:* Father, Robert Emerson Lucas; Mother, Jane Templeton Lucas. *Nationality:* American. *Religion:* Protestant. *Education:* Univ. of Chicago, IL, B.A., 1959; Ph.D., 1964. *Spouse:* Rita Lilli Cohen, married August 29, 1959, divorced 1989. *Children:* Steven, son; Joseph, son *Career:* Univ. of Chicago, IL, Lecturer, 1962–63; Carnegie-Mellon Univ., PA, Professor, 1963–74; Univ. of Chicago, IL, Professor, 1974-.

Selected Publications: Rational Expectations and Econometric Practice. Minneapolis, MN: Univ. of Minnesota Press, 1981 (with T. Sargent); *Studies in Business Cycle Theory.* Cambridge, MA: Massachusetts Institute of Technology Press, 1981; *Models of Business Cycles.* Cambridge, MA: Blackwell, 1989; *Recursive Methods in Economic Dynamics.* Cambridge, MA: Harvard Univ. Press, 1989 (with N. Stokey).

For More Information See: New York Times (October 11, 1995): C1.

Commentary: The Nobel Prize was awarded to Robert Lucas as "the economist who has had the greatest influence on macroeconomic research since 1990." Lucas applied John Muth's insights on rational expectations to monetary theories of the business cycle. He showed that the effect of government's influences on the economy are ameliorated by the fact that workers and firms do not react automatically to government influences. Instead, the consumers shape the economy by their rational expectations as to what the economy will be like in the future. Lucas applied the same analysis of the role of expectations to investment, unemployment, taxation, public debt management, and asset pricing. (B.S.S./J.H.S.)

1996

Mirrlees, James Alexander, Sir 173

Prize: Economics, 1996. *Born:* July 5, 1936; Minnigaff, Scotland. *Parents:* Father: George Barlas MacNab Mirrlees; Mother: Nana Lindsay Purdie Mirrlees. *Nationality:* Scottish. *Religion:* Probably Christian. *Education:* Cambridge Univ., England, B.A., 1959; Univ. of Edinburgh, Scotland, M.A., 1957; Cambridge Univ., England, Ph.D., 1963. *Spouse:* Gillian Marjorie Hughes, married July 29, 1961, died November 1993. *Children:* Catriona, daughter; Fiona, daughter.

Career: Univ. of Cambridge, England, Professor, 1963–68; Univ. of Oxford, England, Professor, 1968–95; Univ. of Cambridge, England, Professor, 1995-.

Selected Publications: Manual of Industrial Project Analysis in Developing Countries, Vol. II: Social Cost Benefit Analysis. Paris: OECD, 1969 (with I.M.D. Little). *Project Appraisal and Planning for Developing Countries.* New York: Basic Books, 1974 (with I.M.D. Little). "Private Constant Returns and Public Shadow Prices," *Review of Economic Studies* (1976) (with P. Diamond). *Welfare, Incentives, and Taxation.* Oxford: Oxford University press, 2000.

For More Information See: New York Times (October 9, 1996): D1.

Commentary: James Mirrlees and William Vickrey shared the Nobel Prize "for their fundamental contributions to the economic theory of incentives under asymmetric information." Based on Vickrey's work on how income taxation can be balanced between efficiency and equity, Mirrlees identified the condition known as "single crossing" which greatly simplified the problem and solved it in such a way as to allow individuals to reveal information without harming their self-interest. As noted by the Nobel Committee, "By applying this principle, it becomes much easier to design optimal contracts and other solutions to incentive problems." (L.S.S.)

Vickrey, William Spencer   174

Prize: Economics, 1996. *Born:* June 21, 1914; Victoria, British Columbia, Canada. *Death:* October 11, 1996; White Plains, NY. *Parents:* Father, Charles Vernon Vickrey; Mother, Ada Eliza Spencer Vickrey. *Nationality:* Canadian; later American citizen. *Religion:* Quaker. *Education:* Yale Univ., CT, B.A., 1935; Columbia Univ., NY, M.A., 1937; Columbia Univ., NY, Ph.D., 1947. *Spouse:* Cecile Montez Thompson, married July 21, 1951. *Children:* None. *Career:* National Resources Planning Board, Washington, D.C., Economist, 1937–38; 20th Century Fund, Washington, D.C., Researcher, 1939–40; U.S. Treasury Department, Washington, D.C., Economist, 1941–43; Civilian Public Service Assignee, 1943–46; Columbia Univ., NY, Professor, 1946–81.

Selected Publications: Agenda for Progressive Taxation. New York: Ronald Press, 1947. "Pricing of Urban Transportation," *American Economic Review* 53, 2 (May 1963): 452–65. *Metastatistics and Macroeconomics.* New York: Harcourt, Brace, 1964. *Microstatistics.* New York: Harcourt Brace, 1964. *Public Economics.* Cambridge: Cambridge University Press, 1994.

For More Information See: New York Times (October 9, 1996): D1. *New York Times* (October 12, 1996): A1.

Commentary: William Vickrey shared the Nobel Prize with James Mirrlees "for their fundamental contributions to the economic theory of incentives under asymmetric information." Vickrey's research indicated that a progressive tax schedule would have an impact on the productivity of the individual and the incomplete knowledge that the government had about each person's incentive to work. He solved the income taxation problem in priniciple but was unable to solve it mathematically. It was Mirrlees who solved the problem twenty-five years later. Vickrey is also known for his work on auctions, especially second-price or Vickrey auctions, where the highest bidder gets to buy the item at the

second highest price, thus ensuring that the bidder will place a truthful bid in terms of what he is actually willing to pay. (L.S.S.)

1997

Merton, Robert C.   175

Prize: Economics, 1997. *Born:* July 31, 1944; New York, NY. *Parents:* Father, Robert K. Merton; Mother, Suzanne Carhart Merton. *Nationality:* American. *Religion:* Methodist/Quaker background. *Education:* Columbia Univ., NY, B.S., 1966; California Institute of Technology, M.S., 1967; Massachusetts Institute of Technology, Ph.D., 1970. *Spouse:* June Rose, married 1966, separated. *Children:* Samantha J., daughter; Robert F., son; Paul J., son. *Career:* Massachusetts Institute of Technology, MA, Professor, 1969–88; Harvard Univ., MA, Professor, 1988-; Long-Term Capital Management, CT, Principal and Co-founder, 1993–99. *Other Awards:* Leo Melamed Prize, 1983; Roger Murray Prize, 1985, 1986; International INA-National Academy of Lincei Prize, 1993; FORCE Award, 1993; Financial Engineer of the Year Award, 1993; Pupin Medal, 1998; Derivatives Hall of Fame, 1998; Distinguished Alumni Award, California Institute of Technology, 1999; MFD Lifetime Achievement Award, 1999.

Selected Publications: "Theory of Rational Option Pricing," *Bell Journal of Economics and Management Science* 4 (1973): 141–183. *Continuous-Time Finance.* Cambridge, MA; Oxford: Basil-Blackwell, 1990, rev. ed. 1992, 1998. *Cases in Financial Engineering.* New York: Prentice-Hall, 1995. *Global Financial System.* Boston: Harvard University Press, 1995. *Finance.* Upper Saddle River, NJ: Prentice-Hall, 2000 (with Zvi Bodie).

For More Information See: New York Times (October 15, 1997): D1. *New York Times* (November 14, 1998): A1.

Commentary: Robert C. Merton and Myron Scholes shared the Nobel Prize "for a new method to determine the value of derivatives." Merton was able to expand on the work done by Scholes and the late Fischer Black in developing a new formula for valuing stock options now used in stock markets all over the world. This formula took into account the risk factors that could affect the value of a stock and included it in the price of the stock. This formulation has had a great impact on the growth of markets for derivative securities. (L.S.S.)

Scholes, Myron S.   176

Prize: Economics, 1997. *Born:* July 1, 1941; Timmins, Ontario, Canada. *Parents:* No record found. *Nationality:* Canadian; later American citizen. *Religion:* No record found. *Education:* McMaster Univ., Canada, B.A., 1962; McMaster Univ., Canada, M.B.A., 1964; Univ. of Chicago, IL, Ph.D., 1969. *Spouse:* married previously, no name, date; Jan Blaustein, married October 4, 1998. *Children:* Anne, daughter; Sara, daughter. *Career:* Univ. of Chicago, IL, Professor, 1967–68; Massachusetts Institute of Technology, MA, Professor, 1968–73; Univ. of Chicago, IL, Professor, 1973–83; Stanford Univ., CA, Professor, 1983–96; Long-Term Capital Management, CT, Principal and Co-Founder, 1994–98.

Selected Publications: "The Pricing of Options and Corporate Liabilities," *Journal of Political Economy* 81

(1973): 637–54 (with F. Black). *Taxes and Business Strategy: A Planning Approach*. Englewood Cliffs, NJ: Prentice-Hall, 1992 (with Mark A. Wolfson).

For More Information See: Maclean's 110 (October 27, 1997): 40. *New York Times* (October 15, 1997): D1. *New York Times* (November 14, 1998): A1.

Commentary: Myron Scholes and Robert C. Merton were awarded the Nobel Prize for determining a new formula that allows investors to more accurately determine the value of a stock. Scholes, the late Fischer Black, and Merton developed the Black-Scholes formula that allows an investor to lower the risk of changes in the price of stocks at some point in the future. This formula had an immediate impact in the growth of options markets worldwide and has "generated new types of financial instruments and facilitated more efficient risk management in society." (L.S.S.)

1998

Sen, Amartya Kumar 177

Prize: Economics, 1998. *Born:* November 3, 1933; Santiniketan, India. *Parents:* Father, Ashutosh Sen; Mother, Amita Sen. *Nationality:* Indian; later British and American resident. *Religion:* Hindu. *Education:* Calcutta Univ., India, B.A., 1953; Cambridge Univ., England, B.A., 1955; Cambridge Univ., England, Ph.D., 1958. *Spouse:* Nabaneeta Dev, married 1960, divorced 1974; Eva Colorni, married 1977, died 1985; Emma Rothschild, married 1991. *Children:* Antara; Nandana; Indrani; Kabir, son. *Career:* Jadavpur Univ., India, Professor, 1956–58; Cambridge Univ., England, Fellow, 1957–63; Delhi Univ., India, Professor, 1963–71; London School of Economics, England, Professor, 1971–77; Oxford Univ., England, Professor, 1977–88; Harvard Univ., MA, Professor, 1988–98; Trinity College, England, Master, 1998-. *Other Awards:* Mahalanobis Prize, 1976; Agnelli International Prize, 1990; Feinstein World Hunger Award, 1990.

Selected Publications: Choice of Techniques. Oxford: Blackwell, 1960. *Collective Choice and Social Welfare.* San Francisco: Holden-Day, 1970. *Behaviour and the Concept of Preference.* London: London School of Economics, 1971. *On Economic Inequality.* New York: Norton, 1973; New York: Oxford University Press, 1997, enl. ed. *Poverty and Famines.* New York: Oxford University Press, 1981. *Choice, Welfare, and Measurement.* Cambridge, MA: MIT Press, 1982. *Resources, Values and Development.* Cambridge, MA: Harvard University Press, 1984. *Hunger and Public Action.* New York: Oxford University Press, 1989 (with Jean Dreze). *Inequality Reexamined.* Cambridge, MA: Harvard University Press, 1992. *Development as Freedom.* New York: Knopf, 1999.

For More Information See: Economist (October 17, 1998): 87. *Foreign Affairs* (January-February 2000): 163. *New York Times* (October 15, 1998): C1. *Time* (October 26, 1998): 69.

Commentary: Amartya Sen won the Prize for his "contributions to welfare economics." His work on poverty and the real causes of famines has led to real change in how governments deal with famines. Among his major contributions is the development of a poverty index that looks at the distribution of income for those below the poverty line. Another major contribution is his analysis of the various

social and economic factors that contribute to the causes of famines which can occur even food supplies are not significantly lower. The Committee also noted that Sen "has restored an ethical dimension to the discussion of vital economic problems." (L.S.S.)

1999

Mundell, Robert Alexander 178

Prize: Economics, 1999. *Born:* October 24, 1932; Kingston, Ontario, Canada. *Parents:* Father, William C. Mundell; Mother, Lila Knifton Mundell. *Nationality:* Canadian; later American resident. *Religion:* Probably Christian. *Education:* Univ. of British Columbia, Canada, B.A., 1953; Massachusetts Institute of Technology, Ph.D., 1956. *Spouse:* Barbara Scheff, married, October 14, 1957, divorced 1972; Valerie Matsios, married, no date. *Children:* William Andrew, son; Paul Alexander, son; Nicholas, son; Robin Leslie, daughter. *Career:* Univ. of Chicago, IL, Researcher, 1956–57; Univ. of British Columbia, Canada, Professor, 1957–58; Stanford Univ., CA, Professor, 1958–59; Johns Hopkins Univ., Italy, Professor, 1959–61; International Monetary Fund, Washington, DC, Researcher, 1961–63; McGill Univ., Canada, Professor, 1963–64; Brookings Institution, Washington, DC, Professor, 1964–65; Univ. of Chicago, IL, Professor, 1965–71; Univ. of Waterloo, Canada, Professor, 1972–74; Columbia Univ., Professor, 1974-. *Other Awards:* Jacques Rueff Medal, 1983.

Selected Publications: "A Theory of Optimal Currency Areas," *American Economic Review* 51 (1961): 657–65. "Capital Mobility and Stabilization Policy under Fixed and Flexible Exchange Rates," *Canadian Journal of Economics* 29 (1963): 475–485. *International Monetary System.* Montreal: Canadian Trade Committee, 1965. *International Economics.* New York: Macmillan, 1968. *Man and Economics* New York: McGraw Hill, 1968. *Monetary Theory.* Pacific Palisades, CA: Goodyear Publishing, 1971.

For More Information See: Forbes (November 15, 1999): 39. *Maclean's* (October 25, 1999): 46+. *New York Times* (October 14, 1999): C1.

Commentary: Robert Mundell was awarded the Prize "for his analysis of monetary and fiscal policy under different rate regimes and his analysis of optimum currency areas." Mundell demonstrated the impact of the exchange rate regime where "under a floating exchange rate, monetary policy becomes powerful and fiscal policy powerless, whereas the opposite is true under a fixed exchange rate." Mundell's theories on supply side economics became a cornerstone of President Ronald Reagan's fiscal policy. He was also influential in the development of the common European currency, the euro. (L.S.S.)

2000

Heckman, James Joseph 179

Prize: Economics, 2000. *Born:* April 19, 1944; Chicago, IL. *Parents:* Father, John Jacob Heckman; Mother, Bernice Irene Medley Heckman. *Nationality:* American. *Religion:* No record found. *Education:* Colorado College, CO, A.B., 1965; Princeton Univ., NJ, M.A., 1968; Princeton Univ., NJ, Ph.D., 1971; Yale Univ., CT, M.A., 1989. *Spouse:* Lynn Pettler, married 1979. *Children:* Jonathan Jacob, son; Alma Rachel, daughter. *Career:* Columbia Univ., NY, Professor,

1970–74; Univ. of Chicago, IL, Professor, 1973-. *Other Awards:* Guggenheim Fellow, 1978–79; John Bates Clark Medal, 1983; L. Benezet Alumni Prize (Colorado College), 1985.

Selected Publications: Longitudinal Analysis of Labor Market Data. Cambridge; New York: Cambridge University Press, 1985 (with Burton Singer). "Selection Bias and Self-Selection," in P. Newman, M. Milgate and J. Eatwell (eds.), *The New Palgrave—A Dictionary of Economics.* New York: Macmillan, 1987. "Assessing the Case for Social Experiments," *Journal of Economic Perspectives* 9 (1995): 85–110 (with J. Smith). *Evaluating Social Programs.* Chicago: Chicago University Press, 2000. *Incentives in Government Bureaucracies.* Chicago: Upjohn, 2000.

For More Information See: Business Week (October 23, 2000): 48. *Economist* 357 (October 14, 2000): 94. *New York Times* (October 12, 2000): C1.

Commentary: James Heckman shared the Nobel Prize for "his development of theory and methods for analyzing selective samples" in the field of microeconometrics. Heckman developed appropriate statistical methods for studying selective samples, or microdata, that allow the study of large groups of individuals, households or companies. (L.S.S.)

McFadden, Daniel Little   180

Prize: Economics, 2000. *Born:* July 29, 1937; Raleigh, NC. *Parents:* Father, Robert S. McFadden; Mother, Alice Little McFadden. *Nationality:* American. *Religion:* No record found. *Education:* Univ. of Minnesota, B.S., 1957; Univ. of Minnesota, MN, Ph.D., 1962. *Spouse:* Beverlee Tito Simboli, married December 15, 1962. *Children:* Nina, daughter; Robert, son; Raymond, son. *Career:* Univ. of Minnesota, MN, Professor, 1957–62; Univ. of Pittsburgh, PA, Professor, 1962–63; Univ. of California, Berkeley, CA, Professor, 1963–79; Massachusetts Institute of Technology, MA, Professor, 1979–90; Univ. of California, Berkeley, CA, Professor, 1990-. *Other Awards:* John Bates Clark Medal, 1975; Frisch Medal, 1986; Nemmers Prize, 2000.

Selected Publications: Urban Travel Demand. Amsterdam; New York: North-Holland, 1975. *Production Economics.* Amsterdam; New York: North-Holland, 1978 (with M.A. Fuss). *Structural Analysis of Discrete Data with Econometric Applications.* Cambridge, MA: MIT Press, 1981. *Microeconomic Modeling and Policy Analysis.* Orlando: Academic Press, 1984 (with T.G. Cowing).

For More Information See: Business Week (October 23, 2000):48. *Economist* 357 (October 14, 2000):94. *New York Times* (October 12, 2000): C1.

Commentary: Daniel McFadden was cited by the Nobel Committee "for his development of theory and methods for analyzing discrete choice" in microeconometrics. He developed statistical methods for studying discrete choice that has transformed empirical research in this area. His methods have been used to study transportation models and to evaluate changes in communication systems, such as San Francisco's BART system and telephone service for the elderly. (L.S.S.)

Literature

1901

Prudhomme, René-François-Armend (Sully Prudhomme, René-François-Armend)   181

Prize: Literature, 1901. *Born:* March 16, 1839; Paris, France. *Death:* September 6, 1907; Châtenay, France. *Parents:* Father, M. Sully Prudhomme; Mother, Clotilde Caillat Sully Prudhomme. *Nationality:* French. *Religion:* Catholic. *Education:* Lycée Bonaparte, France, Bachelier ès Sciences, 1856. *Spouse:* None. *Children:* None. *Career:* Paris, France, Clerk, 1859–60; Writer.

Selected Publications: Les Solitudes: Poèsies. Paris: A. Lemerre, 1869. *Poèsie, 1865–88.* Paris: A. Lemerre, 1883–88. *Le Prisme, Poèsies Diverses.* Paris: A. Lemerre, 1886. *Psychologie du Arbitre de Definitions Fondamentales: Vocabulaire Logiquement Ordonné des Idées les Plus Generals et des Idées les Plus Abstraites.* Paris: A. Lemerre, 1896. *Oeuvres de Sully Prudhomme.* Paris: A. Lemerre, 1900–01. *Epaves.* Paris: A. Lemerre, 1908. *Patrie et Humanité (Essai de Solution Collective).* Paris: Edition de "La Revue," 1913. *Journal Intime: Lettres-Pensée.* Paris: A. Lemerre, 1922.

For More Information See: Columbia Dictionary of Modern European Literature. New York: Columbia Univ. Press, 1947, 791. Esteve, Edmond. *Sully Prudhomme.* Paris: Boivin, 1925.

Commentary: René Sully-Prudhomme, French poet, was the recipient of the first Nobel Prize for literature. His work is generally considered to fall into two stylistic groups. The earlier is lyrical, typified by his most famous poem, "Vase Brisé," which was published in his first book of poems, *Stances et Poèmes* (1865). Later in his life, Sully-Prudhomme's poetry grew increasingly abstract and concerned with philosophic and didactic issues. Sully-Prudhomme was given the Nobel Prize "in special recognition of his poetic composition, which gives evidence of lofty idealism, artistic perfection, and a rare combination of the qualities of both heart and intellect." (S.W.C.)

1902

Björnson, Björnstjerne Martinius   182

Prize: Literature, 1902. *Born:* December 8, 1832; Kvikne, Norway. *Death:* April 26, 1910; Paris, France. *Parents:* Father, Peder Björnson; Mother, Inger Elise Nordraak Björnson. *Nationality:* Norwegian. *Religion:* Freethinker; from Lutheran background. *Education:* No college degrees. *Spouse:* Karoline Reimers, married 1857. *Children:* Björn, son; Bergljot, daughter. *Career: Morgenbladet*, Theater Critic, 1854–56; *Illustreret Folkeblad*, Editor, 1856; *Bergensposten*, Editor, 1858; *Aftenbladet*, Editor, 1859–60; *Norsk Folkeblad*, Editor, 1866–71. *Other Awards:* Norwegian Government's Author's Salary, first recipient, 1863.

Selected Publications: Synnöve Solbakken. Kristiania: Dahl, 1857 (*Synnöve Solbakken.* Tr. by Julie Sutter. New York: Macmillan, 1912). *Sigurd Slembe.* Copenhagen: Gyldendal, 1862 (*Sigurd Slembe.* Tr. by William Morton Payne. Boston: Houghton, Mifflin & Co., 1888). *En Gead Gutt.* Copenhagen: Gyldendal, 1868. *Arnl jot Gelline.* Copenhagen: Gyldendal, 1870. *Digte og Sange.* Copenhagen: Gyldendal, 1870 (*Poems and Songs.* Tr. by Arthur Hubbel Palmer. New York: American-Scandinavian Foundation, 1915). *Sigurd Jorsalfar* (*Sigurd the Crusader*). Copenhagen: Gyldendal, 1872. *Over Aevne* (Volume I, 1883) and *Over Aevne* (Volume II, 1895). Copenhagen: Gyldendal, 1883–95 (*Beyond Our Power* (Volume I)). *Modern Continental Plays.* Tr. by Edwin Bjorkman. Ed. by S.M. Tucker. New York, 1929 and *Beyond Human Might* (Volume II). Tr. by Edwin Bjorkman. *Nobel Prize Library* (volume on Beckett, Björnson, Buck, Bunin). New York: Gregory, 1971, 85–136. *Når den ny Vin Blomstrer.* Gyldendal, 1909 (*When the New Wine Blooms.* Tr. by Lee M. Hollander. Boston: R.G. Badger, 1911).

For More Information See: Anker, Öyvind. *Björnstjerne Björnson: The Man and His Work* (with Björnson's *Modern Norwegian Literature*). Follebu: Aulestad, 1955. Beyer, Harald. *A History of Norwegian Literature.* Tr. by Einar Haugen. New York: New York Univ. Press, 1970. Brandes, Georg Morris Cohen. *Henrik Ibsen: A Critical Study with a 42-Page Essay on Björnstjerne Björnson.* London: Macmillan, 1899; New York: Arno Press, 1977. Payne, William Morton. *Björnstjerne Björnson, 1832–1910.* Chicago: McClurg, 1910.

Commentary: Björnstjerne Björnson was 71 years old when he received the Nobel Prize as "a tribute to his noble, magnificent, and versatile work as a poet, which has always been distinguished by both the freshness of its inspiration and the rare purity of its spirit." Besides poetry, he wrote numerous novels and plays, ranging from early peasant stories and historical dramas to contemporary works. His most famous poem is the Norwegian national anthem. An untiring writer, orator, and champion of the oppressed, Björnson was always involved in public debate and surrounded by controversy. Even today his status as author is rivaled by the memory of his fearless and flamboyant personality. (S.O.)

Mommsen, Christian Matthias Theodor   183

Prize: Literature, 1902. *Born:* November 30, 1817; Garding, Schleswig, Germany. *Death:* November 1, 1903; Berlin-Charlottenburg, Germany. *Parents:* Father, Jens Mommsen; Mother, Sophie Elisabeth Krumbhaur Mommsen. *Nationality:* German. *Religion:* Atheist; from Protestant background. *Education:* Universität zu Kiel, Germany, Doctor of Law, 1843. *Spouse:* Marie Auguste Reimer, married 1854. *Children:* Marie, daughter; Lisbet, daughter; Käthe, daughter; Hildegard, daughter; Adelheid, daughter; Luise, daughter; Anna, daughter; Wolfgang, son; Karl, son; Kurt, son; Ernst, son; Oswald, son; Konrad, son; Hans, son; Max, son; Otto, son. *Career:* Danish Government Traveling Fellowship, 1844–46; *Schleswig-Holsteinische Zeitung,* Editor, 1848; Univ. of Leipzig, Germany, Professor, 1848–51; Univ. of Zürich, Switzerland, Professor, 1852–54; Univ. of Breslau, Germany, Professor, 1854–58; Königlich Preussischen Akademie der Wissenschaften, Professor, 1858–61; Univ. of Berlin, Germany, Professor, 1861–1903.

Selected Publications: Inscriptiones regni Neapolitani Latinae. Leipzig, Germany: G. Wigand, 1852. *Romische Geschichte.* Berlin: Weidmann, 1854–85 (*History of Rome.* Volumes I-III. Tr. by W.P. Dickson. New York: Scribner's, 1862–75; *The Provinces of the Roman Empire.* Volume V. Tr. by W.P. Dickson. London: Bentley, 1886). *Geschichte der Römische Munzwesen.* Berlin: Weidmann, 1860. *Römisches Staatsrecht.* Leipzig, Germany: S. Hirzel, 1871–88. *Römisches Strafrecht.* Leipzig, Germany: Duncker und Humblot, 1899. *Gesammelte Schriften* (*Collected Writings*). Berlin: Weidmann, 1905–13.

For More Information See: Fowler, W. Warde, "Theodor Mommsen: His Life and Work." In *Roman Essays and Interpretations.* Oxford: Clarendon Press, 1920, 250–68. Hartmann, Ludo Moritz. *Theodor Mommsen: Eine Biographische Skizze.* Gotha, Germany: F. A. Perthes, 1908. Wikert, Lothar. *Theodor Mommsen: Eine Biographie.* Frankfurt: V. Klosterman, 1958–80.

Commentary: The Nobel Committee cited Theodor Mommsen as "the greatest living master of historical writing, with special reference to his monumental work, *History of Rome.*" In this work, he demonstrated unparalleled ability to combine minute detail with a sweeping breadth of view, and passionate feeling with sober critical judgment. Particularly memorable are his battle scenes and character portraits which, though thoroughly historical, are painted with consummate artistic skill. His other scholarly achievements include his work as an editor of the *Corpus Inscriptionum Latinarum,* a collection of all known Latin inscriptions. Mommsen was not only chiefly responsible for organizing this publication, which extended the range of research on Roman civilization immeasurably, but was also its most important contributor. A researcher of Herculean productivity who was also intimately involved in the political life and thought of his time, Mommsen ranks as one of the greatest minds of the nineteenth century. (H.J.W.)

1904

Echegaray Y Eizaguirre, José   184
Prize: Literature, 1904. *Born:* April 19, 1832; Madrid, Spain. *Death:* September 14, 1916; Madrid, Spain. *Parents:* Father, José Echegary y Lacosta; Mother, Manuela Eizaguirre Chaler. *Nationality:* Spanish. *Religion:* Freethinker; from Catholic background. *Education:* Escuela de Caminos, Spain, engineering degree, 1853. *Spouse:* Ana Perfecta Estrada, married 1857. *Children:* 1 daughter. *Career:* Escuela de Caminos, Madrid, Spain, Professor, 1854–68; Political posts and Writer, 1868–1916. *Other Awards:* Cortina Award, Real Academia Espanola de La Lengua, Spain, 1892; Grand Cross of Alfonso XII, 1904; Premio Echegaray, Royal Academy of the Exact, Physical and Natural Sciences, 1907; Knight of the Golden Fleece; Grand Cordon of the Legion of Honor; Grand Cross of San Mauricio and San Lazaro, Italy.

Selected Publications: O Locura o Santidad, Drama en Tres Actos y en Drosa. Madrid: J.M. Duncazcal, 1877 (*Madman or Saint.* Tr. by H. Lynch. Boston: L. Wolfe, 1895). *El Gran Galeoto, Drama en Tres Actos y en Verso, Precedido de un Dialogo en Prosa.* Madrid: J. Rodrignes, 1881 (*The Great Galeoto, a Drama in Four Acts: a Prologue.* Tr. by Jacob F. Fassett. Boston: R. G. Badger, 1914). *El Loco Dios; Drama en Cuatro Actos, en Prosa.* Madrid: Velasco, 1900 (*The Madman Divine, a Prose Drama in Four Acts.* Tr. by Elizabeth Howard West. Boston: Poet Lore, 1908).

For More Information See: Matias, Julio. *Echegaray-Su Vida y Obra.* Madrid: E.P.S.A., 1970. *Oxford Companion to Spanish Literature.* Oxford: Clarendon Press, 1978, 176.

Commentary: The Nobel Prize was given to José Echegaray "in recognition of the numerous and brilliant compositions which in an individual and original manner have revived the great traditions of the Spanish drama." Echegaray excelled as a professor of mathematics, as a high political figure in the Spanish government and as a leader in Spanish drama. Remembered as a dramatist, his output included a dozen competent works in science. It wasn't until early middle age that he turned to writing plays; in the 30 following years, he produced more than 60 works in the melodramatic vein; his greatest strength lay in his power to create and maintain suspense and to stimulate the imagination with stage effects. (D.C.)

Mistral, Frederic   185
Prize: Literature, 1904. *Born:* September 8, 1830; Maillane, Bouches-du-Rhone, France. *Death:* March 25, 1914; Maillane, France. *Parents:* Father, François Mistral; Mother, Adelaide Poulinet Mistral. *Nationality:* French. *Religion:* Catholic. *Education:* Univ. of Aix-en-Provence, France, licence en droit, 1851. *Spouse:* Marie Riviére, married 1876. *Children:* None. *Career:* Writer. *Other Awards:* French Academy Prize, 1861; Reynaud Prize, Institute of France.

Selected Publications: Mireio, Poémes Provençau de Frederic Mistral. Avignon, France: J. Roumanille, 1859 (*Mireille, A Pastoral Epic of Provence from the Provencal of F. Mistral.* Tr. by H. Crichton. London: Macmillan, 1868). *Calendau.* Avignon, France: J. Roumanille, 1867. *La Reine Jeanne: Tragedie Provençale en Cinq Actes.* Paris: A. Lemerre, 1879. *Lou Tresor d'ou Felibridge ou Dictionaire Provençal-Français.* Aix-en-Provence, France: Veue Remondet-Aubin, 1879–1887. *Nerte, Nouvelle Provençale.* Paris: Hachette, 1884. *Le poème du Rhône, xii Chantes: Texte, Provençal et Traduction Française.* Paris: A. Lemerre, 1897 (*The Poem of the Rhone.* Tr. by M.B. Jones. Claremont, CA: Claremont College Press, 1914).

For More Information See: Downer, Charles. *Frederic Mistral.* New York: Columbia Univ. Press, 1901. Edwards, T. *The Lion of Arles.* New York: Fordham Univ. Press, 1964. *Memoirs of Frederic Mistral.* Tr. by George Wicks. New York: New Directions, 1986. *Memoirs of Mistral.* Tr. by Constance Maud. London: E. Arnold, 1907.

Commentary: The Nobel Award was conferred on Frederic Mistral "in recognition of the fresh originality and true artistic genius of his poetry, which faithfully mirrors the native spirit of his people, and of his important work as a

Provençal philologist." Mistral's love of Provence translated itself into an outpouring of poetry about its people and its natural beauties, as well as the founding of the Association of Provençal Poets, whose members standardized the language and presented it in dictionary form. (P.K.)

1905

Sienkiewicz, Henryk Adam Aleksander Pius (Litwos) 186

Prize: Literature, 1905. *Born:* May 5, 1846; Wola Okrzejska, Lithuania. *Death:* November 15, 1916; Vevey, Switzerland. *Parents:* Father, Jozef Sienkiewicz; Mother, Stefania Cieciszowska Sienkiewicz. *Nationality:* Polish. *Religion:* Catholic. *Education:* No college degrees. *Spouse:* Maria Szetkiewicz, married 1881, died October 19, 1885; Maria Romanowska, married 1893, separated shortly thereafter, marriage later annulled; Maria Babska, married May 5, 1904. *Children:* Henryk Jozef, son; Jadwiga, daughter. *Career:* Writer, Journalist, and Editor. *Other Awards:* Oblegorek Estate, received as national gift, 1900.

Selected Publications: Dziela. Sixty-volume collective edition. Ed. by Julian Krzyzanowski. Warsaw: Pantsworog Instytut Wydawniczy, 1947–55. Contains Polish versions of all below. *Janko Muzykant*. 1879 (*Yanko, the Musician and Other Stories*. Tr. by Jeremiah Curtin. Boston: Little, Brown & Co., 1893). *Ogniem i Mieczem*. 1884 (*With Fire and Sword: An Historical Novel of Poland and Russia*. Tr. by Jeremiah Curtin. Boston: Little, Brown & Co., 1890). *Potop*. 1886 (*The Deluge: An Historical Novel of Poland, Sweden, and Russia*. Tr. by Jeremiah Curtin. Boston: Little, Brown & Co., 1891). *Pan Wolodyjowski*. 1888 (*Pan Michael: An Historical Novel of Poland, the Ukraine, and Turkey*. Tr. by Jeremiah Curtin. Boston: Little, Brown and & Co., 1893). *Bez Dogmatu*. 1891 (*Without Dogma*. Tr. by Iza Young. Boston: Little, Brown & Co., 1893). *Rodzina Polanieckich*. 1894 (*Children of the Soil*. Tr. by Jeremiah Curtin. Boston: Little, Brown & Co., 1895). *Quo Vadis*. 1895 (*Quo Vadis*. Tr. by Jeremiah Curtin. Boston: Little, Brown & Co., 1896). *Na Polu Chwaly*. 1906 (*The Field of Glory: An Historical Novel*. Tr. by Henry Britoff. New York: J.S. Ogilvie Publishing Co., 1906). *Wiry*. 1910 (*Whirlpools*. Tr. by Max A. Drezmal. Boston: Little, Brown & Co., 1910). *W Pustyni i w Puszczy*. 1912 (*In Desert and Wilderness*. Tr. by Max A. Drezmal. Boston: Little, Brown & Co., 1912).

For More Information See: Gardher, Monica. *The Patriot Novelist of Poland*. New York: E.P. Dutton, 1926. Giergielewicz, Mieczyslaw. *Henryk Sienkiewicz*. New York: Twayne Publishers, 1968. *Modern Slavic Literatures: A Library of Literary Criticism*. New York: Frederick Ungar Publishing Co., 1976 (Volume 2), 394–99.

Commentary: Henryk Sienkiewicz's award was "because of his outstanding merits as an epic writer," with a style distinguished by naive and striking metaphors. In his historical novels, Sienkiewicz maintained the objectivity of an historian while demonstrating uncompromising loyalty to his country and fellow Poles. Writing about Poland's past, Sienkiewicz inspired faith in the country's future. With remarkable insight and rich imagination he created characters that belong in the gallery of immortal characters of world literature. (S.R.)

1906

Carducci, Giosuè Alessandro Guiseppe 187

Prize: Literature, 1906. *Born:* June 27, 1835; Valdicastello, Italy. *Death:* February 16, 1907; Bologna, Italy. *Parents:* Father, Michele Carducci; Mother, Idegonde Celli Carducci. *Nationality:* Italian. *Religion:* Anti-church; from Catholic background. *Education:* Univ. of Pisa, Italy, Ph.D., 1855. *Spouse:* Elvira Manicucci, married 1859. *Children:* Beatrice, daughter; Laura, daughter; Dante, son; Liberta, daughter. *Career:* Univ. of Bologna, Italy, Professor, 1860–1904.

Selected Publications: Levia Gravia (*Light and Heavy*). Pistoia Tip, Italy: Niccolai e Quarteroi, 1868. *Odi Barbare* (*The Barbarian Odes*). Bologna: Presso Nicola Zanichelli, 1877 (*The Barbarian Odes of Giosuè Carducci*. Tr. by W.F. Smith et al. Menasha, WI: George Bante Co., 1939). *Giambi ed Epodi* (*Iambics and Epodes di Giosue Carducci 1867–1872*). Bologna: N. Zanichelli, 1882 (*Political and satiric verse of Giosue Carducci*. Tr. by W.F. Smith. Colorado Springs, CO: Private Printing, 1942). *Rime Nuove* (*New Rhymes*). Bologna: N. Zanichelli, 1887 (*The New Lyrics of Giosue Carducci*. Tr. by W.F. Smith. Colorado Springs, CO: private printing, 1942). *Bozzetti e Scherme*. Bologna: Carducci, 1889. *Primi Saggi*. Bologna: Carducci, 1889. *Confessioni e Battaglie* (*Confessions and Battles*. Bologna: Carducci, 1890). *Giambi ed Epodi e Rime*. Bologna: N. Zanichelli, 1894. *Studi Saggi e Discorsi*. Bologna: Carducci, 1898. *Su Ludovico Aristo e Taquarto Tasso: Studi*. Bologna: Carducci, 1905. *Archelogia Poetica*. Bologna: N. Zanichelli, 1908. *Edizione Nazionale Delle Opere di Giosuè Carducci*. Bologna: N. Zanichelli, 1935–40.

For More Information See: Bailey, John. *Carducci*. Oxford: Clarendon, 1926. *Columbia Dictionary of Modern European Literature*. New York: Columbia Univ. Press, 1947, 143–44. Sontag, Susan. *Under the Sign of Saturn*. London: Writers and Readers, 1980.

Commentary: Giosuè Carducci, Italian poet, politician, and literary historian, was awarded the Nobel Prize "not only in consideration of his deep learning and critical research, but above all as a tribute to the creative energy, freshness of style, and lyrical force which characterize his poetic masterpieces." An ardent patriot known for his radical opinions, Carducci strove in his poetry to fuse the modern with the ancient. He was viewed as the greatest figure in Italian literature of his time. (S.W.C.)

1907

Kipling, Joseph Rudyard 188

Prize: Literature, 1907. *Born:* December 30, 1865; Bombay, India. *Death:* January 18, 1936; London, England. *Parents:* Father, John Lockwood Kipling; Mother, Alice MacDonald Kipling. *Nationality:* British. *Religion:* Methodist. *Education:* No college degrees. *Spouse:* Caroline Starr Bolestier, married 1892. *Children:* Josephine, daughter; Elsie, daughter; John, son. *Career: Civil and Military Gazette*, India, Editor, 1882–87; *Pioneer*, India, Editor, 1887–89; Writer. *Other Awards:* Order of Merit, 1916, 1921, 1924 (refused); Gold Medal, 1926.

Selected Publications: Barrack Room Ballads and Other Verses. Leipzig, Germany: Heinemann and Balestier, 1892. *The Jungle Book. The Second Jungle Book*. Garden City, NY: Doubleday, Page, 1895. *From Sea to Sea: Letters of*

Travel. New York: Scribner's, 1900. *Kim.* Leipzig, Germany: B. Tauchnitz, 1901. *Just So Stories for Little Children.* Leipzig, Germany: B. Tauchnitz, 1902. *The Five Nations.* Leipzig, Germany: B. Tauchnitz, 1903. *Puck of Pook's Hill.* Leipzig, Germany: B. Tauchnitz, 1906. *Soldier Stories.* Garden City, NY: Doubleday, Page, 1920.

For More Information See: Amis, Kingsley. *Rudyard Kipling and His World.* New York: Scribner's, 1975. Clemens, William Montgomery. *A Ken of Kipling Being a Biographical Sketch of Rudyard Kipling.* Toronto: G.N. Norang, 1899. Dobree, Bonamie. *Rudyard Kipling: Realist and Fabulist.* New York: Oxford Univ. Press, 1967. Laski, Marhanita. *From Palm to Pine: Rudyard Kipling Abroad and at Home.* New York: Facts on File, 1987. Lycett, Andrew. *Rudyard Kipling.* London: Weisenfeld and Nicolson, 1999. *Something of Myself. An Autobiography.* London: Macmillan, 1937.

Commentary: Rudyard Kipling received the Nobel Prize "in consideration of the power of observation, originality of imagination, and also the manly strength in the art of perception and delineation that characterize the writings of this world-renowned author." Kipling, only 42 years of age, was the first English person to receive the award. The author's early fame and critical acclaim were products of his stories and poems of colonial India. His patriotism and support of British colonialism, however, brought him disapproval and critical dismissal, although his stories remained favorites with the British and with international readers. Kipling's poetry ranged from music hall ballads to serious poems for public occasions (*Recessional*, 1897). His beloved works for children include such titles as *Kim* (1901), *Just So Stories for Little Children* (1902), and *Puck of Pook's Hill* (1906). Kipling is remembered as one of England's greatest short story writers, a genuinely popular poet, and a classic author for children. (A.D.J.)

1908

Eucken, Rudolph Christoph   **189**
Prize: Literature, 1908. *Born:* January 5, 1846; Aurich, Ostfriesland, Germany. *Death:* September 15, 1926; Jena, Germany. *Parents:* Father, Ammo Becker Eucken; Mother, Ida Maria Gitterman Eucken. *Nationality:* German. *Religion:* Freethinker; from Lutheran background. *Education:* Univ. of Göttingen, Germany, Dr. Phil., 1866. *Spouse:* Irene Passow, married 1882. *Children:* Arnold Thomas, son; Walter, son; 1 daughter. *Career:* Germany, Schoolteacher, 1867–71; Univ. of Basel, Switzerland, Professor, 1871–74; Univ. of Jena, Germany, Professor, 1874–1920.

Selected Publications: Geschichte und Kritik der Grundbegriffe der Gegenwart. Leipzig, Germany: Veit & Comp., 1878 (*The Fundamental Concepts of Modern Philosophic Thought.* Tr. by M. Stuart Phelps. New York: Appleton & Co., 1880). *Grundlinien Einer Neuen Lebensanschauung.* Leipzig, Germany: Veit, 1907 (*Life's Basis and Life's Ideal.* Tr. by Alan G. Widgery. London: Black, 1911). *Der Sinn und Wert des Lebens.* Leipzig, Germany: Quelle & Meyer, 1908 (*The Meaning and Value of Life.* Tr. by Lucy Judge Gibson and W.R. Boyce Gibson. London: Black, 1916). *Können Wir Noch Christen Sein?* Leipzig, Germany: Veit, 1911 (*Can We Still Be Christians?* Tr. by Lucy Judge Gibson. New York: Macmillan, 1914). *Ethics and Modern*

Thought: A Theory of Their Relations. New York: Putnam, 1913.

For More Information See: Booth, M. *Rudolph Eucken.* London: T.F. Unwin, 1913. Hermann, Emily. *Eucken and Bergson: Their Significance for Christian Thought.* Boston: Pilgrim Press, 1912. Raeber, Thomas. "Rudolph Christoph Eucken." In *Neue Deutsche Biographie* (Volume 4), 670–72. Berlin: Duncker & Humblot, 1959.

Commentary: Rudolph Eucken did not receive the Nobel Prize for poetry or fiction but "in recognition of his earnest search for truth, his penetrating power of thought, the warmth and strength of presentation with which in his numerous works he has vindicated and developed an idealistic philosophy of life." He diagnosed the malaise of his age as a spiritual confusion and provided a constructive response in his writings. One of his most influential works is *The Meaning and Value of Life.* His philosophy stresses "activism" and spirituality as a creative and renovating force. (S.O.)

1909

Lagerlöf, Selma Ottilian Lovisa   **190**
Prize: Literature, 1909. *Born:* November 20, 1858; Ostra Emtervik, Marbacka Farm, Varmland, Sweden. *Death:* March 16, 1940; Marbacka, Sweden. *Parents:* Father, Erik Gustaf Lagerlöf; Mother, Louisa Elizabeth Wallrock Lagerlöf. *Nationality:* Swedish. *Religion:* Freethinker; from Christian, most probably Lutheran, background. *Education:* Royal Woman's Superior Training College, Sweden, graduate, 1885. *Spouse:* None. *Children:* None. *Career:* Girls' High School, Landskrona, Sweden, Teacher, 1885–95. *Other Awards:* Gold Medal, Swedish Academy, 1904.

Selected Publications: Gösta Berling's Saga. Stockholm: Bonnier, 1891 (*The Story of Gösta Berling.* Tr. by Pauline Flach. Garden City, NY: Doubleday, Page, 1917). *Antikrists Mirakler.* Stockholm: Bonnier, 1897 (*The Miracles of Antichrist.* Tr. by Pauline Flach. Boston: Little, Brown, 1910). *Jerusalem.* Stockholm: Bonnier, 1901–02 (Tr. by Velma Swanston Howard. Garden City, NY: Doubleday, 1915). *Nils Holgerssons underbara Resa Gennom Sverige.* Stockholm: Bonnier, 1906 (*The Wonderful Adventures of Nils.* Tr. by Velma Swanston Howard. Garden City, NY: Doubleday, 1907). *Nils Holgersson 2.* Stockholm: Bonnier, 1907 (*The Further Adventures of Nils.* Tr. by Velma Swanston Howard. New York: Grosset and Dunlap, 1911). *Tosen Från Stormyrtorpet och Andra Sagor.* Göteborg, Sweden: Ahlen and Akerlund, 1908 (*The Girl from the Marsh Croft.* Tr. by Velma Swanston Howard. Boston: Little, Brown and Co., 1912).

For More Information See: The Diary of Selma Lagerlöf. Tr. by Velma Swanston Howard. Garden City, NY: Doubleday, Doran, 1936. Edstrom, Vivi. *Selma Lagerlöf.* Boston: Twayne, 1984. Larsen, Hanna. *Selma Lagerlöf.* New York: Doubleday, Doran, 1936. *Memories of My Childhood.* Tr. by Velma Swanston Howard. Garden City, NY: Doubleday, Doran, 1934. *Something About the Author.* Detroit, MI: Gale, 1979 (Volume 15), 160–74.

Commentary: Selma Lagerlöf won the Nobel Prize "in appreciation of the lofty idealism, vivid imagination, and spiritual perception that characterize her writings." The first woman to win the prize for literature, her works were in contrast to the prevailing Swedish writers' realism of her day. The Swedish educator, novelist, short story writer, poet, biographer, autobiographer, and dramatist was the leading figure in the romantic revival in Swedish literature. (L.B.)

1910

Heyse, Paul Johann Ludwig von   **191**
Prize: Literature, 1910. *Born:* March 15, 1830; Berlin, Germany. *Death:* April 2, 1914; Munich, Germany. *Parents:* Father, Karl Ludwig Heyse; Mother, Julie Saaling Heyse. *Nationality:* German. *Religion:* Protestant and Jewish. *Education:* Univ. of Bonn, Germany, doctorate, 1852. *Spouse:* Margaretha Kugler, married May 15, 1854, died 1862; Anna Schubart, married 1867. *Children:* 3 sons; 3 daughters. *Career:* King Maximilian II of Bavaria, Germany, Court Poet, 1854–1914. *Other Awards:* Schiller Prize, Germany, 1884.

Selected Publications: L'Arrabbiata. Berlin: Hertz, 1853 (*L'Arrabbiata and Other Tales.* Tr. by Mary Wilson. New York: Leypold and Holt, 1867). *Kinder der Welt.* 2 volumes. Berlin: Hertz, 1872 (*Children of the World.* New York: Munro, 1883). *Im Paradiese.* 3 volumes. Berlin: Hertz, 1875 (*In Paradise.* New York: Appleton, 1878). *Der Weinhüter.* In *Novellen.* 7 volumes. Berlin: Hertz, 1882. *Selected Stories.* Chicago: Schick, 1886. *Merlin.* Berlin: Hertz, 1892.

For More Information See: Bianquis, Genevieve. "The Life and Works of Payl Heyse." In *Nobel Prize Library.* New York: Gregory, 1971, 347–53. Brandes, Georg. *Creative Spirits of the Nineteenth Century.* Tr. by Rasmas B. Anderson. New York: Crowell, 1923. *Jugenderinnerungen und Bekenntnisse (Memories of My Youth and Confessions).* Berlin: Hertz, 1900.

Commentary: Paul Heyse's Nobel award was "as a tribute to the consummate artistry, permeated with idealism, which he has demonstrated during his long and productive career as a lyric poet, dramatist, novelist, and writer of world-renowned short stories." He was a prolific writer of novellas, plays, poems, novels, and translated works, as attested to by the 38-volume edition of works completed between 1871 and 1914. Although liberal and progressive, his creative work was in traditional forms considered old-fashioned by the naturalists. He excelled particularly in his tightly constructed novellas and developed this genre to a mastery rarely matched. (S.O.)

1911

Maeterlinck, Mauritius Polydorus Maria
Bernardus (Maeterlinck, Maurice)   **192**
Prize: Literature, 1911. *Born:* August 29, 1862; Ghent, Belgium. *Death:* May 6, 1949; Nice, France. *Parents:* Father, Polydore Maeterlinck; Mother, Mathilde Colette Françoise Van den Bossche Maeterlinck. *Nationality:* Belgian. *Religion:* Agnostic; from Catholic background. *Education:* Jesuit Collége de Sainte-Barbe, Belgium, baccalaureate, 1881; Univ. of Ghent, Belgium, law degree, 1885. *Spouse:* Companion, Georgette Le Blanc, 1895–1918; Renée Dahon, married 1919. *Children:* 1 stillborn child. *Career:* Belgium, Attorney, 1886–89; Writer thereafter. *Other Awards:* Triennial Prize for Dramatic Literature, Belgium, 1891 (refused), 1903; Grand Officer of the Ordre

de Léopold, Belgium, 1920; made Count, 1932; Medal of the Order of St. James of the Sword, Portugal, 1939.

Selected Publications: La Princesse Maleine. Paris: Lacomblez, 1891 (*The Princess Maleine.* Tr. by Gerard Harry. London: W. Heinemann, 1892). *Pelleas et Melisande.* Brussels: P. Lacomblez, 1892 (*Pelleas and Melisanda.* Tr. by Laurence Alma Tadem. London: G. Allen & Unwin, 1915). *Aglavaine et Selysette.* Paris: Societé du Mercure de France, 1896 (*Aglavaine and Selysette: A Drama in Five Acts.* Tr. by Alfred Sutro. London: G. Richards, 1897). *Les Aveugles.* Brussels: Lacomblez, 1897 (*Buried Temple.* Tr. by Alfred Sutro. New York: Dodd, Mead, and Company, 1902). *La Sagesse et la Destinée.* Paris: Bibliothéque-Charpentier, E. Fasquelle, 1898 (*Wisdom and Destiny.* Tr. by Alfred Sutro. Dodd, Mead, and Company, 1898). *Mona Vanna.* Paris: Fasquelle, 1902 (Tr. by Alfred Sutro. London: G. Allen, 1904). *L'oiseau Bleu: Féerie en Cinq Actes et Dix Tableau.* Paris: Charpentier et Fasquelle, 1909 (*The Blue Bird: A Fairy Play in Five Acts.* Tr. by Alexander Teixeira de Mattos. London: Methuen, 1909). *La Vie des Abeilles.* Paris: Charpentier, 1912 (*The Life of the Ant.* Tr. by Bernard Miall. New York: John Day, 1930).

For More Information See: Andrieu, Jean-Marie. *Maeterlinck.* Paris: Éditions Universitaires, 1962. *Encyclopedia of World Literature in the 20th Century.* New York: Ungar Publishing, 1969 (Volume 2), 367–68. Halls, W.D. *Maurice Maeterlinck: A Study of His Life and Thought.* Oxford: Clarendon Press, 1960. Knapp, Bettina. *Maurice Maeterlinck.* Boston: Twayne, 1975.

Commentary: Maurice Maeterlinck received the prize in honor of "his diverse literary activity and especially his dramatic works, which are outstanding for their richness of imagination and for poetic realism, which sometimes in the dim form of the play of legend display a deep intimacy of feeling, and also in a mysterious way appeal to the reader's sentiment and sense of foreboding." Maeterlinck first achieved fame for his symbolist dramas, in which Death seemed triumphant. Late in the 1890s, his works showed a more optimistic attitude, and after 1900, he rejected symbolism, turning to a more realistic style as he wrote of moral and philosophical problems. The Committee's reference to Maeterlinck's diversity also took note of his poems and famous essays such as *Wisdom and Destiny* (1898) and *The Life of the Bees* (1901). (H.L.F.)

1912

Hauptmann, Gerhart Johann   **193**
Prize: Literature, 1912. *Born:* November 15, 1862; Bad Salzbrunn, Silesia, Germany. *Death:* June 8, 1946; Agnetendorf, Silesia, Germany. *Parents:* Father, Robert Hauptmann; Mother, Marie Straehler Hauptmann. *Nationality:* German. *Religion:* Rejected organized Christianity; from Protestant background. *Education:* No college degrees. *Spouse:* Marie Thienemann, married 1885, divorced 1895; Margarete Marschalk, married 1904. *Children:* Ivo, son; Eckart, son; Klaus, son; Bonvenuto, son. *Career:* Germany, Sculptor and Writer. *Other Awards:* Gullparzer Prize, Austria, 1896, 1898, 1900; Pour Le Mérite, Peace, 1924; Goethe Prize, 1932.

Selected Publications: Vor Sonnenaufgang. Berlin: Fischer, 1889 (*Before Sunrise.* Tr. by James Joyce. San

Marino, CA: Huntington Library, 1978). *Die Weber.* Berlin: Fischer, 1892 (*The Weavers.* Tr. by Mary Morison. New York: Huebsch, 1911). *Der Biberpelz, eine Diebskomödie.* Berlin: Fischer, 1893 (*The Beaver Coat: A Thieves' Comedy.* Tr. by Ludwig Lewisohn. In *Contemporary Drama: European Plays.* Ed. by E.B. Watson. New York, 1931). *Der Narr in Christo Emanuel Quint.* Berlin: Fischer, 1910 (*The Fool in Christ: Emanuel Quint.* Tr. by T. Seltzer. New York: Viking, 1926). *Die Ratten: Berliner Tragikomödie.* Berlin: Fischer, 1911 (*The Rats.* Tr. by Ludwig Lewisohn. In *Modern Continental Plays.* Ed. by S.M. Tucker. New York: Harper & Bros., 1929, 415–68). *The Dramatic Works.* 7 volumes. New York: Huebsch, 1912–17. *Der Ketzer von Soana.* Berlin: Fischer, 1918 (*The Heretic of Soana.* Tr. by Bayard Quincy Morgan. 2d ed. London: Calder, 1960). *Die Atriden-Tetralogie.* Berlin: Suhrkamp, 1949. *Three Plays: The Weavers, Hannele, the Beavercoat.* Tr. by Horst Frenz and Miles Waggoner. New York: Ungar, 1977.

For More Information See: Behl, Carl Fr. Wm. *Gerhart Hauptmann: His Life and Works.* Tr. by Helen Taubert. Würzburg: Holzner, 1956. *Encyclopedia of World Biography.* New York: McGraw-Hill, 1973, 135–37. Garten, Hugh F. *Gerhart Hauptmann.* New Haven, CT: Yale Univ. Press, 1954. Maurer, Warren R. *Gerhart Hauptmann.* Boston: Hall, 1982. Maurer, W. *Understanding Gerhart Hauptmann.* Columbia, SC: Univ. of South Carolina Press, 1992. *Twentieth Century Authors.* New York: H.W. Wilson, 1942, 625–27. Mellen, P. *Gerhart Hauptmann.* New York: P. Lang, 1983.

Commentary: Gerhart Hauptmann was awarded the Nobel Prize "primarily in recognition of his fruitful, varied, and outstanding production in the realm of dramatic art." At that time he was famous internationally for his naturalist plays, which voice a strong social compassion. Later works reflect his lifelong preoccupation with religious studies, philosophy, and ancient Greece. (S.O.)

1913

Tagore, Rabindranath, Sir (Thakura, Ravindranatha)   194

Prize: Literature, 1913. *Born:* May 7, 1861; Calcutta, India. *Death:* August 7, 1941; Calcutta, India. *Parents:* Father, Debendranath Marashi; Mother, Sarada Devi. *Nationality:* Indian. *Religion:* "Pirali" Brahmin. *Education:* No college degrees. *Spouse:* Bhavatarini Benimadhav Raichaudhuri, married 1936. *Children:* Madhurilata, daughter; Rathindranath, son; 1 other son. *Career:* Writer, Poet, Landowner, and Activist. *Other Awards:* Knighthood, 1915.

Selected Publications: Gitanjali (Song Offerings). London: The India Society, 1912. *The Gardener.* London: Macmillan, 1913. *Glimpses of Bengal Life.* Tr. by Rajani Ranjan. Madras, India: G.A. Natesan, 1913. *Sadhana (Essays and Lectures).* London: Macmillan, 1913. *The King of the Dark Chamber.* Tr. by K.C. Sen. London: Macmillan, 1914. *The Fugitive.* Sankiniketan, India: Sankiniketan Press, 1919. *Gora.* Tr. by W.W. Pearson. London: Macmillan, 1924. *The Child.* London: Allen & Unwin, 1931. *The Religion of Man.* London: Allen & Unwin, 1931. *Collected Poems and Plays of Rabindranath Tagore.* London: Macmillan, 1936. *Farewell, My Friend.* Tr. by Krishna Kripalani. London: The New India Publishing Co., 1946. *A Flight of Swans.* Tr. by Aurobindo Bose. London: John Murray, 1955. *Letters from Russia.* Tr. by Sasadhar Sinha. Calcutta: Visva-Bharati, 1960.

For More Information See: Gnatyuk, D. *Tagore, India and the Soviet Union.* Columbia, MO: South Asia Books, 1986. Kripalani, Krishna. *Rabindranath Tagore: A Biography.* New York: Grove Press, 1962. *My Boyhood Days* (autobiography). Tr. by Marjorie Sykes. Sankiniketan, India: Visva-Bharati, 1940. Sykes, Marjorie. *Rabindranath Tagore.* London: Longmans, 1947. Thomson, Edward John. *Rabindranath Tagore: His Life and Works.* New York: Haskell House, 1974. *Twentieth Century Authors.* New York: H.W. Wilson, 1942, 1381–82.

Commentary: Rabindranath Tagore received the Nobel "because of his profoundly sensitive, fresh and beautiful verse, by which, with consummate skill, he has made his poetic thought, expressed in his own English words, a part of the literature of the West." Although noted for his poetry, because of its "rhythmically balanced style" and "taste in the choice of words," Tagore was also an accomplished playwright, novelist, short-story writer, essayist, musician, and artist. In all his output, he displayed the wisdom and religious mysticism of his Indian background. Tagore was also well known as an educator and a politician. (J.H.S.)

1915

Rolland, Romain (Saint Just)   195

Prize: Literature, 1915. *Born:* January 29, 1866; Clamecy, Nievre, France. *Death:* December 30, 1944; Vezelay, France. *Parents:* Father, Romain Edmé Paul Émile Rolland; Mother, Antoinette Marie Courot Rolland. *Nationality:* French. *Religion:* Catholic. *Education:* École Normale, France, Agrégation d'histoire, 1889; École Française d'Archéologie, Italy, Docteur-ès-Lettres, 1895. *Spouse:* Clotilde Bréal, married October 31, 1892, divorced May 1901; Veuve Marie Koudachev, married 1934. *Children:* None. *Career:* École Normale Superieure, Paris, France, Professor, 1895–1900; Sorbonne, Paris, France, Professor, 1900–12. *Other Awards:* Grand Prix, French Academy, 1913; Goethe Medal, Germany, 1933 (refused).

Selected Publications: Les Loups. Paris: Albin Michel, 1898 (*The Wolves.* Tr. by Barrett H. Clark. New York: Random House, 1937). *Le Quatorze Juillet.* Paris: Cahier de la Quinzaine, 1902 (*The Fourteenth of July.* Tr. by Barrett H. Clark. New York: H. Holt and Company, 1918). *Beethoven.* Paris: Fischbacher, 1903 (*Beethoven.* Tr. by B. Constance Hull. New York: H. Holt and Company, 1917). *Le Théâtre du Peuple.* Paris: Suresnes, 1903 (*The People's Theatre.* Tr. by Barrett H. Clark. New York: H. Holt and Company, 1918). *Jean-Christopher.* 10 volumes. Paris: Ollendorff, 1904–12 (Tr. by Gilbert Cannan. New York: H. Holt and Company, 1910–13). *Michel-Ange.* Paris: Librairie Plon, 1906. *Danton.* Paris: Librairie Ollendorff, 1909 (*Danton.* Tr. by Katherine Miller. New York: H. Holt and Company, 1919). *Colas Breugnon.* Paris: Albin Michel, 1918 (*Colas Breugnon.* Tr. by Katherine Miller. New York: H. Holt and Company, 1919).

For More Information See: Francis, R.A. *Romain Rolland.* Oxford: Berg, 1999. Starr, William. *Romain Rolland.* Paris: Hague, 1971. Zweig, Stefan. *Romain Rolland.* New

York: Haskell, 1970. Zweig, Stefan. *Romain Rolland: The Man and His Works.* Salem, NH: Ayer Co., 1973.

Commentary: The citation to Romain Rolland noted "a tribute to the lofty idealism of his literary production and to the sympathy and love of truth with which he has described different types of human beings." His backgrounds in history, literature, and music produced writing of noteworthy character in all three fields, especially the biographical material on such greats as Handel, Beethoven, Michelangelo, Gandhi, and Tolstoi. The same background helped to produce his most memorable work, *Jean Christophe.* In addition, Rolland was involved in theater and in a lifelong quest for peace among nations. (P.K.)

1916

Von Heidenstam, Carl Gustaf Verner 196

Prize: Literature, 1916. *Born:* July 6, 1859; Olshammer, Sweden. *Death:* May 20, 1940; Övralid, Sweden. *Parents:* Father, Nils Gustaf von Heidenstam; Mother, Magdalena Rytterskjöld von Heidenstam. *Nationality:* Swedish. *Religion:* Atheist; from Christian background. *Education:* No college degrees. *Spouse:* Emilia Uggla, married 1880, died 1883; Oldj Wiberg, married 1886, divorced 1888; Greta Sjoberg, married 1889. *Children:* None. *Career:* Writer. *Other Awards:* Henrik Steffens Prize, 1938.

Selected Publications: Valfart Och Vandringsår (Pilgrimage: The Wander Years). Stockholm: A. Bonnier, 1888. *Endymion.* Stockholm: F. Hegel & Son, 1889. *Renassans.* Stockholm: A. Bonnier, 1889. *Hans Alienus.* Stockholm: A. Bonnier, 1892. *Dikter (Poems).* Stockholm: A. Bonnier, 1895. *Karolinerna Berattelser.* Stockholm: A. Bonnier, 1897–98 (*The Charles Men.* Tr. by Charles W. Stork. New York: American Scandinavian Foundation, 1920). *Sankt Goran Och Drahen (Saint George and the Dragon).* Stockholm: A. Bonnier, 1900. *Heliga Birgittas Pilgrimsfard (Saint Bridget's Pilgrimage).* Stockholm: A. Bonnier, 1901. *Ett Folk (One People).* Stockholm: A. Bonnier, 1902. *Folkungatradet. Folke Filbyter Berattelse.* Stockholm: A. Bonnier, 1905 (*The Tree of the Folkungs.* Tr. by Arthur G. Chater. London: Glydendal, 1925). *Folkungatradet Bjalboarfvet (The Bjalbo Inheritance).* Stockholm: A. Bonnier, 1907. *Svenskarna Och Deras Havdingar.* Stockholm: A. Bonnier, 1908–10 (*The Swedes and Their Chieftains.* Tr. by Charles W. Stork. New York: American Scandinavian Foundation, 1925). *Nya Dikter (New Poems).* Stockholm: A. Bonnier, 1915.

For More Information See: Cyclopedia of World Authors. New York: Harper and Row, 1958, 495–96. Gustafson, Alrik. *History of Swedish Literature.* Minneapolis, MN: Univ. of Minneapolis Press, 1961. *Twentieth Century Authors.* New York: H.W. Wilson, 1942, 663–64.

Commentary: Verner von Heidenstam was the recipient of the Nobel Prize "in recognition of his significance as the leading representative of a new era in our literature." Von Heidenstam broke with the Swedish realistic school of gloomy poetry and prose and, using his studies of painting and interest in travel as the source, produced a literature of explosive beauty, filled with an enjoyment of life and of the Swedish countryside and history. As noted in the Nobel presentation, he is "a manly poet and a master of the lyric genre." (J.H.S.)

1917

Gjellerup, Karl Adolph (Epigonos) 197

Prize: Literature, 1917. *Born:* June 2, 1857; Praestö, Roholte, Denmark. *Death:* October 13, 1919; Klotzsche, Germany. *Parents:* Father, Ryde Carl Adolph Gjellerup; Mother, Anna Johanne Fibiger Gjellerup. *Nationality:* Danish. *Religion:* Atheist; from Lutheran background. *Education:* Univ. of Copenhagen, Denmark, B.D., 1878. *Spouse:* Eugenia Anna Caroline Heusinger, married 1887. *Children:* None. *Career:* Writer. *Other Awards:* Poet's Pension, Denmark, 1889.

Selected Publications: En Idealist (An Idealist). Copenhagen: R.A. Reitzel, 1878. *Germanerness Loerling (The Teuton's Apprentice).* Copenhagen: A. Schau, 1882. *Brynhild.* Copenhagen: A. Schau, 1884. *Minna.* Copenhagen: P.G. Philipsens, 1889 (Tr. by C.L. Nielsen. London: W. Heinemann, 1913). *Mollen (The Mill).* Copenhagen: Gyldendal, 1896. *Pilgrimmen Kamanita.* Copenhagen: Gyldendal, 1906 (*The Pilgrim Kamanita.* Tr. by John Logie. London: W. Heinemann, 1911). *Den Fuldentes Husfru (The Wife of the Perfect One).* Copenhagen: Glydendalske Boghandel, 1907. *Verdens Vandrerne (World Wanderers).* Copenhagen: Gyldendal, 1910.

For More Information See: European Authors, 1000–1900. New York: H.W. Wilson, 1967, 330–31. *Karl Gjellerup, Der Dichter und Denker; sein Leben in Selbstzeugnissen und Briefen.* Leipzig, Germany: Quelle and Meyer, 1923. Nørregård, Georg. *Karl Gjellerup: en biografi.* Copenhagen: C.A. Reitzelsforlag, 1988.

Commentary: Karl Gjellerup became a Nobel laureate "for his many-sided, rich and inspired writing with high ideals." He is typical of late-nineteenth-century writers trying to discover meaning in a life without Christianity, turning first to an artistic defense of atheism and naturalism, and later developing a more humanistic and idealistic vision. Gjellerup moved from Lutheran to atheist/naturalist to Buddhism and mystical Christianity. Few of his works were translated and he has been considered by some undeservedly forgotten, by others "the dullest writer of the century." (M.F.L.)

Pontoppidan, Henrik 198

Prize: Literature, 1917. *Born:* July 24, 1857; Frederica, Jutland, Denmark. *Death:* August 21, 1943; Charlottenlund, Denmark. *Parents:* Father, Dines Pontoppidan; Mother, M. Marie Kirstina Oxenboll Pontoppidan. *Nationality:* Danish. *Religion:* Freethinker; from Lutheran background. *Education:* No college degrees. *Spouse:* Mette Marie Hansen, married December 1881, divorced 1892; Antoinette Cecilia Kofoed, married April 9, 1892. *Children:* None. *Career:* Folk High School, Denmark, Teacher, 1879–82.

Selected Publications: Stalkkede Vinger (Clipped Wings). Copenhagen: Andr. Schous Forlag, 1881. *Spogelser (Ghosts).* Copenhagen: Gyldendalske Boghandel Forlag, 1888. *Skyer (Clouds).* Copenhagen: Gyldendalske Boghandel Forlag, 1890. *Det Forjaettede Land.* Copenhagen: Philipsen, 1892 (*The Promised Land.* Tr. by Ms. Edgar Lucas. London: J.M. Dent, 1896). *Emmanuel.* Tr. by Mrs. Edgar Lucas. London: J.M. Dent, 1896. *Lykke-Per (Lucky Peter).* Copenhagen: Det Nordiske Forlag, 1898–1904. *Kjobenhavn Kristiania.* Copenhagen: Gyldendalske Bohgandel Forlag, 1907. *De Dodes Rige (The Kingdom of the Dead).* Copenhagen: Gyldendalske

Boghandel, 1917. *Mand's Himmerig* (*Man's Heaven*). Copenhagen: Hyldendal, Norkiske Forlag, 1927.

For More Information See: Masterplots Cyclopedia of World Authors. New York: Salem Press, 1958, 852–53. Mitchell, P. *Henrik Pontoppidan.* Boston: Twayne, 1984.

Commentary: Henrik Pontoppidan received the Nobel Prize "for his profuse descriptions of Danish life of today" and is recognized as the classic Danish novelist, especially for his trilogy of *The Promised Land,* which dealt with Danish life in the countryside; *Lucky Peter,* which treated Danish life in Copenhagen; and *The Kingdom of the Dead,* a pessimistic social novel of Danish life in the early twentieth century. Beginning as a naturalist, he ended as a philosophical and psychological novelist searching for enduring values. (C.R.L.)

1918

Karlfeldt, Erik Axel   **199**

Prize: Literature, 1918 (refused); Literature, 1931 [SEE REF] (posthumous). *Born:* July 20, 1864; Folkarna, Sweden. *Death:* April 8, 1931; Stockholm, Sweden. *Parents:* Father, Erik Erikson Janson; Mother, Anna Stina Jansdotter. *Nationality:* Swedish. *Religion:* Lutheran. *Education:* Univ. of Uppsala, Sweden, licentiate, 1898. *Spouse:* Gerda Holmberg, married 1916. *Children:* 2 daughters. *Career:* Djursholm Grammar School, Teacher, 1893–96; Stockholm, Sweden, Newspaper Reporter, 1896–98; Royal Library, Stockholm, Sweden, Librarian, 1898–1903; Agricultural Academy, Sweden, Librarian, 1903–05.

Selected Publications: Vidmarks och Karlekvisor. Stockholm: J. Seligman, 1906. *Flora och Pomona.* Stockholm: Wahlstrom & Widstrand, 1906. *Fridolins Visor och Andra Dikter.* Stockholm: Wahlstrom & Widstrand, 1914. *Flora och Bellona; Dikter.* Stockholm: Wahlstrom & Widstrand, 1918. *Hosthorn; Dikter.* Stockholm: Wahlstrom & Widstrand, 1927.

For More Information See: Columbia Dictionary of Modern European Literature. New York: Columbia Univ. Press, 1947, 436–37. Gustafson, Alrik. *A History of Swedish Literature.* Minneapolis, MN: Univ. of Minnesota Press, 1961. *Twentieth Century Authors.* New York: H.W. Wilson, 1942, 746.

Commentary: Erik Karlfeldt won the prize in 1918, but refused it, instead devoting himself to the affairs of the Academy as member and secretary from 1904 until his death. He was awarded a second prize posthumously in 1931 for his body of poetry. The presentation talked about representing " . . . our character with a style and a genuineness that we should like to be ours . . . " and about singing " . . . with singular power and exquisite charm of the tradition of our people. . . . " (P.K.)

1919

Spitteler, Carl Friedrich Georg (Felix Tan'-dem)   **200**

Prize: Literature, 1919. *Born:* April 24, 1845; Liesthal, Switzerland. *Death:* December 28, 1924; Lucerne, Switzerland. *Parents:* Father, Carl Spitteler; Mother, Anna Dorothea Brodbeck. *Nationality:* Swiss. *Religion:* Rejected doctrine; from Protestant background. *Education:* Univ. of Basel,

Switzerland, theology degree, 1870. *Spouse:* Marie Oden Hooff, married 1883. *Children:* 2 daughters. *Career:* Saint Petersburg, Russia, Private Tutor, 1871–79; Neuveville Schools, Berne, Switzerland, Teacher, 1881–85; *Grenzpost,* Basel, Switzerland, Reporter, 1885–86; *Neue Zurcher Zeitung,* Reporter, 1890–92.

Selected Publications: Lachende Wahrheiten. Leipzig, Germany: E. Diederichs, 1898 (*Laughing Truths.* Tr. by James F. Muirhead. New York: G.P. Putnam's Sons, 1927). *Der Olympischer Frühling* (*Olympian Spring*). Leipzig, Germany: E. Diederichs, 1900–05. *Glockenlieder* (*Bell Songs*). Jena, Germany: E. Diederichs, 1906. *Imago.* Jena, Germany: E. Diederichs, 1906. *Prometheus und Epimetheus.* Jena, Germany: E. Diederichs, 1906 (*Prometheus and Epimetheus.* Tr. by James F. Muirhead. New York: Scribner's, 1931). *Die Madchenfeinde.* Jena, Germany: E. Diederichs, 1907 (*Two Little Misogynists.* Tr. by Mme. la Vicomtesse Le Roquette-Buisson. New York: H. Hold, 1922). *Meine Fruhesten Erlebnisse* (*My Earliest Experiences*). Jena, Germany: E. Diederichs, 1914. *Prometheus der Dulder.* Jena, Germany: E. Diederichs, 1924.

For More Information See: Boesche, A. *The Life and Works of Carl Spitteler.* Albany, NY: J.B. Lyon, 1913–14. "Carl Spitteler." *The London Mercury* 16 (1927): 53–61. *Columbia Dictionary of Modern European Literature.* New York: Columbia Univ. Press, 1947, 775–76.

Commentary: Carl Spitteler was awarded the Nobel Prize "in special appreciation of his epic, *Olympischer Frühling.*" It was compared to the writings of Homer and to *Faust* by the presenter. Spitteler's work is notable for its blend of idealistic hope in the individual and pessimistic view of the world as a whole. (C.C. and J.H.S.)

1920

Hamsun, Knut (Hamsund, Knud Pedersen)   **201**

Prize: Literature, 1920. *Born:* August 4, 1859; Lom, Norway. *Death:* February 19, 1952; Nörholmen, Norway. *Parents:* Father, Peder Pedersen Hamsund; Mother, Tora Olsdatter Garmostraeet Hamsund. *Nationality:* Norwegian. *Religion:* Rejected organized Christianity; from Lutheran background. *Education:* No college degrees. *Spouse:* Bergljot Beck, married 1898, divorced 1906; Marie Andersen, married 1908. *Children:* Victoria, daughter; Arild, son; Tore, son; Ellinor, daughter; Cecilia, daughter. *Career:* World Traveler early in life; Farmer and Writer in adult life. *Other Awards:* Goethe Prize, 1934 (accepted medal, refused money).

Selected Publications: Sult. Copenhagen: Jörgensen, 1890 (*Hunger.* Tr. by George Egerton. London: Smithers, 1899). *Pan.* Copenhagen: Philipsen, 1894 (*Pan.* Tr. by W.W. Worster. London: Gyldendal, 1920). *Victoria, en Kaerligheds Historie.* Kristiania: Cammermeyer, 1898 (*Victoria: A Love Story.* Tr. by Oliver Stallybrass. New York: Farrar, Straus & Giroux, 1969). *Markens Gröde.* Kristiania: Gyldendal, 1920 (*Growth of the Soil.* Tr. by W.W. Worster. New York: Knopf, 1923). *Landstrykere.* Oslo: Gyldendal, 1927 (*Wayfarers.* Tr. by James McFarlane. New York: Farrar, Straus & Giroux, 1980). *August.* Oslo: Gyldendal, 1930 (*August.* Tr. by Eugene Gay-Tifft. New York: Coward-McCann, 1931). *Men livet lever.* Oslo: Gyldendal, 1933 (*The Road Leads On.* Tr. by Eugene Gay-Tifft. New York: Coward-McCann, 1934).

For More Information See: Buttry, Dolores. "Knut Hamsun: A Scandinavian Rousseau." Ph.D. diss. Univ. of Illinois at Urbana-Champaign, 1978. Ferguson, Robert. *Enigma: The Life of Knut Hamsun.* New York: Farrar, Straus & Giroux, 1987. Ostby, Arvid. *Knut Hamsun: En bibliografi.* Oslo: Gyldendal, 1972. Naess, Harald. *Knut Hamsun.* Boston: Twayne, 1984. *Paa gjengrodde stier.* Oslo: Gyldendal, 1949 (Memoirs) (*On Overgrown Paths.* Tr. by Carl L. Anderson. New York: Paul Ericksson, 1967).

Commentary: Knut Hamsun received the Nobel Award "for his monumental work, *Growth of the Soil*," which depicted an archetypal pioneer farmer, the love of nature, and the simple life. His output of poetry, short stories, and novels reflects his development from a restless vagabond to farmer and family man. Because of his reverence for everything German, his countrymen's admiration for him cooled after the Nazi occupation of Norway. He remains more respected abroad than in his home country. (S.O.)

1921

France, Anatole (Thibault, Jacques Anatole-François) 202

Prize: Literature, 1921. *Born:* April 16, 1844; Paris, France. *Death:* October 12, 1924; La Bechéllerie, France. *Parents:* Father, François-Noël Thibault; Mother, Antoinette Gallas Thibault. *Nationality:* French. *Religion:* "Neo-pagan"; from Catholic background. *Education:* Collège Stanislas, France, baccalauréat, 1864. *Spouse:* Marie-Valérie Guérin de Sauville, married April 28, 1877, divorced August 3, 1893; Leontine Arman de Caillavet, lived with, 1888–1910; Marie-Héloïse Laprévotte, married 1920. *Children:* Suzanne, daughter. *Career:* Bibliothéque du Sénat, Librarian, 1876–90; France, Free-lance Journalist, 1862–77; *Le Temps*, Editor, 1888.

Selected Publications: Le Crime de Sylvestre Bonnard, membre de l'Institute. Paris: Calmann-Lévy, 1881 (*Crime of Sylvester Bonnard.* Tr. by Lafcadio Hearn. New York: Dodd-Mead, 1918). *Thais.* Paris: Calmann-Lévy, 1890 (*Thais.* Tr. by Robert Douglas. New York: Macmillan, 1929). *L'Étui de Nacre.* Paris: Calmann-Lévy, 1892 (*The Mother of Pearl.* Tr. by Frederic Chapman. London: John Lane, 1908). *La Rotisserie de la Reine Pedauque.* Paris: Calmann-Lévy, 1893 (*At the Sign of the Reine Pedauque.* Tr. by Wilfred Jackson, London: John Lane, 1912). *Le Lys Rouge.* Paris: Calmann-Lévy, 1899 (*The Red Lily.* Tr. by Wilfred Stephens. London: John Lane Company, 1912). *Sur la Pièrre Blanche.* Paris: Calmann-Lévy, c 1900 (*The White Stone.* Tr. by Charles E. Roche. London: John Lane, 1909–23). *L'île des Pinqouins.* Paris: Calmann-Lévy, 1908 (*Penquin Island.* Tr. by A.W. Evans. New York: Grosset & Dunlap, 1909). *Les Dieux ont Soif.* New York: Macmillan; Paris: Calmann-Lévy, 1912 (*The Gods are Athirst.* Tr. by Alfred Allison. London: John Lane, 1913). *La Revolte des Anges.* Paris: Calmann-Lévy, 1914 (*The Revolt of the Angels.* Tr. by Mrs. Wilfred Jackson. New York: John Lane, 1914). *Histoire Contémporaine.* Paris: Calmann-Lévy, 1920–21. *La Vie en Fleur.* Paris: Calmann-Lévy, 1922 (*The Bloom of Life.* Tr. by James Lewis May. New York: Dodd, Mead & Co., n.d.). *Works of Anatole France in English Translation.* Ed. by Frederic Chapman. 39 volumes. New York: John Lane Co., 1928.

For More Information See: Axelrad, Jacob. *Anatole France: A Life Without Illusions, 1844–1924.* New York: Harper, 1944. Dargan, Edwin Preston. *Anatole France (1844–1896).* New York: Oxford Univ. Press, 1937. Jefferson, Carter. *Anatole France: The Politics of Skepticism.* New Brunswick, NJ: Rutgers Univ. Press, 1965. Sareil, Jean. *Anatole France et Voltaire.* Geneva: Droz, 1961. Tylden-Wright, David. *Anatole France.* New York: Walker & Co., 1967. Virtanen, Reino. *Anatole France.* New York: Twayne, 1968.

Commentary: The award to Anatole France was given "in recognition of his splendid activity as an author—an activity marked by noble style, large hearted humanity, charm and French spirit." This activity covered a span of more than five decades, from publication of his first book, *Alfred de Vigny*, in 1868, to *La Vie en Fleur*, in 1922. During this period France labored as novelist, critic, reviewer, essayist, and editor. In this diverse work he displayed a rich erudition, a subtle irony, and a constant strain of skepticism. By the end of the 1890s, he was the leading French literary figure. Within a few years after his death, however, there was a reaction against his work—partly literary, partly political—from which his reputation has never recovered. As one scholar puts it: He "offers an interesting case of great fame followed by abrupt decline." (G.K.)

1922

Benavente y Martinez, Jacinto 203

Prize: Literature, 1922. *Born:* August 12, 1866; Madrid, Spain. *Death:* July 14, 1954; Madrid, Spain. *Parents:* Father, Mariano Benavente y Gonzáles; Mother, Venancia Martinez. *Nationality:* Spanish. *Religion:* Catholic. *Education:* No college degrees. *Spouse:* None. *Children:* None. *Career:* Writer, Editor, Theatrical Worker. *Other Awards:* Gran Cruz de Alphonso XIII, Spain, 1923.

Selected Publications: El Nido Ajeno (The Intruder). (Premiered October 6, 1894). *La Noche del Sabado.* Barcelona: Editorial Cisne, 1903 (*Saturday Night.* Tr. by John Garrett Underhill. Boston: R.G. Badger, 1918). *Los Intereses Creados (Bonds of Interest).* (Premiered December 9, 1907). In *Los Intereses Creados.* Madrid: Anaya, 1965, 5–28. *Senora Ama (The Lady of the House).* (Premiered February 22, 1908). *La Fuerza Brutta.* Barcelona: Teatralia, 1909 (*Brute Force.* Tr. by John Garrett Underhill. New York: S. French, 1935). *El Principe Que Todo Lo Aprendio en Los Libros.* San Juan: Editorial Teresa Martinez, 1909 (*The Prince Who Learned Everything Out of Books.* Tr. by John Garrett Underhill. Boston: R.G. Badger, 1919). *La Malquerida (The Ill-Beloved).* (Premiered December 12, 1913). *Pepa Doncel (Don Juan's Servant).* Madrid: Hernando, 1928. *La Honradez de la Cerradura (The Secret of the Keyhole).* Buenos Aires: Espasa-Calpe Argentina, 1943. *Su Amante Esposa (An Enchanted Hour).* Madrid: Aguilar, 1951.

For More Information See: Encyclopedia of World Literature. Englewood Cliffs, NJ: Salem Press, 1958 (Volume 1), 117–18. Penuelas, Marcelino. *Jacinto Benavente.* Tr. by Kay Engler. New York: Twayne, 1968. Starkie, Walter. *Jacinto Benavente.* New York: H. Milford, 1982.

Commentary: The Nobel Prize was awarded to Jacinto Benavente y Martinez for "the talent that he has shown, as a continuator of the illustrious traditions of Spanish drama."

Essayist and literary critic, Benavente is best remembered for his theatre, throughout which the theme of love is most important. In his vast and productive literary life, his preoccupation was to show that love was the definitive and certain way to reach sincere kindness, truth, and justice. His best and most popular plays, *The Bonds of Interest* (1907), *The Lady of the House* (1908), and *The Passion Flower* (1913), attest to this goal. (F.R.P.)

1923

Yeats, William Butler   **204**
Prize: Literature, 1923. *Born:* June 13, 1865; Dublin, Ireland. *Death:* January 28, 1939; Cap Martin, France. *Parents:* Father, John Butler Yeats; Mother, Susan Pollexfen Yeats. *Nationality:* Irish. *Religion:* Anti-religious; from Protestant (Church of Ireland) background. *Education:* No college degrees. *Spouse:* Georgie Hyde-Lees, married October 21, 1917. *Children:* Ann Butler, daughter; Michael, son. *Career: Beltaine*, Editor, 1899–1900; *Samhain*, Editor, 1901–08; *The Arrow*, Editor, 1908–09; Abbey Theatre, Dublin, Ireland, Director, 1904–39. *Other Awards:* Royal Academy Prize, 1899; Knighthood, 1915 (refused).

Selected Publications: The Celtic Twilight. Men and Women, Ghouls and Faeries. London: Lawrence and Bullen, 1893. *The Wind among the Reeds.* London: John Lane, 1899. *The Collected Works.* 8 volumes. London: Chapman & Hall, 1908. *Responsibilities, and Other Poems.* London: Macmillan and Co., 1916. *Essays.* London: Macmillan and Co., 1924. *The Tower.* London: Macmillan and Co., 1928. *The Winding Stair.* New York: The Foundation Press, 1929. *The Collected Poems.* London: Macmillan and Co., 1933. *The Collected Plays.* London: Macmillan and Co., 1934. *Last Poems and Plays.* London: Macmillan and Co., 1940.

For More Information See: Cowell, Raymond. *W.B. Yeats.* New York: Arco, 1970. Donoghue, D. *William Butler Yeats.* New York: Ecco, 1989. Ellman, Richard. *Yeats: The Man and the Masks.* New York: Norton, 1948. Jeffares, Alexander. *W.B. Yeats: Man and Poet.* New York: Barnes and Noble, 1966. Ronsley, J. *Yeats' Autobiography: Life as a Symbolic Pattern.* Cambridge, MA: Harvard Univ. Press, 1968. *W. B. Yeats.* New York: St. Martin's Press, 1995.

Commentary: William Butler Yeats received the Nobel Prize "for his consistently emotional poetry, which in the strictest artistic form expresses a people's spirit." He went on to become what many critics consider the most important poet of the twentieth century, integrating into his poetry and plays lifelong concerns with theosophy, symbolism, Irish folklore, the Irish cause, and occultism. His contributions extended to development of the arts and to personal involvement in the politics of the Irish cause. (L.P.)

1924

Reymont, Wladyslaw Stanislaw (Rejment, Wladyslaw Stanislaw)   **205**
Prize: Literature, 1924. *Born:* May 7, 1867; Kobiele Weilkie, Poland. *Death:* December 5, 1925; Warsaw, Poland. *Parents:* Father, Jozef Rejment; Mother, Antonia Kupcynska Rejment. *Nationality:* Polish. *Religion:* Catholic. *Education:* No college degrees. *Spouse:* None. *Children:* None. *Career:* Writer.

Selected Publications: The Commedienne. Tr. by Edmund Obecny. New York: G.P. Putman's Sons, 1920. *The Peasants.* Tr. by Michael H. Dziewicki. 4 volumes. New York: Knopf, 1924–25. *The Promised Land.* Tr. by Michael H. Dziewicki. 2 volumes. New York: Knopf, 1927.

For More Information See: Columbia Dictionary of Modern European Literature. New York: Columbia Press, 1947, 671–72. Krzyzanowski, Jerzy K. *Wladyslaw Stanislaw Reymont.* New York: Twayne, 1972.

Commentary: Wladyslaw Reymont received the Nobel Prize "for his great national epic, *The Peasants*," which described in imaginative form the rural life and landscape of Poland. His early work was naturalistic and gradually developed into the blend of realism and symbolism that characterized *The Peasants* and later work. (J.H.S.)

1925

Shaw, George Bernard   **206**
Prize: Literature, 1925. *Born:* July 26, 1856; Dublin, Ireland. *Death:* November 2, 1950; Hertfordshire, England. *Parents:* Father, George Carr Shaw; Mother, Elizabeth Gurly Shaw. *Nationality:* Irish. *Religion:* Antifundamentalist; from Christian background. *Education:* No college degrees. *Spouse:* Charlotte Payne-Townshend, married 1898. *Children:* None. *Career:* Edison Telephone Company, London, England, Clerk, 1879–80; *Star*, Critic, 1888–90; *The World*, Critic, 1890–94; *Saturday Review*, Critic, 1895–98; Writer. *Other Awards:* Order of Merit (refused).

Selected Publications: Widowers' Houses: A Comedy. London: Henry, 1893. *The Devil's Disciple: A Melodrama in Three Acts.* London: Grant Richards, 1901. *Mrs. Warren's Profession: A Play in Four Acts.* London: Grant Richards, 1902. *Man and Superman.* Cambridge, MA: The University Press, 1903. *Arms and the Man: A Pleasant Play.* New York: Brentano's, 1905. *Caesar and Cleopatra: A History.* London: Constable, 1905. *Candida: A Mystery.* London: Constable, 1905. *The Philanderer: An Unpleasant Play.* New York: Brentano's, 1905. *Captain Brassbound's Conversion: An Adventure.* London: Constable, 1906. *Major Barbara.* New York: Brentano's, 1907. *The Doctor's Dilemma.* New York: Brentano's, 1911. *Pygmalion: A Play in Five Acts.* London: Constable, 1912. *Heartbreak House.* Leipzig, Germany: Tauchnitz, 1921. *Back to Methuselah: A Metabiological Pentateuch.* London: Constable, 1921. *The Apple Cart: A Political Extravaganza.* London: Constable, 1930. *The Political Madhouse in America and Nearer Home: A Lecture.* London: Constable, 1933.

For More Information See: Chappelow, Allan. *Shaw the Villager and Human Being: A Biographical Symposium.* New York: Macmillan, 1962. *G.B. Shaw: An Annotated Bibliograpy of Writings about Him.* J.P. Wearing, ed. De Kalb, IL: Northern Illinois Univ. Press, 1986–87. Harris, Frank. *Bernard Shaw.* Garden City, NY: Garden City Publishing Company, Inc., 1931. Henderson, Archibald. *George Bernard Shaw: Man of the Century.* New York: Appleton-Century Crofts, 1956. Holroyd, M. *Bernard Shaw.* New York: Random House, 1988–92.

Commentary: George Bernard Shaw was the Nobel recipient "for his work which is marked by both idealism and humanity, its stimulating satire often being infused with a singular poetic beauty." Shaw's writings owed much to his lifelong espousal of socialism and his impressive knowledge of music, drama, philosophy, and biology. He was not only a great playwright, but a brilliant music and drama critic, a noted essayist, and a novelist of some repute. (J.L. and J.H.S.)

1926

Deledda, Grazia (Madesani, Grazia)   **207**
Prize: Literature, 1926. *Born:* September 27, 1871; Nuoro, Sardinia, Italy. *Death:* August 16, 1936; Cervia, Italy. *Parents:* Father, Giovantonio Deledda; Mother, Chrisceda Cambosu Deledda. *Nationality:* Italian. *Religion:* Catholic. *Education:* No college degrees. *Spouse:* Palmiro Madesani; married January 11, 1900. *Children:* Sardus, son; Franz, son. *Career:* Writer.

Selected Publications: Il Vecchio della Montagna (The Old Man of the Mountain). Milan: Fratelli Treves, 1900. *Elias Portolu: Romanzo*. Milan: Fratelli Treves, 1903. *Cenere: Romanzo*. Rome: Nuova Antologia, 1904 (*Ashes: A Sardinian Story*. Tr. by Helen Hester Colvell. London: J. Lane, 1908). *L'Edera: Romanzo (The Ivy)*. Rome: Nuova Antologia, 1908. *Chiaroscuro: Novella (Light and Dark)*. Milan: Fratelli Treves, 1912. *Il Fanciulla Nascosto (The Hidden Boy)*. Milan: Fratelli Treves, 1915. *La Madre: Romanzo*. Milan: Fratelli Treves, 1920 (*The Mother*. Tr. by Mary G. Steegmann. New York: Macmillan, 1928).

For More Information See: Balducci, Carolyn. *A Self-Made Woman*. Boston: Houghton-Mifflin, 1975. Mundula, Mercede. *Grazia Deledda*. Rome: A.F. Forniggini, 1929.

Commentary: The Academy recognized Grazia Deledda "for her idealistically inspired writings which with plastic clarity picture the life on her native island and with depth and sympathy deal with human problems in general." Deledda's earlier material revolved around the life and the customs of Sardinia, with theme a less important part of the writing. Gradually, and more powerfully in her later works, her only message—"everything is hatred, blood and pain; but, perhaps, everything will be conquered one day by means of love and good will"—emerges in her writings. (J.H.S.)

1927

Bergson, Henri Louis   **208**
Prize: Literature, 1927. *Born:* October 18, 1859; Paris, France. *Death:* January 4, 1941; Paris, France. *Parents:* Father, Varsovie Michael Bergson; Mother, Katharine Levinson Bergson. *Nationality:* French. *Religion:* Jewish. *Education:* École Normale Supérieure, France, Licencié és Lettres, 1881; Univ. of Paris, France, Docteur-és-Lettres, 1889. *Spouse:* Louise Neuburger, married 1891. *Children:* Jeanne Bergson, daughter. *Career:* Lycée of Angers, France, Professor, 1881–83; Lycée of Clermont-Ferrand, France, Professor, 1883–88; College Rollin and Lycée Henry IV, France, Professor, 1888–98; École Normale Supérieure, France, Professor, 1898–1900; Collège de France, Professor, 1900–18. *Other Awards:* Nicholas Murray Butler Gold Medal, 1940.

Selected Publications: Essai Sur les Données Immédiates de la Conscience. Paris: Félix Alcan, 1889 (*Time and Free Will: An Essay on the Immediate Data of Consciousness*. Tr. by F.L. Pogson. New York: Macmillan, 1910). *Matiére et*

Mémoire: Essai Sur la Relation du Corps Avec L'Spirit. Paris: Félix Alcan, 1896 (*Matter and Memory*. Tr. by Nancy Paul and W. Scott Palmer. New York: Macmillan, 1911). *Le Rire: Essai Sur la Signification du Comique*. Paris: Félix Alcan, 1900 (*Laughter: An Essay on the Meaning of the Comic*. Tr. by Cloudesly Brereton and Fred Rothwell. New York: Macmillan, 1911). "Introduction à la Métaphysique." *Revue de Métaphysique et de Morale* (29 Janvier 1903): 1–36. *L'Evolution Creatrice*. Paris: Félix Alcan, 1907 (*Creative Evolution*. Tr. by Arthur Mitchell. New York: Holt and Co., 1911). *L'Energie Spirituelle*. Paris: Félix Alcan, 1919 (*Mind Energy, Lectures and Essays*. Tr. by H. Wildon Carr. London: Macmillan and Co., 1920). *Durée et Simultaneite*. Paris: Félix Alcan, 1922 (*Duration and Simultaneity, with Reference to Einstein's Theory*. Tr. by Leon Jacobson. New York: Bobbs-Merrill, 1966). *Les Deux Sources de la Morale et de la Religion*. Paris: Félix Alcan, 1932 (*The Two Sources of Morality and Religion*. Tr. by Ashley Andra, Cloudesly Brereton, and W. Horsfal Carter. London: Macmillan and Co., 1935).

For More Information See: Alexander, Ian W. *Bergson, Philosopher of Reflection*. New York: Hillary House, 1957. Gunter, Pete A.Y., ed. *Henri Bergson: A Bibliography*. Bowling Green, OH: Bowling Green State Univ., 1986. LeRoy, Edouard. *The New Philosophy of Henri Bergson*. New York: Holt, 1913.

Commentary: Although Henri Bergson's Nobel Prize has been linked in the public mind with his masterwork *Creative Evolution*, the prize was awarded him for the full scope of his writings, which provided a forum for new ideas in aesthetics, psychology, biology, and philosophy. The citation read "in recognition of his rich and vitalizing ideas and the brilliant skill with which they are presented." In the first three decades of the twentieth century, Bergson's books, translated into more than 20 languages, extended his influence throughout the world. (P.A.G.)

1928

Undset, Sigrid   **209**
Prize: Literature, 1928. *Born:* May 20, 1882; Kalundborg, Denmark. *Death:* June 10, 1949; Lillehammer, Norway. *Parents:* Father, Ingvald Martin Undset; Mother, Anna Charlotte Gyth Undset. *Nationality:* Danish; later Norwegian citizen. *Religion:* Catholic; from Lutheran background. *Education:* No college degrees. *Spouse:* Anders Castus Svarstad, married 1912, divorced 1925. *Children:* Anders, son; Maren Charlotte, daughter; Hans, son. *Career:* Secretary, 1898–1909; Writer. *Other Awards:* Grand Cross of the Order of St. Olaf, Norway, 1947.

Selected Publications: Viga Ljot og Vigdis: Roman. Olten, Denmark: Walter, 1909 (*Gunnar's Daughter*. Tr. by Arthur G. Chater. London: Cassell, 1931). *Vaaren (Spring)*. Oslo: H. Aschehoug, 1914. *Kristin Lavansdatter*. 3 volumes. Oslo: H. Aschehoug, 1920–22. *Fru Marta Oulie*. Oslo: H. Aschehoug, 1921. *Olav Audunsson: Hestviken*. 2 volumes. Oslo: H. Aschehoug, 1925. *Olav Audunsson og Hans Börn*. Oslo: H. Aschehoug, 1927. *Gymnadenia*. Oslo: H. Aschehoug, 1929 (*The Wild Orchid*. Tr. by Arthur G. Chater. New York: Alfred A. Knopf, 1931). *Den Braendende Busk*. Oslo: H. Aschehoug, 1930 (*The Burning Bush*. Tr. by

Arthur G. Chater. London: Cassell, 1932). *Elleve år*. Oslo: H. Aschehoug, 1934 (*The Longest Years*. Tr. by Arthur G. Chater. New York: A.A. Knopf, 1935). *Madam Dorthe*. Frankfurt am Main: Buchergilde, 1939 (*Madam Dorothea*. Tr. by Arthur G. Chater. 2 volumes. New York: A.A. Knopf, 1940).

For More Information See: Bayerschmidt, Carl. *Sigrid Undset*. New York: Twayne Publishers, 1970. Brundale, M. *Sigrid Undset*. New York: St. Martin's Press, 1988. *Encyclopedia of World Literature in the 20th Century*. New York: Ungar Publishing, 1971 (Volume 3), 451–52.

Commentary: Sigrid Undset's prize was awarded "mainly in view of her splendid descriptions of Scandinavian life in the Middle Ages." Her early novels dealt with the problems of young women in a man's world looking for meaning in life. Her psychological insights and religious convictions were then turned to the writing of the historical sagas cited by the Committee. Throughout her writing career, Undset continued to explore women's role and the erotic life. (J.H.S.)

1929

Mann, Paul Thomas   210

Prize: Literature, 1929. *Born:* June 6, 1875; Lübeck, Germany. *Death:* August 12, 1955; Zürich, Switzerland. *Parents:* Father, Johann Heinrich Mann; Mother, Julia da Silva-Bruhns Mann. *Nationality:* German; later Czechoslovakian and American citizen. *Religion:* Protestant. *Education:* No college degrees. *Spouse:* Katja Pringsheim, married 1905. *Children:* Erika Julia Hedwig, daughter; Monika, daughter; Elisabeth Veronika, daughter; Klaus Heinrich, son; Angelus Gottfried, son; Michael Thomas, son. *Career:* Writer. *Other Awards:* Prussian Academy of Arts, 1926; Medal of Service, American Academy of Arts and Letters, 1949; Goethe Prize, Frankfurt, Germany, 1949; Goethe Prize, Weimar, Germany, 1949; Pegasus Medallion, American Academy of Art and Literature, 1950; Antonio Feltrinelli Prize, Academia Nazionale dei Lincei, 1952; Cross of the Legion of Honor, France, 1952.

Selected Publications: Buddenbrooks. Berlin: S. Fischer, 1901. *Der Tod in Venedig*. Munich: Hyperion Verlag Hans von Weber, 1912 (*Death in Venice*. London: Martin Secker, 1928). *Der Zauberberg*. Berlin: S. Fischer, 1924 (*The Magic Mountain*. New York: Knopf, 1927). *Joseph und Seine Brüder*. Berlin: S. Fischer, 1933 (*Joseph and His Brothers*. Tr. by H.T. Lowe-Porter. New York: A.A. Knopf, 1934). *Doktor Faustus*. Frankfurt: S. Fischer, 1947 (*Doctor Faustus*. Tr. by H.T. Lowe-Porter, New York: Modern Library, 1948). *Confessions of Felix Krull, Confidence Man*. Tr. by Denver Lindley. New York: New American Library, 1957.

For More Information See: Berendsohn, Walter. *Thomas Mann*. University, AL: Univ. of Alabama Press, 1973. Bürgin, Hans, and Mayer, Hans-Otto. *Thomas Mann: A Chronicle of His Life*. Tr. by Eugene Dobson. University, AL: Alabama Univ. Press, 1969. Feuerlicht, Ignace. *Thomas Mann*. New York: Twayne, 1968. Hayman, R. *Thomas Mann*. New York: Scribner's, 1995.

Commentary: When Thomas Mann's award cited "his great novel, *Buddenbrooks*, which in the course of the years has found greater and greater recognition as a classic work

of the present day," nearly half of his writing career remained before him and many of his greatest works had not yet been written. A study of the decline of four generations of a German family, the novel expressed Nietzchean themes of the rift between health and will on one hand, and the artist and sensitivity on the other. This theme was further developed in other works such as *Death in Venice*. *The Magic Mountain* paralleled a young man's musings on death with World War I Germany, as later *Doctor Faustus* found parallels between a possessed composer and Germany under the Nazis. Political essays opposing the Nazis forced him to leave Germany in the '30s. He also wrote many essays on literary figures. In his Nobel acceptance speech, Mann said he put the prize "at the feet of my country and people . . . dedicated to the German soul," and throughout his exile Mann expressed that soul at its best, with his love for family, intellectualism, satiric bent, and humanity. (E.B.)

1930

Lewis, Harry Sinclair   211

Prize: Literature, 1930. *Born:* February 7, 1885; Sauk Centre, MN. *Death:* January 10, 1951; Rome, Italy. *Parents:* Father, Emmet J. Lewis; Mother, Emma Kermott Lewis. *Nationality:* American. *Religion:* Areligious; from Congregationalist background. *Education:* Yale Univ., CT, A.B., 1908. *Spouse:* Grace Hegger, married 1914, divorced 1925; Dorothy Thompson, married 1928, divorced 1942. *Children:* Wells, son; Michael, son. *Career: New Haven (CT) Journal and Courier, San Francisco (CA) Evening Bulletin*, Reporter, 1908–10; George H. Doran Co., Editor, 1910–14. *Other Awards:* Pulitzer Prize, 1926 (refused).

Selected Publications: Main Street. New York: Harcourt, Brace, 1920. *Babbitt*. New York: P.F. Collier, 1922. *Arrowsmith*. New York: Harcourt, Brace, 1925. *Elmer Gantry*. New York: Harcourt, Brace, 1927. *Dodsworth*. New York: Harcourt, Brace, 1929. *It Can't Happen Here*. New York: P.F. Collier, 1935. *Cass Timberlane*. New York: P.F. Collier, 1945. *Kingsblood Royal*. New York: Random House, 1947.

For More Information See: Bucco, Martin, ed. *Critical Essays on Sinclair Lewis*. Boston: G.K. Hall, 1986. Gribstein, Sheldon. *Sinclair Lewis*. New York: Twayne Publishers, 1962. Schorer, Mark. *Sinclair Lewis: An American Life*. New York: McGraw-Hill, 1961. Van Doren, Carl. *Sinclair Lewis: A Biographical Sketch*. Garden City, NY: Doubleday, Doran, 1933.

Commentary: Sinclair Lewis's citation reads "for his great and living art of painting life, with a talent for creating types, with wit and humor," but as the first American recipient, his award also represented the international recognition of modern American writing. Lewis's five novels published in the 1920s created from his background a mythical world with density and vitality and provided a framework for his attacks on those values he both understood and scorned. Although Lewis wrote before and after, he was scarcely noticed by critics and readers except for the work he produced in the 20s. (J.S.)

1931

Karlfeldt, Erik Axel *See* entry 199

1932

Galsworthy, John 212

Prize: Literature, 1932. *Born:* August 14, 1867; Kingston Hill, Surrey, England. *Death:* January 31, 1933; Grove Lodge, Hampstead, London, England. *Parents:* Father, John Galsworthy; Mother, Blanche Bailey Bartleet. *Nationality:* British. *Religion:* No organized religion; from Anglican background. *Education:* Oxford Univ., England, Bachelor in Law, 1890. *Spouse:* Ada Cooper, married September 23, 1905. *Children:* None. *Career:* Independently wealthy, Writer. *Other Awards:* Knighthood, 1918 (refused); Les Palmes D'Or, Belgium, 1919; Order of Merit, 1929.

Selected Publications: From the Four Winds. London: T. Fisher Unwin, 1897. *Jocelyn.* London: Duckworth and Co., 1898. *The Island Farisees.* London: W. Heinemann, 1904. *The Man of Property.* London: W. Heinemann, 1906. *Fraternity.* Leipzig, Germany: B. Tauchnitz, 1909. *Plays: The Silver Box: Joy: Strife.* London: Duckworth and Co., 1909. *The Silver Box.* New York; London: G.P. Putnam's Sons, 1909. *Justice: A Tragedy in Four Acts.* London: Duckworth and Co., 1910. *Strife: A Drama in Three Acts.* London: Duckworth and Co., 1910. *The Pigeon: A Fantasy in Three Acts.* London: Duckworth and Co., 1912. *The Dark Flower.* London: W. Heinemann, 1913. *The Fugitive: A Play in Four Acts.* London: Duckworth and Co., 1913. *The Freelands.* London: W. Heinemann, 1915. *Beyond.* London: W. Heinemann, 1917. *Saint's Progress.* London: W. Heinemann, 1919. *Villa Rubein, and Other Stories.* London: W. Heinemann, 1923. *A Modern Comedy.* New York: C. Scribner's Sons, 1924–28. *Flowering Wilderness.* London: W. Heinemann, 1932.

For More Information See: Barker, Dudley. *The Man of Principle: A View of John Galsworthy.* Toronto: W. Heinemann, 1963. *Dictionary of Literary Biography.* Detroit, MI: Gale Research, 1985 (Volume 34), 153–74. Dupré, Catherine. *John Galsworthy: A Biography.* London: Collins, 1976. Gindin, J. *John Galsworthy: Life and Art.* Ann Arbor, MI: Univ. of Michigan Press, 1987. Marrot, H.V. *The Life and Letters of John Galsworthy.* London: W. Heinemann, 1935.

Commentary: John Galsworthy's award was for "his distinguished art of narration," with *The Forsyte Saga* (1922) being singled out for attention. The first work in this trilogy was *The Man of Property* (1906), which satirized the Forsyte family for their obsession with property; to this he added two other novels, *In Chancery* (1920) and *To Let* (1921). Galsworthy was also a successful playwright, frequently defending the underprivileged and condemning the British system of justice for its harshness; the play *Justice* (1910) so impressed Home Secretary Winston Churchill that he immediately initiated reforms in the prison system. (H.L.F.)

1933

Bunin, Ivan Alexeievich 213

Prize: Literature, 1933. *Born:* October 22, 1870; Voronezh, Russia. *Death:* November 8, 1953; Paris, France. *Parents:* Father, Aleksej Nikolaevic Bunin; Mother, Ljudmila Aleksandrovna Cubarova Bunin. *Nationality:* Russian; later French resident. *Religion:* Eastern Orthodox. *Education:*

No college degrees. *Spouse:* Anna Nikolaevna Cakni, married September 23, 1898, divorced 1902; Vera Nikolaevna Muromceva, married 1922. *Children:* Nicholas, son; Alexei, son; Ludmilla Chubarova, daughter. *Career:* Writer. *Other Awards:* Pushkin Prize, Russia, 1903.

Selected Publications: The Dreams of Chang. Tr. by Bernard Gilbert Guerney. New York: A.A. Knopf, 1923. *The Village.* Tr. by Isabel F. Hapgood. London: M. Secker, 1923. *Mitya's Love.* Tr. by Madelaine Boyd. New York: Holt, 1926. *The Gentleman from San Francisco.* Tr. by Bernard Gilbert Guerney. New York: A.A. Knopf, 1927. *Well of Days.* Tr. by Gleb Struve and Hamish Miles. London: Hogarth Press, 1933. *Elaghin Affair.* Tr. by Bernard Gilbert Guerney. New York: Funk and Wagnalls, 1935. *Dark Avenues.* Tr. by Richard Hare. London: J. Lehmann, 1949. *Memories and Portraits.* Tr. by Vera Traill and Robin Chancellor. London: J. Lehmann, 1951.

For More Information See: Connolly, Julian W. *Ivan Bunin.* Boston: Twayne, 1982. Marullo, T. *Ivan Bunin.* Chicago: Ivan R. Dee, 1993. *Twentieth-Century Russian Literature.* London: Feffer and Simons, 1974, 31–32. Woodward, J. *Ivan Bunin.* Chapel Hill, NC: Univ. of North Carolina Press, 1980.

Commentary: Ivan Bunin won the Nobel Prize "for the strict artistry with which he has carried on the classical Russian traditions in prose writing." An accomplished translator and writer of both prose and poetry, his work was laden with symbolism and the recurrent themes of the uselessness of vanity and the nobility of human spirit. His most quoted work remains *The Gentleman from San Francisco.* (C.C. and J.H.S.)

1934

Pirandello, Luigi 214

Prize: Literature, 1934. *Born:* June 28, 1867; Girgenti, Sicily. *Death:* December 10, 1936; Rome, Italy. *Parents:* Father, Stefano Pirandello; Mother, Caterina Ricci-Gramitto Pirandello. *Nationality:* Italian. *Religion:* Catholic. *Education:* Univ. of Bonn, Germany, Dr. Phil., 1891. *Spouse:* Marie Antonietta Portulano, married January 27, 1894. *Children:* Stefano, son; Fausto, son; Lietta, daughter. *Career:* Writer, 1891–98; R. Instituto Superiore di Majistero Femminile, Rome, Italy, Professor, 1898–1921; Teatro d'Arte di Roma, Italy, Director, 1925–28.

Selected Publications: Erma Bifronte (Two-Faced Erma). Milan, Italy: Fratelli Treves, 1906. *L'Escula (The Outcasts).* Milan, Italy: Treves, 1908. *Co si e (Se vi pare).* Rome: Nuova Antologia, 1918 (*Right You Are, If You Think You Are.* Tr. by Arthur Livingston. New York: Rialto Service Bureau, 1927). *Maschere Nude.* Milan, Italy: Fratelli Treves, 1918–20. *Ciascuno a Suo Modo.* Florence, Italy: R. Bemporad, 1920 (*Each in His Own Way.* Tr. by J.M. Dent. New York: E.P. Dutton & Co., 1923). *Sie Personnaggi in Cerca d'Autore.* Florence, Italy: R. Bemporad, 1921 (*Six Characters in Search of an Author.* Tr. by Frederick May. London: Heinemann, 1954). *Enrico IV.* Florence, Italy: R. Bemporad, 1922 (*Henry IV.* Tr. by J.M. Dent, New York: Dutton, 1923). *Collected Plays.* London: J. Calder, 1988–92.

For More Information See: Caputi, A. *Pirandello and the Crisis of Modern Consciousness.* Champaign, IL: Univ. of Illinois Press, 1988. Guidice, Gaspare. *Pirandello: A*

Biography. New York: Oxford Univ. Press, 1975. Ragusa, Olga. *Luigi Pirandello.* New York: Columbia Univ. Press, 1968.

Commentary: "For his bold and ingenious revival of Italian dramatic and scenic art," Luigi Pirandello received the Nobel Prize. Pirandello's influence as a modern dramatist was not confined to the Italian theater. He was recognized as a major international figure in the theater of the twentieth century for his innovative techniques of philosophical and psychological drama, and he produced notable works as dramatist, novelist, short story writer, poet, and critic. (A.D.J.)

1936

O'Neill, Eugene Gladstone   **215**
Prize: Literature, 1936. *Born:* October 16, 1888; New York, NY. *Death:* November 27, 1953; Boston, MA. *Parents:* Father, James O'Neill; Mother, Ella Quinlan O'Neill. *Nationality:* American. *Religion:* Catholic. *Education:* No college degrees. *Spouse:* Kathleen Jenkins, married October 4, 1909, divorced 1912; Agnes Boulton, married April 12, 1918, divorced July 1929; Carlotta Monterey, married July 1929. *Children:* Eugene Gladstone, son; Shane Rudreighe, son; Oona, daughter. *Career:* New England, Clerical and Manual Laborer, 1907–12; *New London (CT) Telegraph*, Reporter, 1912. *Other Awards:* Pulitzer Prize, 1920; Pulitzer Prize, 1922; Gold Medal, National Institute of Arts and Letters, 1923; Pulitzer Prize, 1928; Pulitzer Prize, 1957 (posthumous).

Selected Publications: Beyond the Horizon. 1920. *The Emperor Jones.* 1920. *Anna Christie.* 1921. *The Hairy Ape.* 1922. *Desire Under the Elms.* 1924. *The Great God Brown.* 1925. *Strange Interlude.* 1928. *Mourning Becomes Electra.* 1931. *Ah, Wilderness!* 1933. *The Iceman Cometh.* 1938. *A Moon for the Misbegotten.* 1943. *A Long Day's Journey into Night.* 1955.

For More Information See: American Writers: A Collection of Literary Biographies. New York: Charles Scribner's Sons, 1974 (Volume III), 385–408. Berlin, N. *Eugene O'Neill.* New York: Grove Press, 1982. Bogard, T., and Bryer, J., eds. *Selected Letters of Eugene O'Neill.* New Haven, CT: Yale Univ. Press, 1988. Skinner, Richard Dana. *Eugene O'Neill: A Poet's Quest.* New York: Longman's, Green, 1935. Winther, S.K. *Eugene O'Neill: A Critical Study.* New York: Russell, 1961.

Commentary: The Nobel Prize was awarded to Eugene O'Neill "for dramatic works of vital energy, sincerity and intensity of feeling, stamped with an original conception of tragedy." Although there has been disagreement with that evaluation, the corpus of O'Neill's work now seems to justify that selection of an important and memorable American dramatist whose influential dramas have been read, translated, and acted out around the world. (C.B.)

1937

Martin du Gard, Roger   **216**
Prize: Literature, 1937. *Born:* March 22, 1881; Neuilly-sur-Seine, France. *Death:* August 22, 1958; Belleme, France. *Parents:* Father, Paul Martin du Gard; Mother, Madeleine Winy Martin du Gard. *Nationality:* French. *Religion:*

No organized religion; from Catholic background. *Education:* École des Chartres, France, baccalauréat, 1906. *Spouse:* Helene Foucault, married February 1906. *Children:* Christiane, daughter. *Career:* Writer.

Selected Publications: Devener. Paris: Société d'Editions Litteraire et Artistique, 1908. *Jean Barois.* Paris: Edition de la Nouvelle Revue Française, 1913 (*Jean Barois.* Tr. by Stuart Gilbert. New York: Viking, 1949). *Les Thibaults.* 8 volumes. Paris: Gallimard, 1922–40. *Vieille France.* Paris: Gallimard, 1933 (*The Postman.* Tr. by John Russell. New York: Viking, 1955). *Note sur André Gide, 1913–1951.* Paris: Gallimard, 1951 (*Recollections of Andre Gide.* Tr. by John Russell. New York: Viking, 1953).

For More Information See: O'Nan, M. *Roger Martin du Gard Centennial.* Brockport, NY: State University of New York, 1981. *The Oxford Companion to French Literature.* Oxford: Clarendon Press, 1959, 458–59. Savage, Catherine. *Roger Martin du Gard.* New York: Twayne Publishers, 1968.

Commentary: Roger Martin du Gard, novelist and playwright, received his Nobel Prize "for the artistic vigor and truthfulness with which he has pictured human contrasts as well as some fundamental aspects of contemporary life in the series of novels entitled *Les Thibault*." The eight-part novel is one of a genre called the "roman-fleuve," a popular novelistic style of French writers in the twentieth century characterized by basing a collection of novels around a central character or theme. Martin du Gard's works illustrate his ability to observe and describe human nature with precision and detail, making his novels realistic psychological studies. His works are marked by central themes of turmoil caused by illness, suffering and death, evil, and loss of faith, all reflecting his own early religious upbringing and subsequent abandonment of his religion. (S.C.)

1938

Buck, Pearl Comfort Sydenstricker   **217**
Prize: Literature, 1938. *Born:* June 26, 1892; Hillsboro, WV. *Death:* March 6, 1973; Danby, VT. *Parents:* Father, Absalom Andrew Sydenstricker; Mother, Caroline Stulting Sydenstricker. *Nationality:* American. *Religion:* Presbyterian. *Education:* Randolph-Macon College, VA, A.B., 1914; Cornell Univ., NY, M.A., 1926. *Spouse:* John Lossing Buck, married 1917, divorced 1935; Richard John Walsh, married 1935. *Children:* Carol, daughter; legally adopted children include Janice, daughter; Richard, son; John, son; Edgar, son; Jean, daughter; Henrietta, daughter; Theresa, daughter; Chieko, daughter; Johanna, daughter. *Career:* Univ. of Nanking, China, Intermittent Instructor, 1921–31. *Other Awards:* Laura Messenger Prize, Cornell Univ., 1926; Pulitzer Prize, 1931; Howells Medal, American Academy of Arts and Letters, 1935.

Selected Publications: East Wind, West Wind. New York: John Day, 1930. *The Good Earth.* New York: John Day, 1931. *Sons.* New York: John Day, 1932. *The Mother.* New York: John Day, 1934. *A House Divided.* New York: John Day, 1935. *The Exile.* New York: John Day, 1936. *Fighting Angel.* New York: John Day, 1936. *The Patriot.* New York: John Day, 1939. *Dragon Seed.* New York: John Day, 1941. *A Bridge for Passing.* New York: John Day, 1962.

For More Information See: Conn, Peter J. *Pearl S. Buck.* Cambridge: Cambridge University Press, 1996. Doyl, Paul A. *Pearl S. Buck.* New York: Twayne, 1965. Harris, Theodore. *Pearl S. Buck: A Biography.* 2 volumes. New York: John Day, 1969–71. LaFarge, A. *Pearl Buck.* New York: Chelsea House, 1988.

Commentary: Pearl Buck won the Nobel Prize "for her rich and genuine epic pictures of Chinese life, and for her masterly biographies." She saw herself as an interpreter of the nature of China and its people, among whom she lived, and brought into focus in her novels the conflict between the old and the new and the problems faced by Chinese women in both the old and new world. (V.V.M.)

1939

Sillanpää, Frans Eemil (Taata)   218
Prize: Literature, 1939. *Born:* September 16, 1888; Hämeen Kyro, Finland. *Death:* June 3, 1964; Helsinki, Finland. *Parents:* Father, Frans Henrik Koskinen Sillanpää; Mother, Louisa Vilhelmüna Iisaksdottor Sillanpää. *Nationality:* Finnish. *Religion:* Most probably Christian/Protestant. *Education:* No college degrees. *Spouse:* Sigrid Maria Salomäki, married September 11, 1916, died April 1939; Anna Armia von Hertzen, married November 1939. *Children:* 8 children. *Career:* Writer. *Other Awards:* Finnish State Pension, 1919; Aleksis Kivi Prize, 1937; Kordelin Foundation Prize, 1938; Frenckell Foundation Prize, 1938.

Selected Publications: Hiltu ja Ragner (Hiltu and Ranger). Porvoo, Finland: Soderström, 1923. *Hurskhas Kurjuus.* Helsinki: Otava, 1930 (*Meek Heritage.* Tr. by Alex Matson. London: Putnam, 1938). *Nuorena Nukkunut.* Helsinki: Otava, 1931 (*The Maid Silja: The History of the Last Offshoot of an Old Family Tree.* Tr. by Alexander Matson. New York: The Macmillan Co., 1933). *Ihmiset Suviyossa, eepillinen sarja.* Helsinki: Otava, 1934 (*People in a Summer Night: An Epic Suite.* Tr. by Alexander Matson. Madison, WI: Univ. of Wisconsin Press, 1966). *Manniskor i Sommarnatten (A Man's Way).* Stockholm: Holger Schildt, 1935. *Miehentie Ahrolan Talon Oloista Paavon Isännyyden Vakiintuessa.* Helsinki: Otava, 1948.

For More Information See: Ahokas, J. *A History of Finnish Literature.* Bloomington, IN: Indiana Univ. Press, 1973. *Encyclopedia of World Literature in the Twentieth Century.* New York: Frederick Publishing, 1975 (Volume 3), 273–74. *Twentieth Century Authors.* New York: H.W. Wilson, 1942, 1286–88.

Commentary: Frans Sillanpää received the Nobel "for his deep comprehension and exquisite art in painting the nature of his country and the life of its peasants in their mutual relations." The Finnish novelist and short-story writer wrote around elemental themes about the life and struggles of his people, and was a favorite both in Finland and Sweden before receiving world-wide acclaim. (J.H.S.)

1944

Jensen, Johannes Vilhelm (Lykke, Ivar)   219
Prize: Literature, 1944. *Born:* January 20, 1873; Farso, Denmark. *Death:* November 25, 1950; Copenhagen, Denmark. *Parents:* Father, Hans Jensen; Mother, Marie Kirstine Jensen. *Nationality:* Danish. *Religion:* Freethinker; from Lutheran background. *Education:* Univ. of Copenhagen, Denmark, M.D., 1896. *Spouse:* Else Marie Ulrik, married 1904. *Children:* 3 sons. *Career:* Writer.

Selected Publications: Himmerlandshistorier (Himmerland Stories). Copenhagen: Gyldendal, 1898–1910. *Madame d'Ora.* Copenhagen: Gyldendal, 1904. *Hjulet (The Wheel).* Copenhagen: Gyldendal, 1905. *Den Lange Rejse.* Copenhagen: Gyldendal, 1908–22 (*The Long Journey.* Tr. by Arthur Chater. London: Gyldendal, 1922).

For More Information See: Columbia Dictionary of Modern European Literature. New York: Columbia Univ. Press, 1947, 544–45. Kujoory, Parvin. "Johannes Vilhelm Jensen," in *Book of Days.* Ann Arbor, MI: Pierian Press, 1988. Rossel, Sven H. *Johannes V. Jensen.* Boston: Twayne, 1984. *Twentieth Century Authors.* New York: H.W. Wilson, 1942, 723–24.

Commentary: Johannes Jensen received the Nobel Prize "for the rare strength and fertility of his poetic imagination, with which is combined an intellectual curiosity of wide scope and a bold, freshly creative style." Jensen was notable for his epic historical and imaginative prose, particularly the multivolume *Himmerlandshistorier* and *Den Lange Rejse.* He was also recognized as an accomplished poet, translator, essayist, and a lucid advocate of Darwin's theories. (P.K.)

1945

Mistral, Gabriela (Godoy Alcayaga, Lucila)   220
Prize: Literature, 1945. *Born:* April 7, 1889; Vicuna, Chile. *Death:* January 10, 1957; New York, NY. *Parents:* Father, Jeronimo Godoy Villanueva; Mother, Petronila Alcayaga de Molina. *Nationality:* Chilean. *Religion:* Catholic. *Education:* Pedagogical College, Chile, teacher's training, 1909. *Spouse:* None. *Children:* Juan Miguel Godoy, son (adopted). *Career:* Liceo de Antofagasta, Chile, Teacher and Administrator, 1911–12; Liceo de los Andes, Chile, Teacher and Administrator, 1912–18; Liceo de Punte Arenas, Chile, Teacher and Administrator, 1918–20; Liceo de Temuco, Chile, Teacher and Administrator, 1920–21; Ministry of Education, Mexico, Adviser, 1922–24; Writer, Lecturer, and Diplomat thereafter. *Other Awards:* Laurel Wreath and Gold Crown, Writer's Society, Santiago, Chile, 1914; Chilean National Prize, 1951.

Selected Publications: Desolaçion (Despair). New York: Spanish Institute, 1922. *Ternura (Tenderness).* Madrid: Satunio Calleja, 1924. *Tala (Ravage).* Buenos Aires: SUR, 1938. *Lagar (The Wine Press).* Santiago: Editorial del Pacifico, 1954.

For More Information See: Castleman, W. *Beauty and the Mission of the Teacher.* Smithtown, NY: Exposition Press, 1982. De Vazquez, Margot Arce. *Gabriela Mistral: The Poet and Her Work.* Tr. by Helene Masslo Anderson. New York: New York Univ. Press, 1964. Gazarian-Gautier, Marie-Lise. *Gabriela Mistral: The Teacher from the Valley of Elqui.* Chicago: Franciscan Herald Press, 1975.

Commentary: The Nobel Academy cited Gabriela Mistral "for her lyric poetry which, inspired by powerful emotions, has made her name a symbol of the idealistic aspirations of the entire Latin American world." Her despair on the loss of her lover through suicide led to her first powerful poetry, *Desolaçion,* her love for children to *Ternura* and *Tala.* In addition, Mistral was a guiding force in education in Chile and Mexico and a gifted Chilean diplomat in several countries and in international activities. (D.K.)

1946

Hesse, Herman (Lauscher, Hermann; Sinclair, Emil)   221

Prize: Literature, 1946. *Born:* July 2, 1877; Calw, Germany. *Death:* August 9, 1962; Montagnola, Switzerland. *Parents:* Father, Johannes Hesse; Mother, Marie Gundert Hesse. *Nationality:* German; later Swiss citizen. *Religion:* Lutheran. *Education:* No college degrees. *Spouse:* Marie Bernoulli, married 1904, divorced 1923; Ruth Wenger, married January 1924, divorced 1927; Ninon Ausländer Dolbin, married November 1931. *Children:* Bruno, son; Heiner, son; Martin, son. *Career:* Clock Factory, Calw, Germany, Apprentice, 1894; Tübingen, Germany, Bookseller, 1895–99. *Other Awards:* Bauernfeld Prize, Vienna, 1904; Fontane Prize, 1920 (refused); Keller Prize, Zürich, 1936; Goethe Prize, Frankfurt, 1946; Raabe Prize, Brunswick, Germany, 1950; German Book Trade Peace Prize, 1955; Knight of the Order Pour le Merite, Germany, 1955.

Selected Publications: Peter Camenzind. Berlin: S. Fischer, 1904 (Tr. by Michael Roloff. New York: Farrar, Straus, 1968). *Unterm Rad.* Berlin: S. Fischer, 1906 (*Beneath the Wheel.* Tr. by Michael Roloff. New York: Farrar, Straus, 1968). *Gertrude.* Munich: A. Langen, 1910 (Tr. by Ralph Manheim. New York: Farrar, Straus, 1970). *Rosshalde.* Berlin: S. Fischer, 1914 (Tr. by Ralph Manheim. New York: Farrar, Straus, 1970). *Knulp: Drei Geschichten aus dem Leben Knulps.* Berlin: S. Fischer, 1915 (*Three Tales from the Life of Knulp.* Tr. by Ralph Manheim. New York: Farrar, Straus, 1971). *Maerchen.* Berlin: S. Fischer, 1918 (*Strange News from Another Star and Other Tales.* Tr. by Denver Lindley. New York: Farrar, Straus, 1971). *Demian.* Berlin: S. Fischer, 1919 (Tr. by Michael Roloff and Michael Lebeck. New York: Harper, 1965). *Klingsors Letzter Sommer.* Berlin: S. Fischer, 1920 (*Klingsor's Last Summer.* Tr. by Richard Winston and Clara Winston. New York: Farrar, Straus, 1970). *Wanderung, Aufzeichnungen.* Berlin: S. Fischer, 1920 (*Wandering: Notes and Sketches.* Tr. by James Wright. New York: Farrar, Straus, 1972). *Siddhartha.* Berlin: S. Fischer, 1922 (Tr. by Hilda Rosner. New York: New Directions, 1951). *Der Steppenwolf.* Berlin: S. Fischer, 1927 (*Steppenwolf.* Tr. by Basil Creighton. New York: Holt, 1970). *Narziss und Goldmund.* Berlin: S. Fischer, 1930 (*Narcissus and Goldmund.* Tr. by Ursula Molinaro. New York: Farrar, Straus, 1968). *Die Morgenlandfahrt: Eine Erzaehlung.* Berlin: S. Fischer, 1932 (*The Journey to the East.* Tr. by Hilda Rosner. New York: Farrar, Straus, 1968). *Das Glasperlenspiel: Versuch einer Lebensbeschreibung des Magister Ludi Josef Knecht samt Knechts hintelassenen Schriften.* Zürich: Fretz & Wasmuth, 1943 (*Magister Ludi: The Glass Bead Game.* Tr. by Richard Winston and Clara Winston. New York: Holt, 1969). *Krieg und Frieden: Betrachtungen zu Krieg und Politik seit dem Jahre 1914.* Zürich: Fretz & Wasmuth, 1949 (*If the War Goes on: Reflections on War and Politics.* Tr. by Ralph Manheim. New York: Farrar, Straus, 1971). *My Belief: Essays on Life and Art.* Ed. by Theodore Ziolkowski, Tr. by Denver Lindley and Ralph Manheim. New York: Farrar, Straus, 1974. *Hours in the Garden and Other Poems* (Tr. by Rika Lesser. New York: Farrar, Straus, 1979).

For More Information See: Contemporary Authors Permanent Series. Detroit, MI: Gale Research, 1978 (Volume 2), 252–60. Freedman, Ralph. *Hermann Hesse, Pilgrim of Crisis.* New York: Pantheon, 1978. Mileck, Joseph. *Hermann Hesse, Life and Art.* Berkeley, CA: Univ. of California Press, 1978. Stelzig, E. *Herman Hesse's Fiction of the Self.* Princeton, NJ: Princeton Univ. Press, 1988.

Commentary: Herman Hesse's award was "for his inspired writings which, while growing in boldness and penetration, exemplify the classical humanitarian ideals and high qualities of style." His work, which examined the theme of man's search for his essential, true self as it conflicts with the world, and mirrored the stages of his own life, was nominated for the award by Thomas Mann. (M.K.)

1947

Gide, André Paul Guillaume   222

Prize: Literature, 1947. *Born:* November 22, 1869; Paris, France. *Death:* February 19, 1951; Paris, France. *Parents:* Father, Paul Gide; Mother, Juliette Rondeaux. *Nationality:* French. *Religion:* Protestant; from Huguenot background. *Education:* École Alsaçienne, France, baccalauréat, 1889. *Spouse:* Madeleine Rondeaux, married 1895. *Children:* Catherine, daughter. *Career: La Nouvelle Revue Française,* Founder and Editor, 1908–41.

Selected Publications: L'Immoraliste. Paris: Merceure de France, 1902 (*The Immoralist.* Tr. by Dorothy Bussy. New York: A.A. Knopf, 1930). *La Porte Étroite.* Paris: Merceure de France, 1909 (*Strait Is the Gate.* Tr. by Dorothy Bussy. New York: A.A. Knopf, 1924). *Les Caves du Vatican.* Paris: Librarie Stock, 1914 (*The Vatican Swindle.* Tr. by Dorothy Bussy. New York: A.A. Knopf, 1925). *La Symphonie Pastorale.* Paris: Éditions de La Nouvelle Revue Française, 1919 (*The Pastoral Symphony.* Tr. by Dorothy Bussy. New York: A.A. Knopf, 1925). *Les Faux-Monnayeurs.* Paris: Éditions de La Nouvelle Revue Française, 1925 (*The Counterfeiters.* Tr. by Dorothy Bussy. New York: A.A. Knopf, 1927). O'Brien, Justin. *The Journals of André Gide.* 2 Volumes. Evanston, IL: Northwestern Univ. Press, 1987.

For More Information See: "André Gide." *Saturday Review* (November 29, 1947): 20. Brèe, Germaine. *Gide.* New Brunswick, NJ: Rutgers Univ. Press, 1963. Cordle, T. *Andre Gide.* New York: Twayne Publishers, 1993. Guérard, Albert J. *André Gide.* 2d ed. Cambridge, MA: Harvard Univ. Press, 1969. O'Brien, Justin. "The Barely Posthumous Gide." *Saturday Review* (March 22, 1952): 21, 41–42. O'Brien, Justin. *Portrait of André Gide: A Critical Biography.* New York: A.A. Knopf, 1953. Sheridan, Alan. *André Gide: A Life in the Present.* London: Hamish Hamilton, 1998.

Commentary: André Gide wrote over 50 volumes of novels, plays, poems, translations, criticism, journals, and travel books. Not surprisingly, the Nobel award was given not for any one work but "for his comprehensive and artistically significant writings, in which human problems and conditions have been presented with a fearless love of truth and keen psychological insight." Although Gide has had a broad and diverse influence on the twentieth-century French novel, he remains better known as an "emancipator of the mind" who, discontented with himself and the world, fought against social and moral conventions while insisting on rigorous personal honesty and authentic affirmation of the individual. (E.E.G.)

1948

Eliot, Thomas Stearns   223

Prize: Literature, 1948. *Born:* September 26, 1888; St. Louis, MO. *Death:* January 4, 1965; London, England. *Parents:* Father, Henry Ware Eliot; Mother, Charlotte Champe Stearns Eliot. *Nationality:* American; later British citizen. *Religion:* Anglican; from Unitarian background. *Education:* Harvard Univ., MA, B.A., 1909; Harvard Univ., MA, M.A., 1910. *Spouse:* Vivienne Haigh-Wood, married June 26, 1915, separated 1932, died 1947; Valerie Fletcher, married January 10, 1957. *Children:* None. *Career:* High Wycombe and Highgate, Teacher, 1915–16; *Egoist*, Editor, 1917–19; Lloyds Bank, Clerk, 1917–23; *Criterion*, Editor, 1922–39; Faber and Gwyer, Editor and Director, 1925–65. *Other Awards:* Order of Merit, 1948; French Legion of Honor, 1948; Hanseatic Goethe Prize, 1954; Dante Medal, 1959; German Order of Merit, 1959; United States Medal of Freedom, 1964.

Selected Publications: The Waste Land. New York: Boni and Liveright, 1922. *Ash-Wednesday.* London: Faber & Faber Ltd., 1930. *Murder in the Cathedral.* London: Faber & Faber Ltd., 1935. *Four Quartets.* New York: Harcourt, Brace and Co., 1943. *The Cocktail Party.* London: Faber & Faber Ltd., 1950. *The Letters of T.S. Eliot.* San Diego, CA: Harbrace, 1988.

For More Information See: Gilbert, Sandra. *T.S. Eliot.* Atlantic Highlands, NJ: Humanities, 1989. Gordon, Lyndall. *T.S. Eliot: An Imperfect Life.* New York: Norton, 1998. Headings, Philip. *T.S. Eliot.* New York: Twayne, 1964. Margolis, John D. *T.S. Eliot's Intellectual Development, 1922–1939.* Chicago: Univ. of Chicago Press, 1972. Mattheissen, Francis O. *The Achievement of T.S. Eliot: An Essay on the Nature of Poetry.* 3d edition. New York: Oxford Univ. Press, 1958.

Commentary: T.S. Eliot's Nobel was "for his outstanding pioneer contribution to present-day poetry." An individualist throughout his lifetime, Eliot pioneered many techniques in his poetry that developed as a result of his life experience and the influence of such writers as Laforgue, the Elizabethans, Gautier, and others. His early pessimistic writings were later tempered by his increasing understanding and elaboration of the relationships among religion, politics, and culture. (G.K.)

1949

Faulkner, William Cuthbert   224

Prize: Literature, 1949. *Born:* September 25, 1897; New Albany, MS. *Death:* July 6, 1962; Oxford, MS. *Parents:* Father, Murry C. Faulkner; Mother, Maud Butler Faulkner. *Nationality:* American. *Religion:* Episcopalian. *Education:* No college degrees. *Spouse:* Estelle Oldham Franklin, married June 20, 1929. *Children:* Alabama, daughter; Jill, daughter. *Career:* First National Bank, Oxford, MS, Clerk, 1915; Winchester Repeating Arms, New Haven, CT, Clerk, 1918; Royal Air Force, Canada, Cadet, 1918; Bookstore, NY, Clerk, 1921; Oxford, MS, Postmaster, 1921–24; Power

Company, Oxford, MS, Night Superintendent, 1929. *Other Awards:* Howells Medal for Fiction, American Academy of Arts and Letters, 1950; National Book Award for Fiction, 1951; Member of the French Legion of Honor, 1951; National Book Award for Fiction, 1955; Pulitzer Prize, 1955, 1963; Silver Medal of the Greek Academy, 1957; Gold Medal for Fiction, National Institute of Arts and Letters, 1962.

Selected Publications: Sartoris. New York: Grosset & Dunlap, 1929. *The Sound and the Fury.* New York: J. Cape and H. Smith, 1929. *As I Lay Dying.* New York: J. Cape and H. Smith, 1930. *Sanctuary.* New York: J. Cape and H. Smith, 1930. *Light in August.* New York: H. Smith and R. Hass, 1932. *Absalom, Absalom!* London: Chatto and Windus, 1934. *The Hamlet.* London: Chatto and Windus, 1940. *Intruder in the Dust.* New York: The Modern Library, 1948.

For More Information See: Blotner, Joseph. *Faulkner: A Biography.* 2 volumes. New York: Random House, 1974. *Contemporary Authors.* Detroit, MI: Gale Research, 1979 (Volumes 81–84), 157–65. Gray, Richard J. *The Life of William Faulkner: A Critical Biography.* Oxford; Cambridge, MA: Blackwell, 1994. Karl, Frederick. *Biography of William Faulkner.* New York: Weidenfeld, 1988. Sensibar, Judith. *Faulkner's Poetry: A Bibliographical Guide.* Ann Arbor, MI: UMI Research Press, 1988.

Commentary: The award to William Faulkner was "for his powerful and artistically unique contribution to the modern American novel." In the presentation, Gustaf Hellstroem called Faulkner "the unrivalled master of all living British and American novelists as a deep psychologist" and "the greatest experimentalist among twentieth-century novelists." He used the setting and characters of fictional Yoknapatawpha County in Mississippi to expound his philosophy of the suffering and overall dignity of man. (J.F.K.)

1950

Russell, Bertrand Arthur William   225

Prize: Literature, 1950. *Born:* May 18, 1872; Monmouthshire, Wales. *Death:* February 3, 1970; Merionethshire, Wales. *Parents:* Father, John Russell; Mother, Katharine Stanley Russell. *Nationality:* British. *Religion:* Agnostic; from Anglican background. *Education:* Cambridge Univ., England, M.A., 1894. *Spouse:* Alys Pearsall Smith, married 1894, divorced 1921; Dora Winifred Black, married 1921, divorced 1935; Patricia Helen Spence, married 1936, divorced 1952; Edith Finch, married 1952. *Children:* John Conrad, son; Katharine Jane, daughter; Conrad Sabastian Robert, son. *Career:* Cambridge Univ., England, Professor, 1894–16; National Univ. of Peking, China, Professor, 1920–21; Beacon Hill School, England, Founder and Director, 1927–32; Univ. of California, Los Angeles, Professor, 1939–40; Barnes Foundation, Merion, PA, Lecturer, 1941–42. *Other Awards:* Nicholas Murray Butler Medal, 1915; Sylvester Medal, London, 1934; Order of Merit, England, 1949; Pears Cyclopedia Prize, London, 1955; Kalinga Prize, UNESCO, 1957; Sonning Prize, Denmark, 1960.

Selected Publications: The Principles of Mathematics. Cambridge: Cambridge Univ. Press, 1903. *Principia Mathematica.* 3 volumes. Cambridge: Cambridge Univ. Press, 1910–13. *The Problems of Philosophy.* New York:

Holt, 1912. *Our Knowledge of the External World as a Field for Scientific Method in Philosophy.* Chicago: Open Court, 1914. *The Analysis of Mind.* New York: Macmillan, 1921. *The Analysis of Matter.* New York: Harcourt, 1927. *Marriage and Morals.* New York: Liveright, 1929. *Education and the Modern World.* New York: Norton, 1932. *Religion and Science.* New York: Holt, 1935. *An Inquiry into Meaning and Truth.* New York: Norton, 1940. *A History of Western Philosophy and Its Connection with Political and Social Circumstances from the Earliest Times to the Present Day.* New York: Simon & Schuster, 1945. *Authority and the Individual.* New York: Simon & Schuster, 1948. *Human Knowledge: Its Scope and Limits.* New York: Simon & Schuster, 1948. *My Philosophical Development.* New York: Simon & Schuster, 1959. Blackwell, K. *A Bibliography of Bertrand Russell.* London: Routledge, 1994.

For More Information See: Ayer, A.J. *Bertrand Russell.* Ann Arbor, MI: Univ. of Michigan Press, 1988. Clark, Ronald. *Bertrand Russell.* New York: Thames and Hudson, 1981. Kuntz, Paul G. *Bertrand Russell.* New York: Twayne, 1986. Russell, Bertrand. *The Autobiography of Bertrand Russell.* 2 volumes. Boston: Little, Brown, 1967–68. Russell, Bertrand. *The Autobiography of Bertrand Russell, 1944–1969.* New York: Simon & Schuster, 1969.

Commentary: Bertrand Russell was granted the Nobel Prize "in recognition of his varied and significant writings, in which he champions humanitarian ideals and freedom of thought." He could have claimed worldwide impact for his work in mathematics, history, philosophy, education, or politics, but his greatest impact was in the model he set for the world of an individual who felt a responsibility for the welfare of the whole and spoke out, unafraid, in defense of his three passions: "the longing for love, the search for knowledge, and unbearable pity for the suffering of mankind." (M.K.)

1951

Lagerkvist, Pär Fabian 226
Prize: Literature, 1951. ***Born:*** May 23, 1891; Vaxjo, Sweden. ***Death:*** July 11, 1974; Stockholm, Sweden. ***Parents:*** Father, Anders Johan Lagerkvist; Mother, Johanna Blad Lagerkvist. ***Nationality:*** Swedish. ***Religion:*** Atheist; from Protestant background. ***Education:*** No college degrees. ***Spouse:*** Karen Dagmar Johanne Sorensen, married 1918, divorced 1925; Elaine Luella Hallberg, married 1925. ***Children:*** None. ***Career:*** Writer. ***Other Awards:*** Samfundet Prize, Sweden, 1928; Sante-Beuve Prize, 1946; Prix du Meilleur Livre Etranger, 1951; Ameties Francaises Award, France, 1956.

Selected Publications: *Det Eviga Leendet.* Stockholm: Bonniers, 1920 (*The Eternal Smile.* Tr. by Denys Harding and Eric Masterton. Cambridge: Fraser, 1934). *Bödeln.* Stockholm: Bonniers, 1933 (*The Hangman.* Tr. by Denys Harding and Eric Masterton. Cambridge: Fraser, 1934). *Mannen Utan Själ.* Stockholm: Bonniers, 1936 (*The Man Without a Soul.* Tr. by Helge Kokeritz in *Scandinavian Plays of the Twentieth Century*, First Series. Princeton, NJ: Princeton Univ. Press, 1944). *Barabbas.* Stockholm: Bonniers, 1950 (*Barabbas.* Tr. by Ann Blair. New York: Random House, 1951). *Sibyllan.* Stockholm: Bonniers, 1956 (*The Sibyl.* Tr. by Naomi Walford. New York: Random House,

1958). *Pilgrim Pa Havet.* Stockholm: Bonniers, 1962 (*Pilgrim at Sea.* Tr. by Naomi Walford. New York: Random House, 1964). *Mariamne.* Stockholm: Bonniers, 1967 (*Herod and Mariamne.* Tr. by Naomi Walford. New York: A.A. Knopf, 1968).

For More Information See: *Current Biography Yearbook.* New York: H.W. Wilson, 1952, 321–24. Spector, Robert Donald. *Par Lagerkvist.* New York: Twayne, 1973. Syoberg, Leif. *Par Lagerkvist.* New York: Columbia Univ. Press, 1976.

Commentary: Pär Lagerkvist, equally heralded as a dramatist and novelist, won the Nobel Prize "for the artistic vigor and true independence of mind with which he endeavors in his poetry to find answers to the eternal questions confronting mankind." Early in his writings, perhaps in rebellion against his conservative and religious upbringing, Lagerkvist focused pessimistically on themes such as the cruelty of humankind, humanity's cosmic loneliness, and the futility of hope/love. Later, although his works continued to contain corrupt characters, he tempered pessimism with hope and visions of morality. (J.H.S.)

1952

Mauriac, François 227
Prize: Literature, 1952. ***Born:*** October 11, 1885; Bordeaux, France. ***Death:*** September 1, 1970; Paris, France. ***Parents:*** Father, Jean-Paul Mauriac; Mother, Marguerite Coiffard Mauriac. ***Nationality:*** French. ***Religion:*** Catholic. ***Education:*** Univ. of Bordeaux, France, Licence és Lettres, 1904. ***Spouse:*** Jeanne Lafont, married June 3, 1913. ***Children:*** Claude, son; Claire, daughter; Luce, daughter; Jean, son. ***Career:*** Writer. ***Other Awards:*** Grand Prix du Roman, L'Académie Française, 1926.

Selected Publications: *L'Enfant Chargé de Chaines.* Paris: Grasset, 1913 (*Young Man in Chains.* Tr. by Gerard Hopkins. London: Eyre and Spottiswoode, 1961). *La Robe Prétexte.* Paris: Grasset, 1914 (*The Stuff of Youth.* Tr. by Gerard Hopkins. London: Eyre and Spottiswoode, 1960). *La Chair et le Sang.* Paris: Emile-Paul, 1920 (*Flesh and Blood.* Tr. by Gerard Hopkins. London: Eyre and Spottiswoode, 1954). *Le Baiser au Lépreux.* Paris: Grasset, 1922 (*A Kiss for the Leper.* Tr. by Gerard Hopkins. London: Eyre and Spottiswoode, 1950). *Le Désert de L'Amour.* Paris: Grasset, 1925 (*The Desert of Love.* Tr. by Gerard Hopkins. London: Eyre and Spottiswoode, 1949). *Ce Qui Était Perdu.* Paris: Grasset, 1930 (*That Which Was Lost.* Tr. by J.H. McEwen. London: Eyre and Spottiswoode, 1950). *Le Mystère Frontenac.* Paris: Grasset, 1933 (*Frontenac Mystery.* Tr. by Gerard Hopkins. London: Eyre and Spottiswoode, 1961). *Les Anges Noirs.* Paris: Grasset, 1936 (*The Dark Angels.* Tr. by Gerard Hopkins. London: Eyre and Spottiswoode, 1950). *Asmodée.* Paris: Grasset, 1938 (*Asmodée or the Intruder.* Tr. by Basil Bartlett. London: Secker and Warburg, 1939). *La Pharisienne.* Paris: Grasset, 1941 (*A Woman of the Pharisees.* Tr. by Gerard Hopkins. New York: Farrar, Straus, 1946). *L'Agneau.* Paris: Flammarion, 1954 (*The Lamb.* Tr. by Gerard Hopkins. London: Eyre and Spottiswoode, 1955).

For More Information See: Alyn, Marc. *François Mauriac.* Paris: P. Seghers, 1960. Jenkins, Cecil. *Mauriac.* London: Oliver and Boyd, 1965. Smith, Maxwell Austin. *Francóis Mauriac.* New York: Twayne Publishers, 1970.

Commentary: François Mauriac received his Nobel "for the deep spiritual insight and the artistic intensity with which he has in his novels penetrated the drama of human life." Though known primarily as a novelist, Mauriac also was a successful playwright, biographer, poet, and journalist. His novels deal with psychological struggles of good versus evil and weaknesses of the flesh versus the spirit. The religious overtones of Mauriac's semi-autobiographical novels are the result of a pious upbringing, which would later cause him to be identified as a Catholic novelist. In addition to his full-length fictional works, he also published two volumes of short stories, four plays, four books of poetry, a number of volumes of literary criticism, and several biographies (most notably *De Gaulle*—1964, *La Vie de Jesus*—1936, and *La Vie de Racine*—1928). (S.C.)

1953

Churchill, Winston Leonard Spencer, Sir   228
Prize: Literature, 1953. *Born:* November 30, 1874; Blenheim Palace, England. *Death:* January 24, 1965; London, England. *Parents:* Father, Randolph Spencer Churchill; Mother, Jennie Jerome Churchill. *Nationality:* British. *Religion:* Anglican. *Education:* Royal Military College, England, baccalaureate, 1895. *Spouse:* Clementine Ogilvy Hozier, married September 12, 1908. *Children:* Diana, daughter; Randolph Frederick Edward Spencer, son; Sarah, daughter; Mary, daughter; Marigold Frances, daughter. *Career:* Great Britain, various military and governmental posts up through Prime Minister, 1898–1955. *Other Awards:* Literary Award, *Sunday Times*, 1938, 1949; Man of the Year, *Time*, 1949; Charlemagne Prize, 1955; Freedom House Award, United States, 1955; Williamsburg Award, 1955; Humanitarian Award, 1954, 1956; Sonning Foundation Award, Denmark, 1959; Companion of Literature Prize, United Kingdom Royal Society, 1961; Theodore Herzl Award, Zionist Organization of America, 1964.

Selected Publications: The River War: An Historical Account of the Reconquest of the Sudan. London: Eyre & Spottiswood, 1899. *Lord Randolph Churchill.* London: Macmillan, 1906. *The World Crisis.* 4 volumes. London: T. Butterworth, 1923–29. *Marlborough, His Life and Times.* 4 volumes. London: G.G. Harrap, 1933–38. *The Second World War.* 6 volumes. Boston: Houghton-Mifflin, 1948–53. *A History of the English-Speaking Peoples.* 4 volumes. New York: Dodd, Mead, 1956–58. *My Early Life.* New York: Scribner's, 1987.

For More Information See: Broad, Lewis. *Winston Churchill: A Biography.* 2 volumes. New York: Hawthorn Books, 1958–63. Churchill, Randolph Spencer. *Winston S. Churchill.* Boston: Houghton-Mifflin, 1966. Pelling, Henry. *Winston Churchill.* New York: Dutton, 1974. Robbins, K. *Churchill.* London: Longman, 1992. Schoenfeld, Maxwell. *Sir Winston Churchill.* Melbourne, FL: Krieger, 1986.

Commentary: Winston Churchill's Nobel Award was "for his mastery of historical and biographical description as well as for brilliant oratory in defending exalted human values." It was a fitting tribute to an heroic soldier, an ingenious politician, a tirelessly intelligent organizer and manager, and an international political figure, who managed to leave, despite all of his other activities, an impressive

output of writings of magnificent quality for future generations. (N.L.)

1954

Hemingway, Ernest Miller   229
Prize: Literature, 1954. *Born:* July 21, 1899; Oak Park, IL. *Death:* July 2, 1961; Ketchum, ID. *Parents:* Father, Clarence Edmonds Hemingway; Mother, Grace Hall Hemingway. *Nationality:* American. *Religion:* Catholic. *Education:* No college degrees. *Spouse:* Hadley Richardson, married September 3, 1921, divorced January 27, 1927; Pauline Pfeiffer, married May 10, 1927, divorced November 4, 1940; Martha Gellhorn, married November 21, 1940, divorced December 21, 1945; Mary Welsh, married March 14, 1946. *Children:* John Hadley Nicanor, son; Patrick, son; Gregory Hancock, son. *Career: Kansas City Star*, Reporter, 1917–18; American Red Cross, Ambulance Driver in Italy, 1918; *Toronto Star Weekly*, Canada, Writer, 1920; *Cooperative Commonwealth*, Writer, 1921; *Toronto Star*, Canada, Correspondent, 1922–24; North American Newspaper Alliance, Correspondent in Spain, 1937–38; *PM*, Correspondent, 1941; *Colliers*, Correspondent, 1944. *Other Awards:* Pulitzer Prize, 1952.

Selected Publications: The Sun Also Rises. New York: Grosset & Dunlap, 1926. *A Farewell to Arms.* New York: Scribner's, 1927. *Death in the Afternoon.* New York: Scribner's, 1932. *For Whom the Bell Tolls.* Garden City, NJ: Sun Dial Press, 1940. *The Old Man and the Sea.* London: Jonathan Cape, 1952. *A Moveable Feast.* New York: Scribner's, 1964.

For More Information See: Baker, Carlos. *Ernest Hemingway: A Life Story.* New York: Macmillan, 1988. Griffin, Peter. *Along with Youth: Hemingway, the Early Years.* New York: Oxford Univ. Press, 1988. Hemingway, Gregory. *Papa: A Personal Memoir.* New York: Paragon, 1988. Mellon, J. *Hemingway.* Boston: Houghton Mifflin, 1992.

Commentary: The Nobel Prize citation commended Ernest Hemingway for his "powerful, stylemaking mastery of the art of modern narration, most recently displayed in *The Old Man and the Sea*, and for his influence on contemporary style." His early work was described as "brutal, cynical, and callous," but the citation also spoke of his "heroic pathos" that formed "the basic element of his awareness of life," and of his "manly love of danger and adventure." Hemingway was praised for his "natural admiration for every individual who fights the good fight in a world of reality overshadowed by violence and death." (J.K.)

1955

Laxness, Halldór Kiljan (Gudjonsson, Halldór)   230
Prize: Literature, 1955. *Born:* April 23, 1902; Reykjavik, Iceland. *Death:* February 8, 1998; Reykjavik, Iceland. *Parents:* Father, Gudjon Helgi Helgason; Mother, Sigridur Halldordottir. *Nationality:* Icelandic. *Religion:* Christian by birth; Catholic in young manhood; devoted to the class struggle later; with no religious affiliation. *Education:* No college degrees. *Spouse:* Ingibjorg Einarsdottir, married May 1, 1930, divorced 1940; Audur Sveinsdottir, married December 24, 1945. *Children:* Sigridur, daughter; Gudny, daughter; Einar, son. *Career:* Writer. *Other Awards:* Stalin

Prize, 1953; Literature Prize, International Peace Movement, 1953; Sonning Prize, 1969.

Selected Publications: *Vafarinn Mikli fra Kasmir* (*The Great Weaver from Kashmir*). Reykjavik: Acta, 1927. *Altydubokin* (*The Book of the People*). Reykjavik: Alpyouflokkurin, 1929. *Pu Vinvidur Hreini* (*O Thou Pure Vine*). Reykjavik: Bokadeild, Menningarsjoos, 1931. *Fuglinn i Fjorunni* (*The Bird on the Beach*). Reykjavik: Bokadeild, Menningarsjoos, 1932. *Salka Valka*. Copenhagen: Steen Hasselbach, 1934 (Tr. by F. H. Lyon. London: Allen and Unwin, 1963). *Sjalfstaett Folk*. 2 volumes. Reykjavik: E.P. Briem, 1934–35 (*Independent People*. Tr. by J.A. Thompson. London: Allen and Unwin, 1945). *Ljos Heimsins* (*The Light of the World*). Reykjavik: Heimskringla, 1937. *Atomstodin*. Reykjavik: Helgafell, 1948 (*The Atom Station*. Tr. by M. Magnusson. London: Methuen and Company, 1961). *Gerpla*. Reykjavik: Helgafell, 1952 (*The Happy Warriors*. Tr. by K. John. London: Methuen and Company, 1958). *Paradisarheimt*. Reykjavik: Helgafell, 1960 (*Paradise Reclaimed*. Tr. by M. Magnusson. London: Methuen and Company, 1962).

For More Information See: Hallberg, Peter. *Halldor Laxness*. New York: Twayne Publishers, 1971. *New York Times* (February 10, 1998):Sect. D, 22. *Twentieth Century Authors. First Supplement*. New York: H.W. Wilson, 1955, 561–62.

Commentary: The Academy cited Halldór Laxness "for his vivid epic power, which has renewed the great narrative art of Iceland." All of Laxness's important books have Icelandic themes and explore social and sometimes political issues, which relates to his own strong positive feelings about his country and its language, as well as to his lifelong struggles with personal religious and political beliefs. (J.H.S.)

1956

Jiménez, Juan Ramón 231

Prize: Literature, 1956. **Born:** December 24, 1881; Moguer, Spain. **Death:** May 29, 1958; San Juan, Puerto Rico. **Parents:** Father, Víctor Jiménez y Jiménez; Mother, Purificación Mantecón y López Parejo. **Nationality:** Spanish. **Religion:** Catholic. **Education:** Colegio de los Jesuitas del Puerto de Santa María de Cádiz, Spain, bachillerato, 1896. **Spouse:** Zenobia Camprubí Aymar, married 1916. **Children:** None. **Career:** Writer.

Selected Publications: *Almas de Violeta* (*Violet Souls*). Madrid: Tipografia Moderna, 1900. *Ninflas* (*Water Lilies*). Madrid: Tipografia Moderna, 1900. *Arias Tristes* (*Sad Airs*). Madrid: Fernando Fe, 1903. *Rimas* (*Rhymes*). Madrid: Fernando Fe, 1903. *Jardines Lejanos* (*Distant Gardens*). Madrid: Fernando Fe, 1904. *Elejías Puras*. (*Pure Elegies*). Madrid: Revista de Archivas, 1908. *Pastorales* (*Pastorals*). Madrid: Biblioteca Renacimiento, 1911. *La Soledad Sonora* (*The Sonorous Solitude*). Madrid: Revista de Archives, 1911. *Platero y Yo*. Madrid: La Lectura, 1914 (*Platero and I*. Tr. by William and Mary Roberts. Oxford: Dolphin, 1956). *Estio* (*Summer*). Madrid: Calleja, 1916. *Sonetos Esperituales* (*Spiritual Sonnets*). Madrid: Colleja, 1917. *Diario de Un Poeta Recién Casado* (*Diary of a Newly-Wed Poet*). Madrid: Calleja, 1917. *Espanoles de Tres Mundos* (*Spaniards of Three Worlds*). Buenos Aires: Losada, 1942. *Animal de Fondo* (*Animal of Depth*). Buenos Aires: Pleamar, 1949.

Selected Writings. Tr. by H.R. Hays. New York: Farrar, Straus and Cudahy, 1957. *Three Hundred Poems*. Tr. by Eloise Roach. Austin, TX: Univ. of Texas Press, 1962.

For More Information See: Fogelquist, Donald F. *Juan Ramón Jiménez*. Boston: Twayne Publishers, 1976. Grafias, Francisco. *Juan Ramón Jiménez*. Madrid: Taurus Ediciones, 1958. Young, Howard. *Juan Ramón Jiménez*. New York: Columbia Univ. Press, 1967.

Commentary: The Nobel Prize was granted to Juan Ramón Jiménez "for his lyrical poetry which constitutes an inspiring example in the Spanish language of spirituality and artistic poetry." Influenced by Bécquer, Darío, and other modernists, as well as by French symbolists, Jiménez created his own unique style—metaphysical, abstract, pure, lyrical, and spiritual. His work, in turn, greatly influenced many Hispanic poets—Alberti, Guillén, Salinas, Lorca, Mistral. (M.G.R.)

1957

Camus, Albert 232

Prize: Literature, 1957. **Born:** November 7, 1913; Mondovi, Algeria. **Death:** January 4, 1960; Petit-Villeblevin, France. **Parents:** Father, Lucien Camus; Mother, Catherine Sintes Camus. **Nationality:** French. **Religion:** "Atheistic Humanist;" from Christian background. **Education:** Univ. of Algiers, Algeria, Diplôme d'études superieurs, 1936. **Spouse:** Simone Hie, married June 16, 1936, divorced 1940; Francine Faure, married December 3, 1940. **Children:** Jean, son; Catherine, daughter. **Career:** Théâtre du Travail, France, Actor, Writer, Producer, 1935–38; *Alger-Républicain*, Algiers, Journalist, 1938–40; *Paris-Soir*, France, Journalist, 1940; Oran, Algeria Public School, Teacher, 1941–42; Paris, France, Freelance Journalist, 1942–45; *Combat*, Paris, France, Editor, 1944–47; Éditions Gallimard, Reader, 1943–60. **Other Awards:** Medal of the Liberation, French Government, 1946; Prix des Critiques, 1947; Legion of Honor (refused).

Selected Publications: *L'Étranger*. Paris: Gallimard, 1942 (*The Stranger*. Tr. by Stuart Gilbert. New York: A. Knopf, 1946). *Le Mythe de Sisyphe*. Paris: Gallimard, 1942 (*The Myth of Sisyphus*. Tr. by Justin O'Brien. London: H. Hamilton, 1955). *La Peste*. Paris: Gallimard, 1947 (*The Plague*. Tr. by Stuart Gilbert. New York: A. Knopf, 1948). *L'Homme Révolté*. Paris: Gallimard, 1951 (*The Rebel*. Tr. by Anthony Bower. New York: A. Knopf, 1954). *La Chute*. Paris: Gallimard, 1956 (*The Fall*. Tr. by Justin O'Brien. New York: A. Knopf, 1957). *L'Exil et Le Royaume*. Paris: Gallimard, 1957 (*Exile and the Kingdom*. Tr. by Justin O'Brien. New York: A. Knopf, 1958).

For More Information See: Brée, Germaine. *Camus*. New Brunswick, NJ: Rutgers Univ. Press, 1972. Camus, Albert. *Notebooks 1935–1942*. New York: Alfred A. Knopf, 1963. Lottman, Herbert. *Albert Camus, a Biography*. Garden City, NY: Doubleday, 1979. Thody, Philip. *Albert Camus*. New York: St. Martin's Press, 1988.

Commentary: Albert Camus was awarded the Nobel Prize "for his important literary production, which with clear-sighted earnestness illuminates the problems of the human conscience in our times." His work expressed the concerns of his generation and the moral climate of the mid-twentieth century. Confronted with war's atrocities, Camus expressed despair but looked beyond nihilism to find a reason for human existence and the possibility of happiness. (K.G.)

1958

Pasternak, Boris Leonidovich 233

Prize: Literature, 1958 (refused). *Born:* February 10, 1890; Moscow, Russia. *Death:* May 30, 1960; Peredelkino, USSR. *Parents:* Father, Leonid Ossipovich Pasternak; Mother, Rosa Isodornovna Kaufman Pasternak. *Nationality:* Russian. *Religion:* Jewish. *Education:* Moscow Univ., USSR, baccalaureate, 1913. *Spouse:* Evgeniia Vladimirovna Lourie, married 1922, divorced 1931; Zinaida Nikolaevna Neuhaus Ereemeev, married 1934. *Children:* Evgenii Borisovich, son; Leonid Borisovich, son. *Career:* Moscow, Russia, Tutor, 1914–16; Moscow, Russia, Clerk, 1916–17; Soviet Commissariat for Education, USSR, Librarian, 1918; Writers Bookshop, Moscow, USSR, Salesclerk, 1921; Commissariat of Foreign Affairs, Librarian, 1924; Translator, 1932–43. *Other Awards:* Bancarella Prize, 1958.

Selected Publications: The Collected Prose Works. Arranged by Stefan Schimanski. London: L. Drummond, 1945. *Doctor Zhivago.* Tr. by Max Hayward and Manya Harari. New York: Pantheon, 1958. *The Last Summer.* Tr. by George Reavy. New York: Avon Book Division, Hearst Corp., 1959. *The Poetry of Boris Pasternak, 1914–1960.* Tr. by George Reavy. New York: Putnam, 1960. *The Blind Beauty.* Tr. by Max Hayward and Manya Harari. New York: Harcourt, Brace & World, 1969.

For More Information See: An Essay in Autobiography. Tr. by Manya Harari. London: Collins & Harvill Press, 1959. Conquest, Robert. *Pasternak: A Biography.* New York: Octagon Books, 1979. de Mallac, Guy. *Boris Pasternak: His Life and Art.* Norman, OK: Univ. of Oklahoma Press, 1981. Fleishman, Lazar, ed. *Boris Pasternak and His Times.* Oakland, CA: Berkeley Slavic, 1988. Hingley, Robert. *Pasternak: A Biography.* New York: Knopf, 1983. *I Remember: Sketch for an Autobiography.* Tr. by David Magarshack. Cambridge, MA: Harvard Univ. Press, 1983. Sendich, M. *Boris Pasternak.* New York: G. K. Hall, 1994.

Commentary: The Committee cited Boris Pasternak "for his important achievement both in contemporary lyrical poetry and in the field of the great Russian epic tradition." Some felt that the award was based solely on *Doctor Zhivago*, but the importance of Pasternak's poetry is underscored by the fact that he was also nominated in 1953. Anders Oesterling, permanent secretary of the Academy, compared Pasternak's novel to Tolstoy's *War and Peace* and spoke of the book's "pure and powerful genius." He also said that the award was in honor of Pasternak's courage in producing a work of such independence: "It is indeed a great achievement to have been able to complete under difficult circumstances a work of such dignity, high above all political party frontiers and rather anti-political in its entirely humane outlook." (D.V.)

1959

Quasimodo, Salvatore 234

Prize: Literature, 1959. *Born:* August 20, 1901; Modica, Sicily, Italy. *Death:* June 14, 1968; Naples, Italy. *Parents:* Father, Gaetano Quasimodo; Mother, Clotilde Ragusa Quasimodo. *Nationality:* Italian. *Religion:* Catholic. *Education:* No college degrees. *Spouse:* Bice Donetti; married 1920, died 1948; Maria Cumani, married 1948. *Children:* Orietta, daughter; Alessandro, son. *Career:* Italian Ministry of Public Works, Engineer, 1926–38; *Il Tempo*, Editor, 1938–40; Giuseppe Verdi Conservatory of Music, Milan, Italy, Professor, 1941–64. *Other Awards:* Florentine Prize, Italy, 1932; Etna-Taormina International Poetry Prize, 1953; Viareggio Prize, 1958.

Selected Publications: Edè Subito Sera. Milan: Mondadori, 1942. *Giorno Dopo Giorno.* Milan: Mondadori, 1947. *La Vita Non è Sogno.* Milan: Mondadori, 1949. *Il Falso e Vero Verde.* Milan: Schwarz, 1954. *La Terra Impareggiabile.* Milan: Mondadori, 1958. *Selected Writings of Salvatore Quasimodo.* Tr. by Allen Mandelbaum. New York: Farrar, Straus & Cudahy, 1960.

For More Information See: Contemporary Authors, Permanent Series. Detroit, MI: Gale, 1975 (Volume 1), 524–25. *Current Biography Yearbook.* New York: H.W. Wilson, 1960, 325–27.

Commentary: Salvatore Quasimodo, Italian poet and translator, was awarded the Nobel Prize "for his lyrical poetry, which with classical fire expresses the tragic experience of life in our times." In the 1930s, he was considered to be a leader of the Italian hermetic poetry movement. After World War II, his poetry, while retaining classical imagery and themes, became an instrument for social and political reform. It is this later poetry that the Nobel Committee expressly cited in awarding the prize. (S.W.C.)

1960

Saint-John Perse (Léger, Marie-Rene Auguste Alexis Saint-Léger) 235

Prize: Literature, 1960. *Born:* May 31, 1887; Saint-Léger-les-Feuilles, French West Indies. *Death:* September 20, 1975; Giens, France. *Parents:* Father, Amedée Léger; Mother, Françoise-Renée Dormoy Léger. *Nationality:* French. *Religion:* Spiritualist; from Protestant background. *Education:* Univ. of Bordeaux, France, Licencié in Law, 1908. *Spouse:* Dorothy Milburn Russell, married 1958. *Children:* None. *Career:* French Government Positions, 1914–40; United States Library of Congress, Consultant, 1941–45. *Other Awards:* Grand Officer of Legion of Honor; Knight of the Grand Cross of the British Empire; Award of Merit, American Academy of Arts and Letters, 1950; Grand Prix National des Letters, 1959; Grand Prix International de Poésie, Belgium, 1959.

Selected Publications: Éloges. Paris: Gallimard, 1911 (*Eulogies and Other Poems.* Tr. by Louise Varese. New York: Norton, 1944). *Anabase.* Paris: Gallimard, 1924 (*Anabasis.* Tr. by T.S. Eliot. London: Faber, 1930). *Exil, Suivi de Poémes a L'Étrangere, Pluies, Neiges.* Paris: Gallimard, 1945 (*Exile, and Other Poems.* Tr. by Denis Devlin. New York: Pantheon, 1949). *Vents.* Paris: Gallimard, 1946 (*Winds.* Tr. by Hugh Chisholm. New York: Pantheon, 1952). *Amers.* Paris: NRF, 1953 (*Seamarks.* Tr. by Wallace Fowlie. New York: Pantheon, 1958).

For More Information See: Galand, Rene. *Saint-John Perse.* New York: Twayne, 1972. Knodel, Arthur. *Saint-John Perse: A Study of His Poetry.* Edinburgh: Edinburgh

Univ. Press, 1966. Ostrovsky, Erica. *Under the Sign of Ambiguity*. New York: New York Univ. Press, 1985. Sacotte, M. *Saint-John Perse*. Paris: P. Belfond, 1991.

Commentary: Saint-John Perse's Nobel was "for the soaring flight and the evocative imagery of his poetry, which in a visionary fashion reflects the conditions of our times." His impressive diplomatic career and the destruction of his manuscripts by the Nazis left a rather small total body of work. Never closely allied with any school of poetry though a friend of many poets, Saint-John Perse began by evoking his childhood by the tropical sea. *Anabasis* continues the exotic background, in his own words "a poem of personal and public solitude in the midst of action." *Exile* deals with more personal subjects in a nevertheless epic fashion; *Winds*, too, is epic, and like *Anabasis* can be read on another level as about literature's ability to make passing time eternal. *Seamarks* pictures human life centered about the sea and features a discussion between Man and Woman concerning human life, love, and eternity. Little-known in or out of France, Saint-John Perse is an author whose work is not easy but is extremely rewarding for those who will live with it and absorb its grand scope, its clarity of image, and its levels of meaning. (E.B.)

1961

Andrić, Ivo   236

Prize: Literature, 1961. *Born:* October 10, 1892; Dolac, Yugoslavia. *Death:* March 13, 1975; Belgrade, Yugoslavia. *Parents:* Father, Antun Andrić; Mother, Katarina Pejic Andrić. *Nationality:* Yugoslavian. *Religion:* Eastern Orthodox. *Education:* Univ. of Graz, Austria, Ph.D., 1923. *Spouse:* Milica Babic, married 1959. *Children:* None. *Career:* Yugoslavian Diplomatic Service, 1923–41; Yugoslavian Politics, 1946–52. *Other Awards:* Prize for Life Work, Yugoslavia.

Selected Publications: Gospodica (*The Woman from Sarajevo*). Sarajevo, Yugoslavia: Sjetlost, 1945. *Travnick Hronika* (*Bosnian Chronicle*). Belgrade: Drez. Izdavacki Zavad Jugoslavije, 1945. *Na Drini Cuprija*. Sarajevo, Yugoslavia: Sjetlost, 1947 (*The Bridge on the Drina*. Tr. by Lovett F. Edwards. London: George Allen & Unwin, Ltd., 1959). *Prokleta Avlija*. Belgrade: Prosveta, 1954 (*Devil's Yard*. Tr. by Kenneth Johnstone. New York: Grove Press, 1962).

For More Information See: Contemporary Literary Criticism. Detroit, MI: Gale, 1978 (Volume 8), 19–22. Hawkesworth, Celia. *Ivo Andrić*. London: Athlone Press, 1980. Juricic, Zelimir. *The Man and the Artist: Essays on Ivo Andrić*. Lenham, MD: Univ. Press of America, 1986. Singh Mukerji, V. *Ivo Andrić*. Jefferson, NC: McFarland, 1990.

Commentary: The Nobel Prize was presented to Ivo Andrić "for the epic force with which he has traced themes and depicted human destinies from his country's history." Especially in his Bosnian trilogy, Andrić presented the panorama of Serbian history and life, from the sixteenth-century action around the bridge in *The Bridge on the Drina* to the rivalry between the Austrian and French consuls in Travnick of the Napoleonic Wars in *Bosnian Story* and finally to the psychological study of the merchant's daughter in the present-day *The Woman from Sarajevo*. (K.C.)

1962

Steinbeck, John Ernst   237

Prize: Literature, 1962. *Born:* February 27, 1902; Salinas, California. *Death:* December 28, 1968; New York, NY. *Parents:* Father, John Ernst Steinbeck; Mother, Olive Hamilton Steinbeck. *Nationality:* American. *Religion:* Protestant. *Education:* No college degrees. *Spouse:* Carol Henning, married 1930, divorced 1943; Gwyn Conger, married 1943, divorced 1949; Elaine Scott, married 1950. *Children:* Tom, son; John, son. *Career:* Writer and Free-lance Journalist. *Other Awards:* Gold Medal, Commonwealth Club of California, 1936, 1937, 1940; Circle Silver Plaque, New York Drama Critics, 1938; Pulitzer Prize, 1940.

Selected Publications: To a God Unknown. New York: Covici-Freide, 1933. *Tortilla Flat*. New York: Covici-Freide, 1935. *In Dubious Battle*. New York: Covici-Freide, 1936. *Of Mice and Men*. New York: Covici-Freide, 1937. *The Red Pony*. New York: Viking Press, 1937. *The Grapes of Wrath*. New York: Viking Press, 1939. *The Forgotten Village*. New York: Viking Press, 1941. *The Moon Is Down*. New York: Viking Press, 1942. *The Pearl*. New York: Viking Press, 1947. *East of Eden*. New York: Viking Press, 1952. *Sweet Thursday*. New York: Viking Press, 1954. *Once There Was a War*. New York: Viking Press, 1958. *The Winter of Our Discontent*. New York: Viking Press, 1961. *The Short Novels of John Steinbeck*. New York: Viking Press, 1963. Harmon, Robert B. *Steinbeck Bibliography: An Annotated Guide*. Metuchen, NJ: Scarecrow, 1987.

For More Information See: Bloom, Harold. *John Steinbeck*. New York: Chelsea, 1987. Fensch, Thomas, ed. *Conversations with Steinbeck*. Jackson, MS: Univ. of Mississippi, 1988. Fontenrose, Joseph. *John Steinbeck*. New York: Barnes & Noble, 1963. French, Warren. *John Steinbeck*. Boston: Twayne Publishers, 1961. Parini, J. *John Steinbeck*. New York: H. Holt, 1995.

Commentary: John Steinbeck was cited by the Academy "for his one and at the same time realistic and imaginative writings distinguished as they are by a sympathetic humour and a social perception." An author whose critical acclaim seemed to rise or fall almost with each literary contribution, Steinbeck appeared to be most in his element when writing about "the simple joy of life." The Nobel jurors cited his "great feeling for nature—the tilled soil, the wasteland, the mountains and the ocean coasts" in his writing. The American proletariat was the model for Steinbeck's most memorable characters and formed the nucleus around which some of his most recognized themes revolved—such topics as the Depression, realities of nature, responsibility and human suffering, moral neutrality, and eccentric loneliness. (J.H.S.)

1963

Seferis, Giorgos (Seferiádis, Yorgos)   238

Prize: Literature, 1963. *Born:* February 29, 1900; Smyrna, Turkey. *Death:* September 20, 1971; Athens, Greece. *Parents:* Father, Stelios Seferiádis; Mother, Dhespo Tinekidhis Seferiádis. *Nationality:* Greek. *Religion:* Eastern Orthodox. *Education:* Univ. of Paris-Sorbonne, France, law degree, 1924. *Spouse:* Maria Zannou, married 1941. *Children:* None. *Career:* Greek Diplomat, 1931–62.

Selected Publications: Six Poems from the Greek of Sikelianos and Seferis. Tr. by L. Durell. Athens: Rhodes,

1946. *The King of Asine and Other Poems*. Tr. by B. Spencer, N. Valaoritis, and L. Durell. London: Lehmann, 1948. *Poems*. Tr. by Rex Warner. London: Bodley Head, 1960. *Collected Poems, 1924–1955*. Tr. by Edmund Keeley and Philip Sherrard. Princeton, NJ: Princeton Univ. Press, 1967. *Three Secret Poems*. Tr. by Walter Kaiser. Cambridge, MA: Harvard Univ. Press, 1969.

For More Information See: Current Biography Yearbook. New York: H.W. Wilson, 1964, 402–04. *Days of 1945–1951: A Poet's Journal*. Tr. by Athan Anagnostopoulos. Cambridge, MA: Harvard Univ. Press, 1974. Tsatsou, I. *My Brother, George Seferis*. St. Paul, MN: North Central Publishing, 1982.

Commentary: Giorgos Seferis was cited by the Academy for "the unique thought and style and beauty of his language, which has become a lasting symbol of all that is indestructible in the Hellenic acceptance of life." In his poetry, Seferis immortalized the glory and the pain of the Greek experience, investigating in depth the themes of modern tensions, war, exile, and nostalgia. In his life's work, meanwhile, the poet carried forward the history of Greece in a series of important diplomatic posts held over a period of 31 years. (J.H.S.)

1964

Sartre, Jean-Paul Charles Aymard   239

Prize: Literature, 1964 (refused). *Born:* June 21, 1905; Paris, France. *Death:* April 15, 1980; Paris, France. *Parents:* Father, Jean Baptiste Sartre; Mother, Anne Marie Schweitzer. *Nationality:* French. *Religion:* Atheist in adult years; from Lutheran/Catholic background. *Education:* École Normale Supérieure, France, "Agrege de philosophie," 1929. *Spouse:* Unmarried, but lived with life-long companion Simone De Beauvoir for almost 50 years. *Children:* None; but legally adopted his editorial assistant, Miss Arlette Kaim. *Career:* French Army, Sergeant, 1929–31; Lycée du Havre, France, Professor, 1931–33; Institute Français, Berlin, Germany, Teaching Fellow, 1933–34; Lycée de Laon, France, Professor, 1936–37; Lycée Pasteur de Neuilly-sur-Seine, France, Professor, 1937–39; French Army, 1939–41; Lycée Condorcet, France, Professor, 1941–44; *Les Temps Moderne*, Paris, France, Editor, 1944–80. *Other Awards:* French Popular Novel Prize, 1940; Legion d'honneur (refused), 1945; New York Drama Critics Award, 1947; French Grand Novel Prize, 1950; Omega Prize, Italy, 1950.

Selected Publications: La Nausée. Paris: Gallimard, 1938 (*Nausea*. Tr. by R. Baldick. Harmondsworth, England: Penguin, 1965). *L'imagination*. Paris: F. Alcan, 1939 (*Imagination*. Tr. by F. Williams. Ann Arbor, MI: Univ. of Michigan Press, 1962). *Le Mur*. Paris: Gallimard, 1939 (*The Wall*. Tr. by L. Alexander. Norfolk, CT: Penguin 1948). *L'imaginaire: Psychologie Phenomenologie*. Paris: Gallimard, 1940 (*The Psychology of Imagination*. Tr. by B. Frechtman. New York: Philosophical Library, 1948). *L'être et le Néant: Essais d'Ontologie Phenomenologique*. Paris: Gallimard, 1943 (*Being and Nothingness: An Essay on Phenomenological Ontology*. New York: Philosophical Library, 1956). *Huis clos*. Paris: Gallimard, 1943 (*In Camera*. Tr. by S. Gilbert. New York: Alfred A. Knopf, 1946. Also Tr. as *No Exit* by P. Bowles. New York, 1958). *Les Chemins de la Liberté*. Paris: Gallimard, 1945–49, comprising: 1. *L'âge de Raison, Roman*, 1945 (*The Age of Reason*.

Tr. by E. Sutton. New York: Alfred A. Knopf, 1947); 2. *Le Sursis*, 1945 (*The Reprieve*. Tr. by E. Sutton. London: Hamish Hamilton, 1947); 3. *La Mort dans l'Âme*, 1949 (*Iron in the Soul*. Tr. by G. Hopkins. London: Hamish Hamilton, 1950). *Mort sans Sépalture*. Lausanne: Marguerat, 1946 (*Men without Shadows*. Tr. by Kitty Black. London: H. Hamilton, 1949). *Les Mouches*. Paris: Gallimard, 1946 (*The Flies*. Tr. by S. Gilbert. New York: Alfred A. Knopf, 1946). *La Putain Respectueuse*. Paris: Nagel, 1946 (*The Respectful Prostitute*. Tr. by K. Black. London: Hamish Hamilton, 1949). *Réflexion sur la Question Juive*. Paris: Morihien, 1946 (*Portrait of the Anti-Semite*. Tr. by Mary Guggenheim. New York: Partisan Review, 1946). *Situations*, 9 volumes (collected articles and criticism). Paris: Gallimard, 1947–72 (*What is Literature?* Tr. by B. Frechtman. New York: Philosophical Library, 1949—from *Situation III*). *Literary and Philosophical Essays*. (Tr by A. Michelson. London: Rider, 1955—selections). *Situations*. (Tr. by B. Eisler. London: Fawcitt, 1965—*Situations IV*). *Les Jeux sont Faits*. French and European Publications, 1947 (*The Chips are Down*. Tr. by L. Vares. New York: Lear, 1948). *L'engrenage*. Paris: Nagel, 1948 (*In the Mesh*. Tr. by M. Savill. London: A. Dakers). *Les Mains Sales*. Paris: Gallimard, 1948 (*Dirty Hands*. Tr. by L. Abel. New York: Vintage Books, 1949). *Le Diable et le bon Dieu*. Paris: Gallimard, 1951 (*Lucifer and the Lord*. Tr. by Kitty Black. London: H. Hamilton, 1953). *Les Séquestrés d'Altona*. Paris: Gallimard, 1955 (*The Condemned of Altona*. Tr. by G. and S. Leeson. New York: Vintage Books, 1961). *Les Mots*. Paris: Gallimard, 1964 (*Words*. Tr. by I. Clephane. London: H. Hamilton, 1964).

For More Information See: de Beauvoir, S. *Adieux: A Farewell to Sartre*. New York: Pantheon, 1984. Hayman, Ronald. *Sartre*. New York: Simon & Schuster, 1987. Howells, C. *The Cambridge Companion to Sartre*. Cambridge, England: Cambridge Univ. Press, 1992. Suhl, Benjamin. *Jean-Paul Sartre: The Philosopher as Literary Critic*. New York: Columbia Univ. Press, 1970. Thody, Philip Malcolm. *Sartre: A Biographical Introduction*. New York: Scribner's, 1972.

Commentary: The award to Jean-Paul Sartre was "for his work which, rich in ideas and filled with the spirit of freedom and the quest for truth, has exerted a far-reaching influence on our age." Although Sartre is primarily known for his contributions in the areas of drama and psychological biography, he is equally well known for his notable contributions in literary criticism, political journalism, and philosophy. Probably most know him for his development of the philosophy of existentialism and for the play *No Exit* (1947), still frequently read in college literature courses. (P.K.)

1965

Sholokhov, Mikhail Aleksandrovich   240

Prize: Literature, 1965. *Born:* May 24, 1905; Veshenskaya, Rostov, Russia. *Death:* February 21, 1984; Veshenskaya, Rostov, USSR. *Parents:* Father, Aleksander Mikhailovich Sholokhov; Mother, Anastasiya Danilovna Chernikova Sholokhov. *Nationality:* Russian. *Religion:* Atheist; from

Eastern Orthodox background. *Education:* No college degrees. *Spouse:* Maria Petrovna Gromoslakskaya, married 1923. *Children:* 4 children. *Career:* Soviet Army, 1918–22; Moscow, USSR, Manual Laborer, 1922–26; Writer and Politician thereafter. *Other Awards:* Stalin Prize, 1941; Order of the Fatherland; Lenin Prize, 1960; Hero of Socialist Labor, 1967; Order of Lenin, 8 times.

Selected Publications: Nakhalenof. Moscow: n.p., 1925. *Lazorevaya Steppe.* Moscow: n.p., 1925. *Donskie Rasskazy.* Originally published in 1925. Available through Moscow: Gosud. Izd-vo, Khudozh Lit-ry, 1958 (*Tales of the Don.* Tr. by H.C. Stevens. New York: Knopf, 1962). *Tikhii Don.* Originally published, 1926–40. Available through Moscow: Gosud. Izd-vo, Khudozh Lit-ry, 1945 (Translation of volumes 1 and 2 by Stephen Garry published as *And Quiet Flows the Don.* New York: Putman, 1934; translation of volumes 3 and 4 by Stephen Garry published as *The Don Flows Home to the Sea.* New York: Putman, 1940). *Seeds of Tomorrow.* Tr. by Stephen Garry. New York: Knopf, 1935. *Nauka Nenavisti.* Originally published in 1942. Available through Moscow: Sovremennik, 1975 (*Hate.* Moscow: Foreign Language Publishing House, 1942). *Oni Srazhalis' Za Rodinu.* Volume 1. Moscow: Pravda, 1943. *Shornik Statei.* Leningrad: Izdvo Leningradskogo Universiteta, 1956. *Sobraine Sochinenii.* 8 volumes. Moscow: Goslitzdat, 1956–60. *Sud'ba Cheloveka.* Moscow: Gos. Izd-vo Khudozh, Lit-ry, 1957 (*The Fate of Man.* Tr. by Robert Daglish. Moscow: Foreign Languages Press, 1957). *Harvest on the Don.* Tr. by H.C. Stevens. New York: Putnam, 1960. *Rannie Rasskazy.* Moscow: Sovetskaiia Rossia, 1961. *Pleswns, Romans.* Moscow: Riga, 1961. *Put'dorozhen'ka.* Moscow: Molodaia Gvardiia, 1962. *Slovo o Rodine.* Moscow: n.p., 1965. *Izbrannoe.* Moscow: Molodaia Gvardiia, 1968. *Po Veleniiu Dushi.* Moscow: Molodaia Gvardiia, 1970 (*At the Bidding of the Heart.* Tr. by Olga Shartse. Progress Publishers, 1973). *Rosii v Serdtse.* Moscow: Sovremennik, 1975. *Slovo k Molodym.* Moscow: n.p., 1975. *Stories.* Moscow: Progress Publishers, 1975.

For More Information See: Ermolaev, Herman. *Mikhail Sholokhov and His Art.* Princeton, NJ: Princeton Univ. Press, 1982. Slonim, Marc. *Soviet Russian Literature, 1917–77.* New York: Oxford Univ. Press, 1977, 188–97. Stewart, D. *Mikhail Sholokhov: A Critical Introduction.* Ann Arbor, MI: Univ. of Michigan Press, 1967.

Commentary: Mikhail Sholokhov's award was for "artistic strength and honesty when depicting a historical epoch in the life of the Russian people." His major work, *The Quiet Don* (a 1934 work which took him 14 years to write and which is published in the U.S. as *Quiet Flows the Don*), is an epic novel steeped heavily in nineteenth century realism. The work, an outstanding representative of the so-called "proletarian" current in Russian literature, has been compared by some to *War and Peace*, and it was instrumental in his becoming, at age 50, the most renowned writer in the Soviet Union. The struggle between the old and the new, the difficulty in choosing between white and red Russia, dominates his work. Sholokhov was often a controversial figure in the Kremlin because his position was so high that he could afford to be very outspoken. (D.S. and R.P.)

1966

Agnon, Shmuel Yosef (Czaczkes, Shmuel Yosef)   241

Prize: Literature, 1966. *Born:* July 17, 1888; Buczacz, Galicia (Austria). *Death:* February 17, 1970; Rehovat, Israel. *Parents:* Father, Shalom Czaczkes; Mother, Esther Farb Czaczkes. *Nationality:* Austrian; later Israeli citizen. *Religion:* Jewish. *Education:* No college degrees. *Spouse:* Esther Marx, married 1920. *Children:* Emuna, daughter; Hemdat, son. *Career:* Israel, Governmental Agency Secretary, 1907–13. *Other Awards:* Ussishkin Prize, 1950; Bialik Prize, Israel, 1954, 1958.

Selected Publications: Hakhnasat Kalah. Berlin: Schocken, 1931 (*The Bridal Canopy.* Tr. by I.M. Lask. New York: Doubleday, 1937). "Sefer Hamaasim" (*The Book of Deeds*). *Davar (Musaf)* VII (April 20, 1932). "Pat Shlema." *Moznayim* IV (January 5, 1933): 50–53. In *A Whole Loaf.* Tr. by I.M. Lask. Jerusalem: Schocken, 1958, 316–31. *Oreach Nata Lalun.* In *Kol Sippurav* (Volume VII). Berlin: Schocken, 1939 (*Wayfarer Stopped for a Night.* Tr. by R. Alter. *Mosaic* II (Winter 1961): 37–41). *Shevuat Emunim.* Jerusalem: Schocken, 1943 ("Betrothed." In *Two Tales.* Tr. by W. Lever. New York: Schocken, 1966). *Temol Shilshom (Only Yesterday).* In *Kol Sipurav* (Volume IX). Berlin: Schocken, 1945. *Kol Sipurav (Collected Works).* 11 volumes. Berlin: Schocken, 1931–53.

For More Information See: Aberbach, David. *At the Handles of the Lock.* London: Oxford Univ. Press, 1984. Band, Arnold J. *Nostalgia and Nightmare.* Berkeley, CA: Univ. of California Press, 1968. *Contemporary Authors. Permanent Series.* Detroit, MI: Gale, 1978 (Volume 2), 16–18. Fisch, Harold. *S.Y. Agnon.* New York: Frederick Ungar, 1975. Shaked, Gershon. *Shmuel Yosef Agnon: A Revolutionary Tradition.* New York: New York Univ. Press, 1989.

Commentary: "For his profoundly distinctive narrative art with motifs from the life of the Jewish people," S.Y. Agnon was given the Nobel Prize. Over six decades, Agnon produced poems, stories, and novels that first lovingly and simply told of the life of the Jewish communities in Eastern Europe and later introduced overtones of fantasy and nightmare in the Kafka tradition. His *The Bridal Canopy* has been referred to as a Hebrew *Don Quixote.* Agnon also produced critically acclaimed books on the Days of Awe, the giving of the Torah, and Hassidic lore. (J.H.S.)

Sachs, Leonie Nelly   242

Prize: Literature, 1966. *Born:* December 10, 1891; Berlin, Germany. *Death:* May 12, 1970; Stockholm, Sweden. *Parents:* Father, William Sachs; Mother, Margaretha Karger. *Nationality:* German; later Swedish citizen. *Religion:* Jewish. *Education:* No college degrees. *Spouse:* None. *Children:* None. *Career:* Berlin, Germany and Stockholm, Sweden, Translator. *Other Awards:* Kulturpreis der Deutschen Industrie, 1959; Jahrespring Literary Prize, 1959; Annette von Droste-Hülshoff Prize, 1960; 1st Nelly Sachs Prize for Literature, 1961; Peace Prize, German Bookseller's Association, 1966.

Selected Publications: Eli: Ein Mysterienspiel vom Leiden Israels. Stockholm: Walter A. Berendsohn, 1943 (*Eli: A Mystery Play of the Sufferings of Israel.* Tr. by Christopher Holme. New York: Kurt Bernheim, 1970). *In den Wohnungen des Todes* (*In the Habitations of Death*). Berlin: Aufbau-Verlag, 1947. *Sternverdunkelung* (*Eclipse of the Stars*). Amsterdam: Berman-Fischer, 1949. *Und Neimand Weiss Weiter* (*And Noone Knows Where to Go*). Hamburg: Heinrich Ellerman, 1957. *Flucht und Verwandlung* (*Flight and Metamorphosis*). Stuttgart, Germany: Deutsche Verlags-Anstalt, 1959. *Fahrt ins Staublose* (*Journey to the Beyond*). Frankfurt: Suhrkamp Verlag, 1961. *Zerchen im Sand* (*Signs in the Sand*). Frankfurt: Suhrkamp Verlag, 1962. *O the Chimneys. Selected Poems, Including the Verse Play, "Eli."* Tr. by Michael Hamburger, Christopher Holme, Ruth and Matthew Mead, and Michael Raloff. New York: Farrar, Straus and Giroux, 1967.

For More Information See: Hermann, Armin. *German Nobel Prizewinners.* Munich: Heinz Moos Verlagsgesellschaft, 1968, 32, 39, 40. Opfell, Olga S. *The Lady Laureates.* Metuchen, NJ: Scarecrow Press, 1978, 135–46. St. Andrew, B. "The Forces of Life." *Humanist* 45 (January/February 1985): 31.

Commentary: The Holocaust, from which she escaped, transformed Nelly Sachs from a minor German poet writing rhymed forms about nature and mythological figures to a powerful voice that reached into the hearts of the world with echoes of Jewish mysticism in works that were her "mute outcry" against her people's sufferings. Her later work identified Jewish suffering with the suffering of all humanity and led to a final message of forgiveness, peace, and hope resting in new generations. The Committee cited her "for her outstanding lyrical and dramatic writings, which interpret Israel's destiny with touching strength." (J.H.S.)

1967

Asturias, Miguel Angel 243

Prize: Literature, 1967. *Born:* October 19, 1899; Guatemala City, Guatemala. *Death:* June 9, 1974; Madrid, Spain. *Parents:* Father, Ernesto Asturias; Mother, Maria Rosales de Asturias. *Nationality:* Guatemalan. *Religion:* Most probably Christian/Catholic. *Education:* San Carlos Univ., Guatemala, law degree, 1923. *Spouse:* Clemencia Amado, married 1939, divorced 1947; Blanca Mora y Araujo, married (no date found). *Children:* Rodrigo, son; Miguel Angel, son. *Career:* Guatemala, Newspaper Correspondent, 1923–33; Writer/Diplomat. *Other Awards:* Chavez Prize, 1923; Prix Sylla Monsegur, Paris, 1931; Lenin Peace Prize, 1966.

Selected Publications: Leyendas de Guatemala. Madrid: Ediciones Oriente, 1930. *El Señor Presidente.* Mexico City: Editorial Costa-Amic, 1946 (*The President.* Tr. by Frances Partridge. London: V. Gollancz, 1963). *Viento Fuerte.* Buenos Aires: Losada, 1950 (*The Cyclone.* Tr. by Dawin Flahall and Claribel Alegaria. London: Owen, 1967). *Bolívar.* Guatemala City: Editorial Landiver, 1961. *Emulo Lipolidan Fantomina por Miguel Angel Asturias.* Guatemala City: Editorial Landiver, 1961. *Mulata de Tal.* Buenos Aires: Editorial Losada, 1963 (*Mulata.* Tr. by Gregory Ratassa. New York: Delacorte Press, 1967).

For More Information See: Callan, Richard. *Miguel Angel Asturias.* New York: Twayne, 1970. *Current Biography Yearbook.* New York: H.W. Wilson, 1975, 35–38.

Commentary: Miguel Asturias received the Nobel "for his highly colored writings, rooted in a national individuality and Indian traditions." In his many novels, stories, poems, and plays, Asturias displayed his concern for the South American Indian traditions, mythology, and folklore; the national identity for which he fought; and the compassion for the underdog in which he believed. His writing was a true reflection of his beliefs, which led to many years in exile because of his opposition to dictatorships in power in his native Guatemala. (J.H.S.)

1968

Kawabata, Yasunari 244

Prize: Literature, 1968. *Born:* June 11, 1899; Osaka, Japan. *Death:* April 16, 1972; Zushi, Japan. *Parents:* Father, Eikichi Kawabata; Mother, Gen Kawabata. *Nationality:* Japanese. *Religion:* From Buddhist background. *Education:* Tokyo Imperial Univ., Japan, baccalaureate, 1924. *Spouse:* Matsubayashi Hideko, married (common law) 1926, (formally) 1931. *Children:* 1 daughter. *Career:* Japan, Writer and Editor. *Other Awards:* Bungei Konwa Kai Prize, 1937; Geijutsuin-sho Literary Prize, 1952; Noma Literary Prize, 1954; Goethe Medal, Germany, 1959; Ordre des Arts et Lettres, France, 1960; French Prix du Meilleur Livre Etranger, 1961; Cultural Medal, Japan, 1961; Akutagawa Prize.

Selected Publications: Yukiguni (*Snow Country*). Tr. by Edward G. Seidensticker. New York: Knopf, 1956. *Sembazuru* (*Thousand Cranes*). Tr. by Edward G. Seidensticker. New York: Knopf, 1959. *Nemureru bijo* (*The House of the Sleeping Beauties and Other Stories*). Tr. by Edward G. Seidensticker. Tokyo: Kodansha International, 1969. *Yama No Oto* (*The Sound of the Mountain*). Tr. by Edward G. Seidensticker. New York: Knopf, 1970. *Meijin* (*The Master of Go*). Tr. by Edward G. Seidensticker. New York: Knopf, 1972. *Utsukshisa To Kanashimi To* (*Beauty and Sadness*). Tr. by Howard Hibbett. New York: Knopf, 1975.

For More Information See: Buckstead, Richard. *Kawabata and the Divided Self.* Taiwan: China Printing, 1972. *Contemporary Authors.* Detroit, MI: Gale Research, 1980 (Volume 93–96), 265–68. *Current Biography Yearbook.* New York: H.W. Wilson, 1969, 231–33. Gesell, V. *Three Modern Novelists.* Tokyo, Japan: Kodansha International, 1993.

Commentary: The award to Yasunari Kawabata was "for his narrative mastership, which with sensibility expresses the essence of the Japanese mind." The first Japanese writer to win the Nobel Prize in literature, Kawabata rejected earlier experiments with the "automatic writing" of Gertrude Stein as well as the "stream of consciousness" method of James Joyce in favor of a more traditional Japanese style of writing that is lyrical and deceptively simple. Kawabata's works are characteristically melancholic and deal with such major themes as alienation, guilt, love, old age, and the acceptance of death. Prior to winning the Nobel Prize, Kawabata was virtually unknown outside of Japan. His winning of the award surprised many Western critics, who were often puzzled by the episodic structure found in his impressionistic novels. (K.M.)

1969

Beckett, Samuel Barclay 245

Prize: Literature, 1969. *Born:* April 13, 1906; Dublin, Ireland. *Death:* December 22, 1989; Paris, France. *Parents:*

Father, William Frank Beckett; Mother, Mary Roe Beckett. *Nationality:* Irish; later French resident. *Religion:* Protestant. *Education:* Trinity College, Ireland, B.A., 1927; Trinity College, Ireland, M.A., 1931. *Spouse:* Suzanne Dechevaux-Dumesnil, married March 25, 1961. *Children:* None. *Career:* Campbell College, Belfast, Ireland, Professor, 1927–28; École Normale Supérieure, Paris, France, Professor, 1928–31; Trinity College, Dublin, Ireland, Professor, 1931–32; Writer. *Other Awards:* Evening Standard Award, 1955; Obie Award, 1958, 1960, 1962, 1964; Italia Prize, 1959, 1957; International Publishers Prize, 1961; Prix Formentor, 1961; Prix Filmcritice, 1965; Tours Film Prize, 1966; Grand Priz National du Theatre, France, 1975.

Selected Publications: En Attendant Godot. Paris: Edition de Minuit, 1952 (*Waiting for Godot.* London: Faber, 1956). *Malloy.* Paris: Olympia Press, 1955. *Malone Dies.* New York: Grove Press, 1956. *All That Falls.* New York: Grove Press, 1957. *Murphy.* New York: Grove Press, 1957. *Proust.* New York: Grove Press, 1957. *The Unnamable.* New York: Grove Press, 1958. *Watt.* Paris: Olympic Press, 1958. *Endgame.* London: Faber, 1959. *Krapp's Last Tape, and Embers.* London: Faber, 1959. *Happy Days.* New York: Grove Press, 1961. *More Pricks than Kicks.* London: Calder & Boyars, 1966. *No's Knife: Collected Shorter Prose, 1945–1966.* London: Calder & Boyars, 1967. *Collected Works.* New York: Grove Press, 1970. *First Love and Other Shorts.* New York: Grove Press, 1974. *The Complete Dramatic Works.* London: Faber, 1986. *Malloy Malone Dies Unnameable.* New York: Grove, 1989.

For More Information See: Bair, Dierdre. *Samuel Beckett: A Biography.* New York: Harcourt, 1978. Ben-Zvi, Linda. *Samuel Beckett.* Boston: Twayne, 1986. Brater, E. *Why Beckett.* New York: Thames and Hudson, 1989. Gordon, Lois G. *The World of Samuel Beckett, 1906–1946.* New Haven: Yale University Press, 1996. Kennedy, Andrew. *Samuel Beckett.* Cambridge, England: Cambridge Univ. Press, 1989. Lyons, Charles. *Samuel Beckett.* New York: Grove Press, 1983. Tindall, William York. *Samuel Beckett.* New York: Columbia Univ. Press, 1964.

Commentary: Samuel Beckett's Nobel citation recognized him "for introducing new forms to the novel and the drama." Known for his contributions to the theater of the absurd, Beckett himself said "The major sin is the sin of being born." His works portrayed life as "buzzing confusion all around us" centered on Beckett's view of human beings' futile existence. His characters buzz away their existence in pointless, absurd, confusing activity. They exist in settings and engage in discussions from which the only hope for relief is a return to a prefetal nothingness. Using parables to define human beings' completely rudderless spiritual desolation, Beckett conveys the absurdity of life by showing reality as nothingness and theater—a representation of life—as absurd. (J.H.S.)

1970

Solzhenitsyn, Alexander   246

Prize: Literature, 1970. *Born:* December 11, 1918; Kislorodsk, USSR. *Parents:* Father, Isai Solzhenitsyn; Mother, Taisya Zakharovna Shcherbak Solzhenitsyn. *Nationality:* Russian; later American resident. *Religion:* Eastern Orthodox. *Education:* Rostov Univ., USSR,

baccalaureate, 1941. *Spouse:* Natalya Reshetovskaya, married April 27, 1940, divorced 1949, remarried 1956, redivorced 1972; Natalya Svetlova, married 1973. *Children:* Yermoli, son; Ignat, son; Stephan, son. *Career:* Secondary School, USSR, Teacher, 1941; Soviet Army, 1941–45; Prisoner, Exile, Writer, 1945-. *Other Awards:* Lenin Prize Nomination, 1964; Prix du Meilleur Livre Etranger, France, 1969; Freedoms Foundation Award, 1976; Templeton Prize, 1983; Medal of Honor for Literature, National Arts Club, 1993.

Selected Publications: Odin den' Ivana Denisovicha Matrenin Dvor. Paris: YMCA Press, 1973 (first published in 1963) (*One Day in the Life of Ivan Denisovich.* Tr. by Ralph Parker. New York: Dutton, 1963). *V Kruge Pervom.* Paris: YMCA Press, 1968 (*First Circle.* Tr. by Thomas P. Whitney. New York: Harper and Row, 1968). *Rakovyĭ Korpus.* Paris: YMCA Press, 1969 (*Cancer Ward. Sobranie Sochinenii.* (Collected Works). 5 volumes. Frankfurt: Possev Verlag, 1969–70. Tr. by Nicholas Bethel and David Burg. New York: Farrar, Straus and Giroux, 1969). *August Chetyrnadtsatogo.* Paris: YMCA Press, 1971 (*August 1914.* Tr. by Michael Glenny. New York: Farrar, Straus and Giroux, 1972). *Arkhipelag Gulag.* Paris: YMCA Press, 1973 (*Gulag Archipelago.* Tr. by Thomas Whitney. New York: Harper and Row, 1974–78). *Victory Celebrations, Prisoners, The Love Girl and Innocent: Three Plays.* Tr. by Helen Rap and Nancy Thomas. New York: Farrar, Straus, and Giroux, 1983. *The Red Wheel: A Narrative, Indiscreet Period of Time.* Tr. by H.T. Willets. London: Bodley Head, 1989.

For More Information See: Contemporary Authors. Detroit, MI: Gale Research, 1978 (Volume 69–72), 543–50. *Current Biography Yearbook.* New York: H.W. Wilson, 1988, 534–38. Scammel, Michael. *Solzhenitsyn.* New York: W.W. Norton, 1984. Thomas, D.M. *Alexander Solzhenitsyn: A Century in His Life.* New York: St. Martin's Press, 1998.

Commentary: Alexander Solzhenitsyn's Nobel Award was "for the ethical force with which he has pursued the indispensable traditions of Russian literature." Both his written work and his personal life—rooted in his own country, his own people, his own religion—embody the heritage of the great Russian novelists—like Dostoevsky in his prison experiences and in his spiritual conversion, like Tolstoy in his moral approach to literature and life, and like both in the immense range of his work. (T.S.K.)

1971

Neruda, Pablo (Eliecer Neftali Reyes y Basoalto, Ricardo)   247

Prize: Literature, 1971. *Born:* July 12, 1904; Parral, Chile. *Death:* September 23, 1973; Santiago, Chile. *Parents:* Father, José del Carmen Reyes; Mother, Rosa de Basoalto. *Nationality:* Chilean. *Religion:* Christian background. *Education:* No college degrees. *Spouse:* Marie Antonieta Maruca Hagenaar Vogelzanz, married 1930, separated 1936; Delia del Carril, married 1934; Matilde Urrutia, married 1955. *Children:* Malva Marina, daughter. *Career:* Diplomat/Writer. *Other Awards:* Premio Municipal de Poesia, Chile, 1944; Order of the Aztec Eagle, Mexico, 1946; International Peace Prize, 1950; Stalin Peace Prize, 1953.

Selected Publications: Veinte Poemas de Amor y Una Cancion Desesperada. Santiago: Nascimento, 1924 (*Twenty*

Poems: A Disdaining Song. Tr. by W.S. Merwin. New York: Grossman, 1970). *Residencia en la Tierra*. Madrid: Ediciones del Arbol, 1935 (*Residence on Earth*. Tr. by Angel Flores. New York: New Directions, 1947). *Espana en el Corazo* (*Spain in the Heart*). Santiago: Ediciones Ercilla, 1937. *Canto General*. Santiago: n.p., 1950 (*General Song*. Tr. by Nathaniel Tarn. New York: Farrar, Straus & Giroux, 1967). *Odas Elementales*. Buenos Aires: Editorial Losada, 1954 (*The Elementary Odes of Pablo Neruda*. Tr. by Carlos Lozano. New York: Las Americas, 1961). *Bestiario; Bestiary; a Poem*. Tr. by Elsa Neuberger. New York: Harcourt, 1965.

For More Information See: Agosin, Marjorie. *Pablo Neruda*. Boston: Twayne, 1986. Duran, Manuel, and Safir, Margery. *Earth Tones: The Poetry of Pablo Neruda*. Bloomington, IN: Indiana Univ. Press, 1981. *Memoirs*. Tr. by Hardie St. Martin. New York: Farrar, Straus, and Giroux, 1977. Teitelboim, V. *Neruda*. Austin, TX: Univ. of Texas Press, 1991.

Commentary: Pablo Neruda won the Nobel Prize for "a poetry that, with the action of an elementary force, brings alive a continent's destiny and dreams." His work, utilizing surrealist techniques and exploring his inner self against the broad background of South America, was critically acclaimed throughout his career. He also was a force in the political arena as a Chilean diplomat and through his deep commitment to Communism. (J.H.S.)

1972

Böll, Heinrich 248

Prize: Literature, 1972. *Born:* December 21, 1917; Cologne, Germany. *Death:* July 16, 1985; Bornheim-Merten, Germany. *Parents:* Father, Viktor Böll; Mother, Maria Hermanns Böll. *Nationality:* German. *Religion:* Catholic. *Education:* No college degrees. *Spouse:* Annemarie Cech, married 1942. *Children:* Christoph, son; Raimund, son; René, son; Vincent, son. *Career:* Bonn, Germany, Bookshop Apprentice, 1937–38; Germany, Civilian Labor Service, 1938–39; Germany, Army, 1939–45. *Other Awards:* Prize of "Group 47," Bad Dürkheim, 1951; René-Schickele Prize, 1952; German Critics Prize, 1953; Southern German Narrator Prize, 1953; Prize of the *Tribune de Paris*, 1955; Eduard-von-der-Heydt Prize, Wuppertal, 1958; Prize of the State of Nordrhein-Westfalen, 1959; Charles-Veillon Prize, 1960; Literary Prize of the City of Cologne, 1961; Literary Prize Isola d'Elba, Italy, 1965; Premio Calabria, 1966; Georg-Büchner Prize, 1967; Carl-von-Ossietzky Medal, International League for Human Rights, 1974.

Selected Publications: Und Sagte Kein Einziges Wort. Cologne: Kiepenheuer and Witsch, 1953 (*And Never Said a Word*. Tr. by Leila Vennewitz. New York: McGraw-Hill, 1978). *Haus ohne Hüter*. Cologne: Kiepenheuer and Witsch, 1954 (*The Unguarded House*. Tr. by Mervyn Savill. London: Arco, 1957). *Billard um Halbzehn*. Cologne: Kiepenheuer and Witsch, 1959 (*Billiards at Half-Past Nine*. New York: McGraw-Hill, 1973). *Ansichten eines Clowns*. Cologne: Kiepenheuer and Witsch, 1963 (*The Clown*. Tr. by Leila Vennewitz. New York: McGraw-Hill, 1965). *Gruppenbild mit Dame*. Cologne: Kiepenheuer and Witsch, 1971 (*Group Portrait with Lady*. Tr. by Leila Vennewitz. New York: McGraw-Hill, 1973). *Fürsorgliche Belagerung*. Cologne: Kiepenheuer and Witsch, 1979 (*The Safety Net*.

Tr. by Leila Vennewitz. New York: Penguin, 1983). *Die Verwundung und Andrere Fruhe Erzahlungen*. Bornheim-Merten, Germany: Lamuv Verlag, 1983 (*The Casualty*. Tr. by Leila Vennwitz. New York: Norton, 1986). *The Stories of Heinrich Böll*. Tr. by Leila Vennwitz. New York: Knopf, 1986.

For More Information See: Conard, Robert C. *Heinrich Böll*. Boston: Twayne Publishers, 1981. Friedrichsmeyer, Erhard. *The Major Works of Heinrich Böll: A Critical Commentary*. New York: Monarch Press, 1974. Macpherson, Enid. *A Student's Guide to Böll*. London: Heinemann, 1972. Reid, James H. *Heinrich Böll: Withdrawal and Re-emergence*. London: Oswald Wolff, 1973. Reid, J. *A German for His Time*. New York: St. Martin's, 1988. Yuill, W.E., "Heinrich Böll." In *Essays on Contemporary German Literature*, edited by Brian Keith-Smith, London: Oswald Wolff, 1966, 141–58.

Commentary: Heinrich Böll received the award for his "literary works, which represent a renewal of the German literary tradition and which combine a clear vision of contemporary history with an art of representation characterized by sensitivity as well as emotional penetration." Set in modern Germany, but symbolic of conditions throughout the world, Böll's works exhibit a steadfast humanitarianism, which is marked by unwavering compassion for the victims of society as well as by resolute condemnation of the various individuals, groups and economic, historical, political, or social forces which in his opinion precipitated the widespread human suffering of this century. (W.L.N.)

1973

White, Patrick Victor Martindale 249

Prize: Literature, 1973. *Born:* May 28, 1912; London, England. *Death:* September 30, 1990; Sydney, Australia. *Parents:* Father, Victor Martindale White; Mother, Ruth Withycombe White. *Nationality:* Australian. *Religion:* No organized religion; from Anglican background. *Education:* Cambridge Univ., England, B.A., 1935. *Spouse:* None. *Children:* None. *Career:* Royal Air Force, 1940–45, Writer. *Other Awards:* Gold Medal, Australian Literary Society, 1940, 1956; Miles Franklin Award, 1958, 1962; W.H. Smith and Son Literary Award, 1959; Brotherhood Award, National Conference of Christians and Jews, 1962.

Selected Publications: Happy Valley. London: Harrap, 1939. *The Living and the Dead*. New York: Viking, 1941. *The Aunt's Story*. New York: Viking, 1948. *The Tree of Man*. New York: Viking, 1955. *The Burnt Ones*. London: Eyre & Spottiswoode, 1957. *Voss*. London: Eyre & Spottiswoode, 1957. *Riders in the Chariot*. New York: Viking, 1961. *The Solis Mandala*. New York: Viking, 1966. *The Vivisector*. New York: Viking, 1970. *The Eye of the Storm*. New York: J. Cape, 1973. *The Cockatoos: Shorter Novels and Stories*. New York: J. Cape, 1974. *A Fringe of Leaves*. New York: J. Cape, 1976. *Flaws in the Glass*. New York: Viking, 1982. *Memoirs of Many in One*. New York: Penguin, 1988.

For More Information See: Colmer, John. *Patrick White*. New York: Methuen Inc., 1984. Lawson, Alan. *Patrick White*. New York: Oxford Univ. Press, 1974. Marr, D. *Patrick White*. New York: Knopf, 1992. Weigel, John. *Patrick White*. Boston: Twayne, 1983.

Commentary: The Nobel presentation noted that Patrick White's work "for the first time has given the continent of Australia an authentic voice that carries across the world" by creating "Epic and Psychological narrative art which has introduced a new continent in Literature." The Royal Academy concluded by saying his works "show White's unbroken creative power, an ever deeper restlessness and seeking urge, an onslaught against vital problems that have never ceased to engage him and a wrestling with the language in order to extract all its power and nuances, to the verge of the unobtainable." (D.E.S.)

1974

Johnson, Eyvind Olof Verner   250
Prize: Literature, 1974. *Born:* July 29, 1900; Overlulea, Sweden. *Death:* August 25, 1976; Stockholm, Sweden. *Parents:* Father, Olof Johnson; Mother, Cevia Gustafsdotter Johnson. *Nationality:* Swedish. *Religion:* Most probably Christian/Protestant. *Education:* No college degrees. *Spouse:* Aase Christoffersen, married 1927, died 1938; Cilla Frankenhaeuser, married 1940. *Children:* Tore, son; Maria, daughter; Anders, daughter. *Career:* Writer. *Other Awards:* Samfundet De Nio's Award, 1936; Swedish Academy Award, 1944; Nordic Council Prize for Literature, Helsinki, 1962.

Selected Publications: An En Gang, Kapten (Once More, Captain). Stockholm: A. Bonnier, 1934. *Nu Var Det, 1914.* Stockholm: A. Bonnier, 1934 (*1914.* Tr. by Mary Sandbach. New York: Adama Books, 1970). *Grupp Krilon (Krilon's Group).* Stockholm: A. Bonnier, 1941. *Krilon's Resa (Krilon's Journey).* Stockholm: A. Bonnier, 1942. *Krilon Sjalv (Krilon Himself).* Stockholm: A. Bonnier, 1943. *Strandernas Svall.* Stockholm: A. Bonnier, 1946 (*Return to Ithaca.* Tr. by M.A. Michael. New York: Thames & Hudson, 1952). *Romantisk Berattelse (Romantic Tale).* Stockholm: A. Bonnier, 1955. *Tidens Gang (The Course of Time).* Stockholm: A. Bonnier, 1955. *Hans Naades Tid.* Stockholm: A. Bonnier, 1960 (*The Days of His Grace.* Tr. by Elspeth Harley Schubert. New York: Vanguard, 1968). *Livsdagen Lang (Life's Long Day).* Stockholm: A. Bonnier, 1964. *Favel Ansam (Favel Alone).* Stockholm: A. Bonnier, 1968.

For More Information See: Contemporary Authors. Detroit, MI: Gale Research, 1978 (Volume 73–76), 317–18. Orton, G. *Eyvind Johnson.* New York: Twayne, 1972.

Commentary: Eyvind Johnson received the Nobel Prize for "a narrative art, far-seeing in lands and ages." Many objected at the time because his reputation was national rather than international. Johnson's writings fell into several periods. His novels and short stories first explored socialism and world reform, moved to representations of Swedish life with psychological and intellectually questioning overtones, and, with the growth of Naziism, became pleas for freedom and against dictatorship. Johnson devoted considerable time after 1945 to representing Sweden in UNESCO activities. (J.H.S.)

Martinson, Harry Edmund   251
Prize: Literature, 1974. *Born:* May 6, 1904; Jamshog, Sweden. *Death:* February 11, 1978; Stockholm, Sweden. *Parents:* Father, Martin Olofsson; Mother, Betty Olofsson. *Nationality:* Swedish. *Religion:* Lutheran background; with Taoist orientation. *Education:* No college degrees. *Spouse:*

Moa Swartz, married 1929, divorced 1940; Ingrid Lindcrantz, married 1942. *Children:* None. *Career:* Seaman, 1918–27; Writer. *Other Awards:* Henrik Steffins Prize, 1972.

Selected Publications: Kap Faerval. Stockholm: A. Bonnier, 1933 (*Cape Farewell.* Tr. by Naomi Walford. New York: Putnam, 1934). *Naesslorna Blomma.* Stockholm: A. Bonnier, 1935 (*Flowering Nettle.* Tr. by Naomi Walford. New York: Cresset, 1935). *Verlighet Till Dods (Realism Unto Death).* Stockholm: P.A. Norstedt and Soner, 1940. *Passad (Trade Wind).* Stockholm: A. Bonnier, 1945. *Vagen Till Klockrile.* Stockholm: A. Bonnier, 1948 (*The Road.* Tr. by M.A. Michael. New York: J. Cape, 1955). *Cikada (Cicada).* Stockholm: A. Bonnier, 1953. *Aniara.* Stockholm: A. Bonnier, 1956 (*Aniara.* Tr. by Hugh McDiarmid and Elspeth Harley Shubert. New York: Knopf, 1963). *Wild Bouquet: Nature Poems.* Tr. by William Smith and Leif Sjoberg. Kansas City, MO: Univ. of Missouri, 1985.

For More Information See: Encyclopedia of World Literature in the Twentieth Century. New York: Frederick Ungar Publishing Co., 1964 (Volume 2), 387–88. Holm, I. *Harry Martinson: Myster Malningar Motiv.* Stockholm: A. Bonnier, 1960. Kristensen, Tom. *Harry Martinson, den Fribaarne Fyrboder.* Copenhagen: Glydendal, 1941.

Commentary: Harry Martinson—poet, novelist, dramatist, and essayist—shared the Nobel Prize for "writings that catch the dewdrops and reflect the cosmos." His award was looked upon as Swedish nationalism at the time, since his international reputation was slight. Martinson's early work dealt with his hardships as a child and his extensive travels, and exhibited his lack of education and acquaintance with standard writing forms, while capturing the imagination with its unorthodox qualities. The primitivism of his early work matured into the philosophical, cosmic nature of his later efforts, which dealt with the disorientation of modern humanity and have been called "a unique contribution to poetic science fiction." (J.H.S.)

1975

Montale, Eugenio   252
Prize: Literature, 1975. *Born:* October 12, 1896; Genoa, Italy. *Death:* September 12, 1981; Milan, Italy. *Parents:* Father, Domenico Montale; Mother, Guiseppina Ricci Montale. *Nationality:* Italian. *Religion:* Catholic. *Education:* No college degrees. *Spouse:* Drusilla Tanzi, married 1950, died 1963. *Children:* None. *Career:* Writer, Editor, Critic, Translator. *Other Awards:* Antico Fattore Poetry Prize, Italy, 1932; Premio Manzotto, Italy, 1956; Dante Medal, Italy, 1959; Feltrinelli Prize, Italy, 1962; Calouste Gulbenkian Prize, Paris, 1971.

Selected Publications: Ossi Di Seppia. Turin, Italy: Gobetti, 1925 (*Cuttlefish Bones.* Tr. by Edith Farnsworth. Chicago: Regnery, 1970). *La Occasioni.* Turin, Italy: Einaudi, 1939. *Finistere.* Lugano, Italy: Quaredeni di Lugano, 1943. *La Bufera e Alto.* Venice: Edizione Nero Pozza, 1956 (*The Storm and Other Things.* Tr. by Edith Farnsworth. Chicago: Regnery, 1970). *La Farfalla di Dinard.* Venice: Nero Puzzo, 1956 (*The Butterfly of Dinard.* Tr. by G. Singh. Lexington, KY: Kentucky Univ. Press, 1971). *Xenia* (bilingual). Tr. by G. Singh. Los Angeles: Black Sparrow Press, 1970. *Satura.* Milan: Mondadori, 1971 (*Satura and Diario del '71-'72* (selections). Tr. by G. Singh. New York: New Directions

Publishing Corp., 1976). *Nel Nostro Tempo*. Rome: Rizzoli Editore, 1972 (*Poets in our Time*. Tr. by Alastair Hamilton. New York: Urizen Books, 1976). *The Storm and Other Things*. Tr. by William Arrowsmith. New York: Norton, 1986. *The Occasions*. Tr. by William Arrowsmith. New York: Norton, 1987. *Poems*. Milan, Italy: Mondadori, 1991.

For More Information See: Becker, Jared. *Eugenio Montale*. Boston: Twayne, 1986. *Current Biography Yearbook*. New York: H.W. Wilson, 1976, 265–68. Singh, Ghan Shyam. *Eugenio Montale: A Critical Study of His Poetry, Prose, and Criticism*. New Haven, CT: Yale Univ. Press, 1973. West, Rebecca. *Eugenio Montale: Poet on the Edge*. Cambridge, MA.: Harvard Univ. Press, 1981.

Commentary: Eugenio Montale, Italian poet, translator, and journalist, was cited by the Academy, which noted that his "poetry with great artistic sensitivity, has interpreted human values under the sign of an outlook on life with no illusions." His poetic output of five volumes of poetry at the time of the prize, although small, has ranked him as one of the world's great poets. His public involvement as a journalist in serving as a conscience for his generation is also worthy of note. (A.N.)

1976

Bellow, Saul 253

Prize: Literature, 1976. *Born:* June 10, 1915; Lachine, Quebec, Canada. *Parents:* Father, Abraham Bellow; Mother, Liza Gordon Bellow. *Nationality:* Canadian; later American citizen. *Religion:* Jewish. *Education:* Northwestern Univ., IL, B.S., 1937. *Spouse:* Anita Goshkin, married December 31, 1937, divorced 1955; Alexandra Tschacbasov, married February 1, 1956, divorced 1956; Susan Glassman, married December 10, 1961, divorced 1968; Alexandra Ionescu Tulcea, married October 1974, divorced 1986; Janis Freedman, married September 1989. *Children:* Gregory, son; Adam, son; Daniel, son. *Career:* Pestalozzi-Froebel Teachers College, Chicago, IL, Professor, 1938–42; *Encyclopedia Britannica*, Editor, 1943–46; Univ. of Minnesota, Professor, 1946–49; New York Univ., Professor, 1950–52; Princeton Univ., NJ, Fellow, 1952–53; Bard College, NY, Professor, 1953–54; Univ. of Minnesota, Professor, 1954–59; Univ. of Chicago, Professor, 1962-. *Other Awards:* Guggenheim Fellowship, 1948, 1955; National Institute of Arts and Letters Award, 1952; American Academy Grant, 1952; National Book Award, 1954, 1964, 1970; O. Henry Prize, 1956, 1980; Ford Grant, 1959; Friends of Literature Fiction Award, 1960; James L. Dow Award, 1964; Prix International de Literature, 1965; Jewish Heritage Award, 1968; Croix de Chevalier, France, 1968; Formentor Prize, 1970; Pulitzer Prize, 1976; Neil Gunn International Fellowship, 1977; American Academy Arts & Letters Gold Medal, 1977; Emerson Thoreau Medal, 1977; Brandeis Univ. Creative Arts Award, 1978; Medal of Honor for Literature, National Arts Club, 1978; Malaparte Literature Award, 1984; Premio Scanno Literature Award, Italy, 1988; National Medal of Arts, 1988; Lifetime Achievement Award, National Book Award, 1990; Lifetime Cultural Achievement Award, YIVO Institute for Jewish Research, 1996; Lifetime Achievemnt Award, *New Yorker*, 2000.

Selected Publications: *Dangling Man*. New York: Vanguard, 1944. *The Victim*. New York: Vanguard, 1947.

Adventures of Augie March. New York: Viking Press, 1953. *Seize the Day, and Three Short Stories*. New York: Viking Press, 1956. *Henderson, the Rain King*. New York: Viking Press, 1959. *Herzog*. New York: Viking Press, 1964. *The Last Analysis*. New York: Viking Press, 1965. *Mosby's Memories and Other Stories*. New York: Viking Press, 1968. *Mr. Sammler's Planet*. New York: Viking Press, 1970. *Humboldt's Gift*. New York: Viking Press, 1975. *The Dean's December*. New York: Harper, 1981. *Him with His Foot in His Mouth and Other Stories*. New York: Harper and Row, 1984. *To Jerusalem and Back: A Personal Account*. New York: Penguin, 1985. *More Die of Heartbreak*. New York: Morrow, 1987. *The Theft*. New York: Penguin, 1989. *Something to Remember Me By*. New York: Viking, 1991; *It All Adds Up*. New York: Viking, 1994.

For More Information See: Atlas, James. *Bellow: A Biography*. New York: Random House, 2000. Clayton, John J. *Saul Bellow: In Defense of Man*. Bloomington, IN: Indiana Univ. Press, 1979. Cohen, Sara B. *Saul Bellow's Enigmatic Laughter*. Urbana, IL: Univ. of Illinois Press, 1974. *Contemporary Authors*. Detroit, MI: Gale Research, 1969 (Volume 5–8 First Revision), 94–96. Kiernan, Robert. *Saul Bellow*. New York: Continuum, 1989. Miller, Ruth. *Saul Bellow*. New York: St. Martin's Press, 1991. Tanner, Tony. *Saul Bellow*. Edinburgh: Oliver and Boyd, 1965.

Commentary: Saul Bellow received the Nobel Prize in literature "for the human understanding and subtle analysis of contemporary culture that are combined in his works." At the time of the award Bellow had written seven major novels, one novella, and a number of short stories as well as essays and plays. This serious novelist of the post-World War II generation was speaking for the humanistic purposes of the novel. The prize recognized Bellow's "exuberant ideas, flashing irony . . . and burning compassion" in his depiction of modern man as one "who keeps trying to find a foothold during his wanderings in our tottering world, one who can never relinquish his faith that the value of life depends on its dignity not its success." (C.B.)

1977

Aleixandre y Merlo, Vicente Pio Marcelino Cirilo 254

Prize: Literature, 1977. *Born:* April 26, 1898; Seville, Spain. *Death:* December 14, 1984; Madrid, Spain. *Parents:* Father, Cirilo Aleixandre Ballester; Mother, Elvira Merlo Garcia de Pruneda. *Nationality:* Spanish. *Religion:* Catholic. *Education:* Univ. of Madrid, Spain, law degree, 1919; Univ. of Madrid, Spain, Diploma in Business Administration, 1919. *Spouse:* None. *Children:* None. *Career:* Central School of Commerce, Madrid, Spain, Professor, 1919–21; Residentia de Estudiantes, Madrid, Spain, Professor, 1921–22; Writer, 1922-. *Other Awards:* National Prize for Literature, Spain, 1933; Spanish Critics Prize, 1969; Ceraud Cross of Order of Carlos III, 1977.

Selected Publications: *Ambito, 1924–1927*. Malaga, Spain: Impresa Sur, 1928. *Espadas Como Labios, 1930–31*. Madrid: Espasa-Calpe, 1932. *Pasion de la Tierra*. Mexico City: Fabula, 1935. *Sombra del Paradiso*. Madrid: Adan, 1944 (*Shadow of Paradise*. Tr. by Hugh Harter. Berkeley, CA: Univ. of California Press, 1987). *Mundo a Solas*. Madrid: Clan, 1950. *Nacimiento Ultimo*. Madrid: Insula, 1953. *Es*

Un Vasto Dominio. Madrid: Revista del Occidente, 1962. *Poemas de la Consumacion.* Barcelona: Plaza y Janes, 1968. *Dialogos del Conocimiento.* Barcelona: Plaza y Janes, 1974. *Poemas Paradisiacos.* Madrid: Editiones Catedra, 1981. *A Longing for the Night: Selected Poems of Vicente Aleixandre.* Lewis Hyde, ed. Tr. by Stephen Kessler, et. al. Port Townsend, WA: Copper Canyon Press, 1985.

For More Information See: Daydi-Tolson, Santiago, ed. *Vicente Aleixandre: A Critical Appraisal.* Ypsilanti, MI: Bilingual Press, 1981. Luis, Leopoldo. *Vida y Obra de Vicente Aleixandre.* Madrid: Espasa-Calpe, 1978. Schwartz, Kessel. *Vicente Aleixandre.* New York: Twayne Publishers, 1970.

Commentary: The Nobel Prize was granted to Vicente Aleixandre "for a creative poetic writing which illuminates men's condition in the cosmos and present-day society, at the same time representing the great renewal of the traditions of Spanish poetry between the wars." Aleixandre was highly admired in Spain and in Latin America as a lifelong poet of the people, beginning with his membership in the so-called Poetic Group of 1927, with roots in both the Spanish lyric tradition and in modernism. His poems are free verse and deal with love, death, and eternity. Most of his early poems were sad love poems, but later, his writings rose above the early pessimistic emptiness. (D.C.)

1978

Singer, Isaac Bashevis　　　　　　　　　　255

Prize: Literature, 1978. *Born:* July 14, 1904; Leoncin (some sources say Radzymin), Poland. *Death:* July 24, 1991; Miami, FL. *Parents:* Father, Pinchas Mendel Singer; Mother, Bathsheba Zylberman Singer. *Nationality:* Polish; later American citizen. *Religion:* Jewish. *Education:* No college degrees. *Spouse:* Runya (Rachel), married 1927 (?), divorced 1935; Alma Haimann, married February 14, 1940. *Children:* Israel, son. *Career:* Writer. *Other Awards:* Louis Lamed Prize, 1950, 1956; American Academy Award, 1959; Harry and Ethel Daroff Memorial Fiction Award, 1963; Epstein Fiction Award, 1963; National Endowment for the Arts Grant, 1966, 1967; *Playboy* Magazine Award, 1967; Newbery Honor Book Award, 1967, 1968; Bancarella Prize, 1968; Brandeis Univ. Creative Arts Medal, 1970; National Book Award, 1970, 1974; Poses Creative Arts Award, 1970; Agnon Gold Medal, 1975; Handel Medallion, 1986; Gold Medal, Academy Arts & Letters, 1989.

Selected Publications: The Family Moskat. New York: Knopf, 1950. *Satan in Goray.* New York: Noonday, 1955. *The Magician of Lublin.* New York: Noonday, 1960. *The Slave.* New York: Farrar, Straus, 1962. *Zlateh the Goat and Other Stories.* New York: Harper, 1966. *The Fearsome Inn.* New York: Scribner's, 1967. *The Manor.* New York: Farrar, Straus, 1967. *Mazel and Schlimazel.* New York: Farrar, Straus, 1967. *When Schlemiel Went to Warsaw and Other Stories.* New York: Farrar, Straus, 1968. *The Estate.* New York: Farrar, Straus, 1969. *Joseph and Koza.* New York: Farrar, Straus, 1970. *Alone in the Wild Forest.* New York: Farrar, Straus, 1971. *Topsy Turvy Emperor of China.* New York: Harper, 1971. *Enemies: A Love Story.* New York: Farrar, Straus, 1972. *The Fools of Chelm and Their History.* New York: Farrar, Straus, 1973. *Naftali the Storyteller and*

His Horse, Sus, and Other Stories. New York: Farrar, Straus, 1976. *Tale of Three Wishes.* New York: Farrar, Straus, 1976. *Shosha.* New York: Farrar, Straus, 1978. *Stories for Children.* New York: Farrar, Straus, 1985. *The Image and Other Stories.* New York: Farrar, Straus, 1985. *The Death of Methuselah and Other Stories.* New York: Farrar, Straus, 1988. *The King of the Fields.* New York: Farrar, Straus, 1988. *Scum.* New York: Farrar, Straus, 1994.

For More Information See: Alexander, Edward. *Isaac Bashevis Singer.* Boston: Twayne Publishers, 1980. Benedict, Ito. *Portraits in Print.* New York: Columbia Univ. Press, 1991. *Bibliography of Isaac Bashevis Singer, 1924–49.* David Miller, ed. New York: P. Lang, 1983. *Current Biography Yearbook.* New York: H.W. Wilson, 1969, 402–04. Hadda, Janet. *Isaac Bashevis Singer: A Life.* New York: Oxford University Press, 1997. Kresh, Paul. *Isaac Bashevis Singer.* New York: Lode Star, 1984. *New York Times Biographical Service* (July 25, 1991): 736.

Commentary: Isaac Bashevis Singer received the Nobel Prize "for his impassioned narrative art which, with roots in a Polish-Jewish cultural tradition, brings universal human conditions to life." Singer's writings bring to life the shtetl world of East European Jewry in his time of growth and maturing. Based on his own childhood, adolescence, and youthful and mature experiences, his writings vividly portray "the clash between tradition and renewal, between otherworldliness and pious mysticism on the one hand, free thought, doubt, and nihilism on the other." His adult works have been supplemented by a much-loved and admired set of children's books and stories, which have endeared him to children and adults alike. (J.V.)

1979

Elytis, Odysseus (Alepoudelis)　　　　　　256

Prize: Literature, 1979. *Born:* November 2, 1911; Crete, Greece. *Death:* March 18, 1996; Athens, Greece. *Parents:* Father, Panayiotis Alepoudelis; Mother, Maria Alepoudelis. *Nationality:* Greek. *Religion:* Eastern Orthodox. *Education:* No college degrees. *Spouse:* None. *Children:* None. *Career: Kathimerini,* Athens, Greece, Art Critic, 1946–48; Writer. *Other Awards:* National Poetry Prize, 1960; National Book Award, 1960; Order of the Phoenix, 1965; Benson Silver Medal, Royal Society of Literature, 1981.

Selected Publications: To Axion Esti. Athens: Ikaros, 1959 (*The Axion Esti of Odysseus Elytis.* Tr. by Edmund Keeley and George Savadis. Pittsburgh, PA: Univ. of Pittsburgh Press, 1974). *O Ilios Oiliatorus.* Athens: Ikaros, 1971 (*The Sovereign Sun: Selected Poems.* Tr. by Kimon Friar. Philadelphia, PA: Temple Univ. Press, 1974). *To Fotodhendro Ke i Dhekati Tetarti Omorfia* (*The Light Tree and the Fourteenth Beauty*). Athens: Ikaros, 1971. *O Fillomandis* (*The Leaf Diviner*). Athens: Asterias, 1973. *Anihta Hartia* (*Open Book*). Athens: Asterias, 1974. *Maria Nefeli: Shiniko Püma.* Athens: Ikaros, 1978 (*Maria Nefephele.* New York: Houghton-Mifflin, 1981). *Mikros Nautilos.* Athens, Greece: Ikaros Ekdotikettetaipeia, 1986 (*The Little Mariner.* Tr. by Olga Brovmas. Port Townsend, WA: Copper Canyon, 1988).

For More Information See: Contemporary Authors. Detroit, MI: Gale, 1981 (Volume 102), 171–73. *Current Biography Yearbook.* New York: H.W. Wilson, 1980, 94–96.

Commentary: The Academy praised Odysseus Elytis's "poetry, which against the background of Greek tradition, depicts with sensuous strength and intellectual clearsightedness modern man's struggle for freedom and creativity." It was further noted that by "its combination of fresh sensuous flexibility and strictly disciplined implacability in the face of all compulsion, Elytis's poetry gives shape to its distinctiveness, which is not only very personal but also represents the traditions of the Greek People." (D.E.S.)

1980

Milosz, Czeslaw 257

Prize: Literature, 1980. *Born:* June 30, 1911; Seteiniai, Lithuania. *Parents:* Father, Aleksander Milosz; Mother, Weronika Kunat Milosz. *Nationality:* Polish; later American citizen. *Religion:* Catholic. *Education:* Univ. of Wilno, Poland, Master Juris, 1934. *Spouse:* Janina (Janka) Dluska, married January 1, 1944. *Children:* Anthony, son; John Peter, son. *Career:* Polish National Radio, Programmer, 1935–39; Polish Foreign Affairs Ministry, Diplomat, 1945–50; Univ. of California, Berkeley, Professor, 1960–78. *Other Awards:* Polish Writers Union Award, 1934; Prix Litteraire Europeen, Les Guildes du Livre, Geneva, 1953; Marian Kister Literary Award, 1967; Jurzykowski Foundation Award for Creative Work, 1968; Polish PEN Club Award for Poetry Translations, 1974; Neustadt International Prize for Literature, Univ. of Oklahoma, 1978.

Selected Publications: Trzy Zimy (Three Winters). Warsaw: Wilno, 1936. *Ocalenie (Rescue).* Cracow: Spoldzielnia Wydawnicza "Cytelnik," 1945. *Zdobycie Wladzy.* Paris: Instytut Literacki, 1953 (*The Seizure of Power.* Tr. by Celina Viennaiewska. New York: Criterion Books, 1955). *Zniewolony Umysl.* Paris: Institut Littéraire, 1953 (*The Captive Mind.* Tr. by Jane Zielonko. New York: Knopf, 1953). *Dolina Issy.* Paris: Institut Littéraire, 1955 (*The Issa Valley.* Tr. by Louis Iribarne. New York: Farrar, Straus & Giroux, 1981). *Swiatlo Dzienne (Daylight).* Paris: Institut Littéraire, 1955. *Traktat Poetycki (Poetic Treatise).* Paris: Institut Littéraire, 1957. *Rodzinna Europa.* Paris: Institut Littéraire, 1958 (*Native Realm: A Search for Self-Definition.* Tr. by Catherine S. Leach. Garden City, NY: Doubleday, 1968). *Widzenia Nad Zatoka.* Paris: Institut Littéraire, 1969 (*Visions from San Francisco Bay.* Tr. by Riczard Lourie. New York: Farrar, Straus & Giroux, 1982). *Prywatne Obowiazki (Private Obligations).* Paris: Institut Littéraire, 1972. *Emperor of the Earth: Modes of Eccentric Vision.* Berkeley: Univ. of California Press, 1977. *Ziemia Ulro (The Land of Ulro).* Paris: Institut Littéraire, 1977. *Bells in Winter.* New York: Ecco Press, 1978. *Czeslaw Milosz, an International Bibliography, 1930–1980.* Ann Arbor, MI: Univ. of Michigan, 1983. *The Separate Notebooks.* Tr. by Robert Hass and Robert Pinsky. New York: Ecco Press, 1987. *The Collected Poems, 1937–1987.* New York: Ecco Press, 1988. *A Year of the Hunter.* New York: Farrar, Straus and Giroux, 1994. *Roadside Dog.* Tr. By Robert Hass. New York: Farrar, Straus & Giroux, 1998. *Milosz's ABC's.* Tr. By Madeline G. Levine. New York: Farrar, Straus & Giroux, 2001.

For More Information See: Beginning with My Streets. New York: Farrar, Straus and Giroux, 1991. *Current Biography Yearbook.* New York: H.W. Wilson, 1981, 305–08.

Modern Slavic Literatures: A Library of Literary Criticism. New York: Frederick Ungar Publishing Co., 1976 (Volume 2), 340–46. *Native Realm: A Search for Self-Definition.* Tr. by Catherine S. Leach. Berkeley, CA: Univ. of California Press, 1981.

Commentary: Czeslaw Milosz's award was for voicing "with uncompromising clearsightedness . . . man's exposed condition in a world of severe conflicts." Milosz is an exiled writer, "a stranger for whom physical exile is really a reflection of a . . . spiritual exile applying to humanity in general." His works as a poet, novelist, essayist, translator, critic, and literary scholar are of great historical, sociological, political, and spiritual value. Having experienced the devastation of Hitler's Naziism and the repression of Russian communism, he depicts in his writing the meanness and cruelty of the world; but his writing, of itself, is an expression of hope. (S.R.)

1981

Canetti, Elias 258

Prize: Literature, 1981. *Born:* July 25, 1905; Russe, Bulgaria. *Death:* August 14, 1994; Zürich, Switzerland. *Parents:* Father, Jacques Canetti; Mother, Mathilde Arditti. *Nationality:* Bulgarian; later Austrian resident and British citizen. *Religion:* Jewish. *Education:* Univ. of Vienna, Austria, D.Sc., 1929. *Spouse:* Venetia Taubner-Calderón, married February 26, 1934, died 1963; Hera Buschor, married 1971. *Children:* Johanna, daughter. *Career:* France, Writer and Freelance Journalist. *Other Awards:* Prix International, Paris, 1949; Author's Prize, Vienna, 1966; Deutscher Kritikerpreis, Berlin, 1967; Austrian Prize for Literature, 1968; Georg Büchner Prize, Munich, 1972; Franz Nabl Prize, Graz, 1975; Nelly Sachs Prize, Dortmund, 1975; Gottfried Keller Prize, Zurich, 1977; Hebel Preis, 1980; Premio Europa Prato, Italy, 1980; Kafka Prize, Austria, 1981.

Selected Publications: Die Komödie der Eitelkeit. Munich: W. Weismann, 1934 (*Comedy of Vanity and Life-Terms.* Tr. by Getta Honegger. New York: Performing Arts, 1983). *Die Blendung.* Vienna: H. Reichner, 1935 (*Auto-da-Fé.* Tr. by C.V. Wedgwood. London: J. Cape, 1946). *Masse und Macht.* Dusseldorf, West Germany: Claasen, 1962 (*Crowds and Power.* Tr. by Carol Stewart. New York: Viking, 1962). *Die Andere Prozess: Kafka's Briefe an Felice.* Munich: Hanser, 1969 (*Kafka's Other Trial: The Letters of Felice.* Tr. by Christopher Middleton. New York: Schocken Books, 1974). *Die Ohrenzeuge: 50 Charaktere.* Munich: Hanser, 1974 (*Earwitness: Fifty Characters.* Tr. by Joachim Neugroschel. New York: Seabury, 1979). *Das Gewissen der Worte.* Munich: Hanser, 1975 (*The Conscience of Words.* Tr. by Joachim Neugroschel. New York: Continuum, 1979). *The Plays of Elias Canetti.* Tr. by Getta Honegger. New York: Farrar, Straus and Giroux, 1984. *Der ohrenzeuge: funfzig charaktere.* Frankfurt: Ullstein, 1974 (*Earwitness: Fifty Characters.* Tr. by Joachim Neugroschel. New York: Seabury, 1979). *Das Augenspiel.* Munich: C. Hanser, 1985 (*The Play of the Eyes.* Tr. by Ralph Manheim. New York: Farrar, Straus and Giroux, 1986). *Geheimherz der Uhr.* Munich: C. Hanser, 1987 (*The Secret Heart of the Clock.* Tr. by Joel Agee. New York: Farrar, Straus and Giroux, 1989).

For More Information See: *Current Biography Yearbook.* New York: H.W. Wilson, 1983, 48–51. Sontag, Susan. *Under the Sign of Saturn.* New York: Farrar, 1980, 181–204. *Die Gerettete Zunge. Geschichte einer Jugend.* Munich: Hanser, 1977 (*The Tongue Set Free.* Tr. by Joachim Neugroschel. New York: Seabury, 1979). *Die Fackel im Ohr.* Munich: Hanser, 1980 (*The Torch in My Ear.* Tr. by Joachim Neugroschel. London: Farrar, 1982). *Memoirs of Elias Canetti.* New York: Farrar, Straus and Giroux, 1999. *World Authors.* New York: H.W. Wilson, 1975, 270–72.

Commentary: The Nobel Prize was awarded to Elias Canetti for "writings marked by a broad outlook, a wealth of ideas and artistic power." The modest and humble Canetti paradoxically spent a lifetime studying and writing about power. The Bulgarian-born writer's first languages were Spanish and Ladino; his education was in the sciences (a doctorate in Chemistry) in Britain, Germany, Switzerland, and Austria; and he identified himself as a "Viennese" writer, following the traditions of Goethe and the circle of writers he knew and admired (Brecht, Broch, Kafka, and Kraus). This author was relatively unknown to the English-speaking world until the Nobel Prize was granted in 1981. His most cited works are the nightmarish *Auto-da-Fé,* written in the Kafka tradition of horror and comedy imbedded in a story simply told, and his "life work," *Crowds and Power,* with its paranoic ruler, which has been referred to as "the nearest thing to a book of wisdom we are likely to get in the twentieth century." (J.H.S.)

1982

García Márquez, Gabriel José   259

Prize: Literature, 1982. *Born:* March 6, 1928; Aracataca, Colombia. *Parents:* Father, Gabriel Eligio Garcia; Mother, Luisa Santiaga Márquez Iguaràn. *Nationality:* Colombian. *Religion:* No organized religion; from Catholic background. *Education:* No college degrees. *Spouse:* Mercedes Barcha, married March, 1958. *Children:* Rodrigo, son; Gonzalo, son. *Career:* El Heraldo, Barranquilla, Colombia, Journalist, 1950–54; *El Espectador,* Bogota, Colombia, Rome, Italy, and Paris, France, Journalist, 1954–55; Europe, Free-lance Journalist, 1956–57; *Momento,* Caracas, Venezuela, Journalist, 1957–59; *Premsa Latina,* Bogota, Colombia and Havana, Cuba, Journalist, 1959–61; Mexico City, Free-lance Editor, Screenwriter, Copywriter, 1961–65; Mexico City and Barcelona, Spain, Writer, 1965-. *Other Awards:* Colombian Association of Writers and Artists Award, 1954; Premio Literario Esso, Colombia, 1961; Premio Chianciano, Italy, 1969; Prix du Meilleur Livre Etranger, France, 1969; Romulo Gallegos Prize, Venezuela, 1971; Books Abro ad, Neustadt International Prize for Literature, 1972; *Los Angeles Times* Book Prize, 1988; Serfin Prize, 1989

Selected Publications: La Hojarasca. Bogota: Ediciones S.L.B., 1955 (*Leaf Storm, and Other Stories.* Tr. by Gregory Rabassa. New York: Harper & Row, 1978). *El Coronel No Tiene Quien Le Escriba.* Medellin: Aqirre, 1961 (*No One Writes to the Colonel, and Other Stories.* Tr. by J.S. Bernstein. New York: Harper & Row, 1979). *La Mala Hora.* Madrid: 1962 (*The Evil Hour.* Tr. by Gregory Rabassa. New York: Harper & Row, 1979). *Cien Anos de Soledad.* Buenos Aires: Editorial Sudamericana, 1967 (*One Hundred Years of*

Solitude. Tr. by Gregory Rabassa. New York: Harper & Row, 1970). *Relato de un naufrago.* Bogota, Colombia: Ovaja Negra, 1979 (*The Story of a Shipwrecked Sailor.* Tr. by Randolph Hogan. New York: Alfred A. Knopf, 1986). *Collected Stories.* 1st ed. New York: Harper and Row, 1984. *Amor en los tiempos del colera.* Bogota, Colombia: Ovaja Negra, 1985 (*Love in the Time of Cholera.* Tr. by Edith Grossman. New York: Alfred A. Knopf, 1988). *Bibliographic Guide to Gabriel Garcia Márquez, 1979–1985.* Comp. by Margaret Eustella Fau and Nelly Sfeir de Gonzalez. Westport, CT: Greenwood Press, 1986.

For More Information See: Bell-Villada, G. *Garcia Márquez.* Chapel Hill, NC: Univ. of North Carolina Press, 1990. Kennedy, William. "The Yellow Trolley Car in Barcelona: A Profile of Gabriel Garcia Márquez." *The Atlantic* 231 (January 1973): 50–59. McMurray, Robert R. *Gabriel Garcia Márquez.* New York: Ungar, 1984. Williams, Raymond L. *Gabriel Garcia Márquez.* Boston: G.K. Hall, 1984. McNerney, Kathleen. *Understanding Gabriel Garcia Márquez.* Columbia, SC: Univ. of South Carolina Press, 1989.

Commentary: Gabriel García Márquez was awarded the Nobel Prize "for his novels and short stories, in which the fantastic and the realistic are combined in a richly composed world of imagination, reflecting a continent's life and conflicts." The fictional world created by García Márquez centers around the jungle town of Macondo, which reappears in many novels and stories, including his outstanding achievement *One Hundred Years of Solitude.* The central themes of solitude, time, and death are portrayed through comedy, surrealism, and mythical allegory. García Márquez is committed politically to the side of the poor and, in addition to his literary works, has been very active as a journalist writing on politics and the arts. (K.G.)

1983

Golding, William Gerald   260

Prize: Literature, 1983. *Born:* September 19, 1911; St. Columb, Cornwall, England. *Death:* June 19, 1993; Perranarworthal, Trur, England. *Parents:* Father, Alec A. Golding; Mother, Mildred A. Golding. *Nationality:* British. *Religion:* Belongs to no organized church; from Christian background. *Education:* Oxford Univ., England, B.A., 1935. *Spouse:* Ann Brookfield, married 1939. *Children:* David, son; Judith, daughter. *Career:* Bishop Wordsworth's School, England, Teacher, 1939–40; British Navy, 1940–45; Bishop Wordsworth's School, England, Teacher, 1945–61; Hollins College, VA, Writer-In-Residence, 1961–62; Writer, 1962–93. *Other Awards:* Commander, Order of the British Empire, 1965; Booker Prize, 1979; Black Memorial Award, 1980; Booker McConnell Prize, 1981; Knighthood, 1988.

Selected Publications: Lord of the Flies. London: Faber and Faber, 1954. *The Inheritors.* London: Faber and Faber, 1955. *Pincher Martin.* London: Faber and Faber, 1956. *Free Fall.* London: Faber and Faber, 1959. *The Spire.* London: Faber and Faber, 1964. *Darkness Visible.* London: Faber and Faber, 1979. *Rites of Passage.* London: Faber and Faber, 1980. *The Paperman.* New York: Farrar, Straus and Giroux, 1984. *An Egyptian Journal.* London: Faber, 1985. *Fire Down Below.* London, Boston: Faber, 1986. *Close*

Quarters. London: Faber, 1987. *Double Tongue*. New York: Farrar, Straus & Giroux, 1995.

For More Information See: *Contemporary Authors New Revision Series*. Detroit, MI: Gale Research, 1984 (Volume 13), 219–26. Dick, Bernard. *William Golding*. Boston: Twayne, 1987. Friedman, L. *William Golding*. New York: Continuum, 1993. Hynes, Samuel. *William Golding*. New York: Columbia Univ. Press, 1964. Kinkead-Weekes, Mark, and Gregor, Dan. *William Golding: A Critical Study*. London: Faber and Faber, 1983.

Commentary: The body of William Golding's works, which "illustrate the human condition in the world today" and demonstrate that "evil springs from the depth of man himself," won him the Nobel Prize. *Lord of the Flies*, the novel that brought him literary recognition, shows a group of English schoolboys on a deserted island reverting to primal savagery; in his other novels, Golding, who has been called an allegorist and fabulist, develops the theme of humans' tendency toward evil. (J.A.)

1984

Seifert, Jaroslav   261

Prize: Literature, 1984. *Born:* September 23, 1901; Prague, Czechoslovakia. *Death:* January 10, 1986; Prague, Czechoslovakia. *Parents:* Father, Antonin Seifert; Mother, Marie Seifert. *Nationality:* Czechoslovakian. *Religion:* Catholic. *Education:* No college degrees. *Spouse:* Marie Ulrichova, married 1928. *Children:* Jana, daughter; Jaroslav, son. *Career:* Prague, Czechoslovakia, Writer/Journalist, 1921; *Srěatec*, Editor, 1922–25; *KSČ Reflektor*, Editor, 1927–29; *Nová scéna*, Editor, 1929–31; *Pestré květy*, Editor, 1931–33; *Ranni noviny*, Editor, 1933–39; *Národní práce*, Editor, 1939–45; *Práce*, Editor, 1945–49; Writer, 1949–86. *Other Awards:* Czechoslovak State Prize, 1936, 1955, 1968; Union of Czechoslovak Writers Publishing House Prize, 1966; Czechoslovak National Artist, 1967.

Selected Publications: *Jablko z Klína* (*An Apple from the Lap*). Prague: Melantrich, 1933. *Ruce Venušing* (*The Hands of Venus*). Toronto: Sixty-Eight Publishers, 1934. (Also Prague: Melantrich, 1936). *Zhasněti Světla* (*Put Out the Lights*). Prague: Fr. Borovy, 1940. *Světlem Oděná* (*Dressed in Light*). Prague: Nákl. Fr. Borovéha, 1940. *Ruka a Plamen* (*The Hand and the Flame*). Praze: F. Borovy, 1943. *Kammený Most* (*The Stone Bridge*). Prague: Fr. Borovy, 1944. *Prilba Hlíny* (*The Helmut of Clay*). Praze: Práce, 1945. *Mozart v Praze*. Praze, Jarsoslav Pica, 1948. (*Mozart in Prague* (no record found), 1970). *Pisěn o Viktorce*. Praze: Ceskoslovensky spisovatel, 1950. *Maminka* (*Mother*). Prague: Ceskoslovensky Spisovatel, 1955. *Odlévání Zvonú*. Praze: Ceskoslovensky spis, 1967 (*The Casting of the Bells*. Tr. by Tom O'Grady and Paul Jagasich. Iowa City, IA: The Spirit That Moves Us Press, 1983). *Koncert no Ostrově* (*Concert on the Island*). Prague: Ceskoslovensky spisovatel, 1967. *Morový Sloup*. Cologne: Index, 1977 (*The Plague Monument*. Tr. by Lyn Coffin. New York: Czechoslovak Society of Arts and Sciences, 1980). *Destník z Picadilly*. Prague: Cs. spis, 1979 (*Umbrella from Picadilly*. Tr. by Ewald Osers. San Francisco, CA: Parsons Books, 1984). *Selected Poetry of Jaroslav Seifert*. Tr. by Ewald Osers and George Gibian. New York: Macmillan, 1987.

For More Information See: "Czech Poet Wins Nobel Prize for Literature." *Publisher's Weekly* (October 26, 1984): 26–27. French, Alfred. *The Poets of Prague*. London: Oxford Univ. Press, 1969, 20–35. Iggers, W.A. "The World of Jaroslav Seifert." *World Literature Today* (Winter 1986): 8–12. Skvorecky, Josef. "Czech Mate." *The New Republic* (February 18, 1985): 27–32. *Všecky Krásy Sveta* ("*Memoirs: All the Beauties of the World*"). Praha: Ceskoslovenský Spisovatel, 1982.

Commentary: The Nobel announcement cited Jaroslav Seifert's work, which "endowed with freshness, sensuality and rich inventiveness, provides a liberating image of the indomitable spirit and versatility of man." Seifert's defense of and call for greater freedom is also noted in that "he conjures up another world than that of tyranny and desolation—a world that exists both here and now, although it may be hidden from our view and bound in chains, and one that exists in our dreams and our will and our art and our indomitable spirit. His poetry is a kind of maieutics—an act of deliverance." (D.W.)

1985

Simon, Claude Eugene Henri   262

Prize: Literature, 1985. *Born:* October 10, 1913; Tananarive, Madagascar. *Parents:* Father, Louis d'Antoine Simon; Mother, Suzanne Denamiel Simon. *Nationality:* French. *Religion:* Christian. *Education:* No college degrees. *Spouse:* Yvonne Ducing, married 1951, divorced (no date found); Rhea Axelos Karavas, married May 29, 1978. *Children:* None. *Career:* Writer. *Other Awards:* Prix de l'Express, 1961; Prix Medicis, 1967.

Selected Publications: *Le Tricheur* (*The Cheat*). Paris: Éditions de Minuit, 1945. *La Corde Raide* (*The Tightrope*). Paris: Éditions de Minuit, 1947. *Gulliver*. Paris: Calmann-Lévy, 1952. *Le Sacre du Printemps* (*The Annointment of Spring*). Paris: Calmann-Lévy, 1952. *Le Vent, Tentative de Restitution d'un Retable Baroque* (*The Wind*). Paris: Éditions de Minuit, 1957. *L'Herbe* (*The Grass*). Paris: Éditions de Minuit, 1958. *La Route des Flandres* (*The Flanders Road*). Paris: Éditions de Minuit, 1960. *Le Palace* (*The Palace*). Paris: Éditions de Minuit, 1962. *Histoire*. Paris: Éditions de Minuit, 1967. *La Bataille de Pharsale* (*The Battle of Pharsalus*). Paris: Éditions de Minuit, 1969. *Orion Aveugle* (*Blind Orion*). Geneva: Editions Albert Skira, 1970. *Les Corps Conducteurs* (*Conducting Bodies*). Paris: Éditions de Minuit, 1971. *Triptyque*. Paris: Éditions de Minuit, 1973. *Leçon de Choses* (*Lesson in Things*). Paris: Éditions de Minuit, 1975. *Claude Simon, New Directions: Collected Papers*. Ed. by Alastair B. Duncan. Edinburgh: Scottish Academic Press, 1985. *L'Invitation*. Paris: Éditions de Minuit, 1987. *The Georgics*. London: John Calder, 1989. *The Acacia*. New York: Pantheon Books, 1991.

For More Information See: Britton, Celia. *Claude Simon*. New York: Cambridge Univ. Press, 1987. Duffy, Jean. *Reading Between the Lines*. Liverpool: Liverpool University Press, 1998. Fletcher, John. *Claude Simon*. London: Calder and Boyars, 1975. Jimenez-Fajardo, Salvador. *Claude Simon*. Boston: Twayne, 1975.

Commentary: Claude Simon was cited by the Academy because he "in his novels combines the poet's and the painter's creativeness with a deepened awareness of time in the depiction of the human condition." Simon combined his lifelong interest in painting with linguistic and literary experimentation to become a leader among French experimentalist novelists, basing his work on remembered images, especially of war. Although Simon's initial works contained long, involved sentences, many parentheses, and present participles, his later works were composed of short sentences that require careful reading for emotional and literal comprehension. (J.H.S.)

1986

Soyinka, Wole (Akinwande Oluwole Soyinka)   263

Prize: Literature, 1986. *Born:* July 13, 1934; Abeokuta, Nigeria. *Parents:* Father, Samuel Ayodele Soyinka; Mother, Grace Eniola Soyinka. *Nationality:* Nigerian. *Religion:* From African/Anglican background. *Education:* Univ. of Leeds, England, B.A., 1959. *Spouse:* Barbara Dickson, married 1958; Olayide Idowu, married 1963. *Children:* 1 son; 3 daughters. *Career:* Royal Court Theatre, London, Play Reader, 1957–59; Univ. of Ibadan, Nigeria, Research Fellow, 1960–61; Univ. of Ife, Nigeria, Professor, 1962–64; Univ. of Lagos, Nigeria, Professor, 1965–67; Political Prisoner, 1967–69; Univ. of Ibadan, Nigeria, Professor, 1969–72; Univ. of Ife, Nigeria, Professor, 1973–87; Cornell Univ., New York, Professor, 1988–91; *Transition*, Editor, 1991–2000; Univ. of Nevada, Las Vegas, Professor, 2000-. *Other Awards:* John Whiting Drama Prize, 1966; Dakar Negro Arts Festival Award, 1966; Jock Campbell Award, 1968; Prisoner of Conscience, 1969; Jock Campbell-New Statesman Literature Award, 1969; Leopold Sedan Senghor Award, 1986; Enrico Mattei Award, 1986.

Selected Publications: Indare and Other Poems. New York: Hill and Wang, 1968. *Three Short Plays: The Swamp Dwellers, The Trials of Brother Jero, The Strong Breed.* London: Oxford Univ. Press, 1969. *The Interpreters.* New York: Collier Books, 1970. *Season of Anomy.* New York: The Third Press, 1974. *Myth, Literature and the African World.* New York: Cambridge Univ. Press, 1976. *Opera Wonyosi.* Bloomington: Indiana Univ. Press, 1981. *A Play of Giants.* New York: Methuen, 1984. *Requiem for a Futurologist.* London: R. Collings, 1985. *Wole Soyinka: A Bibliography.* Westport, CT: Greenwood, 1986. *Mandela's Earth and Other Poems.* New York: Random House, 1988. *The Open Sore of a Continent.* Oxford: Oxford Univ. Press, 1996.

For More Information See: Ake: The Years of Childhood. New York: Random House, 1981. Gibbs, James. *Wole Soyinka.* Basingstoke, England: Macmillan, 1986. *Ibadan: A Memoir.* London: Methuen, 1994. Jones, Eldred. *Wole Soyinka.* New York: Twayne, 1973. Jones, Eldred. *The Writings of Wole Soyinka.* London: Currey, 1988. *The Man Died.* New York: Harper & Row, 1972. Wright, Derek. *Wole Soyinka.* Fredericton, N.B.: York Press, 1996.

Commentary: The Academy cited Wole Soyinka as a writer "who in a wide cultural perspective and with poetic overtones fashions the drama of existence." The first African author to win a Nobel, Soyinka's works portray a fusion between African and European influences, conventions, and artistic/thematic devices. Starting as a writer of light satirical

verse, he moved to drama, and developed a set of writings concerned with the road that leads to the reality of death. Death-on-the-road is for Soyinka a type of self-sacrifice aiming at "progress" toward reality—a theme that he acted out in his real-life arrest and imprisonment. His post-prison writings emphasize his activist role: the protagonist of freedom against tyranny. (P.K./J.H.S.)

1987

Brodsky, Joseph Alexandrovich (Iosif Alexandrovich)   264

Prize: Literature, 1987. *Born:* May 24, 1940; Leningrad, USSR. *Death:* January 28, 1996; Brooklyn, NY. *Parents:* Father, Alexander I. Brodsky; Mother, Maria M. Volpert Brodsky. *Nationality:* Russian; later American citizen. *Religion:* Jewish. *Spouse:* Maria, no date. *Children:* Andrei, son; Anna, daughter. *Career:* Univ. of Michigan, Poet-in-Residence and Professor, 1972–73, 1974–80; Queens College, City Univ. of New York, Professor, 1973–74; Mt. Holyoke College, MA, Professor, 1981–96; U.S. Poet Laureate, 1991–92. *Other Awards:* Premio Mondello, Italy, 1979; MacArthur Foundation Fellow, 1981; National Book Critics Circle Award, 1986.

Selected Publications: Stikhotvoreniia i poemi (Verses and Poems. Washington DC: Inter-Language Literary Associates, 1965). *Elegy to John Donne and Other Poems.* Tr. by Nicholas Bethell. London: Longmans Green, 1967. *Ostanovka v pustyne (A Stop in the Desert.* New York: Chekhov Publishing Co., 1970). *Selected Poems.* Tr. by George L. Kline. New York: Harper & Row, 1973. *Konets prekrasnoi epokhi: stikhotvoreniia 1964–71.* Ann Arbor, MI: Ardis, 1977. *Chast'rechi: stikhotvoreniia 1972–76.* Ann Arbor, MI: Ardis, 1977 (*A Part of Speech.* [Collected Poems] Tr. by Richard Wilbur, Anthony Hecht, George Kline, et al. New York: Farrar, Straus & Giroux, 1980). *Rimskie elegii.* New York: Russica, 1982 (*Roman Elegies* [bilingual edition]. New York: Farrar, Straus & Giroux, 1984). *Less Than One: Selected Essays.* New York: Farrar, Straus & Giroux, 1986. *Urania* (poems). Ann Arbor, MI: Ardis Publishers, 1987. *To Urania.* New York: Farrar, Straus & Giroux, 1988. *Marbles.* New York: Farrar, Straus, & Giroux, 1989. *Watermark.* New York: Farrar, Straus & Giroux, 1992. *On Grief and Reason.* New York: Farrar, Straus & Giroux, 1996. *Discovery.* New York: Farrar, Straus & Giroux, 1999.

For More Information See: Benedict, Helen. "Flight from Predictability: Joseph Brodsky." *The Antioch Review.* 43 (Winter 1985): 9–21. Benedict, H. *Portraits in Print.* New York: Columbia Univ. Press, 1991. *Current Biography Yearbook.* New York: H.W. Wilson, 1982, 51–54. Tavis, Anne. "A Journey from Petersburg to Stockholm: Preliminary Biography of Joseph Brodsky." *Slavic Review* 47 (Fall 1988): 499–501.

Commentary: At the age of 47, Joseph Brodsky, the second youngest person to receive the Nobel in literature, was praised by the Academy for his "all-embracing authorship imbued with clarity of thought and poetic intensity." Born in the USSR and a recognized poet there before his political imprisonment, Brodsky, who came to the U.S. in 1972, is equally at home with Russian and English, revealing a broad range of interests related to both countries in his poetry, which the Academy cited for its "luminous intensity." (P.K./J.H.S.)

1988

Mahfouz, Naguib (Mahfuz, Najib; Abdel Aziz Al-Sabilgi)   **265**

Prize: Literature, 1988. **Born:** December 11, 1911(?); Cairo, Egypt. *Parents:* Father, Abdel Aziz Ibrahim Mahfouz; Mother, Fatma Mostapha Mahfouz. *Nationality:* Egyptian. *Religion:* Muslim. *Education:* Univ. of Cairo, Egypt, B.A., 1934. *Spouse:* Attiyat-Allah, married September 27, 1954. *Children:* Umm Kalthum, daughter; Fatima, daughter. *Career:* Government Employee, 1934–72. *Other Awards:* Egyptian State Prize, 1956; Great Nile Collar, State Prize for Literature, 1957; National Film Prize, 1962; National Prize for Letters, Egypt, 1970; Collar of the Republic, 1972.

Selected Publications: Zugag-al-Midagg. Al Qahirah: Maktabat Misr, 1946 (*Midaq Alley.* Tr. by Trevor le Gassick. Washington, DC: Three Continents Press, 1981). *Bedaya Wa Nehaya.* Al Qahirah: Maktabat Misr, 1949 (*The Beginning and the End.* Tr. by Ramses H. Awad. Cairo: American Univ. of Cairo, 1985). *Al Less Wa al Kalib.* Al Qahirah: Maktabat Misr, 1961 (*Thief and the Dogs.* Tr. by Trevor le Gassick. Cairo: American Univ. of Cairo, 1984). *Awlad Harettna.* Beirut: Car al Adab, 1962 (*The Children of Gebelawi.* Tr. by Philip Stewart. London: Heinemann, 1981). *Al Seman Wa El Khareef.* Al Qahirah: Dar Masser, 1962 (*Autumn Quail.* Tr. by John Rodenbeck. Cairo: American Univ. of Cairo, 1985). *El Shahadh.* Al Qahirah: Maktabat Misr, 1965 (*The Beggar.* Tr. by Kristin Walker Henry and Nariman Khales Naili al-Warraki. Cairo: American Univ. of Cairo, 1986). *Miramar.* Al Qahirah: Maktabat Misr, 1967 (*Miramar.* Tr. by Fatma Mousa-Mahmoud. London: Heinemann, 1978). *God's World: An Anthology of Short Stories.* Tr. by Akef Abadir and Roger Allen. Minneapolis: Bibliotheca Islamica, 1973. *Hadret El Muhtaram.* Al Qahirah: Maktabat Misr, 1975 (*Respected Sir.* Tr. by Rasheed El Enany. London: Quartet, 1986). *Yawm qutila alzaim (The Assassination of a Leader.)* Al Qahirah: Maktabat Misr, 1985. *Hadith al-Sabah wa-al-masa (Morning and Evening Chatting.)* Al Qahirah: Maktabat Misr, 1987. *Sabah al-ward* (short stories.) Al Qahirah: Maktabat Misr, 1987. *Qushtumur.* Al Qahirah: Maktabat Misr, 1989. *Children of the Alley.* (Tr. By Peter Theroux) New York: Doubleday, 1996. *Akhenaten: Dweller in Truth.* (Tr. by Tagreid Abu-Hassabo) New York: Doubleday/Anchor, 2000.

For More Information See: Al-Ghitani, Jamal. *Nijib Mahfuz-Yatadhakkar.* Beirut: Dar Al-Masirah, 1980. *Autobiography.* New York: Doubleday, 1997. *Current Biography Yearbook.* New York: H.W. Wilson, 1989, 365–69. Milson, Menahem. *Najib Mahfouz.* New York: St. Martin's Press, 1998. Peled, Mattityahu. *Religion, My Own: The Literary Works of Najib Mahfuz.* New Brunswick, NJ: Transaction Books, 1983.

Commentary: The Nobel for Literature was granted to Naguib Mahfouz because his writing "through works rich in nuance—now clear-sightedly realistic, now evocatively ambiguous—has formed an Arabian narrative art that applies to all mankind." The prolific laureate, a master in the art of the novel, short story, play, and screenplay, was particularly recognized for his introduction of the novel form in Egypt, and for his impact on the field of screenwriting. His early attempts at historical fiction gave way to a succession of realistic novels, followed by writings that embraced measures of realism, modernism, and the realm of "symbolist-absurd." But no matter the form, all his writings are imbedded in the Egyptian experience. Mahfouz was also recognized for his friendship with Israel, especially at a time when such friendship was both discouraged and dangerous. (P.K./J.H.S.)

1989

Cela, Camilo José (Don Camilo, Matilde Verdu)   **266**

Prize: Literature, 1989. **Born:** May 11, 1916; Iria Flavia, La Coruna, Spain. *Parents:* Father, Camilo Cela; Mother, Camila Emmanuela Trulock Bertorini Cela. *Nationality:* Spanish. *Religion:* Catholic. *Education:* No college degrees. *Spouse:* Maria del Rosario Conde Picavea, married March 12, 1944, divorced 1989; Maria Castano, married 1991. *Children:* Camilo Jose, son. *Career:* Writer; *Papeles de Son Armadans* (literary monthly), Publisher, 1956–79. *Other Awards:* Premio de la Critica, 1955; National Prize for Literature, Spain, 1984; Premio Principe de Asturias, 1987.

Selected Publications: La Familia de Pascual Duarte. Barcelona: Ediciones Destino, 1942 (*Family of Pascual Duarte.* Tr. by Anthony Kerrigan. London: Eyre and Spottiswoode, 1946). *Pabellon de reposo.* Madrid: Afrodisio Aguado, 1943 (*Rest Home.* Tr. by Herma Briffault. New York: Las Americas Publishing, 1961). *Nuevas andanzas y desventuras de Lazarillo de Tormes.* Madrid: Ediciones La Nava, 1944. *Las Botas de siete leguas: Viaje a la Alcarria, con los versos de su cancionero, cada uno en su debido lugar.* Madrid: Revista de Occidente, 1948 (*Journey to the Alcarria.* Tr. by Frances M. Lopez-Morrilos. Madison: Univ. of Wisconsin Press, 1964). *Caminos inciertos: La Colmena.* Buenos Aires: Emece Editores, 1951 (*The Hives.* Tr. by J.M. Cohen and Arturo Berea. New York: Farrar, Straus, 1953). *Mrs. Caldwell habla con su hijo.* Barcelona: Ediciones Destino, 1953 (*Mrs. Caldwell Speaks to Her Son.* Tr. by Jerome S. Berstein. Ithaca, NY: Cornell Univ. Press, 1968). *Nuevas escanas matritenses.* Madrid: Alfguara, 1965. *Homenaje al Bosco, I: El carro de heno; el inventor de la guillotina.* Baleares, Spain: Papelas de Son Armadans, 1969. *El Huevo del Juicio.* Barcelona: Seix Barral, 1993.

For More Information See: Charlebois, Lucille C. *Understanding Camilio Jose Cela.* Columbia, S.C.: Univ. of South Carolina Press, 1997. *Contemporary Authors.* Detroit, MI: Gale Research Co., 1977, 160–63. Foster, David. *Forms of the Novel in the Work of Camilo Jose Cela.* Columbia: Univ. of Missouri Press, 1967. McPheeters, D.W. *Camilo Jose Cela,* Boston: Twayne, 1969.

Commentary: The Academy cited Camilo Cela for his "rich and intensive prose, which with restrained compassion forms a challenging vision of man's vulnerability." The versatile author of ten novels and sixty other works—essays, short stories, poetry, and travel books—reintroduced the Spanish audience to the novel. Cela also experimented with openness of the novel structure, with a focus on realism and exploration of the "darker side of life," and with fragmented chronology. About the novel, Cela said, "Anything goes . . . as long as it's told with common sense." (P.K./J.H.S.)

1990

Paz, Octavio   267

Prize: Literature, 1990. *Born:* March 31, 1914; Mexico City, Mexico. *Death:* April 19, 1998; Mexico City, Mexico. *Parents:* Father, Octavio Paz; Mother, Josephina Lozano Paz. *Nationality:* Mexican. *Religion:* Atheist, from Catholic background. *Spouse:* Elena Garro, married 1937, divorced, no date; Marie-Jose Tramini, married 1964. *Children:* Elena, daughter *Career:* Writer; various Mexican government positions, 1945–68. *Other Awards:* Grand Prix International de Poesie, Belgium, 1963; Critics Prize, Spain, 1977; National Prize for Letters, Mexico, 1977; Jerusalem Prize, 1977; Grand Golden Eagle International Festival, Paris, 1979; Grand Aigle d'Or, Nice, 1979; Premio Ollin Yoliztli, 1980; Cervantes Prize, 1981; Neustadt Prize, 1982; German Book Trade Peace Prize, 1984; Mexico Heinse Medal, 1984; Gran Cruz de Alfonso X el Sabrio, 1986; T.S. Eliot Award, 1987; Tocqueville Prize, 1988.

Selected Publications: The Labyrinth of Solitude. New York: Grove, 1961. *Sun Stone.* New York: New Directions, 1963. *Alternating Current.* New York: Viking, 1973. *Conjunctions and Disjunctions.* New York: Viking, 1973. *One Earth, Four or Five Worlds.* San Diego, CA: Harcourt Brace Jovanovich, 1985. *Collected Poems, 1957–87.* New York: New Directions, 1987. *Sor Juana: Or, The Traps of Faith.* Cambridge, MA: Harvard Univ. Press, 1988. *The Other Voice: Essays on Modern Poetry.* New York: Harcourt Brace, 1991. *Essays on Mexican Art.* New York: Harcourt Brace, 1993. *The Double Flame: Essays on Love and Eroticism.* New York: Harcourt Brace, 1995.

For More Information See: Contemporary Authors. Detroit: Gale Research, 1978, Vol. 73–76, 491–92. *Itinerary.* New York: Harcourt, 1999. *New York Times* (October 12, 1990): B1. Wilson, J. *Octavio Paz.* Boston: Twayne, 1986.

Commentary: The Nobel Prize in Literature was granted to Octavio Paz, the first Mexican writer to win, "for impassioned writing with wide horizons, characterized by sensuous intelligence and humanistic integrity." A political commentator, a diplomat, and an accomplished essayist and poet, Paz was a force in Mexico throughout his life, dealing in his writings and actions with societal reality and "surrealistically inspired thoughts." (J.H.S.)

1991

Gordimer, Nadine   268

Prize: Literature, 1991. *Born:* November 20, 1923; Springs, South Africa. *Parents:* Father, Isidore Gordimer; Mother, Nan Myers Gordimer. *Nationality:* South African. *Religion:* Jewish. *Education:* No college degrees. *Spouse:* Gerald Gavronsky, married March 6, 1949, divorced 1952; Reinhold Cassirer, married January 29, 1954. *Children:* Orianne, daughter; Hugo, son. *Career:* Writer. *Other Awards:* Smith Award, 1961; Pringle Award, 1969; Black Award, 1973; Booker Prize, 1974; CNA Award, 1974, 1979, 1981, 1991; Grand Aigle d'Or, 1975; Commonwealth Award for Distinguished Service in Literature, 1981; MLA Award,

1982; Sachs Prize, 1985; Malaparte Award, 1986; Bennet Award, 1986; Benson Medal, 1990.

Selected Publications: A World of Strangers. London: Cape, 1958, 1976; *Selected Stories.* Harmonsworth: Penguin, 1975; *Berger's Daughter.* New York: Viking Press, 1979; *July's People.* New York: Viking Press, 1981; *A Sport of Nature.* New York: Knopf, 1987; *Crimes of Conscience.* Oxford: Heinemann International, 1991; *Three in a Bed: Fiction, Morals, and Politics.* Bennington, VT: Bennington College, 1991; *Legal Fictions: Short Stories about Lawyers and the Law.* Woodstock, NY: Overlook Press, 1992; *Why Haven't You Written: Selected Stories, 1950–1972.* New York: Penguin Books, 1993; *The Lying Days.* New York: Penguin Books, 1994; *My Son's Story.* New York: Farrar, Straus & Giroux, 1994; *No One to Accompany Me.* New York: Farrar, Straus & Giroux, 1994; *Playboy Stories: The Best of Forty Years of Short Fiction.* New York: Dutton, 1994.

For More Information See: Contemporary Authors. Detroit, MI: Gale Research, 1991. Driver, Dorothy. *Nadine Gordimer: A Bibliography of Primary and Secondary Sources, 1937–1992.* New Providence, NJ: K. G. Saur, 1994. Head, Dominic. *Nadine Gordimer.* New York: Cambridge University Press, 1994. Oliphant, A.W. & Gordimer, N. *A Writing Life.* London; New York: Viking, 1998. Temple-Thurston, Barbara. *Nadine Gordimer Revisited.* New York: Twayne, 1999.

Commentary: Nadine Gordimer, the first South African to win the Nobel Prize, was cited because her "continual involvement on behalf of literature and free speech in a police state where censorship and persecution of books and people exist [has] made her the doyenne of South African letters." Gordimer's writings portray the trauma of racial segregation in South Africa, reflecting the changes in the life of the region since 1949. Her themes are predominantly concerned with the effects of the political situation, taboos, and restrictions on individual lives and sensibilities—effects that result in fear and distrust. (P.K.)

1992

Walcott, Derek Alton   269

Prize: Literature, 1992. *Born:* January 23, 1930; Castries, St. Lucia, West Indies. *Parents:* Father, Warwick Walcott; Mother, Alix Walcott. *Nationality:* Jamaican. *Religion:* Protestant. *Education:* Univ. of West Indies, Jamaica, B.A., 1953. *Spouse:* Fay Morton, married 1954, divorced 1959; Margaret Ruth Maillard, married 1962, divorced (no date); Norline Metivier, married (no date), divorced (no date). *Children:* Peter, son; 2 daughters. *Career:* Writer; Trinidad Theatre Workshop, Director, 1959–76. *Other Awards:* Jamaica Prize, 1958; Guinness Award, 1961; Royal Society Award, 1964; W. H. Heinemann Award, 1966, 1983; Cholmondeley Award, 1969; Obie Award, 1971; Jock Campbell/New Statesman Prize, 1974; International Writer's Prize, Welsh Arts Council, 1979; MacArthur Foundation Award, 1981; L.A. Times Book Review Prize, 1986; Queen Elizabeth II Gold Medal, 1988; W.H. Smith Literary Award, 1991; St. Lucia Cross, 1993.

Selected Publications: Poems. Kingston, Jamaica: City Printery, 1953; *In a Green Night: Poems 1948–1960.* London: Jonathan Cape, 1962; *Selected Poems.* New York:

Farrar, Straus & Giroux, 1964; *Castaway and Other Poems.* London: Jonathan Cape, 1965; *Dream on Monkey Mountain and Other Plays.* New York: Farrar, Straus & Giroux, 1970; *Another Life.* New York: Farrar, Straus & Giroux, 1973; *Sea Grapes.* New York: Farrar, Straus & Giroux, 1976; *Joker of Seville & O Babylon.* New York: Farrar, Straus & Giroux, 1978; *The Fortunate Traveler.* New York: Farrar, Straus & Giroux, 1981; *Midsummer.* New York: Farrar, Straus & Giroux, 1984; *The Arkansas Testament* [three plays]. New York: Farrar, Straus & Giroux, 1990. *The Odyssey: A Stage Version.* New York: Farrar, Straus & Giroux, 1993; *The Antilles: Fragments of Epic Poetry.* New York: Farrar, Straus & Giroux, 1993; *Tiepolo's Hound.* New York: Farrar, 2000.

For More Information See: Brown, Stewart. *The Art of Derek Walcott.* Chester Springs, PA: Dufour Edition, 1991. *Dictionary of Literary Biography Yearbook, 1981.* Detroit: Gale, 1982. Hamner, Robert D. *Critical Perspectives on Derek Walcott.* Washington, DC: Three Continents Press, 1993. King, Bruce. *Derek Walcott.* Oxford; New York: Oxford Univ. Press, 2000.

Commentary: Poet and playwright, painter and journalist, Derek Walcott won the Nobel Prize for the "melodious and sensitive style" in his "poetic oeuvre of great luminosity, sustained by historical vision, the outcome of multicultural commitment." His writings embody the cultural diversity of the Indies, the strange and exotic island life, evoking the darkness of colonialism, slavery, and exile. Though he uses the idioms and rhythms of Caribbean dialects, he "achieves a universal resonance in his connection of the Caribbean situation with those of the exploited peoples everywhere." The Academy noted that "in him, West Indian culture has found its great poet." (P.K.)

1993

Morrison, Toni (Chloe Anthony Wofford)   270

Prize: Literature, 1993. ***Born:*** February 18, 1931; Lorain, OH. ***Parents:*** Father, George Wofford; Mother, Ramah Willis Wofford. ***Nationality:*** American. ***Religion:*** Christian. ***Education:*** Howard Univ., Washington, DC, B.A., 1953; Cornell Univ., NY, M.A., 1955. ***Spouse:*** Harold Morrison, married 1958, divorced 1964. ***Children:*** Harold Ford, son; Slade Kevin, son. ***Career:*** Texas Southern Univ., Professor, 1955–1957; Howard Univ., Washington, DC, Professor, 1957–64; Random House, NY, Editor, 1965–84; State Univ. of New York at Albany, NY, Professor, 1984–89; Princeton Univ., NJ, Professor, 1989- ***Other Awards:*** Ohioana Book Award, 1975; National Book Critics Circle Award, 1977; New York State Governor's Art Award, 1986; Kennedy Award, 1988; Pulitzer Prize, 1988; Melcher Book Award, 1988; National Book Foundation Medal, 1996.

Selected Publications: *The Bluest Eye.* New York: Holt, Rinehart and Winston, 1969; *Sula.* New York: Knopf, 1973; *Song of Solomon,* New York: Knopf, 1977; *Pathways to the Gods: The Mystery of the Indies Lines.* New York: Harper & Row, 1978; *Tar Baby.* New York: Knopf, 1987; *Beloved.* New York: Knopf, 1987; *Jazz.* New York: Random House, 1992; *Playing in the Dark: Whiteness and the Literary Imagination.* Cambridge, MA: Harvard Univ. Press, 1993; *Sexual Offending against Children: Assessment and Treatment of Male Abusers.* New York: Routledge, 1994.

For More Information See: Bjork, P. *The Novels of Toni Morrison.* New York: P. Lang, 1992; Rigney, B. *The Voices of Toni Morrison.* Columbus, OH: Ohio State Univ. Press, 1991; Samuel, W. *Toni Morrison.* Boston: Twayne Publishers, 1990; Taylor-Guthrie, D. *Conversations with Toni Morrison.* Jackson, MS: Univ. Press of Mississippi, 1994.

Commentary: In granting the Nobel Prize to Toni Morrison, the Academy described her as "a literary artist of the first rank . . . characterized by visionary force and poetic import [that] gives life to an essential aspect of American reality." Morrison's fiction is a mixture of fantasy and realism, drawing on folklore, myth, and legend, and juxtaposing black humanity and white cultural values. She has been described as the "high priestess of village literature," revealing the black experience in all its facets. The Academy noted that she "delves into the language itself, a language she wants to liberate from the fetters of race, and she addresses us with the luster of poetry." (P.K.)

1994

Oe, Kenzaburo   271

Prize: Literature, 1994. ***Born:*** January 31, 1935; Ose Village, Shikoku, Japan. ***Parents:*** Father, Kotaro Oe; Mother, Koseki Oe. ***Nationality:*** Japanese. ***Religion:*** Agnostic. ***Education:*** Tokyo Univ., Japan, B.A., 1960. ***Spouse:*** Yukari Itami, married February 1960. ***Children:*** Hikari, son; Natsumiko, daughter; Sakurao, son ***Career:*** Writer, 1952-. ***Other Awards:*** May Festival Prize, 1954; Akutagawa Prize, 1958; Shinchosha Literary Prize, 1964; Tanizaki Prize, 1967; Noma Prize, 1969, 1973; Osaragi Jiro Award, 1983; Europelia Arts Festival Prize, 1989.

Selected Publications: *Shiiku,* 1958 (*The Catch.* Tr. by John Bester in *The Shadow of Sunrise,* ed. Saeki Shoichi, Palo Alto, CA: Stanford Univ. Press, 1966); *Kojinteki na taiken* (*A Personal Matter.* New York: Grove Press, 1969); *Man'en gannen no futtoboru,* 1967; *The Silent Cry.* Tr. by John Bester. Tokyo: Kodansha International, 1974; *Teach Us to Outgrow Our Madness.* Tr. by John Nathan. New York: Grove Press, 1977; *Fire and Ashes: Short Stories about Hiroshima and Nagasaki.* London: Readers International, 1985; *The Crazy Iris and Other Stories of the Atomic Aftermath.* New York: Grove Press, 1985; *Pinchi ranna chosho,* 1976; *The Pinch Runner Memorandum.* Tr. by Michiko N. Wilson and Michael K. Wilson. Armonk, NY: M. E. Sharpe, 1994; *A Quiet Life.* Tr. By Kunioki Yanagishita and William Wetherall. New York: Grove Press, 1996.

For More Information See: Cameron, Lindsley. *The Music of Light.* New York: Free Press, 1998. *New York Times Biographical Service* (October 14, 1994): 1516. Wilson, Michiko N. *The Marginal World of Oe, Kenzaburo: A Study in Times and Techniques.* Armonk, NY: M. E. Sharpe, 1986. *World Authors, 1980–85.* New York: H. W. Wilson, 1991, 655–8.

Commentary: Kenzaburo Oe, the Japanese "uncompromising avant-gardist," won the Nobel for his works in which "poetic force creates an imagined world where life and myth condense to form a disconcerting picture of the human predicament today." Influenced by the war, Hiroshima, and the birth of a brain-damaged son, Oe's work moves from his early writings of innocence overshadowed by a life of alienation, to semi-autobiographical considerations of past and present, and finally to mixtures of Japanese and Western intellectual traditions. Oe summarizes his work as "writing about the dignity of human beings." (P.K.)

1995

Heaney, Seamus Justin   **272**

Prize: Literature, 1995. *Born:* April 13, 1939; Mossbawn, County Derry, Northern Ireland. *Parents:* Father, Patrick Heaney; Mother, Margaret Kathleen McCann Heaney. *Nationality:* Irish. *Religion:* Catholic. *Education:* Queen's Univ., Ireland, B.A., 1961. *Spouse:* Marie Devlin, married August 1965. *Children:* Christopher, son; Michael, son; Catherine, daughter. *Career:* Poet, 1960-; Ballymurphy Schools, Ireland, Teacher, 1962–63; St. Joseph's College of Education, Ireland, Lecturer, 1963–66; Queen's Univ., Ireland, Lecturer, 1966–72; Freelance Writer, 1972–75; Carysfort College, Ireland, Lecturer, 1976–82; Harvard Univ., MA, Professor, 1982–92. *Other Awards:* Gregory Award, 1966; Cholomondely Award, 1967; Maugham Award, 1968; Faber Prize, 1968; Irish Academy of Letters Award, 1971; Devlin Prize, 1973; American-Irish Foundation Award, 1975; E.M. Forster Award, 1975; Smith Award, 1976; Cooper Award, 1976; Bennett Award, 1982; Whitbread Award, 1987, 1996, 1999; Lannam Award, 1990; Mondello Prize, 1993; Irish Literature Poetry Prize, 1999.

Selected Publications: Death of a Naturalist. London: Faber, 1966; *Door into the Dark.* London: Faber, 1969; *Wintering Out.* London: Faber, 1972; *North.* London: Faber, 1975; *Field Work.* London: Faber, 1979; *Poems, 1965–1975.* New York: Farrar, Straus & Giroux, 1980; *Preoccupations: Selected Prose, 1968–1978.* New York: Farrar, Straus & Giroux, 1980; *Station Island.* New York: Farrar, Straus & Giroux, 1984; *The Haw Lantern.* New York: Farrar, Straus & Giroux, 1987; *Selected Poems, 1966–1987.* New York, NY: Farrar, Straus & Giroux, 1990; *Spirit Level.* New York: Farrar, Straus, 1996; *Opened Ground: Selected Poems, 1966–1996.* New York: Farrar, Straus, 1998; *Beowulf* Tr. New York: Farrar, Straus, 2000. *Electric Light.* London: Faber & Faber, 2001.

For More Information See: Allen, M. ed. *Seamus Heaney.* New York: St. Martin's Press, 1997; Buttel, R. *Seamus Henry.* Lewisburg, PA: Bucknell Univ. Press, 1975; *Contemporary Authors. New Revision Series.* Detroit, MI: Gale Research, 1989, Volume 25; *Contemporary Literary Criticism.* Detroit, MI: Gale Research, 1993, Volume 74; *New York Times* (October 6, 1995): B1.

Commentary: Seamus Henry, "the guardian spirit of Irish poetry," received the Nobel Prize "for works of lyrical beauty and ethical depth, which exalt everyday miracles and the living past." The Laureate, in his poetry, searches for Irish origins and identities, including his personal origins and identity. Characterized by sensuous language, sexual metaphors, and natural images, Heaney's work also shows his concern about poetry's relevance in the confused and difficult world in which he finds himself. (P.K./J.H.S.)

1996

Szymborska, Wislawa   **273**

Prize: Literature, 1996. *Born:* July 2, 1923; Prowent-Bnin, Kornik, Poland. *Parents:* No record found. *Nationality:* Polish. *Religion:* No record found. *Education:* No college degrees. *Spouse:* Adam Wlodek, married, no date, divorced, no date; Kornel Flipowicz, married, no date, died, early 1990s. *Children:* None. *Career:* Poet; *Zycie Literackie* (Literary Life), Editorial Staff, 1953–81. *Other Awards:* Cracow Literary Prize, 1954; Polish Ministry of Culture Prize, 1963; Knight's Cross, Order of Polonia Restitute, 1974; Gold Cross of Merit, 1955; Goethe Prize, 1991; Herder Prize, 1995; Polish PEN Poetry Award, 1996.

Selected Publications: Questions Put to Myself, 1954. *Calling Out to Yeti.* 1957. *Sól (Salt).* Warszawa: Panstwowy Instytut Wydawniczy, 1962. *No End of Fun*, 1967. *Sounds, Feelings, Thoughts* (Tr. M.J. Krynski and R.A. Maguire). Princeton, NJ: Princeton University Press, 1981. *The People on a Bridge* (Tr. A. Czerniawski). London; Boston: Forest Books, 1986. *The End and the Beginning*, 1993. *View with a Grain of Sand* (Tr. S. Baranczak and C. Cavanagh). New York: Harcourt, 1995. *Nic dwa razy.* Krakow: Wydawnm 1997 (*Nothing Twice.* Tr. S. Baranczak and C. Cavanaugh). *Poems New and Collected, 1957–1997* (Tr. S. Baranczak and C. Cavanagh). New York: Harcourt, 1998. *Miracle Fair* (Tr. J. Trzeciak). New York: Norton, 2001.

For More Information See: New York Times (October 4, 1996): C5. *New York Times Magazine* (December 1, 1996): 46+.

Commentary: Wislawa Szymborska won the Nobel Prize "for poetry that with ironic precision allows the historical and biological context to come to light in fragments of human reality." A quiet, shy, yet witty person, she has been described as the "Mozart of poetry, not without justice in view of her wealth of inspiration and the veritable ease with which her words seem to fall in place." Disclaiming her early work which embraced social realism, she now writes primarily of ordinary life and relationships. (L.S.S.)

1997

Fo, Dario   **274**

Prize: Literature, 1997. *Born:* March 26, 1926; San Giano, Lombardy, Italy. *Parents:* Father, Felice Fo; Mother, Pina Rota Fo. *Nationality:* Italian. *Religion:* No record found. *Education:* No college degrees. *Spouse:* Franca Rame, married June 24, 1954. *Children:* Jacopo, son; three other children *Career:* Playwright and Actor; La Comune Theatre Collective, Italy, Founder, 1970–73; Nuova Scena, Italy, Co-founder, 1968; Fo-Rame Company, Co-founder, 1957–69. *Other Awards:* Sonning Award, 1981; Premio Eduardo, 1986; Obie Award, 1987; Agro Dolce Prize, 1988.

Selected Publications: Teatro Comico. Milano: Garzanti, 1962. *Mistero Buffo* (Tr. *The Comic Mysteries.* London: Methuen, 1988. Tr. Ed Emery.), 1969. *Morte accidentale di un anarchio* (Tr. *Accidental Death of an Anarchist.* London: Methuen, 1994). Torino: Einaudi, 1974 (Tr. Gavin Richards). *Tutta casa, letto e chiesa* (with F. Rame). Verona: Bertani, 1978 (Tr. *All House, Bed and Church*). *Le Commedie di Dario Fo.* 6 volumes. Torino: Einaudi, 1974, reprinted, 1984. *Tricks of the Trade* (Tr.*Manuale minimo dell'attore.* London: Methuen, 1991 (Tr. by J. Farrell). *The Virtuous Burglars.* London: Methuen, 1992. *Plays*, 2 vols. London: Methuen, 1994. *The Pope and the Witch* (*Papa e la strega.* Tr. by Ed Emery). London: Oberon, 1997.

For More Information See: Behan, Tom. *Dario Fo.* London; Sterling, VA: Pluto Press, 2000. *Contemporary*

Literary Criticism. Detroit: Gale, v.32, 1985; vol. 109, 1998. Mitchell, Tony. *Dario Fo.* London: Methuen, 1984, 1999. *New York Times* (October 10, 1997): A1.

Commentary: Known primarily as an actor and clown, but also a playwright, Dario Fo was awarded the Nobel Prize as one "who emulates the jesters of the Middle Ages in scourging authority and upholding the dignity of the downtrodden." A controversial award denounced by the Vatican, the Swedish Academy noted his 1969 work "Mistero Buffo" ("Comic Mystery") and the "Morte accidentale di un anarchio" ("Accidental Death of an Anarchist," 1970) as major examples that "open our eyes to abuses and injustices in society and also the wider historical perspective in which they can be placed. Fo is an extremely serious satirist with a multifaceted oeuvre." (L.S.S.)

1998

Saramago, José   275

Prize: Literature, 1998. *Born:* November 16, 1922; Azinhaya, Portugal. *Parents:* Father, José de Sousa; Mother, Maria da Piedade. *Nationality:* Portuguese. *Religion:* Communist. *Education:* No college degrees. *Spouse:* Ilda Reis, married 1944, divorced 1970; Pilar del Rio, married 1988. *Children:* Violante Matos, daughter. *Career:* Writer. *Other Awards:* Association of Portuguese Critics Prize, 1979; Lisbon Literary Prize, 1980; Premio Cidade de Lisboa, 1980; Portuguese PEN Prize, 1982, 1984; Premio PEN Club Portugê, 1983, 1984; Grinzane Cavour Prize, 1987; Mondello Prize, 1992; Flaiano Prize, 1992; Brancatti Prize, 1992; Independent Foreign Fiction Prize, 1993; Portuguese Association of Writers Prize, 1993; Premio Vida Literaria, 1993; Luis de Camoes Prize, 1995; Portuguese Society of Authors Prize, 1995.

Selected Publications: Land of Sin, 1947. *Manual de pintura e caligrafia* (*Manual of Painting and Calligraphy.* Tr. G. Pontiero. Manchester: Carcanet, 1994), Sao Paulo: Moraes,1976. *Levantado do chao* (*Raised From the Ground*), Lisbon: Caminho,1980. *Memorial do convento* (*Memoirs of the Convent*), Lisbon: Caminho, 1982 (Tr. G.Pontiero as *Baltasar and Blimunda.* San Diego: Harcourt, 1987). *The Year of the Death of Ricardo Reis,* New York: Harcourt,1991 (Tr.*O ano da morte de Ricardo Reis* by G. Pontiero. Lisbon: Caminho, 1984). *The Gospel According to Jesus Christ* (*O Evangelho Segundo Jesus Cristo,* Lisbon: Caminho,1991) New York: Harcourt, 1994 (Tr. G. Pontiero. *The Stone Raft* New York: Harcourt, 1994 (Tr. G. Pontiero. *A jangada de pedra.* Lisbon: Caminho, 1984). *History of the Siege of Lisbon* (*Historia do cerco de Lisboa.* Lisbon: Caminho, 1989). New York: Harcourt Brace, 1996 (Tr. G. Pontiero). *Blindness: A Novel.* New York: Harcourt Brace, 1998. *All the Names* (*Todos os Nomes*). New York: Harcourt:, 2000 (Tr. M.J. Costa). *Journey to Portugal* (*Viagem a Portugal*). New York: Harcourt, 2001 (Tr. A. Hopkinson and N. Caister).

For More Information See: New York Times (October 9, 1998): A12. *New York Times* (December 3, 1998): E1. *Paris Review* 40 (Winter, 1998): 54–73.

Commentary: José Saramago, "who with parables sustained by imagination, compassion and irony continually enables us once again to apprehend an elusory reality" was the first Portuese to be awarded the prize for literature. His success as a writer came late in life, at the age of 60, with the publication of "Baltasar and Blimunda." This novel is described as having "a historical, a social and an individual perspective. The insight and wealth of imagination to which it gives expression is characteristic of Saramago's works as a whole." (L.S.S.)

1999

Grass, Günter Wilhelm   276

Prize: Literature, 1999. *Born:* October 16, 1927; Free City of Danzig, Germany (now Gdansk, Poland). *Parents:* Father, Willy Grass; Mother, Helena Knoff Grass. *Nationality:* German. *Religion:* Catholic. *Education:* No college degrees. *Spouse:* Anna Margareta Schwarz Grass, married 1954, divorced no date; Utte Grunert, married 1979. *Children:* Franz, son; Raoul, son; Laura, daughter, Bruno, son; Malte, stepson; Hans, stepson. *Career:* Writer. *Other Awards:* Suddeutscher Rund Funk Lyrikpreis, 1955; Preisder Gruppe 47, 1958; City of Bremen Literary Prize, 1959; German Critics Prize, 1960; Foreign Book Prize, France, 1962; Buchner Prize, 1965; Fontaine Prize, 1968; Berliner Fontane Aeis, 1969; Heuss Prize, 1969; Mondello Prize, 1977; Carl von Ossiersky Medal, 1977; International Literatur Award, 1978; Viareggio-Versilia Prize, 1978; Majakowski Medal, 1978; Vienna Literature Prize, 1980; Feltrinelli Prize, 1982; Leonhard Frank Ring, 1988; Karel Capek Prize, 1994.

Selected Publications: The Tin Drum (*Die Blechtrommel.* Darmstadt: Luchterhand, 1959). (Tr. R. Manheim) New York: Vintage, 1962. *Cat and Mouse* (*Katz und Maus.* Darmstadt: Luchterhand, 1961.) (Tr. R. Manheim) San Diego: Harcourt Brace, 1963. *Dog Years* (*Hundejahre.* Darmstadt: Luchterhand, 1963). (Tr. R. Manheim.) New York: Harcourt, 1965. *The Plebeians Rehearse the Uprising.* (*Die Plebejer proben den Aufstand*). (Tr. R. Manheim.) New York: Harcourt Brace, 1966. *Four Plays.* New York: Harcourt, Brace & World, 1967. *Speak out! Speeches, Open Letters, Commentaries.* (Tr. R. Manheim.) London: Secker & Warburg, 1969. *Local Anaesthetic* (*Oertlich betacubt.* Darmstadt: Luchterhand, 1969). (Tr. R. Manheim.) New York: Harcourt, 1970. *From the Diary of a Snail* (*Aus dem Tagebuch einer Schnecke.* Darmstadt: Luchterhand, 1972). (Tr. R. Manheim.) New York: Harcourt Brace Jovanovich, 1973. *In the Egg and Other Poems* (*Der Butt.* Darmstadt: Luchterhand, 1977). (Tr. by M. Hamburger and C. Middleton.) New York: Harcourt Brace Jovanovich, 1977. *The Meeting at Telgte* (*Das Treffen in Telgte.* Darmstadt: Luchterhand, 1978). (Tr. R. Manheim.) New York: Harcourt Brace Jovanovich, 1981. *The Flounder.* (Tr. R. Manheim.) New York: Harcourt Brace Jovanovich, 1978. *Headbirths, or, the Germans are Dying Out* (*Kopfgeburten; oder Die Deutschen sterben aus*). (Tr. R. Manheim.) New York: Harcourt Brace Jovanovich, 1982. *The Rat* (*Die Raettin.* Tr. R. Manheim.) San Diego: Harcourt Brace Jovanovich, 1987. *Show Your Tongue* (*Zunge Zeigen*). (Tr. J. E. Woods.) San Diego: Harcourt Brace Jovanovich, 1987. *Two States One Nation?* (*Deutscher Lastenausgleich*). (Tr. R. Winston with A.S. Wensinger.) San Diego: Harcourt Brace Jovanovich, 1990. *The Call of the Toad* (*Unkenrufe*). (Tr. R. Manheim.) New York: Harcourt Brace Jovanovich, 1992. *My Century* (*Meine Jahrhundert*). (Tr. M. H. Heim.) New York: Harcourt Brace,

1999. *Too Far Afield* (*Ein Weites Feld*). New York: Harcourt, 2000 (Tr. K. Winston).

For More Information See: Brandes, Ute Thoss. *Guenter Grass*. Berlin: Edition Colloquium, 1998. Hollington, Michael. *Guenter Grass*. New York: Marion Boyars, 1980. *New York Times* (October 1, 1999): A13. O'Neill, Patrick. *Guenter Grass Revisited*. Boston: Twayne, 1999. Preece, Julian. *Guenter Grass*. New York: St. Martin's Press, 2000.

Commentary: Günter Grass, "Whose frolicsome black fables portray the forgotten face of history" was awarded the Nobel Prize in literature. "The Tin Drum," for which Grass is most famous, "Cat and Mouse" and "The Dog Years" make up the "Danzig Trilogy" in which he recreates the horror of the Nazi years and the exploration of Germany's national identity. His later works "confirm the author's position as the great prober of the history of this century." His works explore the intertwined roots of good and evil against the political background of the 20th Century. (L.S.S.)

2000

Xingjian, Gao   277

Prize: Literature, 2000. *Born:* January 4, 1940; Ganzhou, Jiangxi, China. *Parents:* Father: Bank official; Mother: Amateur actress (No further record found). *Nationality:* Chinese; later French citizen. *Religion:* No record found. *Education:* Beijing College, China, B.A., 1962. *Spouse:* Married, no date, dissolved, no date; no further record found. *Children:* No record found. *Career:* Writer. *Other*

Awards: Chevalier de l'Ordre des Arts et des Lettres, 1992; Prix Communauté française de Belgique, 1994; Prix du Nouvel An chinois, 1997. $11*Premier essai sur les techniques du roman moderne/A Preliminary Discussion of the Art of Modern Fiction*. 1981. *Signal d'alarme/Signal Alarm*, 1982. *Arrêt de bus/Bus Stop*, 1983. *L'Homme sauvage/Wild Man*, 1985. *Pigeon Called Red Beak*, 1985. *Collected Plays*, 1985. *In Search of a Modern Form of Dramatic Representation*, 1987. *Between Life and Death. The Other Shore* (Tr. Gilbert C.F. Fong). Hong Kong: Chinese University Press, 1999. *Soul Mountain*. (Tr. Mabel Lee) Sydney, Australia: HarperCollins, 1999; New York: HarperCollins, 2000. *La fuite/Fugitives*. Carnieres-Morlanwelz: Lansman, 2000. *Le Livre d'un homme seul/One Man's Bible*. La Tour d'Aigues: Editions de l'Aube, 2000.

For More Information See: *New York Times* (October 13, 2000): A5. *New York Times* (October 18, 2000): A4. *New Times Magazine* (December 10, 2000): 51.

Commentary: The first Chinese language writer to win the Nobel Prize in literature received the award "for an oeuvre of universal validity, bitter insights and linguistic ingenuity, which has opened new paths for the Chinese novel and drama." Exiled from his homeland and now a French citizen, his work has been banned in China. His literature "is born anew from the struggle of the individual to survive the history of the masses" and reflects the influence of Western drama from the works of Artaud, Brecht and Beckett. (L.S.S.)

Medicine and Physiology

1901

von Behring, Emil Adolph   **278**

Prize: Medicine and Physiology, 1901. *Born:* March 15, 1854; Hansdorf, Germany. *Death:* March 31, 1917; Marburg, Germany. *Parents:* Father, August Georg Behring; Mother, Augustine Zech Behring. *Nationality:* German. *Religion:* Agnostic; most probably from Protestant background. *Education:* Friedrich-Wilhelms Univ., Germany, M.D., 1878; Friedrich-Wilhelms Univ., Germany, Ph.D., 1880. *Spouse:* Elsie Spinola, married 1896. *Children:* 6 sons. *Career:* Charité Hospital, Berlin, Germany, Intern, 1880–81; Prussian Army, Surgeon, 1881–87; Academy for Military Medicine, Berlin, Germany, Professor, 1888–89; Institute of Hygiene, Berlin, Germany, Researcher, 1889–93; Univ. of Halle, Germany, Professor, 1894–95; Univ. of Marburg, Germany, Professor and Administrator, 1895–1917. *Other Awards:* Officer, Legion of Honor, 1895; Prize, Paris Académie d' Medicine, 1895; Prize, Institute of France, 1895; Nobility, Prussia, 1901; Iron Cross, Germany, World War I.

Selected Publications: "Über das Zustandekommen der Diptherie-Immunität und der Tetanus-Immunität bei Thieren." *Deutsche Medizinische Wochenschrift* 16 (1890): 113–14 (with S. Kitasato). *Gesammelte Abhandlungen zur Atiologischen Therapie von Ansteckenden Krankheiten.* Leipzig, Germany: Thieme, 1893. *Gesammelte Abhandlungen. Nene Folge.* Bonn: A. Marcus and E. Webers, 1915.

For More Information See: Dictionary of Scientific Biography. New York: Scribner's, 1970 (Volume 1), 574–78. Macnalty, A.S. "Emil von Behring." *British Medical Journal* 1 (1954): 668–70. Unger, Hellmuth. *Emil von Behring, Sein Lebenswerk Als Vovergangliches Erbe.* Hamburg: Hoffmann und Campe, 1948. Zeiss, Heinz, and Bieling, R., *Behring, Gestalt und Werk.* Berlin: Grunewald, B. Schultz, 1940.

Commentary: The Nobel citation for Emil von Behring reads "for his work on serum therapy, especially its application against diptheria, by which he has opened a new road in the domain of medical science and thereby placed in the hands of the physician a victorious weapon against illness and death." Von Behring is considered one of the founders of immunology, introduced the term "antitoxin," and successfully used antitoxins against diphtheria, tetanus, and bovine tuberculosis. (L.W.)

1902

Ross, Ronald, Sir   **279**

Prize: Medicine and Physiology, 1902. *Born:* May 13, 1857; Almora, India. *Death:* September 16, 1932; London, England. *Parents:* Father, Campbell Claye Grant Ross; Mother, Matilda Charlotte Elderton Ross. *Nationality:* British. *Religion:* Anglican. *Education:* St. Bartholomew's Medical School Hospital, England, MRCS diploma (medical degree), 1879. *Spouse:* Rosa Bessie Bloxam, married April 25, 1889. *Children:* Charles Claye, son; Dorothy, daughter; Sylvia, daughter; Ronald, son. *Career:* Indian Medical Service, Doctor, 1881–99; School of Tropical Medicine, Liverpool, England, Professor, 1899–1917; London, England, Physician, 1917–23; Hospital for Tropical Diseases, Ross Institute, London, England, Director, 1923–32. *Other Awards:* Parke Gold Medal, 1895; Cameron Prize, 1901; Royal Medal, Royal Society, 1909; Knighthood, 1911.

Selected Publications: "On Some Peculiar Pigmented Cells Found in Two Mosquitoes Fed on Malarial Blood." *British Medical Journal* 2 (1897): 1786–88. *The Prevention of Malaria.* London: J. Murray, 1910. *Studies on Malaria.* London: J. Murray, 1928.

For More Information See: Dictionary of Scientific Biography. New York: Scribner's, 1975 (Volume 11), 555–57. Megroz, R.L. *Ronald Ross, Discoverer and Creator.* London: Allen and Unwin, 1931. Nye, E.R. and Gibson, Mary E. *Ronald Ross: Malariologist and Polymath.* New York: St. Martin's Press, 1997. Ross, Sir Ronald. *Memoirs, with a Full Account of the Great Malaria Problem and Its Solution.* London: J. Murray, 1923.

Commentary: Ronald Ross's Nobel Prize came for his work on malaria. His research proved that the Anopheles mosquito was the intermediate host in malaria's transmission, and he later developed the methods for destroying the mosquito. Ross was also an accomplished doctor, mathematician, author, editor, musician, and composer. (R.K.)

1903

Finsen, Niels Ryberg   **280**

Prize: Medicine and Physiology, 1903. *Born:* December 15, 1860; Thorshavn, Denmark. *Death:* September 24, 1904; Copenhagen, Denmark. *Parents:* Father, Hannes Steingrin Finsen; Mother, Johanne Froman Finsen. *Nationality:* Danish. *Religion:* Lutheran. *Education:* Univ. of Copenhagen, Denmark, M.D., 1890. *Spouse:* Ingeborg Balslev, married 1892. *Children:* Halldor, son; Gudrun, daughter; Valgerda, daughter. *Career:* Univ. of Copenhagen, Denmark, Professor, 1890–93; Finsen Ray Institute, Copenhagen, Denmark, Founder and Director, 1896–1904. *Other Awards:* Knight of the Order of Dannebrog, 1899; Danish Gold Medal for Merit; Cameron Prize, Univ. of Edinburgh, Scotland, 1904.

Selected Publications: "Red Light Treatment of Smallpox." *British Medical Journal* 2 (1895): 1412–14. *Om Anvendelse i Medicinen af Koncentrede Kemiske Lysstraaler* (On the use in medicine of concentrated chemical rays). Copenhagen: F. Hegel and Son, 1896. *Phototherapy.* London: E. Arnold, 1901. *Om Bekaempelse af Lupus Vulgaris Med Rede Gōrelse for de i Danmark Opnaaede Resultater.* Copenhagen: Gyldendalske Boghandels Forlag, 1902. *Die Bekampfung des Lupus Vulgaris.* Jena, Germany: G. Fischer, 1903.

For More Information See: De Kruif, Paul. *Men Against Death*. New York: Harcourt, Brace, 1934, 283–99. *Dictionary of Scientific Biography*. New York: Scribner's, 1970 (Volume 4), 620–21.

Commentary: The Nobel Prize was awarded to Niels Finsen "in recognition of his treatment of disease, especially lupus vulgaris, with concentrated light rays, whereby he opened up new channels for the art of medicine." His frail health and short years prevented further successes, but Finsen's discovery that the bactericidal effect of sunlight was due to the blue, violet, and ultraviolet portions of the spectrum; his development of the instrumentation and the mechanism for screening out heat; and his applications to treatment of disease states left a valuable legacy. (B.I.M.)

1904

Pavlov, Ivan Petrovich   **281**

Prize: Medicine and Physiology, 1904. *Born:* September 27, 1849; Ryazan, Russia. *Death:* February 27, 1936; Leningrad, USSR. *Parents:* Father, Pyotr Dmitrievich Pavlov; Mother, Varvara Ivanova Pavlov. *Nationality:* Russian. *Religion:* Agnostic; from Eastern Orthodox background. *Education:* Military Medical Academy, Russia, graduate, 1879; Military Medical Academy, Russia, M.D., 1883. *Spouse:* Serafina Vasilievna Karchevskaya, married May 1, 1881. *Children:* Mirchik, son; Vladmir, son; Vera, daughter; Victor, son; Vsevolod, son. *Career:* Military Medical Academy, St. Petersburg, Russia, Professor, 1888–1924; Institute of Experimental Medicine, St. Petersburg, Russia, Director, 1891–1936. *Other Awards:* Gold Medal, Univ. of St. Petersburg, Russia, 1875; Copley Medal, Royal Society, 1915.

Selected Publications: The Work of the Digestive Glands. Philadelphia: J.B. Lippincott, 1910. *Conditioned Reflexes*. London: Oxford Univ. Press, 1927. *Polnoe Sobranie Sochineny* (complete collected works) Moscow: Academy of Sciences, USSR, 1954.

For More Information See: Babkin, Boris P. *Pavlov: A Biography*. Chicago: Univ. of Chicago Press, 1949. *Dictionary of Scientific Biography*. New York: Scribner's, 1974 (Volume 10), 431–36. Gray, J.A. *Ivan Pavlov*. New York: Penguin, 1981. Parry, Albert. *The Russian Scientist*. New York: Macmillan, 1973, 78–89.

Commentary: The Nobel Award citation to Ivan Pavlov read "in recognition of his work on the physiology of digestion, by which, in essential respects, he has transformed and enlarged our knowledge of the subject." During his long career, Pavlov contributed impressively to the understanding of the heart, of blood circulation, and of digestion, but his name today is remembered principally for the concept of "conditioned reflexes," discovered while studying the digestive process. (L.W.)

1905

Koch, Heinrich Hermann Robert   **282**

Prize: Medicine and Physiology, 1905. *Born:* December 11, 1843; Clausthal, Germany. *Death:* May 27, 1910; Baden-Baden, Germany. *Parents:* Father, Hermann Koch; Mother, Mathilde Julie Henriette Biewend Koch. *Nationality:* German. *Religion:* Lutheran. *Education:* Univ. of Göttingen, Germany, M.D., 1866. *Spouse:* Emmy Adolfine Josefine Fraatz, married July 1867, divorced 1893; Hedwig Freiberg, married 1893. *Children:* Gertrud, daughter. *Career:* Hamburg, Germany, Doctor, 1866; Lagenhagen Lunatic Asylum, Germany, Doctor, 1866–68; Poznan, Germany, Doctor, 1868; Rakwitz, Germany, Doctor, 1869; German Army, Doctor, 1870–71; Wollstein, Germany, Doctor, 1872–80; Health Department, Berlin, Germany, Doctor, 1880–85; Berlin Univ., Germany, Professor and Administrator, 1885–90; Institute for Infectious Diseases, Berlin, Germany, Director, 1891–1904. *Other Awards:* Harben Medal, 1901; Prussian Order Pour le Mérite, 1906; Robert Koch Medal, 1908.

Selected Publications: Investigations into the Etiology of Traumatic Infective Diseases. London: The New Sydenham Society, 1880. "Etiology of Turberculosis." *American Review of Tuberculosis* 25 (1932): 285–323. "Etiology of Anthrax, Bases on the Ontogeny of the Anthrax Bacillus." *Medical Classics* 2 (1937–38): 787–820. "Methods for Studying, Preserving and Photographing Bacteria." In *Microbiology Contributions from 1776–1908*. New Brunswick, NJ: Rutgers Univ. Press, 1960, 67–73.

For More Information See: Barlowe, C. *Robert Koch*. Portland, OR: Heron Books, 1971. *Dictionary of Scientific Biography*. New York: Scribner's 1973 (Volume 7), 420–35. Brock, Thomas D. *Robert Koch*. New York: Springer-Verlag, 1988.

Commentary: For his work on tuberculosis, Robert Koch was awarded the Nobel Prize. Koch is regarded as the founder of modern medical bacteriology, in recognition of his discoveries as well as development of rigorous research methods. His most important work included proving that anthrax, tuberculosis, and cholera were caused by bacteria. (L.W.)

1906

Golgi, Camillo   **283**

Prize: Medicine and Physiology, 1906. *Born:* July 7, 1843; Corteno, Italy. *Death:* January 21, 1926; Pavia, Italy. *Parents:* Father, Alessandro Golgi; Mother, Carolina Papini Golgi. *Nationality:* Italian. *Religion:* Christian. *Education:* Univ. of Padua, Italy, M.D., 1865. *Spouse:* Lina Aletti, married October 28, 1877. *Children:* Carolina, niece (adopted). *Career:* Pavia, Italy, Doctor and Researcher, 1865–72; Univ. of Pavia, Italy, Professor, 1875–78; Univ. of Siena, Italy, Professor, 1879–80; Univ. of Pavia, Italy, Professor, 1880–1918.

Selected Publications: Opera Omnia (collected works) 4 volumes. Milan: U. Hoepli, 1903–29.

For More Information See: Chorobski, J. "Camillo Golgi, 1843–1926." *Archives of Neurology* (Chicago) 33 (1935): 163–70. *Dictionary of Scientific Biography*. New York: Scribner's, 1973 (Volume 5), 459–61. Mazzarello, Paolo, Henry A. Buchtel and Aldo Badiani. *The Hidden Structure: A Scientific Biography of Camillo Golgi*. Oxford; New York: Oxford University Press, 1999.

Commentary: Camillo Golgi shared the Nobel Prize for "work on the structure of the nervous system." A prominent neurohistologist, pathologist, and malariologist, his major contributions are usually listed as the development of a staining technique using silver (the Golgi method) for nerve substances, the portrayal of the cytoplasmic reticular substance of nerve and other cells, and the investigation of the fever curve as related to the parasite development in malaria. (R.K.)

Ramón y Cajal, Santiago   284

Prize: Medicine and Physiology, 1906. *Born:* May 1, 1852; Petilla de Aragón, Spain. *Death:* October 18, 1934; Madrid, Spain. *Parents:* Father, Justo Ramón y Casasús Cajal; Mother, Antonia Cajal. *Nationality:* Spanish. *Religion:* Catholic. *Education:* Univ. of Zaragoza, Spain, licentiate in medicine, 1873; Univ. of Zaragoza, Spain, doctorate in medicine, 1877. *Spouse:* Silveria Fananás García, married 1880. *Children:* Paula, daughter; Fe, daughter; Pilar, daughter; Santiago, son; Jorge, son; Luis, son. *Career:* Army Medical Service, 1874–76; Univ. of Zaragoza, Spain, Professor, 1876–83; Univ. of Valencia, Spain, Professor, 1883–87; Univ. of Barcelona, Spain, Professor, 1887–92; Univ. of Madrid, Spain, Professor, 1892–1922; Institute Cajal, Madrid, Researcher, 1922–34. *Other Awards:* Fauvelle Prize, 1896; Rubio Prize, 1897; Moscow Prize, 1900; Martinez y Molina Prize, 1902; Helmholtz Gold Medal, 1905; Echegaray Medal, 1922.

Selected Publications: Manual de Anatomia Pathologica General. Madrid: Moya, 1896. *Textura del Systema Nervioso del Hombre y de los Vertebrados.* Madrid: Moya, 1899–1904. *Degeneration and Regeneration of the Nervous System.* Tr. by Raoul M. Day. London: Oxford Univ. Press, 1928.

For More Information See: Cannon, Dorothy F. *Explorer of the Human Brain: The Life of Santiago Ramón y Cajal. 1852–1934.* New York: Schuman, 1949. *Dictionary of Scientific Biography.* New York: Scribner's, 1975 (Volume 11), 273–76. *Obituary Notices of Fellows of the Royal Society,* Cambridge: Royal Society, 1932–35 (Volume 1), 425–41. Ramón y Cajal, Santiago. *Recollections of My Life.* Cambridge, MA: Massachusetts Institute of Technology, 1966.

Commentary: Santiago Ramón y Cajal was awarded the Nobel Prize for his work on the structure of the nervous system. His major contributions were in adapting Golgi's silver nitrate staining techniques to thick sections of embryonic material, in formulating theories of nervous system structure and nerve impulse transmission, and in explaining the areas of traumatic degeneration and regeneration of nervous structures. He was also a notable author and Spanish statesman, always concerned about the status of Spain and the Spanish language. (A.C.)

1907

Laveran, Charles Louis Alphonse   285

Prize: Medicine and Physiology, 1907. *Born:* June 18, 1845; Paris, France. *Death:* May 18, 1922; Paris, France. *Parents:* Father, Louis Laveran; Mother, no record found. *Nationality:* French. *Religion:* Christian. *Education:* Univ. of Strasbourg, France, M.D., 1867. *Spouse:* Married, 1885. *Children:* No record found. *Career:* French Army, Surgeon, 1870–96; Pasteur Institute, Paris, France, Researcher, 1897–1922. *Other Awards:* Breant Prize, 1884; Jenner Medal, 1902; Moscow Prize, 1906; Commander of Legion of Honor, 1912.

Selected Publications: Traite des Fieures Palustres avec la Description des Microbes du Paludisme. Paris: O. Doin, 1884. *Du Paludisme et de Son Hematozoaire.* Paris: G. Masson, 1891. *Les Hematozoaires de L'Homme et des Animaux.* Paris: Rueff, 1895. *Trypanosome et Trypanoso-miases.* Paris: Masson, 1912.

For More Information See: Dictionary of Scientific Biography. New York: Scribner's, 1973 (Volume 8), 65–66. "Le Professeur Laveran." *Bulletin de la Société de Pathologie Exotique* 15 (1922): 373–78.

Commentary: Charles Laveran was cited "for his work on the part played by protozoa in the generation of disease." His early observation, that protozoa caused malaria, was followed by careful study of the trypanosome diseases of cattle and human sleeping sickness. (D.W.)

1908

Ehrlich, Paul   286

Prize: Medicine and Physiology, 1908. *Born:* March 14, 1854; Strehlen, Germany. *Death:* August 20, 1915; Bad Homburg, Germany. *Parents:* Father, Ismar Ehrlich; Mother, Rosa Weigert Ehrlich. *Nationality:* German. *Religion:* Jewish. *Education:* Univ. of Leipzig, Germany, M.D., 1878. *Spouse:* Hedwig Pinkus, married 1883. *Children:* Steffa, daughter; Marianne, daughter. *Career:* Charité Hospital and Univ. of Berlin, Germany, Doctor and Researcher, 1878–87; Robert Koch Institute, Berlin, Germany, Researcher and Administrator, 1890–95; State Institute for the Investigation and Control of Serum, Stieglitz, Germany, Director, 1896–99; Royal Institute for Experimental Therapy, Frankfurt, Germany, Director, 1899–1915. *Other Awards:* Geheimer Obermedizinalrat, 1907; Privy Councilor, 1911; Liebig Medal, Society of German Chemists, 1911; Cameron Prize, Edinburgh, 1914.

Selected Publications: The Collected Papers of Paul Ehrlich. Ed. by F. Himmelwert. New York: Pergamon Press, 1956–58.

For More Information See: Baumler, E. *Paul Ehrlich.* New York: Holmes and Meier, 1984. *Dictionary of Scientific Biography.* New York: Scribner's, 1971 (Volume 4), 295–305. Marquandt, Martha. *Paul Ehrlich.* New York: Henry Schuman, 1951.

Commentary: Paul Ehrlich was awarded the Nobel Prize "in recognition of his work on immunity," specifically the work which led to a diphtheria antitoxin serum dosage which could be safely used in clinical practice. In the process, he developed a method for measuring the effectiveness of sera that was widely adopted, and a theory of immunity. His work in histology produced tissue-staining techniques that were also acclaimed. But the work for which he is remembered is in the field of chemotherapy, particularly his treatment of syphilis with the arsenic compound, Number 606. (L.W.)

Metchnikoff, Elie (Mechnikov, Ilya Ilyich)   287

Prize: Medicine and Physiology, 1908. *Born:* May 15, 1845; Kharkov, Russia. *Death:* July 15, 1916; Paris, France. *Parents:* Father, Ilya Ivanovich Mechnikov; Mother, Emilia Nevakhovich Mechnikov. *Nationality:* Russian; later French resident. *Religion:* Jewish; with record of unsuccessful conversion to Lutheranism as a child; mother was Jewish; father was not. *Education:* Univ. of Kharkov, Russia, graduate, 1864; Univ. of St. Petersburg, Russia, M.S., 1867; Univ. of St. Petersburg, Russia, doctorate, 1868. *Spouse:* Lyudmilla Fedorovich, married 1868, died 1873; Olga Belokopytova, married 1875. *Children:* None. *Career:* Univ. of Odessa, Russia, Professor, 1867–69; Univ. of St. Petersburg, Russia, Professor, 1870; Univ. of Novorossiia, Russia, Professor, 1870–72; Messina, Sicily, Researcher, 1882–86; Bacteriological Institute, Odessa, Russia, Director, 1886–87; Pasteur Institute, Paris, France, Administrator to Director, 1888–1916. *Other Awards:* Copley Medal, 1908.

Selected Publications: Lectures on the Comparative Pathology of Inflammation, Delivered at the Pasteur Institute in 1891. London: K. Pau, Trench, Trubner and Co., 1893. *Immunity in Infectious Diseases.* Cambridge: Cambridge Univ. Press, 1907. *The Prolongation of Life: Optimistic Studies.* New York: G.P. Putnam's Sons, 1912. *The Nature of Man: Studies in Optimistic Philosophy.* London: Watts and Company, 1938.

For More Information See: Dictionary of Scientific Biography. New York: Scribner's, 1973 (Volume 9), 331–35. Mechnikov, Olga. *The Life of Elie Metchnikoff, 1845–1916.* New York: Houghton-Mifflin, 1921. Tauber, A. *Metchnikoff and the Origins of Immunology.* New York: Oxford Univ. Press, 1991.

Commentary: Elie Metchnikoff was cited by the Academy for his "work on immunity," especially for the formulation of the "cellular" theory of immunity, which states that certain cells of the body (phagocytes) are able to capture and destroy bacteria which have invaded the body. His early career produced important discoveries in comparative anatomy, establishing an evolutionary link between invertebrates and vertebrates. His later career led to an increasing interest by scientists in the process of aging, especially in the role diet and body bacterial processes played. (L.W.)

1909

Kocher, Emil Theodor 288

Prize: Medicine and Physiology, 1909. *Born:* August 25, 1841; Berne, Switzerland. *Death:* July 27, 1917; Berne, Switzerland. *Parents:* Father, Jacob Alexander Kocher; Mother, Maria Wermuth Kocher. *Nationality:* Swiss. *Religion:* Protestant. *Education:* Univ. of Berne, Switzerland, M.D., 1869. *Spouse:* Marie Witschi-Courant, married 1869. *Children:* 3 sons. *Career:* Univ. of Berne, Switzerland, Professor, 1872–1911.

Selected Publications: Chirurgische Operationslehre. Jena, Germany: G. Fischer, 1892. *Operative Surgery.* New York: W. Wood and Co., 1894. *Vorlesungen über Chirurgische Infektionskrankheiten.* 2 volumes. Basel, Switzerland: C. Sallman, 1895–1909 (with E. Tavel).

For More Information See: A Biographical Dictionary of Scientists. New York: Wiley, 1969, 295–96. Boni, T. *Theodor Kocher, 1841–1917.* Berne: Huber, 1991. Bonjour, Edgar. *Theodor Kocher.* Berne: P. Haupt, 1981.

Commentary: Emil Kocher won the Nobel Prize "for his work on the physiology, pathology and surgery of the thyroid gland." Kocher also was a pioneer in aseptic methods and in surgery of many types. (C.E. and D.W.)

1910

Kossel, Karl Martin Leonhard Albrecht 289

Prize: Medicine and Physiology, 1910. *Born:* September 16, 1853; Rostock, Germany. *Death:* July 5, 1927; Heidelberg, Germany. *Parents:* Father, Albrecht Kossel; Mother, Clara Jeppe Kossel. *Nationality:* German. *Religion:* Christian. *Education:* Univ. of Strasbourg, France, M.D., 1878. *Spouse:* Luise Holtzmann, married 1886. *Children:* Walther, son; 1 daughter. *Career:* Univ. of Strasbourg, France, Professor, 1877–83; Berlin Physiological Institute, Germany, Director, 1883–87; Univ. of Berlin, Germany, Professor, 1887–95; Univ. of Marburg, Germany, Professor, 1895–1901; Univ. of Heidelberg, Germany, Professor and Administrator, 1901–27.

Selected Publications: Leitfaden für Medicinisch-Chemische Kurse. Berlin: Fischer Medecin, 1888. *Die Gewebe des Menschlichen Körpers und Ihre Mikroskopische Untersuchung.* Brunswick, Germany; Herald Braha, 1889 (with W. Behrens and P. Schiefferdecker). *The Protamines and Histones.* New York: Longmans, Green and Co., 1928.

For More Information See: "Albrecht Kossel zum Gedächtnis." *Hoppe-Seyler's Zeitschrift für Physiologische Chemie* 177 (1928): 1–14. *Dictionary of Scientific Biography.* New York: Scribner's, 1973 (Volume 7), 466–68.

Commentary: Albrecht Kossel was the Nobel Award recipient "in recognition of the contributions to the chemistry of the cell made through his work on proteins, including the nucleic substances." Kossel separated nucleoproteins into two parts—a protein and a nucleic acid composed of sugar, phosphoric acid, and nitrogen-containing compounds. He later found that the sugar was a hexose. His writings foresaw the modern investigations of nucleic acids as the storers and transmitters of genetic information. (L.W.)

1911

Gullstrand, Allvar 290

Prize: Medicine and Physiology, 1911. *Born:* June 5, 1862; Landskrona, Sweden. *Death:* July 21, 1930; Uppsala, Sweden. *Parents:* Father, Pehr Alfred Gullstrand; Mother, Sophia Matilda Korsell Gullstrand. *Nationality:* Swedish. *Religion:* Most probably Christian/Protestant. *Education:* Royal Caroline Institute, Sweden, M.D., 1888; Royal Caroline Institute, Sweden, Ph.D., 1890. *Spouse:* Signe Christina Breitholz, married 1885. *Children:* 1 daughter. *Career:* Royal Caroline Institute, Stockholm, Sweden, Lecturer, 1892–94; Univ. of Uppsala, Sweden, Professor, 1894–1930. *Other Awards:* Grafe Medal, Deutsche Opthalmologische Gesellschaft, 1927.

Selected Publications: Allgemeine Theorie der Monochromatischen Aberrationen und Ihre Nachsten Ergebnisse für die Opththalmologie. Uppsala, Sweden: Berling, 1900. *Die Optische Abbildung in Heterogenen Medien und die Dioptrik der Kristallinge des Menschen.* Uppsala, Switzerland: Almquist & Wiksells, 1908. *Einführung in die Methoden der Dioptrik des Auges des Menschen.* Leipzig, Germany: S. Hirzil, 1911.

For More Information See: "Allvar Gullstrand." *Zeitschift für Opthalmologische Optik* 18 (1930): 129–34. *Dictionary of Scientific Biography.* New York: Scribner's, 1972 (Volume 5), 590–91.

Commentary: The Nobel Prize was awarded to Allvar Gullstrand "for his work on the dioptrics of the eye." With a sound medical and scientific background, he explained mathematically and physiologically the basis of the operation of the eye, with special attention to accommodation and astigmatism. He also was an active writer in the area of geometrical optics and an inventor of note of several optical instruments. (R.R.)

1912

Carrel, Alexis   291

Prize: Medicine and Physiology, 1912. *Born:* June 28, 1873; Sainte Foy-les-Lyon, France. *Death:* November 5, 1944; Paris, France. *Parents:* Father, Alexis Carrel-Billiard; Mother, Anne Marie Ricard Carrel. *Nationality:* French; later American resident. *Religion:* Catholic. *Education:* Univ. of Lyons, France, Bachelor of Letters, 1889; Univ. of Lyons, France, Bachelor of Science, 1890; Univ. of Lyons, France, M.D., 1900. *Spouse:* Anne-Marie Laure Gourley de la Motte de Meyrie, married 1913. *Children:* None. *Career:* Lyons Hospital, France, Intern, 1896–1900; Univ. of Lyons, France, Professor, 1900–02; Univ. of Chicago, IL, Researcher, 1905–06; Rockefeller Institute, NY, Researcher, 1906–44. *Other Awards:* Legion d'Honneur, France; Nordhoff-Jung Prize for Cancer Research, 1930; Newman Foundation Award, Univ. of Illinois, 1937; Rotary Club of New York Service Award, 1939.

Selected Publications: *Treatment of Infected Wounds.* New York: Hoeber, 1917 (with George Dehelly). *The Culture of Organs.* New York: Hoeber, 1938 (with Charles A. Lindbergh). *Man, the Unknown.* New York: Harper and Brothers, 1939.

For More Information See: *Dictionary of Scientific Biography.* New York, Scribner's, 1971 (Volume 3), 90–91. Malanin, T.I. *Surgery and Life: The Extraordinary Career of Alexis Carrel.* New York: Harcourt, Brace, Jovanovich, 1979. May, A. *The Two Lions of Lyons.* Rockville, MD: Kabel Publishers, 1992. Soupalt, Robert. *Alexis Carrel, 1873–1944.* Paris: Plon, 1952.

Commentary: The Academy cited Alexis Carrel "for his work on vascular suturing, and on the grafting of blood vessels and organs." In addition to his notable medical work, Carrel was a philosopher and philosophical writer. In later life, he headed the Vichy government's Carrel Foundation for the Study of Human Problems. (B.I.M.)

1913

Richet, Charles Robert   292

Prize: Medicine and Physiology, 1913. *Born:* August 26, 1850; Paris, France. *Death:* December 4, 1935; Paris, France. *Parents:* Father, Alfred Richet; Mother, Eugenie Renouard Richet. *Nationality:* French. *Religion:* Catholic. *Education:* Univ. of Paris, France, M.D., 1877; Univ. of Paris, France, D.Sc., 1878. *Spouse:* Amélie Aubry, married 1877. *Children:* Georges, son; Jacques, son; Charles, son; Albert, son; Alfred, son; Louise, daughter; Adele, daughter. *Career:* Collège de France, Paris, Professor, 1876–87; Univ. of Paris, France, Professor, 1887–1927. *Other Awards:* French Biological Society Institute Award, 1879; Cross of the Legion of Honor, 1926.

Selected Publications: *Physiology and Histology of the Cerebral Convolutions.* New York: W. Wood and Co., 1879. *La Chaleur Animale.* Paris: F. Alcan, 1889. *Dictionnaire de Physiologie.* 10 volumes. Paris: F. Alcan, 1895–1928 (with P. Langlois and L. Lapicque). *Traité de Métapsychique.* Paris: F. Alcan, 1923.

For More Information See: *Biographical Dictionary of Scientists.* New York: Wiley, 1969, 443. *Dictionary of Scientific Biography.* New York: Scribner's, 1975 (Volume 11), 425–32. Wolf, S. *Brain, Mind, and Medicine.* New Brunswick, NJ: Transaction Publishers, 1993.

Commentary: Charles Richet received the Nobel Prize "in recognition of his work on anaphylaxis," the study of hypersensitivity induced by foreign "bodies" injected into the body. His work led to much of our knowledge of allergic reactions. Richet also studied and wrote extensively on clairvoyance, telepathy, and other psychological phenomena; was an ardent student of aeronautics; author of several literary works; and an active pacifist. (R.K.)

1914

Bárány, Robert   293

Prize: Medicine and Physiology, 1914. *Born:* April 22, 1876; Vienna, Austria. *Death:* April 8, 1936; Uppsala, Sweden. *Parents:* Father, Ignaz Bárány; Mother, Marie Hock Bárány. *Nationality:* Austrian; later Swedish resident. *Religion:* Jewish. *Education:* Univ. of Vienna, Austria, M.D., 1900. *Spouse:* Ida Berger, married 1909. *Children:* 2 sons; 1 daughter. *Career:* Univ. of Vienna, Austria, Professor and Researcher, 1903–14; Austrian Army, 1914–17; Univ. of Uppsala, Sweden, Professor and Administrator, 1917–36. *Other Awards:* Politzer Prize, 1912; Belgian Academy of Sciences Prize, 1913; ERB Medal, German Neurological Society, 1913; Guyot Prize, 1914; Swedish Medical Society Medal, 1925.

Selected Publications: *Untersuchungen über den Vestibular-Apparat des Ohres.* Berlin: O. Coblentz, 1906. *Physiologie und Pathologie des Bogengang-Apparatus beim Menschen.* Leipzig, Germany: F. Deuticke, 1907. *Funktionelle Prüfung des Vestibular-Apparatus.* Jena, Germany: G. Fischer, 1911 (with K. Wittmaack). *Die Radikaloperation des Ohres ohne Gehoergangsplastik.* Leipzig, Germany: F. Deuticke, 1923.

For More Information See: *Dictionary of Scientific Biography.* New York: Scribner's, 1971 (Volume 1), 446–47. Joas, Gunter. *Robert Barany (1876–1936): Leben und Werk.* Frankfurt am Main; New York: P. Lang, 1996. Wodak, Ernst. *Der Báránysche Zeigeversuch.* Berlin: Urban and Schwarzenberg, 1927.

Commentary: Robert Bárány was granted the Nobel Prize "for his work on the physiology and pathology of the vestibular apparatus." This founder of the medicine of the ear also studied the brain in depth. (B.I.M.)

1919

Bordet, Jules Jean Baptiste Vincent   294

Prize: Medicine and Physiology, 1919. *Born:* June 13, 1870; Soignies, Belgium. *Death:* April 6, 1961; Brussels, Belgium. *Parents:* Father, Charles Bordet; Mother,

Célestine Vandenabeele Bordet. *Nationality:* Belgian. *Religion:* Christian. *Education:* Univ. of Brussels, Belgium, M.D., 1892. *Spouse:* Marthe Levoz, married 1899. *Children:* Simone, daughter; Marguerite, daughter; Paul, son. *Career:* Middlekerke Hospital, Belgium, Physician, 1892–94; Institut Pasteur, Paris, France, Researcher, 1894–1901; Institut Pasteur de Brabant, Univ. of Brussels, Belgium, Professor and Administrator, 1901–40. *Other Awards:* Prix de la Vaille, Paris, 1911; Hansen Prize, 1913; Pasteur Medal, Swedish Medical Society, 1913.

Selected Publications: Studies in Immunity. New York: Wiley, 1909 (with others). *Traité de l'Immunité dans les Maladies Infectieuses.* Paris: Masson et cie, 1920. *Infection et immunité.* Paris: Flammarion, 1947.

For More Information See: Biographical Memoirs of the Fellows of the Royal Society. London: Royal Society, 1962 (Volume 8), 18–25. *Dictionary of Scientific Biography.* New York: Scribner's, 1971 (Volume 2), 300–01.

Commentary: Jules Bordet received the Nobel Prize "for his discoveries in regard to immunity." His work ranged from the elaboration of the constituents of immune serum to the uses of that research in diagnosing various disease states, and from the discovery of the whooping cough bacillus to studies of blood coagulation and bacteriophages. (L.W.)

1920

Krogh, Schack August Steenberg   295

Prize: Medicine and Physiology, 1920. *Born:* November 15, 1874; Grenaa, Jutland, Denmark. *Death:* September 13, 1949; Copenhagen, Denmark. *Parents:* Father, Viggo Krogh; Mother, Marie Drechmann Krogh. *Nationality:* Danish. *Religion:* Most probably Christian/Protestant. *Education:* Univ. of Copenhagen, Denmark, M.Sc., 1899; Univ. of Copenhagen, Denmark, Ph.D., 1903. *Spouse:* Birte Marie Jörgensen, married 1905. *Children:* Erik, son; Bodie, daughter; Ellen, daughter; Agnes, daughter. *Career:* Univ. of Copenhagen, Denmark, Professor, 1899–1949. *Other Awards:* Seegan Prize, Vienna Academy of Sciences, 1906; Baly Medal, Royal College of Physicians, London, 1945.

Selected Publications: Meddelelser fra Akademiet for de Tekniske Videnskaber 1 (1949): 39–50 (complete works).

For More Information See: Dictionary of Scientific Biography. New York: Scribner's, 1973 (Volume 7), 501–04. Rehberg, Brandt. "August Krogh, November 15, 1874-September 13, 1949." Schmidt-Nielsen, B. *August and Marie Krogh.* New York: Oxford Univ. Press, 1995. *Yale Journal of Biology and Medicine* 24 (1951): 83–102.

Commentary: August Krogh's Nobel Prize was presented "for his discovery of the regulation of the motor mechanism of capillaries." His studies of respiration led him to the discovery that the capillaries of the muscles were open during muscular work and partially closed during rest. He later wrote about the importance of capillary control to the economy of the body, and the role of muscles and hormones in capillary control. (B.I.M.)

1922

Hill, Archibald Vivian   296

Prize: Medicine and Physiology, 1922. *Born:* September 26, 1886; Bristol, Gloucestershire, England. *Death:* June 3, 1977; Cambridge, England. *Parents:* Father, Jonathan Hill; Mother, Ada Priscilla Rumney Hill. *Nationality:* British. *Religion:* Anglican. *Education:* Cambridge Univ., England, M.A., 1906; Cambridge Univ., England, Sc.D., 1907. *Spouse:* Margaret Neville Keynes, married June 18, 1913. *Children:* Mary Eglantyne, daughter; David Keynes, son; Janet Rumney, daughter; Maurice Neville, son. *Career:* British Army, 1914–19; Univ. of Manchester, England, Professor, 1920–23; Univ. of London, England, Professor, 1923–51. *Other Awards:* Order of the British Empire, 1918; Royal Medal, 1926; Officer of the British Empire, 1927; Medal of Freedom with Silver Palm, U.S., 1947; Companion of Honour, Britain, 1948; Copley Medal, 1948; Chevalier of Legion of Honor, 1950.

Selected Publications: Muscular Activity. Baltimore: Williams and Wilkins, 1926. *Living Machinery.* New York: Harcourt Brace, 1927. *Muscular Movement in Man.* New York: McGraw-Hill, 1927. *Trails and Trials in Physiology.* Baltimore, MD: Williams and Wilkins, 1965.

For More Information See: Biographical Memoirs of the Fellows of the Royal Society. London: Royal Society, 1978 (Volume 24), 71–149. *Perspectives in Biology and Medicine* 14 (1977): 27–42.

Commentary: Archibald Hill was cited by the Academy "for his discovery relating to the production of heat in the muscles." His other activities included service as a member of Parliament and as a member of the Scientific Advisory Committee in England during the Second World War. (B.I.M.)

Meyerhof, Otto Fritz   297

Prize: Medicine and Physiology, 1922. *Born:* April 12, 1884; Hanover, Germany. *Death:* October 6, 1951; Philadelphia, PA. *Parents:* Father, Felix Meyerhof; Mother, Bettina May Meyerhof. *Nationality:* German; later American citizen. *Religion:* Jewish. *Education:* Univ. of Heidelberg, Germany, M.D., 1909. *Spouse:* Hedwig Schallenberg, married June 4, 1914. *Children:* George Geoffrey, son; Walter Ernst, son; Bettina Ida, daughter. *Career:* Univ. of Heidelberg, Germany, Researcher, 1909–11; Univ. of Kiel, Germany, Professor, 1912–24; Kaiser Wilhelm Institute of Biologie, Berlin-Dahlem, Germany, Researcher, 1924–29; Kaiser Wilhelm Institute of Physiology, Heidelberg, Germany, Director, 1929–38; Research Centre Nationale, Paris, France, Director, 1938–40; Univ. of Pennsylvania, Professor, 1940–51.

Selected Publications: Chemical Dynamics of Life Phenomena. London: J.B. Lippincott, 1924. *Die Chemischen Vorgänge in Muskel.* Berlin: J. Springer, 1930. *Chimie de la Contraction Musculaire.* Bordeaux: Delmas, 1932.

For More Information See: Biographical Memoirs. National Academy of Sciences. New York: Columbia Univ. Press, 1960 (Volume 34), 152–82. *Dictionary of Scientific Biography.* New York: Scribner's, 1974 (Volume 9), 359.

Commentary: Otto Meyerhof received his Nobel "for his discovery of the fixed relationship between the consumption of oxygen and the metabolism of lactic acid in the muscle." His later studies led to recognition of the similarity of chemical pathways in many biological systems and of the key role in muscle contraction played by adenosine triphosphate. (B.I.M.)

1923

Banting, Frederick Grant, Sir 298

Prize: Medicine and Physiology, 1923. *Born:* November 4, 1891; Alliston, Ontario, Canada. *Death:* February 21, 1941; Newfoundland, Canada. *Parents:* Father, William Thompson Banting; Mother, Margaret Grant Banting. *Nationality:* Canadian. *Religion:* Methodist. *Education:* Victoria College, Canada, M.B., 1916; Univ. of Toronto, Canada, M.D., 1922. *Spouse:* Marion Robertson, married 1924, divorced 1932; Henrietta Ball, married 1939. *Children:* William Robertson, son. *Career:* Western Ontario Univ., London, Canada, Researcher, 1920–21; Univ. of Toronto, Canada, Professor, 1921–41. *Other Awards:* Starr Gold Medal, Univ. of Toronto, Canada, 1922; George Armstrong Peters Prize, Univ. of Toronto, Canada, 1922; John Scott Medal, American Philosophical Society, 1923; Charles Mickle Fellowship, Univ. of Toronto, Canada, 1923; Reeve Prize, Univ. of Toronto, Canada, 1923; Rosenberger Gold Medal, Chicago, IL, 1924; Cameron Prize, Edinburgh, Scotland, 1927; Flavelle Medal, Royal Society of Canada, 1931; Knighthood, 1934; Apothecaries' Medal, London, Canada, 1934.

Selected Publications: "Internal Secretion of Pancreas." *Journal of Laboratory and Clinical Medicine* 7 (February 1922): 251–326 (with C.H. Best). "Pancreatic Extracts in Diabetes." *Journal of the Canadian Medical Association* 12 (March 1922): 141–46 (with others). "Effect of Pancreatic Extract (Insulin) on Normal Rabbits." *American Journal of Physiology* 62 (September 1922): 162–76. "Insulin in Treatment of Diabetes Mellitus." *Journal of Metabolic Research* 2 (November-December 1922): 547–604 (with W.R. Campbell and A.A. Fletcher).

For More Information See: Bliss, M. *Banting.* Toronto, Canada: Univ. of Toronto Press, 1992. *Dictionary of National Biography.* London: Oxford Univ. Press, 1959, 54–55. *Dictionary of Scientific Biography.* New York: Scribner's, 1970 (Volume 1), 440–43. Harris, Seale. *Banting's Miracle: The Story of the Discoverer of Insulin.* Philadelphia, PA: Lippincott, 1946. *Obituary Notices of Fellows of the Royal Society.* Cambridge: Royal Society, 1942–44 (Volume 4), 21–26. Stevenson, Lloyd. *Sir Frederick Banting.* Toronto: Ryerson Press, 1946.

Commentary: The award to Sir Frederick Banting was "for the discovery of insulin." In collaboration with C.H. Best, J. MacLeod, and J.B. Collip, Banting ligated the pancreatic ducts of dogs and subsequently removed the pancreas. The now-diabetic dogs were given an intravenous solution prepared from the degenerated pancreas, resulting in a reduced blood sugar. Purification of the active substance yielded insulin, which has saved thousands of lives since its introduction in 1922. Banting's later work included research in cancer, coronary thrombosis, silicosis, and altitude sickness. (D.J.S.)

Macleod, John James Rickard 299

Prize: Medicine and Physiology, 1923. *Born:* September 6, 1876; Cluny, Scotland. *Death:* March 16, 1935; Aberdeen, Scotland. *Parents:* Father, Reverend Robert MacLeod; Mother, Jane Guthrie McWalter MacLeod. *Nationality:* Scottish. *Religion:* Presbyterian. *Education:* Marischal College, Scotland, M.B., 1898; Marischal College, Scotland, Ch.B., 1898; Cambridge Univ., England, D.P.H., 1902.

Spouse: Mary Watson McWalter, married 1903. *Children:* None. *Career:* Western Reserve Univ., Cleveland, OH, Professor, 1903–18; Univ. of Toronto, Canada, Professor and Administrator, 1918–28; Univ. of Aberdeen, Scotland, Professor, 1928–35. *Other Awards:* Cameron Prize, Univ. of Edinburgh, Scotland, 1923.

Selected Publications: Practical Physiology. London: E. Arnold, 1902 (with others). *Recent Advances in Physiology.* New York: Longmans, Green, 1906 (with Leonard Hill). *Diabetes: Its Pathological Physiology.* New York: Longmans, Green, 1913. *Fundamentals of Human Physiology.* St. Louis: C.V. Mosby, 1916 (with R.G. Pearce). *Physiology and Biochemistry in Modern Medicine.* St. Louis: C.V. Mosby, 1918 (with R.G. Pearce). *Carbohydrate Metabolism and Insulin.* New York: Longmans, Green, 1926.

For More Information See: Best, C.H. "The Late John James Rickard Macleod, M.B., Ch.B., LL.D., F.R.C.P." *Canadian Medical Association Journal* 32 (1935): 556. *Dictionary of Scientific Biography.* New York: Scribner's, 1973 (Volume 8), 614–15. *Obituary Notices of Fellows of the Royal Society.* Cambridge: Royal Society, 1932–35 (Volume 1), 585–89. Williams, M. *John James Rickard MacLeod.* Edinburgh, Scotland: Royal College of Physicians, 1993.

Commentary: John MacLeod shared the Nobel Prize with Frederick Banting "for the discovery of insulin." Originally concerned with studies of respiration, his interests turned to experimental glycosuria and carbohydrate metabolism. Together with Banting, a new surgeon in his academic department, and C.H. Best, a student in his classes, he carried out the insulin work in the early 20s. His long career continued in further investigations of carbohydrate metabolism and respiration. (C.S.)

1924

Einthoven, Willem 300

Prize: Medicine and Physiology, 1924. *Born:* May 22, 1860; Semarang, Dutch East Indies. *Death:* September 29, 1927; Leiden, Netherlands. *Parents:* Father, Jacob Einthoven; Mother, Louise M.M.C. de Vogel Einthoven. *Nationality:* Dutch. *Religion:* Jewish. *Education:* Univ. of Utrecht, Netherlands, Ph.D., 1885. *Spouse:* Frédérique Jeanne Louise de Vogel, married 1886. *Children:* Augusta, daughter; Louise, daughter; Willem, son; Johanna, daughter. *Career:* Univ. of Leiden, Netherlands, Professor, 1885–1927.

Selected Publications: Stereoscopie door Kleurverschil. Utrecht, Netherlands: Utrechtsche Drukkerij, 1885. *Over de Beteekenis der Electrophysiologie als een Ouderdeel Van de Leer der Levensverrichtingen.* Leiden, Netherlands: Brill, 1906. *Das Saitengalvenometer und die Messung der Aktionsströme des Herzens.* Stockholm: Norstedt, 1926.

For More Information See: Dictionary of Scientific Biography. New York: Scribner's, 1971 (Volume 4), 333–35. Hogenwerf, S. *Leven en Werken van Willem Einthoven.* n.p.: Hoorn, 1925. Snellen, H. *Willem Einthoven.* Boston: Klvwer Academic Publishers, 1995.

Commentary: Willem Einthoven received the Nobel "for his discovery of the mechanism of the electrocardiogram." His knowledge of both physics and medicine led to the development of the string galvanometer and other medically oriented equipment, and extension of his work to the measurement of action currents of the cervical sympathetic nerve and of the heart. (R.K.)

1926

Fibiger, Johannes Andreas Grib   **301**
Prize: Medicine and Physiology, 1926. *Born:* April 23, 1867; Silkeborg, Denmark. *Death:* January 30, 1928; Copenhagen, Denmark. *Parents:* Father, C.E.A. Fibiger; Mother, Elfride Muller Fibiger. *Nationality:* Danish. *Religion:* Lutheran. *Education:* Univ. of Copenhagen, Denmark, baccalaureate, 1883; Univ. of Copenhagen, Denmark, M.D., 1890; Univ. of Copenhagen, Denmark, Ph.D., 1895. *Spouse:* Mathilde Fibiger, married 1894. *Children:* None. *Career:* Univ. of Copenhagen, Denmark, Researcher, 1891–94; Blegdams Hospital for Contagious Diseases, Copenhagen, Denmark, Physician, 1894–97; Univ. of Copenhagen, Denmark, Professor, 1897–1928. *Other Awards:* Nordhoff-Jung Cancer Prize, 1927.

Selected Publications: Bakteriologiske Studier over Diphtheri. Copenhagen: det Schulothecke Forlag, 1895. *Investigations on the Spiroptera Cancer.* Copenhagen: Andr. Fred. Host and Son, Bianco Lunos Bogtrykkeri, 1918–19. *Experimental Production of Tar Cancer in White Mice.* Copenhagen: Andr. Fred. Host and Son, Bianco Lunos Bogtrykkeri, 1921 (with Fridtjof Bang). *Investigations Upon Immunisation against Metastasis Formation in Experimental Cancer.* Copenhagen: Andr. Fred. Host and Son, Bianco Lunos Bogtrykkeri, 1927 (with Paul Moller).

For More Information See: Meisen, V. *Prominent Danish Scientists.* Copenhagen: Levin and Munkegaard, 1932. Secher, K. *Johannes Fibiger.* Copenhagen: Nordisk Vorlag, 1947.

Commentary: The Academy cited Johannes Fibiger "for his discovery of the *Spiroptera* carcinoma." Fibiger published extensively in this area and was the first to study artificially produced cancer. (B.I.M.)

1927

Wagner von Jauregg, Julius   **302**
Prize: Medicine and Physiology, 1927. *Born:* March 7, 1857; Wels, Austria. *Death:* September 27, 1940; Vienna, Austria. *Parents:* Father, Adolf Johann Wagner von Jauregg; Mother, Ludovika Ranzoni von Jauregg. *Nationality:* Austrian. *Religion:* Christian. *Education:* Univ. of Vienna, Austria, Ph.D., 1880. *Spouse:* Anna Koch, married 1899. *Children:* Julia, daughter; Theodor, son. *Career:* Univ. of Vienna, Austria, Professor, 1881–1928. *Other Awards:* Cameron Prize, 1935; Gold Medal, American Committee for Research on Syphilis, 1937.

Selected Publications: "Über die Einwirkung Fieberhafter Erkrankungen auf Psychosen." *Jahrbuch für Psychiatrie und Neurologie* 7 (1887): 94–131. "Zur Reform des Irrenwesens." *Viennaer Klinische Wochenschrift* 14 (1901): 293–96. *Myxöden und Kretinismus.* Leipzig, Germany: F. Deuticke, 1915. "Über die Einwirkung der Malaria auf die Progressive Paralyse." *Psychiatrischneurologische Wochenschrift* 20 (1918–19): 132–34. *Fieber und Infektionstherapie.* Vienna: Verlag für Medizin, Weidmann, 1936.

For More Information See: Dictionary of Scientific Biography. New York: Scribner's, 1976 (Volume 14), 114–16.

Grosse Nervenärzte. Stuttgart, Germany: G. Thieme, 1956, 254–66. Whitrow, Magda. *Julius Wagner-Jauregg (1857–1940).* London: Smith-Gordon, 1993.

Commentary: Julius Wagner von Jauregg was granted the Nobel Prize "for his discovery of the therapeutic value of malaria inoculation in the treatment of dementiaparalytica." His long career included other notable work in the areas of the vagus nerve, the thyroid gland, cretinism, and insane patient treatment. (R.K.)

1928

Nicolle, Charles Jules Henri   **303**
Prize: Medicine and Physiology, 1928. *Born:* September 21, 1866; Rouen, France. *Death:* February 28, 1936; Tunis, Tunisia. *Parents:* Father, Dr. Eugène Nicolle; Mother, no record found. *Nationality:* French; later Tunisian resident. *Religion:* Christian. *Education:* Rouen School of Medicine, France, M.D., 1893. *Spouse:* Alice Avice, married 1893. *Children:* Marcelle, son; Pierre, son. *Career:* Rouen School of Medicine, France, Professor, 1895–1903; Pasteur Institute, Tunis, Tunisia, Director, 1903–36. *Other Awards:* Prix Montyon, 1909, 1912, 1914; Prix Osiris, 1927; Gold Medal, Tunis, 1928.

Selected Publications: "Recherches Experimentales sur le Typhus Exanthématique." *Annales de l'Institut Pasteur* 24 (1910): 243–75; 25 (1911): 97–144; 26 (1912): 250–80, 332–35. *Naissance, Vie et Mort des Maladies Infectieuses.* Paris: F. Alcan, 1930. *Biologie de l'Invention.* Paris: F. Alcan, 1932. *Destindes Maladies Infectieuses.* Paris: Presses Universitaires de France, 1939.

For More Information See: Dictionary of Scientific Biography. New York: Scribner's, 1978 (Supplement), 453–55. Lot, G. *Charles Nicolle et la Biologie Conquerante.* Paris: Seghers, 1961.

Commentary: The Academy cited Charles Nicolle for his work on typhus, which proved the infectious nature of the blood of typhus fever patients and the transmission of typhus fever by the body louse. Nicolle also demonstrated that serum from patients with measles, typhus fever, or undulant fever could protect uninfected persons from the disease. (R.K.)

1929

Eijkman, Christiaan   **304**
Prize: Medicine and Physiology, 1929. *Born:* August 11, 1858; Nijkerk, Netherlands. *Death:* November 5, 1930; Utrecht, Netherlands. *Parents:* Father, Christiaan Eijkman; Mother, Johanna Alida Pool Eijkman. *Nationality:* Dutch. *Religion:* Christian. *Education:* Univ. of Amsterdam, Netherlands, M.D., 1883. *Spouse:* Aaltje Wigeri van Edema, married 1883, died 1886; Berthe Julie Louise van der Kemp, married 1888. *Children:* Pieter Hendrik, son. *Career:* Dutch Army, 1886–87; Medical School, Java, Indonesia, Director, 1888–96; Univ. of Utrecht, Netherlands, Professor, 1896–1928. *Other Awards:* John Scott Medal, Philadelphia, 1923.

Selected Publications: Specifieke Antistoffen. Haarlem, Netherlands: de Erven F. Bohn, 1901. *Onzichtbare Smetstoffen.* Haarlem, Netherlands: de Erven F. Bohn, 1904. *Een en Ander over Voeding.* Haarlem, Netherlands: de

Erven F. Bohn, 1906. *Hygiënische Strijdvragen*. Rotterdam: W.L. and J. Brusse, 1907.

For More Information See: Dictionary of Scientific Biography. New York: Scribner's, 1971 (Volume 4), 310–12. Jansen, Barend Coenraad. *Het Levenswerk van Christiaan Eijkman, 1858–1930*. Haarlem, Netherlands: de Erven F. Bohn, 1959. *Polyneuritis in Chickens or the Origins of Vitamin Research*. New Brunswick, NJ: Hoffman-LaRoche, 1990.

Commentary: Christiaan Eijkman won the Nobel "for his discovery of the antineuritic vitamin," by study of the effect of polishings from polished rice on a beri-beri-like disease in fowl. He also studied the physiology of tropical residents and conducted fermentation tests and testing for the colon bacillus in water. (R.K.)

Hopkins, Frederick Gowland, Sir   305

Prize: Medicine and Physiology, 1929. *Born:* June 30, 1861; Eastbourne, Sussex, England. *Death:* May 16, 1947; Cambridge, England. *Parents:* Father, Frederick Hopkins; Mother, Elizabeth Gowland Hopkins. *Nationality:* British. *Religion:* Anglican. *Education:* Univ. of London, England, B.Sc., 1890; Univ. of London, England, M.B., 1894. *Spouse:* Jessie Anne Stevens, married 1898. *Children:* Barbara Holmes, daughter; Jacquetta Hawkes, daughter; 1 son. *Career:* Guy's Hospital, London, England, Researcher, 1894–97; Cambridge Univ., England, Professor, 1898–1943. *Other Awards:* Baly Medal, Royal College of Physicians, 1915; Royal Medal, Royal Society, 1918; Cameron Prize, Univ. of Edinburgh, Scotland, 1922; Knighthood, 1925; Copley Medal, 1926; Albert Medal, 1934; Order of Merit, 1935; Harben Medal, 1937.

Selected Publications: Hopkins and Biochemistry, 1861–1947. Cambridge: W. Heffer, 1949.

For More Information See: Baldwin, Ernest. *Gowland Hopkins*. London: VandenBerghs, 1961. *Dictionary of Scientific Biography*. New York: Scribner's, 1972 (Volume 6), 498–502. *Obituary Notices of Fellows of the Royal Society*. Cambridge: Royal Society, 1948–49 (Volume 6), 115–45.

Commentary: Frederick Hopkins received the Nobel "for his discovery of the growth-stimulating vitamins." Hopkins's work on nutrition was pioneering in that field, but he also contributed to the study of muscle metabolism, glutathione, and uric acid. (R.K.)

1930

Landsteiner, Karl   306

Prize: Medicine and Physiology, 1930. *Born:* June 14, 1868; Vienna, Austria. *Death:* June 26, 1943; New York, NY. *Parents:* Father, Leopold Landsteiner; Mother, Fanny Hess Landsteiner. *Nationality:* Austrian; later American citizen. *Religion:* Catholic; from Jewish background. *Education:* Univ. of Vienna, Austria, M.D., 1891. *Spouse:* Helen Wlatso, married 1916. *Children:* Ernst Karl, son. *Career:* Univ. of Vienna, Austria, Professor, 1896–98; Pathological-Anatomical Institute, Vienna, Austria, Researcher, 1898–1907; Wilhelmina Hospital, Vienna, Austria, Physician, 1908–19; R.K. Zickenhuis Hospital, The Hague, Netherlands, Physician, 1919–22; Rockefeller Institute, NY, Researcher, 1922–43. *Other Awards:* Chevalier

Legion of Honor, France; Hans Aronson Foundation Prize, Berlin, 1926; Paul Ehrlich Gold Medal, 1930; Dutch Red Cross Medal, 1933; Cameron Prize, Univ. of Edinburgh, Scotland, 1938.

Selected Publications: Die Spezifizität der Serologischen Reaktionen. Berlin: Julius Springer, 1933.

For More Information See: Dictionary of Scientific Biography. New York: Scribner's, 1973 (Volume 7), 622–25. *Obituary Notices of Fellows of the Royal Society of London*. London: Royal Society, 1947 (Volume 5), 295–324. Speiser, Paul. *Karl Landsteiner*. Vienna: Hallenek Brothers, 1961.

Commentary: Karl Landsteiner was awarded the Nobel Prize "for his discovery of the human blood groups," but his work ranged across chemistry, bacteriology, immunology, and pathology, with important work in each. His efforts in the study of poliomyelitis and syphilis were especially notable. (R.K.)

1931

Warburg, Otto Heinrich   307

Prize: Medicine and Physiology, 1931. *Born:* October 8, 1883; Freiburg, Germany. *Death:* August 1, 1970; Berlin, Germany. *Parents:* Father, Emil Gabriel Warburg; Mother, Elizabeth Gaertner Warburg. *Nationality:* German. *Religion:* Jewish. *Education:* Univ. of Berlin, Germany, Dr. der Chemie, 1906; Univ. of Heidelberg, Germany, Dr. der Medizin, 1911. *Spouse:* None. *Children:* None. *Career:* Kaiser-Wilhelm Institute, Germany, Professor, 1913–70. *Other Awards:* Paul Ehrlich Prize, 1962; Nordhoff-Jung Prize; Schneider Prize; Gold Medal, Univ. of Würzburg; German Order of Merit; Freedom of the City of Berlin.

Selected Publications: Über den Stoffwechsel der Tumoren. Berlin: Springer, 1926 (*The Metabolism of Tumours*. Tr. by Frank Dickens. London: Constable, 1930). *Über die Katalytischen Wirkungen der Lebendigen Substanz*. Berlin: Springer, 1928. *Schwermetalle als Wirkungsgruppen von Fermenten*. Berlin: W. Saenger, 1948. *Wasserstoffübertragende Fermente*. Berlin: W. Saenger, 1948. *The Prime Cause and Prevention of Cancer*. Würzburg, Germany: K. Triltsch, 1969.

For More Information See: Biographical Memoirs of the Fellows of the Royal Society. London: Royal Society, 1972 (Volume 18), 629–99. *Dictionary of Scientific Biography*. New York: Scribner's, 1976 (Volume 14), 172–77. Krebs, Hans A. *The Excitement and Fascination of Science*. Palo Alto, CA: Annual Reviews, Inc., 1965, Vol. 1, 531–44. *Otto Warburg: Biochemist and Eccentric*. New York: Oxford Univ. Press, 1981. Werner, P. *Ein Genie Irrt Seltener—Otto Heinrich Warburg*. Berlin: Akademie Verlag, 1991.

Commentary: In a career spanning 65 years and over 500 papers, Otto Warburg distinguished himself as probably the greatest biochemist of this century. His Nobel Prize was awarded for the discovery of "the nature and mode of action of the respiratory enzyme" (cytochrome oxidase's action in cellular respiration). Other major research areas included photosynthesis and the metabolism, prevention, and treatment of cancer. Possibly as important as his research was the fact that Warburg worked with and helped develop three future Nobel Prize winners: Otto Meyerhof, Hans Krelos, and Hugo Theorell, sustaining a legacy which would even further enhance our understanding of the essence of life. (D.J.S.)

1932

Adrian, Edgar Douglas, Baron   308

Prize: Medicine and Physiology, 1932. *Born:* November 30, 1889; London, England. *Death:* August 4, 1977; London, England. *Parents:* Father, Alfred Douglas Adrian; Mother, Flora Lavinia Barton Adrian. *Nationality:* British. *Religion:* Protestant; from Huguenot background. *Education:* Cambridge Univ., England, M.A., 1911; Cambridge Univ., England, M.D., 1915. *Spouse:* Hester Agnes Pinsent, married June 15, 1923. *Children:* Anne, daughter; Jennet, daughter; Richard Hume, son. *Career:* British Army, 1916–19; Cambridge Univ., England, Professor and Administrator, 1920–75. *Other Awards:* Baly Medal, 1929; Royal Medal, Royal Society, 1934; Order of Merit, England, 1942; Copley Medal, Royal Society, 1946; Hughlings Jackson Medal, Royal Society of Medicine, 1947; Gold Medal, Royal Society of Medicine, 1950; Albert Gold Medal, Royal Society of Arts, 1953; Harben Medal, 1955; Made Baron, 1955; Chevalier Legion of Honour, France, 1956; Sherrington Memorial Medal, 1957; Medal for Distinguished Merit, British Medical Association, 1958; Jephcott Medal, Royal Society of Medicine, 1963.

Selected Publications: The Basis of Sensation. New York: W.W. Norton, 1928. *Mechanism of Nervous Action.* Philadelphia, PA: Univ. of Pennsylvania Press, 1932. *Physical Background of Perception.* Oxford: Clarendon Press, 1947.

For More Information See: Biographical Memoirs of the Fellows of the Royal Society. London: Royal Society, 1979 (Volume 25), 1–73. *Current Biography Yearbook.* New York: H.W. Wilson, 1955, 1–3.

Commentary: Edgar Adrian's shared Nobel was for his "discoveries regarding the function of the neurons" in sending nerve messages. His work led to the development of the techniques of electroencephalography. (R.K.)

Sherrington, Charles Scott, Sir   309

Prize: Medicine and Physiology, 1932. *Born:* November 27, 1857; London, England. *Death:* March 4, 1952; Eastbourne, Sussex, England. *Parents:* Father, James Norton Sherrington; Mother, Anne Brookes Sherrington. *Nationality:* British. *Religion:* Anglican. *Education:* Cambridge Univ., England, M.B., 1885. *Spouse:* Ethel Mary Wright, married 1892. *Children:* Carr E.R., son. *Career:* Koch Laboratory, Berlin, Germany, Researcher, 1886–87; St. Thomas Hospital, London, England, Physician, 1887–90; Univ. of London, England, Professor and Administrator, 1891–94; Univ. of Liverpool, England, Professor, 1895–1913; Oxford Univ., England, Professor, 1913–35; Univ. of Edinburgh, Scotland, Professor, 1936–38. *Other Awards:* Royal Medal, Royal Society, 1905; Knighthood, 1922; Order of Merit, England, 1924; Baly Gold Medal; Retzius Gold Medal, Royal Swedish Academy; Copley Medal, 1927.

Selected Publications: The Integrative Action of the Nervous System. New Haven, CT: Yale Univ. Press, 1906. *Man on His Nature.* London: Cambridge Univ. Press, 1940. *Selected Writings of Sir Charles Sherrington.* Oxford: Oxford Univ. Press, 1979.

For More Information See: Dictionary of Scientific Biography. New York: Scribner's, 1975 (Volume 12), 395–402. Eccles, John C., and Gibson, William C. *Sherrington. His Life and Thought.* New York: Springer International, 1979. *Obituary Notices of Fellows of the Royal Society.* Cambridge: Royal Society, 1952 (Volume 21), 241–70.

Commentary: Charles Sherrington shared the Nobel Prize for "discoveries regarding the function of the neurons" in the activity of the brain and spinal cord. Although his life's work was in this field, his writings show a broader scope, including poetry and the history of medicine. (R.K.)

1933

Morgan, Thomas Hunt   310

Prize: Medicine and Physiology, 1933. *Born:* September 25, 1866; Lexington, KY. *Death:* December 4, 1945; Pasadena, CA. *Parents:* Father, Charlton Hunt Morgan; Mother, Ellen Key Howard Morgan. *Nationality:* American. *Religion:* Episcopalian. *Education:* State College of Kentucky, B.S., 1886; State College of Kentucky, M.S., 1888; Johns Hopkins Univ., MD, M.D., Ph.D., 1890. *Spouse:* Lilian V. Sampson, married June 4, 1904. *Children:* Lilian Vaughn, daughter; Isabel Merrick, daughter; Edith Sampson, daughter; Howard Key, son. *Career:* Bryn Mawr College, PA, Professor, 1891–1903; Columbia Univ., NY, Professor, 1904–28; California Institute of Technology, Professor, 1928–45. *Other Awards:* Darwin Medal, 1924; Copley Medal, 1939.

Selected Publications: Regeneration. New York: Macmillan, 1901. *Heredity and Sex.* New York: Columbia Univ. Press, 1913. *The Scientific Basis of Evolution.* London: Faber and Faber, 1932. *The Theory of the Gene.* New Haven, CT: Yale Univ. Press, 1932.

For More Information See: Allan, Garland E. *Thomas Hunt Morgan: The Man and His Science.* Princeton, NJ: Princeton Univ. Press, 1978. Barahona, A. *El Hombre de las Moscas; Thomas H. Morgan.* Mexico City: Pangea, 1992. *Biographical Memoirs. National Academy of Sciences.* New York: Columbia Univ. Press, 1959 (Volume 33), 383–436. *Dictionary of Scientific Biography.* New York: Scribner's, 1974 (Volume 9), 515–26.

Commentary: Thomas Morgan received the Nobel "for his discoveries concerning the function of the chromosome in the transmission of heredity." His life's work on the fruit fly, *Drosophila melanogaster*, led to a broad understanding of genetic principles. (R.K.)

1934

Minot, George Richards   311

Prize: Medicine and Physiology, 1934. *Born:* December 2, 1885; Boston, MA. *Death:* February 25, 1950; Brookline, MA. *Parents:* Father, James Jackson Minot; Mother, Elizabeth Whitney Minot. *Nationality:* American. *Religion:* Unitarian. *Education:* Harvard Univ., MA, B.A., 1908; Harvard Univ., MA, M.D., 1912. *Spouse:* Marian Linzee Weld, married June 29, 1915. *Children:* Marian Linzee, daughter; Elizabeth Whitney, daughter; Charles Sedgwick, son. *Career:* Massachusetts General Hospital, Boston, Physician, 1912–13; Johns Hopkins Univ., Baltimore, MD, Researcher,

1913–15; Massachusetts General Hospital, Boston, Physician, 1915–23; Peter Bent Brigham Hospital, MA, Physician, 1923–28; Collis P. Huntington Memorial Hospital, MA, Physician and Administrator, 1923–28; Harvard Univ., MA, Professor and Administrator, 1928–50. *Other Awards:* Kober Gold Medal, Association of American Physicians, 1928; Cameron Prize, Univ. of Edinburgh, Scotland, 1930; Gold Medal, National Institute of Social Sciences, 1930; Gold Medal and Award, Popular Science Monthly, 1930; Moxon Medal, Royal College of Physicians, 1933; John Scott Medal, Philadelphia, 1935; Scroll Award, Association of Grocery Manufacturers of America, 1936.

Selected Publications: "Development of Liver Therapy in Pernicious Anemia." *Lancet* 1 (1935): 361–64. *Pathological Physiology and Clinical Description of the Anemias.* New York: Oxford Univ. Press, 1936.

For More Information See: Biographical Memoirs: National Academy of Sciences. New York: Columbia Univ. Press, 1974 (Volume 45), 336–83. *Dictionary of Scientific Biography.* New York: Scribner's (Volume 9), 1974, 416–17. Rackemann, F.M. *The Inquisitive Physician: The Life and Times of George Richards Minot.* Cambridge, MA: Harvard Univ. Press, 1956.

Commentary: George Minot shared the Nobel Prize for "discoveries concerning liver therapy against anemias." Minot's work in anemia and pernicious anemia was only part of his work in blood disorders and was in addition to research in such varied areas as cancer, arthritis, and dietary deficiencies. (R.K.)

Murphy, William Parry   312

Prize: Medicine and Physiology, 1934. *Born:* February 6, 1892; Stoughton, WI. *Death:* October 9, 1987; Brookline, MA. *Parents:* Father, Thomas Francis Murphy; Mother, Rose Anna Parry Murphy. *Nationality:* American. *Religion:* Congregationalist. *Education:* Univ. of Oregon, A.B., 1914; Harvard Univ., MA, M.D., 1920. *Spouse:* Pearl Harriet Adams, married September 10, 1919. *Children:* Priscilla Adams, daughter; William Parry, Jr., son. *Career:* U.S. Army, 1917–18; Rhode Island Hospital, Physician, 1920–22; Peter Bent Brigham Hospital, MA, Physician and Researcher, 1922–58. *Other Awards:* Cameron Prize, Univ. of Edinburgh, Scotland, 1930; Commander Order of White Rose First Rank, Finland, 1934; Bronze Medal for Science Exhibit, American Medical Association, 1934; Gold Medal, Humane Society of Massachusetts, 1935; National Order of Merit Carlos J. Finlay, Cuba, 1952; Distinguished Achievement Award, Boston, MA, 1965; International Bicentennial Symposium Award, 1972; Gold Badge, Massachusetts Medical Society, 1973; Paul Harris Fellow Award, 1980.

Selected Publications: Anemia in Practice: Pernicious Anemia. Philadelphia, PA: W.B. Saunders, 1939.

For More Information See: Asimov's Biographical Encyclopedia of Science and Technology. Garden City, NY: Doubleday, 1964, 507. *National Cyclopedia of American Biography.* New York: James T. White, 1946 (Volume G), 358–59.

Commentary: William Murphy's shared Nobel was for "discoveries concerning liver therapy against anemias." His work with Minot on pernicious anemia is noted as his most important contribution. (R.K.)

Whipple, George Hoyt   313

Prize: Medicine and Physiology, 1934. *Born:* August 28, 1878; Ashland, NH. *Death:* February 1, 1976; Rochester, NY. *Parents:* Father, Ashley Cooper Whipple; Mother, Frances Anna Hoyt Whipple. *Nationality:* American. *Religion:* Baptist/Episcopalian background. *Education:* Yale Univ., CT, A.B., 1900; Johns Hopkins Univ., MD, M.D., 1905. *Spouse:* Katherine Ball Waring, married June 24, 1914. *Children:* Barbara, daughter; George Hoyt, son. *Career:* Holbrook School, NY, Teacher, 1901; Johns Hopkins Univ., MD, Professor, 1902–14; Univ. of California, San Francisco, Professor and Administrator, 1914–21; Univ. of Rochester, NY, Professor and Administrator, 1921–55. *Other Awards:* Warren Triennial Prize, 1910; Popular Science Monthly Award, 1929; William Wood Gerhard Gold Medal, 1934; Charles Mickle Fellowship, Univ. of Toronto, Canada, 1938; Kober Medal, Georgetown Univ., 1939; Rochester Civic Medal, NY, 1943; Certificate of Honor, European Society for Hematology, 1959; Gold-Headed Cane Award, American Association of Pathologists and Bacteriologists, 1961; Kovalenko Medal, National Academy of Sciences, 1962; Distinguished Service Award, American Medical Association, 1973; President's Medal, Univ. of Rochester, NY, 1975.

Selected Publications: "Icterus. A Rapid Change of Hemoglobin to Bile Pigments in the Circulation Outside the Liver." *Journal of Experimental Medicine* 17 (1913): 612–35 (with C.W. Hooper). "Blood Regeneration Following Simple Anemia. IV. Influence of Meat, Liver, and Various Extractives, Alone or Combined with Standard Diets." *American Journal of Physiology* 53 (1920): 236–62 (with C.W. Hooper and F.S. Robscheit). "Pigment Metabolism and Regeneration of Hemoglobin in the Body." *Archives of Internal Medicine* 29 (1922): 711–31. "Blood Regeneration in Severe Anemia. 14. A Liver Fraction Potent in Pernicious Anemia Fed Alone and Combined with Whole Liver, Liver Ash and Fresh Bile." *Journal of Experimental Medicine* 49 (1929): 215–27 (with F.S. Robscheit-Robbins). *The Dynamic Equilibrium of Body Proteins. Hemoglobin, Plasma Proteins, Organ and Tissue Proteins.* Springfield, IL: Thomas, 1956.

For More Information See: Biographical Memoirs of National Academy of Sciences. Washington, DC: National Academy, 1995 (Volume 66). Corner, George W. *George Hoyt Whipple and His Friends.* Philadelphia, PA: Lippincott, 1963. *Perspectives in Biology and Medicine* 2 (Spring 1959): 253–89.

Commentary: George Whipple shared his Nobel Prize for "discoveries concerning liver therapy against anemia." In a long and fruitful career, his work on anemia in dogs was landmark, but he also did notable work on bile and bile pigments, black water fever, intestinal obstructions, plasma protein regeneration, and iron metabolism. (R.K.)

1935

Spemann, Hans   314

Prize: Medicine and Physiology, 1935. *Born:* June 27, 1869; Stuttgart, Würtenberg, Germany. *Death:* September 12, 1941; Freiburg-im-Breisgau, Baden, Germany. *Parents:* Father, Johann Willhelm Spemann; Mother, Lisinka

Hoffmann Spemann. *Nationality:* German. *Religion:* Protestant. *Education:* Univ. of Würzburg, Germany, doctorate, 1895. *Spouse:* Clara Binder, married 1895. *Children:* Fritz, son; Rudo, son. *Career:* Univ. of Würzburg, Germany, Researcher, 1894–1908; Univ. of Rostock, Germany, Professor, 1908–13; Kaiser Wilhelm Institute of Biology, Berlin-Dahlem, Germany, Director, 1914–18; Univ. of Freiburg-im-Breisgau, Germany, Professor, 1919–35.

Selected Publications: Experimentelle Beiträge zu einer Theorie der Entwicklung. Berlin: J. Springer, 1936 (*Embryonic Development and Induction.* New Haven, CT: Yale Univ. Press, 1938).

For More Information See: Dictionary of Scientific Biography. Scribner's, 1975 (Volume 12), 567–69. Mangold, Otto. *Hans Spemann, ein Meister der Entwicklungsphysiologie, sein Leben und sein Werk.* Stuttgart, Germany: Wissenschaftlich Verlagsgesellschaft, 1953. Spemann, Hans. *Forschung und Leben, Erinnerungen.* Stuttgart, Germany: J. Engelhorns Nacht, 1943.

Commentary: Hans Spemann was awarded the Nobel Prize "for his discovery of the organizer effect in embryonic development." By developing techniques that permitted implanting embryo sections into another embryo, Spemann was able to show that certain parts of the embryo, which contained specific chemicals, could induce further development, while others could not. (R.K.)

1936

Dale, Henry Hallett, Sir   315

Prize: Medicine and Physiology, 1936. *Born:* June 9, 1875; London, England. *Death:* July 23, 1968; Cambridge, England. *Parents:* Father, Charles James Dale; Mother, Frances Ann Hallett Dale. *Nationality:* British. *Religion:* Methodist. *Education:* Cambridge Univ., England, B.S., 1898; Cambridge Univ., England, B. Chir., 1903; Cambridge Univ., England, M.D., 1909. *Spouse:* Ellen Harriet Hallett, married November 5, 1904. *Children:* Robert Henry, son; Alison Sarah, daughter; Elinor Mary, daughter. *Career:* Wellcome Physiological Research Laboratories, England, Director, 1904–14; National Institute for Medical Research, Hampstead, England, Researcher and Administrator, 1914–42; Royal Institution of Great Britain, Director, 1942–46. *Other Awards:* Gedge Prize, Cambridge Univ., England, 1900; Walsingham Medal, Cambridge Univ., England, 1900; Raymond Horton Smith Prize, 1909; Baly Medal, Royal College of Physicians, 1921; Cameron Prize, Univ. of Edinburgh, Scotland, 1926; Medal of the Society of Apothecaries, 1932; Harrison Memorial Medal, Pharmaceutical Society of Great Britain, 1932; Knighthood, 1932; Addingham Medal, William Hoffmann Wood Trust, Leeds, England, 1935; Royal Medal, Royal Society, 1936; Copley Medal, Royal Society, 1937; Fothergillian Medal, Medical Society of London, 1938; Harben Gold Medal, Royal Institute of Public Health and Hygiene, 1943; Danbury Memorial Medal, Pharmaceutical Society of Great Britain, 1943; Dr. Bimala Churn Law Gold Medal, Indian Association for the Cultivation of Science, 1943; Order of Merit, 1944; USA Medal of Freedom with Silver Palm, 1947; Grand Croix de l'Ordre de la Couronne

of Belgium, 1949; Pour le Mérite, West Germany, 1955; Gold Medal of Honour, Canadian Pharmaceutical Manufacturer's Association, 1955; Gold Albert Medal, Royal Society of the Arts, 1956; Schmiedeberg-Plakette, German Pharmacological Society, 1962.

Selected Publications: Adventures in Physiology. London: Pergammon Press, 1953. *An Autumn Gleaning.* London: Pergammon Press, 1954.

For More Information See: Biographical Memoirs of the Fellows of the Royal Society. London: Royal Society, 1970 (Volume 16), 77–174. *Dictionary of Scientific Biography.* New York: Scribner's, 1978 (Supplement I), 104–07.

Commentary: Henry Dale shared the Nobel Prize for "discoveries relating to the chemical transmission of nerve impulses." His two major research interests were derived from studies of the action of adrenaline and acetylcholine (chemical transmission of nerve impulses) and studies of the action of histamine (response of the organism and its tissues to various external assaults). (R.K.)

Loewi, Otto   316

Prize: Medicine and Physiology, 1936. *Born:* June 3, 1873; Frankfurt-am-Main, Germany. *Death:* December 25, 1961; New York, NY. *Parents:* Father, Jacob Loewi; Mother, Anna Willstädter Loewi. *Nationality:* German; later American citizen. *Religion:* Jewish. *Education:* Univ. of Strasbourg, France, M.D., 1896. *Spouse:* Gulda Goldschmiedt, married April 5, 1908. *Children:* Harold, son; Victor, son; Geoffrey W., son; Anna, daughter. *Career:* City Hospital, Frankfurt, Germany, Researcher, 1897–98; Univ. of Marburg, Germany, Professor, 1898–1904; Univ. of Vienna, Austria, Professor, 1905–09; Univ. of Graz, Austria, Professor, 1909–38; Univ. of Brussels, Belgium, Professor, 1938–39; New York Univ., Professor, 1940–61. *Other Awards:* Austrian Distinguished Order for Art and Science, 1936; Cameron Prize, Univ. of Edinburgh, Scotland, 1944.

Selected Publications: "The Humoral Transmission of Nervous Impulse." *Harvey Lectures* 28 (1934): 218–33. "The Ferrier Lecture on Problems Connected with the Principle of Humoral Transmission of Nervous Impulses." *Proceedings of the Royal Society* 118B (1935): 299–316. "Die Chemische Übertragung der Nervwirkung." *Schweizerische Medizinische Wochenschrift* 67 (1937): 850–55. "The Edward Gamaliel Janeway Lectures: Aspects of the Transmission of Nervous Impulse." *Journal of the Mount Sinai Hospital* 12 (1945): 803–16, 851–65.

For More Information See: Biographical Memoirs of the Fellows of the Royal Society. London: Royal Society, 1962 (Volume 8), 67–89. *Dictionary of Scientific Biography.* New York: Scribner's, 1973 (Volume 8), 451–56. Lembeck, Fred, and Giere, Wolfgang. *The Excitement and Fascination of Science.* Palo Alto, CA: Annual Reviews, Inc., 1965, Vol. 1, 269–78. *Otto Loewi: Ein Lebensbild in Dokumenten.* New York: Springer, 1968.

Commentary: Otto Loewi's shared Nobel Prize was for "discoveries relating to chemical transmission of nerve impulses." He also produced significant papers on metabolism, the heart, the kidney, the action of insulin, and cocaine's effect on adrenalin. (R.K.)

1937

Szent-Györgyi, Albert von Nagyrapolt **317**

Prize: Medicine and Physiology, 1937. *Born:* September 16, 1893; Budapest, Hungary. *Death:* October 22, 1986; Woods Hole, MA. *Parents:* Father, Nicholas Szent-Györgyi; Mother, Josephine Lenhossek Szent-Györgyi. *Nationality:* Hungarian; later American citizen. *Religion:* Belonged to no organized church. *Education:* Univ. of Budapest, Hungary, M.D., 1917; Cambridge Univ., England, Ph.D., 1927. *Spouse:* Cornelia Demeny, married 1917; Marta Borbiro, married 1941; Marcia Houston, married 1975. *Children:* Cornelia, daughter. *Career:* Austro-Hungarian Army, 1914–18; Researcher at various universities (Prague, Czechoslovakia; Berlin, Germany; Hamburg, Germany; Leiden, Netherlands; Liége, Belgium; Groningen, Germany; Budapest, Hungary; Minnesota; Cambridge, England), 1919–30; Univ. of Szeged, Hungary, Professor and Administrator, 1931–45; Univ. of Budapest, Hungary, Professor, 1945–47; Marine Biology Laboratories, Woods Hole, MA, Director, 1947–75; National Foundation for Cancer Research, Woods Hole, MA, Director, 1975–86. *Other Awards:* Cameron Prize, Univ. of Edinburgh, Scotland, 1946; Lasker Award, American Heart Association, 1954.

Selected Publications: On Oxidation, Fermentation, Vitamins, Health and Disease. Baltimore, MD: Williams and Wilkins, 1939. *Chemistry of Muscular Contraction.* New York: Academic Press, 1947. *Bioelectronics.* New York: Academic Press, 1968. *The Living State and Cancer.* New York: M. Dekker, 1978. *Essays and Scientific Papers of Albert Szent-Györgyi.* Szeged, Hungary: Albert Szent-Györgyi Medical Univ., 1991.

For More Information See: Current Biography Yearbook. New York: H.W. Wilson, 1955, 596–99. *Encyclopedia of World Biography.* New York: McGraw-Hill, 1973 (Volume 10), 314–16. *The Excitement and Fascination of Science.* Palo Alto, CA: Annual Reviews, Inc., 1965, Vol. 1, 461–74. "Lost in the Twentieth Century." *Annual Review of Biochemistry* 32 (1963): 1–14. Szabo, T. *Albert Szent-György and Szeged.* Szeged, Hungary: Szote Nyomba, 1993.

Commentary: Albert Szent-Györgyi was granted the Nobel Prize "for his discoveries in connection with the biological combustion processes, with especial reference to Vitamin C and the catalysis of fumaric acid." A prolific researcher and writer, Szent-Györgyi made significant contributions as well in discovering Vitamin P, in the biochemistry of muscular contraction, in isolation of ATP, and in the study of cancer. (M.L.)

1938

Heymans, Corneille Jean François **318**

Prize: Medicine and Physiology, 1938. *Born:* March 28, 1892; Ghent, Belgium. *Death:* July 18, 1968; Knokke, Belgium. *Parents:* Father, Jean-François Heymans; Mother, Marie-Henriette Henning Heymans. *Nationality:* Belgian. *Religion:* Catholic. *Education:* Univ. of Ghent, Belgium, M.D., 1920. *Spouse:* Bertha May, married January 18, 1921. *Children:* Pierre, son; Marie-Henriette, daughter; Jean, son; Berthe, daughter. *Career:* Univ. of Ghent, Belgium, Professor, 1923–68. *Other Awards:* Alvarenga Prize, Académie Royale de Médecine, Belgium; Gluge Prize,

Académie Royal des Sciences, Belgium; Prix Quinquennal de Médecine du Gouvernement, Belgium; Pius XI Prize, Pontifica Academia Scientiarum, Rome; Purkinje Prize, Academy of Medicine, Czechoslovakia; Bourceret Prize, Académie de Médecine de Paris, France; Monthyon Prize, Institut de France; Schmiedeberg Plakette, Deutsche Pharmakologische Gesellschaft, Germany; Cyon Prize; Academy of Sciences, Bologna, Italy; Burgi Prize, Univ. of Bern, Switzerland.

Selected Publications: The Cartiod Sinus and Other Reflexogenic Vasosensitive Zones. Paris: Press of French Universities, 1929. *Introduction to the Regulation of Blood Pressure and Heart Rate.* Springfield, IL: Thomas, 1950. *Reflexogenic Areas of the Cardiovascular System.* London: Churchill, 1958 (with E. Neil).

For More Information See: A Biographical History of Medicine. New York: Grune and Stratton, 1970, 984–86. *Corneel Heymanns: A Collective Biography.* Ghent, Belgium: Archives Internationales de Pharmacodynamie et de Therapie, 1972. *The Excitement and Fascination of Science.* Palo Alto, CA: Annual Reviews, Inc., 1965, Vol. 1, 163–76.

Commentary: Corneille Heymans won the Nobel Prize "for his discovery of the role played by the sinus and aortic mechanisms in the regulation of respiration." This was accomplished by development of new techniques for physiologic investigation, such as cross-circulation (where the carotid artery and jugular vein of one animal were used to perfuse blood in another animal unconnected except for the nerves involved). (M.L. and C.E.)

1939

Domagk, Gerhard **319**

Prize: Medicine and Physiology, 1939 (refused). *Born:* October 30, 1895; Lagow, Brandenburg, Germany. *Death:* April 24, 1964; Beirberg, Württenburg, Baden, Germany. *Parents:* Father, Paul Domagk; Mother, Martha Reimer Domagk. *Nationality:* German. *Religion:* Christian. *Education:* Univ. of Kiel, Germany, M.D., 1921. *Spouse:* Gertrude Strübe, married 1925. *Children:* Hildegarde, daughter; 3 sons. *Career:* German Army, 1914–18; Univ. of Greifswald, Germany, Professor, 1921–25; Univ. of Müenster, Germany, Professor, 1925–64; I.G. Farberindustrie, Elberfeld, Germany, Director of Research, 1928–64. *Other Awards:* Emil Fischer Memorial Plaque, 1937; Gold Medal of the Paris Exposition, 1938; Paul Ehrlich Gold Medal, 1939; Cameron Prize, Univ. of Edinburgh, Scotland, 1939; Von Klebelsberg Award, Univ. of Szeged, Hungary.

Selected Publications: "Ein Beitrag zur Chemotherapie der Bakteriellen Infektionen." *Deutsche Medizinische Wochenschrift* 61 (1935): 250–53. *Chemotherapie Bakterieller Infektionen.* Leipzig, Germany: Hirzel, 1940 (with F. Hegler). *Pathologische Anatomie und Chemotherapie der Infektionskrankenheiten.* Stuttgart, Germany: Thieme, 1947. *Chemotherapie der Tuberkulose mit Thiosemikarbazonen.* Stuttgart, Germany: Thieme, 1950.

For More Information See: Biographical Memoirs of the Fellows of the Royal Society. London: Royal Society, 1964 (Volume 10), 39–50. *Dictionary of Scientific Biography.* New York: Scribner's, 1971 (Volume 4), 153–56.

Commentary: Gerhard Domagk received the Nobel Prize "for his discovery of the antibacterial effects of prontosil," one of the sulfonamide compounds. It was used against many disease states successfully, and led to the preparation of many related sulfonamides. Domagk continued to work to find medically effective drugs, first for tuberculosis, later for cancer. (C.E.)

1943

Dam, Carl Peter Henrik   320
Prize: Medicine and Physiology, 1943. *Born:* February 21, 1895; Copenhagen, Denmark. *Death:* April 18, 1976; Copenhagen, Denmark. *Parents:* Father, Emil Dam; Mother, Emilie Peterson Dam. *Nationality:* Danish. *Religion:* Christian. *Education:* Polytechnic Institute, Denmark, M.S., 1920; Univ. of Copenhagen, Denmark, D.Sc., 1934. *Spouse:* Inger Olsen, married July 15, 1924. *Children:* None. *Career:* Royal School of Agriculture and Veterinary Medicine, Copenhagen, Denmark, Professor, 1920–23; Univ. of Copenhagen, Denmark, Professor, 1923–41; Univ. of Rochester, NY, Researcher, 1942–45; Rockefeller Institute for Medical Research, NY, Researcher, 1945–48; Polytechnic Institute, Copenhagen, Denmark, Professor, 1948–65. *Other Awards:* Christian Bohr Award in Physiology, 1939; Norman Medal, German Fat Research Society, 1960.

Selected Publications: Some Studies on Vitamin E. Copenhagen: E. Munksgaard, 1941. "Vitamin K, Its Chemistry and Physiology." *Advances in Enzymology* 2 (1942): 285. "Medical Aspects of Vitamin K." *Lancet* 63 (1943): 353.

For More Information See: Current Biography Yearbook. New York: H.W. Wilson, 1949, 134–36. *Dictionary of Scientific Biography.* Supplement II. New York: Scribner's, 1990, 196–202. *Modern Scientists and Engineers.* New York: McGraw-Hill, 1980 (Volume 1), 258–59.

Commentary: Henrik Dam was cited by the Academy "for his discovery of vitamin K," the blood coagulation factor. Dam's work also included research in cholesterol metabolism, vitamin E, lipids, growth factors, and gallstone formation. (C.E.)

Doisy, Edward Adelbert   321
Prize: Medicine and Physiology, 1943. *Born:* November 13, 1893; Hume, IL. *Death:* October 23, 1986; St. Louis, MO. *Parents:* Father, Edward Perez Doisy; Mother, Ada Alley Doisy. *Nationality:* American. *Religion:* Congregationalist. *Education:* Univ. of Illinois, A.B., 1914; Univ. of Illinois, M.S., 1916; Harvard Univ., MA, Ph.D., 1920. *Spouse:* Alice Ackert, married July 20, 1918, died August 1964; Margaret McCormick, married April 19, 1965. *Children:* Edward Adelbert, son; Robert A., son; Philip P., son; Richard J., son. *Career:* Harvard Univ., MA, Researcher, 1915–17; U.S. Army, 1917–19; Washington Univ., MO, Professor, 1919–23; St. Louis Univ., MO, Professor, 1923–65. *Other Awards:* Gold Medal, St. Louis Medical Society, 1935; Philip A. Conne Medal, Chemist's Club of New York, 1935; St. Louis Civic Award, 1939; Willard Gibbs Award, American Chemical Society, 1941; American Pharmaceutical Manufacturing Association Award, 1942; Squibb Award, 1944; Fleur de Lis, St. Louis Univ., MO, 1951; Commercial Solvent Award, 1952; Illini Achievement Award, Univ. of Illinois, 1958; Barren Foundation Medal, 1972.

Selected Publications: "The Constitution and Synthesis of Vitamin K1." *Journal of Biological Chemistry* 131 (1939): 357–69 (with others). "The Isolation of Vitamin K1." *Journal of Biological Chemistry* 130 (1939): 219–34 (with others). "The Isolation of Vitamin K2." *Journal of Biological Chemistry* 131 (1939): 327–44 (with others). *Female Sex Hormones.* Philadelphia, PA: Univ. of Pennsylvania Press, 1941 (with others).

For More Information See: Current Biography Yearbook. New York: H.W. Wilson, 1949, 161–62. *Modern Scientists and Engineers.* New York: McGraw-Hill, 1980 (Volume 1), 298–99.

Commentary: Edward Doisy was granted the Nobel Prize "for his discovery of the chemical nature of vitamin K." In addition to synthesis isolation, and characterization of the K vitamins, Doisy also worked with metabolism, endocrinology, insulin, blood buffers, ovarian hormones, and estrogens. (K.F.)

1944

Erlanger, Joseph   322
Prize: Medicine and Physiology, 1944. *Born:* January 5, 1874; San Francisco, CA. *Death:* December 5, 1965; St. Louis, MO. *Parents:* Father, Herman Erlanger; Mother, Sarah Galinger Erlanger. *Nationality:* American. *Religion:* Jewish. *Education:* Univ. of California, B.S., 1895; Johns Hopkins Univ., MD, M.D., 1899. *Spouse:* Aimee Hirstel, married June 21, 1906. *Children:* Margaret, daughter; Ruth Josephine, daughter; Herman, son. *Career:* Johns Hopkins Univ., MD, Professor, 1899–1906; Univ. of Wisconsin, Professor, 1906–10; Washington Univ., MO, Professor, 1910–65.

Selected Publications: "A Study of the Metabolism in Dogs with Shortened Small Intestines." *American Journal of Physiology* 6 (1901): 1–30 (with A.W. Hewlett). "On the Physiology of Heart-Block in Mammals, with Especial Reference to the Causation of Stokes-Adams Disease." *Journal of Experimental Medicine* 7 (1905): 676–724. "Studies in Blood Pressure Estimation by Indirect Methods. I. The Mechanism of the Oscillatory Methods." *American Journal of Physiology* 39 (1916): 401–46. "The Compound Nature of the Action Current of Nerve as Disclosed by the Cathode Ray Oscillograph." *American Journal of Physiology* 70 (1924): 624–66 (with H.S. Gasser).

For More Information See: Biographical Memoirs. National Academy of Sciences. New York: Columbia Univ. Press, 1970 (Volume 41), 111–39. *Dictionary of Scientific Biography.* New York: Scribner's, 1971 (Volume 4), 397–99. *The Excitement and Fascination of Science.* Palo Alto, CA: Annual Reviews, Inc., 1965, Vol. 1, 93–106. "A Physiologist Reminisces." *Annual Review of Physiology* 26 (1964): 1–14.

Commentary: Joseph Erlanger shared his Nobel for "discoveries regarding the highly differentiated functions of single nerve fibers." His career included work on circulation and cardiac physiology, blood pressure and blood volume, neurophysiology, and treatment of wound shock. (B.R.W.)

Gasser, Herbert Spencer   323
Prize: Medicine and Physiology, 1944. *Born:* July 5, 1888; Platteville, WI. *Death:* May 11, 1963; New York, NY. *Parents:* Father, Herman Gasser; Mother, Elizabeth Griswold

Gasser. *Nationality:* American. *Religion:* Jewish. *Education:* Univ. of Wisconsin, A.B., 1910; Univ. of Wisconsin, A.M., 1911; Johns Hopkins Univ., MD, M.D., 1915. *Spouse:* None. *Children:* None. *Career:* Univ. of Wisconsin, Professor, 1911–16; Washington Univ., MO, Professor, 1916–31; Cornell Univ., NY, Professor, 1931–35; Rockefeller Institute for Medical Research, NY, Professor and Administrator, 1935–63. *Other Awards:* Kober Medal, American Association of Physicians, 1954.

Selected Publications: "A Study of the Mechanism by Which Muscular Exercise Produces Acceleration of the Heart." *American Journal of Physiology* 34 (1914): 48–71 (with W.J. Meek). "An Experimental Study of Surgical Shock." *Journal of the American Medical Association* 69 (1917): 2089–92 (with J. Erlanger and B.L. Elliott). "The Compound Nature of the Action Current of Nerve as Disclosed by the Cathode Ray Oscillograph." *American Journal of Physiology* 70 (1924): 624–66 (with J. Erlanger). "The Classification of Nerve Fibers." *Ohio Journal of Science* 41 (1941): 145–59.

For More Information See: Biographical Memoirs of the Fellows of the Royal Society. Cambridge: Royal Society, 1964 (Volume 10), 75–82. *Dictionary of Scientific Biography.* New York: Scribner's, 1972 (Volume 5), 290–91. *Herbert Spencer Gasser, 1888–1963: An Autobiographical Memoir.* New York: Academic Press, 1964.

Commentary: Herbert Gasser shared his Nobel Prize for "discoveries regarding the highly differentiated functions of single nerve fibers." Gasser's major work was accomplished with Joseph Erlanger, in wound shock, blood volume, and in neurophysiology, but his later work on nerve fibers helped to clarify many problems in that field. (B.R.W.)

1945

Chain, Ernst Boris, Sir   324

Prize: Medicine and Physiology, 1945. *Born:* June 19, 1906; Berlin, Germany. *Death:* August 12, 1979; Mulranny, County Mayo, Ireland. *Parents:* Father, Michael Chain; Mother, Margarete Eisner Chain. *Nationality:* German; later Italian resident and British citizen. *Religion:* Jewish. *Education:* Friedrich-Wilhelms Univ., Germany, Ph.D., 1930. *Spouse:* Anne Beloff, married 1948. *Children:* Benjamin, son; Daniel, son; Judith, daughter. *Career:* Charite Hospital, Berlin, Germany, Researcher, 1930–33; Cambridge Univ., England, Researcher, 1933–35; Oxford Univ., England, Professor, 1935–48; Instituto Superiore di Sanita, Rome, Italy, Professor and Administrator, 1948–61; Univ. of London, England, Professor, 1961–73. *Other Awards:* Silver Berzelius Medal, Swedish Medical Society, 1946; Pasteur Medal, Institut Pasteur and Société de Chimie Biologique, 1946; Harmsworth Memorial Fund, 1946; Paul Ehrlich Centenary Prize, 1954; Gold Medal for Therapeutics, Worshipful Society of Apothecaries, England, 1957; Knighthood, 1969; Marotta Medal, Societa Chimica Italiana, 1972; Carl Neuberg Medal, 1972; Hamburg Memorial Medal, Germany, 1972; Heymans Memorial Medal, 1974.

Selected Publications: "Penicillin as a Chemotherapeutic Agent." *Lancet* 239 (1940): 226–28 (with others). "Further Observations on Penicillin." *Lancet* 241 (1941): 177–89 (with others). *Antibiotics: A Survey of Penicillin, Streptomycin and other Antimicrobial Substances from Fungi,* *Actinomycetes, Bacteria and Plants.* London: Oxford Univ. Press, 1949 (with others).

For More Information See: Biographical Encyclopedia of Scientists. New York: Facts on File, 1981, 140. *Biographical Memoirs of the Fellows of the Royal Society.* London: Royal Society, 1983 (Volume 29), 42–91. Clark, R.W. *The Life of Ernst Chain.* New York: St. Martin Press, 1985.

Commentary: Ernst Chain shared the Nobel "for the discovery of penicillin and its curative effect in various infectious diseases." Chain participated in the research that demonstrated the structure of penicillin and used it in successful clinical trials. Other notable work included that on penicillinase, tumor metabolism, and insulin action. (B.I.M.)

Fleming, Alexander, Sir   325

Prize: Medicine and Physiology, 1945. *Born:* August 6, 1881; Lochfield Farm, Ayrshire, Scotland. *Death:* March 11, 1955; London, England. *Parents:* Father, Hugh Fleming; Mother, Grace Morton Fleming. *Nationality:* Scottish. *Religion:* Presbyterian. *Education:* Univ. of London, England, M.D., 1903. *Spouse:* Sarah Marion McElroy, married December 1915, died 1949; Amalia Cotsouris Voureka, married April 1953. *Children:* Robert, son. *Career:* Shipping Company, London, Clerk, 1897–1901; St. Mary's Hospital, London, England, Physician and Researcher, 1906–55. *Other Awards:* Gold Medal, Univ. of London, England, 1908; Cheadle Medal, 1908; John Scott Medal, Philadelphia, PA, 1944; Knighthood, 1944; Cameron Prize, Univ. of Edinburgh, Scotland, 1945; Louis Pasteur Medal, 1947; Medal for Merit, United States, 1947.

Selected Publications: "On the Use of Salvarsan in the Treatment of Syphilis." *Lancet* 1 (1911): 1631–34. "On a Remarkable Bacteriolytic Substance Found in Secretions and Tissues." *Proceedings of the Royal Society* 93B (1922): 306–17. "On the Antibacterial Action of Cultures of a *Penicillium,* with Special Reference to Their Use in the Isolation of *B. Influenzae.*" *British Journal of Experimental Pathology* 10 (1929): 226–36. "Penicillin: Its Discovery, Development, and Uses in the Field of Medicine and Surgery." *Journal of the Royal Institute of Public Health and Hygiene* 8 (1945): 36–49, 63–71, 93–105. *Chemotherapy: Yesterday, Today, and Tomorrow.* Cambridge: Cambridge Univ. Press, 1946. Shipton, R. *Bibliography of Sir Alexander Fleming.* 1881–1955. London: St. Mary's Hospital Medical School, 1993.

For More Information See: Bennett, P. *Alexander Fleming.* Boston: Wayland, 1992. *Dictionary of Scientific Biography.* New York: Scribner's, 1972 (Volume 5), 28–31. Ludovici, Laurence J. *Fleming, Discoverer of Penicillin.* London: A. Dakers, 1952. Macfarlane, Gwyn. *Alexander Fleming: The Man and the Myth.* Cambridge, MA: Harvard Univ. Press, 1984. Maurois, Andre. *The Life of Sir Alexander Fleming, Discoverer of Penicillin.* New York: Dutton, 1959.

Commentary: Alexander Fleming received the Nobel Prize "for the discovery of penicillin," which had occurred in 1928. Fleming shared the prize with Florey and Chain, who, after having discovered Fleming's published work on the *Penicillium* mold, had purified penicillin, produced it in quantity, and used it successfully in the treatment of disease. Fleming's work continued with important contributions in the areas of blood chemistry, antiseptics, lysozyme, and antibiotics. (H.L.F.)

Florey, Howard Walter, Sir   326

Prize: Medicine and Physiology, 1945. *Born:* September 24, 1898; Adelaide, Australia. *Death:* February 21, 1968; Oxford, England. *Parents:* Father, Joseph Florey; Mother, Bertha Mary Wadham Florey. *Nationality:* Australian; later British resident. *Religion:* Christian/Protestant. *Education:* Adelaide Univ., Australia, B.S., 1921; Adelaide Univ., Australia, M.B., 1921; Oxford Univ., England, B.Sc., 1924; Oxford Univ., England, M.A., 1924; Cambridge Univ., England, Ph.D., 1927. *Spouse:* Mary Ethel Reed, married 1926, died 1966; Margaret Augusta Fremantle Jennings, married 1967. *Children:* Charles, son; Poquita, daughter. *Career:* Cambridge Univ., England, Professor, 1926–31; Univ. of Sheffield, England, Professor, 1931–35; Oxford Univ., England, Professor and Administrator, 1935–65; Australian National Univ., Canberra, Chancellor, 1965–68. *Other Awards:* Knighthood, 1944; Lister Medal, Royal College of Surgeons, 1945; Cameron Prize, Univ. of Edinburgh, Scotland, 1945; Berzelius Silver Medal, Swedish Medical Society, 1945; Commander of the Legion of Honor, 1946; Harmsworth Memorial Award, 1946; Albert Gold Medal, Royal Society of the Arts, 1946; Medal in Therapeutics, Society of Apothecaries, London, England, 1946; Gold Medal, Royal Society of Medicine, 1947; Medal for Merit, United States, 1948; Addingham Gold Medal, 1949; Copley Medal, Royal Society, 1951; Royal Medal, 1951; Gold Medal, British Medical Association, 1964; Lomonossov Medal, USSR Academy of Sciences, 1964.

Selected Publications: "The Secretion of Mucus by the Colon." *British Journal of Experimental Pathology* 11 (1930): 348–61. "Some Properties of Mucus, with Special Reference to Its Antibacterial Functions." *British Journal of Experimental Pathology* 11 (1930): 192–208 (with N.E. Goldsworthy). "Penicillin as a Chemotherapeutic Agent." *Lancet* 239 (1940): 226–28 (with others). "Further Observations on Penicillin." *Lancet* 241 (1941): 177–88 (with others). *Antibiotics: A Survey of Penicillin, Streptomycin, and Other Antimicrobial Substances from Fungi, Actinomycetes, Bacteria and Plants.* London: Oxford Univ. Press, 1949.

For More Information See: Biographical Memoirs of the Fellows of the Royal Society. London: Royal Society, 17 (1971): 255–302. Chase, D. *Howard Florey, The Man Who Developed Penicillin.* South Melbourne, Australia: Macmillan Australia, 1991. *Dictionary of Scientific Biography.* New York: Scribner's, 1972 (Volume 5), 41–44. McFarlane, R.G. *Howard Florey.* London: Oxford Univ. Press, 1979.

Commentary: Howard Florey shared the Nobel Prize "for the discovery of penicillin and its curative effects in various infectious diseases." His joint research elaborated the structure of penicillin and used it in successful clinical trials. Florey did notable work also in mucous secretions, the cell's role in inflammation, the action of lysozyme, and the development of atherosclerosis. (R.K.)

1946

Muller, Hermann Joseph   327

Prize: Medicine and Physiology, 1946. *Born:* December 21, 1890; New York, NY. *Death:* April 5, 1967; Indianapolis, IN. *Parents:* Father, Hermann Joseph Muller; Mother, Frances Louise Lyons Muller. *Nationality:* American. *Religion:* Unitarian; from Jewish/Catholic background. *Education:* Columbia Univ., NY, B.A., 1910; Columbia Univ., NY, M.A., 1911; Columbia Univ., NY, Ph.D., 1916. *Spouse:* Jessie Marie Jacobs, married June 11, 1923, divorced 1934; Dorothea Johanna Kantorowicz, married May 20, 1939. *Children:* David Eugene, son; Helen Juliette, daughter. *Career:* Cornell Univ., NY, Professor, 1911–12; Columbia Univ., NY, Professor, 1912–15; Rice Institute, TX, Professor, 1915–18; Columbia Univ., NY, Professor, 1918–20; Univ. of Texas, Professor, 1920–36; Soviet Academy of Sciences Institute of Genetics, USSR, Researcher, 1933–37; Univ. of Edinburgh, Scotland, Professor, 1937–40; Amherst College, MA, Professor, 1940–45; Indiana Univ., Professor, 1945–67. *Other Awards:* Cleveland Research Prize, American Association for the Advancement of Science, 1927; Kimber Award in Genetics, US National Academy of Sciences, 1955; Virchow Medal, Virchow Society of New York, 1956; Darwin Medal, Linnean Society of London, 1958; Darwin Medal, Deutsche Akademie Naturforscher Leopoldina, 1959; Alexander Hamilton Award, Columbia Univ., NY, 1960; Humanist of the Year, Humanist Association, 1963; City of Hope Medical Centre Research Citation, 1964.

Selected Publications: "Artificial Transmutation of the Gene." *Science* 66 (1927): 84–87. *Out of the Night: A Biologist's View of the Future.* London: V. Gollancz, 1936. *Genetics, Medicine and Man.* Ithaca, NY: Cornell Univ. Press, 1947 (with C.C. Little and L.H. Snyder). *Studies in Genetics: The Selected Papers of H.J. Muller.* Bloomington, IN: Indiana Univ. Press, 1962.

For More Information See: Biographical Memoirs of the Fellows of the Royal Society. London: Royal Society, 1968 (Volume 14), 349–89. Carlson, E.A. *Genes, Radiation and Society: The Life and Work of H.J. Muller.* Ithaca, NY: Cornell Univ. Press, 1981. *Dictionary of Scientific Biography.* New York: Scribner's, 1974 (Volume 9), 564–65.

Commentary: Hermann Muller was given the Nobel "for the discovery of the production of mutations by means of x-ray irradiation." His work and writings led to much research on artificial mutation of organisms and to much discussion of the effects of atomic fission. Muller's writings also include papers on genetics, blood transfusion, and the psychological studies of identical twins raised in different environments. (R.K.)

1947

Cori, Carl Ferdinand   328

Prize: Medicine and Physiology, 1947. *Born:* December 5, 1896; Prague, Czechoslovakia. *Death:* October 20, 1984; Cambridge, MA. *Parents:* Father, Carl Isidor Cori; Mother, Maria Lippich Cori. *Nationality:* Czechoslovakian; later American citizen. *Religion:* Christian. *Education:* German Univ. of Prague, Czechoslovakia, M.D., 1920. *Spouse:* Gerty Theresa Radnitz, married August 5, 1920, died October 26, 1957; Anne Fitzgerald Jones, married March 23,

1960. *Children:* Carl Thomas, son. *Career:* Univ. of Graz, Austria, Researcher, 1920–21; State Institute for the Study of Malignant Disease, Buffalo, NY, Researcher, 1922–31; Washington Univ., St. Louis, MO, Professor, 1931–66; Harvard Univ., MA, Professor, 1966–84. *Other Awards:* Midwest Award, American Chemical Society, 1946; Lasker Award, 1946; Squibb Award, 1947; Sugar Research Foundation Award, 1947, 1950; Willard Gibbs Medal, American Chemical Society, 1948.

Selected Publications: "Mammalian Carbohydrate Metabolism." *Physiological Reviews* 11 (April 1931). "The Formation of Hexosephosphate Esters in Frog Muscle." *Journal of Biological Chemistry* 116 (1936): 119–28 (with G.T. Cori). "Crystalline Muscle Phosphorylase. III. Kinetics." *Journal of Biological Chemistry* 151 (1943): 39–55 (with A.A. Green and G.T. Cori). "The Enzymatic Conversion of Phosphorylase a to b." *Journal of Biological Chemistry* 158 (1945): 321–32 (with G.T. Cori). "Glucose 6-Phosphatase of the Liver in Glycogen Storage Disease." *Journal of Biological Chemistry* 199 (1952): 661–67 (with G.T. Cori).

For More Information See: Biographical Memoirs of the Fellows of the Royal Society. London: Royal Society, 1986 (Volume 32), 65. *Current Biography Yearbook* New York: H.W. Wilson, 1947, 135–37. Houssay, B.A. "Carl F. and Gerty T. Cori." *Biochimica et Biophysica Acta* 20 (1956): 11–16. *Biographical Memoirs. National Academy of Sciences.* Washington, D.C.: National Academy Press, 1992, Volume 61, 111.

Commentary: Carl Cori, with his wife and colaureate, Gerty, were honored with the Nobel Prize "for their discovery of the course of the catalytic conversion of glycogen." The Coris elucidated the process by which animal starch (glycogen) is converted into utilizable sugar and isolated the enzyme, phosphorylase, which is integral to the process. The laureates also made significant contributions in the studies of sugar utilization and the effects of insulin and epinephrine, tumor glycolysis, carbohydrate metabolism, and the action of pituitary extracts. (B.A. and R.K.)

Cori, Gerty Theresa Radnitz   329

Prize: Medicine and Physiology, 1947. *Born:* August 15, 1896; Prague, Czechoslovakia. *Death:* October 26, 1957; St. Louis, MO. *Parents:* Father, Otto Radnitz; Mother, Martha Neustadt Radnitz. *Nationality:* Czechoslovakian; later American citizen. *Religion:* Jewish. *Education:* German Univ. of Prague, Czechoslovakia, M.D., 1920. *Spouse:* Carl Ferdinand Cori, married August 5, 1920. *Children:* Carl Thomas, son. *Career:* Children's Hospital, Vienna, Austria, Researcher, 1920–22; State Institute for the Study of Malignant Diseases, Buffalo, NY, Researcher, 1922–31; Washington Univ., St. Louis, MO, Professor, 1931–57. *Other Awards:* Midwest Award, American Chemical Society, 1946; Squibb Award, 1947; Garvan Medal, 1948; Sugar Research Prize, National Academy of Sciences, 1950; Borden Award, Association of Medical Colleges.

Selected Publications: "The Formation of Hexosephosphate Esters in Frog Muscle." *Journal of Biological Chemistry* 116 (1936): 119–28 (with C.F. Cori). "Crystalline Muscle Phosphorylase. II. Prosthetic Group." *Journal of Biological*

Chemistry 151 (1943): 31–38. (with A.A. Green). "Crystalline Muscle Phosphorylase. III. Kinetics." *Journal of Biological Chemistry* 151 (1943): 39–55 (with A.A. Green and C.F. Cori). "The Enzymatic Conversion of Phosphorylase a to b." *Journal of Biological Chemistry* 158 (1945): 321–32 (with C.F. Cori). "Action of Amylo-1,6-Glycosidase and Phosphorylase on Glycogen and Amylopectin." *Journal of Biological Chemistry* 188 (1951): 17–29 (with J. Larner). "Glucose 6-Phosphatase of the Liver in Glycogen Storage Disease." *Journal of Biological Chemistry* 199 (1952): 661–67 (with C.F. Cori). "Glycogen Structure and Enzyme Deficiencies in Glycogen Storage Disease." *Harvey Lectures* 48 (1952–53): 145–71.

For More Information See: Cori, C.F. "The Call of Science." *Annual Review of Biochemistry* 38 (1969): 1–20. *Current Biography Yearbook.* New York: H.W. Wilson, 1947, 135–37. *Dictionary of Scientific Biography.* New York: Scribner's, 1971 (Volume 3), 415–16. Houssay, B.A. "Carl F. and Gerty T. Cori." *Biochimica et Biophysica Acta* 20 (1956): 11–16. *Biographical Memoirs. National Academy of Sciences.* Washington, DC: National Academy Press, 1990, Volume 61, 111.

Commentary: Gerty Cori, with her husband and colaureate, Carl, were honored with the Nobel Prize "for their discovery of the course of the catalytic conversion of glycogen." The Coris elucidated the process by which animal starch (glycogen) is converted into usable sugar and isolated the enzyme, phosporylase, which is integral to the process. The Coris also made significant contributions in the study of sugar utilization and the effects of insulin and epinephrine, tumor glycolysis, carbohydrate metabolism, and the action of pituitary extracts. (B.A. and R.K.)

Houssay, Bernardo Alberto   330

Prize: Medicine and Physiology, 1947. *Born:* April 10, 1887; Buenos Aires, Argentina. *Death:* September 27, 1971; Buenos Aires, Argentina. *Parents:* Father, Alberto Houssay; Mother, Clara Laffont Houssay. *Nationality:* Argentinian. *Religion:* Christian. *Education:* Univ. of Buenos Aires, Argentina, Pharmacy Degree, 1904; Univ. of Buenos Aires, Argentina, Doctorate in Medicine, 1910. *Spouse:* Maria Angelica Catan, married December 22, 1920. *Children:* Alberto Bernardo, son; Hector Emilio Jose, son; Raul Horacio, son. *Career:* Univ. of Buenos Aires, Argentina, Professor, 1907–69. *Other Awards:* National Award of Sciences, Buenos Aires, Argentina, 1923; Charles Mickle Fellowship, Toronto, Canada, 1945; Banting Medal, American Diabetes Association, 1946; Research Award, American Pharmaceutical Manufacturers' Association, 1947; Baly Medal, Royal College of Physicians, England, 1947; James Cook Medal; Sydney Medal, 1948; Dale Medal, Society for Endocrinology, England, 1960; Weizmann Prize, 1967.

Selected Publications: "Carbohydrate Metabolism." *New England Journal of Medicine* 214 (1936): 971. "The Hypophysis and Metabolism." *New England Journal of Medicine* 214 (1936): 961. "Diabetes as a Disturbance of Endocrine Regulation." *American Journal of Medical Science* 193 (1937): 581. "Advancement of Knowledge of the Role of the Hypophysis in Carbohydrate Metabolism During the Last Twenty-Five Years." *Endocrinology* 30 (1942): 884.

For More Information See: *Biographical Memoirs of the Fellows of the Royal Society.* London: Royal Society, 1974 (Volume 20), 247–70. Cereijido, M. *La Nuca de Houssay.* Buenos Aires: Fondo de Cultura Economica, 1990. *Current Biography Yearbook.* New York: H.W. Wilson, 1948, 295–97. *The Excitement and Fascination of Science.* Palo Alto, CA: Annual Reviews, Inc., 1965, Vol. 1, 205–16.

Commentary: Argentinian scientist and activist Bernardo Houssay was recognized by the Academy "for his discovery of the part played by the hormone of the anterior pituitary lobe in the metabolism of sugars." Although Houssay's major interest was in the endocrine glands and the pituitary, his research produced significant results on the physiology of circulation and respiration, the process of immunity, the nervous system, digestion, and snake and spider venoms. He was also recognized as an activist leader in the promotion of democracy, education, and scientific research in Argentina. (B.S.S.)

1948

Müller, Paul Hermann   331

Prize: Medicine and Physiology, 1948. *Born:* January 12, 1899; Olten, Switzerland. *Death:* October 13, 1965; Basel, Switzerland. *Parents:* Father, Gottlieb Müller; Mother, Fanny Leypoldt Müller. *Nationality:* Swiss. *Religion:* Evangelical. *Education:* Univ. of Basel, Switzerland, doctorate, 1925. *Spouse:* Friedel Rugsegger, married October 6, 1927. *Children:* Henry, son; Niklaus, son; Margaret, daughter. *Career:* Lonza Power Plant, Switzerland, Researcher, 1916–17; J.R. Geigy Company, Basel, Switzerland, Researcher, 1925–65.

Selected Publications: "Über Konstitution und Toxische Wirkung von Naturlichen und Neuen Synthetischen. Insektentotenden Stoffen." *Helvetica Chimica Acta* 27 (1944): 899–928 (with P. Lauger and H. Martin). "Über Zusammenhange Zwischen Konstitution und Insektizider Werkung. I." *Helvetica Chimica Acta* 29 (1946): 1560–80.

For More Information See: *Current Biography Yearbook.* New York: H.W. Wilson, 1945, 340–42. *Dictionary of Scientific Biography.* New York: Scribner's, 1974 (Volume 9), 576–77.

Commentary: Paul Müller's Nobel was granted "for his discovery of the high efficiency of DDT as a contact poison against several arthropods." Müller's original research on plant pigments and natural tanning agents led him to the research on disinfectants and pesticides that resulted in his discovery of the effectiveness of DDT as an insecticide. It was later used in tropical areas and in the fight against malaria and typhus. Müller's original articles included a warning about the stability of DDT, which later proved to be warranted when large accumulations of DDT were found in biological organisms. (M.D.C.)

1949

Egas Moniz, Antonio Caetano Abreu Freire   332

Prize: Medicine and Physiology, 1949. *Born:* November 29, 1874; Avanca, Portugal. *Death:* December 13, 1955; Lisbon, Portugal. *Parents:* Father, Fernando De Pina Rezende Abreu; Mother, Maria de Rosario de Almeida e Sousa. *Nationality:* Portuguese. *Religion:* Catholic. *Education:* Univ. of Coimbra, Portugal, M.D., 1899. *Spouse:* Elvira de Macedo Dias, married 1902. *Children:* None. *Career:* Univ. of Coimbra, Portugal, Professor, 1902–11; Univ. of Lisbon, Portugal, Professor, 1911–55. *Other Awards:* Grand Cross of Isabel la Catolica, Spain; Instrucao Publica, Portugal; Santiago de Espada; Commander, Legion of Honour.

Selected Publications: *Diagnostic des Tumeurs Cérébrales et Epreuve de L'Encephalographie Arterielle.* Paris: Masson, 1931. *A Vida Sexual (Fisiologia e Patologia).* Lisbon: Abrantes, 1931. *L'Angiographie Cérébrale, Ses Applications et Résultats en Anatomie, Physiologie et Clinique.* Paris: Masson, 1934. *Cérébrale Arteriographie und Phlebographie.* Berlin: J. Springer, 1940.

For More Information See: *Dictionary of Scientific Biography.* New York: Scribner's, 1971 (Volume 4), 286–87. "Egas Moniz, 1874–1955." *Journal of the International College of Surgeons* 36 (1961): 261–71.

Commentary: Egas Moniz was cited by the Academy "for his discovery of the therapeutic value of leucotomy in certain psychoses." His earlier work was concerned with cerebral angiography, a method of studying blood circulation in the brain. In addition, he was an active and important member of the political scene in Portugal throughout his lifetime. (A.C.)

Hess, Walter Rudolph   333

Prize: Medicine and Physiology, 1949. *Born:* March 17, 1881; Frauenfeld, Switzerland. *Death:* August 12, 1973; Locarno, Switzerland. *Parents:* Father, Clemen Hess; Mother, Gertrud Fischer Saxon Hess. *Nationality:* Swiss. *Religion:* Christian. *Education:* Univ. of Zürich, Switzerland, M.D., 1906. *Spouse:* Louise Sandmeyer, married 1909. *Children:* Gertrud, daughter; Rudolph, son. *Career:* Zürich, Switzerland, Physician, 1905–12; Bonn, Germany, Physician, 1913–17; Univ. of Zürich, Switzerland, Professor and Administrator, 1917–51. *Other Awards:* Marcel Benorst Prize, Switzerland, 1933; Ludwig Medal, German Society for Circulation Research, 1938.

Selected Publications: *Die Funktionelle Organisation des Vegetativen Nervensystems.* Basel, Switzerland: B. Schwabe, 1948. *The Functional Organization of the Diencephalon.* New York: Grune and Stratton, 1957. *The Biology of Mind.* Chicago: Univ. of Chicago Press, 1964. *Biological Order and Brain Organization: Selected Works of W.R. Hess.* New York: Springer-Verlag, 1981.

For More Information See: Ingle, D.J. *A Dozen Doctors.* Chicago: Univ. of Chicago Press, 1963. *Modern Scientists and Engineers.* New York: McGraw-Hill, 1980 (Volume 2), 52. "W.R. Hess: The Control of the Autonomic Nervous System by the Hypothalamus." *The Lancet* 1 (March 17, 1951): 627–29.

Commentary: Walter Hess received the Nobel "for his discovery of the functional organization of the interbrain as a coordinator of the activities of the internal organs," using strictly localized stimuli as the investigating tool. He also worked in the areas of blood pressure and viscosity and in respiratory function. (R.K.)

1950

Hench, Philip Showalter   334

Prize: Medicine and Physiology, 1950. *Born:* February 28, 1896; Pittsburgh, PA. *Death:* March 30, 1965; Ocho Rios,

Jamaica. *Parents:* Father, Jacob Bixler Hench; Mother, Clara John Showalter Hench. *Nationality:* American. *Religion:* Presbyterian. *Education:* Lafayette College, PA, A.B., 1916; Univ. of Pittsburgh, PA, M.D., 1920; Univ. of Minnesota, M.Sc., 1931. *Spouse:* Mary Genevieve Kahler, married July 14, 1927. *Children:* Mary Showalter, daughter; Susan Kahler, daughter; Philip Kahler, son; John Bixler, son. *Career:* St. Francis Hospital, Pittsburgh, PA, Physician, 1920–21; Univ. of Minnesota, Professor, 1921–57. *Other Awards:* Heberden Medal, London, 1942; Lasker Award, American Public Health Association, 1949; Page One Award, Newspaper Guild of New York, 1950; Passano Foundation Award, 1950; Scientific Award, American Pharmaceutical Manufacturers Association, 1950; Special Citation, American Rheumatism Association, 1951; Pennsylvania Ambassador Award, 1951; Northwestern Univ. Centennial Award, 1951; Award of Merit, Masonic Foundation, 1951; Criss Award, 1951; Honor Award, Mississippi Valley Medical Society, 1952; Order of Carlos Finlay, Cuba.

Selected Publications: Chronic Arthritis: Chronic Infectious Arthritis, Chronic Senescent Arthritis, Gout. Baltimore, MD: The Williams and Wilkins Company, 1940. "Effects of Cortisone Acetate and Pituitary ACTH on Rheumatoid Arthritis, Rheumatic Fever, and Certain Other Conditions." *Archives of Internal Medicine* 85 (1950): 545–666 (with E. Kendall). *Cortisone, Hydrocortisone, and Corticotropin (ACTH) in the Treatment of Rheumatoid Arthritis.* Basel, Switzerland: Geigy, 1954.

For More Information See: Current Biography Yearbook. New York: H.W. Wilson, 1950, 230–32. *Modern Scientists and Engineers.* New York: McGraw-Hill, 1980 (Volume 2), 42–43. Rowntree, L.G. *Amid Masters of the Twentieth Century Medicine.* Springfield, IL: C.C. Thomas, 1958.

Commentary: Philip Hench shared the Nobel Prize for "discoveries relating to the hormones of the adrenal cortex, their structure, and biological effects." His use of cortisone in the treatment of arthritis, a disease in which he was an acknowledged expert, led to his receiving the award. Hench was also a scholar of the history of yellow fever. (B.W.)

Kendall, Edward Calvin 335

Prize: Medicine and Physiology, 1950. *Born:* March 8, 1886; Norwalk, CT. *Death:* May 4, 1972; Rahway, NJ. *Parents:* Father, George Stanley Kendall; Mother, Eva Frances Abbott Kendall. *Nationality:* American. *Religion:* Congregationalist. *Education:* Columbia Univ., NY, B.S., 1908; Columbia Univ., NY, M.S., 1909; Columbia Univ., NY, Ph.D., 1910. *Spouse:* Rebecca Kennedy, married December 30, 1915. *Children:* Hugh, son; Roy, son; Norman, son; Elizabeth, daughter. *Career:* Parke, Davis, and Co., Detroit, MI, Researcher, 1910–11; St. Luke's Hospital, NY, Researcher, 1911–14; Univ. of Minnesota, Professor and Administrator, 1914–51. *Other Awards:* John Scott Prize and Premium, Philadelphia, 1921; Chandler Medal, Columbia Univ., NY, 1925; Squibb Award for Outstanding Research in Endocrinology, 1945; Lasker Award, American Public Health Association, 1949; Page One Award, Newspaper Guild of NY, 1950; John Phillips Memorial Award, American College of Physicians, 1950; Research Corporation Award, Research Corporation of NY, 1950; Remsen Memorial Award, MD section of American Chemical Society,

1950; Research Award, American Pharmaceutical Manufacturers Association, 1950; Edgar F. Smith Award, American Chemical Society, 1950; Passano Award, 1950; Medal of Honor, Canadian Pharmaceutical Manufacturers Association, 1950; Dr. C.C. Criss Award, 1951; Award of Merit, Masonic Foundation for Medical Research and Humane Welfare, 1951; Cameron Award, Univ. of Edinburgh, Scotland, 1951; Heberden Society Award, London, 1951; Kober Award, Association of American Physicians, 1952; Alexander Hamilton Medal, Alumni of Columbia College, 1961; Scientific Achievement Award, American Medical Association, 1965.

Selected Publications: "The Isolation in Crystalline Form of the Compound Containing Iodin Which Occurs in the Thyroid: Its Chemical Nature and Physiological Activity." *Transactions of the Association of American Physicians* 30 (1914): 420–49. *Oxidative Catalysis.* New York: Columbia Univ. Press, 1925. "The Identification of a Substance Which Possesses the Qualitative Action of Cortin." *Journal of Biological Chemistry* 116 (1936): 267–76. "Effects of Cortisone Acetate and Pituitary ACTH on Rheumatoid Arthritis, Rheumatic Fever, and Certain Other Conditions." *Archives of Internal Medicine* 85 (1950): 545–666 (with P. Hench).

For More Information See: Biographical Memoirs. National Academy of Sciences. Washington, DC: National Academy of Sciences, 1975 (Volume 48), 249–92. *Dictionary of Scientific Biography.* New York: Scribner's, 1978 (Supplement I), 258–59.

Commentary: Edward Kendall shared the Nobel Prize for "discoveries relating to the hormones of the adrenal cortex, their structure, and biological effects." In addition to his research on cortisone and its therapeutic effects, Kendall also did notable work on thyroxine and thyroid extracts, oxidation in animals, and the action of amylases. (B.W.)

Reichstein, Tadeus 336

Prize: Medicine and Physiology, 1950. *Born:* July 20, 1897; Wloclawek, Poland. *Death:* August 1, 1996; Basel, Switzerland. *Parents:* Father, Isidor Reichstein; Mother, Gustava Brockman Reichstein. *Nationality:* Polish; later Swiss citizen. *Religion:* Jewish. *Education:* Eidenössische Technische Hochschule, Switzerland, B.S., 1920; Eidenössische Technische Hochschule, Switzerland, Ph.D., 1922. *Spouse:* Louise Henriette Quarls Van Ufford, married July 21, 1927. *Children:* Ruth, daughter. *Career:* Eidenössische Technische Hochschule, Switzerland, Professor, 1922–38; Univ. of Basel, Switzerland, Professor and Administrator, 1938–87. *Other Awards:* Cameron Award, Univ. of Edinburgh, Scotland, 1951; Copley Medal, Royal Society, 1968.

Selected Publications: Über das Offenkettige Tropin und Einige Seiner Homologen. Weida i. Thür, Germany: Thomas & Hubert, 1924. "Die Hormone der Nebennierenrinde." In *Handbuch der Biologischen Arbeitsmethoden,* by Emil Abderhalden. Berlin, 1938 (Volume 5), 1367–1439. "The Hormones of the Adrenal Cortex." In *Vitamins and Hormones.* New York: Academic Press, 1943, 346–414 (with C.W. Shoppee).

For More Information See: Current Biography Yearbook. New York: H.W. Wilson, 1951, 512–14. "Tadeus Reichstein." *Journal of Chemical Education* 26 (1949): 529–30.

Commentary: Tadeus Reichstein shared the Nobel Prize for "discoveries relating to the hormones of the adrenal cortex, their structure, and biological effects." Prior to his work on the hormones of the adrenal cortex, Reichstein researched the composition of roasted coffee and coffee, along with synthesized Vitamin C, and studied plant glycosides. The isolation of cortisone and the discovery of its therapeutic value were the end results of the Nobel Prize-winning work. (R.K.)

1951

Theiler, Max 337
Prize: Medicine and Physiology, 1951. *Born:* January 30, 1899; Pretoria, South Africa. *Death:* August 11, 1972; New Haven, CT. *Parents:* Father, Sir Arnold Theiler; Mother, Emma Jegge Theiler. *Nationality:* South African; later American resident. *Religion:* Most probably Christian/Protestant. *Education:* Univ. of London, England, M.D., 1922. *Spouse:* Lillian Graham, married February 18, 1928. *Children:* Elizabeth, daughter. *Career:* Harvard Univ., MA, Professor, 1922–30; Rockefeller Foundation, NY, Researcher and Administrator, 1930–64; Yale Univ., New Haven, CT, Professor, 1964–67; Rockefeller Foundation, NY, Researcher, 1967–72. *Other Awards:* Chalmers Medal, Royal Society of Tropical Medicine and Hygiene, England, 1939; Flattery Medal, Harvard Univ., MA, 1945; Lasker Award, American Public Health Association, 1949.

Selected Publications: "Studies on the Action of Yellow Fever Virus in Mice." *Annals of Tropical Medicine and Parasitology* 24 (1930): 249–72. "The Effect of Prolonged Cultivation in Vitro upon the Pathogenicity of Yellow Fever Virus." *Journal of Experimental Medicine* 65 (1937): 767–86. *Yellow Fever.* Chapter 2. New York: McGraw-Hill, 1951. *The Anthropod-Borne Viruses of Vertebrates: An Account of the Rockefeller Foundation Virus Program.* New Haven, CT: Yale Univ. Press, 1973.

For More Information See: Biographical Encyclopedia of Scientists. New York: Facts on File, 1981, 778–79. *Current Biography Yearbook.* New York: H.W. Wilson, 1952, 586–87.

Commentary: Max Theiler won the Nobel "for his discoveries concerning yellow fever and how to combat it." His contributions to yellow fever research included the theory of transmission, the introduction of a new experimental animal (mice), and the development of a vaccine. During his long career, he also worked on amoebic dysentery, rat bite fever, dengue fever, and Japanese encephalitis. (M.D.C.)

1952

Waksman, Selman Abraham 338
Prize: Medicine and Physiology, 1952. *Born:* July 2, 1888; Priluka, Ukraine, Russia. *Death:* August 16, 1973; Hyannis, MA. *Parents:* Father, Jacob Waksman; Mother, Fradia London Waksman. *Nationality:* Russian; later American citizen. *Religion:* Jewish. *Education:* Rutgers Univ., NJ, B.Sc., 1915; Rutgers Univ., NJ, M.Sc., 1916; Univ. of California, Ph.D., 1918. *Spouse:* Bertha Deborah Mitnick, married August 5, 1916. *Children:* Byron H., son. *Career:* Rutgers Univ., NJ, Professor, 1918–58. *Other Awards:* Nitrate of Soda Research Award, 1930; Passano Foundation

Award, 1947; Award of the Carlsberg Laboratories, Denmark, 1948; New Jersey Agricultural Society Medal, 1948; Lasker Award, American Public Health Association, 1948; Emil Christian Hanson Medal, 1948; Leeuwenhoek Medal, Netherlands Academy of Sciences, 1950; Henrietta Szold Award, 1950; Commander, French Legion of Honour, 1950; British Shalom Humanitarian Award, 1952; Order of Merit of the Rising Sun, Japan, 1952; Great Cross of Public Health, Spain, 1954; St. Vincent Award for Medical Sciences, Academy of Sciences of Torino, Italy, 1954; Instituto Curlo Forlanini Medal, 1959; American Trudeau Medal, 1961; Commendatore Order of Southern Cross of Brazil, 1963.

Selected Publications: Enzymes: Properties, Distribution, Methods and Applications. Baltimore, MD: Williams and Wilkins, 1926 (with W.C. Davison). *Humus: Origin, Chemical Composition, and Importance in Nature.* Baltimore, MD: Williams and Wilkins, 1936. *Neomycin: Its Nature, Formation, Isolation and Practical Application.* New Brunswick, NJ: Rutgers Univ. Press, 1953. *The Actinomycetes.* 3 volumes. Baltimore, MD: Williams and Wilkins, 1959–62. *Scientific Contributions of Selman A. Waksman; Selected Articles Published in Honor of His 80th Birthday.* New Brunswick, NJ: Rutgers Univ. Press, 1968.

For More Information See: National Cyclopedia of American Biography. New York: James T. White, 1960 (Volume I), 312–13. Waksman, Selman. *My Life with the Microbes.* New York: Simon and Schuster, 1954.

Commentary: The Academy cited Selman Waksman "for his discovery of streptomycin, the first antibiotic effective against tuberculosis." His other research was concerned with the microbiology in soil and sea; investigation of organic matter decomposition in various soils; the study of bacteria, fungi, and actinomycetes; and the transformation of nitrogen and carbon compounds. (R.K.)

1953

Krebs, Hans Adolf, Sir 339
Prize: Medicine and Physiology, 1953. *Born:* August 25, 1900; Hildesheim, Germany. *Death:* November 22, 1981; Oxford, England. *Parents:* Father, Georg Krebs; Mother, Alma Davidson Krebs. *Nationality:* German; later British citizen. *Religion:* Jewish. *Education:* Univ. of Hamburg, Germany, M.D., 1925; Cambridge Univ., England, M.S., 1934. *Spouse:* Margaret Cicely Fieldhouse, married 1938. *Children:* Paul, son; John, son; Helen, daughter. *Career:* Kaiser Wilhelm Institute, Berlin, Germany, Researcher, 1926–30; Municipal Hospital, Altona, Germany, Physician, 1930–32; Univ. of Freiberg, Germany, Professor, 1932–33; Cambridge Univ., England, Professor, 1933–35; Univ. of Sheffield, England, Professor, 1935–54; Oxford Univ., England, Professor, 1954–67. *Other Awards:* Lasker Award, 1953; Royal Medal, Royal Society, 1954; Gold Medal, Netherlands Society for Physics, Medical Science and Surgery, 1958; Knighthood, 1958; Copley Medal, 1961.

Selected Publications: "Metabolism of Acetoacetic Acid in Animal Tissues." *Nature* 154 (August 12, 1944): 209–10 (with L. V. Eggleston). "Urea Synthesis in Mammalian

Liver." *Nature* (June 14, 1947): 808–09 (with others). "Tricarboxylic Acid Cycle." *Harvey Lectures* 44 (1950): 165–99. "A Survey of the Energy Transformations in Living Matter." *Ergcbn. Physiol. Biol. Chem. Exp. Pharmak* 49 (1957): 212 (with H. Kornberg). *The Metabolic Roles of Citrate*. London: Academic Press, 1968. *Essays in Cell Metabolism*. New York: Wiley, 1970.

For More Information See: Biographical Memoirs. Royal Society of London. London: Royal Society, 1984 (Volume 30), 349. *Current Biography Yearbook*. New York: H.W. Wilson, 1954, 384–85. Holmes, F. *Hans Krebs*. New York: Oxford Univ. Press, 1991–93. *Reminiscences and Reflections*. New York: Oxford Univ. Press, 1982.

Commentary: Hans Krebs's Nobel Prize was granted "for his discovery of the citric acid cycle," now known as the Krebs cycle, which noted the oxidation of pyruvic acid to carbon dioxide and water. Other metabolic paths, especially energy-related (which were major interests), included the ornithine cycle of urea synthesis in liver and the glyoxalate cycle of fat metabolism. (J.E.H.)

Lipmann, Fritz Albert 340

Prize: Medicine and Physiology, 1953. *Born:* June 12, 1899; Königsburg, Germany. *Death:* July 24, 1986; Poughkeepsie, NY. *Parents:* Father, Leopold Lipmann; Mother, Gertrude Lachmanski Lipmann. *Nationality:* German; later American citizen. *Religion:* Jewish. *Education:* Univ. of Berlin, Germany, M.D., 1924; Univ. of Berlin, Germany, Ph.D., 1927. *Spouse:* Elfreda M. Hall, married June 23, 1931. *Children:* Stephen Hall, son. *Career:* Kaiser Wilhelm Institute, Berlin and Heidelberg, Germany, Researcher, 1927–30; Fischer's Laboratory, Berlin, Germany, Researcher, 1930–31; Rockefeller Institute for Medical Research, NY, Researcher, 1931–32; Carlsburg Foundation, Copenhagen, Denmark, Researcher, 1932–39; Cornell Univ., Ithaca, NY, Researcher, 1939–41; Massachusetts General Hospital, Boston, Researcher and Administrator, 1941–57; Harvard Univ., MA, Professor, 1949–57; Rockefeller Univ., NY, Professor, 1957–86. *Other Awards:* Carl Neuberg Medal, 1948; Mead Johnson and Company Award, 1948; National Medal of Science, 1966.

Selected Publications: "Fermentation of Phosphogluconic Acid." *Nature* (October 3, 1936): 588–89. "Colored Intermediate on Reduction of Vitamin B1." *Nature* (November 13, 1937): 849. "Coupling Between Pyruvic Acid Dehydrogenation and Adenylic Acid Phosphorylation." *Nature* (February 18, 1939): 281. "Biosynthetic Mechanisms." *Harvey Lectures* 44 (1950): 99–123.

For More Information See: Current Biography Yearbook. New York: H.W. Wilson, 1954, 413–14. *The Excitement and Fascination of Science*. Palo Alto, CA: Annual Reviews, Inc., 1990, Vol. 3, Part 1, 383–415. *Wanderings of a Biochemist*. New York: Wiley, 1971.

Commentary: Fritz Lipmann received the Nobel Prize "for his discovery of Coenzyme A and its importance for intermediary metabolism." Lipmann's major work was in the classification of energy-producing phosphates, but his research endeavors also included work with the thyroid gland, fibroblasts and the Pasteur effect, glycolysis in embryo cell metabolism, and the mechanism of peptide and protein synthesis. (R.K.)

1954

Enders, John Franklin 341

Prize: Medicine and Physiology, 1954. *Born:* February 10, 1897; West Hartford, CT. *Death:* September 8, 1985; Waterford, CT. *Parents:* Father, John Ostrom Enders; Mother, Harriet Goulden Whitmore Enders. *Nationality:* American. *Religion:* Protestant. *Education:* Yale Univ., CT, A.B., 1920; Harvard Univ., MA, M.A., 1922; Harvard Univ., MA, Ph.D., 1930. *Spouse:* Sarah Frances Bennett, married September 17, 1927, died 1943; Carolyn Keane, married May 12, 1951. *Children:* John Ostrom II, son; Sarah Steffian, daughter; William Edmund Keane, stepson. *Career:* U.S. Army, 1917–20; Harvard Univ., MA, Professor, 1929–77. *Other Awards:* Commander, Order National de la Republic de Haute Volta; Passano Foundation Award, 1953; Lasker Award, 1954; Kimball Award, 1954; Kyer Award, U.S. Public Health Service, 1955; Chapin Award, 1955; Bruce Award, American College of Physicians, 1956; Cameron Prize, Univ. of Edinburgh, Scotland, 1960; Howard Taylor Ricketts Memorial Award, Univ. of Chicago, 1962; New England Israel Freedom Award, 1962; Robert Koch Medal, Germany, 1962; Science Achievement Award, American Medical Association, 1963; Presidential Medal of Freedom, 1963.

Selected Publications: Immunity: Principles and Application in Medicine and Public Health. New York: Macmillan, 1939 (with Hans Zinsser and Leroy D. Fothergill). "Cultivation of the Lansing Strain of Poliomyelitis Virus in Cultures of Various Human Embryonic Tissues." *Science* 109 (January 28, 1949): 85–87. "Mumps." In *Viraland Ricketsial Infections of Man*. Philadelphia, PA: Lippincott, 1959, 780–89.

For More Information See: Biographical Memoirs of the Fellows of the Royal Society. London: Royal Society, 1987 (Volume 33), 211. *Biographical Encyclopedia of Scientists*. New York: Facts on File, 1981, 239. *Current Biography Yearbook*. New York: H.W. Wilson, 1955, 182–84.

Commentary: John Enders shared the Nobel Prize for "discovery of the ability of the poliomyelitis virus to grow in cultures of different tissues." He pioneered work in virus study and vaccine development that eventually led to safe vaccines for polio, measles, German measles, and mumps. Enders also worked in the areas of cancer and genetics. (R.K.)

Robbins, Frederick Chapman 342

Prize: Medicine and Physiology, 1954. *Born:* August 25, 1916; Auburn, AL. *Parents:* Father, Dr. William Jacob Robbins; Mother, Christine F. Chapman. *Nationality:* American. *Religion:* Presbyterian background. *Education:* Univ. of Missouri, B.A., 1936; Univ. of Missouri, B.S., 1938; Harvard Univ., MA, M.D., 1940. *Spouse:* Alice Havemeyer Northrop, married June 19, 1948. *Children:* Alice, daughter; Louise, daughter. *Career:* Children's Hospital, Boston, MA, Physician, 1946–52; Harvard Univ., MA, Professor, 1950–52; Case Western Reserve Univ., OH, Professor and Administrator, 1952–80; Institute of Medicine, Bethesda, MD, Researcher, 1980–85. *Other Awards:* Bronze Star, 1945; Mead Johnson Prize, 1953; Medical Mutual Honor Award, 1969; Ohio Governor's Award, 1971; Abraham Flexner Award, 1987.

Selected Publications: "Cultivation of the Lansing Strain of Poliomyelitis Virus in Cultures of Various Human Embryonic Tissues." *Science* 109 (January 28, 1949): 85–87 (with T.H. Weller and J.F. Enders). *Proceedings of the Society for Experimental Biology and Medicine* 72 (1949): 153–55 (with T.H. Weller and J.F. Enders). "Studies of the Cultivation of Poliomyelitis Viruses in Tissue Culture. I. The Propagation of Poliomyelitis Viruses in Suspended Cell Cultures of Various Human Tissues." *Journal of Immunology* 69 (1952): 645–71 (with others).

For More Information See: Biographical Encyclopedia of Scientists. New York: Facts on File, 1981, 682. *Current Biography Yearbook.* New York: H.W. Wilson, 1955, 182–84.

Commentary: Frederick Robbins received the Nobel for "discovery of the ability of the poliomyelitis virus to grow in cultures of different tissues." His research efforts also included work on the parasitic microorganisms causing Q fever. (R.K.)

Weller, Thomas Huckle 343

Prize: Medicine and Physiology, 1954. *Born:* June 15, 1915; Ann Arbor, MI. *Parents:* Father, Carl Vernon Weller; Mother, Elsie Huckle Weller. *Nationality:* American. *Religion:* Most probably Christian. *Education:* Univ. of Michigan, B.S., 1936; Univ. of Michigan, M.S., 1937; Harvard Univ., MA, M.D., 1940. *Spouse:* Kathleen R. Fahey, married August 18, 1945. *Children:* Peter Fahey, son; Robert Andrew, son; Nancy Kathleen, daughter; Janet Louise, daughter. *Career:* Harvard Univ., MA, Professor and Administrator, 1940–85. *Other Awards:* E. Mead Johnson Award, American Academy of Pediatrics, 1953; Kimble Methodology Award, 1954; George Ledlie Prize, 1963; Weinstein Cerebral Palsy Award, 1973; Bristol Award, Infectious Diseases Society of America, 1980; Gold Medal, Univ. of Costa Rica, 1984; First Science Achievement Award, VZV Research Foundation, 1993; Walter Reed Medal, American Society of Tropical Medicine, 1996.

Selected Publications: "Cultivation of the Lansing Strain of Poliomyelitis Virus in Cultures of Various Human Embryonic Tissues." *Science* 109 (January 28, 1949): 85–87 (with F.C. Robbins and J.F. Enders). *Proceedings of the Society for Experimental Biology and Medicine* 72 (1949): 153–55 (with F.C. Robbins and J.F. Enders). "Studies of the Cultivation of Poliomyelitis Viruses in Tissue Culture. I. The Propagation of Poliomyelitis Viruses in Suspended Cell Cultures of Various Human Tissues." *Journal of Immunology* 69 (1952): 645–71 (with others).

For More Information See: Biographical Encyclopedia of Scientists. New York: Facts on File, 1981, 834. *Current Biography Yearbook.* New York: H.W. Wilson, 1955, 182–84.

Commentary: Thomas Weller's Nobel was shared for "discovery of the ability of the poliomyelitis virus to grow in cultures of different tissues." Prior to this research, Weller had grown both rubella and chicken-pox viruses in tissue cultures. His work led to the development of a successful polio vaccine. (R.K.)

1955

Theorell, Axel Hugo Theodor 344

Prize: Medicine and Physiology, 1955. *Born:* July 6, 1903; Linköping, Sweden. *Death:* August 15, 1982; Stockholm,

Sweden. *Parents:* Father, Thure Theorell; Mother, Armida Bill Theorell. *Nationality:* Swedish. *Religion:* Lutheran. *Education:* Univ. of Stockholm, Sweden, Bachelor of Medicine, 1924; Univ. of Stockholm, Sweden, M.D., 1930. *Spouse:* Elin Margit Elisabeth Alenius, married 1931. *Children:* Klas, son; Henning, son; Tores, son; Eva Kristina, daughter, died 1935. *Career:* Univ. of Uppsala, Sweden, Professor, 1930–36; Nobel Medical Institute, Stockholm, Sweden, Professor and Administrator, 1937–70. *Other Awards:* First Class Commander, Royal Order of North Star; Legion d'Honneur, France; Officer, Order Southern Cross, Brazil.

Selected Publications: "The Heme-Protein Linkage in Hemoglobin and in Horseradish Peroxidase." Arkiv Kemi Mineral. Geol. 16A (1943): 1–18. "Catalases and Peroxidases." In *The Enzymes.* New York: Academic Press, 1951, 397–427. "Function and Structure of Liver Alcohol Dehydrogenase." *Harvey Lectures* 61 (1967): 17–41. "Introduction to Mechanisms of Enzyme Actions." In *Metabolic Regulation and Enzyme Action.* London: Academic Press, 1970, 179–80. "My Life with Proteins and Prosthetic Groups." In *Proteolysis and Physiological Regulation.* New York: Academic, 1975, 1–27.

For More Information See: Biographical Memoirs of the Fellows of the Royal Society. London: Royal Society, 1983 (Volume 29), 585–621. *Current Biography Yearbook.* New York: H.W. Wilson, 1956, 622–24.

Commentary: Axel Theorell won the Nobel Prize "for his discoveries concerning the nature and mode of action of oxidation enzymes." In pioneer research, he found that the yellow enzyme isolated from yeast consists of two parts, the first an enzyme of vitamin B2 plus a phosphate group, the second a protein apoenzyme. He further elaborated on the mechanism by which the coenzyme oxidizes glucose. Theorell also studied Cytochrome C, isolated crystalline myoglobin, and researched alcohol dehydrogenase, which resulted in the development of blood tests for alcohol levels. (R.K.)

1956

Cournand, André Frédéric 345

Prize: Medicine and Physiology, 1956. *Born:* September 24, 1895; Paris, France. *Death:* February 19, 1988; Great Barrington, MA. *Parents:* Father, Jules Cournand; Mother, Marguerite Weber Cournand. *Nationality:* French; later American citizen. *Religion:* Agnostic; from a Christian background. *Education:* Univ. of Paris-Sorbonne, France, B.A., 1913; Univ. of Paris-Sorbonne, France, P.C.B., 1914; Univ. of Paris, France, M.D., 1930. *Spouse:* Sibylle Blumer, married 1924, died 1959; Ruth Fabian, married 1963, died 1973; Beatrice Bishop Berle, married August 29, 1975. *Children:* Muriel, daughter; Marie-Eve, daughter; Marie Claire, daughter; Pierre, son (adopted). *Career:* French Army, 1915–19; Columbia Univ., NY, Professor and Researcher, 1930–64. *Other Awards:* Croix de Guerre, France; Silver Medal, Univ. of Paris, France, 1930; Anders Retzius Silver Medal, Swedish Society of Internal Medicine, 1946; Lasker Award, 1949; John Phillips Memorial Award, American College of Physicians, 1952; Gold Medal, Royal Academy of Medicine, Belgium, 1956; Jiminiz Diaz Prize, 1970.

Selected Publications: "Catheterization of the Right Auricle in Man." *Proceedings of the Society for Experimental Biology and Medicine* 46 (1941): 462–66. *Cardiac Catheterization in Congenital Heart Disease: A Clinical and Physiological Study in Infants and Children.* New York: Commonwealth Fund, 1949 (with J.S. Baldwin and A. Himmelstein). *Pulmonary Circulation: Historical Background and Present Day Status of Knowledge in Man.* Leiden, Netherlands: Universitaire Pers, 1959.

For More Information See: Current Biography Yearbook. New York: H.W. Wilson, 1957, 117–19. *From Roots to Late Budding: The Intellectual Adventures of a Medical Student.* New York: Gardner Press, 1985.

Commentary: André Cournand shared the Nobel for "discoveries concerning heart catheterization and pathological changes in the circulatory systems." Cournand's work with Dickinson Richards was the product of a lifelong interest in the heart and lung systems of the body. His later interests extended to the history of science and scientific ethics and psychology. (R.K.)

Forssmann, Werner Theodor Otto 346

Prize: Medicine and Physiology, 1956. *Born:* August 29, 1904; Berlin, Germany. *Death:* June 1, 1979; Schopfheim, Germany. *Parents:* Father, Julius Forssmann; Mother, Emmy Hindenberg Forssmann. *Nationality:* German. *Religion:* Evangelical. *Education:* Univ. of Berlin, Germany, M.D., 1929. *Spouse:* Elsbet Engel, married 1933. *Children:* Klaus, son; Knut, son; Jorg, son; Wolf, son; Bernd, son; Renate, daughter. *Career:* Augusta Viktoria Hospital, Eberswalde, Germany, Physician, 1929–30; Ferdinand Sauerbruch Clinic, Berlin, Germany, Physician and Researcher, 1931–32; City Hospital, Dresden, Germany, Physician and Researcher, 1933–38; German Army, Physician, 1939–45; Bad Kreuznach, Germany, Physician, 1946–58; Dusseldorf Evangelical Hospital, Germany, Physician, 1958–79. *Other Awards:* Leibniz Medal, German Academy of Sciences, 1954; Grosses Bundesverdienst Kreuz, 1958, 1964; Gold Medal, Societa Medico Chirurgica di Ferrara, 1968; Ordentliches Mitglied der Rheinisch-Westfallschoen Akademie der Wissenschaften des Landes Nordrhein Westfalen, 1968; Commander, Ordre des Palmes Academiques, 1971.

Selected Publications: "Die Sondierung des Rechten Herzens." *Klinische Wochenschrift* 8 (1929): 2085–87. "Technik und Praktische Bedentung der Herzkatheterung fur die Funktionelle Diagnostik und die Therapie von Herz- und Lungenerkrankungen." *Med. Klin., Berl* 48 (October 30, 1953): 1614–20 (with W. Bolt and H. Rink).

For More Information See: Current Biography Yearbook. New York: H.W. Wilson, 1957, 190–92. *Selbstversuch: Erinnerungen Eines Chirurgen.* Düsseldorf, Germany: Droste, 1972 (*Experiments on Myself: Memoirs of a Surgeon in Germany.* Tr. by Hilary Davies. New York: St. Martin's Press, 1974).

Commentary: Werner Forssmann received the Nobel in recognition of "discoveries concerning heart catheterization and pathological changes in the circulatory system." He researched and introduced the process that was later developed further by Richards and Cournand. He specialized both in work and in research as a heart and pulmonary surgeon and urologist. (R.K.)

Richards, Dickinson Woodruff 347

Prize: Medicine and Physiology, 1956. *Born:* October 30, 1895; Orange, NJ. *Death:* February 23, 1973; Lakeville, CT. *Parents:* Father, Dickinson Woodruff Richards; Mother, Sally Lambert Richards. *Nationality:* American. *Religion:* Presbyterian. *Education:* Yale Univ., CT, A.B., 1917; Columbia Univ., NY, M.A., 1922; Columbia Univ., NY, M.D., 1923. *Spouse:* Constance B. Riley, married September 19, 1931. *Children:* Ida E., daughter; Ann H., daughter; Constance L., daughter; Gertrude W., daughter. *Career:* Presbyterian Hospital, NY, Physician, 1923–27; National Institute for Medical Research, London, England, Researcher, 1927–28; Columbia Univ., NY, Professor, 1928–73. *Other Awards:* Chevalier Legion of Honor, France.

Selected Publications: "The Circulation in Traumatic Shock in Man." *Harvey Lectures* 39 (1943–44): 217. "Cardiac Output by the Catheterization Technique in Various Clinical Conditions." *Federation Proceedings* 4 (1945): 215. "Contributions of Right Heart Catheterization to the Physiology of Congestive Heart Failure." *American Journal of Medicine* 3 (1947): 434.

For More Information See: Current Biography Yearbook. New York: H.W. Wilson, 1957, 457–59. *The National Cyclopedia of American Biography.* New York: James T. White, 1960 (Volume I), 336–37.

Commentary: Dickinson Richards shared the Nobel for "discoveries concerning heart catheterization and pathological changes in the circulatory systems." Richards's work with Andre Cournand made feasible the application of the method earlier devised by Werner Forssmann. Throughout a long career, he continued to investigate the problems of pulmonary and cardiac physiology and the diagnosis of clinical disorders in these systems. (R.K.)

1957

Bovet, Daniel 348

Prize: Medicine and Physiology, 1957. *Born:* March 23, 1907; Neuchatel, Switzerland. *Death:* April 9, 1992; Rome, Italy. *Parents:* Father, Pierre Bovet; Mother, Amy Babut Bovet. *Nationality:* Swiss; later Italian citizen. *Religion:* From Calvinist background. *Education:* Univ. of Geneva, Switzerland, M.S., 1927; Univ. of Geneva, Switzerland, D.Sc., 1929. *Spouse:* Filomena Nitti, married March 19, 1938. *Children:* 2 daughters; Danièle, son. *Career:* Institut Pasteur, Paris, France, Researcher, 1929–47; Instituto Superiore di Sanita, Rome, Italy, Researcher, 1947–64; Univ. of Sassari, Italy, Professor, 1964–71; Rome Univ., Italy, Professor, 1971–77. *Other Awards:* Martin Damourette Prize, France, 1936; General Muteau Prize, Italy, 1941; Chevalier de la Legion d'Honneur, 1946; Burgi Prize, Switzerland, 1949; Addingham Gold Medal, England, 1952; Order of Merit, Italy, 1959.

Selected Publications: Structure Chimique et Activité Pharmacodynamique du Systeme Nerveux Vegetatif. Basel, Switzerland: Karger, 1948 (with F. Bovet-Nitti). *Curare and Curare-like Agents.* Amsterdam: Elsevier Publishing Co., 1959 (with F. Bovet-Nitti and G.B. Marini-Bettolo). *Controlling Drugs.* San Francisco, CA: Jossey-Bass, 1974 (with others).

For More Information See: Biographical Encyclopedia of Scientists. New York: Facts on File, 1981, 98–99. Biographical Memoirs of the Fellows of the Royal Society. London: Royal Society, 1994 (Volume 39), 59. Current Biography Yearbook. New York: H.W. Wilson, 1958, 55–56.

Commentary: Daniele Bovet was granted the Nobel "for his discoveries relating to synthetic compounds that inhibit the action of certain body substances, and especially their action on the vascular system and the skeletal muscles." Among his contributions was pioneer work on the sulfanilimids, antihistamines, curare-like anesthetics, brain-influencing drugs, and oxytocic substances. (A.N.)

1958

Beadle, George Wells 349

Prize: Medicine and Physiology, 1958. *Born:* October 22, 1903; Wahoo, NE. *Death:* June 9, 1989; Pomona, CA. *Parents:* Father, Chauncey Elmer Beadle; Mother, Hattie Albro Beadle. *Nationality:* American. *Religion:* Most probably Christian/Protestant. *Education:* Univ. of Nebraska, B.S., 1926; Univ. of Nebraska, M.S., 1927; Cornell Univ., NY, Ph.D., 1931. *Spouse:* Marion Cecile Hill, married August 22, 1928, divorced 1953; Muriel McClure Burnett, married August 12, 1953. *Children:* David, son. *Career:* Cornell Univ., Ithaca, NY, Researcher, 1926–31; California Institute of Technology, Professor, 1931–35; Institut de Biologie, Paris, France, Researcher, 1935; Harvard Univ., MA, Professor, 1936–37; Stanford Univ., CA, Professor, 1937–46; California Institute of Technology, Professor, 1946–61; Univ. of Chicago, IL, Professor and Administrator, 1961–75. *Other Awards:* Lasker Award, American Public Health Association, 1950; Dyer Award, 1951; Emil C. Hansen Prize, Denmark, 1953; Albert Einstein Commemorative Award in Science, 1958; National Award of American Cancer Society, 1959; Kimber Genetics Award, National Academy of Science, 1960; Priestley Memorial Award, 1967; Donald Forsha Jones Medal, 1972.

Selected Publications: An Introduction to Genetics. Philadelphia, PA: W.B. Saunders, 1939 (with A.H. Sturtevant). The Language of the Gene. London: Univ. of London Press, 1960. Genetics and Modern Biology. Philadelphia, PA: American Philosophical Society, 1963. The Language of Life. New York: Doubleday, 1966 (with M.M. Beadle).

For More Information See: Current Biography Yearbook. New York: H.W. Wilson, 1956, 37–39. National Cyclopedia of American Biography. New York: James T. White, 1964 (Current Volume J), 372–73. New York Times Biographical Service (June 12, 1989): 531. Biographical Memoirs. National Academy of Sciences. Washington, DC: National Academy Press, 1990, Volume 59, 27.

Commentary: George Beadle shared the Nobel Prize for "fundamental contributions in the field of biochemical and microbial genetics." His genetic studies progressed from maize to Drosophila to Neurospora crassa, the red bread mold. In the studies of *Neurospora*, Beadle found mutations by irradiation that could be reversed by Vitamin B6 additions and concluded that specific genes controlled chemical synthesis in cells. The research for which the Nobel was awarded laid the foundations of biochemical genetics. (P.M.)

Lederberg, Joshua 350

Prize: Medicine and Physiology, 1958. *Born:* May 23, 1925; Montclair, NJ. *Parents:* Father, Zwi Hirsch Lederberg; Mother, Esther Goldenbaum Lederberg. *Nationality:* American. *Religion:* Jewish. *Education:* Columbia Univ., NY, B.A., 1944; Yale Univ., CT, Ph.D., 1947. *Spouse:* Esther Miriam Zimmer, married 1946, divorced 1968; Marguerite Stein Kirsch, married April 5, 1968. *Children:* David, son; Anne, daughter. *Career:* Univ. of Wisconsin, Professor, 1947–58; Stanford Univ., CA, Professor and Administrator, 1958–78; Rockefeller Univ., NY, President, 1978–90; Professor Emeritus, 1990-. *Other Awards:* Eli Lilly Award, 1953; Pasteur Award, Society of Illinois Bacteriologists, 1956; Procter Prize, 1982. National Medal of Science, 1989; Alan Newell Award, ACM, 1996; John Stearns Award, New York Academy of Medicine, 1996; Maxwell Finland Award, NCIN, 1997.

Selected Publications: Papers in Microbial Genetics. Madison, WI: Univ. of Wisconsin Press, 1952. "Viruses, Genes and Cells." Bacteriological Reviews 21 (1957): 133–39. "Bacterial Reproduction." Harvey Lectures 53 (1959): 69–82. Tables and Algorithms for Calculating Functional Groups of Organic Molecules in High Mass Spectrometry. Palo Alto, CA: Stanford Univ. Press, 1964.

For More Information See: Biographical Encyclopedia of Scientists. New York: Facts on File, 1981, 479–80. Current Biography Yearbook. New York: H.W. Wilson, 1959, 251–52. The Excitement and Fascination of Science. Palo Alto, CA: Annual Reviews, Inc., 1990, Vol. 3, Part 1, 893–915.

Commentary: Joshua Lederberg's Nobel was granted "for his discoveries concerning genetic recombination and the organization of the genetic material of bacteria." His studies showed that, in some cases, bacteria were sexual, based on the work with *Escherichio coli*. Lederberg also studied bacterial transduction—genetic information transfer across barriers by *Salmonella*—that led to the later work in genetic engineering. (J.C.)

Tatum, Edward Lawrie 351

Prize: Medicine and Physiology, 1958. *Born:* December 14, 1909; Boulder, CO. *Death:* November 5, 1975; New York, NY. *Parents:* Father, Arthur Lawrie Tatum; Mother, Mabel Webb Tatum. *Nationality:* American. *Religion:* From Quaker background. *Education:* Univ. of Wisconsin, A.B., 1931; Univ. of Wisconsin, M.A., 1932; Univ. of Wisconsin, Ph.D., 1934. *Spouse:* June Alton, married July 28, 1934, divorced 1956; Viola Kantor, married December 16, 1956, died April 21, 1974; Elsie Berglund, married 1974. *Children:* Margaret Carol, daughter; Barbara Ann, daughter. *Career:* Univ. of Wisconsin, Researcher, 1935; Univ. of Utrecht, Netherlands, Researcher, 1936–37; Stanford Univ., CA, Professor, 1937–45; Yale Univ., New Haven, CT, Professor, 1948–56; Stanford Univ., CA, Professor, 1956–57; Rockefeller Institute, NY, Professor, 1957–75. *Other Awards:* Remsen Award, American Chemical Society, 1953.

Selected Publications: "Genetic Control of Biochemical Reactions in Neurospora." Proceedings of the National Academy of Sciences 27 (1941): 499–506 (with G. Beadle). "Genetic Control of Biochemical Reactions in Neurospora: An Aminobenzoicless Mutant." Proceedings of the National

Academy of Sciences 28 (1942): 234–64 (with G. Beadle). "Gene Recombination in the Bacterium Escherichia Coli." *Journal of Bacteriology* 53 (1947): 673–84 (with J. Lederberg). "Sex in Bacteria: Genetic Studies, 1945–1952." *Science* 118 (1953): 169–74 (with J. Lederberg).

For More Information See: Current Biography Yearbook. New York: H.W. Wilson, 1959, 437–39. *The Excitement and Fascination of Science.* Palo Alto, CA: Annual Reviews, Inc., 1990, Vol. 3, Part 1, 775–79. *National Cyclopedia of American Biography.* New York: James T. White, 1964 (Current Volume J): 475. *Biographical Memoirs. National Academy of Sciences.* Washington, DC: National Academy Press, 1990, Volume 59, 357.

Commentary: Edward Tatum shared the Nobel Prize "for discovering that genes act by regulating specific chemical processes." His career included work on the nutrition and metabolism of Drosophila, on inherited defects in eye pigment development in Drosophila, on mutation and hereditary characteristic transmission in relation to genes in *Neurospora crassa*, on biochemical mutations and nutrition of *Escherichia coli*, and on genetic recombination. (P.M.)

1959

Kornberg, Arthur   352

Prize: Medicine and Physiology, 1959. *Born:* March 3, 1918; Brooklyn, NY. *Parents:* Father, Joseph Kornberg; Mother, Lena Katz Kornberg. *Nationality:* American. *Religion:* Jewish. *Education:* City College of New York, B.S., 1937; Univ. of Rochester, NY, M.D., 1941. *Spouse:* Sylvy R. Levy, married November 21, 1943, died 1986; Charlene Walsh Levering, married 1988, died 1995. *Children:* Roger David, son; Thomas Bill, son; Kenneth Andrew, son. *Career:* National Institutes of Health, MD, Researcher, 1942–52; Washington Univ., MO, Professor, 1953–59; Stanford Univ., CA, Professor, 1959–88. *Other Awards:* Paul-Lewis Laboratory Award, American Chemical Society, 1951; Silver Medal, Federal Security Agency, 1952; Lucy Wortham James Award, James Ewing Society, 1968; Max Berg Award, 1968; Science Achievement Award, American Medical Association, 1968; Borden Award, American Association of Medical Colleges, 1968; Albert Gallatin Medal, New York Univ., 1970; J.M. Russell Medal, 1970; National Medal of Science, United States, 1980; Gairdner Foundation International Award, 1995.

Selected Publications: Harvey Lectures 53 (1957–58): 83. *Enzymatic Synthesis of DNA.* New York: Wiley, 1961. "Enzymatic Synthesis of DNA. XXIII. Synthesis of Circular Replicative Form of Phage Phi X174DNA." *Proceedings of the National Academy of Sciences* 58 (1967): 1723–30 (with M. Goulian). "Enzymatic Synthesis of DNA. XXIV. Synthesis of Infectious Phage Phi X174DNA." *Proceedings of the National Academy of Sciences* 58 (1967): 2321–28 (with M. Goulian and R. Sinsheimer). *DNA Replication.* New York: W.H. Freeman, 1980.

For More Information See: Current Biography Yearbook. New York: H.W. Wilson, 1968, 210–12. *For the Love of Enzymes.* Cambridge, MA: Harvard Univ. Press, 1991. *New York Times* (October 16, 1959): 1.

Commentary: Arthur Kornberg won the Nobel Prize for his contributions "to the discovery of the mechanisms in the biological synthesis of ribonucleic acid and deoxyribonucleic acid." At the beginning of his career, Kornberg studied the mechanisms of formation of important coenzymes (flavin adenine dinucleotide and nicotinamide adenine dinucleotide). This led to the discovery of the enzyme DNA polymerase, which catalyzes formation of short DNA molecules. Kornberg's later research centered around reactions in the Krebs cycle and on phospholipid synthesis. (R.K.)

Ochoa, Severo   353

Prize: Medicine and Physiology, 1959. *Born:* September 24, 1905; Luarca, Spain. *Death:* November 1, 1993; Madrid, Spain. *Parents:* Father, Severo Ochoa; Mother, Carmen de Albornoz Ochoa. *Nationality:* Spanish; later American citizen. *Religion:* Christian. *Education:* Malaga College, Spain, B.A., 1921; Univ. of Madrid, Spain, M.D., 1929. *Spouse:* Carmen Garcia Cobian, married July 8, 1931, died 1986. *Children:* None. *Career:* Kaiser-Wilhelm Institute, Berlin, Germany, Researcher, 1929–37; Marine Biological Laboratory, England, Researcher, 1937; Univ. of Oxford, England, Researcher, 1938–40; Washington Univ., MO, Researcher, 1941–42; New York Univ., Professor, 1942–75; Roche Institute of Molecular Biology, NJ, Researcher, 1975–85. *Other Awards:* Neuberg Medal Award, Society of European Chemists, 1951; Charles Meyer Price Award, Societé de Chimie Biologique, 1955; Borden Award, Association of American Medical Colleges, 1958; New York Univ. Medal, 1960; Order of the Rising Sun, 2nd Class Gold Medal, Japan, 1967; Quevedo Gold Medal, Spain, 1969; Albert Gallatin Medal, 1970; National Medal of Science, 1979.

Selected Publications: "Enzymatic Synthesis and Breakdown of Polynucleotides; Polynucleotide Phosphorylase." *Journal of the American Chemical Society* 77 (1955): 3165–66 (with M. Grunberg-Manago). "Enzymatic Synthesis of Nucleic Acidlike Polynucleotides." *Science* 122 (1955): 907–10 (with M. Grunberg-Manago and P.J. Ortiz). "Small Polyribonucleotides with 5^1 Phosphomonoester End-Groups." *Science* 123 (1956): 415–17 (with L.A. Heppel and P.J. Ortiz). *La Clare Genetica, Base Quimica de la Herencia.* Barcelona, Spain: Real Academia de Ciencias y Artes de Barcelona, 1964. *Macromolecules: Biosynthesis and Function.* New York: Academic Press, 1970. *Viruses, Oncogenes, and Cancer.* New York: Karger, 1985.

For More Information See: Current Biography Yearbook. New York: H.W. Wilson, 1962, 327–29. *The Excitement and Fascination of Science.* Palo Alto, CA: Annual Reviews, Inc., 1990, Vol. 3, Part 1, 291–320. Gomez-Santos, M. *Severo Ochoa.* Madrid: Piramida, 1993. *Science* (October 23, 1959): 1099–1100.

Commentary: Severo Ochoa shared the Nobel Prize for his contributions "to the discovery of the mechanisms in the biological synthesis of ribonucleic acid and deoxyribonucleic acid." His research on high-energy phosphates and their role in the body's energy processes resulted in the discovery and application of the enzyme polynucleotide phosphorylase, which catalyzes the synthesis of RNA. Ochoa also studied enzyme catalysis of reactions in the Krebs cycle. (J.C.)

1960

Burnet, Frank MacFarlane, Sir   354

Prize: Medicine and Physiology, 1960. *Born:* September 3, 1899; Traralgon, Victoria, Australia. *Death:* August 31, 1985; Melbourne, Australia. *Parents:* Father, Frank Burnet; Mother, Hadassah Pollock MacKay Burnet. *Nationality:* Australian. *Religion:* Presbyterian. *Education:* Melbourne Univ., Australia, M.A., 1922; Melbourne Univ., Australia, M.D., 1923; Univ. of London, England, Ph.D., 1928. *Spouse:* Edith Linda Marston Druce, married July 10, 1928, died 1973; Hazel Foletta Jenkin, married 1976. *Children:* Ian, son; Elizabeth, daughter; Deborah, daughter. *Career:* Melbourne Hospital, Australia, Physician, 1923–24; Lister Institute, London, England, Researcher, 1926–27; Walter and Eliza Hall Institute for Medical Research, Melbourne, Australia, Physician and Administrator, 1928–65. *Other Awards:* Royal Medal, Royal Society, 1947; Knighthood, 1951; Lasker Award, 1952; Von Behring Prize, Marburg Univ., Germany, 1952; Galen Medal, Society of Apothecaries, 1958; Copley Medal, Royal Society, 1959.

Selected Publications: Biological Aspects of Infectious Disease. New York: Macmillan, 1940. *Virus as Organism.* Cambridge, MA: Harvard Univ. Press, 1945. *Principles of Animal Virology.* New York: Academic Press, 1955. *Clonal Selection: Theory of Acquired Immunity.* Nashville, TN: Vanderbilt Univ. Press, 1959. *Immunology, Aging and Cancer.* San Francisco, CA: W.H. Freeman, 1976.

For More Information See: Biographical Memoirs of the Fellows of the Royal Society. London: Royal Society, 1987 (Volume 33), 100–162. *Changing Patterns: an Atypical Autobiography.* New York: American Elsevier, 1968. "Fifty Years On." *British Medical Journal* 2 (1964): 1091. Norry, R. *Virus Hunter in Australia.* Melbourne, Australia: Nelson, 1966. Sexton, C. *The Seeds of Time.* Oxford, England: Oxford Univ. Press, 1991.

Commentary: MacFarlane Burnet shared the Nobel "for the discovery of acquired immunological tolerance," for which he provided the hypothesis that was the impetus for the experimentation by Sir Peter Medawar. His work on the agglutinins of typhoid fever, his research on influenza virus and other virus biology, and his studies of haemagglutination should also be mentioned. (B.I.M.)

Medawar, Peter Brian, Sir   355

Prize: Medicine and Physiology, 1960. *Born:* February 28, 1915; Rio de Janeiro, Brazil. *Death:* October 2, 1987; London, England. *Parents:* Father, Nicholas Medawar; Mother, Edith Muriel Dowling Medawar. *Nationality:* British. *Religion:* Christian. *Education:* Oxford Univ., England, B.A., 1935; Oxford Univ., England, M.A., 1939; Oxford Univ., England, D.Sci., 1945. *Spouse:* Jean Shinglewood Taylor, married February 27, 1937. *Children:* Caroline, daughter; Louise, daughter; Charles, son; Alexander, son. *Career:* Oxford Univ., England, Researcher, 1938–47; Birmingham Univ., England, Professor and Administrator, 1947–51; Univ. of London, England, Professor and Administrator, 1951–62; National Institute for Medical Research, Mill Hill, England, Director, 1962–71; Clinical Research Centre, England, Researcher, 1971–87. *Other Awards:* Edward Chapman Research Prize, 1938; Royal Medal, Royal Society, 1959; Knighthood, 1965; Copley

Medal, Royal Society, 1969; Hamilton Fairley Medal, Royal College of Physicians, 1971; Order of Merit, 1981.

Selected Publications: The Future of Man. New York: Basic Books, 1960. "Transplantation of Tissues and Organs." *British Medical Bulletin* 27 (1965). *The Life Science: Current Ideas of Biology.* New York: Harper & Row, 1977 (with J.S. Medawar). *Advice to a Young Scientist: Scientific Papers on Growth, Aging, Wound Healing and Transplantation.* New York: Harper Colophon Books, 1981.

For More Information See: Biographical Memoirs of the Fellows of the Royal Society. London: Royal Society, 1990 (Volume 35), 282–301. *Current Biography Yearbook.* New York: H.W. Wilson, 1961, 303–05. Medawar, J. *A Very Decided Preference.* New York: W. W. Norton Co., 1990. *Memoir of a Thinking Radish: An Autobiography.* Oxford, England: Oxford Univ. Press, 1986.

Commentary: Peter Medawar shared the Nobel "for the discovery of acquired immunological tolerance," for which he provided the experimental evidence to support MacFarlane Burnet's hypothesis. He also carried out research in the areas of growth, aging, and cellular transformations and contributed notable writings on the philosophy of science. (R.K.)

1961

Von Békésy, Georg   356

Prize: Medicine and Physiology, 1961. *Born:* June 3, 1899; Budapest, Hungary. *Death:* June 13, 1972; Honolulu, HI. *Parents:* Father, Alexander Von Békésy; Mother, Paula Mazaly Von Békésy. *Nationality:* Hungarian; later American citizen. *Religion:* Christian. *Education:* Univ. of Budapest, Hungary, Ph.D., 1923. *Spouse:* None. *Children:* None. *Career:* Hungarian Telephone System, Communications Engineer, 1923–46; Karolinska Institute, Stockholm, Sweden, Researcher, 1946–47; Harvard Univ., MA, Professor, 1947–66; Univ. of Hawaii, Professor, 1966–72. *Other Awards:* Denker Prize, 1931; Leibniz Medal, Akademie der Wissenschaften, Berlin, Germany, 1937; Academy Award, Academy of Science, Budapest, Hungary, 1946; Shambaugh Prize, 1950; Howard Crosby Warren Medal, Society of Experimental Psychologists, 1955; Gold Medal, American Otological Society, 1957; Achievement Award, Deafness Research Foundation, 1961; Gold Medal, Acoustical Society of America, 1961.

Selected Publications: Experiments in Hearing. New York: McGraw-Hill, 1960 (collection of his papers). *Sensory Inhibition.* Princeton, NJ: Princeton Univ. Press, 1967.

For More Information See: Biographical Encyclopedia of Scientists. New York: Facts on File, 1981, 60. *Biographical Memoirs of the National Academy of Sciences.* Washington, DC: National Academy of Sciences, 1979, 25–49. *Current Biography Yearbook.* New York: H.W. Wilson, 1962, 36–38. Daniel, J. *Békésy Gyorgy.* Budapest, Hungary: Akademiai Kaido, 1990. *The Excitement and Fascination of Science.* Palo Alto, CA: Annual Reviews, Inc., 1978, Vol. 2, 657–72.

Commentary: Georg Von Békésy won the Nobel for his "discoveries concerning the physical mechanisms of stimulation within the cochlea," which permitted the explanation of how persons distinguished between sounds. His entire career was devoted to the ear, including the development of instrumentation as well as experimentation. Von Békésy's work was instrumental in advances in measuring deafness, in surgery of the ear, and in working toward restoring hearing. (R.K.)

1962

Crick, Francis Harry Compton 357

Prize: Medicine and Physiology, 1962. *Born:* June 8, 1916; Northhampton, England. *Parents:* Father, Harry Crick; Mother, Annie Elizabeth Wilkins Crick. *Nationality:* British. *Religion:* Atheist; from Congregationalist background. *Education:* Univ. of London, England, B.Sc., 1937; Cambridge Univ., England, Ph.D., 1954. *Spouse:* Ruth Doreen Dodd, married 1940, divorced 1947; Odile Speed, married 1949. *Children:* Michael, son; Gabrielle, daughter; Jacqueline, daughter. *Career:* British Admiralty, Researcher, 1939–47; Strangeways Research Laboratory, Cambridge, England, Researcher, 1947–49; Cambridge Univ., England, Professor, 1949–77; Salk Institute for Biological Studies, San Diego, CA, Professor, 1977-. *Other Awards:* Warren Triennial Prize, 1959; Albert Lasker Award, 1960; Prix Charles Leopold Mayer, French Academy of Sciences, 1961; Research Corporation Award, 1961; Gairdner Foundation Medal, 1962; Royal Medal, Royal Society, 1972; Copley Medal, Royal Society, 1975; Michelson-Morley Award, Cleveland, OH, 1981; Benjamin P. Cheney Medal, 1986; Golden Plate Award, 1987; Albert Medal, Royal Society of the Arts, 1987; Order of Merit, 1991; Philadelphia Liberty Medal, 2000.

Selected Publications: "Structure for Deoxyribose Nucleic Acid." *Nature* 171 (April 25, 1953): 737. "Genetical Implications of the Structure of Deoxyribonucleic Acid." *Nature* 171 (May 30, 1953): 964–67. *The Genetic Code. III.* San Francisco: W.H. Freeman, 1966. *Of Molecules and Men.* Seattle: Univ. of Washington Press, 1966. *Life Itself: Its Origin and Nature.* New York: Simon and Schuster, 1981.

For More Information See: Asimov's Biographical Encyclopedia of Science and Technology. Garden City, NY: Doubleday, 1982, 859-61. *Biographical Encyclopedia of Scientists.* New York: Facts on File, 1981, 168–69. *Current Biography Yearbook.* New York: H.W. Wilson, 1983, 68–71. Newton, D. *James Watson and Francis Crick.* New York: Facts on File, 1992.

Commentary: Francis Crick won the Nobel Prize for his work leading to "discoveries concerning the structure of nucleic acids and its significance for information transfer in living material." Originally a physicist who worked on problems of radar and magnetic mines, he entered molecular biology with his colaureate, James Watson, in work which defined the molecular structure of DNA, and explained how it replicated. Crick continued to work on the understanding of the genetic code, proposed the existence of transfer RNAs, and formulated the "central dogma" of molecular genetics. His later research focused on the brain. (R.K.)

Watson, James Dewey 358

Prize: Medicine and Physiology, 1962. *Born:* April 6, 1928; Chicago, IL. *Parents:* Father, James Dewey Watson; Mother, Jean Mitchell Watson. *Nationality:* American. *Religion:* From Episcopalian/Catholic background. *Education:* Univ. of Chicago, IL, B.S., 1947; Univ. of Chicago, IL, Ph. B., 1947; Indiana Univ., Ph.D., 1950. *Spouse:* Elizabeth Lewis,

married 1968. *Children:* Duncan James, son; Rufus Robert, son. *Career:* Univ. of Copenhagen, Denmark, Researcher, 1950–51; Cambridge Univ., England, Researcher, 1951–53; California Institute of Technology, Researcher, 1953–55; Harvard Univ., MA, Professor, 1955–76; Cold Spring Harbor Laboratory, NY, Director, 1968–93, President, 1994-. *Other Awards:* John Collins Warren Prize, Massachusetts General Hospital, 1959; Eli Lilly Award, American Chemical Society, 1959; Albert Lasker Prize, American Public Health Association, 1960; Research Corporation Prize, 1962; Carty Medal, National Academy of Sciences, 1971; Presidential Medal of Freedom, 1977, 1989; Kaul Foundation Award, 1993; Copley Medal, 1993; National Biotechnology Venture Award, 1993; Charles A. Dana Award, 1994; Lomonosov Medal, 1995; National Medal of Science, 1997; Philadelphia Liberty Medal, 2000.

Selected Publications: "Structure for Deoxyribase Nucleic Acid." *Nature* 171 (April 25, 1953): 737. "Genetical Implications of the Structure of Deoxyribonucleic Acid." *Nature* 171 (May 30, 1953): 964–67. *Molecular Biology of the Gene.* Menlo Park, CA: W.A. Benjamin, 1965. *The DNA Story.* San Francisco: W.H. Freeman, 1981 (with J. Tooze). *The Molecular Biology of the Cell.* New York: Garland, 1983 (with others).

For More Information See: Baldwin, J. *DNA Pioneer.* New York: Walker and Co., 1994. *Current Biography Yearbook.* New York: H.W. Wilson, 1963, 458–60. *The Double Helix.* New York: Atheneum, 1968. *New York Times* (April 7, 1998): F1.

Commentary: James Watson shared the Nobel Prize for his contributions to "discoveries concerning the structure of nucleic acids and its significance for information transfer in living material." His landmark collaboration with his colaureate, Francis Crick, resulted in the presentation of a model for the structure of DNA and in the discussion of its genetic implications. In addition, Watson performed notable studies on the molecular structure of viruses and on protein biosynthesis. (R.K.)

Wilkins, Maurice Hugh Frederick 359

Prize: Medicine and Physiology, 1962. *Born:* December 15, 1916; Pongaroa, New Zealand. *Parents:* Father, Edgar Henry Wilkins; Mother, Eveline Constance Jane Whittaker Wilkins. *Nationality:* British. *Religion:* Agnostic; from Protestant/Agnostic Buddhist background. *Education:* Cambridge Univ., England, B.A., 1938; Cambridge Univ., England, Ph.D., 1940. *Spouse:* Patricia Ann Chidgey, married March 12, 1959. *Children:* Sarah Fenella, daughter; Emily Lucy Una, daughter; George Hugh, son; William Henry, son. *Career:* Univ. of California, Berkeley, Researcher, 1944; St. Andrews Univ., Scotland, Professor, 1945; Univ. of London, England, Professor and Administrator, 1946–81. *Other Awards:* Albert Lasker Award, American Public Health Association, 1960; Companion of the British Empire, 1962; T.F. Ryan Roentgen Prize, 1997.

Selected Publications: "Crystallinity in Sperm Heads: Molecular Structure of Nucleoprotein in Vivo." *Biochim. Biophys. Act* 10 (1953): 192–93 (with J.T. Randall). "The Molecular Configuration of Deoxyribonucleic Acid. I. X-ray Diffraction Study of a Crystalline Form of the Lithium Salts." *Journal of Molecular Biology* 2 (1960): 19 (with others). "The Molecular Structure of Deoxyribonucleic Acid

(DNA).” *J. Chim. Phys* 58 (1961): 891–98. “Determination of the Helical Configuration of Ribonucleic Acid Molecules by X-ray Diffraction Study of Crystalline Amino-acid Transfer Ribonucleic Acid.” *Nature* 194 (1962): 1014 (with others).

For More Information See: Current Biography Yearbook. New York: H.W. Wilson, 1963, 465–66. Johnson, S. and Mertens, T.R. “An Interview with Nobel Laureate Maurice Wilkins.” *American Biology Teacher* 51 (March 1989): 151–53.

Commentary: Maurice Wilkins’s Nobel Prize was for his research contributing to the “discoveries concerning the structure of nucleic acids and its significance for information transfer in living material.” Wilkins began his career as a physicist, working successively on the luminescence of solids, the theory of phosphorescence, radar, and the separation of uranium isotopes. His biophysical research started with the genetic effects of ultrasonic waves, moved to ultraviolet microspectrophotometric study of nucleic acids and viruses, and finally to the laureate work on x-ray diffraction of DNA and later RNA. (R.K.)

1963

Eccles, John Carew, Sir   360

Prize: Medicine and Physiology, 1963. *Born:* January 27, 1903; Melbourne, Australia. *Death:* May 2, 1997; Contra, Switzerland. *Parents:* Father, William James Eccles; Mother, Mary Carew Eccles. *Nationality:* Australian; later British and American resident. *Religion:* Catholic. *Education:* Melbourne Univ., Australia, B.S., 1925; Melbourne Univ., Australia, M.B., 1925; Oxford Univ., England, M.A., 1929; Oxford Univ., England, Ph.D., 1929. *Spouse:* Irene Miller, married July 3, 1928, divorced 1968; Helena Táboríková, married April 27, 1968. *Children:* Rosamond, daughter; Alice, daughter; Mary, daughter; Judith, daughter; Frances, daughter; Peter, son; William, son; John son; Richard, son. *Career:* Oxford Univ., England, Professor, 1934–37; Kanematsu Memorial Institute of Pathology, Sydney, Australia, Director, 1937–44; Univ. of Otago, Dunedin, New Zealand, Professor, 1944–51; Australian National Univ., Canberra, Australia, Professor, 1951–66; Institute for Biomedical Research, IL, Researcher, 1966–68; State Univ. of NY at Buffalo, Professor and Administrator, 1968–75. *Other Awards:* Gotch Memorial Prize, 1927; Rolleston Memorial Prize, 1932; Knighthood, 1958; Baly Medal, 1961; Cothenius Medal, Deutsche Akademie der Naturforscher Leopoldina, 1963.

Selected Publications: Reflex Activity of the Spinal Cord. London: Oxford Univ. Press, 1938. *The Neurophysiological Basis of Mind.* Oxford: Clarendon Press, 1965. *The Cerebellum as a Neuronal Machine.* Berlin: Springer-Verlag, 1967. *The Physiology of Nerve Cells.* Baltimore, MD: Johns Hopkins Press, 1968. *The Inhibitory Pathways of the Central Nervous System.* Liverpool: Liverpool Univ. Press, 1969.

For More Information See: Current Biography Yearbook. New York: H.W. Wilson, 1972, 119–22. Robinson, John. *100 Most Important People in the World Today.* New York: Putnam, 1970, 237–40.

Commentary: John Eccles was cited by the Academy for establishing the relationship between inhibition of nerve cells and repolarization of a cell’s membrane, much of which work grew out of the findings of his corecipients, Andrew Huxley and Alan Hodgkin. Eccles’s other significant contributions were in the areas of brain research, nerve impulses, and neuromuscular transmissions. (R.K.)

Hodgkin, Alan Lloyd, Sir   361

Prize: Medicine and Physiology, 1963. *Born:* February 5, 1914; Danbury, Oxfordshire, England. *Death:* December 20, 1998; Cambridge, England. *Parents:* Father, George L. Hodgkin; Mother, Mary F. Wilson Hodgkin. *Nationality:* British. *Religion:* Most probably Christian/Protestant. *Education:* Cambridge Univ., England, M.A., Sc.D., 1936. *Spouse:* Marion de Kay Rous, married 1944. *Children:* Deborah, daughter; Sarah, daughter; Rachel, daughter; Jonathan, son. *Career:* Air Ministry and Ministry of Aircraft Production, England, Scientific Officer, 1939–45; Cambridge Univ., England, Professor and Administrator, 1945–52; Royal Society, England, Foulerton Research Professor, 1952–69; Cambridge Univ., England, Professor and Administrator, 1970–84. *Other Awards:* Baly Medal, 1955; Royal Medal, Royal Society, 1958; Copley Medal, 1965; Knighthood, 1972; Order of Merit, 1973; Lord Crook Medal, 1983; Helmerich Prize, 1988.

Selected Publications: “Ionic Currents Underlying the Activity in the Giant Axon of the Squid.” *Arch. Sci. Physiol* 3 (1949): 129–50 (with A. Huxley and B. Katz). “Properties of Nerve Axons. I. Movement of Sodium and Potassium Ions during Nervous Activity.” *Cold Spring Harbor Symposia on Quantitative Biology* 17 (1952): 43–52 (with A. Huxley). “Movement of Radioactive Potassium and Membrane Current in a Giant Axon.” *Journal of Physiology (London)* 121 (1953): 403–14 (with A. Huxley). *The Conduction of the Nervous Impulse.* Liverpool: Liverpool Univ. Press, 1971. *The Pursuit of Nature: Informal Essays on the History of Physiology.* Cambridge: Cambridge Univ. Press, 1977.

For More Information See: Biographical Encyclopedia of Scientists. New York: Facts on File, 1981, 386. *Chance and Design: Reminiscences of Science in Peace and War.* Cambridge: Cambridge University Press, 1992. *Science* 142 (October 25, 1963): 468–70.

Commentary: Alan Hodgkin’s Nobel Prize was shared for studies of the ionic mechanisms involved in excitation and inhibition in peripheral and central portions of the nerve cell membrane. The discoveries stemmed from “elegant experiments” that measured the potential across the membrane with activity and without, and explained those measurements as related to sodium concentrations. The sodium hypothesis was later proven by many researchers. Hodgkin also did notable work on muscles and vision. (B.I.M.)

Huxley, Andrew Fielding, Sir   362

Prize: Medicine and Physiology, 1963. *Born:* November 22, 1917; London, England. *Parents:* Father, Leonard Huxley; Mother, Rosalind Bruce Huxley. *Nationality:* British. *Religion:* Agnostic; from Christian background. *Education:* Cambridge Univ., England, B.A., 1938; Cambridge Univ., England, M.A., 1941. *Spouse:* Jocelyn Richenda Gammell Pease, married July 5, 1947. *Children:* Eleanor Bruce, daughter; Henrietta Catherine, daughter; Clare Marjory

Pease, daughter; Camilla Rosalind, daughter; Janet Rachel, daughter; Stewart Leonard, son. *Career:* Plymouth Marine Biology Laboratory, MA, Researcher, 1939–40; Cambridge Univ., England, Professor and Administrator, 1941–60; Univ. of London, England, Professor, 1960–83; Cambridge Univ., England, Professor and Administrator, 1983-. *Other Awards:* Copley Medal, Royal Society, 1973; Knighthood, 1974; Order of Merit, 1983.

Selected Publications: "Ionic Currents Underlying the Activity in the Giant Axon of the Squid." *Arch. Sci. Physiol* 3 (1949): 129–50 (with A. Hodgkin and B. Katz). "Properties of Nerve Axons. I. Movement of Sodium and Potassium Ions during Nervous Activity." *Cold Spring Harbor Symposia on Quantitative Biology* 17 (1952): 43–52 (with A. Hodgkin). "Movement of Radioactive Potassium and Membrane Current in a Giant Axon." *Journal of Physiology (London)* 121 (1953): 403–14 (with A. Hodgkin). *Reflections on Muscle*. Princeton, NJ: Princeton Univ. Press, 1980.

For More Information See: Biographical Encyclopedia of Scientists. New York: Facts on File, 1981, 404. *Science* 142 (October 25, 1963): 468–70.

Commentary: Andrew Huxley shared the Nobel Prize for studies of the ionic mechanisms involved in excitation and inhibition in peripheral and central portions of the nerve cell membrane. His earlier formulation of the hypothesis that, during activity, the nerve membrane potential was controlled by sodium levels, was proven to be true by his own studies; studies of others also proved this. Huxley's research extended into muscular contraction and the development of the interference microscope and the ultramicrotome. (R.K.)

1964

Bloch, Konrad Emil   363

Prize: Medicine and Physiology, 1964. *Born:* January 12, 1912; Neisse, Germany. *Death:* October 15, 2000; Burlington, MA. *Parents:* Father, Frederick D. Bloch; Mother, Hedwig Striemer Bloch. *Nationality:* German; later American citizen. *Religion:* Jewish. *Education:* Technische Hochschule, Germany, Chem. Eng., 1934; Columbia Univ., NY, Ph.D., 1938. *Spouse:* Lore Teutsch, married February 15, 1941. *Children:* Peter, son; Susan, daughter. *Career:* Columbia Univ., NY, Professor, 1939–46; Univ. of Chicago, IL, Professor, 1946–54; Harvard Univ., MA, Professor, 1954–82. *Other Awards:* Medal, Société de Chimie Biologique, 1958; Fritzsche Award, American Chemical Society, 1964; Distinguished Service Award, Univ. of Chicago School of Medicine, IL, 1964; Centennial Science Award, Univ. of Notre Dame, IN, 1965; Cardano Medal, Lombardy Academy of Sciences, 1965; Ernst Guenther Award, 1965; William Lloyd Evans Award, Ohio State Univ., 1968; National Medal of Science, 1988.

Selected Publications: "Biological Conversion of Cholesterol to Cholic Acid." *Journal of Biological Chemistry* 149 (1943): 511–17 (with B. Berg and D. Rittenberg). "The Utilization of AcOH for Fatty Acid Synthesis." *Journal of Biological Chemistry* 154 (1944): 311–12 (with D. Rittenberg). "Biosynthesis of Squaline." *Journal of Biological Chemistry* 200 (1953): 129–34 (with R.G. Langdon). *Lipide Metabolism*. New York: Wiley, 1960. *Blondes in Venetian Paintings, the Nine-Banded Armadillo, and other essays in Biochemistry*. New Haven: Yale University Press, 1994.

For More Information See: The Excitement and Fascination of Science. Palo Alto, CA: Annual Reviews, Inc., 1990, Vol. 3, Part 1, 495–513. *New York Times* (October 16, 1964): 1, 3. *Science* 146 (October 23, 1964): 504–06. *New York Times* (October 18, 2000): C23.

Commentary: Konrad Bloch shared the Nobel Prize for his "contributions to understanding the mechanism and regulation of cholesterol and fatty acid metabolism." Bloch's early research showed that acetic acid was a major precursor of cholesterol in rats, and he continued to work on explaining the steps in the biosynthesis of sterols, first following the metabolism of acetic acid to squalene, then proposing the cyclization of squalene to lanosterol, and then working on the intermediates of lanosterol conversion to cholesterol. Bloch also made notable contributions in the study of the biosynthesis of glutathione and of the metabolism of the fatty acids. (R.K.)

Lynen, Feodor Felix Konrad   364

Prize: Medicine and Physiology, 1964. *Born:* April 6, 1911; Munich, Germany. *Death:* August 6, 1979; Munich, Germany. *Parents:* Father, Wilhelm L. Lynen; Mother, Frieda Prym Lynen. *Nationality:* German. *Religion:* Lutheran. *Education:* Univ. of Munich, Germany, Dr. Phil., 1937. *Spouse:* Eva Wieland Lynen, married May 14, 1937. *Children:* Peter, son; Heinrich, son; Annemarie, daughter; Susanne, daughter; Eva-Marie, daughter. *Career:* Univ. of Munich, Germany, Professor, 1942–79. *Other Awards:* Neuberg Medal, American Society of European Chemists and Pharmacists, 1954; Justus von Liebig Medal, Gesellschaft Deutscher Chemiker, 1955; Carus Medal, Deutsche Akademie der Naturforscher Leopoldina, 1961; Otto Warburg Medal, Gesellschaft für Physiologische Chemie, 1963; Norman Medaille, Deutsche Gesellschaft für Fettnissenschaft, 1967.

Selected Publications: "Acetyl Coenzyme A and the Fatty Acid Cycle." *Harvey Lecture Series* 48 (1953): 210–44. "Der Fettsaurecyclus." *Angewandte Chemie* 67 (1955): 463–70. "Phosphatkreislauf und Pasteur-Effekt." *Proceedings of the International Symposium on Enzyme Chemistry, Tokyo and Kyoto* (1957): 25–34. "Biosynthesis of Fatty Acids." *Proceedings of the Symposium on Drugs Affecting Lipid Metabolism* (1961): 3–15. "Cholesterol und Arteriosklerose." *Naturwiss. Rundschau* 25 (1972): 382–87.

For More Information See: Biographical Memoirs of the Fellows of the Royal Society. London: Royal Society, 1982 (Volume 28), 261. *Current Biography Yearbook*. New York: H.W. Wilson, 1967, 263–65. *Die Aktivierte Essigsaure und Ihre Folgen: Autobiograph*. New York: de Gruyter, 1976.

Commentary: The Nobel Prize was awarded to Feodor Lynen for his "contributions to understanding the mechanism and regulation of cholesterol and fatty acid metabolism." His research on cholesterol, in particular, helped clarify its role as a possible cause of diseases of the heart and the circulatory system. Lynen studied the enzymatic steps of the fatty acid cycle, the role of biotin in fatty substance metabolism, fermentation, the citric acid cycle, phosphorization/oxidation, and the regulation of metabolic rates. (R.K.)

1965

Jacob, François   365

Prize: Medicine and Physiology, 1965. *Born:* June 17, 1920; Nancy, France. *Parents:* Father, Simon Jacob; Mother, Therese Franck Jacob. *Nationality:* French. *Religion:* Jewish. *Education:* Lycée Carnot, France, baccalauréat, 1938; Univ. of Paris, France, M.D., 1947; Univ. of Paris, France, B.S., 1951; Univ. of Paris, France, D.Sc., 1954. *Spouse:* Lysiane Bloch, married November 27, 1947, died 1984. *Children:* Pierre, son; Laurent, son; Henri, son; Odile, daughter. *Career:* French Army, 1940–45; Institut Pasteur, Paris, France, Researcher and Administrator, 1950–92. *Other Awards:* Bronze Medal, French National Scientific Research Center, 1955; Essee Prize, Anti-Cancer League, 1958; Prix Charles Leopold Mayer, Académie des Sciences, 1962; Croix de la Liberation; Grand Croix; Legion d'Honneur.

Selected Publications: "Genetic Regulatory Mechanisms in the Synthesis of Proteins." *Journal of Molecular Biology* 3 (1961): 356 (with Jacques Monod). "On the Regulation of Gene Activity: Beta-Galactosidase Formation in E. Coli." *Cold Spring Harbor Symposia on Quantitative Biology* 26 (1961): 207 (with Jacques Monod). *Sexuality and Genetics of Bacteria.* New York: Academic Press, 1961 (with E. Wollman). "Telenomic Mechanism's Cellular Metabolism, Growth and Differentiation." *Cold Spring Harbor Symposia on Quantitative Biology* 26 (1961): 394–95 (with Jacques Monod).

For More Information See: Current Biography Yearbook. New York: H.W. Wilson, 1966, 191–93. *Of Flies, Mice and Men.* Tr. Giselle Weiss. Cambridge, MA: Harvard University Press, 1998. *Science* 150 (October 22, 1965): 462–63. *The Statue Within.* Paris: Seuil, 1990.

Commentary: Francois Jacob shared the Nobel Prize with Jacques Monod and André Lwoff for his contributions "to our knowledge of the fundamental processes in living matter which form the bases for such phenomena as adaptation, reproduction and evolution." Jacob's major contributions came in his explanation of the genetic basis of lysogenic bacteria through inherited sexual differences, in his elucidation of the action of regulator genes which control the behavior of structural and operator genes in enzyme synthesis, and in his work on messenger RNA. (B.S.S.)

Lwoff, André Michel   366

Prize: Medicine and Physiology, 1965. *Born:* May 8, 1902; Allier, France. *Death:* September 30, 1994; Paris, France. *Parents:* Father, Salomon Lwoff; Mother, Marie Siminovitch Lwoff. *Nationality:* French. *Religion:* Jewish. *Education:* Univ. of Paris, France, Licencie es Sciences, 1921; Univ. of Paris, France, M.D., 1927; Univ. of Paris, France, D.Sc., 1932. *Spouse:* Marguerite Bourdaleix, married December 5, 1925. *Children:* None. *Career:* Institut Pasteur, Paris, France, Researcher and Administrator, 1921–68; Cancer Research Institute, Villejuif, France, Researcher and Administrator, 1968–72. *Other Awards:* Medaille de la Resistance, France; Commander Legion d'Honneur, France; Lallemont Award, Académie des Sciences; Noury Award,

Académie des Sciences; Longchampt Award, Académie des Sciences; Chaussier Award, Académie des Sciences; Petit d'Ormoy, France; Charles Leopold Mayer Foundation Prize; Leeuwenhoek Medal, Royal Netherlands Academy of Sciences and Arts, 1960; Keilin Medal, British Biochemical Society, 1964; Einstein Award, 1967.

Selected Publications: L'Evolution Physiologique. Paris: Hermann, 1944. *The Kinetosomes in Development, Reproduction, and Evolution.* New York: Wiley, 1950. *Problems of Morphogenesis in Ciliates.* New York: Wiley, 1950. *Biochemistry and Physiology of Protozoa.* New York: Academic Press, 1951–64. *Biological Order.* Cambridge, MA: Massachusetts Institute of Technology Press, 1962.

For More Information See: Asimov's Biographical Encyclopedia of Science and Technology. Garden City, NY: Doubleday, 1982, 787. Debré, P. *Jacques Monod.* Paris: Flammarion, 1996. *The Excitement and Fascination of Science.* Palo Alto, CA: Annual Reviews, Inc., 1978, Vol. 2, 301–26. *New York Times* (October 15, 1965): 1, 36. *New York Times Biographical Serivce* (October 5, 1994): 1520. *Science* 150 (October 22, 1965): 462–63.

Commentary: André Lwoff was honored, together with his colaureates François Jacob and Jacques Monod, for his contributions "to our knowledge of the fundamental processes in living matter which form the bases for such phenomena as adaptation, reproduction, and evolution." Lwoff was active first in elucidating the morphology and biology of the ciliate protozoa, with particular attention paid to how cell structures are genetically continued. He was also a major contributor in the areas of the biology of viruses, the genetics of bacteria, and the mechanisms by which viruses are replicated in the course of a viral infection. (B.S.S.)

Monod, Jacques Lucien   367

Prize: Medicine and Physiology, 1965. *Born:* February 9, 1910; Paris, France. *Death:* May 31, 1976; Cannes, France. *Parents:* Father, Lucien Monod; Mother, Charlotte Todd MacGregor Monod. *Nationality:* French. *Religion:* Protestant. *Education:* Univ. of Paris, France, B.S., 1931; Univ. of Paris, France, D.Sc., 1941. *Spouse:* Odette Bruhl, married 1938. *Children:* Olivier, son; Philippe, son. *Career:* Univ. of Paris, France, Professor, 1931–41; Pasteur Institute, Paris, France, Researcher and Administrator, 1945–76. *Other Awards:* Montyon Physiology Prize, Paris Académie des Sciences, 1955; Louis Rapkine Medal, London, England, 1958; Chevalier de l'Ordre des Palmes Academiques, 1961; Charles Leopold Mayer Prize, Académie des Sciences, 1962; Officer de la Legion d'Honneur, 1963.

Selected Publications: "Genetic Regulatory Mechanisms in the Synthesis of Proteins." *Journal of Molecular Biology* 3 (1961): 356 (with François Jacob). "On the Regulation of Gene Activity: Beta Galactosidase Formation in E. Coli." *Cold Spring Harbor Symposia on Quantitative Biology* 26 (1961): 207 (with François Jacob). "Teleonomic Mechanism's Cellular Metabolism, Growth and Differentiation." *Cold Spring Harbor Symposia on Quantitative Biology* 26 (1961): 394–95 (with François Jacob). *Chance and Necessity.* New York: Random House, 1971.

For More Information See: Current Biography Yearbook. New York: H.W. Wilson, 1971, 277–79. *Dictionary of Scientific Biography.* Supplement II. New York: Scribner's, 1990, 636–49. *Science* 150 (October 22, 1965): 462–63.

Commentary: Jacques Monod shared the Nobel Prize with François Jacob and André Lwoff for his contributions "to our knowledge of the fundamental processes in living matter which form the bases for such phenomena as adaptation, reproduction, and evolution." The subject research elucidated the mechanism by which genes manufacture the proteins necessary for individual development. Monod studied protein metabolism, specifically the synthesis of the bacterial enzyme Beta-galactosidase and its role as a catalyst. He was also a part of the work that identified messenger RNA and its role in protein production and introduced the concept of the operon (working gene cluster). Monod is recognized as well as a philosopher of science. (B.S.S.)

1966

Huggins, Charles Brenton 368

Prize: Medicine and Physiology, 1966. *Born:* September 22, 1901; Halifax, Nova Scotia, Canada. *Death:* January 12, 1997; Chicago, IL. *Parents:* Father, Charles Edward Huggins; Mother, Bessie Spencer Huggins. *Nationality:* Canadian; later American citizen. *Religion:* Baptist. *Education:* Acadia Univ., Canada, B.A., 1920; Harvard Univ., MA, M.D., 1924. *Spouse:* Margaret Wellman, married July 29, 1927, died 1983. *Children:* Charles Edward, son; Emily Wellman Fine, daughter. *Career:* Univ. of Michigan Medical School, Surgery Intern and Instructor, 1924–27; Univ. of Chicago Medical School, IL, Professor and Administrator, 1927–72; Acadia Univ., Nova Scotia, Chancellor, 1972–79. *Other Awards:* Gold Medal, American Medical Association, 1936, 1940; Charles L. Meyer Award, National Academy Sciences, 1943; Award for Research, American Urological Association, 1948; Francis Amory Award, 1948; Gold Medal, Société Internationale d'Urologie, 1948; American Cancer Society Award, 1953; Bertner Award, M.D. Anderson Hospital, TX, 1953; American Pharmaceutical Manufacturers Award, 1953; Gold Medal, American Association of Genito-Urinary Surgeons, 1955; Borden Award, Association of American Medical Colleges, 1955; Comfort Cruikshank Award, Middlesex Hospital, London, 1957; Cameron Prize, Edinburgh Univ., 1958; Valentine Prize, New York Academy of Medicine, 1962; Hunter Award, American Therapeutic Society, 1962; Lasker Award for Medical Research, 1963; Gold Medal for Research, Rudolph Virchow Society, 1964; Laurea Award, American Urological Society, 1969; Gold Medal in Therapeutics, Worshipful Society of Apothecaries of London, 1966; Gairdner Award, Toronto, 1966; Chicago Medical Society Award, 1967; Centennial Medal, Acadia Univ., Nova Scotia, 1967; Hamilton Award, Illinois Medical Society, 1967; Bigelow Medal, Boston Surgical Society, 1967; Sheen Award, American Medical Association, 1970; Distinguished Service Award, American Society of Abdominal Surgeons, 1972; Franklin Medal, 1985; Sesquicentennial Commemorative Award, National Library of Medicine, 1986.

Selected Publications: "The Business of Discovery in the Medical Sciences." *Journal of the American Medical Association* 194 (December 13, 1965): 1211–15. "Endocrine-Induced Regression of Cancers." *Science* 156 (1967): 1050–54. *Experimental Leukemia and Mammary Cancer: Induction, Prevention and Cure.* Chicago: Univ. of Chicago Press, 1979.

For More Information See: Current Biography Yearbook. New York: H.W. Wilson, 1965, 205–08. Talalay, Paul. "The Scientific Contributions of Charles Brenton Huggins." *Journal of the American Medical Association* 192 (June 28, 1965): 1137–40.

Commentary: The Nobel Prize went to Charles Huggins "for his discoveries concerning hormonal treatment of prostate cancer," recognizing 25 years of painstaking investigation of the relationship between hormones and cancer. Huggins first found that androgens (male hormones) can stimulate prostatic cancer, whereas castration or estrogens (female hormones) frequently have the opposite effect. The effectiveness of antiandrogenic treatment was soon confirmed and adopted. Huggins has worked since on producing variants of natural hormones that have little or no feminizing effect. (S.D.S.)

Rous, Francis Peyton 369

Prize: Medicine and Physiology, 1966. *Born:* October 5, 1879; Baltimore, MD. *Death:* February 16, 1970; New York, NY. *Parents:* Father, Charles Rous; Mother, Frances Anderson Wood Rous. *Nationality:* American. *Religion:* Christian/Protestant. *Education:* Johns Hopkins Univ., MD, B.A., 1900; Johns Hopkins Univ., MD, M.A., 1901; Johns Hopkins Univ., MD, M.D., 1905. *Spouse:* Marion Eckford de Kay, married June 15, 1915. *Children:* Marion de Kay, daughter; Ellen de Kay, daughter; Phoebe de Kay, daughter. *Career:* Univ. of Michigan, Professor, 1906–08; Rockefeller Institute, NY, Professor, 1909–45. *Other Awards:* John Scott Medal, Philadelphia, PA, 1927; Walker Prize, Royal College of Surgeons, London, 1941; Kobler Medal, Association of American Physicians, 1953; Bertner Foundation Award, Univ. of Texas, 1954; Jessie Stevenson Kovalenko Award, National Academy of Sciences, 1954; Distinguished Service Award, American Cancer Society, 1957; Lasker Foundation Award, 1958; Karl Landsteiner Award, American Association of Blood Banks, 1958; New York Academy of Medicine Medal, 1959; Judd Award, Memorial Center for Cancer, NY, 1959; United Nations Prize, 1962; Gold-Headed Cane, American Association of Pathologists and Bacteriologists, 1964; National Medal of Science, United States, 1966; Paul Ehrlich-Ludwig Darmstaedter Prize, West Germany, 1966; Gold Medal, British Royal Society of Medicine, 1966; Cleveland Medal, American Cancer Society, 1966.

Selected Publications: "A Sarcoma of the Fowl Transmissible by an Agent Separable from the Tumor Cells." *Journal of Experimental Medicine* 13 (1911): 397–411. "Transmission of a Malignant New Growth by Means of a Cell-Free Filtrate." *Journal of the American Medical Association* 56 (1911): 198. *The Modern Dance of Death.* London: Cambridge Univ. Press, 1929. "The Virus Tumors and the Tumor Problem." *American Journal of Cancer* 28 (1936): 233–71. "Surmise and Fact on the Nature of Cancer." *Nature* 183 (1959): 1357–61.

For More Information See: Biographical Memoirs of the Fellows of the Royal Society. London: Royal Society, 1971 (Volume 17), 643–62. *Biographical Memoirs of the National Academy of Sciences.* Washington, DC: National Academy of Sciences, 1976 (Volume 48), 275–306. *Current Biography Yearbook.* New York: H.W. Wilson, 1967, 354–57.

A Notable Career in Finding Out: Peyton Rous. New York: Rockefeller Univ. Press, 1971.

Commentary: Peyton Rous's work on tumor-inducing viruses in chickens earned him the Nobel Prize, 55 years after the original report. Rous did notable work also in the fields of blood preservation, the liver and its connection with the biliary system, the gall bladder, and culture techniques for viruses and cells. (R.K.)

1967

Granit, Ragnar Arthur   370
Prize: Medicine and Physiology, 1967. *Born:* October 30, 1900; Helsinki, Finland. *Death:* March 12, 1991; Stockholm, Sweden. *Parents:* Father, Arthur W. Granit; Mother, Albertina Helena Malmberg Granit. *Nationality:* Finnish; later Swedish citizen. *Religion:* Lutheran. *Education:* Helsinki Univ., Finland, M.S., 1923; Helsinki Univ., Finland, M.D., 1927. *Spouse:* Baroness Marguerite E. Bruun, married October 2, 1929. *Children:* Michael, son. *Career:* Pennsylvania Univ., Philadelphia, Fellow, 1929–31; Helsinki Univ., Finland, Professor, 1932–40; Royal Caroline Institute, Stockholm, Sweden, Professor, 1940–67. *Other Awards:* Lunsgaard Gold Medal, 1938; Jubilee Medal, Swedish Society of Physicians, 1947; Björkén Prize, Uppsala Univ., 1948; Retzius Gold Medal, 1957; Donders Medal, 1957; 3rd International St. Vincent Prize, 1961; Jahre Prize, Oslo Univ., Norway, 1961; Sherrington Memorial Gold Medal, 1967; Purkinje Gold Medal, 1969.

Selected Publications: On the Correlation of Some Sensory and Physiological Phenomena of Vision. London: George Putman, 1938. *Sensory Mechanisms of the Retina*. New York: Hafner, 1963. *Receptors and Sensory Perception*. Westport, CT: Greenwood Press, 1975. *The Purposive Brain*. Cambridge, MA: Massachusetts Institute of Technology Press, 1980.

For More Information See: Hur det Kom Sig (A Memoir). n.p., 1983. *Science* (October 27, 1967): 468–71.

Commentary: Ragnar Granit shared the Nobel Prize for his research which illuminated the electrical properties of vision by studying wavelength discrimination by the eye. His pioneer discovery that light waves both excite and inhibit the electric impulse discharge stimulated much research. Granit's other contributions are in the areas of electrical control of nerves in muscle tissues and nerve impulse transmission of pain and touch. (B.I.M.)

Hartline, Haldan Keffer   371
Prize: Medicine and Physiology, 1967. *Born:* December 22, 1903; Bloomsburg, PA. *Death:* March 17, 1983; Fallston, MD. *Parents:* Father, Daniel Schollenberger Hartline; Mother, Harriet Franklin Keffer Hartline. *Nationality:* American. *Religion:* Protestant. *Education:* Lafayette College, PA, B.S., 1923; Johns Hopkins Univ., MD, M.D., 1927. *Spouse:* Mary Elizabeth Kraus, married April 11, 1936. *Children:* Daniel Keffer, son; Peter Haldan, son; Frederick Flanders, son. *Career:* Johns Hopkins Univ., Baltimore, MD, Researcher, 1927–29; Univ. of Pennsylvania, Professor, 1929–49; Johns Hopkins Univ., Baltimore, MD, Professor, 1949–53; Rockefeller Univ., NY, Professor, 1953–74. *Other Awards:* William H. Howell Award, 1927; Howard Crosby

Warren Medal, 1948; A.A. Michelson Award, Case Institute, 1964; Lighthouse Award, New York City, 1969; George Washington Kidd Award, 1982.

Selected Publications: Studies on Excitation and Inhibition in the Retina: A Collection of Papers from the Laboratories of H. Keffer Hartline. New York: Rockefeller Univ. Press, 1974.

For More Information See: Biographical Encyclopedia of Scientists. New York: Facts on File, 1981, 355. *Biographical Memoirs of the Fellows of the Royal Society*. London: Royal Society, 1985 (Volume 31), 261. *Science* 158 (October 27, 1967): 471–73.

Commentary: Haldan Hartline's research on the mechanisms by which we see won him the Nobel Prize. Early in his career, he found that in the process of vision, changes occur in the electrical potential of the retina. By studying individual nerve fibers in the eye of the crab, Hartline demonstrated that the intensity of light affected the speed of the electric impulses generated, and that faint light's effect was cumulated over time. In further research with vertebrates and crabs, he demonstrated complex interactions of the nerve cells and fibers of the eye that helped to explain the intricacies of vision. (B.I.M.)

Wald, George   372
Prize: Medicine and Physiology, 1967. *Born:* November 18, 1906; New York, NY. *Death:* April 12, 1997; Cambridge, MA. *Parents:* Father, Isaac Wald; Mother, Ernestine Rosenmann Wald. *Nationality:* American. *Religion:* Jewish. *Education:* New York Univ., B.S., 1927; Columbia Univ., NY, M.A., 1928; Columbia Univ., NY, Ph.D., 1932. *Spouse:* Frances Kingsley, married May 15, 1931, divorced 1957; Ruth Hubbard, married 1958. *Children:* Elijah, son; Michael, son; David, son; Deborah, daughter. *Career:* National Research Council Fellow, 1932–34; Harvard Univ., MA, Professor, 1934–77. *Other Awards:* Eli Lilly Prize, American Chemical Society, 1939; Lasker Award, American Public Health Association, 1953; Proctor Medal, Association for Research in Ophthalmology, 1955; Rumford Medal, American Academy of Arts and Sciences, 1959; Ives Medal, Optical Society of America, 1966; Paul Karrer Medal, Univ. of Zürich, Switzerland, 1967; T. Duckett Jones Award, Helen Hay Whitney Foundation, 1967; Bradford Washburn Medal, Boston Museum Society, 1968; Max Berg Award, 1969; Priestley Medal, Dickinson College, 1970.

Selected Publications: General Education in a Free Society. Cambridge, MA: Harvard Univ. Press, 1945. *Twenty-Six Afternoons of Biology*. Reading, MA: Addison-Wesley, 1966. *Visual Pigments and Photoreceptors: Review and Outlook*. New York: Academic Press, 1974.

For More Information See: Current Biography Yearbook. New York: H.W. Wilson, 1968, 412–14. "George Wald: The Man, the Speech." *New York Times Magazine* (August 17, 1969): 28–29+.

Commentary: George Wald's share of the Nobel Prize was for his research on the chemical processes that allow pigments in the retina of the eye to convert light into vision. Wald's original research showed that the eye rod pigment was made up of the protein opsin and retinene, a Vitamin A compound. Light striking the pigment separated the two components and produced an energy burst that moved along the retina's nerve network. In later work, Wald showed that the eye cones contained three pigments corresponding to the three primary colors, which could be used to explain many phenomena, including color blindness. (B.I.M.)

1968

Holley, Robert William 373

Prize: Medicine and Physiology, 1968. *Born:* January 28, 1922; Urbana, IL. *Death:* February 11, 1993; Los Gatos, CA. *Parents:* Father, Charles Elmer Holley; Mother, Viola Esther Wolfe Holley. *Nationality:* American. *Religion:* Unitarian. *Education:* Univ. of Illinois, A.B., 1942; Cornell Univ., NY, Ph.D., 1947. *Spouse:* Anne Lenore Dworkin, married March 3, 1945. *Children:* Frederick, son. *Career:* Washington State College, Researcher, 1947–48; Cornell Univ., Ithaca, NY, Professor, 1948–66; Salk Institute of Biological Studies, La Jolla, CA, Researcher, 1966–93. *Other Awards:* Distinguished Service Award, U.S. Department of Agriculture, 1965; Lasker Award, 1965; U.S. Steel Foundation Award, National Academy of Sciences, 1967.

Selected Publications: "A New Method for Sequence Determination of Large Olegonucleotides." *Biochem. Biophys. Res. Commun.* 17 (1964): 389–94 (with others). "Structure of a Ribonucleic Acid." *Science* 147 (1965): 1462–65 (with others). "Structure of an Alanine Transfer Ribonucleic Acid." *Journal of the American Medical Association* 194 (1965): 868–71. "Experimental Approaches to the Determination of the Nucleotide Sequences of Large Oligonucleotides and Small Nucleic Acids." *Progr. Nucl. Acid Res. Mol. Biol.* (1968): 37–47.

For More Information See: Current Biography Yearbook. New York: H.W. Wilson, 1967, 172–74. *New York Times Biographical Service* (February 14, 1993): 230. *Science* 162 (October 25, 1968): 433–36.

Commentary: Robert Holley shared the Nobel Prize for his development of techniques for determining the structure of nucleic acids and for his determination of the complete nucleotide sequence of the alanine transfer ribonucleic acids. His continued research refined techniques, prepared other candidates for study, and elaborated further structures. His later research included work on factors affecting cell division. (K.F.)

Khorana, Har Gobind 374

Prize: Medicine and Physiology, 1968. *Born:* January 9, 1922; Raipur, India. *Parents:* Father, Shri Ganpat Rai Khorana; Mother, Shrimat Krishna Devi Khorana. *Nationality:* Indian; later American citizen. *Religion:* Hindu. *Education:* Punjab Univ., India, B.Sc., 1943; Punjab Univ., India, M.Sc., 1945; Liverpool Univ., England, Ph.D., 1948. *Spouse:* Esther Elizabeth Sibler, married 1952. *Children:* Julia, daughter; Emily Anne, daughter; Dave Roy, son. *Career:* Federal Institute of Technology, Zürich, Switzerland, Researcher, 1948–49; Cambridge Univ., England, Researcher, 1950–52; Univ. of British Columbia, Canada, Administrator, 1952–60; Univ. of Wisconsin, Professor and Administrator, 1960–70; Massachusetts Institute of Technology, Professor, 1970–97. *Other Awards:* Merck Award, Chemical Institute of Canada, 1958; Gold Medal, Professional Institute of Public Service of Canada, 1960; Dannie-Heinneman Preiz, Göttingen, Germany, 1967; Remsen

Award, Johns Hopkins Univ., 1968; American Chemical Society Award, 1968; Louisa Gross Horowitz Prize, 1968; Lasker Award, 1968; Gibbs Medal, American Chemical Society, 1974. Gairdner Foundation Award, 1980; National Medal of Science, 1987; Kayser Award, 1987.

Selected Publications: Some Recent Developments in the Chemistry of Phosphate Esters of Biological Interest. New York: Wiley, 1961. "Studies on Polynucleotides. LXVII. Initiation of Protein Synthesis in Vitro as Studied by Using Ribopolynucleotides with Repeating Nucleotide Sequences as Messengers." *Journal of Molecular Biology* 25 (1967): 275–98 (with others). "Synthesis of Transfer RNA Genes." *Advan. Biosci* (1971): 89–102.

For More Information See: Current Biography Yearbook. New York: H.W. Wilson, 1970, 222–24. *Science* 162 (October 25, 1968): 433–36.

Commentary: Har Khorana received the Nobel Award for his work in the genetics area. He succeeded first in synthesizing polynucleotides and extended Nirenberg's nitrocellulose binding technique by testing each of the 64 possible ribonucleotides. This work was followed by other proofs of parts of the genetic code. Prior to his work in genetics, Khorana had done valuable research on alkaloids and on the synthesis of Coenzyme A. After receiving the Nobel, Khorana succeeded in an even more striking accomplishment—the synthesis of an artificial gene. (K.F.)

Nirenberg, Marshall Warren 375

Prize: Medicine and Physiology, 1968. *Born:* April 10, 1927; New York, NY. *Parents:* Father, Harry Edward Nirenberg; Mother, Minerva Bykowsky Nirenberg. *Nationality:* American. *Religion:* Jewish. *Education:* Univ. of Florida, B.S., 1948; Univ. of Florida, M.S., 1952; Univ. of Michigan, Ph.D., 1957. *Spouse:* Perola Zaltzman, married July 14, 1961. *Children:* None. *Career:* National Institutes of Health, Bethesda, MD, Researcher and Administrator, 1957-. *Other Awards:* Molecular Biology Award, National Academy of Sciences, 1962; Biological Sciences Award, Washington Academy of Sciences, 1962; Paul Lewis Award, American Chemical Society, 1963; Modern Medicine Award, 1963; Medal, Department of Health, Education and Welfare, 1964; Harrison Howe Award, American Chemical Society, 1964; National Medal of Sciences, 1965; Hildebrand Award, American Chemical Society, 1966; Research Corporation Award, 1966; Gairdner Foundation Award of Merit, Canada, 1967; Prix Charles Leopold Meyer, French Academy of Sciences, 1967; A.C.P. Award, 1967; Franklin Medal, Franklin Institute, 1968; Lasker Award, 1968; Priestly Award, 1968; Louisa Gross Horowitz Prize, 1968.

Selected Publications: "The Genetic Code." *Scientific American* 208 (March 1963): 80–94. "RNA Code and Protein Synthesis." *Cold Spring Symposium on Quantitative Biology* (1966): 11–24 (with others). "Genetic Memory." *Journal of the American Medical Association* 206 (1968): 1973–77.

For More Information See: Current Biography Yearbook. New York: H.W. Wilson, 1965, 305–07. Robinson, Donald. *100 Most Important People in the World Today.* New York: Putnam, 1970, 204–06.

Commentary: Marshall Nirenberg won the Nobel Prize for his development of the procedure for deciphering the genetic code in living cells. He was then able to reveal the exact order of amino acids in protein synthesis as directed by the information stored in DNA (deoxyribonucleic acid). (K.F.)

1969

Delbrück, Max   376

Prize: Medicine and Physiology, 1969. *Born:* September 4, 1906; Berlin, Germany. *Death:* March 10, 1981; Pasadena, CA. *Parents:* Father, Hans Delbrück; Mother, Lina Thiersch Delbrück. *Nationality:* German; later American citizen. *Religion:* Protestant. *Education:* Univ. of Göttingen, Germany, Ph.D., 1930. *Spouse:* Mary Adaline Bruce, married August 2, 1941. *Children:* Jonathan, son; Nicola, daughter; Tobias, son; Ludina, daughter. *Career:* Kaiser Wilhelm Institute, Berlin, Germany, Researcher, 1932–37; California Institute of Technology, Researcher, 1937–39; Vanderbilt Univ., TN, Professor, 1940–47; California Institute of Technology, Professor, 1947–76. *Other Awards:* Kimber Medal, National Academy of Sciences; Louisa Gross Horowitz Prize, 1969.

Selected Publications: "Mutation of Bacteria from Virus-Sensitive to Virus-Resistant." *Genetics* 28 (1943): 491–511 (with S. Luria). "Induced Mutations in Bacterial Viruses." *Cold Spring Harbor Symposia on Quantitative Biology* 11 (1946): 33–37. *Über Vererbungschemie.* Cologne: Westdeutscher Verlag, 1963.

For More Information See: Biographical Memoirs of the Fellows of the Royal Society. London: Royal Society, 1982 (Volume 28), 59–60. Fischer, E.P. and Lipson, C. *Thinking about Science: Max Delbrück and the Origins of Molecular Biology.* New York: Norton, 1988.

Commentary: Max Delbrück was awarded the Nobel Prize for his share in the "discoveries concerning the replication mechanism and the genetic structure of viruses." Originally a physicist, Delbrück became interested in bacteriophages. He pioneered the use of the plaque technique to study bacteriophage replication and discovered that bacteriophages produced multiple offspring while destroying their hosts. He also showed that genetic material from two different viruses could combine into a third form. His career later turned to the study of sensory physiology. (K.F.)

Hershey, Alfred Day   377

Prize: Medicine and Physiology, 1969. *Born:* December 4, 1908; Owosso, MI. *Death:* May 22, 1997; Syosset, NY. *Parents:* Father, Robert Day Hershey; Mother, Alma Wilbur Hershey. *Nationality:* American. *Religion:* Christian/Protestant. *Education:* Michigan State Univ., B.S., 1930; Michigan State Univ., Ph.D., 1934. *Spouse:* Harriet Davidson, married November 15, 1946. *Children:* Peter Manning, son. *Career:* Washington Univ., MO, Professor, 1934–50; Carnegie Institute at Cold Spring Harbor, NY, Researcher and Administrator, 1950–74. *Other Awards:* Lasker Award, American Public Health Association, 1958; Kimber Genetics Award, National Academy of Sciences, 1965.

Selected Publications: "Reproduction of Bacteriophage." *International Review of Cytology* 1 (1952): 119–34. "Nucleic Acid Economy in Bacteria Infected with Bacteriophage T2. II. Phage Precursor Nucleic Acid." *Journal of General Physiology* 37 (1953): 1–23. "Upper Limit to the Protein Content of the Germinal Substance of Bacteriophage T2." *Virology* 1 (1955): 108–27.

For More Information See: Biographical Encyclopedia of Scientists. New York: Facts on File, 1981, 370. *Current Biography Yearbook.* New York: H.W. Wilson, 1970, 175–77. *Science* (October 24, 1969): 479–81. Stahl, F.W. and Hershey, A.D. *We Can Sleep Later: Alfred D. Hershey and the Origins of Molecular Biology.* Cold Spring Harbor, NY: Cold Spring Harbor Laboratory Press, 2000.

Commentary: Alfred Hershey shared the Nobel Prize for his work in "discoveries concerning the replication mechanism and the genetic structure of viruses." He was instrumental in demonstrating that spontaneous mutations occurred in both bacteriophages and the cells with which they interacted; that the genetic material of different viruses could combine; and that the nucleic acid, not its associated protein, carried genetic information. His early research was on the chemistry of Brucella bacteria and in the area of immunology. Hershey also worked on the development of vaccines for various childhood diseases. (K.F.)

Luria, Salvador Edward   378

Prize: Medicine and Physiology, 1969. *Born:* August 13, 1912; Turin, Italy. *Death:* February 6, 1991; Lexington, MA. *Parents:* Father, David Luria; Mother, Ester Sacerdote Luria. *Nationality:* Italian; later American citizen. *Religion:* Jewish. *Education:* Univ. of Turin, Italy, M.D., 1935. *Spouse:* Zella Hurwitz, married April 18, 1945. *Children:* Daniel, son. *Career:* Italian Army, 1935–38; Institute of Radium, Paris, France, Researcher, 1938–40; Columbia Univ., NY, Researcher, 1940–42; Indiana Univ., Professor, 1943–50; Univ. of Illinois, Professor, 1950–59; Massachusetts Institute of Technology, Professor and Administrator, 1959–78. *Other Awards:* Lepetit Prize, 1935; Lenghi Prize, Academia Nazionale Lincei, 1965; Louisa Gross Horowitz Prize, Columbia Univ., 1969; National Book Award, 1974.

Selected Publications: "Mutation of Bacteria from Virus-Sensitive to Virus-Resistant." *Genetics* 28 (1943): 491–511 (with M. Delbrück). *The Multiplication of Viruses.* Vienna: Springer, 1958. *The Recognition of DNA in Bacteria.* San Francisco, CA: W.H. Freeman, 1969. *A View of Life.* Menlo Park, CA: Benjamin Cummings, 1981 (with S. Gould and S. Singer).

For More Information See: Current Biography Yearbook. New York: H.W. Wilson, 1970, 258–60. *A Slot Machine, A Broken Test Tube* (autobiography). New York: Harper & Row, 1984. *New York Times Biographical Service* (February 7, 1991): 108.

Commentary: Salvador Luria shared the Nobel Prize for his part in "discoveries concerning the replication mechanism and the genetic structure of viruses." Luria, working with Delbrück, developed techniques for purifying viruses and discovered that generations of viruses mutate, and that during bacteriophage growth, spontaneous mutations occurred in both the bacteriophages and in the host bacterial cells. He also worked on the phenomena of lysogeny and transduction, as well as being a social conscience of the scientific community, championing a variety of causes. (A.N.)

1970

Axelrod, Julius 379

Prize: Medicine and Physiology, 1970. *Born:* May 30, 1912; New York, NY. *Parents:* Father, Isadore Axelrod; Mother, Molly Liechtling Axelrod. *Nationality:* American. *Religion:* Jewish. *Education:* City College of New York, B.S., 1933; New York Univ., M.A., 1941; George Washington Univ., Washington, DC, Ph.D., 1955. *Spouse:* Sally Taub, married August 30, 1938. *Children:* Paul Mark, son; Alfred Nathan, son. *Career:* New York Univ., Researcher, 1933–49; National Institutes of Health, MD, Researcher and Administrator, 1950–96. *Other Awards:* Meritorious Research Award, Association for Research on Nervous and Mental Diseases, 1965; Gairdner Award, 1967; Alumni Distinguished Achievement Award, George Washington Univ., 1968; Claude Bernard Professorship and Award, Univ. of Montreal, 1969; Distinguished Service Award, 1970; Distinguished Service Award, Modern Medicine Magazine, 1970; Albert Einstein Award, Yeshiva Univ., 1971; Rudolph Virchow Medal, 1971; Myrtle Wreath Award, Hadassah, 1972; Torald Sollmann Award, American Society of Pharmacology and Experimental Therapeutics, 1973. Leibniz Medal, 1984; Salmon Medal, 1989; Thudicum Medal, 1989; Gerard Medal, 1991.

Selected Publications: "Reduction in the Accumulation of Norepinephrine 3H in Experimental Hypertension." *Life Science* 5 (1966): 2283–91 (with others). "Control of Catechol Amine Metabolism." *Progress in Endocrinology, International Congress of Endocrinology, 3rd* (1968): 286–93. *The Pineal.* New York: Academic Press, 1968 (with R. Wurthman and D. Kelly). "Biochemical Pharmacology of Catechol Amines and Its Clinical Implications." *Transactions of the American Neurological Association* 96 (1972): 179–86.

For More Information See: People 11 (February 5, 1979): 24. *Science* (October 23, 1970): 422–23.

Commentary: Julius Axelrod shared the Nobel Prize for his role in developing the available knowledge about humoral transmitters in sympathetic nerves. Axelrod used tagged epinephrine and norepinephrine to show that the injected drugs equilibrated with the pool of transmitters in the nerve channels. He studied the action of many drugs and proved that their action was due to the changes they caused in the storage of neurotransmitters. Axelrod also studied the role of two enzymes which degrade the catecholamines, of which norepinephrine is one. With Bernard Brodie, he was responsible for the widely used drug Tylenol. (K.F.)

Katz, Bernard, Sir 380

Prize: Medicine and Physiology, 1970. *Born:* March 26, 1911; Leipzig, Germany. *Parents:* Father, Max N. Katz; Mother, Eugenie Rabinowitz Katz. *Nationality:* German; later British citizen. *Religion:* Jewish. *Education:* Univ. of Leipzig, Germany, M.D., 1934; Univ. of London, England, Ph.D., 1938. *Spouse:* Marguerite Penly, married October 27, 1945. *Children:* David, son; Jonathan, son. *Career:* Sydney Hospital, Australia, Physician, 1939–42; British Army, 1942–45; Univ. of London, England, Professor and Administrator, 1946–78. *Other Awards:* Garten Prize, Univ. of Leipzig, 1934; Feldberg Foundation Award, 1965; Baly Medal, Royal College of Physicians, 1967; Copley Medal, Royal Society, 1967; Knighthood, 1969; Cothenius Medal, Deutsche Akademie der Naturforscher Leopoldina, 1989.

Selected Publications: Electric Excitation of Nerve: A Review. London: Oxford Univ. Press, 1939. *How Cells Communicate.* San Francisco: W.H. Freeman, 1961. *Nerve, Muscle, and Synapse.* New York: McGraw-Hill, 1966. *The Release of Neural Transmitter Substance.* Springfield, IL: Thomas, 1969.

For More Information See: New York Times Biographical Service (October 1970): 2589. *Science* 170 (October 23, 1970): 422–24.

Commentary: Bernard Katz shared the Nobel Prize for his contribution to the knowledge of the mechanisms involved in the release of transmitter substances from nerve terminals. Katz discovered that there was a potential present at a neuromuscular junction even after stimulation and proposed the quantum hypothesis (that nerve endings secrete acetylcholine in quanta, and that stimulation enormously increases the quanta released). He also researched the effects of sodium, potassium, and calcium on activity in the junction. (K.F.)

Von Euler, Ulf Svante 381

Prize: Medicine and Physiology, 1970. *Born:* February 7, 1905; Stockholm, Sweden. *Death:* March 10, 1983; Stockholm, Sweden. *Parents:* Father, Hans von Euler-Chelpin; Mother, Astrid Cleve von Euler. *Nationality:* Swedish. *Religion:* Protestant. *Education:* Karolinska Institute, Sweden, M.D., 1930. *Spouse:* Jane Sodenstierna, married April 12, 1930, divorced 1957; Dagmar Cronstedt, married August 20, 1958. *Children:* Leo, son; Christopher, son; Ursula, daughter; Marie, daughter. *Career:* Karolinska Institute, Sweden, Professor and Administrator, 1930–71. *Other Awards:* Commander, Order of the North Star, Sweden; Cruzeiro do Sul, Brazil, 1952; Palmes Academiques, France; Gairdner Award, 1961; Jahre Prize, 1965; Stouffer Prize, 1967; Grand Cross al Merito Civil, Spain, 1979.

Selected Publications: "Hypertension after Bilateral Nephrectomy in the Rat." *Nature* 160 (1947): 905 (with E. Braun-Menendez). *Noradrenaline: Chemistry, Physiology, Pharmacology, and Clinical Aspects.* Springfield, IL: Thomas, 1956. *Prostaglandins.* New York: Academic Press, 1968. *Release and Uptake Functions in Adrenergic Nerve Granules.* Liverpool: Liverpool Univ. Press, 1982.

For More Information See: Biographical Encyclopedia of Scientists. New York: Facts on File, 1981, 815. *Biographical Memoirs of the Fellows of the Royal Society.* London: Royal Society, 1985 (Volume 31), 143–70. *The Excitement and Fascination of Science.* Palo Alto, CA: Annual Reviews, Inc., 1978, Vol. 2, 675–86.

Commentary: Ulf von Euler was awarded the Nobel Prize for his contribution to knowledge concerning humoral transmitters in sympathetic nerves. Von Euler was responsible for isolation and identification of norepinephrine as the transmitter in the sympathetic nervous system and elaboration of its role in stress conditions. He also found that stimulation of the nerve to the adrenal gland produced increased adrenal epinephrine and isolated and characterized the norepinephrine storage units in nerves. Von Euler, early in his career, discovered prostaglandin, which would later become a much-studied entity. (K.F.)

1971

Sutherland, Earl Wilbur, Jr.   **382**
Prize: Medicine and Physiology, 1971. *Born:* November 19, 1915; Burlingame, KS. *Death:* March 9, 1974; Miami, FL. *Parents:* Father, Earl Wilbur Sutherland; Mother, Edith Hartshorn Sutherland. *Nationality:* American. *Religion:* Protestant. *Education:* Washburn College, KS, B.S., 1937; Washington Univ., MO, M.D., 1942. *Spouse:* Mildred Rice, married 1937, divorced 1962; Claudia Sebeste Smith, married 1963. *Children:* 2 sons; 2 daughters. *Career:* Washington Univ., MO, Professor, 1940–42; United States Army, 1942–45; Washington Univ., MO, Professor, 1945–53; Case Western Reserve Univ., OH, Professor, 1953–63; Vanderbilt Univ., TN, Professor, 1963–73; Univ. of Miami, FL, Professor, 1973–74. *Other Awards:* Torald Sollman Award, 1969; Dickson Prize in Medicine, 1970; Lasker Award, 1970; Achievement Award, American Heart Association, 1971; National Medal of Science, United States, 1973.

Selected Publications: "Hormonal Regulatory Mechanisms." *Proceedings of the Third International Congress of Biochemistry.* New York: Academic Press, 1955, 318–27. "The Properties of an Adenine Ribonucleotide Produced with Cellular Particles, ATP, Mg++, and Epinephrine or Glucagon." *Journal of the American Chemical Society* 79 (1957): 3068 (with T.W. Rall). "Formation of a Cyclic Adenine Ribonucleotide by Tissue Particles." *Journal of Biological Chemistry* 232 (1958): 1065–76 (with T.W. Rall). "The Biological Role of Adenosine 3^1, 5^1-Phosphate." *Harvey Lecture Series.* New York: Academic Press, 1962 (Volume 57), 17–33. "The Role of Cyclic 3^1, 5Á-AMP in Responses to Catecholamines and Other Hormones." *Pharmacological Reviews* 18 (1966): 145–61 (with G.A. Robison). *Cyclic AMP.* New York: Academic Press, 1971 (with G.A. Robison and R.W. Butcher).

For More Information See: Biographical Memoirs of the National Academy of Sciences. Washington, DC: National Academy of Sciences, 1978 (Volume 49), 319–50. *Time* 98 (October 25, 1971): 63.

Commentary: Earl Sutherland received the Nobel Prize for "his long study of hormones, the chemical substances that regulate virtually every body function." During his career, he investigated the regulation of carbohydrate metabolism by the hormone adrenaline interaction with phosphorylase, the role of the cyclic AMP intermediate in hormonal activities, and the involvement of cyclic AMP in transmission of genetic information and in abnormal cell growth. (B.I.M.)

1972

Edelman, Gerald Maurice   **383**
Prize: Medicine and Physiology, 1972. *Born:* July 1, 1929; New York, NY. *Parents:* Father, Edward Edelman; Mother, Anna Freedman Edelman. *Nationality:* American. *Religion:* Jewish. *Education:* Ursinus College, PA, B.S., 1950; Univ. of Pennsylvania, M.D., 1954; Rockefeller Univ., NY, Ph.D., 1960. *Spouse:* Maxine Morrison, married June 11, 1950. *Children:* Eric, son; David, son; Judith, daughter. *Career:* Rockefeller Univ., NY, Professor and Administrator, 1957–92. Scripps Research Institute, CA, Researcher, 1992-. *Other Awards:* Spencer Morris Award, Univ. of Pennsylvania, 1954; Eli Lilly Award, 1965; Annual Alumni

Award, Ursinus College, 1969; Albert Einstein Commemorative Award, Yeshiva Univ., 1974; Buchman Memorial Award, California Institute of Technology, 1975; Rabbi Shai Schaknai Memorial Prize, Hebrew Univ., 1977; Regents Medal, New York State, 1984; Sesquicentennial Commemorative Award, National Library of Medicine, 1986; Neurath Prize, 1986; Vogt Award, 1988; Personnalite de l'annee, Paris, 1990; Warren Prize, 1992.

Selected Publications: "The Structure and Function of Antibodies." *Scientific American* 223 (August 1970): 34–42. *Cellular Selection and Regulation in the Immune Response.* New York: Raven Press, 1974. *Molecular Machinery of the Membrane.* Cambridge, MA: Massachusetts Institute of Technology Press, 1975. *Dynamic Aspects of Neocortical Function.* New York: Wiley, 1985 (with E. Gall and W. Cowan). *Molecular Basis of Neural Development.* New York: Wiley, 1985 (with E. Gall and W. Cowan). *Bright Air, Brilliant Fire.* New York: Basic Books, 1992.

For More Information See: Current Biography Yearbook. New York: H. W. Wilson, 1995, 9. *New York Times* (May 22, 1988): Section 6, 16–19. *Science* 178 (October 27, 1972): 384–86.

Commentary: Gerald Edelman shared the Nobel Prize for his research on the chemical structure of antibodies. His dissertation used Rodney Porter's methods to cleave and study the structure of human immunoglobulins. Later research led to the cleavage of the large molecules into component polypeptide chains, using urea. Edelman reported two different polypeptides and different antigen-binding properties, which stimulated much of the later work in this field. He also succeeded in determining the structure of human myeloma protein. His later studies focused on brain function and embryology. (B.I.M.)

Porter, Rodney Robert   **384**
Prize: Medicine and Physiology, 1972. *Born:* October 8, 1917; Liverpool, England. *Death:* September 6, 1985; Winchester, England. *Parents:* Father, Joseph L. Porter; Mother, Isobel M. Porter. *Nationality:* British. *Religion:* Protestant. *Education:* Liverpool Univ., England, B.S., 1939; Cambridge Univ., England, Ph.D., 1948. *Spouse:* Julia Frances New, married 1948. *Children:* Nigel, son; Tim, son; Susan, daughter; Ruth, daughter; Helen, daughter. *Career:* National Institute for Medical Research, London, England, Researcher, 1949–60; London Univ., England, Professor, 1960–67; Oxford Univ., England, Professor, 1967–85. *Other Awards:* Award of Merit, Gairdner Foundation, 1966; Ciba Medal, Biochemistry Society, 1967; Karl Landsteiner Memorial Award, American Association of Blood Banks, 1968; Royal Medal, Royal Society, 1973.

Selected Publications: Defence and Recognition. Baltimore, MD: University Park Press, 1973. *Chemical Aspects of Immunology.* Burlington, NC: Carolina Biological Supply Company, 1976. *Contemporary Topics in Molecular Immunology.* Volume 6, New York: Plenum Press, 1976 (with G. Ada). *Biochemistry and Genetics of Complement: A Discussion.* London: Royal Society, 1984.

For More Information See: Biographical Memoirs of the Fellows of the Royal Society. London: Royal Society, 1987 (Volume 33): 433. *New Scientist* (October 19, 1972): 142–43. *New York Times Biographical Service* (1972): 1779. *Science* 178 (October 27, 1972): 384–86.

Commentary: Rodney Porter won the Nobel Prize for his research on the chemical structure of antibodies. He developed the method of selective cleavage with enzymes and succeeded in separating antibodies into two different parts with the enzyme papain. The activities of the two parts fit the known bivalency of immunoglobulin G. Later, Porter separated rabbit immunoglobulin polypeptides and developed the four-chain model for immunoglobulin G structure. (R.K.)

1973

Frisch, Karl von   385
Prize: Medicine and Physiology, 1973. *Born:* November 20, 1886; Vienna, Austria. *Death:* June 12, 1982; Munich, Germany. *Parents:* Father, Anton Ritter von Frisch; Mother, Marie Exner von Frisch. *Nationality:* Austrian. *Religion:* Catholic. *Education:* Univ. of Munich, Germany, Ph.D., 1910. *Spouse:* Margaret Mohr, married July 20, 1917. *Children:* Johanna, daughter; Maria, daughter; Helene, daughter; Otto, son. *Career:* Univ. of Munich, Germany, Professor, 1910–14; Döbling Hospital, Vienna, Austria, Physician, 1914–19; Univ. of Munich, Germany, Professor, 1912–21; Univ. of Rostock, Germany, Professor, 1921–23; Univ. of Breslau, Poland, Professor, 1923–25; Univ. of Munich, Germany, Administrator, 1925–46; Univ. of Graz, Austria, Professor and Administrator, 1946–50; Univ. of Munich, Germany, Professor, 1950–58. *Other Awards:* Orden Pour le Merite für Wissenschaften und Kunste, 1952; Magellan Prize, American Philosophical Society, 1956; Kalinga Prize, UNESCO, 1959; Balzan Prize, 1963.

Selected Publications: The Dancing Bees: An Account of the Life and Senses of the Honeybee. New York: Harcourt, Brace, 1955. *Man and the Living World.* New York: Harcourt, 1963. *Bees: Their Vision, Chemical Senses and Language.* Ithaca, NY: Cornell Univ. Press, 1972. *Animal Architecture.* New York: Van Nostrand Reinhold, 1983.

For More Information See: A Biologist Remembers. New York: Pergamon, 1967. *Current Biography Yearbook.* New York: H.W. Wilson, 1974, 130–33. "Karl von Frisch." *Biographical Memoirs of the Fellows of the Royal Society.* London: Royal Society, 1983 (Volume 29), 197–200.

Commentary: Karl von Frisch was awarded the Nobel Prize for his work in ethology (the study of animal behavior). He used conditioned reflex studies to show that bees distinguished among colors and could communicate their findings. Previously, von Frisch had shown that fish could distinguish among colors, light intensities, and sound levels. (B.I.M.)

Lorenz, Konrad Zacharias   386
Prize: Medicine and Physiology, 1973. *Born:* November 7, 1903; Vienna, Austria. *Death:* February 27, 1989; Altenburg, Austria. *Parents:* Father, Adolf Lorenz; Mother, Emma Lecher Lorenz. *Nationality:* Austrian. *Religion:* Catholic. *Education:* Univ. of Vienna, Austria, M.D., 1928; Univ. of Vienna, Austria, Ph.D., 1933. *Spouse:* Margarethe "Gretl" Gebhardt, married June 24, 1927. *Children:* Agnes, daughter; Dagmar, daughter; Thomas, son. *Career:* Univ. of Vienna, Austria, Professor, 1928–40; Univ. of Königsberg, Germany, Professor, 1940–42; German Army, 1942–44; Soviet Armenia, Prisoner of War, 1944–48; Institute of Comparative Ethology, Altenberg, Austria, Administrator,

1949–51; Max Planck Foundation, Germany, Administrator, 1951–73; Austrian Academy of Science, Administrator, 1973–82. *Other Awards:* Gold Medal, Zoological Society of New York, 1955; City Prize, Vienna, 1959; Gold Bölsche Medal, 1962; Austrian Distinction for Science and Art, 1964; Prix Mondial, Cino de Duca, 1969; Kalinga Prize, UNESCO, 1970; Order Pour le Mérite; Grosses Verdienstkreuz, 1974; Bayerischer Verdienstorden, 1974.

Selected Publications: On Aggression. New York: Harcourt, Brace and World, 1966. *Evolution and Modification of Behavior.* Chicago: Univ. of Chicago Press, 1967. *Studies in Animal and Human Behavior.* Cambridge, MA: Harvard Univ. Press, 1970–71.

For More Information See: Current Biography Yearbook. New York: H.W. Wilson, 1977, 274–77. Evans, Richard. *Konrad Lorenz: The Man and His Ideas.* New York: Harcourt, Brace, Jovanovich, 1975. Lorenz, K. and Mündl, K.L. *On Life and Living: Konrad Lorenz in Conversation with Kurt Mündl.* New York: St. Martin's, 1990. Wukelits, F. *Konrad Lorenz.* Munich: Piper, 1990.

Commentary: Konrad Lorenz shared the Nobel Prize for his work in ethology (the comparative study of the behavior of animals in their natural environment). He worked mostly with birds, particularly geese, and was especially well known for his study of aggressive behavior, of imprinting (the programed action of following the first moving object seen after hatching), and of the effects of isolation and overcrowding on young primates. (B.I.M.)

Tinbergen, Nikolaas   387
Prize: Medicine and Physiology, 1973. *Born:* April 15, 1907; The Hague, Netherlands. *Death:* December 21, 1988; Oxford, England. *Parents:* Father, Dirk Cornelus Tinbergen; Mother, Jeannette Van Eek Tinbergen. *Nationality:* Dutch; later British citizen. *Religion:* Agnostic; from Protestant background. *Education:* Univ. of Leiden, Netherlands, Ph.D., 1932. *Spouse:* Elisabeth "Lies" Amelie Rutten, married April 14, 1932. *Children:* Jacob, son; Catharina, daughter; Dirk, son; Jannetje, daughter; Gerardina, daughter. *Career:* Univ. of Leiden, Netherlands, Professor, 1933–49; German Prisoner of War, 1945–47; Oxford Univ., England, Professor, 1949–74. *Other Awards:* Bölsche Medal, 1969; Italia Prize for TV Documentaries, 1969; Godman-Salvin Medal, British Ornithologists Union, 1969; Jan Swammerdam Medal, 1973.

Selected Publications: The Animal in Its World: Explorations of an Ethologist, 1932–72 (collected papers). Cambridge, MA: Harvard Univ. Press, 1972–73. *Early Childhood Autism: An Ethological Approach.* Berlin: P. Parry, 1972 (with E.A. Tinbergen).

For More Information See: Biographical Memoirs of the Fellows of the Royal Society. London: Royal Society, 1990 (Volume 36): 549. *Current Biography Yearbook.* New York: H.W. Wilson, 1975, 414–16. *Psychology Today* (March 1974): 68–71. Röll, d.R. and Kofod, Margaret. *The World of Instinct: Niko Tinbergen and the Rise of Ethology in the Netherlands (1920–1950).* Assen: Van Gorcum, 2000.

Commentary: Nikolaas Tinbergen received the Nobel for his studies of animal behavior, in acknowledgement of the importance of ethological research to the understanding of human behavior. Best known for his studies of the habits of gulls, Tinbergen also researched the homing instincts of digger wasps, the mating rituals of sticklebacks, and the color adaptations of butterflies. His later studies of autism in children were also noteworthy. (B.I.M.)

1974

Claude, Albert 388

Prize: Medicine and Physiology, 1974. *Born:* August 24, 1898; Longlier (now Luxembourg), Belgium. *Death:* May 22, 1983; Brussels, Belgium. *Parents:* Father, Florentin Joseph Claude; Mother, Marie-Glaudicine Wautriquant Claude. *Nationality:* Belgian; later American citizen. *Religion:* Catholic. *Education:* Univ. of Liège, Belgium, M.D., 1928. *Spouse:* Joy Gilder, married June 20, 1935, divorced. *Children:* Philippa, daughter. *Career:* Rockefeller Univ., NY, Professor, 1929–72; Univ. of Belgium, Professor, 1948–70; Institute Jules Bordet, Brussels, Belgium, 1948–71; Catholic University, Louvain, Professor, 1972–83. *Other Awards:* British War Medal, 1918; Interallied Medal, 1918; Grand Cordon de l'Ordre de Leopold II, Belgium; Prize Fonds National de la Recherche Scientifique, 1965; Medal, Belgian Academie of Medicine; Louisa G. Horowitz Prize, Columbia Univ., 1970; Paul Ehrlich Award, 1971; Ludwig Darmstaedter Prize, 1971.

Selected Publications: "Fractionation of Chicken Tumor Extracts by Highspeed Centrifugation." *American Journal of Cancer* 30 (1937): 742–45. "Distribution of Nucleic Acids in the Cell and the Morphological Constitution of Cytoplasm." *Biological Symposia* 10 (1943): 111–29. "Fractionation of Mammalian Liver Cells by Differential Centrifugation. I and II." *Journal of Experimental Medicine* 84 (1946): 51–89. "The Nature of the Golgi Apparatus. I and II." *Journal of Morphology* 85 (1949): 35–111 (with G. Palade).

For More Information See: Biographical Encyclopedia *of Scientists.* New York: Facts on File, 1981, 151. *New Scientist* (October 24, 1974): 255–56. *Science* 186 (November 8, 1974): 516–20.

Commentary: Albert Claude won the Nobel Prize for his contributions to the research on the structure and function of the internal components of cells. Claude discovered early that cell components could be separated in a centrifuge and developed the procedures and studied the fractions for several different cells and tissues. He also used electron microscopy to study cell structure. (R.K.)

de Duvé, Christian René Marie Joseph 389

Prize: Medicine and Physiology, 1974. *Born:* October 2, 1917; Thames Ditton, England. *Parents:* Father, Alphonse de Duvé; Mother, Madaleine Pungs de Duvé. *Nationality:* Belgian; later American resident. *Religion:* Catholic. *Education:* Univ. of Louvain, Belgium, M.D., 1941; Univ. of Louvain, Belgium, M.Sc., 1946; Univ. of Louvain, Belgium, Ph.D., 1945. *Spouse:* Janine Herman, married September 30, 1943. *Children:* Thierry, son; Alain, son; Anne, daughter; Françoise, daughter. *Career:* Univ. of Louvain, Belgium, Professor, 1947–85; Rockefeller Univ., NY, Professor, 1962–88. *Other Awards:* Prix des Alumni, 1949; Prix Pfizer, 1957; Prix Francqui, 1960; Prix Quinquennal, Belge des Sciences Médicales, Belgium, 1967; International Award of Merit, Gairdner Foundation, Canada, 1967; Dr. H.P. Heineken Prijs, Netherlands, 1973; Grand Cross, Order

of Leopold II, 1975; Harden Award, 1978; Theobald Smith Award, 1981; Jimenez Diaz Award, 1985; E.B. Wilson Award, 1989.

Selected Publications: "Cytochrome Oxidase and Acid Phosphatase of Isolated Mitochondria." *Congr. Intern. Biochim.*, Resumes Communs., 2e Congr., Paris (1952): 278 (with F. Appelmans and R. Wattiaux). "Lysosomes, a New Group of Cytoplasmic Particles." *Subcellular Particles, Symposium, Woods Hole, MA* (1958): 128–58. "Lysosomes and Chemotherapy." *Biological Approaches to Cancer Chemotherapy* (1960): 101–12. *A Guided Tour of the Living Cell.* New York: Scientific American Books, 1984. *Vital Dust.* New York: Basic, 1995.

For More Information See: New York Times Biographi-*cal Service* (October 1974): 1405. *Science* 186 (November 8, 1974): 516–20.

Commentary: Christian de Duvé shared the Nobel Prize for his contributions to research on the structure and function of the internal components of cells. Using electron microscopy and biochemical analyses, de Duvé identified and discussed in detail two cytoplasmic enzyme-containing units—the lysosome and peroxisome. His later research also involved work on the relationships of lysosomes and storage diseases in man, on lysosomes in cell pathology, and on drug-lysosome interactions. (B.I.M.)

Palade, George Emil 390

Prize: Medicine and Physiology, 1974. *Born:* November 19, 1912; Jassi, Rumania. *Parents:* Father, Emil Palade; Mother, Constana Cantemir Palade. *Nationality:* Romanian; later American citizen. *Religion:* Greek Orthodox. *Education:* Univ. of Bucharest, Rumania, M.D., 1940. *Spouse:* Irina Malaxa, married June 12, 1941, died 1969; Marilyn Farquhar, married 1970. *Children:* Philip Theodore, son; Georgia Teodora, daughter. *Career:* Univ. of Bucharest, Rumania, Professor, 1935–45; Rockefeller Univ., NY, Professor, 1946–72; Yale Univ., CT, Professor, 1972–90; Univ. of California, San Diego, Professor, 1990-. *Other Awards:* Passano Award, American Medical Association, 1964; Lasker Award, 1966; Gairdner Special Award, 1967; Horowitz Prize, 1970; Warren Prize, Massachusetts General Hospital; National Medal of Science, 1986.

Selected Publications: "The Nature of the Golgi Apparatus. I and II." *Journal of Morphology* 85 (1949): 35–111 (with A. Claude). "Liver Microsomes. An Integrated Morphological and Biochemical Study." *J. Biophys. Biochem. Cytol.* 2 (1956): 171–200 (with P. Siekovitz). "Pancreatic Microsomes. An Integrated Morphological and Biochemical Study." *J. Biophys. Biochem. Cytol* 2 (1956): 671–90 (with P. Siekovitz). "Functional Changes in the Structure of Cell Components." *Subcellular Particles, Symposium, Woods Hole, MA* (1958): 64–80.

For More Information See: Current Biography Year-*book.* New York: H.W. Wilson, 1967, 324–26. *Science* 186 (November 8, 1974): 516–20.

Commentary: George Palade shared the Nobel Prize for his contributions to research on the structure and function of the internal components of cells. Palade used and refined the available techniques of electron microscopy and sedimentation to isolate purified cell functions and study their biochemical nature. His introduction of osmium tetroxide as a fixative made electron microscopy a viable technique for the studies. Palade also studied the synthesis of enzymes on ribosomes and the pathways of resulting protein and provided the first detailed studies of mitochondrial fine structure. (B.I.M.)

1975

Baltimore, David 391

Prize: Medicine and Physiology, 1975. *Born:* March 7, 1938; New York, NY. *Parents:* Father, Richard I. Baltimore; Mother, Gertrude Lipschitz Baltimore. *Nationality:* American. *Religion:* Jewish. *Education:* Swarthmore College, PA, B.A., 1960; Rockefeller Univ., NY, Ph.D., 1964. *Spouse:* Alice S. Huang, married October 5, 1968. *Children:* Lauren Rachel, daughter. *Career:* Albert Einstein College of Medicine, NY, Researcher, 1964–65; Salk Institute, CA, Researcher, 1965–68; Massachusetts Institute of Technology, Professor and Administrator, 1968–90; Rockefeller Univ., NY, Professor, 1990–94; Massachusetts Institute of Technology, Professor, 1994–97; California Institute of Technology, Administrator, 1997-. *Other Awards:* Gustav Stern Award, 1970; Warren Triennial Prize, Massachusetts General Hospital, 1971; Eli Lilly Award, 1971; U.S. Steel Foundation Award, 1974; Gairdner Foundation Annual Award, 1974; National Medal of Science, 1999.

Selected Publications: "Viral RNA-Dependent DNA Polymerase." *Nature (London)* 226 (1970): 1211–13. "RNA-Directed DNA Synthesis and RNA Tumor Viruses." *Advances in Virus Research* 17 (1972): 51–94. *Animal Virology.* New York: Academic Press, 1976 (with others). *Activation and Regulation of Immunoglobin Synthesis in Malignant B Cells.* Copenhagen: Munksgaard, 1979 (with others).

For More Information See: *Current Biography Yearbook.* New York: H.W. Wilson, 1983, 25–28. *Science* 190 (November 14, 1975): 650, 712–13.

Commentary: David Baltimore received the Nobel Prize for his contributions to the "discoveries concerning the interaction between tumor viruses and the genetic material of the cell." He and Howard Temin independently arrived at an explanation of DNA synthesis in RNA tumor viruses through the proposal of a reverse transcriptase enzyme which allowed DNA synthesis to proceed by copying the RNA element. The theory, although controversial, was later accepted. Baltimore began his career working on RNA virus replication and moved on to polio virus and leukemia virus research later. His partial synthesis of a mammalian hemoglobin gene led to his activity in support of limitations of genetic engineering research. He also worked successfully in synthetic vaccine research. (B.I.M.)

Dulbecco, Renato 392

Prize: Medicine and Physiology, 1975. *Born:* February 22, 1914; Catanzaro, Italy. *Parents:* Father, Leonardo Dulbecco; Mother, Maria Virdia Dulbecco. *Nationality:* Italian; later American citizen. *Religion:* Catholic. *Education:* Univ. of Torino, Italy, M.D., 1936. *Spouse:* Giuseppina Salvo, married June 1, 1940, divorced 1963; Maureen Rutherford Muir, married July 17, 1963. *Children:* Peter Leonard, son; Maria Vittoria, daughter; Fiona Linsey, daughter. *Career:* Univ. of Torino, Italy, Researcher, 1936–47; Indiana Univ., Researcher, 1947–49; California Institute of Technology, Professor, 1949–63; Salk Institute, CA, Researcher, 1963–71;

Imperial Cancer Research Fund, London, England, Administrator, 1971–77; Salk Institute, CA, Professor and Administrator, 1977–92. *Other Awards:* John Scott Award, City of Philadelphia, PA, 1958; Kimball Award, Conference of Public Health Laboratory Directors, 1959; Albert and Mary Lasker Basic Medical Research Award, 1964; Howard Taylor Ricketts Award, 1965; Paul Ehrlich-Ludwig Darmstaedter Prize, 1967; Horowitz Prize, Columbia Univ., 1973; Selman Waksman Award, National Academy of Sciences, 1974; Man of the Year, London, 1975; Targo d'oro, Villa San Giovanni, 1978; Italian-American of the Year, San Diego, CA, 1978; Decorated Grand Officiale, Italian Republic, 1981; Mandel Gold Medal, Czechoslovak Academy of Sciences, 1982; Via de Condotti Prize, 1990; Natale Di Roma Prize, 1993; Columbus Prize, 1993.

Selected Publications: *The Induction of Cancer by Viruses.* San Francisco: W.H. Freeman, 1967. *The Biology of Small DNA-Tumor Viruses.* New York: MSS Information Corp., 1974. *Induction of Host Systems, Integration and Excision.* Cambridge, MA: Cambridge Univ. Press, 1975. *Virology.* Hagerstown, MD: Harper and Row, 1980 (with Howard Ginsberg).

For More Information See: *Biographical Encyclopedia of Scientists.* New York: Facts on File, 1981, 219. *New Scientist* (October 23, 1975): 219–20. *New York Times Bibliographic Service* (October 1975): 1266–67. *Science* 190 (November 14, 1975): 650, 712–13. *Scienza, Vita e Aventura.* Paris: Plow, 1990.

Commentary: Renato Dulbecco's Nobel was awarded for his contributions to the "discoveries concerning the interaction between tumor viruses and the genetic material of the cell." He developed many of the techniques used by researchers to study the molecular biology of animal viruses, including those used by his colaureates, who had both worked under him. Dulbecco also did pioneer work on gene transformation by DNA tumor viruses. (B.I.M.)

Temin, Howard Martin 393

Prize: Medicine and Physiology, 1975. *Born:* December 10, 1934; Philadelphia, PA. *Death:* February 9, 1994; Madison, WI. *Parents:* Father, Henry Temin; Mother, Annette Lehman Temin. *Nationality:* American. *Religion:* Jewish. *Education:* Swarthmore College, PA, B.A., 1955; California Institute of Technology, Ph.D., 1959. *Spouse:* Rayla Greenberg, married May 27, 1962. *Children:* Sara Beth, daughter; Miriam Judith, daughter. *Career:* California Institute of Technology, Researcher, 1959–60; Univ. of Wisconsin, Professor, 1960–94. *Other Awards:* Warren Triennial Prize, Massachusetts General Hospital, 1971; Special Commendation, Medical Society of Wisconsin, 1971; PAP Award, Papanicolaou Institute, 1972; Bertner Award, M.D. Anderson Hospital and Tumor Institute, 1972; U.S. Steel Foundation Award, 1972; Waksman Award, Theobald Smith Society, 1972; Griffuel Prize, Association of Developmental Recherche Cancer, Villejuif, France, 1972; Award in Enzyme Chemistry, American Chemical Society, 1973; Award for Distinguished Achievement, Modern Medicine, 1973; Gairdner Foundation International Award, 1974; Albert Lasker Award, 1974; Lucy Wortham James Award, Society of Surgical Oncologists, 1976; Alumni Distinguished Service Award, California Institute of Technology, 1976; Gruber Award, American Academy of Dermatology, 1981; Hilldale

Award, Univ. of Wisconsin, 1986; National Medal of Science, 1992.

Selected Publications: "Participation of Deoxyribonucleic Acid (DNA) in Rous Sarcoma Virus Production." *Virology* 22 (1964): 486–94. "Carcinogenesis by Avian Sarcoma Viruses. III. The Differential Effect of Serum and Polyanions on Multiplication of Uninfected and Converted Cells." *Journal of the National Cancer Institute* 37 (1966): 167–75. *RNA-Directed DNA Synthesis.* San Francisco: W.H. Freeman, 1972. "RNA-Directed DNA Synthesis and RNA Tumor Viruses." *Advances in Virus Research* 17 (1972): 51–94 (with D. Baltimore).

For More Information See: Biographical Encyclopedia of Scientists. New York: Facts on File, 1981, 776–77. *New Scientist* (October 23, 1975): 219–20. *New York Times Biographical Service* (February 11, 1994): 226. *Science* 190 (November 14, 1975): 650, 712–13.

Commentary: Howard Temin shared the Nobel Prize for his contributions to the "discoveries concerning the interaction between tumor viruses and the genetic material of the cell." He and David Baltimore independently proposed an explanation of the DNA synthesis in RNA tumor viruses. The theory of the reverse transcriptase enzyme said that the DNA synthesis proceeded by copying the RNA element. The theory, contrary to the "central dogma" of molecular biology at that time, was later accepted. Temin worked with Rous sarcoma virus, beginning with graduate work that developed a reproducible assay in vitro for the tumor virus. (B.I.M.)

1976

Blumberg, Baruch Samuel   394

Prize: Medicine and Physiology, 1976. *Born:* July 28, 1925; New York, NY. *Parents:* Father, Meyer Blumberg; Mother, Ida Simonoff Blumberg. *Nationality:* American. *Religion:* Jewish. *Education:* Union College, NY, B.S., 1946; Columbia Univ., NY, M.D., 1951; Oxford Univ., England, Ph.D., 1957. *Spouse:* Jean Liebesman, married April 4, 1954. *Children:* George Micah Connor, son; Noah Francis Baruch, son; Jane Emily, daughter; Anne Francesca, daughter. *Career:* National Institutes of Health, MD, Administrator, 1957–64; Institute for Cancer Research, PA, Administrator, 1964-; Univ. of Pennsylvania, Professor, 1977–99; NASA Astrobiology Institute, CA, Administrator, 1999-. *Other Awards:* Albion O. Berstein Award, Medical Society of the State of New York, 1969; Grand Scientific Award, Phi Lambda Kappa, 1972; Annual Award, Eastern Pennsylvania Branch of the American Society for Microbiology, 1972; Eppinger Prize, Univ. of Freiburg, Germany, 1973; Passano Award, 1974; Distinguished Achievement Award, Modern Medicine, 1975; Gairdner Foundation International Award, 1975; Karl Landsteiner Memorial Award, American Association of Blood Banks, 1975; Scopus Award, American Friends of Hebrew University, 1977; Strittmatter Award, Philadelphia County Medical Society, 1980. Distinguished Service Award, Pennsylvania Medical Society, 1982; Zubrow Award, 1986; McGovern Award, 1988; Blundell Award, 1989; Huxley Medal, 1989; Governor's Award, Commonwealth of Pennsylvania, 1989; Gold Medal, Canadian Liver Foundation, 1990; Mudd Award, 1990; National Inventor

Hall of Fame, 1993; Showa Emperor Memorial Award, Japan, 1994.

Selected Publications: Conference on Genetic Polymorphisms and Geographic Variations in Disease. Proceedings. New York: Grune & Stratton, 1962. *Australia Antigen and Hepatitis.* Cleveland, OH: Chemical Rubber Co., 1972 (with others). *Primary Hepatocellular Carcinoma and Hepatitis B Virus.* Chicago: Yearbook Medical Publishers, 1982. *Hepatitis B: The Virus, the Disease, and the Vaccine.* New York: Plenum Press, 1984 (with K. Eisenstein and I. Milman).

For More Information See: Current Biography Yearbook. New York: H.W. Wilson, 1977, 72–74. *Science* 194 (November 26, 1976): 928–29.

Commentary: The Academy cited Barry Blumberg for his work in "discoveries concerning mechanisms involved in the origin and spread of infectious diseases." Blumberg identified Australia antigen as the indicator in the blood of the presence of hepatitis-B, which became the basis for the test for screening out hepatitis-B carriers among blood donors and for vaccine work. His career-long research dealt with how and why people of different backgrounds react differently to disease. (B.I.M.)

Gajdusek, Daniel Carleton   395

Prize: Medicine and Physiology, 1976. *Born:* September 9, 1923; Yonkers, NY. *Parents:* Father, Karl A. Gajdusek; Mother, Ottilia Dobroczki Gajdusek. *Nationality:* American. *Religion:* Catholic. *Education:* Univ. of Rochester, NY, B.S., 1943; Harvard Univ., MA, M.D., 1946. *Spouse:* None. *Children:* 58 adopted children. *Career:* Columbia Presbyterian Medical Center, NY, Physician, 1946–47; Pediatrics Children's Hospital, OH, Physician, 1947–48; Harvard Univ., MA, Researcher, 1949–52; Walter Reed Army Institute of Research, Washington, DC, Researcher, 1952–53; Institute Pasteur, Iran, Researcher, 1954–55; Walter and Eliza Hall Institute of Medical Research, Australia, Researcher, 1955–57; National Institutes of Health, MD, Administrator, 1958–97. *Other Awards:* E. Meade Johnson Award, American Academy of Pediatrics, 1963; Superior Service Award, National Institutes of Health, 1970; Distinguished Service Award, Department of Health, Education and Welfare, 1975; Professor Lucian Dautrebande Prize, Belgium, 1976; Cotzias Prize, American Academy of Neurology, 1979.

Selected Publications: Journals. Study of Child Growth and Development of Disease Patterns in Primitive Cultures. Bethesda, MD: National Institute of Neurological Diseases and Blindness, 1963. *Slow Latent and Temperate Virus Infections.* Bethesda, MD: National Institute of Health, 1965 (with C. Gibbs, Jr., and M. Alpers). *Genetic Studies in Relation to Kuru.* Chicago: Univ. of Chicago Press, 1972–75 (with others). *Kuru.* New York: Raven Press, 1981 (with J. Farquhar).

For More Information See: Current Biography Yearbook. New York: H.W. Wilson, 1981, 156–59. *Science* 194 (November 26, 1976): 928–29. Hammond, A., ed. *A Passion to Know.* New York: Scribner's, 1984, 11–22.

Commentary: Carleton Gajdusek was recognized for his "discoveries concerning mechanisms involved in the origin and spread of infectious diseases," especially for his intensive study of kuru, a brain disease in New Guinea, that showed that slow virus infections were possible in humans, and discovered a new group of viruses, apparently pieces of genetically active nucleic acid bound to fragments of plasma membrane. His work included research in many other medical problems in primitive isolated populations as well as contributions to anthropology and comparative child behavior. (B.I.M.)

1977

Guillemin, Roger Charles Louis 396

Prize: Medicine and Physiology, 1977. *Born:* January 11, 1924; Dijon, France. *Parents:* Father, Raymond Guillemin; Mother, Blanche Rigollot Guillemin. *Nationality:* French; later American citizen. *Religion:* Agnostic; from Catholic background. *Education:* Univ. of Dijon, France, B.A., 1941; Univ. of Dijon, France, B.Sc., 1942; Faculty of Medicine, Lyons, France, M.D., 1949; Univ. of Montreal, Canada, Ph.D., 1953. *Spouse:* Lucienne Jeanne Billard, married March 22, 1951. *Children:* Chantal, daughter; François, son; Claire, daughter; Helene, daughter; Elizabeth, daughter; Cecile, daughter. *Career:* Baylor Univ., Texas, Professor, 1953–70; Salk Institute, CA, Professor, 1970–89; Whittier Institute, CA, Researcher, 1989–97; Salk Institute, CA, Professor, 1997-. *Other Awards:* Bonneau and La Caze Awards, Académie des Sciences, 1957, 1960; Legion of Honor, France, 1974; Gairdner International Award, 1974; Lasker Foundation Award, 1975; Dickson Foundation Award, 1975; Dickson Prize, 1976; Passano Award, 1976; Schmitt Medal, 1977; National Medal of Science, USA, 1977; Barren Gold Medal, USA, 1979; Dale Medal, Society for Endocrinology, England, 1980; Ellen Browning Scripps Society Medal, 1988; Distinguished Scientist Award, National Diabetes Research Coalition.

Selected Publications: "Humoral Hypothalamic Control of the Anterior Pituitary. A Study which Combined Tissue Cultures." *Endocrinology* 57 (1955): 599 (with Barry Rosenberg). "Hypothalamic Control of the Anterior Pituitary, Study with Tissue Culture Techniques." *Federation Proceedings* 14 (1955): 211. "The Adenohypophysis and Its Hypothalamic Control." *Annual Review of Physiology* 29 (1967): 313. *The Hormones of the Hypothalamus.* San Francisco: W.H. Freeman Co., 1972 (with R. Burgus). "Control of Adenohypophysial Functions by Peptides of the Central Nervous System." *The Harvey Lectures* 71 (1975–76). "Purification, Isolation, and Primary Structure of the Hypothalamic Luteinizing Hormone-releasing Factor of Ovine Origin—a Historical Account." *American Journal of Obstetrics and Gynecology* 129 (1977): 214. *The Brain as an Endocrine Organ.* Cambridge, MA: Massachusetts Institute of Technology Press, 1978. *Hypothalamic Control of Pituitary Functions: The Growth Hormone Releasing Factor.* Liverpool: Liverpool Univ. Press, 1985. *Pioneers in Neuroendocrinology II.* New York: Plenum Press, 1978, 351. *Science* 198 (November 11, 1977): 594–95. Wade, Nicholas. *The Nobel Duel.* New York: Doubleday, 1981.

Commentary: Roger Guillemin was recognized, with his colaureates, for his work that "opened new vistas within biological and medical research far outside the border of their own spheres of interest." Guillemin's research, both with and independent of Andrew Schally, led to an understanding of the production of peptide hormones in the brain. The two identified and synthesized three brain hormones (thyrotropin-releasing factor, luteinizing-hormone releasing factor, and growth hormone inhibiting factor) that are used by the hypothalamus to direct the release of pituitary hormones. Research on understanding the brain's part in body chemistry and the understanding of the brain's role have been enormously increased as a result of their efforts. (R.K.)

Schally, Andrew Victor 397

Prize: Medicine and Physiology, 1977. *Born:* November 30, 1926; Wilno, Poland. *Parents:* Father, Casimir Peter Schally; Mother, Maria Lacka Schally. *Nationality:* Polish; later Canadian and American citizen. *Religion:* Most probably Christian. *Education:* McGill Univ., Canada, B.Sc., 1955; McGill Univ., Canada, Ph.D., 1957. *Spouse:* Margaret Rachel White, married May 14, 1956, divorced (no date found); Ana Maria de Medeiros Comaru, married August 1976. *Children:* Karen, daughter; Gordon, son. *Career:* Baylor Univ., Texas, Professor, 1957–62; VA Hospital, New Orleans, LA, Administrator, 1962-; Tulane Univ., New Orleans, LA, Professor, 1962-. *Other Awards:* Director's Award, VA Hospital, New Orleans, LA, 1968; Van Meter Prize, American Thyroid Association, 1969; Ayerst-Squibb Award, Endocrine Society, 1970; William S. Middleton Award, VA Hospital, New Orleans, LA, 1970; Charles Mickle Award, Univ. of Toronto, 1974; Gairdner International Award, 1974; Edward T. Tyler Award, 1975; Borden Award, Association of Medical Colleges and Borden Company Foundation, 1975; Lasker Award, 1975; Laude Award, 1975; Award, Spanish Pharmaceutical Society, 1977; Medal of Scientific Merit, Federal Univ. of Ceara, Brazil, 1977; First Diploma of Merit of St. Luke, Foundation of Social Pioneers, Rio de Janeiro, 1977.

Selected Publications: "The Release of Cortico-tropin by Anterior Pituitary Tissue in Vitro." *Canadian Journal of Biochemistry and Physiology* 33 (1955): 408 (with M. Saffran). "Stimulation of the Release of Corticotropin from the Adenohypophysis by a Neurohypophysial Factor." *Canadian Journal of Biochemistry and Physiology* 57 (1955): 439 (with M. Saffran). "Isolation of Thyrotropin Releasing Factor (TRF) from Porcine Hypothalamus." *Biochemical and Biophysical Research Communications* 25 (1966): 165 (with others). "Purification of Thyrotropic Hormone Releasing Factor from Bovine Hypothalamus." *Endocrinolgy* 78 (1966): 726 (with others). "The Amino Acid Sequence of a Peptide with Growth Hormone Releasing Activity Isolated from Porcine Hypothalamus." *Journal of Biological Chemistry* 246 (1971): 6647 (with others). *The Hypothalamus and Pituitary in Health and Disease.* Springfield, IL: Thomas, 1972 (with W. Locke). *Pioneers in Neuroendocrinology II.* New York: Plenum Press, 1978, 351. *Science* 198 (November 11, 1977): 594–95. Wade, Nicholas. *The Nobel Duel.* New York: Doubleday, 1981.

Commentary: The Academy cited Andrew Schally and his colaureates for work that "opened new vistas within biological and medical research far outside the border of their own spheres of interest," specifically that research which contributed to the understanding of the production of peptide hormones in the brain. Schally identified and synthesized, along with his colaureate, Roger Guillemin, three brain hormones (thyrotropin-releasing factor, luteinizing-hormone-releasing factor, and growth hormone release inhibiting factor) that the hypothalamus uses to direct the release of pituitary hormones. The resultant understanding of the brain's role in body chemistry and the research therein has been enormously increased as a result of their efforts. (R.K.)

Yalow, Rosalyn Sussman   **398**

Prize: Medicine and Physiology, 1977. *Born:* July 19, 1921; New York, NY. *Parents:* Father, Simon Sussman; Mother, Clara Zipper Sussman. *Nationality:* American. *Religion:* Jewish. *Education:* Hunter College, NY, A.B., 1941; Univ. of Illinois, M.S., 1942; Univ. of Illinois, Ph.D., 1945. *Spouse:* A. Aaron Yalow, married June 6, 1943. *Children:* Benjamin, son; Elanna, daughter. *Career:* Hunter College, NY, Professor, 1946–50; VA Hospital, NY, Researcher and Administrator, 1950–80; Montefiore Medical Center, NY, Administrator, 1980–85; Mount Sinai School of Medicine, NY, Professor, 1968–79, 1986-; Albert Einstein College of Medicine, Professor, 1979–85. *Other Awards:* William S. Middleton Medical Research Award, Veterans Administration, 1960; Eli Lilly Award, American Diabetes Association, 1961; Federal Woman's Award, 1961; Van Slyke Award, American Association of Clinical Chemists, 1968; Award, American College of Physicians, 1971; Dickson Prize, University of Pittsburgh, PA, 1971; Howard Taylor Ricketts Award, University of Chicago, IL, 1971; Gairdner Foundation International Award, 1971; Commemorative Medallion, American Diabetes Association, 1972; Koch Award, Endocrine Society, 1972; Bernstein Award, Medical Society of the State of New York, 1974; Boehringer-Manheim Corporation Award, American Association of Clinical Chemists, 1975; Science Achievement Award, American Medical Association, 1975; Exceptional Service Award, Veterans Administration, 1975; A. Cressy Morrison Award, New York Academy of Sciences, 1975; Distinguished Achievement Award, Modern Medicine, 1976; Lasker Award, 1976; La Madonnina International Prize, Milan, 1977; Golden Plate Award, American Academy Achievement, 1977; G. von Hevesy Medal, 1978; Rosalyn S. Yalow Research and Development Award, American Diabetes Association, 1978; Banting Medal, 1978; Torch of Learning Award, American Friends of Hebrew University, 1978; Virchow Gold Medal, Virchow-Pirquet Medical Society, 1978; Gratum Genus Humanum Gold Medal, World Federation of Nuclear Medicine or Biology, 1978; Jacobi Medallion, Mount Sinai School of Medicine, 1978; Jubilee Medal, College of New Rochelle, 1978; Exceptional Service Award, Veterans Administration, 1978; Sarasota Medical Award, 1979; Gold Medal, Phi Lambda Kappa, 1980; Achievement in Life Award, Encyclopedia Britannica, 1980; Theobald Smith Award, 1982; John and Samuel Bard Award, Bard College, 1982; Distinguished Research Award, Dallas Association of Retarded Citizens, 1982; Georg Charles de Henesy Nuclear Medicine Pioneer Award, 1986; National Medal of Science, 1988. Sachar Medallion, 1989.

Selected Publications: Peptide Hormones. New York: American Elsevier, 1973 (with S.A. Berson). *Methods in Radioimmunoassay of Peptide Hormones.* New York: American Elsevier, 1976. *Basic Research and Clinical Medicine.* New York: McGraw-Hill, 1981 (with others). *Radioimmunoassay.* New York: Van Nostrand-Reinhold, 1984.

For More Information See: Current Biography Yearbook. New York: H.W. Wilson, 1978, 458–60. "Madame Curie from the Bronx." *New York Times Magazine* (April 9, 1978): 29–31+. Straus, Eugene. *Rosalyn Yalow, Nobel Laureate.* New York: Plenum, 1998.

Commentary: Rosalyn Yalow shared the Nobel for her contributions to the discovery and development of radioimmunoassay, a technique which employs radioactive isotopes to detect and measure the levels of insulin and hormones in the blood and body tissues. Yalow's work indicated that diabetes in adults led to an increase of the insulin level, but the sugar-metabolizing action of the insulin was blocked. Radioimmunoassays have been used to test donors' blood for hepatitis virus; to test antibiotic action; and to diagnose thyroid disease, hypertension, hormone-secreting cancers, drug abuse, reproductive failures, and other growth disorders. (R.K.)

1978

Arber, Werner   **399**

Prize: Medicine and Physiology, 1978. *Born:* June 3, 1929; Granichen, Switzerland. *Parents:* Father, Julius Arber; Mother, Maria Arber. *Nationality:* Swiss. *Religion:* Protestant. *Education:* Univ. of Geneva, Switzerland, Ph.D., 1958. *Spouse:* Antonia, married June 3, 1966. *Children:* Silvia, daughter; Caroline, daughter. *Career:* Univ. of Southern California, Researcher, 1958–59; Univ. of Geneva, Switzerland, Professor, 1960–70; Univ. of California, Berkeley, Professor, 1970–71; Univ. of Basel, Switzerland, Professor, 1971–96.

Selected Publications: "Biological Specificities of Deoxyribonucleic Acid." *Pathol. Microbiol.* 25 (1962): 668–81. "Host-Controlled Restriction and Modification of Bacteriophage." *Symp. Soc. Gen. Microbiol.* 18 (1968): 295–314. "DNA Modification and Restriction." *Prog. Nucleic Acid Res. Mol. Biol.* 14 (1974): 1–37. *Genetic Manipulation: Impact on Men and Society.* New York: Cambridge Univ. Press, 1984.

For More Information See: Asimov's Biographical Encyclopedia of Science and Technology. Garden City, NY: Doubleday, 888–89. *Science* 202 (December 8, 1978): 1069–71.

Commentary: Werner Arber shared the Nobel Prize for his contributions to "the discovery of restriction enzymes and their application to problems of molecular genetics." Arber began to research the molecular basis of the host-controlled variation among bacterial viruses and found that modification involved DNA changes and restriction DNA degradation. His model, later experimentally confirmed, stated that DNA contained specific sites recognizable and cleavable by restriction endonucleases with specificities characteristic of the bacterial strain. The bacterium can methylate within the DNA molecule, protecting it from cleavage, but producing modification. Arber's colaureates (and others) extended his work. (R.K.)

Nathans, Daniel   **400**

Prize: Medicine and Physiology, 1978. *Born:* October 30, 1928; Wilmington, DE. *Death:* November 16, 1999; Baltimore, MD. *Parents:* Father, Samuel Nathans; Mother, Sarah Levitan Nathans. *Nationality:* American. *Religion:* Jewish. *Education:* Univ. of Delaware, B.S., 1950; Washington

Univ., MO, M.D., 1954. *Spouse:* Joanne E. Gomberg, married March 4, 1956. *Children:* Eli, son; Jeremy, son; Benjamin, son. *Career:* Columbia Presbyterian Medical Center, NY, Physician, 1954–59; Rockefeller Univ., NY, Professor, 1959–62; Johns Hopkins Univ., MD, Professor and Administrator, 1962–80; Howard Hughes Medical Institute, CA, Researcher, 1980–96. *Other Awards:* National Medal of Science, 1993.

Selected Publications: "Purification of a Supernatant Factor that Stimulates Amino Acid Transfer from Soluble Ribonucleic Acid to Protein." *Annals of the New York Academy of Sciences* 88 (1960): 718–21. "Cell-free Protein Synthesis Directed by Coliphage MS2 RNA: Synthesis of Intact Viral Coat Protein and Other Products." *Journal of Molecular Biology* 13 (1965): 521–31. "Natural RNA Coding of Bacterial Protein Synthesis." *Methods of Enzymology* 12 (1968): 787–91. "Restriction Endonucleases in the Analysis and Restructuring of DNA Molecules." *Annual Review of Biochemistry* 44 (1975): 273–93 (with H.O. Smith).

For More Information See: Biographical Encyclopedia of Scientists. New York: Facts on File, 1981, 584–85. *Science* 202 (December 8, 1978): 1069–71.

Commentary: Daniel Nathans shared the Nobel Prize for his contribution to the "development of restriction endonucleases, enzymes that can be used to study genetic organization and to manipulate DNA for genetic engineering." Nathans used restriction enzymes to break up the monkey cancer virus SV40 and was able to map the SV40 genes. His techniques were used by others to map various DNA molecules. Nathans also described other possible applications, including the recombinant DNA technique that was the subject of much controversy about potential dangers and benefits in the world's scientific community. (A.D.)

Smith, Hamilton Othanel 401

Prize: Medicine and Physiology, 1978. *Born:* August 23, 1931; New York, NY. *Parents:* Father, Tommie Harkey Smith; Mother, Bunnie Othanel Smith. *Nationality:* American. *Religion:* From Baptist background. *Education:* Univ. of California, Berkeley, A.B., 1952; Johns Hopkins Univ., MD, M.D., 1956. *Spouse:* Elizabeth Anne Bolton, married May 25, 1957. *Children:* Joel, son; Barry, son; Dirk, son; Kirsten, daughter; Bryan, son. *Career:* Barnes Hospital, MO, Physician, 1956–57; U.S. Navy, 1957–59; Henry Ford Hospital, MI, Physician, 1959–62; Univ. of Michigan, Researcher, 1962–67; Johns Hopkins Univ., MD, Professor, 1967-. *Other Awards:* Guggenheim Fellow, 1975–76.

Selected Publications: "A Restriction Enzyme from Hemophilus Influenzae: I. Purification and General Properties." *Journal of Molecular Biology* 51 (1970): 379 (with K.W. Wilcox). "A Restriction Enzyme from Hemophilus Influenzae: II. Base Sequence of the Recognition Site." *Journal of Molecular Biology* 51 (1970): 393. "Restriction Endonucleases in the Analysis and Restructuring of DNA Molecules." *Annual Review of Biochemistry* 44 (1975): 273–93 (with D. Nathans).

For More Information See: Biographical Encyclopedia of Scientists. New York: Facts on File, 1981, 737–38. *Science* 202 (December 8, 1978): 1069–71.

Commentary: The Academy cited Hamilton Smith for his research on "the discovery of restriction enzymes and their application to problems of molecular genetics." Smith purified and characterized the first specific restriction endonuclease, from Hemophilus influenzae. He also interested his colaureate, Daniel Nathans, in applying the restriction enzyme in "chopping" experiments and supplied the requisite endonuclease to him. (R.K.)

1979

Cormack, Allan MacLeod 402

Prize: Medicine and Physiology, 1979. *Born:* February 23, 1924; Johannesburg, South Africa. *Death:* May 7, 1998; Winchester, MA. *Parents:* Father, George Cormack; Mother, Amelia MacLeod Cormack. *Nationality:* South African; later American citizen. *Religion:* Christian. *Education:* Univ. of Cape Town, South Africa, B.Sc., 1944; Univ. of Cape Town, South Africa, M.Sc., 1945. *Spouse:* Barbara Jeanne Seavey, married January 6, 1950. *Children:* Margaret Jean, daughter; Jean Barbara, daughter; Robert Allan Seavey, Jr., son. *Career:* Univ. of Cape Town, Rondebosch, South Africa, Professor, 1946–56; Harvard Univ., MA, Researcher, 1956–57; Tufts Univ., MA, Professor, 1957–94. *Other Awards:* Ballou Medal, Tufts Univ., 1978; Honorable Mention, Swedish Radiological Society, 1979; Medal of Merit, Univ. of Cape Town, South Africa, 1980; Hogg Medal, 1981; National Medal of Science, 1990.

Selected Publications: "Representation of a Function by Its Line Integrals, with Some Radiological Applications." *Journal of Applied Physics* 34 (September 1963): 2722–27. "Representation of a Function by Its Line Integrals, with Some Radiological Applications II. *Journal of Applied Physics* 35 (October 1964): 2908–13. "Small-Angle Scattering of 143-mev Polarized Protons." *Nuclear Physics* 56 (1964): 46–64 (with J.N. Palmieri and D.J. Steinberg). "Measurement of Cross Sections with Neutrons as Targets." *Physical Review* 138 (1965): 823–30 (with M.W. Shapiro and A. M. Koehler).

For More Information See: Physics Today 32 (December 1979): 19–20. *Science* 206 (November 30, 1979): 1060–62. *Son of the Angel.* Boston: B. Benacerraf, 1990.

Commentary: The Nobel Prize was awarded to Allan Cormack for his contributions to "the invention of the x-ray diagnostic technique, computerized axial tomography." Cormack developed the equations necessary for image reconstruction, the process in which x-ray projections of a sample taken at a variety of different angles are combined, using the computer, to reconstruct the image being viewed. Computer-assisted tomography (CAT) has become a most valuable addition to medical diagnostic techniques. (R.K.)

Hounsfield, Godfrey Newbold, Sir 403

Prize: Medicine and Physiology, 1979. *Born:* August 28, 1919; Newark, England. *Parents:* Father, Thomas Hounsfield; Mother, no record found. *Nationality:* British. *Religion:* Christian. *Education:* City and Guilds College, England, Radio Communications Qualification, 1938; Faraday House Electrical Engineering College, England, Degree in Electrical and Mechanical Engineering, 1951. *Spouse:* None. *Children:* None. *Career:* Thorn EMI Limited, Middlesex, England, Researcher and Administrator, 1951-. *Other Awards:* MacRobert Award, 1972; Barclay Prize, British

Institute of Radiology, 1974; Willhelm Exner Medal, Austrian Industrial Association, 1974; Ziedses des Plantes Medal, Physikalisch-Medizinische Gesellschaft, Würzburg, Germany, 1974; Prince Philip Medal Award, City and Guilds of London Institute, 1975; ANS Radiation Award, Georgia Institute of Technology, 1975; Lasker Award, 1975; Duddell Bronze Medal, Institute of Physics, 1976; Golden Plate Award, American Academy of Achievement, 1976; Churchill Gold Medal, 1976; Gairdner Foundation Award, 1976; Reginald Mitchell Gold Medal, Stoke-on-Trent Association of Engineers, 1976; Ambrogino d'Oro Award, City of Milan, 1980; Deutsche Roentgen Plakette, Deutsche Roentgen Museum, 1980; Order British Empire, 1976; Knighthood, 1981.

Selected Publications: "Magnetic Films for Information Storage." *British Patent 1083673* (September 20, 1967) (with P.H. Brown). "Computerized Transverse Axial Scanning (Tomography)." *British Journal of Radiology* 46 (1973): 1016.

For More Information See: Current Biography Yearbook. New York: H.W. Wilson, 1980, 153–55. *Physics Today* 32 (December 1979): 19–20. *Science* 206 (November 30, 1979): 1060–62.

Commentary: Godfrey Hounsfield shared the Nobel Prize for his contributions "to the development of the x-ray scanning system, computerized axial tomography." Hounsfield designed the apparatus that would permit image reconstruction, the process in which x-ray projections of a sample taken at a variety of different angles are combined, using the computer, to reconstruct the image being viewed. The process has revolutionized medical diagnostic techniques employing x-ray methods. Hounsfield was also responsible for significant developments in radar systems, computer design, and large-capacity memory storage in computers, and continues his research in noninvasive medical diagnostic techniques. (R.K.)

1980

Benacerraf, Baruj   404

Prize: Medicine and Physiology, 1980. *Born:* October 29, 1920; Caracas, Venezuela. *Parents:* Father, Abraham Benacerraf; Mother, Henrietta Lasry Benacerraf. *Nationality:* Venezuelan; later American citizen. *Religion:* No organized religion; from Jewish background. *Education:* Lycée Janson, France, baccalauréat, 1940; Columbia Univ., NY, B.S., 1942; Medical College of Virginia, M.D., 1945. *Spouse:* Annette Dreyfus, married March 24, 1943. *Children:* Beryl, daughter. *Career:* Queens General Hospital, NY, Physician, 1945–46; United States Army, 1946–48; Columbia Univ., NY, Researcher, 1948–50; Centre National de Recherche Scientique, France, Administrator, 1950–56; New York Univ., Professor, 1956–68; National Institutes of Health, MD, Administrator, 1968–70; Harvard Univ., MA, Professor and Administrator, 1970–91. *Other Awards:* Rabbi Shai Schacknai Prize, Hebrew Univ. of Jerusalem, 1974; T. Duckett Jones Memorial Award, Helen Jay Whitney Foundation, 1976; Waterford Award, 1980; National Medal of Science, 1990.

Selected Publications: "Studies on Hypersensitivity. III. The Relation between Delayed Reactivity to the Picryl Group of Conjugates and Contact Sensitivity." *Immunology* 2 (1959): 219–29 (with P.G.H. Gell). "Studies on Hypersensitivity. IV. The Relation between Contact and Delayed Sensitivity: A Study on the Specificity of Cellular Immune Reactions." *Journal of Experimental Medicine* 113 (1961): 571–85 (with P.G.H. Gell). "Antigenicity of Altered Autologous Proteins, a Mechanism of Autoimmune Reactions." *Annals of the New York Academy of Sciences* 124 (1965): 126–32. *Textbook of Immunology.* Baltimore, MD: Williams and Wilkins, 1979. *Immunogenetics and Immune Regulation.* New York: Masson Publications, 1982.

For More Information See: From Caracas to Stockholm: A Life in Medicine. Amherst, NY: Prometheus, 1998. *New York Times Biographical Service* (October 1980): 1358–59. *Science* 210 (November 7, 1980): 621–23.

Commentary: Baruj Benacerraf shared the Nobel Prize for his contributions to the explanation of the "genetically determined structures of the cell surface that regulate immunological reactions." Benacerraf found that the genes located in the major histocompatibility complex (MHC), which plays a major role in transplant rejection, control the immune cell interactions that are responsible for a human immune response. Benacerraf continues to research the complex system needed for controlling immune responses. (R.K.)

Dausset, Jean Baptiste Gabriel Joachim   405

Prize: Medicine and Physiology, 1980. *Born:* October 19, 1916; Toulouse, France. *Parents:* Father, Henri Pierre Jules Dausset; Mother, Elizabeth Brullard Dausset. *Nationality:* French. *Religion:* Agnostic; from Christian background. *Education:* Lycee Michelet, France, A.B., 1939; Univ. of Paris, France, M.D., 1943. *Spouse:* Rosita Mayoral Lopez, married March 17, 1962. *Children:* Henri, son; Irene, daughter. *Career:* National Blood Transfusion Center, France, Administrator, 1946–63; Univ. of Paris, France, Professor, 1958–77; Collége de France, Professor, 1977–87; Hopital Saint-Louis, Paris, France, Administrator and Researcher, 1969–84; Human Polymorphism Study Center, 1984-. *Other Awards:* Grand Prix des Sciences Chimiques et Naturelles, 1967; d'Argent Medal, 1967; Grand Prix Scientifique, Ville de Paris, 1968; Prix Cognac-Jay, 1969; Stratton Lecture Award, International Hematology Society, 1970; Karl Landsteiner Award, American Association of Blood Banks, 1971; Gairdner Foundation Prize, 1977; Koch Foundation Prize, 1978; Wolf Foundation Prize, 1978. Honda Prize, 1987.

Selected Publications: Immuno-Hematologie Biologique et Clinique. Paris: Flammarion, 1956. *Tissue Typing.* New York: S. Karger, 1966. *Advances in Transplantation.* New York: Williams and Wilkins, 1968. *Human Transplantation.* Orlando, FL: Grune and Stratton, 1968. *Tissue Typing Today.* Orlando, FL: Grune and Stratton, 1971. *Histocompatibility Testing.* New York: Williams and Wilkins, 1973. *Histocompatibility.* San Diego, CA: Academic Press, 1976 (with G. Snell and S. Nathanson). *Immunology.* New York: Academic Press, 1980 (with M. Fougereau). *A Modern Illustration of Experimental Medicine in Action.* New York: Elsevier/North-Holland, 1980 (with Felix Rapaport).

For More Information See: Current Biography Yearbook. New York: H.W. Wilson, 1981, 108–11. *Science* 210 (November 7, 1980): 621–23.

Commentary: Jean Dausset received the Nobel Prize for work that led to the explanation of "the genetically determined structures of the cell surface that regulate immunological reactions." Dausset first established the existence in humans of the major histocompatibility complex (MHC), which plays a major role in transplant rejection, and led the way to more success in organ transplants, as well as to research on individual susceptibility to infections, diseases, and tumors. His research stemmed from his previous work with blood-replacement transfusion methods. He was also responsible for developing later systems for classification of antigens. (R.K.)

Snell, George Davis   406

Prize: Medicine and Physiology, 1980. *Born:* December 19, 1903; Bradford, MA. *Death:* June 6, 1996; Bar Harbor, ME. *Parents:* Father, Cullen Bryant Snell; Mother, Katherine Davis Snell. *Nationality:* American. *Religion:* Congregationalist. *Education:* Dartmouth College, NH, B.S., 1926; Harvard Univ., MA, M.S., 1928; Harvard Univ., MA, Sc.D., 1930. *Spouse:* Rhoda Carson, married July 28, 1937, died 1994. *Children:* Thomas Carleton, son; Roy Carson, son; Peter Garland, son. *Career:* Dartmouth College, NH, Professor, 1929–30; Brown Univ., RI, Professor, 1930–31; Univ. of Texas, Researcher, 1931–33; Washington Univ., MO, Professor, 1933–35; Jackson Laboratory, Bar Harbor, ME, Researcher, 1935–73. *Other Awards:* Hektoen Silver Medal, American Medical Association, 1955; Bertner Foundation Award, 1962; Griffin Award, Animal Care Panel, 1962; Gregor Mendel Award, Czechoslovak Academy of Sciences, 1967; Gairdner Foundation Award, 1976; Wolf Prize, 1978; Award, National Institute for Arthritis and Infectious Disease, National Cancer Institute, 1978.

Selected Publications: The Biology of the Laboratory Mouse. Philadelphia, PA: The Blakiston Co., 1941. *Cell Surface Antigens: Studies in Mammals Other Than Man.* New York: MSS Information Corporation, 1973 (with others). *Genetic and Biological Aspects of Histocompatibility Antigens.* Copenhagen: Munksgaard, 1973 (with others). *Histocompatibility.* New York: Academic Press, 1976 (with J. Dausset and S. Nathanson).

For More Information See: Current Biography Yearbook. New York: H.W. Wilson, 1986, 533–36. *Science* 210 (November 7, 1980): 621–23.

Commentary: The Nobel Prize was awarded to George Snell for his work on the "genetically determined structures of the cell surface that regulate immunological reactions." Snell's research started with the x-ray induction of mutations in mice and progressed to the breeding of congenic mice, mice that are genetically identical except for a single genetic region. Snell found 10 loci that controlled graft resistance, but one (named Histocompatibility II or H-2) was paramount in determining graft acceptance. It later came to be known as the major histocompatibility complex (MHC), worked on by his colaureates as well. (R.K.)

1981

Hubel, David Hunter   407

Prize: Medicine and Physiology, 1981. *Born:* February 27, 1926; Windsor, Ontario, Canada. *Parents:* Father, Jesse Hervey Hubel; Mother, Elsie M. Hunter Hubel. *Nationality:*

Canadian; later American citizen. *Religion:* Unitarian. *Education:* McGill Univ., Canada, B.Sc., 1947; McGill Univ., Canada, M.D., 1951. *Spouse:* Shirley Ruth Izzard, married June 20, 1953. *Children:* Carl Andrew, son; Eric David, son; Paul Matthew, son. *Career:* Montreal Neurological Institute, Canada, Physician, 1952–54; Johns Hopkins Univ., MD, Physician, 1954–59; Harvard Univ., MA, Professor, 1959-. *Other Awards:* Trustees Research to Prevent Blindness Award, 1971; Lewis S. Rosenstiel Award, Brandeis Univ., MA, 1972; Friedenwald Award, Association for Research in Vision and Ophthalmology, 1975; Karl Spencer Lashley Prize, American Philosophical Society, 1977; Louisa Gross Horowitz Prize, Columbia Univ., NY, 1978; Dickson Prize, Univ. of Pittsburgh, PA, 1979; Ledlie Prize, Harvard Univ., MA, 1980; Kayser Award, 1989; Outstanding Science Leadership Award, 1990; City of Medicine Award, 1990; Glen A. Fry Medal, 1991; Gerard Award, 1993; Charles F. Prentice Medal, 1993; Helen Keller Prize, 1995.

Selected Publications: "Receptive Fields of Single Neurones in the Cat's Striate Cortex." *Journal of Physiology* 148 (1959): 574–91 (with T.N. Wiesel). "Receptive Fields, Binocular Interaction and Functional Architecture in the Cat's Visual Cortex." *Journal of Physiology* 160 (1962): 106–54 (with T.N. Wiesel). "Receptive Fields and Functional Architecture in Two Nonstriate Visual Areas (18 and 19) of the Cat." *Journal of Neurophysiology* 28 (1965): 229–89 (with T.N. Wiesel). "Receptive Fields and Functional Architecture of Monkey Striate Cortex." *Journal of Physiology* 195 (1968): 215–43 (with T.N. Wiesel). "The Visual Cortex of Normal and Deprived Monkeys." *American Scientist* 67 (1979): 532–43.

For More Information See: New York Times Biographical Service (October 1981): 1362. *Science* 214 (October 30, 1981): 518–20.

Commentary: David Hubel was honored by the Academy for his work on "information processing in the visual system." He discovered, with his fellow laureate Torsten Wiesel, that each neuron in the visual system responds best to a particular stimulus and that a complicated arrangement of cells operates to make vision work. In related research, the team made discoveries relating to binocular vision and the importance of early visual stimulation for proper development. (P.P.H.)

Sperry, Roger Wolcott   408

Prize: Medicine and Physiology, 1981. *Born:* August 20, 1913; Hartford, CT. *Death:* April 17, 1994; Pasadena, CA. *Parents:* Father, Francis Bushnell Sperry; Mother, Florence Kramer Sperry. *Nationality:* American. *Religion:* Christian. *Education:* Oberlin College, OH, B.A., 1935; Oberlin College, OH, M.A., 1937; Univ. of Chicago, IL, Ph.D., 1941. *Spouse:* Norma Gay Deupree, married December 28, 1949. *Children:* Glenn Michael (Tad), son; Janeth Hope, daughter. *Career:* Harvard Univ., MA, Researcher, 1941–46; Univ. of Chicago, IL, Professor, 1946–53; California Institute of Technology, Professor, 1954–84. *Other Awards:* Oberlin College Alumni Citation, 1954; Howard Crosby Warren Medal, Society for Experimental Psychology, 1969; Distinguished Scientist/Contribution Award, American Psychological Association, 1971; California Scientist of the Year, 1972; William Thomas Wakeman Research Award,

National Paraplegic Foundation, 1972; Passano Foundation Award, 1973; Claude Bernard Science Journalism Award, 1975; Karl Lashley Award, American Philosophical Society, 1976; Albert Lasker Award, 1979; Ralph Gerard Prize, 1979; Wolf Foundation Prize, 1979; Distinguished Service Award, International Visual Literacy Association, 1979; Golden Plate Award, American Academy of Achievement, 1980; Realia Award, 1986; Mentor Society Award, 1987; National Medal of Science, 1989.

Selected Publications: "Neurology and the Mind-Brain Problem." *American Scientist* 40 (1952): 291. "On the Neural Basis of the Conditioned Response." *British Journal of Animal Behavior* 3 (1955): 41. "Cerebral Organization and Behavior." *Science* 133 (1961): 1749. "Chemoaffinity in the Orderly Growth of Nerve Fiber Patterns of Connection." *Proceedings of the National Academy of Sciences U.S.A.* 50 (1963): 703. "Mental Unity Following Surgical Disconnection of the Cerebral Hemispheres." *Harvey Lectures* 62 (1968): 293–322. *Science and Moral Priority.* New York: Columbia Univ. Press, 1983.

For More Information See: *American Psychologist* 50 (November 1, 1995): 940–41. *Current Biography Yearbook.* New York: H.W. Wilson, 1986, 53–56. Finger, Stanley. *Minds Behind the Brain.* New York: Oxford University Press, 2000. *New York Times Biographical Service* (April 10, 1994): 561. *Science* 214 (October 30, 1981): 517–18.

Commentary: Roger Sperry was cited by the Academy for his split-brain research that separated and identified the functions of the left and right hemispheres of the brain. However, the Nobel Prize also recognized Sperry's relentless pursuit over 40 years for a better understanding of the conscious processes and functions of the human brain through studies in at least three major areas: developmental neurobiology, experimental psychobiology, and human split-brain studies. His later research concentrated on the emotional and social components of the two-sided brain. (D.T.)

Wiesel, Torsten N. 409

Prize: Medicine and Physiology, 1981. *Born:* June 3, 1924; Uppsala, Sweden. *Parents:* Father, Fritz Samuel Wiesel; Mother, Anna-Lisa Elisabet Bentzer Wiesel. *Nationality:* Swedish; later American citizen. *Religion:* From Protestant background. *Education:* Karolinska Institute, Sweden, M.D., 1954. *Spouse:* Teiri Stenhammer, married 1956, divorced 1970; Ann Grace Yee, married 1973, divorced 1981; Jean Stein, married 1995. *Children:* Sara Elisabet, daughter. *Career:* Karolinska Institute, Sweden, Professor, 1954–55; Johns Hopkins Univ., MD, Professor, 1955–59; Harvard Univ., MA, Professor, 1959–83; Rockefeller Univ., NY, Professor and Administrator, 1983-. *Other Awards:* Jules Stein Award, Trustees for Prevention of Blindness, 1971; Lewis S. Rosenstiel Prize, Brandeis Univ., MA, 1972; Friedenwald Award, Trustees of Association for Research in Vision and Ophthalmology, 1975; Lashley Prize, American Philosophical Society, 1977; Louisa Gross Horwitz Prize, Columbia Univ., NY, 1978; Dickson Prize, Univ. of Pittsburgh, PA, 1979; Ledlie Prize, Harvard Univ., 1980; W.H. Helmerich III Award, 1989.

Selected Publications: "Receptive Fields of Single Neurones in the Cat's Striate Cortex." *Journal of Physiology* 148 (1959): 574–91 (with D.H. Hubel). "Receptive Fields, Binocular Interaction and Functional Architecture in the Cat's Visual Cortex." *Journal of Physiology* 160 (1962): 106–54 (with D.H. Hubel). "Receptive Fields and Functional Architecture in Two Nonstriate Visual Areas (18 and 19) of the Cat." *Journal of Neurophysiology* 28 (1965): 229–89 (with D.H. Hubel). "Receptive Fields and Functional Architecture of Monkey Striate Cortex." *Journal of Physiology* 195 (1968): 215–43 (with D.H. Hubel). "Anatomical Demonstration of Orientation Columns in Macaque Monkey." *Journal of Comparative Neurology* 177 (1978): 361–80 (with D.H. Hubel and M.P. Stryker).

For More Information See: Avedon, John F. *Wings for the Mad Flight.* New York: Doubleday, 1991. *New York Times Biographical Service* (October 1981): 1451. *Science* 214 (October 30, 1981): 518–20.

Commentary: Torsten Wiesel shared the Nobel Prize for his work on "information processing in the visual system." With his fellow laureate, D.H. Hubel, he demonstrated that individual neurons respond to specific stimuli and that the cells are organized in columns. Studies of the "ocular dominance columns" showed that the visual response is better to stimulation presented to the dominant eye. Wiesel and Hubel also related ocular dominance to early visual stimulation. (P.P.H.)

1982

Bergström, Sune Karl 410

Prize: Medicine and Physiology, 1982. *Born:* January 10, 1916; Stockholm, Sweden. *Parents:* Father, Sverker Bergström; Mother, Wera Wistrand Bergström. *Nationality:* Swedish. *Religion:* Christian. *Education:* Karolinska Institute, Sweden, D. Med. Sci., 1944; Karolinska Institute, Sweden, M.D., 1944. *Spouse:* Maj Gernandt, married July 30, 1943. *Children:* 1 son. *Career:* Columbia Univ., NY, Researcher, 1940–41; Squibb Institute, NJ, Researcher, 1941–42; Nobel Institute, Stockholm, Sweden, Researcher, 1942–46; Basel Univ., Switzerland, Researcher, 1946–47; Univ. of Lund, Sweden, Professor, 1947–58; Karolinska Institute, Sweden, Professor and Administrator, 1958–80. *Other Awards:* Anders Jahre Prize, 1972; Gairdner Award, 1972; Louisa Gross Horwitz Prize, Columbia Univ., NY, 1975; Francis Amory Prize, 1975; Lasker Award, 1977; Laser Basic Medical Research Award, 1977; Robert A. Welch Award, 1980.

Selected Publications: *Prostaglandins: Proceedings of the Second Nobel Symposium, Stockholm, June 1966.* New York: Interscience Publishers, 1967 (with Bengt Samuelsson). *Third Conference on Prostaglandins in Fertility Control, January 17–20, 1972.* Stockholm: Karolinska Institutet, 1972 (with K. Green and B. Samuelsson). *Report from the Meeting of the Prostaglandin Task Force Steering Committee, Chapel Hill, June 8–10, 1972, Stockholm, October 2–3, 1972, Geneva, February 26–28, 1973.* Stockholm: Karolinska Institutet, 1973. *Prostacyclin.* New York: Raven Press, 1979 (with John R. Vane).

For More Information See: *New Scientist* 96 (November 14, 1982): 82–83. *Science* 218 (November 19, 1982): 765–68.

Commentary: Sune Bergström won the Nobel Prize for his work on the "discoveries concerning prostaglandins and related biologically active substances." Bergström's work began when he found that exceedingly small amounts of the prostaglandins investigated by Ulf von Euler retained very high activity on muscles and in lowering blood pressure. He succeeded later in the isolation and characterization of the structures of the prostaglandins and in the determination that their biosynthetic origin was arachidonic acid. The availability of prostaglandins for research greatly stimulated this field. (R.K.)

Samuelsson, Bengt Ingemar   411

Prize: Medicine and Physiology, 1982. *Born:* May 21, 1934; Halmstad, Sweden. *Parents:* Father, Anders Samuelsson; Mother, Kristina Nilsson Samuelsson. *Nationality:* Swedish. *Religion:* Christian. *Education:* Karolinska Institute, Sweden, D. Med. Sci., 1960; Karolinska Institute, Sweden, M.D., 1961. *Spouse:* Inga Karin Bergstein, married August 19, 1958. *Children:* Bo, son; Elisabet, daughter; Astrid, daughter. *Career:* Karolinska Institute, Sweden, Professor and Administrator, 1961–66; Royal Veterinary College, Sweden, Professor, 1967–72; Karolinska Institute, Sweden, Professor and Administrator, 1973–95. *Other Awards:* A. Jahres Award, Oslo Univ., 1970; Louisa Gross Horwitz Prize, Columbia Univ., 1975; Lasker Award, 1977; Ciba-Geigy Drew Award, 1980; Lewis Rosenstiel Award, 1981; Gairdner Foundation Award, 1981; Swedish Medical Association Jubilee Award, 1981; Heinrich Wieland Prize, 1981; Medical Chemistry Award, 1982; Waterford Bio-Medical Science Award, 1982; International Association of Allergology and Clinical Immunology Award, 1982; Bror Holmberg Medal, 1982; Abraham White Science Achievement Award, 1984; Gregory Pincus Memorial Award, 1984; Charles E. Culpepper Award, 1985; Supelco Award, 1985; Abraham White Award, 1990; City of Medicine Award, 1992; Maria Theresa Medal, 1996; Medicus Magnus Medal, 1997.

Selected Publications: Prostaglandins: Proceedings of the Second Nobel Symposium, Stockholm, June 1966. New York: Interscience Publishers, 1967 (with S. Bergstrom). *Third Conference on Prostaglandins in Fertility Control, January 17–20, 1972.* Stockholm: Karolinska Institutet, 1972 (with K. Green and S. Bergstrom).

For More Information See: New Scientist 96 (November 14, 1982): 82–83. *Science* 218 (November 19, 1982): 765–68.

Commentary: Bengt Samuelsson was awarded the Nobel Prize for his efforts in the "discoveries concerning prostaglandins and related biologically active substances." Samuelsson, working along with his colaureate Sune Bergström, was given credit for structural work, for the detailed description of the role of arachidonic acid, and for clarifying the biosynthetic process that produced the prostaglandins. Samuelsson also discovered thromboxanes, which help blood to clot, and leukotrienes, involved in asthma. (R.K.)

Vane, John Robert   412

Prize: Medicine and Physiology, 1982. *Born:* March 29, 1927; Tardebigg, Worcestershire, England. *Parents:* Father, Maurice Vane; Mother, Frances Florence Fisher Vane. *Nationality:* British. *Religion:* Most probably Christian. *Education:* Univ. of Birmingham, England, B.Sc., 1946; Oxford Univ., England, B.Sc., 1949; Oxford Univ., England, D.Phil., 1953. *Spouse:* Elizabeth Daphne Page, married April 4, 1948. *Children:* Nicola, daughter; Miranda, daughter. *Career:* Yale Univ., CT, Professor, 1953–55; Univ. of London, England, Professor, 1955–73; Wellcome Laboratories, England, Researcher and Administrator, 1973–85; St. Bartholomew's Hospital Medical College, London, Board of Directors, 1986–97. *Other Awards:* Lasker Award, 1977; Baly Medal, Royal College of Physicians, 1977; Joseph J. Bunim Medal, 1979; Nuffield Gold Medal, 1980; Peter Debye Prize, Univ. of Maastricht, Netherlands, 1980; Feldberg Foundation Prize, 1980; Ciba Geigy Drew Award, Drew Univ., NJ, 1980; Dale Medal, Society of Endocrinology, 1981; Galen Medal, Apothecaries' Society, 1983; Biological Council Medal, 1983; Louis Pasteur Foundation Prize, CA, 1984; National Headache Foundation Award, 1988; Royal Medal, 1989; Hamburg Gold Medal, 1996.

Selected Publications: Prostaglandin Synthetase Inhibitors—Their Effects on Physiological Functions and Pathological States. New York: Raven Press, 1974 (with H. Robinson). *Metabolic Functions of the Lung.* New York: Dekker, 1977 (with Y.S. Bakhle). *Inflammation.* New York: Springer Verlag, 1978 (with S.H. Ferreira). *Anti-Inflammatory Drugs.* New York: Springer Verlag, 1979. *Prostacyclin.* New York: Raven Press, 1979 (with S. Bergstrom). *Interactions Between Platelets and Vessel Walls.* Great Neck, NY: Scholium International, 1981 (with G.V.R. Bonn). *Prostacyclin in Health and Disease.* Edinburgh: Royal College of Physicians, 1982.

For More Information See: Current Biography Yearbook New York: H.W. Wilson, 1986, 575–78. *New Scientist* 96 (November 14, 1982): 82–83. *Science* 218 (November 19, 1982): 765–68.

Commentary: John Vane shared the Nobel for his contributions to the "discoveries concerning prostaglandins and related biologically active substances." Vane used the dynamic bioassay method he had developed working with the angiotensins to differentiate the various prostaglandins. He investigated prostaglandin release during anaphylaxis in perfused guinea pig lung and then demonstrated that the release of a contracting substance could be halted with anti-inflammatory drugs. Vane's explanation that aspirin and related drugs acted by inhibiting arachidonic acid conversion to prostaglandins stimulated extensive research on the role of prostaglandins in all sorts of biological systems. (R.K.)

1983

McClintock, Barbara   413

Prize: Medicine and Physiology, 1983. *Born:* June 16, 1902; Hartford, CT. *Death:* September 2, 1992; Huntington, NY. *Parents:* Father, Thomas Henry McClintock; Mother, Sara Handy McClintock. *Nationality:* American. *Religion:* Congregationalist. *Education:* Cornell Univ., NY, B.S., 1923; Cornell Univ., NY, M.A., 1925; Cornell Univ., NY, Ph.D., 1927. *Spouse:* None. *Children:* None. *Career:* Cornell Univ., NY, Researcher, 1924–31; California Institute of Technology, Researcher, 1931–33; Univ. of Freiburg, Germany, Researcher, 1933–34; Cornell Univ., NY, Researcher, 1934–36; Univ. of Missouri, Columbia, Professor, 1936–41;

Carnegie Institution of Washington at Cold Spring Harbor Laboratory, NY, Researcher, 1941–85. *Other Awards:* Achievement Award, AAUW, 1947; Merit Award, Botany Society of America, 1957; Kimber Award, National Academy of Sciences, 1967; National Medal of Science, 1970; Rosenstiel Award, 1978; Freeman Foundation Award, 1978; MacArthur Foundation Prize, 1981; Thomas Hunt Morgan Medal, 1981; Lasker Award, 1981; Wolf Foundation Prize, Israel, 1981; Horwitz Prize, Columbia Univ., 1982; Mayer Prize, 1982.

Selected Publications: "A Correlation of Cytological and Genetical Crossing Over in Zea Mays." *Proceedings of the National Academy of Sciences* 17 (August 1931): 492–97 (with H. Creighton). "The Relation of a Particular Chromosomal Element to the Development of the Nucleoli in Zea Mays." *A. Zellforsch. U. Mikr. Anat* 21 (1934): 294–328. "Mutable Loci in Maize." *Carnegie Institution of Washington Yearbook* 48 (1949): 142–43.

For More Information See: Current Biography Yearbook. New York: H.W. Wilson, 1984, 262–65. Federoff, N. and Botstein, D. *The Dynamic Genome.* Cold Spring Harbor, NY: Cold Spring Harbor Laboratory Press, 1992. Keller, E. *A Feeling for the Organism: The Life and Work of Barbara McClintock.* San Francisco: Freeman, 1983. Kittredge, M. *Barbara McClintock.* New York: Chelsea House Publishers, 1991. *Biographical Memoirs of the Fellows of the Royal Society.* London: Royal Society, 1994 (Volume 40): 265.

Commentary: Barbara McClintock received the Nobel Prize for "discovery of mobile genetic elements of profound importance for our understanding of the organization and function of genes. She carried out this research alone and at a time when her contemporaries were not yet able to realize the generality and significance of her findings." Her early experiments proved that chromosomes exchange genetic information and physical material in crossing over during cell division. Her later work on corn showed that portions of DNA that control other genes can move between chromosome sites. (R.K.)

1984

Jerne, Niels Kaj 414
Prize: Medicine and Physiology, 1984. *Born:* December 23, 1911; London, England. *Death:* October 7, 1994; Pont du Gard, France. *Parents:* Father, Hans Jessen Jerne; Mother, Else Marie Lindberg Jerne. *Nationality:* British; later Danish citizen and Swiss resident. *Religion:* Christian. *Education:* Univ. of Rotterdam, Netherlands, B.A., 1928; Univ. of Copenhagen, Denmark, doctorate in medicine, 1951. *Spouse:* Ursula Alexandra Kohl, married 1964. *Children:* 2 sons. *Career:* Danish State Serum Institute, Researcher, 1943–56; California Institute of Technology, Researcher, 1954–55; World Health Organization, Geneva, Switzerland, Chief Medical Officer, 1956–62; Univ. of Pittsburgh, PA, Professor and Administrator, 1962–66; Paul Ehrlich Institute, Frankfurt, Germany, Director, 1966–69; Basel Institute for Immunology, Switzerland, Director, 1969–80; Pasteur Institute, Professor, 1981–82. *Other Awards:* Waterford Bio-Medical Science Award, 1978; Marcel Benoist Prize, Berne, Switzerland, 1979; Paul Ehrlich Prize, Frankfurt, Germany, 1982.

Selected Publications: "Immunological Speculation." *Annual Review of Microbiology* 14 (1960): 341–58. "Antibody Formation and Immunological Memory." *Macromolecular Behavior* (1966): 151–57. "Regulation of Antibody Synthesis." *Transplant.* Organum Geweben, Int. Symp., Bad Hamburg v.d. H., Ger. (1966): 81–89. "The Immune System." *Scientific American* 229 (July 1973): 52–60.

For More Information See: New Scientist 104 (October 18, 1984): 3–5. *Science* 226 (November 30, 1984): 1025–28. *New York Times Biographical Service* (October 8, 1994): 1537.

Commentary: Niels Jerne, cited as the "leading theoretician in immunology during the last 30 years," was recognized for three theories that propelled the science of immunology forward. The first (1955) opposed the view that the body created antibodies as needed and instead proposed that the body contained all the antibodies needed to fight infection. The second (1966) explained how a type of immune-system cell, the T lymphocyte, develops in the thymus gland and learns its function. The network theory (1973) postulated that the immune system was a self-regulating functional network of interacting antibodies and lymphocytes. (R.K.)

Köhler, Georges J.F. 415
Prize: Medicine and Physiology, 1984. *Born:* April 17, 1946; Munich, Germany. *Death:* March 1, 1995; Freiburg, Germany. *Parents:* No record found. *Nationality:* German. *Religion:* Christian. *Education:* Univ. of Freiburg, Germany, B.A., 1971, Ph.D., 1974. *Spouse:* Claudia Köhler *Children:* 3 children *Career:* Cambridge Univ., England, Researcher, 1974–76; Basel Institute for Immunology, Switzerland, Researcher, 1976–84; Max Planck Institute for Immune Biology, Freiburg, Germany, Director, 1985–95. *Other Awards:* Lasker Award, 1984

Selected Publications: "Continuous Culture of Fused Cells Secreting Antibody of Predefined Specificity." *Nature (London)* 256 (1975): 495–97 (with C. Milstein). "Immunoglobulin Production by Lymphocyte Hybridomas." *European Journal of Immunology* 8 (1978): 82–88 (with H. Hengartner and M.J. Shulman). "Immunoglobulin Chain Loss in Hybridoma Lines." *Proceedings of the National Academy of Sciences USA* 77 (1980): 2197–99. "The Technique of Hybridoma Production." *Immunological Methods* 2 (1981): 285–98. "Resistance of Mice Deficient in IL-4 to Retrovirus-Induced Immunodeficiency Syndrome." *Science* 262 (October 8, 1993): 240–42.

For More Information See: New York Times (4 March 1995): A26. *New York Times Biographical Service* (October 16, 1984): 1339. *Science* 226 (November 30, 1984): 1025–28.

Commentary: The Nobel Prize went to Georges J.F. Köhler and his co-laureate, César Milstein, for their "pioneering contributions to the theory and techniques of immunology." Köhler helped to develop the techniques for producing monoclonal antibodies, antibodies which have a specific affinity for certain sites in the body that might permit them, for example, to attack diseased cells but leave healthy cells intact. The techniques have been said to lay the basis for medical advances such as cancer treatment and the detection of acquired immune deficiency syndrome (AIDS). (R.K.)

Milstein, César   **416**

Prize: Medicine and Physiology, 1984. *Born:* October 8, 1927; Bahia Blanca, Argentina. *Parents:* Father, Lázaro Milstein; Mother, Máxima Milstein. *Nationality:* Argentinian; later British citizen. *Religion:* Agnostic; from Jewish background. *Education:* Univ. of Buenos Aires, Argentina, Licenciado en Ciencias Quimicas, 1952; Univ. of Buenos Aires, Argentina, Doctor en Quimica, 1957; Cambridge Univ., England, Ph.D., 1960. *Spouse:* Celia Prilleltensky, married 1953. *Children:* None. *Career:* Cambridge Univ., England, Researcher, 1960–61; National Institute of Microbiology, Buenos Aires, Argentina, Researcher, 1961–63; Cambridge Univ., England, Researcher and Administrator, 1963–95. *Other Awards:* Silver Jubilee Medal, 1977; Ciba Medal, Biochemistry Society, 1978; Rosenstiel Medal, 1979; Avery-Landsteiner Preis, 1979; Rosenberg Prize, 1979; Mattia Award, 1979; Louisa Gross Horwitz Prize, Columbia Univ., NY, 1980; Koch Preis, 1980; Wolf Prize, 1980; Wellcome Foundation Medal, 1980; Jimencz Diaz Medal, 1981; William Bate Hardy Prize, Cambridge Philosophical Society, England, 1981; Sloan Prize, General Motors Cancer Research Foundation, 1981; Gairdner Award, 1981; Madonnina Award, 1981; Krebs Medal, 1981; Brown-Hazen Memorial Award, 1982; Lynen Medal, 1982; Forteza Medal, 1982; Pressman Memorial Award, 1982; Biochemical Analysis Prize, 1982; Landsteiner Award, 1982; Allergology and Clinical Immunology Award, 1982; Shacknai Memorial Prize, 1982; Royal Medal, Royal Society, 1982; Franklin Medal, 1983; Albert Lasker Award, 1984; Dale Medal, England, 1984. Copley Medal, 1989.

Selected Publications: "Expansion and Contraction in the Evolution of Immunoglobulin Gene Pools." Progr. Immunol., Int. Congr. Immunol., 1st (1971): 33–45 (with J. Svasti). "Clonal Variants of Myeloma Cells." *Prog. Immunol., Proc. Intern Congr. Immunol., 2nd* 1 (1974): 173–82 (with others). "Continuous Cultures of Fused Cells Secreting Antibody of Predefined Specificity." *Nature (London)* 256 (1975): 495–97 (with G. Koehler). "Immunoglobulin Genes in a Mouse Myeloma and in Mutant Clones." *Miami Winter Symposium* 9 (1975): 131–52 (with others).

For More Information See: Ahmad, F. *From Gene to Protein.* New York: Academic Press, 1982. *New York Times Biographical Service* (October 16, 1984): 1361. *Science* 226 (November 30, 1984): 1025–28.

Commentary: César Milstein shared the Nobel Prize for "pioneering contributions to the theory and techniques of immunology," which were said to lay the basis for advances in medical areas such as cancer treatment and the detection of acquired immune deficiency syndrome (AIDS). In work with his colaureate, Georges J. F. Koehler, Milstein developed the techniques for producing monoclonal antibodies, antibodies with a specific affinity for certain sites in the body that might find diseased cells but leave healthy cells intact. (R.K.)

1985

Brown, Michael Stuart   **417**

Prize: Medicine and Physiology, 1985. *Born:* April 13, 1941; New York, NY. *Parents:* Father, Harvey Brown; Mother, Evelyn Katz Brown. *Nationality:* American. *Religion:* Jewish. *Education:* Univ. of Pennsylvania, B.A., 1962;

Univ. of Pennsylvania, M.D., 1966. *Spouse:* Alice Lapin, married June 21, 1964. *Children:* Elizabeth Jane, daughter; Sara Ellen, daughter. *Career:* Massachusetts General Hospital, Boston, Physician, 1966–68; National Institutes of Health, MD, Researcher, 1968–71; Univ. of Texas Health Science Center, Dallas, Professor, 1971-. *Other Awards:* Wieland Prize, 1974; Pfizer Award, American Chemical Society, 1976; A.O. Bernstein Award, 1977; Passano Award, 1978; Lounsbery Award, National Academy of Sciences, USA, 1979; Gairdner Foundation Award, 1981; New York Academy of Sciences Award, 1981; Lita Annenberg Hazen Award, 1982; Horwitz Prize, Columbia Univ., NY, 1984; Mattia Award, 1984; Distinguished Research Award, Association of American Medical Colleges, 1984; 3M Life Sciences Award, 1985; William Allan Award, 1985; Lasker Award, 1985; National Medal of Science, 1988.

Selected Publications: "Binding and Degradation of Low Density Lipoproteins by Cultured Human Fibroblasts: Comparison of Cells from a Normal Subject and from a Patient with Homozygous Familial Hypercholesterolemia." *Journal of Biological Chemistry* 249 (1974): 5153–62 (with J.L. Goldstein). "Development of a Cell Culture System for Study of the Basic Defect in Familial Hypercholesterolemia." In *Atherosclerosis III: Proceedings of the Third International Symposium.* Berlin: Springer-Verlag, 1974, 422–25 (with J.L. Goldstein). "Expression of the Familial Hypercholesterolemia Gene in Heterozygotes: Model for a Dominant Disorder in Man." *Transactions of the Association of American Physicians* 87 (1974): 120–31 (with J.L. Goldstein). "Familial Hypercholesterolemia: A Genetic Regulatory Defect in Cholesterol Metabolism." *American Journal of Medicine* 58 (1975): 147–50 (with J.L. Goldstein).

For More Information See: New York Times (October 15, 1985): C 1,3. *Science* 231 (January 10, 1986): 126–29. Magill, F. *Nobel Prize Winners: Physiology or Medicine.* Pasadena, CA: Salem Press, 1991, 1480–91.

Commentary: Michael Brown and Joseph Goldstein shared the Nobel Prize for their discoveries which "revolutionized our knowledge about the regulation of cholesterol metabolism and the treatment of diseases caused by abnormally elevated cholesterol levels in the blood." Brown's early work included study of the role of enzymes in the chemistry of the digestive system and of cholesterol production. The Nobel work centered on the causes of familial hypercholesterolemia and the discovery that human body cells have surface receptors which process bloodstream particles that carry cholesterol. (B.S.S.)

Goldstein, Joseph Leonard   **418**

Prize: Medicine and Physiology, 1985. *Born:* April 18, 1940; Sumter, SC. *Parents:* Father, Isadore E. Goldstein; Mother, Fannie Alpert Goldstein. *Nationality:* American. *Religion:* Jewish. *Education:* Washington and Lee Univ., VA, B.S., 1962; Southwestern Medical School, Univ. of Texas, M.D., 1966. *Spouse:* None. *Children:* None. *Career:* Massachusetts General Hospital, Boston, Physician, 1966–68; National Institutes of Health, MD, Researcher, 1968–70; Univ. of Washington, Seattle, Researcher, 1970–72; Univ. of Texas Health Science Center, Dallas, Professor, 1972-. *Other Awards:* Heinrich-Wieland Prize, 1974; Pfizer Award, American Chemical Society, 1976; A.O. Bernstein Award, 1977; Passano Award, 1978; Lounsbery Award, National

Academy of Sciences, USA, 1979; Gairdner Foundation Award, 1981; Award, New York Academy of Sciences, 1981; Lita Annenberg Hazen Award, 1982; Louisa Gross Horwitz Award, Columbia Univ., NY, 1984; V.D. Mattia Award, 1984; Distinguished Research Award, Association of American Medical Colleges, 1984; Research Achievement Award, American Heart Association, 1984; 3M Life Sciences Award, 1984; William Allan Award, 1985; Lasker Award, 1985; ACP Award, 1986; Trustees' Medal, Massachusetts General Hospital, 1986; National Medal of Science, 1988.

Selected Publications: "Familial Hypercholesterolemia: Identification of a Defect in the Regulation of 3-hydroxy-3-methylglutaryl Coenzyme A Reductase Activity Associated with Overproduction of Cholesterol." *Proceedings National Academy of Sciences USA* 70 (1973): 2804–08 (with M.S. Brown). "Expression of the Familial Hypercholesterolemia Gene in Heterozygotes: Mechanism for a Dominant Disorder in Man." *Science* 185 (1974): 61–63 (with M.S. Brown). "Homozygous Familial Hypercholesterolemia: Specificity of the Biochemical Defect in Cultured Cells and Feasibility of Prenatal Detection." *American Journal of Human Genetics* 26 (1974): 199–206 (with M.J.E. Harrod and M.S. Brown). "Familial Hypercholesterolemia: Biochemical, Genetic, and Pathophysiological Considerations." *Advances in Internal Medicine* 20 (1975): 273–96 (with M.S. Brown).

For More Information See: Current Biography Yearbook. New York: H.W. Wilson, 1987, 208–11. *New York Times* (October 15, 1985): C 1,3. *Science* 231 (January 10, 1986): 126–29. Magill, F. *Nobel Prize Winners: Physiology or Medicine.* Pasadena, CA: Salem Press, 1991, 1480–91.

Commentary: Joseph Goldstein shared the Nobel Prize with Michael Brown for his discoveries which "revolutionized our knowledge about the regulation of cholesterol metabolism and the treatment of diseases caused by abnormally elevated cholesterol levels in the blood." His early work included study of the genetic code and the genetic aspects of heart disease. The Nobel work centered on the causes of familial hypercholesterolemia and the discovery that human body cells have surface receptors that process bloodstream particles that carry cholesterol. (B.S.S.)

1986

Cohen, Stanley Harold   419

Prize: Medicine and Physiology, 1986. *Born:* November 17, 1922; Brooklyn, NY. *Parents:* Father, Louis Cohen; Mother, Fannie Feitel Cohen. *Nationality:* American. *Religion:* Jewish. *Education:* Brooklyn College, NY, B.A., 1943; Oberlin College, OH, M.A., 1945; Univ. of Michigan, Ph.D., 1948. *Spouse:* Olivia Barbara Larson, married 1951, divorced (no date); Jan Elizabeth Jordan, married 1981. *Children:* Burt Bishop, son; Kenneth Larson, son; Cary, son. *Career:* Univ. of Colorado, Professor, 1948–52; Washington Univ., MO, Professor, 1952–59; Vanderbilt Univ., TN, Professor, 1959-. *Other Awards:* William Thomson Wakeman Award, 1974; Earl Sutherland Research Prize, 1977; Albion O. Bernstein Award, 1978; H.P. Robertson Memorial Award, 1981; Lewis S. Rosentiel Award, 1982; Alfred P. Sloan Award, 1982; Louisa Gross Horwitz Prize, 1983; Lila Gruber Memorial Cancer Research Award, 1983; Bertner Award, 1983; Gairdner Foundation International

Award, 1985; Fred Conrad Koch Award, 1986; National Medal of Science, 1986; Albert Lasker Award, 1986; Franklin Medal, 1987; Albert A. Michaelson Award, 1987.

Selected Publications: "Nerve Growth-stimulating Factor Isolated from Sarcomas 37 and 180." *Proceedings of the National Academy of Science. United States* 40 (1954): 1014–18. "A Nerve Growth-stimulating Factor Isolated from Snake Venom." *Proceedings of the National Academy of Science. United States* 42 (1956): 571–74. "Purification and Properties of a Nerve Growth-promoting Factor Isolated from Mouse Sarcoma 180." *Cancer Research* 17 (1957): 15–20. "Isolation of a Mouse Submaxillary Gland Protein Accelerating Incisor Eruption and Eyelid Opening in the New-Born Animal." *Journal of Biological Chemistry* 237 (1962): 1555–62. "Isolation and Biological Effects of an Epidermal Growth-stimulating Protein." *National Cancer Institute Monograph* 13 (1964): 13–27.

For More Information See: New York Times (October 14, 1986): A1, C3. *Science* 234 (1986): 543–44. Magill, F. *Nobel Prize Winners: Physiology or Medicine.* Pasadena, CA: Salem Press, 1991, 1495–1503.

Commentary: Stanley Cohen received the Nobel Prize for "discoveries which are of fundamental importance for our understanding of the mechanisms which regulate cell and organ growth." With Rita Levi-Montalcini, he identified the proteins that controlled the growth of cells in the nervous system (the nerve growth factor NGF). Later, he found a second growth factor, the epidermal growth factor (EGF), purified it, determined its amino acid sequence, and studied the binding of EGF to receptors on the surface of the cell. (G.R./B.S.S.)

Levi-Montalcini, Rita   420

Prize: Medicine and Physiology, 1986. *Born:* April 22, 1909; Turin, Italy. *Parents:* Father, Adamo Levi; Mother, Adele Montalcini Levi. *Nationality:* Italian; later American citizen. *Religion:* Jewish. *Education:* Univ. of Turin, Italy, M.D., 1936. *Spouse:* None. *Children:* None. *Career:* Univ. of Turin, Italy, Researcher, 1936–38, 1945–47; Allied Health Service, Italy, Researcher, 1944–45; Washington Univ., St Louis, MO, Professor, 1947–77; Institute of Cell Biology, Italy, Researcher, 1969–81. *Other Awards:* Max Weinstein Award, 1962; Feltrinelli Prize, 1969; Golden Plate Award, 1970; Ibico-Reggino Award, 1970; William Wakeman Award, 1974; International St. Vincent's Award, 1979; Knights of Humanity Award, 1979; Lewis Rosenstiel Award, 1982; Louisa Horwitz Prize, 1983; Albert Lasker Award, 1986; Gold Medal for Science, Rome, 1986; National Medal of Science (U.S.), 1987; Thudicum Award, 1987; Gold Medal, Minister of Public Health, Rome, 1988.

Selected Publications: "The Nerve Growth Factor." *Scientific American* 240 (1979): 68–77. *Molecular Aspects of Neurobiology.* New York: Springer-Verlag, 1986. "The Nerve-Growth Factor 35 Years Later." *Science* 237 (1987): 1154–61.

For More Information See: "The Heart and Mind of a Genius." *Vogue* 177 (1987): 480+. *In Praise of Imperfection: My Life and Work.* New York: Basic Books, 1988. "Interview—Rita Levi-Montalcini." *Omni* 10 (1988): 70–72.

Commentary: The prize for medicine and physiology was granted to Rita Levi-Montalcini for "discoveries which are of fundamental importance for our understanding of the mechanisms which regulate cell and organ growth." The laureate identified proteins that controlled the growth of cells in the nervous system (the nerve growth factor NGF). The work on nerve-cell growth continued throughout her career, with significant impact on basic research on several diseases, including cancer, Parkinson's disease, and Alzheimer's disease. (G.R./B.S.S.)

1987

Tonegawa, Susumu   421

Prize: Medicine and Physiology, 1987. *Born:* September 5, 1939; Nagoya, Japan. *Parents:* Father, Tsutomu Tonegawa; Mother Miyuko Masuko Tonegawa. *Nationality:* Japanese; later U.S. resident. *Religion:* No record found. *Education:* Kyoto Imperial Univ., Japan, B.S., 1963; Univ. of California, San Diego, Ph.D., 1968. *Spouse:* Kyoko, no other record; Mayumi Yoshinari, married September 28, 1985. *Children:* Hidde, son; Hanna, daughter; Satto, son. *Career:* Univ. of California, San Diego, Researcher, 1968–69; Salk Institute, CA, Researcher, 1969–70; Basel Institute for Immunology, Switzerland, Researcher, 1971–81; Massachusetts Institute of Technology, Professor, 1981-. *Other Awards:* Cloetta Prize, 1978; Warren Triennial Prize, 1980; Genetics Grand Prize, Japan, 1981; Avery Landsteiner Prize, 1981; Asahi Prize, 1982; Louisa Gross Horwitz Prize, 1982; Gairdner Award, 1983; V.D. Mattia Award, 1983; Bunka Kunsho Order of Culture, Japan, 1984; Robert Koch Prize, 1986; Bristol-Myers Award, 1986; Lasker Award, 1987; Rabbi Shai Shacknai Memorial Prize, 1989; Order of the Southern Cross, Brazil, 1991.

Selected Publications: "Genetic Transcription Directed by the b$_2$ Region of Lambda Bacteriophage." *Proceedings of the National Academy of Science. United States* 61 (1968): 1320–27. "Evidence for Somatic Generation of Antibody Diversity." *Proceedings of the National Academy of Science. United States* 71 (1974): 4027–31. "The Molecules of the Immune System." *Scientific American* 253 (1985): 122–31. "Antibody and T-Cell Receptors." *Journal of the American Medical Association* 259 (1988): 1845–47.

For More Information See: New York Times (October 13, 1987): C1. *Science* 238 (1987): 484–85. Magill, F. *Nobel Prize Winners: Physiology or Medicine.* Pasadena, CA: Salem Press, 1991, 1519–26.

Commentary: Susumu Tonegawa became the first Japanese recipient of the Nobel in Medicine and Physiology for his discovery of "the genetic principle for generation of antibody diversity." The laureate's research solved the puzzle presented by the very large number of antibodies that resulted in the human body in response to varying conditions, from a limited number of genes. Tonegawa showed that the body's immune system cells could reorganize the genes in response to an attack by a hostile organism to produce an antibody with a unique structure that could selectively attack the invasive condition. (G.R./B.S.S.)

1988

Black, James Whyte, Sir   422

Prize: Medicine and Physiology, 1988. *Born:* June 14, 1924; Uddingston, Scotland. *Parents:* Father, Walter Black; Mother, Catherine Whyte Black. *Nationality:* British. *Religion:* Nonpracticing Protestant. *Education:* Univ. of St.

Andrews, Scotland, M.D., 1946. *Spouse:* Hilary Vaughn, married 1946, died 1986. *Children:* Stephanie, daughter. *Career:* Univ. of St. Andrews, Scotland, Professor, 1946–47; Univ. of Malaya, Singapore, Professor, 1947–50; Univ. of Glasgow, Scotland, Professor, 1950–58; Imperial Chemical Industries, England, Researcher, 1958–64; Smith, Kline and French, England, Researcher, 1964–73; University College, England, Professor, 1973–77; Wellcome Research Lab, England, Researcher, 1977–84; King's College Hospital Medical School, England, Professor, 1984-; Dundee Univ., Scotland, Chancellor, 1992-. *Other Awards:* Lasker Award, 1976; Mullard Award, Royal Society, 1978; Knighted, 1981.

Selected Publications: "A New Adrenergic Betareceptor Antagonist." *Lancet* (1964): 1080. "Definition and Antagonism of Histamine H2-Receptors." *Nature* 236 (1972): 385–90. "An Analysis of the Depressor Responses to Histamine in the Cat and Dog: Involvement of Both H1- and H2-Receptors." *British Journal Pharmacology* 54 (1975): 319–24. *The Medicine You Take.* London: Fontana, 1978.

For More Information See: New York Times (October 18, 1988): A1, C17. *Science* 242 (1988): 516–17. Meijler, F. *Journal of the American College of Cardiology* 13 (March 1989): 769. *Nobel Prize Winners: Physiology or Medicine.* Pasadena, CA: Salem Press, 1991, 1529–37.

Commentary: The sharing of the Nobel by James Black was for his part in the "discoveries of important principles for drug treatment (creating a) rational method for designing new compounds." Black studied the reactions of chemicals with receptors in the body located on the surface of nerve and muscle cells. The research enabled him to design drugs of two types, both useful in the treatment of certain abnormal states—beta-blockers (propanol) employed in the treatment of heart disease and high blood pressure, and H-2 receptor-antagonists (cimetidine) employed in treatment of stomach and duodenal ulcers. (G.R./B.S.S.)

Elion, Gertrude Belle   423

Prize: Medicine and Physiology, 1988. *Born:* January 23, 1918; New York, NY. *Death:* February 21, 1999; Chapel Hill, NC. *Parents:* Father, Robert Elion; Mother, Bertha Cohen Elion. *Nationality:* American. *Religion:* Jewish. *Education:* Hunter College, NY, A.B., 1937; New York Univ., M.S., 1941. *Spouse:* None. *Children:* None. *Career:* New York City, Teacher, 1941–42; Quaker Maid Company, NY, Researcher, 1942–43; Johnson and Johnson, NJ, Researcher, 1943–44; Burroughs Wellcome Company, NY and NC, Researcher, 1944–83; Duke Univ., NC, Professor, 1983–99. *Other Awards:* Garvan Medal, 1968; President's Medal, Hunter College, NY, 1970; Distinguished Chemist Award, NC, 1981; Judd Award, 1983; Cain Award, 1984; Bertner Award, 1989; Medal of Honor, American Chemical Society, 1990; Third Century Award, 1990; Discoverers Award, 1990; City of Medicine Award, Durham, NC, 1990; National Inventors Hall of Fame, 1991; National Medal of Science, 1991; Higuchi Memorial Award, 1995; Ronald H. Brown American Innovator Award, 1996; Lifetime Achievement Award, Lemelson-MIT, 1997.

Selected Publications: "Detection of Agents which Interfere with the Immune Response." *Proceedings for the Society for Experimental Biology and Medicine* 107 (1961):

796–99. "A Summary of Investigations with 6-[(1-methyl-4-nitro-r-imidazolyl) thio] Purine." *Cancer Chemotherapy Report* 14 (1961): 93–98. "The Purine Path to Chemotherapy." *Science* 244 (1989): 41–47.

For More Information See: New York Times (October 18, 1988): A1, C17. *Science* 242 (1988): 516–17. *Current Biography Yearbook.* New York: H.W. Wilson, March 1995, 14; St. Pierre, S. *Gertrude Elion.* Vero Beach, FL: Rourke Enterprises, 1993.

Commentary: The Nobel prize was shared by Gertrude Elion for her part in the "discoveries of important principles for drug treatment [creating a] rational method for designing new compounds." She and her colaureate Hitchings researched the differences in structure and action of normal and abnormal cells. The research enabled them to design drugs that selectively operate against various disease states, among them leukemia (6-mercaptopurine and thioguanine), malaria (pyrimethamine), gout (allopurinol), urinary and respiratory infections (trimethoprim), and autoimmune disorders (azathioprine). (G.R./B.S.S.)

Hitchings, George Herbert, Jr.   424

Prize: Medicine and Physiology, 1988. *Born:* April 18, 1905; Hoquiam, WA. *Death:* February 27, 1998; Chapel Hill, NC. *Parents:* Father, George Herbert Hitchings, Sr.; Mother, Lillian Mathews Hitchings. *Nationality:* American. *Religion:* From Methodist/Episcopal background. *Education:* Univ. of Washington, B.S., 1927; Univ. of Washington, M.S., 1928; Harvard Univ., MA, Ph.D., 1933. *Spouse:* Beverly Reimer, married June 24, 1933, died 1985; Joyce Shaver, married February 9, 1989. *Children:* Laramie Ruth, daughter, Thomas Eldridge, son. *Career:* Harvard Univ., MA, Professor, 1933–39; Western Reserve Univ., OH, Professor, 1939–42; Burroughs-Wellcome, NY & NC, Researcher, 1942–75. *Other Awards:* Gairdner Award, 1968; Gregor Mendel Medal, 1968; Passano Award, 1969; de Villier Award, 1969; Purkinje Medal, 1971; Cameron Prize, 1972; Medicinal Chemistry Award, 1972; Bertner Foundation Award, 1974; Mullard Medal, 1976; Papanicolaou Award, 1979; Governor's Award, NC, 1980; C. Chester Stock Medal, 1981; Oscar B. Hunter Award, 1984; Alfred Burger Award, 1984; Lekow Medal, Poland, 1988; Albert Schweitzer Prize, 1989; American Association for Cancer Research Award, 1989; Golden Plate Award, American Academy of Achievement, 1989; City of Medicine Award, Durham, NC, 1990; NC Distinguished Chemist Award, 1991; Civic Honor Award, Durham, NC, 1991; Medal of Honor, Technical Univ., Gdansk, Poland, 1993.

Selected Publications: "Pyrimethamine: The Use of an Antimetabolite in the Chemotherapy of Malaria and Other Infections." *Clinical Pharmacology and Therapeutics* 1 (1960): 570–89. "Suppression of the Immune Response by Drugs in Combination." *Proceedings for the Society for Experimental Biological Medicine* 111 (1962): 334–37. "Chemical Suppression of the Immune Response." *Pharmacology Review* 15 (1963): 365–405.

For More Information See: New York Times (October 18, 1988): A1, C17. *Science* 242 (1988): 516–17. *New York Times Magazine* (January 29, 1989): 28.

Commentary: George Hitchings shared the Nobel for his part in the "discoveries of important principles for drug treatment [creating a] rational method for designing new compounds." He and his colaureate Elion researched the differences in structure and action of normal and abnormal cells. The research enabled them to design drugs that selectively operate against various disease states, among them leukemia (6-mercaptopurine and thioguanine), malaria (pyrimethamine), gout (allopurinol), urinary and respiratory infections (trimethoprim), and autoimmune disorders (azathioprine). (G.R./B.S.S.)

1989

Bishop, John Michael   425

Prize: Medicine and Physiology, 1989. *Born:* February 22, 1936; York, PA. *Parents:* Father, John Schwartz Bishop; Mother, Carrie Rutledge Grey Bishop. *Nationality:* American. *Religion:* No religious affiliation; from Lutheran background. *Education:* Gettysburg College, PA, B.A., 1957; Harvard Univ., MA, M.D., 1962. *Spouse:* Kathryn Ione Putman, married June 18, 1959. *Children:* Dylan Michael Dwight, son; Eliot John Putman, son. *Career:* Massachusetts General Hospital, Resident, 1962–64; National Institutes of Health, MD, Researcher, 1964–68; Univ. of California, San Francisco, Professor and Administrator, 1968-. *Other Awards:* Biomedical Research Award, American Association of Medical Colleges, 1981; Lasker Award, 1982; Passano Award, 1983; Armand Hammer Award, 1984; General Motors Foundation Award, 1984; Gairdner Foundation Award, 1984; Medal of Honor, American Cancer Society, 1985; American College of Physicians Award, 1987; Warren Triennial Prize, no date; Lila Gruber Award, no date; Dickson Prize, no date.

Selected Publications: "DNA related to the Transforming Gene(s) of Avian Sarcoma Viruses is Present in Normal Avian DNA." *Nature* 260 (March 11, 1976): 170–73. "Oncogenes." *Scientific American* 246 (March, 1982): 80–91. "Amplification of N-myc in Untreated Human Neuroblastomas Correlates with Advance Disease State." *Science* 224 (June 8, 1984): 1121–24. "The Molecular Genetics of Cancer." *Science* 235 (January 16, 1987): 305–12.

For More Information See: Chemical and Engineering News 67 (October 16, 1989): 6–8. *Scientific American* 261 (December 1989): 34–36.

Commentary: The Nobel was shared by J. Michael Bishop "for the discovery that the oncogenes of the animal tumour viruses are derived from cellular genes (proto-oncogenes)." Bishop's research showed that viral oncogenes (cancer-causing genes associated with a virus) were produced from altered cellular genes that the virus had picked up, rather than from viral genes themselves. The discovery affected the nature of research on the normal growth of cells and on the growth of tumors. (G.R./B.S.S.)

Varmus, Harold Eliot   426

Prize: Medicine and Physiology, 1989. *Born:* December 18, 1939; Oceanside, NY. *Parents:* Father, Frank Varmus; Mother, Beatrice Barasch Varmus. *Nationality:* American. *Religion:* From Jewish background. *Education:* Amherst College, MA, B.A., 1961; Harvard Univ., MA, M.A., 1962; Columbia Univ., NY, M.D., 1966. *Spouse:* Constance Louise Casey, married October 25, 1969. *Children:* Jacob Carey, son; Christopher Issac, son. *Career:* Presbyterian Hospital, NY, Resident, 1966–68; National Institutes of

Health, MD, Researcher, 1968–70; Univ. of California, San Francisco, Professor, 1970–93; National Institutes of Health, MD, Director, 1993–99; Memorial Sloan-Kettering Cancer Center, NY, President, 2000-. *Other Awards:* Lasker Award, 1982; Passano Award, 1983; Alfred Sloan Award, 1984; Armand Hammer Prize, 1984; Shubitz Prize, 1984; Gairdner Foundation Award, 1984; American College of Physicians Award, 1987.

Selected Publications: "DNA Related to the Transforming Gene(s) of Avian Sarcoma Viruses is Present in Normal Avian DNA." *Nature* 260 (March 11, 1976): 170–73. "Amplification of N-myc in Untreated Human Neuroblastomas Correlates with Advanced Disease State." *Science* 224 (June 8, 1984): 1121–25. "Oncogenes and Transcriptional Control." *Science* 238 (December 4, 1987): 1337–40. *Genes and the Biology of Cancer* (with R. Weinberg). New York: Scientific American Library, 1993.

For More Information See: *Chemical and Engineering News* 67 (October 16, 1989): 6–8; *Scientific American* 261 (December 1989): 34–36.

Commentary: Harold Varmus shared the Nobel "for the discovery that the oncogenes of animal tumour viruses are derived from cellular genes (proto-oncogenes)." Varmus's research showed that viral oncogenes (cancer-causing genes associated with a virus) were produced from altered cellular genes that the virus had picked up, rather than from viral genes themselves. The discovery affected the nature of research on the normal growth of cells and on the growth of tumors. (G.R./B.S.S.)

1990

Murray, Joseph E.   **427**

Prize: Medicine and Physiology, 1990. *Born:* April 1, 1919; Milford, MA. *Parents:* Father, William Andrew Murray; Mother, Mary DePasquale Murray. *Nationality:* American. *Religion:* Catholic. *Education:* Holy Cross College, MA, A.B., 1940; Harvard Univ., MA, M.D., 1943. *Spouse:* Virginia Link, married June 2, 1945. *Children:* Virginia, daughter; Margaret, daughter; Joseph, son; Katherine, daughter; Thomas, son; Richard, son. *Career:* Medical practice, 1943–86; Brigham & Women's Hospital, MA, Surgeon, 1951–86; Children's Hospital Medical Center, MA, Surgeon, 1972–85; Harvard Medical School, MA, Professor, 1970–86. *Other Awards:* American Academy of Arts & Sciences Award, 1962; Gold Medal, International Society of Surgeons, 1963; Sabin Award, 1994; Lifetime Achievement Award, Massachusetts Medical Society, 1998.

Selected Publications: "Organ Transplantation: Status and a Look into the Future." *New York Journal of Medicine* 61 (October 1, 1961): 3245–48. "Organ Transplantation—The Kidney and the Skin." *Southern Medical Journal* 55 (September 1962): 890–93. "Prolonged Survival of Human-Kidney Homografts by Immunosuppressive Drug Therapy." *New Eng. J. Med.* 268 (June 13, 1963): 1315–23.

For More Information See: *New York Times* (October 9, 1990): A1. Magill, F. *Nobel Prize Winners: Physiology or Medicine.* Pasadena, CA: Salem Press, 1991, 588–97.

Commentary: The Nobel in Medicine and Physiology was granted to Joseph E. Murray for work that "proved to a doubting world that it was possible to transplant organs to save the lives of dying patients." Murray was the first to

perform kidney transplants. His work was later used in the general practice of organ transplants. The laureate was also active in the area of plastic surgery. (B.S.S.)

Thomas, Edward Donnall   **428**

Prize: Medicine and Physiology, 1990. *Born:* March 15, 1920; Mart, TX. *Parents:* Father, Edward E. Thomas; Mother, Angie Hill Donnall Thomas. *Nationality:* American. *Religion:* Christian. *Education:* Univ. of Texas, Austin, B.A., 1941; Univ. of Texas, Austin, M.A., 1943; Harvard Univ., MA, M.D., 1946. *Spouse:* Dorothy Martin, married December 20, 1942. *Children:* Edward Donnall, Jr., son; Jeffery A., son; Elaine, daughter. *Career:* Medical practice, 1946–90; U.S. Army, Doctor, 1948–50; Harvard Medical School, MA, Professor 1953–55; Columbia Univ., NY, Professor, 1955–63; Univ. of Washington, Professor, 1963–90. *Other Awards:* McIntyre Award, 1975; Levine Award, 1979; National Award for Basic Science, 1980; Kettering Prize, 1981; de Villiers Award, 1983; Landsteiner Award, 1987; Fox Award, 1990; Gairdner Foundation Award, 1990; National Medal of Science, 1990; Kober Medal, 1992.

Selected Publications: "Supralethal Whole Body Irradiation and Isologous Marrow Transplantation in Man." *Journal of Clinical Investigation* 38 (October 1959): 1709–16. "Irradiation and Marrow Infusion in Leukemia. Observations in Five Patients with Acute Leukemia Treated by Whole Body Exposures of 1400 to 2000 Roentgens and Infusions of Marrow." *Archives of Internal Medicine* (Chicago) 107 (June 1961): 829–45. "Transplantation of Marrow and Whole Organs." *Canadian Medical Association Journal* 86 (March 10, 1962): 435–44.

For More Information See: *New York Times* (October 9, 1990): A1. Magill, F. *Nobel Prize Winners: Physiology or Medicine.* Pasadena, CA: Salem Press, 1991, 588–97.

Commentary: E. Donnall Thomas was awarded the Nobel for work that "proved to a doubting world that it was possible to transplant organs to save the lives of dying patients." Thomas's recognition was for his work with bone marrow transplants in leukemia treatment, but he was active in the areas of hematology, biochemical medicine, and irradiation biology as well. (B.S.S.)

1991

Neher, Erwin   **429**

Prize: Medicine and Physiology, 1991. *Born:* March 20, 1944; Landsberg, Germany. *Parents:* Father, Franz Xaver Neher; Mother, Elizabeth Pfeiffer Neher. *Nationality:* German. *Religion:* Catholic. *Education:* Institute of Technology, Germany, B.S., 1965; Univ. of Wisconsin, M.S., 1967; Institute of Technology, Germany, Ph.D., 1970. *Spouse:* Eva-Marie Ruhr, married December 26, 1978. *Children:* Richard, son; Benjamin, son; Sigmund, son; Carola, daughter; Margret, daughter. *Career:* Max Planck Institut für Psychiatrie, Munich, Germany, Researcher, 1970–72; Yale Univ., Researcher, 1975–76; Max Planck Institut für Biophysikalische Chemie, Gottingen, Germany, Researcher and Administrator, 1972–75, 1976-. *Other Awards:* Nernst-Haber-Rodenstein Award, 1977; Feldberg Foundation Award, 1979; Harold Lampert Award, 1982; K.C. Cole Award, 1982; Spenser Award, 1983; Louisa Gross Horwitz Award, 1986; Leibniz Award, 1986; Schunck Prize, 1986; Gairdner

Foundation Award, 1989; Hans Helmut Vits Prize, 1990; Bristol-Myers Squibb Research Award, 1990; Gerard Prize, 1991.

Selected Publications: "Single-channel Currents Recorded from Membrane of Denervated Frog Muscle Fibres." *Nature* 260 (1976): 799 (with B. Sakmann); "Noise Analysis of Drug-Induced Voltage Clamp Currents in Denervated Frog Muscle Fibers." *J. Physiol. (London)* 258 (1976): 705–29 (with B. Sakmann); *Single Channel Recording.* New York: Plenum Press, 1983 (with B. Sakmann).

For More Information See: Chemical and Engineering News 69 (October 14, 1991): 4; *Science* 254 (October 18, 1991): 380.

Commentary: Erwin Neher shared the Nobel with Bert Sakmann for "their discoveries concerning the function of single ion channels in cells." The two devised a tiny electrode (a patch clamp electrode) which could be used to identify the activity of ion channels (a type of membrane protein) in permitting ion flow across a cell membrane. Ion channel studies have been instrumental in work to explain diseases like cystic fibrosis, diabetes, epilepsy, and neuromuscular disorders. (B.S.S./J.H.S.)

Sakmann, Bert   430

Prize: Medicine and Physiology, 1991. *Born:* June 12, 1942; Stuttgart, Germany. *Parents:* Father, Berthold Sakmann; Mother, Annemarie Schaeffer Sakmann. *Nationality:* German. *Religion:* Protestant. *Education:* Univ. of Munich, Germany, B.A., 1967; Univ. of Göttingen, Germany, M.D., 1974. *Spouse:* Christiane Wulfert, married 1970. *Children:* Bernhard, son; Kaspar, son; Sophie, daughter. *Career:* Max Planck Institut für Psychiatrie, Munich, Germany, Researcher, 1969–70; University College, England, Researcher, 1970–73; Max Planck Institut für Biophysikalische Chemie, Göttingen, Germany, Researcher, 1974–89; Max Planck Institut, Heidelberg, Germany, Researcher, 1989-. *Other Awards:* Nernst Prize, 1977; Feldberg Foundation Prize, 1979; Magnes Award, 1982; Spencer Award, 1983; Louisa Gross Horwitz Prize, 1986; Gairdner Foundation Award, 1989; Harvey Prize, Technion, 1991.

Selected Publications: "Single-channel Currents Recorded from Membrane of Denervated Frog Muscle Fibres." *Nature* 260 (1976): 799 (with E. Neher); "Noise Analysis of Drug-Induced Voltage Clamp Currents in Denervated Frog Muscle Fibers." *J. Physiol. (London)* 258 (1976): 705–29 (with E. Neher); *Single Channel Recording.* New York: Plenum Press, 1983 (with E. Neher); "The Patch Clamp Technique," *Scientific American* (March 1992): 44–51.

For More Information See: Chemical and Engineering News 69 (October 14, 1991): 4; *Science* 254 (October 18, 1991): 380.

Commentary: Bert Sakmann shared the Nobel with Erwin Neher for "their discoveries concerning the function of single ion channels in cells." The two devised a tiny electrode (a patch clamp electrode) which could be used to identify the activity of ion channels (a type of membrane protein) in permitting ion flow across a cell membrane. Ion channel studies have been instrumental in work to explain diseases like cystic fibrosis, diabetes, epilepsy, and neuromuscular disorders. (B.S.S./J.H.S.)

1992

Fischer, Edmond Henri   431

Prize: Medicine and Physiology, 1992. *Born:* April 6, 1920; Shanghai, China. *Parents:* Father, Oscar Fischer; Mother, Renee Tapernoux Fischer. *Nationality:* Chinese/French; came to U.S. in 1953. *Religion:* None. *Education:* Univ. of Geneva, Switzerland, licensure, 1943; diploma, 1944; Ph.D., 1947. *Spouse:* Nelly Gagnaux, married, no date, died 1961; Beverly B. Bullock, married October, 1963 *Children:* François Louis, son; Henri Pierre, son; Paula Danlicker Tubbs, stepdaughter *Career:* Univ. of Geneva, Switzerland, Docent, 1950–53; California Institute of Technology, Professor, 1953–54; Univ. of Washington, Professor, 1954–90 *Other Awards:* Werner Medal, 1952; Lederle Award, 1956–59; Passano Foundation Award, 1988; Beering Award, 1991; Priz Jaubert, no date.

Selected Publications: "Phosphorylase Activity of Skeletal-muscle Extracts." *J. Biol. Chem.* 216 ((1955): 113–20 (with E. Krebs); "Conversion of Phosphorylase b to Phosphorylase a in Muscle Extracts." *J. Biol. Chem.* 216 (1955): 121–32 (with E. Krebs); "Phosphorylase b-to-a Converting Enzyme of Rabbit Skeletal Muscle." *Biochem. et Biophys. Acta* 20 (1956): 150–7 (with E. Krebs).

For More Information See: Chemical and Engineering News 70 (October 19, 1992): 6; *Science* 258 (October 23, 1992): 542.

Commentary: Edmond Fischer and Edwin Krebs jointly received the Nobel Prize for their identification of the process that regulates many metabolic systems. The Coris, Nobel Prize winners in 1947, had shown that phosphorylase allowed glucose to be released from glycogen, which, in turn, provided energy for muscle cells. Fischer and Krebs found an enzyme, a protein kinase, that activates the phosphorylase by removing a phosphate group from ATP and placing it on the phosphorylase. The phosphorylase is deactivated by removing a phosphate group with the enzyme protein phosphatase. Inappropriately phosphorylated proteins have been implicated in many disease states, including cancer, diabetes, and muscular dystrophy. (B.S.S./J.H.S.)

Krebs, Edwin Gerhard   432

Prize: Medicine and Physiology, 1992. *Born:* June 6, 1918; Lansing, IA. *Parents:* Father, William Carl Krebs; Mother, Louise Helena Stegeman Krebs. *Nationality:* American. *Religion:* Presbyterian. *Education:* Univ. of Illinois, A.B., 1940; Washington Univ., MO, M.D., 1943. *Spouse:* Virginia Deedy Frech, married March 10, 1945. *Children:* Sally, daughter; Robert, son; Martha, daughter *Career:* Washington Univ. of St. Louis, MO, Researcher, 1946–48; Univ. of Washington, Professor, 1948–68; Univ. of California, Davis, Professor, 1968–76; Univ. of Washington, Professor, 1976–90. *Other Awards:* Gairdner Foundation Award, 1978; Thorn Award, 1983; American Heart Association Award, 1987; Passano Award, 1988; 3M Award, 1989; Lasker Award, 1989; Horwitz Award, 1989; Ciba-Geigy-Drew Award, 1991; Beering Award, 1991; Welch Award, 1991; Alumni Achievement Award, Univ. of Illinois, 1992; Kaul Foundation Award, 1996.

Selected Publications: "Phosphorylase Activity of Skeletal-muscle Extracts." *J. Biol. Chem.* 216 (1955): 113–120 (with E. Fischer); "Conversion of Phosphorylase b to Phosphorylase a in Muscle Extracts." *J. Biol. Chem.* 216

(1955): 121–32 (with E. Fischer); "Phosphorylase b-to-a Converting Enzyme of Rabbit Skeletal Muscle." *Biochim. et Biophys. Acta* 20 (1956): 150–7 (with E. Fischer).

For More Information See: Chemical and Engineering News 70 (October 19, 1992): 6; *Science* 258 (October 23, 1992): 542.

Commentary: Edwin Krebs and Edmond Fischer jointly received the Nobel Prize for their identification of the process that regulates many metabolic systems. The Coris, Nobel Prize winners in 1947, had shown that phosphorylase allows glucose to be released from glycogen, thus providing energy for muscle cells. Fischer and Krebs found an enzyme, a protein kinase, which activates the phosphorylase by removing a phosphate group from ATP and placing it on the phosphorylase. The phosphorylase is deactivated by removing a phosphate group with the enzyme protein phosphatase. Inappropriately phosphorylated proteins have been implicated in many disease states, including cancer, diabetes, and muscular dystrophy. (B.S.S./J.H.S.)

1993

Roberts, Richard John   433

Prize: Medicine and Physiology, 1993. *Born:* September 6, 1943; Derby, England. *Parents:* Father, John Walter Roberts; Mother, Edna Wilhelmina Allsop Roberts. *Nationality:* English; emigrated to U.S. 1969. *Religion:* Atheist, from Anglican background. *Education:* Sheffield Univ., England, B.S. 1965; Ph.D. 1968. *Spouse:* Elizabeth Dyson, married August 21, 1965, died August 7, 1985; Jean E. Michaelis Tagliabue, married February 14, 1986. *Children:* Alison, daughter; Andrew, son; Amanda, daughter; Christopher, son. *Career:* Harvard Univ., MA, Researcher, 1969–72; Cold Spring Harbor Laboratory, NY, Researcher, 1972–92; New England Biolabs, MA, Researcher, 1992-.

Selected Publications: "Restriction Endonucleases." *CRC Crit. Rev. Biochem.* 4 (1976): 123–64; "The Role of Restriction Endonucleases in Genetic Engineering." *Miles Int. Symp. Ser.* 10 (1977): 21–32; "The Spliced Messenger RNAs of Adenoviru-2. "*Proc. FEBS Meet.* 51 (1978): 245–53.

For More Information See: Chemical and Engineering News 71 (October 18, 1993): 7; *New Scientist* 14 (October 16, 1993): 4.

Commentary: Richard Roberts shared his Nobel with Phillip Sharp for their independent discovery of "split genes." Roberts and Sharp discovered that gene strands in cells are interrupted by nonsense segments of DNA which do not contain genetic codes. They also discovered that messenger RNA molecules remove the nonsense segments and read in appropriate genetic segments. The Academy noted that "the discovery of split genes has been of fundamental importance for today's basic research in biology, as well as for more medically oriented research concerning the development of cancer and other diseases." (B.S.S./J.H.S.)

Sharp, Phillip Allen   434

Prize: Medicine and Physiology, 1993. *Born:* June 6, 1944; Falmouth, KY. *Parents:* Father, Joseph Walter Sharp; Mother, Katherin Colvin Sharp. *Nationality:* American. *Religion:* Congregationalist. *Education:* Union College, KY, B.A., 1966; Univ. of Illinois, Ph.D. 1969. *Spouse:* Ann Christine

Holcombe, married August 29, 1964. *Children:* Christine Alynn, daughter; Sarah Katherine, daughter; Helena Holcombe, daughter. *Career:* California Institute of Technology, CA, Researcher, 1969–71; Cold Spring Harbor Laboratory, NY, Researcher, 1971–74; Massachusetts Institute of Technology, Professor, 1974–99. *Other Awards:* National Academy of Science Award, 1980; U.S. Steel Foundation Award, 1980; Eli Lilly Award, 1980; Ricketts Award, 1985; Sloan Prize, 1986; Gairdner Foundation Award, 1986; New York Academy of Sciences Award, 1986; Horwitz Prize, 1988; Lasker Award, 1988; Dickson Prize, 1990; Franklin Medal, 1999.

Selected Publications: "Speculations on RNA Splicing." *Cell* 23 (1981): 643–6; "Adenovirus Late Transcriptional Unit." *Perspect. Virol.* 11 (1981): 9–30; *DNA Tumor Viruses.* Cold Spring Harbor, NY: Cold Spring Harbor Laboratory, 1986.

For More Information See: Chemical and Engineering News 71 (October 18, 1993): 7; *New Scientist* 14 (October 16, 1993): 4.

Commentary: Phillip Sharp was granted the Nobel with Richard Roberts for their independent discovery of "split genes." They found that gene strands in cells are interrupted by nonsense segments of DNA which do not contain genetic codes. They also discovered that messenger RNA molecules remove the nonsense segments and read in appropriate genetic segments. The Committee noted that "the discovery of split genes has been of fundamental importance for today's basic research in biology, as well as for more medically oriented research concerning the development of cancer and other diseases." (B.S.S./J.H.S.)

1994

Gilman, Alfred Goodman   435

Prize: Medicine and Physiology, 1994. *Born:* July 1, 1941; New Haven, CT. *Parents:* Father, Alfred Gilman; Mother, Mabel Schmidt Gilman. *Nationality:* American. *Religion:* Most probably Christian. *Education:* Yale Univ., CT, B.S., 1962; Case Western Reserve Univ., OH, M.D., Ph.D., 1969. *Spouse:* Kathryn Hedlund, married September 21, 1963. *Children:* Amy, daughter; Anne, daughter; Edward, son. *Career:* National Institutes of Health, MD, Researcher, 1969–71; Univ. of Virginia, Professor, 1971–81; Univ. of Texas Southwestern Medical Center, Professor, 1981–97; Yale Univ., CT, Professor, 1997-. *Other Awards:* J.J. Abel Award, 1975; Paulsson Award, 1982; Gairdner Foundation Award, 1984; Lounsbery Award, 1987; Lasker Award, 1989; Passano Award, 1990; Waterford Award, 1990; American Heart Association Prize, 1990; Beering Award, 1990; L.S. Goodman Award, 1990; Alfred Gilman Award, 1990; CIBA-Geigy-Drew Award, 1991; American Academy Achievement Award, 1995; American Cancer Society Medal, 1995; ACP Award, 1995; Sollman Award, 1997.

Selected Publications: "Resolution, Characterization, and Partial Purification of Components of Catecholamine-sensitive Adenylate Cyclase." *NIH Publication* NIH-80–2017 (1980): 157–72; "Guanine Nucleotide-binding Regulatory Proteins and Dual Control of Adenylate Cyclase." *J. Clin. Invest.* 93 (1984): 1–4; "G Proteins and Dual Control of Adenylate Cyclase." *Cell* 36 (1984): 577–9.

For More Information See: *Chemical and Engineering News* 72 (October 17, 1994): 4; *New York Times Biographical Service* (1994): 1562.

Commentary: The Nobel Prize was granted to Alfred Gilman in recognition of his identification of the G-proteins described earlier by his colaureate, Martin Rodbell. G-proteins are the substances activated in a cell when hormones or neurotransmitters carrying messages from another cell meet the cell's receptors. The G-proteins then activate another intermediary. Gilman's work with cancerous cells has been extended to other disease states and has been instrumental in interpreting the modes of action in sight, smell, and taste. (B.S.S./J.H.S.)

Rodbell, Martin   436

Prize: Medicine and Physiology, 1994. *Born:* December 1, 1925; Baltimore, MD. *Death:* December 7, 1998; Chapel Hill, NC. *Parents:* Father, Milton William Rodbell; Mother, Shirley Helen Abrams Rodbell. *Nationality:* American. *Religion:* None; from Jewish background. *Education:* Johns Hopkins Univ., MD, B.A., 1949; Univ. of Washington, Ph.D., 1954. *Spouse:* Barbara Charlotte Ledermann, married September 10, 1950. *Children:* Paul, son; Suzanne, daughter; Andrew, son; Phillip, son. *Career:* Univ. of Illinois, IL, Researcher, 1954–56; National Institutes of Health, MD and NC, Researcher, 1956–94. *Other Awards:* NIH Duistinguished Service Award, 1973; Health and Human Services Superior Service Award, 1974; Gairdner Foundation Award, 1984; Jacobeus Award, 1973; Lounsbery Award, 1987.

Selected Publications: "Cell Surface Receptor Sites." *Curr. Top. Biochem.* (1972): 187–218; "Problem of Identifying the Glucagon Receptor." *Fed. Proc., FASEB* 32 (1973): 1854–8; "Molecular Mechanisms of Hormone Receptors." *Neurosci. Res. Program Bull.* 11 (1973): 211–15, 271–94.

For More Information See: *Chemical and Engineering News* 72 (October 17, 1994): 4; *New York Times* (December 11, 1998): B15; *New York Times Biographical Service* (1994): 1562.

Commentary: Martin Rodbell received the Nobel Prize for his research on G-proteins, the substances that are activated in a cell when hormones or neurotransmitters carrying messages from another cell meet the cell's receptors. The G-proteins complete the messages between cells by activating another intermediary. The action of G-proteins has been shown to be a contributor to the understanding of some cancers, hereditary glandular disorders, diabetes, and alcoholism. (B.S.S./J.H.S.)

1995

Lewis, Edward B.   437

Prize: Medicine and Physiology, 1995. *Born:* May 20, 1918; Wilkes-Barre, PA. *Parents:* Father, Edward B. Lewis; Mother, Laura Histed Lewis. *Nationality:* American. *Religion:* Non-practicing. *Education:* Univ. of Minnesota, BA, 1939; California Institute of Technology, M.S., 1943; Ph.D., 1942. *Spouse:* Pamela Harrah, married September 26, 1946. *Children:* Hugh, son; Glenn, son; Keith, son. *Career:* U.S. Army Air Force, Doctor, 1942–45; California Institute of Technology, Professor, 1946–88. *Other Awards:* Thomas Hunt Morgan Medal, 1983; Gairdner Foundation Award,

1987; Wolf Foundation Prize, 1989; Rosenstiel Award, 1990; National Medal of Science, 1990; Lasker Award, 1991; Horwitz Prize, 1992.

Selected Publications: "The Relation of Repeats to Position Effect in Drosophila." *Genetics* 30 (1945): 137–66; "Germinal and Somatic Reversion of the Ivory Mutant in Drosophila." *Genetics* 44 (1959): 522–31; "A Gene Complex Controlling Segmentation in Drosophilia." *Nature* 276 (1978): 565–70; "Clusters of Master Control Genes Regulate the Development of Higher Organisms." *JAMA* 267 (1992): 1524–31.

For More Information See: *New York Times* (October 10, 1995): B5.

Commentary: Edward Lewis shared the Nobel Prize with Christiane Nusslein-Volhard and Eric Wieschaus for work that "achieved a breakthrough that will explain congenital malformation in man. . . . [It] is likely that [the same] mutations are responsible for some of the early spontaneous abortions in [humans] and for some of the about 40 percent of the congenital malformations that develop due to unknown reasons." In work that started in the 40s, Lewis used radiation to destroy genes in Drosophila, a type of fruit fly, and identified unusual mutants. He discovered that each gene controlled the development of a different segment of the fruit fly's body and that the genes were lined up along the chromosomes in the order of the parts of the body they controlled. (B.S.S./J.H.S.)

Nusslein-Volhard, Christiane   438

Prize: Medicine and Physiology, 1995. *Born:* October 20, 1942; Magdeburg, Germany. *Parents:* Father, Rolf Volhard; Mother, Brigitte Haas Volhard. *Nationality:* German. *Religion:* Most probably Christian. *Education:* Univ. of Tübingen, Germany, Diploma, 1968, Ph.D., 1973. *Spouse:* No record found. *Children:* No record found. *Career:* Max Planck Institute, Tubingen, Germany, Researcher, 1972–75; Biozentrum Basel, Switzerland, Researcher, 1975–76; Univ. of Freiburg, Germany, Researcher, 1976–77; European Molecular Biology Laboratory, Germany, Researcher, 1978–80; Max Planck Institute, Tubingen, Germany, Professor and Administrator, 1981-. *Other Awards:* Leibniz Prize, 1986; Vogt Prize, 1986; Forderpreis, 1986; Carus Medal, 1989; Rosenstiel Medal, 1990; Lasker Prize, 1991; Louisa Gross Horwitz Prize, 1992; Priz Louis Jeantet, 1992; Otto Bayer Prize, 1992; Alfred Sloan Prize, 1992; Mendel Medal, 1992; Warburg Medal, 1992; Schering Prize, 1993; Krebs Medal, 1993; Bertner Award, 1993.

Selected Publications: "Mutations Affecting Segment Number and Polarity in Drosophila." *Nature* 287 (1980):795–801 (with E. Wieschaus). "Determination of the Embryonic Axes of Drosophila." *Dev. Suppl.* (1991): 1–10; "The Formation of the Embryonic Axes in Drosophila." *Cancer* 71 (1993): 3189–93.

For More Information See: *New York Times* (October 10, 1995): B5. *New York Times Magazine* (October 12, 1997): 42+.

Commentary: Christiane Nusslein-Volhard shared the Nobel with Edward Lewis and Eric Wieschaus for work that "achieved a breakthrough that will explain congenital malformations in man. . . . [It] is likely that [the same] mutations are responsible for some of the early spontaneous abortions in [humans] and for some of the about 40 percent of the congenital malformations that develop due to unknown reasons." Lewis, in the 40s, had formulated the concept of the existence of clusters of genes which controlled development of the fruit fly's body. Nusslein-Volhard and Wieschaus, in the 80s, extended Lewis's work, searching for mutations that controlled the early stages of development. They identified the genes that cause the fertilized egg to develop into an ordered pattern of segments which eventually determine the shape of the fruit fly. (B.S.S./J.H.S.)

Wieschaus, Eric F.   439

Prize: Medicine and Physiology, 1995. *Born:* June 8, 1947; South Bend, IN. *Parents:* Father, Leroy Joseph Wieschaus; Mother, Marcella Carner Wieschaus. *Nationality:* American. *Religion:* None; from Catholic background. *Education:* Univ. of Notre Dame, IN, B.S., 1969; Yale Univ., CT, Ph.D., 1974. *Spouse:* Gertrude (Trudi) Schupbach, married April 11, 1982. *Children:* Ingrid, daughter; Eleanor, daughter; Laura, daughter. *Career:* Univ. of Zürich, Switzerland, Researcher, 1975–78; European Molecular Biology Laboratory, Germany, Researcher, 1978–81; Princeton Univ., NJ, Professor, 1981-. *Other Awards:* John Spangler Niclaus Prize, 1974; NIH Merit Award, 1989; Genetics Society of American Prize, 1995.

Selected Publications: "The Development and Function of the Female Germ Line in Drosophila." *Dev. Biol.* 68 (1979): 29–46; "Mutations Affecting Segment Number and Polarity in Drosophila." *Nature* 287 (1980): 795–801 (with C. Nusslein-Volhard); "Ortho Dental Activity is Required for the Development of Medial Structures in the Larval and Adult Epidermis of Drosophila." *Development* 115 (1992):801–11; "Embryonic Transcription and the Control of Developmental Pathways," *Genetics* (1996).

For More Information See: *New York Times* (October 10, 1995): B5.

Commentary: Eric Wieschaus shared the Nobel with Christiane Nusslein-Volhard and Edward Lewis for work that "achieved a breakthrough that will explain congenital malformations in man. . . . [It] is likely that [the same] mutations are responsible for some of the early spontaneous abortions in [humans] and for some of the about 40 percent of the congenital malformations that develop due to unknown reasons." Lewis, in the 40s, had formulated the concept of the existence of clusters of genes which controlled development of the fruit fly's body. Wieschaus and Nusslein-Volhard, in the 80s, extended Lewis's work, searching for mutations that controlled the early stages of development. They identified the genes that cause the fertilized egg to develop into an ordered pattern of segments which eventually determine the shape of the fruit fly. (B.S.S./J.H.S.)

1996

Doherty, Peter Charles   440

Prize: Medicine and Physiology, 1996. *Born:* October 15, 1940; Brisbane, Queensland, Australia. *Parents:* Father, Eric C. Doherty; Mother, Linda Byford Doherty. *Nationality:* Australian; later American resident. *Religion:* Methodist. *Education:* Univ. of Queensland, Australia, B.V.Sc., 1962; Univ. of Queensland, Australia, M.V.Sc., 1966; Univ.

of Edinburgh, Scotland, Ph.D., 1970. *Spouse:* Penelope Stephens, married 1965. *Children:* James, son; Michael, son. *Career:* Animal Research Institute, Australia, Veterinarian Officer, 1963–67; Moredun Research Institute, Scotland, Scientific Officer, 1967–71; Australian National Univ., Australia, Professor and Researcher, 1972–75; Wistar Institute, PA, Professor, 1975–82; Australian National Univ., Australia, Administrator, 1982–88; St. Jude Children's Research Hospital, TN, Researcher and Administrator, 1988-. *Other Awards:* Paul Ehrlich Prize, 1983; Gairdner Foundation Award, 1986; Lasker Award, 1995; Australian of the Year Award, 1997.

Selected Publications: "Immunological Surveillance Against Altered Self Components by Sensitized T Lymphocytes in Lymphocytic Choriomeningitis," *Nature* 251 (October 11, 1974): 547–48 (with R.M. Zinkernagel). "Restriction of in vitro T cell-mediated cytotoxicty in lymphocytic choriomeningitis within a syngenic and semiallogeneic system," 248 *Nature* (1974): 701–02 (with R.M. Zinkernagel). "Cell-mediated cytoxicity," *Cell* (November 19, 1993): 607–12. "Evasion of Host Immune Responses by Tumours and Viruses" (with R.A. Tripp and J.W. Sixby) in *Ciba Foundation Symposium* (1994): 245–46, 256–60. "The Discovery of MHC Restriction," *Immunology Today* (January 1997): 14–17 (with R.M. Zinkernagel).

For More Information See: *Lancet* 356 (July 8, 2000): 172. *New York Times* (October 8, 1996): C6.

Commentary: Peter Doherty shared the Nobel Prize for discovering how "the immune system recognizes virus-infected cells." He and Rolf Zinkernagel found that "white blood cells had to recognize both the virus and certain self molecules in order to kill the virus-infected cells." This discovery has been highly relevant to clinical medicine and has been especially useful in studying the effects of autoimmune reactions in diseases such as multiple sclerosis and diabetes. (L.S.S.)

Zinkernagel, Rolf Martin   441

Prize: Medicine and Physiology, 1996. *Born:* January 6, 1944; Basel, Switzerland. *Parents:* Father, Robert W. Zinkernagel; Mother, Suzanne Staehlin Zinkernagel. *Nationality:* Swiss. *Religion:* No record found. *Education:* Univ. of Basel, Switzerland, M.D., 1968; Australian National Univ., Australia, Ph.D., 1975. *Spouse:* Kathrin G. Ludin, married November 11, 1968. *Children:* Christine, daughter; Annelies, daughter; Martin, son. *Career:* Claraspital, Switzerland, Intern, 1968–69; Univ. of Basel, Switzerland, Researcher, 1969–70; Univ. of Lausanne, Switzerland, Researcher, 1971–73; Australian National Univ., Australia, Researcher, 1973–75; Scripps Univ., CA, Professor, 1975–79; Univ. of Zurich, Switzerland, Professor, 1979-. *Other Awards:* Cloetta Stiftung Award, 1981; Jung Stiftung Award, 1982; Paul Ehrlich Prize, 1983; Mack-Forster Prize, 1985; Gairdner Foundation Award, 1986; Christoforo Colombo Award, 1992; Lasker Award, 1995.

Selected Publications: "Immunological Surveillance Against Altered Self Components by Sensitized T Lymphocytes in Lymphocytic Choriomeningitis," *Nature* 251 (October 11, 1974): 547–48 (with P.C. Doherty). "Restriction of in vitro T cell-mediated cytotoxicty in lymphocytic choriomeningitis within a syngenic and semiallogeneic system," 248 *Nature* (1974): 701–02 (with P.C. Doherty).

"Cytotoxic T Cells Learn Specificity for Self H-2 During Differentiation in the Thymus," *Nature* (January 19, 1978): 251–53. "The Discovery of MHC Restriction," *Immunology Today* (January 1997): 14–17 (with P.C. Doherty).

For More Information See: Lancet 356 (July 8, 2000): 172. *New York Times* (October 8, 1996): C6.

Commentary: Rolf Zinkernagel shared the Nobel Prize with Peter Doherty for their "discoveries concerning the specificity of the cell mediated immune defence." In their studies of mice they found that "infected mice developed killer T-lymphocytes, which in a test-tube could kill virus-infected cells" but were not able to do so from another strain of infected mice. Thus infected cells had to display both the virus and self molecules indicating they were from the infected animal. This discovery had an immediate impact on immunological research in inflammatory diseases. (L.S.S.)

1997

Prusiner, Stanley Ben   **442**
Prize: Medicine and Physiology, 1997. *Born:* May 28, 1942; Des Moines, IA. *Parents:* Father, Lawrence Albert Prusiner; Mother, Miriam Spigel Prusiner. *Nationality:* American. *Religion:* Jewish. *Education:* Univ. of Pennsylvania, PA, A.B., 1964; Univ. of Pennsylvania, M.D., 1968. *Spouse:* Sandra Lee Turk, married October 18, 1970. *Children:* Helen Chloe, daughter; Leah Anne, daughter *Career:* Univ. of California, San Francisco, CA, Intern and Resident, 1968–74; Univ. of California, San Francisco, CA, Professor, 1974- ; Univ. of California, Berkeley, CA, Professor, 1979- *Other Awards:* Williams Basic Sciences Research Award, 1968; Cotzias Award, 1987; Potamkin Prize, 1991; Medical Research Award, Metropolitan Life Foundation, 1992; Christopher Columbus Award, NIH, 1992; Dana Award, 1992; Dickson Prize, 1992; Max Planck Award, 1992; von Humboldt Award, 1992; Gairdner Foundation Award, 1993; Lounsbery Award, 1993; Presidential Award, American Academy of Neurology, 1993; Bristol-Myers Squibb Distinguished Achievement Award, 1994; Lasker Award, 1994; Caledonian Research Prize, 1995; Paul Ehrlich Award, 1995; Darmstaedter Award, 1995; Paul Hoch Award, 1995; Wolf Prize, 1996; ICN Virology Prize, 1996; Soriano Award, 1996; Pasarow Award, 1996; Leopold-Mayer Prize, 1996; Keio International Prize, 1996; Baxter Award, 1996; Amgen Award, 1997; Louisa Gross Horwitz Prize, 1997; K.J. Zulch Prize, 1997; Distinguished Achievement Award, American Academy of Neurology, 1998; Franklin Medal, 1998; Jubilee Medal, Swedish Medical Society, 1998.

Selected Publications: Prion Diseases of Humans and Animals. New York: Ellis Horwood, 1992. "Evidence for Isolate Specified Allotypic Interactions between the Cellular and Scrapie Prion Proteins in Congenic and Transgenic Mice," *Proceedings of the National Academy of Sciences* 91 (1994): 5690–5694 (with others). "The Prion Diseases," *Scientific American* 272 (1995): 70–77. *Prions, Prions, Prions.* Berlin: Springer, 1996 (with others). *Prion Biology and Diseases.* Cold Spring Harbor, NY: Cold Spring Harbor Laboratory Press, 1999.

For More Information See: Current Biography. New York: H.W. Wilson, 1997, Vol. 58, 440–44. *New York Times* (October 7, 1997): A1. Taubes, Gary. "The Game of the

Name Is Fame. But Is It Science?" *Discover* (December 1986): 44–56.

Commentary: Stanley Prusiner was awarded the Nobel Prize for his discovery of "Prions—a new biological principle of infection." Prions are proteins that have the ability to change their shape by folding and "result in the formation of harmful particles, the causative agents of several deadly brain diseases of the dementia type in humans and animals." Prusiner's work has led to new understandings of dementia-type diseases such as Alzheimer's disease, variants of Creutzfeldt-Jakob disease (CJD) and mad-cow disease. (L.S.S.)

1998

Furchgott, Robert Francis   **443**
Prize: Medicine and Physiology, 1998. *Born:* June 4, 1916; Charleston, SC. *Parents:* No record found. *Nationality:* American. *Religion:* Jewish. *Education:* Univ. of North Carolina, NC, B.S., 1937; Northwestern Univ., IL, Ph.D., 1940. *Spouse:* Lenore, married 1941, died 1983; Magaret, married, no date. *Children:* 3 children. *Career:* Cornell Univ. NY, Researcher and Professor, 1940–49; Washington Univ., MO, Professor, 1949–56; State Univ. of New York Health Science Center, NY, Professor and Administrator, 1956–90. *Other Awards:* Goodman & Gilman Award, 1984; CIBA Award, 1988; American Heart Association Research Achievement Award, 1990; Bristol-Myers-Squibb Award, 1991; Gairdner Foundation Award, 1991; New York Academy of Medicine Medal, 1992; Roussel-Uclaf Prize, 1993; Wellcome Gold Medal, 1995; ASPET Award, 1996; Pincus Award, 1996; Lasker Award, 1996; Lucian Award, 1997.

Selected Publications: "The role of endothelium in the responses of vascular smooth muscle to drugs," *Annual Rev Pharmacol Toxicol.* 24 (1984):175–97. "Evidence for endothelium-dependent vasodilation of resistance vessels by acetylcholine," *Blood Vessels* 24, 3(1987):145–9 (with others). "Endothelium-derived relaxing factor: discovery, early studies, and identification as nitric oxide," Biusci Rep. 19, 4 (August 1999): 235–51.

For More Information See: Lancet 356 (July 22, 2000): 346. *New York Times* (October 13, 1998): A14.

Commentary: Robert Furchgott shared the Nobel Prize for his discovery of the signal molecule EDRF, the endothelium-derived relaxing factor. Furchgott discovered that the same drug could provide contradictory results by sometimes contracting and sometimes dilating. He thought the contradictory results might depend on whether the surface cells (the endothelium) in the blood vessels were intact or damaged. He demonstrated that "acetylcholine dilated blood vessels only if the endothelium was intact. He concluded that blood vessels are dilated because the endothelial cells produce an unknown signal molecule that makes smooth muscle cells relax." He later discovered that nitric oxide (NO) was the EDRF factor. (L.S.S.)

Ignarro, Louis J.   **444**
Prize: Medicine and Physiology, 1998. *Born:* May 31, 1941; Brooklyn, NY. *Parents:* No record found. *Nationality:* American. *Religion:* No record found. *Education:* Columbia Univ., NY, B.A., 1962; Univ. of Minnesota, Ph.D., 1966. *Spouse:* Married, no date, divorced 1985; Sharon Elizabeth Williams, married July, 1997. *Children:* Heather,

daughter. *Career:* National Institutes of Health, MD, Researcher, 1966–68; Geigy Pharmaceuticals, NJ, Researcher, 1968–73; Tulane Univ., LA, Professor, 1973–85; Univ. of California, Los Angeles, CA, Professor, 1985-. *Other Awards:* Merck Research Award, 1974; USPHS Research Career Development Award, 1975–80; Schleider Foundation Award, 1973–76; Lilly Research Award, 1978.

Selected Publications: "Endothelium-derived relaxing factor produced and released from artery and vein is nitric oxide," *Proceedings of the National Academy of Sciences* 84 (December 1987):9265–9 (with others). "Endothelium-derived relaxing factor and nitric oxide possess identical pharmacologic properties as relaxants of bovine arterial and venous smooth muscle," *J Pharmacol Exp Ther.* 246 (July 1988):218–26 (with others). *Nitric Oxide.* San Diego: Academic Press, 1995 (with F. Murad). *Nitric Oxide.* San Diego: Academic Press, 2000.

For More Information See: Lancet 356 (July 22, 2000): 346. *New York Times* (October 13, 1998): A14.

Commentary: Louis Ignarro shared the Nobel Prize for his discovery concerning "nitric oxide as a signalling molecule in the cardiovascular system." Ignarro identified nitric oxide (NO) as the endothelial factor in a "brilliant series of analyses . . . together with and independently of Robert Furchgott, that EDRF was identical to NO." (L.S.S.)

Murad, Ferid (Fred)   445

Prize: Medicine and Physiology, 1998. *Born:* September 14, 1936; Whiting, IN. *Parents:* Father, Jabir (John) Murad Ejupi; Mother, Herietta Josephine Bowman Murad. *Nationality:* American. *Religion:* Episcopalian. *Education:* DePauw Univ., IN, B.A., 1958; Case Western Reserve Univ., OH, M.D., 1965; Case Western Reserve Univ., OH, Ph.D., 1965. *Spouse:* Carol Ann Leopold, married June 21, 1958. *Children:* Christine, daughter; Marianne, daughter; Carrie, daughter; Julie, daughter; Joseph, son. *Career:* Massachusetts General Hospital, MA, Intern and Resident, 1965–67; National Institutes of Health, MD, Researcher, 1967–70; Univ. of Virginia, VA, Professor, 1970–81; Stanford Univ., CA, Professor, 1981–88; Abbott Labs, IL, Administrator, 1988–93; Molecular Geriatrics Corporation, IL, President and CEO, 1993–95; Univ. of Texas-Houston, TX, Professor, 1997-. *Other Awards:* CIBA Award, 1988; Lasker Award, 1996; AAMC Award for Distinguished Research in the Biomedical Sciences, 2000.

Selected Publications: Pharmacological Basis of Therapeutics, 7th ed., 1985. *Cyclic GMP.* San Diego: Academic Press, 1994. *Nitric Oxide.* San Diego: Academic Press, 1995 (with L.J. Ignarro).

For More Information See: Lancet 356 (July 22, 2000): 346. *New York Times* (October 13, 1998): A14.

Commentary: Ferid Murad shared the Nobel Prize for his discovery that nitroglycerin and related vasodilating compounds release "nitric oxide, which relaxes smooth muscle cells." His discovery has led to new drugs to treat heart disease, impotence, shock and lung disease. (L.S.S.)

1999

Blobel, Günter   446

Prize: Medicine and Physiology, 1999. *Born:* May 21, 1936; Waltersdorf, Silesia, Germany. *Parents:* No record found. *Nationality:* German; later American citizen. *Religion:* Lutheran. *Education:* Univ. of Tubingen, Germany, M.D., 1960; Univ. of Wisconsin-Madison, WI, Ph.D., 1967. *Spouse:* Laura Maioglio, married, no date. *Children:* None *Career:* Rockefeller Univ., NY, Researcher, 1967–69; Rockefeller Univ. NY, Professor, 1969-. *Other Awards:* U.S. Steel Award, 1978; Lounsbery Award, 1983; Gairdner Foundation Award, 1982; Warburg Medal, 1983; Wilson Medal, 1986; Mattia Award, 1986; Horwitz Prize, 1987; Waterford Biomedical Science Award, 1989; Lasker Award, 1993; King Faisal International Prize, 1996; New York City Mayor's Award for Excellence in Science and Technology, 1997; Massry Prize, 1999; CIBA-Drew Award, 1995; Max-Planck Forschungspreis, 1992; Ellis Island Medal of Honor, 2000.

Selected Publications: "Gene gating: a hypothesis," *Proceedings of the National Academy of Sciences* 82 (1985):8527–8529. "Kap104p: A karyopherin involved in the nuclear transport of messenger RNA binding proteins," *Science* 274 (1996):624–627 (with JD Aitchison and MP Rout). "Nuclear protein import: Ran-GTP dissociates the karyopherin alpha beta heterodimer by displacing alpha from an overlapping binding site on beta," *Proceedings of the National Academy of Sciences* 93 (1996):7059–7 (with J. Moroianu and A. Radu.)

For More Information See: New York Times (October 12, 1999): B1. *Science News* (October 16, 1999): 1363. *Scientific American* 282 (May 2000): 38–40.

Commentary: Günter Blobel won the Nobel Prize for his discovery that "proteins have intrinsic signals that govern their transport and localization in the cell." Blobel showed that each protein "carries in its structure the information needed to specify its proper location in the cell." His "signal hypothesis" postulated that "proteins secreted out of the cell contain an intrinsic signal that governs them to and across membranes." It is as if the proteins have an "address tag" that determines its correct location in the body. This discovery has had a tremendous impact on research in modern cell biology. (L.S.S.)

2000

Carlsson, Arvid   447

Prize: Medicine and Physiology, 2000. *Born:* January 25, 1923; Uppsala, Sweden. *Parents:* No record found. *Nationality:* Swedish. *Religion:* No record found. *Education:* Univ. of Lund, Sweden, M.D., 1951. *Spouse:* No record found. *Children:* No record found. *Career:* Univ. of Lund, Sweden, Professor, 1951–56; Göteborg Univ., Sweden, Professor, 1959–89. *Other Awards:* Magnus Blix Prize, 1947; James Parkinson Award, 1970; Pehr Dubb Gold Medal, 1970; Anders Jahre Prize, 1974; Stanley R. Dean Award, 1975; Anna-Monika Stiftung Prize, 1975; Wolf Prize, 1979; Björkénska Priset, 1981; Gairdner Foundation Award, 1982; Bristol-Myers Award, 1989; Paul Hoch Prize, 1990; Fred Springer Award, 1990; William K. Warren Schizophrenia Research Award, 1991; Open Mind Award in Psychiatry, 1992; Julius Axelrod Medal, 1992; Japan Prize, 1994; Lieber Prize, 1994; Lundbeck Foundation Research Prize, 1995; Pasarow Foundation Gold Medal, Society of Biological Psychiatry, 1998; Gold Medal, Univ. of Bari, Italy, 1999; Feltrinelli International Award, 1999.

Selected Publications: "Birth of neuropsychopharmacology-impact on brain research," *Brain Research Bulletin* 50 (November 15-December 1999): 363.

For More Information See: New York Times (October 10, 2000): A22. *Time* 156 (October 23, 2000): 78.

Commentary: Arvid Carlsson shared the Nobel Prize for his discovery "that dopamine is a transmitter in the brain and that it has great importance for our ability to control movements." His research led to the development of L-dopa, used in the treatment of Parkinson's disease. The drug converts to dopamine in the brain and helps regularize the patient's motor behavior. His discoveries have also had "great importance for the treatment of depression, which is one of our most common diseases" and a "new generation of antidepressive drugs." (L.S.S.)

Greengard, Paul   448

Prize: Medicine and Physiology, 2000. *Born:* December 11, 1925; New York NY. *Parents:* No record found. *Nationality:* American. *Religion:* No record found. *Education:* Hamilton College, NY, A.B., 1948; Johns Hopkins Univ., MD, Ph.D., 1953. *Spouse:* Married, no further record found. *Children:* 3 children. *Career:* Univ. of London, England, Researcher, 1953–54; Cambridge Univ., Researcher, 1954–56; National Institutes of Health, MD, Researcher, 1956–58; CIBA-Geigy Research Laboratories, Administrator, 1958–67; Yale Univ. CT, Professor, 1968–83; Rockefeller Univ., NY, Professor, 1983-. *Other Awards:* Dickson Prize, 1977; CIBA-Geigy Drew Award, 1979; New York Academy of Sciences Award, 1980; Pfizer Biomedical Research Award, 1986; 3M Life Sciences Award, 1987; Mental Health Research Achievement Award, 1987; Bristol-Myers Award, 1989; National Academy of Sciences Award in the Neurosciences, 1991; Goodman & Gilman Award, 1992; Lashley Prize, 1993; Gerard Prize, 1994; Thudichum Medal, 1996; Lieber Prize, 1996; Dana Foundation Award, 1997; Metropolitan Life Foundation Award, 1998; Ellison Medical Foundation Award, 1999; Mayor of New York City's Award for Excellence in Science and Technology, 1999.

Selected Publications: Cyclic Nucleotides, Phosphorylated Proteins, and Neuronal Function. New York: Raven Press, 1978. *Protein Phosphorylation in the Nervous System.* New York: Wiley, 1984 (with E.J. Nestler).

For More Information See: New York Times (October 10, 2000): A22.

Commentary: Paul Greengard is a co-winner of the Nobel Prize for his discovery of "how dopamine and a number of other transmitters exert their action in the nervous system." This transmission signals a "slow synaptic transmission" which results in changes in the nerve cells that can last from a few seconds to hours. His work pioneered the field of signal transduction. (L.S.S.)

Kandel, Eric Richard   449

Prize: Medicine and Physiology, 2000. *Born:* November 7, 1929; Vienna, Austria. *Parents:* No record found. *Nationality:* Austrian; later American citizen. *Religion:* Jewish. *Education:* Harvard Univ., MA, B.A., 1952; New York Univ., M.D., 1956. *Spouse:* Married, 1956, no further record found. *Children:* 2 children. *Career:* Montefiore Hospital, NY, Intern, 1956–57; National Institutes of Health, MD, Researcher, 1957–60; Harvard Medical School, MA, Resident and Staff Psychiatrist, 1960–65; New York Univ., NY, Professor, 1965–74; Columbia Univ., NY, Professor, 1974-. *Other Awards:* Henry L. Moses Research Award, 1959; Hofheimer Prize, 1977; Lucy G. Moses Prize, 1977; Solomon A. Berson Medical Alumni Achievement Award, 1979; Lashley Prize, 1981; Dickson Prize, 1982; Lasker Award, 1983; Rosenstiel Award, 1984; Howard Crosby Warren Medal, 1984; American Association of Medical Colleges Award, 1985; Gairdner Foundation Award, 1987; National Medal of Science, 1988; Gold Medal for Scientific Merit, 1988; Distinguished Service Award of the American Psychiatric Association, 1989; American College of Physicians Award in Basic Science, 1989; Bristol-Myers-Squibb Award, 1991; Warren Triennial Prize, 1992; Jean-Louis Signoret Prize, 1992; Harvey Prize, 1993; F.O. Schmitt Medal, 1993; Mayor's Award for Excellence in Science and Technology, New York City, 1994; Stevens Triennial Prize, 1995; New York Academy of Medicine Award, 1996; Gerard Prize, 1997; Charles A. Dana Award, 1997; Wolf Prize, 1999.

Selected Publications: Behavioral Biology of Aplysia. San Francisco: W.H. Freeman, 1979. *Memory: From Mind to Molecules.* New York: Scientific American Library, 1999 (with L.R. Squire).

For More Information See: Lancet 356 (October 7, 2000): 1250. *New York Times* (October 10, 2000): A22.

Commentary: Eric Kandel shared the Nobel Prize for his discoveries of how "the efficiency of synapses can be modified, and which molecular mechanisms that take part." Using the sea slug as his model, Kandel was able to demonstrate that "short term memory, as well as long term memory in the sea slug is located at the synapse." Kandel's research increases the possibilities of new drugs being developed to treat different types of dementia and improve memory function. (L.S.S.)

Peace

1901

Dunant, Jean Henri   450

Prize: Peace, 1901. *Born:* May 8, 1828; Geneva, Switzerland. *Death:* October 30, 1910; Heiden, Switzerland. *Parents:* Father, Jean Jacques Dunant; Mother, Anne Antoinette Colladon Dunant. *Nationality:* Swiss. *Religion:* Anti-church; from Calvinist background. *Education:* No college degrees. *Spouse:* None. *Children:* None. *Career:* Colonies Suisses de Setif, President, 1853–58; Société Anonyme des Moulins de Mons-Djemila, President, 1858–60; Société de l'Omnium Algerien Destine a Favoriser le Developpement de l'Industrie, du Commerce et de l'Agriculture en Algerie, President, 1860–66; Compagnie Algerienne, President, 1866–67. *Other Awards:* Order of Saint Maurice and Saint Lazarus, Italy, 1860; Chevalier of the Legion of Honor, France, 1865; Binet-Fendt Prize, Switzerland, 1897; Order of the Crown, Prussia, 1897; Order of Christ, Portugal, 1897; Stuttgart Medal, Germany, 1908.

Selected Publications: L'Empire de Charlemagne Rétabli ou le Saint-Empire Romain Reconstitué par Napoleon III. Geneva: Fick, 1859. *Memorandum au Sujet de la Société Financiere et Industrielle des Moulins de Mons-Djémila en Algérie.* Paris: n.p., 1859. *Un Souvenir de Solferino.* Geneva: Fick, 1862 (*A Memory of Solferino.* Tr. by D.H. Wright. London: Cassell, 1947). *Project de Société Internationale pour la Renovation de l'Orient.* Paris: n.p., 1866. *Bibliothéque Internationale Universelle.* Paris: n.p., 1867. *Les Prisonniers de Guerre.* Geneva: Improv. H. Jarrys, 1915 (with reproduction of original 1867 edition).

For More Information See: Durand, R. *Henry Dunant und die Ostschwerz.* Geneva: Swit. Societe Henry Dunant, 1992. Gumpert, Martin. *Dunant: The Story of the Red Cross.* New York: Blue Ribbon Books, 1942. Hart, Ellen. *Man Born to Live. Life and Work of Henry Dunant.* London: Victor Gollancz, 1953. *Memoires.* Ed. by Bernard Gagnebin. Geneva: n.p., 1970.

Commentary: Henri Dunant shared the first Peace Prize for his work in organizing the Geneva Conventions of 1863 and 1864 and the International Red Cross, which those conventions produced. His memoir of the Battle of Solferino in 1859 stirred Europe as the experience had stirred him. Dunant found himself transformed by the horrors of war as he personally ministered to hundreds of the wounded in the Chiesa Maggiore, a church overlooking the Lombard Plain, which was the site of the battle. His anguished plea for neutralization of the wounded and medical care for friend and foe alike formed the nexus for the Conventions and for Geneva's International Committee of Five, which Gustave Moynier headed and Dunant served as secretary. Though based on his Red Cross efforts, Dunant's prize could have resulted from his longtime devotion to international efforts at human amelioration, including the establishment of a YMCA, the fight to establish a Jewish homeland in Palestine, and championing of the ideas of international arbitration, disarmament, a world court, a universal library, abolition of slavery, and humane treatment for prisoners of war. (R.G.)

Passy, Frederic   451

Prize: Peace, 1901. *Born:* May 20, 1822; Paris, France. *Death:* June 12, 1912; Neuilly-sur-Seine, France. *Parents:* No record found. *Nationality:* French. *Religion:* Protestant; from Catholic background. *Education:* Univ. of Paris, France, law degree, 1846. *Spouse:* Married, no record found. *Children:* Paul Edouard, son; others, no record found. *Career:* French governmental positions, 1847–49, 1881–89; Writer and Lecturer on Economics.

Selected Publications: Melanges Economiques. Paris: Guillaumin, 1857. *Histoire du Travail.* Paris: H. Bellaire, 1873. "The Advance of the Peace Movement throughout the World." *American Monthly Review of Reviews* 17 (February 1898): 183–88. *Pour la Paix: Notes et Documents.* Paris: Charpentier, 1909.

For More Information See: Biographical Dictionary of Modern Peace Leaders. Westport, CT: Greenwood, 1985, 730–32. Passy, Paul. *Un Apotre de la Paix: La Vide Fredric Passy.* Paris: n.p., 1927.

Commentary: Frederic Passy won the Nobel Prize for his efforts over 50 years in the peace movement, for which he became known as the apostle of peace. He was instrumental in forming national and international leagues to further the cause of peace. In his legislative efforts in France, he was an advocate of labor, disarmament arbitration, and free trade, and an opponent of colonialism. Passy was also an acknowledged scholar of economics. (R.G.)

1902

Ducommun, Elie   452

Prize: Peace, 1902. *Born:* February 19, 1833; Geneva, Switzerland. *Death:* December 7, 1906; Berne, Switzerland. *Parents:* Father, Jules Ducommun; Mother, Octavie Mattey Ducommun. *Nationality:* Swiss. *Religion:* Most probably Christian. *Education:* No college degrees. *Spouse:* Adele Ducommun, married 1857. *Children:* No record found. *Career:* Geneva Public Schools, Switzerland, Teacher, 1855–57; Journalist and Writer, 1857–1906; political posts, 1855–75; Jura-Bern-Lucern Railroad, Switzerland, Secretary-General, 1875–1903.

Selected Publications: Precis Historique du Mouvement en Faveur de la Paix. Berne, Switzerland: 1899. "The Permanent International Bureau of Peace." *The Independent* 55 (March 19, 1903): 660–61. *Derniers Sourires: Poesies Precedees d'une Notice Biographique.* Berne, Switzerland: 1908.

For More Information See: Biographical Dictionary of Modern Peace Leaders. Westport, CT: Greenwood Press,

1985, 228–29. *Dictionnaire Historique et Biographique de la Suisse.* Neuchatel, Switzerland: Administration du Dictionnaire Historique et Biographique de la Suisse, 1921–33. *The Independent* 55 (March 5, 1903): 554–57.

Commentary: Elie Ducommun received the Nobel Prize for his work as "the untiring and skillful director of the Berne Peace Bureau and therefore head of the united work of all the peace societies of the world." Although a respected journalist, businessperson, and poet, much of his energy and time was devoted to the cause of peace. He attended many of the meetings which were called on the topic and edited several journals devoted to peace. Ducommun also was an important political figure in Switzerland. (B.S.S.)

Gobat, Charles Albert   453

Prize: Peace, 1902. *Born:* May 21, 1843; Tramelan, Switzerland. *Death:* March 16, 1914; Berne, Switzerland. *Parents:* No record found. *Nationality:* Swiss. *Religion:* Protestant. *Education:* Heidelberg Univ., Germany, Doctor of Law, 1867. *Spouse:* None. *Children:* None. *Career:* Berne, Switzerland, Attorney, 1867–82; Berne Univ., Switzerland, Professor, 1882–1912.

Selected Publications: La Republique de Berne et la France Pendant les Guerres de Religion d'apres des Documents Inedits. Paris: Gedalge, 1891. *Histoire de la Suisse Racontee au Peuple.* Neuchatel, Switzerland: F. Zahn, 1899. *Le Cauchemar de l'Europe.* Paris: Le Soudier, 1911.

For More Information See: London Times (March 17, 1914): 10c. *New York Times* (March 17, 1914): 11+.

Commentary: Lawyer and statesman Charles Gobat shared the Nobel for "his general efforts for Peace, and his work as President of the fourth conference of the Interparliamentarian Union at Berne in 1892." After winning the Nobel, Gobat's role in the struggle for peace became even greater. In 1904, he came to America to lead the Inter-Parliamentary Conference in St. Louis, MO. A firm believer in arbitration, he called on the United States to intervene in the Russo-Japanese War. As president of the Berne International Peace Bureau from 1906 and administrative head of the Interparliamentary Union from 1892, he was simultaneously director of the two largest peace organizations in the world. Gobat died "with his boots on" while addressing a meeting of the International Peace Bureau. (K.N.M.)

1903

Cremer, William Randal, Sir   454

Prize: Peace, 1903. *Born:* March 18, 1828; Fareham, Wiltshire, England. *Death:* July 22, 1908; London, England. *Parents:* Father, George Cremer; Mother, Harriet Tutte Cremer. *Nationality:* British. *Religion:* Methodist. *Education:* No college degrees. *Spouse:* Charlotte Wilson, married 1860, died 1876; Lucy Coombes, married 1877. *Children:* None. *Career:* England, Carpenter and Trade Union Organizer/Worker, 1843–85; British Parliament Member, 1885–1908. *Other Awards:* Cross of the Legion of Honor, England, 1890; Commander of the Norwegian Order of Saint Olav, 1904; Knighthood, 1907.

Selected Publications: The Arbitrator, Journal of the International Arbitration League, Editor and Contributor, 1889–1908.

For More Information See: Dictionary of National Biography: Twentieth Century Supplement, 1901–1911. London: Oxford Univ. Press, 1912, 441–42. Evans, Howard. *Sir Randal Cremer: His Life and Works.* London: T. Fisher Unwin, 1909.

Commentary: William Cremer earned the Nobel Prize for his intensive work in the peace movement and his belief in international arbitration in achieving world peace. His initial efforts, in 1887, led to the drafting of a treaty of international arbitration and to the formation of the Interparliamentary Union for International Courts of Arbitrations after the treaty was not accepted by Britain and the United States in 1889. He had established the precursor of the Interparliamentary Union—the Workmen's Peace Association—in 1870. Later called the International Arbitration League, this organization (and Cremer) formulated the plan for a high court of nations, which eventually materialized in the Hague Tribunal. (D.P.)

1904

Institute of International Law (Institut de Droit International)   455

Prize: Peace, 1904. *Founded:* 1873 in Gent, Belgium

Commentary: This represented the first Nobel Prize given to an institution and was awarded for the Institute's efforts in establishing the law of nations as a "collective scientific action," by a permanent scholarly institution that aspired "to serve as . . . the legal conscience of the civilized world." (G.N.W.)

1905

von Suttner, Bertha Felicie Sophie Kinsky   456

Prize: Peace, 1905. *Born:* June 9, 1843; Prague, Austria. *Death:* June 21, 1914; Vienna, Austria. *Parents:* Father, Count Franz Joseph Kinsky; Mother, Sophie Wilhelmine Körner Kinsky. *Nationality:* Austrian. *Religion:* Areligious; from Catholic background. *Education:* No college degrees. *Spouse:* Arthur Gundaccar von Suttner, married 1876. *Children:* None. *Career: Die Waffen nieder,* Editor, 1892–99.

Selected Publications: Die Waffen nieder. Dresden, Germany: E. Pierson, 1889 (*Lay Down Your Arms: The Autobiography of Martha von Tilling.* Tr. by T. Holmes. New York: Garland Publishing, 1972). *Memoiren von Bertha von Suttner.* Stuttgart, Germany: Deutsche Verlags-Anstalt, 1909 (*Memoirs of Bertha von Suttner: Records of an Eventful Life.* New York: Garland Publishing, 1972). *Der Kampf um die Vermeidung des Weltkrieges: Randglossen aus zwei Jahrzehnten zu den Ereignissen vor der Katastrophe (1892–1900 und 1907–1914).* Zürich: Orell Fussli, 1917.

For More Information See: Kempf, Beatrix. *Woman for Peace: The Life of Bertha von Suttner.* Park Ridge, NJ: Noyes Press, 1973. Lengyel, Emil. *And All Her Paths Were Peace: The Life of Bertha von Suttner.* Nashville, TN: T. Nelson, 1975. Opfell, Olga S. *The Lady Laureates.* Metuchen, NJ: Scarecrow Press, 1978, 1–17. Hamann, B. *Bertha von Suttner.* Munich: Ger Pyser, 1991.

Commentary: The Nobel Peace Prize was awarded to Bertha von Suttner "for her sincere peace activities." Her emergence on the international scene began with publication of *Lay Down Your Arms,* which exposed the cruel realities of war, rather than its glory, heroism, and patriotism. Throughout her life, she popularized the quest for peace through her writings—novels, correspondence, newspaper articles (she was one of the first female political journalists); through the pacifist journal she edited; through her activities in peace societies and at international conferences; and through lecturing in Europe and the United States. (M.A.V.C.)

1906

Roosevelt, Theodore   457

Prize: Peace, 1906. *Born:* October 27, 1858; New York, NY. *Death:* January 6, 1919; Oyster Bay, NY. *Parents:* Father, Theodore Roosevelt; Mother, Martha Bulloch Roosevelt. *Nationality:* American. *Religion:* Presbyterian. *Education:* Harvard Univ., MA, A.B., 1880. *Spouse:* Alice Hathaway Lee, married October 27, 1880, died February 14, 1884; Edith Kermit Carow, married December 2, 1886. *Children:* Alice Lee, daughter; Theodore, son; Kermit, son; Ethel Carow, daughter; Archibald Bulloch, son; Quentin, son. *Career:* New York Assembly, Member, 1882–84; U.S. Civil Service Commission, 1889–95; New York City, Police Commissioner, 1895; Department of the Navy, Assistant Secretary, 1897–98; U.S. Army, 1898; State of New York, Governor, 1899–1901; U.S. President, 1901–09.

Selected Publications: The Naval War of 1812. New York: G.P. Putnam and Sons, 1882. *Hunting Trips of a Ranchman.* Upper Saddle River, NJ: Literature House Gregg Press, 1885. *The Winning of the West 1769–1807.* 4 volumes. New York: G.P. Putnam and Sons, 1889–96. *Oliver Cromwell* New York: Scribner's Sons, 1901. *History as Literature, and Other Essays.* New York: Scribner's Sons, 1913.

For More Information See: Bishop, Joseph Bucklin. *Theodore Roosevelt and His Time Shown in His Own Letters.* 2 volumes. New York: Scribner's, 1920. *Dictionary of American Biography.* 1935 ed. New York: Scribner's (Volume 16), 135–44. Morris, Edmund. *The Rise of Theodore Roosevelt.* New York: Coward, McCann and Geoghegan, 1979. Roosevelt, Theodore. *Theodore Roosevelt: An Autobiography.* New York: Scribner's, 1913.

Commentary: Theodore Roosevelt's mediation of the Russo-Japanese War at a peace conference in Portsmouth, New Hampshire, and his intervention in the dispute between Britain, Germany, and France concerning the roles to be played in Morocco won him the Nobel Peace Prize. He was the first American and the first head of state to win the prize. But his contributions to America and the world neither began nor ended with those events. He is noted as a progressive president who attempted to control trusts, to conserve natural resources, to protect labor, and to provide a "square deal" for all. His foreign policies led most importantly to the securing of the Panama Canal Zone and building of the Canal, and to the expansion of the Monroe Doctrine by statement of the Roosevelt Corollary. (S.W.)

1907

Moneta, Ernesto Teodoro   458

Prize: Peace, 1907. *Born:* September 20, 1833; Milan, Italy. *Death:* February 10, 1918; Milan, Italy. *Parents:* Father, Carlo Aurelio Moneta; Mother, Giuseppina Muzio Moneta. *Nationality:* Italian. *Religion:* Catholic. *Education:* No college degrees. *Spouse:* Ersilia Caglio, married 1874. *Children:* 2 sons. *Career:* Italy, Traveler, Soldier, Political Activist, 1848–66; *Il Secolo,* Editor, 1866–98; *La Vita Internazionale,* Publisher, 1898–1918.

Selected Publications: Patria i Umanita. Milan: Sonzogno, 1899. *Le Guerre, le Insurrezioni e la Pace nel Secolo Decimonono.* 4 volumes. Milan: Societe Tip. Editrice Popolare, 1903–10. *La Nostra Pace.* Milan: Bellini, 1909.

For More Information See: Combi, Maria. *Ernesto Teodoro Moneta: Premio Nobel per la Pace.* Milan: Mursia, 1968. Pinardi, Giuseppe. *La Carriere d'un Pacifiste: E.T. Moneta.* Le Havre, France: L'Universel, 1904.

Commentary: Ernesto Moneta, a "militant pacifist," won the Nobel Prize for his work in founding the Lombard Peace Union in 1887, his peace conferences in Italy, and his role in presiding over the International Peace Congress in Milan in 1906. A rugged Italian soldier in campaigns between 1848 and 1866, Moneta advocated fighting for freedom in Italy while working continuously for peace. He was also well known for remarkable journalistic skill in a variety of publishing ventures. (S.M.)

Renault, Louis   459

Prize: Peace, 1907. *Born:* May 21, 1843; Autun, Saône-et-Loire, France. *Death:* February 8, 1918; Barbizon, France. *Parents:* No record found. *Nationality:* French. *Religion:* Most probably Christian/Protestant. *Education:* Univ. of Dijon, France, bachelor's degree, 1861; Univ. of Paris, France, doctorate in law, 1868. *Spouse:* Juliette Thiaffait, married February 22, 1873. *Children:* 4 daughters (2 survived, Germaine and Marie); 1 son. *Career:* Univ. of Dijon, France, Professor, 1868–73; Univ. of Paris, France, Professor, 1873–1918.

Selected Publications: Précis de Droit Commercial. 2 volumes. Paris: F. Pinchon, 1884–85. *Manuel de Droit Commercial.* Paris: F. Pinchon, 1887. *Traité de Droit Commercial.* 8 volumes. Paris: F. Pinchon, 1889–99.

For More Information See: Encyclopedia of the Social Sciences. New York: Macmillan, 1937 (Volume 13), 287–88. Fauchille, Paul. *Louis Renault.* Paris: A. Pedone, 1918. Scott, James. "In Memoriam: Louis Renault." In *American Journal of International Law* 12 (July 1918), 606–10.

Commentary: Louis Renault, French jurist, scholar, diplomat, and judge, won the Nobel Prize for his efforts as "principal worker" at the Hague Peace Conferences in 1899 and 1907. Although the conferences did not succeed in limiting armaments, they did establish the Hague Permanent Court of Arbitration, which provided an avenue for peaceful resolution of disputes between countries. Renault is also considered to be the founder of international law as a legal science in France. (M.J.H.)

1908

Arnoldson, Klas Pontus   460

Prize: Peace, 1908. *Born:* October 27, 1844; Goteborg, Sweden. *Death:* February 20, 1916; Stockholm, Sweden. *Parents:* Father, Olaf Andersson Arnoldson; Mother, Inga Hagbom von Seth Arnoldson. *Nationality:* Swedish. *Religion:* Christian/Protestant; with Unitarian views. *Education:* No college degrees. *Spouse:* Eva Bernhardina Wahlgren, married May 15, 1869, dissolved April 7, 1903; Edit Viktoria

Blomskold, married May 4, 1903. *Children:* No record found. *Career:* Railroad Worker, 1860–81; Swedish Parliament, 1882–87; Political Activist, Writer, and Peace Worker, 1888–1916.

Selected Publications: Ar Varldsfred Majlig. Stockholm: Froleen, 1890 (*Pax Mundi.* London: Swan Sonnenschein, 1890). *Religionen i Forskningens Ljus* (*Religion in the Light of Research*). Sundsvall, Sweden: Forlagsforeningen Fria Ordet, 1891. *Seklernas Hopp* (*Hope of the Centuries*). Stockholm: Wilhelmsson, 1901. *Maria Magdalena.* Stockholm: Bohlin, 1903.

For More Information See: Svenson, Axel. *En Lifsgerning for Freden: Nagra Erinrande Ord Pa K.P. Arnoldson Sixtioarsdag den 27 Oktober 1904.* Stockholm: n.p., 1904. *Svenst Biografiskt Lexikon.* Stockholm: Albert Bonniers Forlag, 1920 (Volume 2), 248–53.

Commentary: Klas Arnoldson was granted the Nobel Prize for 35 years of working for peace. His outstanding contributions in this regard, in addition to his influential writings, were the founding of the Swedish Society of Arbitration and Peace, the accomplishment of a peaceful separation of Norway and Sweden, and the willingness of Sweden to consider permanent neutrality. Arnoldson was also a powerful member of the Swedish Parliament for many years. (B.S.S.)

Bajer, Fredrik   461

Prize: Peace, 1908. *Born:* April 21, 1837; Vester Egede, Denmark. *Death:* January 22, 1922; Copenhagen, Denmark. *Parents:* Father, Alfred Bayer; Mother, Cecilie Luise Crone Bayer. *Nationality:* Danish. *Religion:* Protestant. *Education:* No college degrees. *Spouse:* Pauline Matilde Schluter, married October 8, 1867. *Children:* No record found. *Career:* Danish Army, 1856–65; Writer and Teacher, 1865–72; Politician and Writer, 1872–95.

Selected Publications: Nordiske Neutralitetsforbund. Copenhagen: Studentersamfund Forlag, 1885. *Tactics for the Friends of Peace.* Tr. by P.H. Peckover. Wisbech, England: Poyser, 1891. *Idéen til Nordens, Saerlig Danmarks, Vedvarende Neutralitet.* Copenhagen: 1900. *A Serious Drama of Modern History: How Danish Slesvig Was Lost.* Tr. by P.H. Peckover. London: Peace Society, 1907. *Nordens, Saerlig Denmarks, Neutralitet under Krimkrigen.* Copenhagen: Schultz, 1914.

For More Information See: Dansk Biografisk Leksikon. Copenhagen: J.H. Schultz Forlag, 1933 (Volume II), 34–39. Schou, August. *Histoire de l'Internationalisme III: Du Congres de Vienne Jusqu'a la Premiere Guerre Mondiale.* Oslo: Aschehoug, 1963.

Commentary: Fredrik Bajer's political and writing activities in support of peace won him the Nobel Prize. An accomplished military figure in his early years, Bajer became an outstanding spokesperson for arbitration and peace later. He was also an outstanding figure in Danish education, a leading spokesperson for women's equality, and a fervent promoter of Scandinavian unity. (B.S.S.)

1909

Beernaert, Auguste Marie François   462

Prize: Peace, 1909. *Born:* July 26, 1829; Ostend, Belgium. *Death:* October 6, 1912; Lucerne, Switzerland. *Parents:* Father, Bernard Beernaert; Mother, Euphrosine-Josepha Royon Beernaert. *Nationality:* Belgian. *Religion:* Catholic. *Education:* Univ. of Louvain, Belgium, Doctor of Law, 1851. *Spouse:* Mathilde-Wilhelmine-Marie Borel, married August 6, 1870. *Children:* None. *Career:* Brussels, Belgium, Attorney, 1853–73; Belgian and international politics, 1873–1907.

Selected Publications: De l'État de l'Enseignement du Droit en France et en Allemagne: Rapport Adressé à M. le Ministre de l'Intérieur. Brussels: Lesigne, 1854. *Discours Prononcé à l'Occasion de l'Inauguration des Quais d'Anvers, le 26 Juillet 1885.* Paris: Chaix, 1885.

For More Information See: Carton de Wiart, Henri. *Beernaert et Son Temps.* Brussels: La Renaissance du Livre, 1945. Carton de Wiart, Henri. "Notice sur Auguste Beernaert," *Annuaire de l'Académic Royale de Belgique* 105 (1939): 293–364. *Notices: Biographiques & Bibliographiques.* Brussels: Hayez, Imprimeur de L'Academie Royale de Belgique, 1909, 315–25.

Commentary: Auguste Beernaert was awarded the Nobel Prize for his untiring efforts for peace in the last third of his long, active life. He was a prominent member of all the peace conferences from 1889 until his death in 1912, his work with the Mexican question in 1902 and enemy property inviolability in 1907 being especially noteworthy. Early in his career he was also instrumental in introducing general suffrage and efficient elections in Belgium and in the establishment of the Belgian Congo. (L.S.)

d'Estournelles, Paul Henri Benjamin Balleut de Constant, Baron   463

Prize: Peace, 1909. *Born:* November 22, 1852; La Fleche, Sarthe, France. *Death:* May 15, 1924; Bordeaux, France. *Parents:* Father, Léonce Balluet d'Estournelles; Mother, Louise de Constant d'Estournelles. *Nationality:* French. *Religion:* Catholic. *Education:* Lycée Louis le Grand, France, licence in law, 1875. *Spouse:* Daisy Sedwick-Barant, married 1885. *Children:* 2 sons; 3 daughters. *Career:* French diplomatic corps and political establishment, 1876–1924. *Other Awards:* Officer of the Legion of Honor, France.

Selected Publications: La Rapprôchement Francoallemand. Paris: Delagrave, 1909. *America and Her Problems.* New York: Macmillan, 1915. *Les Reparations: Les Ruines de Fargniers et la Dotation Carnegie.* La Flèche, Sarthe, France: La Conciliation Internationale, 1922.

For More Information See: Biographical Dictionary of Modern Peace Leaders. Westport, CT: Greenwood Press, 1985, 265–66. Wild, Adolph. *Baron d'Estournelles de Constant (1852–1924).* Hamburg: Stiftung Europa-Kolleg, 1973.

Commentary: Founder of the Association for International Conciliation in 1905, Paul d'Estournelles received the Nobel Prize for his services to the cause of international peace and goodwill. His talents in arbitration among nations were notable and were used in avoiding confrontation between France and Britain in the 1893 Siam/French Siam border dispute and in numerous arbitrations and/or treaties involving France, Britain, and Germany. d'Estournelles founded the Conciliation Internationale and worked with Andrew Carnegie toward peace. (C.B.B.)

1910

Permanent International Peace Bureau (Bureau International Permanent de la Paix)   464

Prize: Peace, 1910. *Founded:* 1891 in Bern, Switzerland

Commentary: Prior to 1914, the Permanent International Peace Bureau was the headquarters of the popular peace movement, i.e., it served as "an international bureau of arbitration and disarmament." Nearly winning the award each of the first 10 years of the prize, the Peace Bureau's turn finally came in 1910 when the committee declared the selection "entirely in the spirit of Alfred Nobel's plan; he wanted his money to be used to support, accelerate, and promote the peace movement." (G.N.W.)

1911

Asser, Tobias Michael Carel   465

Prize: Peace, 1911. *Born:* April 29, 1838; Amsterdam, Netherlands. *Death:* July 29, 1913; The Hague, Netherlands. *Parents:* Father, Carel Daniel Asser; Mother, Rosette Henry Godefroi-Asser. *Nationality:* Dutch. *Religion:* Jewish. *Education:* Atheneum, Netherlands, Doctor of Laws, 1860. *Spouse:* Johanna Ernestina Asser, married 1864. *Children:* 3 sons; 1 daughter. *Career:* Univ. of Amsterdam, Netherlands, Professor, 1862–93. *Other Awards:* Recipient of decorations from the governments of Holland, Austria, Italy, and Belgium.

Selected Publications: Schets van Het Nederlandsch Handelsrecht. Haarlem, Netherlands: Erven F. Bohn, 1873. *Schets van Het International Privaatrecht.* Haarlem, Netherlands: Erven F. Bohn, 1880.

For More Information See: The Jewish Encyclopedia. New York: Funk and Wagnalls, 1925 (Volume 2), 229. "Tobias Asser." In *Jaarboeken der Koninklyke Akademie.* Amsterdam: G.G. Vander Post, 1914.

Commentary: Tobias Asser was recognized by the Committee as a "practical legal statesman" and "pioneer in the field of international legal relations." An authority on international law, he believed that peace depended on a uniformity in international private law which nations could emulate in their national legislation. To this end, he persuaded the Dutch government to convene and presided over four conferences at The Hague on international private law (1893, 1894, 1900, 1904). He was one of the founders of the Institute of International Law and the Review of International Law and Comparative Legislation. (D.S.)

Fried, Alfred Hermann   466

Prize: Peace, 1911. *Born:* November 11, 1864; Vienna, Austria. *Death:* May 6, 1921; Vienna, Austria. *Parents:* Father, Samuel Fried; Mother, Bertha Engel Fried. *Nationality:* Austrian. *Religion:* Jewish. *Education:* No college degrees. *Spouse:* Gertrud Gnadenfeld, married 1889; Martha Hollander (no date found); Therese Volandt, married 1908. *Children:* No record found. *Career:* Austria, Bookdealer and Publisher.

Selected Publications: Handbuch der Friedensbewegung. Vienna; Leipzig, Germany: Oesterveichische Friendensgesellschaft, 1905. *Die Grundlogen des Revolutionaeren Pacifismus.* Tübingen, Germany: Mohr Reichenbachsche Buchhandlung, 1908. *Der Kaiser und der Weltfrieden.* Berlin: Maritima, Verlagsges, 1910. *Der Weltprotest gegen den Versailler Frieden.* Leipzig, Germany: P. Reinhold, 1920.

For More Information See: Encyclopedia Judaica. Jerusalem: Macmillan, 1971 (Volume 7), 171. Goldscheid, R. *Alfred Fried.* Leipzig, Germany: P. Reinhold, 1922.

Commentary: Alfred Fried was recognized by the Committee as perhaps "the most industrious literary pacifist in the past twenty years." Trained as a bookseller, Fried believed that the existing international anarchy would decrease and disappear if international legal and political organizations could be established. To this end, he founded the German and Austrian Peace Societies and edited and published several pacifist periodicals in both Germany and Austria. He worked closely with pacifist Bertha von Suttner (Nobel Peace Prize winner in 1905). Accused of high treason in Austria for his pacifist work, he emigrated to Switzerland to work with prisoners of war. (D.S.)

1912

Root, Elihu   467

Prize: Peace, 1912. *Born:* February 15, 1845; Clinton, NY. *Death:* February 7, 1937; New York, NY. *Parents:* Father, Oren Root; Mother, Nancy Whitney Buttrick Root. *Nationality:* American. *Religion:* Protestant. *Education:* Hamilton College, NY, A.B., 1864; New York Univ., law degree, 1867. *Spouse:* Clara Frances Wales, married January 1878. *Children:* Edith, daughter; Elihu, Jr., son; Edward Wales, son. *Career:* New York, Attorney, 1867–99; United States political offices, 1899–1915. *Other Awards:* Roosevelt Medal, 1924; Woodrow Wilson Foundation Medal, 1926; Civic Forum Medal, 1927; Eleanor van Rensselaer Fairfax Medal, 1930.

Selected Publications: The Citizen's Part in Government. New Haven, CT: Yale Univ. Press, 1907. *Experiments in Government and the Essentials of the Constitution.* Princeton, NJ: Princeton Univ. Press, 1913. *Addresses on American Government and Citizenship.* Cambridge, MA: Harvard Univ. Press, 1916. *Addresses on International Subjects.* Cambridge, MA: Harvard Univ. Press, 1916. *Military and Colonial Policy of the U.S.* Cambridge, MA: Harvard Univ. Press, 1916. *Latin America and the U.S.* Cambridge, MA: Harvard Univ. Press, 1917. *Miscellaneous Addresses.* Cambridge, MA: Harvard Univ. Press, 1917. *Men and Policies.* Cambridge, MA: Harvard Univ. Press, 1925.

For More Information See: Jessup, Philip C. *Elihu Root.* New York: Dodd, Mead and Co., 1938. Leopold, Richard W. *Elihu Root and the Conservative Tradition.* Boston: Little, Brown and Co., 1954. *The National Cyclopedia of American Biography.* New York: J.T. White and Co., 1937 (Volume 26), 1–5.

Commentary: Elihu Root won the Nobel Prize for a number of efforts that were applauded by the Academy, including his championing of the Taft proposal for an unconditional arbitration treaty with Britain, his support of no special privileges for American shipping in the Panama Canal, and his presidency of the Carnegie Peace Foundation. In addition to his peace efforts, Root served his country well in many years of public service, with notable successes in organizing US involvement in Cuba and the Philippines after the Spanish-American War, in promoting understanding between South American countries and between the countries of South and North America, and in dealing with Japan in the dispute over the status of Japanese immigrants. (B.S.)

1913

La Fontaine, Henri Marie   468
Prize: Peace, 1913. *Born:* April 22, 1854; Brussels, Belgium. *Death:* May 14, 1943; Brussels, Belgium. *Parents:* Father, Alfred LaFontaine; Mother, Marie Philips LaFontaine. *Nationality:* Belgian. *Religion:* Christian. *Education:* Univ. of Brussels, Belgium, law doctorate, 1877. *Spouse:* Mathilde Augustine Isabelle Lhoest, married 1903. *Children:* No record found. *Career:* Attorney, 1877–93; Univ. of Brussels, Belgium, Professor, and Belgian Senator, 1894–1940.

Selected Publications: Des Droits et Obligations des Entrepreneurs de Travaux Publics Nationaux, Provinciaux, et Communaux. Brussels: Ferdinand Larcier, 1885. *La Femme et le Barreau.* Brussels: Ferdinand Larcier, 1901. *Histoire Sommaire et Chronologique des Arbitrages Internationaux (1794–1900).* Brussels: Bureau de la Revue de Droit International et de Législation Comparée, 1902. *Bibliographie de la Paix et de l'Arbitrage International.* Brussels: Institut International de Bibliographie, 1904. *The Great Solution: Magnissima Charta.* Boston: World Peace Foundation, 1916.

For More Information See: Biographical Dictionary of Modern Peace Leaders. Westport, CT: Greenwood Press, 1985, 538–39. *Biographie Nationale.* Brussels: Bruylant, 1973–74 (Volume 38): cols. 213–21.

Commentary: For his efforts at establishing and furthering the principles of international cooperation and understanding among the peoples of the world, Henri La Fontaine was awarded the Nobel Prize. His early support of the idea of a world bibliography and a universal index to information, in order to bring about understanding among the nations, led to his lifelong devotion to the principle of bringing freedom to the whole world. The goal, he felt, would be achieved by "the great solution," a "magnissima charta" which would create a "United States of the World." (F.L.T.)

1917

International Committee of the Red Cross (Comité International de la Croix-Rouge)   469
Prize: Peace, 1917. *Founded:* 1863 in Geneva, Switzerland
Commentary: The ICRC received the only Peace Prize awarded during the First World War. The Prize was awarded for the help the ICRC gave to prisoners of war by serving as an intermediary between the prisoners and the country that had captured them, by providing them communications across battle lines, and by dispatching delegates to inspect conditions in the camps. In addition to these achievements, the ICRC also distributed relief supplies and monitored combatants' accomidations of the established rules of warfare. (G.N.W.)

1919

Wilson, Thomas Woodrow   470
Prize: Peace, 1919. *Born:* December 28, 1856; Staunton, VA. *Death:* February 3, 1924; Washington, DC. *Parents:* Father, Joseph Ruggles Wilson; Mother, Jessie Janet Woodrow Wilson. *Nationality:* American. *Religion:* Presbyterian. *Education:* Princeton Univ., NJ, B.A., 1879; Univ. of Virginia, LLB., 1881; Johns Hopkins Univ., MD, Ph.D., 1886. *Spouse:* Ellen Louise Axson, married June 24, 1885, died August 6, 1914; Edith Bolling Galt, married December 18, 1915. *Children:* Margaret Woodrow, daughter; Jessie Woodrow, daughter; Eleanor Randolph, daughter. *Career:* Atlanta, GA, Attorney, 1882–83; Bryn Mawr College, PA, Professor, 1885–88; Wesleyan Univ., Middletown, CT, Professor, 1888–90; Princeton Univ., NJ, Professor and President, 1890–1910; New Jersey, Governor, 1911–13; U.S. President, 1913–21.

Selected Publications: Congressional Government. New York: Meridian Books, 1902. *A History of the American People.* 5 volumes. New York: Harper and Brothers, 1902. *Constitutional Government in the United States.* New York: Columbia Univ. Press, 1908. *The New Freedom.* New York: Doubleday, Page, and Company, 1913. *A Day of Dedication: The Essential Writings and Speeches of Woodrow Wilson.* Edited with an introduction by Alan Fried. New York: Macmillan, 1965.

For More Information See: Baker, Ray Stannard. *Woodrow Wilson: Life and Letters.* 8 volumes. Garden City, NY: Doubleday, Doran and Co., 1927–39. Blum, John Morton. *Woodrow Wilson and the Politics of Morality.* Boston: Little, Brown, 1956. Buehrig, Edward Henry. *Wilson's Foreign Policy in Perspective.* Bloomington, IN: Indiana Univ. Press, 1957. *Encyclopedia of American Biography.* New York: Harper & Row, 1974, 1214–17. *Encyclopedia of World Biography.* New York: McGraw-Hill, 1973, 403–06. Link, Arthur Stanley. *Woodrow Wilson.* 5 volumes. Princeton, NJ: Princeton Univ. Press, 1947–65. White, William Allen. *Woodrow Wilson.* Boston: Houghton-Mifflin, 1924.

Commentary: The Nobel Peace Prize was awarded to Woodrow Wilson "for his sincere attempts at peace negotiations"; this statement has been generally thought to refer to his "Fourteen Points" speech to Congress that was aimed at securing a lasting peace at the end of the First World War and was instrumental in the establishment of the League of Nations. President Wilson's efforts to ensure peace in the world followed a long academic career as a writer and teacher of political science, as president of Princeton University, as governor of New Jersey, and as President of the United States, enacting major bills dealing with areas such as tariffs, banking, and anti-trust legislation. (D.B.)

1920

Bourgeois, Léon-Victor Auguste   471
Prize: Peace, 1920. *Born:* May 29, 1851; Paris, France. *Death:* September 29, 1925; Epernay, France. *Parents:* Father, Marie Victor Bourgeois; Mother, Augustine Elise Hinoult Bourgeois. *Nationality:* French. *Religion:* Catholic. *Education:* Univ. of Paris, France, Docteur en Droit, 1875. *Spouse:* No record found. *Children:* No record found. *Career:* French Public Offices, 1876–1923.

Selected Publications: Solidarité. Paris: A. Colin, 1896. *L'Education de la Démocratie Française.* Paris: E. Cornély, 1897. *Le Declaration des Droits de l'Homme.* Paris: E. Cornély, 1902. *Pour la Société des Nations.* Paris: Bibliothèque Charpentier, 1910. *La Pacte de 1919 et la Société des Nations.* Paris: Bibliothèque Charpentier/E. Fasquelle, 1919. *L'Oeuvre de la Société des Nations, 1920–1923.* Paris: Payot, 1923.

For More Information See: Hamburger, M. *Léon Bourgeois, 1851–1925.* Paris: Librairie des Sciences Politiques et Sociales, 1932. Minnich, Lawrence A. "Social Problems and Political Alignments in France, 1893–1898: Leon Bourgeois and Solidarity." (Ph.D. dissertation, Cornell Univ., 1949).

Commentary: Léon Bourgeois was awarded the Nobel Prize in recognition of his status as the spiritual father of the League of Nations, in that he drafted the original document which described such an organization. In addition to his yeoman efforts for the League, Bourgeois devoted his life to the service of France, occupying a series of major offices and spearheading major reforms in education, finances, and the conduct of government. (B.L.)

1921

Branting, Karl Hjalmar   472

Prize: Peace, 1921. *Born:* November 23, 1860; Stockholm, Sweden. *Death:* February 24, 1925; Stockholm, Sweden. *Parents:* Father, Lars Gabriel Branting; Mother, Emerentia Maria Charlotta Georgii Branting. *Nationality:* Swedish. *Religion:* Most probably Christian/Protestant. *Education:* Univ. of Uppsala, Sweden, baccalaureate, 1882. *Spouse:* Anna Matilda Charlotta Jaderin, married April 4, 1884. *Children:* No record found. *Career:* Stockholm Observatory, Sweden, Astronomer, 1882–84; *Tiden*, Editor, 1884–86; *Socialdemokraten*, Editor, 1886–1917; Political Activist and Prime Minister, 1889–1925.

Selected Publications: Socialdemokratiens Arhundrade. 2 volumes. Stockholm: Aktiebolaget Ljus, 1904–06. *Varfor det var Ratt Antaga Pensionforsakringslagen.* Stockholm: Tidens Forlag, 1913. *Den Politiska Krisen: Dess Innebord, Uppkomst och Forsta Forlopp.* Stockholm: Tidens Forlag, 1914. *Tal och Skrifter i Urval.* Stockholm: Tidens Forlag, 1927–30.

For More Information See: Branting, Anna. *Min Langa Resa: Boken om Hjalmar Och Mig.* Stockholm: Meden, 1945. Hoglund, Zeth. *Hjalmar Branting.* Stockholm: Folket i Bilds Forlag, 1949. *Svenskt Biografiskt Lexikon.* Stockholm: Albert Bonniers Forlag, 1926 (Volume 6), 14–37.

Commentary: Hjalmar Branting won the Nobel Prize for his lifelong commitment to constitutional pacifism and the activities in which he involved himself as a result. He was a fervent supporter of Swedish neutrality and saw the role of Sweden as arbitrator and conciliator in international disputes. An involved worker for and at the League of Nations, Branting participated in many disarmament debates, was involved actively in the settlement of the Greek-Italian conflict of 1923 and the British-Turkish dispute in 1924, and helped in the drafting of the Geneva Protocol for international security. Branting was also the father of socialism in Sweden and served in the Parliament from 1886 until his death, including three terms as Prime Minister. (B.S.S.)

Lange, Christian Lous   473

Prize: Peace, 1921. *Born:* September 17, 1869; Stavanger, Norway. *Death:* December 11, 1938; Oslo, Norway. *Parents:* Father, Halvard Lange; Mother, Thora Marie Lous. *Nationality:* Norwegian. *Religion:* Most probably Christian/Protestant. *Education:* Univ. of Oslo, Norway, M.A., 1893; Univ. of Oslo, Norway, Ph.D., 1919. *Spouse:* Bertha Manthey, married December 27, 1894. *Children:* 3 sons; 2 daughters. *Career:* Writer, Journalist, and Political Activist, 1893–1938.

Selected Publications: Den Europaeiske Borgerkrig. Oslo: Aschehoug, 1915. *The Conditions of a Lasting Peace.* Oslo: Interparliamentary Union, 1917. *Histoire de l'Internationalisme.* 3 volumes. Oslo: Aschehoug, 1919, 1954, 1963.

For More Information See: Falnes, Oscar J. "Christian L. Lange and His Work for Peace." *American-Scandinavian Review* 57 (1969): 266–74. *Norsk Biografisk Leksikon.* Oslo: Aschehoug, 1938 (Volume 8), 172–74.

Commentary: A leader in the practice of internationalism, both in words and action, Christian Lange received the Nobel Prize for a lifetime focused on peace and international affairs. Lange was a founder and officer of the Interparliamentary Union and of the Norwegian Nobel Institute. His work for the Union was especially noteworthy. He also participated actively in two international peace conferences and was a delegate to the League of Nations from its founding until his death. In addition, he was a leader of liberal thought, fighting for free speech, free trade, universal suffrage, and the rights of labor. (B.S.S.)

1922

Nansen, Fridtjof   474

Prize: Peace, 1922. *Born:* October 10, 1861; Store fróen, Vestre Aker, Norway. *Death:* May 13, 1930; Polhogda, Norway. *Parents:* Father, Baldur Nansen; Mother, Adelaide Wedel Jarlsberg Nansen. *Nationality:* Norwegian. *Religion:* Agnostic; from Lutheran background. *Education:* Univ. of Kristiania, Norway, Dr. Philos., 1888. *Spouse:* Eva Sars, married 1889, died 1907; Sigrunn Munthe Sandberg, married 1919. *Children:* Liv, daughter; Irmelin, daughter; Odd, son; Kåre, son; Asmund, son. *Career:* Bergen Museum, Norway, Curator, 1882–87; Greenland Expedition Leader, 1888–89; Kristiania Zootomic Collection, Norway, Curator, 1889–93; Polar Expedition Leader, 1893–96; Univ. of Kristiania, Norway, Professor, 1897–1919. *Other Awards:* Jaachim Friele's Gold Medal; Vega Medal, Sweden, 1889.

Selected Publications: Eskimo Life. London: Longmans, 1893. *Farthest North.* New York: Harper, 1897. *In Northern Mists.* New York: Stokes, 1911.

For More Information See: Christensen, C.A.R. *Fridtjof Nansen.* Oslo, Norway: Fabritius, 1961. Sorensen, Jon. *Fridtjof Nansen.* New York: W.W. Norton, 1932. Sorenson, O. *Fridtjof Nansen.* Oslo: Universittetsforlaget, 1993.

Commentary: Fridtjof Nansen received the Nobel Prize "for his activities in behalf of peace and science." A Renaissance man with accomplishments in zoology, anatomy, geology, oceanography, anthropology, and art, he gained early fame as a polar explorer and, during the first few years after Norway's independence in 1905, as a statesman. It was, however, as a delegate to the League of Nations that he began his crusade against suffering and for peace. For instance, he personally organized the repatriation of over 425,000 prisoners of war after World War I, assisted the Armenians, and helped save millions of Russians from starvation. And with a "Nansen passport," political refugees and displaced persons gained an internationally recognized document of identification enabling them to apply for admission to a new home country. Nansen's service to humanity affected countless lives all over the world. (S.O.)

1925

Chamberlain, Joseph Austen, Sir   475
Prize: Peace, 1925. *Born:* October 16, 1863; Birmingham, England. *Death:* March 16, 1937; London, England. *Parents:* Father, Joseph Chamberlain; Mother, Harriet Kenrick Chamberlain. *Nationality:* British. *Religion:* Anglican. *Education:* Cambridge Univ., England, baccalaureate, 1885. *Spouse:* Ivy Muriel Dundas, married 1906. *Children:* Diane, daughter; Joseph, son; Lawrence Endicott, son. *Career:* Britain, Member of Parliament and other posts, 1892–1937. *Other Awards:* Knighthood, 1925.

Selected Publications: Peace in Our Time. London: Allan, 1928. *The Permanent Bases of Foreign Policy.* New York: Council of Foreign Relations, 1931 (with others). *Down the Years.* London: Cassell, 1935. *Politics from the Inside, an Epistolary Chronicle, 1906–1914.* London: Cassell, 1936. *Seen in Passing.* London: Cassell, 1937.

For More Information See: Dutton, David. *Austen Chamberlain: Gentleman in Politics.* London: Transaction Books, 1987. Petrie, Sir Charles. *Life and Letters of the Rt. Hon. Sir Austen Chamberlain.* 2 volumes. London: Cassell, 1939–40.

Commentary: Austen Chamberlain received the Nobel Prize for his work on the Locarno Pacts of 1925, an activity highly acclaimed also in England. The Locarno Treaty, of which he was the principal architect, set to rest many of the hatreds of World War I by guaranteeing the frontiers of Western Europe, establishing the idea of collective security, and preparing the way for Germany's entrance into the League of Nations. In his 45 years of office, Chamberlain also was responsible for many advances in fiscal policy and for establishing future patterns for dealings with China and Egypt. (F.L.T.)

Dawes, Charles Gates   476
Prize: Peace, 1925. *Born:* August 27, 1865; Marietta, OH. *Death:* April 23, 1951; Evanston, IL. *Parents:* Father, Rufus R. Dawes; Mother, Mary Beman Gates Dawes. *Nationality:* American. *Religion:* Most probably Christian/Protestant. *Education:* Marietta College, OH, B.A., 1884; Cincinnati Law School, OH, L.L.B., 1886; Marietta College, OH, M.A., 1887. *Spouse:* Carol D. Blymyer, married 1889. *Children:* Rufus Fearing, son; Dana McCutcheon, son; Carolyn, daughter; Virginia, daughter. *Career:* Lincoln, NE, Attorney, 1887–94; Utility business development, 1894–97; United States, Comptroller of Currency, 1897–1901; Central Trust Co., Chicago, IL, President and Chair, 1902–25; United States Government, positions to Vice President, 1925–35. *Other Awards:* Distinguished Service Medal,

United States; Companion of the Bath, England; Commander of S.S. Maurice and Lazarus, Italy; Order of Leopold, Belgium, 1919; Commander Legion d'Honneur, France, 1919.

Selected Publications: The Banking System of the United States and Its Relation to the Money and Business of the Country. Chicago: Rand-McNally, 1894. *Notes as Vice President.* Boston: Little, Brown and Company, 1935. *A Journal of Reparations.* London: Macmillan, 1939.

For More Information See: Dictionary of American Biography. Supplement 5. New York: Scribner's, 1977, 159–60. Timmons, Bascom. *Portrait of an American: Charles G. Dawes.* New York: Henry Holt, 1953.

Commentary: Charles Dawes was the Nobel recipient for his work in drafting the Dawes Plan. The apotheosis of American capitalism, Dawes acquired wealth and public influence as an innovative financier and Republican Party stalwart. From McKinley's administration to Hoover's, he held varied federal executive and diplomatic positions, capping his career as Coolidge's vice president from 1929–31. A picturesque figure, possessed of an unusual "dramatic sense" and a penchant for "direct action," Dawes chaired the Reparations Committee of Experts, convened in 1924 to resolve the crisis which threatened peace in Europe, and he popularized its report. An imaginative agreement among the former combatants to settle German reparations payments, the Dawes Plan broke the impasse among the European powers, extending back to 1914, and seemed to lay the foundations for their economic recovery. (S.W.)

1926

Briand, Aristide   477
Prize: Peace, 1926. *Born:* March 28, 1862; Nantes, France. *Death:* March 7, 1932; Paris, France. *Parents:* Father, Pierre-Guillaume Briand; Mother, Magdeleine Boucheau Briand. *Nationality:* French. *Religion:* Christian. *Education:* Univ. of Paris, France, law degree, 1881. *Spouse:* None. *Children:* None. *Career:* Attorney, Journalist, political office through Premier (12 times), 1881–1932.

Selected Publications: Journalist efforts appeared in *Le Peuple, La Lanterne, La Petite Republique,* and *L'Humanité,* 1901–32.

For More Information See: Aubert, Alfred. *Briand.* Paris: Chiron, 1928. Baumont, Maurice. *Aristide Briand: Diplomat and Idealist.* Göttingen, Germany: Munsterschmidt, 1966. Suarez, Georges. *Briand, sa Vie, son Oeuvre.* 6 volumes. Paris: Plon, 1938–52. Thomson, Valentine. *Briand: Man of Peace.* New York: Covici-Friede, 1930. Vercours. *Moi Aristide Briand.* Brussels: Editions Complexe, 1991.

Commentary: The great French politician, Aristide Briand, a member of 21 cabinets and 12 times Premier of France, shared the Nobel Prize for his work on the Locarno Pacts of 1925, which included treaties, guarantees, and nonaggression agreements that involved Germany, France, Poland, Belgium, and Czechoslovakia. A lifelong enemy of war, Briand nonetheless led France through a critical period in World War I but returned to peace efforts after the war. Locarno represented a peak in his performance in this regard and was followed by an even greater victory, the signing by 15 nations of the Kellogg-Briand Pact in 1928, which established arbitration as a viable concept and renounced war.

Briand also proposed, in 1930, the concept of a European Union. In addition to his other efforts, Briand was noted as a supporter of labor unions and as the man who guided the Government Commission that wrote the law separating church and state, won its passage in the Chamber, and enforced it as the Cabinet Minister of Public Instruction and Worship. (B.S.S.)

Stresemann, Gustav   478

Prize: Peace, 1926. *Born:* May 10, 1878; Berlin, Germany. *Death:* October 3, 1929; Berlin, Germany. *Parents:* Father, Ernst Stresemann; Mother, no record found. *Nationality:* German. *Religion:* Lutheran. *Education:* Univ. of Berlin, Germany, Ph.D., 1900; Univ. of Leipzig, Germany, Ph.D., 1902. *Spouse:* Kāthe Kleefeld, married 1906. *Children:* Gert Wolfgang, son; Haus Joachim, son. *Career:* German and international political offices, 1900–29. *Other Awards:* Deutscher Ring, Foreign Institute.

Selected Publications: Essays and Speeches. Freeport, NY: Books for Libraries Press, 1930.

For More Information See: Olden, Rudolf. *Stresemann.* New York: E.P. Dutton, 1930. Turner, Henry. *Stresemann and the Politics of the Weimer Republic.* Princeton, NJ: Princeton Univ. Press, 1963. Von Rheinbaben, Rochus. *Stresemann: The Man and the Statesman.* New York: D. Appleton, 1929.

Commentary: Gustav Stresemann was awarded the Nobel Prize for his successful efforts on behalf of peace. Stresemann's involvement in German politics after World War I was characterized by his attempt to reestablish order and peace. He succeeded in curbing the rampant inflation, and was involved in the negotiations leading to the Dawes Plan, the Locarno Pact, and the admission of Germany to the League of Nations. Stresemann strove to alleviate the harsh conditions imposed upon Germany after World War I, while improving relations internationally, especially with France. He was the most prominent and influential statesman of the Weimar Republic and respected abroad as a man of goodwill. (S.O.)

1927

Buisson, Ferdinand Edouard   479

Prize: Peace, 1927. *Born:* December 20, 1841; Paris, France. *Death:* February 16, 1932; Thieuloy-Saint-Antoine, France. *Parents:* Father, Pierre Buisson; Mother, Adele Aurelie de Aibeaucourt Buisson. *Nationality:* French. *Religion:* Protestant. *Education:* Univ. of Paris, France, Ph.D., 1892. *Spouse:* No name found, married 1866. *Children:* 2 sons, 1 daughter. *Career:* Academie de Neuchatel, Switzerland, Professor, 1866–70; French government positions, 1870–96; Sorbonne Univ., Paris, France, Professor, 1896–1901; French government and international positions, 1902–26.

Selected Publications: Le Christianisme Liberal. Paris: J. Chenbuliez, 1865. *Dictionnaire de Pedagogie et d'Instruction Primarie.* Paris: Hachette, 1878–87.

For More Information See: Dictionnaire de Biographie Française. Paris: Librairie Letouzey, 1956 (Volume 7), 645–46. Loeffel, Laurence. *Ferdinand Buisson: Apotre de l'école Laïque.* Paris: Hachette Education, 1999. Talbott, John E. *The Politics of Educational Reform in France,* *1918–1940.* Princeton, NJ: Princeton Univ. Press, 1969, 57–59, 75–77, 106–07.

Commentary: Ferdinand Buisson has been called "the world's most persistent pacifist," and in the Nobel presentation statement, his prominence as a progressive educator and statesman was also acknowledged in that " . . . great organized work for peace must be preceded by the education of the people. . . . " Buisson dedicated his life to peace by working consistently toward reconciliation between former adversary nations, France and Germany, in particular and through his efforts to reverse the Dreyfus decision; his advocacy of universal suffrage; and by helping to found human rights and peace organizations, La Ligue Internationale de la Paix et de la Liberté (1867) and La Ligue des Droits des Hommes (1898). (C.B.B.)

Quidde, Ludwig   480

Prize: Peace, 1927. *Born:* March 23, 1858; Bremen, Germany. *Death:* March 4, 1941; Geneva, Switzerland. *Parents:* No record found. *Nationality:* German. *Religion:* Most probably Christian/Protestant. *Education:* Univ. of Strasbourg, France, and; Univ. of Göttingen, Germany, Ph.D., no date. *Spouse:* Margarethe Jacobson, married 1882. *Children:* None. *Career:* Independently wealthy, but served in various political, editorial, and societal roles.

Selected Publications: Caligula: Eine Studie Über Römischen Caesarenwahnsinn. Leipzig, Germany: Wilhelm Friedrich, 1894. "Shall There Be a Germany Irredenta?" *Living Age* 302 (September 6, 1919): 583–85. *Die Schuldfrage.* Berlin: Schwetschke, 1922. "The Future of Germany." *Living Age* 321 (April 5, 1924): 635–38.

For More Information See: Taube, Utz-Friedebert. *Ludwig Quidde: Ein Beitrag Zur Geschichte des Demokratischen Gedankens in Deutschland.* Kallmünz über Regensburg: Lassleben, 1963. Wehberg, Hans. *Ludwig Quidde: Ein Deutscher Demokrat und Vorkämpfer der Völkersverständigung.* Offenbach am Main: Ballwerk, 1948.

Commentary: Ludwig Quidde received the Nobel Prize in recognition of his "long and arduous service in the course of peace." His publication of *Caligula* in 1894, seen as an attack on the Kaiser, led to his jailing and subsequent lifelong involvement in pacifist movements. During his career, he founded the Munich Peace Society, opposed German policies in 1914 and fled to Switzerland, wrote against secret military training in Germany in the 20s (and was again jailed), and was forced into exile a second time on Hitler's assumption of power in 1933. (S.K.A.)

1929

Kellogg, Frank Billings   481

Prize: Peace, 1929. *Born:* December 22, 1856; Potsdam, NY. *Death:* December 21, 1937; St. Paul, MN. *Parents:* Father, Asa F. Kellogg; Mother, Abigail Billings Kellogg. *Nationality:* American. *Religion:* Christian. *Spouse:* Clara M. Cook, married 1886. *Children:* None. *Career:* Minnesota, Attorney, 1877–1916; Senator from Minnesota, 1917–23; Ambassador to Great Britain, 1924–25; Secretary of State, 1925–29; Minnesota, Attorney, 1929–37; Permanent Court of International Justice, Judge, 1930–35. *Other Awards:* Grand Cross French Legion of Honor, 1929; Order of Olive Branch of Argentina, 1930.

Selected Publications: Lincoln and Roosevelt. St. Paul, MN: McGill Warner, 1908; *The Paris Peace Pact.* New York: World Alliance for International Friendship Through the Churches, 1928.

For More Information See: Bryn-Jones, David. *Frank B. Kellogg: A Biography.* New York: G.P. Putnam's Sons, 1937. Ellis, L. Ethan. *Frank B. Kellogg and American Foreign Relations, 1925–1929.* New Brunswick, NJ: Rutgers Univ. Press, 1961. Ferrell, Robert H. *Peace in Their Time: The Origins of the Kellogg-Briand Pact.* New Haven, CT: Yale Univ. Press, 1952. *The McGraw-Hill Encyclopedia of World Biography.* New York: McGraw-Hill Book Company, 1973 (Volume 6), 157–58.

Commentary: Frank Kellogg won the Nobel Prize for his efforts in concluding the Pact of Paris (Kellogg-Briand Treaty) in 1928. The treaty, which Kellogg moved from a proposed bilateral agreement with France to one that involved all the major nations of the world, outlawed war as an instrument of national policy. During Kellogg's tenure as secretary of state, he also improved U.S. relations with Mexico, contributed to settlement of a territorial dispute between Chile and Peru, and sought the end of a revolution in Nicaragua. He signed 80 treaties, including conciliation treaties with all of the Latin American countries except Argentina and with 15 other nations. He also concluded 19 arbitration treaties. (W.K.)

1930

Söderblom, Nathan (Söderblom, Lars Olof Jonathan)   **482**
Prize: Peace, 1930. *Born:* January 15, 1866; Trönö, Sweden. *Death:* July 12, 1931; Uppsala, Sweden. *Parents:* Father, Jonas Söderblom; Mother, Sophia Blume Söderblom. *Nationality:* Swedish. *Religion:* Lutheran. *Education:* Univ. of Uppsala, Sweden, B.A., 1886; Univ. of Paris-Sorbonne, France, Doctor of Theology, 1901. *Spouse:* Anna Forsell, married 1897. *Children:* 7 sons; 3 daughters. *Career:* Swedish Church, positions to Archbishop, 1894–1901; Univ. of Uppsala, Sweden, Professor, 1901–12; Univ. of Leipzig, Germany, Professor, 1912–14.

Selected Publications: Die Religionen der Erde (The Religions of the World). Halle, Germany: Gebauer-Schwetschke, 1905. *Einführung in die Religionsgeschichte (Introduction to the History of Religion).* Leipzig, Germany: Quelle and Meyer, 1920. *Christian Fellowship.* New York: Fleming H. Revell, 1923.

For More Information See: Encyclopedia of World Biography. New York: McGraw Hill, 1973 (Volume 10), 120–21. Sundkler, Bengt. *Nathan Söderblom: His Life and Work.* Lynd, Sweden: Gleerup, 1968.

Commentary: Swedish theologian Nathan Söderblom was awarded the 1930 Nobel Prize for "his promotion of international understanding." An outspoken pacifist and leader in the ecumenical movement, he authored numerous theological works. Söderblom's dissertation, *La Vie Future d'Apres le Mazdaisme,* established him as a religious scholar. Perhaps his outstanding success was the realization of the Universal Christian Conference on Life and Work in 1925. (L.S.)

1931

Addams, Laura Jane   **483**
Prize: Peace, 1931. *Born:* September 6, 1860; Cedarville, IL. *Death:* May 21, 1935; Chicago, IL. *Parents:* Father, John Huy Addams; Mother, Sarah Weber Addams. *Nationality:* American. *Religion:* Presbyterian. *Education:* Rockford Female Seminary, IL, A.B., 1882. *Spouse:* None. *Children:* None. *Career:* Hull House, Chicago, IL, Founder and Director, 1889–1935. *Other Awards:* Thomas Prize, Bryn Mawr College, 1931; Pictorial Reviews Annual Achievement Award, 1931; American Education Award, National Education Association, 1935.

Selected Publications: Democracy and Social Ethics. New York: Macmillan, 1902. *Newer Ideals of Peace.* New York: Macmillan, 1907. *The Spirit of Youth and the City Streets.* New York: Macmillan, 1909. *The Excellent Becomes the Permanent.* New York: Macmillan, 1932.

For More Information See: Addams, Jane. *The Second Twenty Years at Hull House.* New York: Macmillan, 1930. Addams, Jane. *Twenty Years at Hull House.* New York: Macmillan, 1910. Farrell, John C. *Beloved Lady: A History of Jane Addams' Ideas on Reform and Peace.* Baltimore, MD: Johns Hopkins Press, 1967. Levine, Daniel. *Jane Addams and the Liberal Tradition.* Stevens Point, WI: Worzalla Publishing Co., 1971. Polikoff, Barbara Garland. *With One Bold Act: The Story of Jame Addams.* Chicago: Boswell Books, 1999.

Commentary: Both 1931 recipients of the Peace Prize, Jane Addams and Nicholas Murray Butler were cited by the committee for a lifetime spent "in trying to raise the ideal of peace in their people and in the whole world." The committee further noted for Jane Addams that "we also pay homage to the work which women can do for the cause of peace and fraternity among nations" and that "for twenty-five years she has been the faithful spokesman of the idea of peace." Her most notable contributions were the establishment of the internationally famous settlement house, Chicago's Hull House, and her work with the National American Woman Suffrage Association and the Women's International League for Peace and Freedom. (M.K.)

Butler, Nicholas Murray   **484**
Prize: Peace, 1931. *Born:* April 2, 1862; Elizabeth, NJ. *Death:* December 7, 1947; New York, NY. *Parents:* Father, Henry Leny Butler; Mother, Mary J. Murray Butler. *Nationality:* American. *Religion:* Episcopalian. *Education:* Columbia Univ., NY, A.B., 1882; Columbia Univ., NY, A.M., 1883; Columbia Univ., NY, Ph.D., 1884. *Spouse:* Susanna Edwards Schyler, married 1887, died 1903; Kate La Montagne, married 1907. *Children:* 1 daughter. *Career:* Columbia Univ., NY, Professor and Administrator, 1885–1945. *Other Awards:* Goethe Gold Medal, 1932; Grand Cross of the Legion of Honor, 1937; Alexander Hamilton Award, 1947.

Selected Publications: The International Mind: An Argument for the Judicial Settlement of International Disputes. New York: Scribner's, 1912. *Building the American Nation: An Essay of Interpretation.* New York: Scribner's, 1923. *The Path to Peace: Essays and Addresses on Peace and Its Making.* New York: Scribner's, 1930. *The Family of Nations: Its Need and Its Problems. Essays and Addresses.* New York: Scribner's, 1938. *Why War? Essays and Addresses on*

War and Peace. New York: Scribner's, 1940. *Liberty-Equality-Fraternity: Essays and Addresses on the Problems of Today and Tomorrow*. New York: Scribner's, 1942. *The World Today: Essays and Addresses*. New York: Scribner's, 1946.

For More Information See: Across the Busy Years: Recollections and Reflections. 2 volumes. New York: Scribner's, 1939–40. *Current Biography Yearbook*. New York: H.W. Wilson, 1940, 130–32. Marrin, Albert. *Nicholas Murray Butler*. Boston: Twayne, 1976.

Commentary: Nicholas Murray Butler—educator, innovative university administrator, and political activist in the Republican party—won the Nobel because "during his twenty-five years of work for peace Dr. Butler has shown almost matchless strength and indefatigable energy." Through his long association with the Carnegie Endowment for International Peace he achieved world-wide influence for his ideas. Friend to the world's statesmen, in 1930 he personally gained the support of Pope Pius XI for the Kellogg-Briand pact outlawing war as an instrument of national policy. (F.L.T.)

1933

Angell, Norman, Sir (Lane, Ralph Norman Angell) 485

Prize: Peace, 1933. *Born:* December 26, 1874; Holbeach, Lincolnshire, England. *Death:* October 7, 1967; Croydon, Surrey, England. *Parents:* Father, Thomas Angell Lane; Mother, Mary Ann Brittain Lane. *Nationality:* British. *Religion:* Anglican. *Education:* No college degrees. *Spouse:* Beatrice Cuvellier, married 1898. *Children:* None. *Career:* Writer and Journalist. *Other Awards:* Knighthood, 1931.

Selected Publications: Patriotism Under Three Flags. London: Unwin, 1903. *The Great Illusion.* London: Heinemann, 1910. *The Fruits of Victory.* London: Collins, 1921. *The Unseen Assassins.* London: Hamish Hamilton, 1932. *Peace with the Dictators?* London: Hamish Hamilton, 1938. *The Steep Places.* London: Hamish Hamilton, 1947.

For More Information See: After All: The Autobiography of Norman Angell. New York: Farrar, Straus and Young, 1952. Marrin, Albert. *Sir Norman Angell.* Boston: Twayne, 1979.

Commentary: Journalist, author, and activist, Norman Angell was awarded the Nobel Prize for his writings on peace. In 1909, he published a pamphlet which was expanded to become his most famous work, *The Great Illusion*. The book preached what was to be his continuing theme, the futility of wars of conquest as a means to achieve economic benefits and human happiness. Denounced by many during World War I as an unpatriotic pacifist, he worked steadfastly during and after the war for international cooperation through collective security. In 1932, he published *The Unseen Assassins*, a masterful and timely analysis of the issues of war and peace. Opposed to war, Angell did, however, believe that the fascist dictators should be resisted in defense of freedom. He worked against the policy of appeasement and supported the war effort during World War II. After the war, he promoted a union of the Western democracies and the international control of atomic energy. (F.L.T.)

1934

Henderson, Arthur 486

Prize: Peace, 1934. *Born:* September 13, 1863; Glasgow, Scotland. *Death:* October 20, 1935; London, England. *Parents:* Father, David Henderson; Mother, no record found. *Nationality:* British. *Religion:* Methodist. *Education:* No college degrees. *Spouse:* Eleanor Percy Watson, married 1888. *Children:* David, son; William Watson, son; Arthur, Jr., son; Eleanor, daughter. *Career:* Foundry Worker and Union Officer, England, 1875–1903; Darlington, England, Mayor, 1903; British Parliament, Member, 1903–35. *Other Awards:* Wateler Peace Prize, Carnegie Foundation, 1933.

Selected Publications: British Finance and Prussian Militarism. New York: Hodder and Stoughton, 1917. *The Aims of Labor.* London: Headley, 1919. *Report of the Labour Commission to Ireland.* London: The Labour Party, 1921. *Consolidating World Peace.* Oxford: Clarendon Press, 1931.

For More Information See: The Dictionary of National Biography, 1931–1940. London: Oxford Univ. Press, 1949, 417–20. Hamilton, Mary. *Arthur Henderson.* London: W. Heinemann, 1938. Wrigley, C. *Arthur Henderson.* Cardiff, Wales: GPC Books, 1990.

Commentary: Arthur Henderson was awarded the Nobel prize in recognition of the role he played as president of the League of Nation's World Disarmament Conference. During his years as president, his tireless efforts, bolstered by his firm conviction in a world commonwealth, were responsible for holding together this conference long after it had become apparent that it was doomed to failure by the rapid growth of nationalism that preceded World War II. Although Henderson's dedication to the cause of world peace was to have little influence, his other achievements were to have far-reaching effects. The greater part of his life was dedicated to the establishment, and success, of a strong British working class party; today he is remembered as a founding father of the Labour Party. (E.G.)

1935

Ossietzky, Carl von 487

Prize: Peace, 1935. *Born:* October 3, 1889; Hamburg, Germany. *Death:* May 4, 1938; Berlin, Germany. *Parents:* Father, Carl Ignatius von Ossietzky; Mother, Rosalie Marie Pratska von Ossietzky. *Nationality:* German. *Religion:* Christian. *Education:* No college degrees. *Spouse:* Maud Woods, married May 22, 1914. *Children:* Rosalinde, daughter. *Career:* Germany, Journalist, 1918–38.

Selected Publications: Schriften (Writings). 2 volumes. Berlin: Aufbau, 1966.

For More Information See: Frei, Bruno. *Carl v. Ossietzky: Ritter ohne Furcht und Tadel.* Berlin: Aufbau, 1966. Grossman, Kurt R. *Ossietzky: Ein Deutscher Patriot.* Munich: Kindler, 1963. Ossietzky, Maud von. *Maud v. Ossietzky Erzahlt: Ein Lebensbild.* Berlin: Buchverlag der Morgen, 1966. Kraiker, G. *Carl von Ossietzky.* Reinbeck, Germany: Rowholt, 1994.

Commentary: The Academy cited Carl von Ossietzky for "his valuable contribution to the cause of peace" but noted his value as "a symbol of the struggle for peace rather than its champion." An accomplished journalist dedicated to liberalism, Ossietzky became a confirmed fighter for peace after his sad experiences as a soldier in World War I. He was a leader of the German Peace Society for many years, but his major contributions took the form of brilliant essays in a number of journals. It was as a symbol, however, that he became an international force. Beginning in 1926, he fearlessly exposed German military activities, which led to his imprisonment several times. His attacks on Hitlerism and Nazi policies, beginning in 1933, led to his banishment to concentration camp life until his death. Ossietzky's receipt of the Prize, which he was prevented from accepting, resulted in Hitler's decree that no German in the future could accept any Nobel Prize. (B.S.S.)

1936

Saavedra Lamas, Carlos   488

Prize: Peace, 1936. *Born:* November 1, 1878; Buenos Aires, Argentina. *Death:* May 5, 1959; Buenos Aires, Argentina. *Parents:* Father, Mariano Saavedra Zavaleta; Mother, Luisa Lamas. *Nationality:* Argentinian. *Religion:* Christian. *Education:* National Univ., Argentina, Doctorate of Laws, 1903. *Spouse:* Rosa Saenz Pena, married 1903. *Children:* Carlos Roque, son. *Career:* Univ. of La Plata and Univ. of Buenos Aires, Argentina, Professor and Administrator (to President), 1903–46; concurrently served in a number of political posts. *Other Awards:* International Medal, Pan-American Society, NY, 1933; Star of the German Red Cross, 1936; Grand Cross of the Legion of Honor, France.

Selected Publications: Traites Internationaux de Type Social: Les Conventions sur L'Emigration et le Travail Perspective Qu'elles Offrent aux Pays Sud-Americains et Specialement a la Republique Argentine. Paris: Pedone, 1924. *Centro de Legislacion Social y del Trabajo.* Buenos Aires: Imprenta de la Universidad, 1927. *La Crise de la Codification et de la Doctrine Argentine de Droit International.* Paris: Pedone, 1931. *Codigo Nacional del Trabajo.* 3 volumes. Buenos Aires: Roldan, 1933.

For More Information See: Encyclopedia of World Biography. New York: McGraw-Hill, 1973 (Volume 9), 346–47. Oro Maini, Atilio del. *Carlos Saavedra Lamas.* Buenos Aires: Anales de la Academia Nacional de Derecho y Ciencias Sociales, 1960. Fraga, R. *Carlos Saavedra Lamas.* Buenos Aires: Editorial Centro de Estudios Union, 1991.

Commentary: In a dual career as a distinguished professor of law and political leader, Carlos Saavedra Lamas earned the Nobel Prize through his espousal of an Antiwar Pact born in Latin America and submitted to the League of Nations, as well as for his work in the League of Nations. Saavedra Lamas had served Argentina in a number of important posts from 1906–32, sponsoring legislation that clarified policies on water rights, agriculture, immigration, and finances. His international prominence began in 1932 when, as foreign minister, he succeeded in ending the Chaco War between Paraguay and Bolivia; he also developed the foundation for the South American Antiwar Pact, which he presented first to the American nations and later to the League of Nations. He was President of the League in 1936. (R.A.)

1937

Cecil, Edgar Algernon Robert Gascoyne, Sir   489

Prize: Peace, 1937. *Born:* September 14, 1864; London, England. *Death:* November 24, 1958; Turnbridge Wells, England. *Parents:* Father, Robert Arthur Talbot Cecil; Mother, Georgiana Alderson Cecil. *Nationality:* British. *Religion:* Anglican. *Education:* Oxford Univ., England, baccalaureate, 1881; law degree, 1884. *Spouse:* Eleanor Lambton, married 1889. *Children:* None. *Career:* Private Secretary, 1886–88; Attorney, 1888–1906; British Parliament and other political positions, 1906–27. *Other Awards:* Knighthood, 1923.

Selected Publications: Our National Church. London: F. Warne & Co., 1913 (with H. J. Clayton). *The Moral Basis of the League of Nations.* London: Lindsey Press, 1923. *The Co-operation of Nations.* London: Univ. of London Press, 1928. *The Way of Peace.* London: P. Allan & Co., 1928. *All the Way.* London: Hodder & Stoughton, 1949.

For More Information See: A Great Experiment: An Autobiography. New York: Oxford Univ. Press, 1941. Jackson, Jere Langdon. "Apostle of the League: Lord Robert Cecil and the Fight for the League of Nations, 1916–1924." (Ph.D. dissertation, Univ. of North Carolina at Chapel Hill, 1974).

Commentary: Robert Cecil was awarded the Nobel Prize for his work as one of the architects of the League of Nations and as its faithful defender. The League occupied much of his life, while at the same time he served his country in a variety of important government posts. Cecil had the distinction of being an important figure in the founding of the League, in its history throughout its existence, and in the final meetings in Geneva in 1946, when he said "The League is dead; long live the United Nations." (B.L.)

1938

Nansen International Office of Refugees (Office International Nansen pour les Réfugiés)   490

Prize: Peace, 1938. *Founded:* 1921 in Geneva, Switzerland

Commentary: An international aid organization established by Fridtjof Nansen in 1921 and authorized by the League of Nations in 1930, the International Office of Refugees closed its doors December 31, 1938. With the League in full decline, the committee decided to give the award to the League's Office of Refugees. Whatever the political difficulties of the world's first international organization of nations, the committee wanted to call attention to how effective it had been in carrying out humanitarian work. (G.N.W)

1944

International Committee of the Red Cross (Comité International de la Croix-Rouge)   491

Prize: Peace, 1944. *Founded:* 1863 in Geneva, Switzerland

Commentary: The ICRC received its second Peace Prize for its humanitarian activities during World War II and, according to the committee, for "rescuing in the dark storm of war the idea of human solidarity and respect for the dignity of every human being—precisely at a time when the real or alleged necessities of war push moral values into the background."

1945

Hull, Cordell   492

Prize: Peace, 1945. *Born:* October 2, 1871; Overton County, TN. *Death:* July 23, 1955; Bethesda, MD. *Parents:* Father, William Hull; Mother, Elizabeth Riley Hull. *Nationality:* American. *Religion:* Protestant. *Education:* Cumberland Univ., TN, law degree, 1891. *Spouse:* Rose Frances Witz Whitney, married 1917. *Children:* None. *Career:* Tennessee, House of Representatives, Member, 1893–97; Tennessee, Infantry Captain, 1898–99; Attorney, 1899–1903; Tennessee, Judge, 1903–07; United States, House of Representatives, Member, 1907–31; United States, Senator, 1931–33; United States, Secretary of State, 1933–44. *Other Awards:* Woodrow Wilson Medal, 1937; Theodore Roosevelt Distinguished Service Medal, 1945.

Selected Publications: Economic Barriers to Peace. New York: Woodrow Wilson Foundation, 1937.

For More Information See: Hinton, Harold B. *Cordell Hull: A Biography.* Garden City, NY: Doubleday, Doran and Company, 1942. *The Memoirs of Cordell Hull.* 2 volumes. New York: The Macmillan Company, 1948. Pratt, Julius. *Cordell Hull, 1933–44.* 2 volumes. New York: Cooper Square Publishers, 1964.

Commentary: The award to Cordell Hull was "for his long and indefatigable work for understanding between nations." Hull was cited for his prominent role in laying the groundwork for the United Nations as an organization dedicated to the maintenance of peace following World War II. The Nobel Committee also recognized Hull's lifelong efforts at lowering trade barriers as a means to improve international relations and remove one of the causes of war; and his promotion of peace among the nations of the American continents through the implementation of Franklin D. Roosevelt's "good neighbor policy." (G.S.)

1946

Balch, Emily Greene   493

Prize: Peace, 1946. *Born:* January 8, 1867; Boston, MA. *Death:* January 7, 1961; Cambridge, MA. *Parents:* Father, Francis Vergnies Balch; Mother, Ellen Noyes Balch. *Nationality:* American. *Religion:* Unitarian. *Education:* Bryn Mawr College, PA, A.B., 1889. *Spouse:* None. *Children:* None. *Career:* Children's Aid Society, Boston, MA, Social Worker, 1891; Denison House Settlement, Boston, MA, Headworker, 1892–93; Wellesley College, MA, Professor, 1896–1918; *The Nation*, NY, Editor, 1918–19.

Selected Publications: Public Assistance of the Poor in France. Baltimore, MD: American Economic Association, 1893. *Our Slavic Fellow Citizens.* New York: Charities Publication Committee, 1910. *Approaches to the Great Settlement.* New York: B.W. Huebsch, 1918. *The Miracle of Living.* New York: Island Press, 1941.

For More Information See: Current Biography Yearbook. New York: H.W. Wilson, 1948, 32–34. Randall, Mercedes M. *Improper Bostonian: Emily Greene Balch.* New York: Twayne Publishers, 1964.

Commentary: The Nobel Award to Emily Greene Balch recognized her important contributions as a leader of the international women's movement for peace. Her activism began in 1915 when she served as a delegate to the International Congress of Women, and later as an official spokesperson to the then-neutral Scandinavian countries, Russia, and the United States. She continued her work as a founder, officer, and lifelong worker of the Women's International League for Peace and Freedom. In 1919, after 22 years of her teaching, Wellesley College declined to reappoint her because of her pacifist views. (J.M.S.)

Mott, John R.   494

Prize: Peace, 1946. *Born:* May 25, 1865; Livingston Manor, NY. *Death:* January 31, 1955; Orlando, FL. *Parents:* Father, John Stitt Mott; Mother, Elmira Dodge Mott. *Nationality:* American. *Religion:* Methodist. *Education:* Cornell Univ., NY, Ph.B., 1888. *Spouse:* Leila Ada White, married November 26, 1891; died September 28, 1952; Agnes Peter, married July 28, 1953. *Children:* John Livingstone, son; Irene, daughter; Frederick Dodge, son; Eleanor, daughter. *Career:* Young Men's Christian Association, Administrator, 1888–1931. *Other Awards:* Distinguished Service Medal, United States, 1919; Order of the Crown, Siam, 1919; Chevalier, French Legion of Honor, 1919; Chevalier, Order of the Crown of Italy, 1920; Imperial Order of the Sacred Treasure, Japan, 1920 and 1929; Star of the Hungarian Red Cross, 1923; Order of Polona Restituta, Poland, 1924; Order of the Holy Sepulchre, Jerusalem, 1924; Order of the Savior, Greece, 1924; Order of the White Lion, Czechoslovakia, 1930; Order of the Jade, China, 1938; Order of the White Rose, Finland, 1946; Prince Carl Medal, Sweden, 1946; Commander's Cross, Order of Merit of the Federated Republic of Germany, 1954.

Selected Publications: Liberating the Lay Forces of Christianity. New York: Macmillan, 1932. *Five Decades and a Forward View.* New York: Harper and Brothers, 1939. *Addresses and Papers.* 6 volumes. New York: Association Press, 1946–1947.

For More Information See: Current Biography Yearbook. New York: H.W. Wilson, 1947, 453–56. *Dictionary of American Biography. Supplement 5 (1951–1955).* New York: Scribner's, 1977, 506–08. Hopkins, Charles Howard. *John R. Mott, 1865–1955: A Biography.* Grand Rapids, MI: Eerdmans, 1979.

Commentary: John Mott was neither a politician nor an active participant in peace organizations but was awarded the Nobel Prize for his steadfast commitment to spreading the word of Christ, as well as his inspiration to youth, his leading role in five world church and missionary movements, his demonstrated respect for individual differences, and humanitarian efforts in time of war. A recognized leader of the Christian ecumenical movement and an organizer at his best when dealing with diverse elements, Mott was also instrumental in founding the World Council of Churches. (M.L.L.)

1947

American Friends Service Committee (Quakers)   495

Prize: Peace, 1947. *Founded:* 1672; headquartered in Washington, DC

Commentary: The Peace Prize was divided equally between the American Friends Service Committee and the Friends Service Council for their activities during World War II and afterward, when Quaker volunteers administered relief in the form of food, clothing, ambulance service, and medical care to many nations of people on more than one continent. (G.N.W.)

Friends Service Council   496
Prize: Peace, 1947. *Founded:* 1647 in London, England

Commentary: The Peace Prize was divided equally between the Friends Service Council and the American Friends Service Committee for their activities during World War II and afterward, when Quaker volunteers administered relief in the form of food, clothing, ambulance service, and medical care to many nations of people on more than one continent. (G.N.W.)

1949

Orr, John Boyd (Orr, Boyd, Lord)   497
Prize: Peace, 1949. *Born:* September 23, 1880; Kilmaurs, Ayrshire, Scotland. *Death:* June 25, 1971; Brechin, Angus, Scotland. *Parents:* Father, Robert Clark Orr; Mother, Annie Boyd Orr. *Nationality:* Scottish. *Religion:* Presbyterian. *Education:* Glasgow Univ., Scotland, M.A., 1902; Glasgow Univ., Scotland, B.Sc., 1910; Glasgow Univ., Scotland, M.B., Ch.B., 1912; Glasgow Univ., Scotland, M.D., 1914; Glasgow Univ., Scotland, D.Sc., 1920. *Spouse:* Elizabeth Pearson Callum, married 1915. *Children:* Elizabeth Joan, daughter; Helen Ann, daughter; Donald Noel, son. *Career:* British Military Service, 1914–19; Rowett Institute, England, Director and Publisher, 1914–45; Glasgow Univ., Scotland, Rector and Chancellor, 1945–71; Food and Agriculture Organization, United Nations, Director, 1946–48. *Other Awards:* Knighthood, 1935; Raised to peerage, 1948; Legion d'Honneur, 1949; Harben Medal, Royal Institute of Public Health, 1949; Gold Medal, International Federation of Agricultural Producers, 1949; Gold Medal, National Farmers Union of America, 1951; Borden Gold Medal, U.S.A., 1958.

Selected Publications: Food, Health and Income. London: Macmillan, 1936. *Food and the People.* London: Pilot Press, 1943. *The White Man's Dilemma.* London: Allen and Unwin, 1953. *Feast and Famine.* London: Rathbone Books, 1957. *As I Recall: The 1880's to the 1960's.* London: MacGibbon and Kee, 1966.

For More Information See: Current Biography Yearbook. New York: H.W. Wilson Co., 1946, 440–43. Cuthbertson, D.P. "Lord Boyd Orr (1880–1971): A Biographical Sketch." *Journal of Nutrition.* 105 (May 1975): 519–24. Kay, H.D. "John Boyd Orr, Baron Boyd Orr of Brechin Mearns." In *Biographical Memoirs of the Fellows of the Royal Society* (Volume 18), 43–81. London: The Royal Society of London, 1972. *Biographical Memoirs. National Academy of Sciences.* Washington, DC: National Academy Press, 1994, Volume 63, 423.

Commentary: John Boyd Orr was recognized by the Academy for his efforts to eliminate world hunger and to promote global unity and peace. A nutritionist, Orr learned early that it was easier to persuade farmers to feed animals well than it was to convince people of the importance of human nutrition. As the first director-general of the Food and Agriculture Organization, he tried, unsuccessfully, to establish a world food plan. Much of his later life was spent working toward a "United States of the World" that would

allow such a plan to exist. "There can be no peace in the world so long as a large proportion of the population lack the necessities of life . . . ," John Boyd Orr stated in his Nobel lecture. (M.L.L.)

1950

Bunche, Ralph Johnson   498
Prize: Peace, 1950. *Born:* August 7, 1904; Detroit, MI. *Death:* December 9, 1971; New York, NY. *Parents:* Father, Fred Bunche; Mother, Olive Agnes Johnson Bunche. *Nationality:* American. *Religion:* Protestant. *Education:* Univ. of California, Los Angeles, A.B., 1927; Harvard Univ., MA, A.M., 1928; Harvard Univ., MA, Ph.D., 1934. *Spouse:* Ruth Ethel Harris, married June 23, 1930. *Children:* Joan Harris, daughter; Jane Johnson, daughter; Ralph Johnson, Jr., son. *Career:* Howard Univ., Washington, DC, Professor, 1929–41; United States government positions, 1942–47; United Nations positions, 1947–71. *Other Awards:* Spingarn Medal, National Association for the Advancement of Colored People, 1949; Medal of Freedom, 1963.

Selected Publications: A World View of Race. Washington, DC: Associates in Negro Folk Education, 1936. "What America Means to Me." *American Magazine* 149 (February 1950): 19, 122–26. *The Political Status of the Negro in the Age of FDR.* Chicago: Univ. of Chicago Press, 1973.

For More Information See: Current Biography Yearbook. New York: H.W. Wilson, 1948, 77–79. Kugelmass, J.A. *Ralph J. Bunche: Fighter for Peace.* New York: Julian Messner, 1952. Mann, Peggy. *Ralph Bunche: UN Peacemaker.* New York: Coward, McCann and Geoghegan, 1975. Urquhart, B. *Ralph Bunche.* New York: W. W. Norton, 1998.

Commentary: Ralph Bunche earned the Nobel Prize for mediating the war among Israel, Egypt, Jordan, Lebanon, and Syria, a war which had followed the United Nation's plan in 1947 for partitioning Palestine. As personal representative of the UN Secretary General, Bunche accompanied Count Folke Bernadotte, UN mediator, to the Middle East. Following Bernadotte's assassination, Bunche became acting mediator and directed the difficult and complex negotiations between Israeli and Arab delegations which culminated in the signing of armistice agreements between these countries in 1949. Bunche was earlier an outstanding academic, a civil rights activist, and a leading United States government service employee. His career ended with 25 years of service to the United Nations. (D.N.S.)

1951

Jouhaux, Leon   499
Prize: Peace, 1951. *Born:* July 1, 1879; Paris, France. *Death:* April 28, 1954; Paris, France. *Parents:* No record found. *Nationality:* French. *Religion:* Christian. *Education:* No college degrees. *Spouse:* (No first name found) Jouhaux, married (no date found). *Children:* None. *Career:* Match Company, Paris, France, Unskilled Laborer, 1895–1900; Paris, France, Unskilled Laborer, 1900–02; France, Union Activist and Leader, 1902–54. *Other Awards:* Medal of the French Resistance, 1946.

Selected Publications: Georges, B. and others. *Léon Jouhaux dans le movement syndical français.* Paris: Presses universitaires de France, 1979. *The International Federation of Trade Unions and Economic Reconstruction.* Amsterdam: IFTU, 1922. *Le Desarmement.* Paris: Alcan, 1927. *Le Mouvement Syndical en France.* Berlin: Federation Syndicale Internationale, 1931.

For More Information See: Current Biography Yearbook. New York: H.W. Wilson, 1948, 329–31. *Living Age* 352 (July 1937): 419–25. Millet, Raymond. *Jouhaux et la C.G.T.* Paris: Denoel et Steele, 1937.

Commentary: Leon Jouhaux was recognized for his "work and struggle to elevate the working class, and first of all to improve their conditions." He received the Prize "because from his earliest years he has time after time thrown himself into the fight for peace and against war. . . ." Jouhaux, forced into work at a match factory at age 13, became a leader of the French trade-union movement and an officer in the national organization, The Confederation Generale du Travail (C.G.T.) from 1909–51. He used his power to lead the C.G.T. into peace programs which included support of arms limitation, international arbitration, respect for all nationalities, and open treaties. (T.B.)

1952

Schweitzer, Albert   **500**

Prize: Peace, 1952. *Born:* January 14, 1875; Kayersburg, Alsace. *Death:* September 4, 1965; Lambaréné, Gabon, French Equatorial Africa. *Parents:* Father, Louis Schweitzer; Mother, Adele Schillinger Schweitzer. *Nationality:* German; later French resident. *Religion:* Lutheran. *Education:* Univ. of Strasbourg, France, Ph.D., 1899; Univ. of Strasbourg, France, Licentiate, 1900; Univ. of Strasbourg, France, Doctorate in Medicine, 1913. *Spouse:* Helene Bresslau, married June 18, 1912. *Children:* Rhena Fanny Suzanne Schweitzer Eckert Miller, daughter. *Career:* Chapel of St. Nicholas, Strasbourg, France, Preacher, 1899–1900; Univ. of Strasbourg, France, Principal of Theological College, 1901–12; Schweitzer Hospital, Gabon, France, Founder and Director, 1913–65. *Other Awards:* Goethe Memorial Prize, Frankfurt, 1928; Wellcome Medal, Royal African Society, 1952; Grand Gold Medal, Paris, 1955; Pour le Merite, Germany, 1955; Order of Merit, England, 1955.

Selected Publications: J.S. Bach, le musicien-poete. Paris: Costallat, 1905 (Tr. by Ernest Newman. Neptune, NJ: Paganiniana, 1980). *Deutsche und Franzosische Orgelbaukunstund Orgelkunst.* Leipzig, Germany: Breitkopf und Hartel, 1906 (*Organ Playing and Organ Building in France and Germany.* Tr. by William D. Turner, Braintree, MA: Organ Literature). *Von Reimarus zu Wrede.* Tübingen, Germany: J.C.B. Mohr, 1906 (*The Quest of the Historical Jesus: A Critical Study of Its Progress from Reimarus to Wrede.* Tr. by W. Montgomery. New York: Macmillan, 1968). *Zwischen Wasser und Urwald.* Upsala, Sweden: Lindblad Publishing House, 1921 (*On the Edge of the Primeval Forest.* Tr. by C.T. Campion. New York: AMS Press, 1976). *Kultur und Ethik.* Munich: C.H. Beck, 1923 (*Civilization and Ethics.* Tr. by C.T. Campion. London: A. & C. Black, 1923). *Aus Meiner Kindheit und Jugendzeit.* Bern, Switzerland: Paul Haupt, 1924 (*Memoirs of Childhood and Youth.* Tr. by C.T. Campion. New York: Macmillan, 1949). *Die Mystik des Apostels Paulus.* Tübingen, Switzerland: J.C.B. Mohr (Siebeck), 1930 (*The Mysticism of Paul the Apostle.* Tr. by

W. Montgomery. New York: Crossroad, 1968). *Aus Meinem Leben und Denken.* Leipzig, Germany: Felix Meiner, 1931 (*Out of My Life and Thought.* Tr. by C.T. Campion, New York: Holt, 1933).

For More Information See: Brabazon, James. *Albert Schweitzer: A Biography.* New York: Putnam, 1975; Syracuse, NY: Syracuse University Press, 2000 (2nd ed.). Cousins, Norman. *Dr. Schweitzer of Lambaréné.* New York: Harper, 1960. *Current Biography Yearbook.* New York: H.W. Wilson, 1965, 375–78. Schweitzer, Albert. *Memoirs of Childhood and Youth.* Tr. by C.T. Campion. New York: Macmillan, 1949. Schweitzer, Albert. *Out of My Life and Thought.* Tr. by C.T. Campion. New York: Holt, 1933. Seaver, George. *Albert Schweitzer, the Man and his Mind.* New York: Harper, 1955. Bentley, J. *Albert Schweitzer.* New York: HarperCollins, 1992.

Commentary: Albert Schweitzer, musician, theologian, philosopher, and doctor, earned the respect and admiration of the world as a humanitarian, receiving the Nobel Prize for his efforts in behalf of "the Brotherhood of Nations." The author of scholarly books on Bach and theology, a renowned organ builder and organist, he became known to the world as the founder and director of the Schweitzer Hospital in Lambaréné, Gabon, French Equatorial Africa. His "Reverence for Life" philosophy left a profound mark on the world. (M.K.)

1953

Marshall, George Catlett   **501**

Prize: Peace, 1953. *Born:* December 31, 1880; Uniontown, PA. *Death:* October 16, 1959; Bethesda, MD. *Parents:* Father, George Catlett Marshall; Mother, Laura Bradford Marshall. *Nationality:* American. *Religion:* Episcopalian. *Education:* Virginia Military Institute, graduate, 1901. *Spouse:* Elizabeth Carter Coles, married 1902, died 1927; Katharine Tupper Brown, married 1930. *Children:* None. *Career:* U.S. Army and Government Posts, 1902–51. *Other Awards:* Gold Medal, Distinguished Service Medal, and Victory Medal, USA; Croix de Guerre Montenegro; Grand Croix Legion of Honor, France; Officer, Order of the Crown, Italy; Knight Grand Cross, Order of the Bath, England; Order of Suvarov, USSR; Theodore Roosevelt Distinguished Service Medal, 1945; Humanitarian Award, Varieties Clubs, 1947; Freedom House Award, 1947; Gold Medal, National Planning Association, 1949; National Civic Service Award, 1949; New York Board of Trade Award, 1949; Distinguished Public Service Award, Conference of Mayors, 1949; Citizenship Award, Disabled American Veterans, New York Chapter, 1950; Distinguished Service Medal, American Legion, 1951; Four Freedoms Foundation Award, 1952.

Selected Publications: Memories of My Service in the World War, 1917–18. Boston: Houghton-Mifflin, 1976. Bland, Larry I. (ed.), *The Papers of George Catlett Marshall.* Baltimore, MD: Johns Hopkins Univ. Press, 1981–86.

For More Information See: Cray, Ed. *General of the Army: George C. Marshall, Soldier and Statesman.* New York: Cooper Square Press, 2000. Ferrell, Robert H. *George C. Marshall.* New York: Cooper Square Publishers, 1966. Mosley, Leonard. *Marshall, Hero for Our Times.* New

York: Hearst Books, 1982. Pogue, Forrest C. *George C. Marshall*. Multivolume set. New York: Viking Press, 1963-.

Commentary: To later generations, General George Catlett Marshall's selection for the Nobel Peace Prize seems anomalous. The seemingly contradictory selection of a military man, the first ever chosen to receive the Peace Prize, is more apparent than real. While serving as Secretary of State, Marshall promoted peace in the aftermath of the most devastating war in history and received the Nobel honor most probably for the Marshall Plan, which provided American loans and technical assistance to any European states pursuing recovery. Throughout his career, Marshall covered himself in glory, especially as Chief of Staff of the U.S. Army (1939–45), Secretary of State (1947–49), and Secretary of Defense (1950–51). (R.S.L.)

1954

Office of the United Nations High Commissioner for Refugees 502

Prize: Peace, 1954. *Founded:* 1951 by United Nations

Commentary: The Office for Refugees received the Peace Prize for their work for and among refugees. The committee credited the Office with "teaching us that the unfortunate foreigner is one of us, and it makes us understand that the solidarity extending equally to human beings beyond [national] frontiers constitutes the very foundation on which any lasting peace must be built." (G.N.W.)

1957

Pearson, Lester Bowles 503

Prize: Peace, 1957. *Born:* April 23, 1897; Newton Brook, Canada. *Death:* December 27, 1972; Ottawa, Canada. *Parents:* Father, Edwin Arthur Pearson; Mother, Annie Sarah Bowles Pearson. *Nationality:* Canadian. *Religion:* Methodist. *Education:* Univ. of Toronto, Canada, B.A., 1919; Oxford Univ., England, B.A., 1923; Oxford Univ., England, M.A., 1925. *Spouse:* Maryon Elspeth Moody, married 1925. *Children:* Geoffrey Arthur, son; Patricia Lillian Hannah, daughter. *Career:* Univ. of Toronto, Canada, Professor, 1926–28; Canadian Government, positions through Prime Minister, 1928–68. *Other Awards:* Order of Merit, England, 1962; Medallion of Valor, Israel.

Selected Publications: Democracy in World Politics. Princeton, NJ: Princeton Univ. Press, 1955. *Diplomacy in the Nuclear Age.* Cambridge, MA: Harvard Univ. Press, 1959. *Peace in the Family of Man.* New York: Oxford Univ. Press, 1969. *Words and Occasions.* Toronto: Univ. of Toronto Press, 1970.

For More Information See: Bothwell, Robert. *Pearson, His Life and World.* New York: McGraw-Hill, 1978. *Current Biography Yearbook.* New York: H.W. Wilson, 1963, 319–21. *Mike: The Memoirs of the Right Honourable Lester B. Pearson.* Toronto: Univ. of Toronto Press, 1972–75. English, J. *The Life of Lester Pearson: the Worldly Years.* Toronto; London: Vintage Books Canada, 1993 (2 vols.). English, J. *Shadow of Heaven.* London: Vintage UK, 1990.

Commentary: Lester Pearson was the Nobel recipient for lifelong work in pursuit of peace, culminating in his efforts to resolve the Suez Canal Crisis of 1956. An immensely likeable person, quick in mind, and buoyant in spirit, "Mike"

Pearson spent 40 years at the center of Canadian foreign policy development, the first 20 as an increasingly respected professional diplomat, the latter 20 as a successful Liberal Party leader. For nearly 10 years, as Minister for External Affairs (1948–57), he presided over a veritable golden age of Canadian leadership in the postwar quest for world peace, and he culminated his distinguished political career as prime minister (1963–68). Following the combined British, French, and Israeli attack upon Egypt in 1956, Pearson took the lead in United Nations efforts to resolve the Suez Canal Crisis. His long diplomatic experience, familiarity with principal actors, and highly respected "personal qualities" enabled him to fashion a solution acceptable to all parties, ending the armed conflict and restoring peace to the region. (S.W.)

1958

Pire, Dominique, Reverend (François, Georges Charles Clement Ghislain Eugéne) 504

Prize: Peace, 1958. *Born:* February 10, 1910; Dinant, Belgium. *Death:* January 30, 1969; Louvain, Belgium. *Parents:* Father, Georges Pire; Mother, François Laurent Pire. *Nationality:* Belgian. *Religion:* Catholic. *Education:* Colegio Angelico, Italy, Doctor of Sacred Theology, 1936. *Spouse:* None. *Children:* None. *Career:* Dominican Priest, 1934–69; Studium de la Sarte-Huy, Professor, 1937–47; Crusader for the successful settlement of displaced persons, 1947–69. *Other Awards:* Croix de Guerre with palms, Belgium; Croix d'Honneur du Mérite Civique Français; Medaille de la Résistance with crossed swords; Legion d'Honneur, France; Cross of Merit Order of Merit, Germany; Medaille de la Reconnaissance Nationale; Sonning Prize, Denmark, 1964.

Selected Publications: The Story of Father Dominique Pire, Winner of the Nobel Peace Prize, as Told to Hugues Vehenne. Tr. by John L. Skeffington. New York: Dutton, 1961. *Building Peace.* Tr. by Graeme M. Ogg. London: Transworld Publishers, 1967. *Vivre ou Mourir Ensemble.* Brussels: Presses Academiques Europeennes, 1969.

For More Information See: Current Biography Yearbook. New York: H.W. Wilson, 1959, 362–64. Houart, Victor. *The Open Heart: The Inspiring Story of Father Pire and the Europe of the Heart.* Tr. by Mervyn Savill. London: Souvenir Press, 1959. Kent, George. "Father Pire: Nobel Prize Winner." *Catholic World* 189 (April 1959): 26–31.

Commentary: Father Dominique Pire was awarded the Nobel Prize for his work with European refugees. He organized a sponsorship program which put refugee families living in camps in touch with private families elsewhere and founded four homes for elderly refugees and seven European villages for the resettlement of refugees. The international society L'Aide aux Personnes Deplacées (Aid to Displaced Persons) was also established by Father Pire to assist stateless refugees with material and moral support. (J.C.H.)

1959

Noel-Baker, Philip John 505

Prize: Peace, 1959. *Born:* November 1, 1889; London, England. *Death:* October 8, 1982; London, England. *Parents:* Father, Joseph Allen Baker; Mother, Elizabeth B.

Moscrip Baker. *Nationality:* British. *Religion:* Quaker. *Education:* Cambridge Univ., England, baccalaureate, 1912; Cambridge Univ., England, M.A., 1914. *Spouse:* Irene Noel, married 1915. *Children:* Francis Edward, son. *Career:* Ruskin College, England, Vice-Principal, 1914; Cambridge Univ., England, Fellow and War Service, 1915–19; British Government Offices, 1919–24; Univ. of London, England, Professor, 1924–29; British Parliament and Government, various positions, 1929–70. *Other Awards:* Mons Star, 1915; Croce di Guerra, 1918; Howland Prize, Yale Univ., CT, 1934; Silver Medal, 1947; Albert Schweitzer Book Prize, 1960.

Selected Publications: The Geneva Protocol for the Pacific Settlement of International Disputes. London: King, 1925. *Disarmament.* London: Hogarth, 1926. *The League of Nations at Work.* London: Nisbet, 1926. *Disarmament and the Coolidge Conference.* London: Leonard and Virginia Woolf, 1927. *The Private Manufacture of Armaments.* London: Gollancz, 1936. *The Arms Race: A Programme for World Disarmament.* London: Stevens, 1958. *The Way to World Disarmament—Now!* London: Union of Democratic Control, 1963.

For More Information See: Annual Obituary. New York: St. Martin's Press, 1982. Russell, Bertrand. *The Nobel Peace Prize and the Laureates.* Boston: G.K. Hall, 1988, 170–73. "Philip Noel-Baker: A Tribute." *International Relations* 2 (1960): 1–2. Whittaker, D.J. *Fighter for Peace: Philip Noel-Baker, 1889–1982.* York, England: W. Sessions, 1989.

Commentary: Philip Noel-Baker was awarded the Nobel for his contributions as a tireless worker for world peace through disarmament. For 53 years, he worked for peace in his speeches, writings, and participation in every international disarmament conference. His service to Britain was equally impressive, both as an Olympic medal winner and Captain of Britain's team and in a long career in Parliament and a succession of government offices. (A.J. and B.S.S.)

1960

Luthuli, Albert John 506

Prize: Peace, 1960. *Born:* 1898 (?); Rhodesia. *Death:* July 21, 1967; Groutville, South Africa. *Parents:* Father, John Luthuli; Mother, Mtonya Gumede Luthuli. *Nationality:* South African. *Religion:* Congregationalist. *Education:* No college degrees. *Spouse:* Nokukhanya Bhengu, married 1927. *Children:* 2 sons; 5 daughters. *Career:* Adam's Mission Station College, South Africa, Teacher, 1921–36; Abasemakholweni Tribe, South Africa, Chief, 1936–53; African National Congress, President-General, 1953–67. *Other Awards:* United Nations Human Rights Prize, 1968.

Selected Publications: "What I Would Do If I Were Prime Minister." *Ebony* 17 (February 1962): 21–29. *Africa's Freedom.* London: Allen and Unwin, 1964.

For More Information See: Benson, Mary. *Chief Albert Luthuli of South Africa.* London: Oxford Univ. Press, 1963. *Current Biography Yearbook.* New York: H.W. Wilson, 1962, 271–73. *Let My People Go.* New York: McGraw-Hill, 1962. *New York Times* (October 24, 1961): 22.

Commentary: Albert Luthuli (also spelled Lutuli) was cited by the Academy for his leadership in peaceful resistance to apartheid in South Africa, noting that "in his fight against racial discrimination he had always worked for nonviolent methods." A longtime teacher, tribal chieftain, President of the African National Congress, and a leader of Christianity in South Africa, Luthuli was a forceful figure of international stature in affairs within South Africa, despite being harassed and under internal exile for a good part of his career. (B.S.S.)

1961

Hammarskjold, Dag Hjalmar Agne Carl 507

Prize: Peace, 1961 (posthumous). *Born:* July 29, 1905; Jonkoping, Sweden. *Death:* September 17, 1961; Northern Rhodesia. *Parents:* Father, Hjalmar Hammarskjold; Mother, Agnes Almquest Hammarskjold. *Nationality:* Swedish. *Religion:* Lutheran. *Education:* Univ. of Uppsala, Sweden, B.A., 1925; Univ. of Uppsala, Sweden, LLB, 1930; Univ. of Stockholm, Sweden, Ph.D., 1934. *Spouse:* None. *Children:* None. *Career:* Commission on Unemployment, Sweden, Secretary, 1930–34; Bank of Sweden, Secretary, 1935–36; Ministry of Finance, Sweden, 1936–45; Ministry of Foreign Affairs, Sweden, 1946; Organization of European Economic Cooperation, Executive Committee Vice-Chair, 1948–49; General Assembly, U.N., 1949–61.

Selected Publications: The Servant of Peace. New York: Harper & Row, 1962. *Markings.* New York: Knopf, 1964.

For More Information See: Current Biography Yearbook. New York: H.W. Wilson Co., 1953, 241–43. *Encyclopedia of World Biography.* New York: McGraw-Hill, 1973 (Volume 5), 65–66. Stolpe, Sven. *Dag Hammarskjold.* New York: Scribner's Sons, 1966. Thorpe, Deryck. *Hammarskjöld: Man of Peace.* Ilfracombe, England: Stockwell, 1969.

Commentary: Although the award to Dag Hammarskjold did not mention any specific achievement, it was widely speculated at the time that the award was presented posthumously for his work toward peace in the Congo. The recipient drew upon 18 years of distinguished service in the Swedish government and for the Organization for European Economic Cooperation to develop the office of the Secretary General of the United Nations as a nonpolitical arena which could serve as a channel of communication and an impartial consultant in international conflicts. Hammarskjold proved the effectiveness of this philosophy in 1955 when he secured the release of 15 American aviators shot down and held by the Chinese; in his role as mediator during the 1956 Middle East crisis; and during the 1960–61 problems in the new Republic of the Congo. (E.G.)

1962

Pauling, Linus Carl *See* entry **57**

1963

International Committee of the Red Cross (Comité International de la Croix-Rouge) 508

Prize: Peace, 1963. *Founded:* 1863 in Geneva, Switzerland

Commentary: On the 100th anniversary of the founding of the Red Cross, the Peace Prize was divided equally between the ICRC (given to them for a third time) and the League of Red Cross Societies, representing the two major elements of the Red Cross movement. (G.N.W.)

League of Red Cross Societies (Ligue des Sociétés de la Croix-Rouge)   **509**
Prize: Peace, 1963. *Founded:* In Geneva, Switzerland
   Commentary: On the 100th anniversary of the founding of the Red Cross, the Peace Prize was divided equally between the League of Red Cross Societies and the ICRC, representing the two major elements of the Red Cross movement. The League was founded by the American banker and Red Cross leader, Henry P. Davison, to join together the independent, national societies into a federation. (G.N.W.)

1964

King, Martin Luther, Jr.   **510**
Prize: Peace, 1964. *Born:* January 15, 1929; Atlanta, GA. *Death:* April 4, 1968; Memphis, TN. *Parents:* Father, Martin Luther King, Sr.; Mother, Alberta Christine Williams King. *Nationality:* American. *Religion:* Baptist. *Education:* Morehouse College, GA, A.B., 1948; Crozer Theological Seminary, PA, B.D., 1951; Boston Univ., MA, Ph.D., 1955. *Spouse:* Coretta Scott, married June 18, 1953. *Children:* Youlanda Denise, daughter; Martin Luther, III, son; Dexter Scott, son; Bernice Albertine, daughter. *Career:* Ebenezer Baptist Church, Atlanta, GA, Pastor, 1947–54; Dexter Avenue Baptist Church, Montgomery, AL, Pastor, 1954–60; Ebenezer Baptist Church, Atlanta, GA, Pastor, 1960–68. *Other Awards:* Pearl Plafker Award, Crozer Theological Seminary, PA, 1951; Spingarn Medal, National Association for the Advancement of Colored People, 1957; Man of the Year, *Time*, 1963.
   Selected Publications: Stride Toward Freedom. New York: Harper & Row, 1958. *Strength to Love.* New York: Harper & Row, 1963. *Why We Can't Wait.* New York: Harper & Row, 1964. *Where Do We Go from Here: Chaos or Community.* New York: Harper & Row, 1967. *The Trumpet of Conscience.* New York: Harper & Row, 1968.
   For More Information See: Ansboro, John. *Martin Luther King, Jr.: The Making of a Mind.* Maryknoll, NY: Orbis Books, 1982. *Current Biography Yearbook.* New York: H.W. Wilson, 1965, 220–23. King, Coretta Scott. *My Life with Martin Luther King, Jr.* New York: Holt, Rinehart and Winston, 1969. Fairclough, A. *Martin Luther King, Jr.* Athens, GA: Univ. of Georgia Press, 1995.
   Commentary: Nobel recipient Martin Luther King, Jr., received his award for his efforts to bring about integration within the United States without violence. Beginning with the successful boycott of the Montgomery, AL, transit company that ended segregated seating on buses in the community, King led Black Americans into a new era of achievement of civil rights based on a nonviolent philosophy and a return of love for hate. He was also later a leader in the movement to end the Vietnam War. (B.S.)

1965

United Nations Children's Fund (UNICEF)   **511**
Prize: Peace, 1965. *Founded:* 1946 by the United Nations
   Commentary: The Peace Prize was awarded to UNICEF in accord with "the solemn recognition that the welfare of today's children is inseparably linked with the peace of tomorrow's world." UNICEF was established by the United Nations in 1946 to meet the desparate needs of children in postwar Europe for food, clothing, and medical care. (G.N.W.)

1968

Cassin, René-Samuel   **512**
Prize: Peace, 1968. *Born:* October 5, 1887; Bayonne, France. *Death:* February 20, 1976; Paris, France. *Parents:* Father, Henri Cassin; Mother, Gabrielle Dreyfus Cassin. *Nationality:* French. *Religion:* Jewish. *Education:* Univ. of Aix-en-Provence, France, degree in humanities, 1908; Univ. of Aix-en-Provence, France, degree in law, 1908; Univ. of Aix-en-Provence, France, doctorate, 1914. *Spouse:* Simone Yzomard, married 1917, died 1969; Ghislaine Bru, married 1975. *Children:* None. *Career:* Paris, France, Attorney, 1909–14; French Army, 1914–16; Univ. of Aix-en-Provence, France, Professor, 1916–20; Univ. of Lille, France, Professor, 1920–29; Univ. of Paris, France, Professor, 1929–60. *Other Awards:* Human Rights Prize, United Nations, 1968; Goethe Prize, 1973; Grand Croix Legion d'Honneur; Croix de Guerre.
   Selected Publications: La Conception des Droits de L'Etat dans les Successions d'apres le Code Civil Suisse. Paris: Sirey, 1914. *L'Inegalite entre l'Homme et la Femme dans la Legislation Civile.* Marseille: Barlatier, 1919. *Pour la Defense de la Paix.* Paris: n.p., 1936. "How the Charter on Human Rights was Born." *UNESCO Courier* 21 (January 1968): 4–6.
   For More Information See: Encyclopedia Judaica. New York: Macmillan, 1971 (Volume 5), 231. *New York Times* (October 10, 1968): 1, 14. Israel, G. *René Cassin, 1877–1976.* Paris: Desclee de Brower, 1990.
   Commentary: René Cassin was awarded the Nobel Prize "primarily for his contribution to the protection of human worth and the rights of man, as set forth in the Universal Declaration of Human Rights." Renowned as a jurist, humanitarian, and internationalist, Cassin brought to all of his activities a profound respect for human rights. His legal scholarship included notable work on contracts, inheritance, domicile, and the inequality between men and women. He was a major force in French politics during World Wars I and II and especially in his work with Charles DeGaulle. Cassin occupied important positions in France, Europe, and the United Nations throughout his long career. He founded the French Federation of Disabled War Veterans and guided it as well as the High Council for Wards of the Nation for many years. But he will be remembered primarily as a charter member of the United Nations Commission on Human Rights, its chair or vice-chair for much of its existence, and the one most responsible for drafting the Declaration of Human Rights. (T.B. and B.S.S.)

1969

International Labour Organization (ILO)   **513**
Prize: Peace, 1969. *Founded:* 1919 in Geneva, Switzerland
   Commentary: The Peace Prize was awarded to the ILO, the only international organization associated with the League of Nations to outlive it, on its 50th birthday. According to the committee, "There are few organizations that have succeeded to the extent that the ILO has in translating into action the fundamental moral idea on which it is based," namely that peace can only thrive when social justice is

achieved. The ILO has worked to secure agreement among nations to improve the conditions of workers by reducing the length of the working day, giving equal pay for equal work, providing a safe workplace, and supplying health insurance. According to the ILO, their primary concern is to eliminate poverty and hardship everywhere. (G.N.W.)

1970

Borlaug, Norman Ernest 514

Prize: Peace, 1970. *Born:* March 25, 1914; Cresco, IA. *Parents:* Father, Henry O. Borlaug; Mother, Clara Vaala Borlaug. *Nationality:* American. *Religion:* Lutheran. *Education:* Univ. of Minnesota, B.S., 1937; Univ. of Minnesota, M.S., 1940; Univ. of Minnesota, Ph.D., 1941. *Spouse:* Margaret G. Gibson, married September 24, 1937. *Children:* Norma Jean Rhoda, daughter; William Gibson, son. *Career:* E.I. DuPont, DE, Microbiologist, 1942–44; Rockefeller Foundation, NY, Research Scientist and Administrator working primarily in Mexico, 1944–79; Texas A&M Univ., Professor, 1980-. *Other Awards:* E.C. Stakman Award, 1961; Agricultural Editors Association Award, 1967; International Agronomy Award, 1968; Distinguished Service Medal, Pakistan, 1968; Service Award, American Farmers Bureau Federation, 1971; Outstanding Agricultural Achievement Award, World Farm Foundation, 1971; Medal of Merit, Italian Wheat Scientists, 1971; Medal of Freedom, Mexico, 1977.

Selected Publications: The Green Revolution, Peace and Humanity. Washington, DC: Population Reference Bureau, 1971. *The World Food Problem: Present and Future.* Amsterdam, Netherlands: North-Holland, 1972.

For More Information See: Current Biography Yearbook. New York: H.W. Wilson, 1971, 50–52. Paarlberg, Don. *Norman Borlaug: Hunger Fighter.* Washington, DC: Foreign Economic Development Service, 1970.

Commentary: Norman Borlaug was cited by the Nobel Committee for his leadership in the "Green Revolution" in developing countries in that "he has helped to provide bread for a hungry world. We have made this choice in the hope that providing bread will also give the world peace." Borlaug's contribution was finding a high-yield, dwarf, disease-resistant wheat strain, capable of cultivation in a wide range of climatic conditions, to provide relief from famine in developing countries. (M.J.H.)

1971

Brandt, Willy (Frahm, Herbert Ernst Karl) 515

Prize: Peace, 1971. *Born:* December 18, 1913; Lübeck, Germany. *Death:* October 8, 1992; Unkel, Germany. *Parents:* Father, Unknown; Mother, Martha Frahm; Stepfather, Emil Kuhlman. *Nationality:* German; also Norwegian Citizen, 1940–47. *Religion:* Anti-religious; from Christian background. *Education:* No college degrees. *Spouse:* Carlotta Thorkildsen, married 1940, divorced 1948; Rut Hansen Bergaust, married 1948, divorced 1980; Brigitte Seebacher, married 1983. *Children:* Ninja, daughter; Peter, son; Lars, son; Matthias, son. *Career: Lübecker Volksbote,* Reporter, 1927–33; Lübeck, Germany, Shipbroker, 1933–34; Student and miscellaneous activities, 1934–39; Norwegian Army, 1940; Stockholm, Reporter, 1940–48; Berlin, Germany, Political Offices to Mayor and in Social Democratic

Party, 1948–66; Germany, Political Offices to Chancellor, 1966–92. *Other Awards:* Grosskreuz des Verdienstorden der Bundesrepublik Deutschland, 1959; Grand Cross, Order of St. Olaf, Norway, 1960; Freedom Prize, Freedom House Organization, 1961; Man of the Year, *Time,* 1970; Order of Pius IX, Vatican, 1970; Reinhold-Niebuhr Prize, 1972; Aspen Institute for Humanistic Studies Prize, 1973; Gold Medal, B'nai Brith, 1981; Einstein International Peace Prize, 1985; Third World Prize, 1985.

Selected Publications: My Road to Berlin. Garden City, NY: Doubleday, 1960. *The Ordeal of Coexistence.* Cambridge, MA: Harvard Univ. Press, 1963. *A Peace Policy for Europe.* New York: Holt, Rinehart and Winston, 1969. *In Exile: Essays, Reflections and Letters, 1933–47.* Philadelphia, PA: Univ. of Pennsylvania Press, 1971. *People and Politics: The Years 1960–1975.* Boston: Little, Brown, 1978. *Arms and Hunger.* New York: Pantheon Books, 1986.

For More Information See: Binder, David. *The Other German: Willy Brandt's Life & Times.* Washington, DC: New Republic Books, 1975. *Current Biography Yearbook.* New York: H.W. Wilson, 1958, 57–58. Harpprecht, Klaus. *Willy Brandt: Portrait and Self-Portrait.* Los Angeles: Nash Publishing Co., 1971. Prittie, Terence. *Willy Brandt: Portrait of a Statesman.* New York: Schocken Books, 1974. *Willy Brandt: A Political Biography.* New York: St. Martin's, 1997.

Commentary: The Nobel Committee unanimously selected Willy Brandt, citing his "efforts to obtain for the people of West Berlin the fundamental human rights of personal security and full freedom of movement" and his "outstanding efforts in order to create conditions for peace in Europe." In a long and respected career, he fought Naziism, wrote in Norway and Germany, and led postwar Germany back to some measure of economic and political health, working toward normal relations between East and West. (S.K.A.)

1973

Kissinger, Henry Alfred 516

Prize: Peace, 1973. *Born:* May 27, 1923; Fuerth, Germany. *Parents:* Father, Louis Kissinger; Mother, Paula Stern Kissinger. *Nationality:* German; later American citizen. *Religion:* Jewish. *Education:* Harvard Univ., MA, A.B., 1950; Harvard Univ., MA, M.A., 1952; Harvard Univ., MA, Ph.D., 1954. *Spouse:* Ann Fleischer, married February 6, 1949, divorced 1964; Nancy Maginnes, married March 30, 1974. *Children:* Elizabeth, daughter; David, son. *Career:* U.S. Army, 1943–46; Harvard Univ., MA, Professor, 1954–69; U.S. Government, Special Assistant to the President and Secretary of State, 1969–77; Kissinger Associates, Chair, 1978-. *Other Awards:* Woodrow Wilson Book Prize, 1958; Guggenheim Fellowship, 1965–66; Gold Medal, National Institute of Social Sciences, 1972; *Time* Man of the Year, 1972; American Institute for Public Service Award, 1973; Jefferson Award, 1973; Theodore Roosevelt Award, 1973; American Legion Distinguished Service Medal, 1974; Wateler Peace Prize, 1974; Presidential Medal of Freedom, 1977; Medal of Liberty, 1986.

Selected Publications: Nuclear Weapons and Foreign Policy. New York: Harper, 1957. *A World Restored: Metternich, Castlereagh and the Problem of Peace.* Boston:

Houghton-Mifflin, 1957. *The Necessity for Choice: Prospects of American Foreign Policy.* New York: Harper, 1961. *The Troubled Partnership: A Re-Appraisal of the Atlantic Alliance.* New York: McGraw-Hill, 1965. *American Foreign Policy.* 3d ed. New York: Norton, 1977. *White House Years.* Boston: Little, Brown, 1979. *Years of Upheaval.* Boston: Little, Brown, 1982. *Observations: Selected Speeches and Essays, 1982–84.* Boston: Little, Brown, 1985. *Years of Renewal.* New York: Simon & Schuster, 1999.

For More Information See: Current Biography Yearbook. New York: H.W. Wilson Co., 1972, 254–57. Dickson, Peter W. *Kissinger and the Meaning of History.* Cambridge: Cambridge Univ. Press, 1978. *Encyclopedia of American Biography.* New York: Harper & Row, 1974, 623–25. Graubard, Stephen R. *Kissinger: Portrait of a Mind.* New York: Norton, 1973. Hersh, Seymour M. *The Price of Power: Kissinger in the White House.* New York: Summit Books, 1983. Morris, Roger. *Uncertain Greatness: Henry Kissinger and American Foreign Policy.* New York: Harper & Row, 1977. Isaacson, W. *Kissinger.* London: Faber and Faber, 1992.

Commentary: Henry Kissinger received the Nobel Prize for his work in "negotiating an end to the war in Vietnam," together with Le Duc Tho of North Vietnam. The awards generated a storm of protests and led to the resignation of two committee members. Kissinger is known for his scholarly and practical work in international relations and for his development, as a government consultant and secretary of state, of American defense and foreign policy. He is also remembered for his long efforts toward a negotiated peace between Israel and the Arab countries. (D.B.)

Le Duc Tho (Phan Dinh Khai)   517

Prize: Peace, 1973 (refused). *Born:* October 14, 1911; Dich Le, Vietnam. *Death:* October 13, 1990; Hanoi, Vietnam. *Parents:* No record found. *Nationality:* Vietnamese. *Religion:* No record found. *Education:* No college degrees. *Spouse:* Married twice. *Children:* No record found. *Career:* Vietnam, Communist Party Positions, 1930–90.

Selected Publications: No record found.

For More Information See: Current Biography Yearbook. New York: H.W. Wilson, 1975, 235–38. *New York Times Biographical Edition* (October 1973): 1683. *New York Times Biographical Service* (October 14, 1990): 936.

Commentary: Le Duc Tho shared the Nobel Prize with Henry Kissinger for his work in negotiating the Vietnam armistice. He refused the award on the grounds that there was no peace in Vietnam. Others bitterly resented the award made to a man dedicated to communism and to wars of liberation. Though his public presence in the long and arduous sessions of negotiation with Kissinger won him international recognition, Le Duc Tho had been known since 1930 as one of the founders of the Indochinese Communist Party and as a powerful figure in the Vietnamese political arena. (R.J.)

1974

MacBride, Sean   518

Prize: Peace, 1974. *Born:* January 26, 1904; Paris, France. *Death:* January 15, 1988; Dublin, Ireland. *Parents:* Father,

John MacBride; Mother, Maud Gonne MacBride. *Nationality:* Irish. *Religion:* Catholic. *Education:* National Univ. of Ireland, law study, 1937. *Spouse:* Catalina Bulfin, married January 26, 1926, died 1976. *Children:* Tiernan, son; Anna, daughter. *Career:* Irish Republican Army, 1918–24; Ireland, Journalist, 1924–37; Ireland, Attorney, 1937–47; Ireland and United Nations, Attorney and Politician, 1947–88. *Other Awards:* International Gaelic Hall of Fame, 1974; Man of the Year, Irish United Societies, 1975; Lenin International Prize, 1977; Medal of Justice, U.S., 1978; International Institute of Human Rights Medal, 1978; UNESCO Silver Medal, 1980; Dag Hammarskjold Peace Prize, 1981.

Selected Publications: Civil Liberty. n.p., 1948. *Our People—Our Money.* 3 lectures. Dublin: Browne and Nolan, 1949. *Ireland; Economy; Report on Italian Economic Situation.* n.p., 1955. *Report on Current Economic Situation in Western Europe.* n.p., 1956. *The Right to Refuse to Kill.* Geneva: International Peace Bureau, 1971. *Israel in Lebanon.* Hollywood, CA: Evergreen Distr., 1983.

For More Information See: New York Times Biographical Edition. (October 1974): 1459. *Time* 104 (October 21, 1974): 18. Jordan, A. *Sean MacBride.* Dublin: Blackwater Press, 1993.

Commentary: Sean MacBride was awarded the Nobel Prize for his lifelong commitment to rights actions, including his work on human rights, on peace and disarmament, and on the liberation of Namibia from South African rule. MacBride's youthful militancy in the Irish Republican Army, his years as a successful attorney, and his political prowess were invaluable assets in a number of important international posts, including committee responsibilities and officerships in the Council of Ministers of the Council of Europe, the Council of OEEC, the Pan European Union, the International Commission of Jurists, the Council of Minorities Rights Group, the International Peace Bureau, Amnesty International, the U.N. Commission for Namibia, and the UNESCO Study Group on Communication Problems. (T.N.B.)

Sato, Eisaku   519

Prize: Peace, 1974. *Born:* March 27, 1901; Tabuse, Yamaguchi, Japan. *Death:* June 2, 1975; Tokyo, Japan. *Parents:* Father, Hidesuke Sato; Mother, Moyo Sato. *Nationality:* Japanese. *Religion:* Shinto. *Education:* Tokyo Imperial Univ., Japan, law degree, 1924. *Spouse:* Hiroku Sato, married February 25, 1926. *Children:* Ryotaro, son; Shinji, son. *Career:* Japanese Government, posts to Prime Minister, 1924–72.

For More Information See: Current Biography Yearbook. New York: H.W. Wilson Co., 1965, 361–64, and 1975–76, 473. Gray, Tony. *Champions of Peace.* New York: Paddington Press, 1976, 302–05. *New York Times.* June 3, 1975, 1:36.

Commentary: Eisaku Sato was awarded the Nobel Peace Prize for his determined antimilitarism and a "reconciliation policy that contributed to a stabilization of conditions in the Pacific area." His winning of the Nobel Prize capped a 48-year career of service to Japan, including eight years as prime minister. (W.E.W.)

1975

Sakharov, Andrei Dmitriyevich   **520**

Prize: Peace, 1975. *Born:* May 21, 1921; Moscow, USSR. *Death:* December 14, 1989; Moscow, USSR. *Parents:* Father, Dmitri Sakharov; Mother, Ekaterina Sofiano. *Nationality:* Russian. *Religion:* From Russian Orthodox background. *Education:* Moscow State Univ., USSR, B.A., 1942; Lebedev Institute of Physics, Soviet Academy of Sciences, USSR, Ph.D., 1947. *Spouse:* Klaudia Vikhereva, married July 10, 1943, died 1969; Yelena G. Bonner, married January 7, 1972. *Children:* Tatiana Andreyevna, daughter; Lyubov Andreyevna, daughter; Dmitri Andreyevich, son; Tatiana Yankelevich, daughter (from Bonner's first marriage; Alexei Semyenov, son (from Bonner's first marriage) *Career:* Lebedev Institute of Physics, USSR, Professor, 1945–80; Internal Exile, 1980–86. *Other Awards:* Stalin Prize; Order of Socialist Labor Award, 1953, 1956, 1962; Eleanor Roosevelt Peace Award, 1973; Cino del Duca Prize, Univ. of Chicago, 1974; Reinhold Niebohr Prize, Univ. of Chicago, IL, 1974; Order of Lenin, USSR; Fritt Ord Prize, 1980.

Selected Publications: Progress, Coexistence, and Intellectual Freedom. New York: Norton, 1968. *Sakharov Speaks.* New York: Knopf, 1974. *My Country and the World.* New York: Knopf, 1975. *Alarm and Hope.* New York: Vintage Books, 1978. *Collected Scientific Works.* London: Penguin, 1982. *Moscow and Beyond, 1986–1989.* New York: Knopf, 1991.

For More Information See: Babyonyshev, Alexander. *On Sakharov.* New York: Knopf, 1982. Bonner, Yelena G. *Alone Together.* London: Collins Harvill, 1986. *Current Biography Yearbook.* New York: H.W. Wilson, 1971, 361–63. *Memoirs.* London: Hutchinson, 1990.

Commentary: Andrei Sakharov was cited by the Committee in that "Sakharov's fearless personal commitment in upholding the fundamental principles for peace between men is a powerful inspiration for all true work for peace." Sakharov was a brilliant physicist, noted as the father of the Soviet hydrogen bomb, before embarking in the 1960s on his lifelong pursuit of, first, educational and scientific thought reform in the Soviet Union, and, later, intellectual freedom and a democratic socialism that would bring the United States and the Soviet Union together in cooperative efforts. (S.K.)

1976

Corrigan, Mairead   **521**

Prize: Peace, 1976. *Born:* January 27, 1944; Belfast, Northern Ireland. *Parents:* Father, Andrew Corrigan; Mother, Margaret Corrigan. *Nationality:* Irish. *Religion:* Catholic. *Education:* No college degrees. *Spouse:* Jack Maguire, married September 8, 1981. *Children:* 2. *Career:* Textile factory, Belfast, Ireland, Bookkeeper, 1960–65; Guiness Son and Company, Belfast, Ireland, Secretary, 1965–76; Peace People, Founder and Administrator, 1976-. *Other Awards:* Carl von Ossietzky Medal, Berlin, 1976; People's Peace Prize, Norway, 1976; Hall of Fame, United States, 1977.

Selected Publications: "A Mother Pleads for Peace." *Parade* (December 29, 1985) 14–16.

For More Information See: Current Biography Yearbook. New York: H.W. Wilson, 1978, 88–91. Deutsch, Richard. *Mairead Corrigan, Betty Williams.* Translated by Jack Bernard. Woodbury, NY: Barron's, 1977. Hershey, Robert D. "Nobels Go to 2 Ulster Women and to Amnesty International." *New York Times* (October 11, 1977): 1+.

Commentary: The award citation praised both Mairead Corrigan and Betty Williams because they had "acted from a profound conviction that the individual can make a meaningful contribution to peace through constructive reconciliation" and had "paved the way for the strong resistance against violence and misuse of power, which was present in broad circles of the people." Corrigan's impetus for starting the Irish group Peace People came from the killing of three of her nieces and nephews by a car driven by a terrorist who had been shot. After her sister's death, she married her brother-in-law, Jack Maguire. She remains an active worker for peace. (K.J.H.)

Williams, Elizabeth   **522**

Prize: Peace, 1976. *Born:* May 22, 1943; Andersonstown, Belfast, Northern Ireland. *Parents:* No record found. *Nationality:* Irish. *Religion:* Catholic (mother)/Protestant (father) background. *Education:* No college degrees. *Spouse:* Ralph Williams, married June 14, 1961, dissolved, 1982; James T. Perkins, married 1982. *Children:* Paul, son; Deborah, daughter. *Career:* Ireland, Clerk and Waitress, 1961–76; Community of Peace People, Ireland, Leader, 1976-. *Other Awards:* Carl von Ossietsky Medal for Courage, 1976; Norwegian People's Peace Prize, 1976.

Selected Publications: Occasional Writer for *Peace by Peace*, 1976–86.

For More Information See: Current Biography Yearbook. New York: H.W. Wilson, 1979, 434–37. Deutsch, Richard. *Mairead Corrigan, Betty Williams.* Translated by Jack Bernard. Woodbury, NY: Barron's, 1977.

Commentary: Betty Williams shared the Nobel Prize with Mairead Corrigan in recognition of the fact that "their initiative paved the way for the strong resistance against violence and misuse of power which was present in broad circles of the people." Shocked into action by her witnessing of the accidental death in a terrorist incident of Corrigan's three nieces and nephews and the subsequent death of Corrigan's sister, Anne Maguire, Betty Williams, along with Corrigan, launched the organization, Peace People, with the goal of ending the fighting and killing in Ireland. The organization, under Williams's leadership, has remained a force in Ireland and in the world. (T.B.)

1977

Amnesty International   **523**

Prize: Peace, 1977. *Founded:* 1961 in London, England

Commentary: The prize was given to Amnesty International in 1977, the Year of Prisoners of Conscience, "for the contribution the organization has made to protect this group of prisoners against treatment which ignores human rights. With its work for the protection of human rights against degradation, violence, and torture, Amnesty International has contributed to securing a foundation for dignity, and thereby, also for peace in the world." (G.N.W.)

1978

Begin, Menachem Wolfovitch   **524**

Prize: Peace, 1978. *Born:* August 16, 1913; Brest-Litovsk, Poland. *Death:* March 9, 1992; Jerusalem, Israel. *Parents:* Father, Zeev-Dov Begin; Mother, Hassia Kossovsky Begin. *Nationality:* Polish; later Israeli citizen. *Religion:* Jewish. *Education:* Univ. of Warsaw, Poland, Masters of Jurisprudence, 1935. *Spouse:* Aliza Arnold, married 1939, died 1982. *Children:* Benjamin, son; Hassia, daughter; Leah, daughter. *Career:* Betar Zionist Youth Movement, Staff and Administrator, 1929–40; Israeli Affairs and Political Posts to Prime Minister, 1942–83.

   Selected Publications: The Revolt: Story of the Irgun. Tr. by Shmuel Katz. New York: Schuman, 1951. *White Nights: The Story of a Prisoner in Russia.* Tr. by Katy Kaplan. London: MacDonald, 1957. *In the Underground.* Tel Aviv: Hadar, 1975, 1977.

   For More Information See: Current Biography Yearbook. New York: H.W. Wilson Co., 1978, 41–45. Gervasi, Frank Henry. *The Life and Times of Menaham Begin: Rebel to Statesman.* New York: Putnam, 1979. Herschler, Gertrude, and Eckman, Lester S. *Menahem Begin: From Freedom Fighter to Statesman.* New York: Shengold Publishers, 1979. Silver, Eric, *Begin: A Biography.* London: Weidenfeld and Nicolson, 1984. Seidman, H. *Menachem Begin.* New York: Shengold, 1990. *New York Times Biographical Service* (March 10, 1992): 286.

   Commentary: Menachem Begin shared the Nobel Prize for his "contribution to the two frame agreements on peace in the Middle East, and on peace between Egypt and Israel, which were signed at Camp David on September 17, 1978." Begin's entire public career was dedicated to the achievement and perpetuation of a Jewish state, first as a rebel, then as a Knesset hawk, and finally as prime minister and peace negotiator. (I.S.Z.)

El-Sadat, Muhammed Anwar   **525**

Prize: Peace, 1978. *Born:* December 25, 1918; Mit Abul-Kum, Minufiyah Province, Egypt. *Death:* October 6, 1981; Cairo, Egypt. *Parents:* Father, Muhammed El-Sadat; Mother, no record found. *Nationality:* Egyptian. *Religion:* Muslim. *Education:* Royal Military Academy, Egypt, baccalaureate, 1938. *Spouse:* Ekbal Mohammed Madi, married 1938; divorced (no date); Jihan Safwat Raouf, married May 29, 1949. *Children:* By first wife: Rokaya, daughter; Rawia, daughter; Camelia, daughter. By second wife: Gamal, son; Lubna, daughter; Noha, daughter; Jihan, daughter. *Career:* Egyptian Army and Political posts to President, 1938–81. *Other Awards:* Sinai Medal, 1974; Man of the Year, *Time*, 1977; Methodist Peace Prize, 1978.

   Selected Publications: Revolt on the Nile. Tr. by Thomas Graham. London: A. Wingate, 1957. *In Search of Identity: An Autobiography.* New York: Harper & Row, 1978. *Speeches and Interviews by President Anwar el-Sadat.* Cairo: Arab Republic of Egypt, Ministry of Information, 1971–79. *The Public Diary of President Sadat.* Ed. by Raphael Israeli. Leiden, Netherlands: Brill, 1979.

   For More Information See: Current Biography Yearbook. New York: H.W. Wilson Co., 1971, 358–61. Hirst, David, and Beeson, Irene. *Sadat.* London: Faber and Faber, 1981. Narayan, B.K. *Anwar el-Sadat: Man with a Mission.* New Delhi: Vikas Publishers, 1977. Sadat, Camelia. *My*

Father and I. New York: Macmillan, 1985. Finklestone, J. *Anwar Sadat.* Essex, England: Frank Case, 1995.

   Commentary: Anwar Sadat shared the Nobel Prize for his "contribution to the two frame agreements on peace in the Middle East, and on peace between Egypt and Israel, which were signed at Camp David on September 17, 1978." In the wake of the October War of 1973, Sadat increasingly sought conciliation with the Israelis, culminating in his historic trip to Jerusalem in November 1977. Substantive agreements were reached at the Camp David talks and a peace treaty was signed in March 1979. This was the highlight of a career-long involvement in Egyptian military and political life, which included a role in the overthrow of the Farouk monarchy. (I.S.Z.)

1979

Teresa, Mother (Bojaxhiu, Agnes Gonxha)   **526**

Prize: Peace, 1979. *Born:* August 27, 1910; Skopje, Yugoslavia. *Death:* September 5, 1997; Calcutta, India. *Parents:* Father, Nikola Bojaxhiu; Mother, Dranofile Bernai Bojaxhiu. *Nationality:* Yugoslavian; later Indian citizen. *Religion:* Catholic. *Spouse:* None. *Children:* None. *Career:* Sisters of Loretto, Teacher and Principal, 1928–48; Missionaries of Charity, 1948–97. *Other Awards:* Padma Shri Lotus Order, 1962; Magsaysay Prize, 1963; Good Samaritan Prize, 1970; Joseph Kennedy Jr. Foundation Award, 1971; Pope John XXIII Peace Prize, 1971; Jawaharlal Nehru Award of India, 1972; Templeton Prize for Progress in Religion, 1973; Saint Louise de Marillac Award, 1973; Albert Schweitzer Award, 1975; Balzan Award, Italy, 1979; Bharat Ratna Award (Star of India), 1980.

   Selected Publications: Life in the Spirit: Reflections, Meditations, Prayers. New York: Harper & Row, 1983. *A Simple Path.* New York: Ballentine, 1995. *In My Own Words.* Liguori, MO: Liguori Publications, 1996. *No Greater Love.* Novato: CA: New World Library, 1997.

   For More Information See: Current Biography Yearbook. New York: H.W. Wilson, 1973, 403–06. Egan, Eileen. *Such a Vision of the Street.* New York: Doubleday, 1985. Muggeridge, Malcolm. *Something Beautiful for God.* New York: Walker, 1984. Rae, Daphne. *Love Until It Hurts: The Work of Mother Teresa and Her Missionaries of Charity.* New York: Harper & Row, 1981. Spink, Kathryn. *The Miracle of Love: Mother Teresa of Calcutta, Her Missionaries of Charity and Her Co-Workers.* New York: Harper & Row, 1982. Shaw, S. *Mother Theresa of Calcutta.* Ann Arbor, MI: Servant Publications, 1994.

   Commentary: In announcing Mother Teresa of Calcutta as the winner of the 1979 Nobel Peace Prize, the Committee said, "This year, the world has turned its attention to the plight of children and refugees, and these are precisely the categories for whom Mother Teresa has for many years worked so selflessly." As a Sister of Loretto, she taught and was principal of St. Mary's High School in Calcutta for 20 years before being inspired to leave the cloister to work among the destitute, the dying, and the orphaned children in the slums of Calcutta. Since founding her order, the Society of the Missionaries of Charity, in 1950, Mother Teresa's work among the poorest of the poor has spread to 50 Indian cities and more than 25 countries. The order operates schools, hospitals, youth centers, and orphanages, and 53,000 lepers are among the patients treated at medical centers in Africa and Asia. (P.E.J.)

1980

Pérez Esquivel, Adolfo 527

Prize: Peace, 1980. *Born:* November 26, 1931; Buenos Aires, Argentina. *Parents:* No record found. *Nationality:* Argentinian. *Religion:* Catholic. *Education:* National School of Fine Arts, Argentina, graduate, 1956. *Spouse:* Amanda Perez, married 1956. *Children:* Leopoldo, son; 2 other sons. *Career:* Manuel Belgrano Escuela Nacionál de Bellas Artes, Buenos Aires, Argentina, Professor, 1956–73; Service for Justice and Peace in Latin America, Founder and Secretary General, 1973-. *Other Awards:* Premio La Nacion de Escultura; Memorial Juan XXIII, Instituto de Poledogia Victor Seix, Barcelona, Spain, 1977.

Selected Publications: Paz y Justicia, Founder and Editor, 1973-. *Christ in a Poncho.* New York: Orbis Books, 1983.

For More Information See: Current Biography Yearbook. New York: H.W. Wilson, 1981, 321–24. *New York Times Biographical Service* (October 14, 1980): 1455–56. *1980 Vela de Armas.* Mexico City: Las Ediciones del Tiempo, 1980, 315–16, 473.

Commentary: Adolfo Pérez Esquivel was honored as "a spokesman of a revival of respect of human rights . . . having shone a light through the darkness" of Argentina's military rule. Pérez Esquivel left a distinguished career as a sculptor to become a human rights activist and Catholic church lay leader, coordinating human rights efforts in Argentina and in all of Latin America. He was mistreated and jailed by the Argentinian military government for 14 months early in his career without charge or trial but has persisted in his efforts through the Service for Justice and Peace, which he founded, and through a women's group, Las Locas de Mayo. (R.A.)

1981

Office of the United Nations High Commissioner for Refugees 528

Prize: Peace, 1981. *Founded:* 1951 by the United Nations

Commentary: The Peace Prize, awarded in recognition of UNHCR's 30th birthday, was their second award (the first was 1954). The UNHCR provides refugees with legal protection from forced repatriation, physical harm, and unjustified detention, as well as assurances of adequate food, clothing, and shelter. (G.N.W.)

1982

García Robles, Alfonso 529

Prize: Peace, 1982. *Born:* March 20, 1911; Zamora, Michoacan, Mexico. *Death:* September 2, 1991; Mexico City, Mexico. *Parents:* Father, Quirino Garcia; Mother, Teresa Robles Garcia. *Nationality:* Mexican. *Religion:* Catholic. *Education:* Univ. of Mexico, law degree, 1933; Univ. of Paris, France, law degree, 1937; Academy of International Law, Netherlands, law degree, 1938. *Spouse:* Juana Maria de Szyszlo, married 1950. *Children:* Alfonso, son; Fernando, son. *Career:* Mexican Government, various posts in Embassies, United Nations, and in Mexico, 1939–91.

Selected Publications: La Anchura del Mar Territorial. Mexico: Collegio de Mexico, 1966. *Seis Anos de la Política Exterior de Mexico* (*Six Years of Mexican Foreign Policy*). Tlatelolco, Mexico: Secretaria de Relaciones Exteriores, 1976. *La Conferencia de Revision del Tratado Sobre la No Proliferación de las Armas Nucleares* (*The Review Conference on the Non-Proliferation Treaty*). Mexico City: Editorial de El Colegio Nacional, 1977. *338 Dias de Tlatelolco* (*338 Days of Tlatelolco*). Mexico: Fondo de Cultura Economica, 1977.

For More Information See: Christian Century (November 3, 1982): 1097. *New York Times Biographical Service* (October 14, 1982): 1305. *New York Times Biographical Service* (September 4, 1991): 915.

Commentary: The Nobel Prize awarded to Alfonso García Robles was "not only a reward for almost twenty years of work on disarmament, but also vindication of the virtues of patient and methodical negotiation." García Robles's major contribution was the Treaty of Tlatelolco, written to ban nuclear weapons from Latin America in the 60s, and signed by 22 nations. Although dedicated to disarmament, he has also been a national and international spokesperson for Mexico in a number of important government and United Nations posts that date back to 1939. His documents on Mexico's position on the Law of the Sea in the late 50s are notable as well. (R.A.)

Myrdal, Alva Reimer 530

Prize: Peace, 1982. *Born:* January 31, 1902; Uppsala, Sweden. *Death:* February 1, 1986; Stockholm, Sweden. *Parents:* Father, Albert Reimer; Mother, Lova Larsson Reimer. *Nationality:* Swedish. *Religion:* Lutheran. *Education:* Univ. of Stockholm, Sweden, B.A., 1924; Univ. of Uppsala, Sweden, M.A., 1934. *Spouse:* Gunnar Myrdal, married October 8, 1924. *Children:* Jan, son; Sissela Bok, daughter; Kaj Ffolster, daughter. *Career:* Stockholm, Sweden, Teacher, 1924–32; Central Prison, Stockholm, Sweden, Psychologist, 1932–34; Training College for Preschool Teachers, Stockholm, Sweden, Director, 1935–48; United Nations, New York, Administrator, 1949–55; Swedish Government, Ambassador and Minister, 1955–73; Center for the Study of Democratic Institutions, Santa Barbara, CA, Researcher, 1973–74; Massachusetts Institute of Technology, Professor, 1974–75; Wellesley College, MA, Professor, 1976–77; Institute for Research on Poverty, Madison, WI, Researcher, 1977–78. *Other Awards:* West German Peace Prize, 1970; Wateler Prize, Hague Academy of International Peace, 1973; Prize, Royal Swedish Institute of Technology, 1975; Monismanien Prize, 1976; Gold Medal, Royal Swedish Academy of Science, 1977; Albert Einstein Peace Prize, 1980; People's Peace Prize, Norway, 1981; Nehru Award, 1981.

Selected Publications: Crisis in the Population Question. Stockholm: A. Bonnier, 1934 (with Gunnar Myrdal). *Women in the Community.* Copenhagen: TARP, 1943. *Women's Two Roles: Home and Work.* Copenhagen: Routledge and Kegan Paul, 1956. *Our Responsibility for the Poor Peoples: Development Problems at Close View.* Copenhagen: Raben and Sjoegren, 1961. *The Game of Disarmament.* New York: Pantheon, 1977, rev. ed. 1982.

For More Information See: Contemporary Authors. Detroit: Gale, 1978 (Volume 69–72), 448–50. *New York*

Times Biographical Service (October 1982): 1367–68. Bok, S. *Alva Myrdal.* Reading, MA: Addison Wesley Publishing Co., 1991.

Commentary: Alva Myrdal received the Nobel Prize for her obsessive work in the latter part of her life in pursuit of disarmament. Her early career included many years as a teacher and as a director of teachers' colleges in Sweden, while at the same time working with her husband, Gunnar, also a Nobel Prize winner, in their sociological work on the population problem and in general areas of social philosophy. A later interest was the role of women. Appointed to important United Nations and Swedish posts, Myrdal became a force in national and international policy. (J.G.)

1983

Walesa, Lech (Leszek, Michael)   **531**
Prize: Peace, 1983. *Born:* September 29, 1943; Popowo, Poland. *Parents:* Father, Boleslaw Walesa; Mother, Feliksa Walesa. *Nationality:* Polish. *Religion:* Catholic. *Education:* No college degrees. *Spouse:* Miroslawa Danuta Golos Walesa, married November 8, 1969. *Children:* Bogdan, son; Slawomir, son; Przemyslaw, son; Jaroslaw, son; Magdalena, daughter; Anna, daughter; Maria-Victoria, daughter; Brygida, daughter *Career:* Polish Army, 1963–65; Lenin Shipyard, Gdansk, Poland, Electrician, 1966–76; Polish Labor Leader, 1976–90; President of Poland, 1990–95; Lech Walesa Institute Foundation, Poland, Administrator, 1995-. *Other Awards:* Man of the Year, *Time,* 1981; Love International Award, 1981; Freedom Medal, U.S.A., 1981; Medal of Merit, Polish American Congress, 1981; Peace Prize of Arbetet, 1981; Free World Prize, Norway, 1982; International Democracy Award, 1982; Social Justice Award, 1983; American Friendship Medal, 1983; Humanitarian Public Service Medal, 1984; Pro Fide et Patria Medal, Poland, 1985; International Integrity Award, 1986; Philadelphia Liberty Medal, 1989; U.S. Medal of Freedom, 1989; George Meany Human Rights Award, 1989; Path to Peace Award, U.N., 1996

Selected Publications: Birth of Solidarity. New York: St. Martin's Press, 1983. *A Way of Hope.* New York: Holt, 1987. *The Struggle and the Triumph.* New York: Arcade Publishers, 1992.

For More Information See: Ascherson, Neal. *The Book of Lech Welesa.* New York: Simon & Schuster, 1982. Brolewicz, Walter. *My Brother, Lech Walesa.* New York: Tribeca Communications, 1983.*Current Biography Yearbook.* New York: H.W. Wilson, 1981, 436–39. "Lech! Lech! Lech!" *New York Times Magazine* (October 23, 1988): 36–46.

Commentary: Lech Walesa was granted the Nobel Prize for his efforts through negotiation and nonviolent protest to gain the right for Polish workers to organize freely. Walesa was involved in labor unrest almost from his first working day and eventually (in 1976) lost his electrician's position because of his activities. He was one of the founders of the free trade union on the Baltic Coast in 1979, the forerunner of the large union Solidarity, which Walesa has guided since its beginnings. Harassed constantly and jailed by Polish leaders, Walesa remains a symbol to Polish labor and the

Polish people, with his activities "characterized by a determination to solve his country's problems through negotiation and cooperation without resorting to violence." (J.H.S.)

1984

Tutu, Desmond Mpilo   **532**
Prize: Peace, 1984. *Born:* October 7, 1931; Klerksdorp, Witwatersrand, Transvaal, South Africa. *Parents:* Father, Zachariah Tutu; Mother, Aletta Tutu. *Nationality:* South African. *Religion:* Anglican. *Education:* Bantu Normal College, South Africa, Teacher's Diploma, 1953; Univ. of South Africa, B.A., 1954; St. Peter's Theological College, South Africa, L.Th., 1960; King's College (Univ. of London), England, B.D., 1966; King's College (Univ. of London), England, M.Th., 1966. *Spouse:* Leah Nomalizo Shenxane, married July 2, 1955. *Children:* Trevor, son; Naomi, daughter; Mpho, daughter; Theresa Thandi, daughter. *Career:* South Africa, Schoolmaster, 1954–57; Anglican Church, South Africa, Parish Priest and various administrative positions, 1960–96. *Other Awards:* Athena Prize, Onassis Foundation, Greece, 1980; Family of Man Gold Medallion, 1983; M.L. King, Jr. Humanitarian Award, 1984; M.L. King, Jr. Peace Award, 1986; International Integrity Award, 1986; Albert Schweitzer Humanitarian Award, 1988; Third World Prize, 1989; Distinguished Peace Leadership Award, 1990.

Selected Publications: Crying in the Wilderness: The Struggle for Justice in South Africa. London: A.R. Mowbray and Co., 1982. *Hope and Suffering: Sermons and Speeches.* Johannesburg: Skotaville Publishers, 1983. *Rainbow People of God.* New York: Doubleday, 1994. *African Prayer Book.* New York: Doubleday, 1995. *No Future Without Forgiveness.* New York: Doubleday, 1999.

For More Information See: Current Biography Yearbook. New York: H.W. Wilson, January 1985, 40–44. "Gifts Seen and Heard." *Commonweal* III (November 30, 1984): 645–46. Hammer, Joshua. "Urging Nonviolent Change in His Tortured Land: South Africa's Desmond Tutu Wins the Nobel Prize." *People* 22 (December 17, 1984): 185–87. Lantier-Sampson, P. *Desmond Tutu.* Milwaukee: G. Stevens Children's Books, 1991.

Commentary: The Nobel Prize Committee indicated that Bishop Desmond Tutu's recognition "should be regarded not only as a gesture of support to him and to the South African Council of Churches of which he is leader, but also to all individuals and groups in South Africa who, with their concern for human dignity, fraternity and democracy, incite the admiration of the world." Tutu has been outspoken for much of his life against apartheid, South Africa's system of strict race separation. In 1984 and 1985, he became personally involved in intervening to defuse violence and in advocating the withdrawal of foreign investments from South Africa. (P.P.F.)

1985

International Physicians for the Prevention of
   Nuclear War, Inc.   **533**
Prize: Peace, 1985. *Founded:* 1980 in Boston, MA

Commentary: This was one of the most controversial awards in the history of the Prize. According to the committee, the Physicians for the Prevention of Nuclear War "performed a considerable service to mankind by spreading authoritative information and by creating an awareness of the catastrophic consequences of atomic warfare." The award was meant as a message to President Reagan and Secretary Gorbachev, who were to have a summit meeting six weeks later. (G.N.W.)

1986

Wiesel, Elie 534

Prize: Peace, 1986. *Born:* September 30, 1928; Sighet, Romania. *Parents:* Father, Shlomo Wiesel; Mother, Sarah Feig Wiesel. *Nationality:* Romanian; later resident in France; American citizen. *Religion:* Jewish. *Education:* No college degrees. *Spouse:* Marion Erster Rose, married 1969. *Children:* Shlomo-Elisha, son. *Career:* Writer and lecturer; City College, City Univ. of New York, Professor, 1972–76; Boston Univ., MA, Professor, 1976-. *Other Awards:* Prix Rivarol, 1963; Ingram Merrill Award, 1964; Eleanor Roosevelt Memorial Award, 1972; American Liberties Medallion, 1972; Martin Luther King Medallion, City College of New York, 1973; Jewish Book Council Literary Award, 1965, 1973; Rambam Award, 1974; Jewish Heritage Award, 1975; First Spertus International Award, 1976; King Solomon Award, 1977; Humanitarian Award, 1978; Joseph Prize for Human Rights, 1978; Zalman Shazar Award, Israel, 1979; Jabotinsky Medal, 1980; S.Y. Agnon Medal, 1980; International Literary Prize for Peace, 1983; A. Scharansky Humanitarian Award, 1983; Congressional Medal of Achievement, 1985; Anne Frank Award, 1985; Medal of Liberty Award, 1986; Golda Meir Humanitarian Award, 1987; Primo Levi Award, 1992; Presidential Medal of Freedom, 1992; Jewish Book Council Lifetime Literary Achievement Award, 2001.

Selected Publications: Night. New York: Hill and Wang, 1960. *Dawn.* New York: Hill and Wang, 1961. *The Accident.* New York: Hill and Wang, 1962. *The Town Beyond the Wall.* New York: Holt, Rinehart and Winston, 1964. *The Gates of the Forest.* New York: Holt, Rinehart and Winston, 1966. *A Beggar in Jerusalem.* New York: Random House, 1970. *The Oath.* New York, Random House, 1973. *The Fifth Son.* New York: Summit, 1985. *All Rivers Run to the Sea.* New York: Knopf, 1995. *And the Sea is Never Full.* New York: Knopf, 1999.

For More Information See: Abrahamson, Irving. *Against Silence: The Voice and Vision of Elie Wiesel.* New York: Schocken, 1984. Brown, Robert. *Elie Wiesel.* South Bend, IN: Univ. of Notre Dame Press, 1984. Cargas, Harry. *In Conversation with Elie Wiesel.* Mahwah, NJ: Paulist Press, 1976. *A Jew Today.* New York: Random House, 1978. *From the Kingdom of Memory.* New York: Schocken Books, 1995.

Commentary: The Peace Award was granted to Elie Wiesel for his self-accepted mission as "a messenger to mankind: his message is one of peace, atonement and human dignity." Wiesel is a committed Jew who survived two Nazi concentration camps and found himself after years of searching. His autobiographical *Night* (1958) hauntingly evokes images of the Holocaust, explores what it means to be Jewish, and examines the tortuous journey from the living death of the concentration camp to life. In his later writings, the laureate introduced the element of hope, but a hope that is shadowed by the lurking specter of disaster. Wiesel's

mission of helping oppressed minorities extended to various groups and causes throughout the world. (J.H.S.)

1987

Arias Sanchez, Oscar 535

Prize: Peace, 1987. *Born:* September 13, 1941; Heredia, Costa Rica. *Parents:* Father, Juan Rafael Arias Trejos; Mother, Lilian Sanchez. *Nationality:* Costa Rican. *Religion:* Most probably Christian. *Education:* Univ. of Costa Rica, law degree, 1967; London School of Economics, England, doctorate. *Spouse:* Margarita Penon Longora, married 1973. *Children:* Silvia Eugenia, daughter; Oscar Felipe, son. *Career:* Univ. of Costa Rica, Professor, 1969–72; Politician, 1972-. *Other Awards:* Philadelphia Liberty Medal, 1991

Selected Publications: Grupos de Presion en Costa Rica. San Jose, Costa Rica: Editorial Costa Rica, 1971; *Who Governs?* San Jose, Costa Rica: Educa, 1976; *Dawn of a New Political Era.* San Jose, Costa Rica: Presidencia de la Republica, 1987.

For More Information See: Abrams, Irwin. "Behind the Scenes." *Antioch Review* 46 (Summer 1988). *New York Times* (October 14, 1987): A1.

Commentary: Oscar Arias Sanchez was cited by the Academy for his "outstanding contribution to the possible return of stability and peace to a region long torn by strife and civil war." Arias was the impetus behind an agreement that he hoped would end the long-time controversies involving Nicaragua, Guatemala, Costa Rica, El Salvador, and Honduras. This was one of the few times that the Nobel for Peace was awarded in an attempt to promote political initiatives that were deemed positive by the Academy. In this case, the endorsement did not succeed in producing a peaceful or permanent solution to the conflicts in the area. (J.H.S.)

1988

United Nations Peace-Keeping Forces 536

Prize: Peace, 1988. *Founded:* Founded 1948

Commentary: The prize was awarded to the peace keepers in trouble spots around the world. In the committee's eyes, they represented "the manifest will of the community of nations to achieve peace."

1989

Dalai Lama, the Fourteenth (Tsering, Tensin) 537

Prize: Peace, 1989. *Born:* July 6, 1935; Taktser, Tibet. *Parents:* Father, Chujon Tsering; Mother, Dekyi Tsering. *Nationality:* Tibetan. *Religion:* Tibetan Buddhist (Lamaist). *Spouse:* None. *Children:* None. *Career:* Religious and political activist, 1940-.

Selected Publications: My Land and My People. New York: McGraw-Hill, 1962. *The Opening of the Wisdom Eye and the History of the Advancement of Buddhadharma in Tibet.* Bangkok: Social Science Association Press of Thailand, 1968. *The Buddhism of Tibet and the Key to the Middle Way.* New York: Harper & Row, 1975. *Freedom in Exile.* New York: HarperCollins, 1990.

For More Information See: Goodman, Michael H. *The Last Dalai Lama: A Biography.* Boston: Shambhala, 1987.

Gould, Basil. *Report on the Discovery, Recognition, and Installation of the Fourteenth Dalai Lama.* New Delhi, India: n.p., 1941. *The Dalai Lama: A Policy of Kindness.* Ithaca, NY: Snow Lion Publishers, 1993.

Commentary: The Dalai Lama received the Nobel Prize in recognition of his nonviolent campaign to end China's long domination of his homeland. The Nobel committee praised him for "advocating peaceful solution based upon tolerance and mutual respect in order to preserve the historical and cultural heritage of his people." In exile since he fled Chinese occupation forces in 1959, the Dalai Lama traveled around the world, preaching the nonviolent Buddhist philosophy and working for Tibet's future. The Fourteenth Dalai Lama successfully passed all the requisite tests at the age of five, and was confirmed, as the true reincarnation, by the State Oracle of Tibet. (S.L.)

1990

Gorbachev, Mikhail Sergeyevich 538

Prize: Peace, 1990. *Born:* March 2, 1931; Privolnoye, USSR. *Parents:* Father, Sergei Andreevich Gorbachev; Mother, Maria Panteleyvna Gorbacheva. *Nationality:* Russian. *Religion:* No record found. *Education:* Moscow State Univ., USSR, law degree, 1955. *Spouse:* Raisa Maksimovna Gorbacheva, married 1953, died 1999. *Children:* Irina, daughter. *Career:* Communist Party Official and Soviet Politician, 1952–91; President, USSR, 1990–91; International Foundation for Social and Economic and Political Research, Administrator, 1991-. *Other Awards:* Order of Lenin, USSR (3 times); Order of Red Banner of Labor, USSR, 1949; Indira Gandhi Award, 1987; Peace Award, World Methodist Council, 1990; Albert Schweitzer Leadership Award, 1992; Ronald Reagan Freedom Award, 1992.

Selected Publications: The Coming Century of Peace. New York: Eagle Publishing, 1986. *Speeches and Writing.* 2 volumes. New York: Pergamon, 1986–87. *Moratorium.* Moscow: Novosti P.R., 1986. *Perestroika.* New York: Harper & Row, 1988. *Memoirs.* New York: Doubleday, 1996. *On My Country and the World.* New York: Columbia Univ. Press, 2000.

For More Information See: Butson, Thomas. *Gorbachev.* New York: Stein and Day, 1985. Zemtsov, Ilya, and John Farrar. *Gorbachev.* New Brunswick, NJ: Transaction, 1989. Ruge, G. *Gorbachev.* London: Chatto and Windus, 1991.

Commentary: Mikhail Gorbachev won the Nobel for his "decisive contributions [to the] dramatic changes that have taken place in the relationship between East and West." Gorbachev's relaxation of the rigid control policies of previous Soviet leaders allowed the breakdown of the Berlin wall in Germany and the breakdown of more intangible walls between the peoples of the world inside and outside the "Iron Curtain." Gorbachev was equally well known for the two policies of glasnost (openness or political coexistence) and perestroika (a move toward a free market economy). (B.S.S./J.H.S.)

1991

Aung San, Suu Kyi 539

Prize: Peace, 1991. *Born:* June 19, 1945; Rangoon, Burma. *Parents:* Father, Bogyoke Aung San; Mother, Khin Kyi

Aung San. *Nationality:* Burmese. *Religion:* Most probably Buddhist. *Education:* Oxford Univ., England, B.A., 1967. *Spouse:* Michael Vaillancourt Aris, married 1972. *Children:* Alexander, son; Kim, son. *Career:* United Nations, New York, Researcher, 1968–71; Foreign Ministry, Bhutan, Researcher, 1972–74; Indian Institute of Advanced Study, Simla, India, Researcher, 1986–87; National League for Democracy, Rangoon, Burma, Leadership Role, 1988-; House arrest, 1989–95. *Other Awards:* Rafto Memorial Prize, 1990; Sakharov Prize, 1991; Bellisario Prize, 1992; Simon Bolivar Prize, 1992.

Selected Publications: The Political Legacy of Aung San. Ithaca, NY: Cornell Univ., 1972; *Burma and India.* New Delhi, India: Indian Institute of Advanced Study, 1990. *Freedom From Fear.* New York: Penguin, 1991. *Towards a True Refuge.* Oxford: Perpetua Press, 1993. *Voice of Hope.* New York: Seven Stories Press, 1997.

For More Information See: Current Biography Yearbook. New York, NY: H.W. Wilson Co., 1992, 27–31. Parenteau, J. *Prisoner for Peace.* Greensboro, NC: Morgan Reynolds, 1994.

Commentary: Suu Kyi Aung San was under house arrest in Burma when she won the Nobel, recognizing her as "the leader of a democratic opposition that employs nonviolent means to resist a regime characterized by brutality." The Committee noted the desire "to show its support for the many people throughout the world who are striving to attain democracy, human rights, and ethnic conciliation by peaceful means." From August 1988, when she joined a pro-democracy movement in Burma, until July 1989, when she disappeared from sight, Aung San, daughter of a legendary Burmese hero, galvanized the people of Burma into support of democratic reform in a country governed by a military junta since 1962. Aung San was released from house arrest in 1995. She was the first Burmese and second Asian to win the Nobel Prize in Peace. (S.L.)

1992

Menchu Tum, Rigoberta 540

Prize: Peace, 1992. *Born:* 1959; Chimel, Guatemala. *Parents:* Father, Vicente Menchu; Mother, Juana Menchu. *Nationality:* Guatemalan. *Religion:* Christian. *Spouse:* Angel Canil, married January 17, 1998. *Children:* Tz'unun, son. *Career:* Political activist, 1981-; International Goodwill Ambassador, UNESCO, 1996-.

Selected Publications: I, Rigoberta Menchu. New York, NY: Routledge, 1985. *Crossing Borders.* New York: Verso, 1998.

For More Information See: Brill, M. T. *Journey for Peace.* New York: Dutton, 1996. *Current Biography Yearbook.* New York: H.W. Wilson, 1993, 398–402; Lazo, C. *Rigoberta Menchu.* New York: Dillon Press, 1994.

Commentary: Rigoberta Menchu was awarded the Nobel Peace Prize for her work in Guatemala and in the world because she "stands out as a vivid symbol of peace and reconciliation across ethnic, cultural, and social dividing lines." Menchu's life, devoted to the cause of freedom—a cause for which she witnessed the death of those dearest to her—remains an inspiration for all. The Committee noted that "by maintaining a disarming humanity in a brutal world,

Rigoberta Menchu appeals to the best in us. She stands as a uniquely potent symbol of a just struggle." (J.H.S./B.S.S.)

1993

de Klerk, Frederik Willem   541
Prize: Peace, 1993. *Born:* March 18, 1936; Johannesburg, South Africa. *Parents:* Father, Johannes de Klerk; Mother, Hendrina Cornella Coetzer de Klerk. *Nationality:* South African. *Religion:* Dutch Reform. *Education:* Potchefstroon Univ. for Christian Higher Education, South Africa, B.A., L.L.B., 1958. *Spouse:* Marike Willemse, married April 1959, dissolved, no date; Elita Lanaras Georgiadis, married November 1998. *Children:* Willem, son; Jan, son; Susan, daughter. *Career:* Vereeniging Law Firm, South Africa, Lawyer, 1961–72; Various political posts, South Africa, 1972–97; President, South Africa, 1989–94.

Selected Publications: The Last Trek-A New Beginning. New York: St. Martin's, 1999.

For More Information See: de Klerk, W. *F. W. de Klerk.* Johannesburg, South Africa: Jonathan Ball Publishers, 1991; Kamsteeg, A. *F. W. de Klerk.* Cape Town, South Africa: Vlaeberg Publishers, 1990; Ottaway, D. *Chained Together* New York: Times Books, 1993.

Commentary: F. W. de Klerk received the Nobel jointly with Nelson Mandela for their "constructive policy of peace and reconciliation [which] also points the way to the peaceful resolution of similar deep-rooted conflicts elsewhere in the world." de Klerk initiated the efforts toward peace and toward developing a nonracial democracy while Prime Minister of South Africa, although his racial policies prior to this political turnaround, as well as his previous actions, were the subject of much controversy when the award was announced. (B.S.S./J.H.S.)

Mandela, Nelson   542
Prize: Peace, 1993. *Born:* July 18, 1918; Transkei, South Africa. *Parents:* Father, Gadla Henry Mphakanyiswa Mandela; Mother, Nosekeni Fawny Mandela. *Nationality:* South African. *Religion:* Methodist background. *Education:* Univ. of South Africa, law degree, 1942. *Spouse:* Evelyn Ntoko Mase, married 1944, divorced 1958; Nomzamo Winnie Madikizela, married 1958, separated 1992, divorced 1996; Graca Machel, married July 18, 1998. *Children:* Makgatho, son; Makaziwe, daughter; Zeni, daughter; Zindzi, daughter. *Career:* Attorney, 1952–56; Political activity and offices, 1956-; President, Republic of South Africa, 1994–99. *Other Awards:* Nehru Award, 1979; Kreisky Prize, 1981; Bolívar Prize, 1983; Third World Prize, 1986; Human Rights Prize, 1988; Sakharov Prize, 1988; Gaddafi Prize, 1989; Houphouet Prize, 1991; Asturias Prize, 1992; Human Rights Award, American Jewish Congress, 1993; Mandela-Fulbright Prize, 1993.

Selected Publications: No Easy Walk to Freedom. New York: Basic Books, 1965. *Nelson Mandela Speeches.* New York: Pathfinder Press, 1990; *Nelson Mandela Speaks.* New York: Pathfinder Press, 1993.

For More Information See: Long Walk to Freedom. Boston: Little, Brown and Co., 1994; Ottaway, David. *Chained Together.* New York: Times Books, 1993. *The Struggle Is My Life.* New York: Pathfinder Press, 1990. Sampson, A. *Mandela.* New York: Knopf, 1999.

Commentary: Nelson Mandela was jointly awarded the Nobel with F. W. de Klerk for their "constructive policy of peace and reconciliation [which] also points the way to the peaceful resolution of similar deep-rooted conflicts elsewhere in the world." Long imprisoned as a result of his efforts to secure equality for the black community in South Africa, Mandela, after his release, succeeded with de Klerk in developing a nonracial democracy—which Mandela was later elected to head. (B.S.S./J.H.S.)

1994

Arafat, Yasir (Mohammed Abed Ar'ouf Arafat al Qudwa al-Husseini)   543
Prize: Peace, 1994. *Born:* August 24, 1929; Cairo, Egypt. *Parents:* Father, Abd al-Raouf al-Qudwa al-Husseini; Mother, Zahwa Abu Saud. *Nationality:* Palestinian. *Religion:* Muslim. *Education:* Univ. of Cairo, Egypt, B. Engineering, 1956. *Spouse:* Sulia Tawil, married 1991. *Children:* Zahwa, daughter. *Career:* Revolutionary, 1950-. *Other Awards:* Joliot-Curie Gold Medal, 1975

For More Information See: Gowers, Andrew and Tony Walker. *Arafat.* New York: Interlink Publishing Group, 1994; Hart, Alan. *Arafat.* Bloomington, IN: Indiana Univ. Press, 1989; Wallach, Janet and John Wallach. *In the Eyes of the Beholder.* New York: Carol Publishing Group, 1990

Commentary: Yasir Arafat shared the Nobel Prize with Yitzhak Rabin and Shimon Peres for their "substantial contributions to a historic process through which peace and cooperation can replace war and hate" in the Middle East. All three winners labored diligently to develop a document on Palestinian self-rule. The award, however, was the subject of much controversy. One committee member stepped down to protest Arafat's receipt of the Nobel, and there was a series of bloody events in Israel and the West Bank after the award was presented. But the march toward peace initiated by the three continued to move forward, even after the assasination of Rabin in November 1995. (B.S.S./J.H.S.)

Peres, Shimon   544
Prize: Peace, 1994. *Born:* August 16, 1923; Vishneva, Poland. *Parents:* Father, Yitzhak Isaac Peres; Mother, Sarah Persky Peres. *Nationality:* Israeli. *Religion:* Jewish. *Spouse:* Sonia Gellman, married May 1, 1945. *Children:* Jonathan, son; Nechemia, son; Zvia, daughter *Career:* Israeli politician, 1948-. *Other Awards:* Legion of Honor, 1959.

Selected Publications: David's Sling. London: Weidenfeld and Nicolson, 1970; *From these Men.* New York: Wyndham Books, 1979; *The New Middle East.* New York: Holt, 1993.

For More Information See: Golan, Matti. *The Road to Peace.* New York: Warner Books, 1989; *Battling for Peace.* London: Weidenfeld and Nicolson, 1995.

Commentary: Shimon Peres was jointly awarded the Nobel with Yasir Arafat and Yitzhak Rabin for "their substantial contributions to a historic process through which peace and cooperation can replace war and hate" in the Middle East. Peres was a critical architect of the document which attempted to spell out the steps toward Palestinian self-rule. The awards were the subject of much controversy, and after the announcement, a series of bloody events occurred in Israel and the West Bank. Peace efforts continued by all parties, even so. Peres became prime minister of

Israel after Rabin was assassinated in November 1995. (B.S.S./J.H.S.)

Rabin, Yitzhak 545

Prize: Peace, 1994. *Born:* March 1, 1922; Jerusalem, Israel. *Death:* November 4, 1995; Tel Aviv, Israel. *Parents:* Father, Nehemia Rabin; Mother, Rosa Cohen Rabin. *Nationality:* Israeli. *Religion:* Jewish. *Spouse:* Leah Schlossberg, married August 28, 1948. *Children:* Yuval, son; Dalia, daughter. *Career:* Israeli politician and military leader, 1941–1995.

    Selected Publications: Rodef Shalom (Pursuing Peace). Tel-Aviv: Zemorah-Bitan, 1995.

    For More Information See: Current Biography Yearbook. New York: H.W. Wilson, January 1995. *The Rabin Memoirs.* Boston: Little, Brown, 1979 (Berkeley: Univ. of California Press, 1996, expanded ed.). Slater, Robert. *Rabin of Israel.* New York: St. Martin's Press, Inc., 1993.

    Commentary: Yitzhak Rabin, Shimon Peres, and Yasir Arafat shared the Peace Prize for their "substantial contributions to a historic process through which peace and cooperation can replace war and hate" in the Middle East. Rabin, as Prime Minister of Israel, received both praise and blame—praise from those who saw peace as worth any price, and blame from those who foresaw dire consequences from Palestinian self-rule as spelled out in the documents prepared by the three laureates. After the announcement of the awards, a series of bloody events occurred in Israel and the West Bank, but peace efforts continued unabated. Rabin was assassinated in November 1995 by an Israeli student opposed to Rabin's policies of giving up land for peace. (B.S.S./J.H.S.)

1995

Pugwash Conferences on Science and World Affairs 546

Prize: Peace, 1995. *Founded:* 1957 in Pugwash, Nova Scotia.

    Commentary: The Peace Prize was divided equally between the Pugwash Conferences and Joseph Rotblat, one of the conferences' charter members and current presiding officer. In 1955, Rotblat joined Albert Einstein, Bertrand Russell, and six other scientists in signing a manifesto that led to the founding of the annual conferences, which have lobbied to convince governments to discontinue the construction and use of nuclear armaments. The conferences were praised by the committee for recognizing "the responsibility of scientists for their inventions" and for bringing together "scientists and decision makers to collaborate across political divides on constructive proposals for reducing the nuclear threat." (G.N.W.)

Rotblat, Joseph 547

Prize: Peace, 1995. *Born:* November 4, 1908; Warsaw, Poland. *Parents:* Father, Zygmunt Rotblat; Mother, Sonia Rotblat. *Nationality:* Polish, later British citizen. *Religion:* Jewish. *Education:* Free Univ. of Poland, M.A., 1932; Univ. of Warsaw, Poland, Ph.D., 1938; Univ. of Liverpool, England, Ph.D., 1950; Univ. of London, England, D.Sc., 1953. *Spouse:* No record found. *Children:* No record found. *Career:* Univ. of Warsaw, Poland, Researcher, 1933–39; Liverpool Univ., England, Professor, 1939–49; Univ. of

London, England, Professor, 1950–76. *Other Awards:* Russell Society Award, 1983; Order of Merit, Poland, 1987; Einstein Peace Prize, 1992; Bajej Foundation Prize, 1999; Toda Peace Prize, 2000.

    Selected Publications: Scientists, the Arms Race, and Disarmament. Bristol, PA: Taylor and Francis, 1982; *Coexistence, Cooperation, and Common Security.* New York: St. Martin's, 1988; *Striving for Peace, Security, and Development in the World.* River Edge, NJ: World Scientific Publication, 1991.

    For More Information See: New York Times (October 14, 1995): A1.

    Commentary: Joseph Rotblat shared the Nobel with the organization he heads, the Pugwash Conferences on Science and World Affairs, for their continuing effort "to diminish the part played by nuclear arms in international politics, and in the longer run, to eliminate such arms." Rotblat, a refugee from the Holocaust, worked on developing the atomic bomb in the Manhattan Project, but left that effort late in the second World War as a protest. He also left nuclear physics after the war to work on applying physics to medical research. Since that time, he has worked on the cause of peace, along with other prominent scientists, including Bertrand Russell and Albert Einstein. (B.S.S./J.H.S.)

1996

Belo, Carlos Filipe Ximenes 548

Prize: Peace, 1996. *Born:* February 3, 1948; Wailakama, Baucau, East Timor. *Parents:* Father: Domingo Vaz Felipe; Mother: Ermelinda Baptista Felipe. *Nationality:* East Timorese. *Religion:* Catholic. *Education:* Salesian Pontifical Univ., Italy, bachelor's degree in theology, no date. *Spouse:* None. *Children:* None. *Career:* Catholic Priest, 1980-; Catholic Bishop, 1983-.

    Selected Publications: Demi keadilan dan perdamaian. Dili: Komisi Keadilan, 1997 (with others).

    For More Information See: America 175 (December 14, 1996): 6–7. Kohen, Arnold. *From the Place of the Dead.* New York: St. Martin's Press, 1999. *New York Times* (October 12, 1996): A6.

    Commentary: Carlos Belo shared the Nobel Peace Prize with José Ramos-Horta for "their work towards a just and peaceful solution to the conflict in East Timor." Indonesia invaded East Timor in 1975 and "began systematically oppressing the people." Bishop Belo is considered the "foremost representative of the people of East Timor. At the risk of his own life, he has tried to protect his people from infringements by those in power." In making the award to Belo and Ramos-Horta, the Nobel Committee wanted to "honour their sustained and self-sacrificing contributions for a small but oppressed people." (L.S.S.)

Ramos-Horta, José 549

Prize: Peace, 1996. *Born:* December 26, 1949; Dili, East Timor. *Parents:* Father, Francisco Horta; Mother, Natalina Ramos Filipe Horta. *Nationality:* East Timorese. *Religion:* Catholic. *Education:* Antioch College, OH, M.A., 1984. *Spouse:* Ana Pessoa, married 1978, divorced, no date. *Children:* 1 son. *Career:* Political activist; Journalist, 1969–74; Minister for External Affairs, East Timor, 1975;

U.N. Representative from Fretilin, NY, 1976–89; Univ. of New South Wales, Australia, Professor and Administrator, 1990–99; East Timor News Agency, Journalist, 2000-. *Other Awards:* Thorolf Raftol Human Rights Award, 1993; Gleitzman Foundation Award, 1995;

Selected Publications: Funu: The Unfinished Saga of East Timor. Trenton, NJ: Red Sea Press, 1987. *Timor Leste: amanha em Dili.* Lisbon:Dom Quixote, 1994.

For More Information See: Economist 341(December 14, 1996): 34. *New York Times* (October 12, 1996): A6.

Commentary: José Ramos-Horta shared the Nobel Peace Prize with Carlos Belo for "their work towards a just and peaceful solution to the conflict in East Timor." Invaded by Indonesia in 1975, Ramos-Horta fled East Timor. Living in Australia, Ramos-Horta, considered the leading spokesman for the East Timorese cause, was cited for his "significant contribution through the 'reconciliation talks' and by working out a peace plan for the region." In making this award, the Nobel Committee hoped it would "spur efforts to find a diplomatic solution to the conflict in East Timor based on the people's right to self-determination." (L.S.S.)

1997

International Campaign to Ban Landmines (ICBL)   550

Prize: Peace, 1997. *Founded:* 1992; Washington, D.C.

Commentary: The Nobel Peace Prize was awarded jointly to the International Campaign to Ban Landmines (ICBL) and to Jody Williams, the campaign's coordinator, "for their work for the banning and clearing of anti-personnel mines." The ICBL is a network of affiliated organizations "through which it has been possible to express and mediate a broad wave of popular commitment in an unprecedented way. . . . This work has grown into a convincing example of an effective policy for peace." (L.S.S.)

Williams, Jody   551

Prize: Peace, 1997. *Born:* October 9, 1950; Rutland, VT. *Parents:* No record found. *Nationality:* American. *Religion:* No record found. *Education:* Univ. of Vermont, VT, B.A., 1972; School for International Training, VT, M.A., 1976; Johns Hopkins Univ., MD, M.A., 1984. *Spouse:* None. *Children:* None. *Career:* Human Rights Activist; Nicaragua-Honduras Education Project, Washington, DC, Coordinator, 1984–86; Medical Aid for El Salvador, CA, Deputy Director, 1986–92; International Campaign to Ban Landmines, Washington, DC, Founder and Ambassador, 1991–2000. *Other Awards:* None.

Selected Publications: "Social Consequences of Widespread Use of Landmines," *Landmine Symposium.* Montreux, Switzerland: International Committee of the Red Cross, April 1993. *After the Guns Fall Silent.* Washington, D.C.: Vietnam Veterans of American Foundation, 1995 (with Shawn Roberts). "Landmines and Measures to Eliminate Them," *International Review of the Red Cross,* no. 307 (July-August 1995). "The Protection of Children Against Landmines and Unexploded Ordinance" in *Impact of Armed Conflict on Children,* U.N. Document A/51/306, 26 August 1996. "Landmines: Dealing with the Environmental Impact," *Environmental Security* (1997).

For More Information See: Current Biography Yearbook 1998. New York: H.W. Wilson, 1998, 612–14. *Maclean's* 110 (October 10, 1997): 32. *New York Times* (September 20, 1997): A5.

Commentary: The Nobel Peace Prize was awarded jointly to the International Campaign to Ban Landmines (ICBL) and to Jody Williams, the campaign's coordinator, "for their work for the banning and clearing of anti-personnel mines." In just a few short years, Jody Williams and the ICBL began a process that culminated in a treaty to ban landmines that was signed by more than 100 countries, but not the United States, China or Russia in December 1997. The Nobel Committee hoped that the Ottawa process would become a model for similar processes and that "it could prove of decisive importance to the international effort for disarmament and peace." (L.S.S.)

1998

Hume, John   552

Prize: Peace, 1998. *Born:* January 18, 1937; Londonderry, Northern Ireland. *Parents:* Father, Samuel Hume; Mother, Anne Doherty Hume. *Nationality:* Irish. *Religion:* Catholic. *Education:* St. Patrick's College, Ireland, B.A., no date; National Univ. of Ireland, M.A., no date. *Spouse:* Patricia Hone, married December 29, 1960. *Children:* 2 sons; 3 daughters. *Career:* Politician, Northern Ireland, 1969-. *Other Awards:* St. Thomas Moore Award, 1991.

Selected Publications: Personal Views. Dublin: Town House, 1996. *A New Ireland.* Boulder, CO: Roberts Rinehart Publishers, 1997 (with others).

For More Information See: New York Times (October 17, 1998): A7. Routledge, Paul. *John Hume.* London: HarperCollins, 1997. White, Barry. *John Hume: Statesman of the Troubles.* Belfast: Blackstaff Press, 1984.

Commentary: The Nobel Peace Prize was awarded to John Hume and David Trimble "for their efforts to find a peaceful solution to the conflict in Northern Ireland." John Hume was cited as "the clearest and most consistent of Northern Ireland's political leaders in his work for a peaceful solution" which resulted in a peace agreement signed in April 1998. (L.S.S.)

Trimble, William David   553

Prize: Peace, 1998. *Born:* October 15, 1944; Belfast, Northern Ireland. *Parents:* Father, William Trimble; Mother, Ivy Trimble. *Nationality:* Irish. *Religion:* Protestant. *Education:* Queen's Univ., Ireland, law degree, 1968. *Spouse:* 1st wife, married, no date, divorced, no date; Daphne Elizabeth Orr, married, 1978. *Children:* Richard, son; Victoria, daughter; Nicholas, son; Sarah, daughter. *Career:* Irish Politician, 1973-; Queen's Univ., Ireland, Professor, 1968–90.

For More Information See: Current Biography Yearbook 2000. New York: H.W. Wilson, 2000, 561–64. *New York Times* (October 17, 1998): A7.

Commentary: The Nobel Peace Prize was awarded to David Trimble and John Hume "for their efforts to find a peaceful solution to the conflict in Northern Ireland." Trimble "showed great political courage when, at a crucial stage of the process, he advocated solutions which led to the peace agreement." Noting as well the positive contributions of others to the peace process, the Norwegian Nobel Committee cited Trimble for his efforts "towards building up the mutual confidence on which a lasting peace must be based." (L.S.S.)

1999

Médecins Sans Frontières (MSF)   554
Prize: Peace, 1999. *Founded:* 1971; France

Commentary: Médecins Sans Frontières was awarded the Nobel Peace Prize for adhering to "the fundamental principle that all disaster victims, whether the disaster is natural or human in origin, have a right to professional assistance, given as quickly and efficiently as possible." The MSF, also called Doctors Without Borders, is known for humanitarian assistance to all with no regard for politics or national borders. (L.S.S.)

2000

Kim Dae-Jung   555
Prize: Peace, 2000. *Born:* December 3, 1925; Hukwang-ri Haewi-myon, Shinangun, Korea. *Parents:* Father, Kim Un-shik; Mother, Chang Soo-keum. *Nationality:* South Korean. *Religion:* Catholic. *Education:* Kyunghee Univ., South Korea, M.A., 1970; Diplomatic Academy of Foreign Ministry, Russia, Ph.D., 1992. *Spouse:* Cha Yong-ae, married 1944, died 1959; Hee-ho Lee, married May 10, 1962. *Children:* Hong-il, son; Hong-up, son; Hong-gul, son. *Career:* Politician, South Korea, 1954-; President, South Korea, 1998- *Other Awards:* Bruno Kreisky Human Rights Award, 1981; Human Rights Award, North American Coalition for Human Rights in Korea, 1984; George Meany Human Rights Award, 1987; Union Theological Seminary Medal, 1994; Philadelphia Liberty Medal, 1999.

Selected Publications: Mass Participatory Economy in Korea. Lanham, MD: Univ. Press of America, 1971, rev. ed., 1985. *Prison Writings.* Berkeley: Univ. Calif. Press, 1987. *A New Beginning.* Los Angeles: Center for Multiethnic and Transnational Studies, 1996.

For More Information See: Goldstein, Norm. *Kim Dae-jung.* Philadelphia: Chelsea House, 1998. *New York Times* (October 14, 2000): A6.

Commentary: Kim Dae-Jung was awarded the Nobel Peace Prize "for his work for democracy and human rights in South Korea and in East Asia in general, and for peace and reconciliation with North Korea in particular." A former political prisoner, Kim, through his "sunshine policy," has "attempted to overcome more than fifty years of war and hostility between North and South Korea." By awarding the Peace Prize to the South Korean President, the Committee expressed the hope "that the cold war will also come to an end in Korea." (L.S.S.)

Physics

1901

Roentgen, Wilhelm Conrad 556

Prize: Physics, 1901. *Born:* March 27, 1845; Lennep, Germany. *Death:* February 10, 1923; Munich, Germany. *Parents:* Father, Friedrich Conrad Roentgen; Mother, Charlotte Constanze Frowein Roentgen. *Nationality:* German. *Religion:* Lutheran. *Education:* Polytechnic, Switzerland, engineering diploma, 1868; Polytechnic, Switzerland, Ph.D., 1869. *Spouse:* Anna Bertha Ludwig, married January 19, 1872. *Children:* None; but adopted wife's niece, Josephine Bertha. *Career:* Univ. of Zürich, Switzerland, Researcher, 1869; Univ. of Würzburg, Germany, Researcher, 1870–72; Univ. of Strasbourg, Germany, Professor, 1872–75; Agricultural Academy, Hohenheim, Germany, Professor, 1875–76; Univ. of Strasbourg, Germany, Professor, 1876–79; Univ. of Giessen, Germany, Professor, 1879–88; Univ. of Würzburg, Germany, Professor, 1888–1900; Univ. of Munich, Germany, Professor, 1900–23. *Other Awards:* Rumford Medal, Royal Society, 1896; Royal Order of Merit, Bavaria, 1896; Baumgaertner Prize, Vienna Academy, 1896; Elliot-Cresson Medal, Franklin Institute, Philadelphia, PA, 1897; Prize Lacaze, Paris, 1897; Mattencei Medal, Rome, 1897; Otto-Wahlbuch-Stiftung Prize, Hamburg, 1898; Order of Merit of St. Michael, I class, 1900; Silver Medal of Prince Regent Luitpold, 1900; Barnard Medal, Columbia Univ., NY, 1900; Komitur of the Order of the Italian Crown, 1900; Order Pour le Mérite for Science and Art, France, 1911; Helmholtz Medal, Germany, 1919.

Selected Publications: "On a New Kind of Rays, a Preliminary Communication." *Sitzungsberichte Phys.-Med. Ges. Würzburg* (1895): CPhysicsVII. "On a New Kind of Rays, Continued." *Sitzungsberichte Phys.-Med. Ges. Würzburg* (1896): XI. "Further Observations on the Properties of X-rays." *Math. u. Naturw. Mitt. a.d. Sitzungsberichte Preuss. Akad. Wiss., Physik.-Math. Kl.* (1897): 392.

For More Information See: Dictionary of Scientific Biography. New York: Scribner's, 1975 (Volume 11), 529–31. Glasser, Otto. *Dr. W.C. Roentgen.* Springfield, IL: Thomas, 1945. Nitske, W. Robert. *The Life of Wilhelm Conrad Roentgen, Discoverer of the X-ray.* Tucson, AZ: Univ. of Arizona Press, 1971.

Commentary: Wilhelm Roentgen, first recipient of the Nobel Prize in Physics, was cited "in recognition of the extraordinary merit gained by the discovery of the special rays bearing his name." Although the award was made for a single surprise discovery, Roentgen had spent 28 years quietly contributing carefully done work that laid part of the foundation for much of the theory of thermodynamics, mechanics, and electricity. His discovery of X-rays remains his stunning contribution in that it opened the doors to modern physics and, in great measure, to modern surgery and medical treatment. (T.S.)

1902

Lorentz, Hendrik Antoon 557

Prize: Physics, 1902. *Born:* July 18, 1853; Arnhem, Netherlands. *Death:* February 4, 1928; Haarlem, Netherlands. *Parents:* Father, Gerrit Frederik Lorentz; Mother, Geertruida van Ginkel Lorentz. *Nationality:* Dutch. *Religion:* Protestant. *Education:* Univ. of Leiden, Netherlands, B.Sc., 1871; Univ. of Leiden, Netherlands, Ph.D., 1875. *Spouse:* Aletta Kaiser, married 1881. *Children:* Geertruida Luberta, daughter; Johanna Wilhelmina, daughter; Rudolf, son; fourth child died in infancy. *Career:* Univ. of Leiden, Netherlands, Professor, 1878–1912; Teyler Laboratory, Haarlem, Netherlands, Director, 1912–23. *Other Awards:* Rumford Medal, Royal Society, 1908; Copley Medal, Royal Society, 1918.

Selected Publications: Lectures on Theoretical Physica. 8 volumes. London: Macmillan and Co., 1927–31. *H.A. Lorentz, Collected Papers.* 9 volumes. The Hague: M. Nijhoff, 1934–39.

For More Information See: de Haas-Lorentz, G.L. *H.A. Lorentz. Impressions of His Life and Work.* Tr. by Joh. C. Fagginer Auer. Amsterdam: North-Holland Publishing Co., 1957. *Dictionary of Scientific Biography.* New York: Scribner's, 1973 (Volume 8), 487–500.

Commentary: Hendrik Lorentz shared the Nobel Prize with Pieter Zeeman "in recognition of the extraordinary service they rendered by their researches into the influence of magnetism upon radiation phenomena." Beginning with his doctoral work on reflection and refraction of light, Lorentz changed the face of optics and electricity in a long and fruitful career. His first major contribution was a formula relating light velocity to the density and composition of the medium through which it passed. His general theory of the electrical and optical properties of moving bodies followed. Next came the concept of the electron, which paved the way for molecular and quantum theories. Lorentz's work in electromagnetism and motion led to the Einstein theory of relativity. He also pioneered in the science of hydraulics. (A.S.)

Zeeman, Pieter 558

Prize: Physics, 1902. *Born:* May 25, 1865; Zonnemaire Zeeland, Netherlands. *Death:* October 9, 1943; Amsterdam, Netherlands. *Parents:* Father, Catharinus Farandinus Zeeman; Mother, Wilhelmina Worst Zeeman. *Nationality:* Dutch. *Religion:* Lutheran. *Education:* Univ. of Leiden, Netherlands, Ph.D., 1893. *Spouse:* Johanna Elisabeth Lebret, married 1895. *Children:* 3 daughters; 1 son. *Career:* Univ. of Leiden, Netherlands, Professor, 1893–97; Univ. of Amsterdam, Netherlands, Professor, 1897–1935. *Other Awards:* Gold Medal, Netherlands Scientific Society of Haarlem, 1892; Rumford Medal, Royal Society, 1922.

Selected Publications: Researches in Magneto-Optics. London: Macmillan, 1913. *Verhandelingen van Dr. P. Zeeman over Magneto-Optische Verschijnselen.* Leiden,

Netherlands: E. Ijdo, 1921. Velthuys-Bechthold, P. *Inventory of the Papers of Pieter Zeeman.* Haarlem, Netherlands: Rijksarchief in Noord-Holland, 1993.

For More Information See: Dictionary of Scientific Biography. New York: Scribner's, 1973 (Volume 10), 524–26. *Obituary Notices of Fellows of the Royal Society of London* 4 (1944): 591–95.

Commentary: Pieter Zeeman and Hendrik Lorentz received the Nobel Prize "in recognition of the extraordinary service they rendered by their researches into the influence of magnetism upon radiation phenomena." Zeeman devoted his early career to studying the interrelationships between magnetism and light. The Zeeman effect refers to the widening and splitting of spectral lines by a magnetic field and added to the evidence for an electromagnetic theory of light. Zeeman also studied the absorption and motion of electricity in fluids, magnetic fields on the sun's surface, the Doppler effect, the effect of nuclear magnetic moments on spectral lines, and mass spectrography of Ar-38 and Ni-64. (A.S.)

1903

Becquerel, Antoine Henri   559

Prize: Physics, 1903. *Born:* December 15, 1852; Paris, France. *Death:* August 25, 1908; Le Croisic, France. *Parents:* Father, Alexander Edmond Becquerel; Mother, no record found. *Nationality:* French. *Religion:* Most probably Christian. *Education:* École des Pontes-et-Chaussees, France, ingenieur, 1877; École des Pontes-et-Chaussees, France, docteur-es-sciences, 1888. *Spouse:* Lucie-Zoe-Marie Jamin, married 1874, died 1878; Louise-Desiree Lorieux, married 1890. *Children:* Jean, son. *Career:* École Polytechnique, Paris, France, Professor, 1876–1908; concurrently employed at Museum of Natural History, National Administration of Bridges and Highways, and National Conservatory of Arts and Trades. *Other Awards:* Legion of Honour, France, 1900; Rumford Medal, 1908; Barnard Medal, 1908; Helmholtz Medal, 1908.

Selected Publications: "Emission de Radiations Nouvelles par l'Uranium Metallique." *Comptes Rendus de l'Académie des Sciences, Paris* 122 (1896): 1086–88. "Sur Diverses Proprietes des Rayons Uraniques." *Comptes Rendus de l'Académie des Sciences, Paris* 123 (1896): 855–58. "Sur le Rayonnement des Corps Radio-Actifs." *Comptes Rendus de l'Académie des Sciences, Paris* 129 (1899): 1205–07. "Sur la Radioactivite de l'Uranium." *Comptes Rendus de l'Académie des Sciences, Paris* 133 (1901): 977–80. "Recherches sur Une Propriete Nouvelle de la Matiere. Activite Radiante Spontanee ou Radioactivite de la Matiere." *Memories de l'Académie des Sciences, Paris* 46 (1903).

For More Information See: Dictionary of Scientific Biography. New York: Scribner's, 1970 (Volume 1), 558–61. Ranc, Albert. *Henri Becquerel et la Decouverte de la Radioactivite.* Paris: Éditiones de la Liberté, 1946.

Commentary: Henri Becquerel was cited by the Academy "in recognition of the extraordinary services he has rendered by his discovery of spontaneous radioactivity." In addition to that monumental discovery, Becquerel performed pioneer research in the areas of light polarization, light absorption, phosphorescence, and terrestrial magnetism. (B.S.S.)

Curie, Marie (Sklodowska, Maria) *See* entry 11

Curie, Pierre   560

Prize: Physics, 1903. *Born:* May 15, 1859; Paris, France. *Death:* April 19, 1906; Paris, France. *Parents:* Father, Eugene Curie; Mother, Sophie-Claire Depoully Curie. *Nationality:* French. *Religion:* Anticlerical; from Protestant background. *Education:* Univ. of Paris-Sorbonne, France, licence es sciences, 1875; Univ. of Paris-Sorbonne, France, licence in physical sciences, 1877; Univ. of Paris-Sorbonne, France, doctor of science, 1895. *Spouse:* Marie Sklodowska, married July 25, 1895. *Children:* Irene, daughter; Eve, daughter. *Career:* Univ. of Sorbonne, France, Researcher, 1878–82; Univ. of Sorbonne, France, Professor, 1882–1906. *Other Awards:* La Caze Prize, Académie des Sciences, 1901; Davy Medal, Royal Society, 1903; Matteuci Gold Medal, Italian Society of Sciences, 1904.

Selected Publications: Oeuvres de Pierre Curie. Paris: Gauthier-Villars, 1908.

For More Information See: Curie, M. *Pierre Curie.* Tr. by Charlotte and Vernon Kellogg. New York: Macmillan, 1923. *Dictionary of Scientific Biography.* New York: Scribner's, 1971 (Volume 3), 503–08.

Commentary: Pierre Curie shared the Nobel Prize with Marie Curie and A. Becquerel "in recognition of the special services rendered by them in the work they jointly carried out in investigating the phenomena of radiation discovered by Professor Becquerel." Curie was also responsible for pioneer magnetic studies. The Curie point, the temperature at which a substance changes its magnetic properties, is named after him. He also studied the piezo-electric properties of crystals and developed sensitive instrumentation to permit such study. (V.C.)

1904

Strutt, John William (Lord Rayleigh)   561

Prize: Physics, 1904. *Born:* November 12, 1842; Lanford Grove, Essex, England. *Death:* June 30, 1919; Witham, Essex, England. *Parents:* Father, John James Strutt; Mother, Clara Elizabeth La Touche Vicars Strutt. *Nationality:* British. *Religion:* Spiritualist; from Anglican background. *Education:* Cambridge Univ., England, B.A., 1865. *Spouse:* Evelyn Balfour, married 1871. *Children:* Robert John, son; Arthur Charles, son; Julian, son. *Career:* Cambridge Univ., England, Laboratory Director, 1879–84; Royal Institute, England, Professor, 1887–1905; Cambridge Univ., England, Chancellor, 1908–19. *Other Awards:* Royal Medal, 1882; Bressa Prize, Italy, 1891; Hodgkins Prize, Smithsonian, 1895; Matteuci Medal, Italy, 1895; Barnard Medal, Columbia Univ., NY, 1895; Faraday Medal, Chemical Society, 1895; Copley Medal, 1899; Albert Medal, Royal Society of the Arts, 1905; Rumford Medal, 1914; Cresson Medal, Franklin Institute, 1914.

Selected Publications: The Theory of Sound. 2 volumes. London: Macmillan, 1877–78. *Scientific Papers.* 6 volumes. Cambridge: Cambridge Univ. Press, 1899–1920.

For More Information See: Dictionary of Scientific Biography. New York: Scribner's, 1976 (Volume 13), 100–07. Lindsay, Robert. *Lord Rayleigh.* Elmsford, NY: Pergamon, 1970. Strutt, Robert John. *Life of John William Strutt.* Madison: Univ. of Wisconsin Press, 1965.

Commentary: Lord Rayleigh received the Nobel Prize "for his investigations into the density of the most important gases, and for his discovery of argon in connection with these investigations." His success was attributable to both his development of new experimental techniques and his ability to explain the experimental results obtained. In his career, he touched many facets of physics-electricity, optics, capillarity, the gas laws, and sound. Probably his most-remembered contribution is the explanation of why the sky is blue. (L.M.)

1905

Lenard, Philipp Eduard Anton von   **562**
Prize: Physics, 1905. *Born:* June 7, 1862; Pressburg, Hungary. *Death:* May 20, 1947; Messelhausen, Germany. *Parents:* Father, Philipp Lenard; Mother, Antonia Baumann Lenard. *Nationality:* Hungarian; later German citizen. *Religion:* Protestant. *Education:* Univ. of Heidelberg, Germany, Ph.D., 1886. *Spouse:* Katherine Schlehner, married 1897. *Children:* Werner, son; others, no record found. *Career:* Univ. of Heidelberg, Germany, Researcher, 1887–90; Univ. of Bonn, Germany, Researcher, 1891–94; Univ. of Breslau, Germany, Professor, 1894–95; Technische Hochschule, Aachen, Germany, Professor, 1895–96; Univ. of Heidelberg, Germany, Professor, 1896–98; Univ. of Kiel, Germany, Professor, 1898–1907; Univ. of Heidelberg, Germany, Professor, 1907–31. *Other Awards:* Rumford Medal, Royal Society, 1904; Franklin Medal, Franklin Institute, 1905.

Selected Publications: Über Kathodenstrahlen. Leipzig, Germany: J.A. Barth, 1906. *Über Aether und Materie.* Heidelberg, Germany: C. Winter, 1911. *Über Relativitatsprinzip, Aether, Gravitation.* Leipzig, Germany: S. Hirzel, 1920.

For More Information See: Dictionary of Scientific Biography. New York: Scribner's, 1973 (Volume 8), 180–83. *Nobel Prize Winners: Physics.* Pasadena, CA: Salem Press, 1988, Volume 1, 87–95.

Commentary: The Committee cited Philipp Lenard "for his work in connection with cathode rays," in which he studied their magnetic deflection and electrostatic properties. Lenard also made significant contributions to the theory of the structure of atoms, to falling drop theory, to the phenomena of magnetism and luminescence, and to the understanding of spectral lines. His ability to contribute, however, was sadly marred by his lifelong pathological anti-Semitism, which did not allow him to accept the work of the Jewish giants in physics and later made him a willing supporter of Hitler and "Aryan Physics." (M.N.C.)

1906

Thomson, Joseph John, Sir   **563**
Prize: Physics, 1906. *Born:* December 18, 1856; Manchester, England. *Death:* August 30, 1940; Cambridge, England. *Parents:* Father, Joseph James Thomson; Mother, Emma Swindells Thomson. *Nationality:* British. *Religion:* Anglican. *Education:* Owens College, England, engineering degree, 1876; Cambridge Univ., England, B.A., 1880. *Spouse:* Rose Elisabeth Paget, married 1890. *Children:* George Paget, son; Joan, daughter. *Career:* Cambridge Univ., England, Professor, 1883–1918. *Other Awards:* Royal Medal, Royal Society, 1894; Hughes Medal, 1902; Hodgkins Medal, Smithsonian Institution, 1902; Knighthood, 1908; Order of Merit, 1912; Copley Medal, Royal Society, 1914; Franklin Medal, 1923; Scott Medal, 1923; Mescart Medal, Paris, 1927; Guthrie Medal and Prize, 1928; Dalton Medal, 1931; Faraday Medal, Institution of Civil Engineers, 1938.

Selected Publications: A Treatise on the Motion of Vortex Rings. London: Macmillan, 1883. *Elements of the Mathematical Theory of Electricity and Magnetism.* Cambridge: Cambridge Univ. Press, 1895. *The Conduction of Electricity Through Gases.* Cambridge: Cambridge Univ. Press, 1903. *Electricity and Matter.* Westminster, England: Constable, 1904. *The Corpuscular Theory of Matter.* New York: Scribner's, 1907. *Atomic Theory.* Oxford: Clarendon Press, 1914.

For More Information See: Biographical Memoirs of the Fellows of the Royal Society. London: Royal Society, 1939–41 (Volume 3), 587–609. *Dictionary of Scientific Biography.* New York: Scribner's, 1976 (Volume 13), 362–72. *Obituary Notices of Fellows of the Royal Society.* London: Royal Society, 1941 (Volume 3), 587. Rayleigh, Robert J.S. *The Life of J.J. Thomson.* Cambridge: Cambridge Univ. Press, 1943. Thomson, J.J. *Recollections and Reflections.* London: G. Bell, 1936.

Commentary: The Nobel award to J.J. Thomson was "in recognition of his merits for the theoretic and experimental study of the conduction of electricity through gases." During his long career at Cambridge, Thomson established a center for experimental work on the discharge of electricity through gases and on chemical analysis with the aid of positive electric rays. He also carried out significant investigations on the structure of atoms and developed a model of atomic structure which was important to theoretical physics until it was replaced by the Rutherford model in 1913. (S.G.)

1907

Michelson, Albert Abraham   **564**
Prize: Physics, 1907. *Born:* December 19, 1852; Strelno, Germany. *Death:* May 9, 1931; Pasadena, CA. *Parents:* Father, Samuel Michelson; Mother, Rosalie Przlubska Michelson. *Nationality:* German; later American citizen. *Religion:* Jewish. *Education:* United States Naval Academy, MD, baccalaureate, 1873. *Spouse:* Margaret McLean Hemingway, married April 10, 1877, divorced, 1897; Edna Stanton, married December 23, 1899. *Children:* Albert Hemingway, son; Truman, son; Elsa, daughter; Madeline, daughter; Dorothy, daughter; Beatrice, daughter. *Career:* United States Naval Academy, MD, Professor, 1875–79; Germany and France, Student, 1879–82; Case School of Applied Science, Cleveland, OH, Professor, 1883–89; Clark Univ., MA, Professor, 1889–93; Univ. of Chicago, IL, Professor, 1893–1929. *Other Awards:* Rumford Medal, Royal Society, 1889; Grand Prix, Paris Exposition, 1900; Matteuci Medal, Rome, Italy, 1904; Copley Medal, Royal Society, 1907; Elliot Cresson Medal, 1912; Draper Medal, National Academy of Sciences, 1916.

Selected Publications: Velocity of Light. Chicago: Univ. of Chicago Press, 1902 *Light Waves and Their Uses.* Chicago: Univ. of Chicago Press, 1903. *Studies in Optics.* Chicago: Univ. of Chicago Press, 1927.

For More Information See: *Biographical Memoirs.*
National Academy of Sciences. Washington, DC: National
Academy of Sciences, 1938 (Volume 19), 120–47. *Diction-
ary of Scientific Biography.* New York: Scribner's, 1974
(Volume 9), 371–74. Livingston, Dorothy M. *The Master of
Light: A Biography of Albert A. Michelson.* New York:
Scribner's, 1973.

Commentary: Albert Michelson was the recipient of the
Nobel Prize "for his optical precision instruments and the
spectroscopic and metrological investigations carried out
with their aid." Although remembered for his painstaking
measurements of the velocity of light, Michelson also developed the echelon spectrograph and astrophysical spectroscopy, measured the rigidity of the Earth, and was a leader in
producing high-quality optical gratings. (C.G. and L.S.)

1908

Lippmann, Gabriel Jonas   **565**
Prize: Physics, 1908. *Born:* August 16, 1845; Hollerich,
Luxembourg. *Death:* July 13, 1921; at sea. *Parents:* No
record found. *Nationality:* French. *Religion:* Jewish. *Edu-
cation:* Heidelberg Univ., Germany, Ph.D.; Univ. of Paris-
Sorbonne, France, D.Sc., 1875. *Spouse:* (No first name
found) Cherbuliez, married 1888. *Children:* None. *Career:*
Sorbonne Univ., Paris, France, Professor, 1878–1921.

Selected Publications: "Extension du Principe de Carnot
à la Theorie des Phenomenes Electriques." *Comptes Rendus
de l'Académie des Sciences* 82 (1876): 1425. "Photographies
Colorées du Spectre, sur Albumine et sur Gelatine Bichro-
matees." *Comptes Rendus de l'Académie des Sciences* 115
(1892): 575. "Sur un Coelostat." *Comptes Rendus de
l'Académie des Sciences* 120 (1895): 1015.

For More Information See: *Annales de Physique* 16
(1921): 156. *Dictionary of Scientific Biography.* New York:
Scribner's, 1981 (Volume 7), 387–88. Lebon, Ernest. *Gabriel Lippmann.* Paris: Gauthier-Villars, 1911.

Commentary: Gabriel Lippmann was awarded the Nobel
Prize "for his method, based on the interference phenomenon, for reproducing colours photographically." Lippmann
possessed a far-ranging research mind which contributed to
the fundamental principles of optics, photochemistry, electricity, and thermodynamics. In addition to his photographic
work, his development of a sensitive capillary electrometer
and his research with pendulum clocks and astronomical
devices are usually mentioned. (V.A.H.)

1909

Braun, Karl Ferdinand   **566**
Prize: Physics, 1909. *Born:* June 6, 1850; Fulda, Germany.
Death: April 20, 1918; Brooklyn, NY. *Parents:* Father,
Konrad Braun; Mother, Franziska Göhring Braun. *Nationality:* German. *Religion:* Christian. *Education:* Univ. of
Berlin, Germany, Ph.D., 1872. *Spouse:* Amelie Bühler,
married 1885. *Children:* Conrad, son; 1 other son; 2 daughters. *Career:* Univ. of Würzburg, Germany, Researcher,
1872–74; St. Thomas Gymnasium, Leipzig, Germany, Professor, 1874–76; Univ. of Marburg, Germany, Professor,
1876–80; Univ. of Strasbourg, France, Professor, 1880–83;
Technical High School, Karlsruhe, Germany, Professor,
1883–85; Univ. of Tübingen, Germany, Professor, 1885–95;
Univ. of Strasbourg, France, Professor, 1895–1915.

Selected Publications: *Über den Einfluss von Steifigkeit,
Befestigung und Amplitude auf die Schwingungen von Saiten.*
Berlin: Druck von G. Schade, 1872. *Über Elektrische
Kraftübertragung Inbesondere über Drehstrom.* Tübingen,
Germany: H. Laupp'sche Buchhandlung, 1892. *Drahtlose
Telegraphie durch Wasser und Luft.* Leipzig, Germany: Veit
and Co., 1901. *Anleitung für das Photographieren von
Tieren.* Berlin: Deutsche Landwirtschafts-Gesellschaft, 1927.

For More Information See: *Dictionary of Scientific
Biography.* New York: Scribner's, 1970 (Volume 2), 427–28.
Nobel Prize Winners: Physics. Pasadena, CA: Salem Press,
1988, Volume 1, 137–45.

Commentary: Karl Braun was cited by the Academy,
along with his colaureate, Guglielmo Marconi, for "contributions to the development of wireless telegraphy." Braun
refined cathode-ray tubes, invented the oscillograph, and
introduced crystal rectifiers, but he is remembered principally for his modification of the Marconi transmitting system to permit greater range. He also made significant
contributions in his study of the oscillations of strings and
elastic rods, of thermodynamics, and of electricity (specifically, the theory of Ohm's Law and the calculation of the
electromotive force of reversible galvanic elements from
thermal sources). (C.S.)

Marconi, Guglielmo   **567**
Prize: Physics, 1909. *Born:* April 25, 1874; Bologna, Italy.
Death: July 20, 1937; Rome, Italy. *Parents:* Father, Guiseppi
Marconi; Mother, Annie Jameson Marconi. *Nationality:*
Italian. *Religion:* Catholic. *Education:* No college degrees.
Spouse: Beatrice O'Brien, married March 16, 1905, an-
nulled 1924; Maria Cristina Bezzi-Scali, married 1927.
Children: Giulio, son; Degna, daughter; Giola, daughter;
Elettra, daughter. *Career:* Inventor and Entrepreneur, Italy.
Other Awards: Order of Saint Anne, Russia; Commander of
the Order of Saint Maurice and Saint Lazarus, 1902; Grand
Cross of the Order of the Crown of Italy, 1902; Freedom of
the City of Rome, 1903; Grand Cross Order of Alphonso
XII; Grand Cordon Order of the Rising Sun; Albert Medal,
Royal Society of Arts.

Selected Publications: "Wireless Telegraphy." *Proceedings of the Institution of Electrical Engineers* 28 (1899):
273. "Wireless Telegraphy." *Proceedings of the Royal Institution of Great Britain* 16 (1899–1901): 247–56. "Syntonic
Wireless Telegraphy." *Royal Society of Arts Journal* 49
(1901): 505. "The Progress of Electric Space Telegraphy."
Proceedings of the Royal Institution of Great Britain 17
(1902–04): 195–210. "Recent Advances in Wireless Telegraphy." *Proceedings of the Royal Institution of Great Britain*
18 (1905–07): 31–45.

For More Information See: Boinod, B.L. Jacot de,
and Collier, D.M.B. *Marconi: Master of Space.* London:
Hutchinson, 1935. *Dictionary of Scientific Biography.* New
York: Scribner's, 1974 (Volume 9), 98–99. Dunlap, Orrin
E., Jr. *Marconi: The Man and His Wireless.* New York:
Macmillan Publishing Co., 1937. Marconi, Degna. *My Father,
Marconi.* New York: McGraw-Hill Book Co., Inc., 1962.
Birch, B. *Gugliemo Marconi.* New York: Exley, 1990.

Commentary: The Nobel Prize given to Guglielmo
Marconi recognized his "contributions to the development
of wireless telegraphy." A privately educated inventor,
Marconi became the inventor of the first practical system of

wireless telegraphy, working in a laboratory on his father's estate. He spent his lifetime refining the invention, acquiring key patents and forming his own company. Marconi's demonstrations and inventions made possible the electronic communications systems of the modern world. (C.G. and L.S.)

1910

Van der Waals, Johannes Diderik   568

Prize: Physics, 1910. *Born:* November 23, 1837; Leiden, Netherlands. *Death:* March 8, 1923; Amsterdam, Netherlands. *Parents:* Father, Jacobus van der Waals; Mother, Elisabeth van den Burg van der Waals. *Nationality:* Dutch. *Religion:* Christian. *Education:* Leiden Univ., Netherlands, Teaching Certificate, 1865; Leiden Univ., Netherlands, doctorate, 1873. *Spouse:* Anna Magdelana Smit, married 1864. *Children:* Anne Madeleine, daughter; Jacqueline Elisabeth, daughter; Johanna Diderica, daughter; Johannes Diderik, son. *Career:* High school teacher, Deventer, Netherlands, 1864–66; Teacher and Principal, The Hague, Netherlands, 1866–77; Univ. of Amsterdam, Netherlands, Professor, 1877–1907.

Selected Publications: Over de Continuiteit van den Gasen-Vloeistoftoestand. Leiden, Netherlands: A.W. Sijthoff, 1873. *La Continuität des Gasförmigen und Flüssigen Zustandes.* Leipzig, Germany: J.A. Barth, 1881. *Lehrbuch der Thermodynamik in Ihrer Anwendung auf das Gleichgewicht von Systemen mit Gasförmig-flüssigen Phasen.* Leipzig, Germany: Maas und van Suchtelen, 1908. *De Relativiteitstheorie.* Haarlem, Netherlands: F. Bohn, 1923. *Lehrbuch der Thermostatik, das Heisst, des Thermischen Gleich Gewichtes Materieller Systeme.* Leipzig, Germany: J.A. Barth, 1927.

For More Information See: Dictionary of Scientific Biography. New York: Scribner's, 1976 (Volume 14), 109–11. Kipnis, A.A., Avelov, B.E., and Rowlinson, J.S. *Van der Waals and Molecular Sciences.* Oxford: Clarendon Press; New York: Oxford University Press, 1996. Oesper, R.E. "Johannes Diderik van der Waals." *Journal of Chemical Education* 31 (1954): 599.

Commentary: The Academy recognized Johannes Diderik van der Waals "for his work on the equation of state for gases and liquids," which relates pressure, absolute temperature, and volume through the use of three constants. Van der Waals was also well known for his theory of binary solutions and thermodynamic theory of capillarity. (C.S.)

1911

Wien, Wilhelm Carl Werner Otto Fritz Franz   569

Prize: Physics, 1911. *Born:* January 13, 1864; Gaffken, Germany. *Death:* August 30, 1928; Munich, Germany. *Parents:* Father, Carl Wien; Mother, Caroline Gertz Wien. *Nationality:* German. *Religion:* Christian. *Education:* Univ. of Berlin, Germany, Ph.D., 1886. *Spouse:* Luise Mehler, married 1898. *Children:* Waltraut, son; Karl, son; Gerda, daughter; Hildegard, daughter. *Career:* Germany, Landowner, 1886–90; State Physico-Technical Institute, Germany, Researcher, 1890–96; Technische Hochschule, Aachen, Germany, Professor, 1896–99; Univ. of Giessen, Germany,

Professor, 1899–1900; Univ. of Würzburg, Germany, Professor, 1900–20; Univ. of Munich, Germany, Professor, 1920–28.

Selected Publications: Lehrbuch der Hydrodynamik. Leipzig, Germany: S. Hirzel, 1900. *Kanalstrahlen.* Leipzig, Germany: Akademische Verlagsgesellschaft, 1917. *Aus Dem Leben und Wirken eines Physikers.* Leipzig, Germany: J.A. Barth, 1930.

For More Information See: Ausdem Leben und Wirken Eines Physikers. Berlin: Deutsches Verlags, 1930. *Deutsches Biographisches Jahrbuch.* Berlin: Deutsches Verlags, 1931 (Volume 10), 302–10. *Dictionary of Scientific Biography.* New York: Scribner's, 1976 (Volume 14), 337–42. Steenbeck, Max. *Wilhelm Wien und Sein Einfluss auf die Physik Seiner Zeit.* Berlin: Akademie-Verlag, 1964.

Commentary: Wilhelm Wien was awarded the Nobel Prize "for his discoveries regarding the laws governing the radiation of heat." In 1893 he developed the law of displacement which states that the wavelength of radiation emitted from bodies varies with temperature; for instance, moderately hot bodies radiate in the infrared, while extremely hot bodies radiate in the ultraviolet ends of the spectrum. He did further research on black bodies, which absorb all radiation. Although his work in this area proved valid only for short waves, Wien's theories enabled Max Planck to devise the quantum theory. Wien's further researches took him into the areas of cathode rays, canal rays, light diffraction, color of refracted light, metal permeability to light and heat, measurement of high temperatures, and thermodynamics. (M.H.)

1912

Dalén, Nils Gustaf   570

Prize: Physics, 1912. *Born:* November 30, 1869; Stenstorp, Sweden. *Death:* December 9, 1937; Lidingo, Sweden. *Parents:* Father, Anders Johansson Dalén; Mother, Lovisa Andersdotter Dalén. *Nationality:* Swedish. *Religion:* Christian. *Education:* Chalmers Tekniska Högskola, Sweden, Civil Engineering Degree, 1896. *Spouse:* Elma Axelia Persson, married July 13, 1901. *Children:* Gunnar, son; Anders, son; 2 daughters. *Career:* Laval Steam Turbine Co., Sweden, Researcher, 1897–1900; Swedish Carbide and Acetylene Co., Sweden, Administrator and Researcher, 1901–03; Gas Accumulator Co., Engineer and Researcher, 1906–12; Inventor, 1912–37. *Other Awards:* Morehead Medal, International Acetylene Association, 1933.

Selected Publications: Chemische Technologie des Papiers. Leipzig, Germany: J.A. Barth, 1911.

For More Information See: Biographical Encyclopedia of Scientists. New York: Facts on File, 1981, 179. *Svenskt Biografiskt Lexikon.* Stockholm: Albert Bonners Forlag, 1931 (Volume 3), 36–50. Wastberg, Erik. *Gustaf Dalén.* Stockholm: Hokerberg, 1938.

Commentary: The award to Gustaf Dalén was "for his invention of automatic regulators for use in conjunction with gas accumulators for illuminating lighthouses and buoys." His inventions to improve coastal lighting were actually threefold: (1) he discovered a method for storing acetylene gas in small containers without fear of explosion; (2) he constructed an apparatus which allowed one liter of gas to provide thousands of rapid flashes; and (3) he developed a "sunset" or "solar" valve which allowed unstaffed lights to be lit as soon as the sun set and extinguished as soon as the sun rose. This last development made operation of lighthouses and beacons entirely automatic for months at a time. Blinded in an industrial accident in 1912, Dalén was unable to attend the presentation of his award. His research did not stop, though: he was awarded the contract for lighting the Panama Canal, worked with hot air turbines and air compressors, and invented an efficient cooking stove. (M.H.)

1913

Kamerlingh Onnes, Heike   **571**

Prize: Physics, 1913. *Born:* September 21, 1853; Gröningen, Netherlands. *Death:* February 21, 1926; Leiden, Netherlands. *Parents:* Father, Harm Kamerlingh Onnes; Mother, Anne Gerdina Coers Kamerlingh Onnes. *Nationality:* Dutch. *Religion:* Christian. *Education:* Univ. of Gröningen, Netherlands, Candidaats Degree, 1871; Univ. of Heidelberg, Germany, Ph.D., 1879. *Spouse:* Maria Adriana Wilhelmina Elisabeth Bijleveld, married 1887. *Children:* Albert, son. *Career:* Univ. of Leiden, Netherlands, Professor, 1882–1923. *Other Awards:* Rumford Medal, Royal Society, 1912.

Selected Publications: "Algemeene Theorie der Vloeistoffen" (*General Theory of Fluids*). *Verhandelingen der Kon. Akademie van Wetenschappen (Amsterdam)* 21 (1881): 9. "On the Cryogenic Laboratory at Leiden and on the Production of Very Low Temperatures." *Communications from the Laboratory of Physics at the University of Leiden* 14 (1894). "The Liquefaction of Helium." *Communications from the Physical Laboratory at the University of Leiden* 108 (August 1908) (Translated from *Bijvoegsel aan het Verslag van de Gewone Vergadering der Wis-en Naturkundige Afdeeling der Kon. Akademie van Wetenschappen te Amsterdan* (June 1908): 163–79). "Further Experiments with Liquid Helium. D. On the Change of the Electrical Resistance of Pure Metals at Very Low Temperatures, etc. V. The Disappearance of the Resistance of Mercury." *Communications from the Physical Laboratory of the University of Leiden* 122b (May 1911) (Translated from *Verslagen van de Afdeeling Natuurkunde der Kon. Akademie van Wetenschappen te Amsterdam* (May 1911): 81–83). "Further Experiments with Liquid Helium. G. On the Electrical Resistance of Pure Metals, etc. VI. On the Sudden Change in the Rate at Which the Resistance of Mercury Disappears." *Communications from the Physical Laboratory of the University of Leiden* 124c (December 1911) (Translated from *Verslagen van de Afdeeling Natuurkunde der Kon. Akademie van Wetenschappen te Amsterdam* (December 30, 1911): 799–802). "Further Experiments with Liquid Helium. P. On the Lowest Temperature Yet Obtained." *Transactions of the Faraday Society* 18, Part 2 (December 1922). Reprinted in *Communications from the Physical Laboratory of the University of Leiden* 159 (1922): 3–32. *Through Measurement to Knowledge.* London: Kluwer Academic Publishers, 1991.

For More Information See: Dictionary of Scientific Biography. New York: Scribner's, 1973 (Volume 7), 220–22. "Heike Kamerlingh Onnes—1853–1926." *Proceedings of the Royal Society* A113 (January 1927): i-vi.

Commentary: Considered the "father of cryogenics," Heike Kamerlingh Onnes received the Nobel Prize for

"researches on the properties of matter at low temperatures. . . . " Working in his world-renowned laboratory at Leiden and ever-mindful of his motto, "through measuring to knowing," he astonished the scientific community in 1908 by liquifying helium, a feat which opened up the whole field of cryogenics. Continued experimentation in this area brought him to the discovery of the phenomenon of "supraconductivity" (later called superconductivity) in 1911, as well as that of Helium II. Less well known are his efforts during World War I to aid starving children in every country suffering from food shortages. (C.H.W.)

1914

Laue, Max Theodor Felix von   **572**

Prize: Physics, 1914. *Born:* October 9, 1879; Pfaffendorf, Germany. *Death:* April 24, 1960; Berlin, Germany. *Parents:* Father, Julius von Laue; Mother, Minna L. Zerrenner von Laue. *Nationality:* German. *Religion:* Protestant. *Education:* Univ. of Berlin, Germany, Dr. Phil., 1903. *Spouse:* Magdalene Deger, married October 6, 1910. *Children:* Theodor Hermann, son; Hildegard Minna, daughter. *Career:* Univ. of Berlin, Germany, Professor, 1906–09; Univ. of Munich, Germany, Professor, 1909–12; Univ. of Zürich, Switzerland, Professor, 1912–14; Univ. of Frankfurt am Main, Germany, Professor, 1914–18; Univ. of Berlin, Germany, Professor and Administrator, 1919–43; Univ. of Göttingen, Germany, Professor and Administrator, 1946–51; Fritz Haber Institute of Physical Chemistry, Berlin, Germany, Director, 1951–58. *Other Awards:* Max Planck Medal, German Physical Society, 1932; Bimala-Churn-Law Gold Medal, Indian Association for the Cultivation of Science, India, 1950; Knight, Order Pour le Mérite, 1952; Grand Cross with Star for Federal Service, 1953; Officer of the Legion of Honour, France, 1957.

Selected Publications: "Interferenzerscheinungen bei Röntgenstrahlen." *Bayerische Akademie der Wissenschaften zu Munchen. Sitzungsberichte Mathematisch-Physikalischen Klasse* (June 1912): 303–22 (with W. Friedrich and P. Knipping). "Eine Quantitative Prüfung der Theorier fü die Interferenzerscheinungen bei Röntgenstrahlen." *Bayerische Akademie der Wissenschaften zu Munchen. Sitzungsberichte Mathematisch-Physikalischen Klasse* (July 1912): 363–73. *Bayerische Akademie der Wissenschaften zu Munchen. Sitzungsberichte Mathematisch-Physikalischen Klasse* (1913): 971–88. *Über die Auffindung der Röntgenstrahlinterferenzen.* Karlsruhe, Germany: C.F. Müllersche Hofbuchhandlung, 1920. *Die Relativitätstheorie (The Theory of Relativity).* 2 volumes. Braunschweig, Germany: F. Vieweg & Sohn, 1921. *Röntgenstrahlinterferenzen (X-ray Interference).* Leipzig, Germany: Akademische Verlagsgesellschaft, 1941. *Geschichte der Physik.* Bonn: Universitats Verlag, 1946 (*History of Physics.* Tr. by Ralph Oesper. New York: Academic Press, 1950). *Theorie der Supraleitung.* Berlin: Springer, 1947 (*Theory of Superconductivity.* Tr. by Lothar Meyer and William Band. New York: Academic Press, 1952).

For More Information See: Biographical Memoirs of the Fellows of the Royal Society. London: Royal Society, 1960 (Volume 6), 135–56. *Dictionary of Scientific Biography.* New York: Scribner's, 1973 (Volume 8), 50–53.

"My Development as a Physicist: An Autobiography." In *Fifty Years of X-ray Diffraction*, by Peter Paul Ewald, 278–307. Utrecht, Netherlands: N.V.A. Obsthoek's Uitgeversmaatschappÿ, 1962.

Commentary: Max von Laue provided the mathematical formulations in 1912 that demonstrated that a narrow beam of X-rays is diffracted by the orderly array of atoms in a crystal lattice. He won the Nobel award for this "discovery of the diffraction of X-rays in crystals," which was described by Einstein as one of the most beautiful discoveries in physics. It enabled the development of two new branches of science: x-ray crystallography and x-ray spectroscopy. Laue's other important accomplishments both before and after his prize-winning work were his thinking and writings on the theory of relativity and superconductivity. (C.H.W.)

1915

Bragg, William Henry, Sir   573

Prize: Physics, 1915. *Born:* July 2, 1862; Westward, Cumberland, England. *Death:* March 12, 1942; London, England. *Parents:* Father, Robert John Bragg; Mother, Mary Wood Bragg. *Nationality:* British. *Religion:* Anglican. *Education:* Cambridge Univ., England, M.A., 1884. *Spouse:* Gwendoline Todd, married 1889. *Children:* William Lawrence, son; Robert Charles, son; Gwendolyn Mary, daughter. *Career:* Univ. of Adelaide, Australia, Professor, 1885–1909; Leeds Univ., England, Professor, 1909–15; Univ. of London, England, Professor, 1915–25; Royal Institution, England, Professor and Administrator, 1923–42. *Other Awards:* Barnard Gold Medal, Columbia Univ., NY, 1915; Rumford Medal, Royal Society, 1915; Gold Medal, Societa Italiana de Scienze, 1917; Knighthood, 1920; Copley Medal, Royal Society, 1930; Franklin Medal, Franklin Institute, Philadelphia, PA, 1930; Faraday Medal, Institution of Electrical Engineers, 1936; John J. Carty Medal, National Academy of Sciences, 1938; Institute of Metals Medal, 1939.

Selected Publications: Studies in Radioactivity. London: Macmillan, 1912. "X-rays and Crystal Structure." *Science* (December 14, 1914): 795–802. *An Introduction to Crystal Analysis.* London: Bell and Sons, Ltd., 1928. *The Crystalline State.* 4 volumes. London: G. Gell, 1933–53 (with W.L. Bragg). *Atomic Structure of Minerals.* London: Oxford Univ. Press, 1937 (with W.L. Bragg).

For More Information See: Caroe, Gwendolyn M. *William Henry Bragg, 1862–1942.* Cambridge: Cambridge Univ. Press, 1978. *Dictionary of Scientific Biography.* New York: Scribner's, 1970 (Volume 2), 397–400. *Obituary Notices of the Fellows of the Royal Society.* London: Royal Society, 1943 (Volume 4): 277–300.

Commentary: William Henry Bragg and his son, William Lawrence Bragg, were jointly awarded the Nobel Prize "for the value of their contribution to the study of crystal structures by means of x-rays." W.H. Bragg began his career studying the properties of alpha, beta, and gamma rays, contributing greatly to the understanding of radioactivity. He built the first x-ray spectrometer and established the field of x-ray spectroscopy. W.L. Bragg found that the phenomenon of x-ray diffraction in crystals could be treated mathematically, and together with his father determined crystal structures, using the x-ray spectrometer. The Braggs reduced the problem of crystal structure analysis to a standard procedure, and their discoveries and techniques became fundamental to the field of molecular biology as well. (M.N.K.)

Bragg, William Lawrence, Sir   574

Prize: Physics, 1915. *Born:* March 31, 1890; Adelaide, Australia. *Death:* July 1, 1971; Ipswich, England. *Parents:* Father, William Henry Bragg; Mother, Gwendoline Todd Bragg. *Nationality:* British. *Religion:* Anglican. *Education:* Univ. of Adelaide, Australia, M.A., 1908; Cambridge Univ., England, M.A., 1912. *Spouse:* Alice Grace Jenny Hopkinson, married December 1921. *Children:* Stephen, son; David, son; Margaret, daughter; Patience, daughter. *Career:* Cambridge Univ., England, Professor, 1914–15; British Army, 1915–19; Manchester Univ., England, Professor, 1919–37; National Physical Laboratory, England, Director, 1937–38; Cambridge Univ., England, Professor, 1938–53; Royal Institution, England, Professor and Administrator, 1954–65. *Other Awards:* Barnard Gold Medal, Columbia Univ., NY, 1915; Gold Medal, Societa Italiana di Scienze, 1917; Military Cross, 1918; Hughes Medal, Royal Society, 1931; Knighthood, 1941; Royal Medal, Royal Society, 1946; Roebling Medal, Mineral Society of America, 1948; Commander, Order of Leopold of Belgium, 1961.

Selected Publications: X-rays and Crystal Structure. London: G. Bell and Sons, 1915 (with W.H. Bragg). *The Crystalline State.* 4 volumes. London: G. Bell, 1933–53 (with W.H. Bragg). *Atomic Structure of Minerals.* London: Oxford Univ. Press, 1937 (with W.H. Bragg). *The Development of X-Ray Analysis.* London: G. Bell, 1975.

For More Information See: Biographical Memoirs of the Fellows of the Royal Society. London: Royal Society, 1975, 75–143. *Dictionary of Scientific Biography.* New York: Scribner's, 1978 (Volume 15), 61–64. "Reminiscences of Fifty Years of Research." *Proceedings of the Royal Institution of Great Britain* 41 (1966): 92–100. *The Legacy of Sir Lawrence Bragg.* Northwood, Middlesex, England: Science Reviews, Ltd., 1990.

Commentary: William Lawrence Bragg and his father, William Henry Bragg, were jointly awarded the Nobel Prize "for the value of their contribution to the study of crystal structures by means of x-rays." W.L. Bragg found that the phenomenon of x-ray diffraction in crystals, discovered by Von Laue, could be treated mathematically. His simplification of the mathematical method made possible an experimental attack on the problem of crystal structures using the x-ray spectrometer, first constructed by W.H. Bragg. The Braggs reduced the problem of crystal structure analysis to a standard procedure, and their discoveries and techniques became fundamental to the field of molecular biology as well. (M.N.K.)

1917

Barkla, Charles Glover   575

Prize: Physics, 1917. *Born:* June 27, 1877; Widness, Lancashire, England. *Death:* October 23, 1944; Edinburgh, Scotland. *Parents:* Father, John Martin Barkla; Mother, Sarah Glover Barkla. *Nationality:* British. *Religion:* Methodist.

Education: Univ. of Liverpool, England, B.Sc., 1898; Univ. of Liverpool, England, M.Sc., 1899; Cambridge Univ., England, B.A., 1901; Univ. of Liverpool, England, D.Sc., 1904. *Spouse:* Mary Esther Cowell, married 1907. *Children:* Michael, son; 1 other son; 1 daughter. *Career:* Univ. of Liverpool, England, Researcher, 1905–09; Univ. of London, England, Professor, 1909–13; Univ. of Edinburgh, Scotland, Professor, 1913–44. *Other Awards:* Hughes Medal, 1917.

Selected Publications: "Secondary Roentgen Radiation." *Philosophical Magazine*, 6th series, 11 (June 1906): 812–28. "The Spectra of the Fluorescent Roentgen Radiations." *Philosophical Magazine* 22 (September 1911): 396–412. *Radiation and Matter.* Greenock, England: Telegraph Printing Works, 1920.

For More Information See: Dictionary of Scientific Biography. New York: Scribner's, 1970 (Volume 1), 456–59. *Obituary Notices of Fellows of the Royal Society of London.* London: Royal Society, 1947, 341–66. Stephenson, Reginald. "The Scientific Career of Charles Glover Barkla." *American Journal of Physics* 35 (February 1967): 141–52.

Commentary: The Nobel Prize was awarded to Charles Glover Barkla "for his discovery of the characteristic Roentgen radiation of the elements." Barkla showed that when a sample of a chemical element is placed in the path of x-rays, secondary x-rays are emitted. Although some of this emitted radiation is in fact a scattering of primary x-rays, Barkla was able to distinguish a secondary emission which produced a spectrum characteristic of each chemical element involved and could be used to deduce much about the structures of atoms. Barkla's career was almost entirely devoted to the study of Roentgen radiation. (J.L.K.)

1918

Planck, Max Karl Ernst Ludwig   576

Prize: Physics, 1918. *Born:* April 23, 1858; Kiel, Germany. *Death:* October 4, 1947; Göttingen, Germany. *Parents:* Father, Johann Julius Wilhelm Planck; Mother, Emma Patzig Planck. *Nationality:* German. *Religion:* Protestant. *Education:* Univ. of Munich, Germany, Ph.D., 1879. *Spouse:* Marie Merck, married 1885, died 1909; Marga von Hosslin, married 1911. *Children:* Karl, son; Hermann, son; Ernst, son; Margarete, daughter; Emma, daughter. *Career:* Univ. of Munich, Germany, Professor, 1880–85; Univ. of Kiel, Germany, Professor, 1885–89; Univ. of Berlin, Germany, Professor, 1889–1928. *Other Awards:* Copley Medal, Royal Society, 1929.

Selected Publications: Vorlesungen über Thermodynamik. Leipzig, Germany: Veit, 1897. "Zur Theorie des Gesetzes der Energieverteilurg im Normalspektrum." *Verhandlungen der Deutschen Physikalischen Gesellschaft* 2 (1900): 237–45. "Über die Elementarquanta der Materie und der Elektrizitat." *Annalen der Physik* 4 (1901): 564–66. *Vorlesungen über die Theorie der Warmestrahlung.* Leipzig, Germany: Barth, 1906.

For More Information See: Dictionary of Scientific Biography. New York: Scribner's, 1975 (Volume 11), 7–17. Hermann, A. *Max Planck in Selbstzeugnissen und Bilddokumenten.* Hamburg: Rowohlt, 1973. *Obituary Notices of Fellows of the Royal Society.* London: Royal Society,

1948, 160–88. *Max Planck.* Halle/Salle, Germany: Deutsche Akademie der Naturforscher Leopoldina, 1990.

Commentary: Max Planck was awarded the Nobel Prize "for his work on the establishment and development of the theory of elementary quanta." Planck's earliest research was in the thermodynamics of irreversible processes. He later turned to the study of electromagnetic radiation, which represented his major contribution to science. Planck put forth the thesis that a body emits radiation in the form of discrete quanta of energy equal to the frequency times a constant, h, later named Planck's Constant, and thus introduced quantum theory. He also contributed to the development of the theory of relativity, soon after Einstein introduced it. (J.L.K.)

1919

Stark, Johannes   577

Prize: Physics, 1919. *Born:* April 15, 1874; Schickenhof, Bavaria, Germany. *Death:* June 21, 1957; Traunstein, Bavaria, Germany. *Parents:* No record found. *Nationality:* German. *Religion:* Most probably Christian/Protestant. *Education:* Univ. of Munich, Germany, Ph.D., 1897. *Spouse:* Louise Uepler, married (no date found). *Children:* 5 children. *Career:* Univ. of Munich, Germany, Professor, 1897–1900; Univ. of Göttingen, Germany, Professor, 1900–06; Technische Hochschule, Hannover, Germany, Professor, 1906–09; Technische Hochschule, Aachen, Germany, Professor, 1909–17; Univ. of Greifswald, Germany, Professor, 1917–20; Univ. of Würzburg, Germany, Professor, 1920–22. *Other Awards:* Baumgartner Prize, Vienna Academy of Sciences, 1910; Vahlbruch Prize, Göttingen Academy of Sciences, 1914; Matteuci Medal, Rome.

Selected Publications: Die Elektrizität in Gasen. Leipzig, Germany: J.A. Barth, 1902. "Der Doppler-Effekt bei den Kanalstrahlen und die Spektra der Positiven Atomionen." *Physikalische Zeitschrift* 6 (1905): 892–97. "Elementarquantum der Energie, Modell der Negativen und Positiven Elektrizität." *Physikalische Zeitschrift* 8 (1907): 881–84. *Prinzipien der Atomdynamik.* 3 volumes. Leipzig, Germany: S. Hirzel, 1910–15.

For More Information See: Dictionary of Scientific Biography. New York: Scribner's, 1975 (Volume 12), 613–66. *Nobel Prize Winners: Physics.* Pasadena, CA: Salem Press, 1988, Volume 1, 233–41.

Commentary: Johannes Stark's award was "for his discovery of the Doppler effect in canal rays and the splitting of spectral lines in electrical fields." The latter phenomenon became known as the Stark effect and was an early confirmation of the quantum theory of atoms. Stark was an important experimental physicist with a talent for conceptualization. His main area of interest was electrical conduction in gases, and he did valuable speculative work regarding the nature of chemical forces and the problems of atomic and molecular structure. In 1904, Stark founded the *Jahrbuch der Radioaktivität und Elektronik* to publish research papers in the area of particle physics. Stark is also known for his modification of the photo-equivalence law proposed by Albert Einstein in 1906. Now known as the Stark-Einstein law, it states that each molecule involved in a photochemical reaction absorbs only one quantum of the radiation that causes the reaction. (B.L.)

1920

Guillaume, Charles Édouard **578**

Prize: Physics, 1920. *Born:* February 15, 1861; Fleurier, Switzerland. *Death:* June 13, 1938; Sèvres, France. *Parents:* Father, Édouard Guillaume; Mother, no record found. *Nationality:* Swiss; later French resident. *Religion:* Christian. *Education:* Zürich Polytechnic, Switzerland, Ph.D., 1883. *Spouse:* A.M. Taufflieb, married 1888. *Children:* 3 children. *Career:* International Bureau of Weights and Measures, France, Administrator and Researcher, 1883–1936. *Other Awards:* Grand Officer, Legion of Honour.

Selected Publications: Traité Pratique de Thermométrie de Précision. Paris: Gauthier-Villars, 1889. "Recherches sur les Aciers au Nickel. Propriétés Metrologiques." *Comptes Rendus Hebdomadaires des Séances de l'Académie des Sciences* 124 (1897): 752. "Recherches sur les Aciers au Nickel. Propriétés Magnétiques et Déformations Permanentes." *Comptes Rendus Hebdomadaires des Séances de l'Académie des Sciences* 124 (1897): 1515. "Recherches sur les Aciers au Nickel. Dilatations aux Températures Élevées: Résistance Électrique." *Comptes Rendus Hebdomadaires des Séances de l'Académie des Sciences* 125 (1897): 235. "Recherches sur les Aciers au Nickel. Variations de Volumes des Alliages Irréversibles." *Comptes Rendus Hebdomadaires des Séances de l'Académie des Sciences* 126 (1898): 738. Les États de la Matiére. Paris: Société Astronomique de France, 1908.

For More Information See: Dictionary of Scientific Biography. New York: Scribner's, 1972 (Volume 5), 582–83. Nobel Prize Winners: Physics. Pasadena, CA: Salem Press, 1988, Volume 1, 243–51.

Commentary: Charles Édouard Guillaume was awarded the Nobel Prize "in recognition of the service he has rendered to precision measurements in physics by his discovery of anomalies in nickel steel alloys." During his years with the Bureau International des Poids et Mesures, his work was concerned with increasing the precision of standard measures. He was known for discovering Invar, an iron and nickel alloy which has a very small coefficient of expansion in relation to temperature change. Invar is used in clockmaking and, among other precise instruments, surveyors' tapes. Guillaume was also known for redetermining the volume of the liter; for his work on the mercury thermometer; and for discovery of another alloy, elinvar, which does not change its elasticity within a wide temperature change. (B.N.L.)

1921

Einstein, Albert **579**

Prize: Physics, 1921. *Born:* March 14, 1879; Ulm, Germany. *Death:* April 18, 1955; Princeton, NJ. *Parents:* Father, Hermann Einstein; Mother, Pauline Koch Einstein. *Nationality:* German; later Swiss and American citizen. *Religion:* Jewish. *Education:* Univ. of Zürich, Switzerland, Ph.D., 1905. *Spouse:* Mileva Maric, married 1903, divorced 1919; Elsa Lowenthal, married 1919. *Children:* Hans Albert, son; Eduard, son; Lieserl, daughter. *Career:* Swiss Patent Office, Berne, Switzerland, Patent Examiner, 1902–08; Univ. of Zürich, Switzerland, Professor, 1909–11; Karl-Ferdinand Univ., Prague, Austria, Professor, 1911–12; Technische Hochschule, Bern, Switzerland, Professor, 1912–14; Kaiser

Wilhelm Institute, Germany, Director, 1914–33; Princeton Univ., NJ, Professor, 1933–55. *Other Awards:* Barnard Medal, Columbia Univ., 1920; Copley Medal, Royal Society, 1925; Gold Medal, Royal Astronomical Society, 1926; Max Planck Medal, 1929; Franklin Medal, Franklin Institute, Philadelphia, PA, 1935.

Selected Publications: Relativity, The Special and the General Theory: A Popular Exposition. Tr. by Robert W. Lawson. London: Methuen, 1920. The Meaning of Relativity: Four Lectures Delivered at Princeton University, May 1921. Tr. by Edwin Plimpton Adams. London: Methuen, 1921. Investigations on the Theory of the Brownian Movement. Tr. by A.D. Cowper. London: Methuen, 1926. The Evolution of Physics: The Growth of Ideas from Early Concepts to Relativity and Quanta. Written with Leopold Infeld. New York: Simon & Schuster, 1938.

For More Information See: Clark, Ronald W. Einstein: The Life and Times. New York: World Publishing, 1971. Dictionary of Scientific Biography. New York: Scribner's, 1971 (Volume 4), 312–33. Frank, Philipp. Einstein, His Life and Times. Tr. by G. Rosen. New York: A.A. Knopf, 1947. Hoffmann, Banesh, and Dukas, Helen. Albert Einstein—Creator and Rebel. New York: Viking, 1972. Overbye, Dennis. Einstein in Love. New York: Viking, 2000. Reiser, Anton. Albert Einstein, a Biographical Portrait. New York: Boni, 1930. Pais, Abraham. "Subtle Is the Lord": The Science and Life of Albert Einstein. New York: Oxford Univ. Press, 1982. Autobiographical Notes. New York: Simon & Schuster, 1993.

Commentary: Although the theory of relativity is synonymous with Albert Einstein, the Nobel Prize was awarded for his work on the photoelectric effect as described in his 1905 paper "The Quantum Law of the Emission and Absorption of Light" (*Annalen der Physik*). Einstein's Law of the Photoelectric Effect became the basis of quantitative photochemistry. Einstein was nominated for the award every year from 1910–22 except for 1911 and 1915, and the Nobel Prize in 1921 notes his contributions to theoretical physics in the area of quantum theory. Albert Einstein's work changed contemporary thinking and formed the basis for the modern science of physics. (J.S.)

1922

Bohr, Niels Henrik David **580**

Prize: Physics, 1922. *Born:* October 7, 1885; Copenhagen, Denmark. *Death:* November 18, 1962; Copenhagen, Denmark. *Parents:* Father, Christian Bohr; Mother, Ellen Adler Bohr. *Nationality:* Danish. *Religion:* From Jewish background. *Education:* Univ. of Copenhagen, Denmark, baccalaureate, 1907; Univ. of Copenhagen, Denmark, M.S., 1909; Univ. of Copenhagen, Denmark, Ph.D., 1911. *Spouse:* Margrethe Norlund, married August 1, 1912. *Children:* Christian, son; Hans, son; Erik, son; Aage, son; Ernest, son; 1 other son. *Career:* Cambridge Univ., England, Professor, 1911–12; Univ. of Manchester, England, Professor, 1912–13; Univ. of Copenhagen, Denmark, Professor, 1913–14; Victoria Univ., England, Professor, 1914–16; Univ. of Copenhagen, Denmark, Professor and Administrator, 1916–62. *Other Awards:* Gold Medal, Royal Danish Academy of Sciences, 1907; Hughes Medal, Royal Society, 1921; H.C. Oerstad

Medal, Society for the Propagation of Natural Science, 1924; Norwegian Gold Medal, Univ. of Oslo, 1924; Barnard Medal, Columbia Univ., NY, 1925; Mateucci Medal, Societa Italiana della Scienze, Rome, Italy, 1925; Franklin Medal, Franklin Institute, Philadelphia, PA, 1926; Faraday Medal, Chemical Society of London, England, 1930; Planck Medal, Deutsche Physikalische Gesellschaft, 1930; Copley Medal, Royal Society, 1938.

Selected Publications: The Theory of Spectra and Atomic Constitution: Three Essays. Cambridge: Cambridge Univ. Press, 1922. *Atomic Theory and the Description of Nature.* New York: Macmillan, 1934. *Atomic Physics and Human Knowledge.* New York: Wiley, 1958. *Essays, 1958–1962, on Atomic Physics and Human Knowledge.* New York: Interscience, 1963. *On the Constitution of Atoms and Molecules, Papers of 1913 Reprinted from the Philosophical Magazine.* New York: Benjamin, 1963.

For More Information See: Dictionary of Scientific Biography. New York: Scribner's, 1970 (Volume 2), 239–54. Folse, Henry. *The Philosophy of Niels Bohr.* New York: North Holland, 1985. Moore, Ruth E. *Niels Bohr: The Man, His Science, and the World They Changed.* New York: Knopf, 1966. *Niels Bohr, His Life and Work as Seen by His Friends and Colleagues.* Edited by S. Rozental. New York: Wiley, 1967. Spangenburg, R. *Niels Bohr.* New York: Facts on File, 1995.

Commentary: "The investigation of the structure of atoms, and of the radiation emanating from them" were recognized as leading to Niels Bohr's Nobel Prize. Bohr's theories on the existence of stationary states of an atomic system and the transition of the system from one stationary state to another laid the foundation for much of the understanding of the physical and chemical properties of the elements. Bohr provided exemplary leadership throughout his career in the development of the field of quantum physics. (J.N.S.)

1923

Millikan, Robert Andrews 581

Prize: Physics, 1923. *Born:* March 22, 1868; Morrison, IL. *Death:* December 19, 1953; San Marino, CA. *Parents:* Father, Silas Franklin Millikan; Mother, Mary Jane Andrews Millikan. *Nationality:* American. *Religion:* Congregationalist. *Education:* Oberlin College, OH, A.B., 1891; Oberlin College, OH, A.M., 1893; Columbia Univ., NY, Ph.D., 1895. *Spouse:* Greta Irvin Blanchard, married April 10, 1902. *Children:* Clark Blanchard, son; Glenn Allen, son; Max Franklin, son. *Career:* Univ. of Chicago, IL, Professor, 1896–1921; California Institute of Technology, Professor and Administrator, 1921–46. *Other Awards:* Comstock Prize, National Academy of Sciences, 1913; Edison Medal, American Institute of Electrical Engineers, 1922; Hughes Medal, Royal Society, 1923; Faraday Medal, Chemical Society of London, 1924; Matteuci Medal, Societa Italiana della Scienze, 1925; Gold Medal, American Society of Mechanical Engineers, 1926; Messel Medal, Society of Chemical Industry, 1928; Gold Medal, Holland Society, 1928; Gold Medal, Radiological Society of North America, 1930; Gold Medal, Roosevelt Memorial Association, 1932; Newman Medal, 1934; Legion of Honor, France, 1936;

Gold Medal, Franklin Institute, PA, 1937; Gold Medal, Ulster-Irish Association of NY, 1938; Joy Kissen Mookerjee Gold Medal, Indian Association for the Cultivation of Science, 1939; Oersted Medal, American Association of Physics Teachers, 1940; Order of the Jade, China, 1940; Order Al Merito, Chile, 1944.

Selected Publications: "Quantum Theory and Its Relation to Photoelectric Phenomena." *Physik. Z.* 17 (1916): 217–21. *Electron: Its Isolation and Measurement and the Determination of Some of Its Properties.* Chicago: Univ. of Chicago Press, 1917. "Radiation and the Electron." *Nature* 101 (1918): 234–37, 254–57. "High-Frequency Rays of Cosmic Origin." *Science* 62 (1925): 445–48. *Electrons, Protons, Photons, Neutrons and Cosmic Rays.* Chicago: Univ. of Chicago Press, 1935.

For More Information See: The Autobiography of Robert A. Millikan. New York: Prentice-Hall, 1950. *Dictionary of Scientific Biography.* New York: Scribner's, 1974 (Volume 9), 395–400. Kargon, Robert. *The Rise of Robert Millikan.* Ithaca, NY: Cornell Univ. Press, 1982.

Commentary: The Academy honored Robert Millikan "for his work on the elementary charge of electricity and on the photoelectric effect." In addition to his determination of the charge of the electron, his verification of Einstein's photoelectric equation, and his determination of Planck's constant, Millikan contributed major work on Brownian movement, the ultraviolet spectrum, the law of motion of a falling particle, and cosmic radiation. (I.H.G.)

1924

Siegbahn, Karl Manne Georg 582

Prize: Physics, 1924. *Born:* December 3, 1886; Örebro, Sweden. *Death:* September 26, 1978; Stockholm, Sweden. *Parents:* Father, Nils Reinhold Georg Siegbahn; Mother, Emma Sofia Mathilda Zetterberg Siegbahn. *Nationality:* Swedish. *Religion:* Christian. *Education:* Univ. of Lund, Sweden, B.S., 1908; Univ. of Lund, Sweden, Dr.Sc., 1911. *Spouse:* Karin Hoegbom, married 1914. *Children:* Kai, son; Bo, son. *Career:* Univ. of Lund, Sweden, Professor, 1911–23; Univ. of Uppsala, Sweden, Professor, 1923–37; Swedish Royal Academy of Sciences, Professor and Administrator, 1937–64. *Other Awards:* Hughes Medal, Royal Society, 1934; Rumford Medal, Royal Society, 1940; Duddel Medal, Physical Society of London, 1948.

Selected Publications: The Spectroscopy of X-rays (collected papers). London: Oxford Univ. Press, 1925.

For More Information See: Biographical Encyclopedia of Scientists. New York: Facts on File, 1981, 733–34. *Nobel Prize Winners: Physics.* Pasadena, CA: Salem Press, 1988, Volume 1, 283–93. *Biographical Memoirs of the Fellows of the Royal Society.* London: Royal Society, 1991 (Volume 37), 427.

Commentary: Karl Siegbahn received his Nobel Prize "for his discoveries and research in the field of x-ray spectroscopy." After briefly studying electricity and magnetism, Siegbahn developed techniques for accurate measurement of x-ray wavelengths and showed that x-ray spectra were valuable for identification, as well as lending credence to the Bohr ideas of structure. In later research, Siegbahn turned to problems of nuclear physics. (C.S.)

1925

Franck, James 583

Prize: Physics, 1925. *Born:* August 26, 1882; Hamburg, Germany. *Death:* May 21, 1964; Göttingen, Germany. *Parents:* Father, Jacob Franck; Mother, Rebecca Drucker Franck. *Nationality:* German; later American citizen. *Religion:* Jewish. *Education:* Univ. of Berlin, Germany, Ph.D., 1906. *Spouse:* Ingrid Josephson, married December 23, 1906, died 1942; Hertha Sponer, married June 29, 1946. *Children:* Dagmar, daughter; Elisabeth, daughter. *Career:* Univ. of Berlin, Germany, Professor, 1906–18; Kaiser Wilhelm Institute, Germany, Professor, 1918–20; Univ. of Göttingen, Germany, Professor, 1920–33; Univ. of Copenhagen, Denmark, Professor, 1934; Johns Hopkins Univ., MD, Professor, 1935–38; Univ. of Chicago, IL, Professor, 1938–49. *Other Awards:* Max Planck Medal, German Physical Society, 1953; Rumford Medal, American Academy of Arts and Sciences, 1955.

Selected Publications: Anregungen von Quantensprüngen durch Stösse. Berlin: J. Springer, 1926 (with P. Jordan). *Photosynthesis in Plants.* Ames, IA: Iowa State College Press, 1949 (with W.E. Loomis).

For More Information See: Biographical Memoirs of the Fellows of the Royal Society. London: Royal Society, 1965 (Volume 11), 53–74. *Current Biography Yearbook.* New York: H.W. Wilson, 1957, 192–94. *Dictionary of Scientific Biography.* New York: Scribner's, 1972 (Volume 5), 117–18.

Commentary: The award to James Franck was for his contributions to the "discovery of the laws governing the impact of an electron upon an atom." He also was one of the formulators of the Franck-Condon Principle, which permitted the prediction of most-favored vibrational transitions in a bond system. His later work dealt with a model for photosynthesis. Franck was also prominent on the political/moral scene in his objections to the Hitler regime in Germany in the early 30s and in the Franck report of 1945, which was prepared by a group of atomic scientists and which called for an open demonstration of the atomic bomb in an uninhabited locale, rather than its surprise use in Japan. (F.K.)

Hertz, Gustav Ludwig 584

Prize: Physics, 1925. *Born:* July 22, 1887; Hamburg, Germany. *Death:* October 30, 1975; Berlin, Germany. *Parents:* Father, Gustav Hertz; Mother, Augusta Arning Hertz. *Nationality:* German. *Religion:* From Jewish background. *Education:* Univ. of Berlin, Germany, Ph.D., 1911. *Spouse:* Ellen Dihlmann, married 1919, died 1941; Charlotte Jollasse, married 1943. *Children:* Hellmuth, son; Johannes, son. *Career:* Univ. of Berlin, Germany, Researcher, 1913–14; German Army, 1914–17; Univ. of Berlin, Germany, Researcher, 1917–20; Philips Incandescent Lamp Factory, Netherlands, Researcher, 1920–25; Univ. of Halle, Germany, Professor and Administrator, 1925–28; Charlottenburg Technological Univ., Berlin, Germany, Professor and Administrator, 1928–35; Siemens Company, Germany, Researcher and Administrator, 1935–45; Research Laboratory, USSR, Researcher and Administrator, 1945–54; Karl Marx Univ., Leipzig, Germany, Professor and Administrator, 1955–61. *Other Awards:* Max Planck Medal, German Physical Society.

Selected Publications: "Impacts Between Gas Molecules and Slowly Moving Electrons." *Ber. Physike. Geog* (1913): 373–91 (with J. Franck). "A Connection Between Impact Ionization and Electron Affinity." *Verh. Deut. Physik. Geo* 15: 929–34 (with J. Franck). "Collisions Between Electrons and Molecules of Mercury Vapor and the Ionizing Voltage for the Same." *Verh. Deut. Physik. Geo* 16: 457–67. *Lehrbuch der Kernphysik.* 3 volumes. Leipzig, East Germany: B.G. Teubner, 1958–62.

For More Information See: Kuczera, Josef. *Gustav Hertz.* Leipzig: BSB B.G. Teubner, 1985. *Nobel Prize Winners: Physics.* Pasadena, CA: Salem Press, 1988, Volume 1, 305–13. *Physics Today* 29 (January 1976): 83–85.

Commentary: Gustav Hertz shared the Nobel Prize for his contributions to the "discovery of the laws governing the collision of an electron with an atom." Hertz, in his earliest research, worked on the infrared absorption of CO_2 and the ionization potentials of several gases. His study of the relationships between electron energy losses in collisions and spectral lines provided needed data for Bohr to develop his theory of atomic structure and for Planck to develop his ideas on quantum theory. (F.K.)

1926

Perrin, Jean Baptiste 585

Prize: Physics, 1926. *Born:* September 30, 1870; Lille, France. *Death:* April 17, 1942; New York, NY. *Parents:* No record found. *Nationality:* French. *Religion:* Christian. *Education:* École Normale Supérieure, France, D.Sc., 1897. *Spouse:* Henriette Duportal, married 1897. *Children:* Aline, daughter; Francis, son. *Career:* École Normale Superieure, France, Researcher, 1894–97; Univ. of Paris, France, Professor, 1897–1940. *Other Awards:* Joule Prize, Royal Society, 1896; La Caze Prize, French Academy of Sciences, 1914.

Selected Publications: "Rayons Cathodiques et Rayons de Roentgen." *Annales de Chimie et de Physique* 11 (1897): 496–554. *Traite de Chimie Physique. Les Principes.* Paris: Gauthier-Villars, 1903. "Mouvement Brownien et Realite Moleculaire." *Annales de Chimie et de Physique* 18 (1909): 1–114. *Les Atomes.* Paris: Alcan, 1913. *Oeuvres Scientifiques de Jean Perrin.* Paris: Centre National de la Recherche Scientifique, 1950.

For More Information See: Dictionary of Scientific Biography. New York: Scribner's, 1973 (Volume 10), 524–26. Nye, Mary Jo. *Molecular Reality.* London: MacDonald, 1972.

Commentary: Jean Perrin was cited by the Academy "for his work on the discontinuous structure of matter, and especially for his discovery of sedimentation equilibrium." Perrin began his career studying the nature of cathode rays and proved they were negative particles. His further studies were of x-ray effects on gas conductivity, fluorescence, radium disintegration, and sound. But his major work was in the exploration of the world of colloids, during which he further developed the theory of Brownian movement and was able to calculate the value of the Avogadro number (the number of molecules per grammolecule of a gas). Perrin was also responsible for the creation of much of the scientific establishment in France. (A.S.)

1927

Compton, Arthur Holly 586

Prize: Physics, 1927. *Born:* September 10, 1892; Wooster, OH. *Death:* March 15, 1962; Berkeley, CA. *Parents:* Father, Elias Compton; Mother, Otelia Catherine Augspurger Compton. *Nationality:* American. *Religion:* Presbyterian. *Education:* College of Wooster, OH, B.S., 1913; Princeton Univ., NJ, M.A., 1914; Princeton Univ., NJ, Ph.D., 1916. *Spouse:* Betty Charity McCloskey, married June 28, 1916. *Children:* Arthur Alan, son; John Joseph, son. *Career:* Univ. of Minnesota, Professor, 1916–17; Westinghouse Lamp Co., PA, Researcher, 1917–19; Cambridge Univ., England, Researcher, 1919–20; Washington Univ., St. Louis, MO, Professor, 1920–23; Univ. of Chicago, IL, Professor, 1923–45; Washington Univ., St. Louis, MO, Professor and Administrator, 1945–61. *Other Awards:* Rumford Medal, American Academy of Arts and Sciences, 1927; Gold Medal, Radiological Society of North America, 1928; Matteuci Medal, Italian Academy of Sciences, 1933; Franklin Medal, Franklin Institute, PA, 1940; Hughes Medal, Royal Society, 1940; Washington Award, Western Society of Engineers, 1945; Franklin Medal, American Philosophical Society, 1945; Congressional Medal of Merit, 1946.

Selected Publications: "A Quantum Theory of the Scattering of X-Rays by Light Elements." *Physical Review* 21 (1923): 483–502. "Polarization of Secondary X-Rays." *Journal of the Optical Society of America* 8 (1924): 487–91 (with C.F. Hagenow). "X-Ray Spectra from a Ruled Reflection Grating." *Proceedings of the National Academy of Sciences, USA* 11 (1925): 598–601 (with R.L. Doan). *X-Rays and Electrons.* Princeton, NJ: D. Van Nostrand Company, 1926. *X-Rays in Theory and Experiment.* Princeton, NJ: D. Van Nostrand Company, 1935 (with S.K. Allison).

For More Information See: Biographical Memoirs of National Academy of Sciences. Washington, DC: National Academy of Sciences, 1965, 81–110. *The Cosmos of Arthur Holly Compton.* New York: Knopf, 1967. *Dictionary of Scientific Biography.* New York: Scribner's, 1971 (Volume 3), 366–72.

Commentary: Arthur Compton won his Nobel Prize "for his discovery of the effect named after him." The Compton effect referred to the increase of wavelength of x-rays caused by scattering of the incident radiation by electrons. It was important in the developing theories of quantum versus wave nature. Compton also developed the coincidence method for studying x-ray scattering and studied x-ray reflection and polarization, x-ray spectra and wavelength measurement, and geographic variations of cosmic-ray intensity. (I.H.G.)

Wilson, Charles Thomson Rees 587

Prize: Physics, 1927. *Born:* February 14, 1869; Glencorse, Midlothian, Scotland. *Death:* November 15, 1959; Carlops, Peeblesshire, Scotland. *Parents:* Father, John Wilson; Mother, Annie Clark Harper Wilson. *Nationality:* Scottish. *Religion:* Protestant. *Education:* Owens College, England, B.Sc., 1887; Cambridge Univ., England, B.A., 1892. *Spouse:* Jessie Fraser Dick, married 1908. *Children:* 1 son; 2 daughters. *Career:* Cavendish Laboratory, England, Researcher, 1892–96; Bradford Grammar School, Yorkshire, England, Teacher, 1894; Cambridge Univ., England, Professor, 1896–1934. *Other Awards:* Hughes Medal, Royal Society, 1911; Hopkins Prize, Cambridge Philosophical Society, England, 1920; Gunning Prize, Royal Society of Edinburgh, Scotland, 1921; Royal Medal, Royal Society, 1922; Howard Potts Medal, Franklin Institute, 1925; Copley Medal, Royal Society, 1935.

Selected Publications: "A Method of Making Visible the Paths of Ionizing Particles Through a Gas." *Proceedings of the Royal Society of London* Series A. 85 (1911): 285–88. "An Expansion Apparatus for Making Visible the Track of Ionizing Particles in Gases and Some Results Obtained by Its Use." *Proceedings of the Royal Society of London* Series A. 87 (1913): 277–92. "The Acceleration of Beta-Particles in Strong Electrical Fields Such as Those of Thunderclouds." *Proceedings of the Cambridge Philosophical Society* 22 (1925): 534–38.

For More Information See: Biographical Memoirs of the Fellows of the Royal Society. London: Royal Society, 1960 (Volume 6), 269–95. *Dictionary of Scientific Biography.* New York: Scribner's, 1981 (Volume 14), 420–23.

Commentary: The award to Charles Wilson was "for his method of making the paths of electrically charged particles visible by condensation of vapour." He invented the cloud chamber, later referred to as the Wilson Cloud Chamber, which Ernest Rutherford called "the most original apparatus in the whole history of physics." It became vital to the study of radioactivity and the development of nuclear physics. Wilson's work was on condensation phenomena, the conductivity of air, and atmospheric electricity. (F.K.)

1928

Richardson, Owen Willans, Sir 588

Prize: Physics, 1928. *Born:* April 26, 1879; Dewsbury, Yorkshire, England. *Death:* February 15, 1959; Alton, Hampshire, England. *Parents:* Father, Joshua Henry Richardson; Mother, Charlotte Maria Willans Richardson. *Nationality:* British. *Religion:* Anglican. *Education:* Univ. of London, England, B.Sc., 1900; Cambridge Univ., England, M.A., 1904; Univ. of London, England, D.Sc., 1904. *Spouse:* Lilian Maud Wilson, married June 12, 1906, died 1945; Henrietta Maria G. Rupp, married 1948. *Children:* Harold, son; John, son; 1 daughter. *Career:* Cavendish Laboratory, England, Researcher, 1900–06; Princeton Univ., NJ, Professor, 1906–14; Univ. of London, England, Professor, 1914–44. *Other Awards:* Hughes Medal, Royal Society, 1920; Royal Medal, Royal Society, 1930; Knighthood, 1939.

Selected Publications: The Electron Theory of Matter. Cambridge: Cambridge Univ. Press, 1914. *The Emission of Electricity from Hot Bodies.* London: Longmans, Green and Co., 1916. *Molecular Hydrogen and Its Spectrum.* New Haven, CT: Yale Univ. Press, 1934.

For More Information See: Biographical Memoirs of the Fellows of the Royal Society. London: Royal Society, 1959 (Volume 5), 207–15. *Dictionary of Scientific Biography.* New York: Scribner's, 1981 (Volume 11), 419–23.

Commentary: The award to Owen Richardson was "for his work on the thermionic phenomenon and especially for the discovery of the law named after him." "Richardson's Law" or the "Richardson Effect," also known as the "thermionic effect," quantified the theory of electron emission from hot bodies and enabled the development of devices like radio tubes and television tubes. Richardson coined the term "thermion." He also made important contributions through his analysis of the molecular hydrogen spectrum. (F.K.)

1929

Broglie, Louis-Victor Pierre Raymond de   **589**

Prize: Physics, 1929. *Born:* August 15, 1892; Dieppe, France. *Death:* March 19, 1987; Lovveciennes, Yvelines, France. *Parents:* Father, Victor de Broglie; Mother, Pauline d'Armaillé de Broglie. *Nationality:* French. *Religion:* Catholic. *Education:* Univ. of Paris, France, licence in history, 1910; Univ. of Paris, France, licence in science, 1913; Univ. of Paris, France, D.Sc., 1924. *Spouse:* None. *Children:* None. *Career:* Univ. of Paris, France, Professor, 1924–62. *Other Awards:* Henri Poincaré Medal, Académie des Sciences, 1929; Max Planck Medal, German Physical Society, 1938; Kalinga Prize, UNESCO.

Selected Publications: "Recherches sur la Théorie des Quanta." *Annales de Physique* 3 (January-February 1925): 22–128. *La Mécanique Ondulatoire.* Paris: Gauthier-Villars, 1928 (*Selected Papers on Wave Mechanics*. Tr. by W.M. Deans. London: Blackie & Son Limited, 1928 (with L. Brillouin)). *An Introduction to the Study of Wave Mechanics.* Tr. by H.T. Flint. London: Methuen & Co., Ltd., 1930. *Matter and Light: The New Physics.* Tr. by W.H. Johnston. New York: W.W. Norton, 1939. *Non-linear Wave Mechanics: A Causal Interpretation.* Tr. by Arthur J. Knodel and Jack C. Miller. New York: Elsevier, 1960. *The Current Interpretation of Wave Mechanics, a Critical Study.* Tr. by Express Translation Service. New York: Elsevier, 1964.

For More Information See: Current Biography Yearbook. New York: H.W. Wilson, 1955, 67–69. *Modern Scientists and Engineers.* New York: McGraw-Hill, 1980 (Volume 1), 143–44. *Nobel Prize Winners: Physics.* Pasadena, CA: Salem Press, 1988, Volume 1, 361–70. Lochak, G. *Louis de Broglie.* Paris: Flammarion, 1992.

Commentary: Louis de Broglie was awarded the Nobel Prize for his discovery of the wave nature of the electron. He showed that both matter and radiation displayed the properties of both particles and waves, which fit the Einstein theory that matter is merely a form of energy and the two can be converted into each other. Schrödinger and Bohr then used the idea of the wave nature of matter in the development of quantum mechanics. In later work, de Broglie attempted to determine a causal, rather than probabilistic, theory of wave mechanics. As a member of the French Commission on Atomic Energy, he actively promoted the peaceful use of atomic power and was an influence on public opinion toward it in France. (L.A.)

1930

Raman, Chandrasekhara Venkata, Sir   **590**

Prize: Physics, 1930. *Born:* November 7, 1888; Trichinopoly, India. *Death:* November 21, 1970; Bangalore, India. *Parents:* Father, Chandrasekhara Aiyar Raman; Mother, Parvati Ammal Raman. *Nationality:* Indian. *Religion:* Hindu. *Education:* Presidency College, India, B.A., 1902; Presidency College, India, M.A., 1907. *Spouse:* Lokasundari Raman, married June 6, 1907. *Children:* Chandrasekhara, son;

Radhakrishnan, son. *Career:* Indian Finance Department, Researcher, 1907–17; Calcutta Univ., India, Professor, 1917–33; Indian Institute of Science, Bangalore, Professor, 1933–48; Raman Institute of Research, Bangalore, India, Director, 1948–70. *Other Awards:* Knighthood, 1929; Mateucci Medal, Italy, 1929; Hughes Medal, Royal Society, 1930; Franklin Medal, Franklin Institute, PA, 1941.

Selected Publications: "Dynamical Theory of the Motion of Bowed Strings." *Bulletin Indian Association for the Cultivation of Science* 11 (1914). "On the Molecular Scattering of Light in Water and the Color of the Sea." *Proceedings of the Royal Society* 64 (1922). "A New Radiation." *Indian Journal of Physics* 2 (1928): 387. "Crystals and Photons." *Proceedings of the Indian Academy of Science* 13A (1941): 1. *The Physiology of Vision.* Bangalore, India: Indian Academy of Sciences, 1968.

For More Information See: Dictionary of Scientific Biography. New York: Scribner's, 1975 (Volume 11), 264–67. Jayaraman, A. *Chandrasekhara Venkata Raman.* New Delhi: Affiliated East-West Press, 1989. *Nobel Prize Winners: Physics.* Pasadena, CA: Salem Press, 1988, Volume 1, 371–80.

Commentary: Chandrasekhara Venkata Raman was cited by the Academy "for his work on the scattering of light and for the discovery of the effect named after him." Raman discovered that, given the proper circumstances, the light scattered by mercury and other elements and compounds is scattered with a different frequency. He explained the observations, using quantum theory. The Raman effect became a powerful tool for studies of molecular structure and chemical analysis. Raman also contributed major work on the theory of musical instruments, the optics of colloids, electrical and magnetic anisotropy, the physiology of human vision, light diffraction by acoustic waves, x-ray effects on infrared vibrations in light-irradiated crystals, and crystal structure and dynamics. (B.S.S.)

1932

Heisenberg, Werner Karl   **591**

Prize: Physics, 1932. *Born:* December 5, 1901; Würzburg, Germany. *Death:* February 1, 1976; Munich, Germany. *Parents:* Father, August Heisenberg; Mother, Annie Wecklein Heisenberg. *Nationality:* German. *Religion:* Protestant. *Education:* Univ. of Munich, Germany, Ph.D., 1923; Univ. of Göttingen, Germany, Dr. Phil. Habil., 1924. *Spouse:* Elisabeth Schumacher, married April 29, 1937. *Children:* Wolfgang, son; Jochem, son; Martin, son; Anna Maria, daughter; Barbara, daughter; Christine, daughter; Verena, daughter. *Career:* Univ. of Copenhagen, Denmark, Professor, 1924–27; Univ. of Leipzig, Germany, Professor, 1927–41; Univ. of Berlin, Germany, Professor, 1942–45; Univ. of Göttingen, Germany, Professor, 1946–58; Univ. of Munich, Germany, Professor, 1958–70. *Other Awards:* Barnard Medal, Columbia Univ., NY, 1930; Max Planck Medal, German Physical Society, 1933; Grotius Medal, Hugo Grotius Stiftung, 1956; Sigmund Freud Prize, Deutsche Akademie für Sprache und Dichtung, 1970; Niels Bohr Gold Medal, Dansk Ingeniorforening, 1970.

Selected Publications: "Über Quantentheoretische Umdeutung Kinematischer und Mechanischer Beziehungen."

Zeitschrift für Physik 33 (1925): 879–983. "Mehrkörper-problem und Resonanz in der Quantenmechanik." *Zeitschrift für Physik* 38 (1926): 411–26; 41 (1927): 239–67. "Über den Anschaulichen Inhalt der Quantentheoretischen Kinematik und Mechanik." *Zeitschrift für Physik* 43 (1927): 172–98. *The Physical Principles of the Quantum Theory.* Tr. by Carl Eckart and Frank C. Hoyt. Chicago: Univ. of Chicago Press, 1930. *Philosophic Problems of Nuclear Science.* Tr. by F.C. Hayes. New York: Pantheon, 1952. *Physics and Philosophy: The Revolution in Modern Science.* New York: Harper, 1958. *Werner Heisenberg: A Bibliography of His Writings.* Berkeley: University of California Press, 1984.

For More Information See: Biographical Memoirs of the Fellows of the Royal Society. London: Royal Society, 1977 (Volume 22), 213–51. Heisenberg, Elisabeth. *Inner Exile: Recollections of a Life with Werner Heisenberg.* Tr. by Steve Capalari. Boston: Birkhäuser, 1984. Hermann, Armin. *Werner Heisenberg, 1901–1976.* Tr. by Timothy Nevill. Bonn-Bad Godesberg, Germany: Inter Nationes, 1976. Cassidy, D. *Uncertainty.* New York: W. H. Freeman, 1992.

Commentary: Werner Heisenberg received the Nobel Prize "for the creation of quantum mechanics, the application of which has, among other things, led to the discovery of the allotropic forms of hydrogen." He is probably better known for his formulation in 1927 of the uncertainty principle that bears his name, which states that it is impossible *simultaneously* to determine both the position and the momentum of a particle. Heisenberg also investigated problems in ferromagnetism and quantum electrodynamics and was among the first to suggest that the atomic nucleus consisted of protons and neutrons. In later life, he worked on a unified field theory of elementary particles. (L.A.)

1933

Dirac, Paul Adrien Maurice   **592**
Prize: Physics, 1933. *Born:* August 8, 1902; Bristol, England. *Death:* October 20, 1984; Tallahassee, FL. *Parents:* Father, Charles Adrien Ladislas Dirac; Mother, Florence Hannah Holten Dirac. *Nationality:* British; later American resident. *Religion:* Catholic. *Education:* Bristol Univ., England, B.Sc., 1921; Cambridge Univ., England, Ph.D., 1926. *Spouse:* Margit Wigner, married 1937. *Children:* Mary Elizabeth, daughter; Florence Monica, daughter. *Career:* Cambridge Univ., England, Professor, 1927–69; Florida State Univ., Professor, 1971–84. *Other Awards:* Royal Medal, Royal Society, 1939; Copley Medal, Royal Society, 1952; Max Planck Medal, German Institute, 1952.

Selected Publications: The Principles of Quantum Mechanics. London: Clarendon Press, 1930. *The Development of Quantum Theory.* New York: Gordon and Breach Science Publishers, 1971. *Spinors in Hibert Space.* New York: Plenum Press, 1974. *General Theory of Relativity.* New York: Wiley, 1975. *The Selected Works of P. A. M. Dirac.* Cambridge: Cambridge Univ. Press, 1995.

For More Information See: Kursunoglu, Behram N. and Eugene P. Wigner. *Paul Adrien Maurice Dirac.* New York: Cambridge Univ. Press, 1987. *Modern Scientists and Engineers.* New York: McGraw-Hill, 1980 (Volume 1), 292–93. Krage, H. *Dirac.* Cambridge: Cambridge Univ. Press, 1990.

Commentary: Paul Dirac shared the Nobel Prize "for the discovery of new productive forms of atomic theory." His mathematical treatment of electronic properties predicted the existence of positrons, previously unobserved, at an early stage of his career. Dirac continued to develop the new field of quantum mechanics, his great contribution being the Dirac wave equations which included special relativity in the Schrödinger equation. (V.A.H.)

Schrödinger, Erwin   **593**
Prize: Physics, 1933. *Born:* August 12, 1887; Vienna, Austria. *Death:* January 4, 1961; Vienna, Austria. *Parents:* Father, Rudolf Schrödinger; Mother, M. Bauer Schrödinger. *Nationality:* Austrian. *Religion:* Catholic. *Education:* Univ. of Vienna, Austria, Ph.D., 1910. *Spouse:* Annemarie Bertel, married April 6, 1920. *Children:* None. *Career:* Univ. of Vienna, Austria, Researcher, 1910–14; Austrian Army, 1914–20; Univ. of Stuttgart, Germany, Professor, 1920; Univ. of Jena, Germany, Professor, 1920–21; Univ. of Breslau, Germany, Professor, 1921; Univ. of Zürich, Switzerland, Professor, 1921–27; Univ. of Berlin, Germany, Professor, 1927–33; Oxford Univ., England, Researcher, 1933–36; Univ. of Graz, Austria, Professor, 1936–38; Fondation Francqui, Belgium, Professor, 1939–40; Royal Irish Academy, Professor, 1940; Dublin Institute for Advanced Studies, Ireland, Professor, 1940–56; Univ. of Vienna, Austria, Professor, 1956–58. *Other Awards:* Matteuci Medal; Planck Medal.

Selected Publications: "Quantisierung als Eigenwertproblem. Erste Mitteilung." *Ann. Phys.* 79 (1926): 361. "Quantisierung Zweite Mitteilung." *Ann. Phys.* 79 (1926): 489. "Quantisierung Dritte Mitteilung." *Ann. Phys.* 80 (1926): 437. "Quantisierung Vierte Mitteilung." *Ann. Phys.* 81 (1926): 109. *What is Life?* Cambridge: Cambridge Univ. Press, 1945. *Space-Time Structure.* Cambridge: Cambridge Univ. Press, 1950. *Statistical Thermodynamics.* Cambridge: Cambridge Univ. Press, 1952.

For More Information See: Dictionary of Scientific Biography. New York: Scribner's, 1975 (Volume 12), 217–22. Kilmister, C.W. *Schrödinger: A Centenary Celebration of a Polymath.* Cambridge, England: Cambrideg Univ. Press, 1987. "What is Life?" Cambridge: Cambridge Univ. Press, 1992.

Commentary: Erwin Schrödinger was granted the Nobel Prize "for the discovery of new productive forms of atomic theory." Early in his career, Schrödinger worked on specific heats of solids, thermodynamics, atomic spectra, and physiological studies of color, culminating this period with the development of his wave equations. Later he worked on the problem of a unified field theory (of gravitation and electromagnetism) and on other foundational studies in atomic physics. (A.S.)

1935

Chadwick, James, Sir   **594**
Prize: Physics, 1935. *Born:* October 20, 1891; Bollington, England. *Death:* July 24, 1974; Cambridge, England. *Parents:* Father, John Joseph Chadwick; Mother, Anne Mary Knowles Chadwick. *Nationality:* British. *Religion:* Christian. *Education:* Univ. of Manchester, England, baccalaureate,

1911; Univ. of Manchester, England, M.Sc., 1913. *Spouse:* Aileen Stewart-Brown, married 1925. *Children:* 2 daughters. *Career:* Cambridge Univ., England, Researcher, 1919–35; Univ. of Liverpool, England, Professor, 1935–48; Manhattan Project, British Mission, England, Administrator, 1943–48; Cambridge Univ., England, Professor, 1948–59. *Other Awards:* Hughes Medal, Royal Society, 1932; MacKenzie Davidson Medal, 1932; Knighthood, 1945; United States Medal for Merit, 1946; Transenter Medal, 1946; Melchett Medal, 1946; Faraday Medal, Institution of Electrical Engineers, 1950; Copley Medal, Royal Society, 1950; Franklin Medal, Franklin Institute, PA, 1951; Guthrie Medal, 1967.

Selected Publications: Radioactivity and Radioactive Substances. London: Sir Isaac Pitman and Sons, 1921. "The Existence of a Neutron." *Proceedings of the Royal Society of London* A136 (1929): 692–708. *Radiations from Radioactive Substances.* Cambridge: Cambridge Univ. Press, 1930 (with E. Rutherford and C.D. Ellis). "The Neutron." (Bakerian Lecture) *Proceedings of the Royal Society of London* A142 (1933): 1–25. "The Neutron and its Properties." *British Journal of Radiology* 6 (1933): 24–32. "Evidence for a New Type of Disintegration Produced by Neutrons." *Proceedings of the Cambridge Philosophical Society* 30 (1934): 357–64 (with N. Feather and W.T. Davies).

For More Information See: Biographical Memoirs of the Fellows of the Royal Society. London: Royal Society, 1976 (Volume 22), 11–70. Brown, Andrew P. *The Neutron and the Bomb: A Biography of Sir James Chadwick.* Oxford; New York: Oxford University Press, 1997. "Chadwick's Neutron." *Contemporary Physics* 6 (1974): 565–712.

Commentary: James Chadwick's Nobel was granted "for his discovery of the neutron." In a repetition of the Joliot-Curie experiments on alpha-ray bombardment, Chadwick showed that the rays produced traveled at 1/10 the speed of light (too slow to be gamma rays) and that they occasionally struck nitrogen atoms with great force (something a gamma ray could not do). He went on to demonstrate that these rays were neutral and could not be deflected by a magnet; that they were particles and could be absorbed; and that they had a mass of one, like a proton. In discovering the neutron, Chadwick solved the problem of extra mass in the nucleus and laid the groundwork for the release of energy from the atom. He continued to research in the general area of particle bombardment and nuclear structure. (S.H.S.)

1936

Anderson, Carl David 595

Prize: Physics, 1936. *Born:* September 3, 1905; New York, NY. *Death:* January 11, 1991; San Marino, CA. *Parents:* Father, Carl David Anderson; Mother, Emma Adolfina Ajaxson Anderson. *Nationality:* American. *Religion:* Most probably Christian/Protestant. *Education:* California Institute of Technology, B.S., 1927; California Institute of Technology, Ph.D., 1930. *Spouse:* Lorraine Elvira Bergman, married 1946. *Children:* Marshall David Lee, son; David Andrew Keith, son. *Career:* California Institute of Technology, Professor and Administrator, 1930–77. *Other Awards:* Gold Medal, American Institute of the City of New York, 1935; Elliott Cresson Medal, Franklin Institute, PA, 1937; Presidential Certificate of Merit, 1945; John Ericsson Gold Medal, American Society of Swedish Engineers, 1960.

Selected Publications: "Energies and Cosmic-Ray Particles." *Physical Review* (August 15, 1932): 405–21. "Positive Electron." *Physical Review* 43 (March 15, 1933): 491–94. "Cosmic-Ray Positive and Negative Electrons." *Physical Review* 44 (September 1, 1933): 406–16. "Mechanism of Cosmic-Ray Counter Action." *Physical Review* 45 (March 15, 1934): 352–63 (with others). "The Positron." *Nature* 133 (March 1934): 313–16.

For More Information See: Current Biography Yearbook. New York: H.W. Wilson, 1951, 15–17. *The Discovery of Anti-matter: The Autobiography of Carl David Anderson.* Singapore; River Edge, N.J.: World Scientific, 1999. *Nobel Prize Winners: Physics.* Pasadena, CA: Salem Press, Volume 1, 437–47. *New York Times Biographical Service* (January 12, 1991): 26

Commentary: Carl Anderson was recognized by the Academy "for his discovery of the positron." Using a Wilson cloud chamber set in a magnetic field powerful enough to deflect high-energy particles, Anderson photographed charged particles set in motion by cosmic rays. In August 1932, Anderson photographed a charged particle moving upward, and because cosmic rays only move downward, he concluded that this must be a positively charged particle released inside the cloud chamber. The particle appeared to have the mass of an electron, and its ionizing power was too weak to be a proton or alpha particle. Carl Anderson had discovered the positive electron which would become a significant contribution to the understanding of atomic structure. Anderson was also known for his research on cosmic rays and for proving the existence of the meson in 1938. (S.H.S.)

Hess, Victor Franz 596

Prize: Physics, 1936. *Born:* June 24, 1883; Schloss Waldstein, Austria. *Death:* December 17, 1964; Mount Vernon, NY. *Parents:* Father, Vincenz Hess; Mother, Serafine Edle von Grossbauer-Waldstatt Hess. *Nationality:* Austrian; later American citizen. *Religion:* Catholic. *Education:* Univ. of Graz, Austria, Ph.D., 1906. *Spouse:* Mary Berta Waermer Breisky, married 1920, died 1955; Elizabeth Hoencke, married 1955. *Children:* None. *Career:* Univ. of Graz, Austria, Researcher, 1906–08; Vienna Veterinary College, Austria, Professor, 1908–10; Univ. of Vienna, Austria, Professor, 1910–20; Univ. of Graz, Austria, Professor, 1920–21; U.S. Radium Corp., NY, Researcher, 1921–23; Univ. of Graz, Austria, Professor, 1923–31; Univ. of Innsbruck, Austria, Professor, 1931–37; Univ. of Graz, Austria, Professor, 1937–38; Fordham Univ., NY, Professor, 1938–58. *Other Awards:* Lieben Prize, Austrian Academy of Sciences, 1919; Abbe Prize, Carl Zeiss Foundation, 1932.

Selected Publications: Die Elektrische Leitfahigkeit der Atmosphare und Ihre Ursachen. Brunswick, Germany: F. Viewig and Sohn, 1926. *Die Weltraumstrahlung und Ihre Biologischen Wirkungen.* Zürich: Drell Füssli, 1940. "The Discovery of Cosmic Radiation." *Thought* (1940): 1–12. "Work in the USA." *Oesterreichische Hochschulzeitung* (January 15, 1955): 4.

For More Information See: Dictionary of Scientific Biography. New York: Scribner's, 1972 (Volume 6), 354–56.

Nobel Prize Winners: Physics. Pasadena, CA: Salem Press, 1988, Volume 1, 427–35. Wilson, J.G. "Obituary Notice." *Nature* 207 (1965): 352.

Commentary: Victor Hess won the Nobel Prize "for his discovery of cosmic radiation." Hess developed the instrumentation and, in a series of daring ascents in balloons and careful study over a period of many years, showed that there was a source of powerful radiation beyond the galaxy which flooded the earth constantly and produced radiation greater in intensity and power than sources on earth. Hess continued to study cosmic radiation throughout his career. (R.J.)

1937

Davisson, Clinton Joseph   597

Prize: Physics, 1937. *Born:* October 22, 1881; Bloomington, IL. *Death:* February 1, 1958; Charlottesville, VA. *Parents:* Father, Joseph Davisson; Mother, Mary Calvert Davisson. *Nationality:* American. *Religion:* Christian. *Education:* Univ. of Chicago, IL, B.S., 1908; Princeton Univ., NJ, Ph.D., 1911. *Spouse:* Charlotte Sara Richardson, married August 4, 1911. *Children:* Clinton Owen Calvert, son; James Willans, son; Richard Joseph, son; Elizabeth Mary, daughter. *Career:* Carnegie Institute of Technology, Pittsburgh, PA, Professor, 1911–17; Bell Telephone Laboratories, NJ, Researcher, 1917–46; Univ. of Virginia, Charlottesville, Professor, 1947–49. *Other Awards:* Comstock Prize, National Academy of Sciences, U.S., 1928; Elliot Cresson Medal, Franklin Institute, PA, 1931; Hughes Medal, Royal Society, 1935; Alumni Medal, Univ. of Chicago, IL, 1941.

Selected Publications: "Dispersion of Hydrogen and Helium on Bohr's Theory." *Physical Review, 2nd Series* 8 (1916): 20–27. "Scattering of Electrons by Nickel." *Science, New Series* 54 (1921): 522–24 (with C.H. Kunsman). "Thermionic Work Function of Tungsten." *Physical Review, 2nd Series* 20 (1922): 300–30 (with L.H. Germer). "Reflection and Refraction of Electrons by a Crystal of Nickel." *Proceedings of the National Academy of Sciences, USA* 14 (1928): 619–27 (with L.H. Germer).

For More Information See: Biographical Memoirs. National Academy of Sciences. Washington, DC: National Academy of Sciences, 1962 (Volume 36), 51–84. *Dictionary of Scientific Biography.* New York: Scribner's, 1971 (Volume 3), 597–98.

Commentary: Clinton Davisson shared the Nobel Prize with George Paget Thomson "for their experimental discovery of the diffraction of electrons by crystals." Davisson studied electron diffraction by nickel crystals and confirmed the de Broglie theory of the wave nature of particles. At the same time that Davisson was studying electron diffraction, he was also doing landmark research in thermal radiation and thermionics. His later research focused on the theory of electron optics and its application, the theory of electronic devices, and solid state physics. (B.S.S.)

Thomson, George Paget, Sir   598

Prize: Physics, 1937. *Born:* May 3, 1892; Cambridge, England. *Death:* September 10, 1975; Cambridge, England. *Parents:* Father, Joseph John Thomson; Mother, Rose Elisabeth Paget. *Nationality:* British. *Religion:* Anglican. *Education:* Cambridge Univ., England, baccalaureate, 1914.

Spouse: Kathleen Adam Smith, married September 18, 1924. *Children:* John Adam, son; Lilian Clare, daughter; David Paget, son; Rose Buchanan, daughter. *Career:* Cambridge Univ., England, Professor, 1919–22; Univ. of Aberdeen, Scotland, Professor, 1922–30; Imperial College of Science, England, Professor, 1930–52; Cambridge Univ., England, Professor and Administrator, 1952–62. *Other Awards:* Hughes Medal, Royal Society, 1939; Knighthood, 1943; Royal Medal, Royal Society, 1949; Faraday Medal, Institution of Electrical Engineers, 1960.

Selected Publications: The Atom. London: Oxford Univ. Press, 1930 (with J.J. Thomson). *Wave Mechanics of Free Electrons.* New York: McGraw-Hill, 1930. *Theory and Practice of Electron Diffraction.* New York: Macmillan, 1939 (with W. Cochrane). *The Foreseeable Future.* London: Cambridge Univ. Press, 1955. *The Inspiration of Science.* London: Oxford Univ. Press, 1961.

For More Information See: Biographical Memoirs of the Fellows of the Royal Society. London: Royal Society, 1977 (Volume 23), 529–56. *Current Biography Yearbook.* New York: H.W. Wilson, 1947, 635–37.

Commentary: George Thomson was awarded the Nobel Prize "for the experimental discovery of the interference phenomenon in crystals irradiated by electrons," which provided ammunition for those who believed in the wave properties of electrons. He developed the techniques of electron diffraction and moved to the study of nuclear physics, becoming involved in fission studies and the atomic bomb development. (T.M.)

1938

Fermi, Enrico   599

Prize: Physics, 1938. *Born:* September 29, 1901; Rome, Italy. *Death:* November 28, 1954; Chicago, IL. *Parents:* Father, Alberto Fermi; Mother, Ida de Gattis Fermi. *Nationality:* Italian; later American citizen. *Religion:* Agnostic; Jewish sympathies. *Education:* Univ. of Pisa, Italy, Ph.D., 1922. *Spouse:* Laura Capon, married 1928. *Children:* Giulio, son; Nella, daughter. *Career:* Univ. of Florence, Italy, Professor, 1924–26; Univ. of Rome, Italy, Professor, 1926–38; Columbia Univ., NY, Professor, 1939–45; Univ. of Chicago, IL, Professor, 1945–54. *Other Awards:* Hughes Medal, 1942; Franklin Medal, Franklin Institute, PA, 1947; Barnard Gold Medal, Columbia Univ., NY, 1950; Rumford Medal, 1953; Fermi Prize, 1954.

Selected Publications: Collected Papers. 2 volumes. Chicago: Univ. of Chicago Press, 1962–65.

For More Information See: Dictionary of Scientific Biography. New York: Scribner's, 1971 (Volume 4), 576–83. Fermi, Laura. *Atoms in the Family.* Chicago: Univ. of Chicago Press, 1954. Segre, Emilio. *Enrico Fermi, Physicist.* Chicago: Univ. of Chicago Press, 1970. Pontekorvo, B. *Enrico Fermi.* Pordenone, Italy: Edizioni Studio Tesi, 1993.

Commentary: A physicist who was both a theoretician and an experimentalist, Enrico Fermi received the Nobel Prize "for his demonstrations of the existence of new radioactive elements produced by neutron irradiation, and for his related discovery of nuclear reactions brought about by slow neutrons." His accomplishments were foundation points for many branches of physics, including studies of the statistics of particles obeying the exclusion principle, quantum electrodynamics, beta-decay, artificial radioactivity, pion-nucleon collisions, and nuclear chain reactions. (A.N. and B.S.S.)

1939

Lawrence, Ernest Orlando 600

Prize: Physics, 1939. *Born:* August 8, 1901; Canton, SD. *Death:* August 27, 1958; Palo Alto, CA. *Parents:* Father, Carl Gustavus Lawrence; Mother, Gunda Jacobson Lawrence. *Nationality:* American. *Religion:* Lutheran. *Education:* Univ. of South Dakota, B.A., 1922; Univ. of Minnesota, M.A., 1923; Yale Univ., CT, Ph.D., 1925. *Spouse:* Mary Kimberly Blumer, married May 1932. *Children:* John Eric, son; Margaret Bradley, daughter; Mary Kimberley, daughter; Robert Don, son; Barbara Hundale, daughter; Susan, daughter. *Career:* Yale Univ., CT, Professor, 1925–28; Univ. of California, Berkeley, Professor and Administrator, 1928–58. *Other Awards:* Elliot Cresson Medal, Franklin Institute, PA, 1937; Comstock Prize, National Academy of Sciences, U.S., 1937; Hughes Medal, Royal Society, 1937; Duddell Medal, Royal Physical Society, 1940; Faraday Medal, 1952; American Cancer Society Medal, 1954; Enrico Fermi Award, 1957; Sylvanus Thayer Award, 1958.

Selected Publications: "On the Production of High Speed Protons." *Science* 72 (1930): 376–77 (with N.E. Edlefsen). "Disintegration of Lithium by Swiftly Moving Protons." *Physical Review* 42 (1932): 150–51 (with M.S. Livingston and M.G. White). "An Improved Cyclotron." *Science* 86 (1937): 411 (with Donald Cooksey). "High Energy Physics." *American Scientist* 36 (1948): 41–49. "High-Current Accelerators." *Science* 122 (1955): 1127–32.

For More Information See: Biographical Memoirs. National Academy of Sciences. Washington, DC: National Academy of Sciences, 1970 (Volume 41), 251–94. Childs, Herbert. *An American Genius: The Life of Ernest Lawrence.* New York: Dutton, 1968. *Dictionary of Scientific Biography.* New York: Scribner's, 1973 (Volume 8), 93–96.

Commentary: Ernest Lawrence was honored by the Academy "for the invention and development of the cyclotron and for results obtained with it, especially with regard to artificial radioactive elements." The cyclotron permitted nuclear particle acceleration to very high velocities. The particles were used to bombard atoms, leading to many new isotopes and elements, some of which were adapted by Lawrence and his brother to medical and biological applications. Lawrence was a prolific researcher and writer who led the way to many advances. He was an important part of the Atomic Bomb Project and the attempt to suspend atomic-bomb testing. He also contributed in the areas of ionization potentials of metals, measurement of small time intervals, and the measurement of the electron's e/m ratio. (B.S.S.)

1943

Stern, Otto 601

Prize: Physics, 1943. *Born:* February 17, 1888; Sohrau, Germany. *Death:* August 17, 1969; Berkeley, CA. *Parents:* Father, Oskar Stern; Mother, Eugenie Rosenthal Stern. *Nationality:* German; later American citizen. *Religion:* Jewish. *Education:* Univ. of Breslau, Germany, Ph.D., 1912. *Spouse:* None. *Children:* None. *Career:* Technische Hochschule, Zürich, Switzerland, Professor, 1913–14; Univ.

of Frankfürt, Germany, Professor, 1914–21; Univ. of Rostock, Germany, Professor, 1921–22; Univ. of Hamburg, Germany, Professor, 1923–33; Carnegie Institute of Technology, PA, Professor, 1933–45.

Selected Publications: "Zur Kinetischen Theorie des Dampfdrucks Einatomiger Fester Stoffe und über die Entropiekonstante Einatomiger Gase." *Physikalische Zeitschrift* 14 (1913): 629–32. "Die Entropie Fester Losungen." *Annalen der Physik, 4th Series* 49 (1916): 823–41. "Ein Weg zur Experimentellen Prufung der Richtungsquantelung im Magnetfeld." *Zeitschrift für Physik* 7 (1921): 249–53. "Das Magnetische Moment des Silberatoms." *Zeitschrift für Physik* 9 (1922): 353–55 (with W. Gerlach). "Über die Richtungsquantelung im Magnetfeld." *Annalen der Physik, 4th Series* 74 (1924): 673 (with W. Gerlach).

For More Information See: Biographical Memoirs of the National Academy of Sciences. Washington, DC: National Academy of Sciences, 1973, 215–36. *Dictionary of Scientific Biography.* New York: Scribner's, 1976 (Volume 13), 40–43. Estermann, I. *Recent Research in Molecular Beams.* New York: Academic Press, 1959, 1–7.

Commentary: Otto Stern received the Nobel Prize "for his contribution to the development of the molecular ray method and his discovery of the magnetic moment of the proton." Stern's early work was theoretical, in the areas of statistical thermodynamics and quantum theory. As noted in the Academy's citation, Stern's major contribution was in the development of the molecular beam method and its application in studying the characteristics of molecules and atoms. His later research, with Gerlach, was on atom deflection by magnetic field action on the magnetic moment and also on the magnetic moments of subatomic particles. His finding of a proton magnetic moment two to three times larger than expected was a stimulus to much research. Stern also studied the wave nature of atoms and molecules. (B.S.S.)

1944

Rabi, Isidor Isaac 602

Prize: Physics, 1944. *Born:* July 29, 1898; Rymanov, Austria. *Death:* January 11, 1988; New York, NY. *Parents:* Father, David Robert Rabi; Mother, Jennie Teig Rabi. *Nationality:* Austrian; later American citizen. *Religion:* Jewish. *Education:* Columbia Univ., NY, Ph.D., 1927. *Spouse:* Helen Newark, married August 17, 1926. *Children:* Nancy Elizabeth, daughter; Margaret Joella, daughter. *Career:* Columbia Univ., NY, Professor, 1929–67. *Other Awards:* Sigma Xi Semicentennial Prize, 1936; Elliot Cresson Medal, Franklin Institute, PA, 1942; United States Medal for Merit, 1948; King's Medal, England, 1948; Commander, Order of the Southern Cross, Brazil, 1952; Henrietta Szold Award, 1956; Barnard Medal, 1960; Priestley Memorial Award, Dickinson College, PA, 1964; Niels Bohr International Gold Medal, 1967; Atoms for Peace Award, 1967; Tribute of Appreciation, United States State Department, 1978; Pupin Gold Medal, Columbia Univ., 1981; Franklin D. Roosevelt Four Freedoms Medal, 1985; Public Welfare Medal, National Academy of Sciences, 1985; Vannevar Bush Award, 1986; Weizmann Medallion, 1987.

Selected Publications: "The Principal Magnetic Susceptibilities of Crystals." *Physical Review* 29 (1927): 174–85.

"Nuclear Spin in Isotopic Mixtures." *Physical Review* 45 (1934): 334. "A New Method of Measuring Nuclear Magnetic Moment." *Physical Review* 53 (1938): 318 (with others). "Molecular Beam Resonance Method for Measuring Nuclear Magnetic Moments. The Magnetic Moments of 3-LI-6, 3-Li-7, and 9-F-19." *Physical Review* 55 (1939): 526–35 (with others). "The Radiofrequency Spectra of Atoms." *Physical Review* 57 (1940): 765–80 (with P. Kusch and S. Millman). *Science: The Center of Culture.* New York: World Publishing, 1970.

For More Information See: My Life and Times as a Physicist. Claremont, CA: Claremont College, 1960. Rigden, John. *Rabi: Scientist and Citizen.* New York: Basic Books, 1987.

Commentary: Isidor Isaac Rabi won the Nobel Prize for his atomic- and molecular-beam work and for his discovery of the resonance method—a precise means of determining the magnetic moments of fundamental particles. He assisted in the development of radar and the atomic bomb, and his work in defining the properties of atomic nuclei contributed to the invention of the laser, maser, and atomic clock. Rabi is one of the founders of Brookhaven National Laboratory in Upton, New York, and, while a member of UNESCO, he originated the movement that led to the foundation of the international laboratory for high-energy physics in Geneva called CERN. (L.N.W.)

1945

Pauli, Wolfgang Ernst   603

Prize: Physics, 1945. *Born:* April 25, 1900; Vienna, Austria. *Death:* December 15, 1958; Zürich, Switzerland. *Parents:* Father, Wolfgang Joseph Pauli; Mother, Bertha Schutz Pauli. *Nationality:* Austrian; later Swiss citizen. *Religion:* Catholic. *Education:* Univ. of Munich, Germany, Ph.D., 1921. *Spouse:* Kate Deppner, married (no date found), divorced (no date found); Franciska Bertram, married April 4, 1934. *Children:* None. *Career:* Univ. of Göttingen, Germany, Researcher, 1921–22; Univ. of Copenhagen, Denmark, Researcher, 1922–23; Univ. of Hamburg, Germany, Professor, 1923–28; Eidgenossische Technishe Hochschule, Zürich, Switzerland, Professor, 1928–58. *Other Awards:* Lorentz Medaille, 1930; Franklin Medal, 1952; Max Planck Medal, 1958.

Selected Publications: "Relativitatstheorie." *Encyklopadie der Mathematischen Wissenschaften.* Leipzig, Germany: 1921 (Volume 2), 539–775 (*Theory of Relativity*. Tr. by G. Field. New York: Pergamon Press, 1958). "Über den Zusammenhang des Abschlusses der Elektronengruppen im Atom mit der Komplexstruktur der Spektren." *Zeitschrift für Physik* 31 (1925): 765. *Naturerklarung und Psyche.* Zürich: Rascher, 1952 (with C.G. Jung). *Collected Scientific Papers.* Ed. by R. Kronig and V.F. Weisskopf. New York: Interscience Publishers, 1964.

For More Information See: Current Biography Yearbook. New York: H.W. Wilson, 1946, 468, 470. *Dictionary of Scientific Biography.* New York: Scribner's, 1974 (Volume 10), 422–25. *Theoretical Physics in the Twentieth Century: A Memorial Volume to Wolfgang Pauli.* Ed. by Markus Fierz and V.F. Weisskopf. New York: Interscience Publishers, 1960. *Writings on Physics and Philosophy.* Berlin: Springer-Verlag, 1994.

Commentary: Wolfgang Pauli was given the Nobel Prize "for his decisive contribution through his discovery in 1925 of a new law of nature, the exclusion principle, or Pauli Principle." This principle states that no two electrons in the same atom can exist in the same state. It is important in understanding the periodic system of the elements and in all theories of atomic and nuclear structure. Pauli's contributions to modern theoretical physics spanned a lifetime. He studied under Arnold Sommerfeld in Munich and, while only 20 years of age, wrote a 200-page article on the theory of relativity which remains highly regarded today. He did much research in quantum field theory and postulated the neutrino—a subatomic particle—in 1931 to explain energy anomalies in emission of beta particles from atoms. Through his scientific publications, he exerted a decisive influence in the evolution of quantum theory. (L.N.W.)

1946

Bridgman, Percy Williams   604

Prize: Physics, 1946. *Born:* April 21, 1882; Cambridge, MA. *Death:* August 20, 1961; Randolph, NH. *Parents:* Father, Raymond Landon Bridgman; Mother, Ann Maria Williams Bridgman. *Nationality:* American. *Religion:* Most probably Christian. *Education:* Harvard Univ., MA, B.A., 1904; Harvard Univ., MA, M.A., 1905; Harvard Univ., MA, Ph.D., 1908. *Spouse:* Olive Ware, married July 16, 1912. *Children:* Jane, daughter; Robert Ware, son. *Career:* Harvard Univ., MA, Professor, 1908–54. *Other Awards:* Rumford Medal, American Academy of Arts and Sciences, 1929; Cresson Medal, Franklin Institute, Philadelphia, PA, 1932; Comstock Prize, National Academy of Sciences, 1933; Bakhius-Roozeboom Medal, Royal Academy of Sciences, Amsterdam, Netherlands, 1933; Bingham Medal, Society of Rheology; Research Corporation of America Award, 1937.

Selected Publications: The Logic of Modern Physics. New York: Macmillan, 1927. *The Physics of High Pressure.* New York: Macmillan, 1931. *The Nature of Thermodynamics.* Cambridge, MA: Harvard Univ. Press, 1941. *The Thermodynamics of Electrical Phenomena in Metals and a Condensed Collection of Thermodynamic Formulas.* New York: Dover Publications, 1961. *Collected Experimental Papers.* Cambridge, MA: Harvard Univ. Press, 1964.

For More Information See: Biographical Memoirs of the Fellows of the Royal Society. London: Royal Society, 1962 (Volume 8), 26–40. *Dictionary of Scientific Biography.* New York: Scribner's, 1971 (Volume 2), 457–61. *Reflections of a Physicist.* New York: Philosophical Library, 1950. Walter, Maila L. *Science and Cultural Crisis: An Intellectual Biography of Percy Williams Bridgman.* Stanford, CA: Stanford University Press, 1990.

Commentary: Percy Bridgman was awarded the Nobel Prize "for the invention of apparatus for obtaining very high pressures and for discoveries which he made by means of this apparatus in the field of high pressure physics." His development of a chamber capable of withstanding higher pressures than ever before realized opened the way for new experiments of immense scientific value and resulted, with his other work, in major advances in thermodynamics, the properties of matter, crystallography, and electric conduction in metals. He also was responsible for the production of synthetic diamonds by General Electric. In addition to Bridgman's long and distinguished career at Harvard working in high pressure physics, he was also involved in the philosophical aspects of physics, as seen in his works *The Logic of Physics* and *The Nature of Physical Theory*. (S.G.)

1947

Appleton, Edward Victor, Sir   605

Prize: Physics, 1947. *Born:* September 6, 1892; Bradford, England. *Death:* April 21, 1965; Edinburgh, Scotland. *Parents:* Father, Peter Appleton; Mother, Mary Wilcock Appleton. *Nationality:* British. *Religion:* Protestant. *Education:* Cambridge Univ., England, B.A., 1913. *Spouse:* Jessie Longson, married 1915, died 1964; Helen F. Allison, married 1965. *Children:* Marjery, daughter; Rosalind, daughter. *Career:* Cambridge Univ., England, Researcher, 1917–24; London Univ., England, Professor, 1924–36; Cambridge Univ., England, Professor, 1936–49; Univ. of Edinburgh, Scotland, Administrator, 1949–65. *Other Awards:* Knighthood, 1941; Medal of Merit, U.S., 1947; French Legion of Honor, 1947; Albert Medal, Royal Society of Arts, 1950; Gunning Victoria Jubilee Prize, Royal Society, Edinburgh, Scotland, 1960; Medal of Honor, Institute of Radio Engineers of America, 1962.

Selected Publications: "Equivalent Heights of the Atmospheric Ionized Regions in England and America." *Nature* 123 (1929): 445. *The Thermionic Value*. London: Methuen, 1931. *Thermionic Vacuum Tubes*. New York: E.P. Dutton, 1933. "Some Problems of Atmospheric Physics. Atmospheric Ozone." *Journal of the Royal Society of Arts* 85 (1937): 299–307. "New Material for Old." *J. Inst. Civil Engrs. (London)* 8 (1939–40): 448–68.

For More Information See: Biographical Memoirs of the Fellows of the Royal Society. London: Royal Society, 1966 (Volume 12), 1–21. Clark, Ronald William. *Sir Edward Appleton*. Oxford; New York: Pergamon Press, 1971. *Dictionary of Scientific Biography*. New York: Scribner's, 1970 (Volume 1), 195–96.

Commentary: Edward Appleton was awarded the Nobel Prize "for his investigations of the physics of the upper atmosphere, especially for the discovery of the so-called Appleton layer." Appleton first proved the existence of the ionosphere, 60 miles above ground, and his radiolocation experiments led to the development of radar. He later discovered the Appleton layer, 150 miles above ground, and showed that it reflected short waves around the earth. His research introduced the prospects of round-the-world broadcasting. Appleton also helped develop cathode ray oscillography and showed that sunspots emit short radio waves. (B.S.S.)

1948

Blackett, Patrick Maynard Stuart   606

Prize: Physics, 1948. *Born:* November 18, 1897; London, England. *Death:* July 13, 1974; London, England. *Parents:* Father, Arthur Stuart Blackett; Mother, Caroline Frances Maynard Blackett. *Nationality:* British. *Religion:* Anglican. *Education:* Cambridge Univ., England, B.A., 1921; Cambridge Univ., England, M.A., 1923. *Spouse:* Constanza

Bayon, married 1924. *Children:* Giovanna, daughter; Nicholas, son. *Career:* British Navy, 1914–19; Cambridge Univ., England, Professor, 1923–33; Univ. of London, England, Professor, 1933–37; Univ. of Manchester, England, Professor, 1937–53; Imperial College of Science and Technology, London, England, Professor, 1953–65. *Other Awards:* Royal Medal, Royal Society of London, 1940; American Medal for Merit, 1946; Dalton Medal, 1949; Copley Medal, Royal Society, 1956; Order of Merit, 1967.

Selected Publications: "Some Photographs of the Tracks of Penetrating Radiation." *Proceedings of the Royal Society of London* A139 (1934): 699 (with G.P.S. Occhialini). "Some Experiments on the Production of Positive Electrons." *Proceedings of the Royal Society of London* A144 (1934): 235 (with J. Chadwick and G.P.S. Occhialini). *Cosmic Rays. The Halley Lecture*. Oxford: Clarendon Press, 1936. *Military and Political Consequences of Atomic Energy*. London: Turnstile Press, 1948. "The Elementary Particles of Nature." *British Journal of Radiology* 31 (1958): 1.

For More Information See: Biographical Memoirs of the Fellows of the Royal Society. London: Royal Society, 1975 (Volume 21), 1–115. Lovell, Bernard. *PMS Blackett: A Biographical Memoir*. London: Royal Society, 1976.

Commentary: The award to Patrick Maynard Stuart Blackett was for "his development of the Wilson cloud chamber and his discoveries therewith in the field of nuclear physics and cosmic radiation." Blackett's other scientific contributions include the theories of pair production and annihilation radiation, a confirmation of the existence of the positron, the discovery of strange particles, and a new theory explaining the earth's magnetism. He was also active in public affairs and an intense opponent of nuclear weapons. (V.C.)

1949

Yukawa, Hideki   607

Prize: Physics, 1949. *Born:* January 23, 1907; Tokyo, Japan. *Death:* September 8, 1981; Kyoto, Japan. *Parents:* Father, Takuji Ogawa; Mother, Koyuki Ogawa; Adopted by Gen'yo Yukawa and his wife, Michi, in 1932. *Nationality:* Japanese. *Religion:* Buddhist (of the Jodo sect). *Education:* Kyoto Imperial Univ., Japan, M.S., 1929; Osaka Univ., Japan, Doctor of Science, 1938. *Spouse:* Sumiko Yukawa, married April 1932. *Children:* Harumi, son; Takaaki, son. *Career:* Kyoto Imperial Univ., Japan, Professor, 1932–70. *Other Awards:* Imperial Prize, Japan Academy, 1940; Decoration of Cultural Merit, 1943; Lomonosov Gold Medal, 1964; Order of Merit, Germany, 1964; Order of Rising Sun, Japan, 1977.

Selected Publications: "On the Interaction of Elementary Particles. I." *Proceedings of the Physical-Mathematical Society of Japan* 17 (1935): 48. *Introduction to Quantum Mechanics*. Tokyo: Kobundo, 1947. *Introduction to the Theory of Elementary Particles*. 2 volumes. Tokyo: Iwanami Shoten, 1948. *Yukawa Hideki Jishenshu (Selected Works of Hideki Yukawa)*. 5 volumes. Tokyo: Asahi Shimbunsha, 1971. *Creativity and Intuition: A Physicist Looks at East and West*. Tr. by J. Bester. Tokyo: Kodansha International, 1973. *Hideki Yukawa Scientific Works*. Tokyo: Iwanami Shoten, 1979.

For More Information See: Biographical Memoirs of the Royal Society. London: Royal Society, 1983, 661–76. *Tabibito, the Traveler.* (autobiography). Tr. by L. Brown and R. Yoshida. Singapore: World Scientific, 1982.

Commentary: Hideki Yukawa won the Nobel Prize "for his prediction of the existence of mesons on the basis of theoretical work on nuclear forces." His research continued on the meson theory and on the general theory of elementary particles related to the concept of the non-local field. Yukawa's pioneering research on the mesons and their essential properties provided "an enormous stimulus to the theoretical as well as experimental physics." In addition, he was a scientist with a broad vision, well versed in classical literature, and keenly aware of social responsibilities of scientists. As a result, he worked as an activist for peace, a world government, and nuclear disarmament. (J.V.S.)

1950

Powell, Cecil Frank 608

Prize: Physics, 1950. *Born:* December 5, 1903; Tonbridge, Kent, England. *Death:* August 9, 1969; Bellano, Lake Como, Italy. *Parents:* Father, Frank Powell; Mother, Elizabeth Caroline Bisacre Powell. *Nationality:* British. *Religion:* Protestant. *Education:* Cambridge Univ., England, baccalaureate, 1925; Cambridge Univ., England, Ph.D., 1927. *Spouse:* Isobel Therese Artner, married 1932. *Children:* 2 daughters. *Career:* Bristol Univ., England, Professor, 1928–69. *Other Awards:* Charles Vernon Boys Prize, 1947; Hughes Medal, Royal Society, 1949; Rutherford Medal and Prize, 1960; Royal Medal, Royal Society, 1961; Lomonosov Gold Medal, Soviet Academy of Sciences, 1967; Guthrie Medal and Prize, Institute of Physics and Physical Society, 1969.

Selected Publications: The Study of Elementary Particles by the Photographic Method. London: Pergamon Press, 1959. "Cosmic Radiation." *Proceedings of the Institute of Electrical Engineers* 107B (1960): 389–94. "The Role of Pure Science in European Civilization." *Physics Today* 18 (1965): 56–64. "Promise and Problems of Modern Science." *Nature* 216 (1967): 543–46. *Selected Papers of Cecil Frank Powell.* Ed. by E.H.S. Burhop, W.O. Lock, and M.G.K. Menon. Amsterdam: North-Holland, 1972.

For More Information See: Biographical Memoirs of the Fellows of the Royal Society. London: Royal Society, 1971, 541–63. *Dictionary of Scientific Biography.* New York: Scribner's, 1975 (Volume 11), 117–18.

Commentary: C.F. Powell received the Nobel Prize "for his development of the photographic method in the study of nuclear processes and for his discoveries concerning mesons." His work in the use of photographic emulsions to track electrically charged particles began in the 1930s, following his work with Tyndall on ionic mobility in gases. Powell's technique led to the discovery of a new particle, the pi-meson, followed by many successive discoveries of unstable elementary particles. His research school at Bristol played a dominant role in particle physics through 1956. Powell was also committed to the social responsibility of the scientist and to international cooperation, founding the Pugwash Movement for Science and World Affairs, and serving as president of the World Federation of Scientific Workers. (S.G.)

1951

Cockcroft, John Douglas, Sir 609

Prize: Physics, 1951. *Born:* May 27, 1897; Todmorden, Yorkshire, England. *Death:* September 18, 1967; Cambridge, England. *Parents:* Father, John Arthur Cockcroft; Mother, Maude Fielden Cockcroft. *Nationality:* British. *Religion:* Anglican. *Education:* Univ. of Manchester, England, M.Sc.Tech., 1922; Cambridge Univ., England, B.A., 1924; Cambridge Univ., England, Ph.D., 1928. *Spouse:* Eunice Elizabeth Crabtree, married August 26, 1925. *Children:* 4 daughters; 1 son. *Career:* Cambridge Univ., England, Professor, 1928–39; British Government Service, 1939–44; British Atomic Energy Projects, 1944–59; Cambridge Univ., England, Professor, 1959–67. *Other Awards:* Hughes Medal, 1938; American Freedom Medal, 1947; Knighthood, 1948; Chevalier de la Legion d'Honneur, 1950; Royal Medal, Royal Society, 1954; Faraday Medal, 1955; Kelvin Gold Medal, 1956; Niels Bohr International Gold Medal, 1958; Grand Cross, Order of Alfonso X, Spain, 1958; Atoms for Peace Award, 1961.

Selected Publications: "The Design of Coils for the Production of Strong Magnetic Fields." *Philosophical Transactions of the Royal Society* A227 (1928): 317–43. "Experiments with High Velocity Positive Ions." *Proceedings of the Royal Society* A129 (1930): 477–89 (with E.T.S. Walton). "Experiments with High Velocity Positive Ions. I. Further Developments in the Method of Obtaining High Velocity Positive Ions." *Proceedings of the Royal Society* A136 (1932): 619–30 (with E.T.S. Walton). "Experiments with High Velocity Positive Ions. II. The Disintegration of Elements by High Velocity Protons." *Proceedings of the Royal Society* A137 (1932): 229–42.

For More Information See: Biographical Memoirs of the Fellows of the Royal Society. London: Royal Society, 1968 (Volume 14), 139–88. *Dictionary of Scientific Biography.* New York: Scribner's, 1971 (Volume 3), 328–31. Hartcup, Guy, and Allibone, T.E. *Cockcroft and the Atom.* Bristol, England: Adam Hilger, 1984.

Commentary: John Cockcroft shared the Nobel Prize for his "pioneer work on the transmutation of atomic nuclei by artificially accelerated atomic particles." Beginning with his interest in producing intense magnetic fields and low temperatures, Cockcroft soon began to collaborate with his colaureate, E.T.S. Walton, in accelerating protons by high voltages, and also studied radioactivity and elements produced by high-energy protons and deuterons. A gifted administrator, Cockcroft was also involved in wartime research and in the British Atomic Energy Projects. (C.G. and L.S.)

Walton, Ernest Thomas Sinton 610

Prize: Physics, 1951. *Born:* October 6, 1903; Dungarvan, Ireland. *Death:* June 25, 1995; Belfast, Ireland. *Parents:* Father, John Arthur Walton; Mother, Anna Elizabeth Sinton Walton. *Nationality:* Irish. *Religion:* Methodist. *Education:* Methodist College, Ireland, B.A., 1922; Trinity College, Ireland, M.A., 1926; Trinity College, Ireland, M.Sc., 1927; Cambridge Univ., England, Ph.D., 1930. *Spouse:* Winifred Isabel Wilson, married 1934. *Children:* Alan, son; Marian, daughter; Philip, son; Jean, daughter. *Career:* Lord Rutherford's Research Assistant, 1927–34; Trinity College,

Dublin, Ireland, Professor, 1934–74. **Other Awards:** Hughes Medal, Royal Society, 1938.

Selected Publications: "Production of High Speed Electrons by Indirect Means." *Cambridge Philosophical Society Proceedings* (October 1929): 469–81. "Experiments with High Velocity Positive Ions." *Royal Society Proceedings* A (November 3, 1930): 477–89 (with J. Cockcroft). "Transmutation of Lithium and Boron." *Royal Society Proceedings* A (September 1, 1933): 733–42 (with P.I. Dee). "High Velocity Positive Ions, Part 3: Disintegration of Li, B, and C by Diplons." *Royal Society Proceedings* A (May 1, 1934): 704–20 (with J. Cockcroft). "Part 4: Production of Induced Radioactivity by Protons and Diplons." *Royal Society Proceedings* A (January 1, 1935): 225–40 (with J. Cockcroft and C.W. Gilbert).

For More Information See: *Current Biography Yearbook.* New York: H.W. Wilson, 1952, 618–20. *Modern Men of Science.* New York: McGraw-Hill, 1966, 509–10. *Nobel Prize Winners: Physics.* Pasadena, CA: Salem Press, 1988, Volume 2, 591–600. *New York Times Biographical Service* (June 28, 1995): 938.

Commentary: The Academy cited Ernest Walton (along with John Cockcroft) "for their pioneer work on the transmutation of atomic nuclei by artificially accelerated atomic particles." While working for Rutherford at Cambridge, Walton built a linear accelerator which became a prototype for subsequent atom-smashers. Using voltages of about 400 kilowatts, with a proton current of a few microamperes, Walton and Cockcroft were able to bombard lithium atoms with sufficient force to transform each lithium nucleus into two helium nuclei—the first successful transmutation of elements by human means. Their experiments demonstrated the enormous energies available in atomic nuclei and provided the first experimental confirmation of Einstein's equations showing the equivalence of mass and energy. (L.R.S.)

1952

Bloch, Felix   611

Prize: Physics, 1952. **Born:** October 23, 1905; Zürich, Switzerland. **Death:** September 10, 1983; Zürich, Switzerland. **Parents:** Father, Gustav Bloch; Mother, Agnes Mayer Bloch. **Nationality:** Swiss; later American citizen. **Religion:** Jewish. **Education:** Univ. of Leipzig, Germany, Ph.D., 1928. **Spouse:** Lore Clara Misch, married March 14, 1940. **Children:** George, son; Daniel, son; Frank, son; Ruth, daughter. **Career:** Univ. of Zürich, Switzerland, Researcher, 1928–29; Univ. of Utrecht, Netherlands, Researcher, 1929–30; Univ. of Leipzig, Germany, Researcher, 1930–31; Univ. of Copenhagen, Denmark, Researcher, 1931–32; Univ. of Leipzig, Germany, Professor, 1932–33; Stanford Univ., CA, Professor, 1934–71.

Selected Publications: "The Magnetic Moment of the Neutron." *Ann. Inst. Henri Poincare* 8 (1938): 63–78. "Nuclear Induction." *Physical Review* 70 (1946): 460–74. "Chemical Analysis by Nuclear Inductions." *U.S. Patent 2, 561, 481.* July 24, 1951 (with William W. Hansen). "Dynamical Theory of Nuclear Induction. II." *Physical Review* 102 (1956): 104–35.

For More Information See: Chodorow, Marvin. *Felix Bloch and the Twentieth Century Physics.* Houston, TX: Rice Univ. Press, 1980. *Nobel Prize Winners: Physics.* Pasadena, CA: Salem Press, 1988, Volume 2, 601–10.

Commentary: The Academy honored Felix Bloch for his "development of high precision methods in the field of nuclear magnetism and the discoveries which were made through the use of these methods." Bloch introduced the techniques of nuclear magnetic resonance, used initially to measure the magnetic moments of the proton and neutron, but utilized later for analysis of organic molecules. Bloch also was a major figure in research on electron behavior in crystals, the properties of ferromagnetic domains, x-ray phenomena, quantum electrodynamics, and superconductivity. (L.I.S.)

Purcell, Edward Mills   612

Prize: Physics, 1952. **Born:** August 30, 1912; Taylorville, IL. **Death:** March 7, 1997; Cambridge, MA. **Parents:** Father, Edward A. Purcell; Mother, Mary Elizabeth Mills Purcell. **Nationality:** American. **Religion:** Most probably Christian/Protestant. **Education:** Purdue Univ., IN, B.S.E.E., 1933; Harvard Univ., MA, A.M., 1935; Harvard Univ., MA, Ph.D., 1938. **Spouse:** Beth C. Busser, married January 22, 1937. **Children:** Dennis W., son; Frank B., son. **Career:** Harvard Univ., MA, Professor, 1938–40; Massachusetts Institute of Technology, Researcher, 1941–45; Harvard Univ., MA, Professor, 1946–80. **Other Awards:** Oersted Medal, American Association of Physics Teachers, 1968; National Medal of Science, 1980; Harvard Medal, 1986.

Selected Publications: "Relaxation Effects in Nuclear Magnetic Resonance Absorption." *Physical Review* 73 (1948): 679–712 (with N. Bloembergen and R.V. Pound). "Structural Investigations by Means of Nuclear Magnetism. I. Rigid Crystal Lattices." *Journal of Chemical Physics* 17 (1949): 972–81 (with others). "A Precise Determination of the Proton Magnetic Moment in Bohr Magnetons." *Physical Review* 76 (1949): 1262–63 (with J.H. Gardner). "Interactions between Nuclear Spins in Molecules." *Physical Review* 85 (1952): 143–44 (with N.F. Ramsey).

For More Information See: *Current Biography Yearbook.* New York: H.W. Wilson, 1954, 519–21. *Nobel Prize Winners: Physics.* Pasadena, CA: Salem Press, 1988, Volume 2, 611–20.

Commentary: Edward Purcell shared the Nobel Prize for "development of new methods of nuclear magnetic precision measurements and discoveries in connection therewith." He independently discovered a method of measuring nuclear magnetism with radio waves, without affecting the structure being examined. Previous methods, particularly those of I.I. Rabi, depended on vaporizing the substance to be examined. Purcell's method also provided for much more accurate values of nuclear magnetic moments. By 1949, Purcell had completed the research for which he won the prize. He continued to make contributions in the fields of nuclear magnetism, radio astronomy, astrophysics, and biophysics. (M.H.)

1953

Zernike, Frits   613

Prize: Physics, 1953. **Born:** July 16, 1888; Amsterdam, Netherlands. **Death:** March 10, 1966; Naarden, Netherlands. **Parents:** Father, Carl Frederick August Zernike;

Mother, Antje Dieperink Zernike. *Nationality:* Dutch. *Religion:* Protestant. *Education:* Univ. of Amsterdam, Netherlands, Ph.D., 1915. *Spouse:* Dora van Bommel van Vloten, married 1929, died 1944; L. Koperberg-Baanders, married 1954. *Children:* 2 children. *Career:* Univ. of Groningen, Netherlands, Professor, 1913–58. *Other Awards:* Gold Medal, Dutch Society for Sciences, 1912; Rumford Medal, Royal Society, 1952.

Selected Publications: "Die Beugung von Rontgenstrahlen in Flussigkeiten als Effect der Molekulanordnung." *Z. Phys.* 41 (1927): 184 (with J.A. Prins). "Diffraction Theory of the Knife-Edge Test and Its Improved Form, the Phase-Contrast Method." *Mon. Nat. Roy. Astron. Soc.* 94 (1934): 377. "Das Phasenkontrastverfahren bei der Mikroskopschen Beobachtung." *Z. Techn. Phys.* 16 (1935): 454. "The Propagation of Order in Cooperative Phenomena." *Physica* 7 (1940): 565. "A Precision Method for Measuring Small Phase Differences." *Journal of the Optical Society of America* 40 (1950): 326.

For More Information See: Biographical Memoirs of the Fellows of the Royal Society. Cambridge: Royal Society, 1967 (Volume 13), 393–402. *Dictionary of Scientific Biography.* New York: Scribner's, 1976 (Volume 14), 616–17.

Commentary: The Academy cited Frits Zernike "for his demonstration of the phase-contrast method, especially for his invention of the phase-contrast microscope." Zernike was able to show that there were indeed phase differences between incident and refracted light, required by the concept of light as a wave motion. He then used this phenomenon to develop a microscope capable of viewing otherwise invisible particles, such as bacteria and cells. Zernike was also a significant contributor to the development of photography, statistics theory, the galvanometer, and optics. (R.J.)

1954

Born, Max   614

Prize: Physics, 1954. *Born:* December 11, 1882; Breslau, Germany. *Death:* January 5, 1970; Göttingen, Germany. *Parents:* Father, Gustav Born; Mother, Margaretta Kauffman Born. *Nationality:* German; later British citizen. *Religion:* Jewish. *Education:* Univ. of Göttingen, Germany, Ph.D., 1907. *Spouse:* Hedwig Ehrenberg, married August 2, 1913. *Children:* Irene, daughter; Margaret, daughter; Gustav, son. *Career:* Cambridge Univ., England, Researcher, 1907–08; Univ. of Breslau, Germany, Researcher, 1908–09; Univ. of Göttingen, Germany, Professor, 1909–12; Univ. of Chicago, IL, Researcher, 1912–15; Univ. of Berlin, Professor, 1915–19; German Army, 1915–19; Univ. of Frankfurt, Germany, Professor, 1919–21; Univ. of Göttingen, Germany, Professor, 1921–33; Cambridge Univ., England, Professor, 1933–36; Univ. of Edinburgh, Scotland, Professor, 1936–53. *Other Awards:* Stokes Medal, England, 1934; Macdougall-Brisbane and Gunning-Victoria Jubilee Prize, Royal Society of Edinburgh, Scotland, 1945, 1950; Max Planck Medaille, Germany, 1948; Hughes Medal, Royal Society, 1950; Grotius Medal, Munich, Germany, 1956.

Selected Publications: Zur Begrundung der Matrizenmechanik. Stuttgart, Germany: E. Battenberg, 1962. *Zur Statistischen Deutung der Quantentheorie.* 2 volumes. Stuttgart, Germany: E. Battenberg, 1962. *Ausgewoehlte*

Abhandlungen (collected works). 2 volumes. Göttingen, Germany: Vandenhoek and Ruprecht, 1963.

For More Information See: Dictionary of Scientific Biography. New York: Scribner's, 1978 (Volume 15), 39–44. *Mein Leben. Die Errinerungen des Nobelpreistragers.* Munich: Nymphenburger Verlagshandlung, 1975 (*My Life: Recollections of a Nobel Laureate.* New York: Scribner, 1978). *Physics in My Generation.* New York: Pergamon Press, 1956.

Commentary: Max Born was cited by the Academy for his statistical interpretation of the quantum theory. His early work on vibrations and lattice energies in crystals was followed by his pioneer efforts in the areas of quantum theory and matrix mechanics. Born was also a leading figure in the early explanations of the wave-particle ambiguities of physics. (M.N.)

Bothe, Walther Wilhelm Georg   615

Prize: Physics, 1954. *Born:* January 8, 1891; Oranienburg, Germany. *Death:* February 8, 1957; Heidelberg, Germany. *Parents:* Father, Friedrich Bothe; Mother, Charlotte Hartung Bothe. *Nationality:* German. *Religion:* Lutheran. *Education:* Univ. of Berlin, Germany, Ph.D., 1914. *Spouse:* Barbara Below, married July 6, 1920. *Children:* Elena, daughter; Johanna, daughter. *Career:* German Army, 1915–20; Univ. of Berlin, Germany, Professor, 1920–30; Giessen Univ., Germany, Professor, 1930–32; Max Planck Institute, Germany, Researcher and Administrator, 1932–57. *Other Awards:* Order Pour le Mérite, peace class, 1952; Max Planck Prize, 1953; Grossen Verdeinstkreuz Bundesrepublik, 1954.

Selected Publications: "Ein Weg zur Experimentellen Nachprufund der Theorie von Bohr, Kraners und Slater." *Zeitschrift für Physik* 26 (1924): 44. "Über des Wesen des Comptoneffekts." *Zeitschrift für Physik* 32 (1925): 639. *Atlas Typischer Nebelkammerbilder.* Berlin: J. Springer, 1940 (with Wolfgang Gentner). "Das Wesen der Hohenstrahlung." *Zeitschrift für Physik* 56 (1959): 75.

For More Information See: Current Biography Yearbook. New York: H.W. Wilson, 1955, 55–56. *Dictionary of Scientific Biography.* New York: Scribner's, 1973 (Volume 2), 337–39. *Nobel Prize Winners: Physics.* Pasadena, CA: Salem Press, 1988, Volume 2, 643–52.

Commentary: The Nobel Committee honored Walther Bothe for "the coincidence method and his discoveries with this method" and cited him for his leadership in the "new physics." The coincidence method Bothe used was based on the fact that a single particle passing through two or more counters produces pulses from each counter practically coincident in time. The method was used to study angular distribution of cosmic rays, the Compton Effect, and many other physics problems. Bothe also contributed significantly in his research on the corpuscular theory of light, light quanta and interference, and fission products. (M.N.C.)

1955

Kusch, Polycarp   616

Prize: Physics, 1955. *Born:* January 26, 1911; Blankenburg, Germany. *Death:* March 20, 1993; Dallas, TX. *Parents:* Father, John Matthias Kusch; Mother, Henrietta Van der Haas Kusch. *Nationality:* American. *Religion:* Lutheran.

Education: Case Institute of Technology, OH, B.S., 1931; Univ. of Illinois, M.S., 1933; Univ. of Illinois, Ph.D., 1936. *Spouse:* Edith Starr McRoberts, married August 12, 1935, died December 1959; Betty Jane Pezzoni, married 1960. *Children:* Kathryn, daughter; Judith, daughter; Sara, daughter; Diana, daughter; Maria, daughter. *Career:* Univ. of Minnesota, Researcher, 1936–37; Columbia Univ., NY, Professor, 1937–41; Westinghouse Electric and Manufacturing Company, Researcher, 1941–42; Columbia Univ., NY, Researcher, 1942–44; Bell Telephone Laboratories, NJ, Researcher, 1944–46; Columbia Univ., NY, Professor and Administrator, 1946–72; Univ. of Texas at Dallas, Professor, 1972–82. *Other Awards:* Illinois Achievement Award, Univ. of Illinois, 1975.

Selected Publications: "The Radiofrequency Spectra of Atoms." *Physical Review* 57 (1940): 765–80 (with S. Millman and I.I. Rabi). "The Magnetic Moment of the Electron." *Physical Review* 74 (1948): 250–63 (with H.M. Foley). "The Magnetic Moment of the Proton." *Physical Review* 75 (1949): 1481–92 (with H. Taub). "The World of Science and the Scientist's World." *Bulletin of the Atomic Scientists* 24 (October 1968): 38–43. "A Personal View of Science and the Future." In *The Future of Science; 1975 Nobel Conference Organized by Gustavus Adolphus College.* New York: John Wiley & Sons, 1977, 39–55.

For More Information See: Current Biography Yearbook. New York: H.W. Wilson, 1956, 348–50. *National Cyclopedia of American Biography.* New York: James T. White, 1960 (Volume I), 35. *Nobel Prize Winners: Physics.* Pasadena, CA: Salem Press, 1988, Volume 2, 663–72. *New York Times Biographical Service* (March 23, 1993): 401.

Commentary: Polycarp Kusch made careful analyses of the magnetic moment of the electron based on the structure of energy levels in various elements and was, thereby, able to disprove the long-prevailing calculations of Dr. P.M.A. Dirac. These results led to the development of new scientific principles serving as the basis of quantum electrodynamics. The importance of Kusch's "precision determination of the magnetic moment of the electron" merited him the Nobel Prize, which he shared with William Lamb, a colleague who had performed experiments related to Kusch's. In later years Kusch also devoted much effort to promoting science education. (C.H.W.)

Lamb, Willis Eugene, Jr.   617

Prize: Physics, 1955. *Born:* July 12, 1913; Los Angeles, CA. *Parents:* Father, Willis Eugene Lamb; Mother, Marie Helen Metcalf Lamb. *Nationality:* American. *Religion:* No religious affiliation. *Education:* Univ. of California, B.S., 1934; Univ. of California, Ph.D., 1938. *Spouse:* Ursula Schaefer, married June 5, 1939, died 1996; Bruria Kaufman, married November 29, 1996. *Children:* None. *Career:* Columbia Univ., NY, Professor, 1938–51; Stanford Univ., CA, Professor, 1951–56; Oxford Univ., England, Professor, 1956–62; Yale Univ., CT, Professor, 1962–74; Univ. of Arizona, Professor, 1974-. *Other Awards:* Rumford Award, American Academy of Arts, 1953; Research Corporation Award, 1955; Yeshiva Award, 1962.

Selected Publications: "Fine Structure of the Hydrogen Atom by a Microwave Method." *Physical Review* 72 (1947): 241–43 (with Robert C. Retherford). "Formation of Metastable Hydrogen Atoms by Electron Bombardment of

H-2." *Physical Review* 75 (1949): 1332 (with Robert C. Retherford). "The Fine Structure of Singly Ionized Helium." *Physical Review* 78 (1950): 539–50 (with Miriam Skinner). "Fine Structure of n-3 Hydrogen by a Radio-Frequency Method." *Physical Review* 103 (1956): 313–14 (with T.M. Sanders). *Laser Physics.* Reading, MA: Addison-Wesley Publishing Co., 1974 (with M. Sargent and M.O. Scully).

For More Information See: Current Biography Yearbook. New York: H.W. Wilson, 1956, 357–58. *National Cyclopedia of American Biography.* New York: James T. White, 1963 (Volume J), 238. *Nobel Prize Winners: Physics.* Pasadena, CA: Salem Press, 1988, Volume 2, 653–62.

Commentary: Willis Lamb received the Nobel Prize for his "discoveries regarding the hyperfine structure of the hydrogen spectrum." His accurate studies showed that the two possible energy states of hydrogen, rather than being equal as predicted by Dirac, differed by a very small amount. The "Lamb shift" required a revision of the theory of interaction of the electron with electromagnetic radiation. Lamb also contributed significantly in theoretical physics, atomic and nuclear structure, microwave spectroscopy, and maser and laser physics. (L.I.S.)

1956

Bardeen, John   618

Prize: Physics, 1956; Physics, 1972 [SEE REF]. *Born:* May 23, 1908; Madison, WI. *Death:* January 30, 1991; Boston, MA. *Parents:* Father, Charles Russell Bardeen; Mother, Althea Harmer Bardeen. *Nationality:* American. *Religion:* "Hardly any"; from Unitarian/Catholic background. *Education:* Univ. of Wisconsin, B.S., 1928; Univ. of Wisconsin, M.A., 1929; Princeton Univ., NJ, Ph.D., 1936. *Spouse:* Jane Maxwell, married 1938. *Children:* James Maxwell, son; William Allen, son; Elizabeth Ann Bardeen Greytak, daughter. *Career:* Gulf Research and Development, Geophysicist, 1930–33; Harvard Univ., MA, Fellow, 1935–38; Univ. of Minnesota, Professor, 1938–41; U.S. Naval Ordinance Laboratory, Physicist, 1941–45; Bell Telephone Laboratories, NJ, Physicist, 1945–51; Univ. of Illinois, Professor, 1951–75. *Other Awards:* Stuart Ballantine Medal, Franklin Institute, 1952; Buckley Prize, American Physical Society, 1954; John Scott Medal, City of Philadelphia, 1955; Fritz London Award, 1962; Vincent Bendix Award, American Society of Engineering Education, 1966; Michelson-Morley Award, Case Western Reserve Univ., OH, 1968; Medal of Honor, Institute of Electrical and Electronic Engineering, 1971; James Madison Medal, Princeton Univ., NJ, 1973; Franklin Institute Medal, 1975; Presidential Medal of Freedom, 1977; Lomonosov Medal, 1987.

Selected Publications: "Interaction between Electrons and Lattice Vibrations." *Canadian Journal of Physics* 34 (1956): 1171–89. "Research Leading to the Point-Contact Transistor." *Science* 126 (1957): 105–13. "Theory of Superconductivity." *Physical Review* 108 (1957): 1175–204. "Critical Fields and Currents in Superconductors." *Reviews of Modern Physics* 34 (1962): 667–75. "Review of the Present Status of the Theory of Superconductivity." *IBM Journal of Research* 6 (1962): 3–11. "Electron-phonon Interactions and Superconductivity." *Science* 181 (1973): 1209–14. *A Collection of Professor John Bardeen's Publications on*

Semiconductors and Superconductivity. Urbana: Univ. of Illinois Press, 1988.

For More Information See: Modern Men of Science. 2 volumes. New York: McGraw-Hill, 1966–68 (Volume 1), 19–20. Weinraub, Bernard. "Six Americans Win Nobel Prizes in Physics and Chemistry Fields." *New York Times* (October 21, 1972): 1, 14. *Biographical Memoirs of the Fellows of the Royal Society*. London: Royal Society, 1994 (Volume 39): 19.

Commentary: John Bardeen was the third Nobel laureate to win the prize twice and the first to win twice in the same field, the first time (1956) for cooperative research on "semiconductors and . . . discovery of the transistor effect" and the second time (1972) for a cooperative development of a theory of superconductivity. His initial work had been the basis for the emergence of the solid state electronics industry. His later work permitted a theoretical explanation of the disappearance of electrical resistance in materials at temperatures close to absolute zero. (L.M.W.)

Brattain, Walter Houser   619

Prize: Physics, 1956. *Born:* February 10, 1902; Amoy, China. *Death:* October 13, 1987; Seattle, WA. *Parents:* Father, Ross R. Brattain; Mother, Ottilie Houser Brattain. *Nationality:* American. *Religion:* From Quaker background. *Education:* Whitman College, WA, B.S., 1924; Univ. of Oregon, M.A., 1926; Univ. of Minnesota, Ph.D., 1929. *Spouse:* Keren Gilmore, married July 5, 1935, died April 1957; Emma Jane Kirsch Miller, married May 10, 1958. *Children:* William Gilmore, son. *Career:* Bureau of Standards, Washington, DC, Researcher, 1928–29; Bell Telephone Laboratories, NJ, 1929–67; Whitman College, Walla Walla, WA, Professor, 1967–72. *Other Awards:* Stuart Ballantine Medal, Franklin Institute, PA, 1952; John Scott Medal, Philadelphia, PA, 1955; National Inventors Hall of Fame, 1974.

Selected Publications: "Nature of the Forward Current in Germanium Point Contacts." *Physical Review* 74 (1948): 231–32 (with J. Bardeen). "The Transistor, a Semi-Conductor Triode." *Physical Review* 74 (1948): 230–31 (with J. Bardeen). "Physical Principles Involved in Transistor Action." *Physical Review* 75 (1949): 1208–25 (with J. Bardeen). "Surface Properties of Semiconductors." *Science* 126 (1957): 151–53. "The Distribution of Potential Across the Low-Index Crystal Planes of Germanium Contacting on Aqueous Solution." *Proceedings of the National Academy of Sciences* 48 (1962): 2005–12 (with P.J. Boddy).

For More Information See: Current Biography Yearbook. New York: H.W. Wilson, 1957, 68–70. *National Cyclopedia of American Biography*. New York: James T. White, 1960 (Volume 1), 404–05. *Nobel Prize Winners: Physics*. Pasadena, CA: 1988, Volume 2, 695–704. *New York Times Biographical Service* (October 14, 1987): 1040. *Biographical Memoirs. National Academy of Sciences*. Washington, D.C.: National Academy Press, 1994, Volume 63, 69.

Commentary: Walter Houser Brattain shared the Nobel Prize for his "investigations on semiconductors and the discovery of the transistor effect." While engaged in semiconductor research at Bell Laboratories to find a substitute for vacuum tubes in radios, he and his colaureates invented the transistor and showed that certain semiconductors could rectify and amplify currents and voltages. Brattain's contributions to solid state physics also include his work on the photoeffect at the free surface of a semiconductor. During World War II, Brattain worked on the magnetic detection of submarines. (B.N.L.)

Shockley, William Bradford   620

Prize: Physics, 1956. *Born:* February 13, 1910; London, England. *Death:* August 12, 1989; Palo Alto, CA. *Parents:* Father, William Hillman Shockley; Mother, May Bradford Shockley. *Nationality:* American. *Religion:* Atheist; from Protestant background. *Education:* California Institute of Technology, B.S., 1932; Massachusetts Institute of Technology, Ph.D., 1936. *Spouse:* Jean Alberta Bailey, married 1933, divorced 1955; Emily I. Lanning, married 1955. *Children:* Alison, daughter; William, son; Richard, son. *Career:* Bell Telephone Laboratories, NJ, Researcher, 1936–42; United States Navy, Research Director, 1942–44; Bell Telephone Laboratories, NJ, Researcher, 1945–55; Shockley Semiconductor Laboratories, Director, 1955–58; Shockley Transistor Corporation, President, 1958–60; Shockley Transistor Unit, Director, 1960–63; Consultant, 1963–65; Stanford Univ., CA, Professor, 1963–75. *Other Awards:* Medal of Merit, United States, 1946; Morris Leibmann Prize, Institute of Radio Engineers, 1951; O.E. Buckley Prize, American Physical Society, 1953; Comstock Prize, National Academy of Sciences, 1954; Wilhelm Exner Medal, Oesterreichischer Gewerberein, 1963; Holley Medal, American Society of Mechanical Engineers, 1963; Public Service Achievement Award, National Aeronautics and Space Administration, 1969; Gold Medal, Institute of Electrical and Electronics Engineers, 1972; National Inventors Hall of Fame, 1974; Medal of Honor, Institute of Electrical and Electronics Engineers, 1980; California Inventor's Hall of Fame, 1983.

Selected Publications: "Density of Surface States on Silicon Deduced from Contact Potential Measurements." *Physical Review* 72 (1947): 345 (with W. Brattain). "Modulation of Conductance of Thin Films of Semiconductors by Surface Charges." *Physical Review* 74 (1948): 232–33 (with G.L. Pearson). "Investigation of Hole Injection in Transistor Action." *Physical Review* 75 (1949): 691 (with J.R. Haynes). *Electrons and Holes in Semiconductors*. New York: D. Van Nostrand Co., 1950. "The Mobility and Life of Injected Holes and Electrons in Germanium." *Physical Review* 81 (1951): 835–43 (with J.R. Haynes). "Statistics of the Recombinations of Holes and Electrons." *Physical Review* 87 (1952): 835–42 (with W.T. Read).

For More Information See: Current Biography Yearbook. New York: H.W. Wilson, 1953, 569–71. *Modern Men of Science*. New York: McGraw-Hill, 1966, 430. *Nobel Prize Winners: Physics*. Pasadena, CA: Salem Press, Volume 2, 673–82. *New York Times Biographical Service* (August 14, 1989): 776.

Commentary: William Shockley won the Nobel Prize for his "researches on semiconductors and discovery of the transistor effect." Shockley advanced the hypothesis which led the way to the invention of the transistor, which freed electronics from the disadvantages of the vacuum tube, and provided a device which could rectify extremely high-frequency signals with great reliability. In later years, his theories on the genetic differences between races occupied much of his time and were widely criticized. (D.A.K.)

1957

Lee, Tsung-Dao 621

Prize: Physics, 1957. *Born:* November 25, 1926; Shanghai, China. *Parents:* Father, Tsing-Kong Lee; Mother Ming-Chang Chang Lee. *Nationality:* Chinese; later American citizen. *Religion:* No religious affiliation. *Education:* National Chekiang Univ., China, baccalaureate, 1944; Univ. of Chicago, IL, Ph.D., 1950. *Spouse:* Jeanette Hui-Chung Chin, married June 3, 1950. *Children:* James, son; Stephen, son. *Career:* Univ. of California, Berkeley, Researcher, 1950–51; Institute for Advanced Study, Princeton, NJ, Researcher, 1951–53; Columbia Univ., NY, Professor, 1953–60; Institute for Advanced Study, Princeton, NJ, Researcher, 1960–63; Columbia Univ., NY, Professor, 1963-. *Other Awards:* Albert Einstein Commemorative Award in Science, Yeshiva Univ., 1957; Science Award, Newspaper Guild of NY, 1957.

Selected Publications: "Interaction of Mesons with Nucleons and Light Particles." *Physical Review* 75 (1949): 905 (with C.N. Yang and M. Rosenbluth). "Mass Degeneracy of the Heavy Mesons." *Physical Review* 102 (1956): 290–91 (with C.N. Yang). "Question of Parity Conservation in Weak Interactions." *Physical Review* 104 (1956): 254–58 (with C.N. Yang). "Parity Nonconservation and a Two-Component Theory of the Neutrino." *Physical Review* 105 (1957): 1671–75 (with C.N. Yang). "Remarks on Possible Noninvariance under Time Reversal and Charge Conjugation." *Physical Review* 106 (1957): 340–45 (with C.N. Yang). *Particle Physics and Introduction to Field Theory.* New York: Harwood Academic Press, 1981. *T.D. Lee: Selected Papers.* Boston, MA; Birkhauser, 1987.

For More Information See: Current Biography Yearbook. New York: H.W. Wilson, 1958, 240–41. *Physics Teacher* 20 (May 1982), 281–88. *Nobel Prize Winners: Physics.* Pasadena, CA: Salem Press, 1988, Volume 2, 715–25.

Commentary: The award to Tsung-Dao Lee and Chen Ning Yang was "for their penetrating investigation of the so-called parity laws which has led to important discoveries regarding the elementary particles." The parity principle had held that there was no difference between right and left or that the mirror image of a nuclear reaction was identical to the reaction. Lee and Yang could not make the K-meson particles fit this accepted theory. They questioned the underlying theory of symmetry and proposed experiments to check their ideas. In addition to his work on parity nonconservation, Lee's work was noteworthy in the areas of statistical mechanics, nuclear and subnuclear physics, field theory, astrophysics, and turbulence. (F.K.)

Yang, Chen Ning 622

Prize: Physics, 1957. *Born:* September 22, 1922; Hofei, Anwhei, China. *Parents:* Father, Ke Chuan Yang; Mother, Meng Hwa Loh Yang. *Nationality:* Chinese; later American citizen. *Religion:* No religious affiliation; parents are also unaffiliated. *Education:* National Southwest Associated Univ., China, B.Sc., 1942; Tsinghua Univ., China, M.Sc., 1944; Univ. of Chicago, IL, Ph.D., 1948. *Spouse:* Chih Li Tu, married August 26, 1950. *Children:* Franklin, son; Gilbert, son; Eulee, daughter. *Career:* Univ. of Chicago, IL, Professor, 1948–49; Institute for Advanced Study, Princeton, NJ, Professor, 1949–65; State Univ. of New York, Stony Brook, Professor and Administrator, 1965-. *Other Awards:* Albert Einstein Commemorative Award, 1957; Rumford Prize, 1980; National Medal of Science, 1986; Liberty Award, 1986; Franklin Medal, 1993.

Selected Publications: "Interaction of Mesons with Nucleons and Light Particles." *Physical Review* 75 (1949): 905 (with T.D. Lee and M. Rosenbluth). "Reflection Properties of Spin 1/2 Fields and a Universal Fermi-Type Interaction." *Physical Review* 79 (1950): 495–98 (with J. Tiomno). "Mass Degeneracy of the Heavy Mesons." *Physical Review* 102 (1956): 290–91 (with T.D. Lee). "Question of Parity Conservation in Weak Interactions." *Physical Review* 104 (1956): 254–58 (with T.D. Lee). "Parity Nonconservation and a Two-Component Theory of the Neutrino." *Physical Review* 105 (1957): 1671–75 (with T.D. Lee). "Remarks on Possible Noninvariance under Time Reversal and Charge Conjugation." *Physical Review* 106 (1957): 340–45 (with T.D. Lee). *Selected Papers, 1945–80, with Commentary.* San Francisco, CA: W.H. Freeman, 1983.

For More Information See: Biographical Encyclopedia of Scientists. New York: Facts on File, 1981, 866. Liu, C.S. and Yau, Shing-Tung. *Chen Ning Yang: a Great Physicist of the Twentieth Century.* Cambridge, MA: International Press, 1995. *Nobel Prize Winners: Physics.* Pasadena, CA: Salem Press, 1988, Volume 2, 705–13.

Commentary: Chen Ning Yang shared the Nobel Prize with Tsung-Dao Lee "for their penetrating investigation of the so-called parity laws which has led to important discoveries regarding the elementary particles." Yang and Lee could not make K-mesons fit the accepted theory of parity conservation, so they experimented to demonstrate parity nonconservation. In addition to the research on parity nonconservation, Yang's major interests were in the areas of statistical mechanics and symmetry principles. (B.S.S.)

1958

Cherenkov, Pavel Alekseyevich 623

Prize: Physics, 1958. *Born:* July 28, 1904; Novaya Chigla, Russia. *Parents:* Father, Aleksei Cherenkov; Mother, Mariya Cherenkov. *Nationality:* Russian. *Religion:* Most probably Christian/Eastern Orthodox. *Education:* Voronezh Univ., USSR, graduate, 1928; Physics Institute, USSR Academy of Science, Doctorate of Physico-Mathematical Sciences, 1940. *Spouse:* Marya Putintseva, married 1930. *Children:* Aleksei, son; Elena, daughter. *Career:* Lebedev Physic Institute, Moscow, USSR, Researcher and Administrator, 1930-. *Other Awards:* Stalin Prize, 1946; Order of Lenin, 1964.

Selected Publications: "Visible Glow of Pure Liquids under the Influence of Gamma-rays." *Compt. Rend. Acad. Sci. U.R.S.S.* 2 (1934): 451–54. "Visible Radiation Produced by Electrons Moving in a Medium with Velocities Exceeding that of Light." *Physical Review* 52 (1937): 378–79. "Visible Radiation of Pure Liquids under the Action of Fast Electrons." *Bull. Acad. Sci. U.R.S.S., Classe sci. Mat. Nat., Ser. Phys* (1937): 455–91. "Absolute Output of Radiation

Caused by Electrons Moving within a Medium with Super-Light Velocity." *Compt. Rend. Acad. Sci. U.R.S.S.* 21 (1938): 116–21. "Radiation of Electrons Moving with Super-Light Speed." *Trudy Fiz. Inst. Im. P.N. Lebedeva, Akad. Nauk. S.S.S.R.* 2 (1944): 3–62.

For More Information See: Asimov's Biographical Encyclopedia of Science and Technology. Garden City, NY: Doubleday, 1982, 801. *Nobel Prize Winners: Physics.* Pasadena, CA: Salem Press, 1988, Volume 2, 727–34.

Commentary: Pavel Cherenkov shared the Nobel for his work on "the discovery and the interpretation of the Cherenkov effect." Cherenkov observed the emission of blue light from water bombarded by gamma-rays. This Cherenkov effect, produced by charged atomic particles moving at velocities greater then the speed of light, and the Cherenkov detector for observing high-speed particles became standards for work on nuclear physics and cosmic rays. Cherenkov also contributed to the development and construction of electron accelerators and study of photo-nuclear and photo-meson reactions. (G.E.M.)

Frank, Ilya Mikaylovich 624

Prize: Physics, 1958. *Born:* October 23, 1908; Leningrad, Russia. *Death:* June 22, 1990; Moscow, USSR. *Parents:* Father, Mikhail Luydvigovic Frank; Mother, Yelizaveta Mikhailovna Gratsianova Frank. *Nationality:* Russian. *Religion:* No record found. *Education:* Moscow State Univ., USSR, baccalaureate, 1930; Moscow State Univ., USSR, Doctor of Physio-mathematical Sciences, 1935. *Spouse:* Ella Abramovna Beilikhis, married 1937. *Children:* Alexander, son. *Career:* State Optical Institute, USSR, Professor, 1931–34; Lebedev Institute of Physics, USSR, Professor, 1934–90. *Other Awards:* Stalin Prize, 1946, 1954, 1971; Order of Lenin (3); Vavilov Gold Medal, 1979; Lenin Prize.

Selected Publications: "The Excitation Function and the Absorption Curve in the Optical Dissociation of Thallium Iodide." *Physik Z. Sowjetunion* 2 (1932): 319–36. "Coherent Visible Radiation of Fast Electrons Passing through Matter." *Compt. Rend. Acad. Sci. U.R.S.S.* 14 (1937): 109–14 (with I. Tamm). "Visible Radiation of Pure Liquids under the Action of Rapid Electrons." *Bull. Acad. Sci. U.R.R.S., Classe Sci. Math, Nat., Ser. Phys* (1938): 29–30. (with I. Tamm and P.A. Cherenkov). "A New Type of Nuclear Reactions (The Splitting of Uranium and Thorium Nuclei under the Influence of Neutrons)." *Priroda* 9 (1939): 20–27.

For More Information See: Biographical Encyclopedia of Scientists. New York: Facts on File, 1981, 280–81. *Modern Men of Science.* New York: McGraw-Hill, 1966, 182. *Nobel Prize Winners: Physics.* Pasadena, CA: Salem Press, Volume 2, 735–43. *New York Times Biographical Service* (June 25, 1990): 597.

Commentary: The Nobel Prize was shared by Ilya Frank for his contributions to "the discovery and interpretation of the Cherenkov effect." Frank's work on the interpretation of the Cherenkov effect, produced by charged atomic particles moving at velocities greater than the speed of light, made it possible for the Cherenkov effect and Cherenkov detector to become standards for work in nuclear physics and cosmic rays. Frank also carried out significant research on photoluminescence, photochemistry, pair production by gamma-rays, reactions of light nuclei, and nuclear fission by mesons. (G.E.M.)

Tamm, Igor Evgenevich 625

Prize: Physics, 1958. *Born:* July 8, 1895; Vladivostok, Russia. *Death:* April 12, 1971; Moscow, USSR. *Parents:* Father, Evgenij Tamm; Mother, Olga Davidova Tamm. *Nationality:* Russian. *Religion:* Jewish. *Education:* Moscow State Univ., USSR, degree in physics, 1918; Moscow State Univ., USSR, doctorate, 1933. *Spouse:* Natalie Shuskaia, married September 16, 1917. *Children:* Irene, daughter; Eugen, son. *Career:* Crimean Univ., USSR, Professor and Administrator, 1918–20; Odessa Polytechnical Institut, USSR, Professor, 1920–22; Sverdlov Communist Univ., USSR, Professor, 1922–24; Moscow Univ., USSR, Professor and Administrator, 1924–71. *Other Awards:* Order of Lenin 1946, 1953; Order of Red Banner of Labor; Stalin Prize, 1946.

Selected Publications: "Exchange Forces Between Neutrons and Protons, and Fermi's Theory." *Nature* 133 (1934): 981. "Nuclear Magnetic Moments and the Properties of the Neutron." *Nature* 134 (1934): 380. "Izluchenie Elektrona pri Ravnomernom Ovizhenii v Prelomliaiushchei Srede" ("Theory of the Electron in Uniform Motion in a Refracting Medium"). *Trudy Fizicheskago Instituta* 2 (1944): 63. "K Reliativistskoi Teorii Vzaimodeistvia Nuklonov" ("Toward a Relativistic Theory of the Mutual Interaction of Nucleons.") *Zhurnal Eksperimentalnogo i Teoricheskogo Fizika* 24 (1954): 3. "Teorii Magnitnykh Termoiadernykh Reaktsy" ("Theory of Magnetic Thermodynamic Reactors"). *Fizika Plazmy i Problemy Upravliaemykh Termoiadernykh Reaktsy* (1958): 3–19, 31–41. *Osnovy Teorii Elektrichestva (Principles of the Theory of Electricity).* Moscow: n.p., 1966.

For More Information See: Current Biography Yearbook. New York: H.W. Wilson, 1963, 412–14. *Dictionary of Scientific Biography.* New York: Scribner's, 1973 (Volume 13), 239–42. Feinberg, E.L. *Reminiscences About I.E. Tamm.* Moscow: Nauka, 1987. "In Memory of Igor Evgenevich Tamm." *Soviet Physics—Uspekhi* 14 (1972): 669–70.

Commentary: Igor Tamm shared the Nobel Prize for his contributions to the distinguished work on the Cherenkov radiation effect. Tamm and his colaureates developed a theory of the radiation of the electron based on a classical interpretation that a charged particle moving through a medium at a velocity greater than that of light produces an electromagnetic shock-wave effect. Tamm's other work included a quantum theory for acoustical vibrations and light scattering in solid bodies, a theory of light diffusion by free electrons, transistor electronics, the theory of elementary particles, and the theory of gas discharge in a powerful magnetic field. (T.B.)

1959

Chamberlain, Owen 626

Prize: Physics, 1959. *Born:* July 10, 1920; San Francisco, CA. *Parents:* Father, W. Edward Chamberlain; Mother, Genevieve Lucinda Owen Chamberlain. *Nationality:* American. *Religion:* Most probably Christian/Protestant. *Education:* Dartmouth College, NH, B.S., 1941; Univ. of Chicago, IL, Ph.D., 1949. *Spouse:* Babette Cooper, married 1943, divorced 1978; June Steingart, married 1980, died; Senta Pugh, married 1998. *Children:* Karen, daughter; Lynn, daughter; Pia, daughter; Darol, son. *Career:* Manhattan Project, United States, Researcher, 1942–46; Argonne

National Laboratory, Illinois, 1946–48; Univ. of California, Berkeley, Professor, 1948–1989. *Other Awards:* Guggenheim Fellow, 1957; Berkeley Citation, University of California, 1989.

Selected Publications: "Observation of Antiprotons." *Physical Review* 100 (1955): 947–50 (with others). "Antiproton Star Observed in Emulsion." *Physical Review* 101 (1956): 909–10 (with others). "Example of an Antiproton Nucleon Annihilation." *Physical Review* 102 (1956): 921–23 (with others).

For More Information See: Current Biography Yearbook. New York: H.W. Wilson, 1960, 83–85. *Modern Scientists and Engineers.* New York: McGraw-Hill, 1980 (Volume 1), 191. *Nobel Prize Winners: Physics.* Pasadena, CA: Salem Press, Volume 2, 767–75.

Commentary: Owen Chamberlain shared the Nobel Prize for his confirmation of the existence of the antiproton, using the Bevatron particle accelerator. Chamberlain's early work was on the atomic bomb project, alpha particle decay, neutron diffraction, and high-energy nuclear reactions. He also confirmed existence of the antineutron. (V.A.H.)

Segré, Emilio Gino 627

Prize: Physics, 1959. *Born:* February 1, 1905; Rome, Italy. *Death:* April 22, 1989; Lafayette, CA. *Parents:* Father, Giuseppe Segré; Mother, Amelia Treves Segré. *Nationality:* Italian; later American citizen. *Religion:* Jewish. *Education:* Univ. of Rome, Italy, Ph.D., 1928. *Spouse:* Elfriede Spiro, married February 2, 1936, died 1970; Rosa Mines, married February 12, 1972. *Children:* Claudio, son; Amelia, daughter; Fausta, daughter. *Career:* Univ. of Rome, Italy, Professor, 1932–36; Univ. of Palermo, Italy, Researcher, 1936–38; Univ. of California, Berkeley, Researcher, 1938–43; Los Alamos Laboratory of the Manhattan Project, NM, Researcher, 1943–46; Univ. of California, Berkeley, Professor, 1946–72; Univ. of Rome, Italy, Professor, 1974–75. *Other Awards:* Hofmann Medal, German Chemical Society, 1954; Cannizzaro Medal, Academie Nazionale dei Lincei, 1956; Commander of Merit, Republic of Italy, 1959.

Selected Publications: "Observation of Antiprotons." *Physical Review* 100 (1955): 947–50 (with others). "Antiproton Star Observed in Emulsion." *Physical Review* 101 (1956): 909–10 (with others). "Antiprotons." *Nature* 177 (1956): 11–12 (with others). "Proton-Antiproton Elastic and Charge Exchange Scattering at About 120 Mev." *Physical Review* 110 (1958): 994–95 (with others). *Nuclei and Particles.* New York: W.A. Benjamin, 1964. *Enrico Fermi, Physicist.* Chicago: Univ. of Chicago Press, 1970.

For More Information See: Current Biography Yearbook. New York: H.W. Wilson, 1960, 369–71. *Nobel Prize Winners: Physics.* Pasadena, CA: Salem Press, Volume 2, 755–65. *A Mind Always in Motion.* Berkeley, CA: Univ. of California Press, 1993. Segré, Claudio G. *Atoms, Bombs & Eskimo Kisses: a Memoir of Father and Son.* New York: Viking, 1995.

Commentary: For the 1955 discovery of the antiproton, "a nuclear ghost which has haunted the world's physicists for a generation," Emilio Segré was awarded the 1959 Nobel Prize for Physics, along with Owen Chamberlain. The antiproton, a negatively charged proton that destroys itself as well as the matter it strikes, was only one of Segré's discoveries. Included in his research findings throughout his career were the role of the neutron in the splitting of the atom; the discovery of new elements (technetium, astatine, and plutonium-239); and the development of a chemical method for dividing nuclear isomers. Segré's later interests have included writings on the history and contributions of classical and modern physicists. (J.B.T.)

1960

Glaser, Donald Arthur 628

Prize: Physics, 1960. *Born:* September 21, 1926; Cleveland, OH. *Parents:* Father, William Joseph Glaser; Mother, Lena Glaser. *Nationality:* American. *Religion:* Jewish. *Education:* Case Institute of Technology, OH, B.S., 1946; California Institute of Technology, Ph.D., 1950. *Spouse:* Ruth Louise Thompson, married November 28, 1960; divorced 1969. *Children:* William, son; Louise, daughter. *Career:* Univ. of Michigan, Professor, 1949–59; Univ. of California, Berkeley, Professor, 1959-. *Other Awards:* Henry Russel Award, Univ. of Michigan, 1955; Charles Vernon Boys Prize, Institute of Physics, 1958; American Physics Society Prize, 1959; Gold Medal, Case Institute of Technology, 1967; Alumni Distinguished Service Award, California Institute of Technology, 1967; Golden Plate Award, American Academy of Achievement, 1989.

Selected Publications: "Some Effects of Ionizing Radiation on the Formation of Bubbles in Liquids." *Physical Review* 87 (August 15, 1952): 665. "Progress Report on the Development of Bubble Chambers." *Nuovo Cimento Supplement* 11 (1953): 361–68. "Characteristics of Bubble Chambers." *Physical Review* 97 (January 15, 1955): 474–79 (with D.C. Rahm). "Bubble Counting for the Determination of the Velocities of Charged Particles in Bubble Chambers." *Physical Review* 102 (July 15, 1956): 1653–58 (with D.C. Rahm and C. Dodd).

For More Information See: Current Biography Yearbook. New York: H.W. Wilson, 1961, 176–78. *Nobel Prize Winners: Physics.* Pasadena, CA: Salem Press, Volume 2, 777–85.

Commentary: The Academy cited Donald Glaser "for the invention of the bubble chamber." The chamber, built in 1952, allowed the tracing of movement of high-energy atomic particles as they passed through a chamber filled with heated liquid through the track of tiny bubbles (which could be photographed for further study). Bubble chambers have been used to study high-energy particles in the way that cloud chambers have been used to study low-energy particles. Bubble chambers have also played a part in the discovery of new atomic particles (such as the rho and omega minus particles); in visualization of charged particle interaction; and in the study of particle mass, lifetime, and decay modes. Glaser's later interests changed to the application of physics to molecular biology. (S.H.S.)

1961

Hofstadter, Robert 629

Prize: Physics, 1961. *Born:* February 5, 1915; New York, NY. *Death:* November 17, 1990; Stanford, CA. *Parents:* Father, Louis Hofstadter; Mother, Henrietta Koenigsberg Hofstadter. *Nationality:* American. *Religion:* Jewish. *Education:* City College of New York, B.S., 1935; Princeton

Univ., NJ, M.A., 1938; Princeton Univ., NJ, Ph.D., 1938. *Spouse:* Nancy Givan, married May 9, 1942. *Children:* Douglas Richard, son; Laura James, daughter; Mary Hinda, daughter. *Career:* Univ. of Pennsylvania, Researcher, 1939–40; Princeton Univ., NJ, Professor, 1940–41; City College of New York, Professor, 1941–42; National Bureau of Standards, Washington, DC, Researcher, 1942–43; Norden Laboratories Corporation, NY, Researcher, 1943–46; Princeton Univ., NJ, Professor, 1946–50; Stanford Univ., CA, Professor and Administrator, 1950–85. *Other Awards:* Kenyon Prize in Mathematics and Physics, 1935; California Scientist of the Year, 1958; Townsend Harris Medal, City College of New York, 1962; Röntgen Medal, 1985; National Science Medal, 1986; Cultural Foundation Prize, Fiuggi, Italy, 1986.

Selected Publications: "High-Energy Electron Scattering and the Charge Distributions of Selected Nuclei." *Physical Review* 101 (1956): 1131–42 (with B. Hahn and D.G. Ravenhall). *High Energy Electron Scattering Tables.* Stanford, CA: Stanford Univ. Press, 1960 (with Robert C. Herman). *Nuclear and Nucleon Structure.* Stanford, CA: Stanford Univ. Press, 1963. *Nucleon Structure: Proceedings.* Stanford, CA: Stanford Univ. Press, 1964.

For More Information See: Current Biography Yearbook. New York: H.W. Wilson, 1962, 212–14. *Nobel Prize Winners: Physics.* Pasadena, CA: Salem Press, 1988, Volume 2, 787–95. *New York Times Biographical Services* (November 19, 1990): 1098.

Commentary: Robert Hofstadter was cited by the Academy "for his pioneering studies of electron scattering in atomic nuclei and for his thereby achieved discoveries concerning the structure of the nucleons." Among Hofstadter's major contributions were the development of the sodium iodide-thallium scintillation counter for gamma rays and other detectors for neutrons and X-rays; the study of electron scattering, cosmic rays, and cascade showers from high-speed electron interactions; and determination of nuclear charge distributions, the charge and magnetic moments of protons and neutrons, the size and surface thickness of nuclei, and the nucleon form factors. His later studies were in astronomy and coronary angiography. (J.B.T.)

Mössbauer, Rudolf Ludwig   630
Prize: Physics, 1961. *Born:* January 31, 1929; Munich, Germany. *Parents:* Father, Ludwig Mössbauer; Mother, Erna Ernst Mössbauer. *Nationality:* German. *Religion:* Most probably Christian. *Education:* Technische Hochschule, Germany, B.S., 1952; Technische Hochschule, Germany, M.S., 1955; Technische Hochschule, Germany, Ph.D., 1958. *Spouse:* Elizabeth Pritz, married 1957. *Children:* Peter, son; Regine, daughter; 1 other daughter. *Career:* Max Planck Institute, Heidelberg, Germany, Researcher, 1955–57; Institute of Technology, Munich, Germany, Researcher, 1958–60; California Institute of Technology, Researcher and Professor, 1960–64; Technische Universitat, Munich, Germany, Professor and Administrator, 1964–72; Institute Max von Laue, Grenoble, France, Director, 1972–77; Institute of Technology, Munich, Germany, Professor, 1977–97. *Other Awards:* Research Corporation Award, New York, 1960; Roentgen Award, Univ. of Giessen, Germany, 1961; Elliot Cresson Medal, Franklin Institute, PA, 1961; Bavarian Order of Merit, 1962; Guthrie Medal, Institute of Physics,

London, 1974; Lomonosov Gold Medal, 1984; Einstein Medal, 1986.

Selected Publications: "Nuclear Resonance Absorption of Gamma-Rays in Iridium-191." *Naturwissenschaften* 45 (1958): 538–39. "Nuclear Resonance Fluorescence of Gamma-Radiation in Iridium-191." *Z. Physik* 151 (1958): 124–43. "Nuclear Resonance Absorption of Gamma-Rays in Iridium-191." *Z. Naturforsch.* 14a (1959): 211–16. "Nuclear Resonance Absorption of Gamma-Radiation in Re-87 Not Broadened by Doppler Effect." *Z. Physik* 159 (1960): 33–48 (with Herbert W. Wiedemann). "Hyperfine Structure Splitting of Recoil-Free Gamma-Lines." *Z. Physik* 161 (1961): 388–91 (with F.W. Stanek and H.W. Wiedemann).

For More Information See: Current Biography Yearbook. New York: H.W. Wilson, 1962, 306–08. *Nobel Prize Winners: Physics.* Pasadena, CA: Salem Press, 1988, Volume 2, 797–807. *Physics Today* 15 (December 1962): 56.

Commentary: Rudolf Mössbauer won the Nobel Prize "for his researches concerning the resonance absorption of gamma-radiation and his discovery in this connection of the effect which bears his name." Mössbauer's discovery of recoilless nuclear resonance absorption by atoms bound in a solid led to the verification of some predictions of the Einstein theory of relativity and to the possibility of studying small phenomena related to the separation and displacement of nuclear energy levels. The Mössbauer effect has become an important tool of physics, especially in the application known as Mössbauer spectroscopy. (C.N.B.)

1962

Landau, Lev Davidovich   631
Prize: Physics, 1962. *Born:* January 22, 1908; Baku, Russia. *Death:* April 1, 1968; Moscow, USSR. *Parents:* Father, David Llovich Landau; Mother, Lyubov Veniaminovna Garvaki Landau. *Nationality:* Russian. *Religion:* Jewish. *Education:* Leningrad State Univ., USSR, baccalaureate, 1924; Kharkov Institute of Mechanical Engineering, USSR, Ph.D., 1934. *Spouse:* Konkordia Drobantseva, married 1937. *Children:* Igor, son. *Career:* Univ. of Leningrad, USSR, Researcher and Professor, 1931–35; Kharkov Univ., USSR, Researcher and Administrator, 1935–37; Institute of Physical Problems of the USSR Academy of Sciences, USSR, Researcher, 1937–68. *Other Awards:* Fritz London Award, 1960; Lenin Prize, 1962; Stalin Prize (3).

Selected Publications: Teoriia Polia (Field Theory). Moscow: n.p., 1941 (with E. Lifshits). "Teoriia Sverkhtekuchesti Gelia-2" ("Theory of the Superfluidity of Helium II"). *Zhurnal Eksperimentalnoe i Theoreticheskoi Fiziki* 11 (1941): 592. *Kvantovaia Mekhanika (Quantum Mechanics).* Moscow: n.p., 1948 (with E. Lifshits). "O Zakonakh Sokhranenia pri Slabykh Vzaimodeistviakh" ("On the Laws of Conservation in Weak Interactions"). *Zhurnal Eksperimentalnoe i Theoreticheskoi Fiziki* 32 (1957): 2. *Collected Papers of L.D. Landau.* New York: Pergamon, 1965.

For More Information See: Current Biography Yearbook. New York: H.W. Wilson, 1963, 231–33. *Dictionary of Scientific Biography.* New York: Scribner's, 1973 (Volume 7), 616–19. Besserab, M. *Landau.* Moscow: Moskowskii Rabochii, 1990. Livanova, Anna. *Landau, a Great Physicist and Teacher.* Oxford; New York: Pergamon Press, 1980.

Commentary: Lev Landau's work with Helium III at low temperatures won him the Nobel Prize. In the 1950s, building on P.L. Kapitsa's work, he developed mathematical physical theories to explain the behavior of superfluid Helium III at temperatures near absolute zero. Helium at this temperature flows more easily than a gas, and since it does not behave like a solid, liquid, or a gas, it has been called the "fourth" state. He predicted the possibility of sound wave propagation at two different speeds. Landau was also known for his work in quantum mechanics and for fundamental research in magnetism, elasticity, and plasma oscillations. (T.B.)

1963

Jensen, Johannes Hans Daniel   632

Prize: Physics, 1963. *Born:* June 25, 1907; Hamburg, Germany. *Death:* February 11, 1973; Heidelberg, Germany. *Parents:* Father, Karl Jensen; Mother, Helene J. Ohm Jensen. *Nationality:* German. *Religion:* Christian/Protestant. *Education:* Univ. of Hamburg, Germany, Dr. rerum naturalium, 1932. *Spouse:* None. *Children:* None. *Career:* Univ. of Hamburg, Germany, Professor, 1932–41; Hanover Institute of Technology, Germany, Professor, 1941–48; Univ. of Heidelberg, Germany, Professor, 1949–69.

Selected Publications: "Systematics of the Binding Energies of Atomic Nuclei." *Naturwissenschaften* 33 (1946): 249–50 (with H. Steinwedel). "Interpretation of Preferred Nucleon Numbers in the Structure of Atom Nuclei." *Naturwissenschaften* 36 (1949): 153–55 (with H.E. Suess and O. Haxel). "Electromagnetic Effects Due to Spin-Orbit Coupling." *Physical Review* 85 (1952): 1040–41 (with M. Goeppert-Mayer). "Nuclear Structure and Nuclear Transformation." *Zeitschrift für Elektrochemie* 58 (1954): 546–53. *Elementary Theory of Nuclear Shell Structure.* New York: Wiley, 1955 (with M. Goeppert-Mayer).

For More Information See: Modern Men of Science. New York: McGraw-Hill, 1966, 257. *Nobel Prize Winners: Physics.* Pasadena, CA: Salem Press, 1988, Volume 2, 841–49. *Physics Today* 16 (December 1963): 21.

Commentary: The Nobel Committee awarded the Prize to Hans Jensen for his work with Maria Goeppert-Mayer on developing the shell model of the atomic nucleus, citing it as "a most striking advance in the correlation of nuclear properties." According to the Academy, their work "has inspired an ever increasing number of new investigations and has been indispensable for later work, both experimental and theoretical, on atomic nuclei." Jensen also studied the recoil distribution of nuclear radiation, the giant resonance in the nuclear photoeffect, and the gamma-5 invariance of the weak interaction. (M.N.C.)

Mayer, Maria Goeppert   633

Prize: Physics, 1963. *Born:* June 28, 1906; Kattowitz, Poland. *Death:* February 20, 1972; San Diego, CA. *Parents:* Father, Friedrich Goeppert; Mother, Maria Wolff Goeppert. *Nationality:* German; later American citizen. *Religion:* Christian. *Education:* Univ. of Göttingen, Germany, Ph.D., 1930. *Spouse:* Joseph Edward Mayer, married January 19, 1930. *Children:* Maria Anne, daughter; Peter Conrad, son. *Career:* Johns Hopkins Univ., Baltimore, MD, Volunteer Researcher, 1930–39; Columbia Univ., NY, Volunteer Lecturer, 1939–45; Sarah Lawrence College, NY, Professor, 1942–45; Univ. of Chicago, Fermi Institute, IL, Professor, 1946–60; Univ. of California, San Diego, Professor, 1960–72.

Selected Publications: Statistical Mechanics. New York: Wiley, 1940 (with J.E. Mayer). "Nuclear Configurations in the Spin-Orbit Coupling Model." *Physical Review* Series 2, 78 (April 1, 1950): 16–23. "The Structure of the Nucleus." *Scientific American* 184 (March 1951): 22–26. "Electromagnetic Effects Due to Spin-Orbit Coupling." *Physical Review* 85 (1952): 1040–41 (with J.H.D. Jensen). *Elementary Theory of Nuclear Shell Structure.* New York: Wiley, 1955 (with J.H.D. Jensen).

For More Information See: Biographical Memoirs. National Academy of Sciences. Washington, DC: National Academy of Sciences, 1979 (Volume 50), 310–28. Dash, Joan. *A Life of One's Own.* New York: Harper & Row, 1973, 226–369. *Physics Today* 25 (May 1972): 77, 79.

Commentary: Maria Goeppert Mayer was cited, with J. Hans D. Jensen, "for their discoveries concerning nuclear shell structure." Mayer first published evidence that atomic nuclei with 2, 8, 20, 28, 50, 82, or 126 nucleons (protons and/or neutrons) show unusual stability; the integers in this context are known as "magic numbers." Later, independently of Jensen, Mayer demonstrated the theoretical basis for a shell model of atomic nuclei, with each magic number corresponding to a completed nuclear shell. She also worked on the absorption spectra of organic molecules and isotope separation by chemical methods. Mayer and Marie Curie are the only two women who have won a Nobel Prize in Physics. (J.W.)

Wigner, Eugene Paul   634

Prize: Physics, 1963. *Born:* November 17, 1902; Budapest, Hungary. *Death:* January 1, 1995; Princeton, NJ. *Parents:* Father, Anthony Wigner; Mother, Elisabeth Einhorn Wigner. *Nationality:* Hungarian; later American citizen. *Religion:* Jewish. *Education:* Technische Hochschule, Germany, Chemical Engineering Degree, 1924; Technische Hochschule, Germany, Doctorate in Engineering, 1925. *Spouse:* Amelia Z. Frank, married December 23, 1936, died 1937; Mary Annette Wheeler, married June 4, 1941, died November 1977; Eileen C.P. Hamilton, married December 29, 1979. *Children:* David Wheeler, son; Martha Faith, daughter. *Career:* Technische Hochschule, Berlin, Germany, Professor, 1926–27; Univ. of Göttingen, Germany, Professor, 1927–28; Technische Hochschule, Berlin, Germany, Professor, 1928–30; Princeton Univ., NJ, Professor, 1930–36; Univ. of Wisconsin, Professor, 1936–38; Princeton Univ., NJ, Professor, 1938–71. *Other Awards:* Medal of Merit, 1946; Franklin Medal, Franklin Institute, PA, 1950; Enrico Fermi Award; Atoms for Peace Award; Max Planck Medal, German Physical Society, 1961; George Washington Award; Semmelweiss Medal; National Science Medal, 1969; Pfizer Award, 1971; Albert Einstein Award, 1972; Golden Plate Medal; Wigner Medal, 1978; Founders Medal, International Cultural Foundation, 1982; Medal, Hungarian Central Research Institute, 1985; American Preparedness Award, 1985; Lord Foundation Award, 1989.

Selected Publications: Gruppentheorie und Ihre Anwendung auf die Quantenmechanik der Atomspektren. Braunschweig, Germany: Vieweg, 1931 (*Group Theory and Its*

Application to the Quantum Mechanics of Atomic Spectra.
Tr. by J.J. Griffin. New York: Academic Press, 1959).
Nuclear Structure. Princeton, NJ: Princeton Univ. Press,
1958 (with Leonard Eisenbud). *The Physical Theory of
Neutron Chemical Reactors.* Chicago: Univ. of Chicago
Press, 1958 (with Alvin Martin Weinberg). *Symmetries and
Reflections: Scientific Essays of Eugene P. Wigner.* Bloom-
ington, IN: Indiana Univ. Press, 1967. *The Collected Works
of Eugene Paul Wigner.* Berlin, Germany: Springer-Verlag,
1993.

*For More Information See: Current Biography Year-
book.* New York: H.W. Wilson, 1954, 657–59. *McGraw-
Hill Encyclopedia of World Biography.* New York: McGraw-
Hill Book Co., 1973 (Volume 11), 357–58. *Nobel Prize
Winners: Physics.* Pasadena, CA: Salem Press, 1988, Vol-
ume 2, 819–28. *The Recollections of Eugene P. Wigner.*
New York: Plenum Press, 1992.

Commentary: Eugene Paul Wigner, who has been called
one of the great physicists of the twentieth century, shared
the Nobel Prize for "systematically improving and extending the methods of quantum mechanics and applying them
widely." He formulated symmetry principles and with group
theory, applied them in atomic, nuclear, and elementary
particle physics. Wigner worked out the theory of neutron
absorption and showed that nuclear forces did not depend on
electric charge. His work also included research in theories
of chemical reaction rates and the solid state and part of the
design of the first large-scale nuclear reactor in 1943. In the
late 1930s and early 1940s, along with other physicists, he
convinced the U.S. government of the need for an atomic
bomb project. His book *Gruppentheorie und Ihre Anwendung auf die Quantenmechanik der Atomspektren* was widely
used as an advanced text in quantum mechanics. (L.N.W.)

1964

Basov, Nikolai Gennadievich   **635**
Prize: Physics, 1964. *Born:* December 14, 1922; Usman,
USSR. *Parents:* Father, Gennady Fedorovich Basov; Mother,
Zinaida Andreevna Molchanova Basov. *Nationality:* Rus-
sian. *Religion:* Most probably Eastern Orthodox. *Educa-
tion:* Moscow Institute of Engineering Physics, USSR,
Candidaat, 1950; Lebedev Institute of Physics, Soviet Acad-
emy of Sciences, USSR, Ph.D., 1956. *Spouse:* Qsenia
Tikhonova Nasarova, married July 18, 1950. *Children:*
Genadii, son; Dmitrii, son. *Career:* P.N. Lebedev Physical
Institute, Researcher and Administrator, Moscow, USSR,
1950-. *Other Awards:* Lenin Prize, 1959, 1964; Order of
Lenin, 1967, 1969, 1972, 1975, 1982; Gold Medal, Czecho-
slovakian Academy of Sciences, 1975; A. Volta Gold Medal,
Italian Physical Society, 1977; Henkel Gold Medal, 1986;
Kalinga Prize, 1986; Gold Medal, Slovak Academy of
Sciences, 1988; State Prize, USSR, 1989; Lomonosov Gold
Medal, 1990; Teller Medal, 1991.

Selected Publications: "Application of Molecular Beams
to the Radio Spectroscopic Study of the Rotation Spectra of
Molecules." *Zh. Eksp. Teor. Fiz.* 27 (1954): 431–38 (with
A.M. Prokhorov). "Possible Methods of Obtaining Active
Molecules for a Molecular Oscillator." *Soviet Physics-JETP*
1 (1956): 184–85 (with O.N. Krokhin and Y.M. Popov).
"Theory of the Molecular Generator and the Molecular
Power Amplifier." *Zh. Eksp. Teor. Fiz.* 30 (1956): 560–63

(with A.M. Prokhorov). "Generation, Amplification, and
Detection of Infrared and Optical Radiation by Quantum
Mechanical Systems." *Soviet Physics-Uspekhi* 3 (March-
April 1961): 702–28 (with O.N. Krokhin and Y.M. Popov).

For More Information See: New York Times (October
30, 1964): 23. *Nobel Prize Winners: Physics.* Pasadena, CA:
Salem Press, 1988, Volume 2, 859–68. Perlado, J.M. "N.G.
Basov and Laser Technology in the USSR." *Arbor* 121
(1985): 87–97. Zhukova, L.M., et al. *Nikolai Gennadievich
Basov.* Moskva: Izd-vo "Nauka," 1982.

Commentary: Nikolai Gennadievich Basov, together
with his teacher Alexander Prokhorov, was awarded the
Nobel Prize for "basic researches in the field of experimental physics, which led to the discovery of the maser and the
laser." They deduced that quantum mechanics, which governs the behavior of atoms at different energy levels, permits
the amplification of microwaves and light waves. They then
developed principles and refinements for the construction of
first the maser (microwave amplification by stimulated
emission of radiation) and then the laser (optical maser),
starting in 1954. Such devices collect energy waves, amplify
them hundreds of times, and produce a beam whose waves
are almost perfectly parallel with little or no interference or
static. The work was done independently of, and simultaneously with, the work of C.H. Townes, with whom Basov and
Prokhorov shared the 1964 Nobel Prize in Physics. (M.N.K.)

Prokhorov, Alexander Mikhailovich   **636**
Prize: Physics, 1964. *Born:* July 11, 1916; Atherton, Aus-
tralia. *Parents:* Father, Mikhail Ivanovich Prokhorov; Mother,
Mariya Ivanovna Prokhorova. *Nationality:* Australian; later
Russian citizen. *Religion:* Most probably Eastern Orthodox.
Education: Leningrad State Univ., USSR, baccalaureate,
1939; Institute of Physics, Academy of Sciences, USSR,
doctorate, 1948. *Spouse:* Galina Alekseyevna Shelepina,
married 1941. *Children:* Kirill, son. *Career:* Institute of
Physics, Academy of Sciences, USSR, Researcher and
Administrator, 1939-. *Other Awards:* Lenin Prize, 1959;
Order of Lenin; Lomosonov Gold Medal, 1988.

Selected Publications: "Application of Molecular Beams
to the Radio Spectroscopic Study of the Rotation Spectra of
Molecules." *Zh. Eksp. Teor. Fiz.* 27 (1954): 431–38 (with
N.G. Basov). "Theory of the Molecular Generator and the
Molecular Power Amplifier." *Zh. Eksp. Teor. Fiz.* 30 (1956):
560–63 (with N.G. Basov). "Quantum Electronics." *Fiz.
Mat. Spisanie, Bulgar. Akad. Nauk.* 8 (1965): 165–71.
"Quantum Electronics." *Usp. Fiz. Nauk* 85 (1965): 599–604.

*For More Information See: The Great Soviet Encyclo-
pedia.* New York: Macmillan, 1978 (Volume 21), 257. *New
York Times* (October 30, 1964): 23. *Nobel Prize Winners:
Physics.* Pasadena, CA: Salem Press, 1988, Volume 2,
869–79.

Commentary: Alexander Prokhorov won his Nobel for
contributing to a new method for generating electromagnetic
waves using quantum systems and for devising the first
molecular generator using ammonia molecule beams (maser). He later created paramagnetic masers and proposed the
use of ruby in quantum electronics and the concepts of open
resonators and gas dynamic lasers. Prokhorov further investigated the resonance and nonresonance interactions of laser
radiation with matter. (G.E.M.)

Townes, Charles Hard 637

Prize: Physics, 1964. *Born:* July 28, 1915; Greenville, SC. *Parents:* Father, Henry Keith Townes; Mother, Ellen Sumter Hard Townes. *Nationality:* American. *Religion:* Presbyterian. *Education:* Furman Univ., SC, B.A.; Furman Univ., SC, B.S., 1935; Duke Univ., NC, M.A., 1936; California Institute of Technology, Ph.D., 1939. *Spouse:* Frances H. Brown, married May 4, 1941. *Children:* Linda Lewis, daughter; Ellen Screven, daughter; Carla Keith, daughter; Holly Robinson, daughter. *Career:* Bell Telephone Laboratories, NJ, Researcher, 1939–48; Columbia Univ., NY, Professor, 1948–61; Massachusetts Institute of Technology, Professor and Administrator, 1961–67; Univ. of California, Berkeley, Professor, 1967–86. *Other Awards:* Comstock Award, 1959; Stuart Ballantine Medal, 1959, 1962; Thomas Young Medal, 1963; Medal of Honor, IEEE, 1967; Mees Medal, 1968; Distinguished Public Services Medal, NASA, 1969; Wilhelm Exner Award, Austria, 1970; National Inventors Hall of Fame, 1976; Earle K. Plyler Prize, 1977; Niels Bohr International Gold Medal, 1979; National Science Medal, 1983; Engineering and Science Hall of Fame, 1983; Commonwealth Award, 1993; ADION Medal, 1995.

Selected Publications: "Molecular Microwave Oscillator and New Hyperfine Structure in the Microwave Spectrum of NH_3." *Physical Review* Series 2, 95 (July 1, 1954): 282–84 (with J.P. Gordon and H.J. Zeiger). *Microwave Spectroscopy.* New York: McGraw-Hill, 1955 (with A.L. Schawlow). *Quantum Electronics: A Symposium.* New York: Columbia Univ. Press, 1960. *Venus: Strategy for Exploration.* Report of a study by the Space Science Board. C.H. Townes, chair. Washington, DC: National Academy of Sciences, 1970.

For More Information See: Asimov's Biographical Encyclopedia of Science and Technology. Garden City, NY: Doubleday, 855–57. *Current Biography Yearbook.* New York: H.W. Wilson, 1963, 423–25. *A Life in Physics.* Berkeley: Univ. of California Press, 1994.

Commentary: Charles H. Townes was awarded the Nobel Prize "for fundamental work in the field of quantum electronics, which has led to the construction of oscillators and amplifiers based on the maser-laser principle." Townes and two coworkers completed the first successful maser in 1954. It was based on excited ammonia molecules which, when struck by photons of the appropriate energy, were stimulated into emitting additional photons of the same energy. The amount of energy in question was equal to the energy level difference between an excited ammonia molecule and a ground-level ammonia molecule. This quantum of energy falls into the microwave portion of the electromagnetic spectrum—hence, the name of the device m(icrowave) a(mplification by) s(timulated) e(mission of) r(adiation). Townes's later research was in radio and infrared astronomy. (J.W.)

1965

Feynman, Richard Phillips 638

Prize: Physics, 1965. *Born:* May 11, 1918; New York, NY. *Death:* February 15, 1988; Los Angeles, CA. *Parents:* Father, Melville Arthur Feynman; Mother, Lucille Phillips Feynman. *Nationality:* American. *Religion:* Jewish. *Education:* Massachusetts Institute of Technology,

B.S., 1939; Princeton Univ., NJ, Ph.D., 1942. *Spouse:* Arlene H. Greenbaum, married June 29, 1942, died June 1945; Mary Louise Bell, married June 28, 1952; Gweneth Howarth, married 1960. *Children:* Carl, son; Michelle, daughter. *Career:* Princeton Univ. Atomic Bomb Project, NJ, Researcher, 1941–43; Los Alamos Atomic Bomb Project, NM, Researcher, 1943–45; Cornell Univ., NY, Professor, 1945–50; California Institute of Technology, Professor, 1950–88. *Other Awards:* Einstein Award, 1954; Oersted Medal, 1972; Niels Bohr International Gold Medal, 1973.

Selected Publications: Quantum Electrodynamics. Reading, MA: Benjamin/Cummings, Advanced Book Program, 1961. *Theory of Fundamental Processes.* New York: W.A. Benjamin, 1961. *Feynman Lectures on Physics.* 3 volumes. Reading, MA: Addison-Wesley Pub. Co., 1963–69. *Quantum Mechanics and Path Integrals.* New York: McGraw-Hill, 1965. *The Character of Physical Law.* Cambridge, MA: M.I.T. Press, 1967. *Photon Hadron Interactions.* Reading, MA: W.A. Benjamin, 1972. *Statistical Mechanics.* Reading, MA: W. A. Benjamin, 1972.

For More Information See: Current Biography Yearbook. New York: H.W. Wilson, 1955, 205–07. Gribbin, John R. and Mary Gribbin. *Richard Feynman: a Life in Science.* New York: Plume, 1998. *Nobel Prize Winners: Physics.* Pasadena, CA: Salem Press, 1988, Volume 2, 901–10. *Science* 150 (October 29, 1965): 588–89. *Surely You're Joking, Mr. Feynman.* New York: Bantam, 1985. Gleick, J. *Genius.* London: Little Brown, 1992.

Commentary: Richard Feynman, with his two colaureates, shared the Nobel Prize for their development of the theory of quantum electrodynamics. His contributions in scientific work included an important role in the atomic bomb project, the development of a quantum theory of electricity and magnetism, the presentation of the Feynman diagram (for possible particle transformations), and the quantum mechanical explanation of the properties of liquid helium. (B.M.)

Schwinger, Julian Seymour 639

Prize: Physics, 1965. *Born:* February 12, 1918; New York, NY. *Death:* July 16, 1994; Los Angeles, CA. *Parents:* Father, Benjamin Schwinger; Mother, Belle Rosenfeld Schwinger. *Nationality:* American. *Religion:* Jewish. *Education:* Columbia Univ., NY, BA, 1936; Columbia Univ., NY, Ph.D., 1939. *Spouse:* Clarice Carrol, married 1947. *Children:* None. *Career:* Univ. of California, Berkeley, Researcher, 1939–41; Purdue Univ., IN, Professor, 1941–43; Univ. of Chicago, IL, Researcher, 1943; Massachusetts Institute of Technology, Researcher, 1943–45; Harvard Univ., MA, Professor, 1945–72; Univ. of California, Los Angeles, Professor, 1975–88. *Other Awards:* C.L. Mayer Nature of Light Award, 1949; University Medal, Columbia Univ., NY, 1951; Einstein Prize, 1951; National Medal of Science for Physics, 1964; Humbolt Award, 1981; Monie A. Fest Award, 1986; Castiglione di Sicilia Award, 1986; American Academy of Achievement Award, 1987; Alexander Hamilton Medal, 1995 (posthumous).

Selected Publications: "Quantum Electrodynamics." *Physical Review* 74 (November 15, 1948): 39–61. "On Gauge Invariance and Vacuum Polarization." *Physical Review*

82 (1951): 664–79. "A Theory of the Fundamental Interactions." *Annals of Physics* 2 (1957): 407–34. *Quantum Electrodynamics*. New York: Dover, 1958. "Gauge Invariance and Mass II." *Physical Review* 128 (1962): 2425–29. *Particles Sources and Fields*. Reading, MA: Addison-Wesley Pub. Co., 1970.

For More Information See: Current Biography Yearbook. New York: H.W. Wilson, 1967, 379–81. Mehra, Jagdish and others. *Climbing the Mountain: the Scientific Biography of Julian Schwinger*. Oxford: Oxford University Press, 2000. *Nobel Prize Winners: Physics*. Pasadena, CA: Salem Press, 1988, Volume 2, 891–900. *Science* 150 (October 29, 1965): 588–89. Schweber, S. *QED and the Men Who Made It*. Princeton, NJ: Princeton Univ. Press, 1994; *New York Times Biographical Service* (July 20, 1994): 1077.

Commentary: Julian Schwinger and his two colaureates received the Nobel Prize for their development of the theory of quantum electrodynamics. Earlier work by Paul Dirac applied quantum mechanics to an analysis of the electromagnetic field and predicted that particles such as the electron would have an infinite quantity of energy, which contradicted observed fact. Schwinger reworked the mathematics in the theory so that the infinite quantities no longer appeared and made it consistent with observation, capable of predicting the magnetic and other properties of particles and radiation. He later worked on the properties of synchrotron radiation. (J.L.K.)

Tomonaga, Shinichiro   640

Prize: Physics, 1965. *Born:* March 31, 1906; Tokyo, Japan. *Death:* July 8, 1979; Tokyo, Japan. *Parents:* Father, Sanjuro Tomonaga; Mother, Hide Tomonaga. *Nationality:* Japanese. *Religion:* Most probably Buddhist. *Education:* Kyoto Imperial Univ., Japan, B.A., 1929; Tokyo Imperial Univ., Japan, D.Sc., 1939. *Spouse:* Ryoko Sekiguchi, married 1940. *Children:* Atsushi, son; Makoto, son; Shigeko, daughter. *Career:* Tokyo Univ., Japan, Professor, 1939–70. *Other Awards:* Japan Academy Prize, 1948; Lomonosov Medal, Russia, 1964.

Selected Publications: Quantum Mechanics. Tokyo: Misuzu Publishing Company, 1949. (English publication in two volumes. Amsterdam: North-Holland Publishing Company, 1962–66). *Scientific Papers of Tomonaga*. 2 volumes. Tokyo: Misuzu Shobo Publishing Company, 1971–76.

For More Information See: Matsui, M. and others. *Sinitiro Tomonaga: Life of a Japanese Physicist*. Tokyo: MYU, 1995. *Modern Men of Science*. New York: McGraw-Hill, 1966: 483–84. *Nobel Prize Winners: Physics*. Pasadena, CA: Salem Press, 1988, Volume 2, 881–89. Weber, Robert L. *Pioneers of Science, Nobel Prize Winners in Physics*. London: Institute of Physics, 1980, 205–06. Schweber, S. *QED and the Men Who Made It*. Princeton, NJ: Princeton Univ. Press, 1994.

Commentary: The Nobel Prize was awarded to Shinichiro Tomonaga, jointly with Richard Feynman and Julian Schwinger, for his research on a theoretical basis for quantum electrodynamics which was consistent with both observable behavior of particles and the theory of relativity. Tomonaga also worked in the areas of quantum dynamics, the theory of neutrons, and electromagnetics. (D.P.N.)

1966

Kastler, Alfred   641

Prize: Physics, 1966. *Born:* May 3, 1902; Guebwiller, France. *Death:* January 7, 1984; Bandol, France. *Parents:* Father, Frederic Kastler; Mother, Anna Frey Kastler. *Nationality:* French. *Religion:* Most probably Christian. *Education:* École Normale Supérieure, France, Teaching degree, 1926; Univ. of Bordeaux, France, Docteur des Sciences Physiques, 1936. *Spouse:* Elise Cosset, married December 24, 1924. *Children:* Daniel, son; Claude-Yves, son; Mireille, daughter. *Career:* Clermont-Ferrant Univ., France, Professor, 1936–38; Univ. of Bordeaux, France, Professor, 1938–41; École Normale Supérieure, France, Professor, 1941–68; CNRS, France, Director, 1968–72. *Other Awards:* Holweck Prize, London Physical Society, 1954; C.E.K. Mees International Medal, Optical Society of America, 1962; Award in Scientific Research, Academy of Sciences; Science Prize, City of Paris, 1963.

Selected Publications: La Diffusion de la Lumière par les Milieux Troubles. Paris: Hermann, 1952. *Polarisation, Matière et Rayonnement, Volume Jubilaire en l'Honneur d'Alfred Kastler*. Paris: Presses Universitaires de France, 1969. *Cette Etrange Matière*. Paris: Stock, 1976.

For More Information See: Current Biography Yearbook. New York: H.W. Wilson, 1967, 216–18. *New York Times* (November 4, 1966): 1,28. "Notices sur les membres dècèdès: Kastler (Alfred)." Association Amicale des Anciens élèves de l'École Normale Supérieure (*Annuaire*), 1985, 60–65.

Commentary: Alfred Kastler was awarded the Nobel prize for "the discovery and development of optical methods for studying Herzian resonances in atoms." He not only provided a stimulus to further research by other scientists, but his work also resulted in practical applications, namely the developments of the laser, magnetometers, and atomic clocks. The double resonance technique, which uses optical and Herzian resonances (light and radiowaves), and the optical pumping technique to orient atoms and atomic fields made it possible to detect with precision the spectrum of Herzian resonances. Kastler was also well known for his humanitarian, social, and political activities. He took stands against the French occupation of Algeria, against the Soviet treatment of Sakharov and Solzhenitsyn, and against cruel and inhuman treatment of livestock. (J.U.S.)

1967

Bethe, Hans Albrecht   642

Prize: Physics, 1967. *Born:* July 2, 1906; Strassbourg, Germany (now France). *Parents:* Father, Albrecht Theodore Julius Bethe; Mother, Anna Kuhn Bethe. *Nationality:* German; later American citizen. *Religion:* Jewish. *Education:* Goethe Gymnasium, Germany, baccalaureate, 1924; Univ. of Munich, Germany, Ph.D., 1928. *Spouse:* Rose Ewald, married September 14, 1939. *Children:* Henry George, son; Monica, daughter. *Career:* Univ. of Frankfurt, Germany, Professor, 1928–29; Univ. of Stuttgart, Germany, Professor, 1929–30; Univ. of Munich and Univ. of Tübingen, Germany, Professor, 1930–33; Univ. of Manchester, England, Professor, 1933–34; Univ. of Bristol, England, Professor, 1934–35; Cornell Univ., NY, Professor, 1937–75. *Other Awards:* Morrison Prize, New York Academy of Science,

1938; U.S. Medal of Merit, 1946; Draper Medal, National Academy of Sciences, 1948; Max Planck Medal, 1955; Enrico Fermi Prize, 1961; Eddington Medal, Royal Astronomical Society, 1963; National Medal of Science, 1976; Vannevar Bush Award, 1985; Einstein Peace Prize, 1993.

Selected Publications: "Energy Production in Stars." *Physical Review* 55 (1939): 434. *Elementary Nuclear Theory.* New York: John Wiley and Sons, Inc., 1947. *Quantum Mechanics of One- and Two-Electron Atoms.* New York: Plenum Publishing Co., 1958 (with E.E. Salpeter). *Splitting of Atoms in Crystals.* New York: Plenum Publishing Co., 1962. *Intermediate Quantum Mechanics.* San Francisco: Benjamin-Cummings Co., 1968 (with Roman W. Jackiw).

For More Information See: Bernstein, Jeremy. *Hans Bethe: Prophet of Energy.* New York: Basic Books, 1980. *Modern Men of Science.* New York: McGraw Hill, 1966, 37–39. *National Cyclopedia of American Biography.* New York: James T. White, 1960 (Volume I), 320–21. *Nobel Prize Winners: Physics.* Pasadena, CA: Salem Press, Volume 2, 923–34.

Commentary: Hans Bethe won the Nobel Prize for his several contributions to nuclear reaction theory, with special reference to the energy production of stars. He was unique among his contemporaries in making diverse contributions to the field of physics, ranging from fundamental particles to ballistic missiles. Bethe was best known for developing a theoretical description of deuteron fusion and using the carbon cycle as a mechanism to explain the rate of energy production in the sun's interior balanced against surface energy losses. He contributed to the theory of nuclear reactors and developed the first theory of electron-positron pair creation. The early work of Bethe and others led to our present-day understanding of core nuclear reactions in the sun. (G.W.)

1968

Alvarez, Luis Walter   643

Prize: Physics, 1968. *Born:* June 13, 1911; San Francisco, CA. *Death:* September 1, 1988; Berkeley, CA. *Parents:* Father, Walter Clement Alvarez; Mother, Harriet Skidmore Smyth Alvarez. *Nationality:* American. *Religion:* Congregationalist background. *Education:* Univ. of Chicago, IL, B.S., 1932; Univ. of Chicago, IL, M.Sc., 1934; Univ. of Chicago, IL, Ph.D., 1936. *Spouse:* Geraldine Smithwick, married April 15, 1936, divorced 1957; Janet L. Landis, married December 28, 1958. *Children:* Walter S., son; Donald L., son; Jean S., daughter; Helen L., daughter. *Career:* Univ. of California, Berkeley, Professor, 1936–78. *Other Awards:* Collier Trophy, 1946; Medal for Merit, 1948; John Scott Medal, 1953; California Scientist of the Year, 1960; Einstein Medal, 1961; Pioneer Prize, AIEEE, 1963; National Medal of Science, 1964; Michelson Award, 1965; National Inventors Hall of Fame, 1978; Wright Prize, 1981; Rockwell Medal, 1986; Enrico Fermi Award, 1987.

Selected Publications: "The Lifetime of the t-Meson." *Nuovo Cimento* 2 (1955): 344 (with S. Goldhaber). "Catalysis of Nuclear Reactions by u Mesons." *Physical Review* 105 (1957): 1127 (with others). "K-Interactions in Hydrogen." *Nuovo Cimento* 5 (1957): 1026 (with others). "Elastic Scattering of 1.6-Mev Gamma Ray from H, Li, C, and Al Nuclei." *Physical Review* 112 (1958): 1267 (with F.S.

Crawford and M.L. Stevenson). *Strong Interactions.* New York: Academic Press, 1966. "Recent Developments in Particle Physics." *Science* 165 (September 12, 1969): 1071.

For More Information See: Alvarez: *Adventures of a Physicist.* New York: Basic Books, 1987. *Science* 162 (November 8, 1968): 645.

Commentary: The award to Luis Alvarez was for his "decisive contributions to elementary particle physics, in particular the discovery of a large number of resonance states made possible through his development of the technique of using hydrogen bubble chambers and data analysis." He also made important contributions in many other areas of physics: he codiscovered the east-west effect in cosmic rays, demonstrated orbital electron capture by nuclei, collaborated on building the first proton linear accelerator based on the use of cavity resonators, and developed the ground-controlled-approach blind landing system, which uses microwave radar. (C.D.)

1969

Gell-Mann, Murray   644

Prize: Physics, 1969. *Born:* September 15, 1929; New York, NY. *Parents:* Father, Arthur Gell-Mann; Mother, Pauline Reichstein Gell-Mann. *Nationality:* American. *Religion:* Nonbeliever; from Jewish background. *Education:* Yale Univ., CT, B.S., 1948; Massachusetts Institute of Technology, Ph.D., 1951. *Spouse:* J. Margaret Dow, married April 19, 1955, died December 1981; Marcia Southwick, married June 20, 1992. *Children:* Elizabeth, daughter; Nicholas, son; Nicholas Levis, stepson. *Career:* Princeton Univ., NJ, Professor, 1951–52; Univ. of Chicago, IL, Professor, 1952–55; California Institute of Technology, Pasadena, Professor, 1955–93. *Other Awards:* Dannie Heineman Prize, American Physical Society and American Institute of Physics, 1959; E.O. Lawrence Award, 1966; Franklin Medal, Franklin Institute, PA, 1967; Carty Medal, 1968; Research Corporation Award, 1969; Erice Prize, 1990.

Selected Publications: "Isotopic Spin and New Unstable Particles." *Physical Review* 92 (1953): 833. *Lectures on Weak Interactions of Strongly Interacting Particles, Delivered at the Summer School in Theoretical Physics, Bangalore, 1961.* Bombay: Tata Institute of Fundamental Research, 1961. *Lecture Notes on Special Topics in Relativistic Quantum Theory.* Cambridge, MA: Massachusetts Institute of Technology Press, 1963. "A Schematic Model of Baryons and Mesons." *Physics Letters* 8 (February 1, 1964): 214. *The Eightfold Way: A Review with a Collection of Reprints.* New York: W.A. Benjamin, 1964 (with Y. Ne'eman). *The Quark and the Jaguar.* New York: W.H. Freeman, 1994.

For More Information See: Current Biography Yearbook. New York: H.W. Wilson, 1966, 124–66. Johnson, George. *Strange Beauty: Murray Gell-Mann and the Revolution in 20th-Century Physics.* New York: Alfred A. Knopf, 1999. *Science* (November 8, 1969): 715–22.

Commentary: The award to Murray Gell-Mann was "for his contributions and discoveries concerning the classification of elementary particles and their interactions." Gell-Mann's earlier contribution was the introduction of the strangeness principle, which classified the elementary particles in the atomic nucleus, based on properties related to charge and spin. Later, using symmetry group theory, he devised the Eightfold Way, a scheme for classification, based on eight quantum numbers. His predictions of the existences of particles led to many discoveries, including those in the world of quarks. (C.D.)

1970

Alfven, Hannes Olof Gösta   645

Prize: Physics, 1970. *Born:* May 30, 1908; Norrkoeping, Sweden. *Death:* April 2, 1995; Djursholm, Sweden. *Parents:* Father, Johannes Alfven; Mother, Anna-Clara Romanus Alfven. *Nationality:* Swedish. *Religion:* Lutheran. *Education:* Univ. of Uppsala, Sweden, Ph.D., 1934. *Spouse:* Kerstin Maria Erikson, married June 18, 1935. *Children:* Cecilia, daughter; Inger, daughter; Gösta, daughter; Reidun, son; Berenike, son. *Career:* Univ. of Uppsala, Sweden, Professor, 1934–37; Nobel Institute of Physics, Sweden, Researcher, 1937–40; Royal Institute of Technology, Professor, 1940–73; Univ. of California, San Diego, Professor, 1967–88. *Other Awards:* Gold Medal, Royal Astronomical Society, 1967; Lomonosov Gold Medal, Soviet Academy of Sciences, 1971; Franklin Medal, Franklin Institute, PA, 1971; Bowie Gold Medal, 1987; Dirac Medal, 1994.

Selected Publications: Cosmical Electrodynamics. Oxford: Clarendon Press, 1950. *On the Origin of the Solar System.* Oxford: Clarendon Press, 1954. *Cosmical Electrodynamics: Fundamental Principles.* Oxford: Clarendon Press, 1963 (with Carl-Gunne Falthammar). *Worlds-Antiworlds: Antimatter in Cosmology.* San Francisco: W.H. Freeman, 1966. *Structure and Evolutionary History of the Solar System.* Dordrecht, Netherlands: D. Reidel, 1975 (with Gustaf Arrhenius).

For More Information See: New York Times Biographical Edition (October 28, 1970): 2707–08. *Physics Today* 23 (December 1970): 61–63.

Commentary: One of the founders of the field of plasma physics, Hannes Alfven shared the Nobel Prize "for fundamental work in magnetohydrodynamics with fruitful applications in different parts of plasma physics." His work on the motion of electrically conducting fluids in a magnetic field was concerned primarily with geophysics and astrophysics. It led to the development of the concept of "Alfven's waves," transverse hydromagnetic waves transmitted by the plasma. Alfven's work helped provide an understanding of the solar system and was instrumental in the development of controlled thermonuclear reactors and space travel. (J.N.S.)

Néel, Louis Eugene Felix   646

Prize: Physics, 1970. *Born:* November 22, 1904; Lyons, Rhone, France. *Death:* November 17, 2000; Brive-Correze, France. *Parents:* Father, Louis Antoine Néel; Mother, Marie Antoinette Hartmayer Néel. *Nationality:* French. *Religion:* Catholic. *Education:* École Normale Supérieure, France, Agrege de l'Université, 1928; Univ. of Strasbourg, France, Docteur es Sciences, 1932. *Spouse:* Helene Hourticq, married September 14, 1931. *Children:* Marie-Françoise, daughter; Marguerite Guely, daughter; Pierre, son. *Career:* Univ. of Strasbourg, France, Professor, 1928–45; Univ. of Grenoble, France, Professor, 1945–76. *Other Awards:* Prix Holweck, 1952; Gold Medal (C.N.R.S)., 1965; Croix de Guerre, 1940; Grand Croix, Legion d'Honneur.

Selected Publications: Exposés sur l'Energie. Paris: Institute de France, 1978. *Ouevres Scientifique de Louis Néel.* Paris: Centre National de la Recherche Scientifique, 1978. *Selected Works of Louis Néel.* New York: Gordon and Breach, 1988.

For More Information See: New York Times Biographical Edition. (October 28, 1970): 2707–08. *Science* (November 6, 1970): 604–609.

Commentary: Louis Néel received the Nobel Prize "for his pioneering studies of the magnetic properties of solids." His early studies explained antiferromagnetism, the magnetic effect derived from electron alignments in opposite directions. He also studied the magnetic memory of certain mineral deposits which explained observed changes in the Earth's magnetic field. Néel's research on the ferrimagnetics has provided new materials for microwave electronics. (V.A.H.)

1971

Gabor, Dennis   647

Prize: Physics, 1971. *Born:* June 5, 1900; Budapest, Hungary. *Death:* February 8, 1979; London, England. *Parents:* Father, Berthold Gabor; Mother, Adrienne Jacobovits Gabor. *Nationality:* Hungarian; later British citizen. *Religion:* Jewish. *Education:* Technische Hochschule, Germany, diploma, 1924; Technische Hochschule, Germany, Dr. Elect. Eng., 1927. *Spouse:* Marjorie Louise Butler, married August 8, 1936. *Children:* None. *Career:* Siemens and Halske, Berlin, Germany, Researcher, 1927–33; British Thomson-Houston Co., Rugby, England, Researcher, 1934–48; Imperial College, London, England, Professor, 1949–67. *Other Awards:* Thomas Young Medal and Prize, 1967; Cristoforo Columbo Prize, Genoa, Italy, 1967; Rumford Medal, Royal Society, 1968; Michelson Medal, Franklin Institute, PA, 1968; Medal of Honor, Institute of Electrical and Electronics Engineers, 1970; Semmelweis Medal, American Hungarian Medical Association, 1970; Holweck Prize, French Physical Society, 1971; George Washington Award, American Hungarian Studies Foundation, 1973.

Selected Publications: "A New Microscopic Principle." *Nature* (May 15, 1948): 777–78. "Microscopy by Reconstructed Wave-Fronts." *Proceedings of the Royal Society* A197 (1949): 454. "Microscopy by Reconstructed Wave Fronts: II." *Proceedings of the Royal Society* B64 (1951): 244. *Inventing the Future.* New York: Knopf, 1964. *Innovations: Scientific, Technological, and Social.* London: Oxford Univ. Press, 1970.

For More Information See: Biographical Memoirs of the Fellows of the Royal Society. London: Royal Society, 1980 (Volume 26), 107–47. *New York Times* (November 3, 1971): 1, 28.

Commentary: Dennis Gabor was one of the few inventors who received the Nobel Prize, "for his invention and development of holography," a lenseless system of three-dimensional photography. His contributions extended into many other areas—the high-speed cathode ray oscillograph, the shrouded magnetic lens, theories of communication, information theory, the physics of optics, predicting machines, plasmas, gas discharge tubes, and television. Gabor was also a thinker about the discipline of physics itself, writing thoughtfully about its applications and societal issues. (G.W.)

1972

Bardeen, John *See* entry **618**

Cooper, Leon Neil   **648**
Prize: Physics, 1972. *Born:* February 28, 1930; New York, NY. *Parents:* Father, Irving Cooper; Mother, Anna Zola Cooper. *Nationality:* American. *Religion:* Jewish. *Education:* Columbia Univ., NY, A.B., 1951; Columbia Univ., NY, A.M., 1953; Columbia Univ., NY, Ph.D., 1954. *Spouse:* Kay Anne Allard, married May 18, 1969. *Children:* Kathleen, daughter; Coralie, daughter. *Career:* Princeton Univ., NJ, Researcher, 1954–55; Univ. of Illinois, Researcher, 1955–57; Ohio State Univ., Professor, 1957–58; Brown Univ., RI, Professor, 1958–. *Other Awards:* Comstock Prize, National Academy of Science, 1968; Descartes Medal, Académie de Paris, 1977; John Jay Award, Columbia College, New York, 1985; Distinguished Achievement Award, Columbia Univ., 1990; Alexander Hamilton Award, Columbia College, 1995.

Selected Publications: "Microscopic Theory of Superconductivity." *Physical Review* 106 (1957): 162–64 (with J. Bardeen and J.R. Schrieffer). "Theory of Superconductivity." *Physical Review* 108 (1957): 1175–1204 (with J. Bardeen and J.R. Schrieffer). "Specific Heat Measurements and the Energy Gap in Superconductors." *Physical Review Letters* 3 (1959): 17. "Superconductivity in the Neighborhood of Metallic Contacts." *Physical Review Letters* 6 (1961): 689–90. *An Introduction to the Meaning and Structure of Physics.* New York: Harper & Row, 1968. "Origin of the Theory of Superconductivity." *IEEE Transactions on Magnetics MAG-23* (March 1987): 376.

For More Information See: Physics Today 25 (December 1972): 73–75. *Science* 178 (November 3, 1972): 489–91.

Commentary: Leon Cooper shared, with John Bardeen and John Schrieffer, the Nobel Prize for work on the theory of superconductivity. Cooper showed that at low temperatures electrons in a conductor could act in bound pairs (called Cooper pairs). With his colaureates, he demonstrated that the Cooper pair action resulted in no electrical resistance to electron flow through solids. The BCS theory stimulated much work in physics. Cooper also contributed significantly in the areas of nuclear physics, the superfluid state at low temperatures, and the theory of the central nervous system. (P.S.)

Schrieffer, John Robert   **649**
Prize: Physics, 1972. *Born:* May 31, 1931; Oak Park, IL. *Parents:* Father, John Henry Schrieffer; Mother, Louise Anderson Schrieffer. *Nationality:* American. *Religion:* Christian. *Education:* Massachusetts Institute of Technology, B.S., 1953; Univ. of Illinois, M.S., 1954; Univ. of Illinois, Ph.D., 1957. *Spouse:* Anne Grete Thomsen, married December 30, 1960. *Children:* Paul Karsten, son; Anne Bolette, daughter; Anne Regina, daughter. *Career:* Univ. of Chicago, IL, Professor, 1957–59; Univ. of Illinois, Professor, 1959–62; Univ. of Pennsylvania, Professor, 1962–79; Univ. of California, Santa Barbara, Professor, 1979–91; Florida State Univ., Professor, 1992–. *Other Awards:* Buckley Prize,

1968; Comstock Prize, National Academy of Sciences, 1968; John Ericsson Medal, American Society of Swedish Engineers, 1976; Alumni Achievement Award, Univ. of Illinois, 1979; National Medal of Science, 1984.

Selected Publications: "Microscopic Theory of Superconductivity." *Physical Review* 106 (1957): 162–64 (with L.N. Cooper and J. Bardeen). "Theory of Superconductivity." *Physical Review* 108 (1957): 1175–1204 (with J. Bardeen and L.N. Cooper). "Recent Advances in the Theory of Superconductivity." *Physica* 26 (1960): S1–S16. *Theory of Superconductivity.* Reading, MA: W.A. Benjamin, 1964, revised 1983.

For More Information See: Physics Today 25 (December 1972): 73–75. *Science* 178 (November 3, 1972): 489–91.

Commentary: John Schrieffer received the Nobel Prize with his colaureates, John Bardeen and Leon Cooper, for their development of the BCS theory of superconductivity, which related the superconducting state to the bound pair actions of electrons at low temperature in the conductor. His later work has been in the areas of particle physics, metal impurities, spin fluctuations, and chemisorption. (P.S.)

1973

Esaki, Leo   **650**
Prize: Physics, 1973. *Born:* March 12, 1925; Osaka, Japan. *Parents:* Father, Soichiro Esaki; Mother, Niyoko Ito Esaki. *Nationality:* Japanese; later American resident. *Religion:* Buddhist. *Education:* Univ. of Tokyo, Japan, B.S., 1947; Univ. of Tokyo, Japan, Ph.D., 1959. *Spouse:* Masako Araki, married November 21, 1959, divorced; Masako Kondo, married May 31, 1986. *Children:* Eugene Leo, son; Nina Yvonne, daughter; Anna Eileen, daughter. *Career:* Kobe Kogyo Corporation, Japan, Researcher, 1947–56; Sony Corporation, Japan, Researcher, 1956–60; International Business Machines, Researcher, 1960–92; Univ. of Tsukuba, Japan, President, 1992–98. *Other Awards:* Nishina Memorial Award, 1959; Asahi Press Award, 1960; Toyo Rayon Foundation Award, 1961; Morris N. Liebmann Memorial Prize, 1961; Stuart Ballantine Medal, Franklin Institute, PA, 1961; Japan Academy Award, 1965; Order of Culture, Japan, 1974; Science Achievement Award, U.S.-Asia Institute, 1983; International Prize for New Materials, American Physical Society, 1985; IEEE Medal of Honor, 1991; Japan Prize, 1998.

Selected Publications: "Properties of Heavily-Doped Ge and Narrow p-n Junctions." *Solid State Phys. Electronics Telecommun., Proc. Intern. Conf., Brussels* 1 (1958): 514–23. "New Horizons in Semimetal Alloys." *IEEE Spectrum* 3 (1966): 74–80, 85–86. "Tunneling Studies on the Group 5 Semimetals and the 4–6 Semiconductors." *Journal of the Physical Society of Japan*, Supplement 21 (1966): 589–97. "Tunneling in Solids." *Electron. Struct. Solids, Lect. Chania Conf., 2nd* (1968): 1–40.

For More Information See: Modern Men of Science. New York: McGraw-Hill, 1966, 156–57. *New York Times Biographical Edition* (October 24, 1973): 1640. *Science* 182 (November 16, 1973): 701–04.

Commentary: Leo Esaki shared the 1973 prize for his discovery of tunneling in semiconductors. Tunneling is a quantum mechanical effect in which an electron passes through a potential barrier (a solid region), even though classical theory predicted that it could not. His research at the Sony Corporation in the late 1950s led to the creation of the Esaki diode, an important component of solid state physics. Because of its simplicity and sensitivity, it has practical applications in high-speed circuits, such as those in computers, communications networks, and other electronic equipment. Esaki applied a tunneling technique in spectroscopic studies, known as tunneling spectroscopy. (D.P.N.)

Giaever, Ivar   651

Prize: Physics, 1973. *Born:* April 5, 1929; Bergen, Norway. *Parents:* Father, John A. Giaever; Mother, Gudrun M. Skaarud Giaever. *Nationality:* Norwegian; later American citizen. *Religion:* No affiliation; from Lutheran background. *Education:* Norwegian Institute of Technology, Norway, Bachelor of Engineering, 1952; Rensselaer Polytechnical Institute, NY, Ph.D., 1964. *Spouse:* Inger Skramstad, married November 8, 1952. *Children:* John, son; Guri, daughter; Anne Kari, daughter; Trine, daughter. *Career:* Norwegian Army, 1952–53; Norwegian Patent Office, Oslo, Patent Examiner, 1953–54; General Electric Company, Canada, Engineer, 1954–56; General Electric Company, United States, Researcher, 1956–88; Rensselaer Polytechnic, NJ, Professor, 1988-; Univ. of Oslo, Norway, Professor, 1988-. *Other Awards:* Oliver E. Buckley Prize, American Physical Society, 1965; Guggenheim Fellow, 1970; V.K. Zworykin Award, National Academy of Engineering, 1974.

Selected Publications: "Energy Gap in Superconductors Measured by Electron Tunneling." *Physical Review Letters* 5 (1960): 147. "Electron Tunneling between Two Superconductors." *Physical Review Letters* 5 (1960): 464. "Detection of the A.C. Josephson Effect." *Physical Review Letters* 14 (1965): 904. "Magnetic Coupling Between Two Adjacent Superconductors." *Physical Review Letters* 15 (1965): 825.

For More Information See: Nobel Prize Winners: Physics. Pasadena, CA: Salem Press, 1988, Volume 3, 1027–36. *Physics Today* 14 (December 1961): 38–41. *Science* 182 (November 16, 1973): 701–04.

Commentary: Ivar Giaever was cited by the Academy for his work on tunneling effects in semiconductors and superconductors. His research studying the behavior of electrons in solids when a superconducting metal is present laid the foundation for Josephson's discovery of the Josephson effect, which has been heavily applied in microelectronics. Giaever's interest has shifted to biology, and he has studied stress reactions and antibody-antigen reactions while working as a researcher in immunology at General Electric and at the Albany Medical Center. (L.D.)

Josephson, Brian David   652

Prize: Physics, 1973. *Born:* January 4, 1940; Cardiff, Wales. *Parents:* Father, Abraham Josephson; Mother, Mimi Josephson. *Nationality:* British. *Religion:* Jewish. *Education:* Cambridge Univ., England, B.A., 1960; Cambridge Univ., England, M.A., 1964; Cambridge Univ., England, Ph.D., 1964. *Spouse:* Carol Anne Olivier, married 1976. *Children:* 1 daughter. *Career:* Cambridge Univ., England, Professor, 1965-. *Other Awards:* New Scientist Award, 1969; Research Corporation Award, 1969; Fritz London Medal, 1970; Guthrie Medal, 1972; van der Pol Medal, 1972; Elliott Cresson

Medal, 1972; Hughes Medal, 1972; Holweck Medal, 1973; Faraday Medal, 1982; Sir George Thompson Medal, 1984.

Selected Publications: "Potential Differences in the Mixed State of Type II Superconductors." *Physics Letters* 16 (1965): 242–43. "Macroscopic Field Equations for Metals in Equilibrium." *Physical Review* 152 (1966): 211–17. "Inequality for the Specific Heat. I. Derivation." *Proceedings of the Physical Society* 92 (1967): 269–75. "Inequality for the Specific Heat. II. Application to Critical Phenomena." *Proceedings of the Physical Society* 92 (1967): 276–84. "Equation of State Near the Critical Point." *Proceedings of the Physical Society, London (Solid State Physics)* 2 (1969): 1113–15. *Consciousness and the Physical World.* New York: Pergamon Press, 1980.

For More Information See: New York Times (October 24, 1973): 1, 26. *Nobel Prize Winners: Physics.* Pasadena, CA: Salem Press, 1988, Volume 3, 1037–44.

Commentary: Brian Josephson shared the Nobel Prize for work in developing theories that advanced and expanded the world of miniature electronics. Specifically, Josephson was cited by the Academy for his theoretical predictions of the properties of supercurrent through a tunnel barrier, particularly phenomena called "Josephson effects." One of the youngest Nobel laureates, the physicist was only 22 and in graduate school when he made his discoveries while doing research on semiconductivity in 1963. He has contributed significantly to studies of superconductivity, critical phenomena, and the theory of intelligence. (L.D.)

1974

Hewish, Antony   653

Prize: Physics, 1974. *Born:* May 11, 1924; Fowey, England. *Parents:* Father, Ernest William Hewish; Mother, Frances Grace Lanyon Pinch Hewish. *Nationality:* British. *Religion:* Most probably Christian/Protestant. *Education:* Cambridge Univ., England, B.A., 1948; Cambridge Univ., England, M.A., 1950; Cambridge Univ., England, Ph.D., 1952. *Spouse:* Marjorie Elizabeth Catherine Richards, married 1950. *Children:* 1 son; 1 daughter. *Career:* Cambridge Univ., England, Professor, 1952–89. *Other Awards:* Hamilton Prize, Cambridge Univ., England, 1952; Eddington Medal, Royal Astronomical Society, 1969; Charles Vernon Boys Prize, Institute of Physics and Physical Sciences, 1970; Dellinger Gold Medal, International Union of Radio Sciences, 1972; Michelson Medal, Franklin Institute, PA, 1973; Hopkins Prize, Cambridge Philosophical Society, 1973; Holweck Medal and Prize, Institute of Physics and French Physical Society, 1974; Hughes Medal, Royal Society, 1976.

Selected Publications: Seeing Beyond the Visible. London: English Universities Press, 1970. "Small Stars Raise Large Problems." *Physics Bulletin* 25 (1974): 459–61.

For More Information See: Nobel Prize Winners: Physics. Pasadena, CA: Salem Press, 1988, Volume 3, 1053–59. *Science* 186 (November 15, 1974): 620–21.

Commentary: Antony Hewish was honored for his pioneering research in radio astrophysics, which led to the discovery of pulsars (compact radio sources emitting regular pulses). Although questioned by some scientists, Hewish's delay in announcing the discovery allowed principal scientific facts to be established and clarified, averting what has been called the "little green men" speculation. Hewish's earlier research was on radio scintillation, and he was involved in the study of all three types of radio scintillation, i.e., due to radio wave deflection by ionized gases in the interstellar medium, in the interplanetary medium, and in the earth's atmosphere. (D.H.)

Ryle, Martin, Sir   654

Prize: Physics, 1974. *Born:* September 27, 1918; Brighton, England. *Death:* October 14, 1984; Cambridge, England. *Parents:* Father, John A. Ryle; Mother, Miriam Scully Ryle. *Nationality:* British. *Religion:* From Anglican background. *Education:* Oxford Univ., England, baccalaureate, 1939. *Spouse:* Ella Rowena Palmer, married 1947. *Children:* John, son: Alison, daughter; Claire, daughter. *Career:* Telecommunications Research Establishment, England, Researcher, 1939–45; Cambridge Univ., England, Professor and Administrator, 1945–82. *Other Awards:* Hughes Medal, Royal Society, 1954; Van der Pol Gold Medal, International Scientific Radio Union, 1963; Gold Medal, Royal Astronomical Society, 1964; Henry Draper Medal, National Academy of Sciences, U.S.A., 1965; Holweck Prize, 1965; Knighthood, 1966; Morris N. Liebman Award, 1971; Popov Medal, 1971; Faraday Medal, 1971; Michelson Award, 1971; Royal Medal, Royal Society, 1973; Bruce Medal, 1974.

Selected Publications: "The New Cambridge Radio Telescope." *Nature* 194 (May 12, 1962): 517–18. "High-Resolution Observations of the Radio Sources in Cygnus and Cassiopeia." *Nature* 205 (March 27, 1965): 1259–62 (with B. Elsmore and Ann C. Neville). "Observations of Radio Galaxies with the One-Mile Telescope at Cambridge." *Nature* 207 (September 4, 1965): 1024–27 (with B. Elsmore and Ann C. Neville). "The 5-km Radio Telescope at Cambridge." *Nature* 239 (October 20, 1972): 435–38.

For More Information See: New York Times Biographical Edition (October 16, 1974): 1491. *Nobel Prize Winners: Physics.* Pasadena, CA: Salem Press, 1988, Volume 3, 1045–52. *Biographical Memoirs of the Fellows of the Royal Society.* London: Royal Society, 1986 (Volume 32), 495.

Commentary: Martin Ryle shared the Nobel Prize for his creative research in the area of radio astrophysics. Ryle developed the aperture synthesis technique, which combines radiotelescopes with computers to see deeply into space. Using the techniques and instrumentation he developed, Ryle was able to map the skies with a thoroughness previously not possible. His research elucidated the characteristics of radio stars, analyzed the pulsars and eliminated "little green men" conjectures about them, and explained the origin of radio scintillation. His studies have also strengthened the belief in the "big bang" theory of the origination of the universe. (D.H.)

1975

Bohr, Aage Niels   655

Prize: Physics, 1975. *Born:* June 19, 1922; Copenhagen, Denmark. *Parents:* Father, Niels Bohr; Mother, Margrethe Norlund Bohr. *Nationality:* Danish. *Religion:* From Jewish background. *Education:* Univ. of Copenhagen, Denmark, M.S., 1946; Univ. of Copenhagen, Denmark, Ph.D., 1954. *Spouse:* Marietta Bettina Soffer, married March 1950, died

1978; Bente Meyer Scharff, married 1981. *Children:* Vilhelm, son; Tomas, son; Margrethe, daughter. *Career:* Los Alamos Scientific Laboratory, NM, Researcher, 1943–45; Institute for Theoretical Physics, Copenhagen, Researcher, 1946–49; Columbia Univ., New York, Researcher, 1949–50; Univ. of Copenhagen, Denmark, Researcher and Professor, 1950–81; Neils Bohr Institutem Copenhagen, Denmark, Researcher and Administrator, 1962–70; Nordic Institute for Theoretical Physics (Nordita), Administrator, 1975–81. *Other Awards:* Dannie Heineman Prize, American Physical Society and American Institute for Physics, 1960; Pope Pius XI Medal, 1963; Atoms for Peace Award, Ford Motor Company Fund, 1969; H. C. Orsted Medal, 1970; Rutherford Medal and Prize, Institute of Physics, London, 1972; John Price Wetherill Medal, Franklin Institute, PA, 1974; Ole Römer Medal, 1976.

Selected Publications: "On the Quantization of Angular Momenta in Heavy Nuclei." *Physical Review* 81 (January 1, 1951): 134–38. "Nuclear Magnetic Moments and Atomic Hyperfine Structure." *Physical Review* 81 (February 1, 1951): 331–35. *Rotational States of Atomic Nuclei.* Copenhagen: Munksgaard, 1954. *Collective and Individual-Particle Aspects of Nuclear Structure.* Copenhagen: Munksgaard, 1957 (with B. Mottelson). *Nuclear Structure.* 2 volumes. New York: W.A. Benjamin, 1969–75 (with B. Mottelson).

For More Information See: Physics Today 28 (December 1975): 69–71. *Science* 190 (November 28, 1975): 868–70.

Commentary: Aage Bohr shared the Nobel Prize for his contributions to the "discovery of the connection between collective motion and particle motion in the atomic nucleus and the development of the structure of the atomic nucleus based on this connection." Through their own research as well as through their influence on experimental studies pursued at nuclear laboratories throughout the world, Bohr and his colaureate, Ben Mottelson, were instrumental in developing a qualitative and quantitative understanding of the nonspherical (deformed) shape of atomic nuclei postulated in 1950 by their colaureate James Rainwater. Bohr and Mottelson identified the properties of the spheroidal nucleus and provided a clearer picture of nuclear structural dynamics. (J.C.H.)

Mottelson, Benjamin Roy   656

Prize: Physics, 1975. *Born:* July 9, 1926; Chicago, IL. *Parents:* Father, Goodman Mottelson; Mother, Georgia Blum Mottelson. *Nationality:* American; later Danish citizen. *Religion:* Jewish. *Education:* Purdue Univ., IN, B.S., 1947; Harvard Univ., MA, M.A., 1948; Harvard Univ., MA, Ph.D., 1950. *Spouse:* Nancy Jane Reno, married May 31, 1948, died 1975. *Children:* 2 sons; 1 daughter. *Career:* Institute for Theoretical Physics, Denmark, Researcher, 1950–51; U.S. Atomic Energy Commission, Researcher, 1951–53; CERN, Theoretical Study Group, Researcher, 1953–56; Nordic Institute for Theoretical Atomic Physics, Denmark, Professor and Administrator, 1957-.

Selected Publications: Collective and Individual-Particle Aspects of Nuclear Structure. Copenhagen: Munksgaard, 1957 (with A. Bohr). *Lectures on Selected Topics in Nuclear Structure.* Bombay: Tata Institute of Fundamental Research, 1964. *Nuclear Structure.* 2 volumes. New York: W.A. Benjamin, 1969–75 (with A. Bohr). "Elementary Modes of

Excitation in the Nucleus." *Reviews of Modern Physics* 48 (July 1976): 375–83.

For More Information See: Asimov's Biographical Encyclopedia of Science and Technology. Garden City, NY: Doubleday, 1982, 883. *Kraks Blaa Bog 1984.* Copenhagen: Krak, 1985, 754. *Physics Today* 28 (December 1975): 69, 71–72.

Commentary: Ben Mottelson was awarded the Nobel Prize for "the discovery of the connection between collective motion and particle motion in atomic nuclei and the development of the theory of the structure of the atomic nucleus based on this connection." Mottelson and Bohr, paying close attention to new experimental results, found the means to combine two previously discrete models of nuclear structure—the liquid-drop and the nuclear shell models—into one unified theory. (J.W.)

Rainwater, Leo James   657

Prize: Physics, 1975. *Born:* December 9, 1917; Council, ID. *Death:* May 31, 1986; Yonkers, NY. *Parents:* Father, Leo Jasper Rainwater; Mother, Edna Eliza Teague Rainwater. *Nationality:* American. *Religion:* Presbyterian. *Education:* California Institute of Technology, B.S., 1939; Columbia Univ., NY, M.A., 1941; Columbia Univ., NY, Ph.D., 1946. *Spouse:* Emma Louise Smith, married March 7, 1942. *Children:* James Carlton, son; Robert Stephen, son; William George, son; Elizabeth, daughter. *Career:* Columbia Univ., NY, Professor, 1946–82. *Other Awards:* Ernest Orlando Lawrence Memorial Award, Atomic Energy Commission, 1963.

Selected Publications: "Nuclear Energy Level Argument for a Spheroidal Nuclear Model." *Physical Review* 79 (August 10, 1950): 432–34. "Mu-Meson Physics." *Annual Review of Nuclear Science* 7 (1957): 1–30. "Increasing Synchrocyclotron Currents and the Space Charge Limit." *AD 636708* (1965): 1–8.

For More Information See: Nobel Prize Winners: Physics. Pasadena, CA: Salem Press, 1988, Volume 3, 1079–87. *Science* 190 (November 28, 1975): 868–70. *New York Times Biographical Service* (June 3, 1986): 733.

Commentary: James Rainwater and his colaureates, Aage Bohr and Ben Mottelson, shared the Nobel Prize "for their discovery of the connection between collective motion and particle motion in the atomic nucleus and the development of the structure of the atomic nucleus based on this connection." Rainwater postulated the nonspherical (deformed) shape of atomic nuclei, for which Bohr and Mottelson developed a qualitative and quantitative understanding. The work of the three laureates resolved the apparent conflict between the prevailing liquid drop and nuclear shell models of nuclear structure, and provided the base for an understanding of the low-lying states of all nuclei. (J.C.H.)

1976

Richter, Burton   658

Prize: Physics, 1976. *Born:* March 22, 1931; Brooklyn, NY. *Parents:* Father, Abraham Richter; Mother, Fanny Pollack Richter. *Nationality:* American. *Religion:* Jewish. *Education:* Massachusetts Institute of Technology, B.S., 1952; Massachusetts Institute of Technology, Ph.D., 1956. *Spouse:*

Laurose Becker, married July 1, 1960. *Children:* Elizabeth, daughter; Matthew, son. *Career:* Stanford Univ., CA, Professor, 1956–99. *Other Awards:* Ernesto Orlando Lawrence Medal, 1975.

Selected Publications: "Low Mass Anomaly in Photoproduction of Pion Pairs." *Physical Review Letters* 9 (1962): 217–20. *Instabilities in Stored Particle Beams.* Springfield, VA: CFSTI, 1965 (with M. Sands and A.M. Sessler). "High-energy Photoproduction." *U.S. Atomic Energy Commission CONF-670923* (1967): 309–36. "Two-body Photoproduction." *U.S. Atomic Energy Commission SLAC-PUB-501* (1968): 1–57. "Plenary Report on e(+)e(−) Hadrons." *Proceedings of the International Conference on High Energy Physics* 17th (1974): 20–35.

For More Information See: Nobel Prize Winners: Physics. Pasadena, CA: Salem Press, 1988 (Volume 3) 1089–97. *Science* (November 19, 1976): 825–26.

Commentary: Burton Richter's award was for the discovery of a subatomic particle three times heavier than the proton with a life span 10,000 times longer than could be predicted by prior discoveries. These characteristics led to drastic revisions in the quark theories. Richter calls his particle "psi" because "it's the only unassigned Greek letter in particle physics"; colaureate Samuel Ting refers to the particle as "J." The scientific community has not yet resolved the nomenclature. J/psi has been called "the greatest discovery ever in the field of particle physics." The properties of the particle are consistent with a fourth type of quark and support the concept of charm. (R.P.)

Ting, Samuel Chao Chung   659

Prize: Physics, 1976. *Born:* January 27, 1936; Ann Arbor, MI. *Parents:* Father, Kuan Hai Ting; Mother, Tsun-Ying S. Wang Ting. *Nationality:* American. *Religion:* Christian. *Education:* Univ. of Michigan, B.S.E., 1959; Univ. of Michigan, M.S., 1960; Univ. of Michigan, Ph.D., 1962. *Spouse:* Kay Louise Kuhne, married November 23, 1960, no further record; Susan Carol Marks, married April 28, 1985. *Children:* Jeanne Min, daughter; Amy Min, daughter; Christopher M., son. *Career:* Columbia Univ., NY, Professor, 1964–67; Massachusetts Institute of Technology, Professor, 1967-. *Other Awards:* Ernest Orlando Lawrence Award, 1976; A.E. Eringen Medal, 1977; De Gasperi Prize, Italian Republic, 1988; Gold Medal, Brescia, Italy, 1988; Golden Leopard Award, Taormina, 1988; Forum Engelberg Prize, 1996.

Selected Publications: "Timelike Momenta in Quantum Electrodynamics." *Physical Review* 145 (1966): 1018–22 (with Stanley J. Brodsky). "Leptonic Decays of Vector Mesons." *United States Atomic Energy Commission CONF-670923* (1967): 452–83. "Electrodynamics at Small Distances, Leptonic Decays of Vector Mesons, and Photoproduction of Vector Mesons." *Int. Conf. High-Energy Phys., Proc. 14th* (1968): 43–71. "Summary of Photoproduction and Leptonic Decays of Vector Mesons." *United States Atomic Energy Commission DESY-68/29* (1968): 1–18. *The Search for Charm, Beauty and Truth at High Energies.* New York: Plenum Press, 1984 (with G. Bellini).

For More Information See: Physics Today 29 (December 1976): 17+. *Science* 194 (November 19, 1976): 825–26+.

Commentary: Samuel Ting's award was for the discovery of a subatomic particle three times heavier than the proton with a life span 10,000 times longer than could be predicted by prior discoveries. Ting called the particle "J" after the physical symbol for angular momentum; his colaureate Burton Richter referred to the particle as "psi." The discovery of the particle forced revisions in the existent theory of quarks to accommodate the previously predicted charmed quark. Since the discovery, a family of such particles has been found. (R.P.)

1977

Anderson, Philip Warren 660

Prize: Physics, 1977. *Born:* December 13, 1923; Indianapolis, IN. *Parents:* Father, Harry Warren Anderson; Mother, Elsie Osborne Anderson. *Nationality:* American. *Religion:* Christian. *Education:* Harvard Univ., MA, B.S., 1943; Harvard Univ., MA, M.A., 1947; Harvard Univ., MA, Ph.D., 1949. *Spouse:* Joyce Gothwaite, married July 31, 1947. *Children:* Susan Osborne, daughter. *Career:* Bell Telephone Laboratories, NJ, Researcher, 1949–84; Cambridge Univ., England, Professor, 1967–75; Princeton Univ., NJ, Professor, 1975–96. *Other Awards:* Oliver E. Buckley Prize, 1964; Dannie Heineman Prize, 1975; Guthrie Medal, 1978; National Medal of Science, 1982; Centennial Medal, Harvard Univ., 1996; Bardeen Prize, 1997.

Selected Publications: "The Limits of Validity of the Van Vleck-Weisskopf Line Shape Formula." *Physical Review* 76 (1949): 471. "An Approximate Quantum Theory of the Antiferromagnetic Ground State." *Physical Review* 86 (1952): 694–701. "New Method in the Theory of Superconductivity." *Physical Review* 110 (1958): 985–86. "New Approach to the Theory of Superexchange Interactions." *Physical Review* 115 (1959): 2–13. "Generalized B.C.S. States and Aligned Orbital Angular Momentum in the Proposed Low-Temperature Phase of Liquid Helium-3." *Physica* 26 (1960): 5137–42. *Concepts in Solids.* New York: W.A. Benjamin, 1963. *Basic Notions of Condensed Matter Physics.* Menlo Park, CA: Benjamin/Cummings, 1984.

For More Information See: Biographical Encyclopedia of Scientists. New York: Facts on File, 1981, 18–19. *Physics Today* 30 (December 1977): 77–78.

Commentary: Philip Anderson shared the Nobel Prize with John Van Vleck and Nevill Mott "for their fundamental theoretical investigation of the electronic structure of magnetic and disordered systems." Anderson was responsible for a number of important contributions: the pressure broadening of spectral lines; the theory of superexchange; further explanations of antiferromagnetics, ferroelectrics, and superconductors; the model of metals with impurity atoms (the Anderson model); the treatment of impurity migration in crystals (the Anderson localization); discussions of superconductivity and superfluidity; Helium-3 superfluid state treatment; and work on low-temperature properties of glass. (C.T.)

Mott, Nevill Francis, Sir 661

Prize: Physics, 1977. *Born:* September 30, 1905; Leeds, England. *Death:* August 8, 1996; Milton Keynes, England. *Parents:* Father, Charles Francis Mott; Mother, Lilian Mary Reynolds Mott. *Nationality:* British. *Religion:* Anglican.

Education: Cambridge Univ., England, BA, 1927; Cambridge Univ., England, MA, 1930. *Spouse:* Ruth Horder, married March 21, 1930. *Children:* Elizabeth, daughter; Alice, daughter. *Career:* Cambridge Univ., England, Professor, 1930–33; Univ. of Bristol, England, Professor, 1933–54; Cambridge Univ., England, Professor, 1954–71. *Other Awards:* Hughes Medal, 1941; Royal Medal, 1953; Knighthood, 1962; Copley Medal, 1972; Faraday Medal, 1973; Ordre Nationale Mérite, 1977.

Selected Publications: The Theory of Atomic Collisions. Oxford: Clarendon Press, 1933 (with H.S.W. Massey). *The Theory of Properties of Metals and Alloys.* New York: Dover, 1936 (with H. Jones). *Electronic Processes in Ionic Crystals.* Oxford: Clarendon Press, 1948 (with R.W. Gurney).

For More Information See: Davis, E.A. *Neville Mott.* London; Bristol, PA: Taylor & Francis, 1998. A Life in Science. Philadelphia, PA: Taylor and Francis, 1986, 1996. *Physics Today* 30 (December 8, 1977): 77–78. *Science* 198 (November 18, 1977): 713–15.

Commentary: The Nobel Prize was awarded to Nevill Mott, along with his two colaureates, for their "fundamental theoretical investigations of the electronic structure of magnetic and disordered systems." Mott began his career working on the quantum theory of atomic collisions and scattering. His fields of interest were multiple and included significant work on models of the solid state, electronic processes in metal-insulator transitions, the photographic process in relation to surface and defect properties, crystal strength, liquid metals, semiconductors, and glassy semiconductors. (C.T.)

Van Vleck, John Hasbrouck 662

Prize: Physics, 1977. *Born:* March 13, 1899; Middletown, CT. *Death:* October 27, 1980; Cambridge, MA. *Parents:* Father, Edward Burr Van Vleck; Mother, Hester Laurence Raymond Van Vleck. *Nationality:* American. *Religion:* Christian. *Education:* Univ. of Wisconsin, B.S., 1920; Harvard Univ., MA, M.A., 1921; Harvard Univ., MA, Ph.D., 1922. *Spouse:* Abigail June Pearson, married June 10, 1927. *Children:* None. *Career:* Harvard Univ., MA, Professor, 1922–23; Univ. of Minnesota, Professor, 1923–28; Univ. of Wisconsin, Professor, 1928–34; Harvard Univ., MA, Professor, 1934–69. *Other Awards:* Chevalier Legion of Honor, France; Albert A. Michelson Award, Case Institute of Technology, 1963; Irving Langmuir Award, General Electric Foundation, 1965; National Medal of Science, 1966; Distinguished Service Award, Univ. of Wisconsin Alumni Association, 1967; Cresson Medal, Franklin Institute, PA, 1971; Lorentz Medal, Netherlands Academy, 1974.

Selected Publications: "Quantum Theory of the Specific Heat of Hydrogen. I. Relation to the New Mechanics, Band Spectra and Chemical Constants." *Physical Review* 28 (1926): 980–1021. "Dielectric Constants and Magnetic Susceptibilities in the New Quantum Mechanics. Part I. A General Proof of the Langevin-Debye Formula." *Physical Review* 29 (1927): 727–44. "The New Quantum Mechanics." *Chemical Reviews* 5 (1928): 467–507. *The Theory of Electric and Magnetic Susceptibilities.* New York: Oxford Univ. Press, 1932. "The Theory of Antiferromagnetism." *Journal of Chemical Physics* 9 (1941): 85–90.

For More Information See: Biographical Memoirs of the National Academy of Sciences. New York: Columbia

Univ. Press, 1987 (Volume 56), 501–40. *Biographical Memoirs of the National Academy Sciences* Washington, DC: National Academy of Sciences, 1987. *Biographical Memoirs of the Royal Society.* London: Royal Society, 1982 (Volume 28), 627–65.

Commentary: John Van Vleck shared the Nobel Prize for "fundamental theoretical investigations of the electronic structure of magnetic and disordered systems." Van Vleck was specifically cited for his research on electron correlation, which was important in the development of the laser. His early work focused on magnetism, both from the standpoint of classical quantum theory and the new wave mechanics. Van Vleck developed the concept of temperature-independent magnetic susceptibility. He also contributed significantly in the areas of molecular structure and bonding, the properties of an atom or ion in a crystal, and radar and radioastronomy. (C.T.)

1978

Kapitsa, Pyotr Leonidovich   663

Prize: Physics, 1978. *Born:* July 9, 1894; Kronstadt, Russia. *Death:* April 8, 1984; Moscow, USSR. *Parents:* Father, Leonid Petrovich Kapitsa; Mother, Olga Stebnitsckiy Kapitsa. *Nationality:* Russian. *Religion:* Christian. *Education:* Petrograd Polytechnical Institute, USSR, baccalaureate, 1918; Cambridge Univ., England, Ph.D., 1923. *Spouse:* Nadezhda Tschernosvitova, married 1916, died 1920; Anna Alekseyevna Kyrillovna, married 1926. *Children:* Andrei, son; Sergei, son; Ieronim, son; Nadezhda, daughter. *Career:* Petrograd Polytechnical Institute, USSR, Professor, 1918–21; Cambridge Univ., England, Researcher and Professor, 1921–35; USSR Academy of Sciences, Institute for Physical Problems, Director, 1935–46, 1955–84; Physiotechnical Institute, Moscow, USSR, Professor, 1947–84. *Other Awards:* Stalin Prize, 1941, 1943; Faraday Medal, Council of Electrical Engineers of England, 1942; Five Orders of Lenin, 1943; Order of the Red Banner of Labor; Franklin Medal, 1944.

Selected Publications: Collected Papers. Oxford: Oxford Univ. Press, 1946–47. *Elektronika Bol'shikh Moshchnostei.* Moscow: n.p., 1962. *Teoriia, Eksperiment, Praktika (Theory, Experiment, Practice).* Moscow: n.p., 1966.

For More Information See: Badash, Lawrence. *Kapitza, Rutherford and the Kremlin.* New Haven, CT: Yale Univ. Press, 1985. *Peter Kapitza on Life and Science.* New York: Macmillan, 1968. *Science* 202 (December 1, 1978): 960–62. *Kapitza in Cambridge and Moscow.* Amsterdam, Netherlands: North-Holland, 1990.

Commentary: The Nobel Prize was awarded to Pyotr Kapitsa for his work in low temperature physics, including studies of electrical properties of matter and the liquefaction of gases. Kapitsa invented a new method for liquefying gases and studied the unusual properties of flow and conduction of Helium II. His invention of a simple turbine device to substitute oxygen for air in blast furnaces revolutionized the Soviet steel industry. He was also known for his research with ball lightning, standing waves, atomic energy, and space research. Kapitsa's career in the Soviet Union remains shrouded in mystery since his detention there in 1934, when he was director of the Cavendish Laboratory in England. (T.B.)

Penzias, Arno Allan   664

Prize: Physics, 1978. *Born:* April 26, 1933; Munich, Germany. *Parents:* Father, Karl Penzias; Mother, Justine Inge Eisenreich Penzias. *Nationality:* German; later American citizen. *Religion:* Jewish. *Education:* City College of New York, B.S., 1954; Columbia Univ., NY, M.A., 1958; Columbia Univ., NY, Ph.D., 1962. *Spouse:* Anne Pearl Barras, married November 25, 1954; Sherry Chamove Levit, married August 2, 1996. *Children:* David Simon, son; Mindy Gail, daughter; Laurie Ruth, daughter. *Career:* Bell Laboratories, NJ, Researcher and Administrator, 1961–95; Lucent Technologies, Researcher and Administrator, 1995–98; New Enterprise Associates, Administrator, 1998-. *Other Awards:* Henry Draper Medal, 1977; Herschel Medal, 1977; Townsend Harris Medal, 1979; Newman Award, City College of New York, 1983; Joseph Handleman Prize, 1983; Graduate Faculties Alumni Award, Columbia Univ., 1984; Achievement Award, Big Brothers, New York City, 1985; Priestley Award, 1989; Pake Prize, 1990; Pender Award, 1992; New Jersey Science and Technology Medal, 1996.

Selected Publications: "Interstellar Carbon Monoxide, Carbon-13 Monoxide, and Carbon Monoxide-Oxygen-18." *Astrophysics Journal* 165 Part I (1971): L63 (with Keith B. Jefferts and Robert W. Wilson). "Interstellar Carbon Monosulfide." *Astrophysics Journal* 168 Part 2 (1971): L53-L58 (with others). "Interstellar C N Excitation at 2.64 mm." *Physics Review Letters* 28 (1972): 772–75 (with Keith B. Jefferts and Robert W. Wilson). "Millimeter-Wavelength Radio-Astronomy Techniques." *Annu. Rev. Astron. Astrophys* 11 (1973): 51–72 (with C.A. Burrus).

For More Information See: Current Biography Yearbook. New York: H.W. Wilson, 1985, 328–31. *New York Times* (October 18, 1978): 5.

Commentary: Arno Penzias and his colleague, Robert W. Wilson, were awarded the Nobel Prize for their detection of microwave background radiation, which supported the theory that the universe was created by a "big bang" that took place some 20 billion years ago, as opposed to the "Steady State" theory which held that the universe continually expanded and collapsed upon itself. The findings indicated that the universe is an "open" system continually expanding from the initial "bang" until it loses momentum and becomes still and lifeless. Penzias and Wilson continued their research collaboration and discovered large amounts of the fossil element deuterium in the Milky Way galaxy. The team's discoveries have stimulated extensive further research. (B.M.)

Wilson, Robert Woodrow   665

Prize: Physics, 1978. *Born:* January 10, 1936; Houston, TX. *Parents:* Father, Ralph Woodrow Wilson; Mother, Fannie May Willis Wilson. *Nationality:* American. *Religion:* Christian. *Education:* Rice Univ., TX, B.A., 1957; California Institute of Technology, Ph.D., 1962. *Spouse:* Elizabeth Rhoads Sawin, married September 4, 1958. *Children:* Philip Garrett, son; Suzanne Katherine, daughter; Randal Woodrow, son. *Career:* Owens Laboratories, United States, 1962–63; Bell Laboratories, NJ, 1963–95; Smithsonian Astrophysical Laboratory, Cambridge, MA, Researcher, 1995-. *Other Awards:* Henry Draper Medal, Royal Astronomy Society, 1977; Herschel Medal, National Academy of Sciences, 1977.

Selected Publications: "Isotropy of Cosmic Background Radiation at 4080 Megahertz." *Science* 156 (1967): 1100–01 (with A.A. Penzias). "Measurement of the Flux Density of CAS A at 4080 Ma/s." *Astrophysical Journal* 142 (1965): 1149–56 (with A.A. Penzias). "Interstellar CN Excitation at 2.64 mm." *Physics Review Letters* 28 (1972): 772–75 (with A.A. Penzias and K.B. Jefferts).

For More Information See: "The 1978 Nobel Prize in Physics." *Science* 205 (December 1, 1978): 962–65. *Nobel Prize Winners: Physics.* Pasadena, CA: Salem Press, 1988, (Volume 3), 1163–70.

Commentary: Robert Wilson's Nobel Prize was for work that "made it possible to obtain information about cosmic processes that took place a very long time ago, at the time of the creation of the universe." Wilson's studies of radio noise in the sky led to the observation of a ubiquitous background radiation which fit the spectrum of a blackbody at a temperature about 3 degrees K. The discovery lent credence to the "big bang" theory of the beginning of the universe, which would predict such a background. (L.M.)

1979

Glashow, Sheldon Lee 666

Prize: Physics, 1979. *Born:* December 5, 1932; New York, NY. *Parents:* Father, Lewis (Gluchovsky) Glashow; Mother, Bella Rubin Glashow. *Nationality:* American. *Religion:* Jewish. *Education:* Cornell Univ., NY, A.B., 1954; Harvard Univ., MA, M.A., 1955; Harvard Univ., MA, Ph.D., 1958. *Spouse:* Joan Shirley Alexander, married 1972. *Children:* Jason David, son; Jordan, son; Brian Lewis, son; Rebecca Lee, daughter. *Career:* Institute of Theoretical Physics, Copenhagen, Denmark, Researcher, 1958–60; California Institute of Technology, Researcher, 1960–61; Stanford Univ., CA, Professor, 1961–62; Univ. of California, Berkeley, Professor, 1962–66; Harvard Univ., MA, Professor, 1966-; Texas A & M, Professor, 1983-. *Other Awards:* J.R. Oppenheimer Memorial Prize, 1977; George Ledlie Prize, 1978; Castiglione di Silica Prize, 1983; Erice Scientists for Peace Prize, 1991.

Selected Publications: "Symmetries of Strong Interactions." In *Proceedings of the International School of Physics "Enrico Fermi" Course XXXIII, Varenna, 6th-18th July 1964*, pp.189–225. New York: Academic Press, 1966. "Divergencies of Massive Yang-Mills Theories: Higher Groups." *Physical Review D: Particles and Fields* 4 (September 15, 1971): 1918–19 (with J. Iiopoulos). "Toward a Unified Theory: Threads in a Tapestry." *Science* 210 (1980): 1319–23. *The Charm of Physics.* New York: American Institute of Physics, 1991.

For More Information See: Glashow, S.L. and Bova, B. *Interactions.* New York: Warner Books, 1998. *Physics Today* 32 (December 1979): 17–19. *Science* 206 (December 14, 1979): 1290–92.

Commentary: Sheldon Glashow shared the Nobel Prize with Abdus Salam and Steven Weinberg "for their contribution to the theory of the unified weak and electromagnetic interaction between elementary particles, including, *inter alia,* the prediction of the weak neutral current." Glashow extended the Weinberg-Salam theory (which introduced the unity of the electromagnetic interaction and the weak interaction—two of the four fundamental forces) to several elementary particles (among them the baryons and mesons) by defining a new characteristic which he called charm. The concept of charm has been used since in work on the quark theory and in explanations of properties of the J/psi particle. (M.N.)

Salam, Abdus 667

Prize: Physics, 1979. *Born:* January 29, 1926; Jhang, Pakistan. *Death:* November 21, 1996; Oxford, England. *Parents:* Father, Muhammed Hussain; Mother, Hajira Hussain. *Nationality:* Pakistani; later British resident. *Religion:* Muslim. *Education:* Univ. of Punjab, Pakistan, M.A., 1946; Cambridge Univ., England, B.A., 1949; Cambridge Univ., England, Ph.D., 1951; Cambridge Univ., England, D.Sc., 1957. *Spouse:* Amtul Hafeez Begum, married 1949; Louise Johnson, married, no date found. *Children:* Masooda, daughter; Salam, son; 3 other daughters; 1 other son. *Career:* Institute for Advanced Study, Princeton, NJ, Researcher, 1951; Univ. of Punjab, Lahore, Pakistan, Professor, 1951–54; Cambridge Univ., England, Professor, 1954–56; Imperial College, London, England, Professor, 1957–96. *Other Awards:* Hopkins Prize, Cambridge Univ., England, 1957; Adams Prize, 1958; Pride of Performance Award, Pakistan, 1959; Maxwell Medal, Physical Society, London, England, 1961; Hughes Medal, 1964; Oppenheimer Prize and Medal, 1971; Atoms for Peace Award, 1968; Guthrie Medal and Prize, 1976; Sarvadhikary Gold Medal, Calcutta Univ., 1977; Royal Medal, Royal Society, 1978; Matteuci Medal, Academia Nazionale di Lincei, Rome, Italy, 1978; John Tate Medal, American Institute of Physics, 1978; Einstein Medal, 1979; Shri R.D. Birla Award, Indian Physics Association, 1979; Josef Stefan Medal, 1980; Gold Medal, Czechoslovak Academy of Sciences, 1981; Peace Medal, 1981; Lomonosov Gold Medal, 1983; Dayemi International Peace Award, 1986; Edinburgh Medal and Prize, 1989; Erice Science Peace prize, 1989; Copley Medal, 1990; Catalunya International Prize, 1990; Gold Medal, Slovak Academy of Sciences, 1992; d'Oro Prize, 1993; Mazhar-Ali Applied Science Medal, 1992.

Selected Publications: "Gauge Unification of Fundamental Forces." *Proc. Eur. Conf. Part. Phys. (9th)* 2 (1977): 1187–1207. "Gauge Unification of Fundamental Forces." *Proc. Int. Conf. Winter Sch. Front. Theor. Phys.* (1977): 29–35. "Gauge Unification of the Four Fundamental Forces." *Phys. Contemp. Needs* 2 (1978): 419–56. "The Electroweak Force, Grand Unification and Superunification." *Phys. Scr.* 20 (1979): 227–34. *Selected Papers of Abdus Salam.* River Edge, NY: World Scientific, 1994.

For More Information See: Ghani, Abdul. *Abdus Salam* Khanachi, Pakistan: Ma'Aref, 1982. *Physics Today* 32 (December 1979): 17–19. *Science* 206 (December 14, 1979): 1290–92. Singh, J. *Abdus Salam, A Biography.* New York: Penguin Books, 1992.

Commentary: Abdus Salam and his two colaureates, Sheldon Glashow and Steven Weinberg, shared the Nobel Prize "for their contributions to the theory of the unified weak and electromagnetic interaction between elementary particles, including *inter alia* the prediction of the weak neutral current." The Weinberg-Salam theory treated the unification of two of the four fundamental forces (the electromagnetic interaction and the weak interaction) for certain particles and was a major step toward an overall unified field theory. The theory also predicted neutral currents (elementary particle interactions with no exchange of electric charge). Salam continues his work on theories describing the behavior and properties of elementary particles. (L.I.S.)

Weinberg, Steven   668

Prize: Physics, 1979. *Born:* May 3, 1933; New York, NY. *Parents:* Father, Frederick Weinberg; Mother, Eva Israel Weinberg. *Nationality:* American. *Religion:* Jewish. *Education:* Cornell Univ., NY, A.B., 1954; Princeton Univ., NJ, Ph.D., 1957. *Spouse:* Louise Goldwasser, married July 6, 1954. *Children:* Elizabeth, daughter. *Career:* Columbia Univ., NY, Professor, 1957–59; Univ. of California, Berkeley, Professor, 1959–69; Massachusetts Institute of Technology, Professor, 1969–73; Harvard Univ., MA, Professor, 1973–83; Univ. of Texas, Austin, Professor, 1982-. *Other Awards:* J.R. Oppenheimer Prize, 1973; Dannie Heineman Mathematical Physics Prize, 1977; American Institute of Physics—U.S. Steel Foundation Science Writing Award, 1977; Elliot Cresson Medal, Franklin Institute, PA, 1979; Madison Medal, 1991; National Medal of Science, 1991; Andrew Gemant Award, 1997; Piazzi Prize, 1998; Lewis Thomas Prize, 1999.

Selected Publications: Gravitation and Cosmology: Principles and Applications of the General Theory of Relativity. New York: Wiley, 1972. "Recent Progress in Gauge Theories of the Weak, Electromagnetic and Strong Interactions." *Reviews of Modern Physics* 46 (1974): 255–77. *The First Three Minutes: A Modern View of the Origin of the Universe.* New York: Basic Books, 1977. "Limits of Massless Particles." *Physics Letters. B* 96 (1980): 59–62. "Charges from Extra Dimensions." *Physics Letters. B* 125 (1983): 265–69. *The Discovery of Subatomic Particles.* New York: Scientific American Library, 1983. *Quantum Theory of Fields* (3 volumes). Cambridge, England: Cambridge University Press, 1995, 1997, 2000.

For More Information See: Physics Today 32 (December 1979): 17–19. *Science* 206 (December 14, 1979): 1290–92.

Commentary: Steven Weinberg and his two colaureates, Abdus Salam and Sheldon Glashow, shared the Nobel Prize "for their contributions to the theory of the unified weak and electromagnetic interaction between elementary particles, including, *inter alia,* the prediction of the weak neutral current." The Weinberg-Salam theory dealt with the unification of two of the four fundamental forces (the electromagnetic interaction and the weak interaction) for certain particles and was a significant step toward the overall unified field theory. The theory predicted neutral currents (elementary particle interactions with no exchange of electric charge). Weinberg has also written on the problems of astrophysics and cosmology. (M.N.)

1980

Cronin, James Watson   669

Prize: Physics, 1980. *Born:* September 29, 1931; Chicago, IL. *Parents:* Father, James Farley Cronin; Mother, Dorothy Watson Cronin. *Nationality:* American. *Religion:* Christian. *Education:* Southern Methodist Univ., TX, B.S., 1951;

Univ. of Chicago, IL, Ph.D., 1955. *Spouse:* Annette Martin, married September 11, 1954. *Children:* Daniel, son; Emily, daughter; Cathryn, daughter. *Career:* Brookhaven National Laboratory, Researcher, 1955–58; Princeton Univ., NJ, Professor, 1958–71; Univ. of Chicago, IL, Professor, 1971–96. *Other Awards:* Research Corporation Award, 1968; John Price Wetherill Medal, Franklin Institute, PA, 1975; Ernest Orlando Lawrence Award, 1977.

Selected Publications: "Experimental Status of CP Violation." *AEC Accession Number 19428, Report Number ANL-7130* (1965): 17–28. "Coupling Constant Relations for 1 (+/−) and Induced 0 (+/−) Mesons." *Nuovo Cimento* 41A (1966): 380–85 (with Y. Nambu). "Experimental Developments in Weak Interactions." *Proc. Int. Conf. Particles Fields* (1967): 3–20. "Weak Interactions and CP Violation-Experimental." *Int. Conf. High-Energy Phys., Proc., 14th* (1968): 281–303.

For More Information See: New York Times Biographical Service (October 1980): 1374. *Science* 210 (November 7, 1980): 619–21.

Commentary: James Cronin and Val Fitch shared the Nobel Prize for their demonstration that the K-mesons resulting from proton collisions did not obey the absolute principle of symmetry. Specifically, they found that the rates of switching of K-mesons from particle to antiparticle and from antiparticle to particle were different, which represented deviation from the theory of absolute symmetry. Cronin continued his work in the area of the nature and characteristics of elementary particles. (J.N.B.)

Fitch, Val Logsdon   670

Prize: Physics, 1980. *Born:* March 10, 1923; Merriman, NE. *Parents:* Father, Fred B. Fitch; Mother, Frances M. Logsdon Fitch. *Nationality:* American. *Religion:* Christian. *Education:* McGill Univ., Canada, B.Eng., 1948; Columbia Univ., NY, Ph.D., 1954. *Spouse:* Elise Cunningham, married June 11, 1949, died 1972; Daisy Harper Sharp, married August 14, 1976. *Children:* John Craig, son; Alan Peter, son. *Career:* Columbia Univ., NY, Professor, 1953–54; Princeton Univ., NJ, Professor, 1954-. *Other Awards:* Research Corporation Award, 1968; Ernest Orlando Lawrence Award, 1968; John Wetherill Medal, Franklin Institute, PA, 1976; National Medal of Science, 1993.

Selected Publications: "Mass Difference of Neutral K Meson." *Nuovo Cimento* 22 (1961): 1160–70 (with P.A. Piroue and R.B. Perkins). "The K(+) Decay Probability." *Physical Review* 140B (1965): 1088–91 (with C.A. Quarles). "Experiments on Time-Reversal Invariance." *Nucl. Particle Phys. Annu* 1 (1967): 117–20. "Charge Assymetries." *Comments Nucl. Particle Phys* 2 (1968): 6–9.

For More Information See: Physics Today 33 (December 1980): 17–19. *Science* 210 (November 7, 1980): 619–21.

Commentary: Val Fitch shared the Nobel Prize with James Cronin for their discovery that the elementary particles K-mesons, resulting from proton collisions, did not obey the absolute principle of symmetry. Specifically, they found that the rates of switching of K-mesons from particle to antiparticle and from antiparticle to particle were different. This represented a deviation from the theory of absolute symmetry. Fitch continued to work in the area of the nature and characteristics of elementary particles. (J.N.B.)

1981

Bloembergen, Nicolaas   **671**

Prize: Physics, 1981. *Born:* March 11, 1920; Dordrecht, Netherlands. *Parents:* Father, Auke Bloembergen; Mother, Sophia Maria Quint Bloembergen. *Nationality:* Dutch; later American citizen. *Religion:* Dutch Mennonite. *Education:* Univ. of Utrecht, Netherlands, B.A., 1941; Univ. of Utrecht, Netherlands, M.Sc., 1943; Leiden Univ., Netherlands, Ph.D., 1948. *Spouse:* Huberta Deliana Brink, married June 26, 1950. *Children:* Antonia, daughter; Juliana, daughter; Brink, son. *Career:* Kamerlingh Onnes Laboratory, Netherlands, Researcher, 1947–48; Harvard Univ., MA, Professor, 1949–90. *Other Awards:* Guggenheim Fellow, 1957; Buckley Prize, American Physical Society, 1958; Morris Liebman Award, IEEE, 1959; Ballantine Medal, Franklin Institute, PA, 1961; Half Moon Trophy, Netherlands Club, NY, 1972; National Medal of Science, 1974; Lorentz Medal, Royal Dutch Academy, 1979; Frederic Ives Medal, Optical Society of America, 1979; von Humboldt Senior Scientist Award, Munich, Germany, 1980; Medal of Honor, IEEE, 1983; Dirac Medal, Univ. of New South Wales, Australia, 1983; Von Humboldt Medal, 1989.

Selected Publications: Nuclear Magnetic Relaxation. The Hague: M. Nijhoff, 1948. "Nuclear Magnetic Relaxation in Semiconductors." *Physica* 20 (1954): 1130–33. "Proposal for a New-Type Solid-State Maser." *Physical Review* 104 (1956): 324–27. "The Zero-Field Solid-State Maser as a Possible Time Standard." *Quantum Electronics Symposium, High View, New York* (1959): 160–66. *Nonlinear Optics.* Reading, MA: W.A. Benjamin, 1965.

For More Information See: Nobel Prize Winners: Physics. Pasadena, CA: Salem Press, 1988 (Volume 3) 1219–28. *Science* 214 (November 6, 1981): 629–33.

Commentary: Nicolaas Bloembergen shared the Nobel Prize with Arthur Schawlow "for their contribution to the development of laser spectroscopy," the use of laser beams as analytical tools. A number of Bloembergen's major contributions are in the field of nonlinear optics (phenomena that occur when a laser beam is intensive enough to make the target resonate, revealing the spectral properties of entire molecules). He also did pioneering work in the development of the maser. (C.M.)

Schawlow, Arthur Leonard   **672**

Prize: Physics, 1981. *Born:* May 5, 1921; Mt. Vernon, NY. *Death:* April 28, 1999; Palo Alto, CA. *Parents:* Father, Arthur Schawlow; Mother, Helen Mason Schawlow. *Nationality:* American. *Religion:* Congregationalist. *Education:* Univ. of Toronto, Canada, B.A., 1941; Univ. of Toronto, Canada, M.A., 1942; Univ. of Toronto, Canada, Ph.D., 1949. *Spouse:* Aurelia Keith Townes, married May 19, 1951, died 1991. *Children:* Arthur Keith, son; Helen Aurelia, daughter; Edith Ellen, daughter. *Career:* Columbia Univ., NY, Researcher, 1949–51; Bell Telephone Laboratories, NJ, Researcher, 1951–61; Stanford Univ., CA, Professor, 1961–91. *Other Awards:* Ballantine Medal, Franklin Institute, PA, 1962; Thomas Young Medal and Prize, Institution of Physics and the Physics Society of London, England, 1963; Liebmann Prize, IEEE, 1964; California Scientist of the Year, 1973; Frederick Ives Medal, Optical Society of America, 1976; Schawlow Medal, 1982; National Medal of Science, 1991; Arata Award, High Temperature Society,

Japan, 1994; Ronald H. Brown American Innovator Award, 1996; American Inventors Hall of Fame, 1996.

Selected Publications: "Significance of the Results of Microwave Spectroscopy for Nuclear Theory." *Annals of the New York Academy of Sciences* 55 (1952): 955–65. "Infrared and Optical Masers." *Physical Review* 112 (1958): 1940–49 (with Charles H. Townes). "Simultaneous Optical Maser Action in Two Ruby Satellite Lines." *Physical Review Letters* 6 (1961): 605–07 (with G.E. Devlin). *Microwave Spectroscopy.* New York: McGraw-Hill, 1955 (with Charles H. Townes).

For More Information See: Physics Today 34 (December 1981): 17–20. *Science* 214 (November 6, 1981): 629–33. Weber, R.L. *Pioneers of Science: Nobel Winners in Physics.* Bristol: Institute of Physics, 1980, 275–76.

Commentary: Arthur Schawlow shared the Nobel Prize with Nicolaas Bloembergen "for their contribution to the development of laser spectroscopy," the use of laser beams as analytical tools. One of Schawlow's best known applications of laser spectroscopy has been in determining the energy that binds an electron to the proton of a hydrogen atom (the Rydberg constant). Schawlow worked with Charles Townes in maser development and then in extending the maser principle to the optical region. Schawlow's group has researched the applications of the laser in depth since, including the Rydberg constant determination and the observation of the Doppler-free optical spectra of hydrogen. (C.M.)

Siegbahn, Kai Manne Boerje   **673**

Prize: Physics, 1981. *Born:* April 20, 1918; Lund, Sweden. *Parents:* Father, Karl Manne Georg Siegbahn; Mother, Karin Hoegbom Siegbahn. *Nationality:* Swedish. *Religion:* Christian. *Education:* Univ. of Uppsala, Sweden, B.Sc., 1939; Univ. of Uppsala, Sweden, Licentiate of Philosophy, 1942; Univ. of Stockholm, Sweden, Ph.D., 1944. *Spouse:* Anna-Brita Rhedin, married May 23, 1944. *Children:* Per, son; Hans, son; Nils, son. *Career:* Nobel Institute of Physics, Sweden, Researcher, 1942–51; Univ. of Stockholm, Sweden, Professor, 1951–54; Uppsala Univ., Sweden, Professor, 1954–84; Papal Academy of Science, Professor, 1996-. *Other Awards:* Lindblom Prize, 1945; Knight of the Order of the North Star; Bjoerken Prize, 1955, 1977; Celsius Medal, 1962; Sixten Heyman Award, 1971; Harrison Howe Award, 1973; Maurice F. Hasler Award, 1975; Charles Frederick Chandler Medal, 1976; Torbern Bergman Medal, 1979; Pittsburgh Award of Spectroscopy, 1982; Rontgen Medal, 1985; Fiuggi Award, 1986; Humboldt Award, 1986; Premio Castiglione Di Scilia, 1990.

Selected Publications: "β-Ray Spectroscopy in the Precision Range of $1:10^5$." *Nuclear Physics* 1 (1956): 137–59 (with K. Edvarson). *ESCA—Atomic, Molecular and Solid State Structure Studied by Means of Electron Spectroscopy.* Nova Acta Regiae Societatis Scientiarum Upsaliensis, Series IV, Volume 20. Uppsala, Sweden: Almquist and Wiksells Boktryckeri Ab, 1967 (with others). *ESCA—Applied to Free Molecules.* Amsterdam; London: North-Netherlands, 1969 (with others). "ESCA Applied to Liquids." *Journal of Electron Spectroscopy and Related Phenomena* 2 (1973): 319–25 (with Hans Siegbahn). "Electron Spectroscopy for Atoms, Molecules, and Condensed Matter." *Review of Modern Physics* 54 (July 1982): 709–28.

For More Information See: Hecht, J., and Brookfield, R. "Physicists Keep Nobel Prizes in the Family." *New Scientist* 92 (October 22, 1981): 224–25. Hollander, Jack M., and Shirley, David. "The 1981 Nobel Prize in Physics." *Science* 214 (November 6, 1981): 629–31. Sullivan, Walter. "Physics: To the Heart of the Matter." *New York Times* (20 October 1981): Sec. 3, p. 2.

Commentary: Kai Siegbahn received his Nobel Prize in recognition of "his contribution to the development of high-resolution spectroscopy" in developing the technique of ESCA—electron spectroscopy for chemical analysis. He subsequently led a team of researchers who refined the technique and extended its application to gases and liquids in addition to solids. His father, Manne, won the 1924 prize for physics for the development of high-resolution x-ray spectroscopy. (N.R.H.)

1982

Wilson, Kenneth Geddes   674

Prize: Physics, 1982. *Born:* June 8, 1936; Waltham, MA. *Parents:* Father, Edgar Bright Wilson, Jr.; Mother, Emily Fisher Buckingham Wilson. *Nationality:* American. *Religion:* Christian. *Education:* Harvard Univ., MA, B.A., 1956; California Institute of Technology, Ph.D., 1961. *Spouse:* Alison Brown, married October 1982. *Children:* None. *Career:* Harvard Univ., MA, Fellow, 1959–62; Ford Foundation Fellow, 1962–63; Cornell Univ., NY, Professor, 1963–87; Ohio State Univ. OH, Professor, 1988-. *Other Awards:* Heineman Prize, 1973; Boltzmann Medal, 1975; Wolf Prize, 1980; Franklin Medal, 1983; A.C. Eringen Medal, 1984; Rahman Prize, 1993.

Selected Publications: "Renormalization Group and Critical Phenomena. I. Renormalization Group and the Kadanoff Scaling Picture." *Physics Reviews* B4 (November 1, 1971): 3174–83. "Renormalization Group and Critical Phenomena. II. Phase-Space Cell Analysis of Critical Behavior." *Physics Reviews* B4 (November 1, 1971): 3184–205.

For More Information See: *Nobel Prize Winners: Physics.* Pasadena, CA: Salem Press, 1988 (Volume 3), 1253–60. *Physics Today* 35 (December 1982): 17–19.

Commentary: Kenneth Wilson received his award "for his theory for critical phenomena in connection with phase transitions." His further development of the "renormalization group" method, a mathematical technique which allows working with problems that contain mathematical infinities, was applied in investigating various critical phenomena in physical systems, moving toward a general theory. The method is widely applicable to many fields of research. (S.D.)

1983

Chandrasekhar, Subrahmanyan   675

Prize: Physics, 1983. *Born:* October 19, 1910; Lahore, India. *Death:* August 21, 1995; Chicago, IL. *Parents:* Father, Chandrasekhara Subrahmanya Ayyar; Mother, Sitalakshmi Balakrishnan Chandrasekhar. *Nationality:* Indian; later American citizen. *Religion:* Hindu. *Education:* Madras Univ., India, M.A., 1930; Cambridge Univ., England, Ph.D., 1933. *Spouse:* Lalitha Doraiswamy, married

September 1936. *Children:* None. *Career:* Cambridge Univ., England, Professor, 1933–37; Univ. of Chicago, Professor, 1937–86. *Other Awards:* Bruce Medal, Astronomical Society of the Pacific, 1952; Gold Medal, Royal Astronomical Society, 1953; Rumford Medal, American Academy of Arts and Sciences, 1957; S. Ramanujan Medal, 1962; Royal Medal, Royal Society, 1962; National Science Medal, 1966; P. Vibhushan Medal, 1968; Henry Draper Medal, 1971; Smoluchowski Medal, 1973; Dannie Heineman Prize, 1974; Copley Medal, 1984; Tomalla Prize, 1984; Birla Memorial Award, 1984; Vainu Bappu Memorial Award, 1986.

Selected Publications: *An Introduction to the Study of Stellar Structure.* Chicago: Univ. of Chicago Press, 1939. *Principles of Stellar Dynamics.* Chicago: Univ. of Chicago Press, 1942. *Hydrodynamic and Hydromagnetic Stability.* London: Clarendon, 1961. *Ellipsoidal Figures of Equilibrium.* New Haven, CT: Yale Univ. Press, 1969. *The Mathematical Theory of Black Holes.* London: Clarendon, 1983. *Selected Papers*, 6 volumes. Chicago: Univ. of Chicago Press, 1989–90.

For More Information See: *Biographical Memoirs of National Academy of Sciences.* Washington, DC: National Academy of Sciences, 1997, 29–48. *Current Biography Yearbook.* New York: H.W. Wilson, March 1986: 6–9. *New York Times Biographical Service* (October 1973): 1176–77. *Science* 222 (November 25, 1983): 883+. Wali, K. *Chandra.* New Delhi, India: Viking, 1991.

Commentary: In honoring Subrahmanyan Chandrasekhar, the Academy noted his lifetime of scientific contributions, but cited in particular his study of the structure of white dwarfs as his "possibly best-known achievement." In that early work, Chandrasekhar noted that only smaller stars (with a mass less than 1.44 times that of the sun) would stabilize into white dwarfs. Larger stars would continually compress, due to the large gravitational forces and their acceleration of electrons toward the speed of light (relativistic degeneracy). This original work later would be used in the explanation of neutron stars and black holes. Chandrasekhar was also a major contributor in the areas of stellar dynamics, hydromagnetics, and radiative transfer. (B.S.S.)

Fowler, William Alfred   676

Prize: Physics, 1983. *Born:* August 9, 1911; Pittsburgh, PA. *Death:* March 14, 1995; Pasadena, CA. *Parents:* Father, John McLeod Fowler; Mother, Jennie Summers Watson Fowler. *Nationality:* American. *Religion:* Presbyterian. *Education:* Ohio State Univ., B.Eng., 1933; California Institute of Technology, Ph.D., 1936. *Spouse:* Ardiane Foy Olmstead, married August 24, 1940, died 1988; Mary Dutcher, married December 14, 1989. *Children:* Mary Emily Fowler Galowin, daughter; Martha Summers Fowler Schoenemann, daughter. *Career:* California Institute of Technology, Professor and Administrator, 1936–82. *Other Awards:* Naval Ordinance Development Award, United States Navy, 1945; Medal of Merit, 1948; Lamme Medal, Ohio State Univ., 1952; Medal, Univ. Liège, 1955; Scientist of the Year Award, CA, 1958; Barnard Medal, Columbia Univ., NY, 1965; Apollo Achievement Award, National Aeronautics and Space Administration, 1969; Bonner Prize, American Physical Society, 1970; Vetlesen Prize, 1973; National

Medal of Science, 1974; Benjamin Franklin Fellow, Royal Society of the Arts; Eddington Medal, Royal Astronomical Society, 1978; Bruce Gold Medal, Astronomical Society of the Pacific, 1979; Sullivant Medal, Ohio State Univ., 1985; Fowler Award, 1986; Legion d'Honneur, 1989.

Selected Publications: "Synthesis of the Elements in Stars." *Review of Modern Physics* 29 (1957): 547 (with E.M. Burbridge, G.R. Burbridge, and F. Hoyle). *Nucleosynthesis in Massive Stars and Supernovae.* Chicago: Univ. of Chicago Press, 1964 (with F. Hoyle). *Nuclear Astrophysics.* Philadelphia, PA: American Philosophical Society, 1967.

For More Information See: Bulletin of the American Astronomical Society 27, no.4 (1995): 1475–77. *New Scientist* 100 (October 27, 1983): 254–55. *New York Times* (March 16, 1995): B14. *Science* 222 (November 25, 1983): 881–83.

Commentary: William Fowler's shared Nobel Prize was "for his theoretical and experimental studies of the nuclear reactions of importance in the formation of the chemical elements in the universe." Fowler's research led to what is now the generally accepted theory for synthesis of the heavier elements in stellar explosions or supernovas. Together, Fowler and his co-recipient, Subrahmanyan Chandrasekhar, have detailed the steps leading to the synthesis of the entire roster of substances from which stars, planets, and people are formed. (S.D.)

1984

Rubbia, Carlo 677

Prize: Physics, 1984. *Born:* March 31, 1934; Gorizia, Italy. *Parents:* Father, Silvio R. Rubbia; Mother, Bice Liceni Rubbia. *Nationality:* Italian. *Religion:* Catholic. *Education:* Univ. of Pisa, Italy, Ph.D., 1958. *Spouse:* Marissa Romé, married June 27, 1960. *Children:* Laura, daughter; Andre, son. *Career:* European Organization of Nuclear Research, Geneva (CERN), Switzerland, Researcher and Administrator, 1961-; concurrently associated with Harvard Univ., MA, Professor, 1970–89. *Other Awards:* Ledlie Prize, 1985; Jesolo d'Oro, 1986.

Selected Publications: "The Physics of the Proton-Anti-proton Collider." *Proc. HEP83, Int. Europhys. Conf. High Energy Phys.* (1983): 860–79. "The HPW Proton-Decay Experiment." *AIP Conf. Proc.* (1984): 77–88 (with others).

For More Information See: Current Biography Yearbook. New York: H.W. Wilson (June 1985), 26–29. *New York Times* (October 18, 1984): B13. *Science* (January 11, 1985): 131–34. Taubes, Gary. *Nobel Dreams.* New York: Random House, 1986.

Commentary: Carlo Rubbia and Simon van der Meer shared the Nobel Prize for their contributions to the discovery of three subatomic particles that moved physics closer to the ultimate goal of a single theory for all natural forces. The team designed and built a colliding-beam accelerator which permitted observation of the then-hypothetical W(−), W(+), and Z particles. The work of the two laureates confirmed the unification of two of the four basic forces of nature—the electromagnetic force that relates electricity and magnetism and the weak force that controls phenomena like radioactivity. In 1984, Rubbia also announced the discovery of the sixth (top) quark, another long-sought particle. (S.M./B.S.S.)

van der Meer, Simon 678

Prize: Physics, 1984. *Born:* November 24, 1925; The Hague, Netherlands. *Parents:* Father, Pieter van der Meer; Mother, Jetske Groeneveld van der Meer. *Nationality:* Dutch. *Religion:* Agnostic; from Protestant background. *Education:* Technical Univ., Netherlands, physical engineering degree, 1952. *Spouse:* Catharina M. Koopman, married April 26, 1966. *Children:* Esther, daughter; Mathijs, son. *Career:* Dutch Philips Company, Researcher, 1952–56; European Organization for Nuclear Research, Researcher, 1956–90. *Other Awards:* Duddell Medal and Prize, England, 1982.

Selected Publications: "Stochastic Cooling Theory and Devices." *Lawrence Berkeley Laboratory Report LBL-7574* (1978): 93–97. "Stochastic Cooling in the CERN Antiproton Accumulator." *IEEE Trans. Nucl. Sci.* NS28–3 Part I (1981): 1994–98. "Recent Experience with Antiproton Cooling." *IEEE Trans. Nucl. Sci.* 30–4 Part I (1983): 2587–89 (with others). "Antiproton Production and Collection for the CERN Antiproton Accumulator." *IEEE Trans. Nucl. Sci.* 30–4 Part I (1983): 2778–80 (with others).

For More Information See: New York Times (October 18, 1984): B13. *Nobel Prize Winners: Physics.* Pasadena, CA: Salem Press, 1988. Volume 3, 1291–99. *Science* 227 (January 11, 1985): 131–34.

Commentary: Simon van der Meer shared the Nobel Prize with Carlo Rubbia for their contributions to the discovery of three subatomic particles that provided another link in developing a single theory for all natural forces. Van der Meer was the engineering force in the design and construction of a colliding-beam accelerator which permitted observation of the then-hypothetical W(−), W(+), and Z particles. The work of the two laureates confirmed the unification of two of the four basic forces of nature—the electromagnetic force that relates electricity and magnetism and the weak force that controls phenomena like radioactivity. (B.S.S.)

1985

Klitzing, Klaus von 679

Prize: Physics, 1985. *Born:* June 28, 1943; Schroda, Germany. *Parents:* Father, Bogislav von Klitzing; Mother, Anny Ulbrich von Klitzing. *Nationality:* German. *Religion:* Christian. *Education:* Technical Univ., Berlin, Germany, baccalaureate, 1969; Univ. of Würzburg, Germany, Ph.D., 1972. *Spouse:* Renate Falkenberg, married May 27, 1971. *Children:* Andreas, son; Christine, daughter; Thomas, son. *Career:* Univ. of Würzburg, Germany, 1970–78; High Magnetic Field Laboratory, France, Researcher, 1979–80; Technical Univ., Munich, Germany, Professor, 1980–84; Max Planck Institute, Stuttgart, West Germany, Researcher, 1985-. *Other Awards:* Walter-Schottky Prize, 1981; Hewlett Packard Europhysics Prize, 1982.

Selected Publications: "Resonance Structure in the High Field Magnetoresistance of Tellurium." *Solid State Communications* 9 (1971): 1251–54 (with G. Landwehr). "An Observation by Photoconductivity of Strain Splitting of Shallow Bulk Donors Located Near to the Surface in Silicon MOS Devices." *Solid State Communications* 20 (1976): 77–80 (with R.J. Nicholas and R.A. Stradling). "New Method for High-Accuracy Determination of the Fine-Structure Constant Based on Quantized Hall Resistance." *Physical*

Review Letters 45 (1980): 494 (with G. Dorda and M. Pepper). "Electron Spin Resonance on GaAs-Al(x)Ga(1-x) As Heterostructures." *Physical Review Letters* 51 (1983): 130–33 (with D. Stein).

For More Information See: New York Times (October 17, 1985): 1. *Nobel Prize Winners: Physics*. Pasadena, CA: Salem Press, 1988. Volume 3, 1301–11. *Science* 231 (February 21, 1986): 820–22.

Commentary: Klaus von Klitzing received the Nobel Prize for his discovery of the quantized Hall effect, which occurs in semiconductor devices at low temperatures in strong magnetic fields. The discovery not only caused major revision of the theory of electric conduction in strong magnetic fields but also provided a highly accurate laboratory standard of electrical resistance. Von Klitzing also researched the electrical properties of tellurium in strong magnetic fields, silicon inversion layers in strong magnetic fields and unixial stress, and the properties of two-dimensional electron systems. (L.S.S.)

1986

Binnig, Gerd Karl   680

Prize: Physics, 1986. *Born:* July 20, 1947; Frankfurt, West Germany. *Parents:* Father, Karl Franz Binnig; Mother, Ruth Bracke Binnig. *Nationality:* German. *Religion:* No religion. *Education:* Goethe Univ., Germany, Diploma, 1973; Univ. of Frankfurt, Germany, Ph.D., 1978. *Spouse:* Lore Wagler, married 1969. *Children:* Marvin, son; Iris, daughter. *Career:* IBM, Switzerland, Researcher, 1978-. *Other Awards:* Physics Prize, German Physical Society, 1982; Otto Klung Prize, 1983; Hewlett-Packard Europhysics Prize, 1984; King Faisal International Prize, Saudi Arabia, 1984; Elliot Cresson Medal, 1987; Minnie Rosen Award, Ross Univ., New York, 1988; National Inventors Hall of Fame, 1994.

Selected Publications: "Scanning Tunneling Microscopy." *IBM Journal of Research and Development* 30 (1986): 355–69. "Atomic Resolution with Atomic Force Microscope." *Europhysics Letters* 3 (1987): 1281–86. "Scanning Tunneling Microscopy: From Birth to Adolescence." *Review of Modern Physics* 59 (1987): 615–25. "Smectic Liquid Crystal Monolayers on Graphite Observed by STM." *Science* 245 (1989): 43–46.

For More Information See: Nobel Prize Winners: Physics., Volume 3. Pasadena, CA: Salem Press, 1989. *Research and Development* 23 (1986): 37–38. *Science* 234 (1986): 821–22.

Commentary: Gerd Binnig and Heinrich Rohrer shared half the prize in Physics "for their design of the scanning tunnel microscope." Whereas Ernst Ruska's (the third laureate) electron microscope played on the ability to focus a beam of electrons using magnetic fields, the scanning tunnel microscope is based on the electron's wave properties, which result in their tunneling out of "fixed" positions to form an electron cloud. By bringing the very fine tip of the microscope close enough to the sample surface so that the electron clouds of the surface and the tip are touching and applying a voltage, an electric current (tunneling current) is caused to flow. As the tip is moved across the surface, the atomic characteristics of the surface can be measured by the intensity of the current. The technique has been used in studies in semiconductor physics, atomic structure of biological macromolecules, and low-temperature physics. (G.R./ B.S.S.)

Rohrer, Heinrich   681

Prize: Physics, 1986. *Born:* June 6, 1933; Buchs, Switzerland. *Parents:* Father, Hans Heinrich Rohrer; Mother, Katharina Ganpenbein Rohrer. *Nationality:* Swiss. *Religion:* Protestant. *Education:* Federal Institute of Technology, Switzerland, Diploma, 1955; Federal Institute of Technology, Switzerland, Ph.D., 1960. *Spouse:* Rose-Marie Eggar, married 1961. *Children:* Doris Shannon, daughter; Ellen Linda, daughter. *Career:* Swiss Institute of Technology, Switzerland, Researcher, 1960–61; Rutgers Univ., New Jersey, Researcher, 1961–63; IBM, Switzerland, Researcher, 1963–97; Tohoku Univ., Japan, Researcher, 1997-; concurrently, RIKEN, Japan, Researcher, 1997-. *Other Awards:* Hewlett-Packard Europhysics Prize, 1984; King Faisal International Prize, Saudi Arabia, 1984; IBM Fellow, 1986; Elliot Cresson Medal, 1987; National Inventors Hall of Fame, 1994.

Selected Publications: "Scanning Tunneling Microscopy." *IBM Journal of Research and Development* 30 (1986): 355–69. "A Study of Graphite Surface Using the Scanning Tunneling Microscope and Electronic Structure Calculations." *Surface Sciences* 81 (1987): 26–38. "Topography of Defects at Atomic Resolution Using the STM." *Surface Sciences* 181 (1987): 139–44. "Scanning Tunneling Microscopy: From Birth to Adolescence." *Review of Modern Physics* 59 (1987): 615–25.

For More Information See: Nobel Prize Winners: Physics, Volume 3. Pasadena, CA: Salem Press, 1989. *Science* 234 (1986): 821–22. *Science News* 130 (1986): 262–63.

Commentary: Heinrich Rohrer and Gerd Binnig shared half the prize in Physics "for their design of the scanning tunnel microscope." Whereas Ernst Ruska's (the third laureate) electron microscope played on the ability to focus a beam of electrons using magnetic fields, the scanning tunnel microscope is based on the electron's wave properties, which result in their tunneling out of "fixed" positions to form an electron cloud. By bringing the very fine tip of the microscope close enough to the sample surface so that the electron clouds of the surface and the tip are touching, and applying a voltage, an electric current (tunneling current) is caused to flow. As the tip is moved across the surface, the atomic characteristics of the surface can be measured by the intensity of the current. The technique has been used in studies in semiconductor physics, atomic structure of biological macromolecules, and low-temperature physics. (G.R./ B.S.S.)

Ruska, Ernst August Friedrich   682

Prize: Physics, 1986. *Born:* December 25, 1906; Heidelberg, Germany. *Death:* May 30, 1988; Berlin, Germany. *Parents:* Father, Julius Ferdinand Ruska; Mother, Elisabeth Merx Ruska. *Nationality:* German. *Religion:* Protestant. *Education:* Technical Univ., Munich, Germany, Certified engineer, 1931; Technical Univ., Berlin, Germany, Ph.D., 1934. *Spouse:* Irmela Ruth Geigis, married May 15, 1937. *Children:* Ulrich-Ernst, son; Jurgen, son; Irmtraud, daughter. *Career:* Fernseh Corporation, Germany, Engineer, 1933–37; Siemens Company, Germany, Engineer, 1937–56;

Institute of Electron Microscopy, Max Planck Society, Germany, 1956–74. *Other Awards:* Senckenberg Prize, 1939; Leibniz Silver Medal, 1941; Lasker Award, 1960; Paul Ehrlich Prize, 1970; Duddell Medal and Prize, 1975; Cothenius Medal, 1975; Albrecht von Grafe Medal, 1983; Distinguished Scientist Award, Electron Microscopy Society of America, 1985; Robert Koch Gold Medal, 1986; Minni Rosen Award, 1987; Grune Rosette, 1987.

Selected Publications: "The Electron Microscope." *Zeitschrift für Physik* 78 (1932): 318–39. "Images of Metal Forces in the Electron Microscope." *Zeitschrift für Physik* 83 (1933): 187–93. "Images of Surfaces Which Reflect Electrons in the Electron Microscope." *Zeitschrift für Physik* 83 (1933): 492–97. "Magnetic Objective for the Electron Microscope." *Zeitschrift für Physik* 89 (1934): 90–128. *The Early Development of Electron Lenses and Electron Microscopy*. Stuttgart, Germany: S. Hirzel Verlag, 1980.

For More Information See: New York Times (May 31, 1988): D14. *Nobel Prize Winners: Physics*. Pasadena, CA: Salem Press, 1988, Volume 3, 1315–21. *Physics Today* 40 (1987): 17–20. *Science* 234 (1986): 821–22.

Commentary: The Nobel Prize was shared by Ernst Ruska for "fundamental work in electron optics and for the design of the first electron microscope." His first electron microscope, built in 1931, replaced the light beam used in previous microscopy with an accelerated electron beam focused by electromagnets. A more powerful version was completed in 1933 and a commercial, mass-produced version in 1937. The electron microscope made visible the structures of biological entities and molecules. Ruska's work with electron microscopy continued until his death. (G.R./B.S.S.)

1987

Bednorz, Johannes Georg 683

Prize: Physics, 1987. *Born:* May 16, 1950; Neuenkirchen, West Germany. *Parents:* Father, Anton Bednorz; Mother, Elizabeth Bednorz. *Nationality:* West German; resident in Switzerland. *Religion:* Catholic. *Education:* Univ. of Münster, Germany, B.S., 1976; Federal Institute of Technology, Switzerland, Ph.D., 1982. *Spouse:* Mechthild Wennemer, married 1978. *Children:* None. *Career:* IBM, Switzerland, Researcher, 1982-. *Other Awards:* Marcel-Benoist Prize, 1986; Victor Moritz Goldschmidt Prize, 1987; Robert Wichard Pohl Prize, 1987; Fritz London Memorial Award, 1987; Dannie Heineman Prize, 1987; Otto Klung Prize, 1987; Goldschmidt Prize, 1987; APS International Prize, 1988; Minnie Rosen Award, 1988; Hewlett-Packard Europhysics Prize, 1988.

Selected Publications: "Possible High T_c Superconductivity in the Ba-La-Cu-O System." *Zeitschrift für Physik B* 64 (1986): 189–93. "The Discovery of a Class of High Temperature Superconductors." *Science* 237 (1987): 1133–39. "The Discovery of Superconductivity at High Temperature." *Recherche (France)* 19 (January 1988): 52–60.

For More Information See: Nobel Prize Winners: Physics. Pasadena, CA: Salem Press, 1988, Volume 3, 1336–48. *Science* 238 (1987): 481–82.

Commentary: J. Georg Bednorz shared the Nobel Prize for the "discovery of superconductivity in a new class of ceramics at temperatures higher than had previously been thought possible." A relatively recent Ph.D. at the time he received the Nobel, Bednorz was recruited by his colaureate to work on oxides as superconductors because of his recognized talents as a laboratory innovator, both in the areas of equipment and technique. The growth of the crystals in the superconducting experiments and the design of the necessary equipment was, in large part, Bednorz's responsibility. Bednorz was attracted to the project because of his interest in the applications of superconductivity, particularly in the design of superfast trains. (G.R./B.S.S.)

Müller, Karl Alexander 684

Prize: Physics, 1987. *Born:* April 20, 1927; Basel, Switzerland. *Parents:* Father, Paul Rudolph Müller; Mother, Irma Feigenbaum Müller. *Nationality:* Swiss. *Religion:* Protestant. *Education:* Evangelical College, Switzerland, B.A., 1945; Federal Institute of Technology, Switzerland, M.S., 1952; Federal Institute of Technology, Switzerland, Ph.D., 1958. *Spouse:* Ingeborg Marie Louise Winkler, married 1956. *Children:* Erich Rudolf, son; Sylvia Irene, daughter. *Career:* Batelle Institute, Switzerland, Researcher, 1959–63; IBM, Switzerland, Researcher, 1963–85; Independent Researcher, Switzerland, 1985-. *Other Awards:* IBM Fellow, 1982; Marcel-Benoist Foundation Prize, 1986; Fritz London Memorial Award, 1987; Dannie Heineman Prize, 1987; Robert Wichard Pohl Prize, 1987; Hewlett-Packard Europhysics Prize, 1988; APS International Prize, 1988; Minnie Rosen Award, 1988; Special Tsukuba Award, 1989.

Selected Publications: "Inhomogeneous Superconductivity Transitions in Granular Al." *Physical Review Letters* 45 (1980): 832–36. "Possible T_c Superconductivity in the Ba-La-Cu-O System." *Zeitschrift für Physik B* 64 (1986): 189–93. "The Discovery of a Class of High-Temperature Superconductors," *Science* 237 (1987): 1133–39. "The Discovery of Superconductivity at High Temperature." *Recherche (France)* 19 (January 1988): 52–60.

For More Information See: New York Times (October 15, 1987): A14. *Nobel Prize Winners: Physics*. Pasadena, CA: Salem Press, 1988, Volume 3, 1336–48.

Commentary: K. Alex Müller shared the Nobel for the "discovery of superconductivity in a new class of ceramics at temperatures higher than had previously been thought possible." Müller had spent the early part of his career working with oxides and solid state physics, and had observed that oxides with nickel and copper exhibited some degree of superconductivity. His team started out working with an oxide of lanthanum and nickel to which they added aluminum with no success. After tests of many oxides, they found one containing lanthanum, barium, and copper that continued to superconduct up to 35 degrees Kelvin. The discovery revitalized the field of superconductivity. (G.R./B.S.S.)

1988

Lederman, Leon Max 685

Prize: Physics, 1988. *Born:* July 15, 1922; New York, NY. *Parents:* Father, Morris Lederman; Mother, Minna Rosenberg Lederman. *Nationality:* American. *Religion:* Jewish. *Education:* City College of New York, B.S., 1943; Columbia Univ., NY, A.M., 1948; Columbia Univ., NY, Ph.D.,

1951. *Spouse:* Florence Gordon, married September 19, 1945; no further record; Ellen Carr, married September 17, 1981. *Children:* Rena S., daughter; Jesse A., son; Heidi Rachel, daughter. *Career:* Columbia Univ., NY, Professor, 1951–79; Fermi National Accelerator Lab, IL, Administrator, 1979–89; University of Chicago, IL, Professor, 1989–92; Illinois Institute of Technology, Professor, 1992-. *Other Awards:* National Medal of Science, 1965; Townsend Harris Medal, 1973; Elliot Cresson Medal, 1976; Wolf Prize, 1982; Fermi Prize, 1992; President's Award, 1993; Joseph Priestly Award, 1996.

Selected Publications: "The Two-Neutrino Experiment." *Scientific American* 208 (1963): 60–70. *From Quarks to the Cosmos.* New York: Scientific American Library, 1989. *The God Particle.* New York: Houghton Mifflin, 1993.

For More Information See: Nobel Prize Winners: Physics. Pasadena, CA: Salem Press, 1989, Volume 3, 1353–64. *Physics Today* 42 (1989): 17–19. *Science* 242 (1988): 669–70.

Commentary: Leon Lederman won a share of the Nobel for his part in "discovering neutrinos and also for the method used to produce high-energy neutrino streams." His early work with particle accelerators, Wilson cloud chambers, and pi-mesons prepared the colaureate for the collaborative work of studying the neutrino, a subatomic entity with no electric charge. The bombardment of beryllium with protons produced neutrinos that were filtered out to provide a neutrino beam. The team proved that the beam consisted of the neutrino associated with electrons (previously observed) and a second neutrino associated with mu-mesons. The work had far-reaching effects on the theory of fundamental particles. (G.R./B.S.S.)

Schwartz, Melvin   **686**
Prize: Physics, 1988. *Born:* November 2, 1932; New York, NY. *Parents:* Father, Harry Schwartz; Mother, Hannah Shulman Schwartz. *Nationality:* American. *Religion:* Jewish. *Education:* Columbia Univ., NY, B.A., 1953; Columbia Univ., NY, Ph.D., 1958. *Spouse:* Marilyn Fenster, married November 25, 1953. *Children:* David N., son; Diane R., daughter; Betty Lynne, daughter. *Career:* Brookhaven National Laboratories, NY, Researcher, 1956–58; Columbia Univ., NY, Professor, 1958–66; Stanford Univ., CA, Professor, 1966–83; Digital Pathways, CA, President, 1979–91; Columbia Univ., NY, Professor, 1991-. *Other Awards:* Hughes Prize, 1964; Guggenheim Fellow Award, 1968; John Jay Award, Columbia Univ., 1989; Alexander Hamilton Medal, 1995.

Selected Publications: "Observation of High-Energy Neutrino Reactions and the Existence of Two Kinds of Neutrinos." *Physical Reviews Letters* 9 (1962): 36. "Neutrino Physics." *Reports on Progress in Physics* 28 (1965): 61–75. "Search for Intermediate Bosons." *Physical Reviews Letters* 15 (1965): 42. *Principles of Electrodynamics* New York: McGraw-Hill, 1972.

For More Information See: Nobel Prize Winners, Physics. Pasadena, CA: Salem Press, 1989, Volume 3, 1353–64. *Physics Today* 42 (1989): 17–19. *Science* 242 (1988): 669–70.

Commentary: The Nobel Prize was shared by Melvin Schwartz for his part in "discovering neutrinos and also for the method used to produce high-energy neutrino streams." A graduate student in colaureate Steinberger's laboratory, Schwartz is credited with the idea that initiated the work on

neutrinos, subatomic entities with no electric charge previously thought to be associated only with electrons. The experiment, which bombarded beryllium with protons, produced a neutrino beam that contained a second neutrino, associated with mu-mesons. The results stimulated new approaches to the theory of fundamental particles. Schwartz later worked in the area of computer software and systems. (G.R./B.S.S.)

Steinberger, Jack   **687**
Prize: Physics, 1988. *Born:* May 25, 1921; Bad Kissingen, Germany. *Parents:* Father, Ludwig Lazarus Steinberger; Mother, Berta May Steinberger. *Nationality:* German; later American citizen. *Religion:* Jewish. *Education:* Univ. of Chicago, IL, B.S., 1942; Univ. of Chicago, IL, Ph.D., 1948. *Spouse:* Joan Beauregard, married November 17, 1943, divorced 1962; Cynthia Eve Alff, married 1962. *Children:* Joseph, son; Richard, son; Julia Karen, daughter; John Paul, son. *Career:* Univ. of California, Berkeley, Professor, 1949–50; Columbia Univ., NY, Professor 1950–68; European Center for Nuclear Research, Director, Researcher and Administrator, 1968–86; Scuola Normale Superiore, Italy, Professor 1986-. *Other Awards:* National Medal of Science, 1988; Mateuzzi Medal, 1991.

Selected Publications: "Observation of High-Energy Neutrino Reactions and the Existence of Two Kinds of Neutrinos." *Physical Reviews Letters* 9 (1962): 36. "Resonances in Strange-Particle Production." *Physical Reviews* 128 (1962): 1930. "Lifetime of the ω-Meson." *Physical Reviews Letters* 11 (1963): 436.

For More Information See: New York Times (October 20, 1988): B11–12. *Nobel Prize Winners: Physics.* Pasadena, CA: Salem Press, 1989, Volume 3, 1353–64. *Physics Today* 42 (1989): 17–19. *Science* 242 (1988): 669–70.

Commentary: Jack Steinberger shared the Nobel for his part in "discovering neutrinos and also for the method used to produce high-energy neutrino streams." Steinberger began his career studying the "weak interactions" involved in mu-meson interactions with matter. His work with pi-mesons, and with mesons generally, occupied many years. The team efforts with his colaureates proved the existence of a new type of neutrino associated with mu-mesons, and refined the theories of fundamental particles then in existence. His work with neutrinos and mesons has continued throughout his career. (G.R./B.S.S.)

1989

Dehmelt, Hans Georg   **688**
Prize: Physics, 1989. *Born:* September 9, 1922; Görlitz, Germany. *Parents:* Father, Georg Karl Dehmelt; Mother, Asta Ella Klemmt Dehmelt. *Nationality:* German; later American citizen. *Religion:* Christian. *Education:* Univ. of Göttingen, Germany, M.S., 1948; Ph.D., 1950. *Spouse:* Irmgard Lassow, married (no date), died (no date); Diane Elaine Dundore, married November 18, 1989. *Children:* Gerd, son. *Career:* Univ. of Göttingen, Researcher, 1950–52; Duke Univ., NC, Researcher, 1952–55; Univ. of Washington, Seattle, Professor, 1955-. *Other Awards:* Davisson-Germer Prize, 1970; Humbolt Prize, 1974; Basic Research Award, International Society of Magnetic Resonance, 1980; Rumford Prize, 1985; National Medal of Science, 1995.

Selected Publications: "Spin Resonance of Free Electrons Polarized by Exchange Collisisons." *Physical Review* 109 (1958): 381–85. "Spin Resonance of Free Electrons." *Journal of Physical Radium* 19 (1958): 866–71. "Radiofrequency Spectroscopy of Stored Ions. I. Storage." *Advances in Atomic Molecular Physics* 3 (1967): 53–72. "Radiofrequency Spectroscopy of Stored Ions. II. Spectroscopy." *Advances in Atomic Molecular Physics* 5 (1969): 109–54.

For More Information See: New York Times (October 13, 1989): I, 10. *Science* 246 (October 20, 1989): 327–28.

Commentary: The Academy awarded the Nobel to Hans Georg Dehmelt "for developing ways of trapping particles to study them with extreme precision." Dehmelt refined the methods used to trap particles, including those developed by his colaureate Paul, so that atomic measurements could be made more precisely. His most important contribution was the "Penning Trap," a combination of a strong magnetic field and a weak electric field used to trap subatomic particles. The trap was used to determine the electron g-factor, the ratio of the magnetic and angular momenta of the electron. (G.R./B.S.S.)

Paul, Wolfgang   689

Prize: Physics, 1989. *Born:* August 10, 1913, Lorenzkirch, Germany. *Death:* December 6, 1993; Bonn, Germany. *Parents:* Father, Theodor Paul; Mother, Elizabeth Ruppel Paul. *Nationality:* German. *Religion:* Lutheran. *Education:* Technical Univ., Berlin, Germany, Ph.D., 1939. *Spouse:* Liselotte Hirsche, married 1940, died 1977; Doris Waloh-Paul, married 1979. *Children:* Lorenz, son; Stephan, son; Jutta, daughter; Regine, daughter. *Career:* Univ. of Göttingen, Germany, Professor, 1944–52; Univ. of Bonn, Germany, Professor, 1952–83. *Other Awards:* Humboldt Prize 1979; Robert W. Pohl Prize, 1989; Gold Medal, Czech Academy of Sciences, no date.

Selected Publications: "A New Mass Spectrometer Without Magnetic Field." *Z. Naturforsch* 89 (1953): 448–50. "Production of Elementary Particles in the Laboratory." *Naturwissenschaften* 46 (1959): 277–83. "Survey of Methods of Producing Sources of Polarized Protons." *Helvetica Physica Acta Supplement* 6 (1961): 17–25.

For More Information See: New York Times (October 13, 1989): I, 10. *Science* 246 (October 20, 1989): 327–28. *New York Times Biographical Service* (Dec. 8, 1993): 1681.

Commentary: The Nobel prize was shared by Wolfgang Paul "for developing a way of trapping particles to study them with extreme precision." Paul used a hexapole magnetic field as a "lens" for focusing atomic beams, and he developed methods for separating ions by mass distribution that became the basis of the quadrupole mass spectrometer. He also was responsible for the "Paul Trap," a method of isolating ions by radio-frequency radiation. His later work included trapping neutrons electromagnetically and developing nuclear research in Germany. (G.R./B.S.S)

Ramsey, Norman Foster, Jr.   690

Prize: Physics, 1989. *Born:* August 27, 1915; Washington, DC. *Parents:* Father Norman F. Ramsey; Mother, Minna Bauer Ramsey. *Nationality:* American. *Religion:* From Presbyterian background. *Education:* Columbia Univ., NY, A.B., 1935; Cambridge Univ., England, B.A., 1937; Cambridge Univ., England, M.A., 1941; Columbia Univ., NY,

Ph.D., 1940; Cambridge Univ., England, D.Sc., 1954. *Spouse:* Elinor Steadman Jameson, married June 3, 1940, died December, 1983; Ellie A. Welch, married May 11, 1985. *Children:* Margaret, daughter; Patricia, daughter; Janet, daughter; Winifred, daughter. *Career:* Univ. of Illinois, Researcher, 1940–42; Columbia Univ., NY, Professor, 1942–47; Harvard Univ., MA, Professor, 1947–86. *Other Awards:* Presidential Order of Merit, 1947; AEC Award, 1960; E.O. Lawrence Award, 1960; Davisson-Germer Prize, 1974; Medal of Honor, IEEE, 1984; Rabi Prize, 1985; Monte Ferst Award, 1985; Compton Medal, 1986; Oersted Medal, 1988; National Medal of Science, 1988; Pupin Medal, 1992; Science for Peace Prize, 1992; Einstein Medal, 1993; Vannevar Bush Award, 1995; Alexander Hamilton Award, 1995.

Selected Publications: "A New Molecular-Beam Resonance Method." *Physical Review* 76 (1949): 996. "A Molecular-Beam Resonance Method with Separated Oscillating Fields." *Physical Review* 78 (1950): 695–99. "Radiofrequency Spectra of Hydrogen and Deuterium by a New Molecular-Beam Resonance Method." *Physica* 17 (1951): 328–32. *Molecular Beams*. Oxford, England: Clarendon Press, 1956; 2nd ed., 1985.

For More Information See: Current Biography. New York: H.W. Wilson, 1993, 351–53. *New York Times* (October 13, 1989): I, 10. *Science* 246 (October 20, 1989): 327–28.

Commentary: Norman Ramsey received the Nobel "for inventing a method for measuring time on which the current standard of time is measured." Ramsey was cited for his development of a method for studying atomic structure by passing atoms at high speeds through two oscillating electromagnetic fields, thus producing an interference pattern, from which could be deduced atomic structure and behavior. The research lead to the development of the hydrogen maser (and elaboration of details of the hydrogen atom structure), and to the cesium atomic clock, used to define the second of time. The laureate also played an important role in the development of radar and in the study of chemical shifts in nuclear magnetic resonance. (G.R./B.S.S.)

1990

Friedman, Jerome Isaac   691

Prize: Physics, 1990. *Born:* March 28, 1930; Chicago, IL. *Parents:* Father, Selig Friedman; Mother, Lillian Warsaw Friedman. *Nationality:* American. *Religion:* Jewish. *Education:* Univ. of Chicago, IL, A.B., 1950; Univ. of Chicago, IL, M.S., 1953; Univ. of Chicago, IL, Ph.D., 1956. *Spouse:* Tanya Letetsky-Baranovsky, married 1956. *Children:* Ellena, daughter; Joel, son; Martin, son; Sandra, daughter. *Career:* Univ. of Chicago, IL, Researcher, 1956–57; Stanford Univ., CA, Researcher, 1957–60; Massachusetts Institute of Technology, Professor, 1960- . *Other Awards:* Panofsky Prize, 1989.

Selected Publications: "Electron-Proton Elastic Scattering at High Momentum Transfer." *Physical Review Letters* 20 (1968): 292. "High Energy Inelastic Electron-Proton Scattering at Six Degrees and Ten Degrees." *Physical Review Letters* 23 (1969): 930. "Observed Behavior of

Highly Inelastic Electron-Proton Scattering." *Physical Review Letters* 23 (1969): 935.

For More Information See: New York Times (October 18, 1990): A12. *Science* 250 (October 26, 1990): 508–09

Commentary: Jerome Friedman shared the Nobel in Physics for a "breakthrough in our understanding of matter." In an experiment that further elaborated the theory of structure of protons and neutrons, the colaureates bombarded hydrogen and deuterium with high-energy electrons, and confirmed the existence of the theoretically predicted quark, proving that protons and neutrons were not the fundamental particles they were previously assumed to be. The experiments lead to the theory that all the particles thus far observed were combinations of six quarks and six leptons, interacting through the presence of three types of force particles. (B.S.S.)

Kendall, Henry Way   692

Prize: Physics, 1990. *Born:* December 9, 1926; Boston, MA. *Death:* February 15, 1999; Wakulla Springs State Park, FL. *Parents:* Father, Henry P. Kendall; Mother, Evelyn Louise Way Kendall. *Nationality:* American. *Religion:* Christian. *Education:* Amherst College, MA, B.A., 1950; Massachusetts Institute of Technology, Ph.D., 1955. *Spouse:* Ann C.G. Pine, married 1972, divorced 1988. *Children:* None. *Career:* Massachusetts Institute of Technology, Researcher, 1954–56; Stanford Univ., CA, Professor, 1956–61; Massachusetts Institute of Technology, Professor, 1961–99. *Other Awards:* Leo Szilard Award, 1981; Bertrand Russell Society Award, 1982; Panofsky Prize, 1989.

Selected Publications: "Electron-Proton Elastic Scattering at High Momentum Transfer." *Physical Review Letters* 20 (1968): 292. "High-Energy Inelastic Electon-Proton Scattering at Six Degrees and Ten Degrees." *Physical Review Letters* 23 (1969): 930. "Observed Behavior of Highly Inelastic Electron-Proton Scattering." *Physical Review Letters* 23 (1969): 935. *Energy Strategies.* Cambridge, MA: Union of Concerned Scientists, 1980.

For More Information See: New York Times (October 18, 1990): A12. *Science* 250 (October 26, 1990): 508–09.

Commentary: The Academy awarded the Nobel in Physics to Henry Kendall and his colaureates for a "breakthrough in our understanding of matter." In an experiment that further elaborated the theory of structure of protons and neutrons, the colaureates bombarded hydrogen and deuterium with high-energy electrons, and confirmed the existence of the theoretically predicted quark, proving that protons and neutrons were not the fundamental particles they were previously assumed to be. The experiments lead to the theory that all the particles thus far observed were combinations of six quarks and six leptons, interacting through the presence of three types of force particles. Dr. Kendall was also a founder and chair of the Union of Concerned Scientists. (B.S.S.)

Taylor, Richard E.   693

Prize: Physics, 1990. *Born:* November 2, 1929; Medicine Hat, Alberta, Canada. *Parents:* Father, Clarence Richard Taylor; Mother, Delia Alena Brunsdale Taylor. *Nationality:* Canadian; later American resident. *Religion:* Christian. *Education:* Univ. of Alberta, Canada, B.S., 1950; Univ. of Alberta, Canada, M.S., 1952; Stanford Univ., CA, Ph.D.,

1962. *Spouse:* Rita Jean Bonneau, married August 25, 1951. *Children:* Norman Edward, son. *Career:* Boursier Laboratory, France, Researcher, 1958–61; Lawrence Laboratory, CA, Researcher, 1961–62; Stanford Univ., CA, Professor, 1962- . *Other Awards:* von Humboldt Foundation Award, 1981; Panofsky Prize, 1989.

Selected Publications: "Electron-Proton Elastic Scattering at High Momentum Transfer." *Physical Review Letters* 20 (1968): 292. "High-Energy Inelastic Electron-Proton Scattering at Six Degrees and Ten Degrees." *Physical Review Letters* 23 (1969): 930. "Observed Behavior of Highly Inelastic Electron-Proton Scattering." *Physical Review Letters* 23 (1969): 935.

For More Information See: New York Times (October 18, 1990): A12. *Science* 250 (October 26, 1990): 508–09.

Commentary: The Nobel in Physics was shared by Richard Taylor for a "breakthrough in our understanding of matter." In an experiment that further elaborated the theory of structure of protons and neutrons, the colaureates bombarded hydrogen and deuterium with high-energy electrons and confirmed the existence of the theoretically predicted quark, proving that protons and neutrons were not the fundamental particles they were previously assumed to be. The experiments lead to the theory that all the particles thus far observed were combinations of six quarks and six leptons, interacting through the presence of three types of force particles. (B.S.S.)

1991

de Gennes, Pierre-Gilles   694

Prize: Physics, 1991. *Born:* October 24, 1932; Paris, France. *Parents:* Father, Robert de Gennes; Mother, Yvonne Morin-Pons de Gennes. *Nationality:* French. *Religion:* Most probably Christian. *Education:* Lycée Claude-Bernard a Paris, France, B.A., no date; École Normale Supérieure, France, Ph.D., 1958. *Spouse:* Anne-Marie Rouet, married June 3, 1954. *Children:* Christian, son; Dominique, daughter; Christine, daughter. *Career:* Center for Atomic Studies, France, Researcher, 1955–59; French Navy, 1959–61; Univ. of Paris, France, Professor, 1961–71; Collége de France, Professor, 1971-. *Other Awards:* Ampere Prize, 1977; Polymer Chemistry Award, American Chemical Society, 1988; Harvey Prize, 1989; Wolf Prize, 1990; Lorentz Medal (no date); Matteuci Medal (no date).

Selected Publications: The Physics of Liquid Crystals. Oxford, England: Oxford Univ. Press, 1974; *Scaling Concepts in Polymer Physics.* Ithaca, NY: Cornell Univ. Press, 1979; *Simple Views on Condensed Matter.* New York: World Scientific Publishing Co., 1992. *Fragile Objects* (with J. Badoz). New York: Springer-Verlag, 1996.

For More Information See: Chemical and Engineering News 69 (October 21, 1991): 4; *Science* 254 (October 25, 1991): 518.

Commentary: Pierre-Gilles de Gennes received the Nobel Prize for "discovering that methods developed for studying order phenomena in simple systems can be generalized to more complex forms of matter, in particular to liquid crystals and polymers." The Nobelist's studies of condensed matter have included forays into the areas of ferromagnetics and superconductors as well as research into interfaces. (B.S.S./J.H.S.)

1992

Charpak, Georges   695

Prize: Physics, 1992. *Born:* August 1, 1924; Dubrovica, Poland. *Parents:* Father, Maurice Charpak; Mother, Anne Szapiro Charpak. *Nationality:* Born Polish, naturalized French 1946. *Religion:* Jewish. *Education:* École des Mines de Paris, France, B. Engineering, 1948; Collège de France, Ph.D., 1954. *Spouse:* Dominique Vidal, married April 28, 1953. *Children:* Yves, son; Natalie, daughter; Serge, son. *Career:* National Center for Scientific Research, France, Researcher, 1948–59; European Center for Nuclear Research, Switzerland, Researcher, 1959–91. *Other Awards:* Ricard Prize, 1980; Commissariat Prize of Atomic Energy, 1984; High Energy and Particle Physics Prize, European Physical Society, 1989.

Selected Publications: "Recent Progress in Particle Detection." *IEEE Transactions in Nuclear Science* 19 (1972): 152–7; "Multiwire Proportional Chambers." *Report* JINR-D-5805 (1970): 217–50; "Multiwire and Multipurpose Development of Multiwire Proportional Chambers." *CERN Cour* 12 (1972): 362–4; *Research on Particle Imaging Detectors.* River Edge, NJ: World Scientific, 1995.

For More Information See: La Vie a Fil Tendu. Paris, France: O. Jacob, 1993; *New York Times* (October 15, 1992): B14; *Physics Today* 46 (January 1993): 17–20; *Science* 258 (October 23, 1992): 543.

Commentary: The Nobel Prize was awarded to Georges Charpak "for his invention and development of particle detectors, in particular the multiwire proportional chamber." The multiwire proportional chamber replaced the bubble chamber as the instrument used to "see" the tracks of particles resultant from collisions in large accelerators. It allowed researchers to focus on potentially valuable events and eliminates the need for photographs. Charpak later worked with detectors for biomedical uses. He is also noted for his work in the support of scientists living in repressive countries. (B.S.S./J.H.S.)

1993

Hulse, Russell Alan   696

Prize: Physics, 1993. *Born:* November 28, 1950; New York, NY. *Parents:* Father, Alan Earle Hulse; Mother, Betty Joan Wedemeyer Hulse. *Nationality:* American. *Religion:* Most probably Christian. *Education:* Cooper Union, NY, B.S., 1970; Univ. of Massachusetts, M.S., 1972; Ph.D., 1975. *Spouse:* Jeanne Kuhlman, companion. *Children:* No record found. *Career:* National Radio Astronomy Observatory, VA, Researcher, 1975–77; Princeton Univ., NJ, Researcher, 1977-.

Selected Publications: "Discovery of a Pulsar in a Binary System." *Astrophysical Journal* 195 (1975): L51 (with J. H. Taylor); "Charge Exchange as a Recombination Mechanism in High-Temperature Plasmas." *Report PPPL-1633* (1980); "Charge Exchange as a Recombination Mechanism in High-Temperature Plasmas." *J. Phys. B.* 13 (1980): 3895–907.

For More Information See: New York Times (October 12, 1993): B9; *Physics Today* 46 (December 1993): 17; *Science* 262 (October 22, 1993): 507.

Commentary: The Nobel Prize was granted jointly to Russell Hulse and Joseph Taylor for their "discovery of a new type of pulsar, a discovery that has opened up new possibilities for the study of gravitation." Hulse was a graduate student at the time he performed the original observations. He later moved into the area of fusion-energy experimentation. (B.S.S./J.H.S.)

Taylor, Joseph Hooton, Jr.   697

Prize: Physics, 1993. *Born:* March 29, 1941; Philadelphia, PA. *Parents:* Father, Joseph Hooton Taylor; Mother, Sylvia Hathaway Evans Taylor. *Nationality:* American. *Religion:* Quaker. *Education:* Haverford College, PA, B.A., 1963; Harvard Univ., MA, Ph.D., 1968. *Spouse:* Marietta Bisson, married January 3, 1976. *Children:* Jeffrey, son; Rebecca, daughter; Anne-Marie, daughter. *Career:* Univ. of Massachusetts, Professor, 1969–80; Princeton Univ., NJ, Professor and Administrator, 1980-. *Other Awards:* Heineman Prize, 1980; MacArthur Fellow, 1981; Tomalla Foundation Prize, 1985; Draper Medal, 1985; Magellanic Premium Award, 1990; Carty Medal, 1991; Einstein Prize, 1991; Wolf Prize, 1992.

Selected Publications: "Discovery of a Pulsar in a Binary System." *Astrophysical Journal* 195 (1975): L51 (with R. Hulse); "Further Observations of the Binary Pulsar PSR1913+16. "*Astrophysical Journal* 206 (1976): L53; *Pulsars.* San Francisco: W.H. Freeman, 1977; "Further Tests of Relativistic Gravity Using the Binary Pulsar PSR 1913+16. "*Astrophysical Journal* 345 (1989): 434.

For More Information See: New York Times (October 12, 1993): B9; *Physics Today* 46 (December 1993): 17; *Science* 262 (October 22, 1993): 507.

Commentary: Joseph Taylor shared the Nobel Prize with Russell Hulse for their "discovery of a new type of pulsar, a discovery that has opened up new possibilities for the study of gravitation." Taylor later used the radio pulses from the binary pulsar to test Einstein's general theory of relativity, and was the first to report gravity waves. (B.S.S./J.H.S.)

1994

Brockhouse, Bertram Neville   698

Prize: Physics, 1994. *Born:* July 15, 1918; Lethbridge, Alberta, Canada. *Parents:* Father, Israel Bertram Brockhouse; Mother, Mable Emily Neville Brockhouse. *Nationality:* Canadian. *Religion:* Catholic. *Education:* Univ. of British Columbia, Canada, B.A., 1947; Univ. of Toronto, Canada, M.A., 1948, Ph.D., 1950. *Spouse:* Doris Isobel Mary Miller Brockhouse, married May 22, 1948. *Children:* Ann, daughter; Gordon Peter, son; Ian Bertram, son; James Christopher, son; Alice Elizabeth, daughter; Charles Leslie, son. *Career:* Univ. of Toronto, Ontario, Canada, Professor, 1949–50; Atomic Energy of Canada, Researcher, 1950–62; McMaster Univ., Ontario, Canada, Professor, 1962–84. *Other Awards:* Buckley Prize, 1962; Duddell Medal, 1963; Canadian Association of Physics Medal, 1967; Centennial Medal, Canada, 1967; Tory Medal, 1973; Queen's Jubilee Medal, 1977.

Selected Publications: "Resonant Scattering of Slow Neutrons." *Canadian Journal of Physics* 31 (1953):432–52; "Energy Distribution of Neutrons Scattered by Paramagnetic Substances." *Physics Reviews* 99(1955):601–3; "Slow-neutron Spectrometry—a New Tool for the Study of Energy Levels in Condensed Systems." *Physics Reviews* 98(1955):1171.

For More Information See: New York Times Biographical Service (October 13, 1994): 1570; *Physics Today* 47 (December 1994): 17.

Commentary: Bertram Brockhouse received the Nobel Prize in recognition of his "pioneering contributions to the development of neutron scattering techniques for study of condensed matter." His use of neutron beams ("the development of neutron spectroscopy") to study atomic structure allowed him to determine atomic vibrations from the velocities of the deflected neutrons. His elaboration on the theory of phonons was seen by the Committee as leading to "valuable information . . . for use in the development of new materials." (B.S.S./J.H.S.)

Shull, Clifford Glenwood   **699**

Prize: Physics, 1994. *Born:* September 23, 1915; Pittsburgh, PA. *Parents:* Father, David H. Shull; Mother, Daisy I. Bistline Shull. *Nationality:* American. *Religion:* No record found. *Education:* Carnegie Institute of Technology, PA, B.S., 1937; New York Univ., Ph.D., 1941. *Spouse:* Martha-Nuel Summer, married June 19, 1941. *Children:* John C., son; Robert D., son; William F., son. *Career:* Texas Co., NY, Researcher, 1941–46; Oak Ridge National Laboratories, TN, Researcher, 1946–55; Massachusetts Institute of Technology, Professor, 1955–86. *Other Awards:* Buckley Prize, 1956; Carnegie Mellon Univ. Alumni Award, 1968; Humboldt Award, 1979; Tennessee Governor Award, 1986; Aminoff Prize, 1993; Frank Prize, 1993.

Selected Publications: "Determination of X-ray Diffraction Line Widths." *Phys. Rev.* 70 (1946): 679–84; "X-ray Scattering at Small Angles by Finely Divided Solids." *J. Applied Phys.* 18 (1947): 295–313; "Highly Polarized Neutron Beams by Bragg Reflection from Ferromagnetic Crystals." *Phys. Rev.* 81 (1951): 626.

For More Information See: New York Times Biographical Service (1994): 1570; *Physics Today* 47 (December 1994): 17.

Commentary: Clifford Shull was awarded the Nobel Prize for his "pioneering contributions to the development of neutron scattering techniques for studies of condensed matter." By studying the patterns of scattering of the neutrons, the Nobelist was able to determine the position of the atoms in the material being tested. The Nobel Committee noted that, because of Shull's work, "valuable information is being obtained for use in the development of new materials." (B.S.S./J.H.S.)

1995

Perl, Martin L.   **700**

Prize: Physics, 1995. *Born:* June 24, 1927; New York, NY. *Parents:* Father, Oscar Perl; Mother, Fay P. Rosenthal Perl. *Nationality:* American. *Religion:* Jewish. *Education:* Polytechnic Institute of New York, B.A., 1948; Columbia Univ., NY, Ph.D., 1955. *Spouse:* Teri Hoch, married June 19, 1948. *Children:* Jed, son; Matthew, son; Joseph, son; Anne, daughter. *Career:* General Electric, NY, Researcher, 1948–50; Univ. of Michigan, Professor, 1955–63; Stanford Univ., CA, Professor, 1963-. *Other Awards:* Wolf Prize, 1982.

Selected Publications: High Energy Hadron Physics. New York, NY: Wiley, 1974; "Evidence for, and Properties

of the Tau Lepton." *Report 1977, SLAC-PUB-2055, CONF-7710107–1;* "Comments on the Tau Heavy Lepton." *Exp. Meson Spectrosc. Int. Conf., 5th* (1977); 118–31; *Search for New Elementary Particles.* River Edge, NJ: World Scientific, 1992.

For More Information See: New York Times (October 12, 1995): A 12. *Reflections on Experimental Science.* River Edge, NJ: World Scientific, 1996.

Commentary: Martin Perl received the Nobel Prize with Frederick Reines for their discovery of "two of nature's most remarkable subatomic particles." Perl discovered the heavy tau lepton, the first of a new family of subatomic particles, a discovery that is "very important for physicists' confidence in the present theoretical model for understanding the properties of nature's smallest constituents." (B.S.S./J.H.S.)

Reines, Frederick   **701**

Prize: Physics, 1995. *Born:* March 16, 1918; Paterson, NJ. *Death:* August 26, 1998; Orange, CA. *Parents:* Father, Israel Reines; Mother, Gussie R. Cohen Reines. *Nationality:* American. *Religion:* Jewish. *Education:* Stevens Institute of Technology, NJ, B.S., 1939; M.S., 1941; New York Univ., Ph.D., 1944. *Spouse:* Sylvia Samuels, married August 30, 1940. *Children:* Robert G., son; Alisa K., daughter. *Career:* Los Alamos Scientific Laboratory, NM, Researcher, 1944–59; Case Institute of Technology, OH, Professor, 1959–66; Univ. of California, Irvine, Professor, 1966–88. *Other Awards:* Oppenheimer Prize, 1981; National Medal of Science, 1983; Michelson-Morley Award, 1990; Rossi Prize, 1990; Franklin Medal, 1992; Panofsky Prize, 1992.

Selected Publications: "Neutron Spectra from Proton Recoils in Photographic Emulsions." *Phys. Rev.* 74 (1948):1565; "A Proposed Experiment to Detect the Free Neutrino." *Phys. Rev.* 90 (1953): 492–93; "Detection of the Free Neutrino." *Phys. Rev.* 92 (1953): 830–31.

For More Information See: New York Times (October 12, 1995): A12.

Commentary: The Nobel Prize was shared by Frederick Reines and Martin Perl for their discovery of "two of nature's most remarkable subatomic particles." Reines confirmed the existence of the neutrino, one of these subatomic particles, in the 50s. Neutrinos, first predicted by Wolfgang Pauli in the 30s, are created in nature by a variety of cosmic processes. (B.S.S./J.H.S.)

1996

Lee, David Morris   **702**

Prize: Physics, 1996. *Born:* January 20, 1931; Rye, NY. *Parents:* Father, Marvin Lee; Mother, Annette Franks Lee. *Nationality:* American. *Religion:* Jewish. *Education:* Harvard Univ., MA, A.B., 1952; Univ. of Connecticut, CT, M.S., 1955; Yale Univ., CT, Ph.D., 1959. *Spouse:* Dana Thorangkul, married September 7, 1960. *Children:* Eric Bertel, son; James Marvin, son *Career:* Cornell Univ., NY, Professor, 1959-. *Other Awards:* Sir Francis Simon Memorial Prize, 1976; Oliver Buckley Prize, 1981; Wilbur Cross, Medal, 1998.

Selected Publications: "Evidence for a New Phase of Solid He3," *Physical Review Letters* 28 (April 1972):885 (with D.D. Osheroff and R.C. Richardson). "Superfluid

Helium3," *Scientific American* (December 1976): 56–71 (with N. David Mermin). "The Extraordinary Phases of Liquid He3," *Reviews of Modern Physics* 69 (July 1997): 645–65.

For More Information See: New York Times (October 10, 1996): D21. Science News 150 (October 19, 1996): 247.

Commentary: David Lee shared the Nobel Prize with Douglas Osheroff and Robert Richardson "for their discovery of superfluidity in helium-3." By freezing helium-3 to near absolute zero, they discovered that helium-3 atoms "lose all their randomness and move in a coordinated manner in each movement." This means that the liquid loses its viscosity or inner friction and flows without any resistance, thus exhibiting unusual behaviors such as climbing out of a container. (L.S.S.)

Osheroff, Douglas Dean   703

Prize: Physics, 1996. *Born:* August 1, 1945; Aberdeen, WA. *Parents:* Father, William Osheroff; Mother, Bessie Anne Ondov Osheroff. *Nationality:* American. *Religion:* From Jewish/Lutheran background. *Education:* California Institute of Technology, B.S., 1967; Cornell Univ., NY, M.S., 1969; Cornell Univ., NY, Ph.D., 1973. *Spouse:* Phyllis S.K. Liu, married August 14, 1970. *Children:* None. *Career:* Bell Labs, NY, Researcher and Administrator, 1972–87; Stanford Univ., CA, Professor, 1987-. *Other Awards:* Simon Memorial Prize, 1976; Oliver E. Buckley Prize, 1981; MacArthur Fellow, 1981.

Selected Publications: "Evidence for a New Phase of Solid He3," *Physical Review Letters* 28 (April 1972):885 (with D.M. Lee and R.C. Richardson). "Novel Magnetic Properties of Solid Helium-3," *Physics Today* (February 1987): 34 (with M.C. Cross).

For More Information See: New York Times (October 10, 1996): D21. Science News 150 (October 19, 1996): 247.

Commentary: Douglas Osheroff shared the Nobel Prize with David Lee and Robert Richardson for "their discovery of superfluidity in helium-3." Actually looking for a phase transition in frozen helium-3 ice, it was Osheroff who noticed "the small extra jumps in the curve measured" and, after further tests, the three colaureates decided it was a "true effect." The discovery of the unusual properties of these very cold, or quantum, liquids has enabled researchers to further describe matter at the microscopic level. (L.S.S.)

Richardson, Robert Coleman   704

Prize: Physics, 1996. *Born:* June 26, 1937; Washington, D.C. *Parents:* Father, Robert Franklin Richardson; Mother, Lois Price Richardson. *Nationality:* American. *Religion:* Probably Christian. *Education:* Virginia Polytechnic Institute, VA, B.S., 1958; Virginia Polytechnic Institute, VA, M.S., 1960; Duke Univ., NC, Ph.D., 1966. *Spouse:* Betty Marilyn McCarthy, married September 2, 1962 *Children:* Jennifer, daughter; Pamela, daughter *Career:* Cornell Univ. NY, Researcher, 1966–67; Cornell Univ., NY, Professor, 1968-. *Other Awards:* Simon Memorial Prize, 1976; Oliver E. Buckley Prize, 1981.

Selected Publications: "Evidence for a New Phase of Solid He3," *Physical Review Letters* 28 (April 1972):885 (with D.D. Osheroff and D.M. Lee). "Low Temperature Science—What Remains for the Physicist?" *Physics Today* (August 1981): 46. *Experimental Techniques in Condensed Matter Physics at Low Temperature* (With E.N. Smith). NY: Addison-Wesley, 1988.

For More Information See: New York Times (October 10, 1996): D21. Science News 150 (October 19, 1996): 247.

Commentary: Robert Richardson shared the Nobel Prize with David Lee and Douglas Osheroff for discovering the superfluid properties of helium-3. By lowering the temperature of helium-3 to near absolute zero, they discovered the unexpected property of its atoms losing their randomness and instead, moving in a coordinated manner. "This causes the liquid to lack all inner friction: It can overflow a cup, flow out through very small holes, and exhibits a whole series of other non-classical effects. . . . One thing these show is that the quantum laws of microphysics sometimes directly govern the behaviour of macroscopic bodies also." (L.S.S.)

1997

Chu, Steven   705

Prize: Physics, 1997. *Born:* February 28, 1948; St. Louis, MO. *Parents:* Father, Ju Chin Chu; Mother, Ching Chen Li Chu. *Nationality:* American. *Religion:* No record found. *Education:* Univ. of Rochester, NY, B.S., A.B., 1970; Univ. of California, Berkeley, Ph.D., 1976. *Spouse:* Married, no date, divorced, no date; no further record found. *Children:* Geoffrey, son; Michael, son. *Career:* Univ. of California, Berkeley, CA, Researcher, 1976–78; Bell Labs, (later AT&T Bell Labs) NJ, Researcher, 1978–87; Stanford Univ., CA, Professor, 1987-. *Other Awards:* Broida Prize, 1987; A.L. Schawlow Prize, 1994; William F. Meggers Award, 1994; von Humboldt Award, 1995; Science for Art Prize, 1995; King Faisal Prize, 1993; APS/AAPT Richtmyer Memorial Prize, 1990.

Selected Publications: "Laser Manipulation of Atoms and Particles," *Science* 253 (August 23, 1991): 861–66. "Laser Trapping of Neutral Particles," *Scientific American* 71 (February 1992).

For More Information See: American Scientist 86 (January/February 1998): 22–5. New York Times (October 16, 1997): A16. New York Times (June 30, 1998): F1.

Commentary: Steven Chu shared the Nobel Prize for the "development of methods to cool and trap atoms with laser light." Chu used lasers to chill atoms to near absolute zero and to slow them down in a kind of "atom trap." The laser light forms a thick liquid called optical molasses that holds the atoms so they can be studied. These new methods of study have added to our knowledge of the relationship between radiation and matter and have "opened the way to a deeper understanding of the quantum-physical behaviour of gases at low temperatures." (L.S.S.)

Cohen-Tannoudji, Claude Nessim   706

Prize: Physics, 1997. *Born:* April 1, 1933; Constantine, Algeria, France. *Parents:* Father, Abraham Cohen-Tannoudji; Mother, Sarah Sebba Cohen-Tannoudji. *Nationality:* French. *Religion:* Jewish. *Education:* École Normale Supérieure, France, Aggregation, 1957; Univ. de Paris, France, Ph.D., 1962. *Spouse:* Jacqueline Veyrat, married November 24, 1958. *Children:* Alain, son; Joëlle, daughter; Michel, son. *Career:* Centre National La Recherche Scientifique, France, Researcher, 1960–64; Univ. de Paris, France, Professor,

1964–73; Collège de France, France, Professor, 1973-. *Other Awards:* Julius Edgar Lilienfeld Prize, 1992; Charles Hard Townes Medal, 1993; Harvey Prize, 1996; Gold Medal, CNRS, 1996.

Selected Publications: Photons and Atoms. New York: Wiley, 1989, 1997 (with others). "New Mechanisms for Laser Cooling," *Physics Today* (October 1990): 33–40 (with W.D. Phillips). *Atoms in Electromagnetic Fields.* River Edge, NJ: World Scientific, 1994. *Quantum Mechanics.* New York: Wiley, 1993, 2 vols. (with others).

For More Information See: Science (May 26, 1995): 1212–14. *New York Times* (October 16, 1997): A16.

Commentary: Claude Cohen-Tannoudji shared the Nobel Prize for refining the methods of cooling atoms based on the "use of the Doppler effect and which converts the slowest atoms to a dark state." He was able to combine this method with laser cooling to break the recoil limit of helium atoms and slow them down to a speed of only about 2cm/second. (L.S.S.)

Phillips, William Daniel   707

Prize: Physics, 1997. *Born:* November 5, 1948; Wilkes-Barre, PA. *Parents:* Father, William Cornelius Phillips; Mother, Mary Catherine Savine Phillips. *Nationality:* American. *Religion:* Methodist. *Education:* Juniata College, PA, B.S., 1970; Massachusetts Institute of Technology, Ph.D., 1976. *Spouse:* Jane Van Wynen, married June 20, 1970 *Children:* Catherine, daughter; Christine, daughter *Career:* Massachusetts Institute of Technology, MA, Researcher, 1970–78; National Institute of Standards and Technology, MD, Researcher, 1978-. *Other Awards:* Outstanding Young Scientist, Maryland, 1982; Gold Medal, U.S. Department of Commerce, 1993; Michelson Medal, 1996; Schawlow Prize, 1998; Gold Medal, Pennsylvania Society, 1999; Oested Medal, 2000.

Selected Publications: "Cooling and Trapping Atoms," *Scientific American* (March 1987): 36–44 (with H.J. Metcalf). "New Mechanisms for Laser Cooling," *Physics Today* (October 1990): 33–40 (with C.N. Cohen-Tannoudji). "Laser Manipulation of Atoms and Ions" in *Proceedings of the International School of Physics "Enrico Fermi,"* vol. 118. Amsterdam; New York: North-Holland, 1992.

For More Information See: New York Times (October 16, 1997): A16.

Commentary: William Phillips shared the Nobel Prize for his development of a "Zeeman slower, a coil with a varying magnetic field, along the axis of which atoms could be retarded by an opposed laser beam." With the successful laser cooling of atoms, Phillips was able to develop new methods of studying the temperature of atoms, achieving temperatures six times lower than the theoretically calculated Doppler limit. (L.S.S.)

1998

Laughlin, Robert B.   708

Prize: Physics, 1998. *Born:* November 1, 1950; Visalia, CA. *Parents:* No record found. *Nationality:* American. *Religion:* Christian. *Education:* Univ. of California, Berkeley, A.B., 1972; Massachusetts Institute of Technology, Ph.D., 1979. *Spouse:* Anita Rhona Perry, married April 22, 1979. *Children:* Nathaniel David, son; Todd William, son.

Career: Bell Telephone Labs, NJ, Researcher, 1979–81; Lawrence Livermore National Laboratory, CA, Researcher, 1981–85; Stanford Univ., CA, Professor, 1985-. *Other Awards:* E.O. Lawrence Award, 1985; Oliver E. Buckley Prize, 1986; Franklin Medal, 1998.

Selected Publications: "Quantized Hall Conductivity in two dimensions," *Physical Review B* 23 (15 May 1981): 5632–3. "Excitons in the fractional quantum Hall effect," *Physica B&C* 126 (November 1984): 254–59. "Fractional-statistics gas with spin and stability of the superfluid state," *Physical Review B* 48 (October 1, 1993): 10382–90.

For More Information See: New York Times (October 14, 1998): A16.

Commentary: Robert Laughlin won the Nobel Prize for explaining the discovery of the fractional quantum Hall effect discovered by Horst Störmer and Daniel Tsui. Laughlin showed that "the electrons in a powerful magnetic field can condense to form a kind of quantum fluid related to the quantum fluids that occur in superconductivity and in liquid helium." Laughlin's quantum fluid has the unusual property of being composed of composite particles called quasiparticles that have the ability to explain Störmer's and Tsui's results. This discovery led to the further understanding of quantum physics. (L.S.S.)

Störmer, Horst Ludwig   709

Prize: Physics, 1998. *Born:* April 6, 1949; Frankfurt-am-Main, Germany. *Parents:* Father, Karl-Ludwig Stömer; Mother, Marie Ihrig Stömer. *Nationality:* German; later American resident. *Religion:* Probably Christian. *Education:* Goethe-Universitaet, Germany, B.S., no date; M.S., no date; Univ. of Stuttgart, Germany, Ph.D., 1977. *Spouse:* Dominique A. Parchet, married 1982. *Children:* None. *Career:* AT&T Bell Labs (now Lucent Technologies), NJ, Researcher and Administrator, 1977–97; Columbia Univ., NY, Professor, 1998-. *Other Awards:* Buckley Prize, 1984; Otto Klung Prize, 1985; Franklin Medal, 1998; Legion d' Honneur, France and Germany, 1999; Mayor's Award for Excellence in Science and Technology, New York City, 2001.

Selected Publications: "The Fractional Quantum Hall Effect," *Science* (June 22, 1990): 1510 (with J.P. Eisenstein). "Composite Fermions," *Physics News* (1994); American Institute of Physics, 1995 (with D. Tsui).

For More Information See: New York Times (October 14, 1998): A16. *Science* (October 23, 1998).

Commentary: Horst Störmer shared the Nobel Prize with Daniel Tsui and Robert Laughlin "for their discovery of a new form of quantum fluid with fractionally charged excitations." Störmer and Tsui, in their studies of the quantum Hall effect and using more powerful magnetic fields and lower temperatures, discovered a new step in the Hall resistance that was three times higher than that identified by von Klitzing (Physics, 1985). Additional steps were discovered, both above and between the integers. This was called the "fractional quantum Hall" effect because the new heights can all be expressed with the same earlier constant but now divided by different fractions. (L.S.S.)

Tsui, Daniel Chee   710

Prize: Physics, 1998. *Born:* February 28, 1938; Henan, China. *Parents:* No record found. *Nationality:* Chinese;

later American citizen. *Religion:* Lutheran. *Education:* Augustana College, IL, B.A., 1961; Univ. of Chicago, IL, M.S., 1967; Univ. of Chicago, IL, Ph.D., 1967. *Spouse:* Linda Varland, married 1964. *Children:* 2 children. *Career:* Univ. of Chicago, IL, Researcher, 1967–68; Bell Labs, NJ, Researcher, 1968–82; Princeton Univ., NJ, Professor, 1982-. *Other Awards:* Buckley Prize, 1984; Franklin Medal, 1998.

Selected Publications: "The Fractional Quantum Hall Effect," *IEEE Journal of Quantum Electronics* 22 (1986). "Composite Fermions," *Physics News* (1994); American Instiue of Physics, 1995 (with H. Störmer).

For More Information See: *New York Times* (October 14, 1998): A16. *Notable Twentieth Century Scientists.* Detroit: Gale, 1995, 2051–52.

Commentary: Daniel Tsui was a colaureate with Horst Störmer and Robert Laughlin "for discovering that electrons acting together in strong magnetic fields can form new types of 'particles', with charges that are fractions of electron charges." This discovery allows researchers to understand more thoroughly the "general inner structure and dynamics of matter." (L.S.S.)

1999

't Hooft, Gerardus 711

Prize: Physics, 1999. *Born:* July 5, 1946; Den Helder, the Netherlands. *Parents:* Father, Hendrik 't Hooft; Mother, Margaretha Agnes van Kampen 't Hooft. *Nationality:* Dutch. *Religion:* Probably Christian. *Education:* Rijksuniversiteit Utrecht, Netherlands, candidaatsexamen, 1966; doctoral examen, 1969; Ph.D., 1972. *Spouse:* Albertha Anje Schik, married July 1, 1972. *Children:* Saskia Anne, daughter; Ellen Marga, daughter. *Career:* European Center for Nuclear Research, Switzerland, Researcher, 1972–74; Univ. of Utrecht, Netherlands, Professor, 1974-. *Other Awards:* Winkler Prins Prize, 1974; Akzo Prize, 1977; Lorentz Medal, 1986; Dannie Heineman Prize, 1979; Wolf Prize, 1981; Pius XI Medal, 1983; Franklin Medal, 1995; Spinoza Premium, 1995; Gian Carlo Wick Medal, 1997; Oskar Klein Silver Medal, 1999; High Energy Physics Prize, 1999.

Selected Publications: "Gauge Theories of the Forces Between Elementary Particles," *Scientific American* (June 1980): 90. *In Search of the Ultimate Building Blocks* (Tr. *Bouwstenen van de Schepping*). Cambridge: Cambridge University Press, 1997.

For More Information See: *New York Times* (October 13, 1999): A8. *New York Times* (October 17, 1999): Section 4, 6.

Commentary: Gerardus 't Hooft shared the Nobel Prize with his former teacher, Martinus Veltman, "for elucidating the quantum structure of electroweak interactions in physics." Using Veltman's work as a basis, 't Hooft was able to find the "key to renormalizing electroweak theory, reconciling the infinities" that often were produced as a result of some calculations. He also "deepened the understanding of how, in the early moments of creation, the two forces (electromagnetism and the weak force) might have come unraveled." The agent for this is the Higgs particle, still undiscovered until new, more powerful, accelerators become available. (L.S.S.)

Veltman, Martinus J.G. 712

Prize: Physics, 1999. *Born:* 1931; the Netherlands. *Parents:* No record found. *Nationality:* Dutch; later American resident. *Religion:* Probably Christian. *Education:* Univ. of Utrecht, the Netherlands, Ph.D., 1963. *Spouse:* Married, no further record found. *Children:* None. *Career:* CERN, Switzerland, Researcher, 1963–66; Univ. of Utrecht, Netherlands, Professor, 1966–81; Univ. of Michigan, MI, Professor, 1981–97. *Other Awards:* von Humboldt Award, 1989; Fifth Physica Lezing, 1990; Dutch Order of the Lion of Queen Beatrix, 1992; High Energy and Particle Physics Prize, 1993; P.A.M. Dirac Medal and Prize, 1996.

Selected Publications: "The Higgs Boson," *Scientific American* (November 1986): 88. *Diagrammatica.* Cambridge, MA: Cambridge University Press, 1994.

For More Information See: *Economist* (October 16, 1999). *New York Times* (October 13, 1999): A8. *New York Times* (October 17, 1999): Section 4, 6.

Commentary: Martinus Veltman shared the Nobel Prize with his former student Gerardus 't Hooft for "having placed particle physics theory on a firmer mathematical foundation." Calculations using the electroweak theory would sometimes produce infinite answers. 't Hooft and Veltman developed detailed calculations that place the electroweak theory on a firmer mathematical understanding that eliminates the infinite answers in certain circumstances. These calculations have led to the discovery of the top quark, the latest elementary particle to be discovered. (L.S.S.)

2000

Alferov, Zhores I. 713

Prize: Physics, 2000. *Born:* March 15, 1930; Vitebsk, Byelorussia, USSR. *Parents:* Father, Ivan Karpovich Alferov; Mother, Anna Vladimirovna Rosenblum Alferov. *Nationality:* Russian. *Religion:* No record found. *Education:* Electrotechnical Institute, USSR, Engineering degree, 1952; Ioffe Physico-Technical Institute, USSR, Science and Technology degree, 1961; Ioffe Physico-Technical Institute, USSR, D.Sci., 1970. *Spouse:* Tamara Georgievna Darscaya, married November 11, 1967. *Children:* Ivan Zhoresovich, son; 1 daughter. *Career:* Ioffe Physico-Technical Institute, Russia, Researcher and Administrator, 1953-. *Other Awards:* Ballantine Medal, 1971; Lenin Prize, 1972; Hewlett-Packard Europhysics Prize, 1978; State Prize, USSR, 1984; GaAs Symposium Award, 1987; H. Welker Medal, 1987; A.P. Karpinskii Prize, 1989; Ioffe Prize, 1996; Nicholas Holonyak, Jr. Award, 2000.

Selected Publications: "The History and Future of Semiconductor Heterostructures from the Point of View of a Russian Scientist," *Physica Scripta* T68 (1996):32.

For More Information See: *New York Times* (October 11, 2000): A16. *New York Times* (October 12, 2000): A3.

Commentary: Zhores Alferov and his colaureate, Herbert Kroemer, were awarded the Nobel Prize "for developing semiconductor heterostructures used in high-speed and opto-electronics." Their invention has led to the development of fast transistors that are used in modern telecommunications. Heterostructures, such as semiconductors, are used in radio link satellites, mobile telephones, fibre-optic cables, CD players, bar-code readers and laser pointers. Alferov was also the first to develop a heterostructure laser, which made fibre-optic communication viable. (L.S.S.)

Kilby, Jack St. Clair   714

Prize: Physics, 2000. *Born:* November 8, 1923; Jefferson City, MO. *Parents:* Father, Hubert St. Clair Kilby; Mother, Vina Freitag Kilby. *Nationality:* American. *Religion:* Probably Christian. *Education:* Univ. of Illinois, BSEE, 1947; Univ. of Wisconsin, WI, M.S., 1950. *Spouse:* Barbara Annegers, married June 27, 1948. *Children:* Ann, daughter; Janet Lee, daughter. *Career:* Globe-Union, Inc., WI, Program Manager, 1947–58; Texas Instruments, TX, Administrator and Researcher, 1958–70; Inventor, TX, 1970–78; Texas A&M Univ. TX, Professor, 1978–84. *Other Awards:* Sarnoff Medal, 1966; Ballentine Medal, 1967; National Medal of Science, 1969; Alumni Achievement Award, Univ. of Illinois, 1974; Zworykin Medal, 1975; Brunetti Award, 1978; Consumer Electronics Award, IEEE, 1980; National Inventors Hall of Fame, 1982; Holley Medal, 1982, 1989; IEEE Medal of Honor, 1986; Haggerty Innovation Award, 1987; Draper Prize, 1989; National Medal of Technology, 1990; Kyoto Prize, 1993.

Selected Publications: "Invention of the Integrated Circuit," *IEEE Transactions on Electronic Devices* ED-23, #7 (July 1976): 648. "The Individual Inventor," *IEEE Transactions on Consumer Electronics* (February 1979).

For More Information See: New York Times (October 11, 2000): A16. *Notable Twentieth Century Scientists.* Detroit: Gale, 1995, 1094–96.

Commentary: Jack Kilby shared the Nobel Prize "for his part in the invention of the integrated circuit." Ten years after the first transistor, Jack Kilby built the first integrated circuit, the microchip, that led, among many other items, to the invention of the pocket calculator and personal computers. His research helped lay the "foundations of modern information technology" and the development of the field of microelectronics. (L.S.S.)

Kroemer, Herbert   715

Prize: Physics, 2000. *Born:* August 25, 1928; Weimar, Germany. *Parents:* No record found. *Nationality:* German; later American resident. *Religion:* No record found. *Education:* Univ. of Göttingen, Germany, Diplom-Physiker, 1951; Univ. of Göttingen, Germany, Ph.D., 1952. *Spouse:* No record found. *Children:* No record found. *Career:* Univ. of California, Santa Barbara, CA, Professor, 1976-. *Other Awards:* J.J. Ebers Award, 1973; Heinrich Welker Medal, 1982; Jack Morton Award, 1986; von Humboldt Award, 1994.

Selected Publications: "A Proposed Class of Heterojunction Injection Lasers," *Proc. IEEE* 51 (1963): 1782–83. "Heterostructure Bipolar Transistors and Integrated Circuits," *Proc. IEEE* 70 (1982): 13–25. *Quantum Mechanics.* Englewood Cliffs, NJ: Prentice Hall, 1994. "Band Offsets and Chemical Bonding: The Basis for Heterostructure Applications," *Physica Scripta* T68 (1996):10.

For More Information See: New York Times (October 11, 2000): A16.

Commentary: Herbert Kroemer shared the Nobel Prize with Zhores Alferov for their contributions to information technology and telecommunications. Kroemer first proposed a heterostructure transistor that improved upon the conventional transistors then in use "particularly for current amplification and high-frequency applications." Independently of each other, the two researchers also proposed the principle of the heterostructure laser. (L.S.S.)

Name Index

Note: Numbers refer to entry accession numbers located in the upper right-hand corner of each entry.

Education Index

Nationality or Citizenship Index

Note: Asterisks indicate names indexed under more than one nationality or citizenship category.

Religion Index

About the Editor

LOUISE S. SHERBY is Associate Dean and Chief Librarian at Hunter College in New York City. Her articles have appeared in *College & Research Libraries News, Journal of Academic Librarianship,* and *The Reference Librarian.* She also is the author of chapters in *Essays From the New England Academic Librarians' Writing Seminar, The Basic Business Library: Core Resources,* and *Library Education and Leadership.* She is a co-editor of *P.G. Wodehouse: A Comprehensive Bibliography and Checklist* and was an Associate Editor for the previous editions of *The Who's Who of Nobel Prize Winners.*